INDIANA

RULES OF COURT

VOLUME III – LOCAL

2014

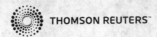
THOMSON REUTERS

Mat #41258955

ISBN: 978–0–314–65398–7

PREFACE

Indiana Rules of Court, Volume III – Local, 2014, includes rules and associated material governing practice before the Indiana local courts. It replaces the 2013 edition and any accompanying supplements. It is current with amendments received through November 1, 2013.

For additional information or research assistance call the West reference attorneys at 1–800–REF–ATTY (1–800–733–2889). Contact West's editorial department directly with your questions and suggestions by e-mail at west.editor@thomson.com.

THE PUBLISHER

December, 2013

THOMSON REUTERS PROVIEW™

This title is one of many now available on your tablet as an eBook.

Take your research mobile. Powered by the Thomson Reuters ProView™ app, our eBooks deliver the same trusted content as your print resources, but in a compact, on-the-go format.

ProView eBooks are designed for the way you work. You can add your own notes and highlights to the text, and all of your annotations will transfer electronically to every new edition of your eBook.

You can also instantly verify primary authority with built-in links to WestlawNext® and KeyCite®, so you can be confident that you're accessing the most current and accurate information.

To find out more about ProView eBooks and available discounts, call 1-800-344-5009.

TABLE OF CONTENTS

———

TABLE OF CONTENTS

TABLE OF CONTENTS

*

LOCAL CIVIL RULES OF THE ALLEN SUPERIOR & CIRCUIT COURT

Adopted September 8, 2000, Effective November 1, 2000

Including Amendments Received Through November 1, 2013

Research Notes

Annotations to the Local Civil Rules of the Allen Superior & Circuit Court are available in West's Annotated Indiana Code, *Title 34 Appendix.*

These rules may be searched electronically on Westlaw *in the IN-RULES database; updates to these rules may be found on* Westlaw *in IN-RULESUPDATES. For search tips and a summary of database content, consult the* Westlaw Scope Screens *for each database.*

LR02 Rule AR00-1. Applicability and Citation of Rules

A. Scope. The following rules shall apply to cases filed in Allen Superior Court Civil Division or the Allen Circuit Court (herein after referred to as "Court"), these rules shall not apply to any other cases. Nothing in these rules shall limit the general jurisdiction of any judge.

B. Citation. These rules may be cited as L.R. _____. The Indiana Rules of Trial Procedure are hereinafter referred to as T.R. _____.

Adopted as Superior Civil Rule 1 Sept. 8, 2000, effective Nov. 1, 2000. Renumbered as Superior and Circuit Civil Rule AR00-1, and amended effective Dec. 7, 2006. Amended Oct. 3, 2008, effective Jan. 1, 2009.

LR02-TR Rule 4-1. Service of Process

(A) Procedure for Service of Process.

(1) By Mail. When service by certified mail is requested, the party shall not prepare envelopes, but shall furnish for each party to be served, the originals and three copies of prepared summons, complaints, notices or subpoenas to the Clerk, who shall prepare the envelopes using the addresses furnished. Proper postage and return receipt request card will be furnished by the Clerk. Upon receipt of the return, the Clerk shall insert the return with the pleadings in the packet.

(2) By Sheriff. When Sheriff service is requested, the party shall furnish for each party to be served, the original and three copies of prepared summons, complaints, notices or subpoenas to the Clerk, who will forward the documents to the Sheriff for proper service.

(B) Summons and Complaint Served Together—Exceptions. The summons and complaint shall be served as provided by the Trial Rule 4(E) except as may otherwise be provided by statute or other Trial Rule.

Adopted as Superior Civil Rule 2 Sept. 8, 2000, effective Nov. 1, 2000. Renumbered as Superior and Circuit Civil Rule 4-1, and amended effective Dec. 7, 2006.

LR02-TR Rule 3.1-1. Appearances

(A) Written Appearance Form. An attorney entering an appearance on behalf of any party shall file a written appearance as provided in T.R. 3.1 and serve a copy on all parties of record.

(B) Filing Appearance. Appearance shall be filed with the Clerk, who shall file-stamp the same and shall enter the attorney's name and the date of such appearance on the chronological case summary. In addition, the Clerk shall note such attorney's name, address, or box number, and phone number on the chronological case summary. It shall be the duty of attorneys to see that their appearance is properly filed and entered.

(C) Party Appearing Without an Attorney. When a party to an action appears without an attorney, the party shall give, and the Clerk shall note on the chronological case summary of the case, a name, a mailing address and phone number of the party to which notices and communications concerning the case may be delivered and mailed pursuant to T.R. 5 (B).

(D) Address Changes. It shall be the duty of all attorneys who have entered their written appearance and of all parties who are not represented by an attorney, to notify the Court through the Clerk of any change of their mailing addresses and phone numbers. Such notification shall be in writing filed separately for each case to which the change applies and served upon other parties to each case or their attorneys of record.

(E) Proof of Mailing. Certificates of service or proof of mailing of pleadings concerning any case shall be deemed sufficient proof of service if such pleadings were mailed to the last known address of a party or attorney noted upon the chronological case summary of a case.

Adopted as Superior Civil Rule 3 Sept. 8, 2000, effective Nov. 1, 2000. Renumbered as Superior and Circuit Civil Rule 3.1-1, and amended effective Dec. 7, 2006.

LR02-TR Rule 3.1-2. Withdrawal of Appearance

(A) Procedure for Withdrawal. A request to withdraw an appearance shall be in writing and by leave of Court. Permission to withdraw shall be given only after the withdrawing attorney has given his client at least ten (10) days written notice of his intention to withdraw and has filed a copy of such notice with the Court; or upon a simultaneous or prior entering of appearance by counsel for said client. Once a case has been assigned to a judge, no motion to withdraw appearance shall be granted except by the judge to whom the case has been assigned.

(B) Contents of Notice. Any notice of intention to withdraw shall include an explanation to the client as follows:

(1) the present status of the case.

(2) the date or dates of scheduled hearings and any other pending matters;

(3) advice that the provisions in Local Rule 3C and 3D apply to the client after withdrawal of counsel;

(4) the expectation of the Indiana common law that, as an unrepresented party, the client will be held to the same standard of conduct as an attorney licensed to practice in the State of Indiana; and

(5) the prejudice which might result from failure of the client to act promptly or to secure new counsel.

(6) an attorney, in compliance of T.R. 3.1(E), shall certify the last known address and telephone number of the party, subject to the confidentiality provisions of T.R. 3.1(A)(8) and (D).

Adopted as Superior Civil Rule 4 Sept. 8, 2000, effective Nov. 1, 2000. Amended and effective Oct. 1, 2003; renumbered as Superior and Circuit Civil Rule 3.1-2, and amended effective Dec. 7, 2006.

LR02-TR Rule 5-1. Consent to Alternate Service

A. Courthouse Boxes. Any Allen County Attorney or any Allen County law firm may, without charge, maintain an assigned Courthouse box in the library of the Allen County Courthouse for receipt of notices, pleadings, process orders, or other communications from the Court, the Clerk, and other attorneys or law firms.

B. How Assigned. Courthouse boxes shall be assigned only after the attorney or law firm has filed with the Law Librarian a Consent to Alternate Service (Appendix A).

C. Effect of Consent. Deposits made in any assigned box of notices, pleadings, process, orders, or other communications made shall be deemed to constitute and be accepted as service equivalent to service by first class mail under Trial Rule 6(E).

D. Form of Deposit to Box. Any papers served under this rule by the Court, Clerk, or other attorneys or firm of attorney shall be placed in an envelope with the name of the intended receiving attorney on it and the current box number on the outside thereof.

E. Revocation of Consent. Consent to Alternate Service under this rule shall remain valid until a written revocation has been filed with the Law Librarian.

F. Index. An index of those attorneys and firms consenting to alternate service shall be located near the boxes. The Law Librarian shall be responsible for assigning boxes and maintaining a file of consents and of revocations of consents to alternate service.

G. If an attorney revokes consent to alternate service, that attorney shall notify the Courts and all counsel of record in any matter that the revoking attorney has an appearance filed.

Adopted as Superior Civil Rule 5 Sept. 8, 2000, effective Nov. 1, 2000. Renumbered as Superior and Circuit Civil Rule 5-1, and amended effective Dec. 7, 2006. Amended Oct. 3, 2008, effective Jan. 1, 2009.

LR02-TR Rule 8-1. Preparation of Pleadings

All pleadings shall be in accordance with the provisions of the Indiana Rules of Trial Procedure. For the purpose of uniformity and convenience, the following requirements shall also be observed:

(A) Form. Such pleadings must be printed on white paper. The lines shall be double spaced except for quotations, which shall be indented and single-spaced. Handwritten pleadings may be accepted for filing in the discretion of the Court. Photocopies are acceptable if legible.

(B) Margins and Binding. Margins shall be 1-1 ½ inches on the left side and ½ inch on the right. Binding or stapling shall be at the top left and at no other place. Covers or backing shall not be used.

(C) Signature. All pleadings to be signed by an attorney shall contain the written signature of the individual attorney, the attorney's printed name, Supreme Court Attorney Number, the name of the attorney's law firm, the attorney's address, telephone number, and a designation of the party for whom the attorney appears.

The following is recommended:

John Doe, #284-703

Doe, Rowe and Smith

2222 Blackburn Building

Fort Wayne, Indiana 46802

(260) 555-1212

Attorney for Defendant

Neither printed signatures, nor facsimile signatures shall be accepted on original documents. Facsimile signatures are permitted on copies.

Adopted as Superior Civil Rule 6 Sept. 8, 2000, effective Nov. 1, 2000. Renumbered as Superior and Circuit Civil Rule 8-1, and amended effective Dec. 7, 2006.

LR02-TR Rule 77-1. Filing

(A) Flat Filing. The files of the Clerk of the Court shall be kept under the "flat filing" system. All pleadings presented for filing with the Clerk or Court shall be flat and unfolded. Only the original of any pleading shall be placed in the Court file.

(B) Filing Pleadings, File-Stamped Copies. A copy of any pleading required to be served under Trial Rule 5 upon counsel of record or the adverse party shall be file-stamped.

Adopted as Superior Civil Rule 7 Sept. 8, 2000, effective Nov. 1, 2000. Renumbered as Superior and Circuit Civil Rule 77-1, and amended effective Dec. 7, 2006.

LR02-TR Rule 59-1. Default Judgments

(A) Written Instruments. Where a case is based on a written negotiable instrument, the original of the instrument must be produced for cancellation when obtaining judgment thereon. If the only instrument produced is a photocopy including the photocopy of the signature of the defendant, an affidavit by plaintiff that the original of such instrument cannot be found

or produced shall be filed before judgment will be issued thereon.

(B) Application for Judgment. Where an appearance has been entered for a party, the party entitled to a judgment shall file an "Application for Judgment" pursuant to Trial Rule 55(B). The movant will set the application for hearing and give notice of such application and hearing on the party's attorney who is in default.

(C) Affidavit of Non-Military Service. No default judgment shall be entered unless there has been filed an affidavit or other evidence, satisfactory to the Court, of non-military service.

Adopted as Superior Civil Rule 8 Sept. 8, 2000, effective Nov. 1, 2000. Renumbered as Superior and Circuit Civil Rule 59-1, and amended effective Dec. 7, 2006.

LR02-TR Rule 7-1. Motions in Civil Court

A. Setting Motions for Hearing. Except for the motions described in TR7–1E below, all motions shall be set for hearing. It shall be the responsibility of the moving party to request the date of such hearing from the Judicial Assistant, or if the case has already been assigned to a Judge, from the Judicial Law Clerk of the assigned Judge.

B. Motions to Correct Error. It shall be discretionary with the Judge before whom the case is pending whether a hearing shall be held on a motion to correct error.

C. Motions to Amend Pleadings. All motions to amend pleadings shall contain a written representation of the moving party's attorney that said attorney advised opposing counsel of the substance of the motion and that opposing counsel either consents or objects to the motion or that the motion may be submitted for ruling by the Court without hearing or briefing. Upon being advised of opposing counsel's objection, the moving party's attorney shall request a date for hearing, as prescribed in TR7–1A above.

D. Motions Not Likely to Require Hearing. At the time of filing, the following motions, along with the court packet, shall be brought to the attention of the Judicial Assistant or Law Clerk of the Judge.

(1) Motion for Enlargement of Time

(2) Motion to Dismiss complaint by Plaintiff when no answer has been filed

(3) Motion to Dismiss Counterclaim by Defendant when no reply has been filed

(4) Motion to amend any pleading Such motions shall be summarily granted or denied *ex parte* unless the assigned Judge, determines that a hearing should be scheduled.

E. Briefs and Memoranda Regarding Motions. If a party desires to file a brief or memorandum in support of any motion, such brief or memorandum shall be filed simultaneously with the motion, and a copy shall be promptly served upon the adverse party.

F. Motions to Strike or to Insert New Matter. Subject to Trial Rule 12(F), every motion to insert new matter or to strike out any part or parts of any pleading, deposition, report, order or other document in a case shall be made in writing and shall set forth the words sought to be inserted or stricken. Each set of words to be inserted or stricken shall be in a separate specification and each specification shall be numbered consecutively.

G. Motions to Reconsider Rulings. A motion to reconsider a ruling of the Court on any pleading or motion must be in writing and must be served personally upon the ruling Judge. If a motion to reconsider is set for hearing by the Judicial Assistant or by the Judicial Law Clerk of the Judge, the five (5) day automatic denial time period contained in T.R. 53.4 shall not apply.

H. Discovery Dispute Motions. The Court expects complete compliance with T.R. 26(F).

I. Responsibility for Notice. It shall be the responsibility of the moving party to give notice to all other parties of hearings scheduled on motions.

Adopted as Superior Civil Rule 9 Sept. 8, 2000, effective Nov. 1, 2000. Amended and effective Oct. 1, 2003; renumbered as Superior and Circuit Civil Rule 7-1, and amended effective Dec. 7, 2006. Amended Oct. 3, 2008, effective Jan. 1, 2009.

LR02 Rule TR00-1. Proposed Orders

A. Matters in which Proposed Orders Required. Prior to entry by the Court of orders granting motions or applications, the moving party or applicant (or his or her attorney) shall, unless the Court directs otherwise, furnish the Court with proposed orders in the following matters:

(1) for enlargement of time

(2) for continuance

(3) for default judgment

(4) to compel discovery

(5) of dismissal

(6) for appointment of receiver

(7) for appointment of guardian

(8) for immediate possession of real estate

(9) for immediate possession of personal property

(10) for petition for certification of interlocutory appeals

(11) for staying further proceedings by reason of bankruptcy, appeal, or other cognizable grounds

(12) for notice of hearing

(13) for extensions of dispositive motion filing deadlines and the resetting of hearings thereon

(14) such other orders, judgments, or decrees as the Court may direct

This rule does not apply to judgments on general verdicts of the jury or upon a decision announced by the Court.

B. Form. Any proposed order shall be a document that is separate and apart from the motion or application to which it relates and shall contain a caption showing the name of the court, the case number assigned to the case and the title of the case as shown by the complaint. If there are multiple parties, the title may be shortened to include only the first name plaintiff and defendant with appropriate indication that there are additional parties. The proposed order shall be on white paper, 8 ½″ × 11″ in size, and each page shall be numbered. On the last page of the proposed order there shall be a line for the signature of the judge under which shall be typed "Judge, Allen Superior Court" or "Judge, Allen Circuit Court", whichever is applicable, to the left of which shall be the following: "Dated _____". To allow space for the Clerk to make entries on the proposed order to show compliance with the notice requirements of TR 72(D), the lower 4 inches of the last page of the proposed order shall be left blank. The proposed order shall also include a prepared proof of notice, under T.R. 72(D). The proof of notice shall conform to the following format:

NOTICE IS TO BE GIVEN BY:

__COURT __ CLERK __ PARTY __ OTHER

PROOF OF NOTICE UNDER TRIAL RULE 72 (D)

A copy of this entry was served either by mail to the address of record, deposited in the Court's attorney's distribution box, distributed personally upon the persons and/or filed as listed below:

Insert Name and address or court's attorney distribution box number, of all Pro Se Parties and Attorneys of Record.

Court Packet—2

DATE OF NOTICE: _____

INITIALS OF PERSON WHO NOTIFIED PARTIES:

__COURT __ CLERK __ PARTY __ OTHER

NOTE: When a party provides notice under this section said party shall complete all portions of the prepared proof of notice.

C. Copies. All proposed orders shall be submitted in an original plus a number of copies equal to one more than the number of pro se parties and attorneys of record contained in the prepared proof of notice under T.R. 72 (D) required above.

D. Proposed Orders on Motions for Summary Judgment. Proposed orders on motions for summary judgment may contain the language called for in T.R. 56 (C) that there is not just reason for delay and directs entry of final judgment as to less than all the issues, claims or parties.

Adopted as Superior Civil Rule 10 Sept. 8, 2000, effective Nov. 1, 2000. Renumbered as Superior and Circuit Civil Rule TR00-1, and amended effective Dec. 7, 2006. Amended Oct. 3, 2008, effective Jan. 1, 2009.

LR02-TR Rule 53.1-1.   Failure to Rule — Informal Procedure

In the event a Judge fails to set a motion or hearing or fails to rule on a motion within the time period specified in Trial Rule 53.1(A), and if no action has been taken as provided in Trial Rule 53.1(D) or (E), an interested party may seek that an informal resolution be attempted as to such Judge's failure through *ex parte* request made to the Administrative Judge of the Civil Division, the Court Executive of the Allen Superior Court, or the Judge or Court Administrator of the Allen Circuit Court.

Adopted as Superior Civil Rule 11 Sept. 8, 2000, effective Nov. 1, 2000. Renumbered as Superior and Circuit Civil Rule 53.1-1, and amended effective Dec. 7, 2006. Amended Oct. 3, 2008, effective Jan. 1, 2009.

LR02-TR Rule 53.5-1.   Continuances Civil

A.   Motion. A motion for continuance, unless made during trial, shall be in writing, state with particularity the grounds and be verified, with copies of such requests served upon opposing counsel unless the Court directs otherwise.

B.   Party to Suit Signing Requirement. The Court, in its discretion, may require any written motion or stipulation for continuance to be signed by the party requesting the continuance in addition to signature of attorney so moving.

C.   By Stipulation of Counsel. Stipulation to continue the hearing of any pending matter shall state with particularity the grounds for the continuance and be signed by all attorneys of record.

D.   Time for Filing. Motions or Stipulations for Continuance shall be filed as soon after the cause for continuance or delay is discovered by the party seeking same, and no later than seven (7) days before date set, unless the reason therefore is shown by affidavit to have occurred within said seven (7) day period.

E.   Court's Discretion. The Court in its discretion may grant or deny a motion or stipulation for continuance.

F.   Rescheduling. All matters continued shall be rescheduled.

Adopted as Superior Civil Rule 12 Sept. 8, 2000, effective Nov. 1, 2000. Renumbered as Superior and Circuit Civil Rule 53.5-1, and amended effective Dec. 7, 2006. Amended Oct. 3, 2008, effective Jan. 1, 2009.

LR02 Rule AR00-2. Assignment of Cases to Judges for Cases Filed in the Allen Superior Court

A. The Administrative Judge of the Civil Division of the Allen Superior Court shall assign case types within the Division on a bi-annual basis pursuant to I.C. 33–33–2–31.

B. In addition to the assignments under LR02–AR00–2(A), the Administrative Judge or his/her designee may assign cases to a particular Judge upon filing. After a case has been assigned to a particular Judge, all matters pertaining to that case shall be heard and determined by the assigned Judge.

C. At the time of filing, the Administrative Judge may also set a Case Management Conference. Notice of the Case Management Conference will be included with the pleading served with the summons in the case.

D.   Unassigned Cases. Prior to assignment of the case to a particular Judge, any matter in the case may be scheduled for hearing or disposition before any of the Judges of the Civil Division.

Adopted as Superior Civil Rule 13 Sept. 8, 2000, effective Nov. 1, 2000. Renumbered as Superior and Circuit Civil Rule AR00-2, and amended effective Dec. 7, 2006. Amended Oct. 3, 2008, effective Jan. 1, 2009.

LR02 Rule TR00-2. Admissions, Stipulations and Agreements

Admissions, stipulations and agreements concerning the proceedings in a case will not be enforced, unless submitted in writing or made of record.

Adopted as Superior Civil Rule 14 Sept. 8, 2000, effective Nov. 1, 2000. Renumbered as Superior and Circuit Civil Rule TR00-2, and amended effective Dec. 7, 2006.

LR02 Rule AR00-3.   Retrieval/Destruction of Exhibits

After a case is decided and no appeal is timely taken, or after the applicable retention period under State Law, the court reporter may give notice in writing to the party or party's attorney who introduced an exhibit at trial specifying a time within which the exhibit must be removed from the custody of the court reporter. If the party or attorney does not retrieve the exhibit within the time indicated, the reporter may dispose of same and the party shall be charged with any expenses of disposition.

Adopted as Superior Civil Rule 15, Sept. 8, 2000, effective Nov. 1, 2000. Renumbered as Superior and Circuit Civil Rule AR00-3, and amended effective Dec. 7, 2006.

LR02 Rule TR00-3.   Attorney's Fees

(a) [1] No order granting a request for attorney fees shall be made unless such fees are allowable under applicable law and there has been evidence furnished by testimony of an attorney, or by affidavit of an attorney. Such testimony or affidavit shall describe the services rendered in order to establish to the Court's satisfaction the amount of time expended (or to be expended in the matter), the fact that such services and time were or are reasonably necessary considering the nature and complexity of the matter, the experience or expertise of the attorney seeking an attorney fee award, the usual and customary charges, and the reasonableness of the fees sought.

Judicial notice of reasonable fees shall not be taken. In any event, the award of attorney fees shall be within the sound discretion of the Court.

Adopted as Superior Civil Rule 16, Sept. 8, 2000, effective Nov. 1, 2000. Renumbered as Superior and Circuit Civil Rule TR00-3, and amended effective Dec. 7, 2006.

1 There is no Subd. (b) in this rule.

LR02-TR Rule 69-1. Proceedings Supplemental

A. Ten Day Rule. Except for good cause shown, a motion for proceedings supplemental may not be filed until ten (10) calendar days have elapsed since the date of judgment.

B. One Year Rule. Except upon good cause shown, no proceedings supplemental may pend for more than one (1) year period from the date of its filing. At the end of said one (1) year period, the proceedings supplemental shall be dismissed. Except upon good cause shown, no judgment creditor may file more than four (4) proceedings supplemental per year against any individual judgment debtor in a given case.

C. Bank Interrogatories. Except by order of the Court for good cause shown, judgment creditors may not submit garnishment interrogatories to more than two (2) banking institutions for each hearing on proceedings supplemental.

D. Conduct of Hearings. Unless the judgment creditor is represented by an attorney at the proceedings supplemental hearing, the hearing shall be conducted by an officer of the Court. If no attorney appears on behalf of the judgment creditor after 15 minutes of the scheduled hearing time, the proceedings supplemental shall be dismissed and no garnishment order shall issue.

E. Proceedings Supplemental During Pendency of Garnishment Order. If a garnishment order has been issued and remains unsatisfied, additional proceedings supplemental directed to the judgment debtor or to an additional garnishee defendant may be filed only by order of the Court for good cause shown.

F. Default on Proceedings Supplemental. The Court shall permit each party a fifteen (15) minute grace period to appear for any proceedings supplemental hearing. After the fifteen (15) minute grace period has elapsed:

(1) if the judgment debtor has failed to appear, a judgment creditor who appears shall be entitled to apply for appropriate proceedings supplemental sanctions; or

(2) if the judgment debtor has appeared within the grace period and the judgment creditor or his attorney fails to appear or to commence to conduct the proceedings supplemental interview, the judg-

ment debtor may leave without risk of sanction for failure to appear.

Adopted as Superior Civil Rule 17, Sept. 8, 2000, effective Nov. 1, 2000. Renumbered as Superior and Circuit Civil Rule 69-1, and amended effective Dec. 7, 2006. Amended Oct. 3, 2008, effective Jan. 1, 2009.

LR02-TR Rule 69-2. Court Orders to Appear (COTA)

A. General Use. Judgment creditors may request the Court to issue a Court order to appear (COTA) to judgment debtor(s) only when:

(1) an active proceedings supplemental is pending against the judgment debtor;

(2) the hearing date set for the COTA is within sixty (60) days of the date on which the COTA is issued; and

(3) good cause exists for the COTA and is shown on the record at the time the COTA is requested.

B. Good Cause. "Good cause" under TR69–2A(3) shall include but not be limited to cases in which:

(1) the judgment debtor fails to produce documents as previously ordered by the Court;

(2) the judgment debtor indicates intended relocation with new address presently unknown;

(3) there is a reasonable certainty that the judgment debtor's financial status will substantially change within sixty (60) days.

C. COTA's and Garnishment Orders. When a garnishment order has been issued, no pending COTA will be enforced, and no COTA will issue to the judgment debtor, except by order of the Court for good cause shown.

D. Failure to Appear on COTA. Upon proof of service and a judgment debtor's failure to appear on the date and time set by the COTA, the judgment creditor may file contempt proceedings under TR69–3.

E. Agreements to Appear Without COTA. In any proceedings supplemental, the parties may agree to reset a hearing without use of a COTA. If after such agreement either party fails to appear at the reset hearing, the underlying proceedings supplemental shall be dismissed and no sanctions shall be available for such failure to appear.

Adopted as Superior Civil Rule 18, Sept. 8, 2000, effective Nov. 1, 2000. Renumbered as Superior and Circuit Civil Rule 69-2, and amended effective Dec. 7, 2006. Amended Oct. 3, 2008, effective Jan. 1, 2009.

LR02-TR Rule 69-3. Contempt/Rule to Show Cause/Body Attachment

A. Contempt. Upon failure of a judgment, debtor or garnishee defendant to appear as ordered for a scheduled hearing, the judgment creditor may file a contempt citation as to said person. Said contempt citation must be filed within thirty (30) days of the failure to appear.

B. Body Attachment. Body attachment shall be requested and issued only when:

(1) The judgment debtor or garnishee defendant previously ordered to appear for a scheduled hearing was personally served with notice of a contempt hearing;

(2) The judgment debtor fails to appear at the contempt hearing;

(3) The request for body attachment is filed within thirty (30) days of the contempt hearing at issue; and

(4) The judgment creditor properly completes and files all pleadings and forms from time to time required by the Court. Said pleadings and forms currently include for each judgment debtor:

(a) one (1) Request for Body Attachment;

(b) at least three (3) Writs of Attachment which must include a statement setting a bond for release; (The bond amount should be set at the lesser of $500.00 or the total amount remaining unpaid on the judgment including costs and interest.)

(c) and the Warrant Information Card, including the judgment debtor's social security number or date of birth.

C. Procedure for Contacting Judgment Creditor When Attached Person is in Custody. When the judgment creditor under TR69–3 requests the issuance of a body attachment, and as needed at any time thereafter, said creditor shall file with the Court any telephone numbers (not to exceed three (3)) at which the Court may notify the creditor of the attached person's appearance in custody. Upon such appearance in custody, the Court, to the best of its ability and consistent with the continued performance of its daily responsibilities shall:

(1) Attempt to contact the creditor at the telephone numbers on file with the Court; and

(2) Thereby notify the creditor of a time later during the same Court business day at which the attached person will be brought before the Court for questioning by said creditor.

If the judgment creditor does not appear within two (2) hours of having been contacted by the Court, the attached person shall be released and the underlying proceedings supplemental dismissed.

D. Expiration and Recall of Body Attachments.

(1) *Expiration.* Body Attachments expire on year after issuance.

(2) *Recall.* If during the pendency of a Body Attachment, the judgment creditor desires to recall said body attachment, said judgment creditor shall;

(a) appear personally or by attorney and move on the record for recall of the Body Attachment; and

(b) state on the record the reason for the desired recall.

Upon the recall of a Body Attachment, the underlying proceedings supplemental shall be dismissed.

Adopted as Superior Civil Rule 19, Sept. 8, 2000, effective Nov. 1, 2000. Renumbered as Superior and Circuit Civil Rule 69-3, and amended effective Dec. 7, 2006. Amended Oct. 3, 2008, effective Jan. 1, 2009.

LR02-TR Rule 69-4. Garnishment

A. General Procedure. A garnishment order shall not issue with respect to a judgment debtor's wage or other property without:

(1) An active proceedings supplemental as to the judgment debtor or waiver of notice by said judgment debtor;

(2) Service on the garnishee defendant of the proceedings supplemental by

(a) Certified mail,

(b) Sheriff's service, or

(c) Private process server; and

(3) return of answered interrogatories, other verification of employment by the garnishee defendant, or failure to answer interrogatories after notice.

B. Voluntary Garnishments. In instances where a judgment debtor has entered a voluntary agreement for periodic payments to satisfy the judgment and has further consented to garnishment upon default, notwithstanding the terms of the agreement, no garnishment order shall issue unless:

(1) an active proceeding supplemental is pending against the judgment debtor and the garnishee defendant;

(2) the judgment debtor's employment by said garnishee defendant has been verified as set forth in TR69–4(A) on the record within three (3) months prior to the date on which judgment creditor requests issuance of the garnishment order; and

(3) the judgment creditor represents on the record the default of judgment debtor.

C. Stay. In instances where a judgment creditor has stayed a garnishment order which has been issued and served on a garnisheed defendant, said judgment creditor shall lose any priority over pending, but later issued, garnishment orders pertaining to the judgment debtor's wages.

D. Release. Upon receipt by the judgment creditor or by the Clerk on the judgment creditor's behalf of monies sufficient to fully satisfy the judgment, any accrued interest and costs, the judgment creditor shall immediately obtain a court order releasing the applicable garnishment order and shall forward a copy to the garnishee defendant(s).

Adopted as Superior Civil Rule 20, Sept. 8, 2000, effective Nov. 1, 2000. Renumbered as Superior and Circuit Civil Rule 69-4, and amended effective Dec. 7, 2006. Amended Oct. 3, 2008, effective Jan. 1, 2009.

LR02-AR Rule 00-4. Authority of Attorneys' Employees

A. In General. Generally, attorneys' employees who have not been admitted to practice law in Indiana but who assist their employers in Courthouse activities (herein called "legal assistants"), shall be limited to the performance of tasks which do not require the exercise of legal discretion or judgment that affects the legal rights of any person.

B. Trust Account Deposits. Only one legal assistant per law firm shall have the authority to obtain trust account deposits at the Allen County Clerk's Office in the name of his or her employer firm. The employer law firm shall submit a letter to the Clerk of the Allen Circuit and Superior Courts (See Appendix "B" to these rules) stating that:

1. Such employee is authorized to obtain trust account deposits at the Allen County Clerk's Office in the name of his employer; and

2. Such employer fully releases the Clerk of the Allen Circuit and Superior Courts and all employees of said Clerk of any liability for paying any such funds by check, naming said employer as payee, to any such designated employee, unless such law office has previously notified in writing the Clerk of the Allen Circuit and Superior Courts that such employee's authority to act on behalf of said law office has been terminated.

C. Legal Documents. All pleadings which the legal assistant presents or files at the Courthouse must contain an attorney's signature, as the attorney for a party, or a statement affixed indicating that the documents were prepared by said attorney.

D. Permitted Acts. Such an employee shall be limited to the following acts:

(1) To file, and obtain orders on all motions described in TR00–1(A).

(2) To set Pre–Trial Conferences and all other hearing dates except trials.

(3) To examine pleadings and chronological case summary sheets and make copies thereof within the Courthouse.

(4) At the discretion of the Court, to obtain approval of orders of the Court from the Judge's Law Clerk for:

(a) Notice of hearings

(b) Orders to appear and answer interrogatories on the filing of the Verified Motion for Proceedings Supplemental

(c) Stipulations signed and approved by all parties of record.

(d) Motions to Withdraw Appearance.

E. Acts Not Permitted. Such employee shall not have the authority to perform any acts not specified in LR02–AR00–4(D).

F. Termination of Authority. Each employer law firm shall be responsible for notifying in writing the Law Librarian of the termination or revocation of any legal assistant's authority to act on behalf of the law office as covered by this rule.

Adopted as Superior Civil Rule 21, Sept. 8, 2000, effective Nov. 1, 2000. Renumbered as Superior and Circuit Civil Rule 00-4, and amended effective Dec. 7, 2006. Amended Oct. 3, 2008, effective Jan. 1, 2009.

LR02-AR Rule 00-5. Conflicts

The Indiana Rules of Trial Procedure shall govern in the event of any conflict with the Local Rules of the Allen County Courts.

Adopted as Superior Civil Rule 22, Sept. 8, 2000, effective Nov. 1, 2000. Renumbered as Superior and Circuit Civil Rule 00-5, and amended effective Dec. 7, 2006. Amended Oct. 3, 2008, effective Jan. 1, 2009.

LR02-AR00 Rule 6. Attorney and Personal Representative Fee Guidelines for Decedents' Estates

ATTORNEY FEES–ESTATES

Preamble

The Allen Superior Court, Civil Division has adopted these guidelines in an effort to achieve the following objectives:

(A) Establish uniformity in determining a fair and reasonable fee for supervised estates;

(B) Provide a guideline to assist the Court in determining fair and reasonable fees;

(C) Furnish a guideline to attorneys so they can discuss fees that may be reasonably incurred with their clients at the onset of administration;

(D) Assist the legal profession to arrive at a fair and reasonable fee for the estate work.

Every attorney and personal representative has an obligation to request a fee which is fair and reasonable for the work performed, taking into account those provisions of the Rules of Professional Conduct applicable to attorneys admitted to practice law in the State of Indiana. Except under extraordinary circumstances, a request for fees should not exceed these guidelines. In an uncomplicated estate, fees should be less than those listed in the schedule, and fees must always bear a reasonable relationship to the services rendered.

1. **PRINCIPLES APPLICABLE TO FEE DETERMINATIONS**

Although fee guidelines have been promulgated by the Court for probate matters, it is important that your attention be directed to certain criteria as they pertain to these guidelines as follows:

(A) The time and labor required, the novelty, complexity, or difficulty of the questions involved, the skill required to perform the services properly, including a determination as to how much of the attorney's time was devoted to ministerial functions;

(B)   The nature and extent of the responsibilities assumed by the attorney and the results obtained, including the considerations of the identity of the personal representative and the character of the probate and non-probate transferred assets;

(C)   The sufficiency of assets properly available to pay for legal services, and whether the attorney's duties are expanded by the existence of non-probate assets because of their inclusion for tax purposes, both federal and state;

(D)   The timeliness with which the necessary services are performed consistent with statutory requirements, the Court's rules of procedure and applicable Rules of Professional Conduct.

Attorneys are urged to discuss their fee and that of the personal representative at the time they are retained in all probate matters.

2.   **ATTORNEY FEE GUIDELINES**

I.   **Administration:**

Gross estate services are considered to normally include: probating the Will, opening of the estate, qualifying the personal representative, preparing and filing the Inventory, paying claims, collecting assets, preparing and filing non-extraordinary petitions, preparing and filing of Fiduciary Income Tax Return, preparing and filing all tax returns and schedules, obtaining Court Orders thereon, and paying the taxes, preparing and filing the Final Report, obtaining Order approving same, distributing assets, obtaining discharge of the personal representative, and preparing and serving all notices on interested parties throughout the proceedings. This list shall not be considered to be exclusive.

(A)   Gross Estate –Minimum Fee of $500.00 Plus:
Up to $100,000. not to exceed 6%
Next $100,000. not to exceed 4%
Next $100,000. not to exceed 3%
Next $100,000. not to exceed 2%
Over $400,000. not to exceed 1%

(B)   Miscellaneous—Extraordinary Services:

(1)   Sale of Real Estate . . . . Hourly Rate.

(2)   Indiana Inheritance Tax Schedule—
(Preparation and filing only).
(To be applied only to non-administered property).
One percent (1%) of the first $100,000 of the non-administered assets of gross estate as determined for Indiana Inheritance Tax purpose, plus ¾ of 1% of the next $150,000 of non–administered assets of said gross estate.
½ of one percent (1%) on all non-administered assets of said gross estate in excess of $250,000.

(3)   Federal Estate Tax Returns—(To be applied only if return required because of non-administered property, to be based only on assets not listed on Indiana Inheritance Tax Schedule). A base fee of $750.00 or one percent (1%) of the first $100,000.00. Of the non-administered assets of the said gross estate as determined for Federal Estate Tax purposes plus: ¾ of one percent (1%) of the next $150,000. of non-administered assets of said gross estate, plus ½ of one percent (1%) on all non-administered assets of said gross estate in excess of $250,000.

(4)   Ex parte Petitions not included under I. $200.00

(5)   Other than as provided above . . . . . Hourly Rate. (Attorney's expertise in probate matters will be considered by the Court in determining the applicable hourly rate).

II.   **Wrongful Death Administration:**

The Court recognizes that in most instances a retainer or contingent fee agreement is an appropriate method by which legal services can be provided in wrongful death claims. Accordingly, fees shall be allowed under such agreements if at the time of settlement of the claim, it is shown to the Court's satisfaction:

(A)   That the personal representative was, prior to entering such agreement, fully informed as to all aspects of the arrangement.

(B)   That the agreement is fair and reasonable.

(C)   That the fee sought is fair and reasonable.

III.   **In General:**

(A)   Extraordinary Fee Requests

Fee petitions requesting extraordinary fees must set forth services rendered with specificity. Extraordinary service may include: sale of personal property, sale of real property, partial distributions, will contest actions, contesting claims, adjusting tax matters, contested hearings, petitions for instructions, heirship determinations, generating additional income for the estate, etc.

All such petitions will be set for hearing, with notice to all interested parties. If all interested parties sign a waiver and consent stating they have been advised the additional fee request exceeds the Court's guidelines and that the services as detailed are extraordinary, the Court may, in its discretion, determine if a hearing is required.
An acceptable form of waiver is attached.

(B)   Unsupervised Estates

The Court will not determine and allow fees in an unsupervised administration.

(C)   Filing of Fee Petition

Before any fee is paid a petition for allowance of such fee shall be filed and determined by the Court. A request for fees will be considered only under the following circumstances:

(1)   When the Inheritance Tax Petition is ready to be filed, or

(2)   When a petition to find no tax due has been approved, or

(3)   When necessary for purposes of an estate fiduciary income tax deduction, or

(4)   Under extraordinary circumstances.

(D)   Payment of Fees

Except where payment has been authorized under C.3 or C.4 above, fees are payable one half (1/2) upon approval of fee petition and one half (1/2) upon approval of the Final Report.

WAIVER AND CONSENT TO ALLOWANCE OF FEES IN EXCESS OF GUIDELINES

The waiver and consent is not to be merely a pro forma waiver and consent, but is to be in substantially the following form:

IMPORTANT: PLEASE READ BEFORE SIGNING!

WAIVER AND CONSENT

The undersigned, an interested party in the Estate of _____ understands that:

(A)   The maximum fee ordinarily allowed by the Court for legal services in this Estate would amount to $ _____;

(B)   The Attorney has requested fees in the amount of $ _____, alleging that extraordinary and unusual services have been performed.

The undersigned, being fully advised, now consents to the allowance of the requested fee, waives any notice of hearing on the Petition and requests that the Court allow fees in the amount of $ _____.

Dated _____   _____
                                  Devisee/Heir

3.   **PERSONAL REPRESENTATIVE FEES**

I.   **Professional:**

The Court will approve their applicable prevailing rate, provided:

(A)   Said rates are on file with and approved by the Court.

(B)   The rate results in a reasonable fee in light of all circumstances.

(C)   A description of services rendered in support of a request for fees is filed.

II.   **Non–Professional:**

Fees may be allowed not to exceed one half (1/2) the fee allowed the attorney, provided:

(A)   Said fee is reasonable in light of all circumstances.

(B)   A description of services rendered, including time spent with hourly Rate in support of said request is filed.

III.   **Attorney:**

The Court recommends that attorneys not assume the dual role of attorney and personal representative in the same estate. When the attorney does serve as the personal representative, an additional amount not to exceed one-third (1/3) of the attorney fee may be allowed, provided:

(A)   Said fee is reasonable in light of all circumstances.

(B)   A description of services rendered, including time spent with hourly rate in support of said request is filed.

IV.   **In General:**

The Court will apply the same procedures to the allowance and drawing of fees and to a personal representative's extraordinary fee request as it does to attorney fee requests.

Adopted as Superior Civil Attorney Fee Guidelines, effective Aug. 15, 1990. Renumbered as Superior and Circuit Civil Rule 6, and amended effective Dec. 7, 2006.

LR02–TR Rule 79–01. Selection of A Special Judge Pursuant to TR 79(H)

A. Appointment by Clerk.

If a special judge is not appointed pursuant to TR 79(D), the Clerk of the Court shall select a special judge (on a rotating basis) from a list consisting of judicial officers eligible under TR 79(J).

B. Certification to the Supreme Court.

In cases in which no judge is eligible to serve as special judge or the particular circumstances of a case warrant selection of a special judge by the Indiana Supreme Court, the appropriate Allen County Judge may certify the case to the Indiana Supreme Court for appointment of a special judge.

Adopted effective March 15, 2011. Amended effective Sept. 1, 2013.

APPENDICES

Appendix A.   Consent to Alternate Service

CONSENT TO ALTERNATE SERVICE

The undersigned, as an individual practitioner or for and on behalf of the law firm below, hereby consents to service of any notice, pleading, process, order or other communication by deposit of the same in an assigned Courthouse box by:

    (a) Allen Superior Court or Allen Circuit Court

    (b) Clerk, as to matter with Allen Superior Court or Allen Circuit Court;

    (c) Other Attorneys and law firms.

"Deposit" pursuant to this Consent shall constitute and be accepted as 1st class mail under Trial Rule 6(E). Any papers served under this Consent shall be placed in an envelope with the name of receiving attorney and current box number on the outside thereof. The Consent shall remain valid until revoked in writing. The Consent or revocation will be effective upon filing with the Law Librarian of Courts.

This Consent shall also apply to any attorneys who become associates with the undersigned law firm after the date of this consent.

The undersigned agree(s) to notify the Allen Superior Court Executive or Allen Circuit Court Executive promptly of any changes in the list of attorneys designated in the Consent.

DATED: _____

_____   _____
(Individual Practitioner)   (Firm Name)
                By: _____
                    Managing or Senior Partner

List of Attorneys in Law Firm Hereby Consenting:

_____   _____

_____   _____

_____   _____

_____   _____

_____   _____

_____   _____

(File with the Law Librarian in the Allen County Courthouse.)

Adopted as Superior Civil Appendix A, Sept. 8, 2000, effective Nov. 1, 2000. Renumbered as Superior and Circuit Civil Appendix A, and amended effective Dec. 7, 2006.

Appendix B.   Release of Clerk for Payment of Trust Account Deposits to the Clerk of the Allen County Superior and Circuit Courts

RELEASE OF CLERK FOR PAYMENT OF TRUST ACCOUNT DEPOSITS TO THE CLERK OF THE ALLEN COUNTY SUPERIOR AND CIRCUIT COURTS

Please be advised that _____, an employee of our law firm, is authorized to obtain trust account deposits at the Allen County Clerk's office in the name of his/her employer. The law firm fully releases the Clerk of the Allen Superior and Circuit Court and all employees, of said Clerk for paying any such funds by check, naming said employer as payee to above named employee, unless we have previously notified you in writing that such employee's authority to act on behalf of our law office has been terminated.

Law Firm Of: _____

    By: _____
           Attorney Name and #

STATE OF INDIANA, COUNTY OF ALLEN, SS:

Subscribed and sworn to before me, a Notary Public in and for said County and State, this _____ day of _____, 20 ___.

My Commission Expires: _____

_____
Notary Public

Adopted as Superior Civil Appendix B, Sept. 8, 2000, effective Nov. 1, 2000. Renumbered as Superior and Circuit Civil Appendix B, and amended effective Dec. 7, 2006.

Appendix C.   Final Pre-trial Order

FINAL PRE–TRIAL ORDER

STATE OF INDIANA	)		IN THE COURTS
	)		
	)	SS:	
COUNTY OF ALLEN	)		CASE NUMBER:
	)		
PLAINTIFF _____	)		FINAL
vs.	)		PRE–TRIAL ORDER
	)		
	)		
	)		
	)		
DEFENDANT _____	)		

The parties submit this FINAL PRE–TRIAL ORDER:

A.   Jurisdiction.

B.   Status of the Record.

C.   Motions.

D.   Discovery.

E.   Contested Issues.

F.   Stipulations. (e.g. facts, liability, damages, admissibility of dispositions, capacity of parties.)

G.   Contentions of the Plaintiff(s).

H.   Contentions of the Defendant(s).

I.   Exhibits.

    (1) Plaintiff(s) exhibits may include any or all of the following: (which have been numbered and submitted to Defendant(s) for examination):

    (2) Defendant(s) exhibits may include any or all of the following: (which have been lettered and submitted to Plaintiff(s) for examination):

    (3) The authenticity of all exhibits has been stipulated except the following:

    (4) The relevancy and materiality of all exhibits has been stipulated except for the following:

J.   Witnesses.

    (1) The names, addresses and telephone numbers of Plaintiff(s) witnesses are as follows:

    (2) The names, addresses and telephone numbers of Defendant(s) witnesses are as follows:

K.   Order.

    (1) Reasonable opportunity has been afforded counsel for corrections or additions prior to approval and signing by the Court. Subject to any corrections and additions that may be made as a result of the Status Conference with the Court, this Pre–Trial Order when filed with and approved by the Court before the commencement of the trial, shall control the course of the trial and may not be amended except by order of Court to prevent manifest injustice. All pleadings shall be deemed to be merged herein.

L.   **Settlement.**

The parties have discussed settlement and are prepared to discuss the status of settlement negotiations with the Court.

M.   **Trial.**

The trial will be to (Court) a (Jury). Length of the trial is _____ day(s). The Court has set the trial for _____.

Plaintiff(s)
By: _____

Defendant(s)
By: _____

Approved and made an Order of the Court, dated: _____

_____
Judge

Adopted as Superior Civil Appendix C, Sept. 8, 2000, effective Nov. 1, 2000. Renumbered as Superior and Circuit Civil Appendix C, and amended effective Dec. 7, 2006.

LOCAL RULES OF THE SMALL CLAIMS DIVISION OF ALLEN SUPERIOR COURT—CIVIL DIVISION

Adoptive Effective January 1, 1988

Including Amendments Received Through November 1, 2013

Research Notes

Annotations to the Local Rules of the Small Claims Division of Allen Superior Court—Civil Division are available in West's Annotated Indiana Code, *Title 34 Appendix.*

These rules may be searched electronically on Westlaw *in the IN-RULES database; updates to these rules may be found on Westlaw in IN-RULESUPDATES. For search tips and a summary of database content, consult the Westlaw Scope Screens for each database.*

LR02-SC Rule 01-1. Scope

(A) Scope. These rules shall govern the procedure and practice of the Small Claims Division, Allen Superior Court — Civil Division.

(B) Citation. These rules may be cited as LR02-SC ___. The small claims rules promulgated by the Indiana Supreme Court are hereinafter referred to as S.C. ___; and the Indiana Rules of Trial Procedure are hereinafter referred to as T.R. ___.

Adopted as Rule 1, effective Jan. 1, 1988. Amended and renumbered as Rule 01-1, Dec. 7, 2006, effective Jan. 1, 2007.

LR02-SC00 Rule 2. General Procedure

(A) Conflict of Rules. All proceedings in the Allen Superior Court, Small Claims Division shall be governed by the Small Claims Rules promulgated from time to time by the Indiana Supreme Court, and the local rules set forth herein. In instances where these local rules conflict with the rules promulgated by the Indiana Supreme Court, the latter shall control.

(B) Tender of Completed Documents and Proper Costs. Parties or their attorneys are solely responsible to tender to the Court any documents desired to be filed in complete and correct form, together with proper costs, as determined by the Clerk. Neither the Court nor the Clerk will be responsible for delays or deadlines missed due to the tender of incomplete or incorrect documents, or improper costs.

(C) Entries. Parties or their attorneys are solely responsible to secure entries on their packets from the law clerk, scheduling clerk, or Judicial Officer on the scheduled date of hearing or other activity. Packets remaining after the scheduled time for hearing or other activity will receive the entry, "No one appears", unless dismissal or judgment LR02-TR41-8 or LR02-TR60-9 is appropriate.

(D) Misplaced Packets. If parties or their attorneys are unable, after receiving assistance from the Clerk and/or Court, to locate a packet for an entry to be made, said parties or attorneys shall tender the document(s) sought to be filed or make a written record of the entry desired, which shall be initialed and dated for said purpose by any Court employee except the receptionist. No later request for a *nunc pro tunc* or other corrective entry will be considered without such supporting record.

(E) Notice Required to Obtain Court's Packets. The Clerk shall retrieve as many as three (3) packets per party or per attorney per day. Any party or attorney desiring to review more than three (3) packets in one day shall submit to the Clerk a written list of the cause numbers of the packets desired, or a completed Clerk's pull card for each packet desired, in chronological order to the Clerk at least one (1) full business day prior to the date upon which the packets are to be reviewed.

(F) Appearance by Husband or Wife. Except for hearings on proceedings supplemental or by contrary order of the Court, appearance in any cause by a party's spouse shall be considered the appearance of the party upon said spouse's representation on the record that the party and the appearing spouse are currently married and living together.

(G) Parties' Current Addresses. Notices from the Court will be sent to the parties at the most recent addresses contained in the Court's packet. The parties are therefore solely responsible to maintain their current address in all packets concerning them.

Adopted effective Jan. 1, 1988. Amended Dec. 7, 2006, effective Jan. 1, 2007.

LR02-SC Rule 00-3. Forms

(A) Court's Forms. The Court shall from time to time, and with the consultation of the Clerk, draft forms for use of litigants, the Clerk, and the Court in small claims actions.

(B) No Other Forms. Originals or photocopies of the forms described in LR02-SC00-3(A) shall be acceptable for filing. Any other form or photocopy thereof presented to the Clerk shall be accepted for filing only if such form receives prior approval of the Judicial Officer and the Civil Division of the Allen Superior Court, and in such instance, blank forms identical to that submitted and approved shall be immediately provided to the Clerk and to the Judicial Officer for future reference and comparison.

Adopted as Rule 3, effective Jan. 1, 1988. Amended and renumbered as Rule 00-3, Dec. 7, 2006, effective Jan. 1, 2007.

LR02-AR Rule 00-7. Hearing Calendars

(A) General Procedure. Upon the filing of the notice of claim, the plaintiff may schedule the first hearing of said claim on the accounts calendar or Judicial Officer's calendar.

(B) Accounts Calendar. If the notice of claim is set for first hearing on the accounts calendar, no party is expected to be prepared for trial on the merits at the first hearing, and the setting shall serve as an opportunity for the parties to meet and informally resolve their dispute. However, a party's failure to appear for first hearing on the accounts calendar may be cause for entry of default judgment or dismissal against said party.

(C) Judicial Officer's Calendars. If the notice of claim is set for first hearing on the Judicial Officer's calendar, all parties are expected to be prepared for trial on the merits at the first hearing. The parties are responsible for reserving the appropriate amount of time for trial on the Judicial Officer's calendar.

(D) Change of Calendar. At the time any continuance is granted, hearing on the cause may be rescheduled to a calendar different than the calendar on which it was originally set. However, if such a calendar change is made, the party making the calendar change shall notify the opposing party of the change.

Adopted as Rule 4, effective Jan. 1, 1988. Amended and renumbered as Rule 00-7, Dec. 7, 2006, effective Jan. 1, 2007.

LR02-TR Rule 76-1. Change of Judge

(A) General Procedure. A change of Judicial Officer shall be granted as provided by statute and by the Indiana Rules of Trial Procedure, except that the Judicial Officer of the Small Claims Division may be included on the panel named. The Court shall set a time within which the parties are to strike that does not exceed fourteen (14) days.

(B) Striking. The party filing the motion shall strike first. After the non-moving party strikes, the remaining judicial officer shall be appointed to hear the case. The case shall then be set on that officer's calendar. If a party fails to strike within the time set, said party shall not be entitled to a change of judge, or shall be subject to the Court's arbitrary assignment of the case to one of the two remaining judicial officers, as appropriate.

Adopted as Rule 5, effective Jan. 1, 1988. Amended and renumbered as Rule 76-1, Dec. 7, 2006, effective Jan. 1, 2007.

LR02-SC Rule 5-1. Counterclaims Outside Small Claims Division Jurisdiction

(A) Counterclaims in Excess of the Court's Monetary Jurisdiction. A defendant who has a counterclaim in excess of the monetary jurisdiction of the Small Claims Division who does not wish to waive the excess of the claim, must file this claim in a timely fashion as a separate action on the plenary docket of the Allen Superior Court, Civil Division, or in any other Court of competent jurisdiction. Either party may then file a motion for consolidation pursuant to T.R. 21(B) in both pending actions.

(B) Counterclaims Outside the Court's Subject Matter Jurisdiction. A defendant who has a counterclaim outside the subject matter jurisdiction of the Small Claims Division must file his claim in a timely fashion as a separate action on the plenary docket of the Allen Superior Court, Civil Division, or in any other Court of competent jurisdiction. Either party may then file a motion for consolidation pursuant to T.R. 21(B) in both pending actions.

Adopted as Rule 6, effective Jan. 1, 1988. Amended and renumbered as Rule 5-1, Dec. 7, 2006, effective Jan. 1, 2007.

LR2-TR Rule 53.5-3. Continuances

(A) General Rule. Except as provided in LR2-TR53.5-7(B) and (D) below, each party to an action may be granted one (1) continuance of right and without showing good cause. A continuance under this subsection shall not be granted within seven (7) days of the trial, unless approved by a Judicial Officer. All motions for continuances must be made in person or by the party's attorney who has filed a written appearance on behalf of said party. The party or attorney obtaining the continuance shall notify any opposing party in a timely fashion.

(B) Possession of Real Estate or Personal Property. No continuance will be granted to a defendant where the action involves the issue of possession of real estate or personal property, except on good cause shown and upon approval by a Judicial Officer.

(C) Agreed Continuance. Any action may be continued by agreement of the parties.

(D) Proceedings Supplemental. No motion for continuance of a proceedings supplemental hearing will be granted, except by agreement of the parties, or on good cause shown and upon approval by a Judicial Officer.

(E) Sanctions for Failure to Notify. Where notice of a continuance has not been timely given, the Court may assess sanctions which may include, but are not limited to, reasonable attorney's fees, lost wages and other costs for each party and necessary witness appearing due to lack of notice. Motions for sanctions shall be heard as a part of the trial on the merits.

Adopted as Rule 7, effective Jan. 1, 1988. Amended effective May 1, 1992; amended and renumbered as Rule 53.5-3, Dec. 7, 2006, effective Jan. 1, 2007.

LR02-TR Rule 41-1. Dismissal of Actions

(A) Dismissal by Plaintiff. Any claim may be dismissed by the plaintiff at any time before judgment has been entered unless a counterclaim or motion for summary judgment has been filed by a defendant.

(B) Dismissal by Stipulation. Any claim may be dismissed by filing a stipulation of dismissal signed by all parties to the claim.

(C) Dismissal by Court. The cause or any pending pleadings in the cause may be dismissed with or without prejudice upon order of the Court, including by way of illustration and not of limitation, as follows:

(1) the cause has not been reduced to judgment and where there has been no action on the case for a period of sixty (60) days; provided however, that no such cause shall be dismissed without notice and hearing; or

(2) a proceedings supplemental pleading has been filed and there is no action on the day on which the proceedings supplemental is set for hearing, or for sixty (60) days thereafter.

Adopted as Rule 8, effective Jan. 1, 1988. Amended and renumbered as Rule 41-1, Dec. 7, 2006, effective Jan. 1, 2007.

LR02-TR Rule 60-1. Default

(A) Pre-Judgment Grace Period. The Court shall permit each party a twenty (20) minute grace period to appear for any prejudgment accounts or trial calendar setting, or for any other matter not pertaining to a proceeding supplemental hearing.

(B) Default of Defendant and Default Affidavit. Upon the failure of a defendant to appear at the initial hearing or at a trial on the merits, the plaintiff(s) shall be entitled to judgment on the merits against said defendant. In addition to any other applicable requirements of Indiana law, the plaintiff or plaintiff's(s') attorney shall sign and file a completed "Affidavit for Judgment by Default" form furnished by the Court.

(C) Default of Plaintiff. Upon the failure of a plaintiff to appear at the initial hearing or at a trial on the merits, the cause shall be dismissed without prejudice and default judgment shall be entered for the defendant against the plaintiff on any timely-filed counterclaim. Upon plaintiff's failure to appear at the initial hearing or at a trial on the merits in a subsequent cause based on the same facts as the cause earlier dismissed without prejudice, said subsequent cause shall be dismissed with prejudice and default judgment shall be entered for the defendant against the plaintiff on any timely-filed counterclaim.

(D) Letter Notice for Inadequate Service. Where a plaintiff has received return of service which discloses less than ten (10) days notice to a defendant of a hearing on the Accounts Calendar or a Trial Calendar, and said defendant fails to appear for said hearing, the plaintiff shall not be entitled to entry of default. If the plaintiff wishes to proceed, the plaintiff shall notify the defendant of a new calendar setting by first class mail to the address at which service was obtained. Such notice is sufficient if said notice is sent and the hearing set so as to comply with T.R. 6 and S.C. 2.

(E) Setting Aside Default Judgment. A default judgment may be set aside according to the procedures set forth in S.C. 10(C) and T.R. 60(B). Forms for this purpose are available from the Court upon request.

(1) *Expedited Hearing.* An expedited hearing on such a motion to set aside default judgment shall be set on the Judicial Officer's calendar.

(2) *Stay of Collection Proceedings.* In any cause in which a motion to set aside default judgment has been filed, collection proceedings as to the judgment debtor filing the motion will not be stayed unless a motion to stay such proceedings is filed and granted pursuant to T.R. 62(B).

(F) Default on Proceedings Supplemental. The Court shall permit each party a thirty (30) minute grace period to appear for any proceedings supplemental hearing. After the thirty (30) minute grace period has elapsed:

(1) a judgment creditor shall be entitled to apply for appropriate proceedings supplemental sanctions; or

(2) a judgment debtor appearing for the proceedings supplemental hearing shall be entitled to leave without risk of sanction for failure to appear.

A judgment debtor so appearing is entitled to leave without risk of sanction for failure to appear even if the judgment creditor or its attorney is present for the proceedings supplemental hearing, if said judgment debtor has not been called for the proceedings supplemental interview within the grace period. However, a judgment creditor's failure to conduct the proceedings supplemental interview within the grace period shall not bar the judgment creditor from filing a garnishment order against the judgment debtor's wages if appropriate under LR02-TR69-17. For this purpose, the grace period shall begin at the time of the scheduled hearing or trial or at the time the judgment debtor registers with the Court's receptionist, whichever is later.

Adopted as Rule 9, effective Jan. 1, 1988. Amended effective May 1, 1992; amended and renumbered as Rule 60-1, Dec. 7, 2006, effective Jan. 1, 2007.

LR02-TR Rule 00-8. Attorney Fees

Evidence Required to Support Award. The amount of attorney fees awarded shall be within the sound discretion of the Court. No attorney fees shall be awarded unless:

(1) provided for by written agreement(s) between the parties; or

(2) according to applicable statute(s) or common law. Proof of such fees shall be in the form of sworn testimony from, or the affidavit of, the attorney(s) whose services are being proved.

Adopted as Rule 10, effective Jan. 1, 1988. Amended and renumbered as Rule 00-8, Dec. 7, 2006, effective Jan. 1, 2007.

LR02-TR00 Rule 9. Judgments for Payment of Money

In General. Judgments for payment of money shall be enforceable according to the Indiana Rules of Trial Procedure and applicable statutes.

Adopted as Rule 11, effective Jan. 1, 1988. Amended and renumbered as Rule 00-9, Dec. 7, 2006, effective Jan. 1, 2007.

LR02-SC Rule 2-1. Judgments for Possession of Real Estate or Personal Property

(A) Bifurcated Judgment and Expedited Hearing on Possession. Judgments in actions involving the issue of possession of real estate or personal property shall be bifurcated. The initial hearing on possession issues shall be set in an expedited setting on the Judicial Officer's calendar. A final judgment for possession of the real estate or personal property shall be entered at the initial hearing and a judgment for back rent and/or other damages, if any, shall be entered at a subsequent hearing.

(B) Notice to Tenant. Unless the landlord shall file the pleadings and bond set forth in I.C. § 32–6–1.5–1, *et seq.*, notice to a tenant shall be ten (10) days as required by S.C. 2.

(C) Disposition of Tenant's(s') Remaining Personal Property. If a tenant leaves personal property of value in or about the demised premises under circumstances which reasonably show abandonment of said personal property, the landlord may dispose of said property by:

(1) removing said property from the premises using reasonable care and storing it in a location reasonably secure from damage of any kind; and

(2) immediately notifying tenant by first class mail to tenant's last known address, with a copy thereof retained by the landlord, that the property is so stored, that storage charges (if any, but not to exceed $3.00 per day) are accruing, and that the property is available to tenant upon reasonable notice to landlord at a reasonable time for a period at least two (2) weeks from the date said letter notice is mailed to tenant. Said notice shall also contain landlord's telephone number, and an address at which, and reasonable time during which, landlord can be contacted during the two (2) week time period.

(3) If at the expiration of the two (2) week retrieval period, tenant has not contacted landlord to arrange an imminent and mutually convenient date and time for retrieval of tenant's personal property, landlord may dispose of said property in a reasonable manner, including the destruction of apparently valueless property and the private sale or donation of property of value. Proceeds from any sale and credit for any donation shall first be applied to reduce any accrued storage charges and then to reduce any alleged back rent or damages beyond normal wear and tear established by the Court.

Adopted as Rule 12, effective Jan. 1, 1988. Amended and renumbered as Rule 2-1, Dec. 7, 2006, effective Jan. 1, 2007.

LR02-SC Rule 11-1. Release of Judgment

(A) Release of Judgment. When any judgment has been fully paid and satisfied, including any interest and all costs, and the judgment creditor has received all of said monies or they are available in the Clerk's office, said judgment creditor shall immediately release the judgment against the debtor by personally executing such release on the judgment record of the Clerk, or by causing such release to be filed with the Clerk.

(B) Failure to Release Judgment. Upon a judgment creditor's failure to release a judgment allegedly fully paid and satisfied, the affected debtor may:

(1) proceed to notify the judgment creditor and file suit for penalties as set forth in I.C. § 32–8–1–2; or

(2) move on the record of the cause in which the judgment was entered to have said judgment deemed satisfied pursuant to T.R. 13(M), upon which motion notice shall issue and hearing shall be held by the Court.

(C) Release of Judgment. Upon payment in full, including accrued interest, the Clerk shall notify the judgment creditor and shall require him or her to file a Release of Judgment. If the judgment creditor fails to file a Release of Judgment within thirty (30) days of the issuance of the notice, the Clerk shall enter on the Chronological Case Summary that the judgment has been satisfied, the Plaintiff has failed to release judgment pursuant to Court directive, and the Clerk shall enter a Release of Judgment in the judgment docket. *Adopted as Rule 13, effective Jan. 1, 1988. Amended and renumbered as Rule 11-1, Dec. 7, 2006, effective Jan. 1, 2007.*

LR02-TR69 Rule 5. Proceedings Supplemental

(A) General Procedure. Proceedings supplemental to execution shall be governed by T.R. 69(E) of the Indiana Rules of Trial Procedure and applicable statutes.

(B) Ten Day Rule. A motion for proceedings supplemental may not be filed until ten (10) calendar days have elapsed since the date of judgment except by order of the Court for good cause shown.

(C) One Year Rule. Except by order of the Court for good cause shown, no proceedings supplemental may pend for more than six (6) months from the date of its filing, and no judgment creditor may file more than four (4) proceedings supplemental per year against any individual judgment debtor in a given cause. At the end of said six (6) month period, any pending proceedings supplemental shall be dismissed.

(D) Hearing. Unless a party specifically requests otherwise and sets the hearing accordingly, all hearings on proceedings supplemental will be set on the accounts calendar.

(E) Bank Interrogatories. Except by order of the Court for good cause shown, judgment creditors may not submit garnishment interrogatories to more than two (2) banking institutions for each hearing on proceedings supplemental.

(F) Conduct of Hearings. Unless the judgment creditor is represented by an attorney at the proceedings supplemental hearing, said hearing shall be conducted by an officer of the Court.

(G) Completion of Interview Forms. At each proceedings supplemental hearing, the attorney or the Court's officer conducting the hearing shall complete and file with the Court a proceedings supplemental interview form provided by the Court based on the judgment debtor's testimony at said hearing. At its completion and prior to its filing, the judgment debtor shall be given the opportunity to review and sign said form in acknowledgment of its accuracy.

(H) Proceedings Supplemental During Pendency of Garnishment Order. If a garnishment order has been issued and remains unsatisfied, additional proceedings supplemental directed to the judgment debtor or to an additional garnishee defendant may be filed only by order of the Court for good cause shown. *Adopted as Rule 14, effective Jan. 1, 1988. Amended and renumbered as Rule 5, Dec. 7, 2006, effective Jan. 1, 2007.*

LR02-TR69 Rule 6.   Court Orders to Appear

(A) General Use. Judgment creditors may request the Court to issue an order to appear (COTA) to judgment debtor(s) only when:

(1) an active proceedings supplemental is pending against the judgment debtor;

(2) the hearing date set for the COTA is within sixty (60) days of the date on which the COTA is issued; and

(3) good cause exists for the COTA and is shown on the record at the time the COTA is requested.

(B) Good Cause. "Good cause" under LR02-TR69-15(A)(3) shall include but not be limited to:

(1) the judgment debtor failed to produce documents as previously ordered by the Court;

(2) the judgment debtor has indicated intended relocation with new address presently unknown;

(3) there is a reasonable certainty that the judgment debtor's financial status will substantially change within sixty (60) days.

(C) COTAs and Garnishment Orders. When a garnishment order has issued, no pending COTA will be enforced, and no COTA will issue to the judgment debtor, except by order of the Court for good cause shown.

(D) Failure to Appear on COTA. Upon a judgment debtor's failure to appear on the date and time set by the COTA, the judgment creditor may file contempt proceedings under LR02-TR00-16.

(E) Agreements to Appear Without COTA. In any proceedings supplemental, the parties may agree to reset a hearing without use of a COTA. If after such agreement either party fails to appear at the reset hearing, the underlying proceedings supplemental shall be dismissed and no sanctions shall be available for such failure to appear.

Adopted as Rule 15, effective Jan. 1, 1988. Amended and renumbered as Rule 2-1, Dec. 7, 2006, effective Jan. 1, 2007.

LR02-TR00 Rule 10. Contempt/Rule to Show Cause/Body Attachment

(A) Contempt. Upon failure of a judgment, debtor or garnishee defendant to appear as ordered for a scheduled hearing, the judgment creditor may file a contempt citation as to said person. Said contempt citation must be filed within thirty (30) days of the failure to appear.

(B) Body Attachment. Body attachment shall be requested and issued only when:

(1) the judgment debtor or garnishee defendant previously ordered to appear for a scheduled hearing was personally served with a contempt citation and failed to appear for the contempt hearing;

(2) the request for body attachment is filed within thirty (30) days of the contempt hearing at issue; and

(3) the judgment creditor properly completes and files all pleadings and forms from time to time required by the Court. Said pleadings and forms currently include for each judgment debtor:

(a) one (1) Request for Body Attachment;

(b) at least three (3) Writs of Attachment which must include a statement setting a bond for release; (The bond amount should be set at the lesser of $500.00 or the total amount remaining unpaid on the judgment including costs and interest.)

(c) and the Warrant Information Card, including the judgment debtor's social security number or date of birth.

Adopted as Rule 16, effective Jan. 1, 1988. Amended Aug. 29, 1997, effective Oct. 1, 1997; amended and renumbered as Rule 10, Dec. 7, 2006, effective Jan. 1, 2007.

LR02-TR Rule 69-7.   Garnishment

(A) General Procedure. All garnishment proceedings shall comply with T.R. 69(E) and applicable statutes.

(B) Requirements for Garnishment Order to Issue. A garnishment order shall not issue with respect to a judgment debtor's wage or other property without:

(1) an active proceedings supplemental as to the judgment debtor or waiver of notice by said judgment debtor;

(2) service on the garnishee-defendant of the proceedings supplemental by

(a) certified mail, or refusal thereof,

(b) Sheriff's service, or

(c) private process server; and

(3) return of answered interrogatories, other verification of employment by the garnishee-defendant, or failure to answer interrogatories after notice.

(C) Voluntary Garnishments. In instances where a judgment debtor has entered a voluntary agreement for periodic payments to satisfy judgment and has further consented to garnishment upon default, notwithstanding the terms of the agreement, no garnishment order shall issue unless:

(1) an active proceeding supplemental is pending against the judgment debtor and the garnishee-defendant;

(2) the judgment debtor's employment by said garnishee-defendant has been verified as set forth in LR02-TR69-17(A) and (B) on the record within three (3) months prior to the date on which judgment creditor requests issuance of the garnishment order; and

(3) the judgment creditor represents on the record the default of judgment debtor.

(D) Stay. In instances where a garnishment order has been issued and served on a garnishee-defendant, if the judgment creditor then stays said order, said judgment creditor shall lose any priority over pending but later garnishment orders pertaining to the judgment debtor's wages.

(E) Release. Upon receipt by the judgment creditor or by the Clerk on the judgment creditor's behalf of monies sufficient to fully satisfy the judgment, and accrued interest and costs, the judgment creditor shall immediately obtain a court order releasing the applicable garnishment order and shall forward a copy to the garnishee-defendant(s).

Adopted as Rule 17, effective Jan. 1, 1988. Amended and renumbered as Rule 69-7, Dec. 7, 2006, effective Jan. 1, 2007.

LR02-TR Rule 69-8.   Post-Judgment Orders to Self-Employed and Other Judgment Debtor(s)

(A) General Procedure. Post-judgment orders to self-employed and other judgment debtors are available pursuant to T.R. 69(E) and I.C. § 34–1–44–7 upon the filing of a verified motion for proceedings supplemental by the judgment creditor.

(B) Hearing Before Judicial Officer. All motions for a court order requiring the judgment debtor(s) to apply specified or unspecified property towards the satisfaction of the judgment pursuant to T.R. 69(E)(3) or I.C. § 34–1–44–7 shall be set for hearing before the Judicial Officer.

Adopted as Rule 18, effective Jan. 1, 1988. Amended and renumbered as Rule 69-8, Dec. 7, 2006, effective Jan. 1, 2007.

LR02-TR Rule 70-1.   Writs

(A) General Procedure. Writs to enforce the Court's orders or in aid of its jurisdiction are generally available as set forth in T.R. 70(A) and Title 34 of Indiana Code.

(B) Writs of Execution for Delivery of Possession of Real Estate. Except by order of the Court for good cause shown, no writ of execution for delivery of possession of real estate shall issue before one (1) calendar week has expired after entry of the underlying judgment by the Court.

Adopted as Rule 19, effective Jan. 1, 1988. Amended and renumbered as Rule 70-1, Dec. 7, 2006, effective Jan. 1, 2007.

LR02-SC00 Rule 4.   Bankruptcy

(A) [1] **Bankruptcy of Judgment Debtor.** All Court action, including pending collection proceedings, will be stayed as to any judgment debtor:

(1) who files with the Court in each relevant action one (1) copy of the bankruptcy court's notice of relief; or

(2) whose attorney files with the Court in each relevant action a motion for stay reciting the prior filing of bankruptcy by the judgment debtor and resultant stay of all proceedings by the bankruptcy

court, including the cause number and court of the bankruptcy.

Adopted as Rule 20, effective Jan. 1, 1988. Amended and renumbered as Rule 4, Dec. 7, 2006, effective Jan. 1, 2007.

1 There is no Subd. (B) in this rule.

ALLEN CIRCUIT AND SUPERIOR COURT FAMILY LAW LOCAL RULES

Adopted Effective May 1, 2007

Including Amendments Received Through November 1, 2013

Research Notes

Annotations to the Allen County Family Law Local Rules are available in West's Annotated Indiana Code, *Title 34 Appendix.*

These rules may be searched electronically on Westlaw in the IN-RULES database; updates to these rules may be found on Westlaw in IN-RULESUPDATES. For search tips and a summary of database content, consult the Westlaw Scope Screens for each database.

LR02–TR1 Rule 700.   Application

Unless otherwise specifically provided herein, these local rules shall apply to Allen Superior and Circuit Court cases involving family law matters (DR, JP, JD, JC, JS, JM, RS and AD case file types).

Adopted effective May 1, 2007.

LR02–TR4 Rule 701.   Summons

In all relevant family law matters, the initiating party shall use a form of summons that includes all required information as set out in Trial Rule 4(c).

Adopted effective May 1, 2007.

LR02–TR3.1 Rule 702.   Appearances

In addition to that information required by Trial Rule 3.1 and 11, and specifically pursuant to Trial Rule 3.1(A)(7), all parties are required to provide the following information so that Court personnel may identify those cases that may be suitable for treatment as a Family Court Proceeding: Whether the party, the party's children, or the other parent of the party's children have pending in any jurisdiction a case involving child custody, parenting time (visitation), child support, divorce, paternity, juvenile delinquency, child abuse or neglect, domestic violence or adoption.

Adopted effective May 1, 2007.

LR02–TR3.1 Rule 703. Withdrawal of Appearance and Termination of Attorney–Client Relationship

(1) **Procedure for Withdrawal.** Unless otherwise ordered by the Court, a motion to withdraw appearance shall be in writing and filed with the Court only after the withdrawing attorney has given the client at least ten (10) days written notice of the intention to withdraw. The notice shall be sent to the client by first class mail to the client's last known address. Pursuant to Trial Rule 3.1 (E), the attorney shall certify in the motion the last known address and telephone number of the client, subject to the confidentiality provisions of Trial Rule 3.1 (A) (8) and (D). A copy of the written notice shall be filed with the motion unless another attorney has filed a written appearance on behalf of the client. After a case has been assigned to a judicial officer, any motion to withdraw appearance shall only be ruled upon by the judicial officer to whom the case has been assigned.

(2) **Contents of Notice.** Any notice of intention to withdraw shall include an explanation to the client as follows:

1. the present status of the case;

2. the date or dates of scheduled hearings and any other pending matters;

3. advice that after withdrawal of counsel, the client must keep the Court advised of the client's mailing address and telephone number.

4. the expectation of the Indiana common law that, as an unrepresented party, the client will be held to the same standard of conduct as an attorney licensed to practice in the State of Indiana; and;

5. that the client should act promptly to secure new counsel;

(3) **Automatic Withdrawal.** After the entry of a final Decree or Order that resolves all pending issues, each attorney shall be deemed to have withdrawn his or her appearance upon the occurrence of one of the following events:

(3.1) The expiration of time within which an appeal of such Decree or Order may be preserved or perfected pursuant to the Indiana Rules of Trial Procedure and/or the Indiana Rules of Appellate Procedure if no appeal is filed; or

(3.2) The conclusion of any appeal of such Decree or Order commenced pursuant to the Indiana Rules of Trial Procedure and/or the Indiana Rules of Appellate Procedure, provided the Trial Court is notified in writing that the appeal is concluded.

(4) **Subsequent Filings and Notices.** After withdrawal of an attorney's appearance made in the conformity of these rules, the service of any motion, pleading, or notice of hearing upon any party shall be made upon that party pursuant to Trial Rule 5. A copy of any pleading, motion, or notice of hearing served upon previous counsel who has withdrawn or is deemed to have withdrawn under this Rule shall be considered a matter of professional courtesy only, and is not adequate service of process on the previously represented party.

Adopted effective May 1, 2007.

LR02–TR58 Rule 704. Preparation of Stipulated Orders

(1) If the parties reach an agreement on any or all issues, the terms of that agreement shall be set out in a written document signed by the parties and/or their counsel, if any. If the State of Indiana has intervened in a case or if a guardian ad litem has been appointed in a case, the State of Indiana or guardian ad litem are parties for purposes of consistency to any such agreement. The agreement shall conspicuously inform the Court whether the hearing set upon the issue(s) (noting the date and time of the hearing) should or should not be removed from the Court calendar, or that no hearing is set upon the issue(s). The signed agreement shall be filed with the Court, submitted with a separate proposed Order that includes the relevant portions of the signed agreement in imperative form. The proposed Order shall include instructions regarding the distribution and delivery of the Order, pursuant to Trial Rule 72(D).

(2) Any party submitting a proposed Order, Decree or Marital Settlement Agreement to the Court for approval, must submit an original and at least four (4) copies of each document.

Adopted effective May 1, 2007.

LR02–TR34 Rule 705. Copying Charges for a Non–party

(1) If a non-party to a case provides documents in response to a Trial Rule 34(C) request for production of documents a charge of $.25 per page shall be presumed reasonable. If the non-party assesses a labor charge under subsection (2), the non-party may not charge for the first ten (10) pages of requested documents.

(2) A non-party may collect a $15.00 labor charge in addition to the per page charge allowed under subsection (1).

Adopted effective May 1, 2007.

LR02–TR7 Rule 706. Motions

(1) It is the responsibility of the party that files a motion to schedule the motion for hearing on the Court's calendar. If the parties agree that the Court should rule on the motion without a hearing, then the parties shall file a stipulation requesting the Court to rule on the motion without a hearing.

(2) If a motion is set for hearing, notice of the hearing shall be given within the time limits provided by Trial Rule 6(D). Any written response to a motion set for hearing shall be filed within the time limits provided in Trial Rule 5(A), unless the hearing is set

within ten days or less from the date the motion was filed, in which case the response may be filed at or before the hearing. Any other pending motion or motions may be heard at the same time as the previously scheduled motion, if time permits, and subject to notice of hearing being served on the opposing party or parties pursuant to the provisions of Trial Rule 6 (D).

Adopted effective May 1, 2007.

LR02–TR33 Rule 707. Interrogatories

(1) Interrogatories shall be tailored specifically to the cause in which they are served and numbered consecutively to facilitate response.

(2) A party who has been served with interrogatories may file a motion to strike specific interrogatories as excessive, oppressive or repetitive, after fully complying with Trial Rule 26(F). The motion shall be set for hearing and does not serve to extend the time for answering interrogatories which are not in dispute.

(3) Answers and objections to interrogatories under Trial Rule 31 or 33 shall set forth in full the interrogatories being answered or objected to immediately preceding the answer or objection.

Adopted effective May 1, 2007.

LR02–TR30 Rule 708. Opening Filed Depositions

Unless otherwise ordered by the Court, the Clerk, at any time after a deposition is filed, shall open such deposition upon request of the Court, a member of the Court's staff, or a party or his attorney, after first endorsing on the back thereof, the name of the person at whose request the deposition is opened and the date of opening.

Adopted effective May 1, 2007.

LR02–TR37 Rule 709. Resolution of Discovery Disputes

(1) The Court will strictly enforce the informal resolution of discovery disputes in accordance with Trial Rule 26(F). The Court may deny any discovery motion filed pursuant to Trial Rule 27 through 37, if the party filing the motion has not complied with the requirements of Trial Rule 26 (F).

(2) Upon strict compliance with Trial Rule 26(F), the Court may compel or limit discovery or enter any appropriate sanction, or may set the matter for hearing upon the Court's summary or other appropriate calendar.

Adopted effective May 1, 2007.

LR02–TR26 Rule 710. Financial Declaration Form

(1) **Requirement.** In all relevant family law matters, (except support matters enforced by the State), including dissolution, separation, paternity, post-decree and support proceedings (excepting provisional hearings), the parties shall simultaneously exchange Financial Declaration Forms seven (7) days prior to any hearing. The Financial Declaration Form shall be submitted to the Court during the hearing. The Financial Declaration Forms shall be in a format approved by the Court. These time limits may be amended by the Court for good cause shown.

(2) **Exceptions.** The Financial Declaration Form need not be exchanged or filed if:

(2.1) The Court approves the parties' written agreement to waive the exchange;

(2.2) The parties have executed a written agreement that settles all financial issues;

(2.3) The proceeding is one in which the service is by publication and there is no response; or,

(2.4) The proceeding is post-decree and concerns issues without financial implications.

(3) **Admissibility.** Subject to specific evidentiary challenges, the Financial Declaration Form shall be admissible into evidence during the hearing. The submission of the Financial Declaration Form shall not prohibit any other relevant discovery permitted under the Indiana Rules of Trial Procedure.

(4) **Financial Declaration –Mandatory Discovery.** The exchange of Financial Declaration Forms constitutes mandatory discovery, and Trial Rule 37 sanctions are applicable. Additionally, pursuant to Trial Rules 26 (E) (2) and (3), the Financial Declaration Form shall be supplemented if additional information becomes available.

Adopted effective May 1, 2007.

LR02–TR26 Rule 711. Provisional Orders and Modification of Support

At least three (3) business days before a scheduled hearing regarding provisional orders or modification of child support (except support matters enforced by the State), each party shall deliver to all other parties to the case the following materials:

1. Their three (3) most recent pay stubs for all employers;

2. Their most recent W–2s, 1099s, and federal income tax returns with all schedules and attachments;

3. Documentation regarding work related child care expenses;

4. Documentation regarding health insurance premiums;

5. Documentation regarding child support orders for other children;

6. Proposed Child Support Obligation Worksheets; and

7. Any exhibit or document that each party intends to submit to the Court.

Adopted effective May 1, 2007.

LR02–TR26 Rule 712. Exchange of Appraisals: Mandatory Discovery

At least sixty (60) days prior to the final hearing the parties shall exchange copies of all real estate and personal property appraisals that will be offered into evidence at the final hearing.

Adopted effective May 1, 2007.

LR02–TR47 Rule 713. Juries

If a jury is required in a family law matter, the local rules for civil practice in Allen County regarding jury practice and management shall govern.

Adopted effective May 1, 2007.

LR02–TR43 Rule 714. Exhibits

(1) After being marked for identification, exhibits, that are offered or admitted into evidence shall be placed in custody of the Court Reporter unless otherwise ordered by the Court.

(2) After a case is decided and no appeal is taken, or after all appeals are exhausted, an attorney may request in writing the return of the exhibits which are the property of their client. A detailed receipt by shall be filed by the Court Reporter evidencing the return of any exhibits. If no request is made within 90 days after the above stated period, the Court Reporter may, with Court approval, dispose of the exhibits.

Adopted effective May 1, 2007.

LR02–TR42 Rule 715. Multiplicity of Dissolution of Marriage Actions

In its discretion, the Court may continue a hearing in any action for dissolution of marriage until all other cases for dissolution of marriage pending between the same parties in any Court have been dismissed.

Adopted effective May 1, 2007.

LR02–TR58 Rule 716. Duties of Attorneys

(1) Counsel shall prepare proposed orders as may be required by the Court, such as orders granting or denying routine motions and agreements.

(2) Proposed orders and proposed findings of fact and conclusions of law shall be served upon the opposing party or counsel, consistent with Trial Rule 5.

(3) Counsel of record shall keep themselves informed of all action and filings made in all matters pending before the Court.

(4) All proposed Qualified Domestic Relations Orders (QDRO) shall be signed by all parties or their attorneys, and when possible pre-approved by the Plan Administrator. Any dispute regarding a proposed QDRO shall be set for hearing upon request of a party.

Adopted effective May 1, 2007.

LR02–TR4 Rule 717. Alternate Service

(1) This rule shall apply only to the service of papers regarding matters under the jurisdiction of the Court.

(2) All notices, orders, pleadings, process, or other communications from the Court or Clerk to attorneys shall be deemed served upon deposit in the box assigned to said attorney, provided a consent to such alternate service is on file with the Court Executive/Administrator.

(3) All notices, orders, pleadings, process or other communication between attorneys may be served by deposit in the box assigned to the receiving attorney, provided a consent to such alternate service is on file with the Court Executive/Administrator.

(4) Such alternate service shall constitute and be accepted as personal service.

(5) Trial Rule 6(E) shall apply to all alternate service allowing the receiving party a three day time extension for response or compliance thereto.

Adopted effective May 1, 2007.

LR02–FL00 Rule 718. Attorney Fees

(1) All requests for attorney fees shall be presented to the Court by way of affidavit or oral testimony, as the Court allows. The affidavit shall be admitted into evidence subject to cross-examination. In addition, the affidavit shall have attached to it a billing statement which includes an itemization of services, the total fee for the services, payments received for the services, and the account balance.

(2) In assessing preliminary attorney fee awards, the Court may determine the award by comparing the gross incomes of the respective parties and such other financial and non-financial matters as the Court deems appropriate.

(3) An award of additional preliminary attorney fees, expert witness fees, and similar expenses may be granted upon proof of extensive discovery, significant negotiations, preparation of more than the usual number of documents, the preparation for or the conduct of contested preliminary matters or final hearings, the complexity of the case, or other factors necessitating such an award.

(4) The Court may enter an order making funds available for payment of preliminary attorney fees, while reserving for trial whether such an order represents either an award against a party or advancement in favor of the requesting party.

(5) In contempt matters where attorney fees are requested, counsel shall provide the Court with appropriate evidence of time, services and value rendered as part of the fee request. Said evidence may be made by affidavit.

Adopted effective May 1, 2007.

LR02–TR65 Rule 719. Temporary Restraining Orders

(1) Temporary Restraining Order–Marital Property

Upon the filing of a verified petition for dissolution of marriage or verified petition for legal separation, the Court will issue the following temporary restraining order with respect to marital property:

Petitioner and Respondent are both enjoined from transferring, encumbering, concealing, selling or otherwise disposing of any joint property of the parties or asset of the marriage except in the usual course of business or for the necessities of life, without the written agreement of both parties or the permission of the Court.

(2) Temporary Restraining Order–Relocation of Children

Upon the filing of a verified petition for dissolution of marriage or verified petition for legal separation, the Court will issue the following temporary restraining order with respect to the relocation of children from the marriage:

Petitioner and Respondent are both enjoined from removing any child of the parties then residing in the State of Indiana from the State with the intent to deprive the Court of jurisdiction over such child without the prior written consent of all parties or the permission of the Court.

(3) Preparation Of Temporary Restraining Order

At the time if the filing of a verified petition for dissolution of marriage or verified petition for legal separation, Petitioner or Petitioner's counsel shall submit to the Court a proposed temporary restraining order for issuance by the Court. The proposed order shall be in a format that has been approved by the Court.

(4) Request for Hearing

Any party may file a motion for modification or termination of a temporary restraining order issued by the Court pursuant to this Rule. A motion for modification or termination of a temporary restraining order will be given an expedited hearing by the Court.

Adopted effective May 1, 2007.

LR02–TR65 Rule 720. Motions Alleging Emergencies

(1) Trial Rule 65(B)(1) and (2), and current case law, including *In Re: Anonymous*, 726 N.E.2d 566 (Ind. 2005), shall govern all motions alleging an emergency where Court action is sought without notice. Strict construction and application of Trial Rule 65(B) shall be required.

(2) Emergency relief may also be sought upon notice. The Court will review such motions and may set them upon summary hearing or other expedited calendar.

Adopted effective May 1, 2007.

LR02–TR65 Rule 721. Orders For Protection

(1) A Petition For An Order For Protection And Request For A Hearing shall be filed in the Allen Superior Court Small Claims Division.

(2) Pursuant to I.C. 34–26–5–6 (4), If a person who petitions for an ex parte order for protection also has a pending case involving:

1. the respondent; or

2. a child of the petitioner and respondent;

the Court that has been petitioned for relief shall immediately consider the ex parte petition and then transfer the Protective Order case to the Court in which the other case is pending.

(3) The Protective Order cause of action shall be maintained with the pending JP, DR, JC, JT, JS, JM, RS or JD cause of action. However, the cases are not consolidated.

(4) All pleadings, hearings, and orders pertaining to a Protective Order shall be in the Protective Order cause of action. An attorney who also represents a party in a related Family Law case must file a separate written appearance in the Protective Order case.

Adopted effective May 1, 2007.

LR02–TR16 Rule 722. Case Management

(1) An initial Case Management Conference (CMC) shall be set in every case where at least one-half day of trial is sought. When either party requests a Case Management Conference, the CMC shall typically be scheduled to occur within 30 days of the request. Absent leave of Court, trial dates for those matters of at least one-half day will not be assigned until after the CMC is held and after mediation had occurred. Trial dates for such cases will be assigned at a Pre Trial Conference (PTC).

(2) At the Case Management Conference, the Court will address and very likely order mediation, discuss family law arbitration, inquire of the matters at issue, discuss discovery, and schedule a Pre Trial Conference. Absent leave of Court, mediation must occur before the PTC is conducted.

(3) Should the case not be resolved at mediation, then at the PTC, the Court will inquire of the matters at issue, schedule primary and/or secondary trial dates, schedule a Final PTC, and establish discovery and other deadlines.

(4) Hearings requiring less than one-half day may be set upon request without a CMC. However, if the case involves matters where mediation is required regardless of the length of the hearing, such as one involving any issue concerning parenting time (e.g., parenting time modification, custody modification, contempt regarding parenting time, child support modifi-

cation where the number of overnights is at issue) mediation must occur prior to the hearing unless prior leave of Court is otherwise obtained. When mediation is required for hearings of less than one-half day, the moving party shall also file a motion for mediation prior to, or with the notice of hearing.

(5) Case Management Conferences may be set in any matter and at any procedural phase if helpful to assist the parties and the Court in efficient management of the case. Parties represented by counsel need not personally appear at the CMC or PTC unless otherwise ordered by the Court. The party requesting the CMC shall submit a "Notice of Case Management Conference" (similar to a Notice of Hearing) when requesting the date for the CMC.

(6) Cooperative Divorce. Parties formally engaging in the Cooperative Divorce process shall be provided priority settings for Case Management Conferences and will be afforded other such procedural assistance as appropriate to assist in expediting their cooperative process.

Adopted effective May 1, 2007.

LR02–TR73 Rule 723. Hearings

(1) Hearings will be limited to the time scheduled on the calendar, and it shall be the responsibility of the moving party to ensure adequate time is reserved for the completion of the hearing. Should the parties be unable to complete the hearing within the scheduled time, the hearing will be continued and reset on the calendar, unless otherwise directed by the Court. In the event a party files subsequent motions after the matter is set for hearing, the subsequent motions will be heard only if time permits. If time does not permit the subsequent motions to be heard, the motions shall be reset.

(2) Not all family relations hearings are electronically recorded. It is the parties' responsibility to request an electronic recording if they desire the same. Absent such a request, the recording might not be made.

(3) At a hearing for provisional orders, a party may elect to present evidence in a summary manner or by direct testimony. If evidence is presented in a summary manner, then the party presenting the evidence shall be sworn under oath and verify the representations made by counsel. The rules of evidence with respect to hearsay shall apply unless waived by the parties. If an attorney makes a representation by an individual who is not a party during a summary presentation of evidence, that individual must be present to verify the statement. At a provisional order hearing each party shall be allotted one-half of the total hearing time, with the initiating party having the right to reserve a portion of their allotted time for rebuttal.

(4) Protective Order hearings shall not be heard in summary manner absent leave of Court. However,

Protective Order hearings must be concluded in the time allotted. The Court may set parameters to ensure the timely conclusion of the hearing.

(5) Subject to approval by the Court, the parties by agreement may present evidence at any hearing in a summary manner consistent with the procedures used for a provisional orders hearing.

Adopted effective May 1, 2007.

LR02–TR53.5 Rule 724. Continuances

A Motion to Continue a hearing, unless made orally at the commencement of a trial, shall be in writing, shall state with particularity the grounds, shall recite whether the other party objects or consents to the motion, and shall be verified, and shall be served upon opposing counsel or pro se party. When opposed, such motion shall be scheduled on the calendar by the moving party for argument. If the verified motion provides that the date of the hearing sought to be continued was not cleared on the calendar of all attorneys of record at the time of scheduling, the motion may be granted without a hearing.

Adopted effective May 1, 2007.

LR02–FL00 Rule 725. Appointment and Duties of Guardian Ad Litems in DR and JP Cases

(1) **Definition of Guardian Ad Litem.** An individual appointed by the Court pursuant to I.C. 31–15–6–1; I.C. 31–17–6–1 or by Order of the Court. See Also I.C. 31–9–2–50.

(2) **Appointment.** When the Court is required by statute, or when the Court, in its discretion, finds that it is appropriate to do so, the Court shall appoint a guardian ad litem. The guardian ad litem shall be a party to the proceeding.

(3) **Duties.** The guardian ad litem's duties shall include:

(3.1) Performance of all duties required by law, which include to represent and protect the best interests of the child(ren); and

(3.2) When possible, submit a written report of the guardian ad litem's findings and recommendations to the Court prior to the matter being heard by the Court. The attorneys and pro se litigants shall receive a copy of the report in accordance with Trial Rule 5.

(4) **Fees.** All guardian ad litem fees must be submitted to the Court for approval. The Court may order the parties to pay a retainer to the guardian ad litem to be held in trust pending approval of guardian ad litem fees. The amount of the retainer and allocation of payment between the parties shall be determined by the Court based upon all relevant factors. The Court may order an additional retainer or fees to be paid by the parties to the guardian ad litem during the pendency of the case, and the Court may reallocate the parties' share of the total guardian ad litem

fees at the conclusion of the case or other appropriate time.

(5) Term of Service. The guardian ad litem shall serve until discharged by Court order. The guardian ad litem may at anytime petition for removal from service. The parties may also petition for removal of the guardian ad litem. It shall be within the Court's discretion whether just cause exists for such removal.

Adopted effective May 1, 2007.

LR02–TR35 Rule 726. Custodial Evaluation

(1) When a custodial evaluation is ordered by the Court, the Court shall direct the parties to fully cooperate with the custodial evaluator, and contact the custodial evaluator to arrange for the evaluation appointment(s).

(2) A custodial evaluator shall be deemed to be appointed pursuant to I.C. 31–17–2–10, unless otherwise ordered by the Court.

Adopted effective May 1, 2007.

LR02–FL00 Rule 727. Adoption of Family Court Rules

Adoption of Family Court Rules of the Indiana Supreme Court are adopted as a whole by the Allen Superior Court and the Allen Circuit Court and shall be applicable to all cases designated as a Family Court Proceeding in the Family Court. Cases pending before the Allen Superior Court Criminal Division are not bound by Family Court Rules.

Adopted effective May 1, 2007.

LR002–FL00 Rule 728. Family Court Definitions

(1) **Family Court.** "Family Court" is the court or courts before which cases involving a family or household are linked together for purposes of case coordination. The individual cases maintain their separate integrity and separate docket number, but may be given a common Family Court designation. The individual cases may all be transferred to one judge, or may remain in the separate courts in which they were originally filed.

(2) **Family Court Proceeding.** A "Family Court Proceeding" is comprised of the individual cases of the family or household which have been assigned to Family Court.

Adopted effective May 1, 2007.

LR02–FL00 Rule 729. Exercise Of Jurisdiction

With the consent of the judge presiding over each affected case, the Family Court may exercise jurisdiction over any case involving the family at the same time it exercises jurisdiction over a juvenile case (Child In Need of Services, Delinquency, Status, and Paternity) involving the family.

Adopted effective May 1, 2007.

LR02–FL00 Rule 730. Concurrent Hearings

With the consent of the judge presiding over each affected case, the Family Court may, in the Court's discretion, set hearings on related cases to be heard concurrently, take evidence on the related cases at these hearings, and rule on the admissibility of evidence for each cause separately as needed to adequately preserve the record for appeal. This rule applies only when the cases are pending before the same judicial officer.

Adopted effective May 1, 2007.

LR02–FL00 Rule 731. Designation of Family Court and Change of Judge for Cause

(1) Once notice is sent to the parties that a case has been selected for Family Court, no motion for change of venue from the judge may be granted except to the extent permitted by Indiana Trial Rule 76.

(2) Within ten (10) days after notice is sent that a case has been selected for Family Court, a party may object for cause to the Family Court designation.

(3) A motion for change of venue from the judge in any matters arising in the Family Court proceeding or any future cases joined in the Family Court Proceeding after the initial selection of cases, shall be granted only for cause.

(4) If a special judge is appointed, all current and future cases in the Family Court Proceeding may be assigned to the special judge.

Adopted effective May 1, 2007.

LR02–FL00 Rule 732. Judicial Notice and Access to Records

(1) **Notice of Case Assignment.** Within a reasonable time after a case is assigned to Family Court, the Court shall provide to all parties in the Family Court proceeding a list of all cases that have been assigned to that Family Court proceeding.

(2) **Judicial Notice.** Any Court having jurisdiction over a case assigned to Family Court may take judicial notice of any relevant orders or Chronological Case Summary (CCS) entry issued by any Indiana Circuit, Superior, County, or Probate Court. If a Court takes judicial notice of: a Court order, the Court shall provide a copy of that Court order; or a CCS or CCS entry(s), the Court shall provide a copy of the entire CCS. The Court shall provide copies of the order or CCS to the parties to the case at or before the time judicial notice is taken.

(3) **Access to Records** Parties to a Family Court Proceeding shall have access to all cases within the Family Court Proceeding, with the exception of confidential cases or records to which they are not a party. Parties may seek access to the confidential cases or records in another case within the Family Court Proceeding in which they are not a party, by written petition based on relevancy and need. Confidential records shall retain their confidential status and the

Family Court shall direct that confidential records not be included in the public record of the proceedings.

Adopted effective May 1, 2007.

LR02–FL00 Rule 733. Alternative Dispute Resolution

(1) If a case pending before the Court involves parenting time issues, the Indiana 'Parenting Time Guidelines require mediation unless otherwise ordered by the Court.

(2) In all family relations cases the parties shall participate in mediation prior to scheduling any matter requiring a hearing of one half day or longer, unless otherwise ordered by the Court.

(3) Consistent with A.D.R. Rule 2.2, any party may file a motion for mediation at any time.

(4) The parties are encouraged to stipulate to the selection of a mediator. If the parties are unable to do so, the Court shall appoint the mediator, or the Court shall name a panel of three from the Court's approved mediation list, from which the parties shall strike, with the moving party striking first, and the entire selection process to be completed within 30 days.

(5) The Indiana Rules for Alternate Dispute Resolution shall apply in all respects to all family law mediation.

(6) Unless otherwise agreed by the parties, or ordered by the Court, the mediator's fee shall be allocated between the parties on a income shares model basis. In the event of settlement within three (3) days of the scheduled mediation date, the mediator may charge a fee for two (2) hours of time. Each party shall pay their portion of the mediation fees and costs within thirty (30) days after the close of mediation. If a party fails to appear for the mediation or fails to participate in good faith during mediation, the entire cost of the mediation may be assessed against that party.

Adopted effective May 1, 2007.

LR02–FL00 Rule 734. Pending Criminal Domestic Violence Litigation Disclosure

Prior to any hearing or within thirty (30) days after service of a petition seeking relief in a family law matter, whichever shall first occur, each party shall file a written disclosure of any criminal proceedings pending against them as well as any pending civil proceedings in which allegations of spousal abuse, child abuse or domestic violence have been made against either or both parties. The written disclosure shall include the name and location of the Court in which the case is pending, the case number, the names of the parties involved and a brief summary of the nature and procedural status of the other legal proceeding.

Adopted effective May 1, 2007.

LR02–FL00 Rule 735. Transitional and Problem Solving Parenting Classes

It is in the best interest of minor children for the Court to encourage cooperation and conciliation between parents. In all dissolution of marriage and legal separation proceedings involving children under the age of seventeen (17) years, each party shall be ordered to attend Court approved educational programs which are designed to teach effective parenting and parent communication skills unless Court waives the request upon good cause being provided to the Court.

In all paternity proceedings involving children under the age of seventeen (17) years, each party may be ordered to attend Court approved educational programs which are designed to teach effective parenting and parent communication skills. Each party who has been ordered to attend such a program must file a Certificate of Completion with the Court.

Information concerning the name and location of the Court approved organizations providing these classes can be obtained from the Court.

Failure to comply with this rule may subject the non-complying party to Contempt of Court proceedings and other appropriate sanctions.

Adopted effective May 1, 2007.

LR02–JV00 Rule 736. Children in Need of Services—Preliminary Inquiry Hearings

Procedure—In all cases in which the court is to determine whether to authorize a petition, the court shall conduct a hearing to consider the preliminary inquiry and evidence of probable cause to believe a child is a child in need of services. If probable cause is found and a petition is authorized, the court shall schedule an Initial Hearing and order the parties to participate in facilitation. From the evidence and reports presented the court shall:

Enter an order for the detention of the child or to release the child to the child's parent, guardian or custodian under the supervision of the Department of Child Services;

Consider and determine whether to enter a provisional order for the care, treatment and rehabilitation of the child, the parent, guardian, and/or custodian;

Determine whether the child and/or the parent, guardian, and/or custodian should be ordered to complete a mental health assessment and or psychological evaluation;

Determine whether the child and/or the parent, guardian, and /or custodian should be referred for services through the court's Mental Health Specialty Track; and,

Enter findings as to whether the state has made reasonable efforts to prevent the removal of the child from the home or whether exigent circumstances precluded the opportunity to provide services to the parent, guardian or custodian.

Facilitation—At the court's discretion, the court may order that a preliminary hearing be first addressed in facilitation in the manner as set forth herein.

Adopted effective May 1, 2007.

LR02–JV00 Rule 737. Children in Need of Services—Facilitation of Initial Hearings and Dispositional Hearings

Facilitation—Immediately preceding the Initial Hearing on a petition to adjudicate a child to be a child in need of services, or at a time otherwise directed by the court, a facilitation shall be conducted.

Facilitation defined—Facilitation is a confidential process in which a neutral third person, appointed by the court, acts to encourage and to assist the parties in achieving a non-adversarial resolution to the allegations set forth in the petition alleging the child to be a child in need of services. The facilitator assists the parties in problem identification and resolution. During the facilitation process, the parties may agree to orally amend the allegations of the petition and the terms of the proposed plan for parent participation. The facilitator will assist the parties in resolving issues regarding the child's placement; the plan for visitation by the parent, guardian, and/or custodian; the responsibilities, duties and requisite services for the family's care, treatment and rehabilitation; the roles of other individuals in the family's rehabilitation; and other matters relative insuring the child's protection and best interests.

Participants to the facilitation—The parent, guardian, and/or custodian; the attorney representing the parent, guardian, and or custodian; the guardian ad litem or court appointed special advocate; the county Department of Child Services shall participate in the facilitation process. The child shall attend the facilitation if the child's guardian ad litem or court appointed special advocate believes it is in the child's best interests to attend and believes the child to be of suitable age and maturity to participate. The child's relatives; the foster parent; persons providing support for the parent, guardian or custodian; and/or other persons who have significant or caretaking relationships to the child may be in attendance at the facilitation unless excluded by the court. Facilitations are not otherwise open to the public except as may be approved by the court for the purposes of training or research.

Facilitation Procedure—All cases pending an Initial Hearing shall be first submitted for facilitation.

All parties are required to mediate the issues in good faith but are not compelled to reach an agreement.

The facilitator shall first determine whether the parties named in the petition have been apprised of their rights. Any request for the appointment of pauper counsel shall be completed in writing on a form prescribed by the court and submitted to a judge or magistrate for a ruling prior to the start of the facilitation.

The facilitator shall explain the process and identify the issues that are to be discussed in facilitation.

Each allegation of the petition alleging the child to be a child in need of services shall be reviewed. Parties shall be given an opportunity to explain their position with regard to each allegation. Where appropriate and, by agreement of the parties, the allegation may be amended.

Once the petition is facilitated, the facilitator shall assist the participants in determining the nature and types of services in which the child or parent, guardian, custodian, or other person should be required to participate. Agreements reported to the court following facilitation must be based on the autonomous decisions of the parties and not the decisions of the facilitator.

The facilitator shall orally present the facilitation report to the court at the Initial Hearing and, if appropriate, the Dispositional Hearing. The report shall include a recitation of the parties' respective admissions and denials to the allegations of the petition, the parties' agreement for provisional orders, parent participation plan and/or dispositional decree and a statement of unresolved issues.

At the Initial Hearing, the court will confirm with the parties and the participants the terms of the facilitated agreement. The court may adopt the parties' agreement as orders of the court if it determines the agreement is in the best interests of the child. Issues that are not resolved through facilitation or not adopted as an order of the court may be referred back by the court for additional facilitation, may be resolved by order of the court based on a summary presentation, or may be scheduled by the court for a subsequent hearing or fact finding.

The rules of evidence do not apply in facilitation.

Termination of Facilitation

The facilitator may terminate facilitation whenever the facilitator believes that continuation of the process would harm or prejudice the child or one or more of the parties. The facilitator may bifurcate the process whenever the facilitator determines that due to a party's history of domestic violence would impede another party's ability to openly discuss issues should the other person be present.

Confidentiality

Statements and issues discussed in facilitation are confidential and may not be used as statements against interest or otherwise against a party in any Initial Hearing, fact finding, or pending or impending civil or criminal trial unless consent by the declarant is given. Facilitators shall not be subject to process requiring the disclosure of any matter discussed during the facilitation, but rather, such matter shall be considered confidential and privileged in nature. The confidentiality requirement may not be waived by the parties, and an objection to the obtaining of testimony or physical evidence from facilitation may be made by any party or by the facilitators.

Qualification of Facilitators

All facilitators shall be appointed by the court. In determining the appointment of a facilitator, the court may require the following training to be completed:

A series of court-approved classes or seminars on the principles of Family Group Decision Making and/or dependency mediation as offered by the court, the American Humane Association, model courts designated by the National Council of Juvenile and Family Court Judges; or dependency mediation courses that may be offered by the Association of Family and Conciliation Courts;

Classes or seminars on the law governing children in need of services;

Classes or seminars on issues related to poverty, racial and cultural diversity, strength based practices, and positive youth development; and,

In addition to the foregoing, the court may require a facilitator to complete Alternative Dispute Resolution training as set forth in Alternative Dispute Resolution Rule 2.5

Appointment of Pauper Counsel

Any party requesting appointment of pauper council in any case shall complete a questionnaire prescribed by the court that requests information regarding the applicant's employment, earnings, financial resources, education, training, age, family composition, disabilities, or other information necessary for the court to consider the applicant's eligibility for the appointment of pauper counsel. After considering the complexities of the factual and legal issues in this case, the likelihood of the applicant's ability to prevail on the merits of the case, the ability of the applicant to investigate and present the applicant's claims and/or defenses without an attorney, and the opportunity for facilitation/mediation, the court will enter findings and order that determines whether the applicant is indigent and whether the applicant has sufficient means to defend or prosecute the case. Based on its findings, the court may appoint pauper counsel who will be fully or partially compensated by the court. The court may require the applicant to pay and be responsible for all or part of the pauper counsel's fees.

Attorney Guardian ad Litem and Pauper Counsel Fees –

Services by attorneys appointed by the court to serve as pauper counsel or as a guardian ad litem shall be deemed quasi pro bono and shall be paid upon submission of a claim for services as restricted by the court's fee schedule. The fee schedule will be based upon an hourly fee as set forth in the court's order of appointment. With the exception of costs of copying and postage, any fees or costs not set out in the fee schedule must be pre-approved by the court. By acceptance of appointment, the court appointed counsel agrees to abide by the fee schedule established by the court and further agrees to timely submit all claims for payment. Claims for payment should be submitted on the day services are rendered unless other arrangements are made with the court. Any claims for fees not submitted within thirty (30) days from the date the services were rendered will be deemed waived and such services will be regarded as rendered entirely pro bono.

Adopted effective May 1, 2007.

LR02–DR00 Rule 738.   Adoptions

(1) A final hearing shall be scheduled by the Court on its own motion or at the requests of any party only after the Court has examined the court file and determined that all conditions precedent to finalization have been met.

(2) All other adoption matters shall be disposed of in accordance with the Indiana Rules of Trial Procedure and the applicable Indiana Code.

Adopted effective May 1, 2007.

LR02–JV00   Rule   739. ALLEN   SUPERIOR COURT PATERNITY PROCEDURES:

(1) All Superior Court paternity filings shall be filed at the Allen County Juvenile Center.

(2) The Court may order the State of Indiana to file all its paternity pleadings within the existing case management system of the Allen County Juvenile Center.

(3) The child must always be a party. Each child must be listed on their own Verified Petition and the caption should reflect the child's full legal name, by next friend.

(4) Prior to a paternity trial, the Court may order all parties to submit to DNA testing. In the event of DNA exclusion, the court may assess the costs of DNA testing to the Petitioner.

(5) In the event that custody or parenting time issues are presented for Court consideration, the Court on its own motion or on the motion of any party, may order a party to submit to a parenting inventory, skill, risk, and/or needs assessment.

Adopted May 1, 2007.

LR02–JV00 Rule 740. JUVENILE DELINQUENCY PROCEEDINGS:

(1) The Court may order the State of Indiana and the Office of the Public Defender to file its pleadings within the existing case management system of the Allen County Juvenile Center.

(2) If a child is detained in secure detention, a Probable Cause and Detention Review shall be conducted within 48 hours, including weekends and holidays.

Adopted effective May 1, 2007.

JOINT LOCAL RULE OF THE ALLEN CIRCUIT AND SUPERIOR COURTS FOR THE APPOINTMENT OF SPECIAL JUDGES

Adopted Effective October 1, 1995

Including Amendments Received Through November 1, 2013

Research Notes

Annotations to the Joint Local Rule of the Allen Circuit and Superior Courts for the Appointment of Special Judges are available in West's Annotated Indiana Code, Title 34 Appendix.

These rules may be searched electronically on Westlaw *in the* IN-RULES *database; updates to these rules may be found on* Westlaw *in* IN-RULESUPDATES. *For search tips and a summary of database content, consult the Westlaw Scope Screens for each database.*

Rule
LR02-AR00 Rule 9. Appointment of Special Judges

LR02-AR00 Rule 9. Appointment of Special Judges

(A) In the event a regular Judge or any court in Allen County disqualifies himself or herself from a ease, other than a felony or misdemeanor case, under Trial Rule 79(C) or in the event a special judge, selected pursuant to the provisions of Trial Rule 79(1)), (El, or (F)[1], refuses or fails to accept his or her appointment as special judge, then the regular judge of the Allen Circuit Court or Allen Superior Court before whom the case is pending shall appoint at random from those eligible judges set forth below a special judge to thereafter preside over the case, subject to the limitations and procedures set forth in Trial Rule 79(1)[2].

(B) Unless they have previously served in the case, those judges subject to such random selection as special judges in cases, exclusive of felony and misdemeanor eases, shall be:

1. The regular Judge of the Allen Circuit Court

2. The four (4) regular Judges of the Allen Superior Court

3. The two (2) regular judges of the Allen Superior Court-Family Relations Division.

4. The regular Judge of the DeKalb Circuit Court

5. The regular Judge of the Huntington Circuit ('(Silt[3]

6. The regular Judge of the Huntington Superior Court

7. The regular Judge of the Whitley Circuit Court

8. The regular Judge of the Whitley Superior Court

9. The regular Judge of the Noble Circuit Court

10. The regular Judge of the Noble Superior Court

11. The regular Judge of the Noble County Court

(C) Upon such selection and appointment, the new special judge and parties to the litigation shall be promptly notified by the judge before whom the case was pending.

(D) In the event none of the judges listed in Paragraph B of this Local Rule is eligible to serve as special judge in the case or special circumstances of the ease warrant selection of a special judge by the Indiana Supreme Court pursuant to Trial Rule 79(K), the judge before whom the case is pending shall promptly certify that fact to the Indiana Supreme Court.

(E) This Rule shall be effective October 1, 1995.

(F) This Rule shall not apply to the selection, assignment or reassignment of special judges in felony and misdemeanor cases in Allen County. The assignment and reassignment of judges as special judges in felony and misdemeanor cases in Allen County shall be governed by the joint Local Rule of the Allen Circuit and Superior Court Criminal Division as approved by the Indiana Supreme Court on July 27, 1995.

Adopted effective Oct. 1, 1995. Renumbered as Rule 9, and amended effective Dec. 7, 2006.

[1] So in original. Should probably read: "Trial Rule 79(D), (E), or (F)".

[2] So in original. Should probably read: "Trial Rule 79(D)".

[3] So in original. Should probably read: "Huntington Circuit Court".

LOCAL CRIMINAL RULES OF THE ALLEN SUPERIOR & CIRCUIT COURT

Effective January 1, 1995

Including Amendments Received Through November 1, 2013

Research Notes

Annotations to the Local Criminal Rules of the Allen Superior & Circuit Court are available in West's Annotated Indiana Code, Title 34 Appendix.

These rules may be searched electronically on Westlaw in the IN-RULES database; updates to these rules may be found on Westlaw in IN-RULESUPDATES. For search tips and a summary of database content, consult the Westlaw Scope Screens for each database.

LR02-TR Rule 81-1.   Scope of the Rules

These rules are adopted pursuant to the authority of Indiana Rules of Trial Procedure, T.R. 81, and are intended to supplement those rules as well as the Indiana Rules of Criminal Procedure. They shall govern the practice and procedure in all cases in the Courts, Criminal Division, and shall be construed to secure the just, speedy and efficient determination of every action.

Adopted as Superior Criminal Rule 1, effective Jan. 1, 1995. Renumbered as Superior and Circuit Criminal Rule 81-1, and amended effective Dec. 7, 2006.

LR02–CR Rule 2.2–1.   Assignment of Criminal Cases

Pursuant to CR 2.2 Effective January 1, 2005, Criminal cases filed in Allen County, Indiana shall be before the Court herein designated as follows:

(A) Original Assignments–Charged by Information.

1.   All Criminal cases filed by information, charging an offense of:

a) Operating a Motor Vehicle With Lifetime Suspension, a Class C Felony, I.C. 9–30–10–17;

b) Operating While Intoxicated, a Class D felony, I.C. 9–30–5–3;

c) Operating Vehicle as Habitual Traffic Violator, a Class D felony I.C. 9–30–10–16;

d) Criminal Non–Support of Dependents, I.C. 35–46–1–5 through I.C. 35–46–1–7; shall be filed before the Allen Circuit Court.

2.   All other criminal cases, filed by Information, other than those filed before the Allen Circuit Court pursuant to Paragraph 1 above, shall be filed in the Allen Superior Court, Criminal Division.

3.   Unless pendent to a felony, all misdemeanors shall be filed in the Misdemeanor and Traffic Division of the Allen Superior Court, Criminal Division.

4.   Within the Allen Superior Court, Criminal Division, felony offenses shall be filed as follows:

a) Two (2) Judges shall preside over all Murder, Class A, B and C felonies, excluding Drug cases.

b) One (1) Judge shall preside over all Class D Felonies, and over all Drug cases not assigned to the Drug Court Intervention Program.

5.   Designation of Judges to the categories, referred to in Section 4(a) & (b), shall be by Order of the Judges of the Allen Superior Court, Criminal Division, to be made on or before May 1, 1995 and annually prior to January 1 each year thereafter.

(B) Original Assignment–Indictment By Grand Jury. All criminal prosecutions, investigated and by True Bill returned as a Grand Jury indictment, shall be filed in the respective Criminal Courts of Allen County as provided in Paragraph A above.

(C) Assignment By Transfer. Transfers of cases may be made between the Allen Circuit Court and the Allen Superior Court, Criminal Division, at the discretion of and with the consent of respective Judges of said Courts to accommodate the respective work load of said judges. Said transfers shall be made pursuant to I.C. 33–33–2–25 and I.C. 33–33–2–26.

Transfers of individual cases may be made among Judges of the Allen Superior Court, Criminal Division, at the discretion of and with the consent of said Judges to accommodate the respective work loads of said Judges.

(D) Assignment by Change of Venue [CR 12(B)]. In the event of disqualification, recusal, or other change of Judge, the case shall be reassigned in random order in equal numbers to one of the Judges exercising Felony or Misdemeanor jurisdiction in Allen County. A Judge who previously served in the case is not eligible for reassignment.

In the event no Judge is available for reassignment of a Felony or Misdemeanor case, such case shall be certified to the Indiana Supreme Court for the appointment of a Special Judge. In the event the Judge presiding in a Felony or Misdemeanor case concludes that the unique circumstances presented in such proceeding require appointment by the Indiana Supreme Court of a Special Judge, the presiding Judge may request the Indiana Supreme Court for such appointment.

(E) Miscellaneous. Cases dismissed and re-filed shall be filed or assigned to the Judge presiding at the time of the dismissal, regardless of the foregoing rules of assignment.

This rule may be modified upon order and notice of a minimum of 30 days by the Allen Circuit Court or the majority of the Judges of the Allen Superior Court, Criminal Division. Following such an order of modification, should the Judges of the Allen Circuit and Allen Superior Court, Criminal Division fail to adopt a new plan pursuant to CR2.2 within 30 days, the Supreme Court of Indiana shall be notified.

Adopted effective April 11, 1995. Amended Sept. 29, 2004, effective Jan. 1, 2005; amended Sept. 28, 2010, effective Jan. 1, 2011.

LR02-CR Rule 2.1-1. Court Appearances

(A) If an arrested person is released from custody or admitted to bail prior to his first court appearance, he shall personally appear in court forthwith or at such other time as competent authority may direct.

(B) Upon the first appearance of the defendant, the court shall inform the defendant of the charge pending against him and of his rights as required by IC 35–33–7–5.

(C) The court may allow the defendant reasonable time and opportunity to consult counsel.

(D) The court may admit the defendant to bail as provided by law, or by court rule or order.

(E) The court shall fix a time for the defendant's next court appearance which shall be the omnibus hearing unless otherwise ordered.

(F) In all felony cases, the defendant is required to appear personally for appointment of counsel, waivers of right, initial hearing, omnibus hearing, plea, trial setting, trial, and such other times as the court may direct.

(G) In all misdemeanor cases, the defendant is required to appear personally at the initial hearing, guilty plea, waivers of right, unless a written waiver is provided, and jury verification.

Adopted as Superior Criminal Rule 2, effective Jan. 1, 1995. Renumbered as Superior and Circuit Criminal Rule 2.1-1, and amended effective Dec. 7, 2006.

LR02-CR Rule 00-1. Appointed Counsel

(A) A defendant, who is financially unable to obtain counsel, and who is not charged with an infraction or ordinance violation, is entitled to appointed counsel in accordance with this rule.

(B) If a defendant states that he is financially unable to obtain counsel, the court shall cause the defendant's financial circumstances to be investigated.

(C) If the court's investigation reveals that the defendant is indigent, the court shall appoint the Allen County Public Defender to represent the defendant.

(D) Notwithstanding the provisions of this rule, the court may, in the interest of justice, appoint counsel for any person at any stage of any proceedings.

Adopted as Superior Criminal Rule 3, effective Jan. 1, 1995. Renumbered as Superior and Circuit Criminal Rule 00-1, and amended effective Dec. 7, 2006.

LR02-CR Rule 2.1-2. Appearance of Counsel

(A) Any attorney representing a defendant shall appear for such defendant immediately upon being retained or appointed, by signing and filing an appearance in writing with the court containing his name, attorney number, address and telephone number and shall serve a copy of said appearance on the Deputy Prosecuting Attorney assigned to the cause or to the office of the Prosecuting Attorney.

(B) At such time as the Office of the Prosecuting Attorney assigns a case to a Deputy Prosecuting Attorney, that Deputy Prosecuting Attorney shall file a written appearance in the same form as set out above, and shall serve a copy of the appearance on counsel for the defendant.

Adopted as Superior Criminal Rule 4, effective Jan. 1, 1995. Renumbered as Superior and Circuit Criminal Rule 2.1-2, and amended effective Dec. 7, 2006.

LR02-TR Rule 3.1-3. Withdrawal of Counsel

(A) Permission of the court is required to withdraw the appearance of counsel for a defendant. IC 35–36–8–2 shall govern the granting of such permission.

(B) Counsel desiring to withdraw their appearance shall notify the defendant of such intention, in writing, not less than ten (10) days prior to the counsel's filing of such motion. Counsel shall further send notice of the filing of said motion to the defendant, which notice shall indicate the date, time and place of said hearing. It shall be sent by first class mail and shall inform the defendant of the necessity to be present. A copy of said notice shall be attached to counsel's Motion to Withdraw. No withdrawal of appearance shall be granted unless said procedure is followed.

Adopted as Superior Criminal Rule 5, effective Jan. 1, 1995. Renumbered as Superior and Circuit Criminal Rule 3.1-3, and amended effective Dec. 7, 2006.

LR02-CR Rule 10-1.   Initial Hearing and Plea

(A) Initial hearings shall be conducted pursuant to and in accordance with IC 35–33–7–5 et seq.

(B) Guilty pleas shall be conducted pursuant to and in accordance with IC 35–35–1–1 et seq.

(C) All guilty pleas with a plea agreement must be finalized and a plea entered not later than 1:30 p.m. of the last business day prior to the jury trial date. No plea agreement will be considered by the court after that date. The court will deny all requests for a continuance based on the need for further plea negotiations.

Adopted as Superior Criminal Rule 6, effective Jan. 1, 1995. Renumbered as Superior and Circuit Criminal Rule 10-1, and amended effective Dec. 7, 2006.

LR02-TR00 Rule 4.   Trial Setting

Setting of trials on the same date with different Judges is prohibited. Multiple settings for the same trial date with the same Judge is allowed.

Adopted as Superior Criminal Rule 7, effective Jan. 1, 1995. Renumbered as Superior and Circuit Criminal Rule 4, and amended effective Dec. 7, 2006.

LR02-CR Rule 10-2.   Trial

(A) If the defendant pleads not guilty, the court shall determine whether a jury trial is waived and shall fix a time for the trial. The date of trial shall be fixed at such time as will afford the defendant a reasonable opportunity for preparation and for representation by counsel if desired.

(B) A verbatim record shall be taken in all trials.

Adopted as Superior Criminal Rule 8, effective Jan. 1, 1995. Renumbered as Superior and Circuit Criminal Rule 10-2, and amended effective Dec. 7, 2006.

LR02-TR Rule 51-1.   Jury Instructions

(A) All requests for jury instructions tendered in accordance with Criminal Rule 8 and Trial Rule 51 of the Indiana Rules of Trial Procedure must be submitted to the court, with citations of authority, not later than the day prior to the trial. Parties are encouraged to utilize the Indiana Pattern Jury Instructions wherever possible.

(B) Exceptions to this requirement will be made only when the matters on which the instruction is sought could not have been reasonably anticipated in advance of the trial. Proposed instructions need not be exchanged by counsel until after the evidence has been submitted.

Adopted as Superior Criminal Rule 9, effective Jan. 1, 1995. Renumbered as Superior and Circuit Criminal Rule 51-1, and amended effective Dec. 7, 2006.

LR02-TR Rule 7-2.   Motions for Criminal Court

(A) The Court encourages the early filing of motions so that they can be ruled upon prior to the day of trial.

(B) An application to the court for an order shall be by motion. A motion other than one made during the trial or hearing shall be in writing. Unless otherwise provided by law or rule, only the original copy of a motion need be filed. It shall state the grounds upon which it is made and set forth the relief or order sought. It may be supported by affidavit. It shall be accompanied by a memorandum of law in support thereof. It shall be signed by an attorney of record or the defendant personally and shall clearly identify the name, attorney number and address of any attorney filing the same. A rubber stamp or facsimile signature on the original copy shall not be acceptable.

(C) All motions requiring a hearing before the court shall be set on the court calendar by the moving party after first consulting with opposing counsel. Any motion requiring a hearing before the court which is not set for hearing on the court calendar by the moving party shall be summarily denied.

(D) A proposed form of order shall accompany all motions.

Adopted as Superior Criminal Rule 10, effective Jan. 1, 1995. Renumbered as Superior and Circuit Criminal Rule 7-2, and amended effective Dec. 7, 2006.

LR02-TR Rule 53.5-2.   Continuances Criminal

Upon motion of any party, the court may grant a continuance only upon a showing of good cause and only for so long as necessary, taking into account not only the request or consent of the prosecution or defendant, but also the public interest in the prompt disposition of the case. All motions seeking a continuance shall be heard by the court and shall therefore be set for hearing in accordance with Rule 10(C)[1] above.

Adopted as Superior Criminal Rule 11, effective Jan. 1, 1995. Renumbered as Superior and Circuit Criminal Rule 53.5-2, and amended effective Dec. 7, 2006.

1 So in original. Should probably read: "Rule 7-2(C)".

LR02-CR Rule 00-2.   Failure to Appear [1]

If a defendant fails to appear before the court when summoned or otherwise ordered by the court to appear, the court may summarily issue a warrant for his immediate arrest and appearance before the court.

Adopted as Superior Criminal Rule 12, effective Jan. 1, 1995. Renumbered as Superior and Circuit Criminal Rule 00-2, and amended effective Dec. 7, 2006.

1 There are two Rules 00-2 in this set of rules.

LR02-TR Rule 26-1. Pre-Trial Discovery

In all felony cases, the court has entered the following General Order concerning pre-trial discovery:

(A) The State shall disclose to the defendant the following material and information on or before thirty (30) days following the Initial Hearing.

(1) The names and last known addresses of persons whom the State may call as witnesses, together with

(a) their relevant written or recorded statements;

(b) memoranda containing substantially verbatim reports of their oral statements (if any memoranda exist);

(c) memoranda reporting or summarizing oral statements (if such memoranda exist);

(d) a brief statement indicating the nature of each witness' involvement in the case; such statements may be no more than a reference to statements described in paragraphs (A)(1), (a), (b), or (c) above.

(2) Any written or recorded statements and the substance of any oral statements made by the accused or by a co-defendant, and a list of witnesses to the making and acknowledgement of such statements.

(3) A transcript of the recorded grand jury testimony of persons whom the prosecuting attorney may call as witnesses at a hearing or trial. A typed transcript of said testimony shall be provided if it is available.

(4) Any reports or statements of experts, made in connection with the particular case, including results of physical or mental examinations and of scientific tests, experiments or comparisons.

(5) Any books, papers, documents, photographs, or tangible objects which the prosecuting attorney intends to use in the hearing or trial or which were obtained from or belong to the accused, together with the location of such items and an indication of appropriate means for defense counsel's examination of same. Under circumstances where chain of custody issues are readily apparent, such as drug cases, such chain shall be provided to the extent available on the disclosure date provided above and shall be supplemented:

(a) upon defendant's written request;

(b) by pre-trial conference; and

(c) thereafter as ordered to complete such chain.

(6) Any record of prior criminal convictions which may be used for impeachment of the persons whom the State intends to call as witnesses at the hearing or trial.

(7) A copy of any written agreement and the complete substance of any oral agreement made by the State with

(a) any witnesses to secure their testimony or

(b) any co-defendant or other person charged arising out of the same incident.

(8) Any evidence which tends to negate the guilt of the accused as to the crime charged or tends to reduce the class of the act alleged or which would tend to mitigate his punishment.

(9) Evidence of other crimes which the State intends to use at trial, pursuant to Rule 404, Indiana Rules of Evidence.

(10) Newly discovered material within the above categories shall be provided to opposing counsel as soon as reasonably possible following discovery of same.

(B)

(1) The State shall perform these obligations in any manner mutually agreeable to the Prosecutor's Office and to defense counsel. The State shall provide legible copies of existing written statements described in paragraphs (A)(1), (2), (3), and (7). Other items shall be provided for examination, testing, copying, photographing, or other proper use either by agreement or at specified reasonable times and places. Defense counsel shall provide reasonable notice of such examination and shall schedule these examinations in cooperation with the State. An application to the court shall be made to obtain copies of audio or videotape. Said application shall state in specific terms the necessity for such copies.

(2) The State shall make a record of compliance with this order not more than five (5) days after the date set out in paragraph (A) above by filing with the court:

(a) its witness list together with the statement described in (A)(1)(d);

(b) a suitable description of memoranda and items provided, but not necessarily by providing copies of all such items to the court; and

(c) an indication of arrangements made for inspection, if any.

(C) Subject to constitutional limitations, and not later than thirty (30) days following the date that the State has provided to the defense the information required under this rule, defense counsel shall inform the State of any defense which counsel intends to present at a hearing or trial and shall furnish the State with the following information within counsel's possession and control:

(1) The names, last known addresses, dates of birth and social security numbers of persons defense counsel intends to call as witnesses.

(2) Any books, papers, documents, photographs, or tangible objects which are intended to be used at a hearing or trial.

(D)

(1) The defense shall perform these obligations in any manner mutually agreeable to the Prosecutor's Office and to defense counsel. Defense shall provide the same documents in a fashion similar to the State's obligations described in (B)(1).

(2) The defense shall make a record of compliance with this order not more than five (5) days after the date set out in paragraph (C) above by filing with the court:

(a) its witness list together with the statement described in (C)(1)(a);

(b) a suitable description of items provided for examination, etc.; and

(c) the statement of defense described in (C).

(E) The court anticipates that compliance will be deemed satisfactory unless failure to comply is brought to the court's attention by Motion to Compel. Sanctions for failure of compliance or violations of orders on Motion to Compel shall be pursuant to Trial Rule 37. Prior to the filing of a Motion to Compel counsel shall comply with the provisions of Trial Rule 26(F).

(F) Nothing herein shall limit any party's right to seek protective orders to avoid destruction or other loss of evidence, or to seek deposition at such times as they may desire.

(G) The court may deny disclosure upon showing that:

(1) There is a substantial risk to any person of physical harm, intimidation, bribery, economic reprisals, or unnecessary annoyance or embarrassment resulting from such disclosure which outweighs any usefulness of the disclosure to counsel.

(2) There is a paramount interest in non-disclosure of an informant's identity and a failure to disclose will not infringe the constitutional rights of the accused. Disclosure of the identity of witnesses to be produced at a hearing or trial will be required.

(3) Such determination of non-disclosure shall be by the court and shall not be within the discretion of the State or defense. Such non-disclosure shall be sought by motion for protective order.

(H) Disclosure shall not be required of:

(1) Any matter otherwise protected by law (however disclosing the identity of juvenile co-defendants or witnesses shall not be barred because of delinquency non-disclosure statutes).

(2) Work product of counsel including memoranda of opinions, theories, or research for themselves or from their legal or in-house investigative staff.

(I) This discovery order is a continuing order through the trial of this cause and no written motion shall normally be required except to compel discovery, for a protective order, or for an extension of time.

(J) Failure of either party to engage in and comply with discovery shall not be excused by the parties' unsuccessful or incomplete efforts to enter into a plea agreement or other resolution of the case unless both parties waive in writing

(1) compliance with this order for a specified period of time and

(2) any speedy trial requirements.

(K) Any cost for reproduction or transcripts under this order shall be borne by the party to whom the information is provided except that as to pauper counsel defendants the costs shall be borne by the State or County.

(L) The time limits for providing discovery materials to opposing counsel set out at (A) and (B) herein shall be reduced to fifteen (15) days in the event that the defendant requests a speedy trial.

(M) Depositions should be scheduled for, and taken at, the Office of the Allen Prosecuting Attorney.

(N) Nothing in this Order shall be in contravention of case law or statute.

Adopted as Superior Criminal Rule 13, effective Jan. 1, 1995. Amended effective March 1, 1996; Feb. 22, 1999, effective July 1, 1999; renumbered as Superior and Circuit Criminal Rule 81-1, and amended effective Dec. 7, 2006.

LR02-CR Rule 00-2.   Motion to Sequester [1]

All motions to sequester a jury shall be filed no later than the 30th day preceding the time fixed for trial or within five (5) days after setting the case for trial, whichever is later.

Adopted as Superior Criminal Rule 14, effective Jan. 1, 1995. Renumbered as Superior and Circuit Criminal Rule 00-2, and amended effective Dec. 7, 2006.

1 There are two Rules 00-2 in this set of rules.

LR02-TR00 Rule 5.   Stipulations

All stipulations must be in writing, signed by all parties or their counsel, signed by the defendant personally, and approved by the court.

Adopted as Superior Criminal Rule 15, effective Jan. 1, 1995. Renumbered as Superior and Circuit Criminal Rule 5, and amended effective Dec. 7, 2006.

LR02-TR Rule 16-1.   Pretrial Conference

At any time after the filing of the indictment or information, the court upon motion of any party or upon its own motion, may order one or more conferences to consider such matters as will promote a fair and expeditious trial. At the conclusion of a conference the court shall prepare and file a memorandum of the matters agreed upon. No admission made by the defendant or his attorney at the conference shall be used against the defendant unless the admissions are reduced to writing and signed by the defendant and his attorney.

Adopted as Superior Criminal Rule 16, effective Jan. 1, 1995. Renumbered as Superior and Circuit Criminal Rule 16-1, and amended effective Dec. 7, 2006.

LR02-TR Rule 47-1. Selection of a Jury Panel

When jury panels have been drawn, the clerk shall cause a questionnaire to be sent to each member of such panels to be answered and returned by such persons. Such completed jury questionnaires are confidential and may only be removed from the files of the clerk or court by an attorney of record giving a proper receipt for a period of twenty-four (24) hours for inspection and copying the same.

Adopted as Superior Criminal Rule 17, effective Jan. 1, 1995. Renumbered as Superior and Circuit Criminal Rule 47-1, and amended effective Dec. 7, 2006.

LR02-CR Rule 00-3. Special Procedures for Misdemeanor and Traffic Division

(A) An attorney may enter his appearance on behalf of a defendant prior to the defendant's next court appearance and secure a one (1) week continuance without appearing before the court.

(B) Defendants requesting counsel (private or public defender) will be granted a continuance of 2 weeks for the purpose of obtaining counsel.

(C) Upon initial appearance, counsel will be entitled, upon request, to a continuance of 2 to 3 weeks for the purpose of investigating the case, discussing potential settlement with the Prosecuting Attorney, etc.

(D) At second appearance, counsel and client **MUST** be prepared to enter a plea (guilty or not guilty) in the case.

(E) Clients **MUST** accompany attorneys at **ALL** court appearances including initial continuances for investigation, trial setting, jury verification, etc.

(F) The defendant must appear personally, or a written waiver signed by the defendant must be filed in order to waive trial by jury.

(G) When a jury trial is requested, a jury verification date shall be set not later than six (6) days prior to the date set for the jury trial. The defendant shall appear personally on that date. Failure of the defendant and his attorney to appear shall result in the jury trial being cancelled and reset for a later date, and defendant being remanded to the custody of the Allen County Sheriff pending trial.

Adopted as Superior Criminal Rule 18, effective Jan. 1, 1995. Renumbered as Superior and Circuit Criminal Rule 00-3, and amended effective Dec. 7, 2006.

LR02-TR00 Rule 6. Procedure Not Otherwise Specified

If no procedure is specially prescribed by these rules, the court may proceed in any lawful manner not inconsistent with these rules or with any applicable constitutional provision, statute, rule of the Supreme Court of Indiana, or local civil rules of the Courts.

Adopted as Superior Criminal Rule 19, effective Jan. 1, 1995. Renumbered as Superior and Circuit Criminal Rule 6, and amended effective Dec. 7, 2006.

LR02-TR00 Rule 7. Service of Notice of Appeal

In addition to filing the Notice of Appeal with the Clerk, the Notice of Appeal shall also be hand-delivered to the Court Reporter for the Judicial Officer from which the appeal is taken.

The Court Reporter shall make a CCS entry acknowledging receipt of the Notice of Appeal.

Adopted as Superior Criminal Rule 20, effective Jan. 1, 1995. Renumbered as Superior and Circuit Criminal Rule 7, and amended effective Dec. 7, 2006.

ALLEN COUNTY LOCAL RULE FOR COURT REPORTER SERVICES

Adopted June 16, 1998, Effective October 30, 1998

Including Amendments Received Through November 1, 2013

Research Notes

Annotations to Allen County Local Rule 2 for Court Reporter Services are available in West's Annotated Indiana Code, *Title 34 Appendix.*

These rules may be searched electronically on Westlaw *in the* IN-RULES *database; updates to these rules may be found on Westlaw in* IN-RULESUPDATES. *For search tips and a summary of database content, consult the Westlaw Scope Screens for each database.*

Rule
LR02-AR00 Rule 1. Rule for Court Reporter Services

LR02-AR00 Rule 1. Rule for Court Reporter Services

Section One. Definitions. The following definitions shall apply under this local rule.

(1) *Court Reporter* is a person who is specifically designated by a court to perform the official court reporting services for the court including preparing a transcript of the record.

(2) *Equipment* means all physical items owned by the court or other governmental entity and used by a court reporter in performing court reporting services. Equipment shall include, but not be limited to, telephones, computer hardware, software programs, disks, tapes, and any other device used for recording and storing, and transcribing electronic data.

(3) *Work space* means that portion of the court's facilities dedicated to each court reporter, including but not limited to actual space in the courtroom and any designated office space.

(4) *Page* means the page unit of transcript which results when a recording is transcribed in the form required by Indiana Rule of Appellate Procedure 7.2

(5) *Recording* means the electronic, mechanical, stenographic or other recording made as required by Indiana Rule of Trial Procedure 74.

(6) *Regular hours worked* means those hours which the court is regularly scheduled to work during any given work week. Depending on the particular court, these hours may vary from court to court within the county but remain the same for each work week.

(7) *Gap hours worked* means those hours worked that are in excess of the regular hours worked but hours not in excess of forty (40) hours per week.

(8) *Overtime hours worked* means those hours worked in excess of forty (40) hours per work week.

(9) *Work week* means a seven (7) consecutive day week that consistently begins and ends on the same days throughout the year; i.e. Sunday through Saturday, Wednesday through Tuesday, Friday through Thursday.

(10) *Court* means the particular court for which the court reporter performs services. Court may also mean all of the courts in Allen County.

(11) *County indigent transcript* means a transcript that is paid for from county funds and is for the use on behalf of a litigant who has been declared indigent by a court.

(12) *State indigent transcript* means a transcript that is paid for from state funds and is for the use on behalf of a litigant who has been declared indigent by a court.

(13) *Private transcript* means a transcript means a transcript, including but not limited to a deposition transcript, that is paid for by a private party.

(14) *Expedited transcript* means a transcript which is requested to be prepared within five (5) working days or less.

Section Two. Salaries and Per Page Fees

(1) Court Reporters shall be paid an annual salary for time spent working under the control, direction and direct supervision of their supervising court during any regular work hours, gap hours or overtime hours. The supervising court shall enter into a written agreement with the court reporters which outlines the manner in which the court reporter is to be compensated for gap and overtime hours; i.e. monetary compensation or compensatory time off regular work hours.

(2) The maximum per page fee a court reporter may charge for the preparation of a county indigent transcript, state indigent transcript, and private practice transcript shall be $3.75; and an expedited rate of $6.50 per page for expedited transcripts. The court reporter shall submit a claim directly to the county for the preparation of any county indigent transcripts.

(3) The maximum fee that a court reporter may charge for copies shall be $1.00 per page.

(4) The minimum fee that a court reporter may charge for transcripts is $35.00.

(5) An additional labor charge approximating the hourly rate based upon the court reporter's annual court compensation may be charged for the time spent binding the transcript and exhibits.

(6) Each court reporter shall report, at least on an annual basis, all transcript fees received for the preparation of either county indigent, state indigent, or private transcripts to the Indiana Supreme Court Division of State Court Administration. The reporting shall be made on forms prescribed by the Division of State Court Administration.

Section Three. Private Practice

(1) [1] If a court reporter elects to engage in private practice through the recording of a deposition and/or preparing of a deposition transcript, and the court reporter desires to utilize the court's equipment, work space and supplies, and the court agrees to the use of court equipment for such purpose, the court reporter shall enter into written agreement which must, at a minimum, designate the following:

a) The reasonable market rate for the use of equipment, work space and supplies;

b) The method by which records are to be kept for the use of equipment, work space and supplies; and

c) The method by which the court reporter is to reimburse the court for the use of the equipment, work space and supplies.

Adopted as Rule 2, June 16, 1998, effective Oct. 30, 1998. Amended March 15, 2002, effective Jan. 1, 2002; renumbered as Rule 1, and amended effective Dec. 7, 2006.

[1] There is no Section Three(2) in this rule.

LOCAL ADMINISTRATIVE RULES OF THE ALLEN SUPERIOR & CIRCUIT COURT

Adoptive December 7, 2006, Effective January 1, 2007

Including Amendments Received Through November 1, 2013

Research Notes

Annotations to the Local Administrative Rules of the Allen Superior & Circuit Court are available in West's Annotated Indiana Code, Title 34 Appendix.

These rules may be searched electronically on Westlaw in the IN-RULES database; updates to these rules may be found on Westlaw in IN-RULESUPDATES. For search tips and a summary of database content, consult the Westlaw Scope Screens for each database.

Rule
LR02–AR1E Rule 1.   Allen County Caseload Allocation Plan

LR02–AR1E Rule 1.   Allen County Caseload Allocation Plan

(A) Domestic Relations (DR) cases with self represented litigants. New cases filed with the Clerk of the Allen Superior and Circuit Court on a Verified Petition for Dissolution of Marriage without legal representation shall be assigned on an alternating basis (every other case) to Superior Court 8 and Circuit Court respectively.

(B) Mortgage Foreclosures (MF).

(1) 10% shall be filed in Circuit Court, and

(2) 90% shall be filed in Superior Court, divided evenly among the four judges of the Civil Division (Superior 1, Superior 2, Superior 3, and Superior 9).

(C) Civil Collections (CC). Civil Collection (CC) cases shall be assigned in the proportion of 100% in Superior Court, divided evenly among the four judges of the Civil Division (Superior 1, Superior 2, Superior 3 and Superior 9).

(D) Criminal Cases:

(1) All felony and misdemeanor cases are allocated as provided By LR02–CR2.2–1.

(2) All infractions (IF), and ordinance violations (OV, OE) shall be filed in Superior Court.

(3) All Superior FD cases shall be allocated as follows: 50% Superior 4, 30% Superior 5 and 20% Superior 6.

(E) Other Civil Cases.

(1) All small claims (SC), mental health (MH), guardianships (GU), estates (EU/ES), trusts (TR),

and protection orders (PO) shall be filed in Superior Court.

(2) Civil plenary (PL) cases may be filed in Circuit Court or Superior Court. Superior PL cases shall be divided equally among Superior 1, Superior 2, Superior 3 and Superior 9.

(3) All MH cases shall be divided equally among Superior 1, Superior 2, Superior 3 and Superior 9.

(F) Civil Tort (CT). 100% civil tort claims (CT) will be filed with the Superior Court, divided equally among Superior 1, Superior 2, Superior 3 and Superior 9.

(G) Civil Miscellaneous (MI). Property tax cases, property forfeiture cases and name change cases shall be filed in Circuit Court. All other civil miscellaneous (MI) cases shall be filed in Superior Court.

(H) Juvenile Cases.

(1) All juvenile CHINS (JC), juvenile delinquency (JD), juvenile status (JS), juvenile termination (JT), juvenile miscellaneous (JM) and adoptions (AD) shall be filed in Superior Court.

(2) Juvenile paternity (JP) cases may be filed in Circuit Court or Superior Court.

(I) Other Family Cases.

(1) Domestic relations (DR) and reciprocal support (RS) cases may be filed in Circuit Court or Superior Court.

(2) Of the DR cases filed in Superior Court 75% shall be filed in Superior 7 and 25% in Superior 8.

Adopted Dec. 7, 2006, effective Jan. 1, 2007. Amended Sept. 30, 2008, effective Jan. 1, 2009; effective Jan. 1, 2011.

BARTHOLOMEW COUNTY RULES SUPPLEMENTING INDIANA RULES OF TRIAL PROCEDURE

Adopted Effective January 1, 2007

Including Amendments Received Through November 1, 2013

Research Notes

These rules may be searched electronically on Westlaw *in the* IN-RULES *database; updates to these rules may be found on Westlaw in* IN-RULESUPDATES. *For search tips and a summary of database content, consult the Westlaw Scope Screens for each database.*

LR03–TR Rule 3.1–1. LEAVE TO WITHDRAW APPEARANCE

(A) Motion to Withdraw. All withdrawals of an appearance must be made in the form of a motion filed with the Court. Permission to withdraw is at the discretion of the Court.

(B) Form of Motion. Motions for leave to withdraw appearance must indicate the client's address in the Certificate of Service and Proposed Order.

(C) Client Notification. An attorney must give his client 10 days written notice of his intention to withdraw unless:

(1) another attorney has filed an appearance for the same party;

(2) the withdrawing attorney indicates in the motion that he or she has been terminated by the client; or,

(3) the appearance of the attorney is deemed withdrawn upon conclusion of an action or matter.

Failure to conform to this rule may result in the denial of the motion to withdraw as counsel. The Court, in its discretion, may decide to grant the motion notwithstanding an attorney's failure to comply with this rule.

(D) Rules of Professional Conduct. All withdrawals of appearance shall comply fully with the provisions of the Rules of Professional Conduct.

Adopted effective Jan. 1, 2007.

LR03–TR Rule 5–1. GENERAL PROVISIONS REGARDING FILING OF PLEADINGS, MOTIONS, AND OTHER PAPERS

(A) Number of Copies. All pleadings, motions, and other papers filed with the Court must be filed with the following number of copies:

(1) an original copy that will be retained by the Court and,

(2) 1 copy for each of the attorneys, or firms, for the opposing party or parties or 1 copy for the

opposing party if he or she is not represented by counsel.

(3) The other parties should receive a file-marked copy. If the pleading is filed by mail, the attorney must also send stamped envelopes for the Court to serve the file-marked copy to the other parties. If the pleading is filed in person, the attorney shall serve the other parties the file-marked copy.

(B) Appearance & Signature Required for Filing. No pleading, motion, or other paper specified in Rule 5, Indiana Rules of Trial Procedure, will be accepted for filing by the Clerk of the Court unless such pleading, motion, or other paper has been signed in accordance with Rule 11, Indiana Rules of Trial Procedure, (if so required) by an attorney who has filed an appearance, in accordance with Rule 3.1, Indiana Rules of Trial Procedure, on behalf of the filing party, or by a party who has filed a pro se appearance. If it is later discovered that a nonconforming pleading or motion has inadvertently been accepted by the Clerk of the Court, upon this discovery, the pleading, motion, or paper may be stricken from the record at the Court's discretion.

(C) Supporting Briefs & Memoranda. If a party desires to file a brief or memoranda in support of a motion, such brief or memoranda must be attached to the motion and simultaneously filed. A supporting brief or memoranda must be attached to all motions filed under Rules 12 and 56 of the Indiana Rules of Trial Procedure.

Adopted effective Jan. 1, 2007.

LR03–TR Rule 5–2. SPECIAL PROVISIONS REGARDING FILING OF PLEADINGS, MOTIONS, AND OTHER PAPERS

(A) Special Judge. When a special judge is selected, a copy of all pending pleadings, motions, and other papers must be mailed or delivered to the office of the special judge with a certificate of forwarding attached and made a part of the original papers. All proposed orders must be forwarded to the special judge as well.

(B) Filing by Mail. When pleadings, motions, or other papers are sent by mail for filing with the Court, the filing attorney or party must include a self-addressed, stamped envelope for the return of documents to the attorney or party. If there are any deficiencies in the pleading, motion, or paper that precludes filing, the Clerk is not responsible for such deficiencies. The Clerk and the Court are under no obligation to inform the filing attorney or party of any deficiencies or to correct any deficiencies.

(C) Filing by Facsimile Transmission. Pleadings, motions, or other papers may not be filed by facsimile transmission.

(D) Case Numbers. Except for the initial pleading (Complaint, etc.), no pleadings shall be accepted by the Clerk or the Court unless it has a Case Number placed prominently on the face of the pleading.

Adopted effective Jan. 1, 2007.

LR03–TR Rule 5–3. FILINGS REQUIRING IMMEDIATE ACTION

If a motion, pleading, or paper requires immediate action, the party shall file the document with the Clerk of the Court and bring the case-file to the Court so that the judge may take immediate action, if he or she so decides in his or her sound discretion.

Adopted effective Jan. 1, 2007.

LR03–TR Rule 5–4. ALTERNATIVE SERVICE—COURTHOUSE BOXES

(A) Courthouse Boxes. Any Bartholomew County attorney or any Bartholomew County law firm may, without charge, maintain an assigned Courthouse box in the library of the Bartholomew County Courthouse for receipt of notices, pleadings, process, orders, or other communications from the Bartholomew County Courts, the Clerk, and other attorneys or law firms which use this service. If a Bartholomew County attorney or law firm declines to consent to receiving service by Courthouse boxes from other attorneys or Courts, then they may not use the boxes to serve other attorneys.

(B) How Assigned. Such Courthouse boxes shall be assigned only after such attorney or law firm has filed with the Circuit Court a Consent to Alternate Service (Form A). Bartholomew Circuit Court shall be responsible for assigning boxes and maintaining a file of consents and of revocations of consents to alternate service.

(C) Effect of Consent. Deposits made in any assigned box of notices, pleadings, process, orders, or other communications made shall be deemed to constitute and be accepted as service equivalent to service by first class mail under Trial Rule 6(E).

(D) Limitations on Firm Use. Members of law firms must all agree to Courthouse box service. If one member of the firm declines to accept service by Courthouse box method, then no other members of that firm may accept service utilizing the Courthouse box.

(E) Revocation of Consent. Consent to Alternate Service under this rule shall remain valid until a written revocation has been filed with the Bartholomew Circuit Court.

Adopted effective Jan. 1, 2007.

LR03–TR Rule 10–1. GENERAL RULES FOR THE FORMAT OF PLEADINGS, MOTIONS, & OTHER PAPERS

(A) Paper Size, Line Spacing, and Margins. All pleadings, motions, and other papers filed with the Court which are to be retained by the Court must:

(1) use white, opaque paper (except those filed on green paper to conform to Administrative Rule 9);

(2) use 8 1/2 by 11–inch paper;

(3) be double-spaced in the main body of the text. Quotations may single-spaced if they are indented. Headings and footnotes may be single-spaced;

(4) have one-inch margins on all four sides. Page numbers may be placed in the margins, but no other text may appear there;

(5) be printed only on the front side of the sheet; and

(6) include page numbers that are centered in the bottom margin of each page.

(B) File Stamp Space. All pleadings shall allow sufficient blank space to the right of the case title to allow the clerk to file stamp the pleading without stamping over the caption or case number. The space shall be a minimum of three inches in width and two and one-half inches in height.

(C) Type Styles. All pleadings, motions, and other papers filed with the Court must be legibly printed in non-cursive or be typed using:

(1) a plain style font;

(2) 12–point font;

(3) black-colored font, and,

(4) contain italics or underlines for case names or where otherwise appropriate according to the Uniform System of Citation. Italics and underlines may also be used for emphasis.

(D) Binding. All pleadings, motions, and other papers filed with the Court must:

(1) be bound so that their pages appear in numerical order;

(2) be stapled or otherwise bound, as opposed to using a paperclip, in the upper-left hand corner.

Adopted effective Jan. 1, 2007.

LR03–TR Rule 10–2. SPECIAL RULES FOR THE FORMAT OF PLEADINGS WITH SPECIAL JUDGE PRESIDING

Special Judge. If the case is before a special judge, all pleadings, motions, and other papers shall contain the following to the right of the case title: "BEFORE SPECIAL JUDGE _____."

Adopted effective Jan. 1, 2007.

LR03–TR Rule 10–3. PREPARED ENTRIES

Entries (Orders) prepared by parties or their counsel are not to be placed on the same document as is the underlying Motion or Petition unless said underlying Motion or Petition is one page in length and the Entry can be placed on that same page. If the Entry can not be placed on the one page, then said Entry is to be placed on a separate sheet of paper and captioned as an Order.

Adopted effective Jan. 1, 2007.

LR03–TR Rule 26–1. NOTICE TO COURT OF SERVING DISCOVERY IN CIVIL TORT CASES

In all CT cases, parties are required to file a "Notice of Discovery Requests" with the Court upon sending another party or entity Requests for Production, Interrogatories, or Requests for Admissions. The Notice of Discovery Requests shall state to whom the discovery request was sent and the date it was sent. It shall also specify the number of Interrogatories, number of Requests for Admission, or number of Requests for Production. The Notice of Discovery Requests shall be no more than one page in length.

Adopted effective Jan. 1, 2007.

LR03–TR Rule 26–2. DISCLOSURE OF EXPERT TESTIMONY IN CT CASES

(A) Each party shall disclose to other parties the identity of any person who may be used at trial to present evidence under Rules 702, 703, or 705 of the Indiana Rules of Evidence.

(B) Except as otherwise stipulated or directed by the Court, this disclosure shall, with respect to a witness who is retained or specially employed to provide expert testimony in the case or whose duties as an employee of the party regularly involve giving expert testimony, be accompanied by a written report prepared and signed by the witness. The report shall contain a complete statement of all opinions to be expressed and the basis and reasons there for; the data or other information considered by the witness in forming the opinions; any exhibits to be used as a summary of or support for the opinions; the qualifications of the witness, including a list of all publications authored by the witness within the preceding ten years; the compensation to be paid for the study and testimony; and a listing of any other cases in which the witness has testified as an expert at trial or by deposition within the preceding four years.

Adopted effective Jan. 1, 2007.

LR03–TR Rule 33–1. INTERROGATORY–LIMITATIONS

A party may not submit more than forty (40) Interrogatories, including subparts, without obtaining permission from the Court.

Adopted effective Jan. 1, 2007.

LR03–TR Rule 40–1. ASSIGNING CASES FOR TRIAL

A case shall be assigned for trial and placed upon the trial calendar by the Court upon written request of a party and notice to all other parties. Except in Small Claims, such request must:

(1) contain the type of trial or hearing requested (e.g. jury trial, bench trial);

(2) contain a good-faith estimate of the time needed for the trial or hearing; and

(3) state when it is expected that all parties will be prepared for trial.

Adopted effective Jan. 1, 2007.

LR03-TR Rule 40-2. MEDIATION REQUIREMENTS IN CIVIL CASES

All Civil cases that will require more than two hours of trial time will be referred to mediation, unless written waiver is granted by the Court. In the event that the parties request a trial setting of two hours or less and the hearing has not concluded within the time allotted, then the Court shall recess the trial and refer the matter to mediation. In its discretion, the Court may hear the balance of the evidence without resort to mediation.

Adopted effective Jan. 1, 2007.

LR03-TR Rule 40-3. SETTLEMENT AND REMOVING THE CASE FROM THE DOCKET

Counsel for the parties shall be responsible for notifying the appropriate Court immediately upon settlement of a case so that the docket can be cleared and a new case set therein.

Adopted effective Jan. 1, 2007.

LR03-TR Rule 53.5-1. GENERAL REQUIREMENTS FOR MOTIONS FOR A CONTINUANCE

(A) Scheduling Conflicts

See LR03-TR53.5- 2(b)

(B) Time. In order for a motion for a continuance to be considered by the Court, it must be Filed:

(1) at least seven (7) days before the court trial or hearing to which the motion pertains, or

(2) at least 10 days before the jury trial to which the motion pertains; or

(3) as controlled by a pretrial conference order.

(C) Information in Motion. Motions for a continuance shall contain the following information:

(1) The date and time of the hearing or trial for which a continuance is being sought;

(2) A good-faith estimate of the time needed for such hearing or trial when rescheduled;

(3) The date and time opposing counsel was notified that the party would be seeking a continuance; and

(4) Whether opposing counsel agrees with or objects to the request.

(D) Procedure for Agreed Continuances.

(1) If the Parties agree to the continuance:

i. The parties shall initiate a conference call with the court reporter for the purpose of reaching an agreed date for the hearing/trial.

ii. Once the parties agree to a date it shall not be continued for any reason. (Emergency continuances will be granted only in exceptional circumstances.)

(2) If the Parties do not agree on the continuance, the Motion shall so state and the matter will be forwarded to the Court for consideration. If granted by the Court, the party requesting the continuance shall initiate the conference call described in subsection (i) above. Subsection (ii) above shall apply once the agreed date is confirmed.

(3) The foregoing provisions apply regardless of whether the parties are represented by counsel.

(4) If a party is unavailable or uncooperative with arranging the conference call, the Court may proceed to reach an agreed date, and the parties will nevertheless be bound by the date reached during the conference call.

Adopted effective Jan. 1, 2007.

LR03-TR Rule 53.5-2. EXCEPTIONS TO THE GENERAL REQUIREMENTS FOR MOTIONS FOR A CONTINUANCE

(A) Domestic Matters. For all domestic matters involving final hearings, modifications, or contested contempt citations in Dissolution or Paternity cases, a motion for continuance upon agreement by all the parties must be signed by the attorneys for both parties with a verification that each attorney has consulted with their client concerning the requested continuance. Failure to have both attorneys sign the motion may result in the denial of the motion by the Court. The Court in its discretion may grant the motion notwithstanding the lack of a party's signature.

(B) Conflicting Trials in Other Courts. When counsel for a party requests a continuance because he or she has a conflicting trial scheduled in another court, the motion for a continuance must be filed within twenty-one (21) days after the case in this Court is set for trial or hearing. The motion must also state the name and case number of the other case, as well as the date that the other court set the conflicting case for trial. Failure to timely file may result in a denial of the motion for a continuance. The Court, in its discretion, may choose to grant the motion notwithstanding the lack of timely filing under exceptional circumstances

Adopted effective Jan. 1, 2007.

LR03-TR Rule 72-1.　COURT HOURS

(A) Normal Court Hours of Operation. The Bartholomew County courts shall be open to the public to conduct business Monday through Friday, legal holidays excluded, from 8:00 a.m. until noon and from 1:00 p.m. until 4:45 p. m.

(B) Exceptions to Normal Court Hours. When unforeseen circumstances occur, the judge of the Court may direct court closing for the day. The Court shall make a reasonable effort to notify litigants scheduled for court that day.

Adopted effective Jan. 1, 2007.

LR03–TR Rule 76–1. ASSIGNING A COURT FOR CASES TRANSFERRED TO THIS COUNTY

(A) Default Court. When a case is transferred to this county without specifying to which Court it is to be transferred, the Clerk of the Court shall docket the case in Circuit Court.

(B) Transfer Specifying a Particular Court. When a case is transferred to this county and the transfer specifies a Court, the Clerk shall docket the case in the specified Court.

Adopted effective Jan. 1, 2007.

LR03–TR Rule 77–1. COSTS FOR OBTAINING COPIES OF ANY PLEADING, ORDER, OR RECORDING

(A) Pleadings and Orders. On the application of any person, the Clerk of the Court shall make copies of any non-confidential pleading or order in the Clerk's custody at the expense of the person so requesting the same.

(B) Recordings. On the application of any person, the court reporter of a Court shall make copies of any non-confidential recording in the court reporter's custody at the expense of the person so requesting the same. The person requesting a recording must complete the REQUEST FOR RECORDING form found at Appendix A herein.

(C) Payment in Advance. All costs shall be paid in advance or at the time of receipt of the copied pleading or order. All costs shall be paid in advance for copied recordings.

Adopted effective Jan. 1, 2007.

LR03–TR Rule 77–2. REMOVAL OF ORIGINAL PLEADINGS, PAPERS, AND RECORDS

No person shall withdraw any original pleading, paper, or record from the custody of the Clerk of the Court or other officer of the Court except upon the order of the judge of the Court.

Adopted effective Jan. 1, 2007.

LR03–TR Rule 79–1. SELECTION OF SPECIAL JUDGES

(A) Agreement Between the Parties. If the parties to an action agree on any particular special judge, and if that selected judge also agrees, then the judge shall serve as special judge in the case.

(B) Absent an Agreement Between the Parties. In the absence of an agreement between the parties as to a particular special judge, the parties may:

(1) agree to have the regular sitting judge appoint a special judge; or

(2) agree to have the regular sitting judge appoint a panel of judges from which they may select the special judge; or

(3) if none of these methods work, the regular sitting judge shall certify to the Supreme Court for naming of a special judge. Normally, the regular sitting judge will appoint a panel of judges from District 11. District 11 includes the following counties: Bartholomew, Brown, Decatur, Jackson, and Jennings.

(C) Appointment after a Special Judge Declines Appointment. If a selected special judge does not accept jurisdiction of the case, then pursuant to Trial Rule 79(H) the judge before whom the case is pending shall appoint an eligible special judge from within District 11. Each regular sitting judge shall maintain a list of all eligible special judges from District 11 and shall appoint them sequentially.

Adopted effective Jan. 1, 2007.

LR03–TR Rule 79–2. FORWARDING OF MATERIALS TO SPECIAL JUDGE

After a special judge has accepted jurisdiction, a copy of the Chronological Case Summary shall be mailed or delivered to the office of that special judge by the Court.

Adopted effective Jan. 1, 2007.

LR03–TR00–TR Rule 00–1. PRO SE LITIGANT RESPONSIBILITIES

Litigants who represent themselves should present their case in the proper way. The Court cannot treat pro se litigants differently than if a lawyer represents litigant. The court and staff cannot assist litigants in a way that would put the other side at a disadvantage. The Court cannot talk to litigants about the case without the other party being present. In some cases, the Court cannot act upon a letters from litigants. Any letter filed with the Court should have the parties' names, the name of the court where the case is filed and the case number on it.

The Court cannot teach litigants the rules of evidence or trial procedure because that would put the other side at a disadvantage. Litigants must follow the rules of evidence and trial procedure when your case is presented. Likewise, it is the litigant's responsibility to be certain that the other party has notice about all court hearings and is served with all papers or documents you file with the court. It is also your responsibility to make certain that any witnesses you want to testify are notified of your hearing.

It is the Court's job to consider the testimony and evidence presented during your hearing determine the facts of your case from that testimony and evidence and then apply the law to those facts. In all cases Courts may only consider testimony and evidence that is properly admitted according to the Indiana Rules of Evidence and the Indiana Rules of Trial Procedure.

Further, the Court may only consider testimony and evidence that is relevant to the issues in the case. *Adopted effective Jan. 1, 2007.*

BARTHOLOMEW COUNTY
FAMILY LAW RULES

Adopted Effective January 1, 2007

Including Amendments Received Through November 1, 2013

Research Notes

These rules may be searched electronically on Westlaw in the IN-RULES database; updates to these rules may be found on Westlaw in IN-RULESUPDATES. For search tips and a summary of database content, consult the Westlaw Scope Screens for each database.

LR03–TR00–FL Rule 1. WITNESS AND EXHIBIT EXCHANGE

In all contested Family Law cases except for provisional hearings, counsel for the parties are to exchange names and addresses of all witnesses as well as actual copies of all exhibits at least seven (7) days prior to trial. They are further ordered to file the list of witnesses and exhibits with the Court at least seven (7) days prior to trial. Failure to include a witness or exhibit shall preclude the witness from testifying or the exhibit from being introduced, unless the Court waives such requirement for good case shown.

Adopted effective Jan. 1, 2007.

LR03–TR00–FL Rule 2. MARITAL BALANCE SHEET FILING

In all contested Dissolution of Marriage cases, counsel for the parties are to file with the Court a marital balance sheet, including date-of-filing asset values and debt values, as well as a proposed property and debt division. Said documents are to be filed at least seven (7) days prior to trial. Failure to comply will result in the Court removing the case from the trial calendar and shall subject the non-complying party to sanctions.

Adopted effective Jan. 1, 2007.

LR03–TR00–FL Rule 3. PARENTING CLASS REQUIREMENTS

(A) All parents who are seeking custody or parenting time with their minor children in Dissolution of Marriage and Paternity actions are required to attend a parenting class prior to the final hearing on the case. Said parenting class shall be "Children First" or an equivalent thereto.

(B) All attorneys who represent parties with minor children in Dissolution of Marriage or Paternity actions shall notify their client of this requirement within seven (7) days of entering their appearance in the case. An attorney who fails to notify their client of this requirement may be sanctioned.

LR03–TR00–FL Rule 4. CONTINUANCES

See LR03–TR53.5–2(a).

Adopted effective Jan. 1, 2007.

LR03–TR00–FL Rule 5. GENERAL PRINCIPALS AND PHILOSOPHIES

(A) Ex Parte Temporary Restraining Orders. Pursuant to Indiana Code 31–1–11.5–7 and Trial Rule 65(E), if a party files the appropriate affidavit and Motion For a Temporary Restraining Order, the Court will issue Orders as follows:

1. Dissipation of Assets — A Joint Order will be granted upon affidavit alleging fear that dissipation will occur.

2. Removal of Other Party From Residence — This will be granted only when:

i) There are specific allegations of past physical violence to the spouse; or,

ii) Person seeking TRO has moved from the marital residence and seeks other party restrained from new residence; or,

iii.) Specific allegations that person sought to be restrained moved from the marital residence at least 7 days prior to the filing of the request.

3. Keep other Party from Your Place of Work— The Court will grant a Joint TRO keeping the both parties from coming to the other's place of work or contacting the other at their place of work upon allegations of fear of harassment.

4. Keep Vehicle in Your Possession—This will be granted upon allegation of fear of removal and allegation that this was normally your vehicle to drive during marriage.

51

5. Keep Tangible Personal Property in Possession—This will be granted only to jointly keep parties from removing items from the marital residence.

6. Temporary Custody of Children—This will only be granted in extremely extraordinary circumstances such as specific allegations of specific significant harm perpetrated by other party. Such harm must rise to the level of prima facie abuse or be criminal in nature.

7. Removing Children from Jurisdiction—The Court will grant a Joint TRO prohibiting both parties from removing the children from the Court's jurisdiction upon allegations of fear of removal.

8. Tendered Order Language—The Order tendered to the Court shall not contain the phrase "and the Court finding the allegations to be true."

(B) Emergency Provisional Hearings. If a provisional hearing is set and the other party moves for a change of venue from the judge, the Court will consider that the matter is an emergency and the hearing will remain on the docket. The hearing will then be held in a bifurcated fashion and the party seeking the provisional order must show that an emergency exists. If there is no showing that an emergency exists, then the second part of the hearing will not take place. The Court will generally consider the need for support or maintenance as an emergency.

(C) Court Costs. If court costs are initially waived, they will be addressed at the Provisional Hearing and/or the Final Hearing.

(D) Required Language in Every Decree.

1. Tax Exemptions ... If a non-custodial parent is granted a child as a dependent for their income taxes, the Decree shall state: "X shall be entitled to claim C as a dependent on his/her state and federal income taxes so long as he/she is current in child support obligations as the end of said tax year. Y shall execute and return to X the necessary tax documents, upon receipt from him/her, on or before January 31st after the close of said taxable calendar year."

2. Payment of Child Support through Withholding Orders ... Income Withholding Orders shall contain the following language. "The Court having issued an Order, ordering X, SS # ___—___—___–2282 (place only the last four numbers of Obligor's Social Security number here) (hereinafter called "Support Obligator") to pay for the benefit of the parties' minor child(ren) in the sum of xxx Dollars ($x.00) per week, and the Court further having determined that said Support Obligor is employed by Y, (address of Employer) (hereinafter called "Income Payor") and regularly receives income from said Income Payor.

And the Court orders that Income Payor, until further order of this Court, is to withhold the following amount of x Dollars ($x.00) from Support Obligor's weekly check and forward same to the Indiana State Central Collection Unit, P.O. Box 6219, Indianapolis, IN, 46206–6219 with Obligators Social Security # ___—___ –2282 (place only the last four numbers of Obligor's Social Security number here) and ISETS # ___ posted on his check, each week.

Said Income Payor may also collect from Support Obligor, for the Income Payor's benefit and upon the decision of said Income Payor, the sum of Two Dollars ($2.00) each time the Income Payor forwards money to the Bartholomew County Clerk.

The Court further orders that this wage withholding order is binding upon the Income Payor until further notice of the Court; that the Support Obligor may recover One Hundred Dollars ($100.00) from the Income Payor in a civil action if the Income Payor discharges, refuses employment, or disciplines the Support Obligor because of this Order; that the Income Payor is liable for any amount that the Income Payor fails to forward to the Clerk of the Bartholomew County Courts; that this order has priority over any claim on the Support Obligor's income except claims for federal, state and local taxes; that said Income Payor may combine payments hereunder with other payments for all Support Obligors in one payment, provided, however, each portion of said payment is identified for each said Support Obligor; that said Income Payor shall comply on a "first come, first serve" basis for any competing withholding orders.

The Court further orders that said Income Payor shall implement the withholding hereunder no later than the first pay period that accrues after fourteen (14) days hereof; and that said Income Payor shall notify the Court if said Support Obligor terminates his employment within ten (10) days thereof, and shall provide the last known address of Support Obligor and name and address of said Support Obligor's new employer, if known."

3. Payment of Child Support through Clerk's Office ... In each case where a party pays child support through the Clerk of the Court, the Decree should state: "X is ordered t o pay $x.00 per week through the Office of the Clerk of this Court, 234 Washington Street, Columbus, IN 47201, by cash, which payments are to commence on the ___ day of _____, 20 ___, and be paid on or before each Friday thereafter. X shall pay any yearly fees that are required by the Bartholomew County Clerk's Office."

(E) Separation Agreement Signature. Separation Agreements should not have a line for the Judge to sign. The proposed Decree of Dissolution should contain language, which incorporates the Separation Agreement into the Decree.

(F) Higher Education—College Expenses. The Court will generally look at the Child's aptitude, the parents and child's ability to pay. Generally, the Court will not delineate higher educational contributions years in advance of attendance. Generally, Court will order contribution based upon in-state school expenses, regardless of which institution of higher education child is attending. Examples of exceptions to limiting contribution to instate costs are 1) where parents both attended a private or out-of-state school, 2) where siblings attended private or out-of-state school, 3) child has an extremely high aptitude, 4) where child has been promised private school or out-of-state school for years, and 5) where private school or out-of-state school offers classes not offered by in-state school and child intends to major in that area of concentration. Generally, the Court will order contribution for a maximum of four years if four years would normally be required for the degree. Generally, Court will order contribution based upon the net costs after subtracting out grants and scholarships that do not have to be paid back. The Court will generally start with a presumption that the child should pay circa twenty (20%) percent of the net costs and that the parents should contribute pursuant to their percentage of earnings for the other eighty (80%) percent. This presumption is general and can be influenced by availability of monies child has from other sources (grandparents' trust fund), parent not working because of subsequent marriage, the child's inability to work because of extracurricular activities, parents' overall level of income, precedent of the way parents' paid for older siblings higher education, etc.

(G) In Camera Interviews. If the Court has an in camera interview with a child, the parties and attorneys are prohibited from discussing that interview with the child afterward. LR03–TR00–FL–6: Automatic Withdrawal of Appearance In Domestic Relation (DR) cases and Paternity (JP) cases, an attorney's Appearance in the case shall automatically be deemed to be withdrawn thirty-five (35) days after the conclusion of the pending action, i.e., Final Decree,

Modification, or Citation. If a new action, i.e., Modification or Citation, is filed more than thirty-five (35) days after the conclusion of a prior action, an attorney will need to re-enter his or her Appearance to represent a party in the new action.

Adopted effective Jan. 1, 2007.

LR03–TR00–FL Rule 6. AUTOMATIC WITHDRAWAL OF APPEARANCE

In Domestic Relation (DR) cases and Paternity (JP) cases, an attorney's Appearance in the case shall automatically be deemed to be withdrawn thirty-five (35) days after the conclusion of the pending action, i.e., Final Decree, Modification, or Citation. If a new action, i.e., Modification or Citation, is filed more than thirty-five (35) days after the conclusion of a prior action, an attorney will need to re-enter his or her Appearance to represent a party in the new action.

Adopted effective Jan. 1, 2007.

LR03–TR00–FL Rule 7. GUARDIANSHIP FILINGS

Separate files with separate case numbers must be opened for each prospective ward.

Adopted effective Jan. 1, 2007.

LR03–TR00–FL Rule 8. OVERPAYMENT OF CHILD SUPPORT

When a child support obligor pays a greater amount of support than what is due, it is the responsibility of the obligor to notify the court having jurisdiction over the child support order, to request a repayment from the county clerk or the child support obligee. When child support is overpaid by reason of a tax refund intercept, account seizure, or other statutory or administrative capture, there is a rebuttable presumption that the overpayment was inadvertent and that the support obligor is entitled to the repayment of the overpaid amount.

Adopted effective July 1, 2008.

BARTHOLOMEW COUNTY RULES SUPPLEMENTING INDIANA RULES OF CRIMINAL PROCEDURE

Adopted Effective January 1, 2007

Including Amendments Received Through November 1, 2013

Research Notes

These rules may be searched electronically on Westlaw *in the* IN–RULES *database; updates to these rules may be found on Westlaw in* IN–RULESUPDATES. *For search tips and a summary of database content, consult the Westlaw Scope Screens for each database.*

LR03–CR00 Rule BOND–1. GENERAL PROVISIONS FOR BONDS

(A) Bond Schedule. Unless otherwise ordered by the Court, the following shall be the amounts set for the bail bonds:

Charge Bond	Amount
Class C Misdemeanors	2,500 Cash
Class B Misdemeanors	$3,500 Cash
Class A Misdemeanors	$5,000 Cash
Class D Felony	$10,000 Cash
Class C Felony (HTV)	$15,000 Cash
Class C Felony	$25,000 Cash
Class B Felony	$75,000 Cash
Class A Felony	$150,000 Cash
Murder	NO BOND

All bonds may be posted in full in cash or ten (10%) percent in cash of the full amount. In the event that an arrest is made without a warrant signed by a judge endorsing a specific bond, the charts above shall establish the bond for a "preliminary charge." In the event that the individual is arrested on more than one "preliminary charge," the bond shall be set in the amount of bond for the most serious offense.

In the event that the arresting officer believes that the above schedule is not appropriate for a specific arrest based upon facts known to the officer or surrounding circumstances, the officer may complete an affidavit in a form substantially conforming to the form attached hereto (Form B) and provide it to the Sheriff's Department and the Sheriff is authorized to hold such arrestee until the sooner of forty-eight (48) hours (excluding weekends and holidays) or until further order of a Judge.

Adopted effective Jan. 1, 2007. Amended effective July 1, 2010.

LR03–CR00 Rule DISCOVERY–1. RECIPROCAL PRE–TRIAL DISCOVERY

(A) How Made. In all criminal cases, mandatory reciprocal pre-trial discovery must be furnished by the State within thirty (30) days of the date of the earlier of the omnibus date or the appearance by an attorney on behalf of the defendant and the defendant's pre-trial discovery must be made within 30 days after the State's production.

(B) State's Mandatory Obligations. The State must furnish the following to the defendant or the attorney for the defendant as though a Request For Production was filed:

(1) the names and last known addresses of persons whom the State may call as witnesses, together with their relevant written or recorded statements;

(2) any written or recorded statements and the substance of any oral statements made by the accused or by a co-defendant, and a list of any witnesses to the making or acknowledgment of such statements;

(3) any reports or statements of experts, made in connection with the particular case, including the results of physical or mental examinations and of scientific tests, experiments or comparisons;

(4) any books, papers, documents, photographs or tangible objects which the prosecuting attorney intends to use in the hearing, or trial, or which were obtained from or belong to the accused;

(5) any record of prior criminal convictions which may be used for impeachment of the persons whom the State intends to call as witnesses at the hearing or trial;

(6) the terms of any agreements made with co-defendants or other State's witnesses to secure their testimony;

(7) any material or information within the State's possession that tends to negate the guilt of the accused as to the offense charged or would tend to reduce the defendant's punishment.

(C) Defendant's Mandatory Obligations. The defendant must furnish to the State the following materials as though a Request For Production was filed:

(1) the names and last known addresses of the persons whom the defendant intends to call as witnesses along with their relevant written or recorded statements, and any record of prior criminal convictions of such witnesses, if known;

(2) any books, papers, documents, photographs, or tangible objects the defendant intends to use as evidence or for impeachment at hearing or trial;

(3) medical, scientific, or expert witness evaluations, statements, reports, or testimony, which may be used at hearing or trial.

(D) Defendant's Obligations Upon Request of the State. Upon request by the State, the defendant must produce the person of the accused, subject to constitutional and statutory limitations, for purposes of:

(1) appearing in a line-up;

(2) speaking for identification by witnesses to an offense;

(3) being fingerprinted;

(4) posing for photos not involving reenactment of a scene;

(5) trying on an article of clothing;

(6) permitting samples of blood, hair, or other materials of his body, which involve no unreasonable intrusion;

(7) providing a sample of the defendant's handwriting; and

(8) submitting to a reasonable physical or medical inspection of the defendant's body.

Whenever the person of the accused is required for the foregoing purposes, reasonable notice shall be given by the State to the accused and his counsel, who shall have a right to be present.

Adopted effective Jan. 1, 2007.

LR03–CR00 Rule PLEA AGREEMENTS–1. DEADLINES

(A) A "Plea Bargain" is defined as an offer by the State to the defendant that sets parameters on the sentence that the Court can impose if accepted by the defendant and approved by the Court.

(B) A "Charge Bargain" is defined as an offer by the State to the defendant that dismisses certain

Counts and/or cases, or reduces the charge to a lesser-included offense.

(C) The State shall notify the defendant in writing at least seven (7) days prior to the pretrial conference of any plea or charge bargain they are offering to the defendant.

(D) Counsel for the defendant shall notify the defendant of each plea offer extended to the defendant.

(E) Counsel for the defendant shall notify the defendant of said offer and shall be prepared to notify the Court at the final pretrial conference as to whether the defendant shall accept or reject said offer.

(F) The Court will not accept a plea bargain after the plea hearing date.

Adopted effective Jan. 1, 2007.

LR03–CR00 Rule INITIAL HEARING–1. WAIVERS

In all C Felony or higher cases and all driving felony cases, the defendant is ordered to be present at the initial hearing. In all other D–felony and misdemeanor cases the defendant is required to be present at the initial hearing unless a Waiver is filed, signed by the defendant and his attorney.

Adopted effective Jan. 1, 2007.

LR03–CR00 Rule WARRANT SIGNATURES–1. AUTHORITY TO SIGN

In the event that a presiding judge in Bartholomew County is not available for any reason to sign an Arrest Warrant or Search Warrant which was filed in the presiding judge's court, then any of the other sitting judges from Circuit, Superior Court 2, the magistrate from Superior Court 2, or the magistrate from Bartholomew Circuit Court may sign the warrant.

Adopted effective Jan. 1, 2007. Amended effective Jan. 1, 2013.

LR03–CR00 Rule LATE PAYMENTS–1. ADDITIONAL FEE

(A) Any defendant found to have:

(1) committed a crime;

(2) violated a statute defining an infraction;

(3) violated an ordinance of a municipal corporation; or

(4) committed a delinquent act; and

(B) The defendant is required to pay:

(1) court costs, including fees;

(2) a fine; or

(3) a civil penalty; and

(C) The defendant is not determined by the Court imposing the court costs, fine, or civil penalty to be indigent; and

(D) The defendant fails to pay to the clerk the costs, fine, or civil penalty in full before the later of the following:

(1) The end of the business day on which the Court enters the conviction or judgment.

(2) The end of the period specified in a payment schedule set for the payment of court costs, fines, and civil penalties under rules adopted for the operation of the Court; then

The defendant shall pay an additional $25.00 fee pursuant to IC 33–37–5–22 and the Clerk of the Court shall collect the late payment fee.

Adopted effective Jan. 1, 2007.

LR03–CR Rule 2.1–1. LEAVE TO WITHDRAW APPEARANCE

(A) Motion to Withdraw. All withdrawals of an appearance must be made in the form of a motion filed with the Court. Permission to withdraw is at the discretion of the Court.

(B) Form of Motion. Motions for leave to withdraw appearance must indicate the client's address in the Certificate of Service and Proposed Order.

(C) Client Notification. An attorney must give his client ten (10) days written notice of his intention to withdraw unless:

(1) another attorney has filed an appearance for the same party;

(2) when the withdrawing attorney indicates in the motion that he or she has been terminated by the client;

(3) when the appearance of the attorney is deemed withdrawn upon conclusion of an action or matter.

Failure to conform to this rule may result in the denial of the motion to withdraw as counsel. The Court, in its discretion, may decide to grant the motion notwithstanding an attorney's failure to comply with this rule.

(D) Rules of Professional Conduct. All withdrawals of appearance shall comply fully with the provisions of the Rules of Professional Conduct.

Adopted effective Jan. 1, 2007.

LR03–CR Rule 2.2–1. GENERAL RULES FOR ASSIGNMENT OF CRIMINAL CASES

(a) Superior Court 2. The following types of cases shall be docketed with Superior Court 2:

(1) all class D, C, and B felonies related to driving offenses;

(2) all classes of misdemeanors; and

(3) all classes of infractions.

(b) Circuit Court. The clerk shall docket the following with the Circuit Court:

(1) all class A–D felonies (except those specifically denoted to be filed in Superior Court) and

(2) all capital offenses.

(c) Superior Court 1. No criminal cases shall be docketed in Superior Court 1. All criminal felonies pending at the end of 2012 shall be transferred to Circuit Court as well as those misdemeanors where the defendant also has a pending felony. All other pending misdemeanors shall be transferred to Superior Court 2. In the event that a Petition to Revoke Probation or a PCR is filed in a Superior Court 1 case during 2013, it will be transferred to Circuit Court and Superior Court 2, depending on whether it involves a felony or a misdemeanor.

(d) Defendants with Multiple Actions. Notwithstanding LR03–CR2.2–1(a) and (b), when a defendant has a case pending against them in Circuit or Superior Court 2, during the pendency of that case, all subsequent criminal actions filed against that defendant shall be assigned to the court where the initial case was assigned.

(e) Co–Defendants. When two or more defendants are charged with felonies as the result of the same underlying set of facts, they shall all be charged in the same court.

(f) Charges Alleging violation of Protective Order. When a defendant is charged with violation of a Protective Order, those charges shall be filed in the court where the protective order is pending except that if the protective order is pending in Superior Court 1, the violation shall be filed in Circuit Court if filed as a felony and in Superior Court 2 if it is filed as a misdemeanor.

(g) Prosecutor's Knowledge of Potential Conflict. In the event the prosecutor has knowledge prior to the filing of a case that a judge should not receive a case because of a conflict, or for some other reason, the prosecutor may request the filing of a case in a specific court by making specific allegations in a written request filed at the time of filing said case. The judge of the Court in which the prosecutor seeks to file said case may approve this request.

Adopted effective Jan. 1, 2007. Amended effective July 1, 2008; July 1, 2010; Jan. 1, 2013

LR03–CR Rule 13–1. TRANSFER OF CASES

(a) In the event of a conflict, Circuit Court shall reassign cases to Superior Court 2.

(b) Intentionally left blank

(c) In the event of a conflict, Superior Court 2 shall reassign cases to Circuit Court.

(d) In the event that no courts in Bartholomew County are available to hear a case, then that case shall be transferred on a rotating basis to a judge of one of the other courts in the district in the following order; Brown Circuit, Jackson Circuit, Jackson Superior No 1, Jennings Circuit, Jennings Superior, Decatur Circuit, and Decatur Superior. A judge shall be skipped in the rotation when such judge is known to the court to be ineligible or disqualified. If a judge is so skipped in the rotation, he or she shall be selected for the next eligible case if the ineligibility has been removed.

(e) In the event that no judge is available for assignment or reassignment, such case shall be certified to the Indiana Supreme Court for the appointment of a special judge.

Adopted effective Jan. 1, 2007. Amended effective July 1, 2008; Jan. 1, 2009; Jan. 1, 2013.

BARTHOLOMEW COUNTY RULES SUPPLEMENTING THE INDIANA ADMINISTRATIVE RULES

Adopted Effective January 1, 2007

Including Amendments Received Through November 1, 2013

Research Notes

These rules may be searched electronically on Westlaw in the IN-RULES database; updates to these rules may be found on Westlaw in IN-RULESUPDATES. For search tips and a summary of database content, consult the Westlaw Scope Screens for each database.

LR03–AR Rule 7–1. EVIDENCE HANDLING, RETENTION AND DESTRUCTION

(A) Civil Cases, Including Adoption, Paternity, and Juvenile Proceedings. All models, diagrams, documents, or material admitted in evidence or pertaining to the case placed in the custody of the court reporter as exhibits shall be taken away by the parties offering them in evidence, except as otherwise ordered by the Court, four (4) months after the case is decided unless an appeal is taken. If an appeal is taken, all such exhibits shall be retained by the court reporter for two (2) years from termination of the appeal, retrial, or subsequent appeal and termination, whichever is later.

The court reporter shall retain the mechanical or electronic records or tapes, shorthand or stenographic notes as provided in Indiana Administrative Rule 7.

(B) Retention Periods for Evidence Introduced in Criminal Misdemeanor, Class D and Class C Felonies and Attempts. Misdemeanor, Class D and C Felonies and Attempts. All models, diagrams, documents, or material admitted in evidence or pertaining to the case placed in the custody of the court reporter as exhibits shall be taken away by the parties offering them in evidence except as otherwise ordered by the Court, three (3) years after the case is dismissed, the defendant is found not guilty, or the defendant is sentenced, unless an appeal is taken. If an appeal is taken, all such exhibits shall be retained by the court reporter for three (3) years from termination of the appeal, retrial, or subsequent appeal and termination, whichever is later, unless an action challenging the conviction or sentence, or post-conviction action, is pending.

The court reporter shall retain the mechanical or electronic records or tapes, shorthand or stenographic notes as provided in Indiana Administrative Rule 7.

(C) Retention Periods for Evidence Introduced in Criminal Class B and A Felonies and Murder Attempts. Class B and A Felonies and Murder and Attempts. All models, diagrams, documents, or material admitted in evidence or pertaining to the case placed in the custody of the court reporter as exhibits shall be taken away by the parties offering them in evidence, except as otherwise ordered by the Court, twenty (20) years after the case is dismissed, the defendant found not guilty, or the defendant is sentenced, unless an appeal is taken. If an appeal is taken, all such exhibits shall be retained by the court reporter for twenty (20) years from termination of the appeal, retrial, or subsequent appeal and termination, whichever is later, unless an action challenging the conviction or sentence, or post-conviction action, is pending.

The court reporter shall retain the mechanical or electronic records or tapes, shorthand or stenographic notes as provided in Indiana Administrative Rule 7.

Courts should be encouraged to photograph as much evidence as possible and courts and parties reminded of the requirements of Appellate Rule 29(B).

(D) Non–documentary and Oversized Exhibits. Non–documentary and oversized exhibits shall not be sent to the Appellate level Court, but shall remain in the custody of the trial court or Administrative Agency during the appeal. Such exhibits shall be briefly identified in the Transcript where they were admitted into evidence. Photographs of any exhibit may be included in the volume of documentary exhibits.

Under no circumstances should drugs, currency, or other dangerous or valuable items be included in appellate records.

(E) Notification and Disposition. In all cases, the Court shall provide actual notice, by mail or through the Bartholomew County Courthouse mailbox system, to all attorneys of record and to parties if unrepresented by counsel, that the evidence will be destroyed by a date certain if not retrieved before that date. Counsel and parties have the duty to keep the Court informed of their current addresses and notice to the last current address shall be sufficient. Court reporters should maintain a log of retained evidence and scheduled disposition date and evidence should be held in a secure area. At the time of removal, the party receiving and removing the evidence shall give a detailed receipt to the court reporter, and the receipt will be made part of the court file.

In all cases, the Court, or the sheriff on the Court's order, should dispose of evidence that is not retaken after notice. The sheriff should be ordered to destroy evidence if its possession is illegal or if it has negligible value. The sheriff should auction evidence of some value with proceeds going to the county general fund. These Rules and their retention periods will take precedence over inconsistent language in statutes. I.C. 35–33–5–5(c)(2).

(F) Biologically Contaminated Evidence. A party who offers biologically contaminated evidence must file a pretrial notice with the trial court and serve all the parties so that the Court can consider the issue and rule appropriately before trial. A party can show contaminated evidence or pass photographs of it to jurors, but no such evidence, however contained, shall be handled or passed to jurors or sent to the Jury Room unless specifically ordered by the Court.

Adopted effective Jan. 1, 2007.

LR03–AR Rule 11–1. PAPER AND FILING REQUIREMENTS

See LR03–TR10–1

Adopted effective Jan. 1, 2007.

LR03–AR Rule 12–1. FAX FILINGS

The Court does not accept facsimile filing unless specifically ordered under exceptional circumstances.

Adopted effective Jan. 1, 2007.

LR03–AR Rule 15–1. RULES GOVERNING COURT REPORTERS AND COUNTY EMPLOYERS

(A) Generally. A court reporter shall be permitted to type transcripts of official court proceedings during regular work hours. County equipment and supplies shall be used for the recording and/or preparation of such transcripts.

(B) Overtime. If the preparation of transcripts requires additional time beyond the normal workweek, the court reporter shall either:

(1) be paid overtime;

(2) be credited with time off from the regular work week; or

(3) be paid per-page rates.

Whether to be paid overtime or credited with time off may be negotiated between the court reporter and the Court and is subject to the decision of the Court.

(C) Salary. A court reporter shall be paid an annual salary for time spent working under the control, direction, and direct supervision of the Court during all regular work hours and overtime hours. Each court, subject to the approval of the Bartholomew County Council, shall set the amount of salary. Such salary shall be based on a regular workweek of forty (40) hours.

(D) Transcripts Prepared for Other Courts. A court reporter may, at the request of another official court reporter, prepare transcripts for another court. Such preparation may not be done during regular workweek hours.

Adopted effective Jan. 1, 2007.

LR03–AR Rule 15–2. RULES GOVERNING COURT REPORTERS AND PRIVATE EMPLOYERS

(A) Definitions. The following definitions shall apply under this local rule.

(1) A court reporter is a person who is specifically designated by a court to perform the official court reporting services for the court including preparing a transcript of the record.

(2) Equipment means all physical items owned by the court or other governmental entity and used by a court reporter in performing court reporting services. Equipment shall include, but not be limited to, telephones, computer hardware, software programs, disks, tapes, and any other device used for recording, storing and transcribing electronic data.

(3) Work space means that portion of the court's facilities dedicated to each court reporter including, but not limited to, actual space in the courtroom and any designated office space.

(4) Page means the page unit of transcript which results when a recording is transcribed in the form required by Indiana Rule of Appellate Procedure 7.2.

(5) Recording means the electronic, mechanical, stenographic or other recording made as required by Indian Rule of Trial Procedure 74.

(6) Regular hours worked means those hours which the court is regularly scheduled to work during any given work week.

(7) Gap hours worked means those hours worked that are in excess of the regular hours worked but hours not in excess of forty (40) hours per work week.

(8) Overtime hours worked means those hours worked that are in excess of forty (40) hours per work week.

(9) Work week means a seven (7) consecutive-day week that consistently begins and ends on the same days throughout the year, i.e., Sunday through Saturday, Wednesday through Tuesday, Friday through Thursday.

(10) Court means the particular court for which the court reporter performs services. Court may also mean all of the courts in Bartholomew County.

(11) County indigent transcript means a transcript that is paid for from County funds and is for the use on behalf of a litigant who has been declared indigent by a court.

(12) State indigent transcript means a transcript that is paid for from State funds and is for the use on behalf of a litigant who has been declared indigent by a court.

(13) Private transcript means a transcript including, but not limited to, a deposition transcript that is paid for by a private party.

(B) Salaries and Per–Page Fees.

(1) Court reporters shall be paid an annual salary for time spent working under the control, direction, and direct supervision of their supervising court during any regular work hours, gap hours, or overtime hours. The supervising court shall enter into a written agreement with the court reporters which outlines the manner in which the court reporter is to be compensated and county reimbursed for use of equipment, if any.

(2) The maximum per-page fee a court reporter may charge for the preparation of a county indigent transcript shall be $4.00. The court reporter shall submit a claim directly to the county for the preparation of any county indigent transcripts.

(3) The maximum per-page fee a court reporter may charge for the preparation of a State indigent transcript shall be $4.00.

(4) The maximum per-page fee a court reporter may charge for the preparation of a private transcript shall be $4.00.

(5) With the court's approval, a court reporter may charge a maximum per-page fee of $5.00 for transcripts requested within five (5) working days and a maximum per-page fee of $6.00 for transcripts requested to be prepared within a twenty-four (24) hour time period (example: a witness' testimony during a jury trial to be used in closing arguments).

(6) A minimum fee of $35.00 for total cost of transcript may be charged for any transcript less than ten (10) pages. This includes, but is not limited to, those that require the court reporter's time in searching tapes, i.e., Bartholomew Superior Court 2 transcripts.

(7) An additional labor charge approximating the hourly rate based upon the court reporter's annual court compensation may be charged for the time spent binding the transcript and the exhibit binders.

(8) The maximum per-page fee a court reporter may charge for a copy of the previously typed transcript shall be $1.00. A copy of a transcript shall include all forms of a transcript including, but not limited to, paper, electronic, and digital.

(9) A reasonable charge for the office supplies required and utilized for the binding and electronic transmission of the transcript is permissible. The costs for these supplies shall be determined pursuant to a Schedule of Transcript Supplies that shall be established and published annually by the judges of Bartholomew County.

(10) A deposit of at least 1/2 of the estimated cost of the completed transcript will be required by the court reporter BEFORE beginning any transcript.

(11) Each court reporter shall report, at least on an annual basis, all transcript fees received for the preparation of either county-indigent or private transcripts to the Indiana Supreme Court Division of State Court Administration. The reporting shall be made on forms prescribed by the Division of State Court Administration.

(12) Disk as Official Record. Upon the filing of a written request or praecipe for transcript, the court reporter shall transcribe any court proceedings requested and produce an original paper transcript along with an electronically-formatted transcript. Multiple disks containing the electronically-formatted transcript shall be prepared and designated as "Original Transcript," "Court Reporter's Copy," and "Court's Copy." Each disk shall be labeled to identify the case number, the names of the parties, the date completed, the court reporter's name, and the disk number if more than one disk is required for a complete transcript. The court's copy of the electronic transcript shall become the official record of the court proceeding in lieu of a paper copy of the transcript and shall be retained in the court where said proceedings were held. The court reporter's copy shall be retained by the court reporter. The original paper transcript along with the disk designated as the original transcript shall be forwarded to the clerk if the transcript was prepared for purposes of appeal. If the transcript was not prepared for purposes of appeal, the original paper transcript shall be delivered to the requesting party.

(C) Private Practice.

(1) If a court reporter elects to engage in private practice through the recording of a deposition and/or preparing of a deposition transcript and the court reporter desires to utilize the court's equipment, work space and supplies, and the Court agrees to the use of the court's equipment for such

purpose, the Court and the court reporter shall enter into a written agreement which must, at a minimum, designate the following:

    a. The reasonable market rate for the use of equipment, work space, and supplies;

    b. The method by which records are to be kept for the use of equipment, work space, and supplies; and

    c. The method by which the court reporter is to reimburse the court for the use of the equipment, work space, and supplies.

(2) If a court reporter elects to engage in private practice through the recording of a deposition and/or preparing of a deposition transcript, all such private practice work shall be conducted outside of regular working hours.

Adopted effective Jan. 1, 2007.

LR03–AR Rule 16–1. ELECTRONIC FILING

The Court does not accept electronic filing unless specifically ordered under exceptional circumstances.

Adopted effective Jan. 1, 2007.

LR03–AR Rule 17–1. CASELOAD PLAN

CRIMINAL CASE FILINGS

See LR03–CR2.2–1

Transfer of Criminal Cases See LR03–CR13–1

CIVIL CASE FILINGS

(A) Infraction cases (except for juvenile non-driving infractions) shall be filed in Superior Court 2.

(B) Ordinance Violation cases may be filed in any court.

(C) Juvenile Chins, Delinquents, Status, Miscellaneous, Juvenile Infractions, and Juvenile Ordinance Violation cases shall be filed in Circuit Court.

(D) Civil Plenary, Reciprocal, Adoption, Estates, Guardianships, Trusts, and Miscellaneous Civil cases may be filed in any court.

(E) Civil Tort cases shall be filed randomly between Circuit, Superior1 and Superior 2 Courts.

(F) Mortgage Foreclosure cases may be filed in either Circuit or Superior 1.

(G) Civil Collection cases filed by a governmental entity shall be filed in Circuit. All other Civil Collection cases shall be filed in Superior 2.

(H) Small Claim cases shall be filed in Superior Court 2.

(I) Mental Health cases shall be filed in Superior 1.

(J) Protective Order cases shall be filed randomly between Superior 1 and Superior 2 Courts with Superior Court 1 receiving one-third (1/3) and Superior Court 2 receiving two-thirds (2/3) of these cases, **unless** there is currently pending a case involving the parties in another Bartholomew County Court, then the protective order case shall be filed in the court where the other cases is pending, **unless** the underlying case is a DR filed in Circuit Court. In that case, the protective order case shall be filed in Superior Court 2 and the DR case shall be transferred to Superior Court 2. Circuit Court shall retain those PO cases where there is currently pending another case in Circuit Court other than a DR case (such as JP, JC, JD, JS, or JT cases).

(K) Paternity cases shall be filed randomly between Circuit and Superior 1.

(L) Domestic Relations cases shall be filed randomly between Superior 1 and Superior 2 Courts with Superior 1 receiving two-thirds (2/3) and Superior 2 receiving one-third (1/3) of these cases.

(M) All Domestic Relations cases open and pending in Circuit Court at the end of 2012 shall be transferred to Superior Court 1. All Circuit Court Domestic Relation cases currently closed, but reopened in 2013 shall be transferred to Superior Court 1.

(N) One–half (1/2) of the Paternity cases open and pending in Circuit Court at the end of 2012 shall be randomly transferred to Superior Court 1. One–half (1/2) of the Paternity cases currently closed, but reopened in 2013 shall be randomly transferred to Superior Court 1.

(O) All Civil Tort cases set for trial during the months of January, February, March, and April of 2013 in Circuit Court shall be transferred to Superior Court 1.

Amended effective Jan. 1, 2013.

Form A. CONSENT TO ALTERNATE SERVICE—COURTHOUSE BOXES

The undersigned, as an individual practitioner or for and on behalf of the law firm below, hereby consents to service of any notice, pleading, process, order or other communication by deposit of the same in an assigned Courthouse box by:

(a) Bartholomew County Courts;

(b) Bartholomew County Clerk;

(c) Other Attorneys and law firms which also consent to alternative service.

"Deposit" pursuant to this Consent shall constitute and be accepted as 1st class mail under Trial Rule 6(E). The Consent shall remain valid until revoked in writing. The Consent or revocation will be effective fourteen days after filing with the Bartholomew Circuit Court.

This Consent shall also apply to any attorneys who become associates with the undersigned law firm after the date of this consent. The undersigned agree(s) to notify the Bartholomew County Courts and Bartholomew County Bar Association promptly of any changes in the list of attorneys designated in the Consent.

DATED:

x _____ (Individual Practitioner) (Firm Name)

By: _____ (Printed)

Managing or Senior Partner

List of Attorneys in Law Firm Hereby Consenting:

_____

_____

_____

_____

(File with the Bartholomew Circuit Court.)

Adopted effective Jan. 1, 2007.

Form B.   Affidavit for Hold for Preliminary Charge

Name:

Home address:

Street

City State Zip Code

Home phone: Work phone

Work address:

Person to notify if not able to contact directly:

Name:

Phone:

AFFIDAVIT FOR HOLD FOR PRELIMINARY CHARGE

The undersigned law enforcement officer makes this affidavit for the purpose of requesting that the sheriff hold the named arrestee, and that said arrestee shall not be allowed to post bond pursuant to the schedule set by the judges of this county and pursuant to the provisions of the BARTHOLOMEW COUNTY COURTS BOND SCHEDULE that states as follows:

The bond schedule is not appropriate for:

Name _____

D.O.B. _____, Soc. Sec. No. _____ in that said arrestee:

____ is not a resident of this community and/or appears to have no significant ties to the community and appears to the undersigned to present a higher than normal risk to fail to return; or

____ is believed to have committed an act which is in violation of a previous court order; or

____ has made threats of violence to this officer or to another person which if carried out would warrant a substantially higher charge and bond, and it appears likely to the undersigned that the arrestee would carry out these threats if permitted to post the standard bond; or

3 2

____ is suspected of additional or more serious charges which will require further investigation, and the bond for the offense for which the arrestee is now held is not likely to be sufficient to assure attendance at proceedings for the suspected offense; or

____ other grounds not set forth above: _____.

_____

_____

_____

____ Victim/officer notification sheet is attached.

I affirm under penalties for perjury that the above is true to the best of my knowledge.

_____

Signature

_____

Print name

VICTIM NOTIFICATION FOR RELEASE OF ARRESTEE

CONFIDENTIAL—DO NOT RELEASE WITHOUT COURT ORDER

Adopted effective Jan. 1, 2007.

BOONE COUNTY LOCAL RULES OF PRACTICE AND PROCEDURE

Adopted Effective June 1, 2006

Including Amendments Received Through November 1, 2013

Research Notes

These rules may be searched electronically on Westlaw *in the* IN-RULES *database; updates to these rules may be found on* Westlaw *in* IN-RULESUPDATES. *For search tips and a summary of database content, consult the Westlaw Scope Screens for each database.*

TRIAL RULES

LR06-TR05-BLR Rule 1. PLEADINGS

A. Filings. All causes — civil, criminal, probate, or small claims — may be commenced by personal filing of original pleadings or filing by mail of original pleadings in the office of the Clerk of Boone County. All other pleadings will be accepted and filed as of the date of receipt; provided, however, that any filing made by registered or certified mail, shall be complete upon mailing. All pleadings shall be filed with the Clerk, not directly to the Courts, unless the Indiana Rules of Procedure provide otherwise. Electronic facsimile transmission ("FAX") are not permitted.

B. Distribution and Service. No pleadings, order or notices, other than those originated by the Court, will be returned or distributed to attorneys, or to the party(ies), if not represented by counsel, by mail unless the Court is provided with stamped, self-addressed return envelopes. Pursuant to Indiana

Rules of Procedure, T.R. 5(B) (1)(d), the Boone County Circuit, Superior I, and Superior II Courts hereby designate the mailboxes in the Boone County Superior I office as a suitable place for service upon local attorneys.

Adopted effective June 1, 2006.

LR06-TR11-BLR Rule 2.   PRO SE LITIGANTS

No pleading or motion shall be accepted for filing from a pro se litigant unless the litigant's current address and phone number appear on the pleading. All notices and responses may be served on said pro se litigant at the current address listed in the Court file.

Adopted effective June 1, 2006.

LR06-TR03.1-BLR Rule 3.   APPEARANCES

A.   Entry of Appearance.

1. Every pleading filed shall clearly identify the name, address and telephone number of the attorney filing the pleading. Any attorney for a party shall first file his formal written Appearance in accordance with Trial Rule 3.1 and Criminal Rule 2.1.

2. Any pleading not signed by at least one attorney appearing of record as required by T.R. 11 of Indiana Rules of Procedure shall not be accepted for filing, or, if inadvertently accepted for filing, shall, upon discovery of the omission, be struck from the record.

3. Neither typewritten signatures nor facsimile signatures shall be accepted on original documents. Facsimile signatures are permitted on copies.

4. The Rule shall not apply to small claims where attorneys are not employed; however, parties shall be required to comply with the Small Claims Statute and Rules of Procedure and Instructions provided by the Clerk of the Court.

5. All pleadings shall be submitted on 8½ × 11 paper and shall be double-spaced (except pre-printed forms).

6. All documents or orders requiring a Judge's signature must be submitted with an original and one copy for the Court, plus one copy for each attorney or prose party, for distribution.

B.   Withdrawal of Appearance.

1. Counsel desiring to withdraw Appearance in any cause other than criminal shall file a petition requesting leave to do so. A proposed order complying with section (A) (6) of this Rule shall be submitted along with said petition. All withdrawals of Appearance shall comply fully with the provisions of Rule 1.16 of the Rules of Professional Conduct.

2. No withdrawal of Appearance shall be granted where the withdrawal would deprive the Court of its jurisdiction over the party.

3. A withdrawal of Appearance when accompanied by the Appearance of other counsel shall constitute

compliance with the requirements of Paragraph (A) (1) of this rule.

Adopted effective June 1, 2006.

LR06-TR53.5-BLR Rule 4.   CONTINUANCES/EN-LARGEMENTS OF TIME

A.   A motion for continuance or a motion for enlargement of time, unless made during the hearing of cause, shall be for cause, in writing, with a copy thereof first served upon opposing counsel. A motion for continuance or enlargement of time, except for an initial motion for thirty (30) additional days to answer or otherwise respond to a civil complaint, must recite that the movant has communicated the intent to file the motion to the opposing side. If the opposing side objects the movant must recite that in the motion. If a movant is unable to determine whether the opposing side objects, that shall be recited and the Court staff may contact the opposing side for the limited purpose of ascertaining any objection.

B.   A motion for continuance must be filed as soon after the cause for continuance is discovered by the moving party.

C.   Continuances of small claims will be granted only at the discretion of the Court and, in no event, less than 3 days prior to trial, unless all parties and the Court concur to the continuance or unless shown by affidavit filed with the Court at least 1 day prior to trial that it is physically impossible to attend trial due to illness or injury. A physician's statement must accompany the affidavit.

D.   All delays and continuances shall be at the cost of the party causing same, except where it is otherwise provided by law.

E.   All motions for continuance must be accompanied by an order, providing appropriate blanks for the Court to reset and comply with Local Rules.

Adopted effective June 1, 2006.

LR06-TR07-BLR Rule 5.   MOTIONS

A.   The time of hearing motions shall be fixed by the Court. Dates of hearing shall not be specified in any submitted Order setting said motion for hearing unless prior authorization shall be obtained from the Judge or Court Reporter. Any party may request oral argument upon a motion, but granting of oral argument is discretionary with the Court.

B.   Dispositive motions, such as motions to dismiss, for judgment on the pleadings, and for summary judgment shall be accompanied by a brief or memorandum and shall include proof of service upon opposing counsel of record. Failure to file opposing briefs or memorandum within time limits established by T.R. 56 or by the Court shall subject a dispositive motion to summary ruling by the Court unless, upon motion of a party or the Court, the matter is set for hearing.

C.   Extensions of time for filing briefs or memorandum shall be granted only by order of the Court.

All requests for extensions of time for filing briefs or memoranda, whether written or oral, shall be accompanied by a proposed order.

D. Motions for more definite statement and to strike shall be accompanied by brief or memorandum. The Court, in its discretion, may direct the filing of an answer, brief or memorandum. Such motions shall be decided by the Court without oral argument unless the court otherwise directs.

E. The Court expects the parties to facilitate discovery in good faith within the time limits established by T.R.26 through T.R. 37, without the necessity of filing a Motion to Compel. A party failing, without good cause, to respond to discovery in a timely manner shall be subject, upon motion, to an order compelling discovery and appropriate sanctions.

Adopted effective June 1, 2006.

LR06-TR26-BLR Rule 6.   DISCOVERY

A.   Interrogatories and Requests for Admission: Form and Limitation of Number.

1. Answers or objections to interrogatories or requests for admissions under Rule 33 and Rule 36 of the Indiana Rules of Civil Procedure shall set forth in full the interrogatory or request for admission being answered or objected to immediately preceding the answer or objection. Objections shall be accompanied by citation of legal authority, if any.

2. No party shall serve on any other party more than 30 interrogatories or requests for admission other than requests relating to the authenticity or genuineness of documents in the aggregate, including subparagraphs, without leave of Court. Subparagraphs shall relate directly to the subject matter of the interrogatory or request for admission. Any party desiring to serve additional interrogatories or requests for admissions shall file a written motion setting forth the proposed additional interrogatories or requests for admissions and the reasons establishing good cause for their use.

3. No interrogatories, requests for admissions, or production in small claims matters shall be permitted unless by authorization from the Court upon petition requesting same and the reasons therefore filed not later than 10 days after service of the complaint on the Defendant.

B.   Depositions. Depositions shall be governed by T.R. 30, and videotape or other mechanically reproduced tapes as allowed by T.R. 74, shall be admissible to the same degree as any other depositions. All videotapes shall be paid for by the moving party and shall not be taxed as costs.

Adopted effective June 1, 2006.

LR06-TR16-BLR Rule 7.   PRE-TRIAL CONFERENCES

A. In all cases, a pre-trial conference will be held upon motion of the parties, or upon direction of the Court.

B. It shall be the duty of counsel for the Plaintiff to arrange for a conference of attorneys in advance of the pre-trial conference with the Court. In the absence of an agreement to the contrary, the conference shall be held in the Court in which the action is pending.

C. At the conclusion of the attorneys' conference, counsel for the parties may cause a written memorandum or suggested pre-trial order to be submitted to the Court at the pre-trial conference. The written memorandum or suggested pre-trial order shall be prepared in such a manner to allow the court to adopt same as the pre-trial order controlling the trial of the case.

D. All matters to be assigned for pre-trial conference shall be assigned a date and time not less than thirty (30) days prior to the date for trial, unless otherwise directed by the Court. Notice of pre-trial assignments shall be given promptly by the Court, either by individual notice or by providing copies of the docket entry or as the Court may direct.

E. In all proceedings before the Court, the attorney appearing must have the actual authority to act on behalf of his client. Any attorney may appear in place of another attorney of the same firm or office, but in all instances the substitute attorney must be fully informed of issues in the case and must be empowered to act.

Adopted effective June 1, 2006.

LR06-TR38-BLR Rule 8.   JURY TRIALS

A. Regularly scheduled jury trials shall begin on Monday mornings at 9:00 a.m. in the Circuit Court, unless otherwise scheduled by the Court. Regularly scheduled jury trials in Superior Court I shall begin Monday mornings at 9:00 a.m., unless otherwise scheduled by the Court. Regularly scheduled jury trials in Superior II shall begin on Tuesday mornings at 9:00 a.m., unless otherwise scheduled by the Court. Counsel and parties will be expected to be present at Court at least $\frac{1}{2}$ hour prior to trial.

B. Three (3) working days before the scheduled trial date (Wednesday for the following Monday settings) all choice settings except first and second choices shall be released from trial readiness at 3:00 p.m. As of two (2) calendar days before the scheduled trial date (Friday for the following Monday settings) and if 2nd choice setting is still 2nd choice, it shall be released from trial readiness at 3:00 p.m.

C. The Courts of Boone County utilize a system of calling prospective jurors by issuance of a form letter at least seven (7) calendar days before a scheduled jury trial, using a two-tier notice for summoning jurors. The jury qualification form and notice will be the first tier and summoning the prospective juror at least one week before service will be the second tier. Prospective jurors are to telephone the Court after 5:00 p.m. the day before the scheduled trial date to ascertain if the trial remains on the Court calendar or has been either continued or resolved. This allows the courts to accept cancellation of trials by agreement of counsel due to settlement, up to 2:00 p.m. the day before the scheduled trial. If the matter is settled after this time, such as the evening before or the morning of the trial, prior to the jury being sworn in for voir dire, then the expense of having jurors appear will be assessed as costs of the case, payable along with filing fees and other costs. Circumstances of a particular trial or the Court's schedule may dictate a modification of this procedure.

Adopted effective June 1, 2006. Amended effective January 4, 2010.

LR06-JR01-BLR Rule 9. JURY TRIAL PROCEDURES

A. Objections/Multiple Counsel. During trial where a party is represented by more than one attorney, only one of such attorneys may be designated to make objections, examine or cross-examine as to any particular witness. This designation may be changed as each witness appears to testify and at each stage of the trial.

B. Multiple Parties. Where there are multiple parties, such parties' participation at trial will be in order named in the pleadings, unless such parties agree otherwise and confirm same with the Court prior to trial.

C. Custody and Disposition of Models and Exhibits. After being marked for identification, models, diagrams, exhibits and material offered or admitted in evidence in any cause pending or tried before the Court shall be placed in custody of the Court Reporter unless otherwise ordered by the Court.

Adopted effective June 1, 2006. Amended effective Jan. 4, 2010.

LR06-CR02.1-BLR Rule 10. CRIMINAL MATTERS

A. Immediately upon being retained in a criminal matter, counsel shall file a written Appearance in the cause with the Court and serve a copy thereof upon the Prosecuting Attorney.

B. Counsel desiring to withdraw Appearance in any criminal matter shall file a Petition requesting leave to do so.

Adopted effective June 1, 2006.

LR06-CR00-BLR Rule 11. CRIMINAL CONTINUANCES

Motions for Continuance in criminal cases shall be governed by LR06-TR53.5-BLR-4 herein.

Adopted effective June 1, 2006.

LR06-TR26-BLR Rule 12. AUTOMATIC CRIMINAL DISCOVERY RULE

A. General Provisions.

1. Upon the entry of an appearance by an attorney for a defendant or a defendant's pro se written appearance, the State shall disclose and furnish all relevant items and information under this Rule to the defendant within thirty (30) days from the date of the appearance, subject to Constitutional limitations and such other limitation as the court may specifically provide by separate order, and the defense shall disclose and furnish all relevant items and information under this rule to the State within thirty (30) days after the State's disclosure.

2. No written motion is required, except:

   a) To compel compliance under this Rule;

   b) For additional discovery not covered under this Rule;

   c) For a protective order seeking exemption from the provisions of this Rule; or

   d) For an extension of time to comply with this Rule.

3. Although each side has a right to full discovery under the terms of this Rule, each side has a corresponding duty to seek out the discovery. Failure to do so may result in the waiver of the right to full discovery under this Rule.

4. All discovery shall be completed on or before the omnibus date unless otherwise extended for good cause shown.

5. The party seeking disclosure or a protective order under this Rule shall include in the party's motion or request a statement showing that the attorney making the motion or request has made a reasonable effort to reach agreement with opposing counsel concerning the matter set forth in the motion or request. In addition, this statement shall recite the date, time and place of this effort to reach agreement, whether the effort was made in person or by telephone and the names of all parties and attorneys participating therein. The court may deny a discovery motion filed by a party who has failed to comply with the requirements of this subsection.

B. State Disclosures.

1. The State shall disclose the following materials and information within its possession or control:

   a) The names and last known addresses of persons whom the State intends to call as witnesses along with copies of their relevant written and/or recorded statements. However, the State may refrain from providing a witness' address under this Rule if the State in good faith believes the disclosure of the witness' address may jeopardize the safety of the witness and the witness' immediate family. If the State does not disclose the witness' address for the reason stated under this Rule, then the State shall make the witness available for deposition or interview by defense counsel upon reasonable notice. Should there be a dispute among the parties concerning the disclosure of a witness' address, counsel shall meet and make a reasonable effort to resolve this dispute before seeking intervention from the court. If an attorney for any party advises the court in writing that an opposing attorney has refused or delayed meeting and discussing the issue of witness address disclosure, the court may take such action as is appropriate;

b) Any written, oral, or recorded statements made by the accused or by a co-defendant, and a list of witnesses to the making and acknowledgment of such statements;

c) If applicable, the State shall provide a copy of those portions of any transcript of grand jury minutes, within the State's possession, which contain the testimony of persons whom the State intends to call as a witness at hearing or at trial. If such transcripts do not exist, the defendant may apply to the court for an order requiring their preparation;

d) Any reports or statements of experts, made in connection with the particular case, including results of physical or mental examinations and of scientific tests, experiments or comparisons;

e) Any books, papers, documents, photographs, or tangible objects that the State intends to use in the hearing or trial or which were obtained from or belong to the accused; and

f) Any record of prior criminal convictions that may be used for impeachment of the persons whom the State intends to call as witnesses at any hearing or trial.

2. The State shall disclose to the defense any material or information within its possession or control that tends to negate the guilt of the accused as to the offense(s) charged or would tend to reduce the punishment for such offense(s).

3. The State may perform these disclosure obligations in any manner mutually agreeable to the State and the defense. Compliance may include a notification to the defense that material and information being disclosed may be inspected, obtained, tested, copied, or photographed at a specified reasonable time and place.

C. Defendant Disclosures.

1. Defendant's counsel (or defendant where the defendant is proceeding pro se) shall furnish the State with the following material and information within his or her possession or control:

a. The names and last known addresses of persons whom the defense intends to call as witnesses along with copies of their relevant written and/or recorded statements. However, the defense may refrain from providing a witness' address under this Rule if the defense in good faith believes the disclosure of the witness' address may jeopardize the safety of the

witness and the witness' immediate family. If the defense does not disclose the witness' address for the reason stated under this Rule, then the defense shall make the witness available for deposition or interview by the State upon reasonable notice. Should there be a dispute among the parties concerning the disclosure of a witness' address, counsel shall meet and make a reasonable effort to resolve this dispute before seeking intervention from the court. If an attorney for any party advises the court in writing that an opposing attorney has refused or delayed meeting and discussing the issue of witness address disclosure, the court may take such action as is appropriate.

b. Any books, papers, documents, photographs, or tangible objects the defense intends to use as evidence at any trial or hearing;

c. Any medical, scientific, or expert witness evaluations, statements, reports, or testimony which may be used at any trial or hearing;

d. Any defense, procedural or substantive, which the defendant intends to make at any hearing or trial; and

e. Any record of prior criminal convictions known to the defendant or defense counsel that may be used for impeachment of the persons whom the defense intends to call at any hearing or trial.

2. After the formal charge has been filed, upon written motion by the State, the court may require the accused, among other things, to:

a. Appear in a line-up;

b. Speak for identification by witnesses to an offense;

c. Be fingerprinted;

d. Pose for photographs not involving re-enactment of a scene;

e. Try on articles of clothing;

f. Allow the taking of specimens of material from under his/her fingernails;

g. Allow the taking of samples of his/her blood, hair and other materials of his/her body that involve no unreasonable intrusion;

h. Provide a sample of his/her handwriting; and

i. Submit to a reasonable physical or mental examination.

Whenever the personal appearance of the accused is required for the foregoing purposes, reasonable notice of the time and place of such appearance shall be given by the State to the accused and his/her counsel, who shall have the right to be present. Provision may be made for appearances for such purposes in an order admitting the accused to bail or providing for his/her release.

D. Additions, Limitations and Protective Orders.

1. *Discretionary Disclosures.* Upon written request and a showing of materiality, the court, in its discretion, may require additional disclosure not otherwise covered by this Rule.

2. *Denial of Disclosure.* The court may deny disclosure required by this rule upon a finding that there is substantial risk to any person of physical harm, intimidation, bribery, economic reprisals or unnecessary annoyance or embarrassment resulting from such disclosure which outweighs any usefulness of the disclosure.

3. *Matters not subject to Disclosure.*

    a) Work Product: Disclosure hereunder shall not be required of legal research or records, correspondence, reports, or memoranda to the extent that they contain the opinions, theories, or conclusions of the State or members of its legal or investigative staff, or of defense counsel or his/her staff;

    b) Informants: Disclosure of an informant's identity shall not be required where there is a paramount interest of non-disclosure and where a failure to disclose will not infringe upon the Constitutional rights of the accused. However, disclosure shall not be denied hereunder of the identity of witnesses to be produced at trial or hearing; and

    c) Any matters protected by law.

4. *Protective Orders.* Either the State or defense may apply for a protective order for non-disclosure of discovery required hereunder or any additional requested discovery.

E. Duty of Supplemental Responses. The State and the defense are under a continuing duty to supplement the discovery disclosures required hereunder as required upon the acquisition of additional information or materials otherwise required to be disclosed hereunder.

Supplementation of disclosures shall be made within a reasonable time after the obligation to supplement arises.

F. Sanctions Upon Failure to Comply. Failure of a party to comply with either the disclosure requirements or the time limits required by this Rule may result in the imposition of sanctions against the noncompliant party. These sanctions may include, but are not limited to, the exclusion of evidence at a trial or hearing.

Adopted effective June 1, 2006.

LR06-CR00-BLR Rule 13. NON-DISCRETIONARY FILING OF CRIMINAL CASES

Effective January 1, 2009, all criminal cases, when filed, shall be assigned by the Clerk to the Circuit, Superior I or Superior II Courts of the Judicial Circuit as follows:

Misdemeanors (cases in which only misdemeanors are charged):

A. Cases in which the only misdemeanor charged is Operator Never Licensed, I.C. 9–24–18–1 shall be assigned to Circuit Court.

B. Cases in which the only misdemeanor charged is Driving While Suspended, I.C. 9–24–19–2 or 9–24–19–3, shall be assigned to Superior Court I.

C. All other I.C. 9 *et. seq.* (Title IX traffic) misdemeanor cases shall be assigned to Superior Court II.

D. All cases charging misdemeanors under I.C. 35–48–4, 35–42–2–1, 35–43–5 and Title VII crimes, alone or in conjunction with other misdemeanor offenses, shall be assigned to Superior Court II.

E. All other misdemeanor cases, not covered by A–D, shall be assigned to Circuit Court.

Felonies:

F. All cases in which one for more felony counts are charged under I.C. 35–36–1–3, 35–36–1–4 or 35–36–1–5 (incest, neglect of a dependent and criminal nonsupport of a child) shall be assigned to Circuit Court.

G. All cases in which the only felony count charged is Driving While Suspended under I.C. 9–24–2–4 shall be assigned to Superior Court I,

H. All felony cases, not covered by paragraph F or G, in which the only felony charged is a charge under I.C. 9 *et. seq.* (a Title IX Traffic offense) shall be assigned to Superior Court II.

I. All felony and misdemeanor operating while intoxicated cases shall be assigned to Superior Court II, no matter what other felony charges may be filed therewith.

J. All felony cases not assigned, pursuant to paragraphs F through I, shall be assigned 50% to Superior Court I, 30% to Circuit Court and 20% to Superior Court II by random draw as provided in paragraph L below.

K. If a case charges both a non-traffic code felony and a misdemeanor, other than an alcohol related misdemeanor, the case shall be considered a felony and assigned pursuant to paragraph J above.

L. The rotation of cases under Paragraph J shall be accomplished by using a set of one hundred balls. The set of balls shall contain 50 balls marked Superior Court I, 30 balls marked Circuit Court, and 20 balls marked Superior Court II. The balls (those selected and those yet to be selected) shall be securely maintained by the Clerk of the Court. Each time a felony case is assigned, pursuant to paragraph J, the Clerk shall draw a ball and assign the case the Court designated on that ball. The ball drawn shall be held by the Clerk with the other balls that have been drawn until all one hundred balls have been drawn. At that point, all one hundred balls shall be returned to the receptacle from which they are drawn and the process shall begin anew. The Clerk shall maintain a log of the balls drawn and the case assignments made. A "selection sheet" shall be placed in each file assigned, pursuant to paragraph J, noting the person who made the draw and the Court to which the case was assigned.

M. If, after assignment, a case is dismissed and later re-filed, it shall be assigned to the Court of original assignment. The purpose of this rule is to comply with Indiana Criminal Rule 2.2., so as to provide a procedure for non-discretionary assignment of criminal cases.

N. In cases assigned, pursuant to paragraph J above, where a charge or charges are filed against one or more that one defendant and such charge or charges arise out of the same factual allegations or same criminal episode, such cases shall be assigned, upon the request of the prosecutor, to the same Court in which the first such case was assigned, pursuant to paragraph J. In such event, the subsequent case or cases shall be assigned to the same court as the first one and another ball shall be removed from the draw for the court to which the subsequent case was assigned.

O. Notwithstanding Item J above, whenever the Defendant is charged in a cause wherein the basis for the charge or charges has resulted/ or results in the filing of a CHINS proceeding in Circuit Court, then such cause shall be transferred to the Circuit Court, upon request by the Prosecutor, the Department of Child Services, or the Court, on its own motion.

P. Notwithstanding any of the foregoing, the Judges of Boone County may agree to transfer any criminal case between or among themselves upon good cause shown by the prosecutor or counsel for the Defendant, or upon their own motion, when in the interests of judicial economy or the interests of justice so require.

Q. In order to comply with Criminal Rule 13 (c), a list of alternative judges shall be maintained in the offices of the Circuit, Superior I and Superior II Courts. On this list shall be contained the names of the regular sitting Judges in the counties contiguous to Boone County. Whenever the appointment of an alternative sitting Judge is ordered by any of the regular sitting judges of the court where the Judge sits, the Judge shall assign the case to one of the Judges on this list on a rotating basis.

R. This rule shall not, under any circumstances, limit or otherwise alter the option of the regular sitting Judge to request the Indiana Supreme Court appoint a Special Judge in accordance with the Criminal Rule 13(d).

Adopted effective June 1, 2006. Amended effective Jan. 1, 2009.

LR06-TR52-BLR Rule 14. SPECIAL FINDINGS OF FACT

In all cases where special finding of facts by the Court is required, counsel of record shall submit to the Court proposed special findings embracing all the facts which they claim to have been proved and the conclusions of law thereon. Such special findings shall be submitted to the Court, pursuant to Trial Rule 52(c), and shall be submitted within such time as directed by the Court.

Adopted effective June 1, 2006.

CRIMINAL BOND SCHEDULE

LR06–CR00–BLR Rule 15. CRIMINAL BAIL

A. In all criminal cases coming within the jurisdiction of the Court and preliminary felony charges filed in the Court, the bail is now fixed as of the first day of each yearly term and each succeeding term hereafter as follows, and these amounts will be the only amounts set for bail for charges to be filed in the Circuit, Superior I and Superior II Courts of Boone County, unless otherwise ordered by the Courts:

OFFENSE/CLASS	SURETY BOND	CASH BOND
MURDER	NONE	NONE
METHAMPHETAMINE (All Meth Related Charges)	$50,000.00	$50,000.00
CLASS A FELONY	$50,000.00	$50,000.00
CLASS B FELONY	$25,000.00	$25,000.00
CLASS C FELONY	$10,000.00	$10,000.00

INDIANA RESIDENTS:

CLASS D FELONY	$5,000.00	$550.00
CLASS A MISDEMEANOR	$5,000.00	$550.00
CLASS B MISDEMEANOR	$4,000.00	$450.00
CLASS C MISDEMEANOR	$2,500.00	$300.00

OUT OF STATE RESIDENTS:

CLASS D FELONY	$15,000.00	$7,500.00
CLASS A MISDEMEANOR	$5,000.00	$2,500.00
CLASS B MISDEMEANOR	$3,000.00	$1,000.00
CLASS C MISDEMEANOR	$2,000.00	$1,000.00

B. **No Bond:** Any person arrested on a charge of **Resisting Law Enforcement, Intimidation, Invasion of Privacy, Class A Misdemeanor or higher Battery (including Sexual Battery and Domestic Battery), Strangulation, or Stalking** shall be detained in custody without bond until initial hearing. Also, as further set forth herein, there is no bond for **Child Molesting or Child Solicitation**. At initial hearing, bond shall be set pursuant to the bond schedule above absent a request from the Prosecuting Attorney for an alternative bond.

C. **No Bond for Certain Sex Offenders Without a Hearing.** Pursuant to I.C. 35–33–8–3.5 any person arrested on any charge

1. (a) who is already an I.C. 35–38–1–7.5 sexually violent predator

and

(b) who is arrested for or charged with one or more of the following:

    i.   Rape

    ii.   Criminal deviate conduct

    iii.   (omitted intentionally)

    iv.   Child exploitation

    v.   Vicarious sexual gratification

    vi.   (omitted intentionally)

    vii.   Child seduction

    viii.   Sexual misconduct with a minor as a class A, B or C felony

    ix.   Incest

    x.   (omitted intentionally)

    xi.   Kidnapping where the alleged victim is less than 18 years of age

    xii.   Criminal confinement where the alleged victim is less than 18 years of age

    xiii.   Possession of child pornography

    xiv.   Promoting prostitution as a class B felony

    xv.   Promoting human trafficking where the alleged victim is less than 18 years of age

    xvi.   Sexual trafficking of a minor

    xvii.   Human trafficking if the victim is less than 18 years of age.

    xviii.   (omitted intentionally)

    xix.   Voluntary manslaughter;

    xx.   An attempt or conspiracy to commit any of the charges listed above in a-t and also (1) attempted child molesting, (2) conspiracy to commit child molesting, (3) attempted child solicitation, (4) conspiracy to commit child solicitation, (5) attempted sexual battery, (6) conspiracy to commit sexual battery, (7) attempted murder, or (8) conspiracy to commit murder;

or

2.   who is charged with child molesting;

or

3.   who is charged with child solicitation

shall be detained in custody without bond until initial hearing.

INSTRUCTIONS TO JAIL OFFICERS

Thus in determining whether a person arrested for or charged with an offense listed in C.1(b)(i.–xx.) of this rule the sheriff's assigned jail officer shall review the public record for sexually violent predators and determine whether the person charged with an offense in (i.–xx.) has previously been found to be a sexually violent predator. If that person has been found to be a sexually violent predator, then they have no bond until a bail hearing. If they have not been found to be a sexually violent predator then they have an initial bond pursuant to schedule listed above depending on the class of the offense charged. (For example, a person charged with class A felony volun-

tary manslaughter who has not been found to be a sexually violent predator would have a bond of $25,000.00 cash or surety. Whereas a person charged with class A felony voluntary manslaughter who has previously been found to be a sexually violent predator would have no bond.

For further clarification, ANY person charged with murder, resisting law enforcement, intimidation, invasion of privacy, battery as a class A misdemeanor or higher, strangulation, stalking, sexual battery, child molesting, or child solicitation shall be detained in custody without bond until an initial hearing.

A. If a person has multiple charges, bond shall be posted on the most serious charge only. If the listed bond amount is inappropriate under the circumstances, the Prosecuting Attorney shall bring such circumstances to the attention of the court by written or oral motion.

B. This bond schedule shall not be applicable in the case of a person who has been arrested for a crime while on probation, parole, bond or released on own recognizance for another offense. In such cases, the person may be detained for a maximum period of fifteen (15) calendar days, during which period the Prosecuting Attorney shall notify the appropriate parole or probation authority, and the Court shall determine the proper amount of bond, if any.

C. Upon issuance of a criminal bench warrant, the amount of bail specified shall be endorsed upon the warrant. The Court may increase or diminish the amount specified or permit the posting of cash bond in lieu of accepting any property or surety bond in any justifiable cause.

D. The Clerk may assess a ten percent (10%) administrative fee per statute on all cash bonds.

E. Applicable to Superior II Only: The schedule of fines and penalties established by Superior II for infraction matters as adopted in September 1, 1981, and as amended April 10, 1984, and as may be subsequently amended by Superior II are now incorporated herein and made a part of this Order.

F. Cash Bonds: All cash bonds shall be posted with the Boone County Clerk or the Boone County Sheriff. Cash bonds may be used to pay fines, court costs, and other financial obligations of the defendant in any Boone County Cause. In addition, the bond may be used to reimburse the county for the cost of court appointed counsel and for an administrative fee as authorized by I.C. 35–33–8–3.2 (a)(2)(B). Unless the Court orders otherwise, when cash bonds are released, they may be released to the person who posted the bond, not necessarily to the Defendant.

G. Bond Reductions: Pre-trial Motions for bond reductions shall be presented to the Court in writing and proper notice of the hearing scheduled thereon shall be given to the Prosecuting Attorney. Notwithstanding any pre-trial motion for bond reduction, at the Initial Hearing a Defendant's bond may be reduced at the discretion of the Judge, with or without the presence of the State of Indiana.

H. Domestic Violence Arrest. Any person arrested and held in custody for a crime of domestic violence (as described in *IC 35–41–1–6.3*) shall be kept in custody and not released for at least eight (8) hours from the time of the arrest. Such a person, regardless of when an initial hearing may be held and bond set, may not be released on bail until at least eight (8) hours from the time of the person's arrest. This rule is promulgated to comply with I.C. 35–33–1–6 and is in conformance therewith

I. Detention of Person Arrested for Alcohol Related Offense. When a person is arrested and held in custody for an alcohol related offense, that person may be detained pending release notwithstanding the posting of bond by the jail pursuant to the following schedule.

[INCORPORATED HEREIN BY REFERENCE AS IF FULLY SET FORTH HEREIN THE TABLE ENTITLED HOURS AFTER INITIAL READING IS TAKEN FROM I.C. 35–33–1–6.]

Note: In order to find when a person will reach the legal blood or breath alcohol level, find the blood or breath alcohol level reading in the left hand column, go across and find where the blood or breath alcohol level reading is an alcohol concentration equivalent (as defined in IC 9–13–2–2.4) to below eight-hundredths (0.08) gram of alcohol per one hundred (100) milliliters of the person's blood or per two hundred ten (210) liters of the person's breath, then read up that column

to find the minimum number of hours before the person can be released.

J. Supersedes: This Bail Bond Schedule supersedes all previous Bail Bond Schedules ordered by the Circuit and Superior Courts of this County.

Adopted effective June 1, 2006. Amended effective Jan. 4, 2010; Oct. 15, 2011.

LR06-CR00-BLR Rule 16. SCHEDULE OF FEES FOR SUPERIOR COURT II ALCOHOL AND DRUG PROGRAM

Assessment	$50.00
Basic Education	$250.00*
Advanced Education	$300.00*
Case Transfer	$50.00
Intensive Correctional Treatment	$400.00
Case Management Fee	$100.00**

* Typically includes assessment
** Case Management Fee may be assessed in the following circumstances:

1. Participant voluntarily enrolled in treatment program prior to sentencing;
2. Participant violated probation and/or had probation extended; or
3. Participant transferred probation to Boone County but will not utilize other services of program.

Adopted effective Jan. 4, 2010.

FAMILY LAW

LR06-FL00-BLR Rule 17. CHILD SUPPORT WORKSHEETS AND CHILDREN COPING WITH DIVORCE WORKSHOP

(1) Parties shall complete an Indiana Child Support Guideline Worksheet on forms adopted by the court and in all contested matters involving child support or disposition of assets. Parties must date and file these forms prior to any hearing or trial. Child Support Worksheets shall be exchanged and filed with the court on the hearing date. Child Support Worksheets must be attached to all proposed orders and decrees addressing child support.

(2) If there are any assets or obligations not disposed of by written agreement between the parties, the litigants must prove the value of the assets and the amount of obligations at the hearing.

(3) In the best interest of all minor children in a divorce action, Petitioner and Respondent shall be required to attend a divorce workshop addressing post-separation parenting and encouraging the ability of parents to enter into agreements concerning child-related matters. To this end, Parties are required to attend the workshop offered through Boone County

Mental Health Association entitled "Helping Children Through the Divorce". Parties are responsible for the payment of the cost of the program, with an allowance for waiver of the fee for indigence. Attendance is mandatory for all parties in a Dissolution of Marriage action if there are unemancipated children under the age of eighteen (18). This course must be completed prior to the Final Hearing. Failure to complete the workshop could result in a party having to show cause why s/he should not be held in Contempt of Court.

Formerly Rule 16, adopted effective June 1, 2006. Renumbered as Rule 17 and amended effective Jan. 4, 2010.

LR06-FL00-BLR Rule 18. PARENTING TIME GUIDELINES

The Indiana Parenting Time Guidelines are hereby adopted by Boone County, together with any and all modifications and/or amendments thereto, effective as of the date said Guidelines determined effective by the Indiana Supreme Court.

Formerly Rule 17, adopted effective June 1, 2006. Renumbered as Rule 18 and amended effective Jan. 4, 2010.

SMALL CLAIMS

LR06-SC00-BLR Rule 19. SMALL CLAIMS

(Applicable to Superior II Only)

Documents Filed With the Court.

1. Written Answers to small claims complaints are not necessary but may be filed by parties or counsel at least ten (10) days prior to trial. In no event will the Court continue a trial setting to permit the filing of an Answer.

2. Counter-claims may be filed not later than ten (10) days prior to trial. Parties are responsible for mailing copies of the counter-claim to the opposing party or counsel at least ten (10) days prior to trial and show proof of mailing by a certificate of service attached to the pleading filed with the Court. Failure to comply with these requirements may result in the Court refusing to hear such counter-claim.

Evidence. Parties are expected to bring with them at the time of trial all exhibits and other physical and documentary evidence they intend to introduce at trial. Failure to do so may result in the Court refusing to consider such evidence.

Adopted effective June 1, 2006.

PROBATE/GUARDIANSHIP

LR06-PR00-BLR   Rule   20. PROBATE   AND GUARDIANSHIP RULES

(Applicable to Superior I Only)

A.[1]   Probate.

1. Where required by law, all Wills must be admitted to Probate.

2. Bond Procedures.

a. If the decedent's Will provides for no bond, the Court may honor the request.

b. If all heirs request no bond or a minimal bond, the Court may honor the request.

c. In all instances, upon petition by an interested person, the Court may require bond to protect creditors, heirs, legatees or devisees.

d. In all other situations, the Court will determine and set the amount of the bond and in no event shall it be less than that required to protect creditors and taxing authorities.

e. Personal surety must meet the requirements of Indiana Code 29-1-11-5.

f. No attorney will be accepted as surety in any bond required to be filed with the Court.

3. In all Guardianships and Supervised Estates, an inventory must be filed with the Court within two (2) months after the appointment of the personal representative or guardian.

4. In all Guardianships and Supervised Estates in which real estate is to be sold, a written professional appraisal setting forth the fair market value thereof must be filed with the Court at the time of filing the petition for sale; unless such an appraisal was filed with the Inventory.

5. Three (3) months and fifteen (15) days after the date of the first published notice to creditors, the personal representative, or his/her attorney, shall examine the Claim Docket and shall allow or disallow each claim filed against the estate.

6. Whenever an estate cannot be closed within one (1) year, an intermediate account shall be filed with the Court within thirty (30) days after expiration of one (1) year and each succeeding year thereafter. Such accounting shall comply with the provisions of Indiana Code 29-1-16-4 and 29-1-16-6. Such accounting shall state the facts showing why the estate cannot be closed. Such accounting shall propose partial distribution of the estate to the extent that partial distribution can be made without prejudice to distributees and claimants. Failure to comply with this rule may be grounds for removal of the personal representative.

7. Inheritance Tax Schedules must be filed in duplicate and where necessary, copies of the Will of the decedent must be attached.

8. In supervised administration, the countersigned receipt, or photocopy thereof, showing payment of the Indiana Inheritance Tax liability in the estate, executed and sealed by the Indiana Department of the State Revenue should be attached to the Final Report at the time of filing, although not required.

9. In all probate matters, the Personal Representative shall sign instructions in the following form: See Attached Boone Local Probate Form A.

Adopted effective June 1, 2006. Amended effective Jan. 4, 2010.

[1] There is no Subd. B. in this rule.

LR06-PR00-BLR   Rule   20A. BOONE   LOCAL PROBATE   FORM   A   (INSTRUCTIONS   TO PERSONAL REPRESENTATIVE)

STATE OF INDIANA	) IN THE BOONE SUPERIOR COURT I
	) SS:
COUNTY OF BOONE	) CAUSE NO. 06D01-___-__-__
IN RE UN/SUPERVISED	)
ESTATE OF:	)
	)

INSTRUCTIONS TO PERSONAL REPRESENTATIVE

You have been appointed PERSONAL REPRESENTATIVE of the Estate of a deceased person. It is important that you understand the significance of the appointment and your responsibilities.

Listed below are some of your duties but not necessarily all of them. These duties are not listed in any order of priority. Ask the attorney for the Estate to fully explain to you each of the items below and to tell you about any other duties you have in your particular circumstances. Although the attorney will probably file all papers with the Court, the ultimate responsibility to see that reports and returns are accurately prepared and filed rests with you. As PERSONAL REPRESENTATIVE, you are required to:

1. Locate all property owned individually or otherwise by the decedent at the date of death; and ascertain the value of such assets as of date of death. Secure all property in safekeeping and maintain adequate insurance coverage; keep records of the assets. If applicable, obtain an appraisal of the property.

2. Inventory any safety deposit box.

3. Keep a separate checking account or other type of transaction account for the Estate and keep a record of all receipts and disbursements. Never commingle Estate funds with any other funds or use them for other than Estate purposes. Accounts and securities which are registered to the Estate should be in your name "as Personal Representative for the Estate of (name of Decedent)." Retain all paid bills and canceled checks or other evidence of disbursement or distribution of any funds or assets of the Estate for the Final Report to the Court.

4. Within two (2) months after you qualify and receive Letters of Personal Representative, you must prepare an Inventory of all property found belonging to the decedent on the date of death and giving values as of the date of death. If administration is supervised it must be filed. If unsupervised, the inventory must be available to heirs and beneficiaries.

5. You may need to obtain Consent to Transfer forms from the County Assessor for accounts and securities in order to transfer such assets.

6. Collect any proceeds of life insurance on the life of the decedent which is payable to the Estate. Obtain Form 712 from the insurance company, if needed for taxes.

7. Have mail forwarded; complete change of address forms at the Post Office.

8. Inspect all documents and personal papers of the decedent and retain anything pertinent to tax reporting, location and value of assets, debts or obligations of or to the decedent, or any other items of significance to administering the final affairs of decedent.

9. Pay all legal debts and funeral bills; however, pay only priority claims timely filed if there is any question of solvency of the Estate. Do not pay bills which are doubtful but refer them for Court determination. Do not make any distribution to any heir or

beneficiary until at least three (3) months after the date of first publication of notice, unless an earlier distribution is allowed by Order of the Court.

10. Prepare and file returns and pay taxes due (or claim any refund) for both State and Federal income taxes for the tax year in which the decedent dies and any prior years, if applicable.

11. Prepare and file the prescribed Schedule for Indiana Inheritance Tax within nine (9) months after date of death. Any tax due must be paid within one (1) year after date of death. Do the same for the Federal Estate Tax, if required, within nine (9) months after date of death.

12. Unless subject to an exception, obtain a federal tax identification number for the Estate. Choose a tax year for the Estate; file Estate income tax returns and pay any tax due for both State and Federal income tax.

13. Make distribution and obtain receipts for distribution.

14. File a Final Account, if supervised administration, or a Closing Statement if unsupervised administration, with receipts for distribution if already made; send a copy thereof to all distributes of the Estate and to all creditors or other claimants whose claims are neither paid nor barred; furnish a full account in writing of the administration to the distributes. File an Affidavit in lieu of vouchers with the Court.

15. File a Supplemental Report with the Court, if ordered to do so, with receipts for the final distribution.

16. Pay court costs and expenses of administration when due.

17. Make payments and distributions to the right persons. The personal representative is responsible for incorrect payments or distribution.

I acknowledge receipt of a copy of the above instructions and will read and follow instructions carefully.

Dated this ___ Day of _____, 20 ___.

Cause No.: 06D01—___—___—___

Estate of: _____

Printed: _____

By: _____   _____
     Personal Representative   Personal Representative

B.[1] Guardianships.

1. In all guardianship matters pertaining to declaring an adult incompetent for any reason, at a minimum, an affidavit by the doctor treating the alleged incompetent must be presented at the time the petition is filed, or on the hearing date. No determination will be made without supporting medical testimony.

2. In all instances in guardianships, a bond shall be required to the full extent to secure the value of

the personal property assets in the guardianship, pursuant to Indiana Code 29–1–19–9.

3. In all guardianship matters, whether pertaining to the appointment of a guardian of a minor child, personal service of process must be demonstrated by the record, pursuant to the rules. No waiver of service signed by the proposed adult incompetent or the representative of the minor child shall be recognized or accepted by the Court.

4. Current reports filed by the guardian of the person must show the present whereabouts of the ward and his/her personal welfare.

5. All Social Security benefits received on behalf of a ward must be included and accounted for in the guardian's accounting.

6. All guardians shall execute and file instructions in the following form: See Attached Boone Local Probate Form B.

Adopted effective June 1, 2006. Amended effective Jan. 4, 2010.

1 There is no Subd. A in this rule.

LR06-PR00-BLR Rule 20B. INSTRUCTIONS TO GUARDIAN

BOONE LOCAL PROBATE FORM B

STATE OF INDIANA   )   IN THE BOONE SUPERIOR COURT I
) SS:
COUNTY OF BOONE   )   CAUSE NO. 06D01–_____–__–_____
IN RE THE GUARDIANSHIP OF)
THE ESTATE OF THE PERSON /)
PERSON AND ESTATE OF   )
_____)

INSTRUCTIONS TO GUARDIAN

You have been appointed the Guardian of an individual, " Protected Person," who, because of some incapacity, is unable to care for his/her own estate and/or personal affairs. It is important that you understand the significance of this appointment and your responsibility as Guardian.

In order to qualify and have your Letters issued to you, you may be required to post a bond in the amount set by the Court and to take an oath to faithfully discharge your duties as Guardian. The bond assures the Court that you will properly protect the assets of the Protected Person.

Listed below are some of your duties, but not necessarily all of them. You are directed to ask the Attorney for the Guardianship to fully explain to you each of the items below and to tell you about the other duties you have in your particular circumstances. Though the attorney will file all papers with the Court, the ultimate responsibility to see that all reports, etc., are accurately and timely prepared and filed, rests with you.

As GUARDIAN of the estate of the Protected Person, you are required to:

1. File with the Court, within ninety (90) days after your appointment, a verified Inventory and Appraisement of all of the property belonging to the Protected Person, unless waived by the Court;

2. File with the Court a verified account of all the income and expenditures of the Guardianship every two (2) years after your appointment, unless waived by the Court;

3. Pay bond premiums as they become due;

4. File a final accounting with the Court upon the termination of the Guardianship, whether due to the death of the Protected Person or for any other reason, unless waived by the Court;

5. Keep all of the assets of the Protected Person separate from your own;

6. Open an account, in your name as Guardian, in which all of the cash assets of the Protected Person are deposited. This account <u>must</u> be used for all payments or disbursements on behalf of the Guardianship and the Protected Person;

7. Obtain approval from the Court to use Guardianship assets.

It is your duty to protect and preserve the Protected Person's property, to account for the use of the property faithfully and to perform all the duties required by law of a Guardian. You may NOT make expenditures or investments from the Guardianship funds without Court authorization.

Guardianship funds must never be commingled with personal funds. A separate account for all Guardianship assets must be kept in your name as Guardian. Accurate accounts must be kept and accurate reports made. Unauthorized use of Guardianship funds can result in your being personally liable for the misuse of those sums.

As GUARDIAN of the personal affairs of the Protected Person, you are required to:

1. Make certain that the physical and mental needs of the Protected Person (food, clothing, shelter, medical attention, education, etc.) are property and adequately provided for;

2. File with the Court a status report as to the physical condition and general welfare of the Protected Person every two (2) years after your appointment.

It is important to understand that you have the same duties and responsibilities concerning the Protected Person whether or not the Protected Person is your relative.

If any questions arise during the Guardianship, you should consult with your attorney immediately.

I authorize my attorney to disclose to the Court any information relating to his or her representation of me a Guardian even if such information would be otherwise confidential.

I acknowledge I have read and understand the above instructions and agree to follow them carefully and further that I have kept a copy for my continued use and review.

Dated: _____, 20 ___
Cause Number: 06D01- ___ –GU- ___
The Guardianship of: _____
By: _____, Guardian

Adopted effective June 1, 2006.

COURT ADMINISTRATION

LR06-AR00-BLR Rule 21.   COURT SESSIONS

The Court shall convene promptly at 8:00 a.m., recess at 12:00 noon, reconvene at 1:00 p.m. and adjourn at 4:00 p.m. each day not a legal holiday. Court shall be in session Monday through Friday as specified above, unless a different time or day is ordered by the Judge of the Court.

In addition to the Court session immediately referred to hereinabove, Superior II and Circuit shall also convene in the first and third Wednesdays of each month beginning at 4:00 p.m. when cases are scheduled for such time and recess upon completion of such matters.

Adopted effective June 1, 2006.   Amended effective Jan. 4, 2010.

LR06-AR00-BLR Rule 22.   COURT CLOSING

(1) When weather conditions or other emergencies arise, the court shall make a reasonable effort to contact the litigants scheduled for court if the Chronological Case Summary has the addresses and telephone numbers of the attorneys or pro se litigants.

(2) The court shall not be responsible for contacting attorneys and pro se litigants if the Chronological Case Summary does not contain a current address where notices and orders are to be sent and a current telephone number where the attorney or pro se litigant can be reached during normal business hours.

Adopted effective June 1, 2006.

LR06-AR15-BLR Rule 23.   COURT REPORTERS

The Local Rule for Court Reporters in the Circuit and Superior Courts of Boone County, is patterned after Model Option 2 of Administrative Rule #15.

A.   Court Reporters shall be paid an annual salary applied for by the Court and approved by the County Council, which salary shall be payment for regular work hours, gap hours, or overtime hours as the case may be, and which salary shall not include payment for the preparation of any transcripts.

B.   The salary shall be based upon a 35–hour work week. Should Court Reporters work gap hours from 35 to 40 hours per week on regular court business, they shall be entitled to overtime at the hourly rate or comp time on an hour-for-hour basis. Should Court Reporters work more than 40 hours in one week on regular court business, the Court Reporters should be paid time-and-a-half or receive comp time at the rate of one-and-a-half times the overtime hours worked.

C.   All transcripts, including indigent transcripts, transcripts done for private attorneys, deposition transcripts or any and all other such transcripts shall be prepared by the Court Reporters on their own time, off the court premises and pursuant to their own private business arrangements. Such transcripts shall be prepared on equipment purchased and owned by the Reporters, on paper obtained and paid for by the Court Reporters, and no materials or machinery belonging to the court shall be used in the preparation of such transcripts.

D.   Occasionally, it will be necessary for a Court Reporter to use the court's recording equipment for the purpose of taking a private deposition.

E.   On a request for a transcript to be produced in an ordinary time frame, Court Reporters may collect a per page rate not to exceed $4.25 and a minimum fee of up to ten times the maximum per page rate;

F.   When parties request an expedited transcript, Court Reporters may collect a per page rate not to exceed $8.50, said rate being subject to negotiation between Court Reporter and requester, depending on circumstances;

G.   Index and Table of Contents pages shall be charged at the same per page rate as is charged for the balance of the transcript;

H.   An additional hourly labor charge based upon the Court Reporter's annual court compensation may be collected for time spend binding the transcript and exhibit binders;

I.   A reasonable charge for office supplies required and utilized for binding and electronic transmission of the Transcript may be collected pursuant to Indiana Rules of Appellate Procedure 28 and 29; the costs of which shall be determined pursuant to a Schedule of Transcript Supplies established and published annually by the Judges.

Adopted effective June 1, 2006.   Amended effective Jan. 1, 2009; Jan. 4, 2010.

LR06-TR63-BLR Rule 24.   PRO-TEM JUDGES

TEMPORARY JUDGES. As needed, a Judge Pro-Tem will be appointed according to schedules provided by the Boone County Bar Association. Such Judge Pro-Tem shall hear provisional matters in dissolutions, final uncontested dissolutions, modification petitions not exceeding one-half hour, proceedings supplemental, contempt/show cause hearings, and other matters at the discretion of the regular Judge. This rule will apply whether the regular Judge is physically present, and whether the regular Judge is conducting other Court business. Said Judges Pro–Tem is hereby designated as "Temporary Judges" pursuant to Indiana Code 33–13–16–1 through 33–13–16–11.

WHEN OTHER JUDGES PRESIDE. Each regular sitting Judge of Circuit Court, Superior Court I or Superior Court II shall be empowered to act as temporary judges in the absence of the regular sitting judge of any other respective Court.

Adopted effective June 1, 2006.

LR06-TR79-BLR Rule 25. COORDINATED LOCAL RULE ON SELECTION OF SPECIAL JUDGE IN CIVIL CASES

209.10 Pursuant to Trial Rule 79(H) of the Indiana Rules of Trial Procedure, the Circuit and Superior Courts of Boone County, in conjunction with the other Courts of Administrative District 12 (Clinton County, Hamilton County, and Tipton County), have adopted the following rule to establish procedures for the selection of special judges in civil cases:

209.20 Within seven (7) days of the notation in the Chronological Case Summary of an order granting a change of judge or an order of disqualification, the parties pursuant to Trial Rule 79(D) may agree to any judge eligible under Trial Rule 79 (J).

209.30 If a special judge is required to be selected under Trial Rule 79(H) then the special judge shall be selected as follows:

209.30.10 If the case was originally filed in a court of record in Hamilton County, then the judge will be selected randomly from among the regular judges and full time judicial officers of Hamilton County subject to all existing local rules regarding case allocation and transfer.

209.30.20 If the case was originally filed in a court of record in Boone, Clinton or Tipton County, then the judge will be selected on a rotating basis from among the regular judges of those counties subject to all local rules in each individual county regarding case allocation and transfer.

209.30.30 If for any reason a judge cannot be selected by the above methods then the special judge shall be selected on a rotating basis from among all the regular judges of the District not already disqualified.

209.40 A special judge selected under **209.30** must accept jurisdiction unless disqualified pursuant to *The Code of Judicial Conduct* or excused from service by the Indiana Supreme Court. The Administrator of Courts for Hamilton County shall maintain a list of the judges eligible for selection under 209.30.20 and a list of the judges eligible for selection under 209.30.30 and shall be contacted by the selecting court each time a judge must be selected from one of those lists. The Administrator of Courts shall provide the name of the next judge on the appropriate list upon a request from the selecting court and then strike the name of the judge selected from that list. The judge selected in this manner shall not be eligible to be selected again from the same list until all other judges have been selected from that list except as required to avoid certification to the Supreme Court.

209.50 In the event that no judicial officer within Administrative District 12 is eligible to serve as special judge or the particular circumstance of the case warrants selection of a special judge by the Indiana Supreme Court, the judge of the Court in which the case is pending shall certify the matter to the Indiana Supreme Court for appointment of a special judge.

Formerly Rule 26, adopted effective June 1, 2006. Renumbered as Rule 25 and amended effective Jan. 4, 2010. Amended effective July 1, 2011; May 15, 2013.

LR06-AR00-BLR Rule 26. UNRULY OR DISRUPTIVE CONDUCT PROHIBITED

The Judges of the Boone County Courts, including any duly appointed Commissioner or Judge Pro Tem, Special Judge or any Judicial Officer and/or any Law Enforcement Official/Courthouse Security Personnel and/or any Court staff have the authority to remove or cause to be removed from the Courts of Boone County, including but not limited to the Courtrooms, offices and Courthouse, any person, whom in their opinion is being unruly, disruptive, disorderly, disrespectful or otherwise using profanity or engaging in conduct with disturbs or hinders the operation of the Courts.

Formerly Rule 27, adopted effective June 1, 2006. Renumbered as Rule 26 and amended effective Jan. 4, 2010.

LR06-AR00-BLR Rule 27. NO WEAPONS OR PERSONAL PROTECTION DEVICES ALLOWED IN THE COURTHOUSE

No guns, knives or weapons of any kind shall be allowed in the Boone County Courthouse except those in the possession of law enforcement officers or other persons duly authorized by the Judges to possess the same in the Courthouse.

No personal protection devices, including body armor, mace, pepper spray, protective clothing, gloves or other such related items shall be allowed in the Courtrooms at any time, except by those in law enforcement officers in the course of their duties or by other persons authorized by the Judges to possess the same in the Courthouse.

Courthouse Security Personnel are authorized to conduct searches of anyone in the Courthouse to insure compliance with this Rule.

Formerly Rule 28, adopted effective June 1, 2006. Renumbered as Rule 27 and amended effective Jan. 4, 2010.

LR06-AR00-BLR Rule 28. PHOTOGRAPHS, BROADCASTING, TELEVISING AND RECORDING PROHIBITED

The Boone Circuit and Superior Courts hereby specifically adopt CANON 3B(13) OF THE INDIANA CODE OF JUDICIAL CONDUCT, ADOPTED BY THE SUPREME COURT OF INDIANA AS FOLLOWS:

"(13) A judge should prohibit broadcasting, televising, recording, or taking photographs in the courtroom and areas immediately adjacent thereto during sessions of court or recesses between sessions, except that a judgment may authorize:

(A) the use of electronic or photographic means for the presentation of evidence, for the perpetuation of a record, or for other purposes of judicial administration;

(B) the broadcasting, televising, recording, or photographing of investitive, ceremonial, or naturalization proceedings;

(C) the photographic or electronic recording and production of appropriate court proceedings under the following conditions:

(1) the means of recording will not distract participants or impair the dignity of the proceedings;

(2) the parties have consented, and the consent to being depicted or recorded has been obtained from each

(3) the reproduction will not be exhibited until after the proceedings has been concluded and all direct appeals have been exhausted; and,

(4) the reproduction will be exhibited only for instructional purposes in educational institutions."

In compliance with this rule, broadcasting, televising, recording and the taking of photographs are prohibited in these areas of each court:

Courtroom

Office of the Judge's Staff

Judge's Chambers

Witness waiting area

The entire third floor is included as a prohibited area, as is the Commissioner's office, the Guardian ad Litem's office and the Video Hearing Room.

The areas immediately outside all entrances to the Superior II Courtroom and the Superior II Jury Deliberation Room.

On a limited basis, photographs may be taken when authorized by the Judges.

Formerly Rule 29, adopted effective June 1, 2006. Renumbered as Rule 28 and amended effective Jan. 4, 2010.

LR06-AR00-BLR Rule 29. CIVILITY

The following standards are designed to encourage us, judges and lawyers alike, to meet our obligations to each other, to litigants and to the system of justice, and thereby achieve the twin goals of civility and professionalism, both of which are hallmarks of a learned profession dedicated to public service.

We expect judges and lawyers will make a mutual and firm commitment to these standards. Voluntary adherence is expected as part of a commitment by all participants to improve the administration of justice.

These standards shall not be used as a basis for litigation or for sanctions or penalties. Nothing in these standards supersedes or detracts from existing disciplinary codes or alters existing standards of conduct against which lawyer negligence may be determined.

These standards should be reviewed and followed by all judges and lawyers participating in any proceeding in the Boone County court system. Copies may be made available to clients to reinforce our obligation to maintain and foster these standards.

Lawyers' Duties to Other Counsel.

1. We will practice our profession with a continuing awareness that our role is to advance the legitimate interests of our clients. In our dealings with others we will not reflect the ill feelings of clients. We will treat all other counsel, parties, and witnesses in a civil and courteous manner, not only in court, but also in all other written and oral communications.

2. We will not, even when called upon by a client to do so, abuse or indulge in offensive conduct directed to other counsel, parties, or witnesses. We will abstain from disparaging personal remarks or acrimony toward other counsel, parties or witnesses. We will treat adverse witnesses and parties with fair consideration.

3. We will not encourage or knowingly authorize any person under our control to engage in conduct that would be improper if we were to engage in such conduct.

4. We will not, absent good cause, attribute bad motives or improper conduct to other counsel or bring the profession into disrepute by unfounded accusations of impropriety.

5. We will not seek court sanctions without first conducting a reasonable investigation and unless fully justified by the circumstances and necessary to protect our client's lawful interests.

6. We will adhere to all express promises and to agreements with other counsel, whether oral or in writing, and will adhere in good faith to all agreements implied by the circumstances or local customs.

7. When we reach an oral understanding on a proposed agreement or a stipulation and decide to commit it to writing, the drafter will endeavor in good faith to state the oral understanding accurately and completely. The drafter will provide the opportunity for review of the writing to other counsel. As drafts are exchanged between or among

counsel, changes from prior drafts will be identified in the draft or otherwise explicitly brought to the attention of other counsel. We will not include in a draft matters to which there has been no agreement without explicitly advising other counsel in writing of the addition.

8. We will endeavor to confer early with other counsel to assess settlement possibilities. We will not falsely hold out the possibility of settlement as a means to adjourn discovery or to delay trial.

9. In civil actions, we will stipulate to relevant matters if they are undisputed and if no good faith advocacy basis exists for not stipulating.

10. We will not use any form of discovery or discovery scheduling as a means of harassment.

11. We will make good faith efforts to resolve by agreement our objections to matters contained in pleadings and discovery requests and objections.

12. We will not time the filing or service of motions or pleadings in any way that unfairly limits another party's opportunity to respond.

13. We will not request an extension of time solely for the purpose of unjustified delay or to obtain a tactical advantage.

14. We will consult other counsel regarding scheduling matters in a good faith effort to avoid scheduling conflicts.

15. We will endeavor to accommodate previously scheduled dates for hearings, depositions, meetings, conferences, vacations, seminars, or other functions that produce good faith calendar conflicts on the part of other counsel. If we have been given an accommodation because of a calendar conflict, we will notify those who have accommodated us as soon as the conflict has been removed.

16. We will notify other counsel and, if appropriate, the court or other persons, at the earliest possible time when hearings, depositions, meetings, or conferences are to be canceled or postponed. Early notice avoids unnecessary travel and expense of counsel and may enable the court to use the previously reserved time for other matters.

17. We will agree to reasonable requests for extension of time and for waiver of procedural formalities, provided our clients' legitimate rights will not be materially or adversely affected.

18. We will not cause any default or dismissal to be entered without first notifying opposing counsel when we know his or her identity.

19. We will take depositions only when actually needed to ascertain facts or information or to perpetuate testimony. We will not take depositions for the purposes of harassment or to increase litigation expenses.

20. We will not engage in any conduct during a deposition that would not be appropriate in the presence of a judge.

21. We will not obstruct questioning during a deposition or object to deposition questions unless necessary under the applicable rules to preserve an objection or privilege for resolution by the court.

22. During depositions we will ask only those questions we reasonably believe are necessary for the prosecution or defense of an action.

23. We will carefully craft document production requests so they are limited to those documents we reasonably believe are necessary for the prosecution or defense of an action. We will not design production requests to place an undue burden or expense on a party.

24. We will respond to document requests reasonably and not strain to interpret the request in an artificially restrictive manner to avoid disclosure of relevant and non-privileged documents. We will not produce documents in a manner designed to hide or obscure the existence of particular documents.

25. We will carefully craft interrogatories so they are limited to those matters we reasonably believe are necessary for the prosecution or defense of an action, and we will not design them to place an undue burden or expense on a party.

26. We will respond to interrogatories reasonably and will not strain to interpret them in an artificially restrictive manner to avoid disclosure of relevant and non-privileged information.

27. We will base our discovery objections on a good faith belief in their merit and will not object solely for the purpose of withholding or delaying the disclosure of relevant information.

28. When a draft order is to be prepared by counsel to reflect a court ruling, we will draft an order that accurately and completely reflects the court's ruling. We will promptly prepare and submit a proposed order to other counsel and attempt to reconcile any differences before the draft order is presented to the court.

29. We will not ascribe a position to another counsel that counsel has not taken or otherwise seek to create an unjustified inference based on counsel's statements or conduct.

30. Unless specifically permitted or invited by the court, we will not send copies of correspondence between counsel to the court.

Lawyers' Duties to the Court.

1. We will speak and write civilly and respectfully in all communications with the court.

2. We will be punctual and prepared for all court appearances so that all hearings, conferences, and trials may commence on time; if delayed, we will notify the court and counsel, if possible.

3. We will be considerate of the time constraints and pressures on the court and court staff inherent in their efforts to administer justice.

4. We will not engage in any conduct that brings disorder or disruption to the courtroom. We will advise our clients and witnesses appearing in court

of the proper conduct expected and required there and, to the best of our ability, prevent our clients and witnesses from creating disorder or disruption.

5.   We will not knowingly misrepresent, mischaracterize, misquote, or miscite facts or authorities in any oral or written communication to the court.

6.   We will not write letters to the court in connection with a pending action, unless invited or permitted by the court.

7.   Before dates for hearings or trials are set, or if that is not feasible, immediately after such date has been set, we will attempt to verify the availability of necessary participants and witnesses so we can promptly notify the court of any likely problems.

8.   We will act and speak civilly to court clerks, court reporters, and secretaries, with awareness that they, too, are an integral part of the judicial system.

Courts' Duties to Lawyers.

1.   We will be courteous, respectful, and civil to lawyers, parties, and witnesses. We will maintain control of the proceedings, recognizing that judges have both the obligation and the authority to insure that all litigation proceedings are conducted in a civil manner.

2.   We will not employ hostile, demeaning, or humiliating words in opinions or in written or oral commendations with lawyers, parties, or witnesses.

3.   We will be punctual in convening all hearings, meetings, and conferences; if delayed, we will notify counsel, if possible.

4.   In scheduling all hearings, meetings and conferences, we will be considerate of time schedules of lawyers, parties, and witnesses.

5.   We will make all reasonable efforts to decide promptly all matters presented to us for decision.

6.   We will give the issues in controversy deliberate, impartial, and studied analysis and consideration.

7.   While endeavoring to resolve disputes efficiently, we will be considerate of the time constraints and pressures imposed on lawyers by the exigencies of litigation practice.

8.   We recognize that a lawyer has a right and a duty to present a cause fully and properly, and that a litigant has a right to a fair and impartial hearing. Within the practical limits of time, we will allow lawyers to present proper arguments and to make a complete and accurate record.

9.   We will not impugn the integrity or professionalism of any lawyer on the basis of the clients whom, or the causes which a lawyer represents.

10.   We will do our best to insure that court personnel act civilly toward lawyers, parties, and witnesses.

11.   We will not adopt procedures that needlessly increase litigation expense.

12.   We will bring to lawyers' attention uncivil conduct which we observe.

Formerly Rule 30, adopted effective June 1, 2006. Renumbered as Rule 29 and amended effective Jan. 4, 2010.

LR06-AR01-BLR Rule 30. BOONE COUNTY'S CASE LOAD PLAN

We, the undersigned Judges of Boone County in compliance with Indiana Administrative Rule 1(E), hereby adopt Local Rule 30 entitled "Boone County's Case Load Plan."

WHEREAS, Indiana Administrative Rule 1(E) requires the Judges of Boone County to implement a caseload allocation plan for the county that ensures an even distribution of judicial workload among the courts of record in the county; and

WHEREAS, the Courts of Boone County, pursuant to Legislative direction and the evolution of time, have acquired certain subject matter expertise that the Judges of Boone County believe should not be altered, but instead should be preserved and enhanced upon, i.e., Circuit Court has exclusive jurisdiction over all juvenile matters, including, but not limited to, Status Offenses, Delinquent Offenses, CHINS proceedings and Paternity matters; Superior I has exclusive jurisdiction over all Estates, Guardianships, Probate matters and Adoptions; and Superior II has exclusive jurisdiction over all Small Claims and certain Alcohol and Drug Offenses;

WHEREAS, the Judges of Boone County have met and discussed Indiana Administrative Rule 1(E) and have established the following plan for allocation of judicial resources within Boone County which maintains the integrity of the courts in Boone County:

IT IS THEREFORE ORDERED by the Judges of Boone County that for calendar year 2009 and beyond, within 60 days of the Supreme Court's issuance of the previous year's Weighted Caseload Report, as reported by the Division of State Court Administration, the report will be reviewed by the Judges to determine whether Boone County's caseload complies with Indiana Administrative Rule 1(E).

To the extent that the difference in utilization of any two (2) Courts of Record exceeds 0.40 percentage points, then the Judges of Boone County agree to alter or modify the distribution of cases in the County to bring each Court within the range of 0.40 percentage points by amending Local Rule 13, Non–Discretionary filing of Criminal Cases. If all the courts of record are within 0.40 percentage points then no action will be taken.

The Judges of Boone County have determined that this method can be implemented with very little administrative effort and that it will have a minimal effect on the Prosecuting Attorney's office and a negligible effect on the Local Bar Association. The statistics for the previous year's criminal filings are readily available and the necessary adjustments can be made very quickly and modifications made to Local Rule 11 can be easily distributed to the Clerk's Office and the Prosecutor's Office.

Consistent with the schedule to be set and monitored by the Indiana Supreme Court Division of State Court Administration (Division), the Boone County Judges will review weighted caseload statistics and submit a new caseload allocation plan or resubmit an existing plan every two (2) years. In addition, an amended Local Rule 13 will be implemented by Boone County Judges, when applicable. Moreover, the Judges of Boone County have agreed to review this Rule every two years to determine whether other adjustments should be made in the distribution of cases in Boone County outside the spectrum of Local Rule 11.

Formerly Rule 31, adopted effective June 1, 2006. Renumbered as Rule 30 and amended effective Jan. 1, 2010.

LR06-AR00-BLR Rule 31. COMPLIANCE WITH RULES

All counsel and/or parties having matters before the Boone Circuit, Superior I or Superior II Courts are presumed to have knowledge of the Courts' Rules and are expected to comply accordingly.

Formerly Rule 32, adopted effective June 1, 2006. Renumbered as Rule 31 and amended effective Jan. 4, 2010.

LR06-AR00-BLR Rule 32. CONFLICTS IN RULES

In the event of conflict between these rules and the Rules of the Supreme Court of Indiana the applicable law or the Rule of the Supreme Court of Indiana shall govern.

Formerly Rule 33, adopted effective June 1, 2006. Renumbered as Rule 32 and amended effective Jan. 4, 2010.

LR06-TR81-BLR Rule 33. NOTICE

Copies of the foregoing Rules shall be certified to the Indiana Supreme Court and the Court of Appeals pursuant to Indiana Rules of Procedure, T.R. 81. Copies of these Rules shall be posted in the Clerk's Office, on the bulletin board in the respective Courts to which these rules apply and a copy of these rules shall at all times be available at counsel tables in open Court of the respective Courts to which the rules apply.

Formerly Rule 34, adopted effective June 1, 2006. Renumbered as Rule 33 and amended effective Jan. 4, 2010.

LOCAL ADMINISTRATIVE RULES OF PRACTICE FOR THE COURTS OF CLARK COUNTY

Adopted July 15, 2009, Effective July 15, 2009

Including Amendments Received Through November 1, 2013

LR10–AR00 Rule 1. APPLICABILITY OF RULES

A. Scope. The following Local Rules of Practice shall apply to cases filed in the Circuit and Superior Courts of Clark County, Indiana.

B. Effective Date. These Rules shall be effective May 1, 2009, and shall supersede the rules currently applied in the Courts.

C. Citation. These Rules may be cited as Local Rule 1 [LR10–AROO–18].

Adopted Aug. 15, 2006, effective Jan. 1, 2007.

LR10–AR00 Rule 2. APPEARANCE AND WITHDRAWAL OF APPEARANCE

A. Initial Appearance. An attorney entering an appearance for any party shall file a written appearance in compliance with Trial Rule 3.1 of the Indiana Rules of Trial Procedure.

B. Withdrawal of Appearance. Except for appearances in estates, guardianships, or criminal matters, an attorney desiring to withdraw an appearance in any other proceeding shall file a written motion requesting leave to withdraw accompanied by a notice of hearing or proof satisfactory to the Court that a notice has been given to the client and all other parties of record at least ten (10) days in advance of the withdrawal date. The actual withdrawal date shall be set forth in the written notice.

C. Withdrawal in Estate, Guardianship, or Criminal Cases. An attorney who desires to withdraw his appearance in an estate, guardianship, or criminal case shall file a written notice requesting leave to withdraw accompanied by a notice of hearing which shall be served upon the personal representative, guardian, or criminal defendant directing the person to appear at the hearing. Proof of the notice shall be submitted to the Court at the time of the hearing.

E.[1] Waiver of Rule. A motion for leave to withdraw an appearance accompanied by a written appearance of successor counsel shall constitute a waiver of the requirements of this rule. Except for appearances in estate, guardianship, or criminal cases, a motion to withdraw appearance accompanied by the written consent of the client shall also constitute a waiver of the requirements of this rule.

Adopted Aug. 15, 2006, effective Jan. 1, 2007.

[1] There is no Subd. D in original.

LR10–AR00 Rule 3. DUTY OF ATTORNEYS TO PREPARE ENTRIES

A. Preparation of Entry. When opposing counsel has appeared in a proceeding, the attorney who has agreed to prepare an entry as requested by the Court shall place on the last page of the entry appropriate signature lines indicating "prepared by" and "reviewed by" and shall submit the entry to opposing counsel for examination. Opposing counsel shall promptly examine the entry when submitted, shall sign the entry, and shall submit the entry to the Court within five (5) days of receiving the entry. If opposing counsel does not agree with the entry, counsel shall advise the Court and request a conference, telephonic or otherwise.

B. Failure to Submit Entry. If opposing counsel shall fail or refuse to sign the entry without advising the Court as to any objections to the entry, the preparing attorney shall submit the entry to the Court advising by letter of opposing counsel's failure or refusal and the Court shall accept the entry without opposing counsel's signature.

C. Failure to Prepare Entry. If an attorney agrees to prepare an entry and then fails to do so within fifteen (15) working days of the Court's request, opposing counsel may prepare the entry and submit the entry to the Court advising the Court by letter of the efforts made to gain preparation of the entry by opposing counsel. Failure of counsel to prepare an entry as agreed may subject counsel to sanctions including the assessment of reasonable attorney fees for the attorney who prepared the entry.

Adopted Aug. 15, 2006, effective Jan. 1, 2007. Amended effective Jan. 24, 2008.

LR10–AR00 Rule 4. FORM AND STYLE OF PLEADINGS FILING OF PLEADINGS

A. Signature Required. Any pleading, motion, brief or paper filed by an attorney but not signed by an attorney admitted to practice in this state shall not be accepted for filing, or, if inadvertently accepted for filing, may upon discovery be stricken from the record by the Court upon its own motion and by an appropriate minute placed on the Chronological Case Summary. This rule does not prohibit the filing of any pleading, motion, brief or paper by a pro se litigant. Pro se litigants are required to adhere to these Local Rules.

B. Paper Size. All pleadings, motions, entries, orders, judgments and other papers shall be filed on letter size [8 1/2 × 11] paper.

C. Identification. Every pleading, motion, brief, and paper shall clearly identify the name, office address, telephone number, and Indiana Supreme Court Attorney Number of the individual attorney or attorneys filing same.

D. Uniform Pleading Header. Every pleading shall have a header in the following style:

IN THE CIRCUIT COURT NO. __ FOR CLARK COUNTY
STATE OF INDIANA

E. Use of Paralegal. All pleadings, motions, briefs and papers may be filed by the attorney's secretary or paralegal.

F. Orders and Entries. All proposed orders and entries shall reflect the name of the preparer under the indication "tendered by", shall be submitted in sufficient number for each person entitled to service, and shall contain a distribution list identifying by name and address each person entitled to service.

F.[1] Use of Special Judge. If a case has a special judge, such fact shall be indicated by the words SPECIAL JUDGE (NAME) placed directly beneath the case number. Unless otherwise directed by a special judge after qualification, a copy of each document filed thereafter in the proceeding shall be served on the Special Judge at his private office or at the Court

where the Special Judge regularly presides and the proof of service may reflect such service.

G. Orders and Judgments by Magistrate. Any Order or Judgment wherein a Magistrate has presided over the case in a criminal matter or Small Claims matter shall contain a signature line for the Magistrate only.

Any final and appealable Order or Judgment granted by a Magistrate in a civil matter, including but not limited to Judgments, Default Judgments, Summary Judgments, Dissolution Decrees, Adoption Orders and Foreclosure Judgments of any kind, shall include a Recommendation by the Magistrate and Approval by the presiding Judge as follows:

Recommended by: _____
Magistrate
Approved by: _____
Judge (Name of Judge)
(Name of Court)

Adopted July 15, 2009, effective July 15, 2009. Amended effective Jan. 1, 2012.

1 Two Subd. F in original.

LR10–AR00 Rule 5. ALLOCATION OF CASES

A. Applicability. This rule shall apply only to those cases filed in the Circuit Courts in Clark County, Indiana. This Rule shall not apply to misdemeanor cases filed in the Jeffersonville City Court or the Clarksville Town Court.

B. Major Felony Cases. Except as otherwise specifically provided for, all cases which include Murder, Class A Felony, Class B Felony, or Class C Felony offenses as the most serious charged shall be assigned on an equal basis between the Judge of the Clark Circuit Court No. 1 and the Clark Circuit Court No. 4. Cases with co-defendants shall be filed in the same court.

C. Misdemeanor and Class D Felony Cases. Except as otherwise specifically provided, all cases having a misdemeanor or Class D Felony as the most serious charge shall be assigned to the Judge of Circuit Court No. 3.

D. Traffic–Related Cases. All cases which include a felony charge relating to traffic or motor vehicles, under Title 9 of the Indiana Code or Indiana Code 35–42–1 (Homicide) shall be assigned to the Judge of Circuit Court No. 3.

E. Controlled Substances Cases. All Class A, Class B, Class C and Class D felony cases which include a charge related to Controlled Substances under Indiana Code 35–48 or Legend Drugs under Indiana Code 16–42 shall be assigned to the Judge of Circuit Court No. 2. All new Class D or multiple Class D Felony cases which include driving offenses shall be assigned to the Judge of Circuit Court No. 3.

F. Juvenile Criminal Cases. All cases which include a misdemeanor or felony charge against a defendant alleged to be under the age of eighteen (18) at the time of the commission of the offense, shall be assigned to the Judge of Circuit Court No. 4.

All cases which include a charge of Contributing to the Delinquency under Indiana Code 35–46–1–8 or Violation of Compulsory School Attendance under Indiana Code 20–8.1–3 shall be assigned to the Judge of Circuit Court No. 4.

G. Attempt, Conspiracy, and Aiding Cases. For purposes of this Rule, when a case includes a charge of Attempt under Indiana Code 35–41–5–1, Conspiracy under Indiana Code 35–41–5–1, or Aiding under Indiana Code 35–41–2–4, proper assignment of the case shall be determined by reference to the substantive offense underlying each charge.

H. Re-filing of Dismissed Cases. In the event a criminal case is dismissed, and thereafter, the same or similar case is filed against the same defendant(s) base upon the same transaction, the case shall be assigned to the judge who entered the Order of Dismissal on the earlier case.

I. Juvenile Paternity Cases. One-half of the Juvenile Paternity cases shall be assigned to the Judge of Circuit Court No. 1. One-half of the Juvenile Paternity cases shall be assigned on an equal basis to the Judges of Circuit Court No. 2 and No. 4.

J. Other Juvenile Cases. All Juvenile CHINS cases, Juvenile Status cases, Juvenile Termination of Parental Rights cases, and Juvenile Miscellaneous cases shall be assigned to the Judge of Circuit Court No. 4.

K. Mortgage Foreclosure and Civil Collection Cases. Mortgage Foreclosure cases shall be assigned on an equal basis to the Judges of Circuit Court No. 1 and Circuit Court No. 2.

L. Civil Tort and Civil Plenary Cases. Civil Tort and Civil Plenary cases shall be assigned on an equal basis to the Judges of Circuit Court No. 1, No. 2 and No. 4.

M. Small Claims Cases. All Small Claims cases shall be assigned to the Judge of Circuit Court No. 3.

N. Mental Health Cases. All Mental Health cases shall be assigned to the Judge of Circuit Court No. 1.

O. Domestic Relations Cases. Domestic Relations cases shall be assigned on an equal basis to the Judges of the Circuit Courts.

P. Reciprocal Support Cases. All Reciprocal Support cases shall be assigned to the Judge of Circuit Court No. 1.

Q. Protective Order Cases. All Protective Order cases shall be assigned to the Judge of Circuit Court No. 2 unless the Protective Order request is associated with a Dissolution of Marriage case filed in another court. In such instance, the Protective Order request shall be assigned to that court.

R. Guardianship and Estate Cases. One-half of the Guardianship cases shall be assigned to the Judge of Circuit Court No. 1 and one-half of the Guardianship cases shall be assigned on an equal basis to the Judges of Clark Circuit Court No. 2 and No. 4. Estate cases (supervised and unsupervised) shall be assigned to the Judge of Circuit Court No. 1.

S. Trust Cases. All Trust cases shall be assigned to the Judge of Circuit Court No. 1.

T. Adoption Cases. All Adoption Cases shall be assigned on an equal basis to the Judges of the Circuit Courts.

U. Family Court Exceptions. This subsection applies to situations of pending CHINS or juvenile delinquency matters in Circuit Court No. 4. Notwithstanding any other provision of this Rule, when a family law case (e. g., dissolution, paternity, guardianship, adoption, reciprocal support) or a modification of an existing family law case involving the same family in the pending CHINS or juvenile delinquency matter is presented to the Clerk for filing, that matter shall be filed in or transferred to Circuit Court No. 4. When a CHINS or juvenile delinquency case is filed in Circuit Court No. 4 after a family law case has been filed in any other court, the judge with jurisdiction over the family law case shall transfer that case to Circuit Court No. 4. The Judge of Circuit Court No. 4 may request a transfer of certain criminal cases where those cases have a direct impact on allocation of parenting time or placement of the child in a pending CHINS or delinquency matter.

V. Exceptions for Defendant with Pending Cases. When a new criminal case filing involves a defendant who has a pending criminal case, other than a Petition to Revoke Probation, the provisions of this subsection shall apply. If a defendant has a pending case in Circuit Court No. 1 or Circuit Court No. 4 and is charged with a new offense that is not (1) a traffic or driving related offense or (2) a felony drug or controlled substance offense, the new case shall be filed where the current case is pending. If a defendant has a pending case in Circuit Court No. 2 or Circuit Court No. 3 that is not (1) a traffic or driving related offense or (2) a felony drug or controlled substance offense, and a new case is filed against that defendant in Circuit Court No. 1 or Circuit Court No. 4, the pending case in the other court shall be transferred to Circuit Court No. 1 or Circuit Court No. 4 upon the filing of the new charge.

W. Transfer of Cases. When a Judge of the Circuit Court deems it appropriate, and consistent with the authority granted to these Courts by statute, any Judge of such Courts may enter an Order, after initial filing, transferring any civil, family or criminal case to the docket of any such other Court in Clark County.

X. Error in Case Assignments. Any error in the assignment of a criminal case shall not constitute grounds for an appeal or post-conviction relief unless actual bias or prejudice of the judge hearing the case is demonstrated

Y. Clerk Management of Case Assignment Process. The Clerk of the Circuit Courts shall, upon the approval of the Judges of each such Court, implement and manage an appropriate, efficient system for distribution of cases described in the foregoing subsections as being the object of assignment "on an equal basis."

Adopted Aug. 15, 2006, effective Jan. 1, 2007. Amended effective July 15, 2009; Jan. 1, 2012.

LR10–AR00 Rule 6. PRE–TRIAL CONFERENCES ASSIGNMENT OF CASES FOR TRIAL

A. Trial Settings. No case shall be assigned for jury trial without the Court having conducted a pre-trial conference or an Initial Hearing in a criminal case.

B. Attendance at Pre-trial Conference. At least one attorney, for each party, admitted to practice in Indiana, shall appear at the pre-trial conference. Attorneys, with court approval, may participate in the pre-trial conference telephonically. An attorney who fails to attend/participate for a pre-trial conference shall be bound by the trial date set by the Court as well as such other matters contained in the Court's Pre–Trial Order.

C. Requests for Bench Trial. The assignment of a case for a bench trial may be accomplished by a motion duly filed and accompanied by a proposed order. The motion shall reflect an estimate of the time required.

Adopted Aug. 15, 2006, effective Jan. 1, 2007.

LR10–AR00 Rule 7. MOTIONS

A. Generally. All written motions shall be filed with (a) a proposed order of the Movant and (b) a proposed order setting the motion for hearing. Any motion not accompanied by these required draft orders may be returned, without action taken, to the filing party until these draft orders are tendered.

B. Time for Responses to Motions. Except when time periods are otherwise provided in Indiana Trial Rules, Criminal Rules or Statutes, it is recommended that any party opposing any written motion filed should file their Response or Objection within ten (10) days after filing of any Motion.

C. Notice/Motion/Order Procedure. In lieu of requesting any hearing on any motion, an attorney may utilize a Notice/Motion/Order procedure for non-dispositive and routine motions. The attorney utilizing this procedure shall also file, at the time of filing a written motion and orders required by subsection A above, a written Notice of Ruling, stating that the Court will rule on the Motion and enter its Order

upon such Motion beginning at 1:30 o'clock p.m. on the Friday (unless a different day and time is required by any individual court). The Notice/Motion/Order pleadings shall be filed and served on the opposing party not later than seven (7) days prior to the date of the scheduled ruling.

Adopted Aug. 15, 2006, effective Jan. 1, 2007. Amended effective Jan. 24, 2008.

LR10–AR00 Rule 8. CONTINUANCES

A. Generally. A motion for continuance of a hearing or trial shall be accompanied by an order which shall contain adequate space for the insertion of a new time and date for rescheduling purposes.

B. Content of Motion/Position of Opposing Party. A Motion for Continuance shall set forth the scheduled date, the reason for the continuance, and the specific length of time the moving party desires the case to be delayed. Every Motion for Continuance must contain a statement of agreement or objection from opposing parties, obtained by the moving party after having made inquiry of opposing parties. Failure to state the position of opposing parties will prevent any court action on a Motion for Continuance.

C. Telephonic Conferences. If parties do not agree on a Motion for Continuance filed, either party may schedule a telephone conference with the Court for the purpose of discussing the motion or the objection.

Adopted Aug. 15, 2006, effective Jan. 1, 2007. Amended effective Jan. 24, 2008.

LR10–AR00 Rule 9. DISCOVERY

A. Scope/Resolution of Disputes. The parties to a case are expected to perform discovery on the manner provided by Indiana Trial Rules, statutes and case decisions. The parties shall conform to all requirements of Rule 26 (F) in attempting to resolve discovery disputes before seeking court intervention upon any such dispute.

B. Use of Form Discovery. No "form" discovery shall be served upon a party unless all discovery requests on such forms are consecutively numbered and applicable to the case.

C. Admissions Format. Answers or objections to requests for admissions filed and served pursuant to Trial Rule 36 shall set forth in full the request for admissions being answered or objected to immediately preceding the answer or objection.

D. Limitation on Interrogatories. The number of interrogatories which may be served pursuant to Trial Rule 33 shall be limited so as to require the answering party to make no more than forty (40) answers, each sub-part of an interrogatory counting as one (1) answer. This limitation does not mean a limit of forty (40) interrogatories and answers for the entire case but rather to each set of interrogatories propounded. Waiver of this limitation will be granted by the Court in cases in which this limitation would work a manifest injustice or would be impractical because of the complexity of the issues in the case.

E. Motion for Waiver of Interrogatory Limit. Each motion requesting a waiver of the above limitation of interrogatories shall contain, as an exhibit, the interrogatories which the party proposes to serve.

Adopted Aug. 15, 2006, effective Jan. 1, 2007.

LR10–AR00 Rule 10.   CONTEMPT/ISSUANCE OF BODY ATTACHMENT

A. Contempt Citation. Whenever a judgment debtor fails to appear as ordered for a scheduled hearing, the judgment creditor may file a contempt citation against the debtor. The citation must be filed within thirty (30) days of the failure to appear.

B. Personal Service Required. If a judgment creditor is desirous of using a body attachment whenever a judgment debtor fails to appear as directed in a contempt citation, the contempt citation must be personally read and served on the debtor with proof of service presented to the Court along with the request for issuance of the body attachment. Leaving a copy at the debtor's residence or place of business is insufficient.

C. Notice to Sheriff. The body attachment must include a Notice to Sheriff which states that "the Judgment Defendant must be served during regular business hours. Do not place in jail. Bring the Judgment Defendant to Court upon service."

Adopted Aug. 15, 2006, effective Jan. 1, 2007.

LR10–AR00 Rule 11.   APPLICABILITY TO FAMILY LAW AND CRIMINAL CASES

These Local Administrative Rules shall generally apply to Family Law cases unless the Family Law Rules provide otherwise. Unless otherwise addressed in published Trial Rules, Rules of Criminal Procedure or in statutes or case decisions, prescribing scope and procedures of matters addressed above, these Local Rules of Practice shall otherwise apply to criminal cases in the Clark Circuit and Superior Courts.

Adopted Aug. 15, 2006, effective Jan. 1, 2007.

LR10–AR00 Rule 12.   APPLICABILITY TO NON–REPRESENTED LITIGANT CASES

These Local Administrative Rules shall apply to all persons who appear in court without the benefit of counsel including cases where the other party appears with or without counsel.

Adopted Aug. 15, 2006, effective Jan. 1, 2007.

LR10–AR00 Rule 13.   APPLICABILITY OF CERTAIN RULES IN SMALL CLAIMS CASES

These Rules shall apply in Small Claims cases, unless otherwise waived by the presiding Judge.

Adopted Aug. 15, 2006, effective Jan. 1, 2007.

LR10–AR00 Rule 14.   COURT REPORTER SERVICES/FEES AND ALCOHOL AND DRUG PROGRAM FEES

A. Definitions. The following definitions shall apply under this Local Rule:

[1] *Court Reporter*—a person who is specifically designated by a court to perform the official court reporting services for the court including preparing a transcript of the record.

[2] *Equipment*—physical items owned by the court or other governmental entity and used by a court reporter in performing court reporting services. Equipment shall include, but not be limited to, telephones, computer hardware, software programs, disks, tapes, and any other device used for recording and storing, and transcribing electronic data.

[3] *Work Space*—that portion of the court's facilities dedicated to each court reporter, including but not limited to actual space in the courtroom and any designated office space.

[4] *Page*—the page unit of transcript which results when a recording is transcribed in the form required by Indiana Rule of Appellate Procedure 7. 2.

[5] *Recording*—the electronic, mechanical, stenographic or other recording made as required by Indiana Rule of Trial Procedure 74.

[6] *Regular Hours Worked*—those hours which the court is regularly scheduled to work during any given work week. Depending on the particular court, these hours may vary from court to court within the county but remain the same for each work week.

[7] *Gap Hours Worked*—those hours worked that are in excess of the regular hours worked but not in excess of forty (40) hours per work week.

[8] *Overtime Hours Worked*—those hours worked in excess of forty (40) hours per work week.

[9] *Work Week*—a seven (7) consecutive day week that consistently begins and ends on the same days throughout the year, i.e. Sunday through Saturday, Wednesday through Tuesday, Friday through Thursday.

[10] *Court*—the particular court for which the court reporter performs services. Court may also mean all the courts in Clark County.

[11] *County Indigent Transcript*—a transcript that is paid for from county funds and is for the use on behalf of a litigant who has been declared indigent by a court.

[12] *State Indigent Transcript*—a transcript that is paid for from state funds and is for the use of a litigant who has been declared indigent by a court.

[13] *Private Transcript*—a transcript, including but not limited to a deposition transcript, which is paid for by a private party.

B. Salaries. Court reporters shall be paid an annual salary for time spent working under the control, direction and direct supervision of their supervising court during any regular work hours, gap hours or overtime hours. The supervising court shall enter into a written agreement with the court reporters which outlines the manner in which the court reporter is to be compensated for gap and overtime hours, i.e. monetary compensation for compensatory time off regular work hours.

C. Per Page Fees. The maximum per page fee a court reporter may charge for the preparation of a county indigent transcript shall be five dollars and fifty cents ($5.50) per page. The court reporter shall submit a claim directly to the county for the preparation of any county indigent transcripts. The maximum per page fee a court reporter may charge for the preparation of a state indigent transcript shall be five dollars and fifty cents ($5.50) per page. The maximum per page fee a court reporter may charge for the preparation of a private transcript shall be five dollars and fifty cents ($5.50) per page. The Index and Table of Contents pages may be charged at the per page rate being charged for the rest of the transcript.

If the Court Reporter is requested to prepare an expedited transcript, the maximum per page fee shall be twelve dollars and fifty cents ($12.50) per page when the transcript the transcript must be prepared within 24 hours or less, and ten dollars ($10.00) per page when the transcript must be prepared within three working days. Index and Table of Contents will be charged at the same rate as the other pages.

D. Minimum Fee. A minimum fee of fifty dollars ($50.00) will be charged for transcripts less than ten (10) pages in length.

E. Binding Fees. An additional labor charge approximating an hourly rate based upon the court reporter's annual court compensation shall be added to the cost of the transcript for the time spent binding the transcript and exhibit binders.

F. Office Supplies. A reasonable charge may be made for the costs of office supplies required and utilized for the preparation of the transcript, the binding of the transcript, and the electronic transmission of the transcript. This charge shall be based upon the Schedule of Transcript Supplies annually established and published by the judges of the courts of record of the county.

G. Annual Report Requirement. Each court reporter shall report, at least on an annual basis, all transcript fees received for the preparation of county indigent, state indigent or private transcripts to the Indiana Supreme Court Division of State Court Administration. The reporting shall be made on forms prescribed by the Division of State Court Administration.

H. Private Practice. If a court reporter elects to engage in private practice through the recording of a deposition and/or preparing a deposition transcript, all such private practice work shall be conducted outside regular working hours.

If a court reporter engages in such private practice and the court reporter desires to utilize the court's equipment, work space and supplies, and the court agrees to the use of the court equipment for such purpose, the court and the court reporter shall enter into a written agreement which must, at a minimum, designate the following:

[1] the reasonable market rate for the use of equipment, work space and supplies;

[2] the method by which records are to be kept for the use of equipment, work space and supplies; and

[3] the method by which the court reporter is to reimburse the court for the use of the equipment, work space and supplies.

I. Disk as Official Record. Upon the filing of a written request or praecipe for transcript, the court reporter shall transcribe any court proceeding requested and produce an original paper transcript along with an electronically formatted transcript. Multiple disks containing the electronically formatted transcript shall be prepared and designated as "Original Transcript" "Court Reporter's Copy" and "Court's Copy." Each disk shall be labeled to identify the case number, the names of the parties, the date completed, the court reporter's name, and the disk number if more than one disk is required for a complete transcript. The court's copy of the electronic transcript shall become the official record of the court proceeding, in lieu of a paper copy of the transcript, and shall be retained in the court where said proceeding was held. The court reporter's copy shall by retained by the court reporter. The original paper transcript along with the disk designated as the original transcript shall be forwarded to the Clerk if the transcript was prepared for purposes of appeal. If the transcript was not prepared for purposes of appeal, the original paper transcript shall be delivered to the requesting party.

J. Alcohol and Drug Program Fees. The schedule of fees set forth under Indiana Code 33–37–4–1 and Indiana Code 35–38–2–1 shall be applicable in all court alcohol and drug program services.

Adopted Aug. 15, 2006, effective Jan. 1, 2007. Amended effective July 15, 2009; Aug. 4, 2011.

LR10–TR79 Rule (H)–15. APPOINTMENT OF SPECIAL JUDGES

A. Selection of Assignment Judge. On or before October 1st of each year, the Judges of the Circuit Courts of Clark County shall meet with the presiding judges of Administrative District 23 for the purpose of selecting a judge designated as the assignment judge who shall serve the Administrative District for a period of twelve (12) months.

B. Section H Appointments. In the event it becomes necessary to appoint a special judge under Section H of Trial Rule 79 of the Indiana Rules of Trial Procedure, the judge before whom the case is pending shall send notice of the need of the appointment of a special judge to the Administrative District's assignment judge who shall then make such assignment within five (5) days of receiving said notice.

C. Method of Assignment. The Administrative District's assignment judge shall select special judges from a roster of the available judges in the Administrative District. The assignments shall be in sequential order beginning with the name of the judge following the last judge so assigned. If, however, a judge is otherwise disqualified to hear a particular case, that judge shall be deemed to be the next in sequence until assigned a case. The assignment judge shall maintain a record of all assignments and shall issue a summary report of the assignments on a quarterly basis.

D. Roster of Available Judges. The roster of available judges in Administrative District 23 shall be maintained by Court designation in the following sequential order and shall include senior judges as available.

(1) Clark Circuit #1

(2) Clark Circuit #2

(3) Clark Circuit #3

(4) Clark Circuit #4

(5) Floyd Circuit

(6) Floyd Superior #1

(7) Floyd Superior #2

(8) Floyd Superior #3

(9) Scott Circuit

(10) Scott Superior

(11) Senior Judges who agree to serve as Special Judge

E. Appointment Order. Upon selecting a special judge, the assignment judge shall prepare an Order of Appointment and forward said Order to the judge before whom the case is pending and enter an Order of Appointment and forward a copy of the Order to the special judge and the attorneys of record.

F. Acceptance of Jurisdiction. The Order of Appointment, when entered on the CCS by the judge before whom the case is pending, shall constitute acceptance of jurisdiction by the appointed special judge unless the judge is otherwise disqualified, and no special appearance, oath or additional evidence of acceptance shall be required.

G. Form of Order. The Order of Appointment shall be in the following form:

IN THE _____ COURT FOR _____
COUNTY
STATE OF INDIANA

(Caption)

ORDER OF APPOINTMENT

Under the provisions of Trial Rule 79(H) of the Indiana Rules of Trial Procedures, the Honorable _____ of the _____ Court of _____ County is hereby appointed to serve as special judge in the above-captioned case.

SO ORDERED AND ASSIGNED THIS __ DAY OF _____, __ BY THE ASSIGNMENT JUDGE FOR THE 23RD JUDICIAL DISTRICT.

_____
Assignment Judge

H. Implementation of Rule. In the event a selected Judge does not accept an appointment to serve as a special Judge under the provisions of section (D), (E) or (F) of Trial Rule 79 of the Indiana Rules of Trial Procedure, the judge before whom the case is pending shall notify the assignment judge of the need for an appointment of a special judge under this local rule.

I. Certification to Supreme Court. If, under the provisions of this rule, no judge is eligible to serve as a special judge in a case, the assignment judge shall notify the judge before whom the case is pending who shall then certify such fact to the Indiana Supreme Court for the appointment of a special judge. If the judge before whom the case is pending is of the opinion that the particular circumstances of a case warrants selection of a special judge by the Indiana Supreme Court, said judge shall certify such facts to the Indiana Supreme Court for the appointment of a special Judge. Under such circumstances this Rule shall not be implemented unless the Indiana Supreme Court declines to appoint a special Judge.

Amended effective July 1, 2011.

LOCAL FAMILY RULES OF PRACTICE FOR THE COURTS OF CLARK COUNTY

Adopted effective January 24, 2008

Including Amendments Received Through November 1, 2013

Research Notes

These rules may be searched electronically on Westlaw *in the* IN-RULES *database; updates to these rules may be found on* Westlaw *in* IN-RULESUPDATES. *For search tips and a summary of database content, consult the Westlaw Scope Screens for each database.*

LR10–FR00 Rule 1. APPLICABILITY OF RULES

A. Scope. These rules shall apply in the Clark County Circuit and Superior Courts in all family law matters.

B. Local Civil Rules. The Local Civil Rules of Practice enacted by the Courts shall be applicable in all family law matters when not in conflict with these Local Family Rules. (Local Civil Rules 12, 13, and 14 dealing with family matters are hereby repealed, the subject matters therein having been incorporated in these Local Family Rules).

C. Effective Date. These local family rules have been effective since March 1, 2000. The amendments consist primarily of the insertion of the words "parenting time" in place of the word "visitation."

D. Citation. These rules shall be cited as Local Family Rule ____.

Adopted effective Jan. 24, 2008.

LR10–FR00 Rule 2. PROVISIONAL ORDERS

A. Content of Provisional Pleading. A motion requesting provisional relief under I.C. 31–15–4–1 must be accompanied by an affidavit setting forth the factual basis and the relief requested. If the relief requested is in the nature of child support or other monetary assistance, the motion must contain information regarding each party's employment status and weekly gross income. When child support is requested, the motion must be accompanied by a Child Support Guideline Worksheet and a Parenting Time Credit Worksheet.

B. Order Scheduling Hearing/Preliminary Hearing. A motion requesting provisional relief must be accompanied by a proposed order for the setting of a hearing. If the provisional request includes relief in the nature of child custody or child support, the Court will set the matter for a preliminary hearing on those issues. The proposed Order scheduling hearings must be in a form consistent with that set forth in the Appendix to these Rules.

C. Procedure in Lieu of Hearing. A movant may waive the hearing requirements of I.C. 31–15–4–4 & 5 through the use of a Notice of Ruling accompanying the motion for provisional relief. The Notice of Ruling shall contain the following:

[1] A waiver of the hearing requirements;

[2] The date for ruling which shall not be less than ten (10) working days from the filing of the motion, the movant's counsel to select the date;

[3] Notice that the Court will consider a written response to the motion filed before the ruling date.

If a response to the motion for provisional relief is filed on or before the ruling date, the Court shall extend the ruling date by five (5) working days to allow the movant to file a reply to the response.

If service of the Summons and Notice of Ruling occurs on a date beyond the selected ruling date, the ruling date shall be automatically extended for ten (10) working days from the date of service and the time limitations for the filing of a response and a reply to the response shall be followed.

D. Request for Hearing. When a waiver of the hearing requirements has been made by the movant for provisional relief, the opposing party may, nonetheless, request hearing dates in accordance with the provisions of I.C. 31–15–4–4 & 5. A request for hearing dates must be filed within ten (10) days of the service of Summons and Notice of Ruling and must be accompanied by a proposed Order scheduling hearings in a form consistent with that set forth in the Appendix to these Rules. A request for hearing shall cancel the Notice of Ruling procedure described in Section C.

E. Effect of Change of Venue. The filing of a motion for a change of venue from the judge by either party shall not divest the court of jurisdiction from issuing a preliminary order on temporary custody, child support or parenting time. A written request for such a determination must be filed within five (5) days of service of the motion for change of venue. The filing of such a request shall be accompanied by a proposed Order for the setting of a preliminary hearing on those issues.

Adopted effective Jan. 24, 2008.

LR00–FR00 Rule 3. FINANCIAL DISCLOSURE STATEMENT

A. Requirement. In all contested dissolution, separation, and paternity actions each party shall prepare and exchange within forty-five (45) days of the filing of the action, a Verified Financial Disclosure Statement in such form consistent with that set forth in the Appendix to these Local Family Rules of Practice. For good cause, the time limit may be extended or shortened.

At the time of the filing of the action, the moving party shall serve a Notice upon the opposing party of the requirement to exchange a Verified Financial Dis-

closure Statement. Such Notice shall be in such form consistent with that set forth in the Appendix to these Local Family Rules of Practice.

B. Exceptions. The Verified Financial Disclosure Statement need not be exchanged if the the[1] parties agree in writing within thirty (30) days of the initial filing to waive exchange, or the proceeding is uncontested, or the proceeding is one in which service is by publication and there is no response.

C. Mandatory Discovery. The exchange of the Verified Financial Disclosure Statement constitutes mandatory discovery, therefore, the Indiana Trial Rule of Procedures, Trial Rule 37 sanctions apply. Additionally, pursuant to Trial Rule 26E(2) and (3) the Statement shall be supplemented if additional material becomes available.

D. Statement Considered Confidential. When a Verified Financial Disclosure Statement is filed with the court, it shall be sealed and designated "**Confidential.**"

Adopted effective Jan. 24, 2008.

LR10–FR00 Rule 4. CHILD SUPPORT USE OF SUPPORT GUIDELINES

A. Contested Hearings. In all hearings involving child support, each party shall submit to the court a Child Support Guideline Worksheet and Parenting Time Credit Worksheet in such form consistent with that set forth in the Indiana Child Support Rules and Guidelines.

B. Settlement Agreements. In all settlement agreements in which child support is established, a Child Support Guideline Worksheet and a Parenting Time Credit Worksheet shall be attached as an exhibit with the affirmation executed by the parties.

C. Deviation from Guidelines. If an agreement of the parties or a court order regarding child support deviates from the Guidelines, an adequate explanation for such a deviation must be set forth in the agreement or the order.

D. Effective Date. All orders establishing or modifying child support shall be effective on the Saturday immediately following the date on which the request for child support was filed unless otherwise provided for by statute.

Adopted effective Jan. 24, 2008.

LR10–FR00 Rule 5. PARENTING TIME

A. Use of Guidelines. Unless the court enters specific orders to the contrary or unless the parties otherwise agree to specific parenting terms, parenting time granted to the non-custodial parent shall be in accordance with the Indiana Parenting Time Guidelines.

B. Availability/Receipt of Guidelines. At the time of the filing of any original action or modification request which includes the issues of child custody and/or parenting time, the party bringing the action shall acquire a copy of the Indiana Parenting Time Guidelines fro the Clerk of the Court and send notice to the other party regarding the use of the Guidelines and the opportunity to obtain a copy of the Guidelines at the Clerk's office. The Clerk of the Court may charge a nominal fee for each copy of the Guidelines distributed. A notice in a form consistent with that set for in Appendix K will be sufficient.

C. Acknowledgment. If the parties acknowledge in writing that they have received a copy of the Indiana Parenting Time Guidelines and adopt the Guidelines as written or otherwise explain any deviation from the Guidelines in a settlement or final decree, it will not be necessary that a copy of the Guidelines be attached to the agreement or decree. A document reflecting the parties' signatures acknowledging receipt of a copy of the Guidelines shall be attached to the agreement or decree with a reference in the agreement.

D. Different Parenting Plan. If the parties adopt a parenting plan which is different from the guidelines, the plan must be set forth in the settlement agreement or dissolution decree.

Adopted effective Jan. 24, 2008.

LR10–FR00 Rule 6. TRANSPARENTING SEMINAR REQUIREMENT

A. Mandatory Attendance. In any dissolution or separation proceeding involving children under the age of eighteen (18) years of age, both parties to the proceedings shall attend and complete the seminar "Transparenting." In any post-dissolution proceeding where custody is in issue, both parties shall attend and complete the seminar unless a party has attended the seminar within the prior two (2) years.

B. Failure to Attend Seminar. A failure to attend and complete the seminar may constitute cause for denial of the granting of the dissolution or the relief requested and a continuance of the matter until attendance has been accomplished. A party, with leave of court, may attend a similar seminar or program.

C. Notice Requirement. At the time of the filing of a dissolution or separation proceeding or a post-dissolution proceeding where custody is in issue, the moving party shall serve a Notice upon the opposing party of the requirement of attendance in the Transparenting Seminar. Such Notice shall be in a form consistent with that set forth in the Appendix to these Local Family Rules of Procedure.

Adopted effective Jan. 24, 2008.

LR10–FR00 Rule 7. TRIAL RULE 65(E) JOINT PRELIMINARY INJUNCTION TEMPORARY RESTRAINING ORDER

RELIEF UNDER TRIAL RULE 65(E)(1)

A. Joint Preliminary Injunction. In accordance with the provisions of Trial Rule 65(E)(1), the court will issue a joint preliminary injunction applicable to both parties upon the filing of a verified petition by either party alleging that injury would result to the moving party if no order were to issue and requesting that both parties be enjoined from:

(a) Transferring, encumbering, concealing or otherwise disposing of any joint property of the parties or assets of the marriage without the written of the parties or permission of the court; and/or,

(b) Removing any child of the parties then residing in the State of Indiana from the State with the intent to deprive the court of jurisdiction over such child without the prior written consent of the parties or permission of the court.

B. Form of Injunction. The moving party shall prepare such order in a form consistent with that set forth in the Appendix to these Local Family Rules of Procedure.

C. Immediate Entry of Injunction. A request for a joint preliminary injunction will be entered in the record by the Clerk of the Court immediately upon filing and without bringing the matter to the attention of the judge or waiting for the judge to sign the original. Attorneys may use the court's signature stamp for the convenience of the Clerk and counsel.

RELIEF UNDER TRIAL RULE 65(E)(2)

D. Temporary Restraining Order. In accordance with the provisions of Trial Rule 65(E)(2), the Court will issue a temporary restraining order against the non-moving party upon the filing of a verified petition by either party alleging that injury would result to the moving party if no order were to issue and seeking to enjoin the non-moving party from:

(a) Abusing, harassing, disturbing the peace, or committing a battery on the moving party or Any child or step-child of the parties; or,

(b) Excluding the non-moving party from the family dwelling or any other place.

E. Specific Allegations Required. The moving party must set forth specific facts in the affidavit supporting the request for relief and the court shall determine from such facts whether such restraining order shall issue ex parte.

F. Form of Restraining Order. The moving party shall prepare such order in a form consistent with that set forth in the Appendix to these Local Family Rules of Practice.

G. Entry Only After Court Approval. The Clerk of the Court shall enter the restraining order in the record only after the judge signs the original order. Attorneys may not use the court's signature stamp until the original is signed by the judge.

STATUS OF TRIAL RULE 65(E) ORDERS

H. No Depository Record Maintained. A joint preliminary injunction and/or a temporary restraining order issued under Trial Rule 65(E) does not qualify for filing in a depository maintained by a law enforcement agency and a violation of the injunction does not constitute a basis of arrest for the offense of Invasion of Privacy. Such status shall be reflected on the order issued.

Adopted effective Jan. 24, 2008.

LR10–FR00 Rule 8. TEMPORARY RESTRAINING ORDERS ISSUED UNDER I.C. 31–15–4–7

RELIEF BASED UPON I.C. 31–15–4–3(1) & (4)

A. Temporary Restraining Order–Property. The court will issue a temporary restraining order against the non-moving party upon the filing of motion accompanied by an affidavit by either party alleging that injury would result to the moving party if no order were to issue and seeking to restrain the non-moving party from:

(a) transferring, encumbering, concealing, or in any way disposing of any property except in the usual course of business or for the necessities of life; and/or,

(b) granting temporary possession of property to either party.

B. Form of Order. The moving party shall prepare such order in a form consistent with that set forth in the Appendix to these Local Family Rules of Practice.

C. Immediate Entry of Order. A request for a temporary restraining order regarding property will be entered in the record by the Clerk of the Court immediately upon filing and without bringing the matter to the attention of the judge or waiting for the judge to sign the original. Attorney's may use the court's signature stamp for the convenience of the Clerk and counsel.

RELIEF BASED UPON I.C. 31–15–4–3(2) & (3)

D. Temporary Restraining Order–Personal. The court will issue a temporary restraining order against the non-moving party upon the filing of a motion accompanied by an affidavit by either party alleging that injury would result to the moving party if no order were to issue and seeking the following relief:

(a) enjoining any party from abusing, harassing, or disturbing the peace of the other party; and/or,

(b) excluding either party from the family dwelling, from the dwelling of the other, or from any other place.

E. Specific Allegations Required. The moving party must set forth specific facts in the affidavit supporting the request for relief and the court shall determine from such facts whether such restraining order shall issue ex parte.

F. Form of Order. The moving party shall prepare such order in form consistent with that set forth in the Appendix to these Local Family Rules of Practice.

G. Entry Only After Court Approval. The Clerk of the Court shall enter the restraining order in the record only after the judge signs the original order. Attorneys may not use the Court's signature stamp until the original is signed by the judge.

STATUS OF ORDERS ISSUED UNDER I.C. 31–15–4–7

G.[1] Temporary Restraining Order–Property. An order protecting property based upon I.C. 31–15–4–3(1) and (4) does not qualify for filing in a depository maintained by a law enforcement agency and a violation of the order does not constitute a basis of arrest for the offense of invasion of privacy. Such status shall be reflected on the order issued.

H. Temporary Restraining Order–Personal. An order protecting a person and/or excluding the other party from a dwelling based upon I.C. 31–15–4–3(2) and (3) does qualify for filing in a depository and a violation of such order may constitute a basis of arrest for the offense of invasion of property. Such status shall be reflected on the order issued.

I. Separate Orders Required. A Temporary Restraining Order—Property and a Temporary Restraining Order–Person requested under I.C. 31–15–4–3 may not be combined under one order and must issue as separate orders.

Adopted effective Jan. 24, 2008.

1 Multiple Subd. G in original.

LR10–FR00 Rule 9. MATTER OF PROTECTIVE ORDERS

A. Requirement upon Filing of Dissolution Petition and Issuance of Restraining Order–Personal. A Protective Order previously issued under I.C. 34–26–5 expires when a Petition For Dissolution of Marriage has been filed and a Temporary Restraining Order has been issued based upon the provisions of I.C. 31–15–4–3(2) or (3). In such event, the Petitioner shall file a Motion to Dismiss Protective Order in the Court where the original Protective Order was issued accompanied by an appropriate Order of Dismissal.

B. Requirement upon Filing of Dissolution Petition Only. When a Petition For Dissolution of Marriage has been filed in one court and the Petitioner has previously acquired a Protective Order issued under I.C. 34–26–5 in a different court, the Petitioner shall file a Motion to Dismiss Protective Order in the Court where the original Protective Order was issued accompanied by an appropriate Order of Dismissal. The Petitioner may simultaneously request the issuance of a protective order under I.C. 31–15–5 or a restraining order under I.C. 31–15–4–3 in the dissolution court, if desired.

C. Specific Request for Protective Order. If a dissolution or separation proceeding is pending, any request for a protective order must be filed in the separate action in the court where the dissolution or separation was filed.

D. Form of Order. The moving party shall prepare such order in a form consistent with that set forth in the Appendix to these Local Family Rules of Practice.

Adopted Jan. 24, 2008. Amended effective .

LR00–FR00 Rule 10. OTHER EX PARTE ORDERS

A. Content of Requests for Emergency Orders. In all motions for ex parte emergency orders in family law matters other than those provided for under Local Family Rules 7 and 8, the motion must be accompanied by an affidavit setting forth specific facts supporting the relief requested and specifically alleging the irreparable injury, loss or damage that would result if the relief requested was not granted.

B. Certificate of Notice Requirement. A Certificate of Notice must accompany such request for an emergency order in which the movant or movant's attorney certifies to the court as follows:

(a) opposing counsel has been notified by telephone prior to the filing of the motion and when notification occurred; or

(b) attempts were made to contact opposing counsel and the nature of those attempts; or

(c) notice to opposing counsel should not be required and the reasons therefore.

A Certificate of Notice will not be required if there is no counsel of record, if counsel of record has withdrawn or if there has been no action pending in the case for at least sixty (60) days and there has been no contact with opposing counsel regarding any matters related to the case.

C. Issuance of Ex Parte Order. The court may, without the necessity of notice or hearing, issue the requested emergency order ex parte upon the court's finding that an emergency exists and that immediate and irreparable injury, loss or damage will occur before an adversarial hearing can be scheduled.

D. Order Scheduling Hearing. If the Court issues an ex parte order granting the emergency relief requested, the matter shall be set for an adversarial hearing as soon as possible. The party granted the emergency shall tender a proposed order for the setting of a hearing date. This order shall include the following language:

"As the recipient of this ex parte order for __(Describe order)__, upon two (2) working days notice to the party who obtained such order (or in such shorter notice as the court may prescribe), you shall be allowed to appear before the court and be heard regarding the issuance of this order"

Adopted effective Jan. 24, 2008.

LR10–FR00 Rule 11. EXPEDITED HEARINGS

A. Nature of Proceeding. An expedited hearing is a proceeding in open court where the evidence is presented in summary narrative fashion by counsel accompanied by the submission of documentary evidence when applicable. The court may question the parties or counsel. Formal rules of evidence and procedure are not applicable. At the conclusion of the hearing, the court shall determine if the facts presented are sufficient to enable the court to make its findings or if a full evidentiary hearing should be required.

B. Hearing by Agreement. At the time of a scheduled evidentiary hearing, the parties may orally agree, on record, to proceed in an expedited basis. Prior to the scheduling of a matter for hearing, the parties may agree in writing to proceed in an expedited basis and a hearing shall be scheduled accordingly. The court shall enforce the agreement unless upon a showing of good cause it would appear that justice would not be served by proceeding in an expedited basis.

C. Discretion of the Court. If at any time the court determines that the matters at issue between the parties would be better resolved at a full evidentiary hearing, the court shall schedule such a hearing. The court may, on its own motion, conduct an expedited hearing to consider and determine any emergency matter or temporary situation until a full evidentiary hearing can be held.

Adopted effective Jan. 24, 2008.

LR10–FR00 Rule 12. FINAL HEARING ON DISSOLUTION OF MARRIAGE

A. Scheduling. A final hearing on a Petition for Dissolution of Marriage shall be set by the court in accordance with Local Rule 8 of the Local Rules of Civil Procedure if the cause is contested. If the cause is not contested, a final hearing shall be held at such time as is mutually convenient to the parties and the court or at such time as generally set by the court for hearings on uncontested matters.

B. Expedited Hearing. An expedited final hearing may be held in accordance with Rule 10 of these Local Family Rules.

C. Notice In Uncontested Action. In an uncontested action, written notice of an intention to proceed to final hearing on a date and time certain shall be given to a party not represented by counsel. The written notice shall be sent to the last known address of the party not represented and proof of service shall not be required, however, a copy of said notice shall be submitted to the court at the time of the final hearing.

D. Summary Disposition/Attachments Required. A summary disposition on a Petition for Dissolution of Marriage shall be entered by the court upon submission of the appropriate documentation to the court in accordance with statutory requirements.

In all summary dispositions in which child support is established, a copy of the child support guideline worksheet shall be attached as an exhibit with the affirmation thereon executed by the parties. In cases where there is a deviation from the child support guidelines, an adequate explanation for the deviation must be set forth.

In all summary dispositions in which guideline parenting time is referenced, a copy of the Parenting Time Guidelines shall be attached as an exhibit. An acknowledgment that both parties have received a copy of the current guidelines will satisfy this requirement.

E. Pro Se Dissolutions. All pro se dissolutions must be heard by the court where the cause of actions has been filed.

Adopted effective Jan. 24, 2008.

LR10–FR00 Rule 13. SUBMISSION OF AGREED MATTERS

A. Written Agreement Required. No agreed matter shall be submitted to the court unless it is in writing and signed by the parties and/or counsel and accompanied with other appropriate documents such as a Decree. However, if the parties reach an agreement just prior to hearing or trial, then the court may accept evidence of that settlement by way of a handwritten entry or on the record followed by the submission of a written agreement within a reasonable time thereafter.

B. Personal Property Disposition. All settlement agreements disposing of the personal property of the parties shall reflect that such personal property has been exchanged and that there are no disputes regarding such disposition.

C. Petition For Modification Required. An agreed modification entry shall not be approved by the court without a petition for modification having been first filed setting forth the reasons for such modification.

D. Pro Se Agreements. All pro se domestic agreements shall require a hearing before the Court.

Adopted effective Jan. 24, 2008.

LR10–FR00 Rule 14. EXHIBIT REQUIREMENTS FOR CONTESTED HEARINGS

In all contested hearings, each party shall submit the following exhibits to the Court, if applicable:

[a] a Child Support Guideline Worksheet.

[b] a Parenting Time Credit Worksheet

[c] a calculation of the child support arrearage.

[d] a listing of the marital assets with an indication of fair market values.

[e] a listing of the marital debts with an indication of the balance due and the minimum monthly payment requirement.

[f] the parties' proposed distribution of marital assets and debts.

Adopted effective Jan. 24, 2008.

LR10–FR00 Rule 15. SERVICE ON REDOCKETED MATTERS

Trial Rule 4 Service Required. Service of process of post-dissolution actions such as petitions for modifications and applications for rule to show cause must be on a party pursuant to Trial Rule 4 of the Indiana Rules of Trial Procedure. Service of process of such actions upon the attorney who represented the party in the underlying dissolution action shall be deemed insufficient.

Adopted effective Jan. 24, 2008.

LR10–FR00 Rule 16. MANDATORY MEDIATION IN PRO SE CASES WITH MINOR CHILDREN

A. Applicability. In all pro se domestic relations cases with children or paternity cases, the parties shall be referred to mediation under the courts' Alternative Dispute Resolution Fund Plan.

B. Disqualification. A litigant shall not be qualified for mediation under the Plan if the litigant is currently charged with or has been convicted of a crime under Indiana Code 35–42 (offenses against the person) or is charged with or has been convicted of a crime in another jurisdiction that is substantially similar to the elements of a crime described in Indiana Code 35–42.

C. Procedure. Upon the filing a pro se case, the Clerk of the Court shall provide the parties with a form entitled Application for Mediation Services and advise the parties to complete the form and take it to the judge of the assigned court. Based upon the parties combined income, the judge will advise the parties of the estimated cost of the mediation, determine the appropriate assignment of the case and, utilizing an Order of Referral to Mediation Services, refer the parties to the Plan Administrator or to a specific mediator.

D. Mediator's Report. Upon the passage of sixty (60) days from the filing of the dissolution or paternity action, the mediator shall submit a Mediator's Report on the form provided along with the mediation agreement or with an indication that the mediation was not successful. The mediator should also submit a claim for services.

Adopted effective Jan. 24, 2008.

Appendix A. Suggested format for proposed Order under Local Family Rule 2

[CAPTION]

ORDER SETTING PROVISIONAL HEARINGS

There having been filed in this cause a motion requesting that a provisional order be issued by the Court, this cause is hereby set for hearing as follows:

(1) On the issue of temporary child custody and/or child support, a preliminary hearing is hereby scheduled to begin at ___ AM/PM on the ___ day of _____, 20 ___.

(2) A regular provisional hearing is hereby scheduled to begin at ___ AM/PM on the ___ day of _____, 20 ___.

SO ORDERED THIS ___ DAY OF _____, 20 ___.

_____
Judge, _____ Court

Ordered tendered by:

Adopted effective Jan. 24, 2008.

Appendix B. Suggested format for Notice requirement under Local Family Rule 3A

NOTICE

YOU ARE HEREBY NOTIFIED THAT YOU MUST SUBMIT YOUR **VERIFIED FINANCIAL DISCLOSURE STATEMENT** WITH THE OPPOSING PARTY WITHIN 45 DAYS OF THE FILING DATE OF THIS CASE.

Adopted effective Jan. 24, 2008.

Appendix C. Suggested format for COPE Notice under Local Family Rule 6C

[CAPTION]

NOTICE OF REQUIREMENT TO ATTEND SEMINAR

TO:

It is a standing Order of the Courts of Clark County, Indiana, that you are required to attend a seminar entitled "Children Cope With Divorce" within forty-five (45) days of the date of the filing of this action.

You failure to attend the seminar could result in the Court finding and holding you in contempt of the Court's Order.

The Seminar which you are ordered to attend is being conducted by the Clark Memorial Hospital. You should contact the Hospital at 1220 Missouri Avenue, Jeffersonville, Indiana, Telephone (812) 283–2198 or 283–2811 for additional information and enrollment in the Seminar.

Dated at Jeffersonville, Indiana, this ___ day of _____, 20 ___.

_____
Clark, Clark _____
Court

Prepared by:

Adopted effective Jan. 24, 2008.

Appendix D. Suggested Order for Trial Rule 65(E)(1) Joint Preliminary Injunction

[CAPTION]

JOINT PRELIMINARY INJUNCTION ISSUED UNDER TRIAL RULE 65(E)(1)

(This Joint Injunction does not qualify for filing with a law enforcement agency and a violation of this Order does not constitute a basis for arrest for invasion of privacy.)

Comes now the Court and finding that an Order should be entered pursuant to the provisions of Trial Rules 65(E)(1), both parties are hereby enjoined from:

(A) Transferring, encumbering, concealing, selling or otherwise disposing of any joint property of the parties or asset of the marriage except in the usual course of business or for the necessities of life, without the written consent of the parties or the permission of the Court; and

(B) Removing any child of the parties now residing in the State of Indiana from the State with intent to deprive the Court of jurisdiction over such child without the prior written consent of all parties or the permission of the Court.

This Order shall remain in effect until the entry of a decree or final order or until modified or dissolved by the Court.

SO ORDERED THIS ___ DAY OF _____, 20 ___.

_____
Judge, _____ Court

Order tendered by:

Adopted effective Jan. 24, 2008.

Appendix E. Suggested Order for Trial Rule 65(E)(2) Temporary Restraining Order

[CAPTION]

TEMPORARY RESTRAINING ORDER ISSUED UNDER TRIAL RULE 65(E)(2)

(This Restraining Order does not qualify for filing with a law enforcement agency and a violation of this Order does not constitute a basis for arrest for invasion of privacy.)

Comes now the Court and having determined that an Order should be entered pursuant to the provisions of Trial Rule 65(E)(2), the (Petitioner/Respondent) is hereby ordered to refrain from:

[ ] Abusing, harassing, disturbing the peace of the (Petitioner/Respondent);

[ ] Committing a battery on the (Petitioner/Respondent);

[ ] Committing a battery on any child or step-child of the parties;

[ ] From coming on or about the family dwelling located at _____

[ ] From coming on or about the (Petitioner's/Respondent's) dwelling located at _____

[ ] From coming on or about such other place, to-wit: _____

This Order shall remain in effect until the entry of a decree or final order or until modified or dissolved by the Court.

SO ORDERED THIS ___ **DAY OF** _____, 20 ___.

_____
Judge, _____ Court

Order tendered by:

Adopted effective Jan. 24, 2008.

Appendix F. Suggested form of Temporary Restraining Order (Property) under I.C. 31–15–4–3(1) & (4)

[CAPTION]

TEMPORARY RESTRAINING ORDER (PROPERTY)
ISSUED UNDER INDIANA CODE 31–15–4–3(1) & (4)

(This Restraining Order does not qualify for filing with a law enforcement agency and a violation of this Order does not constitute a basis for arrest for invasion of privacy.)

Comes now the Court and finding that a Restraining Order should be issued pursuant to the provision of Indian Code 31–15–4–3(1) & (4), the (Petitioner/Respondent) is hereby ordered to refrain from:

(A) Transferring, encumbering, concealing, or in any way disposing of any property except in the usual course of business or for the necessities of life;

(B) Interfering with the (Petitioner's/Respondent's) possession of the following property:

_____

_____

This Order shall remain in effect until entry of a decree or final order or until modified or dissolved by the Court.

SO ORDERED THIS ___ **DAY OF** _____, 20 ___.

_____
Judge, _____ Court

Ordered tendered by:

Adopted effective Jan. 24, 2008.

Appendix G. Suggested form of Temporary Restraining Order (Personal) under I.C. 31–15–4–3(2) & (3)

[CAPTION]

TEMPORARY RESTRAINING ORDER (PERSONAL)
ISSUED UNDER INDIANA CODE 31–15–4–3(2) & (3)

(This Restraining Order qualifies for filing with a law enforcement agency and a violation of this Order may constitute a basis for arrest for invasion of privacy.)

Comes now the Court and finding that a Restraining Order should be issued pursuant to the provisions of Indiana Code 31–15–4–3(2) & (3), the (Petitioner/Respondent) is hereby ordered to refrain from:

[ ] Abusing, harassing, disturbing the peace of the (Petitioner/Respondent);

[ ] From coming on or about the family dwelling located at _____;

[ ] From coming on or about the (Petitioner's/Respondent's) dwelling located at _____;

[ ] From contacting or coming on or about the (Petitioner's/Respondent's) workplace;

[ ] From contacting or coming on or about the school of the parties' children;

[ ] From contacting or coming on or about the daycare center or the babysitter of the parties' children;

[ ] From contacting or coming on or about such other place, to–wit: _____;

This Order shall remain in effect until entry of a final dissolution decree or until further order of the Court.

The Sheriff and the Law Enforcement Agency where the (Petitioner/Respondent) resides shall receive and maintain a copy of this Order in the Protective Order Depository as provided by Indiana Code 5–2–9.

Pursuant to the provisions of Indiana Code 35–46–1–15.1, a Law Enforcement Officer may arrest the person subject to this Order for the Offense of Invasion of Privacy, a Class B Misdemeanor punishable by imprisonment of up to 180 days and a fine of $1,000.00 when the officer has probable cause to believe that such person has violated this Order.

SO ORDERED THIS ___ **DAY OF** _____, 20 ___.

_____
Judge, _____ Court

Order tendered by:

Copies distributed to: (Must include Sheriff)
Adopted effective Jan. 24, 2008.

Appendix H. Suggested form of Protective Order in a Dissolution action (commonly referred to as a Permanent Restraining Order) under I.C. 31–15–5–1 through 11

[CAPTION]

PROTECTIVE ORDER
ISSUED UNDER INDIANA CODE 31–15–5–1 THRU 11

(This Protective Order qualifies for filing with a law enforcement agency and a
violation of this Order may constitute a basis for arrest for invasion of privacy.)

Comes now the Court and finding that a Protective Order should be issued pursuant to the provisions of Indiana Code 31–15–5–1 thru 11, the (Petitioner/Respondent) is hereby ordered to refrain from:

( ) Abusing, harassing, disturbing the peace of the (Petitioner/Respondent);

( ) From coming on or about the family dwelling located at _____;

( ) From coming on or about the (Petitioner's/Respondent's) dwelling located at _____;

( ) From contacting or coming on or about the (Petitioner's/Respondent's) workplace;

( ) From contacting or coming on or about the school of the parties' children;

( ) From contacting or coming about the daycare center or the babysitter of the parties children:

( ) From contacting or coming about such other place, to–wit: _____;

This Order **shall remain in effect for one (1) year** from the date signed and at the request of a party, may be renewed for not more than one (1) year.

The Sheriff and the Law Enforcement Agency where the (Petitioner/Respondent) resides shall receive and maintain a copy of this Order in the Protective Order Depository as provided by Indiana Code 5–2–9.

Pursuant to the provisions of Indiana Code 35–46–1–15.1, a Law Enforcement Officer may arrest the person subject to this Order for the Offense of Invasion of Privacy, a Class B Misdemeanor punishable by imprisonment of up to 180 days and a fine of $1,000.00, when the Officer has probable cause to believe that such person has violated this Order.

SO ORDERED THIS ___ DAY OF _____, 20 ___.

_____
Judge, _____ Court

Order tendered by:

Copies distributed to: (Must include Sheriff)
Adopted effective Jan. 24, 2008.

Appendix I. Suggested format for Financial Disclosure Statement under Local Family Rule 3A

Suggested format for Financial Disclosure Statement under Local Family Rule 3A

IN THE _____ COURT OF CLARK COUNTY

STATE OF INDIANA

IN RE THE MARRIAGE OF

_____,
PETITIONER

AND   CASE NO._____

_____,
RESPONDENT

VERIFIED FINANCIAL DISCLOSURE STATEMENT

NOTICE

YOU ARE HEREBY NOTIFIED THAT YOU MUST SUBMIT YOUR **VERIFIED FINANCIAL DISCLOSURE STATEMENT** WITH THE OPPOSING PARTY WITHIN 45 DAYS OF THE FILING DATE OF THIS CASE.

I. PRELIMINARY INFORMATION

Your Full Name:

Your Address:

Your DOB:

Your SS#:

Date of Marriage:

Date of Physical Separation:

Spouse's Name:

Spouse's SS#:

Spouse's DOB:

Children: Name   Social Security   #Age   Date of Birth

YOU MUST ATTACH COPIES OF:

1. Your two (2) most recent paycheck stubs.
2. Your last Federal Income Tax Return including all schedules.

II. INCOME INFORMATION

A. YOUR EMPLOYMENT

Current Employer

Address of Employer

Medical Insurance   Cost each month to you   Who covered?

Length of Employment

Job Description

Gross Income	Per week	Bi–Weekly	Per month	Year

Net Income	Per week	Bi–Weekly	Per month	Year

B. YOUR EMPLOYMENT HISTORY FOR LAST FIVE (5) YEARS

EMPLOYER	DATES OF EMPLOYMENT	COMPENSATION (per wk/month/year)

C. OTHER INCOME

List other sources of income; including but not limited to Dividends, Earned Interest, Rents, Public Assistance (AFDC), Social Security, Worker's Compensation, Child Support from prior marriage, Military or Other Retirement, Unemployment Compensation, etc.

100

SOURCE	AMOUNTS RECEIVED	REASON FOR ENTITLEMENT

D. FRINGE BENEFITS

Including but not limited to Company Automobile, Health Insurance, Club Memberships, etc.

Type of Benefit	Annual Value

III. PROPERTY

A. MARITAL RESIDENCE (If Owned)

Location/Address	
Date Purchased	
Purchase Price	$
Down Payment	$
Source of Down Payment	
Current Mortgage(s) Balance	$
Monthly Payment	$
Current Fair Market Value	$
1st Mortgage Payable To	
2nd Mortgage Payable To	
Are Taxes Included in Mortgage?	
Is Insurance Included in Mortgage?	

B. OTHER REAL PROPERTY OWNED(THIS MAY INCLUDE CEMETERY PLOTS, UNDEVELOPED LOTS ON LAKES, ETC.)

Location/Address	
Date Purchased	
Purchase Price	$
Down Payment	$
Source of Down Payment	
Current Mortgage Balances	$
Monthly Payment	$
Current Fair Market Value	$
1st Mortgage Payable To	
2nd Mortgage Payable To	
Are Taxes Included in Mortgage?	
Is Insurance Included in Mortgage?	

C. VEHICLES(Automobiles, Boats, Motorcycles, Tractors, Trucks, etc.)

MAKE/MODEL OF VEHICLE	DATE ACQUIRED	PURCHASE PRICE	TITLE WHOSE NAME	WHO DRIVES?	CURRENT VALUE
		$			$

MAKE/MODEL OF VEHICLE	DATE ACQUIRED	PURCHASE PRICE	TITLE WHOSE NAME	WHO DRIVES?	CURRENT VALUE
		$			$
		$			$
		$			$
		$			$

D. OTHER PERSONAL PROPERTY(Household furnishings, Jewelry, tools, lawn furnishings, guns, collections, etc. please list items separately [Attach additional pages if necessary])

DESCRIPTION	DATE ACQUIRED	PURCHAS PRICE	BALANC OWED	PAYMENT	CURRENT VALUE	IF YOU WANT TO RETAIN*
					$	
		$	$	$	$	
		$	$	$	$	
		$	$	$	$	
		$	$	$	$	
		$	$	$	$	
		$	$	$	$	
		$	$	$	$	
		$	$	$	$	
		$	$	$	$	
		$	$	$	$	
		$	$	$	$	
		$	$	$	$	
		$	$	$	$	
		$	$	$	$	
		$	$	$	$	
		$	$	$	$	
		$	$	$	$	
		$	$	$	$	
		$	$	$	$	
		$	$	$	$	
		$	$	$	$	
		$	$	$	$	
		$	$	$	$	
		$	$	$	$	
		$	$	$	$	
		$	$	$	$	
		$	$	$	$	
		$	$	$	$	
		$	$	$	$	
		$	$	$	$	
		$	$	$	$	
		$	$	$	$	
		$	$	$	$	
		$	$	$	$	
		$	$	$	$	
		$	$	$	$	
		$	$	$	$	
		$	$	$	$	

$	$	$	$	
$	$	$	$	

E. BANK OR CREDIT UNION (SAVINGS, CHECKING, MONEY MARKET, CD) TO WHICH YOU AND/OR SPOUSE HAVE/HAD A DIRECT OR INDIRECT INTEREST WITHIN THE LAST YEAR(This includes any bank account to which you or your spouse has deposited money) (FOR BOTH HUSBAND AND WIFE ACCTS)

NAME BANK	WHOSE NAME ON ACCOUNT	TYPE ACCOUNT	ACCOUNT NUMBER	BALANCE DATE OF SEPARATION	CURRENT BALANCE
				$	$
				$	$
				$	$
				$	$

F. STOCKS, BONDS, MUTUAL FUNDS

NAME OF STOCK OR FUND	WHOSE NAME ON ACCOUNT	DATE PURCHASED	NUMBER OF SHARES	CURRENT PRICE PER SHARE	CURRENT VALUE
				$	$
				$	$
				$	$
				$	$
				$	$

G. INSURANCE POLICIES

NAME OF COMPANY	POLICY NUMBER	POLICY HOLDER NAME	BENEFICIARY NAME	FACE VALUE	CASH VALUE
				$	$
				$	$
				$	$

(If you don't know, call your agent)

H. RETIREMENT BENEFITS, 401K, IRA, KEOGH, PENSION, ETC.

COMPANY	TYPE ACCOUNT	ACCOUNT NUMBER	VALUE	OWNER YOU OR SPOUSE
			$	
			$	
			$	
			$	

I. INTEREST IN BUSINESS

NAME OF BUSINESS	TYPE (Corp., Partner, Sole Owner)	% (Percent) OWNED	ESTIMATED VALUE
			$
			$
			$
			$

NAME OF BUSINESS	TYPE (Corp., Partner, Sole Owner)	% (Percent) OWNED	ESTIMATED VALUE

IV. DEBTS (including but not limited to Mortgages, Charge Cards, Loans, Medical Bills, Credit Union, Etc.; attach separate list, if necessary)

NAME OF CREDITOR	MONTHLY PAYMENT	CURRENT BALANCE	(H) HUSBAND (W) WIFE (J) JOINT
1ST MORTGAGE NAME	$	$	
2ND MORTGAGE NAME	$	$	
AUTO (MODEL)	$	$	
AUTO (MODEL)	$	$	
CREDIT CARD:	$	$	
CREDIT CARD:	$	$	
CREDIT CARD:	$	$	
	$	$	
	$	$	
	$	$	
	$	$	
	$	$	
	$	$	
	$	$	
	$	$	
	$	$	
	$	$	
	$	$	
	$	$	
TOTALS	$	$	

V. YOUR ASSETS OWNED PRIOR TO OR RECEIVED DURING THE MARRIAGE THROUGH INHERITANCE OR GIFT(Whether now owned or not) (Show significant assets only)

A. ASSETS OWNED BY YOU PRIOR TO THE MARRIAGE

DESCRIPTION OF ASSET	VALUE AT MARRIAGE	BALANCE OF ANY DEBT AT MARRIAGE	VALUE NOW
	$	$	$
	$	$	$
	$	$	$
	$	$	$
	$	$	$
	$	$	$

B. ASSETS RECEIVED BY YOU DURING THE MARRIAGE BY GIFT OR INHERITANCE

DESCRIPTION	CURRENT VALUATION	RECEIVED FROM
	$	
	$	

DESCRIPTION	CURRENT VALUATION	RECEIVED FROM
	$	
	$	
	$	
	$	
	$	
	$	

VI. SUMMARY OF ASSETS AND DEBTS

ASSET	VALUE
HOME	$
OTHER REAL ESTATE	$
OTHER REAL ESTATE	$
VEHICLE	$
VEHICLE	$
VEHICLE	$
OTHER PERSONAL PROPERTY	$
BANK ACCOUNTS	$
STOCKS, MUTUAL FUNDS	$
INSURANCE—CASH VALUE	$
RETIREMENT	$
BUSINESS INTEREST	$
OTHER	$
TOTAL	$

DEBTS	BALANCE DUE
MORTGAGE(S) ON HOME	$
MORTGAGE(S) ON OTHER REAL ESTATE	$
CAR LOAN	$
CAR LOAN	$
CREDIT CARDS	$
MEDICAL BILLS	$
GENERAL CREDITORS	$
NOTE LOANS	$
OTHER DEBTS	$
TOTAL	$

(ASSETS MINUS DEBTS) TOTAL NET WORTH	$

VERIFICATION & DUTY TO SUPPLEMENT OR AMEND

I affirm, under penalties for perjury, that the foregoing representations are true to the best of my knowledge and belief. Further, I understand that I am under a duty to supplement or amend this VERIFIED FINANCIAL DISCLOSURE STATEMENT prior to trial if I learn that the information which has been provided is either incorrect or that information provided is no longer true.

SO DECLARED this _____ day of _____, 20___.

_____
Signature

CERTIFICATE OF SERVICE

I hereby certify that a true and accurate copy of the foregoing Verified Financial Disclosure Statement was delivered to the opposing party or his/her attorney of record, as set forth below, either in person or by U.S. mail postage prepaid this _____ day of _____, 20(3) 6d:

_____

_____

_____

_____
_____ Signature of Counsel or Pro Se

Adopted effective Jan. 24, 2008.

Appendix J.   Minimum Parenting Guidelines

MINIMUM PARENTING GUIDELINES

It is the goal of the Courts to encourage as much flexibility as possible regarding the exercise of parenting time. These guidelines are intended to advise parents of the *minimum* parenting time to which the non-custodial parent is entitled in most cases. The parents may agree to a schedule differ-ent from these guidelines when it is in the best interests of the children and meets the needs of both parents. Absent an agreement, however, the following parenting time shall be ordered.

1.   The non-custodial parent shall have the follow-ing parenting time with the child or children of the parties except where the children are less than one (1) year old or where geographic distances make compli-ance with these guidelines prohibitive:

[a] On alternating weekends from 6:00 P.M. on Friday until 6:00 P.M. on Sunday,

or

if the child(ren) is regularly attending school then on alternating weekends from 6:00 P.M. on Friday until the beginning of the school day on Monday, the non-custodial parent to advise the custodial parent of the choice by August 15 before the school fall semester and by December 15 before the spring semester.

If the non-custodial parent chooses parenting time through Monday morning he/she shall have that responsibility throughout that semester and shall make certain that the children are in school on time on every Monday morning.

[b] Provided there exists no conflict with school activities, one evening per week from 6:00 P.M. until 8:00 P.M., the evening to be agreed upon by the parties. If the parties cannot agree, the evening shall be Wednesday;

[c] In years ending with an odd number:

[1] The evening before each child's birthday from 6:00 P.M. until 9:00 P. M.;

[2] Memorial Day weekend from 6:00 P.M. on Friday until 6:00 P.M. on Monday;

[3] Independence Day from 6:00 P.M. on July 3 until 6:00 P.M. On July 5;

[4] Thanksgiving holiday from 6:00 P.M. on Wednesday until 6:00 P.M. on Sunday;

[5] From 6:00 P.M. on December 20 until 11:00 P.M. on Christmas Eve; and

[6] Martin Luther King holiday from 6:00 P.M. on the day before until 6:00 P.M. on the holiday.

[d] In years ending with an even number:

[1] On each child's birthday for the entire day until 8:00 P.M. unless a school day, then in such event from the end of school until 8:00 P.M. (The non-custodial parent is further entitled to simulta-neous parenting time with the child's siblings on such day);

[2] Easter weekend from 6:00 P.M. on Friday until 6:00 P.M. on Sunday;

[3] Labor Day weekend from 6:00 P.M. on Friday until 6:00 P.M. on Monday;

[4] During Christmas holidays from 11:00 P.M. on Christmas Eve until 6:00 P.M. on January 1;

[5] From 6:00 P.M. on the evening before the school spring break until 7:00 P.M. on the last day of the school spring break.

[e] On the non-custodial parent's Birthday and Mother's Day or Father's Day, as applicable, from 10:00 A.M. until 6:00 P.M.

Similarly, the custodial parent shall have parent-ing time on the custodial parent's Birthday and Mother's Day or Father's Day, as applicable, when such day conflicts with these guidelines.

[f] In the summertime for **school age children**, for two non-consecutive three (3) week periods dur-ing the summer months, the periods to be agreed upon by the parties on or before May 15th of each year. However, if the summer parenting time is

less than twelve (12) weeks, the vacation time shall be split equally between the parties.

There shall be no weekend parenting time during the exercise of these periods and the custodial parent shall be entitled to similar extended periods without interruption.

[g] In the summertime for **pre-school age children**, for two (2) weeks in the month of June and for two (2) weeks in the month of July, the periods to be agreed upon by the parties on or before May 15th of each year.

[h] Such other parenting time as may be agreed upon between the parties.

Missed Weekend Parenting Time as the Result of Holiday or Other Superseding Time. Whenever the child(ren) is with one of his or her parents for two (2) consecutive weekends, then notwithstanding any other provisions contained within these Guidelines, the parent that did not have physical custody of the child(ren) for these two (2) weekends, shall have the child for the following weekend and the parties shall then re-establish alternate weekend parenting time. The only exception to this provision of the reconfiguration of "alternate weekend parenting time" shall be during those times that either parent is exercising the extended summer parenting time as outlined herein. This provision is not intended to apply when the parents agree to "trade" weekends, unless this is the desire of the parties.

2. Where geographical distances make compliance with these guidelines prohibitive, the non-custodial parent shall have the following parenting time with the child or children of the parties:

[a] One (1) weekend per month beginning at 6:00 P.M. on Friday until 6:00 P.M. on Sunday, the parties to agree on the weekend;

[b] Six (6) consecutive weeks of summer parenting time, the weeks to be agreed upon by the parties on or before May 15th of each year;

[c] One (1) week at spring break beginning at 6:00 P.M. on the Friday the school week ends before spring break until 6:00 P.M. on the Sunday before school resumes;

[d] During odd numbered years, for the Thanksgiving holiday from 6:00 P.M. on Wednesday until 6:00 P.M. on Sunday;

[e] During the Christmas holiday, from 6:00 P.M. on December 25 until 6:00 P.M. on January 1;

[f] Such other parenting time as may be agreed upon by the parties.

3. Where a child is less than one (1) year old, parenting time shall be each week on Saturdays or Sundays, the parties to agree on the day, from 10:00 A.M. until 6:00 P.M. If the child is less than three (3) months old, such period shall be from 2:00 P.M. until 6:00 P.M.

4. The non-custodial parent shall advise the custodial parent forty-eight (48) hours in advance if he or she does not intend to exercise any period of parenting time.

5. Unless prior arrangements are made, the non-custodial parent shall pick up the children] at the times specified and return the children] at the times specified, and the custodial parent shall have the children] ready at the scheduled pick-up time and shall be present at the home to receive the children] at the scheduled return time.

6. The custodial parent shall send with the children sufficient clothing and outer wear appropriate for the season to last the period of parenting time.

7. Each parent shall supply the other with his or her current address and telephone number and shall allow liberal but reasonable telephone and mail privileges with the children.

8. The custodial parent shall inform the non-custodial parent of the children]'s school and/or social functions permitting parental participation within twenty-four (24) hours of notification to the custodial parent of such function, and the non-custodial parent shall be permitted to attend such functions, regardless of when the function occurs.

The opportunity to attend school functions should not be denied the children because the custodial parent is not able to attend. In such instances the children shall be allowed to attend with their non-custodial parent.

9. Each parent shall have rights of access to all providers of services to the children] as well as all medical reports, school reports, and the like, issued by any provider of services, all without the need of consent from either party. The custodial parent, nonetheless, shall take the necessary action with school authorities to list the non-custodial parent as a parent of the children], to authorize the school to release to the non-custodial parent any and all information concerning the children], and to otherwise insure that the non-custodial parent receives copies of all grade reports and any notices regarding the children], including scheduled meetings concerning the children].

10. The custodial parent shall promptly inform the non-custodial parent of any illness of the children] which shall require medical attention.

11. Each parent shall have the right of first refusal for child care or babysitting needs of the other parent whenever either parent has a need for child care or babysitting for a duration of four (4) hours or more. A good faith attempt should be made to inquire of the other parent with as much advanced notice as possible. The other parent is under no obligation to provide the child care or babysitting and if he or she elects to provide the care it shall be a no cost.

12.   The child support obligation of the non-custodial parent shall abate by 50% during any period of parenting time of six (6) consecutive days or longer provided the non-custodial parent is current in the court-ordered support obligation (including ordered arrearage payments, if any).

If, as parents, you agree that it is in the best interests of your children to adopt a schedule different from these guidelines, such an agreement should be in writing and approved and ordered by the Court. Without such approval and order, the Court will not enforce such an agreement should a denial of parenting time occur. Under such circumstances, the Court will enforce guideline parenting time.

Adopted effective Jan. 24, 2008.

DELAWARE CIRCUIT COURT LOCAL RULES OF PRACTICE

Amended Effective May 9, 2006

Including Amendments Received Through November 1, 2013

Research Notes

These rules may be searched electronically on Westlaw in the IN-RULES database; updates to these rules may be found on Westlaw in IN-RULESUPDATES. For search tips and a summary of database content, consult the Westlaw Scope Screens for each database.

LR18–SC00–DLR Rule 0001. Small Claims Practice and Procedure

A. Executing Pleadings. Original Pleadings, including but not limited to the Notice of Claims, Affidavits, Petitions and all Motions, shall be signed by the party filing the same if self represented or by the attorney of record where the party is represented by an attorney.

B. Scheduling.

1. The Clerk of the Court shall schedule an initial trial on the complaint. At the initial trial, the defendant shall admit or deny liability as to the claim.

2. If the defendant fails to appear at an initial trial after proper service, the plaintiff may request judgment. If the plaintiff fails to appear at the initial trial after proper notice, the court may dismiss the action without prejudice.

3. If the defendant appears and admits liability the parties may sign and file an Agreed Judgment.

4. If the defendant appears and denies liability, the court shall set the matter for a bench trial and notify all parties.

C. Attorney Fees. A party requesting attorney's fees shall present to the court a written affidavit detailing the time spent, services rendered, and hourly rate requested.

D. Continuances. A party seeking to continue a hearing date must file a written motion for continuance, and the court may grant the motion if the party seeking the motion shows good cause.

E. Judgments. A party seeking a default judgment shall file an Affidavit of Non–Military Service and Competency.

F. Proceedings Supplemental. If a party does not pay the judgment after its entry, the party seeking payment may file a Motion for Proceedings Supplemental and an Order to Appear in Court and Answer as to Wages, Assets, Property, and Income. The Clerk will provide the proper forms and a hearing date.

G. Bankruptcy Stay. Any party seeking a stay due to a bankruptcy filing should file a Notice to Stay the Proceeding stating that they have included the debt at issue with the bankruptcy court and include the bankruptcy cause number. The Court at that time will calendar the matter for one (1) year to set the matter for dismissal if, in fact, the party has not been discharged in bankruptcy.

H. Releasing Judgments. A party shall file a Release of Judgment with the court after the opposing party has paid a judgment in full.

I. Dismissals. The party who filed a Notice of Claim, Counterclaim, or Cross–Claim may file a written Motion to Dismiss the claim at any time before the court enters a judgment.

J. Hearing Dates Following Dismissal. If the court dismisses a Notice of Claim upon the plaintiff's written request, and if a Counterclaim or Cross–Claim is still pending, the hearing will be held on the Counterclaim or Cross–Claim.

K. Small Claims Manual. The Delaware County Clerk's Office has the Small Claims Manual available in hard copy form and on its website.

Adopted effective June 30, 2000. Renumbered as Rule 003, and amended effective May 9, 2006. Renumbered as Rule 0001, and amended effective Sept. 1, 2012.

LR18–DR00–DLR Rule 0002. Domestic Relation Cases

A. Termination of Representative Capacity. After a court enters a Decree of Dissolution of Marriage, Legal Separation, or Paternity; after a court issues an order permanently modifying custody, or after a court issues an order modifying parenting time or child support, the representative capacity of all attorneys appearing on any party's behalf shall be deemed terminated upon:

1. The court has entered an order withdrawing the attorney's appearance;

2. The time for appealing the order had expired; or

3. Any appeal related to the order has concluded.

B. Service of Pleadings. If a party is not represented by counsel pursuant to Paragraph A above, the opposing party shall serve any pleadings directly to the party pursuant to the Indiana Rules of Trial Procedure.

C. Courtesy Copy. If a party serves a pleading upon an attorney who no longer has a representative capacity in the case pursuant to Paragraph A, the court shall deem that service a courtesy copy only.

Adopted as Local Rule 1990, 1997–1 and 1997–2. Amended effective June 30, 2000; renumbered as Rule 004 and amended effective May 9, 20; renumbered as Rule 0002 and amended effective Sept. 1, 2012.

LR18–JD00–DLR Rule 0003. Discovery and Motions In Limine in Juvenile Delinquency Cases

I. Discovery

A. Duty of the State of Indiana. In all filed juvenile delinquency cases, unless relieved by court order, the prosecuting attorney shall, within thirty (30) days after the initial hearing in any delinquency action filed against the child, furnish the attorney for the child the following:

1. The names and addresses of persons whom the prosecuting attorney intends to call as witnesses at the fact-finding hearing, together with their relevant written or recorded statements.

2. Any written or recorded statements and any summaries of oral statements made by the child herein or any statements of others which contain a declaration of the child.

3. Those portions of the Grand Jury minutes which contain statements of witnesses whom the prosecutor intends to call and directly examine at the fact-finding hearing, which statements are probably within the control of the prosecution and which statements will relate to matters covered in the witness' testimony in this case, for the purpose of cross-examination and impeachment of such witness' credibility.

4. The relevant testimony which is reduced to writing of persons whom the prosecutor intends to call as a witness at the fact-finding hearing, but who did not testify before the Grand Jury.

5. Any reports or statements of experts made in connection with the case, including results of physical or mental examination and of scientific tests, experiments, or comparisons.

6. Any books, papers, documents, photographs or tangible objects, which the prosecuting attorney intends to use at the fact-finding hearing or which were obtained from or belong to the child or his family.

7. Any record or prior criminal convictions of persons whom the prosecutor intends to call as witnesses at the fact-finding hearing.

8. Any declarations against interest made by the child.

9. Any evidence the prosecutor might have, favorable to the child.

10. Copies of any photographs which the prosecution has in its possession which it intends to introduce as evidence.

11. Any description of the child's conduct, if any, that the prosecution intends to introduce as an implied admission.

12. Any promises, rewards, or inducements provided to prosecution witnesses or defense witnesses for the child.

13. Any victim's statement that was recorded or memorialized and that is under the State's control.

14. Any and all medical reports in appropriate cases.

15. That portion of police reports containing substantially verbatim statements of witnesses.

16. The delinquency record of the child, including arrests and adjudications.

17. Evidence of other crimes, wrongs, or acts pursuant to Evidence Rule 404(b).

The State shall also allow counsel for the child to examine any and all physical evidence, whether or not the prosecution intends to present the evidence at the fact-finding hearing, within thirty (30) days after the initial hearing.

B. Duty of Counsel for the Child. In all filed juvenile delinquency cases, unless relieved by court order, counsel for the child shall, within thirty (30) days after receiving the discovery from the State of Indiana in any delinquency action filed against the child, furnish the attorney for the State of Indiana the following:

1. Any reports or results or testimony relative thereto, of physical or mental examination or of scientific tests, experiments or comparisons, or any other reports or statements of experts pertaining to this case.

2. A summary of any special or statutory defense(s), which the child intends to make at a hearing in this cause.

3. Names and last known addresses of persons the child intends to call as witnesses, together with their relevant written or recorded statements, including memoranda reporting or summarizing their oral statements, and any record of prior delinquency adjudication known to the child.

4. Any books, papers, documents, photographs, or tangible objects the child intends to use as evidence or for impeachment at a hearing.

If the child is not represented by an attorney, the above requirements do not apply, and the parties must file written motions with the Court to request discovery.

II. Motions in Limine

In all filed delinquency cases, unless relieved by court order, the following items are excluded from evidence, and the court prohibits any reference at the fact-finding hearing to the following. In addition, counsel and all witnesses may not refer to, mention, or testify about the following:

1. The fact that the child failed to make a statement either orally or in writing at the time of his arrest.

2. Any questioning of the child, or any statements which the child may have made while he was in the custody of the police, absent proof beyond a reasonable doubt that the statements were made freely and voluntarily and after a knowing and intelligent waiver of rights by the child.

3. Any previous arrest or detention of the child which did not result in a delinquency adjudication, or any other alleged offenses, purportedly involving the child, in which he was neither arrested nor charged.

4. Any prior delinquency adjudication of the child, except those which may be used for the purpose of impeachment.

The rule regarding Motions in Limine shall apply to cases in which the Child is not represented by an attorney.

Adopted as Local Rule 10–2003, effective Oct. 21, 2003. Renumbered as Rule 013 and amended effective May 9, 2006; renumbered as Rule 0003 and amended effective Sept. 1, 2012.

LR18–JC00–DLR Rule 0004. Discovery and Motions In Limine in CHINS Cases

I. Discovery

A. Duty of Counsel for the DFC. In all filed CHINS cases, unless relieved by court order, the attorney for the Delaware County Office of Family and Children (hereinafter **DFC**) shall, within thirty (30) days after the initial hearing in any CHINS action filed, furnish the attorney for the parent(s), guardian(s) or custodian(s) (hereinafter **PGC**) the following:

1. The names and addresses of persons whom the **DFC** intends to call as witnesses at the fact-finding hearing, together with their relevant written or recorded statements.

2. Any written or recorded statements and any summaries of oral statements made by the *PGC* herein or any statements of others which contain a declaration of the *PGC*.

3. The relevant testimony which is reduced to writing of persons whom the **DFC** intends to call as a witness at the fact-finding hearing.

4. Any reports or statements of experts made in connection with the case, including results of physical or mental examination and of scientific tests, experiments, or comparisons.

5. Any books, papers, documents, photographs or tangible objects, which the **DFC** intends to use in the fact-finding hearing or which were obtained from or belong to the *PGC*.

6. Any record or prior criminal convictions of persons whom the **DFC** intends to call as witnesses at the fact-finding hearing.

7. Any declarations against interest made by the *PGC*.

8. Any evidence the **DFC** might have, favorable to the *PGC*.

9. Copies of any photographs which the **DFC** has in its possession which it intends to introduce as evidence.

10. Any description of the *PGC's* conduct, if any, that the **DFC** intends to introduce as an implied admission.

11. Any promises, rewards, or inducements provided to **DFC** witnesses or *PGC* witnesses.

12. Any victim's statement that was recorded or memorialized and that is under the **DFC's** control.

13. Any and all medical reports in appropriate cases.

14. That portion of police reports containing substantially verbatim statements of witnesses.

15. The criminal record of the *PGC*, including arrests and convictions.

16. Evidence of other crimes, wrongs, or acts pursuant to Evidence Rule 404(b).

The **DFC** shall also allow counsel for the *PGC* to examine any and all physical evidence, whether or not the **DFC** intends to present the evidence at the fact-finding hearing, within thirty (30) days after the initial hearing.

B. Duty of Counsel for the Parents/Guardians/Custodian. In all filed CHINS cases, unless relieved by court order, counsel for the *PGC* shall, within thirty (30) days after receiving the discovery from the **DFC** in any CHINS action filed against the *PGC*, furnish the attorney for the **DFC** the following:

1. Any reports or results or testimony relative thereto, of physical or mental examination or of scientific tests, experiments or comparisons, or any other reports or statements of experts pertaining to this case.

2. A summary of any special or statutory defense(s), which the *PGC* intends to make at a hearing or fact-finding in this cause.

3. Names and last known addresses of persons the *PGC* intends to call as witnesses, together with their relevant written or recorded statements, including memoranda reporting or summarizing their oral statements, and any record of prior criminal convictions known to the *PGC*.

4. Any books, papers, documents, photographs, or tangible objects the *PGC* intends to use as evidence or for impeachment at a hearing or trial.

If the PGC is not represented by an attorney, the above requirements do not apply, and the parties must file written motions with the Court to request discovery.

II. Motions in Limine

In all filed CHINS cases, unless relieved by court order, the following items are excluded from evidence, and the Court prohibits any reference at fact-finding hearing to the following. In addition, counsel and all witnesses may not refer to, mention, or testify about the following:

1. Any questioning of the *PGC*, or any statements which the *PGC* may have made while he was in the custody of the police, absent proof beyond a reasonable doubt that the statements were made freely and voluntarily and after a knowing and intelligent waiver of rights by the *PGC*.

2. Any previous arrest or detention of the *PGC* which did not result in conviction, or any other alleged offenses, purportedly involving the *PGC*, in which he was neither arrested nor charged.

3. Any prior conviction of the *PGC*, except those which may be used for the purpose of impeachment.

4. The rule regarding Motions in Limine shall apply to cases in which the *PGC* is represented by counsel as well as those cases where the *PGC* is not represented by counsel. The rule regarding Motions in Limine shall apply to cases in which the PGC is not represented by an attorney.

Adopted as Local Rule 10–2003(2), effective Oct. 21, 2003. Renumbered as Rule 014 and amended effective May 9, 2006; renumbered as Rule 0004 and amended effective Sept. 1, 2012.

LR18–CR00–DLR Rule 0005. Discovery and Motions In Limine in Criminal Cases

I. Discovery

A. Duty of the State of Indiana. In all Murder, Class A, class B, class C, and class D Felony cases, unless relieved by court order, the Prosecuting Attorney shall, within thirty (30) days after the initial hearing furnish the attorney for the Defendant the following:

1. The names and addresses of persons whom the Prosecuting Attorney intends to call as witnesses at the trial, together with their relevant written or recorded statements.

2. Any written or recorded statements and any summaries of oral statements made by the accused herein or any statements of others which contain a declaration of the accused.

3. Those portions of the Grand Jury minutes which contain statements of witnesses whom the Prosecutor intends to call and directly examine at trial, which statements are probably within the control of the prosecution and which statements will relate to matters covered in the witness' testimony in this case, for the purpose of cross-examination and impeachment of such witness' credibility.

4. The relevant testimony which is reduced to writing of persons whom the Prosecutor intends to call as a witness at the trial, but who did not testify before the Grand Jury.

5. Any reports or statements of experts made in connection with this case, including results of physical or mental examination and of scientific tests, experiments, or comparisons.

6. Any books, papers, documents, photographs or tangible objects, which the Prosecuting Attorney intends to use in the trial or which were obtained from or belong to the accused or his family.

7. Any record or prior criminal convictions of persons whom the Prosecutor intends to call as witnesses at the trial.

8. Any declarations against interest made by the Defendant.

9. Any evidence the Prosecutor might have, favorable to the Defendant.

10. Copies of any photographs which the prosecution has in its possession which it intends to introduce as evidence.

11. Any description of the Defendant's conduct, if any, that the prosecution intends to introduce as an implied admission.

12. Any promises, rewards, or inducements provided to prosecution witnesses or defense witnesses.

13. Any victim's statement that was recorded or memorialized and that is under the State's control.

14. Any and all medical reports in appropriate cases.

15. That portion of police reports containing substantially verbatim statements of witnesses.

16. The criminal record of the Defendant, including arrests and convictions.

17. Evidence of other crimes, wrongs, or acts pursuant to Evidence Rule 404(b).

The State shall also allow counsel for the Defendant to examine any and all physical evidence, whether or not the prosecution intends to present the evidence at trial, within thirty (30) days after the initial hearing.

B. Duty of Counsel for the Defendant. In all Murder, class A, class B, class C, and class D Felony cases, unless relieved by court order, counsel for the Defendant shall, within thirty (30) days after receiving the discovery from the State of Indiana in any criminal action filed against the Defendant, furnish the attorney for the State of Indiana the following:

1. Any reports or results or testimony relative thereto, of physical or mental examination or of scientific tests, experiments or comparisons, or any other reports or statements of experts pertaining to this case.

2. A summary of any special or statutory defense(s), which Defendant intends to make at a hearing or trial in this cause.

3. Names and last known addresses of persons Defendant intends to call as witnesses, together with their relevant written or recorded statements, including memoranda reporting or summarizing their oral statements, and any record of prior criminal convictions known to the Defendant.

4. Any books, papers, documents, photographs, or tangible objects Defendant intends to use as evidence or for impeachment at a hearing or trial.

C. Duty When Defendant is Not Represented by Counsel. If a Defendant is not represented by an attorney, the above duties do not apply. The parties must file written motions with the court to request discovery.

II. Motions in Limine.

In all Murder, class A, class B, class C, and class D Felony cases, unless relieved by court order, the following items are excluded from evidence, and the Court prohibits any reference at the fact-finding hearing to the following. In addition, counsel and all witnesses may not refer to, mention, or testify about the following:

1. The fact that the Defendant failed to make a statement either orally or in writing at the time of his arrest.

2. Any questioning of the Defendant, or any statements which Defendant may have made while he was in the custody of the police, absent proof beyond a reasonable doubt that the statements were made freely and voluntarily and after a knowing and intelligent waiver of rights by the Defendant.

3. Any previous arrest or detention of the Defendant which did not result in a conviction.

4. Any other alleged offenses, allegedly involving the Defendant, in which he or she was neither arrested nor charged.

5. Any prior conviction of the Defendant, except those which may be used for the purpose of impeachment.

6. The statutory penalty for the offense(s) charged, or any and all included offenses.

The rule regarding Motions in Limine applies in cases where Defendant is represented by counsel, and it also applies to cases where Defendant is not represented by counsel.

Adopted as Local Rule 5–2003, effective June 16, 2003. Renumbered as Rule 011 and amended effective May 9, 2006; renumbered as Rule 0005 and amended effective Sept. 1, 2012.

LR18–CR00–DLR Rule 0006. Criminal Practice and Procedure

A. Assignment of Cases. All felonies charging Murder, class A felony, class B felony, class C felony, or class D felony will be assigned to the appropriate court based upon the month in which the offense is alleged to have occurred.

The following monthly rotation is now established, effective January 1, 2013.

- Circuit Court No. 1—the first month (January 2013)
- Circuit Court No. 2—the second month;
- Circuit Court No. 3—the third month;
- Circuit Court No. 4—the fourth month;
- Circuit Court No. 5—the fifth month;

Thereafter, the monthly rotation among the courts will continue in this sequence until further order.

If a Defendant has allegedly committed multiple offenses in different months, the date of the earliest alleged offense shall control the assignment.

B. Criminal Cases Transferred from Muncie City Court or Yorktown Town Court.

1. Any case transferred from the Muncie City Court or the Yorktown Town Court may be filed in the Division of the Circuit Court that holds the highest pending felony charge, regardless of when the misdemeanor crime was allegedly committed.

2. If no felony cases are pending against the Defendant the misdemeanor will be filed in the

Delaware Circuit Court No. 4 or No. 5 under the following rotation schedule:

- Circuit Court No. 4: January, March, May, July, September and November;
- Circuit Court No. 5: February, April, June, August, October, and December.

3. A "pending" case is a case not yet disposed of by guilty plea, jury trial, bench trial, bench disposition, or dismissal.

C. Transfer and Reassignment. A judge may transfer and reassign to any of the other five Circuit Court judges a pending case, by issuing a written order for transfer, and subject to the receiving court's acceptance.

Lower classes of felonies shall transfer to the court where the case alleging the higher felony offense is pending. A "pending" case is a case not yet disposed by guilty plea, jury trial, bench trial, bench disposition, or dismissal.

D. Filing and Reassignment of class D Felony Cases. A class D felony case may be filed in the Division of the Circuit Court that holds another pending felony charge, regardless of when the class D felony offense was allegedly committed.

If a Defendant charged with a pending class D felony case is later charged with a higher felony, i.e., Murder, class A, class B, or class C felony, the Court with the class D felony case shall transfer the class D felony case to the court with the higher pending felony case, either on its own motion or at a party's request.

A "pending" case is a case not yet disposed of by guilty plea, jury trial, bench trial, bench disposition, or dismissal.

E. Re-filing by the State. In the event the State of Indiana dismisses a case and later re-files that case, the State shall file the case in the court which dismissal was taken.

In the event the State of Indiana dismisses a case, any subsequent related cases filed against such defendant within ninety (90) days shall be assigned to the court from which dismissal was taken.

F. Additional Related Charges. If the State files additional related charges against a Defendant, after the case is initially assigned, the State shall file all additional related charges in the court of initial assignment.

G. Additional Unrelated Charges. Except as to class D felonies, as set out in Section D above, if the State files additional unrelated charges against a Defendant, after the case is initially assigned, the State shall file all unrelated charges in the court based upon the month in which the offense allegedly occurred.

H. Reassignment. If a judge grants a change of judge motion, or should a judge find it necessary to disqualify and assign a different judge to a case, the Clerk shall reassign the case as follows:

- Cases from the Delaware Circuit Court No. 1 shall be reassigned to the Delaware Circuit Court No. 2.
- Cases from the Delaware Circuit Court No. 2 shall be reassigned to the Delaware Circuit Court No. 3.
- Cases from the Delaware Circuit Court No. 3 shall be reassigned to the Delaware Circuit Court No. 4.
- Cases from the Delaware Circuit Court No. 4 shall be reassigned to the Delaware Circuit Court No. 5.
- Cases from the Delaware Circuit Court No. 5 shall be reassigned to the Delaware Circuit Court No. 1.

If the judge to whom the case is assigned cannot assume jurisdiction for any reason, the Clerk shall assign the case to the next judge in the consecutive order as set out above.

Adopted Aug. 27, 2003, effective Aug. 31, 2003. Renumbered as Rule 012 and amended effective May 9, 2006; renumbered as Rule 0006 and amended effective Sept. 1, 2012.

LR18–AR00–DLR Rule 0007.   Bail Schedule

A. Felonies. Except for Class D felonies and misdemeanors, the Clerk may not accept a Ten Percent (10%) cash deposit in lieu of bond, except upon written Order of a Judge.

1. Unless otherwise ordered by the Court, there shall be **NO BOND** for the charges of Murder or Attempted Murder except by the Court after a hearing.

2. For any class A or B felony offense or a class C felony offense involving a deadly weapon or serious bodily injury, bail shall be set by the Court after a hearing.

3. The presumptive bond amount for bail on a class A felony offense (except those involving Dealing in Controlled Substances, including Cocaine and Methamphetamine) shall be Thirty Thousand ($30,000.00).

4. The presumptive bond amount for bail on a class A or B felony offense for Dealing in Cocaine, Dealing in Methamphetamine, or Dealing in a Controlled Substance shall be Fifty Thousand ($50,000.00) total, regardless of the number of dealing offenses charged.

5. The presumptive bond amount for bail on a class B felony shall be Twenty Thousand Dollars ($20,000.00).

6. The presumptive bond amount for bail on a class C felony shall be Ten Thousand Dollars ($10,000.00).

7. The presumptive bond amount for bail on a class D Felony shall be Five Thousand Dollars ($5,000.00). Defendant may post a Ten Percent

(10%) cash deposit in lieu of bond in his or her name only.

8. If the defendant has a prior felony conviction within the last Five (5) Years, bail shall be twice the amount unless otherwise specified in this section.

9. For any person charged with a Murder or a class A, B, or C felony, *and* charged with being an Habitual Offender, bail is to be set at an additional Fifty Thousand Dollars ($50,000.00).

10. For any person charged with a class D felony, *and* charged with being an Habitual Offender, bail is to be set at an additional Ten Thousand Dollars ($10,000.00).

B. Misdemeanors.

1. For class A misdemeanors, bail shall be Two Thousand Five Hundred Dollars ($2,500.00). Defendant may post a Ten Percent (10%) cash deposit in lieu of bond in his or her name only.

2. For class B misdemeanors, bail shall be One Thousand Dollars ($1,000.00). Defendant may post a Ten Percent (10%) cash deposit in lieu of bond in his or her name only.

3. For class C misdemeanors, bail shall be Five Hundred Dollars ($500.00). Defendant may post a Ten Percent (10%) cash deposit in lieu of bond in his or her name only.

C. Other Provisions.

1. Persons shall be held without bond until the Pre–Charge Initial Hearing who are arrested and in which:

    a. the true identity of a defendant is unknown; or

    b. there is good cause to believe the defendant is on probation, home detention/house arrest, parole, on bond, on pre-trial release to probation, or participating in the Forensic Diversion Drug Court Program.

2. Delaware County Jail shall place a Fifteen (15) Day hold on any offender upon request by a Delaware County Probation Officer or a Parole Officer employed by the State of Indiana. If the officer fails to initiate probation or parole revocation proceedings within the Fifteen (15) Day period, the hold shall expire.

3. *Intoxication*: The Sheriff of Delaware County shall not release any person unless such person clearly manifests that they are in a state of sobriety at the time the provisions of this Order would otherwise permit release.

The Sheriff shall hold in custody any person who is under the influence of alcohol or controlled substances until such time it is determined, at the Sheriff's discretion, that the individual may be safely released without danger to self or others.

4. *Domestic Violence*: The Sheriff shall not release a person arrested on a charge involving domestic violence until Twelve (12) Hours has elapsed or until appearance in court, whichever is earlier. After Twelve (12) Hours, the person may post bail (1) pursuant to other provisions in this Bail Order, and (2) after signing a No Contact Agreement protecting the victim. If the person refuses to sign a No Contact Agreement, the Sheriff shall hold the person until brought to court.

5. *Overweight Trucking Violations*: The bail schedule as set out in this Order shall not apply to overweight trucking violations. Bail for such offenses shall be convened by I.C. 9–20–1, et seq.

6. *Full Cash Bond*: When any person proposes to post a full bond in cash or by certified check and the Clerk's Office is not open for business, the Sheriff shall accept the money or certified check and issue a release to the person making the payment. The bond must be placed in the name of the arrested person. The Sheriff shall deposit the money or certified check with the Clerk as soon as possible.

7. *10% Cash Bonds*: The Clerk may not accept a Ten Percent (10%) cash deposit in lieu of bond, except upon written Order of a judge. If the Court approves such a bond, the Clerk may retain as a service fee Ten Percent (10%) of the amount deposited, or Fifty Dollars ($50.00), whichever is the lesser amount when the bond is released at the conclusion of the case.

8. *Amount of Bail on Warrant*: If the bail is set at a probable cause hearing, the amount of bail set by the judge shall be endorsed upon the arrest warrant.

9. *Release of Bond*: The Clerk shall not release a cash bond, except upon a judge's written Order after judgment has been entered and any fines and costs imposed by the Court have been paid and satisfied.

10. This Order shall not be interpreted to limit judicial discretion.

11. If the Delaware County Prosecuting Attorney believes a higher bond is necessary for the safety of witnesses and/or protection of the community, the Prosecutor may request a deviation from the scheduled bond amount.

12. A judge may impose any or all of the following **Conditions of Release:**

    a. Report to the Probation Officer Supervising the Pre–Trial Release Program;

    b. Remain in the supervisory custody of a named responsible person;

    c. Live and stay at a specified address;

    d. Remain in the State of Indiana;

    e. Have no contact with the victim/complaining witness;

    f. Not use or possess alcohol;

g. Not use or possess any controlled substances unless on order of a physician;

h. Submit to drug/alcohol testing at your expense;

i. Remain at residence other than at specified hours for specified purposes;

j. Not possess a firearm or other dangerous weapon;

k. Seek and maintain full time employment/student status;

l. Undergo necessary medical or psychiatric treatment, including drug or alcohol abuse treatment;

m. Commit no criminal offense.

n. Comply with any other condition reasonably calculated to assure appearance in court as required or to assure the safety of any other person and the community.

o. Defendant specifically agrees to waive extradition from any jurisdiction inside or outside the United States, wherever he/she may be found, and also agrees not to contest any effort to return him/her to the State of Indiana.

Adopted effective June 30, 2000. Amended effective Aug. 5, 2004; renumbered as Rule 016 and amended effective May 9, 2006; renumbered as Rule 0007 and amended effective Sept. 1, 2012; amended effective March 5, 2013.

LR18–AR01–DLR Rule 0011. Attorney Fees in Probate Matters

The Delaware Circuit Court has prepared the following guidelines for fees in probate matters in an effort to achieve the following objectives:

1. To establish uniformity in determining a fair and reasonable fee for supervised and unsupervised estates, guardianships, wrongful death actions, and minor's claim settlements in Delaware County, Indiana.

2. To provide a guideline to assist all judges of the Circuit Court of Delaware County in determining fair and reasonable fees.

3. To furnish a guideline to attorneys so that attorneys can forecast to their clients the fees the estate may incur before the administration commences.

4. To assist the legal profession in arriving at a fair and reasonable fee for estate work. This schedule is not a minimum fee schedule but a maximum fee schedule. The Court recognizes that every attorney and personal representative has a right and an obligation to request a fee which is fair and reasonable for the estate work performed, taking into account the provision in the Rules of Professional Conduct which applies to all attorneys admitted to practice in Indiana. Fees should always bear a reasonable relationship to the services rendered. In an uncomplicated estate, a reasonable fee may be less than the maximum fees listed in the following schedule.

In determining an appropriate fee, the attorney, client, and Court should consider the following criteria:

1. The time required; the novelty, complexity, or difficulty of the legal questions involved; and the skill required to perform necessary services properly.

2. Who served as personal representative. The Court may consider how much time the attorney devoted to legal matters and how much time the attorney devoted to ministerial functions during supervision and representation of the personal representative.

3. The character of the probate and non-probate assets which are administered or transferred, including whether non-probate assets exist which must be included for federal or state estate tax purposes, and whether these non-probate assets require more work for the attorney.

4. Whether the probate assets are sufficient to pay for legal services or personal representative fees.

5. Timeliness in performing necessary estate services under statutory requirements, these rules, and the Rules of Professional Conduct.

6. Other factors deemed relevant by the attorney, personal representative, and/or the Court.

Attorney Fee Schedule

I. Administration of the Gross Estate.

A. Gross Estate Services include, but will not necessarily be limited to, opening the estate and qualifying the personal representative; preparing and filing the inventory; collecting assets; paying claims; preparing and filing non-extraordinary petitions (including but not limited to petitions to sell real or personal property, petitions to deliver personal property to beneficiaries, petitions to abandon real or personal property, and petitions for appointment of appraisers); preparing and filing the Inheritance Tax Schedule and obtaining court approval; paying inheritance taxes; preparing and filing the final report; obtaining an order approving the final report; distributing assets to beneficiaries; obtaining discharge of the personal representative; preparing and filing the supplemental report after distribution; and preparing and serving all necessary notices on interested parties, including readily ascertainable creditors of the estate, during the estate proceeding.

B. Gross Estate Value means the fair market value of all assets in the decedent's name and included in the decedent's probate estate.

C. *Maximum Fees for Administering the Gross Estate*: the Court may approve the following maximum fees:

1. *Individual Personal Representative:*

Fair Market Value Of Probate Estate Including Income	Percent Rate For Individual Personal Representative	Percent Rate For Professional Services of Attorney
First $25,000.00	4%	8%
Next $25,000.00	3%	6%
Next $50,000.00	2 ½ %	5%
Next $900,000.00	1 ½ %	3%
Next $1,500,000.00	1%	2%
Excess of $2,500,000.00	½ %	1%

Where the attorney acts as both the attorney and Personal Representative, the above schedule will be applied.

2. *Corporate Personal Representative.*

Fair Market Value Of Probate Estate Including Income	Percent Rate For Individual Personal Representative	Percent Rate For Professional Services of Attorney
First $25,000.00	6%	6%
Next $25,000.00	5%	5%
Next $50,000.00	4%	4%
Next $900,000.00	3%	3%
Next $1,500,000.00	2%	2%
Excess of $2,500,000.00	1 %	1%

D. Non–Probate Assets. Non-probate assets are those assets for which the attorney representing the personal representative may assist the transferee of those assets in distribution. Non-probate assets include, but are not necessarily limited to: assets jointly owned which are transferred outside the estate administration; life insurance proceeds; annuities; retirement benefits payable to a named beneficiary other than the estate; and assets held in trust which are reportable on the federal transfer tax return or would be reportable if such return were required. Fee charges for assisting beneficiaries or transferees in transferring Non–Probate Assets shall conform to the hourly rate provision established by the Court in paragraph E below. Unless the will admitted to probate provides otherwise, fees generated by the attorney in administering Non–Probate Assets should be charged to the beneficiary or transferee, and not to the estate.

E. Additional Fees. Fees computed on the above schedule are intended to cover only the usual and ordinary services that are reasonably anticipated in handling the normal estate. Such fees do not contemplate all work which may become necessary in conjunction with administration, such as will contests; will construction; contested claims; family settlement agreements; death tax complications; determination of heirship; generating additional income for the estate during administration; and other similar matters. The attorney shall detail the request for additional fees in a Petition to the Court for Additional Fees.

The Court will compensate attorneys for work involving extraordinary service at an hourly rate. The attorney's hourly rate should conform to the prevailing hourly rate for legal services provided in Delaware County, Indiana, at the time the attorney provided the extraordinary services. The Court reserves the right to review and adjust the hourly rate request after considering the attorney's expertise and the nature of the extraordinary services provided.

F. Unsupervised Estates. The attorney and personal representative should negotiate fees for handling unsupervised estates. The Court shall not hear the requests for fees unless an objection to the closing statement is timely filed. In the absence of evidence to the contrary, the fees for handling unsupervised estates should not exceed eighty percent (80%) of the above schedules.

G. Petitions and Hearings on Fee Requests. All requests for approval of estate or guardianship fees shall be submitted to the Court in writing, along with an appropriate proposed order.

If the fee requested to administer the Gross Estate conforms to the Guideline in Paragraph I. (C), the Court may waive a hearing on the Petition.

If the petition to approve fees includes a request for additional fees, the Court will schedule a hearing on the petition, unless all interested parties execute a waiver and consent stating they have been advised that the fee request exceeds the Court's guidelines for administering the Gross Estate and that the fee request is for additional services. A proposed waiver and consent form is attached to this fee schedule, and the waiver and consent should be in the same or similar form as the attachment. If a waiver and consent form is filed with the petition for additional fees, the Court, at its discretion, may waive the requirement for hearing on the petition.

II. Wrongful Death Claim Administration.

If a wrongful death claim is settled before trial, the fee should not exceed 33 ⅓ percent of the settlement amount.

If a wrongful death action proceeds to trial by court or by jury, the attorney fee should not exceed 40 percent of the court or jury award.

If a wrongful death action is appealed after trial, the attorney fee should not exceed 50 percent of the court or jury award.

The fee schedule for wrongful death actions does not preclude the attorney from recovering litigation expenses incurred in preparing for trial or in pre-trial discovery proceedings.

III. Guardianship Fees.

Attorneys should charge fees generated in guardianship proceedings at the customary and prevailing hourly rates in Delaware County for opening the guardianship; selling real or personal property; assisting the Guardian in filing the inventory and necessary accounting; and providing professional advice.

Attorneys shall submit petitions to approve attorney fees in writing in all cases, along with an appropriate proposed order. The Court, at its discretion, may require a hearing on the fee request of the attorney or the Guardian.

IV. Fees for Compromising, Settling, or Trying a Minor's Claim.

Fee requests to compromise, settle, or try a minor's claim should not exceed the fee limitations imposed by the Court for representing the client in a wrongful death action; however, the attorney may request reimbursement for suit costs and pre-trial discovery in addition to those fees.

Adopted as Rule 0901 May 28, 2009, effective Jan. 1, 2010. Renumbered as Rule 0011 and amended effective Sept. 1, 2012.

LR18–JR00–DLR Rule 0021. Jury Management

The following local rule regarding jury management is now adopted by the undersigned Judges of Delaware County.

A. Uniform Jury Selection. The jury administrator and the supervising judge under the plan will provide a uniform system of jury selection for the courts ensuring that persons selected for jury service are selected at random from a fair cross section of the population of Delaware County. A computerized jury selection system will be fair and will not violate the rights of persons with respect to impartial and random selection of prospective jurors.

B. Jury Selection Plan. The jury administrator, under the supervision of the supervising judge, shall prepare a written plan for the selection of grand and petit jurors in the county. The plan must be designed to achieve the objectives of, and otherwise comply with Indiana Jury Rules. The Jury Selection Plan of the jury administrator is attached hereto and marked as Delaware County Jury Selection Plan.

C. Master List. The jury administrator shall compile and maintain a master list consisting of the approved Jury Pool Master List for Delaware County.

D. Juror Service. Names must be drawn for juror service quarterly, based on a calendar year commencing in January.

1. The jury administrator shall create and file an alphabetical list of names drawn under this section. The alphabetical list may be in the form of a serial listing or discreet computer record filed together to constitute the alphabetical list. Names may not be added to the alphabetical list, except by order of the court. Neither the names drawn nor any list compiled from the alphabetical list may be disclosed to any person other than by order of the supervising judge.

2. Names must be drawn randomly pursuant to Jury Rule 3.

3. Names drawn from the master list may not be returned to the master list until all nonexempt persons on the master list have been called.

E. Random Drawing of Names.

1. The master list will contain names in a sequential order, such as a numeric sequence, and drawn randomly from the Jury Management System through INCITE.

F. Jury Qualification Form. The provisions of Jury Rule 4 will be followed in that not later than 7 days after the date of the drawing of names from the master list, the jury administrator shall cause to be mailed to each person whose name is drawn a juror qualification form.

1. The form will be designed to reflect the prospective juror's name, address, and age.

2. Whether the prospective juror is a citizen of the United States and a resident of the county; is able to read, speak and understand the English language.

3. Has any physical or mental disability impairing the person's capacity to render satisfactory jury service

4. If a prospective juror is unable to fill out the form, another person may fill out the form for the prospective juror. If the form is completed by a person other than a prospective juror, the form must indicate that another person has done so and the reason for doing so.

5. If it appears there is an omission, ambiguity, or error in a returned form, the jury administrator shall resend the form, instructing the prospective juror to make the necessary addition, clarification, or correction and to return the form to the jury administrator not later than 10 days after its second receipt.

6. A prospective juror who fails to return a completed juror qualification form as instructed may be directed by the jury administrator to immediately appear before the jury administrator to fill out a juror qualification form.

G. Disqualification for jury service. The supervising judge or the jury administrator shall determine solely on the basis of information provided on a juror qualification form or interview with a prospective juror whether the prospective juror is disqualified for jury service.

1. The jury administrator shall enter this determination in the space provided on the juror qualification form or electronically and on the alphabetical list of names drawn from the master list.

2. The ISSUING judge, upon request of a prospective juror, shall determine on the basis of information provided on the juror qualification form, correspondence from the prospective juror, or an interview with the prospective juror whether the prospective juror may be excused from jury service. The jury administrator shall enter this determination in the space provided on the juror qualification form.

3. A person who is not disqualified for jury service may be excused from jury service only upon a showing of undue hardship, extreme inconvenience, or public necessity, until the time of the next drawing when the person is summoned. Appropriate records must be maintained by the jury administrator to facilitate summoning.

H. Exemption. A person who has completed a term of jury service in the twenty-four (24) months preceding the date of the person's summons may claim exemption from jury service.

I. Deferral. The judge or judges' designee may authorize deferral of jury service for up to one (1) year upon a showing of hardship, extreme inconvenience, or necessity. Deferral requests made after the issuance of summons for prospective jury duty must be approved by the Issuing Judge. The Issuing Judge may determine if the deferral request may be made by fax or in person. Deferrals may be given one (1) time per year.

J. Grand Jury. Upon receipt of an order for a grand jury, the jury administrator shall draw at random from the qualified Grand Jury Master List twenty (20) qualified jurors and direct them to appear before the supervising judge. The supervising judge shall randomly select six (6) jurors after explaining to the twenty (20) prospective jurors the duties and responsibilities of a grand jury.

The names of qualified jurors drawn and the contents of the jury qualification forms completed by those jurors may not be made available to the public until the period of service of those jurors has expired. However, attorneys in any cases in which these jurors may serve may have access to the information.

K. Preservation of Record. After the period of service for which names were drawn from the master jury list has expired, and all persons selected to serve as jurors have been discharged, all records and papers compiled and maintained by the jury administrator or the clerk must be preserved by the clerk of the courts for the period prescribed by rule of the Indiana Supreme Court. The records and papers must be available for public inspection at all reasonable times.

Adopted effective Sept. 1, 2012.

LR18–JR00–DLR Rule 0022. Jury Selection Plan

1. The Master Jury List will be created each year during the month of November containing the citizens of Delaware County from Bureau of Motor Vehicles and Indiana Department of Revenue lists for the county eighteen (18) years of age and older. The court administrator will be referred to as the "jury administrator" throughout this plan.

2. To create the Master List, the names of persons from the Bureau of Motor Vehicles and Indiana Department of Revenue lists for the county eighteen (18) years of age and older will be provided by the Indiana

Supreme Court. Data Processing will retrieve the information through the internet website for INCITE.

3. During the first week of the second month of each quarter, the jury administrator will cause a draw of 2,500 names for petit jurors and 100 names for grand jurors from the Master List. Jury Questionnaires will be mailed and processed. A quarterly master list will be kept of all qualified jurors. A separate list of those persons excused from jury service will be maintained in a numerical table.

4. To perfect the issuance of a Venire, the court personnel will submit a Venire Order with the cause number, name of case, the number of names to be called, and the date and time of the trial.

5. Those persons selected from the random draw will be temporarily removed until all non-exempt persons have been called. All persons seated for jury service within the quarter will be removed permanently from the year's list, along with those excused or deferred pursuant to statute.

6. Non-exempt persons who request to be excused from jury service should first initiate the call through the Office of Court Services. Requests not included, per statute, shall be referred to the issuing court.

7. The number of petit jurors that constitutes a panel for criminal C felony and higher shall be fifty (50) names. An *additional* number of names may be issued for specific cases requiring a larger pool of prospective jurors. The number of petit jurors that constitutes a panel for civil cases shall be thirty five (35) along with class D felonies and misdemeanors.

8. The number of grand jurors to be drawn for service will be twenty (20). The procedure for selection shall be the same as the petit jury draw with Data Processing providing the key number and the random selection of numbers to be used.

Adopted as Local Rule 0605 effective March 4, 2008. Renumbered as Rule 0022 and amended effective Sept. 1, 2012.

LR18–AR00–DLR Rule 0031. Executive Organization

A. Board of Judges. The five judges of the Delaware Circuit Court shall constitute the Board of Judges.

B. Presiding Judge. At the annual fall meeting the Board of Judges shall select from among themselves a presiding judge of the court. The presiding judge shall be selected for a minimum term of twelve (12) months, whose one-year term shall begin the following January 1st. If available, the judge whose term as presiding judge has just ended shall serve as acting presiding judge when the presiding judge is unavailable. The presiding judge shall, as delegated by the Board of Judges:

1. Direct preparation of the agenda and minutes of the Board of Judges meetings;

2. Preside over the Board of Judges meetings and call special meetings as necessary;

3. Ensure efficient operation of the court system and compliance with these Rules;

4. Submit the annual budget for the court system, as approved by the Board of Judges, to include operation of the Delaware Circuit Court's Probation Department;

5. Present to the Board of Judges recommendations as to appointments or selections required of a circuit court judge;

6. Direct preparation and circulation of all annual reports for the court system and amendments to these Rules;

7. Maintain and distribute to the other judges policy manuals covering bond schedules, juror excuses, caseload allocation schedules and other matters pertaining to the day-to-day operation of the court system; and

8. Perform other duties as directed by the Board of Judges or as set out in these Rules.

C. Quarterly Meeting. The Board of Judges shall meet the months designated below to make policy decisions, provide educational reports, and review operations of the court system. The Director of Court Services, hereinafter referred to as the "court administrator" will be required to attend these meetings and participate in discussions. The meeting will be held during the months of January, April, July, October, and December on the 3rd Wednesday at Noon. A schedule of said meeting dates will be delivered each January by the Office of Court Services to each judge, chief adult probation officer, chief juvenile probation officer, and CASA Director.

D. Fall Meeting. Each fall (October) the Board of Judges and the court administrator shall attend an extended meeting to discuss:

1. Selection of the next presiding judge;

2. Implementation of the next annual budget as approved by the County Council;

3. Allocation of caseload;

4. The annual reports and performance of the Adult and Juvenile Probation Department, and the Office of Court Services.

E. Decisions. Whenever an action of the entire court is required, including selection of a presiding judge under I.C. 33–33–18, the judges herein shall act in concert. If the judges disagree, the decision of the majority of the judges controls. Local Rules shall be made by a vote of the majority of the Board of Judges.

Adopted as Local Rule 0801 effective May 29, 2008. Renumbered as Rule 0031 and amended effective Sept. 1, 2012.

LR18–AR00–DLR Rule 0032. Caseload Allocation

A. Purpose. First and foremost, the judicial officers of Delaware Circuit Court shall make thoughtful, timely, reasoned and just decisions. The allocation of caseload must reflect this purpose.

B. Procedure. The Board of Judges annually shall:

1. Review and assess literature from the Indiana State Bar Association, the American Bar Association and the National Center for State Courts.

2. Review and consider suggestions made by the Delaware County Bar, the prosecuting attorney, the public defender, and the clerk of courts.

3. Review and analyze the statistics on current workload and case flow within the Delaware Circuit Court.

4. Give due weight to the expertise of each judge, the stress associated with certain caseloads, and the goal of keeping each judge competent in all areas of the law.

5. Analyze whether the current allocation is providing excellent public service. There shall be a presumption in favor of the current allocation in order to preserve public confidence in the system, promote stability for the employees of the court system, and avoid inefficient use of personnel, time and resources to effectuate change.

C. Implementation. The Clerk of Delaware County shall maintain a filing system, by computer or otherwise, implementing the caseload allocation approved by the Board of Judges. The current allocation is contained in the Reallocation and Reassignment of Cases under Local Rule LR18–AR00–DLR–0602. If the caseload allocation is changed by order of the Board of Judges, the presiding judge shall forward the amended allocation to the Clerk of the Supreme Court and Court of Appeals, the State Court Administrator, the Clerk of Delaware Circuit Court, and the President of the Delaware County Bar Association for approval by the Supreme Court.

D. Individual Case Transfer. Nothing in this Rule shall preclude the transfer of an individual case from one division of the Circuit Court to another division to promote efficiency and provide for timely resolution of cases. The transferring judge shall direct the Clerk to resubmit the case for transfer to a specific division as designated in the Local Rules of Criminal, Civil, and Small Claims Procedures. In all Orders of Transfer, provisions shall be made to ensure all applicable costs and fees be allocated to the proper cause of action.

Adopted as Local Rule 0802 effective May 29, 2008. Renumbered as Rule 0032 and amended effective Sept. 1, 2012.

LR18–AR00–DLR Rule 0033. Rules of Practice

A. Purpose. Local rules of practice and procedure now in existence and not inconsistent with Administrative Rules will continue to be in existence. Any new local rule will be promulgated pursuant to Trial Rule 81.

B. Procedure. Each year the Board of Judges shall review the local rules and shall consider changes and additions suggested by the Delaware County Bar, the prosecuting attorney, the public defender, and the clerk of courts. Further, the Board of Judges shall review and assess local rules adopted by other counties and jurisdictions.

C. Adoption. On July 1, 2000, and thereafter as amended, the Local Rules of Practice and Procedure for the Delaware Circuit Court are adopted and effective in all divisions of the Delaware Circuit Court. A copy of the Local Rules shall be forwarded to the Clerk of the Supreme Court and the Court of Appeals, the State Court Administrator, the Prosecuting Attorney, the Clerk, the Public Defender, and the President of the Delaware County Bar Association.

Adopted as Local Rule 0803 effective May 29, 2008. Renumbered as Rule 0033 and amended effective Sept. 1, 2012.

LR18–AR00–DLR Rule 0034. Budgetary Matters

A. Budgets. The Board of Judges shall direct the preparation of one unified budget for all divisions of the Court, the Probation Department and the Office of Court Services to be funded from the county general fund upon approval of the County Council, and a separate budget for Title IV-D Court. The Title IV-D Court shall remain separate and apart from the unified budget. The Board of Judges shall further direct the preparation of additional budgets for programs funded by User Fee income upon approval by the County Council.

B. Annual Procedure. Each year the Board of Judges shall establish a schedule of budget preparation, review and submission with the goal of providing for the effective functioning of the Court, as follows:

1. Each judge, CASA Director, and the chief probation officers shall submit written budget requests to the court administrator. These requests shall be specific and well justified in light of the past year's expenditures and the future needs of the offices. Any request shall be submitted by May 15.

2. The Board of Judges shall meet to review the budget requests from the chief probation officers, the court administrator, and CASA Director to establish budget priorities, and to adopt the annual budgets for submission to the County Council.

3. The budget proposals as adopted by the Board of Judges shall be prepared by the court administrator and signed by the presiding judge for submission to the County Council.

C. Allocation of Resources. The Board of Judges shall establish guidelines for allocation of individual line items in the yearly budget approved by the County Council.

D. Claims. Claims shall be submitted to the Office of Court Services for approval by the court administrator and subsequent submission to the Auditor's Office. The court administrator may approve all proper payroll claims and may approve all purchase, travel and training claims not exceeding maximum amounts set by the Board of Judges from time to time. Any claim exceeding these guidelines must be submitted to the Board of Judges for approval.

E. Transfers Within Budget Categories. If the court administrator determines that a transfer is necessary within budget categories, the court administrator shall direct the Auditor's Office to perfect said transfer, following consultation with the presiding judge.

F. Transfers Between Budget Categories. If the court administrator determines that a transfer between budget categories is necessary, a written proposal shall be submitted to the presiding judge for approval prior to submission to the County Council.

G. Additional Appropriation. If the court administrator determines that an additional appropriation is necessary, a written proposal shall be submitted to the Board of Judges.

H. Mandate. No individual judge shall exercise mandates for the adequate provision of court services, personnel, or other expenditures without consultation with the entire Board of Judges. The Board of Judges may exercise mandate authority upon vote of a majority.

Adopted as Local Rule 0804 effective May 29, 2008. Renumbered as Rule 0034 and amended effective Sept. 1, 2012.

LR18–AR00–DLR Rule 0035. Personnel

A. General Organization. The Delaware Circuit Court employs personnel, as follows:

1. Court Divisions

Official Court Reporter
Assistant Court Reporter
Court Secretary
Court Bailiff
Civil Process Server
Master Commissioner
Juvenile Magistrate

2. Adult Probation Department

1 Chief Adult Probation Officer
1 Assistant Chief Adult Probation Officer
Adult Probation Officers
Secretaries to assist probation officers
User Fee Clerk/Secretary

3. Juvenile Probation Department

1 Chief Juvenile Probation Officer
Juvenile Probation Officers
1 Secretary for Juvenile Probation

1 User Fee Clerk/Secretary for Juvenile Proba-tion

4. **Office of Court Services**

Court Administrator
Administrative Assistant
Jury Administrative Assistant (full time or part-time)

5. **CASA Office**

Director
Volunteer Coordinator
Support Staff (full-time or part-time)

B–1. Court Division. The Delaware Circuit Court shall have five court divisions as follows: Delaware Circuit Court shall become Delaware Circuit Court No. 1; Delaware Superior Court No. 2 shall become Delaware Circuit Court No. 2; Delaware Superior Court No. 1 shall become Delaware Circuit Court No. 3; Delaware Superior Court No. 3 shall become Delaware Circuit Court No. 4; Delaware Superior Court No. 4 shall become Delaware Circuit Court No. 5. Pursuant to IC 33–33–18–7, the judge of each court division shall have the sole authority to employ an official court reporter, an assistant court reporter, court secretary or secretaries, a court bailiff, and civil process servers to serve at the pleasure of the judge.

The Board of Judges shall appoint and employ master commissioners to full-time and/or part-time positions. The commissioner/s will not be entitled to practice law. The appointments will be for a two (2) year term. The duties of the master commissioner/s will be as set out in the Terms of Employment of a Master Commissioner. The juvenile magistrate will be responsible for all juvenile cases, IV–D cases, protective order hearings as requested by sitting judge, civil domestic relation cases and guardianship cases related to CHINS cases.

B–2. Court Divisions—Title IV–D Court. The Board of Judges shall have the sole authority to employ Title IV–D Court personnel and the presiding judge shall have the right to terminate their employment after consulting with the Board of Judges. All employees of the Title IV–D Court serve at the plea-sure of the Board of Judges. As directed by the Board of Judges, the presiding judge shall supervise employees of the Title IV–D Court, and may delegate certain supervisory responsibilities to the staff or designee as set out in the Delaware County Circuit Court Personnel Policy and Procedures.

C–1. Adult Probation Department. The Board of Judges shall have the sole authority to employ Probation Department personnel and to terminate their employment. All employees of the Probation Department serve at the pleasure of the Board of Judges. The Board of Judges shall advertise the position of chief adult probation officer and assistant chief adult probation officer with the Delaware County Adult Probation Department, and interview and

screen applicants for said position. The chief adult probation officer shall advertise any other available probation position and interview and screen applicants as directed by the Board of Judges. The chief proba-tion officer shall provide to the Board of Judges a written summary of qualified applicants, with a recom-mendation of three applicants to be hired by the Board of Judges.

C–2. Juvenile Probation Department. The Board of Judges shall have the sole authority to employ Juvenile Probation Department personnel and the supervising judge exercising juvenile jurisdiction shall have the authority to terminate their employ-ment. All employees of the Juvenile Probation De-partment serve at the pleasure of the Board of Judges. The Board of Judges shall advertise the position of Chief Juvenile Probation Officer, and inter-view and screen applicants for said position. The Chief Juvenile Probation Officer shall advertise any other available probation position and interview and screen applicants as directed by the Board of Judges. The Chief Juvenile Probation Officer shall provide to the Board of Judges a written summary of qualified applicants, with a recommendation of three applicants to be hired by the Board of Judges. As directed by the supervising judge exercising juvenile jurisdiction, the Chief Juvenile Probation Officer shall supervise employees of the Juvenile Probation Department, and may delegate certain supervisory responsibilities to the staff and other employees as set out in the Dela-ware County Circuit Court Personnel Policy and Pro-cedures.

D. Office of Court Services. The Board of Judges shall have the sole authority to employ person-nel in the Office of Court Services and to terminate their employment. The court administrator shall ad-vertise an available position and interview and screen applicants as directed by the Board of Judges. The court administrator shall provide to the presiding judge a written summary of qualified applicants, with the court administrator's recommendation of three applicants to be hired by the Board of Judges. Em-ployees of the Office of Court Services shall be super-vised by the Director of Court Services/Court Admin-istrator.

E. CASA. The Board of Judges shall have the sole authority to employ personnel in the CASA Of-fice. The Director of CASA shall advertise an avail-able position and screen applicants as directed by the Board of Judges. The Director shall provide to the presiding judge a written summary of qualified appli-cants, with the Director's recommendation of three applicants to be hired by the Board of Judges. Em-ployees of the CASA Program shall be supervised by the Director. All applicants will be required to take a skills test.

F. Personnel Policy. The Board of Judges shall maintain a written personnel policy setting forth poli-cies and procedures regarding the recruitment, selection, management, and termination of employees and the conditions and expectations of their employment. Each employee shall be given a copy of the personnel policy when employment begins.

G. Termination. If any employee of the Title IV–D Court, secretarial staff of the Adult Probation Department, CASA Department, or the Juvenile Probation Department is not performing adequately, the designated supervising judge or presiding judge shall notify the Board of Judges in writing that termination of the employee is appropriate. The designated supervising judge or the presiding judge of the designated departments in this Paragraph G shall be authorized to terminate the employee.

Adopted as Local Rule 0805 effective May 29, 2008. Renumbered as Rule 0035 and amended effective Sept. 1, 2012.

LR18–AR00–DLR Rule 0036. Administrative Management

A. Management Team. The court administrator, chief probation officers, and CASA director, and presiding judge shall constitute a management team for administrative issues. The team coordinates personnel policy issues and fiscal issues, identifies issues or procedures that may impact outside specific divisions, maintains consistency on administrative issues among the divisions, and addresses other issues and projects within the discretion of the presiding judge.

Adopted as Local Rule 0806 effective May 29, 2008. Renumbered as Rule 0036 and amended effective Sept. 1, 2012.

LR18–AR00–DLR Rule 0037. Office of Court Services

A. Establishment and Purpose. The Board of Judges has established an Office of Court Services to coordinate jury management records, statistics compilation, court security, financial planning and budget management, case flow management, and public information and education for the Delaware Circuit Court.

B. Director of Court Services—Court Administrator. As directed by the Board of Judges, the court administrator shall prepare and monitor the court's budgets; coordinate continuing education and training for court personnel; assist in researching, defining, developing and implementing new programs and procedures; attend and coordinate Board of Judges meetings, coordinate and implement court security plans and perform other duties as required.

C. Other Personnel. The Board of Judges, through the court administrator, shall hire additional administrative aides, clerical staff and bailiffs as needed to provide services to the Court.

D. Financial Planning and Budget Management. The Office of Court Services shall be responsible for the preparation, monitoring and coordination of all budgets of the Delaware Circuit Court. All required fiscal reports are prepared for review by the Board of Judges. This office serves as primary liaison with the Auditor's Office, and prepares and submits payroll, claims and employee status reports as required. This office oversees maintenance and service of equipment.

E. Jury Management. The Office of Court Services is responsible for all functions pertaining to the provision of jury panels for the divisions of the Delaware Circuit Court.

F. Records Management. The Office of Court Services is responsible for compiling and reporting all statistical information regarding caseloads and case movement in the divisions of the Delaware Circuit Court. A written report summarizing the activity operation of the court shall be delivered to the Board of Judges by March 31 of each year.

G. Court Security. The office will *assist* in obtaining security from the Sheriff's Department for the judges, staff, public, in courtrooms and in court offices, only upon request of court personnel; otherwise, the court bailiff will be responsible for making arrangements for security with the Sheriff's Department.

H. Case Flow Management. The Office of Court Services is responsible for assessing case flow and workload distribution to the divisions of the Delaware Circuit Court, and provides supplemental staff when needed and/or available.

I. Public Information and Education. The Office of Court Services serves as liaison officer between the Delaware County Clerk and the Board of Judges. The Filing Office is the designated reception area of the Delaware County Justice Center. The daily court schedule is compiled and distributed by the Filing Office. All stamped and non-stamped mail is disseminated by the Filing Office. File stamps are maintained in the Filing Office to facilitate receipt of pleadings and correspondence for local attorneys. File stamps are also maintained in the individual court divisions. Mail receptacles are provided in the Office of Court Services for local attorneys to collect daily distribution of court documents. All questions regarding new filings or other procedures regarding the court shall be brought to the attention of the court administrator by the designated representative of the Delaware County Clerk.

Adopted as Local Rule 0807 effective May 29, 2008. Renumbered as Rule 0037 and amended effective Sept. 1, 2012.

LR18–AR00–DLR Rule 0038. Probation Department

A. Establishment and Purpose. As required by Indiana law, the Board of Judges has established a Probation Department to serve all divisions of the Delaware Circuit Court. The Probation Department staff conducts interviews and investigations, prepares Pre–Sentence and Juvenile Reports, and oversees probationers and juveniles for compliance with court orders. These activities are conducted with the goals of rehabilitating offenders and protecting society. Further, the Probation Department develops and maintains community-based alternate correction programs.

B. Chief Adult Probation Officer. As directed by the Board of Judges, the chief adult probation officer shall oversee the efficient operation of the adult probation department; assist in the hiring and discharge of personnel; evaluate and train department employees; compile statistics and create required reports; monitor budget expenditures and outline budget requests; maintain written policies and procedures for the department as provided by the Board of Judges; and perform other duties as required.

B–1. Chief Juvenile Probation Officer. As directed by the Board of Judges, the chief juvenile probation officer shall oversee the efficient operation of the juvenile probation department; assist in the hiring and discharge of personnel; evaluate and train department employees; compile statistics and create required reports; monitor budget expenditures and outline budget requests; maintain written policies and procedures for the department as provided by the Board of Judges; and perform other duties as required.

C. Procedures. The Probation Department shall maintain a written policy, procedure and training manual which sets forth the manner of operation of the department and the duties of each officer or staff member.

D. Statistics and Reports. The Probation Department shall maintain all statistical reports and records required by law and necessary for compliance with grant or program authorities. A written report summarizing the activity and operation of the Probation Department shall be delivered to the Board of Judges by March 31st of each year.

E. Fees and Costs. Court-ordered supervision fees shall be collected by designated staff pursuant to an established system of financial records management. This system, subject to State Board of Accounts audit, shall delineate special funds accounts, maintenance of daily collections and ledgers, and proper deposit and disbursement of funds. An internal audit will be conducted any time the collection clerk or staff responsible for the collection of fees terminates employment.

Adopted as Local Rule 0808 effective May 29, 2008. Renumbered as Rule 0038 and amended effective Sept. 1, 2012.

LR18–AR00–DLR Rule 0041. In Re: Court Reporters

Section One. Definitions. The following definitions shall apply under this local rule:

1. A *court reporter* is a person who is specifically designated by a court to perform the official court reporting services for the court including preparing a transcript of the record.

2. *Equipment* means all physical items owned by the court or other government entity and used by a court reporter in performing court reporting services. Equipment shall include, but not be limited to, telephones, copy machines, fax machines, computer hardware, software programs, disks, tapes and any other device used for recording, storing and transcribing electronic data.

3. *Work space* means that portion of the court's facilities dedicated to each court reporter, including but not limited to actual space in the courtroom and any designated office space.

4. *Page* means the page unit of transcript which results when a recording is transcribed in the form required by Indiana rule of Appellate Procedure 7.2.

5. *Recording* means the electronic, mechanical, stenographic or other recording made as required by Indiana Rule of Trial Procedure 74.

6. *Regular hours worked* means those hours which the court is regularly scheduled to work during any given work week.

7. *Gap hours worked* means those hours worked in excess of the regular hours worked but hours not in excess of forty (40) hours per work week.

8. *Overtime hours* worked means those hours worked in excess of forty (40) hours per work week.

9. *Work week* means a seven (7) consecutive day week that consistently begins and ends on the same days through the year, i.e. Sunday through Saturday, Wednesday through Tuesday, Friday through Thursday.

10. *Court* means the particular court for which the court reporter performs services. Court may also mean all of the courts of record in Delaware County.

11. *County indigent transcript* means a transcript that is paid for from county funds and is for the use on behalf of a litigant who has been declared indigent by a court. The county indigent transcript will also include any requests from the local Prosecutor's Office.

12. *State indigent transcript* means a transcript that is paid for from state funds and is for the use on behalf of a litigant who has been declared indigent by a court.

13. *Private transcript* means a transcript that is paid for by a private party, but not limited to a deposition transcript.

14. *Expedited* means transcripts which are requested to be completed within three (3) days.

15. *Rush/Overnight* means transcripts which are requested to be completed within twenty-four (24) hours.

Section Two. Salaries and Per Page Fees.

1. Court Reporters shall be paid an annual salary for time spent working under the control, direction and direct supervision of their supervising court during any regular work hours, gap hours or

overtime hours. The supervising court shall inform the court reporter the manner in which the court reporter is to be compensated for gap and overtime hours, by receiving compensatory time off regular work hours.

2. The maximum per page fee a court reporter may charge for the preparation of a county indigent transcript shall be $4.00, including cover pages; $1.00 per page for a copy of a transcript provided to the Public Defender's Office or the Prosecutor's Office; and .50¢ per exhibit. The fee for an "expedited" transcript (preparation within three (3) days) on a county case shall be $6.00 per page. The court reporter shall submit a claim voucher to the supervising judge for approval of payment by the county for the preparation of any county indigent transcripts.

3. If a court reporter is requested to prepare an indigent "rush/overnight" transcript (preparation within twenty-four (24) hours or less), the per page fee shall be $7.00.

4. The maximum per page fee a court reporter may charge for the preparation of a State indigent transcript shall be $4.00; and, $1.00 per page for a copy of a transcript; and .50¢ per exhibit. The fee for a State Public Defender requested "expedited" transcript (preparation within three (3) days) on a State indigent case will in no event exceed $6.00 per page. If a court reporter is requested by the State Public Defender to prepare an indigent "rush/overnight" transcript (preparation within twenty-four (24) hours or less), the per page fee shall be $7.00.

5. The maximum per page fee a court reporter may charge for the preparation of a private transcript shall be $4.25 with the court reporter being responsible for expenses as provided in Section Four (4), Paragraph Two (2). The fee for an "expedited" transcript (preparation within three (3) days) on a private case will be agreed upon between the court reporter and party requesting the same but in no event may exceed $6.25 per page. The court reporter may charge up to $1.00 per page for a copy of a transcript *(including a disc copy)*, or $1.00 per page for an exhibit with the court reporter being permitted to use the court system's copy machine outside of regular work hours. If so requested by a party, an "original copy" generated from the computer may be reproduced and charged at one-half (½) the transcript fee.

6. If a court reporter is requested to prepare a private "rush/overnight" transcript (preparation within twenty-four (24) hours or less), the maximum per page fee shall be $7.25.

7. An additional labor charge approximating the hourly rate based upon the court reporter's annual fixed compensation as reflected in the court budget, may be charged for the time spent binding the transcript and exhibit binders. The labor charge shall not exceed two (2) hours, unless unusual circumstances permit the submission of a recapitulation enumerating the hours spent beyond the two (2) hour base.

8. The Index and Table of Contents pages shall be charged at the per page rate being charged for transcript preparation either for county, state or private cases.

9. A minimum fee up to $35.00 per transcript shall be allowed for transcripts under eight (8) pages.

10. The court reporter or designated court employee shall report, at least on an annual basis, all transcript fees received for the preparation of county indigent, state indigent or private transcripts to the Indiana Supreme Court Division of State Court Administration. The reporting shall be made on forms prescribed by the Division of State Court Administration.

11. The preparation of *any* transcript for payment shall not be performed during regular work hours, including but not limited to, transcribing, copying, or other functions related to the compilation of the transcript.

Section Three. Private Practice

1. If a court reporter elects to engage in private practice through the recording of a deposition and/or preparing of a deposition transcript, all such private practice work shall be conducted outside of regular work hours and the court reporter **will not** be allowed to utilize the court equipment to do so.

Section Four. Supplies

1. All supplies for *County or State indigent transcripts*, i.e. transcript paper, binders and copy paper shall be provided through the court system's office supply account.

2. All supplies for *Private transcripts*, i.e. transcript paper, binders and copy paper shall be the responsibility of the court reporter. The court reporter will not be allowed to charge for the cost of such supplies due to the allotted fee approved herein for the preparation of a private transcript.

Adopted as Local Rule 09–2002, effective Sept. 24, 2002. Renumbered as Rule 008 and amended effective May 9, 2006; renumbered as Rule 0041 and amended effective Sept. 1, 2012.

LR18–TR79–DLR Rule 0051. Civil Practice and Procedure

The following local rule regarding selection of special judges where a special judge does not accept a civil case under TR 79(D), is now adopted by the undersigned judges of the Delaware Circuit Court, in conjunction with the other Courts of Administrative District 15.

A. Conflicts by Circuit Court No. 2 Judge in DR (Domestic Relations) and JP (Juvenile Paternity)

cases from Title IV–D Court. In DR (Domestic Relations) and JP (Juvenile Paternity) cases from Title IV–D Court where the Circuit Court No. 2 Judge has a conflict and enters an order of disqualification or recusal, and parties do not agree to a particular special judge pursuant to TR 79(D), the Clerk of Delaware County shall assign the case to the regular sitting Judge in Circuit Court No. 3. If that Judge is unable to serve as set forth in Trial Rule 79 (H), then the Clerk shall select a special judge pursuant to paragraph B or C of this local rule.

B. Assignment—Civil. In civil cases where the appointment of a special judge is required under TR 76, or the presiding judge has disqualified or recused under TR 79(C), and parties do not agree to a particular special judge pursuant to TR 79(D); the regular sitting judge shall direct the Clerk of Delaware County to select (on a rotating basis) one of the judges from the following available panel of judges (omitting the judge from whom the change of venue is being taken):

a. Presiding Judge, Delaware Circuit Court No. 1;

b. Presiding Judge, Delaware Circuit Court No. 2;

c. Presiding Judge, Delaware Circuit Court No. 3;

d. Presiding Judge, Delaware Circuit Court No. 4;

e. Presiding Judge, Delaware Circuit Court No. 5;

f. Presiding Judge, Blackford Circuit Court;

g. Presiding Judge, Blackford Superior Court;

h. Presiding Judge, Henry Circuit Court No. 1

i. Presiding Judge, Henry Circuit Court No. 2;

j. Presiding Judge, Henry Circuit Court No. 3;

k. Presiding Judge, Jay Circuit Court;

l. Presiding Judge, Jay Superior Court;

m. Presiding Judge, Randolph Circuit Court; and

n. Presiding Judge, Randolph Superior Court.

If a special judge selected from the rotating list is ineligible for, disqualified from, or excused from appointment, then the regular sitting judge shall direct the Delaware County Clerk to select (on a rotating basis) the next judge on the list.

In the event that no judicial officer within the above list is eligible to serve as special judge, or if the case's particular circumstances warrant selection of a special judge by the Indiana Supreme Court, the judge of the court in which the case is pending shall certify the matter to the Indiana Supreme Court to appoint a special judge.

C. Assignment—Juvenile. In juvenile cases where the appointment of a special judge is required under TR 76, or the presiding judge has disqualified or recused under TR 79(C), and parties do not agree to a particular special judge pursuant to TR 79(D); the regular sitting judge shall direct the Clerk of Delaware County to select (on a rotating basis) one of the following available judges:

a. Presiding Judge, Blackford Circuit Court;

b. Presiding Judge, Henry Circuit Court No. 1

c. Presiding Judge, Henry Superior Court No. 2;

d. Presiding Judge, Jay Circuit Court; and

e. Presiding Judge, Randolph Circuit Court;

If a special judge selected from the rotating list is ineligible for, disqualified from, or excused from appointment, then the regular sitting judge shall direct the Delaware County Clerk to select (on a rotating basis) the next judge on the list.

In the event that no judicial officer within the above list is eligible to serve as special judge, or if the case's particular circumstances warrant selection of a special judge by the Indiana Supreme Court, the judge of the court in which the case is pending shall certify the matter to the Indiana Supreme Court to appoint a special judge.

D. Maintaining Separate Lists. The Delaware County Clerk shall maintain separate civil and juvenile lists, in the rotation order as set forth in this Rule, from which the clerk may determine the appropriate appointment in civil and juvenile cases.

Adopted as Local Rule 0601 effective March 4, 2008. Amended effective July 1, 2011. Renumbered as Rule 0051 and amended effective Sept. 1, 2012. Amended effective March 29, 2013; June 4, 2013)

LR18–AR00–DLR Rule 0052. Allocation and Assignment of Cases

1. That the Clerk of Delaware County, upon direction of a transfer of any case holding a judgment, garnishment, bail bond, or otherwise, shall within said transfer, perfect the necessary changes to provide for the efficient and accurate accounting of all payments made toward any judgment rendered, including, but not limited to, garnishment payments made through a garnishee defendant, the release of judgments, bail bonds or other matters pertaining to said original cause and the transfer therein. In the perfection of the within Order, the Clerk shall notify interested parties to the action and the garnishee defendant.

Circuit Court No. 1

Criminal: Felonies, which include MR (Murder), FA (class A felony), FB (class B felony), FC (class C felony), FD (class D felony), MC (Miscellaneous Criminal), and misdemeanors in conjunction with Murder, or A, B, C felonies or D felonies.

Civil: PL (Civil Plenary), CC (Civil Collection), CT (Civil Tort), DR (Domestic Relations), MF (Mortgage

Foreclosure), AD (Adoption), MI (Miscellaneous—excluding tax sales), ES, EU, GU, TR (Probate), PO (Protective Orders).

Circuit Court No. 2

Criminal: Felonies, which include MR (Murder), FA (class A felony), FB (class B felony), FC (class C felony), FD (class D felony), MC (Miscellaneous Criminal), and misdemeanors in conjunction with Murder, or A, B, C or D felonies.

Juvenile: JP (Juvenile Paternity), JD (Juvenile Delinquency), JS (Juvenile Status), JM (Juvenile Miscellaneous), JC (Juvenile CHINS), JT (Juvenile Termination)

Civil: PL (Civil Plenary), CC (Civil Collection), CT (Civil Tort), DR (Domestic Relations), MF (Mortgage Foreclosure), AD (Adoption), MI (Miscellaneous—excluding tax sales), RS (Reciprocal Support), PO (Protective Orders).

Circuit Court No. 3

Criminal: Felonies, which include MR (Murder), FA (class A felony), FB (class B felony), FC (class C felony), FD (class D felony), MC (Miscellaneous Criminal), and misdemeanors in conjunction with Murder, or A, B, C or D felonies.

Civil: PL (Civil Plenary), CC (Civil Collection), CT (Civil Tort), DR (Domestic Relations), MF (Mortgage Foreclosure), AD (Adoption), MI (Miscellaneous—excluding tax sales), MH (Mental Health), PO (Protective Orders).

Circuit Court No. 4

Criminal: Felonies which include MR (Murder), FA (class A felony), FB (class B felony), FC (class C felony), FD (class D felony), MC (Miscellaneous Criminal), misdemeanors in conjunction with Murder, or A, B, C, or D felonies, class A Misdemeanors and (IF) Infractions.

Juvenile: NONE

Civil: PL (Civil Plenary), CC (Civil Collection), CT (Civil Tort), DR (Domestic Relations), MF (Mortgage Foreclosure), AD (Adoption), MI (Miscellaneous—excluding tax sales) PO (Protective Order), SC (Small Claims)

Circuit Court No. 5

Criminal: Felonies which include MR (Murder), FA (class A felony), FB (class B felony), FC (class C felony), FD (class D felony), MC (Miscellaneous Criminal), misdemeanors in conjunction with Murder, or A, B, C, or D felonies, class A Misdemeanors and (IF) Infractions.

Juvenile: NONE

Civil: PL (Civil Plenary), CC (Civil Collection), CT (Civil Tort), DR (Domestic Relations), MF (Mortgage Foreclosure), AD (Adoption), MI (Miscellaneous—INCLUDING tax sales), PO (Protective Order), SC (Small Claims), ES, EU, GU, TR (Probate)

2. Assignment of cases as heretofore set out will continue to be subject to all Local Rules regarding non-discretionary assignment of felony and misdemeanor cases.

3. Assignment of cases, effective January 1, 2007, the Clerk of Delaware County shall perfect the following limitation of filings:

a. *(MF) Mortgage Foreclosure*: 100 each court, and then commence again (i.e. when each court has 100 foreclosures, then the limitation will begin again until reached with 200, and etc.)

b. *(CC) Civil Collections*: 200 each court, and then commence again (i.e. when each court has 200 Civil Collections, then the limitation will begin again until reached with 400, and etc.)

c. *(DR) Domestic Relations*: 100 each court, and then commence again (i.e. when each court has 100 Domestic relations, then the limitation will begin again until reached with 200 and etc.)

d. *(PO) Protective Orders*: 100 each court, and then commence again (i.e. when each court has 100 Protective Orders, then the limitation will begin again until reached with 200, and etc.)

e. *(MI) Miscellaneous*: 75 each court, and then commence again (i.e. when each court has 75 Miscellaneous, then the limitation will begin again until reached with 150, then, etc.) Exception: Circuit Court No. 5 will receive all Tax Sale filings regardless of count.

Adopted May 20, 2003, effective June 1, 2003. Renumbered as Rule 010 and amended effective May 9, 2006; amended Oct. 11, 2006, effective Jan. 1, 2007; renumbered as Rule 0052 and amended effective Sept. 1, 2012.

LR18–AR00–DLR Rule 0061. Local Rule Governing the Storage, Processing, Disposition of Drug Forfeitures

The Judges of the Delaware Circuit Court hereby issue the following Local Rule in relation to storing, processing, disposition of drug forfeitures:

A. Assets

1. The assets seized by state, city, county, and town law enforcement officers pursuant to I.C. 34–24–1–1 and I.C. 34–24–1–2 shall be inventoried and kept until adjudication of the civil drug forfeiture case pursuant to I.C. 34–24–1–2. For racketeering forfeitures, see I.C. 34–24–2–2.

2. The State of Indiana shall file the forfeiture action as a miscellaneous civil (MI) action in the Circuit Court Division where the State either has filed or is required to file the related criminal action per Local Rule. If the State does not intend to file a criminal action, the State shall then file the forfeiture as a miscellaneous (MI) action in the court where the criminal case would have been filed.

B. Adjudicated Drug Forfeitures

1. All drug forfeitures must be adjudicated pursuant to I.C. 34–24–1–4. See I.C. 34–24–2–1 *et seq.* for racketeering forfeiture procedures. See I.C. 34–24–1–9 for situations where the prosecuting attorney determines that the evidence should be turned over to the Department of Justice.

2. Pursuant to I.C. 32–24–1–3 (a), if the respondent has filed an answer, the court shall schedule a hearing to determine the legitimacy of the forfeiture by a preponderance of the evidence. Pursuant to I.C. 32–24–1–3(d), if the respondent does not file an answer in a timely manner, the court, upon proper motion, shall enter judgment in favor of the State.

3. As part of any judgment in favor of the state, city, or county, the court shall determine the amount of law enforcement costs, which shall include the costs of the police agencies as well as the costs of prosecuting the civil and criminal actions. See I.C. 34–6–2–73. *"Any excess in value of the proceeds or the money over the law enforcement costs [shall] be forfeited and transferred to the Treasurer of State for deposit in the common school fund."* I.C. 34–24–1–4(d)(2) (D).

C. Non–Cash Assets

1. Non–cash assets may be delivered for a period not to exceed three years to the city, county, or town law enforcement agency, which seized the property. After that period, the property shall be delivered to the Sheriff for public sale. I.C. 34–24–1–4(c).

2. An inventory of such assets should be made (which should correspond with the property booked into the property room), and the property delivered to the Sheriff for the next public sale. Public Sales should occur at least once a year.

3. In each action, the State shall file with the Court a report of the sale of all such property, together with proposed disposition in accord with the original determination of law enforcement costs, including those due the Criminal Justice Institute Grant Fund Program Income Account. The Court shall review and approve the report. The forfeiture order allowing use of non-cash assets shall require the sale thereof and a report to be made to the Court within three years. The cash shall be receipted into the Clerk's trust account for payment into the appropriate general fund account of the city, county, or town, and, when appropriate, to the State Treasurer for the common school fund. Cash ordered forfeited by the Court should likewise be receipted into the Clerk's trust account. When the monies are paid over to the appropriate general fund, the receipt (from the city) or the quietus (from the county) should be filed with the Court, as well as the receipt from the State Treasurer in the case of payment to the Common School Fund. *Note: At present, federal forfeiture funds shared with a local law enforcement agency are to be sent to the governmental unit of which that agency is a part. Disbursement of the funds is to be by the fiscal body of that unit (City Council for Muncie, County Council for Delaware County) in accord with Federal guidelines.*

D. Attorney Fees. The Prosecuting Attorney shall enter into a written compensation agreement with an attorney retained to bring an action under the forfeiture statute. The attorney retained shall not serve as a deputy prosecutor in any county. The compensation agreement may be a contingency fee agreement limited as follows:

1. The contingency fee may not exceed Thirty–Three and One–Third percent (33 1/3 %) of the first Ten Thousand Dollars ($10,000.00) of proceeds or money obtained under a settlement or judgment.

2. The contingency fee may not exceed Twenty Percent (20%) of the part of the proceeds or money obtained under a settlement or judgment that is more than Ten Thousand Dollars ($10,000.00) and less than One Hundred Thousand Dollars ($100,000.00).

3. The contingency fee may not exceed Fifteen Percent (15%) of the part of the proceeds or money obtained under a settlement or judgment that exceeds One Hundred Thousand Dollars ($100,000.00).

4. The contingency fee agreement may establish a minimum fee not to exceed One Hundred Dollars ($100.00).

5. A court may authorize a compensation agreement between the Prosecuting Attorney and an attorney retained to bring an action under this Rule that exceeds the limits established above if the court finds that the issues presented in the particular forfeiture action are unusually complex or time consuming as compared with other forfeiture actions.

6. In any event, the fee in each forfeiture case shall be conditioned on court approval using the factors established in Rule 1.5(a) of the Rules of Professional Conduct.

E. Clerk–Trust Account. The Clerk shall also make quarterly trust fund reports of receipts and disbursements to the courts, the prosecutor, the state, city, county, and town law enforcement agencies, and the fiscal bodies and fiscal officers of the units of government involved.

Adopted as Local Rule 0810 Sept. 26, 2008, effective Oct. 1, 2008. Renumbered as Rule 0061 and amended effective Sept. 1, 2012.

ELKHART COUNTY RULES OF COURT

Adopted Effective October, 2004

Including Amendments Received Through November 1, 2013

Research Notes

These rules may be searched electronically on Westlaw in the IN-RULES database; updates to these rules may be found on Westlaw in IN-RULESUPDATES. For search tips and a summary of database content, consult the Westlaw Scope Screens for each database.

LR20–AR00–NADC Rule 1. DRESS AND CONDUCT

(A) Lawyers and litigants shall be appropriately attired during all court appearances.

(B) Lawyers, litigants, and spectators shall at all times speak and behave in such a manner as to respect the dignity and authority of the Courts, Judges, Commissioners and all judicial personnel, and shall not lean on the bench nor sit on counsel tables

(C) No person shall bring food or beverage into any courtroom without the prior approval of the judge, magistrate or commissioner of that court.

(D) All cell phones, pagers and any other personal electronic devices shall be turned off during all court proceedings.

Adopted effective Oct. 2004. Renumbered as Rule 1, and amended effective March 18, 2005. Amended effective March 1, 2012.

LR20–AR00–NAFC Rule 2. FILING OF CASES

(A) General. All new causes of action shall be docketed with the Clerk of the Court and shall comply with Trial Rule 77 and Administrative Rule 9.

(B) Court Costs. No cause shall be docketed or transferred without payment of the costs of the action, unless otherwise ordered.

1) *Collection of Fee for Late Payment.*

A) A late fee is assessed to the defendant if the defendant has:
- committed a crime;
- violated a statute defining an infraction;
- violated an ordinance of a municipal corporation; or
- committed a delinquent act, and the defendant is required to pay:
  - court costs, including fees;
  - a fine; or
  - a civil penalty, and the defendant is not determined by the court imposing the court costs, fine, or civil penalty to be indigent.

B) If the defendant fails to pay to the clerk the costs, fine, or civil penalty in full before the late of the following:
- The end of the business day on which the court enters the conviction or judgment.
- The end of the period specified by the Court.

C) The fee assessed is $25.00 or, if amended, that sum allowed by I.C. 33–37–7–22.

D) The court may, if the defendant has demonstrated good cause for failure to make a timely payment of court costs, a fine, or a civil penalty may suspend the payment of the late fee.

(C) Assignment of Criminal Cases.

1) Criminal cases shall be filed in specific courts as follows:

    a.   Elkhart Circuit Court

        ☐ All murder charges;

        ☐ All attempted murder cases, except child victim cases

        ☐ All manslaughter cases, except those in which a child is the victim

        ☐ All vehicular homicide cases

        ☐ All robbery cases

        ☐ All reckless homicide cases

        ☐ One-half (1/2) of all Class A, B and C controlled substance sale and possession cases

        ☐ Juvenile cases (Magistrate)

        ☐ Grand Jury cases

    b.   Elkhart Superior Court 1

        ☐ All rape cases, except child victim cases

        ☐ all criminal deviate conduct cases, except child victim cases

        ☐ All sexual battery cases, except child victim cases

        ☐ All criminal recklessness cases, except when a child is the victim

        ☐ All C battery and domestic battery cases, except child victim cases, and except those filed in the three (3) city courts sitting in Elkhart County, Indiana

        ☐ All class B felony cases which are not specifically assigned to a court pursuant to this rule

    c.   Elkhart Superior Court 2

        ☐ All burglary cases

        ☐ All welfare fraud cases

        ☐ All forgery cases

        ☐ All class C felony theft cases

        ☐ All arson cases

        ☐ All class C felony cases which are not specifically assigned to a court pursuant to this rule

    d.   Elkhart Superior Court 3

        ☐ All child victim cases except murder

        ☐ One-half (2) of all class A, B and C controlled substance sale and possession cases

        ☐ All kidnaping and confinement cases

        X All Class A felony cases which are not specifically assigned to a court pursuant to this rule

    e.   Elkhart Superior Court 4

        ☐ One-half (2) of all habitual traffic offender cases and one-third (1/3) of all other class D felony and misdemeanor cases, except non-support cases and those filed in the three (3) city courts sitting in Elkhart County, Indiana.

        ☐ ☐ All infraction and county ordinance cases other than those filed in the aforementioned city courts

    f.   Elkhart Superior Court 5

        ☐ One-half (2) of all habitual traffic offender cases and one-third (1/3) of all other class D felony and misdemeanors, except non-support cases and those cases filed in the aforementioned city courts

    g.   Elkhart Superior Court 6

        ☐ All non-support cases and one-third (1/3) of all class D felony and misdemeanor cases, except habitual traffic offender cases and those cases filed in the aforementioned city courts

2) Should a criminal case be pending in a given court, and should an equally serious or less serious criminal case against the same defendant be received by the Prosecutor's Office for filing, the more recently submitted cases shall be filed in the same court as that in which the existing case is pending. In the event that a criminal charge is pending against a given defendant in a given court, and in the further event that a judgment of conviction or acquittal has not yet been entered in that case, and in the further event that, pursuant to the dictates of this Rule, a criminal charge carrying a more severe penalty is filed in another Elkhart County Court, the criminal charge carrying the less severe penalty shall be transferred to the Court in which the other charge has been filed. All cases originally filed as a lesser offense, and subsequently recharged as murder, shall thereupon be transferred to Circuit Court. All cases which may be filed in more than one court (e.g. Class A, B and C controlled substances cases) shall be filed on a purely rotating basis. The provisions of Rule 2(B)(2) do not apply to domestic battery cases.

3) All cases in which juvenile court jurisdiction is waived to adult court shall be filed in the appropriate court as dictated by this rule.

4) All charges of escape shall be filed in the court which committed the defendant to the facility from which he or she allegedly escaped. All charges of failure to appear shall be filed in the court in which the subject order to appear was entered.

5) After January 1, 2003, in the event that the Judge of the Elkhart Circuit Court recuses himself in a given case due to a real or apparent conflict of interest, that case shall be transferred to the Elkhart Superior Court 3. IN the event that the Judge of the Elkhart Superior Court 3 recuses himself in a given case due to a real or apparent conflict of interest, that case shall be transferred to Elkhart Circuit Court. In the event that the Judge of the Elkhart Superior Court 1 recuses himself in a given case due to a real or apparent conflict of interest, that case shall be transferred to Elkhart Superior Court 2. In the event that the Judge of the Elkhart Superior Court 2 recuses himself in a given case

due to a real or apparent conflict of interest, that case shall be transferred to the Elkhart Superior Court 1. In the event that the Judge of the Elkhart Superior Court 4 recuses herself in a given case due to a real or apparent conflict of interest, that case shall be transferred to Elkhart Superior Court 5. In the event that the Judge of the Elkhart Superior Court 5 recuses himself in a given case due to a real or apparent conflict of interest, that case shall be transferred to Elkhart Superior Court 6. In the event that the Judge of the Elkhart Superior Court 6 recuses himself in a given case due to a real or apparent conflict of interest, that case shall be transferred to Elkhart Superior Court 4.

6) All requests for a jury trial in the Elkhart City Court shall be transferred to Elkhart Superior Court 5.

7) All other city courts receiving requests for jury trial shall be transferred to Elkhart Circuit Court for assignment to an appropriate court or magistrate.

8) All requests for trial de novo shall be referred to Elkhart Circuit Court for assignment to an appropriate court or magistrate.

(D) Assignment of Civil Cases.

1) Civil cases shall be filed in specific courts as follows:

    a. Elkhart Circuit Court

    All civil filings with the exception of mental health cases and small claims.

    Juvenile paternity except those filed in Superior Court 6.

    Juvenile CHINS and termination cases (Elkhart Circuit Court, Juvenile Division).

    b. Elkhart Superior Court 1

    All civil filings with the exception of mental health cases and small claims.

    Juvenile paternity except those filed in Superior Court 6.

    c. Elkhart Superior Court 2

    All civil filings with the exception of guardianships and small claims.

    Juvenile paternity except those filed in Superior Court 6.

    d. Elkhart Superior Court 3

    All civil filings except guardianships and small claims.

    e. Elkhart Superior Court 4

    All civil filings except guardianship, estates, mental health paternity and dissolution cases.

    f. Elkhart Superior Court 5

    All civil filings except guardianships, estates, mental health paternity and dissolution cases.

    g. Elkhart Superior Court 6

    All civil filings except guardianships, estates and mental health.

(E) Transfer & Referral of Cases.

1) Whenever a judge is designated Special Judge in a case filed in another court, the designated Special Judge hereby consents to the transfer of the case and the transferring Court may so note in its order of transfer.

2) A case may be transferred on the court's own motion to a court of equal jurisdiction within Elkhart County. Whenever an action is transferred to another court, the Judge of the transferee court hereby consents to the transfer of the case and the transferring Court may so note in its order of transfer.

3) A case referred to a magistrate shall be referred on specific issue(s) to be heard by the magistrate. Upon entry of an order by the magistrate or approval of an agreement of the parties on said issue(s), the case will be returned to the regular judge of the court.

4) When the Judge of the Elkhart Circuit Court enters an order recusing himself due to a conflict of interest in a felony case, said case shall be assigned to the Senior Judge, as approved by the Indiana Supreme Court. The Senior Judge shall accept and retain jurisdiction for all future proceedings unless disqualified under the Code of Judicial Conduct, excused from service by the Indiana Supreme Court, a specific statute or rule provides to the contrary, or the Senior Judge is unavailable by reason of death, sickness or unwillingness to serve. If further reassignment is required, it shall be in the same manner as set forth in the rules of criminal procedure. Upon recusal, the Clerk shall complete the process for transfer to the Senior Judge. An oath or special order accepting jurisdiction shall NOT be required.

5) If a selected judge cannot serve, reassignment of the case shall be determined by the Administrative Judge for Administrative District 5, in compliance with Indiana Trial Rule 79(H), as adopted by the courts in Administrative District 5.

(F) Delinquent Lists.

1) Any civil case pending for more than six months may be placed upon a "Delinquent List" pursuant to Trial Rule 41(E). Any case so listed shall, after 45 days, be dismissed at the cost of the filing party, except for good cause shown. Any case so dismissed shall be deemed to have been dismissed with prejudice as to all parties, unless otherwise ordered.

2) Any probate matter in which no filing has been made for more than one year may be placed upon a Delinquent List. If no action is taken within 45 days thereafter, the Court may require the personal representative to show cause why the Court should not impose an appropriate sanction against the personal representative.

3) Guardianships shall not be placed upon a delinquent list within two years after the issuance of letters of guardianship, the filing of an inventory, or the filing of a current account.

Adopted effective Oct. 2004. Amended effective Dec. 2004; renumbered as Rule 2, and amended effective March 18, 2005. Amended effective Jan. 9, 2007; March 1, 2012; July 1, 2012.

LR20–TR3.1–NAEA Rule 3. APPEARANCES

(A) Entry of Appearance.

1) Appearances shall be made in writing in the state prescribed appearance form in all cases. An attorney's appearance for a party shall not operate as an automatic enlargement of the time for filing a responsive pleading.

2) Appearances once entered remain on record until final disposition.

3) Appearances of attorneys at initial hearings in the Elkhart Circuit Court Juvenile Division shall continue through case closure, including violation of probation and modification of disposition hearings unless withdrawal of appearance is granted by the Court.

4) Attorney appointed under a CHINS cause number shall be presumed to represent the party under the corresponding Termination cause. The docket shall indicate such representation unless and until the Court is notified otherwise.

(B) Withdrawal of Appearance.

1) An attorney's appearance for a party will be withdrawn if:

    a. Another attorney simultaneously appears for the party;

    b. The attorney provides satisfactory evidence that the party has discharged the attorney; or

    c. The party acquiesces to the withdrawal.

2) In all other circumstances, an attorney seeking permission to withdraw an appearance shall file a written motion stating justification for the withdrawal. The attorney shall give the party 21 days' written notice of the attorney's intention to seek permission to withdraw. This notice shall (1) Inform the party that failure to secure new counsel may result in dismissal of the party's case or in entry of a judgment or ruling against the party, (2) set forth the date of any scheduled hearing or trial, and (3) include any other pertinent information. Except for good cause shown, an appearance will not be withdrawn within twenty-one days prior to commencement of a trial.

3) In keeping with the provisions of the Indiana Rules of Professional Conduct, an attorney's representation of a client in a given cause pending before an Elkhart County court of general jurisdiction shall be deemed concluded upon:

    a. The entry of an order of court withdrawing that attorney's appearance in that matter for that client; or,

    b. Resolution of all issues raised prior to, or during the course of, that representation. For purposes of this Rule, the term "resolution" shall mean entry of a judgment or an appealable order determining such issues. Should an attorney wish to appear in a given cause a second, or subsequent, time, he or she must file a new appearance in conformity with the dictates of Trial Rule 3.1. This rule does not apply to small claims.

Adopted effective Oct. 2004. Renumbered as Rule 3, and amended effective March 18, 2005. Amended effective March 1, 2012.

LR20–TR00–NAFD Rule 4. FILING OF DOCUMENTS

(A) All documents filed with a court, including but not limited to any reports, modification petitions, memos, motions, orders and notices shall be labeled with the assigned sixteen [16] digit cause number of all causes to which such documents are intended to apply.

(B) Appearances and pleadings not requiring immediate action by the Court shall be filed with the Clerk. Filings shall comply fully with the provisions of Trial Rule 77 and Administrative Rule 9 regarding confidentiality, and shall include the names, addresses, phone numbers, dates of birth and Social Security Account Number or Federal Tax Identification Number of the parties.

(C) In civil cases, a party shall file the original of any pleading, motion, or other document plus only such additional copies as may be required for service on other parties. The filing party shall prepare all forms of summons and citations, provide all materials required for service, and shall provide all parties' names, addresses, telephone numbers, Social Security numbers and dates of birth. If the filing party requests a hearing, that party shall also provide an appropriate form of notice.

(D) When a party requests any order other than a protective order, a preliminary injunction or a restraining order, that party shall tender two (2) copies of the requested order plus one (1) for each other party. When a party requests a protective order, a preliminary injunction, or a restraining order, that party shall tender six (6) copies of the requested order.

(E) All motions to dismiss, motions for summary judgment motions for judgment on pleadings, and similar motions shall be accompanied by a memorandum of legal authority. Any response to such motions shall be accompanied by a similar memorandum.

(F) All pleadings filed in a case while assigned to a magistrate must be file-marked in the appropriate court and then delivered to the magistrate's office by the attorney making the filing. The magistrate will make appropriate entries on the chronological case summary (CCS). Upon entry of an order by the magistrate or approval of an agreement of the parties on said issue(s), the case will be returned to the regular judge of the court, and filings thereafter will be filed with the regular judge of the court.

(G) All pre-fact finding hearing motions and pleadings in juvenile delinquency cases shall be in writing and in compliance with the appropriate rules of procedure. All such motions shall be accompanied by a memorandum of authorities. Any responses to such motions shall be accompanied by a memorandum of authorities and shall be filed within seven (7) days if the child is in secure custody; or fourteen (14) days if not in custody upon the filing of such motions. The failure of either party to comply with this rule shall result in the denial of the motion or in the striking of the response, as appropriate.

(H) Preparation of Documents. The lawyer for a party or any party appearing pro se shall be responsible for preparing and filing summons, citations, notices or other documents for which forms may be obtained from the Clerk of the Court. These forms shall include any names, addresses and other descriptive information, such as place of employment, necessary to affect service of said document. Whenever a form of order is required, the parties shall tender to the Court an appropriate form.

(I) Pro Se Filings/Forms. Copies of pro se forms prepared by the Indiana Supreme Court shall be located in the Offices of the Clerk of the Court. Upon request, copies of such forms shall be provided by the Clerk of the Court at the expense of the person requesting said form.

(J) Record of Judgments and Orders. The Record of Judgments and orders shall consist of original orders entered by the Court, all certified by the Judge for each day and placed in appropriate permanent binders.

(K) Copies Documents Furnished by the Clerk. On application of any person, the Clerk of the Court shall copy any pleading or order at the expense of the person requesting the copy. This rule shall not apply to actions to establish paternity, adoptions, juvenile proceedings or other actions which are not a matter of public record.

(L) Withdrawal of Original Material. No person shall withdraw any original pleading, paper, record, model, exhibit, or other document from the custody of the Clerk, except upon order of the Court and upon leaving a proper receipt with the Clerk or other officer.

Adopted effective Oct. 2004. Renumbered as Rule 4, and amended effective March 18, 2005. Amended effective March 1, 2012.

LR20–TR00–NAFD Rule 4.5. FACSIMILE ELECTRONIC FILINGS

No facsimile filings are allowed except with the express prior approval of the Court. If approval is granted, the filing shall be made to the number designated by the Court and the party making the filing shall otherwise comply with Administrative Rule 12. Initial filing of a cause of action by facsimile is not permitted.

Adopted effective March 1, 2012.

LR20–FL00–CVFL Rule 5. DOMESTIC RELATIONS MATTERS INVOLVING MINOR CHILDREN–COOPERATIVE FAMILY PRACTICE

*The Website www.ElkhartFamilyLaw.gov may be accessed through www.ElkhartFamilyLaw.com or www.Elkhart FamilyLaw.org.

(A) Liberal Construction and Application.

(1) The Circuit and Superior Courts of Elkhart County are committed to a cooperative model for the handling of "family cases" by parents, attorneys, and judges. This Rule will be liberally construed and applied to promote the healthy and child-sensitive functioning of families.

(2) "Family cases" are defined as all marital dissolution or separation, paternity and guardianship proceedings involving custody and parenting issues.

(3) The adoption of this Rule does not affect a lawyer's duty to act in compliance with the Indiana Rules of Professional Conduct, particularly the duty to act with reasonable diligence and promptness in representing a client.

(4) All support orders or modifications must be in writing and filed with and approved by the Court or will be invalid.

(B) Case Captioning.

(1) Parties in marital dissolution and separation and paternity cases shall not be captioned or designated as "petitioner," "respondent," "plaintiff," or "defendant."

(2) In marital dissolution and separation cases on the date of the initial filing, all pleadings shall be captioned, "In Re the Marriage of _____, Husband [or Wife], and _____, Wife [or Husband]." The party filing the initial petition shall be named first.

(3) Parties in paternity cases shall be captioned "In Re the Paternity of [name or initials of minor child] and designated as "mother," "putative father," and father."

(C) Duties of Attorneys and Parties in Family Cases.

(1) Attorneys and parties in family cases are expected to act with the courts as co-problem sol-

vers, not mere problem-reporters. Attorneys shall both inform and remind their clients about the judicial expectations of cooperation in family cases, assist their clients to understand and observe these standards, and encourage clients to participate in co-parenting classes, counseling, mediation, and other appropriate problem-solving processes.

(2) In order to establish and maintain an atmosphere which fosters cooperative problem-solving, all parties and attorneys shall:

(a) explore resources which may reduce conflict, build cooperation and protect children;

(b) attempt reasonable cooperative measures before resorting to the court;

(c) avoid disrespectful language and behavior; and,

(d) avoid unnecessary motions or petitions, hearing and arguments.

(3) *Website.* Parties and counsel should visit the court's website link at www.ElkhartFamilyLaw. gov* for more information on the procedures in use in Elkhart County in support of the cooperative handling of family cases.

Commentary

The Circuit and Superior Courts of Elkhart County recognize that conflict in family cases is destructive and often dangerous. Litigating family cases does not end or resolve the conflict; it heightens the conflict. The cooperative model for handling family cases is implemented in order to minimize such conflict and, instead, foster the healthy and child-sensitive functioning of families.

Actions taken in the earliest stages of parents' separation and other family crises, whether those actions are helpful or destructive, often define much of the future of the family case and the family. Attorneys' language and conduct in these earliest days are often crucial to the future course of both the case and the future functioning of the family. Until the case is filed, the courts have no involvement and are powerless to help families. However, at such early stages, attorneys can either set a tone of beneficial cooperation or of destructive conflict for the families they touch.

All too often in family cases the courtroom becomes an arena in which the parties are subjected to criticism, sometimes even ridicule or similar abuse. Such conduct will not be tolerated. Attorneys have an ethical obligation to refrain from abusive conduct and other offensive tactics; to treat all parties, witnesses and all others involved in the legal process with courtesy and respect; and, to refuse to participate in any effort to embarrass or burden someone. The courts consider such conduct to be repugnant. So should the attorneys and all members of the family. Attorneys have an ethical obligation to consult with their clients about the means to be employed and clients normally defer to their attorney's special knowledge and skill in such matters. These rules and comments require that when doing so, the attorney should educate the client about the substantial risk that conflict pres-

ents for members of the family and of the benefits and opportunities for resolution through the cooperative model. Family members who elect to pursue the path of conflict instead of cooperation are not acting in the best interests of the children; and, the courts should consider the decisions made by the parties in this regard as part of its evaluation of the children's best interests and in the allocation of attorney fees.

This cooperative model will require some fundamental changes in the local legal culture, including the manner in which attorneys approach family cases. While fundamental change does not occur overnight, it must begin now. The attorney's primary focus in family cases should be on defusing the underlying source(s) of conflict(s) by helping the family find ways to resolve issues by means which are less destructive than litigation.

As part of the cooperative model, the courts will expect all parties and attorneys to consistently observe:

(a) personal responsibility by acting on one's opportunities to solve problems and improve circumstances rather than merely reporting on the alleged fault in others;

(b) cooperation by sensibly defining and recognizing the best interests of all family members;

(c) courtesy by constant use of respectful language and behavior; and,

(d) focused attention on children's needs, including an awareness that parental conflict is dangerous to children.

As part of their duty to work as co-problem-solvers with the court in all family cases, if safe to do so, attorneys should;

(a) speak with their clients, as early as possible and as often as necessary, about the advantages and judicial expectations of safe cooperation in family cases;

(b) refer clients to all co-parenting classes, counseling, mediation, and other problem- solving processes that appear to counsel to be promising resources for their clients;

(c) work with other counsel to ensure safety in families where domestic violence has been, or reasonably could be, an issue;

(d) work with other counsel in all cases to reduce conflict, build cooperation, and protect children; and,

(e) avoid unnecessary motions and hearings.

Before any scheduled hearing:

(a) An attorney should assess with a client whether the matter can safely be handled cooperatively and without adversarial motions, hearings and other formal proceedings. Unless safety or exceptional circumstances make cooperation unreasonable, counsel should handle the case in ways that avoid adversarial proceedings and maximize the parties' development of cooperative problem-solving.

(b) An attorney should make reasonable efforts to determine if the other spouse, parent, or putative parent is represented or may be seeking representation. Unless doing so might create a

danger or substantial prejudice to the client, or it is otherwise unreasonable to do so, the attorney should:

(i) confer with the other attorney or self represented litigant;

(ii) attempt in good faith to find cooperative resolutions to provisional matters, including peaceful separation, so that unnecessary provisional filings and hearings can be avoided; and,

(iii) refer parents to resources such as co-parent education, co-parent counseling, marital counseling, and mediation that can help them build cooperation.

(c) If both parties elect to be self represented litigants, they shall have the same duties stated above.

(D) Initial and Provisional Hearings. Unless considerations of safety or other good cause make it unreasonable, before the date and time set for an initial or provisional hearing, counsel or self represented litigants shall meet with each other in a good-faith attempt to resolve all matters.

(E) Mandatory Website Work for Parents.

(1) *Dissolution of Marriage.* In all dissolution cases where the parties have any children together under the age of 18, both parties shall complete the work on www.UpToParents.org within 15 days of initial filing or service.

(2) *Legal Separation.* In all separation cases where the parties have any children together under the age of 18, both parties shall complete the work on www.WhileWeHeal.org within 15 days of initial filing or service.

(3) *Paternity.* In all paternity cases, both parents shall complete the work on www.ProudToParent.org within 15 days of the court's finding of paternity.

(4) *Agreed Commitments.* Following completion of the website work required by this rule, the parents shall merge or exchange their chosen Commitments from their website work into a set of Agreed Commitments.

(5) *Proof of Compliance.*

(i) Dissolution of Marriage and Legal Separation. In order to monitor compliance, within 20 days of the initial filing or service of an action for dissolution or separation, each party shall file a verified certification of their completion of the mandatory website work. A sample form is attached as Appendix "A".

(ii) Paternity. In order to monitor compliance, within 20 days of the court's finding of paternity, each party shall file a verified certification of completion of the mandatory website work. A sample form is attached as Appendix "B".

(iii) Failure to Comply. Any party failing to timely file a certification may be subject to a contempt hearing.

Commentary

The rule contemplates that, following completion of the website work required by this rule, the parents shall merge their chosen Commitments from their website work into a set of Agreed Commitments and review those Agreed Commitments before all hearings. If a hearing is held more than a year since the parents' completion of the website work, they should redo the work and again merge their Commitments into a set of Agreed Commitments.

(F) Transparenting and Seasons Class. Information regarding required classes is available on the court's website at www.ElkhartFamilyLaw.gov*.

(1) *Dissolution of Marriage and Legal Separation. Mandatory Attendance.* In all dissolution and separation cases where the parties have any children together under the age of 18, both parties shall complete the Elkhart County Transparenting class. Any children 6 years of age through 17 years of age shall complete the Elkhart County Seasons class. The court may order any party to attend additional parenting, co-parenting, or parenting enrichment classes in post-decree matters.

(2) *Paternity.* Upon adjudication of paternity, the court shall order the parties to attend and complete the Transparenting class unless circumstances prohibit said attendance. Upon adjudication of paternity, where children 6 years of age through 17 years of age are involved, the court shall order that the minor children enroll and complete the Seasons class. In all paternity cases the court may order any party to attend and complete additional parenting, co-parenting, or parenting enrichment class.

(3) *Proof of Compliance.* In all dissolution of marriage and legal separation cases, the parties must enroll in said classes within 15 days of the filing or service of the petition. The agency providing the Transparenting and Seasons classes, pursuant to the order of court, shall provide a list of enrolled participants to each court on a not less than weekly basis.

Commentary

It is recognized that this Rule may not be applicable in Uniform Interstate Family Support Act (UIFSA) cases.

(G) Parenting Plan Proposals.

(1) The Indiana Parenting Time Guidelines provide useful outlines of the **minimum** time each parent should have with the children to maintain frequent, meaningful, and continuing contact with them.

(2) Unless they have already executed and filed an Agreed Parenting Plan, the parties shall each prepare and exchange their written Parenting Plan Proposals utilizing the form attached as Appendix "C". It is anticipated that this exchange of parent-

ing plan proposals shall occur at least two (2) business days before the hearing.

(3) The Parenting Plan Proposals, Agreed Commitments and other results generated as a result of the website work shall be inadmissible as evidence and unenforceable at any hearing or trial. The purpose of the Parenting Plan Proposals, Agreed Commitments and website work is to generate a culture of co-parenting for the long term benefit of families.

(4) In the event the parties agree on only portions of a Parenting Plan, the parties shall submit the agreed upon portions of the Parenting Plan to the Court, and advise the Court of unresolved issues.

Commentary

(1) Children whose parents live apart have special needs above and beyond those of other children, including the need for frequent, meaningful, and continuing contact with both parents. The courts expect separated and divorced parents, if safely possible, to work together to support children's best possible relationships with each parent.

(2) Dedicated parents will do their best to:

(a) Remember that their children's only job is to be children, not their messengers, spies, counselors, confidants, or carriers of their hurt.

(b) Remember that their love for their children is greater than any issue they could have with each other.

(c) Respect each other's parenting time while also being flexible so the children's lives can be as normal as possible.

(d) Pay special attention to keep their appointments and schedules with each other and call promptly if any problems come up.

(e) Educate their extended families and close friends that they need to make peace as well.

(3) Children shall have frequent, meaningful, and continuing contact with each parent. The Indiana Parenting Time Guidelines provide a useful outline of the minimum time that each parent should have with the children. It is the express preference of the Elkhart Circuit and Superior Courts that parenting plans, if safely possible, should:

(a) exceed the Guideline minimums for the non-custodial parent;

(b) fit the particular needs of the family; and,

(c) encourage parents' use of sensibility, flexibility, and reasonableness to allow for cooperative accommodation of special needs and circumstances in family activities.

(4) Whenever parents need resources to reduce conflict, build cooperation, preserve family relationships, or respond to the needs of their children, they and their attorneys (if any), should use all resources that could help them. Such resources include:

(a) redoing the website work from www.UpTo Parents.org, www.WhileWeHeal.org, or www. ProudToParent.org;

(b) additional co-parenting classes, including re-attending the basic class or attending high-conflict classes;

(c) completing a new Parenting Plan Proposal;

(d) mediation;

(e) confidential therapeutic assessment of the parents to develop a set of recommendations for their improved interaction;

(f) individual, joint, family or child counseling;

(g) appointment of a parenting coordinator; and,

(h) any other measure that might protect children, reduce conflict, or build cooperation.

(5) If parents nevertheless continue to have conflict and appear in court without an agreement about the resources they will use, the court may select the resources the parents will be ordered to use.

(H) Protocols after Initial Filing.

(1) *Duties Regarding Conferences.* Except in emergencies or when it is otherwise unreasonable to do so, counsel and self represented litigants shall make a reasonable attempt to have a personal or telephonic conference to resolve any issue before hearing or seeking any other relief through the court. Counsel and self represented litigants contacted for a conference shall make themselves reasonably available. The duty of a personal or telephonic conference shall be continuing.

(2) *Substance of Conference.* In the conference, counsel and self represented litigants shall:

(a) attempt to resolve all matters at issue;

(b) confirm the parties' compliance with paragraphs (E), (F) and (G) of this Rule; and,

(c) discuss the resources they believe the parents could use to resolve current and future issues and to build cooperation, including any resources listed in Commentary paragraph (4) to paragraph (G) of this Rule.

(3) *Cooperation Update—Mandatory.* All motions and pleadings other than the initial filings shall include a statement confirming compliance with items (1) through (2), above, including the date of the required personal or telephonic conference or shall recite the specific reasons for the lack of a conference.

(4) *Failure of Compliance.* Failure to comply with this section may result in the denial of relief or a hearing until compliance is accomplished.

Commentary

Counsel and self represented litigants shall consult in advance of all court hearings and exchange suggestions for the future course of the case that would serve the best interests of all family mem-

bers, except in the limited circumstances described above.

During a status conference:

(1) the attorneys and self represented litigants will report on:

(a) the status of compliance with each provision of this Rule by the parties and their attorneys; and,

(b) parent progress in reducing conflict, building cooperation, preserving family relationships, and responding to the needs of the children.

(2) where beneficial, the families will be referred for any necessary help; and,

(3) the court will consider the future course of the case.

(I) Requirements before Custody Evaluations. Custody evaluations are sometimes divisive and produce less cooperation between parents. Custody evaluations shall be reserved for cases where the parents cannot resolve the issues. No custody evaluation may be requested, ordered or conducted unless and until all cooperative measures (including, but not limited to, co-parenting education, consultation with a parenting coordinator and mediation) have been exhausted, shown to be dangerous, likely to be unsuccessful, or otherwise unreasonable.

All requests for custody evaluations shall be in writing and shall state:

(a) what specific issues are resolved and what specific issues remain unresolved;

(b) what problem solving resources have been used to date (including any co-parenting education, consultation with a parenting coordinator or mediation); and

(c) why no further cooperative measures can be expected to assist the parents in resolving all issues.

The court will not grant or order a custody evaluation except following a status conference in the presence of both parties and their attorneys, if any, during which the court has been satisfied that:

(1) both parties have completed the requirements of paragraphs (E), (F) and (G) above; and,

(2) the use of other resources including those listed in Commentary paragraph (4) to paragraph (G) of this Rule has been carefully considered and reviewed.

(J) Form of Summons.

(1) *Dissolution of Marriage and Legal Separation.* In dissolution and separation cases, the appropriate summons shall be used and shall be substantially the same as the forms which are attached as Appendix "D" or "D–1".

(2) *Paternity.* In paternity cases, the summons shall be substantially the same as the form which is attached as Appendix "E".

(K) Parenting Coordinator.

(1) *Definition.* Parenting Coordination will be in compliance with any Indiana Parenting Coordination Rules adopted by the Judicial Conference of the State of Indiana. The Parenting Coordinator shall make recommendations and work to resolve conflicts between the parents involving only custody and parenting issues. Such recommendations, negotiations, and education shall include strategies for enforcing any shared parenting plan, communication, and parenting time schedule, for minimizing child-related conflicts between the parties, and for eliminating unproductive or harmful behavior patterns by one or both parents. The Court retains exclusive jurisdiction and authority to determine issues of custody and parenting.

(2) *Appointment.* The Parenting Coordinator shall be appointed by the Courts. At any time after the filing of the petition for dissolution of marriage, legal separation or adjudication of paternity, by stipulation of the attorneys or by order of the court, the parties shall utilize the services of a Parenting Coordinator. The Courts shall also maintain a list of approved private parenting coordinators.

(3) *Inadmissibility and Confidentiality.*

(a) The matters and issues discussed with the Parenting Coordinator shall be confidential in nature and in the context of settlement negotiations. The work of the Parenting Coordinator and the discussions of the parties shall be inadmissible as evidence and unenforceable at any hearing or trial, except as provided in paragraph (4).

(b) However, this Rule shall not prohibit the Parenting Coordinator from making recommendations to the Court on other resources available to the parents, the need for a custody evaluation or the appointment of a guardian ad litem.

(4) *Agreements.* The Parenting Coordinator shall file all agreements signed by the parties and the Parenting Coordinator with the Court for approval.

(5) *Costs.* The Court may assess the costs of the Parenting Coordinator to the parties.

(L) Enforcement. Upon the failure of any attorney or self represented litigant to comply with this Rule, the Courts may use, at their discretion, the variety of enforcement mechanisms available to them in the traditional system. These enforcement mechanisms include a finding of contempt, an award of attorney fees, postponement of hearing, denial of any requested relief, and an award of lost wages.

The Court may waive provisions of the Rule when justice so requires.

Commentary

This Rule and the enforcement thereof appear contradictory. However, the benefits of the overall concepts contained in this Rule, as well as the recognized and hoped for long-term advantages of implementing such a process, render its enforcement of vital importance. Families in conflict do not always fit well into the mold of the traditional adversary system. Nevertheless, it must be recognized that an attempt to reshape the model within which family law cases have traditionally occurred will require, on occasion, the use of those enforcement mechanisms which do not fall within a model of cooperation.

The Circuit and Superior Courts of Elkhart County recognize that, in order to utilize and reap the benefits of a cooperative family law system, attorneys and parties must be subject to the enforcement of these Rules, including but not limited to the award of attorney fees and sanctions. The courts also recognize that enforcement requires uniformity and consistent application of this Rule and its enforcement mechanisms.

*The Website www.ElkhartFamilyLaw.gov may be accessed through www.ElkhartFamily Law.com or www.ElkhartFamilyLaw.org.

Adopted effective Oct. 2004. Renumbered as Rule 5, and amended effective March 18, 2005. Amended effective Aug. 1, 2012.

Commentary

This Rule and the enforcement thereof appear contradictory. However, the benefits of the overall concepts contained in this Rule, as well as the recognized and hoped for long-term advantages of implementing such a process, render its enforcement of vital importance. Families in conflict do not always fit well into the mold of the traditional adversary system. Nevertheless, it must be recognized that an attempt to reshape the model within which family law cases have traditionally occurred will require, on occasion, the use of those enforcement mechanisms which do not fall within a model of cooperation.

The Circuit and Superior Courts of Elkhart County recognize that, in order to utilize and reap the benefits of a cooperative family law system, attorneys and parties must be subject to the enforcement of these Rules, including but not limited to the award of attorney fees and sanctions. The courts also recognize that enforcement requires uniformity and consistent application of this Rule and its enforcement mechanisms.

LR20–FL00–CVFL Rule 6. ADDITIONAL DOMESTIC RELATIONS MATTERS

(A) Financial Disclosures.

1) Any party seeking an initial order of child support or spousal maintenance, or the modification of an existing order of support or maintenance, shall, at the first hearing on such request, provide the court and any other party with appropriate verification of that party's current income and childcare expenses.

2) A party seeking an order which deviates from the Child Support Schedule calculation shall set forth facts supporting the deviation. At or before any hearing on a motion for support or maintenance, the responding party shall file a verified statement showing the party's income and childcare expenses.

3) At or before any pretrial conference, both parties shall file and exchange verified financial disclosure statements. In any event a verified financial disclosure statement shall be filed by both parties at least thirty (30) days prior to submission, unless such filing is waived in writing by both parties. Such waiver shall be filed with the court at the time of submission.

4) Any party failing to comply with the provisions of subsection 3 above shall be ordered to pay a sanction of $100.00. If this amount is not paid AND the verified financial disclosure is not tendered to the opposing party within fifteen (15) days of the pretrial conference, the noncomplying party shall forthwith pay a sanction of $200.00. All payments due under this subsection shall be made to the Treasurer of Elkhart County for deposit into the General Fund. Hearings shall be scheduled to monitor compliance. The Court may also impose such other sanctions permitted by statute or rule as it deems appropriate.

(B) Discovery Limitation. No party shall engage in excessive use of interrogatories, motions for production, or requests for admissions.

(C) Attorney Fees.

1) In the absence of contradictory evidence, a reasonable initial attorney fee shall be $1,200.00. Allocation of this fee between the parties shall be calculated through use of the following formula:

    a. Husband's gross income from line I or line 2 of support worksheet (if maintenance is ordered, use line 2). $ _____

    b. Wife's gross income from line 3 or line 4 of support worksheet (if maintenance is ordered use line 4). $ _____

    c. Add lines A and D. $ _____

    d. Divide line A by line C. $ _____

    e. Divide line B by line C. $ _____

    f. Multiply $2,400.00 by line D or line E, whichever is greater. $ _____

    g. Subtract $1,200.00 $1200.00

    h. Line F minus line G. $ _____

The party having the greater income shall pay the amount shown on line H to the attorney for the party having, the lesser income. If the party having, the lesser income is not represented by an attorney, then no attorney fees will be ordered.

2) In the absence of contradictory evidence a reasonable attorney fee for prosecution of a post dissolution rule to show cause shall be a minimum of $400.00 for one court appearance. A minimum of $200.00 will be added for each additional court appearance.

(D) Decree Provisions.

1) Each decree of dissolution of marriage shall contain a provision which requires compliance with the applicable Indiana statute governing relocation of the residence of unemancipated children. That provision shall also make specific reference to that statute in order to assist lay persons in reviewing and copying it.

2) Both parties shall attach to the decree a current Child Support Computation Worksheet.

(E) Two–Party Auction.

1) If the parties are unable to divide personal property and household goods by agreement, the method of division shall be by the private two-party auction, which shall be conducted by the lawyers for the parties or a Magistrate in a timely manner on such terms as (s)he deems appropriate.

2) Either party may initiate a two-party auction at any point in the proceedings upon application to the court. Upon application, the non-possessory party may have reasonable access to the personal property in order to comply with this rule.

3) Prior to the auction, the two parties are ordered to prepare and submit one itemized list of all household goods and personal property noting, items of a separate nature (e.g. premarital, extended family gifts, inheritance, disposed of or disputed items, etc.).

4) A party who intentionally fails to cooperate or participate in the inventory and auction process will be subject to sanctions.

5) At the conclusion of the auction, the Magistrate or lawyer conducting the auction shall immediately provide copies of all pages indicating the auction results to the parties, and the said results shall b promptly be filed with the appropriate court.

Adopted effective Oct. 2004. Renumbered as Rule 6, and amended effective March 18, 2005. Amended effective March 1, 2012.

LR20–FL00–CVDR Rule 7. SUPPORT AND MAINTENANCE STANDARDS

(A) Except in unusual circumstances, the Courts shall follow the schedule of support payments and maintenance set forth in the Indiana Child Support Guidelines, including all explanations and formulas.

(B) Temporary maintenance shall equal 33–1/3% of the parties' combined net income (net income is defined as gross income minus deductions for any other prior court ordered child support, legal duty of support, other orders of maintenance paid, income producing expenses, and federal, state or local taxes paid). Any order for temporary maintenance shall expire ninety (90) days after the date upon which the order becomes effective. A party seeking an extension of an order for temporary maintenance shall file

an appropriate petition and at a hearing shall show good cause for the extension.

(C) Maintenance paid to a party shall be deducted from the payor's income and added to the recipient's income, and determinations of child support and attorney fees obligations shall be based on those incomes as so adjusted.

(D) If both a support order and a maintenance order are entered, the parties shall recalculate support promptly after ninety (90) days so as to reflect the expiration of the maintenance order. The parties shall calculate support during both the maintenance period and thereafter, and shall file the results with the Court.

(E) If the non-custodial parent has continuous custody of one or more of the parties' minor children for a period of seven (7) days or more, the child support shall abate by one-half (2), pro rata, for each child in such continuous custody, until said child or children are returned to the custodial parent. That portion of support attributable to child care expenses for said child or children shall be totally abated.

(F) Medical insurance. Whichever party can provide the most comprehensive policy of medical insurance for the child(ren) at the lowest cost shall provide said insurance. The amount of the insurance premiums shall then be allocated between the parties on the percentage-of-income basis. If the non-custodial parent pays the insurance premiums, that parent shall receive credit against support paid each week in the amount of that parent's allocated portion of medical insurance. If the custodial parent pays the medical insurance premiums, that parent shall receive an additional amount of support each week equal to the non-custodial parent's percentage of medical insurance premiums. For good cause shown, and following a hearing at which both parties are given an opportunity to be present, the Court may in its discretion waive the requirement that medical insurance be provided for the benefit of minor children.

(G) Educational expenses through grade 12. A Guidelines-based support order shall encompass all ordinary educational expenses through the high school level. If appropriate, extraordinary educational expenses for children who have not yet completed high school, including private school tuition and costs of tutoring, shall be determined as an addition to support and shall be divided between the parties in proportion to their respective weekly adjusted incomes.

(H) Educational expenses after grade 12. Post high school educational expenses shall be determined as either an addition to, or in lieu of support. Except in unusual circumstances, an award of such expenses shall be limited to the lesser of:

1) The actual annual expenditures for tuition, room board, books, transportation, fees and miscellaneous expenses for the student; or

2) The annual cost of tuition, room, board, books, transportation, fees, and miscellaneous expenses which would be incurred by an Indiana resident attending the Bloomington campus of Indiana University as a resident student.

The Custodial parent and the child shall be responsible for making, timely applications for all scholarships and grants for which the child might be eligible. Other than in exceptional circumstances, gifts and trust funds intended for college, scholarships and grants shall be deducted from the educational expenses. All educational tax benefits (e.g. Hope Scholarship Credits and Lifetime Learning Credits) shall be applied by the party receiving them to the payment of educational expenses. Thereafter, the child shall be responsible for twenty-five percent (25%) of the remaining expenses, and the balance shall be divided between the parties in proportions to their respective weekly adjusted income. Except in unusual circumstances, the amount of support determined under the Guidelines shall be wholly abated when the child is not in residence. The child shall execute any and all documents, and perform any and all other acts, reasonably necessary to afford both parents access to all available information regarding, grades, attendance, financial awards, grants and scholarships, and school disciplinary matters.

(I) Income Tax Benefits. The parties shall allocate income tax benefits for a minor child equitably, but in such a manner as to maximize tax benefits. A non-custodial party shall claim such tax benefits only if that party shall have paid all support due through the end of the affected calendar year by January 31 of the following year. Both parties shall execute any forms necessary to carry out the requirements of this paragraph. A party's refusal to sign such forms may be punishable by contempt or by imposition of other sanctions, including modification of the current support obligation to recapture any tax benefit lost by the non-custodial parent.

(J) All petitions to abate or modify child support orders which are filed by child support payors shall include a statement of the amount of the arrearage, if any, owed ·by petitioner in child support, and in the payment of the Clerk's annual fee for the collection and distribution of child support.

(K) So long as one or more the parties' children remain unemancipated or the beneficiary of an order for contribution to educational needs, the parties shall, upon request by either of them, exchange verification of income in the form of his or her most recent federal income tax return. Such income tax return shall be complete and include all attachments thereto. Such exchange shall be required no more often than once annually. Such exchange shall be concluded within two weeks of the making of such request. In the event that either party had not filed a federal income tax return for the tax year last concluded, that party shall provide the other with that federal income tax return described above, together with written verification of current income. Such verification may include a paycheck stub disclosing a year-to-date income or a current profit and loss statement reflecting self-employment or partnership income. It is the purpose of this rule to foster the exchange of accurate and complete income information in order to avoid needless litigation. This rule shall be liberally construed in order to achieve those ends.

(L) For purposes of this rule, healthcare expenses shall accumulate on a calendar year basis. The six percent (.06) deductible contemplated by the Rule shall be prorated for the balance of the calendar year in which the first support order in this case is entered, or in which the subject dissolution is granted, whichever is applicable. This proration shall be calculated by multiplying the total child support due from both parents by six percent (.06), dividing the product by three hundred sixty five (365), and multiplying the result by the number of days remaining in the year in question. As a general rule, in the event of a modification of an existing child support order, any resulting change in the six percent (.06) deductible shall become effective at the beginning of the next succeeding calendar year. The trial court may deviate from this general rule in order to avoid manifest injustice.

(M) In all actions in which a child support order remains in effect, either party shall, upon demand, provide the other party with a copy of his or her most recent federal income tax return, together with all schedules and other attachments. The party supplying the aforementioned income tax return may redact any portions thereof which relate solely to the computation of the income of any other person. Nothing in this rule shall require any person to provide more than one such copy during each calendar year; however, nothing in this rule shall infringe upon the right of any person to engage in appropriate discovery pursuant to the Indiana Rules of Trial Procedure.

Adopted effective Oct. 2004. Renumbered as Rule 7, and amended effective March 18, 2005. Amended effective March 1, 2012.

LR20–TR16–NAHT Rule 8.   HEARINGS/TRIALS

(A) Initial Hearings. All judges and magistrates of Elkhart County, Indiana, Courts of general jurisdiction, including regular judges and magistrates, senior judges and judges pro tempre, shall be authorized to conduct initial hearings and other preliminary hearings held in connection with civil and criminal cases filed in all Elkhart County, Indiana, Courts of general jurisdiction.

(B) Status Conferences.

1) At any time after the issues are finally closed on the merits of any civil case, any party may request, or the court on its motion may set, a status conference to set deadlines, facilitate discovery, and discuss settlement and alternative dispute resolution of the case.

2) At the status conference, all counsel shall be prepared to state:

a. Whether all parties have been correctly designated and properly served;

b. Whether a third-party complaint or impleading petition is contemplated;

c. The time reasonably required for completion of discovery;

d. Whether a jury trial has been timely demanded and if so, whether the parties would contemplate waiver of trial by jury;

e. Whether there are any pending motions and whether dispositive motions are contemplated;

f. Whether a separation of claims, defenses, or issues would be desirable and if so, whether discovery should be limited to the claims, defenses, or issues being tried first;

g. The prospects of disposing of the case through settlement, mediation, or other methods of alternative dispute -resolution.

3) At the conclusion of the status conference, the court may establish deadlines for disclosure of witnesses and exhibits to be offered at trial, discovery, amendments to the pleadings, dispositive motions, alternate dispute resolution measures, and any other matters to come before the court. The court may thereupon schedule a pretrial conference or a further status conference.

4) Deadlines established at the status conference shall not be extended, except by agreement of the parties and the Court, or for good cause shown.

(C) Pretrial Conferences.

1) Unless waived by the Court, a pretrial conference shall be held in every civil case. No case shall be set for trial before the pre-trial order is filed.

2) All discovery shall be completed at least five (5) days prior to the pretrial conference, except an examination of the physical or mental condition of a party pursuant to TR 35, which may be ordered at any time prior to trial. Prior to the discovery cutoff date the Court may extend the time for completing discovery upon the filing of a written motion showing good cause for the extension of time.

3) The attorney for each party and each party appearing pro se shall have an independent duty to arrange the conference of the attorneys required by TR 16 8). Unless the attorneys agree otherwise, the conference shall be held in the office of the attorney located closest to the Court in which the case is pending. At this conference, every party shall provide each other party an opportunity to inspect and copy all exhibits. Any plaintiff's proposed exhibits shall be numbered, and any defendant's, proposed exhibits shall be lettered. The attorneys shall explore fully the possibility of settlement and of any further alternative dispute resolution techniques. The attorneys shall also discuss

the length of time probably required for trial of the case and, in any case for which a jury has been requested, the possibility of waiving the jury and trying the case to the Court alone.

4) Following the conference of attorneys, and at least five (5) days before the pre-trial conference, the plaintiff shall file a proposed pre-trial order, signed by counsel for all parties. The proposed order shall cover the following points:

a. The nature of the action;

b. The basis of jurisdiction of the Court;

c. Questions raised by pending motions;

d. Proposed amendments to pleadings;

e. A concise statement of the contentions of each party;

f. A concise statement of undisputed facts;

g. A concise statement of disputed issues of fact;

h. A concise statement of uncontested issues of law;

i. A concise statement of contested issues of law;

j. A numbered list of the names and addresses of each party's witnesses', with expert witnesses designated as such;

k. A numbered or lettered list of trial proposed exhibits of each party, as appropriate;

l. A concise statement of any disagreement regarding rules of law relating to anticipated jury instructions;

m. Appropriateness of ADR processes; and

n. A certification by each attorney or pro se party of compliance with the provisions of TR 16.

5) A pretrial order, once signed by the Court, shall govern the course of the trial. The pretrial order shall not be amended except by consent of the parties and the Court or by further order of the Court to prevent manifest injustice. All pleadings shall be deemed merged into the pretrial order.

6) If the parties fail to timely file any material required to be filed prior to the pretrial conference, the Court may postpone the pretrial conference and take further action as appropriate.

(D) Trial Settings.

1) Except for good cause shown, the parties and counsel involved in any civil jury trial set as a backup trial shall be prepared to begin the trial when scheduled.

2) All attorneys and all parties appearing pro se shall be responsible for discovering the sequence of cases and shall be prepared to try their cases on the date scheduled.

3) Whenever a Court sets a criminal case for trial and the defendant is not then present, the defendant within twenty-one days thereafter shall file a signed written acknowledgment of the trial date or

shall in open court orally acknowledge the trial date.

4) No dispositive motions, including but not limited to motions for summary judgment, shall be filed in any action within one hundred twenty (120) days of a scheduled trial of that action without leave of court. Leave of court may be granted or denied with or without hearing, at the option of the court.

Adopted effective Oct. 2004. Renumbered as Rule 8, and amended effective March 18, 2005. Amended effective March 1, 2012.

LR20–TR00–NATP Rule 9. TRIAL PROCEDURES

(A) Ten days before the commencement of the trial of any criminal case or a civil case which is a first or second setting:

1) Each attorney shall mark for identification and provide opposing counsel an opportunity to inspect and copy all exhibits which that party intends to introduce into evidence during the trial. The proponent of the exhibit shall prepare a proposed stipulation and shall submit it to opposing counsel with the exhibits. All documents stipulated to be admissible shall be prepared so that the court and each juror shall have a packet of stipulated exhibits at the beginning of the trial; and

2) Each party shall provide the court and each opposing counsel a final written list of names and addresses of that party's witnesses, as well as a written list of exhibits. If without just cause the exhibits and lists are not exchanged, stipulated to, or provided, then the exhibits or witnesses shall not be allowed to be used during the trial.

(B) Voir dire examinations shall be conducted first by the Court. Parties may submit to the Court, at least five days prior to the trial, any proposed questions for prospective jurors, which questions shall be asked if the court deems them appropriate. The Court may also grant each party a limited amount of time for additional examination of prospective jurors. The sole purpose of voir dire examination shall be to determine qualifications of prospective jurors.

(C) All challenges to prospective jurors seated in the jury box shall be exercised in writing after the first round of questioning of those prospective jurors. If more than one party peremptorily challenges the same juror, the challenge shall be counted against each party so challenging. At the end of each succeeding round, peremptory challenges may be exercised against only those persons seated after the previous round. Parties may interrogate previously-accepted prospective jurors only as to new matters and may thereafter challenge for cause a previously-accepted prospective juror.

(D) When an objection is made to a question posed to a witness during any jury trial, the person asking

the question shall not state within the hearing of the jury the expected response of the witness.

(E) Only one person shall examine or cross-examine a witness, except by permission of the Court.

(F) A court shall not enforce any admissions, agreements, or stipulations unless they are reduced to writing and either filed with the Court or made a part of the record in open court.

Adopted effective Oct. 2004. Renumbered as Rule 9, and amended effective March 18, 2005. Amended effective March 1, 2012.

LR20–TR51–NAJI Rule 10. JURY INSTRUCTIONS

(A) A court may require a party to submit any proposed instructions either on paper or on a 3.5–inch computer diskette in WordPerfect format.

(B) In any civil case each party shall tender to the court all proposed preliminary and final instructions at least 14 days prior to the trial date.

(C) In any criminal case each party shall tender to the court all proposed preliminary and final instructions at least 3 days prior to the trial date.

(D) The Court may in its discretion permit the parties to submit additional proposed final instructions after the close of the evidence.

(E) Any proposed instruction shall contain a citation of legal authority for the proposed instruction. Indiana Pattern Jury Instructions shall be used wherever applicable. Failure to comply with this rule shall be deemed a waiver by a party of the right to tender instructions.

(F) A party submitting proposed instructions on paper shall submit the proposal in duplicate. One copy of each proposed instruction shall identify the party tendering the instruction and shall contain citations of authority. The other copy of the instruction shall be prepared so as not to identify either the party proposing the instruction or the citation of authority.

(G) A party proposing any instruction shall deliver a copy of such instruction to any other party.

Adopted effective Oct. 2004. Renumbered as Rule 10, and amended effective March 18, 2005. Amended effective March 1, 2012.

LR20–TR00–NACE Rule 11. CUSTODY/DISPOSITION OF EXHIBITS

(A) Any material marked as an exhibit, whether or not admitted into evidence, shall be held in the custody of the Court Reporter, unless otherwise ordered by the Court.

(B) All material placed in the custody of the Court Reporter shall be removed by the offering party, except as otherwise ordered by the Court, within four months after the final disposition of the case. At the time of removal, the party shall give a detailed receipt to the Court Reporter which shall be filed in the record of the case. If a party fails to comply with this rule, the Court may order the destruction or other disposition of the material.

Adopted effective Oct. 2004. Renumbered as Rule 11, and amended effective March 18, 2005. Amended effective March 1, 2012.

LR20–TR00–CVSB Rule 12. SURETY ON BONDS

(A) No attorney, employee or other officer of the Court shall be accepted as surety on bonds in criminal, civil or probate matters.

(B) The Court will require a bond in an amount sufficient to cover all liquid assets of all estates, trusts and guardianships. If any non-liquid assets (such as real estate) become liquid, the bond shall immediately be increased in an amount to cover the additional liquid asset. The bond shall also be in an amount to protect two (2) times the annual income. The bond may be waived in an estate only if a sole heir is also the personal representative and as heir files a waiver of bond or if all adult competent heirs file a waiver of bond, and in a guardianship if the minor's account cannot be withdrawn except by Court order. When two or more persons are appointed personal representative or co-guardians, they may file a joint surety.

(C) Order on Appearance of Criminal Defendants and the Setting of Bail in Criminal Cases.

1. *No Bail Requirement.* If a Court has not established bail in a particular case, no bail shall be set for the following offenses until such time as the person arrested has been brought before a neutral and detached Judge or Magistrate within the County of Elkhart, State of Indiana:

    a. all offenses if the offender is on probation

    b. all felonies

    c. all misdemeanors involving possession or delivery of a firearm as proscribed by I.C. § 35–47 *et seq.*

    d. all misdemeanors involving domestic battery as proscribed by I.C. § 35–42–2–1.3

    e. all misdemeanors involving invasion of privacy as proscribed by I.C. § 35–46–1–15.1

    f. all misdemeanors involving operating while intoxicated proscribed by I.C. § 9–30–5 *et seq.*

2. *Standard bail requirement for non-exempt misdemeanors and exceptions.* A standard bail may be applied for non-exempt misdemeanors in the amount of one-thousand five hundred dollars ($1,500.00) regardless of the number of misdemeanors cited by the arresting law enforcement officer. If the arresting law enforcement officer documents circumstances surrounding the offense which he believes warrant a different amount of bail, he or she may request the person be held without bail until such time as a neutral and detached Judge or Magistrate reviews said facts and set bail.

3. *Consideration of Local Rule 13 for fixing amount of bail.* Except as otherwise provided herein, or in applicable statute or rule, bail in felony and misdemeanor cases shall be fixed by the Judicial officer finding probable cause for the arrest of the defendant. In fixing the amount of bail in a give case, that judicial officer shall consider the Elkhart County Criminal Bail/Bond schedule, as embodied in LR20–CR00–CRBS Rule 13. Notwithstanding the foregoing, it is emphasized that such schedule is advisory in nature, and shall not be construed as limiting the authority of any judicial officer to fix bond in any amount which he or she deems to b e appropriate in any given cause.

4. *Surety requirement.* On all cases involving the posting of bail through a surety, a person shall not be released on bail until the bail bond agent certifies that he or she has verified that the information provided to the bail bond agent regarding identification and address of the person are accurate and reliable.

5. *Notice regarding Initial Hearing.* A person who has posted bail prior to his or her appearance in court for an Initial Hearing shall be informed of his or her Initial Hearing date, time and location, and that failure to appear as directed will result in a revocation of bail and the issuance of an arrest warrant for failure to appear.

6. *Alcohol related charges.* No bail shall be allowed for persons arrested on alcohol related charges if release of said person is otherwise prohibited by law (See I.C. § 35–33–1–6)

7. *Duty of recording bail information.* **All original documentation regarding the posting of bail shall be submitted to the Court where the particular offense is filed and the Clerk of the Court shall be responsible for entering the information on the Chronological Case Summary (CCS).**

If criminal charges have not been filed, the original documentation regarding the posting of bail shall be submitted to the Court that dockets the finding of probable cause for the arrest and shall also be entered by the Clerk of the Court in the CCS.

Adopted effective Oct. 2004. Renumbered as Rule 12, and amended effective March 18, 2005. Amended effective March 1, 2012.

LR20–CR00–CRBS Rule 13. CRIMINAL BAIL/ BOND SCHEDULE

(A) Unless otherwise ordered by a court, bail on felony charges shall be as follows:

FELONY CLASS	SUSPENDIBLE	NONSUSPENDIBLE
A	$150,000.00	$150,000.00
B	75,000.00	75,000.00
C	5,000.00	10,000.00
D	3,000.00	5,000.00

(B) Bail for any misdemeanor shall be $1,500 per charge.

(C) This Bail/Bond Schedule is advisory. It shall be within the discretion of any court to set a bond which is higher or lower than that recommended by the schedule in any given case. Any bail setting shall be reviewable at the instance of any party.

(D) Subject to court approval, a person charged with any class C or class D felony which does not involve the use or possession of a deadly weapon and for which the sentence would apparently be suspendible may be permitted to post with the Clerk of the Court a cash bond in the amount of 10% of the bail as set, provided that:

1) The person has close ties to the local community;

2) The person has not been convicted of an offense;

3) The person agrees to submit to supervision by the pretrial release officer;

4) The bond is posted in the name of the defendant; and

5) The bond shall disclose on its face that it is a personal asset of the defendant and may be subjected to payment-of court-imposed financial obligations

Adopted effective Oct. 2004. Renumbered as Rule 13, and amended effective March 18, 2005. Amended effective March 1, 2012.

LR20–CR00–CRDD Rule 14. CRIMINAL DISCOVERY DISCLOSURE

(A) In any criminal case, each party shall routinely disclose:

1) The names, dates of birth, Social Security Account Numbers, and last-known addresses of all persons whom that party may call as witnesses, together with any written or recorded statements the person may have made, any memoranda containing substantially-verbatim reports of any oral statements the person may have made and summaries of the anticipated testimony of each potential witness;

2) Copies of statements of any co-defendant;

3) Copies of reports of experts made in connection with the case, including results of physical or mental examinations, scientific tests, experiments, or comparisons;

4) Any books, papers, documents, photographs, videotapes, audio recordings, or tangible objects which the party may introduce at hearing or trial; and

5) A record of prior criminal convictions of any witnesses called by that party.

(B) In addition to the matters described in Section A of this Rule, the State shall disclose:

1) Copies of any written or recorded statements made by the defendant, summaries of any oral statements made by the defendant, and a list of witnesses to the making and acknowledgment of such statements; and

2) Any other evidence which tends to negate the guilt of the defendant as to the offense charged or to mitigate the punishment of the defendant upon conviction.

3) In addition to the matters described in Section A of this Rule, the defendant shall disclose any defense, procedural or substantive, which the defendant intends to assert at hearing or trial.

4) A party seeking discovery shall prepare any discovery document so that answers may be made on the original discovery document. Discovery requests and responses shall not be filed with the Court or Clerk unless a dispute arises regarding said discovery.

5) Providing discoverable material shall be a continuing Obligation of all parties and each party shall promptly provide any new material for which disclosure is required under this rule.

6) A court may make more specific orders for additional discovery after a hearing on any appropriate motion filed by either party.

7) A court may exclude from evidence any materials not properly disclosed to the other party and may impose further sanctions for any party's unjustified failure to comply with this rule.

Adopted effective Oct. 2004. Renumbered as Rule 14, and amended effective March 18, 2005. Amended effective March 1, 2012.

LR20–AR15–NACR Rule 15. COURT REPORTERS

Court reporter services in the Elkhart County Courts shall be governed by following local rule.

SECTION ONE: DEFINITIONS The following definitions shall apply under this local rule:

(A) A Court Reporter is a person who is specifically designated by a court to perform the official court reporting services for the Court, including preparing a transcript of record.

(B) Equipment means all physical items owned by the court or other governmental entity and used by a court reporter in performing court reporting services. Equipment $hall include, but not be limited to, telephones, computer hardware, software programs, disks, tapes, and any other device used for recording and storing, and transcribing electronic data.

(C) Work space means that portion of the court's facilities dedicated to each court reporter, including but not limited to actual space in the courtroom and any designated office space.

(D) Page means the page unit of transcript which results when a recording is transcribed in the form required by Indiana Rule of Appellate Procedure 7.2.

(E) Recording means the electronic, mechanical, stenographic or other recording made as required by Indiana Rule of Trial Procedure 74.

(F) Regular hours -worked means those hours which the court is regularly scheduled to work during any given work week. Depending on the particular court, these hours may vary from court to court within the county but remain the same for each work week.

(G) Gap hours worked means those hours worked that are in excess of the regular hours worked but hours not in excess for forty (40) hours per work week.

(H) Overtime hours worked means those hours worked in excess of forty (40) hours per work week.

(I) Work week means a seven (7) consecutive day week that consistently begins and ends on the same days throughout the year, i.e. Sunday through Saturday, Wednesday through Tuesday, Friday through Thursday.

(J) Court means the particular court for which the court reporter performs services.

(K) County indigent transcript means a transcript that is paid for from county funds and is for the use on behalf of a litigant who has been declared indigent by a court.

(L) State indigent transcript means a transcript that is paid for from state funds and is for the use on behalf of a litigant who has been declared indigent by a court.

(M) Private transcript means a transcript, including but not limited to a deposition transcript, that is paid for by a private party.

(N) Expedited or rush transcript is one which is requested for delivery within three days, excluding weekends and holidays.

SECTION TWO: SALARIES AND PER PAGE FEES

(A) Court reporters shall be paid an annual salary for the time spent working under the control, direction and direct supervision of their supervising court during any regular work hours, gap hours or overtime hours. The supervising court shall enter into a written agreement with the court reporters which outlines the manner in which the court reporter is to be compensated for gap and overtime hours; i.e. monetary compensation or compensatory time off regular work hours.

(B) The maximum per page fee a court reporter may charge for the preparation of a county or state indigent transcript shall be $2.80; the court reporter shall submit a claim directly to the county for the preparation of any county indigent transcripts. However, whenever possible, county indigent transcripts

shall be prepared during regular work hours. When prepared during regular work hours, a per page fee shall not be assessed.

(C) The maximum per page fee a court reporter may charge for the preparation of a state indigent transcript shall be $2.80

(D) The maximum per page fee a court reporter may charge for the preparation of a private transcript shall be $2.80,

(E) The maximum per page fee a court reporter may charge for an expedited or rush transcript shall be $5.60.

(F) Each court reporter shall report, at least on an annual basis, all transcript fees for the preparation of either county indigent, state indigent or private transcripts to the Indiana Supreme Court Division of State Court Administration. The reporting shall be made on forms prescribed by the Division of State Court Administration.

SECTION THREE: PRIVATE PRACTICE

(A) If a court reporter elects to engage in private practice through the recording of a deposition and/or preparing of a deposition transcript, and the court reporter desires to utilize the court's equipment, work space and supplies, and the court agrees to the use of the court equipment for such purpose, the court and the court reporter shall enter into a written agreement which must, at a minimum, designate the following:

1) The reasonable market rate for the use of equipment, work space and supplies;

2) The method by which records are to be kept for the use of equipment, work space and supplies; and

3) The method by which the court reporter is to reimburse the court for the use of the equipment, workspace and supplies

(B) If a court reporter elects to engage in a private practice through the recording of a deposition and/or preparing of a deposition transcript, all such private practice work shall be conducted outside of regular working hours.

Adopted effective Oct. 2004. Renumbered as Rule 15, and amended effective March 18, 2005. Amended effective March 1, 2012.

LR20–TR00–NAGC Rule 16. GUARDIAN AD LITEM/CASA

(1) Appointment of Guardian Ad Litem. The Courts of Elkhart County reserve the right to appoint a guardian ad litem to represent the interests of minors and incapacitated persons. An order for appointment of a guardian ad litem may be entered by agreement of the parties and the court or by petition and approval by the court. Guardian ad litem fees shall be ordered paid by the parties in accordance with the percentages of their incomes, unless otherwise agreed to by the parties or the parties are determined to be indigent, in which case the court shall pay the fees at the rate set forth by Elkhart County. Within ten (10) days of the appointment of the guardian ad litem, the parties and/or counsel shall file a guardian ad litem information sheet form and shall serve a copy upon the guardian ad litem. The guardian ad litem shall file a written report with the court and serve copies upon the parties and/or counsel as ordered by the court. The guardian ad litem's appointment shall be considered terminated upon completion of the work required by the court's initial order or upon entry of an order deciding the matters at issue. The appointment may be renewed at a later date by further order of the court.

Henceforth the customary fee for home studies conducted by an employee of the Elkhart County Probation Department shall be Five Hundred Dollars ($500.00). Absent a court order to the contrary, that fee will be divided equally between the parties to the action in which the home study is ordered. The courts of Elkhart county, Indiana, both individually and collectively, reserve the right to enter Orders modifying the fee charged for the preparation of a home study in a give case, and modifying the division of responsibility for payment of that fee between the parties.

(2) Juvenile Court Guardian Ad Litem/CASA. The Court shall appoint a Guardian Ad Litem and/or Court appointed Special Advocate (CASA) to each child involved in the Juvenile Court alleged to be a Child in Need of Services (CHINS), and in each Petition for Termination of Parental Rights. The following procedure shall be followed with respect to such appoints:

1) The CASA shall file a Form of Order with the Court appointing a CASA in each CHINS case. The Form of Order shall indicate the name of the assigned CASA.

2) The Court shall issue an Order appointing a CASA with the filing of all Termination Petitions. The CASA appointed in the corresponding CHINS action shall be appointed to represent the Minor in the Termination cause to provide for continuity in the representation of each child.

Adopted effective Oct. 2004. Renumbered as Rule 16, and amended effective March 18, 2005. Amended effective March 1, 2012.

LR20–AR00–NAMC Rule 17. MAGISTRATE AND IV–D COMMISSIONER GUIDELINES

(A) Magistrate Guidelines. The Courts of Elkhart County adopt the following guidelines regarding use of Magistrates:

1) Any Court may, with or without the consent of the parties, assign to a Magistrate the responsibility to hear specific currently-disputed matters.

2) The Magistrate shall, with reasonable promptness, hear such matters and shall issue to such Court either a report of findings, which may be accompanied by a recommendation for disposition of those matters, or a final order, whichever is appropriate under controlling law. Complaints regarding the timeliness of any disposition shall be made to the referring Court.

3) All filings related to any matter referred to a Magistrate shall be made with the Magistrate.

4) No change of venue from a Magistrate shall be granted. A change of venue from the referring Court may be sought under applicable trial Rules.

5) A Magistrate shall maintain an office which shall be open at all reasonable times during the Elkhart County hours of operation. A Magistrate shall maintain a telephone answering system during any workday periods when the office is not manned.

6) Referral of a matter to a Magistrate shall not operate as an appointment of a special judge, temporary judge or a judge pro tempore.

(B) IV–D Commissioner Guidelines. The IV–D Child Support Court (hereinafter IV–D Court) is established by Elkhart County pursuant to Title IV, Section D, of the Federal Social Security Act for the purpose of providing for paternity establishment, establishment of child support orders, enforcement of child support orders and collection of past due support for Title IV–D Program participants.

1) In all cases in which the Title IV–D Child Support Division of the Elkhart County Prosecutor's Office (hereinafter IV–D Office) has intervened, all child support issues shall be deemed automatically referred to the IV–D Court;

2) Except that felony non-support cases shall remain in Elkhart Superior Court 6 unless Elkhart Superior Court 6 chooses to refer a felony non-support case to the IV–D Court.

3) In a case in which child support issues are deemed automatically referred to the IV–D Court, the underlying cause shall remain in the court in which it was originally filed, unless properly transferred to another court.

4) All new causes filed by the IV–D Office after January 1, 2005 shall be filed in Elkhart Superior Court 6 and the Judge of Elkhart Superior Court 6 shall supervise the administration of the IV–D Court.

5) All cases currently assigned a cause number will retain the original cause number; the IV–D staff will file all pleadings in the Court of origin with sufficient copies for all parties being noticed. All pleadings must include the parties address, dates of birth and social security numbers when preparing and filing orders, the IV–D Office shall tender two copies of the requested order plus one copy for each part

6) The IV–D Office is exempt from filing fees.

Adopted effective Oct. 2004. Renumbered as Rule 17, and amended effective March 18, 2005. Amended effective March 1, 2012.

LR20–JV00–NAJV Rule 18.   CIRCUIT COURT JUVENILE DIVISION

(A) Juvenile Court Detention and Protective Custody Hearings. Such hearings are probable cause hearings and by nature ex parte. Notwithstanding the above:

1) Detention Hearing: Minor allowed to cross-examine and confront witnesses, representation by counsel and presentation of relevant evidence discretionary with Court.

2) Protective Custody Hearing: Minor, parent, guardian or custodian allowed (K)cross-examination and confrontation of witnesses and representation by counsel. Minor, parent, guardian or custodian allowed to make statement of explanation of circumstances surrounding protective custody, presentation of relevant other evidence discretionary with the Court.

(B) Juvenile Court Initial Hearings—Delinquency/CHINS.

1) Initial hearings shall be held pursuant to law.

2) Upon denial of petition, the Court will set the matter for fact finding hearing, unless the parties agree and the Court has sufficient time to hear the same without disruption of the remainder of the Court schedule.

(C) Juvenile Court Dispositional, Modification of Disposition Progress Reports, Placement Review Hearings—Delinquency/CHINS.

1) Parties shall inform the Court within seven (7) days or such time as the Court determines, if the party intends to call witnesses other than Probation or the Division of Family and Children staff at such hearings; and said party shall inform opposing counsel and guardian ad litem or non-represented party within the same time limits.

2) The Court may reschedule such hearings if sufficient time is not available at the scheduled time.

(D) Juvenile Court Waiver of Jurisdiction, Violation of Probation Delinquency and Termination of Parental Rights—Welfare.

1) Initial hearings shall be held on such petitions.

2) Upon denial of same, the Court shall set the matter for fact finding or evidentiary hearing following Rule 11 herein above stated.

3) Upon granting of waiver of jurisdiction, the State shall provide the waiver decree embracing all facts which the party claims is proven and conclusions of law thereon within seventy-two (72) hours of the conclusion of the hearing, in such numbers that the Juvenile Court, the adult Court to which

the minor is waived, Probation Department and minor receive copies.

(E) Juvenile Court Reports, Assessments and Evaluations.

1) All Division of Family and Children, Probation and CASA reports, court ordered assessments and evaluations shall be filed with the Court not later than 4:00 p.m. on the Friday before the scheduled hearing.

2) All such reports shall be served on opposing parties and CASA, if relevant, as soon as such are available, the latest being by 4:00 p.m. on the Friday before the scheduled hearing.

(F) Juvenile Court Scheduling.

1) All scheduling shall be done by Court staff. Specific dates for hearing may be requested, efforts to accommodate such requests shall be made contingent upon availability.

2) The Court shall set fact finding hearings or evidentiary hearings in first and second settings. If a matter is set for hearing and is resolved before the evidentiary hearing, the parties shall notify the Court and all witnesses, probation officers or caseworkers that the matter has been resolved. Any "second setting" shall be prepared proceed to evidentiary hearing with notice of seven (7) days prior to the scheduled setting. All parties shall be responsible for determining the order of cases and shall be prepared to try their cases on the dates scheduled.

(G) Juvenile Court Additional Procedures, Fact Finding or Other Evidentiary Hearings.

1) A writ of attachment for an absent witness shall not be issued unless the party calling said witness files an affidavit showing:

2) The materiality of the testimony of the witness;

3) The expected testimony of the witness; and

4) Certification that the absent witness was served with process more than three (3) days earlier or that for good and sufficient cause the witness was served with process less than three (3) days earlier.

5) Only one attorney for each party shall examine or cross-examine a witness, except by permission of the Court.

6) No person shall withdraw any original pleading, paper, record, model, exhibit or other document from the custody of the Clerk or other officer of the Court having custody thereof, except upon order of the Court and upon leaving a proper receipt with the Clerk or other officer.

7) Counsel for a party shall be responsible for preparing and filing summons, citations, notices or other documents for which forms may be obtained from the Clerk of the Court. These forms shall include any names, addresses and other descriptive

information, such as place of employment, necessary to effect service of said document.

8) CASA's, foster parents, school personnel, Lifeline staff, institutional placement staff and any others the Court may determine will be invited by the Court to give reports and testimony as to a minor at dispositional, progress report, placement review or other hearing where such testimony is admissible under the law.

(H) JUVENILE COURT RULES OF COURTS OF GENERAL JURISDICTION. The Rules of Court promulgated by the Courts of General Jurisdiction are applicable to Juvenile Court unless negated by statute or Juvenile Court Rule.

Adopted effective Oct. 2004. Renumbered as Rule 18, and amended effective March 18, 2005. Amended effective March 1, 2012.

LR20—AR1E Rule 19. CASELOAD ALLOCATION PLAN

One (1) full time Juvenile Magistrate

Two (2) full time Court Magistrates

One (1) part-time (.6) Title IV–D Court Commissioner

Total: 3.6 available

(Based Upon 2010 Projections Supplied by Indiana State Court Administration)

	NEED	ADJUSTMENT OF MAGISTRATE TIME	HAVE (After Adjustment)	UTILIZATION (After Adjustment)
CIRCUIT	3.49		2.01	1.73
SUPERIOR I	2.30		1.30	1.77
SUPERIOR II	1.68	–.54	1.01	1.66
SUPERIOR III	1.42	–.07	1.01	1.40
SUPERIOR IV	1.56		1.08	1.44
SUPERIOR V	1.73		1.15	1.51
SUPERIOR VI	3.76	+ .61	2.46	1.53

Adopted effective Jan. 9, 2007. Amended effective Jan. 1, 2009; Jan. 1, 2011; March 1, 2012; July 1, 2012.

LR20–FL00–CVFL–5 Appendix A. CERTIFICATION OF COMPLIANCE IN DISSOLUTION CASES

The undersigned, as the (select: Wife or Husband) in this cause, does hereby certify that:

On (type date) I completed the mandatory website work as required by the Court and have attached my certificate to confirm the same.

I affirm under the penalties for perjury that the foregoing representations are true.

Date: _____ _____

                     (Type name), (select: Wife or Husband)

Adopted effective March 1, 2012.

LR20–FL00–CVFL–5 Appendix B. CERTIFICATION OF COMPLIANCE IN PATERNITY CASES

The undersigned, as the (select: Mother or Father) in this cause, does hereby certify that:

On (type date) I completed the mandatory website work as required by the Court and have attached my certificate to confirm the same.

I affirm under the penalties for perjury that the foregoing representations are true.

Date: _____ _____

                     (Type name), (select: Mother or Father)

Adopted effective March 1, 2012.

LR20–FL00–CVFL–5 Appendix C. PARENTING PLAN PROPOSAL

In Re The (select: Marriage/Paternity) of: _____

Case No.: _____

(Select Mother's/Father's) Parenting Plan Proposal

Parent's Affirmation

I hereby affirm under the penalties for perjury, that **before** preparing this proposal I have:

1. carefully read the Indiana Parenting Time Guidelines, including the Preamble and General Rules and understand that they reflect the **minimum** parenting time; and,

2. completed all the work assignments for parents at (select: www.UpToParents.org or www.ProudTo Parent.org); and,

3. enrolled in the parenting class required by the court.

Dated: _____, 20 _____

_____
(Select: Mother/Father)

Terms of This Proposal

The following proposal for our children's parenting plan for our children was prepared as part of the effort of both parents to devise a parenting plan to include decision making and living arrangements that will serve to nurture and protect our children as the years progress. This proposal was prepared and is submitted as required by the Elkhart County Rules of Court for cooperative family practice and is part of an effort to compromise and settle these and other issues which now exist between the parents. Unless all of the terms of the following proposal are accepted as shown by the signatures of both parents on page two (2), the following proposal and all of its terms are inadmissible as evidence for any purpose.

Custody

"Legal custody" of children means decision making responsibility for substantial matters that affect a child's life, such as place of residence, school selection and other educational decisions, non-emergency healthcare and religious upbringing. Legal custody of our children shall be as follows:

_____ Joint

_____ Mother

_____ Father

"Physical custody" means where the children primarily reside. Physical custody of our children shall be as follows:

_____ Shared

_____ Mother

_____ Father

Parenting Time Schedule

The time for our children to be with each of us shall be as provided in the Indiana Parenting Time Guidelines as adopted by Elkhart County ("Guidelines").

The following shall be (select: in addition to/excluded from) the time provided in the Guidelines:

Weekdays:

Weekends:

Holidays and Special Days:

Extended Parenting Time/Summer Vacation:

Other provisions of our parenting plan would be:

In the event of disagreement, we will speak to one another first to try to resolve any parenting issues and focus on the children's needs. If we are unable to resolve all the issues, then we will consider the following:

A. Use of a parenting coordinator to work with us.

B. Mediation.

C. Use of other resources such as redoing website work at www.UpToParents. org or www.ProudTo Parent.org; additional co-parenting classes, including re-attending the basic class or attending high-conflict classes; and individual, joint, family or child counseling.

Dated: _____, 20 _____

_____
(Select: Mother/Father)

(attorney's name)
Indiana Attorney No.:
(firm name)
Attorney for (select: Mother/Father)
(address)
(phone number)

ACCEPTANCE

By our signatures, we, as parents, agree to all of the terms set forth above as our Agreed Parenting Plan and acknowledge that this document is now admissible as evidence in court.

_____
(Select: Mother/Father)
Date: _____, 20 _____

(attorney's name)
Indiana Attorney No.: _____
(firm name)
Attorney for (select: Mother/Father)
(address)
(phone number)

_____
(Select: Mother/Father)
Date: _____, 20 _____.

(attorney's name)
Indiana Attorney No.:
(firm name)
Attorney for (select: Mother/Father)
(address)
(phone number)

IT IS SO ORDERED this _____ day of _____, 20 _____.

_____, Judge

Adopted effective March 1, 2012.

LR20–FL00–CVFL–5 Appendix D. SUMMONS AND NOTICE OF HEARING IN DISSOLUTION OF MARRIAGE PROCEEDING

STATE OF INDIANA IN THE (Title of Court)
  SS:
COUNTY OF ELKHART

IN RE THE MARRIAGE OF Case No.
(Name of Filing Party),
  (select: Wife, Husband)

and
(Name of Spouse),
    (select: Wife, Husband)

SUMMONS
AND NOTICE OF HEARING

THE STATE OF INDIANA TO: (name of spouse being served)
                               (address)

Your spouse has filed an action for dissolution of marriage in the Court stated above. The following documents are attached or otherwise served with this Summons:

_____ Petition for Dissolution of Marriage

_____ Petition for Provisional Orders

_____ Petition for Temporary Restraining Order

_____ Temporary Restraining Order

_____ Standing Order for Attendance at Transparenting & Seasons Classes

_____ Chronological Case Summary

_____ Subpoena

_____ Preliminary Injunction

_____ Other _____

If you and your spouse have children together under the age of eighteen (18), Local Court Rules in Elkhart County require that both you and your spouse complete certain specific tasks. You should immediately and carefully review those requirements at the website established by the Court at: www.ElkhartFamilyLaw.org.

THIS IS YOUR OFFICIAL NOTICE that a hearing for provisional orders has been scheduled for _____, 20 _____, at _____ M. before this Court, which is located at [address of Court]. If you wish to hire an attorney to represent you in this matter, it is advisable to do so before that date. If you do not appear for that hearing, a provisional order could be entered by default which could remain in effect until this action is concluded. If child support and/or spousal maintenance are requested, you are required to bring evidence of your weekly gross income (your pay before any deductions) and documents to verify year-to-date income (pay stub or employer statement) and your last income tax return, including all W–2s, 1099s and all accompanying schedules.

If you do not file a written appearance with the Clerk and serve a copy on your spouse or your spouse's attorney, you may not receive notice of any further proceedings in this action. **If you do not make such an appearance, a final decree could be entered by default which grants the relief sought in your spouse's petition after the expiration of sixty (60) days from the date of the filing of the petition.** You are not required to file any written answer to respond to the petition; however, certain grounds for dismissal must be asserted in a timely fashion or are waived; and, if you have a claim for relief against your spouse you may be required to assert such a claim in a written pleading which must be filed with the Clerk and served on your spouse or your spouse's attorney.

The following manner of service of this SUMMONS is hereby designated:

(select): _____ Registered or certified mail (with addressed envelope) postage prepaid, return receipt #
               _____ Sheriff of Elkhart County
               _____ Private service by: _____

Date:

(Name of attorney for Filing Party)   WENDY HUDSON

Indiana Attorney No: (insert)   CLERK, ELKHART CIRCUIT/
                            SUPERIOR COURTS

(firm name)

Attorney for (select: Wife, Husband)

(address)   BY:
                               Deputy Clerk

(phone number)

PREPARATION DATA:

All summons are to be prepared in triplicate with the original of each to be placed in the Court file with two copies available for service. If service is by certified mail a properly addressed envelope shall be provided for the party being served. Certified mail labels and return receipts must also be furnished for each mailing and the cause number must appear on each return receipt, which shall be returnable to the Clerk at the address of the Court.

CLERK'S CERTIFICATE OF MAILING

I hereby certify that on the _____ day of _____, 20 _____, I mailed a copy of this Summons and designated documents to the party being served, _____, by _____ mail, requesting a return receipt, at the address furnished by the filing party.

               WENDY HUDSON
               CLERK, ELKHART CIRCUIT/
               SUPERIOR COURTS

Dated: _____, 20 _____.   BY: _____
                                 Deputy Clerk

RETURN ON SERVICE OF
SUMMONS BY MAIL

I hereby certify that the attached return receipt was received by me showing that the Summons and designated documents mailed to the party being served, _____, was accepted by the party being served on the _____ day of _____, 20 _____.

I hereby certify that the attached return receipt was received by me showing that the Summons and designated documents was returned not accepted on the _____ day of _____, 20 _____.

WENDY HUDSON
CLERK, ELKHART CIRCUIT/
SUPERIOR COURTS

Dated: _____, 20 _____. BY: _____
Deputy Clerk

RETURN OF SERVICE OF SUMMONS BY SHERIFF

I hereby certify that I have served the within Summons and designated documents:

1) By delivering on _____, 20 _____, a copy of this Summons and designated documents to each of the within named person(s).

2) By leaving on _____, 20 _____, for each of the within named person(s) _____ a copy of the Summons and a copy of the designated documents at the respective dwelling house or usual place of abode, _____ in _____, Indiana, with a person of suitable age and discretion residing within, whose usual duties or activities include prompt communication of such information to the person served, or by otherwise leaving such process thereat, and by mailing a copy of the Summons without the designated documents to the said named person(s) at the address listed herein.

3) This Summons came to hand this date, _____, 20 _____. The within named _____ was not found in my bailiwick this date, _____, 20 _____.

ALL DONE IN ELKHART COUNTY, INDIANA.

SHERIFF OF ELKHART
COUNTY, INDIANA
By: _____

SERVICE ACKNOWLEDGED

I hereby acknowledge that I received a copy of this Summons and copies of the designated documents at _____, Indiana, on this date, _____, 20 _____.

_____
(Select: Wife/Husband)

Adopted effective March 1, 2012.

LR20–FL00–CVFL–5 Appendix D–1. SUMMONS IN DISSOLUTION OF MARRIAGE PROCEEDING

STATE OF INDIANA
SS:
COUNTY OF ELKHART

IN THE (Title of Court)

IN RE THE MARRIAGE OF
(Name of Filing Party),
    (select: Wife, Husband)
    and
(Name of Spouse),
    (select: Wife, Husband)

Case No.

Your spouse has filed an action for dissolution of marriage in the Court stated above. The following

documents are attached or otherwise served with this Summons:

_____ Petition for Dissolution of Marriage

_____ Petition for Provisional Orders

_____ Petition for Temporary Restraining Order

_____ Temporary Restraining Order

_____ Standing Order for Attendance at Transparenting & Seasons Classes

_____ Chronological Case Summary

_____ Subpoena

_____ Preliminary Injunction

_____ Other _____

If you and your spouse have children together under the age of eighteen (18), Local Court Rules in Elkhart County require that both you and your spouse complete certain specific tasks. You should immediately and carefully review those requirements at the website established by the Court at: www.ElkhartFamilyLaw.org.

If you do not file a written appearance with the Clerk and serve a copy on your spouse or your spouse's attorney, you may not receive notice of any further proceedings in this action. **If you do not make such an appearance, a final decree could be entered by default which grants the relief sought in your spouse's petition after the expiration of sixty (60) days from the date of the filing of the petition.** You are not required to file any written answer to respond to the petition; however, certain grounds for dismissal must be asserted in a timely fashion or are waived; and, if you have a claim for relief against your spouse you may be required to assert such a claim in a written pleading which must be filed with the Clerk and served on your spouse or your spouse's attorney.

The following manner of service of this SUMMONS is hereby designated:

(select): _____ Registered or certified mail (with addressed envelope) postage prepaid, return receipt #

_____ Sheriff of Elkhart County

_____ Private service by: _____

Date:

(Name of attorney for Filing Party)   WENDY HUDSON
Indiana Attorney No: (insert)   CLERK, ELKHART CIRCUIT/
(firm name)   SUPERIOR
Attorney for (select: Wife, Husband)
(address)   BY:
         Deputy Clerk
(phone number)

PREPARATION DATA:

All summons are to be prepared in triplicate with the original of each to be placed in the Court file with two copies available for service. If service is by certified mail a properly addressed envelope shall be provided for the party being served. Certified mail labels and return receipts must also be furnished for each mailing and the cause number must appear on each return receipt, which shall be returnable to the Clerk at the address of the Court.

CLERK'S CERTIFICATE OF MAILING

I hereby certify that on the _____ day of _____, 20 _____, I mailed a copy of this Summons and designated documents to the party being served, _____, by _____ mail, requesting a return receipt, at the address furnished by the filing party.

> WENDY HUDSON
> CLERK, ELKHART CIRCUIT/
> SUPERIOR COURTS

Dated: _____, 20 _____.   BY: _____
> Deputy Clerk

RETURN ON SERVICE OF SUMMONS BY MAIL

I hereby certify that the attached return receipt was received by me showing that the Summons and designated documents mailed to the party being served, _____, was accepted by the party being served on the _____ day of _____, 20 _____.

I hereby certify that the attached return receipt was received by me showing that the Summons and designated documents was returned not accepted on the _____ day of _____, 20 _____.

> WENDY HUDSON
> CLERK, ELKHART CIRCUIT/
> SUPERIOR COURTS

Dated: _____, 20 _____.   BY: _____
> Deputy Clerk

RETURN OF SERVICE OF SUMMONS BY SHERIFF

I hereby certify that I have served the within Summons and designated documents:

1) By delivering on _____, 20 ___, a copy of this Summons and designated documents to each of the within named person(s).

2) By leaving on _____, 20 ___, for each of the within named person(s) _____ a copy of the Summons and a copy of the designated documents at the respective dwelling house or usual place of abode, _____ in _____, Indiana, with a person of suitable age and discretion residing within, whose usual duties or activities include prompt communication of such information to the person served, or by otherwise leaving such process thereat, and by mailing a copy of the Summons without the designated documents to the said named person(s) at the address listed herein.

3) This Summons came to hand this date, _____, 20 ___. The within named

_____ was not found in my bailiwick this date, _____, 20 ___.

ALL DONE IN ELKHART COUNTY, INDIANA.

> SHERIFF OF ELKHART
> COUNTY, INDIANA
> By: _____

SERVICE ACKNOWLEDGED

I hereby acknowledge that I received a copy of this Summons and copies of the designated documents at _____, Indiana, on this date, _____, 20 _____.

_____
(Select: Wife/Husband)

Adopted effective March 1, 2012.

LR20–FL00–CVFL–5 Appendix E. SUMMONS AND NOTICE OF HEARING IN A PATERNITY CASE

STATE OF INDIANA   IN THE [Title of Court]
                    SS:
COUNTY OF ELKHART

IN THE MATTER OF THE   Case No.
PATERNITY OF
CHILD
Female/Male [Name],

          Mother/Father/Putative Father,

and

[Name]

          Putative Father/Father/Mother
[Child by Next Friend]

SUMMONS
AND NOTICE OF HEARING

THE STATE OF INDIANA TO: [name]
                             [address]
                             [city, state zip]

A paternity action has been filed in the Court stated above. The following documents are attached or otherwise served with this Summons:

_____ Petition for Establishment of Paternity

_____ Petition for Custody

_____ Petition for Child Support

_____ Petition for Parenting Time

_____ Chronological Case Summary

_____ Subpoena

_____ Other _____

Local Rules in Elkhart County require that both parties to this case complete certain specific tasks. You should immediately and carefully review those requirements at the website established by the Court: www.ElkhartFamilyLaw.org

THIS IS YOUR OFFICIAL NOTICE that a Hearing on the issues raised by the designated petitions is scheduled for the _____ day of _____, 20 _____, at _____ o'clock _____.m. at [Address of Court]. If you wish to hire an attorney to represent you in this matter, it is advisable to do so before that date. **If you do not appear for the hearing, a final order could be entered by default determining paternity, custody, parenting time, medical expenses and child support.** If child support is requested, you are required to bring evidence of your weekly gross income (your pay before any deductions) and documents to verify year-to-date income (pay stub or employer statement) and your last income tax return, including all W–2s, 1099s and all accompanying schedules.

If you do not file a written appearance with the Clerk and serve a copy on the other party or the attorney whose name and address is set forth at the bottom of this page, you may not receive notice of any further proceedings in this action. You are not required to file a written response to the petition(s); however, certain grounds for dismissal must be asserted in a timely fashion or are waived. If you have a claim for relief against the person who filed the petition(s), you may be required to assert such a claim in a written pleading which must be filed with the Clerk and served upon the other party or the attorney whose name and address is set forth at the bottom of this page.

The following manner of service of this SUMMONS is hereby designated:

(select): _____ Registered or certified mail (with addressed envelope) postage prepaid, return receipt #
_____ Sheriff of Elkhart County
_____ Private service by: _____

Date:

(Name of attorney for Filing Party)
Indiana Attorney No: (insert)
(firm name)
Attorney for (select: Mother, Father)
(address)

(phone number)

WENDY HUDSON
CLERK, ELKHART CIRCUIT/
SUPERIOR

By: _____
Deputy Clerk

CLERK'S CERTIFICATE OF MAILING

I hereby certify that on the ___ day of _____, 20 ___, I mailed a copy of this Summons and designated documents to the party being served, _____, by _____ mail, requesting a return receipt, at the address furnished by the filing party.

WENDY HUDSON
CLERK, ELKHART CIRCUIT/
SUPERIOR COURTS

Dated: _____, 20 _____. BY: _____
Deputy Clerk

RETURN ON SERVICE OF SUMMONS BY MAIL

I hereby certify that the attached return receipt was received by me showing that the Summons and designated documents mailed to the party being served, _____, was accepted by the party being served on the ___ day of _____, 20 ___.
I hereby certify that the attached return receipt was received by me showing that the Summons and designated documents was returned not accepted on the _____ day of _____, 20 _____.

WENDY HUDSON
CLERK, ELKHART CIRCUIT/
SUPERIOR COURTS

Dated: _____, 20 _____. BY: _____
Deputy Clerk

RETURN OF SERVICE OF SUMMONS BY SHERIFF

I hereby certify that I have served the within Summons and designated documents:

1) By delivering on _____, 20 ___, a copy of this Summons and the designated documents to each of the within named person(s).

2) By leaving on _____, 20 ___, for each of the within named person(s) _____ a copy of the Summons and a copy of the designated documents at the respective dwelling house or usual place of abode, _____ in _____, Indiana, with a person of suitable age and discretion residing within, whose usual duties or activities include prompt communication of such information to the person served, or by otherwise leaving such process thereat, and by mailing a copy of the Summons without the designated documents to the said named person(s) at the address listed herein.

3) This Summons came to hand this date, _____, 20 ___. The within named _____ was not found in my bailiwick this date, _____, 20 ___.

ALL DONE IN ELKHART COUNTY, INDIANA.

SHERIFF OF ELKHART
COUNTY, INDIANA
By: _____

SERVICE ACKNOWLEDGED

I hereby acknowledge that I received a copy of this Summons and copies of the designated documents at _____, Indiana, on this date, _____, 20 _____.

_____
(Select: Mother/Father)

Adopted effective March 1, 2012.

FLOYD COUNTY LOCAL CIVIL RULES OF PRACTICE

Adopted January 30, 2007, Effective January 1, 2007

Including Amendments Received Through November 1, 2013

Research Notes

These rules may be searched electronically on Westlaw *in the* IN-RULES *database; updates to these rules may be found on* Westlaw *in* IN-RULESUPDATES. *For search tips and a summary of database content, consult the Westlaw Scope Screens for each database.*

LR22–TR1 Rule 100. APPLICABILITY OF RULES

A. Scope. The following local rules of practice and procedure shall apply to cases filed in the Circuit and Superior Courts of Floyd County, Indiana, but shall not apply to criminal cases or cases on the Small Claims Docket unless otherwise indicated.

B. Effective Date. These local rules shall be effective January 1, 2009, and shall supersede such rules heretofore enacted by said Courts.

C. Citation. These rules may be cited as Local Rule ____. (LR22–TR00- ____)

D. Purpose. These rules are promulgated pursuant to Trial Rule 81 of the Indiana Rules of Trial Procedure and are intended to supplement the Indiana Rules of Trial Procedure.

Adopted Jan. 30, 2007, effective Jan. 1, 2007. Amended effective Jan. 1, 2009; effective Sept. 1, 2012.

LR22–TR3.1 Rule 101. WITHDRAWAL OF APPEARANCE

A. Withdrawal of Appearance. Excepting appearances in estates and guardianships, an attorney desiring to withdraw his appearance in any other proceeding shall file a written motion requesting leave to do so accompanied by a notice of hearing or proof satisfactory to the Court that at least ten [10] days prior written notice has been given to the client and to all other parties of record in advance of the withdrawal date, which date shall be set forth in the written notice. The motion must contain the address and phone number of the client.

B. Withdrawal in Estate and Guardianship Cases. An attorney desiring to withdraw his appearance in an estate or guardianship shall file a written motion requesting leave to do so accompanied by a notice of hearing which shall be served at least ten [10] days prior to the hearing upon the personal representative or guardian directing said person to appear at the hearing.

C. Waiver of Rule. A motion for leave to withdraw an appearance accompanied by a written appearance of successor counsel and, excepting appearances in estate or guardianship matters, a motion to withdraw an appearance accompanied by a written consent of the client shall constitute a waiver of the requirements of this local rule.

Adopted Jan. 30, 2007, effective Jan. 1, 2007.

LR22–TR3 Rule 102. DUTIES OF ATTORNEYS PREPARATION OF ENTRIES

A. Status of Proceedings. Each attorney appearing of record and each party to a proceeding shall at all times keep themselves informed of the status of the proceeding and shall be particularly bound by hearing dates orally set by the Court from the bench in their presence.

B. Preparation of Entry. When opposing counsel has appeared in a proceeding, the attorney who has agreed to prepare an entry as requested by the Court shall place on the last page of the entry appropriate signature lines indicating "prepared by" and "reviewed by" and shall submit the entry to opposing counsel for examination. Opposing counsel shall promptly examine the entry when submitted, shall sign the entry, and shall submit the entry to the Court within five [5] days of receiving same. If opposing counsel does not agree with the entry, counsel shall advise the Court and request a conference, telephonic or otherwise.

C. Failure to Submit Entry. If opposing counsel shall fail or refuse to submit the entry without advising the Court as to objections thereto within five [5] days of receiving the same, the preparing attorney shall submit the entry to the Court advising the Court by letter of opposing counsel's failure or refusal and the Court shall accept the entry without opposing counsel's signature.

D. Failure to Prepare Entry. If an attorney agrees or is ordered to prepare an entry and then fails to do so within fifteen [15] working days of the Court's request, opposing counsel may prepare the entry and submit same to the Court advising the Court by letter of the efforts made to gain preparation of the entry. Failure of counsel to prepare an entry as agreed or as ordered may subject counsel to sanctions including the assessment of reasonable attorney fees for counsel who prepared the entry.

E. Attorneys Filing Pleadings with Multiple Cause Numbers. If an attorney files a pleading with more than one cause number, they shall provide the Court with enough copies for each case for filing. This applies to Motions, Notices, and Orders.

Adopted Jan. 30, 2007, effective Jan. 1, 2007. Amended Oct. 5, 2009, effective Jan. 1, 2010.

LR22–TR3 Rule 103. PAYMENT OF FEES

A. Initial Fees. Unless the Court has previously entered a written Order waiving the pre-payment of the filing fee in whole or in part, all fees associated with the filing of a case shall be prepaid to the Clerk when the case is filed.

B. Transfer Fees. All fees and costs associated with the transfer of a case to another county or transfer of a case from the small claims docket to the civil plenary docket shall be paid within twenty [20] days of the Order directing transfer and the failure to pay such costs shall result in the rescinding of the Order directing transfer and jurisdiction of the case shall remain with the Court, or the case shall be transferred back to the small claims docket as applicable, unless the Court has entered a written order waiving the pre-payment of the fee in whole or in part.

Adopted Jan. 30, 2007, effective Jan. 1, 2007.

LR22–TR5 Rule 104. PROOF OF SERVICE

A. Trial Rule 5 Requirements. Proof of service of pleadings or papers required to be served by Trial Rule 5 may be made either by:

[1] a certificate of service signed by an attorney of record which certificate shall identify by name and address the person or persons to whom service is directed; or

[2] an acknowledgment of service signed by the party served or the attorney of record if such party is represented by an attorney.

B. Verifying Service of Process. It is the responsibility of counsel and Pro Se parties to verify service of process. Court personnel are not required to review case files to determine if a party has acquired service of process. Counsel and Pro Se parties may access the Chronological Case Summary online or by use of the public access computers located in the office of the Floyd County Clerk to determine if service of process has been acquired. If necessary, Court files may be reviewed to verify service of process.

Adopted Jan. 30, 2007, effective Jan. 1, 2007. Amended effective Sept. 1, 2012.

LR22–TR10 Rule 105. FORM AND STYLE OF PLEADINGS FILING OF PLEADINGS

A. Signature Required. Any pleading, motion, brief or paper not signed by an attorney admitted to practice or a party who is acting pro se, shall not be accepted for filing, or, if inadvertently accepted for filing, shall upon discovery be stricken from the record by the Court upon its own motion.

B. Paper Size. All pleadings, motions, entries, orders, judgments and other papers shall be filed on letter size 8 1/2 × 11] paper.

C. Flat Filing. The files of the Clerk of the Court shall be kept under the flat filing system. All pleadings presented for filing with the Clerk or the Court shall be flat and unfolded.

D. Orders and Entries. Except as required by Local Rule LR22–TR3–102, all proposed orders and entries shall reflect the name of the preparer under the indication "prepared by", shall be submitted in sufficient number for each person entitled to service and shall contain a distribution list identifying by name and address each person entitled to service. The preparer shall provide sufficient pre-stamped pre-addressed envelopes to the court for mailing of the orders or entries.

Adopted Jan. 30, 2007, effective Jan. 1, 2007.

TR22–TR16 Rule 106. PRE-TRIAL CONFERENCES ASSIGNMENT OF CASES FOR TRIAL

A. Court Calendar. A calendar of cases assigned for bench trial or jury trial shall be kept by the Court and the Court Reporter shall enter on the calendar at the direction of the Court, the style, cause number, and the time and date the trial is assigned to commence.

B. Required Pre-Trial Conference. No case shall be assigned for jury trial without the Court having conducted a pre-trial conference thereon and any party or attorney of record desirous of acquiring a jury trial shall first file a motion requesting a pre-trial conference accompanied by a proposed order.

C. Other Pre-Trial Conferences. The Court, in its discretion, may require a pre-trial conference on certain cases to be heard at bench trial and the Court shall, sua sponte, set such cases for conference. Any party or attorney of record desirous of having a pre-trial conference for such cases may file a motion requesting same accompanied by a proposed order.

D. Attendance at Pre-Trial Conference. At least one attorney for each party who is a member of the Indiana Bar and who will participate in the trial shall appear at the pre-trial conference. An attorney who fails to attend a pre-trial conference shall be bound by the trial date set by the Court as well as such other matters as contained in the Court's Pre-Trial Order.

E. Requests for Bench Trial. The assignment of a case for bench trial may be had by motion duly filed and accompanied by a proposed order. Said motion shall reflect an estimate of the trial time required.

F. Trial Assignments. The Court may assign a case for trial by jury on a primary and/or secondary basis. Ten [10] days prior to the scheduled trial date, an attorney whose case has been assigned for trial on a primary basis may file a Certificate of Readiness indicating the intention of proceeding to trial as scheduled. The failure to file such Certificate may result in forfeiture of the primary trial date if an attorney whose case has been assigned on a secondary basis files such Certificate and in such event the case assigned on a secondary basis shall be heard.

G. Certificate of Readiness. If a Certificate of Readiness is filed pursuant to subsection F of this Local Rule, the Certificate shall be served on all parties in a cause and shall contain a certificate of service. The Certificate shall state:

[1] that the cause is at issue;

[2] that discovery has been completed or will be completed by the scheduled trial date; and

[3] that opposing counsel was advised of the party's intention to file the Certificate five (5) days prior to its filing.

Adopted Jan. 30, 2007, effective Jan. 1, 2007.

LR22–TR7 Rule 107. MOTIONS

A. Generally. Excepting motions made during the course of a recorded proceeding, all motions shall be in writing.

B. Proposed Orders Required. Proposed orders shall accompany motions or applications in the following matters:

[1] to enlarge or shorten time

[2] for setting of hearing, conference or trial

[3] for continuance

[4] for default judgment

[5] to compel discovery

[6] to withdraw appearance

[7] for dismissal

[8] for change of venue

[9] for restraining order, temporary injunction

[10] for summary judgment

[11] for such other orders, judgments or decrees as the Court may direct.

C. Hearings Required. Excepting motions to correct error, motions for summary judgment or other motions described in subsection F, subsection G and subsection H of this rule, all motions shall be accompanied by a separate motion requesting a hearing and a proposed order for the scheduling of a hearing date.

D. Notice of Motion and Order. In lieu of the requirement of subsection C of this rule, an attorney may utilize a Notice of Motion and Order for routine matters such as a motion for continuance, motion to amend pleading, motion to shorten time, motion to add parties, motion to compel discovery and the like. The Notice of Motion shall indicate that the Court will rule on the motion and enter its Order beginning at 9:00 A.M. on the Monday which is not less than five [5] working days from the date of the Court's actual receipt of the Notice of Motion.

E. Motion to Correct Error. At any time before the Court has ruled upon a Motion to Correct Error, any party may request a hearing on such Motion by filing a written motion requesting a hearing and a proposed order for the scheduling of a hearing date. It shall be discretionary with the Court whether a hearing shall be held on such Motion to Correct Error.

F. Hearing Not Required. At the time of filing, the following motions shall be summarily granted or denied ex parte unless the Court, in its discretion, determines a hearing on such motion should be scheduled.

[1] Motion for Enlargement of Time [initial request]

[2] Motion to Reconsider [denial of]

[3] Motion for Change of Venue from Judge/County

[4] Motion for Default Judgment

[5] Joint Motion for Continuance

[6] Motion to Dismiss Settled

[7] Motion to Set Hearing/Pre-trial conference/Bench Trial

[8] Motion to Withdraw Appearance excepting in Estate, Guardianship or Criminal Matters which are subject to the provisions of [Local Rule LR22–TR3.1–101 and LR22–CR2.1–201]

[9] Such matters as permitted by statute or Trial Rule.

G. Motions Under Trial Rules 12, 24, 42, and 60. Motions seeking relief under Trial Rules 12, 24, 42, and 60 shall be accompanied by a brief and proof of service upon opposing counsel. An adverse party shall have fifteen [15] days after service of the movant's brief to file an answer brief, and the movant shall have seven [7] days after service to file a reply brief.

Upon expiration of the time provided by the briefing schedule, the proponent of the motion shall file a written request to schedule the matter for hearing.

Adopted Jan. 30, 2007, effective Jan. 1, 2007. Amended effective Sept. 1, 2012.

LR22–TR53.5 Rule 108. CONTINUANCES

A. Generally. A motion for continuance of a hearing or trial shall be accompanied by an order which shall contain adequate space for insertion of a new time and date for re-scheduling purposes.

B. Content of Motion. A motion for continuance shall set forth the scheduled date, the reason for continuance, the specific length of time the moving party desires the cause to be delayed, and reference as to whether opposing counsel agrees or disagrees to a continuance of the scheduled hearing or trial. It shall be the duty of the moving party to obtain a mutually acceptable future date if and when the motion is granted.

C. Timing of Motion. No continuance shall be granted at the request of a party unless a written motion for same is filed not less than ten [10] days prior to the scheduled hearing or trial, unless it is made to appear by affidavit that the facts which are the basis of the motion did not then exist or were not then known by the moving party.

D. Sanctions. All delays and continuances of a cause shall be at the cost of the party causing the same, except where otherwise provided by law, and the adverse party may have such costs taxed and judgment rendered therefore upon motion duly made.

Adopted Jan. 30, 2007, effective Jan. 1, 2007.

LR22–TR52 Rule 109. FINDINGS OF FACT

In all cases where findings of fact by the Court are requested or required, counsel of record shall submit to the Court proposed findings setting forth all facts claimed to have been established and the conclusions of law thereon. The proposed findings and conclusions shall be submitted to the Court on computer disc or by e-mail in the Court's discretion within such time as directed by the Court.

Adopted Jan. 30, 2007, effective Jan. 1, 2007. Amended effective Sept. 1, 2012.

LR22–TR26 Rule 110. DISCOVERY

A. Use of Form Discovery. No "form" discovery shall be served upon a party unless all discovery requests on such forms are consecutively numbered and applicable to the case in which the same are utilized. The intent and purpose of this rule is to prohibit the use of form discovery unless applicable to the case at bar or where the nature of the case or the number of the parties makes the use of such forms necessary and appropriate.

B. Admissions Format. Answers or objections to requests for admissions filed and served pursuant to Trial Rule 36 shall set forth in full the request for admissions being answered or objected to immediately preceding the answer or objection.

C. Motions for Discovery. The Court shall refuse to rule on any and all motions for discovery concerned with the production of documents or things, permission to enter upon land or other property for inspection and other purposes, for physical or mental examination, or to compel discovery provided in Trial Rules 26 through 37, unless moving counsel shall first advise the Court in writing that after personal consultation and sincere attempts to resolve differences with opposing counsel, they are unable to reach an accord. Such written advisement to the Court shall include a history with the date, time and place and the names of all parties and attorneys with whom the effort has been attempted.

D. Limitation on Interrogatories. The number of interrogatories which may be served pursuant to Trial Rule 33 shall be limited so as to require the answering party to make no more than forty [40] answers, each sub-part of an interrogatory counting as one [1] answer. Waiver of this limitation will be granted by order of the Court in cases in which such limitation would work a manifest injustice or would be impractical because of the complexity of the issues of the case. Each motion requesting waiver of this limitation shall contain as an exhibit the interrogatories which the party proposes to serve. This limitation does not mean a limit of forty (40) interrogatories and answers for the entire case but rather to each set of interrogatories propounded.

Adopted Jan. 30, 2007, effective Jan. 1, 2007.

LR22–TR32 Rule 111. PUBLICATION OF DEPOSITIONS

The seal on depositions shall be broken and the deposition deemed published upon filing with the Court. When depositions are utilized in support of, or in opposition to, a motion for summary judgment or other matter, the pleadings and/or memoranda filed in support or opposition to such motion shall make specific reference by page and line or question number to those places in such deposition which purport to demonstrate the presence or absence of material fact.

Adopted Jan. 30, 2007, effective Jan. 1, 2007.

LR22–TR51 Rule 112. JURY INSTRUCTIONS

Proposed final instructions, special or Indiana Model Civil Jury Instructions, shall be submitted on letter size [8 1/2 × 11] paper, double-spaced, with all designations including indications for the Court's disposition placed on the bottom three [3] inches of the instruction.

The parties shall submit a second set of proposed final instructions containing no designation of who submitted them, or other identifying references, and shall contain only the statement of law. This set of jury instructions may be sent with the jury to the jury room for use during deliberations. These instructions shall also be presented to the court on computer disc or by e-mail in the Court's discretion.

Adopted Jan. 30, 2007, effective Jan. 1, 2007. Amended effective Sept. 1, 2012.

LR22–AR15   Rule   113. PRAECIPES/TRAN-SCRIPTS

A. Content. All notice of appeal and requests for transcripts shall be in writing and filed with the Clerk of the Court. Such notices and requests for transcripts relating to trials by jury shall not include *voir dire*, opening statements, and closing statements unless specifically requested.

B. Costs. The party requesting a transcript shall obtain an estimate of the cost of the transcript from the Court Reporter and shall pay a deposit equal to one-half of the estimated cost of the transcript before the transcription process is undertaken by the Court Reporter. The remaining estimated cost of the transcript shall be paid upon notification by the Court Reporter to the requesting party that one-half of the transcript has been completed. The actual total cost of the transcripts shall be paid in full before the transcript is released to the requesting party.

C. Court Reporter Rule (Pursuant to Adm. Rule 15) Definitions. The following definitions shall apply under this local rule:

(1) *Court Reporter* is a person who is specifically designated by a court to perform the official court reporting services for the court including preparing a transcript of the record.

(2) *Equipment* means all physical items owned by the court or other governmental entity and used by a Court Reporter in performing court reporting services. Equipment shall include, but not be limited to, telephones, computer hardware, software programs, disks, tapes and any other device used for recording and storing, and transcribing electronic data.

(3) *Work space* means that portion of the court's facilities dedicated to each Court Reporter, including but not limited to actual space in the courtroom and any designated office space.

(4) *Page* means the page unit of transcript which results when a recording is transcribed in the form

required by Indiana Rule of Appellate Procedure 7.2.

(5) *Recording* means the electronic, mechanical, stenographic or other recording made as required by Indiana Rule of Trial Procedure 74.

(6) *Regular hours worked* means those hours which the court is regularly scheduled to work during any given work week. Depending on the particular court, these hours may vary from court to court within the county but remain the same for each work week.

(7) *Gap hours worked* means those hours worked that are in excess of the regular hours worked but not in excess of forty (40) hours per work week.

(8) *Overtime hours worked* means those hours worked in excess of forty (40) hours per work week.

(9) *Work week* means a seven (7) consecutive day week that consistently begins and ends on the same days throughout the year; *i.e.* Sunday through Saturday, Wednesday through Tuesday, Friday through Thursday.

(10) *Court* means the particular court for which the Court Reporter performs services. Court may also mean all of the courts in Floyd County.

(11) *County indigent transcript* means a transcript that is paid for from county funds and is for the use on behalf of a litigant who has been declared indigent by a court.

(12) *State indigent transcript* means a transcript that is paid for from state funds and is for the use on behalf of a litigant who has been declared indigent by a court.

(13) *Private transcript* means a transcript, including but not limited to a deposition transcript that is paid for by a private party.

SECTION 2

A. Salaries. Court Reporters shall be paid an annual salary for time spent working under the control, direction and direct supervision of their supervising court during any regular work hours, gap hours or overtime hours. The supervising court shall enter into a written agreement with the court reporters which outlines the manner in which the Court Reporter is to be compensated for gap and overtime hours; *i.e.* monetary compensation or compensatory time off regular work hours.

B. Per Page Fees. The Court Reporter shall be compensated at the rate of Five Dollars and Fifty Cents ($5.50) per page for any county indigent, state indigent or private transcripts prepared. The Court Reporter shall submit directly to the county a claim for the preparation of the county indigent transcript as other county claims are submitted.

If the Court Reporter is requested to prepare an expedited transcript, the per page fee shall be Ten Dollars ($10.00) per page where the transcript must be prepared within twenty-four (24) hours or less and Eight Dollars and Fifty Cents ($8.50) per page where the transcript of fifty (50) pages or more and is to be prepared in an expedited fashion, the maximum per page fee shall be Eight Dollars and Fifty Cents ($8.50) per page and shall be prepared within a time frame to be agreed upon between the Court Reporter and the Attorney. Index and Table of Contents will be charged at the same rate as the other pages.

Copies shall be made at the rate of Two Dollars and Seventy-five Cents ($2.75) per page.

C. Minimum Fee. A minimum fee of Fifty Dollars ($50.00) will be charged for transcripts less than ten (10) pages in length.

D. Binding and Disk Fees. An additional fee shall be added to the cost of the transcript for:

(1) The time spent binding the transcript and the exhibit and index volumes at an hourly rate based on one and one-half (1 ½) times the Court Reporter's hourly rate.

(2) The costs of office supplies and utilized for finding and transmission of the transcript pursuant to the Indiana Rules of Appellate Procedure 28 and 29. Said costs shall be pursuant to a Schedule of Transcript Supplies established and published annually by the Courts.

E. Annual Report Requirement. Each Court Reporter shall report, at least on an annual basis, all transcript fees received for the preparation of either county indigent, state indigent or private transcripts to the Indiana Supreme Court Division of State Court Administration. The reporting shall be made on forms prescribed by the Division of State Court Administration.

F. Private Practice. If a Court Reporter elects to engage in private practice through the recording of a deposition and/or preparing a deposition transcript, all such private practice work shall be conducted outside regular working hours.

If a Court Reporter engages in such private practice and the Court Reporter desires to utilize the court's equipment, work space and supplies, and the court agrees to the use of the court equipment for such purpose, the court and the Court Reporter shall enter into a written agreement which must, at a minimum, designate the following:

(1) The reasonable market rate for the use of equipment, work space and supplies.

(2) The method by which records are to be kept for the use of equipment, work space and supplies.

(3) The method by which the Court Report is to reimburse the court for the use of the equipment, work space and supplies.

G. Disk as Official Record. Upon the filing of a notice of appeal or written request for transcript or the Court Reporter shall transcribe any court proceeding requested and produce an original paper transcript along with an electronically formatted transcript.

Multiple disks containing the electronically formatted transcript shall be prepared and designated as "Official Record," "Court Reporter's Copy," "Court's Copy" and "Party Copy." Each disk shall be labeled to identify the case number, the names of the parties, the date completed, the Court Reporter's name, and the disk number if more than one disk is required for a complete transcript. The Court's Copy of the electronic transcript shall become the official record of the court proceeding, in lieu of a paper copy of the transcript, and shall be retained in the court where said proceeding was held. The Court Reporter's Copy shall be retained by the Court Reporter. The original paper transcript along with the disk designated as the Official Record shall be forwarded to the Clerk if the transcript was prepared for purposes of appeal. If the transcript was not prepared for purposes of appeal, the original paper transcript shall be delivered to the requested party.

SECTION 3

A. Assembly of the Clerk's Record. Upon the filing of a notice of appeal, the trial court clerk shall assemble the Clerk's Record. The Clerk's Record shall be bound and secured by using any method which is easy to read and permits easy disassembly for copying.

Adopted Jan. 30, 2007, effective Jan. 1, 2007. Amended Dec. 29, 2008, effective Sept. 1, 2008; Oct. 5, 2009, effective Jan. 1, 2010; Jan. 1, 2012.

LR22–TR00 Rule 114. EX PARTE ORDERS

Ex parte proceedings are highly disfavored. In civil cases the Court may enter orders, ex parte, in those matters as set forth in Local Rule LR22–TR7–107(F).

Upon motion of any party adversely affected by any ex parte proceeding not in conformity with this rule, the Court, after notice and opportunity to be heard, may direct that the party or attorney seeking an ex parte order shall pay to the adversely affected party the reasonable attorneys fees associated with the opposition to the ex parte order.

Adopted Jan. 30, 2007, effective Jan. 1, 2007.

LR22–TR00 Rule 115. SANCTIONS

A. Court Action. When a party or counsel for a party fails to comply with any of these Local Rules, the Court, after advising the party of the noncompliance, may direct the Clerk of the Court to refuse to accept the pleadings or papers to be filed, or, if inadvertently accepted for filing, direct that such pleadings or papers be stricken from the record.

A.[1] Costs. In addition to the foregoing, the Court may order the party or counsel for the party failing to comply with these Local Rules to pay reasonable expenses, including attorneys fees, caused by the failure[1].

Adopted Jan. 30, 2007, effective Jan. 1, 2007.

  1 So in original.

LR22–TR79 Rule 116. APPOINTMENT OF SPECIAL JUDGES

A. Selection of Assignment Judge. On or before October 1st of each year, the Judges of the Circuit and Superior Courts of Floyd County shall meet with the presiding judges of Administrative District 23 for the purpose of selecting a judge designated as the assignment judge who shall serve the Administrative District for a period of twelve (12) months.

B. Section H Appointments. In the event it becomes necessary to appoint a special judge under Section H of Trial Rule 79 of the Indiana Rules of Trial Procedure, the judge before whom the case is pending shall send notice of the need of the appointment of a special judge to the Administrative District's assignment judge who shall then make such assignment within five (5) days of receiving said notice.

C. Method of Assignment. The Administrative District's assignment judge shall select special judges from a roster of the available judges in the Administrative District. The assignments shall be in a sequential order beginning with the name of the judge following the last judge so assigned. If, however, a judge is otherwise disqualified to hear a particular case, that judge shall be deemed to be the next in sequence until assigned a case. The assignment judge shall maintain a record of all assignments and shall issue a summary report of the assignments on a quarterly basis.

D. Roster of Available Judges. The roster of available judges in Administrative District 23 shall be maintained by Court designation in the following sequential order and shall include senior judges as available:

(1) Clark Circuit #1
(2) Clark Circuit #2
(3) Clark Circuit #3
(4) Clark Circuit #4
(5) Floyd Circuit
(6) Floyd Superior #1
(7) Floyd Superior #2
(8) Floyd Superior #3
(9) Scott Circuit
(10) Scott Superior
(11) Senior Judges who agree to serve as Special Judge

E. Appointment Order. Upon selecting a special judge, the assignment judge shall prepare an Order of Appointment and forward said Order to the judge before whom the case is pending and enter an Order of Appointment and forward a copy of the Order to the special judge and the attorneys of record.

F. Acceptance of Jurisdiction. The Order of Appointment, when entered on the CCS by the judge before whom the case is pending, shall constitute acceptance of jurisdiction by the appointed special judge unless the judge is otherwise disqualified, and no special appearance, oath or additional evidence of acceptance shall be required.

G. Implementation of Rule. In the event a selected judge does not accept an appointment to serve as a special judge under the provisions of Section (D), (E) or (F) of Trial Rule 79 of the Indiana Rules of Trial Procedure, the judge before whom the case is pending shall notify the assignment judge of the need for an appointment of a special judge under this local rule.

H. Certification to Supreme Court. If, under the provisions of this Rule, no judge is eligible to serve as a special judge in a case, the assignment judge shall notify the judge before whom the case is pending who shall then certify such fact to the Indiana Supreme Court for the appointment of a special judge.

If the judge before whom the case is pending is of the opinion that the particular circumstances of a case warrants selection of a special judge by the Indiana Supreme Court, said judge shall certify such facts to the Indiana Supreme Court for the appointment of a special judge. Under such circumstance this Rule shall not be implemented unless the Indiana Supreme Court declines to appoint a special judge.

I. Form of Order. The Order of Appointment shall be in the following form:

IN THE _____ COURT FOR _____ COUNTY

STATE OF INDIANA

(CAPTION)

ORDER OF APPOINTMENT

Under the provisions of Trial Rule 79(H) of the Indiana Rules of Trial Procedures, the Honorable _____ of the _____ Court of _____ County is hereby appointed to serve as Special Judge in the above-captioned case.

SO ORDERED AND ASSIGNED this _____ day of _____, 20 ___, BY THE ASSIGNMENT JUDGE FOR THE 23RD JUDICIAL DISTRICT.

_____ Judge _____

Adopted Jan. 30, 2007, effective Jan. 1, 2007. Amended Dec. 29, 2008, effective Jan. 1, 2009; July 1, 2011.

LR22–TR00 Rule 117. ASSIGNMENT OF CASES TO EQUALIZE WORKLOAD BETWEEN COURTS

A. Assignment. The judges of the Circuit and Superior Courts shall meet on or before October 15 of each year to assign cases to review the Caseload Allocation Plan. Different numbers of cases may be assigned to each court based on the caseload statistics received each year from State Court Administration.

B. Transfer. Transfer between the Floyd Circuit Court and the Floyd Superior Courts shall be accomplished pursuant to IC 33–29–1–9 & 10, which allows the judges to transfer cases between courts with mutual consent and to sit on any case in either court with mutual consent.

C. Criminal Cases.

(1) All Murder cases shall be divided equally between the Circuit, Superior #1 and Superior #3 Courts. All Class A, Class B, Class C, Class D Felony and Domestic Battery cases (Misdemeanor and Felony) shall be filed as follows (except as otherwise designated below):

(a) Class A Felonies: 25% shall be filed in the Circuit Court, 50% shall be filed in the Superior Court #1 and 25% shall be filed in the Superior Court #3.

(b) Class B Felonies: 25% shall be filed in the Circuit Court, 50% shall be filed in Superior Court #1, and 25% shall be filed in the Superior Court #3.

(c) Class C Felonies: 25% shall be filed in the Circuit Court, 50% shall be filed in the Superior Court #1, and 25% shall be filed in the Superior Court #3.

(d) Class D Felonies: 25% shall be filed in the Circuit Court, 50% shall be filed in the Superior Court #1, and 25% shall be filed in the Superior Court #3.

(e) Domestic Battery Cases (Misdemeanor and Felony): 25% shall be filed in the Circuit Court, 50% shall be filed in Superior Court #1, and 25% shall be filed in the Superior Court #3.

(2) All Traffic Infractions and Ordinance Violations shall be filed in the Superior Court #2.

(3) All Motor Vehicle Code, Traffic Misdemeanor and Class D Felony Traffic cases shall be filed in Superior Court #2.

(4) All other Misdemeanor offenses, excepting Domestic Violence cases shall be filed in the Superior Court #2 unless the Defendant has a pending case, or is presently on probation, or has a case under advisement, or a case which has been diverted, in the Circuit Court, Superior Court #1, or Superior Court #3. In the event of such occurrence, the new charge shall be filed in the respective Court where the Defendant is on probation or the other case is pending, under advisement or diverted.

D. Civil Cases.

(1) Except as provided by statute, Civil Tort, Civil Plenary, Mortgage Foreclosure, and Miscellaneous cases may be filed on an open basis in the Circuit Court, Superior Court #1, Superior Court #2, or Superior Court #3.

(2) Civil Collection cases $2,500 and over shall be filed as follows:

(a) 50% in Superior Court #1.

(b) 50% in Superior Court #3.

(3) Civil Collections cases under $2,500 shall be filed in Superior Court #2.

E. Protection Order. All Protection Orders shall be filed in Superior Court #3 (See Local Rule LR22–FR00–314 regarding transfer of Protection Order cases).

F. Domestic Relations Cases. All Pro Se Divorces shall be filed in the Superior Court #3. All non-pro se divorces may be filed on an open base in the Circuit Court, Superior Court #1, or Superior Court #3.

G. Small Claims. All Small Claims cases shall be filed in Superior Court #2

H. Mental Health. Mental Health cases may be filed in any of the Floyd County Courts.

I. Juvenile. All JP, JC, JT and JM (CHINS) cases shall be filed in the Circuit Court subject to LR22–TR–00–17(B). All JD, JS, and JM (delinquent) cases shall be filed in Circuit Court subject to LR22–TR00–17 (B).

J. Guardianships and Estates. All Adoptions, Guardianship, Trust and Estate (supervised and unsupervised) cases shall be filed in the Circuit Court.

K. Adult Problem Solving Court Program(s).

(1) Floyd County Problem Solving Court Program(s) shall be established pursuant to IC 33–23–16–11 and in accordance with Floyd County Local Rules to provide specialized services, including: clinical assessment, education, referral for treatment, and service coordination and case management for eligible defendants and probationers, as determined by its written policy and procedures.

(2) Those persons directed to participate in a Floyd County Problem Solving Court Program shall pay the following fees in accordance with IC 33–23–16–23

(a) The program fee, not to exceed one hundred ($100.00) dollars, per admission for initial problem solving court services regardless of the length of participation;

(b) The court service fee, not to exceed fifty ($50.00) dollars per month beginning in the second month of participation and for each month of participation thereafter for the duration of individual's participation; and

(c) The transfer fee, not to exceed twenty-five ($25.00) dollars, transfer to the problem solving court.

(d) Any additional costs associated with recommended treatment.

(3) The clerk of the court shall collect and transmit the program fee within thirty (30) days after the

fees are collected, for deposit by the auditor or fiscal officer in the appropriate user fee fund established under IC 33–37–8.

(4) The day-to-day operation and management of the Floyd County Veterans Treatment Court shall be assigned to Floyd Superior Court 3.

(5) All criminal charges shall be filed as provided for in this rule. However, after a charge has been filed, a judge may refer the defendant to a Problem Solving Court, and if accepted by the Problem Solving Court the Judge may transfer the defendant's case to the Problem Solving Court for admission and disposition in accordance with IC 33–23–16–13, 14 or 15 and the Problem Solving Court policies and procedures.

(6) A Problem Solving Court may initiate and/or accept transfers of individual from another court.

Allocation of user of Magistrate for Purposes of Weighted Caseload Utilization. Circuit Court and Superior Court #2 shall each be allocated two (2) days per week for use of the Magistrate. Superior Court #1 and Superior Court #3 shall each be allocated one-half (1/2) day per week for use of the Magistrate. When reporting quarterly and annual statistics to State Court Administration, it shall be the duty of the Court Reporter of each Court to include the

Adopted Jan. 30, 2007, effective Jan. 1, 2007. Amended Dec. 29, 2008, effective Jan. 1, 2009; Oct. 15, 2009, effective Jan. 1, 2010; July 12, 2012, effective Jan. 1, 2012.

LR22–TR00 Rule 118. CONTEMPT/RULE TO SHOW CAUSE/BODY ATTACHMENT

A. Contempt. Upon failure of a party/person to appear as ordered for any Court proceeding a contempt citation may be filed as to said party/person.

B. Body Attachment. Body Attachment shall be requested and issued only when the party/person previously ordered to appear for a Court proceeding was personally served with notice of a contempt hearing pursuant to I.C. 34–47–4–1.

C. Expiration and Recall of Body Attachments.

(1) *Expiration.* Body Attachments expire one year after issuance.

(2) *Recall.* If during the pendency of a Body Attachment, a party desires to recall said Body Attachment, said party shall file a written notice to recall Body Attachment forthwith stating the reason for the recall.

Adopted Jan. 30, 2007, effective Jan. 1, 2007.

LR 22–AR7–1 Rule 119. EVIDENCE HANDLING, RETENTION AND DESTRUCTION

Preamble

In all cases, the court shall proceed pursuant to these Rules unless the court directs a longer retention period after motion by any party or on its own motion.

(a) Retention Periods for Evidence introduced in Civil Proceedings

Civil Cases, Including Adoption, Paternity, and Juvenile Proceedings. All models, diagrams, documents, or material admitted in evidence or pertaining to the case placed in the custody of the court reporter as exhibits shall be taken away by the parties offering them in evidence, except as otherwise ordered by the court, four (4) months after the case is decided unless an appeal is taken. If an appeal is taken, all such exhibits shall be retained by the court reporter for two (2) years from termination of the appeal, retrial, or subsequent appeal and termination, whichever is later.

The Court reporter shall retain the mechanical or electronic records or tapes, shorthand or stenographic notes as provided in Administrative Rule 7.

(b) Retention Periods for Evidence Introduced in Criminal Misdemeanor, Class D and Class C Felonies and Attempts

Misdemeanor, Class D and C Felonies and Attempts. All models, diagrams, documents, or material admitted in evidence or pertaining to the case placed in the custody of the court reporter as exhibits shall be taken away by the parties offering them in evidence except as otherwise ordered by the court, three (3) years after the case is dismissed, the defendant found not guilty, or the defendant is sentenced, unless an appeal is taken, If an appeal is taken, all such exhibits shall be retained by the court reporter for three (3) years from termination of the appeal, retrial, or subsequent appeal and termination, whichever is later, unless an action challenging the conviction or sentence, or post-conviction action, is pending.

The Court reporter shall retain the mechanical or electronic records or tapes, shorthand or stenographic notes as provided in Administrative Rule 7.

(c) Retention Periods for Evidence Introduced in Criminal Class B and A Felonies and Murder Attempts

Class B and A Felonies and Murder and Attempts. All models, diagrams, documents, or material admitted in evidence or pertaining to the case placed in the custody of the court reporter as exhibits shall be taken away by the parties offering them in evidence, except as otherwise ordered by the court, twenty (20) years after the case is dismissed, the defendant found not guilty, or the defendant is sentenced, unless an appeal is taken. If an appeal is taken, all such exhibits shall be retained by the court reporter for twenty (20) years from termination of the appeal, retrial, or subsequent appeal and termination, whichever is later, unless an action challenging the conviction or sentence, or post-conviction action, is pending.

The court reporter shall retain the mechanical or electronic records or tapes, shorthand or stenographic notes as provided in Administrative Rule 7.

The Courts are encouraged to photograph as much evidence as possible. The courts and parties are reminded of the requirements of Appellate Rule 29(B).

(d) Non-documentary and Oversized Exhibits

Non-documentary and Oversized Exhibits. Non-documentary and oversized exhibits shall not be sent to the Appellate level Court, but shall remain in the custody of the trial court or Administrative Agency during the appeal. Such exhibits shall be briefly identified in the Transcript where they were admitted into evidence. Photographs of any exhibit may be included in the volume of documentary exhibits.

Under no circumstances should drugs, currency, or other dangerous or valuable items be included in appellate records.

(e) Notification and Disposition. In all cases, the court shall provide actual notice, by mail, to all attorneys of record and to parties only if unrepresented by counsel, that the evidence will be destroyed by a date certain if not retrieved before that date. Counsel and parties have the duty to keep the court informed of their current addresses and notice to the last current address shall be sufficient. Court reporters should maintain a log of retained evidence and scheduled disposition date and evidence should be held in a secure area. At the time of removal, a detailed receipt shall be given to the court reporter by the party receiving and removing the evidence, the receipt will be made part of the court file.

In all cases, evidence which is not retaken after notice should be disposed of by the sheriff on the court's order. The sheriff should be ordered to destroy evidence if its possession is illegal or if it has negligible value. Evidence of some value should be auctioned by the sheriff with proceeds going to the county general fund. These Rules and their retention periods will take precedence over inconsistent language in statutes I.C. 35–33–5–5(c)(2).

(f) Biologically Contaminated Evidence. A party who offers biologically contaminated evidence must file a pretrial notice with the trial court and serve all the parties so that the court can consider the issue and rule appropriately before trial. A party can show contaminated evidence or pass photographs of it to jurors, but no such evidence, however, contained, shall be handled or passed to jurors or sent to the Jury Room.

Adopted effective Sept. 1, 2012.

LR22–TR00 Appendix 1. BODY ATTACHMENT

IN THE FLOYD CIRCUIT/SUPERIOR/COUNTY COURT STATE OF INDIANA

_____

PLAINTIFF/PETITIONER

    VS   CAUSE NO: _____

_____

DEFENDANT/RESPONDENT
   WRIT OF BODY ATTACHMENT

    Expiration Date: _____

  TO THE SHERIFF OF FLOYD COUNTY, STATE OF INDIANA:

    You are hereby commanded to attach the body of:
NAME: _____
ADDRESS: _____
             _____

DOB: _____
SS#:   _____

pursuant to IC 34–47–4–2, and forthwith bring him/her before the Judge of the Floyd Circuit/Superior Courts to answer for a Contempt of Court for: [state reason].

BAIL: $ _____   COURT CASH OR SURETY
OR
ESCROW: $ _____   DEPOSITED WITH THE FLOYD COUNTY CLERK
                            [IF CHILD SUPPORT ARREARAGE]

  SO ORDERED this _____ day of _____, 200_.

_____

JUDGE _____
FLOYD CIRCUIT/SUPERIOR COURT

Adopted Jan. 30, 2007, effective Jan. 1, 2007.

FLOYD COUNTY LOCAL CRIMINAL RULES OF PRACTICE

Adopted January 30, 2007, Effective January 1, 2007

Including Amendments Received Through November 1, 2013

Research Notes

These rules may be searched electronically on Westlaw in the IN-RULES database; updates to these rules may be found on Westlaw in IN-RULESUPDATES. For search tips and a summary of database content, consult the Westlaw Scope Screens for each database.

LR22–CR1 Rule 200. APPLICABILITY OF RULES

A. Scope. The following local criminal rules of practice and procedure shall apply to cases filed in the Circuit and Superior Courts of Floyd County, Indiana.

B. Effective Date. These local rules shall be effective January 1, 2012.

C. Citation. These rules may be cited as Local Criminal Rule ___. LR22–CR00– ___)

D. Purpose. These rules are promulgated pursuant to, and are intended to supplement, the Indiana Criminal Rules as adopted by the Indiana Supreme Court.

Adopted Jan. 30, 2007, effective Jan. 1, 2007. Amended effective Jan. 1, 2009.

LR22–CR2.1 Rule 201. WITHDRAWAL OF APPEARANCE

A. Withdrawal of Appearance. An attorney desiring to withdraw his appearance shall file a written motion requesting leave to do so accompanied by a notice of hearing which shall be served upon the defendant directing said person to appear at the hear-

ing, unless incarcerated, in which event the defendant shall be produced in Court for said hearing. The motion must contain the address and phone number of the defendant.

B. Waiver of Rule. A motion for leave to withdraw an appearance accompanied by a written appearance of successor counsel and a written consent of the defendant shall constitute a waiver of the requirements of this local rule.

B.[1] Termination of Appearance. An attorney's representation of a Defendant shall be conclusively presumed to be withdrawn/terminated five (5) days from the expiration of the time within which a Notice of Appeal must be filed.

Adopted Jan. 30, 2007, effective Jan. 1, 2007.

[1] So in original, probably should be "C".

LR22–CR18 Rule 202. DUTIES OF ATTORNEYS PREPARATION OF ENTRIES

A. Status of Proceedings. The Prosecuting Attorney and each attorney appearing of record shall at all times keep themselves informed of the status of the proceeding and shall be particularly bound by hearing dates orally set by the Court from the bench in their presence.

B. Preparation of Entry. When the Prosecuting Attorney or an attorney of record for a defendant has agreed to or has been directed by the Court to prepare an order or entry, such attorney shall place on the last page of the entry appropriate signature lines indicating "prepared by" and "reviewed by" and shall submit the entry to opposing counsel for examination. Opposing counsel shall promptly examine the entry when submitted, shall sign the entry, and shall submit the entry to the Court within five [5] days of receiving same. If opposing counsel shall fail or refuse to sign or submit the order or entry within five (5) days of receiving same without advising the Court and the preparing attorney as to objections thereto, the preparing attorney shall advise the Court by letter of opposing counsel's failure or refusal to sign or submit such order or entry and submit the same to the Court. The Court shall accept such order or entry without opposing counsel's signature unless after examining the record, the Court determines that the same is erroneous.

C. Flat Filing. The files of the Clerk of the Court shall be kept under the flat filing system. All pleadings presented for filing with the Clerk or the Court shall be flat and unfolded.

D. Paper Size. All pleadings, motions, entries, orders, judgments and other papers shall be filed on letter size [8 1/2 × 11] paper.

C¹. Proposed Orders and Entries. All proposed orders and entries shall reflect the name of the preparer under the indication "tendered by", shall be submitted in sufficient number for each person entitled to service and shall contain a distribution list identifying by name and address each person entitled to service. The preparer shall provide sufficient pre-stamped pre-addressed envelopes to the court for mailing of the orders or entries.

D¹. Proposed Orders and Entries. All proposed orders and entries shall reflect the name of the preparer under the indication "tendered by", shall be submitted in sufficient number for each person entitled to service and shall contain a distribution list identifying by name and address each person entitled to service. The preparer shall provide sufficient pre-stamped pre-addressed envelopes to the court for mailing of the orders or entries.

E. Attorneys Filing Pleadings with Multiple Cause Numbers. If an attorney files a pleading with more than one cause number, they shall provide the Court with enough copies for each case for filing. This applies to Motions, Notices, and Orders.

Adopted Jan. 30, 2007, effective Jan. 1, 2007. Amended Oct. 5, 2009, effective Jan. 1, 2010.

¹ So in original.

LR22–TR7 Rule 203. MOTIONS

A. Proposed Orders Required. Proposed orders shall accompany motions in the following matters:

[1] to enlarge or shorten time

[2] for setting of hearing, conference or trial

[3] for continuance

[4] for reduction of bond

[5] for psychiatric examination for competency

[6] to compel discovery

[7] to withdraw appearance

[8] for dismissal

[9] for change of venue

[10] for modification of sentence

[11] for post-conviction relief

[12] for such other orders, judgments or decrees as the Court may direct; and shall comply with Local Rule LR22–CR18–202(E).

B. Hearings Required. Excepting motions to correct error, all motions shall be accompanied by a separate motion requesting a hearing and a proposed order for the scheduling of a hearing date.

C. Generally. Excepting motions made during the course of a recorded proceeding, all motions shall be in writing.

Adopted Jan. 30, 2007, effective Jan. 1, 2007. Amended effective Sept. 1, 2012.

LR22–CR2.2 Rule 204. PRE–TRIAL CONFERENCES OMNIBUS DATE ASSIGNMENT OF CASES FOR TRIAL

A. Court Calendar. A calendar of cases assigned for bench trial or jury trial shall be kept by the Court and the Court Reporter shall enter on the calendar at the direction of the Court, the style, cause number, and the time and date the trial is assigned to commence. In order to comply with Indiana Criminal Rule 4, the Prosecuting Attorney may submit a motion for trial date setting out the requested trial date which the Court will grant unless a congested calendar exists in which event the next available date shall be the trial date.

B. Pre–Trial Conferences and Omnibus Date.

Pre-trial Conferences. The Court, in its discretion, may require a pre-trial conference on certain cases and, *sua sponte*, set such cases for conference. Any party or attorney of record desirous of having a pre-trial conference for any case may file a motion requesting same accompanied by a proposed order.

Omnibus Date. The Omnibus date shall be set by the Court pursuant to the Indiana Criminal Code. All matters required to be resolved, filed or notices given, and all time limits required to be observed, shall be complied with on or before said date as required by the Indiana Criminal Code.

C. Attendance at Pre–Trial Conference and Omnibus Hearing Date. At least one attorney for each defendant who is a member of the Indiana Bar and who will participate in the trial shall appear at the pre-trial conference and omnibus date. The defendant must also be present for any pre-trial conference or omnibus date in the Circuit and Superior Courts. An attorney and a defendant who fails to attend a pre-trial conference or omnibus date shall be bound by the trial date set by the Court as well as such other matters determined at the conference or omnibus date. A bench warrant may be issued in the discretion of the Court for any defendant who fails to attend a pre-trial or omnibus date.

D. Requests for Bench Trial. The assignment of a case for bench trial may be had by motion duly filed and accompanied by a proposed order. Said motion shall reflect an estimate of the trial time required.

Adopted Jan. 30, 2007, effective Jan. 1, 2007. Amended effective Sept. 1, 2012.

LR22–TR53.5 Rule 205. CONTINUANCES

A. Generally. A motion for continuance of a hearing or trial shall be accompanied by a proposed order which shall contain adequate space for insertion of a new time and date for re-scheduling purposes. The proposed order shall comply with Local Criminal Rule LR22–CR18–202.

B. Content of Motion. A motion for continuance shall set forth the scheduled date, the reason for continuance, the specific length of time the moving party desires the cause to be delayed, and reference as to whether opposing counsel agrees or disagrees to a continuance of the scheduled hearing or trial.

C. Timing of Motion. No continuance shall be granted at the request of a party unless a written motion for same is filed not less than fourteen [14] days prior to the scheduled hearing or trial, unless it is made to appear by affidavit that the facts which are the basis of the motion did not then exist or were not then known by the moving party.

Adopted Jan. 30, 2007, effective Jan. 1, 2007.

LR22–CR00 Rule 206. FINDINGS OF FACT

Proposed Findings. In all cases where findings of fact by the Court are requested or required, counsel of record shall submit to the Court proposed findings setting forth all facts claimed to have been established and the conclusions of law thereon. The proposed findings and conclusions shall be submitted to the Court on computer disc or by e-mail in the Court's discretion within such time as directed by the Court.

Adopted Jan. 30, 2007, effective Jan. 1, 2007. Amended effective Sept. 1, 2012.

LR22–CR00 Rule 207. BONDS AND BOND SCHEDULES

A. Bond Schedule. During regular court hours the judge of each court, or magistrate on cases assigned to him in each court, shall determine the bond on all cases filed in that court. The judges of the various courts may, in their discretion, institute and adopt bond schedules. These bond schedules are for the convenience of the court's and sheriff's offices for use after regular court hours. The sheriff's office may assign bonds for any individual arrested based on the nature of the charge per the schedule.

B. Exceptions. The bond may be changed by the judge of the court providing the bond schedule, and the magistrate on cases assigned to him in such court, at any time for any specific case. Any of the other judges and the magistrate may change a bond on any individual after court hours regardless of which court the individual is charged in, if the bond has not already been reviewed by one of the other judges or magistrate.

C. Other Cases. The bond on any case that is not on a bond schedule due to the severity and nature of the offense, may be set by any of the judges and the magistrate after regular court hours. The judges of the courts wherein the case is appropriate to be sent should be contacted first. In the event said judge or judges are unavailable, then a judge of either of the other courts or the magistrate may set the bond. Nevertheless, any judge or the magistrate may assign a bond to any individual case regardless of the offense or where the case will be filed provided none of the other judges or the magistrate have previously reviewed said bond and taken action thereon.

D. Types of Bonds. The following bonds are approved for the courts of Floyd County: Surety, Cash and Ten (10%) percent Bonds posted in the Clerk's Office (Court Cash Bonds).

Adopted Jan. 30, 2007, effective Jan. 1, 2007.

LR22–CR2.2 Rule 208. CASE ASSIGNMENT

A. Application. In the event a case charges both a felony and a misdemeanor, the case shall be considered a felony for the application of this rule.

B. Assignment. For specific case assignment, refer to Local Rule (Civil) LR22–TR00–117 'Assignment of Cases'.

Adopted Jan. 30, 2007, effective Jan. 1, 2007. Amended Dec. 29, 2008, effective Jan. 1, 2009; effective Sept. 1, 2012.

LR22–CR2.3 Rule 209. TRANSFER

A. Transfer Between Courts. Transfer between the Floyd Circuit Court and the Floyd Superior Courts shall be accomplished pursuant to I.C. 33–29–1–9 & 10, which allows the judges to transfer cases between courts with mutual consent and to sit on any case in either court with mutual consent.

Adopted Jan. 30, 2007, effective Jan. 1, 2007. Amended Dec. 29, 2008, effective Jan. 1, 2009.

LR22–CR2.2 Rule 210. REASSIGNMENT

A. Criminal Case Reassigment[1]. In any criminal proceeding in the Floyd Circuit or Superior Courts when a change of judge is granted, or it becomes necessary to assign another judge, the case shall be reassigned on an alternate basis to the Judge of the Floyd Circuit or Superior Courts or a Senior Judge assigned to that court. If a conflict still exists then a Special Judge shall be sequentially selected from an alphabetized alternative list composed of Judges within Indiana Judicial Conference District No. 23.

Adopted Jan. 30, 2007, effective Jan. 1, 2007. Amended Dec. 29, 2008, effective Jan. 1, 2009; effective Sept. 1, 2012.

[1] So in original.

LR22–CR00 Rule 211. WARRANTS

A. Re-Issuance of Warrants. All warrants issued for misdemeanors shall be returned to the issuing court six (6) months from issuance date and shall be reissued at the request of the Prosecuting Attorney. All warrants for felonies shall be returned to the issuing court one (1) year from issuance date. All bench warrants for contempt of court, failure to appear, revocation of probation, etc.; whether felony or misdemeanor, shall be returned to the issuing court one (1) year from issuance date. The court shall then reissue said warrants as it deems necessary.

Adopted Jan. 30, 2007, effective Jan. 1, 2007.

LR22–TR28 Rule 212. DEPOSITIONS

A. Publication. The seal on depositions shall be broken and the deposition deemed published upon filing with the Court. When depositions are utilized, specific reference by page and line or question number to those places in such deposition which purport to demonstrate the presence or absence of material fact shall be provided.

Adopted Jan. 30, 2007, effective Jan. 1, 2007.

LR22–TR51 Rule 213. JURY INSTRUCTIONS

A. Form. Proposed final instructions, special or pattern, shall be submitted on letter size [8 1/2 × 11] paper, double-spaced, with all designations including indications for the Court's disposition placed on the bottom three [3] inches of the instruction. The parties shall submit a second set of proposed final instructions containing no designation of who submitted them, or other identifying references, which shall contain only the statement of law. This set of jury instructions may be sent with the jury to the jury room for use during deliberations. These instructions shall also be presented to the court on computer disc or by e-mail in the Court's discretion.

Adopted Jan. 30, 2007, effective Jan. 1, 2007. Amended effective Sept. 1, 2012.

LR22–CR00 Rule 214. TRANSCRIPT

A. Costs. Costs for a transcript shall be in accordance with the Local Rule (Civil) LR22–AR15–113. The party requesting a transcript shall obtain an estimate of the cost of the transcript from the Court Reporter and shall pay a deposit equal to one-half of the estimated cost of the transcript before the transcription process is undertaken by the Court Reporter. The remaining estimated cost of the transcript shall be paid upon notification by the Court Reporter to the requesting party that one-half of the transcript has been completed. The actual total cost of the transcript shall be paid in full before the transcript is released to the requesting party. Nevertheless, this provision shall not apply to defendants whom the Court has determined to be indigent and unable to pay for the cost of a transcript.

Adopted Jan. 30, 2007, effective Jan. 1, 2007. Amended effective Sept. 1, 2012.

LR22–CR00 Rule 215. SANCTIONS

A. Court Action. When a party or counsel for a party fails to comply with any of these Local Criminal Rules, the Court, after advising the party of the noncompliance, may direct the Clerk of the Court to refuse any pleadings or papers filed in non-compliance with these rules; or, if inadvertently accepted for filing, direct that such pleadings or papers be stricken from the record; or take whatever other appropriate action deemed necessary.

Adopted Jan. 30, 2007, effective Jan. 1, 2007.

LR22–CR00 Rule 216. FLOYD COUNTY SUBSTANCE ABUSE PROGRAM SCHEDULE OF FEES

1. Convictions for Driving While Intoxicated/Reckless Driving amended from Driving While Intoxicated *Includes clinical impression assessment, classes, case management and workbooks.	$400
2. Convictions for Marijuana/Controlled Substance * Includes clinical impression assessment, classes, case management and workbooks.	$400
3. Convictions for other alcohol or substance offense * Includes clinical impression assessment, classes, case management and workbooks.	$250
4. Conditions of Bond (Court Referral) *Includes clinical impression assessment, classes, case management and workbooks.	$250
5. Referral/transfer to another agency-tracking client to completion of the ordered substance abuse program	$100
6. Clinical Impression Assessment and Recommendation	$50
7. Clinical Impression Assessment and Referral to another outpatient agency or in-patient facility *Includes case management tracking the client to completion of the treatment program.	$250
8. Drug Screenings (administered by the Floyd Superior Court #2 Probation Office)	$30

Adopted Jan. 30, 2007, effective Feb. 15, 2007. Amended effective Jan. 1, 2009; Sept. 1, 2012.

FLOYD COUNTY LOCAL FAMILY RULES OF PRACTICE

Adopted January 30, 2007, Effective January 1, 2007

Including Amendments Received Through November 1, 2013

Research Notes

These rules may be searched electronically on Westlaw *in the* IN-RULES *database; updates to these rules may be found on* Westlaw *in* IN-RULESUPDATES. *For search tips and a summary of database content, consult the Westlaw Scope Screens for each database.*

LR22–FR00 Rule 300. APPLICABILITY OF RULES

A. Scope. These rules shall apply in the Floyd County Circuit and Superior Court in all family law matters.

B. Local Civil Rules. The Local Civil Rules of Practice enacted by the Courts shall be applicable in all family law matters when not in conflict with these Local Family Rules.

C. Effective Date. These local family rules shall be effective January 2009.

D. Citation. These rules shall be cited as Local Family Rule ___ (LR22–FR00- ___).

Adopted Jan. 30, 2007, effective Jan. 1, 2007. Amended effective Jan. 1, 2009.

LR22–FR00 Rule 301. PROVISIONAL ORDERS

A. Content of Provisional Pleading. A motion requesting provisional relief under I.C. 31–15–4–1 must be accompanied by an affidavit setting forth the factual basis and the relief requested pursuant to I.C. 31–15–4–2. If the relief requested is in the nature of child support or other monetary assistance, the motion must contain information and documentation regarding each party's employment status and weekly gross income. When child support is requested, the motion must be accompanied by a Child Support Guideline Worksheet.

B. Order Scheduling Hearing/Preliminary Hearing. A motion requesting provisional relief must be accompanied by a proposed order for the setting of a hearing. If the provisional request includes relief in the nature of child custody or child support, the Court will set the matter for a preliminary hearing on those issues.

C. Procedure in Lieu of Hearing. A movant may waive the hearing requirements of I.C. 31–15–4–4 & 5 through the use of a Notice of Ruling accompanying the motion for provisional relief. The Notice of Ruling shall contain the following:

(1) A waiver of the hearing requirements;

(2) The date for ruling which shall not be less than ten (10) working days from the filing of the motion, the movant's counsel to select the date;

(3) Notice that the Court will consider a written response to the Motion filed before the ruling date.

If a response to the motion for provisional relief is filed on or before the ruling date, the Court shall extend the ruling date by five (5) working days to allow the movant to file a reply to the response.

If service of the Summons and Notice of Ruling occurs on a date beyond the selected ruling date, the ruling date shall be automatically extended for ten (10) working days from the date of service and the time limitations for the filing of a response and a reply to the response shall be followed.

D. Request for Hearing. When a waiver of the hearing requirements has been made by the movant for provisional relief, the opposing party may, nonetheless, request hearing dates in accordance with the provisions of I.C. 31–15–4–4 & 5. A request for hearing dates must be filed within ten (10) days of the service of Summons and Notice of Ruling and must be accompanied by a proposed Order for the setting of a hearing. A request for hearing shall cancel the Notice of Ruling procedure described in Section C and the Court shall immediately schedule a hearing.

E. Effect of Change of Venue. The filing of a motion for a change of venue from the Judge by either party shall not divest the Court of jurisdiction from issuing a preliminary order on temporary custody, child support or parenting time. A written request for such a determination must be filed within five (5) days of service on the motion for change of venue. The filing of such a request shall be accompanied by a proposed Order for the setting of a preliminary hearing on those issues.

Adopted Jan. 30, 2007, effective Jan. 1, 2007.

LR22–FR00 Rule 302. FINANCIAL DISCLOSURE FORM

A. Requirement. In all contested dissolution and separation actions, each party shall prepare and exchange within forty -five (45) days of the filing of the action, a Verified Financial Disclosure Form in substantial compliance with the form set forth in the Appendix to these Local Family Rules of Practice. For good cause, the time limit may be extended or shortened by Court Order.

At the time of the filing of the action, the moving party shall serve a Notice upon the opposing party of the requirement to exchange a Verified Financial Disclosure Form. Such Notice shall be in substantial compliance with that set forth in the Appendix to these Local Family Rules of Practice.

B. Exceptions. The Verified Financial Disclosure Form need not be exchanged if the parties agree in writing within thirty (30) days of the initial filing to waive exchange or the proceeding is uncontested, or the proceeding is one in which service is by publication and there is no pro se response by the Respondent or appearance by counsel for Respondent, or upon order of Court waiving such exchange.

C. Mandatory Discovery. The exchange of the Verified Financial Disclosure Form constitutes mandatory discovery, therefore, the Indiana Trial Rule of Procedures, Trial Rule 37 sanctions apply. Additionally, pursuant to Trial Rule 26 E(2) and (3), the Form shall be amended and/or supplemented as required under such rule and imposed by this local rule.

D. Statement Considered Confidential. When a Verified Financial Disclosure Form is filed with the Court, it shall be sealed and designated "**Confidential.**"

Adopted Jan. 30, 2007, effective Jan. 1, 2007. Amended effective Sept. 1, 2012.

LR22–FR00 Rule 303. CHILD SUPPORT USE OF SUPPORT GUIDELINES

A. Contested Hearings. In all hearings involving child support, each party shall submit to the Court an Indiana Child Support Guideline Worksheet in such form consistent with that set forth in the Indiana Child Support Rules and Guidelines.

B. Settlement Agreements. In all settlement agreements in which child support is established, a Child Support Guideline Worksheet shall be attached as an exhibit with the affirmation executed by the parties.

C. Deviation from Guidelines. If an agreement of the parties or a court order regarding child support deviates from the Guidelines, an adequate explanation for such a deviation must be set forth in the agreement or the order.

D. Effective Date. All orders establishing or modifying child support shall be effective on the Friday immediately following the date on which the request for child support was filed unless otherwise provided for by statute, case law or agreement of the parties approved by the Court.

Adopted Jan. 30, 2007, effective Jan. 1, 2007.

LR22–FR00 Rule 304. PARENTING TIME

A. Use of Parenting Time Guidelines. Unless the Court enters specific orders to the contrary or unless the parties otherwise agree parenting time shall be in accordance with the Indiana Parenting Time Guidelines.

B. Settlement Agreement. In all settlement agreements in which parenting time is established, the parties shall certify in such agreement that they have received a copy of such guidelines and have read and understand the same.

Adopted Jan. 30, 2007, effective Jan. 1, 2007.

LR22–FR00 Rule 305. TRANSPARENTING SEMINAR REQUIREMENT

A. Mandatory Attendance. In any dissolution or separation proceeding involving children under the age of eighteen (18) years of age, both parties to the proceedings shall attend and complete the "Transparenting Seminar" or such other program or seminar which the Court may designate. In any post-dissolution proceeding where custody is in issue, both parties shall attend and complete the seminar or program unless a party has completed the seminar or program within the prior two (2) years.

B. Failure to Attend Seminar. A failure to register, attend, and complete the seminar or program may constitute cause for denial of the granting of the dissolution or the relief requested and a continuance of the matter until attendance has been accomplished. A party, with leave of court, may attend another similar seminar or program.

C. Notice Requirement. At the time of the filing of a dissolution or separation proceeding or a post-dissolution proceeding where custody is in issue, the moving party shall serve a Notice upon the opposing party of the requirement of attendance in the "Transparenting Seminar" or other such program.

D. Waiver of Requirement. Upon motion or its own motion, the Court may waive the requirement for either or both parties to attend and complete the seminar.

Adopted Jan. 30, 2007, effective Jan. 1, 2007.

LR22–FR00 Rule 306. RELIEF UNDER TRIAL RULE 65 (E)(1)

A. Temporary Restraining Order. In accordance with the provisions of Trial Rule 65(E)(1), the court will issue a temporary restraining order applicable to both parties upon the filing of a verified petition by either party alleging that injury would result to the moving party if no order were to issue and requesting that both parties be enjoined from:

(1) Transferring, encumbering, concealing or otherwise disposing of any joint property of the parties or assets of the marriage without the written consent of the parties or permission of the court; and/or;

(2) Removing any child of the parties then residing in the State of Indiana from the State with the intent to deprive the court of jurisdiction over such child without the prior written consent of the parties or permission of the court.

B. Form of Temporary Restraining Order. The moving party shall prepare such order in compliance with Trial Rule 65 (E) (1).

C. Immediate Entry of Temporary Restraining Order. A request for a temporary restraining order will be entered in the record by the Clerk of the Court immediately upon filing and without bringing the matter to the attention of the Judge or waiting for the Judge to sign the original. Attorneys may use the Court's signature stamp for the convenience of the Clerk and counsel.

Adopted Jan. 30, 2007, effective Jan. 1, 2007.

LR22–FR00 Rule 307. EX PARTE ORDERS/EMERGENCY RELIEF

A. Requests for Emergency Relief. All requests for emergency relief in family law matters shall comply with the provisions of Indiana Trial Rule 65(B) and I.C. 31–15–4.

B. Court Scrutiny. All requests for emergency relief will be carefully reviewed by the Court giving due regard to the following:

(1) Rule 3.5 of the Rules of Professional Conduct, In the Matter of Anonymous, 729 NE 2d 566, and In the Matter of Anonymous, 786 NE 2d 1185.

(2) Canon 2 Rule 2.9 of the Code of Judicial Conduct and Opinion Canon 3#1–01 issued by the Indiana Commission on Judicial Qualifications.

C. Issuance of Ex Parte Order. The Court may, without the necessity of notice or hearing, issue the requested emergency order *ex parte* upon the Court's finding that an emergency exists and that immediate and irreparable injury, loss or damage will occur before an adversarial hearing can be scheduled.

D. Order Scheduling Hearing. If the Court issues an *ex parte* order granting the emergency relief requested, the matter shall be set for an adversarial hearing as soon as possible. The party granted the emergency relief shall tender a proposed order for the setting of a hearing date. This order shall include the following language:

"As the recipient of this *ex parte* order for _____, upon two (2) working days notice to the party who obtained such order (or in such shorter notice as the court may prescribe), you shall be allowed to appear before the Court and be heard regarding the issuance of this order."

Adopted Jan. 30, 2007, effective Jan. 1, 2007. Amended effective Sept. 1, 2012.

LR22–FR00 Rule 308. EXPEDITED HEARINGS

An expedited hearing is a proceeding in open Court where the evidence is presented in summary narrative fashion by counsel or the parties, pro se, accompanied by the submission of documentary evidence when applicable. The Court may question the parties or counsel. Formal rules of evidence and procedure shall not apply, except that the Court shall endeavor to insure that traditional concepts of trustworthiness of evidence and fundamental fairness are observed.

All requests for enforcement or modification of existing orders and decrees may first be scheduled for an "expedited" hearing. Each party shall bring to the expedited hearing all documentary evidence as required by these Local Rules. All persons seeking relief, and any party opposing the relief sought, are required to attend the expedited hearing. The parties shall first meet in a settlement conference at least thirty (30) minutes prior to the scheduled hearing. If they are unable to agree, the Court will hear and determine the matters at issue between the parties at the expedited hearing.

Any party, in open Court at the commencement of the expedited hearing, may demand an evidentiary hearing at which all rules of trial procedure and evidence will be observed. If such demand is made, the matters then at issue between the parties will be scheduled, heard, and determined at such evidentiary hearing. The Court may, however, conduct an expedited hearing to consider and determine any emergency matters or other necessary temporary orders until the evidentiary hearing can be held. The Court may, on its own motion, either before or after the expedited hearing, decline to determine any issues on the evidence presented at such hearing and shall thereafter scheduled such issues for evidentiary hearing.

Adopted Jan. 30, 2007, effective Jan. 1, 2007.

LR22–FR00 Rule 309.   FINAL HEARING ON DIS-SOLUTION OF MARRIAGE

A.   Scheduling.   A final hearing on a Petition for Dissolution of Marriage shall be set by the Court in accordance with Local Civil Rule LR22–TR16–106(E) if the cause is contested.   If the cause is not contested, a final hearing shall be held at such time as is mutually convenient to the parties and the Court or at such time as generally set by the Court for hearings on uncontested matters.

B.   Expedited Hearing.   Any party may request that the Final Hearing on a Petition for Dissolution of Marriage be held under the procedure for an expedited hearing.   Such request shall be made in writing and filed with the Court.   Unless the other party files, within ten (10) working days, a written objection to proceeding in expedited fashion, the Court will schedule the trial for an expedited hearing under the procedures outlined in Local Family Rule LR22–FR00–308.

C.   Notice in Uncontested Action.   In an uncontested action, written notice of an intention to proceed to final hearing on a date and time certain shall be given to a party not represented by counsel.   The written notice shall be sent to the last known address of the party not represented and proof of service shall not be required, however, a copy of said notice shall be submitted to the Court at the time of the final hearing.

D.   Summary   Disposition/Attachments   Required.   A summary disposition on a Petition for Dissolution of Marriage shall be entered by the Court upon submission of the appropriate documentation to the Court in accordance with statutory requirements.

In all summary dispositions in which child support is established, a copy of the child support guideline worksheet shall be attached as an exhibit with the affirmation thereon executed by the parties.   In cases where there is a deviation from the child support guidelines, an adequate explanation for such a deviation must be set forth in the summary disposition decree.

In all summary dispositions in which parenting time is referenced in the settlement agreement/dissolution decree, the parties shall certify that they have received a copy of the Indiana Parenting Time Guidelines and that they have read and understand the same.

Adopted Jan. 30, 2007, effective Jan. 1, 2007.   Amended effective Sept. 1, 2012.

LR22–FR00   Rule   310. SUBMISSION   OF AGREED MATTERS

No agreed matter shall be submitted to the Court unless it is in writing and signed by the parties and/or counsel and accompanied with other appropriate documents.   However, if the parties reach an agreement just prior to hearing or trial, then the Court may accept evidence of that settlement by way of a hand-written entry or on the record followed by the submission of a written agreement within a reasonable time thereafter.

Adopted Jan. 30, 2007, effective Jan. 1, 2007.

LR22–FR00   Rule   311. EXHIBIT REQUIREMENTS FOR CONTESTED HEARINGS

In all contested hearings, each party shall submit the following exhibits to the Court, if applicable.

(a) A Child Support Guideline Worksheet.

(b) A calculation of the child support arrearage.

(c) A listing of the marital assets with an indication of fair market value.

(d) A listing of the marital debts with an indication of the balance due and the minimum monthly payment requirement.

(e) The parties' proposed distribution of marital assets and debts.

Adopted Jan. 30, 2007, effective Jan. 1, 2007.

LR22–FR00 Rule 312.   SERVICE ON REDOCKETED MATTERS

A.   Trial Rule 4 Service Required.   Service of process on a party in post-dissolution actions, such as petitions for modifications and applications for rule to show cause, must comply with Trial Rule 4 of the Indiana Rules of Trial Procedure.   Service of process upon the attorney who represented the party in the underlying dissolution action shall be deemed insufficient.

B.   Termination of Appearance.   The appearance of an attorney for, and his or her representation of, a party shall be conclusively presumed to be withdrawn or terminated five (5) days from the expiration of the time within which a Notice of Appeal must be filed.

Adopted Jan. 30, 2007, effective Jan. 1, 2007.

LR22–FR00 Rule 313.   CHILD SUPPORT MODIFICATIONS

Unless waived by the parties in writing or by Order of the Court, a hearing on a Petition to Modify a child support obligation established by an Order of Dissolution of Marriage, an Order Establishing Paternity, an Order Decreeing a Legal Separation, or an Order Establishing Child Support Obligation, will not be scheduled until discovery has been completed and notice of compliance is filed with the Court.   The Court shall then schedule a hearing on the pending Petition to Modify.

Adopted Jan. 30, 2007, effective Jan. 1, 2007.

LR22–FR00 Rule 314.   ORDER FOR PROTECTION

A.   Pursuant to Local Rule (Civil) LR22–TR00–117 all Petitions for an Order for Protection must be filed in the Floyd Superior Court #3.

B. Pursuant to I.C. 34–26–5–6(4), if a person who petitions for an ex parte Order for Protection also has a pending case involving:

(1) the respondent; or

(2) a child of the petitioner and the respondent;

Floyd Superior Court #3 shall immediately consider the petition and act thereon and then transfer the Protection Order case to the Court in which the other case is pending.

C. The Protection Order case shall be maintained with the pending DR, RS, JP, JT, JC, JS, JM, JD, or GU case, however, the cases are not consolidated.

D. All pleadings, hearings and orders pertaining to a Protection Order shall be in the Protection Order case. An attorney who also represents a party in a related Family Law case must file a separate written appearance in the Protective Order case.

Adopted effective Nov. 1, 2012.

LR22–FR00 Appendix 1.   FINANCIAL DISCLOSURE FORM

FINANCIAL DISCLOSURE FORM
NOTICE

YOU ARE HEREBY NOTIFIED THAT YOU MUST FILE YOUR **VERIFIED FINANCIAL DISCLOSURE STATEMENT** WITH THE OPPOSING PARTY WITHIN 45 DAYS OF THE FILING DATE OF THIS CASE. FAILURE TO COMPLY WILL RESULT IN YOUR ADMITTING ALL INFORMATION CONTAINED IN THE OPPOSING PARTY'S VERIFIED FINANCIAL DISCLOSURE STATEMENT.

THE **VERIFIED FINANCIAL DISCLOSURE STATEMENTS** CAN BE OBTAINED FROM THE COURT WHERE THIS ACTION IS FILED.

FINANCIAL DISCLOSURE STATEMENT
COMMENTARY

The form included herein is intended to expedite and facilitate the preparation for trial and disposition of contested marriage dissolution cases.

It is for use in all dissolution cases in which distribution of property is an issue. It is intended also to facilitate a full disclosure of all assets of the parties and should be supplemented where necessary to accomplish that purpose. If needed, use additional sheets and attach with appropriate references.

The parties shall stipulate in writing those assets and liabilities and other matters as to which there is no disagreement.

When supplying the information called for, give the actual or, where the nature of the assets requires, the appraised or estimated value (indicating which) of each asset at the date of the final separation of the parties.

If any asset is located outside the jurisdiction of this Court, state where it is located and, if necessary, give details on a separate sheet. Indicate how much of the value of each asset held in joint ownership was contributed by the husband (h) and how much by the wife (w).

The parties shall state under oath that they have made full disclosure of assets and liabilities.

The Court recognizes that this form calls for information that may not be appropriate in every case. In those cases in which it is not totally inappropriate, merely supply information appropriate to the case at hand and indicate those inquiries that are not applicable.

STATE OF INDIANA   )   IN THE FLOYD _____ COURT
) SS: CAUSE NO _____
COUNTY OF FLOYD   )

IN RE THE MARRIAGE OF
_____
Petitioner
            vs
_____
Respondent

VERIFIED FINANCIAL DISCLOSURE STATEMENT

In accordance with Local Rules and Indiana Trial Rules 33 and 34, the undersigned, Petitioner or Respondent, herewith submits the following VERIFIED FINANCIAL DISCLOSURE STATEMENT:

I. **PRELIMINARY INFORMATION**

Full Name _____
Address _____
Date of Birth _____
Social Security No _____

Date of Marriage _____
Spouse's Name _____
Spouse's Social Security No _____
Spouse's Date of Birth _____
Children:

    Name _____ Age _____ DOB _____
    Name _____ Age _____ DOB _____
    Name _____ Age _____ DOB _____
    Name _____ Age _____ DOB _____

Name of Health Care Provider(s): _____ Weekly Cost: _____
Name of Health Insurance Company: _____
    Weekly Cost: Single Plan _____; Family Plan _____
Extraordinary Medical Expenses: _____
Extraordinary Educational Expenses: _____

II. INCOME INFORMATION

A. EMPLOYMENT

Current Employer _____
Address _____
Telephone No _____ Length of Employment _____
Job Description _____

Gross Income   _____   _____   _____   _____
                Per Week   Bi–Weekly   Per Month   Yearly

Net Income   _____   _____   _____   _____
              Per Week   Bi–Weekly   Per Month   Yearly

B. EMPLOYMENT HISTORY FOR LAST 5 YEARS

Employer	Dates of Employment	Compensation (Per/Wk/Mo/Yr)
_____	_____	_____
_____	_____	_____
_____	_____	_____
_____	_____	_____
_____	_____	_____

C. OTHER INCOME

List other sources of income; including but not limited to Dividends, Earned Interest, Rents, Public Assistance (AFDC), Social Security, Worker's Compensation, Child Support from prior marriage, Military or Other Retirement, Unemployment Compensation, etc.

Source	Amounts Received	Reason for Entitlement
_____	_____	_____
_____	_____	_____
_____	_____	_____

Fringe Benefits; including but not limited to Company Automobile, Health Insurance, Club Memberships, Cafeteria Plan, etc.

Type of Benefit	Annual Value
_____	_____

_____   _____
_____   _____
_____   _____

III. **REQUIRED INCOME VERIFICATION**

You are required by the Trial Court to attach the following:
1.   Your three most recent paycheck stubs.
2.   A full and complete copy including schedules of your last Federal Income Tax Return.
3.   The first page of your last State Income Tax Return.

IV. **PROPERTY**

A. MARITAL RESIDENCE

Description _____
_____
Location _____
Date Acquired _____
Purchase Price _____ Down Payment _____
Source of Down Payment _____
Current Indebtedness _____
Monthly Payment _____
Current Fair Market Value _____
B. OTHER REAL PROPERTY

Description _____
_____
Location _____
Date Acquired _____
Purchase Price _____ Down Payment _____
Source of Down Payment _____
Current Indebtedness _____
Monthly Payment _____
Current Fair Market Value _____

C. PERSONAL PROPERTY (Automobiles, Boats, Furnishings, Household Goods, Jewelry, Motorcycles, Tractors, Trucks, etc. [Attach additional pages if necessary])

Description	Date Acquired	Purchase Price	Indebtedness	Payment	Current Value
_____	_____	_____	_____	_____	_____
_____	_____	_____	_____	_____	_____
_____	_____	_____	_____	_____	_____
_____	_____	_____	_____	_____	_____
_____	_____	_____	_____	_____	_____
_____	_____	_____	_____	_____	_____
_____	_____	_____	_____	_____	_____
_____	_____	_____	_____	_____	_____
_____	_____	_____	_____	_____	_____
_____	_____	_____	_____	_____	_____
_____	_____	_____	_____	_____	_____

_____ _____ _____ _____ _____ _____ _____

_____ _____ _____ _____ _____ _____ _____

V. BANK ACCOUNTS TO WHICH THE PETITIONER/RESPONDENT HAS HAD A DIRECT OR INDIRECT INTEREST WITHIN THE LAST 3 YEARS (This includes any bank account to which the Petitioner or Respondent has deposited money)

Name	Description	Account No	Date Opened	Balance Date Separated	Current Balance
_____	_____	_____	_____	_____	_____
_____	_____	_____	_____	_____	_____
_____	_____	_____	_____	_____	_____
_____	_____	_____	_____	_____	_____
_____	_____	_____	_____	_____	_____
_____	_____	_____	_____	_____	_____

VI. STOCKS, BONDS AND CD'S

Name of Depository	Description & No	Date Acquired	Balance Date Separated	Current Balance
_____	_____	_____	_____	_____
_____	_____	_____	_____	_____
_____	_____	_____	_____	_____
_____	_____	_____	_____	_____
_____	_____	_____	_____	_____

VII. INSURANCE POLICIES

Company	Owner	Policy No	Beneficiary	Cash Value	Face Value
_____	_____	_____	_____	_____	_____
_____	_____	_____	_____	_____	_____
_____	_____	_____	_____	_____	_____

VIII. RETIREMENT BENEFITS, IRA, KEOGH, PENSION, ETC.

Company	Type of Plan	Account No	Value
_____	_____	_____	_____
_____	_____	_____	_____
_____	_____	_____	_____
_____	_____	_____	_____

IX. INTEREST IN BUSINESS

Name of Business   Type (Corp, Part., Sole Owner)   % Owned   Estimated Value

_____ _____ _____ _____

_____ _____ _____ _____

_____ _____ _____ _____

X. DEBTS (Including but not limited to Mortgages, Charge Cards, Loans, Credit Union, Etc.; attach separate list if necessary

Creditor	Account No	Monthly Payment	Current Balance	Balance Date of Filing

Total Monthly Payment ....$ _____

Total Debts Owed ....$ _____

XI. MONTHLY EXPENSES

Housing (Rent or Mortgage) _____   Transportation

2nd Mortgage _____   (a) Gas/Oil _____

Gas/Electric _____   (b) Car Repairs _____

Water/Sewer _____   Car Payment _____

Telephone _____   Home Ins. _____

Garbage Pickup _____   Property Tax _____

Food _____   Charge Accounts

Medical (Self) _____   (a) Name _____

Balance _____

Monthly Pmt _____

Medical (Children) _____

Dental (Self) _____   (b) Name _____

Balance _____

Monthly Pmt _____

Dental Children _____

(c) Name _____

Med/Dental Insurance _____ Balance _____
                                    Monthly Pmt _____

Cleaning/Laundry _____
                                    (d) Name _____
Hair Care _____   Balance _____
                                    Monthly Pmt _____

Toiletries _____
                                    (e) Name _____
School Lunch _____   Balance _____
                                    Monthly Pmt _____

School Tuition _____

School Supplies _____   Other _____

Newspaper _____   Other _____

Cablevision _____   Other _____

Total Monthly Expenses $ _____

XII. **ASSETS ACQUIRED PRIOR TO OR DURING THE MARRIAGE OR THROUGH INHERITANCE OR GIFT (Whether now owned or not)**
(Show significant assets only)
A. ASSETS OWNED BY YOU PRIOR TO THE MARRIAGE
(Value as of the date of marriage)

Asset	Gross Value	Less: Lien/ Mortgage	Net Value	Valuation Date
_____	_____	_____	_____	_____
_____	_____	_____	_____	_____
_____	_____	_____	_____	_____
_____	_____	_____	_____	_____
_____	_____	_____	_____	_____

B. ASSETS ACQUIRED BY YOU DURING THE MARRIAGE
(Value as of the date of acquisition)

Asset	Gross Value	Less: Lien/ Mortgage	Net Value	Valuation Date
_____	_____	_____	_____	_____

Acquired from _____

| _____ | _____ | _____ | _____ | _____ |

Acquired from _____

| _____ | _____ | _____ | _____ | _____ |

Acquired from _____

| _____ | _____ | _____ | _____ | _____ |

Acquired from _____

XIII. **SUMMARY OF ASSETS AND LIABILITIES AS OF DATE OF FINAL SEPARATION**

Asset	Husband's Name	Wife's Name	Jointly Held	Total

Family Dwelling   _____ _____ _____ _____

Other Real Property   _____ _____ _____ _____

Bank or Savings Accts   _____ _____ _____ _____

Stocks/Bonds/Securities   _____ _____ _____ _____

Notes & Accts Receivable   _____ _____ _____ _____

Furniture/Motor Vehicles   _____ _____ _____ _____

Life Ins–Cash Surrender Value _____ _____ _____ _____

Retirement Funds–Vested   _____ _____ _____ _____

Business Interests   _____ _____ _____ _____

Other Assets   _____ _____ _____ _____

    Total Assets $_____ $_____ $_____ $_____

    Liabilities
General Creditors   _____ _____ _____ _____

Mortgage on Family Dwelling _____ _____ _____ _____

Mortgages on Other Real Estate _____ _____ _____ _____

Notes to Banks and Others _____ _____ _____ _____

Loans on Insurance Policies _____ _____ _____ _____

Other Liabilities   _____ _____ _____ _____

    Total Liabilities $_____ $_____ $_____ $_____

ASSETS MINUS LIABILITIES $_____ $_____ $_____ $_____

XIV.   PERSONAL STATEMENT REGARDING DIVISION OF PROPERTY

Indiana law presumes that the marital property be split on a 50/50 basis. However, the Judge may order a division which may differ from an exact 50/50 division of your property. Please provide a brief statement as to your reasons, if there be any, why the Court should divide your property on anything other than a 50/50 basis.

_____

_____

XV.   VERIFICATION & DUTY TO SUPPLEMENT OR AMEND

I affirm, under penalties for perjury, that the foregoing representations are true to the best of my knowledge and belief. Further, I understand that I am under a duty to supplement or amend this VERIFIED FINANCIAL DISCLOSURE STATEMENT prior to trial if I learn that the information which has been provided is either incorrect or that the information provided is no longer true.

SO DECLARED this ___ day of _____, ___.

_____
Signature

CERTIFICATE OF SERVICE

I hereby certify that a true and accurate copy of the foregoing Verified Financial Disclosure Statement was this ___ day of _____, ___, delivered to the opposing party or their attorney of record [list names and addresses] either in person, or by U.S. Mail-postage prepaid, or by Courthouse Mailbox.

Petitioner/Respondent by Counsel or Pro se

NOTICE: THIS VERIFIED FINANCIAL DISCLOSURE STATEMENT IS TO BE TREATED AS A REQUEST FOR ADMISSIONS TO THE RECIPIENT. SHOULD THE RECIPIENT FAIL TO PREPARE AND SEND HIS STATEMENT, THEN THE STATEMENTS CONTAINED HEREIN WILL BE DEEMED ADMITTED BY THE COURT.

YOU ARE FURTHER NOTIFIED THAT YOU HAVE 45 DAYS FROM THE DATE OF FILING IN THIS DISSOLUTION ACTION TO DELIVER YOUR VERIFIED FINANCIAL DISCLOSURE STATEMENT.

Adopted Jan. 30, 2007, effective Jan. 1, 2007.

HAMILTON COUNTY LOCAL
ADMINISTRATIVE
RULES

**Adopted as General Rules Effective July 1, 2000, and
as Administrative Rules Effective June 1, 2005**

Including Amendments Received Through November 1, 2013

Research Notes

Annotations to the Hamilton County Local Administrative Rules are available in West's Annotated Indiana Code, *Title 34 Appendix.*

These rules may be searched electronically on WESTLAW *in the* IN-RULES *database; updates to these rules may be found on Westlaw in* IN-RULESUPDATES. *For search tips and a summary of database content, consult the Westlaw Scope Screens for each database.*

LR29–AR00 Rule 101.   Court Hours

101.10   The Hamilton County Circuit and Superior Courts shall be in session Monday through Friday, legal holidays excluded, and during such other hours as each court may, from time to time, direct or otherwise post.

Adopted as General Rule 101, effective July 1, 2000. Renumbered as Administrative Rule 101 and amended effective June 1, 2005; amended effective August 12, 2007.

LR29–AR00 Rule 102.   Court Closing

102.10   When weather conditions or other emergencies arise, any court closing shall be made by the judge of the Court after consultation with County Officials and the Sheriff. The Court shall make a reasonable effort to contact litigants scheduled for court if the Chronological Case Summary has the addresses and telephone numbers of the attorneys or pro se litigants.

102.20   The Court shall not be responsible for contacting attorneys and pro se litigants if the Chronological Case Summary does not contain a current address where notices and orders are to be sent and a current telephone number where the attorney or pro se litigant can be reached during normal business hours.

Adopted as General Rule 102, effective July 1, 2000. Renumbered as Administrative Rule 102 and amended effective June 1, 2005. Amended effective August 12, 2007.

LR29–AR12 Rule 103.   Facsimile Transmissions

103.10   As outlined below, facsimile filing is permitted in the Circuit and Superior Courts of Hamilton County. The Courts authorize the Hamilton County Clerk of Courts to accept pleadings, motions and other papers by electronic facsimile transmission for filing in any case pending before the Courts, subject to the following requirements:

a.   The transmission must be accompanied by a cover sheet meeting the requirements of the Indiana Supreme Court Administrative Rule 12 (D).

b.   The transmission must include any proposed orders as required by LR29–TR77–202.

c.   The transmission may not exceed ten (10) pages in length including the cover sheet and proposed CCS entry.

d.   The sending party must keep and maintain the transmission log required by Indiana Supreme Court Administrative Rule 12(B)(3) and (4).

e.   The electronic facsimile transmission will not be accepted for filing if its filing requires the payment of any fee other than the electronic facsimile transcription fee set forth in paragraph 103.20 of this rule.

f.   If the filing requires the immediate attention of the Judge, it shall so indicate in bold letters in an accompanying transmittal memorandum.

g.   Legibility of documents and timeliness of filing is the responsibility of the sender.

103.20 Pursuant to Ordinance adopted by the Hamilton County Board of Commissioners, the Clerk shall collect an electronic facsimile transcription fee of One Dollar ($1.00) per page, to a maximum of Ten Dollars ($10.00) per transmission, for each electronic facsimile transmission accepted for filing with the Hamilton County Circuit and Superior Courts. The fee shall be assessed against the sending party and shall be paid upon receipt of invoice by that party and at the latest within 30 days of the transmission. In the event the fee is not paid by the sending party within the time limits provided, the court may issue a show-cause order or enter a judgment in the matter. The Clerk may refuse an electronic facsimile transmission from any attorney or *pro se* litigant who has failed to pay these fees within 30 days.

103.30 Electronic facsimile transmissions will be accepted for filing only during the regular business hours as set forth in LR29–AR00–101. Transmissions received by the Hamilton County Clerk after close of business shall be filed effective the next regular business day.

103.40 The Clerk shall accept electronic facsimile transmission filings only if received at the facsimile machine assigned by the Clerk. The telephone number designated to receive such transmissions is 317–776–9727.

103.50 A party shall not send pleadings, motions and other papers by electronic facsimile transmission for filing directly to any Court without that Court'S prior approval to do so.

Adopted as General Rule 113, effective July 1, 2000. Re-numbered as Administrative Rule 103 and amended effective June 1, 2005. Amended effective August 12, 2007; May 1, 2011; January 1, 2012.

LR29–AR00 Rule 104. Plan for Allocation of Judicial Resources

104.10 The Circuit and Superior Courts of Hamilton County have previously adopted various rules concerning the filing of certain types of matters in the Hamilton County Circuit and Superior Courts. Unless changed by addition, amendment and/or deletion, those rules remain in effect. In conjunction with the adoption of this Local Rule and plan, the following Hamilton County Local Rules also affect the allocation of judicial resources: LR29–AR00–105. Protective Orders; LR29–AR00–110. Assignment of Infraction and Ordinance Violation Cases; LR29–TR76–210. Transfer of Small Claims, Infraction and Ordinance Violations Cases and Protective Orders in the Event of Disqualification; LR29–CR00–301. Criminal Random Filing; LR29–CR00–302. Clerk Procedures to Accomplish Criminal Random Filing; LR29–CR00–303. Filing Rule; LR29–CR00–304. Filing Felony Cases Arising From Juvenile Waiver Hearings; LR29–DN01–602. Rules for Trial De Novo Following Civil Judgments; LR29–DN02–603. Rules for Trial De Novo Following Judgments for Infractions or Ordinance Violations; LR29–PR00–702. Filing of Pleadings; and, LR29–JV00–801. Assignment of Juvenile Case Numbers.

104.20 All requests for a prosecutor subpoena shall be filed in Superior Court No. 6.

104.30 Pursuant to IC 33–33–29–8, Superior Courts No. 4, 5, and 6 each have a standard small claims and misdemeanor division.

104.40 The judges of the Courts of record of Hamilton County shall meet at least once annually for the purpose of reviewing the weighted caseload of each court, and at such other times as may be required either by the Courts themselves or to comply with new orders of the Indiana Supreme Court or to comply with the District Plan.

104.50 The judge of the Circuit Court may with the consent of the judge of a receiving Superior Court, transfer any action either filed and/or docketed in the Circuit Court to the Superior Court to be re-docketed and disposed of as if originally filed with the receiving Superior Court. The judge of a Superior Court may, with the consent of the judge of the receiving Circuit Court or other receiving Superior Court, transfer any action either filed and/or docketed in the Superior Court to the Circuit Court or the other Superior Court to be re-docketed and disposed of as if originally filed with the receiving Court.

Adopted as General Rule 116, effective July 1, 2000. Re-numbered as Administrative Rule 104 and amended effective June 1, 2005. Amended effective August 12, 2007; July 1, 2012; April 1, 2013.

LR29–AR00 Rule 105. Protective Orders Under IC 5–2–9–2.1

105.10 Protective Order Filing:

a. All protective orders (PO) shall be filed in Superior Court No. 6.

b. Once the PO has been acted upon, if there is a related dissolution action pending in any other Hamilton County Court, the PO will be transferred to said court and consolidated with said action for hearing purposes.

c. For a change of judge pursuant to Trial Rule 76(B) or 79(C), see LR29–TR76–210.50.

d. From time to time, the Courts may provide orders to assist the Clerk in implementing the Protective Orders Filing procedures.

Adopted as General Rule 110, effective July 1, 2000. Repealed effective July 1, 2002. Adopted as Rule 105, effective August 12, 2007.

LR29–AR00 Rule 106. Fees for the Hamilton County C.A.R.E. Program

106.10 The Judges of Hamilton County have established the following fees for the Hamilton County Court Assisted Rehabilitative Effort ("C.A.R.E.") program:

Case Management . . . . $ 50
Assessment only $150
Assessment and Education
   program . . . . not to exceed $400

Adopted as General Rule 120, effective July 1, 2000. Re-numbered as Administrative Rule 106 and amended effective June 1, 2005. Amended effective August 12, 2007; January 1, 2012.

LR29–AR00 Rule 107. Duplication Fees

107.10 The Judges of the Hamilton County, in order to comply with IC 5–14–3–8, have established the following fees for duplication of audio and video media when permitted by the Court:

Audio Tape $3.00/each
Video Tape $5.00/each
CD $5.00/each

Adopted effective June 1, 2005. Amended effective August 12, 2007.

LR29–AR00 Rule 108. Possession of Deadly Weapons in Court

108.10 No person shall possess a deadly weapon in the Court, court offices, or in the hallways or areas adjacent to such court.

108.20 "Deadly weapon" is defined as follows:

a. A loaded or unloaded firearm;

b. A weapon, device, taser (as defined in IC 35–47–8–3) or electronic stun weapon (as defined in IC 35–47–8–1), equipment, chemical substance, or other material that in the manner it is used, or could ordinarily be used, or is intended to be used, is readily capable of causing serious bodily injury.

108.30 The Hamilton County Sheriff may establish any and all necessary procedures needed to carry out this rule.

108.40 The Hamilton County Sheriff and/or law enforcement officers shall search and seize all deadly weapons in violation of this rule. All seized deadly weapons shall be held by the Sheriff'S Department until further Order of the Court.

108.50 The Hamilton County Sheriff and/or law enforcement officers may detain persons which they have reason to believe possess such deadly weapons in violation of this rule long enough to obtain proper name, address, date of birth and social security number and/or to seize such deadly weapon.

108.60 Any person who possesses a deadly weapon in violation of this rule shall be immediately brought before the Court for a Direct Contempt Hearing.

108.70 This rule does not apply to any law enforcement officer while on active duty and after first obtaining permission from the Judge of the Court in which he/she is to appear and/or Judicial Officer.

Adopted effective June 1, 2005. Amended effective August 12, 2007.

LR29–AR15 Rule 109. COURT REPORTERS AND PROCEDURES

109.10 The Official Court Reporter serving each court has not only the duties assigned by the Court she or he serves but also certain statutory duties. The purpose of this Rule is to establish personnel policies relating to the Court Reporters' special duties.

109.15 Definitions:

a. Court Reporter is a person who is specifically designated by a court to perform the official court reporting services for the Court including preparing a transcript of the record.

b. Equipment means all physical items owned by the Court or other governmental entity and used by a court reporter in performing court reporting services. Equipment shall include, but not be limited to, telephones, computer hardware, software programs, disks, tapes and any other device used for recording and storing, and transcribing electronic data.

c. Work space means that portion of the Court's facilities dedicated to each court reporter, including but not limited to actual space in the courtroom and any designated office space.

d. Page means the page unit of a transcript which results when a recording is transcribed in the form required by Indiana Rule of Appellate Procedure 7.2.

e. Recording means the electronic, mechanical, stenographic or other recording made as required by Indiana Rule of Trial Procedure 74.

f. Regular hours worked means those hours which the Court is regularly scheduled to work during any given work week. Hamilton County required work hours are 37–1/2 per week.

g. Gap hours worked means those hours worked that are in excess of the regular hours worked but hours not in excess of forty (40) hours per work week.

h. Overtime hours worked means those hours worked in excess of forty (40) hours per work week.

i. Work week means a seven (7) consecutive day week that consistently begins and ends on the same days throughout the year, i.e., Sunday through Saturday, Wednesday through Tuesday, Friday through Thursday.

j. Court means the particular court for which the court reporter performs services. Court may also mean a group of courts, i.e., county courts.

k. County indigent transcript means a transcript that is paid for from county funds and is for the use on behalf of a litigant who has been declared indigent by a court.

l. State indigent transcript means a transcript that is paid for from state funds and is for the use on behalf of a litigant who has been declared indigent by a court.

m.   Private transcript means a transcript, including but not limited to a deposition transcript, that is paid for by a private party.

109.20   A court reporter shall be permitted to type transcripts of official court proceedings during county-compensated hours.   Equipment and supplies shall be used for the recording and/or preparation of such transcripts.   If the recording or preparation of such transcripts requires overtime, such court reporter will be either paid overtime or given compensatory time.

109.25   A court reporter shall be paid an annual salary for time spent working under the control, direction, and direct supervision of the court during all regular work hours, gap hours, or overtime hours.

109.30   The amount of the annual salary of each court reporter shall be set by each court subject to the approval of the Hamilton County Council.

109.35   The annual salary paid to the court reporter shall be for a fixed scheduled 37–1/2 regular working hours per week.

109.40   The court reporter shall, if requested or ordered, prepare any transcript during regular working hours.

109.45   In the event that preparing a transcript could not be completed during regular working hours, a court reporter shall be entitled to additional compensation beyond regular salary under the two options set forth below:

a.   Gap hours shall be paid in the amount equal to the hourly rate of the annual salary; and overtime hours shall be paid in the amount of 1–1/2 times the hourly rate of the annual salary; or

b.   Compensatory time off from regular work hours shall be given in the amount equal to the number of gap hours worked; and compensatory time off from regular work hours shall be given in the amount of 1–1/2 times the number of overtime hours worked.

109.50   Each court and each court reporter may freely negotiate between themselves as to which of the two options may be utilized and the Court and court reporter shall enter into a written agreement designating the terms of such agreement.

109.55   A court reporter may charge $4.75 per page for county and state indigent transcripts.   A court reporter shall submit directly to the county a claim for preparation of county indigent transcripts.

109.60   A court reporter may, at the request of another official court reporter, agree to prepare court proceedings of another court.   Such preparation shall not be done on county-compensated hours, but county equipment and supplies may be used.   In addition, a court reporter may do private recording or preparation of depositions, but a court reporter shall not do any recording or preparation of private depositions during county- compensated hours, and county equipment and supplies shall not be used for recording or preparation of such depositions.

109.65   A court reporter may charge a maximum of $4.75 per page for a transcript prepared for a private party; i.e., either a hearing transcript or deposition transcript.

109.70   The court reporter shall report on an annual basis to the State Court Administrator all transcript fees, whether county indigent, state indigent, or private received by the court reporter.

109.75   Modification of this policy may be made to meet the security, scheduling or other unique needs of a particular case.   Any modification shall be by written order of the Court.   An individual requesting modification of this policy should provide the Court a factual and/or legal basis for such request and specifically set forth what items are being requested.

(Form AR15–109)

Adopted as General Rule 119, effective July 1, 2000.   Renumbered as Administrative Rule 109 and amended effective June 1, 2005.   Amended effective Aug. 12, 2007; Nov. 30, 2009, effective Jan. 1, 2010; April 29, 2010, effective Jan. 1, 2010; Sept. 1, 2011, effective Jan. 1, 2012; March 12, 2013, effective April 1, 2013.

LR29–AR00 Rule 110.   Assignment of Infraction (IF) and Ordinance Violation (OV) Case Numbers

110.10   The Clerk shall as near equally as possible assign cause numbers for new filings of all IF and OV case types to Hamilton Superior Courts No. 4, 5, and 6 (i.e., 1/3 in each court).

110.20   The Clerk shall accomplish the above by assigning cause numbers to the courts based upon the first letter of the defendant'S or respondent'S last name or other method as the judges of said courts shall agree.

Adopted and effective August 12, 2007.

LR29–AR00 Rule 111.   Fees for the Hamilton County Drug Court

106.10   The Judges of Hamilton County have established the following fees for the Hamilton County Drug Court:

Administration fee (per admission) $100

Service fee (per month, per referral) .... not to exceed $50

NOTE: Chemical testing fees will be assessed in addition to the Drug Court services fee.

Adopted effective January 1, 2012.

LR29–AR00 Rule 112.   Audio and/or Video Recording of Court Proceedings

112.10   Pursuant to Indiana's Code of Judicial Conduct Rule 2.17, and the inherent authority of the

Court to prevent the disruption of court proceedings, the recording of audio and taking of video or photographs in the courtroom and adjacent hallways is prohibited. The broadcasting, televising, distribution, or possession of any unauthorized photographs or audio and/or video recordings of any court proceedings is also prohibited. The recording of audio and/or taking of video or photographs or the broadcasting, televising, distribution or possession of any such recording, without the prior written approval of the Court, may be punishable as a contempt of court.

112.20 A person who aids, induces, or causes the unauthorized recording of audio and/or taking of video or photographs of court proceedings or a person who broadcasts, televises, distributes or possesses an unauthorized audio or video recording or photograph of a court proceeding is also subject to contempt of court proceedings.

112.30 In order to ensure compliance with and/or to determine if there is a violation of this rule, the Court may order the seizure of any electronic device suspected of containing or being used in the transmission of unauthorized photographs or recordings. In addition to the possible sanctions for contempt, including imposition of a fine and/or commitment to the Hamilton County Jail, the Court may confiscate any audio recording, video recording, or photograph that is in violation of this rule.

Adopted effective July 1, 2012.

LR29–AR07 Rule 113. Custody, Removal, and Disposal of Original Records and Exhibits

113.10   Governed by Local Rules. Except as provided for in Administrative Rule 7, the custody, removal, and disposal of original records and exhibits shall be governed by this rule.

113.20   Time Period for Court Reporter to Maintain Custody. After being marked for identification, all models, diagrams, exhibits and materials (hereinafter "items") offered or admitted into evidence in any case pending or tried in the Hamilton County Circuit and Superior Courts shall be placed in the custody of the Court Reporter and, unless ordered otherwise by the Court, shall not be removed until after the time periods specified below.

a.   *Criminal Cases*:

(1) Misdemeanor, Class C and Class D Felony cases two (2) years after the latest of the following events:

(a) the case is dismissed;

(b) the defendant is found not guilty;

(c) the defendant is sentenced; or

(d) if there was an appeal, the filing of the final order (i.e., the order disposes of all issues) of the reviewing Court in the office of the Clerk.

(2) Class A and Class B Felony and Murder cases twenty (20) years after the latest of the following events:

(a) the case is dismissed;

(b) the defendant is found not guilty;

(c) the defendant is sentenced; or

(d) if there was an appeal, the filing of the final order (i.e., the order disposes of all issues) of the reviewing Court in the office of the Clerk.

b.   *Civil Cases*:

Thirty (30) days after the latest of the following events:

(a) the case is decided; or

(b) if there was an appeal, the filing of the final order (i.e., the order disposes of all issues) of the reviewing Court in the office of the Clerk.

113.30   Time Period for Removal by Parties. Unless ordered otherwise, all items placed in the custody of the Court Reporter shall be removed by the parties or their attorneys who offered them into evidence no later than ninety (90) days after the expiration of the time periods set forth above in subsection 112.20. At the time of removal, a detailed receipt shall be provided by the party removing said items and this receipt will be filed in the case. No motion or order is required prior to the removal of an exhibit pursuant to this subsection.

113.40   Disposal of Un-removed Items. If the parties or their attorneys do not remove the items within the time period set forth in subsection 112.30, the Court may direct disposition or destruction of the items. For all cases decided or otherwise disposed of as to all issues prior to the effective date of this rule, if the parties or their attorneys do not remove the items within sixty (60) days after the effective date of this rule, the Court may direct disposition or destruction.

113.50   Currency and Contraband. Currency exhibits and contraband exhibits, such as controlled substances and weapons, shall be released to the investigative agency at the conclusion of the trial and not placed in the custody of the Court Reporter. A receipt shall be issued and a photograph substituted when such exhibits are released.

113.60   Biologically Contaminated Evidence. A party who offers biologically contaminated evidence must file a pre-trial notice with the Court and serve all the parties so that the Court can consider the issue and rule appropriately before trial.

Adopted effective July 1, 2012.

HAMILTON COUNTY LOCAL TRIAL RULES

**Adopted as General Rules Effective July 1, 2000,
and as Trial Rules Effective June 1, 2005**

Including Amendments Received Through November 1, 2013

Research Notes

Annotations to the Hamilton County Local Trial Rules are available in West's Annotated Indiana Code, *Title 34 Appendix.*

These rules may be searched electronically on Westlaw *in the* IN-RULES *database; updates to these rules may be found on* Westlaw *in* IN-RULESUPDATES. *For search tips and a summary of database content, consult the Westlaw Scope Screens for each database.*

LR29–TR03 Rule 201. Filing of Pleadings and Entry of Appearances

201.10 All pleadings shall be filed with the Hamilton County Clerk with the exception of emergency orders under Trial Rule 65.

201.20 All documents filed in any Hamilton County Court, with the exception of exhibits and existing wills, shall be prepared on paper measuring 8–1/2″ × 11″.

201.30 All attorneys and pro se litigants shall file appearances complying with Trial Rule 3.1.

201.40 Withdrawals of appearances by attorneys shall be permitted only with leave of Court. In both civil and criminal matters, attorneys requesting withdrawal will include in their motion the last known address of their client(s).

201.50 Pursuant to Trial Rule 5(B)(1)(d), the Circuit and Superior Courts of Hamilton County hereby designate the "mail boxes" located in the Clerk's order book office for service of pleadings upon attorneys who have such boxes.

201.60 All pleadings filed with the Court that require a certificate of service shall specifically name the individual party or attorney on whom service has been made, the address, the manner in which service was made and the date when service was made.

201.70 All filings shall be in compliance with the Indiana Rules of Trial Procedure. If the documents received are not in proper form, such deficiencies will not be corrected by court personnel. The Clerk is not required to notify Counsel or litigants of a filing deficiency.

201.80 Filing by facsimile transmission is permitted as set forth in LR29–AR12–103.

Adopted as General Rule 103, effective July 1, 2000. Renumbered as Trial Rule 201 and amended effective June 1, 2005. Amended effective August 12, 2007; January 1, 2012.

LR29–TR77 Rule 202. Proposed Orders

202.10 Each Motion, Petition or other request for relief shall be accompanied by a proposed order. Opposing counsel may submit proposed alternative orders to the Court.

202.20 The Court shall not be required to act on any Motion, Petition or other request for relief unless filed in conformity with these General Rules.

202.30 All proposed orders submitted by counsel pursuant to these General Rules shall meet the following requirements:

a. Contain a complete distribution list of all attorneys and pro se litigants with full addresses.

b. Stamped envelopes appropriately addressed for each attorney of record and/or pro se litigant on the distribution list.

Adopted as General Rule 104, effective July 1, 2000. Renumbered as Trial Rule 202 and amended effective June 1, 2005. Amended effective August 12, 2007; May 1, 2011, effective July 1, 2011; January 1, 2012.

LR29–TR00 Rule 203. Briefs and Memorandums

203.10 Authorities relied upon which are not cited in the Northeastern Reporter system shall be attached to counsel's brief. If the authority is cited for the first time in oral argument, a copy of the authority may be provided to the Court at the time of the argument. Sufficient copies shall be available to provide counsel for each party with a copy.

Adopted as General Rule 114, effective July 1, 2000. Renumbered as Trial Rule 203 and amended effective June 1, 2005. Amended effective August 12, 2007.

LR29–TR79 Rule 204.   Special Judges

204.10 After a special judge is selected, the attorneys or pro se litigants shall add to the caption of all pleadings to the right of the case title the following:

"BEFORE   SPECIAL   JUDGE
_____."

204.20 After a special judge has qualified, a copy of each pleading and Chronological Case Summary entries filed with the Court shall be mailed or delivered to the office of that Special judge by the counsel or pro se litigant with service indicated on the certificate of service.

Adopted as General Rule 105, effective July 1, 2000. Renumbered as Trial Rule 204 and amended effective June 1, 2005. Amended effective August 12, 2007.

LR29–TR00 Rule 205.   Trial Settings

205.10 All requests to schedule trials and hearings shall be in writing and shall contain the following information:

a. Type of trial or hearing (i.e., jury trial, court trial, final hearing in dissolution, etc.).

b. A good-faith estimate of the total court time needed for the trial or hearing.

205.20 Each request under LR29–TR00–205.10 shall be accompanied by a proposed written order with appropriate blanks for date and time and shall further include reference to those items set forth in LR29–TR00–205.10(a) and (b).

205.30 Every opposing attorney or pro se litigant who receives such an order and disputes the estimate of court time needed for the trial or hearing shall notify the Court in writing within ten (10) days of the receipt of the original order and give their own good-faith estimate of the total court time needed.

Adopted as General Rule 106, effective July 1, 2000. Renumbered as Trial Rule 205 and amended effective June 1, 2005. Amended effective August 12, 2007.

LR29–TR53 Rule 206.   Continuances

206.10 Motions for continuance shall be in writing and include the following information:

a. The date and time opposing counsel was advised that a continuance will be requested.

b. Whether opposing counsel agrees with or objects to the request.

c. The date and time of the hearing or trial for which a continuance is being sought.

d. The approximate amount of time needed to elapse before the matter can be heard.

e. A good-faith estimate of the time needed for such hearing or trial when rescheduled.

206.20 Unless good cause is shown, no motions for continuance will be considered unless filed at least five (5) days before a court trial or hearing, and at least ten (10) days before a Jury Trial.

206.30 All motions for continuance shall be accompanied by a proposed order in conformity with LR29–TR77–202 and LR29–TR00–205 containing a space for the Court to set a new date for the hearing or trial.

206.40 When an attorney enters an appearance, it is the attorney's responsibility to review the file and become aware of all previously scheduled hearing dates.

206.50 A signature by an attorney on the request for continuance is certification by that attorney that the client has been notified of the request, agrees to the continuance and to the reason for which the continuance is sought.

Adopted as General Rule 107, effective July 1, 2000. Renumbered as Trial Rule 206 and amended effective June 1, 2005. Amended effective August 12, 2007.

LR29–TR16 Rule 207.   Pre–Trial Conferences

207.10 An attorney who has the authority to stipulate to pre-trial matters shall attend the pre-trial conference.

207.20 The Court may order the parties to provide written pre-trial entries pursuant to Trial Rule 16 at the pre-trial conference.

207.30 The Court may impose sanctions pursuant to Trial Rule 16(k) and Trial Rule 37 for failure to provide written pre-trial entries.

Adopted as General Rule 108, effective July 1, 2000. Renumbered as Trial Rule 207 and amended effective June 1, 2005. Amended effective August 12, 2007.

LR29–TR00 Rule 208.   Trials

208.10 Jury trials shall begin promptly at 9:00 a.m. unless otherwise directed by the Court. The attorneys and the litigants shall report at 8:30 a.m. on the first day of trial or at a time as the Court shall direct.

208.20 The Court reserves the right to require advance settlement conferences.

208.30 Court trials shall begin promptly at the time assigned. The attorneys and the litigants are encouraged to arrive substantially in advance of the scheduled time for the purpose of entering into any last minute stipulations or agreements.

208.40 Trials shall adjourn or conclude between 4:00 p.m. and 4:30 p.m. or as the Court shall direct.

Adopted as General Rule 109, effective July 1, 2000. Renumbered as Trial Rule 208 and amended effective June 1, 2005. Amended effective August 12, 2007.

LR29–TR79 Rule 209. Coordinated Local Rule of the Courts of Hamilton County, Enacted in Compliance With T.R. 79(H)

209.10 Pursuant to Trial Rule 79(H) of the Indiana Rules of Trial Procedure, the Circuit and Superior Courts of Hamilton County, in conjunction with the other Judges of Administrative District 12, i.e., Boone County, Clinton County, and Tipton County, Indiana, have adopted the following rule to establish procedures for the selection of special judges in civil cases. Said rule, as approved by the Supreme Court of Indiana, is as follows:

209.20 Within seven (7) days of the notation in the Chronological Case Summary of an order granting a change of judge or an order of disqualification, the parties, pursuant to Trial Rule 79(D), may agree to any judge eligible under Trial Rule 79(J).

209.30 If a special judge is required to be selected under Trial Rule 79(H) then the special judge shall be selected as follows:

209.30.10 If the case was originally filed in a court of record in Hamilton County, then the judge will be selected randomly from among the regular judges and full time judicial officers of Hamilton County subject to existing local rules regarding case allocation and transfer.

209.30.20 If the case was originally filed in a court of record in Boone, Clinton or Tipton County, then the judge will be selected on a rotating basis from among the regular judges of those counties subject to all local rules in each individual county regarding case allocation and transfer.

209.30.30 If for any reason a judge cannot be selected by the above methods then the special judge shall be selected on a rotating basis from among all the regular judges of the District not already disqualified.

209.40 A special judge selected under 209.30 must accept jurisdiction unless disqualified pursuant to *The Code of Judicial Conduct* or excused from service by the Indiana Supreme Court. The Administrator of Courts for Hamilton County shall maintain a list of the judges eligible for selection under 209.30.20 and a list of the judges eligible for selection under 209.30. 30 and shall be contacted by the selecting court each time a judge must be selected from one of those lists. The Administrator of Courts shall provide the name of the next judge on the appropriate list upon a request from the selecting court and then strike the name of the judge selected from that list. The judge selected in this manner shall not be eligible to be selected again from the same list until all the other judges have been selected from that list except as required to avoid certification to the Indiana Supreme Court.

209.50 In the event that no judicial officer within Administrative District 12 is eligible to serve as a special judge or the particular circumstance of the case warrants selection of a special judge by the Indiana Supreme Court, the judge of the court in which the case is pending shall certify the matter to the Indiana Supreme Court for appointment of a special judge.

Adopted as General Rule 117, effective July 1, 2000. Renumbered as Trial Rule 209 and amended effective June 1, 2005. Amended effective August 12, 2007; July 1, 2011; January 1, 2012; April 1, 2013.

LR29–TR76 Rule 210. Transfer of Small Claims, Infraction and Ordinance Violation Cases in the Event of Disqualification

210.10 For the orderly administration of the small claims, infraction, and ordinance violation dockets of Superior Court No. 4, Superior Court No. 5, and Superior Court No. 6, this Rule shall govern in the event that a judge of a small claims, infraction, or ordinance violation case orders a change of judge pursuant to Trial Rule 76(B) or disqualifies himself or herself pursuant to Trial Rule 79(C).

210.20 In the event that the judge of a small claims, infraction, or ordinance violation case in either Superior Court No. 4, Superior Court No. 5, or Superior Court No. 6 orders a change of judge pursuant to Trial Rule 76(B) or disqualifies himself or herself pursuant to Trial Rule 79(C), a special judge shall be selected by the Clerk by random selection of one of the remaining two (2) courts (i.e., either Superior Court No. 4, Superior Court No. 5, or Superior Court No. 6 as applicable).

210.30 *Protective Orders*: In the event that the judge of Superior Court No. 6 orders a change of judge pursuant to Trial Rule 76(B) or disqualifies himself or herself pursuant to Trial Rule 79(C), a special judge shall be selected by the Clerk by random selection of one of the remaining two (2) courts (i.e., either Superior Court No. 4 or Superior Court No. 5).

Adopted as General Rule 118, effective July 1, 2000. Renumbered as Trial Rule 210 and amended effective June 1, 2005. Amended effective August 12, 2007.

LR29–TR79 Rule 211. Appointment of Special Judge in Superior Court No. 2

211.10 The regular judge of the Hamilton Superior Court No. 2 will be required to disqualify from cases involving family members on a continuing basis, and that, pursuant to Ind. Trial Rule 79(C)(2), appointment of special judges will be required. In the interest of the orderly administration of justice, special judges should be available for such matters on a continuing basis. The Honorable Paul A. Felix is willing to serve in such capacity in Hamilton Superior Court No. 2. In the event the regular judge of the Hamilton Superior Court No.2, the Honorable Daniel J. Pfleging, becomes disqualified, pursuant to Ind. Trial Rule 79(C)(2), in the Hamilton Superior Court No. 2, the Honorable Paul A. Felix is appointed as Special Judge. Should Judge Felix decline to qualify in a particular case, the matter should then be certified to the Indiana Supreme Court pursuant to Ind. Trial Rule 79(H).

Adopted and effective August 12, 2007. Amended effective January 1, 2012.

LR29–TR65 Rule 212. Dissipation of Assets and Removal of Children from the State

212.10 In any Domestic Relations case filed in Hamilton County, the parties shall not, without hearing or security:

a. Transfer, encumber, conceal, sell or otherwise dispose of any joint property of the parties or asset of the marriage except in the usual course of business or for the necessities of life, without the written consent of the parties or the permission of the Court; and/or

b. Remove any child of the parties then residing in the State of Indiana from the State with the intent to deprive the Court of jurisdiction over such child without the prior written consent of all parties or the permission of the Court.

Adopted and effective August 12, 2007.

HAMILTON COUNTY LOCAL CRIMINAL RULES

Adopted Effective July 1, 2000

Including Amendments Received Through November 1, 2013

Research Notes

Annotations to the Hamilton County Local Criminal Rules are available in West's Annotated Indiana Code, *Title 34 Appendix.*

These rules may be searched electronically on Westlaw *in the* IN-RULES *database; updates to these rules may be found on* Westlaw *in* IN-RULESUPDATES. *For search tips and a summary of database content, consult the Westlaw Scope Screens for each database.*

LR29–CR00 Rule 301. Criminal Random Filing

301.10. This Random Filing Rule does not apply to either civil cases or juvenile cases.

301.20. All misdemeanors (except those assigned to Superior Court No. 3 pursuant to Section 301.30 below) shall be randomly filed with 1/3 in Superior Court No. 4, 1/3 in Superior Court No. 5, and 1/3 in Superior Court No. 6 or other method as the judges of said courts shall agree. All class D Felonies (except those assigned to Superior Court No. 3 pursuant to Section 301.30 below) shall be randomly filed with 1/3 in Superior Court No. 4, 1/3 in Superior Court No. 5, and 1/3 in Superior Court No. 6 or other method as the judges of said courts shall agree. Reassignment of these cases shall be achieved by transferring cases originating in Superior Court No. 4 to either Superior Court No. 5 or Superior Court No. 6; transferring cases originating in Superior Court No. 5 to either Superior Court No. 4 or Superior Court No. 6; and, transferring cases originating in Superior Court No. 6 to either Superior Court No. 4 or Superior Court No. 5. In the event a subsequent reassignment is required (and neither Superior Court No. 4, nor Superi-

or Court No. 5, nor Superior Court No. 6 is available) said case assignment shall be achieved by obtaining a new court assignment from all Hamilton County Courts using the Clerk's random assignment procedure.

301.30. Misdemeanor and class D felony battery offenses, strangulation offenses, and invasion of privacy offenses shall be filed in Superior Court No. 3.

301.40. All Murder (MR Case type), Class A (FA Case Type), Class B (FB Case Type), and Class C (FC Case Type)felonies shall be randomly filed per case type with 25% of each case type filed in Circuit Court, Superior Court No. 1, Superior Court No. 2 and Superior Court No. 3.

Reassignment of these cases shall be achieved by obtaining a new court assignment using the Clerk's random assignment procedure of the Courts designated to accept this type of case.

301.50. The Clerk shall use a court-approved procedure which provides a tamper proof method for random assignment consistent with the foregoing paragraphs of this Criminal Rule.

301.60. From time to time, the Courts may provide orders to assist the Clerk in implementing the Criminal Random Filing procedures.

301.70 Pursuant to Indiana Criminal Rule 2.2(c), if a case is dismissed after filing, upon refiling it shall be assigned to the same court where it was originally assigned. Pursuant to Indiana Criminal Rule 2. 2(d), where a change of judge is granted under Indiana Criminal Rule 12(B) or an order of disqualification or recusal is entered, the judge will be selected randomly from among the full-time judicial officers of Hamilton County according to existing local rules regarding case allocation and transfer. If for any reason a judge cannot be selected from among the full-time judicial officers of Hamilton County, then the judge shall be randomly selected from the full-time judicial officers of the contiguous counties and of Administrative District 12. Except for those serving pursuant to Indiana Criminal Rule 12(G)(4), judges previously assigned to the case are ineligible for reassignment. A person appointed to serve as special judge under this subsection must accept jurisdiction in the case unless they are disqualified pursuant to *The Code of Judicial Conduct*, ineligible for service under local rule, or excused from service by the Indiana Supreme Court. The reassignment procedures set forth in this rule shall also apply where a change of judge is granted pursuant to Indiana Post–Conviction Remedy Rule 1.4(b).

301.80. The Clerk shall file subsequent cases against a defendant with a pending case (where a "pending case" is defined under this rule as a criminal case in which there is either no disposition of the charge(s) via a determination of guilt or dismissal or the defendant has not yet been discharged from the sentence imposed, including probation) as follows:

a. When a defendant has a pending case in Circuit Court, Superior Court No. 1, Superior Court No. 2, or Superior Court No. 3, the Clerk shall file any subsequent felony or misdemeanor offenses in the same court as that of the pending case. This paragraph does not apply to D Felony or misdemeanor OWI offenses.

b. When a defendant has a pending case in Superior Court No. 4, or Superior Court No. 5, or Superior Court No. 6, the Clerk shall file any subsequent misdemeanor or class D Felony offenses (except those assigned to Superior Court No. 3 pursuant to Section 301.30) in the same court as that of the pending case.

c. When a defendant's only pending cases are in Superior Court No. 4, or Superior Court No. 5, or Superior Court No. 6, the Clerk shall file any subsequent offenses listed under Sections 301.30 or 301.40 as set forth in Sections 301.30 and 301.40.

d. It shall be the duty of the Prosecuting Attorney or Deputy Prosecuting Attorney to file written notice with the Clerk that a defendant has a pending case that requires the Clerk to follow the filing requirements of this rule.

e. If a conflict arises between Sections 301.30 and 301.80, Sections 301. 30 controls.

f. A Court, at the request of both parties, may transfer a case to another Court where the defendant has a pending case, as defined by this rule, provided that the receiving Court agrees to accept the transfer.

Adopted as Rule 201, effective July 1, 2000. Renumbered as Rule 301 and amended effective June 1, 2005. Amended effective Aug. 12, 2007; Jan. 1, 2009; amended Sept. 1, 2011, effective Jan. 1, 2012; amended effective Jan. 1, 2013; Aug. 19, 2013, effective Jan. 1, 2014.

LR29–CR00 Rule 302. Clerk Procedures to Accomplish Criminal Random Filing

302.10 The Judges of the Hamilton Circuit Court and Hamilton Superior Courts approve the following procedures to be used in the Hamilton County Clerk's office to accomplish the Hamilton County Criminal Random Filing Order.

a. Begin with a set number of cases which is evenly divisible by the applicable number of Hamilton County Courts.

b. Divide the set number of cases by the percentages for each type of case per Court resulting in the number of each type case for each Court which shall equal the percentages.

c. These cases are then pulled and/or selected for individual case number assignment one by one on an impartial random selection basis.

Adopted as Rule 201, effective July 1, 2000. Renumbered as Rule 302 and amended effective June 1, 2005. Amended effective August 12, 2007.

LR29–CR00 Rule 303. Filing Co–Defendants Under Hamilton County Criminal Random Filing Rule

303.10 It is hereby resolved that the following rule applicable to the filing of misdemeanor and felony cases shall be employed in the implementation of the Hamilton County Criminal Random Filing Rule.

a. When the Prosecutor of Hamilton County, individually or through deputy prosecutors, elects to file a felony or misdemeanor case in which two or more individuals or entities are named as Defendants, at the time of the filing of said charges, said Prosecutor or Deputy Prosecutor shall file notice with the Clerk of Hamilton County that said case is to be treated under this rule.

b. Upon receiving notice for treatment of a case under this rule, the Clerk shall take the following action:

(1) First, the Clerk shall randomly select a Court designated to receive the type case being filed under the Random filing rule approved by the Judges of the Hamilton Circuit and Superior Courts,

(2) Second, the first named defendant in the multiple defendant information shall be assigned the next available cause number in the randomly selected Circuit or Superior Court.

(3) Third, the remaining Defendants shall each be assigned the next available cause number in the randomly selected Circuit or Superior Court in the order of their appearance on the charging information.

(4) Fourth, the Clerk shall treat each cause number assigned under this rule as a separate and distinct case, and shall remove from his/her random selection pool the number of cases assigned hereunder in order to maintain the percentage allocations set forth in the Random Filing Rule.

c. Each Defendant's case filed under this rule shall be treated as a separate and distinct case, and Co-defendant's cases will not be consolidated for trial unless said consolidation is approved by separate order of the assigned Judge.

d. The Clerk shall follow this rule only when the State files the co-defendant cases simultaneously.

e. This rule shall remain in full force and effect unless otherwise modified, amended, or repealed by separate written instructions adopted by the Judges of the Hamilton Circuit and Superior Courts.

Adopted as Rule 201, effective July 1, 2000. Renumbered as Rule 303 and amended effective June 1, 2005. Amended effective August 12, 2007.

LR29–CR00 Rule 304. Filing Felony Cases Arising from Juvenile Waiver Hearings Under Hamilton County Random Filing Rule

304.10 The Clerk is ordered to treat new criminal filings which arise from the waiver of a juvenile matter to criminal court as a new criminal matter under the random filing rule and to assign said cause to the Court identified under said rule regardless of which court may have previously exercised juvenile jurisdiction prior to waiver, unless otherwise directed by the waiving court.

Adopted as Rule 201, effective July 1, 2000. Renumbered as Rule 304 and amended effective June 1, 2005. Amended effective August 12, 2007.

LR29–CR00 Rule 305. Appearance Bonds and Release on Personal Recognizance

305.10. Amount of Bond: The Sheriff shall set the initial bond on warrantless arrests according to the Bond Schedule in Appendix A. In setting bonds on warrants, the Courts may use the Bond Schedule in Appendix A as a guideline.

305.20. Separate Bonds: The Circuit and Superior Courts of Hamilton County will only accept appearance bonds written for a single cause number and will not accept lump sum appearance bonds that apply to more than one cause number.

305.30. Conditions of Bond: All appearance bonds posted by defendants and releases on personal recognizance are subject to the following conditions: (a) defendant shall appear in court at all times required by the Court; (b) defendant shall not leave the State of Indiana without the prior written consent of the Court; (c) defendant shall not commit nor be arrested for another criminal offense; (d) defendant shall keep his or her attorney and the Court advised in writing of any change of address within 24 hours of such change; and (e) any other condition ordered by court. Pursuant to IC 35-33-8-3.2(a)(4) a defendant's release may also be conditioned upon refraining from any direct or indirect contact with the alleged victim of an offense or other individual as ordered by the Court. Violation of any condition may result in the Court revoking the defendant's release on bond and issuing a re-arrest warrant.

305.40. Property Bonds: The Circuit and Superior Courts of Hamilton County will grant a defendant's release on a property bond only after notice is sent to the Prosecuting Attorney and a hearing is set to determine whether such a bond is proper.

305.50. Alteration of Bond: If a judicial officer has set the defendant's initial bond, then the judicial officer conducting the initial hearing may not alter the bond. If the Sheriff has initially set the bond according to the Bond Schedule, then the judicial officer who conducts the initial hearing:

a. shall adjust the bond to conform with the actual charges filed by the State;

b. may increase the bond, if an increase is warranted by the circumstances;

c. may reduce the bond, if multiple charges have been filed, to an amount not lower than the highest class bond for one charge (unstacking), if a reduction is warranted by the circumstances; and

d. may release the defendant on his or her own recognizance for medical reasons if recommended by the Sheriff and if notice has been given to the prosecuting attorney.

In all other cases, a Court shall set a motion for a bond reduction for a hearing and the Court shall give notice of the hearing to the prosecuting attorney, defendant's counsel, and such persons required to be notified by law.

Adopted effective June 1, 2005. Amended effective August 12, 2007; January 1, 2012; Jan. 1, 2013.

LR29–CR00 Rule 306. Waiver of Misdemeanor Initial Hearing

306.10 A defendant may waive an initial hearing for one or more misdemeanors only if the defendant is represented by an attorney, the defendant is not incarcerated, and the defendant and attorney comply with this rule.

306.20 If the misdemeanor charges have been filed with the Clerk, the attorney for the defendant must do the following prior to the scheduled initial hearing:

a. Sign a Request for Waiver of Initial Hearing on the [**Form CR00–306**)] approved by the Courts and available at the Magistrate's office; and

b. File a written Appearance, a CCS entry [**Form TR77–202**], and the Request for Waiver of Initial Hearing at the clerk's office. The CCS entry should show the Request for Waiver of Initial Hearing either granted or denied and provide spaces for the Court to fill in the appropriate omnibus date, and dates for any pre-trial and trial settings that the Court would otherwise have set at the initial hearing.

306.30 If the misdemeanor charges have not been filed with the Clerk at the time the attorney wishes to waive the initial hearing, the attorney may do the following:

a. Complete the paperwork required in LR29–CR00–306.20; and

b. Deliver a courtesy copy to the Magistrate's Office along with a copy of the summons for the defendant's scheduled initial hearing date.

306.40 If an attorney attempts to waive the initial hearing prior to the filing of charges as provided in LR29–CR00–306.30, it is the attorney's responsibility to check with the Magistrate on the scheduled initial hearing date to make sure that the required paperwork was placed with the defendant's file. The magistrate and courts will not be responsible if a court issues a warrant for a defendant's failure to appear for an initial hearing after an attorney has attempted to waive the initial hearing prior to the filing of the charge.

Adopted as Rule 202, effective July 1, 2000. Renumbered as Rule 306 and amended effective June 1, 2005. Amended effective August 12, 2007.

LR29–CR00 Rule 307.   Automatic Discovery

307.10   General Provisions:

a. Within thirty (30) days from the entry of an appearance by an attorney for a defendant, or from the formal filing of charges, whichever occurs later, the State shall disclose all relevant items and information under this rule to the defendant, subject to Constitutional limitations and such other limitation as the Court may specifically provide by separate order, and the defendant shall disclose all relevant items and information under this rule to the State within ten (10) days after the State's disclosure. Both parties shall furnish items disclosed and required to be furnished under this Rule within a reasonable time thereafter.

b. No written motion is required, except:

(1) To compel compliance under this rule;

(2) For additional discovery not covered under this rule;

(3) For a protective order seeking exemption from the provisions of this rule; or,

(4) For an extension of time to comply with this rule.

c. Although each side has a right to full discovery under the terms of this rule, each side has a corresponding duty to seek out the discovery. Failure to do so may result in the waiver of the right to full discovery under this rule.

307.20   State Disclosures:

a. The State shall disclose the following materials and information within its possession or control:

(1) The names and last known addresses of persons whom the State intends to call as witnesses along with copies of their relevant written and recorded statements;

(2) Any written, oral, or recorded statements made by the accused or by a co-defendant, and a list of witnesses to the making and acknowledgment of such statements;

(3) If applicable, the State shall disclose the existence of grand jury testimony of any person whom the prosecuting attorney may call as a witness at any trial or hearing in the case. In addition, the State shall provide a copy of those portions of any transcript of grand jury minutes, within the State's possession, which contain the testimony of such witness or witnesses. If such transcripts do not exist, the defendant may apply to the Court for an order requiring their preparation;

(4) Any reports or statements of experts, made in connection with the particular case, including results of physical or mental examinations and of scientific tests, experiments or comparisons;

(5) Any books, papers, documents, photographs, or tangible objects that the prosecuting attorney intends to use in the hearing or trial or which were obtained from or belong to the accused; and

(6) Any record of prior criminal convictions that may be used for impeachment of the persons whom the State intends to call as witnesses at any hearing or trial.

b. The State shall disclose to the defendant(s) any material or information within its possession or control that tends to negate the guilt of the accused as to the offenses charged or would tend to reduce the punishment for such offenses.

c. The State may perform these disclosure obligations in any manner mutually agreeable to the State and the defendant. Compliance may include a notification to the defendant or defense counsel that material and information being disclosed may be inspected, obtained, tested, copied, or photographed at a specified reasonable time and place.

307.30   Defendant Disclosures:

a. Defendant's counsel (or defendant where defendant is preceding pro se) shall furnish the State with the following material and information within his or her possession or control:

(1) The names and last known addresses of persons whom the defendant intends to call as witnesses along with copies of their relevant written and recorded statements;

(2) Any books, papers, documents, photographs, or tangible objects defendant intends to use as evidence at any trial or hearing;

(3) Any medical, scientific, or expert witness evaluations, statements, reports, or testimony which may be used at any trial or hearing;

(4) Any defense, procedural or substantive, which the defendant intends to make at any hearing or trial; and

(5) Any record of prior criminal convictions known to the defendant or defense counsel that may be used for impeachment of the persons

whom the defense intends to call at any hearing or trial.

307.40 Additions, Limitation, and Protective Orders:

a. Discretionary Disclosures: Upon written request and a showing of materiality, the Court, in its discretion, may require additional disclosure not otherwise covered by this rule.

b. Denial of Disclosure: The Court may deny disclosure required by this rule upon a finding that there is substantial risk to any person of physical harm, intimidation, bribery, economic reprisals, or unnecessary annoyance or embarrassment resulting from such disclosure to defendant or counsel.

c. Matters not subject to Disclosure

(1) Work Product: Disclosure hereunder shall not be required of legal research or records, correspondence, reports, or memoranda to the extent that they contain the opinions, theories, or conclusions of the State or members of its legal or investigative staff, or of defense counsel or counsel's legal or investigative staff; and

(2) Informants: Disclosure of an informant's identity shall not be required where there is a paramount interest of non-disclosure and where a failure to disclose will not infringe upon the Constitutional rights of the accused. Disclosure shall not be denied hereunder of the identity of witnesses to be produced at trial or hearing.

(3) Protective Orders: Either the State or defense may apply for a protective order for non-disclosure of discovery required hereunder or any additional requested discovery.

307.50 Duty to Supplement Responses: The State and the defendant are under a continuing duty to supplement the discovery disclosures required hereunder as required upon the acquisition of additional information or materials otherwise required to be disclosed hereunder. Supplementation of disclosures shall be made within a reasonable time after the obligation to supplement arises.

307.60 Sanctions Upon Failure to Comply: Failure of a party to comply with either the disclosure requirements or the time limits required by this rule may result in the imposition of sanctions against the noncompliant party. These sanctions may include, but are not limited to, the exclusion of evidence at a trial or hearing.

Adopted as Rule 204, effective July 1, 2000. Renumbered as Rule 307 and amended effective June 1, 2005. Amended effective August 12, 2007.

LR29–CR00 Rule 308. Late Payment Fee

308.10 Fines, court costs and civil penalties assessed for infractions, violations of municipal ordinances, felonies, misdemeanors or juvenile delinquency and juvenile status offenses are to be paid before 4:30 p.m. on the date they are assessed unless otherwise ordered. An order extending this deadline will be presumed to require payment on or before 4:30 p.m. of the extension deadline date or on the last business day of the extension period if a specific date is not set. If said fine, cost, or penalty is not paid in conformity with this rule or the court order extending the deadline, the Clerk may collect a late fee under IC 33–37–5–22, subject to the Court's authority to suspend said late fee for good cause.

308.20 Notwithstanding the above, a late fee shall not be assessed for any late payment of fine and costs imposed in the night court sessions of Superior Courts 4, 5, and 6 until the Traffic Violations Bureau of those courts has forwarded notice to the Bureau of Motor Vehicles of failure to pay.

Adopted as Rule 205, effective July 1, 2000. Renumbered as Rule 308 and amended effective June 1, 2005. Amended effective Aug. 12, 2007; amended Nov. 30, 2009, effective Jan. 1, 2010.

LR29–CR00 Rule 309. Collection of Probation User Fees

309.10 The Circuit and Superior Courts of Hamilton County direct the Hamilton County Clerk of Courts to be the designee for the Hamilton County Department of Probation Services to collect probation users' fees for probation services provided by the Hamilton County Department of Probation Services and to remit said fees to the proper authorities. This rule shall remain in effect until the Clerk of Hamilton County shall decline to serve as designee or until a majority of said judges determine that such designation should be withdrawn.

Adopted effective June 1, 2005. Amended effective August 12, 2007.

LR29–CR00 Rule 310. Drug Court

310.10 The Hamilton County Drug Court is established to provide specialized services including: clinical assessment, education, referral for treatment, and service coordination and case management for eligible defendants and probationers as determined by its written policies and procedures.

310.20 The day-to-day operation and management of the drug Court shall be assigned to Hamilton County Superior Court No. 6.

310.30 All criminal charges shall be filled as otherwise provided in these rules. However, after a charge has been filed, if a defendant is accepted by Drug Court, a judge may transfer the defendant's case to Drug Court for services in accordance with Drug Court policies and procedures.

310.40 If a probationer is referred to and is accepted by Drug Court, a judge may transfer the case to drug Court and require a probationer to participate in Drug Court in accordance with Drug Court policies and procedures as a condition of probation.

Adopted effective January 1, 2012.

Appendix A.   Hamilton County Bond Schedule

APPENDIX A
TO LR29–CR00–305.10

HAMILTON COUNTY BOND SCHEDULE

SCOPE: This bond schedule applies to all cases to be filed in the Circuit and Superior Courts of this County and in the City of Carmel, City of Noblesville, and Town of Fishers Courts. THE SHERIFF OF HAMILTON COUNTY IS HEREBY ORDERED TO FOLLOW THIS BOND SCHEDULE FOR SETTING BONDS FOR ALL PERSONS ARRESTED WITHOUT WARRANTS FOR CRIMINAL OFFENSES TO BE FILED IN THE ABOVE COURTS:

SFELONIES:		
	MURDER	NO BOND
	HABITUAL OFFENDER	$50,000
	CLASS A	$50,000
	CLASS B	$25,000
	CLASS C	$10,000
	CLASS D	$ 5,000

MISDEMEANORS:		
	CLASS A MISDEMEANOR	$ 2,500
	CLASS B MISDEMEANOR	$ 1,000
	CLASS C MISDEMEANOR	$ 500

EXCEPTIONS: The following are exceptions to the above listed schedule:

Operating While Intoxicated, Second Offense (Class D felony) ... $ 7,500

Operating While Intoxicated Resulting in Serious Bodily Injury (Class D felony) ... $ 7,500

Dealing Marijuana Less Than 30 Grams (Class A misdemeanor) ... $ 3,500

False Reporting or Informing (Class A or B misdemeanor) ... $ 2,500

Leaving the Scene of a Property Damage Accident (Class B or C misdemeanor) ... $ 2,500

Leaving the Scene of a Personal Injury Accident (Class A misdemeanor) ... $ 5,000

Operating While Intoxicated (Class C misdemeanor) ... $ 2,500

Operating a Vehicle With at Least .08 (Class C misdemeanor) ... $ 2,500

Operating a Motorboat While Intoxicated (Class C misdemeanor) ... $ 2,500

Operating a Motorboat With at Least .08 (Class C misdemeanor) ... $ 2,500

Refusal to Identify Self (Class C misdemeanor) ... $ 1,500

Possession of Drug Paraphernalia (Class A misdemeanor) ... $ 1,000

Driving While Suspended (Class A misdemeanor) ... $ 1,000

Public Intoxication (Class B misdemeanor) .. O/R (when alcohol free)

Illegal Cons./Poss./Transp. of Alcohol (Class C misdemeanor) ... O/R (when alcohol free)

EXCEPTIONS FOR OUT–OF–STATE RESIDENTS:
All bond amounts in this bond schedule, whether surety or cash, shall be **doubled** for out-of-state residents.

CASH BONDS PERMITTED: A person may post a cash bond instead of a surety bond as follows:

FELONIES:		
	MURDER	NO BOND
	CLASS A, B, or C..	Same as Bond Schedule
	CLASS D	One–half (½) of the Bond Schedule

MISDEMEANORS:		
	CLASS A, B, or C..One–half (½) of the Bond Schedule	

All cash bonds shall be posted with the Hamilton County Sheriff or the Hamilton County Clerk only after the person posting the bond has signed the Cash Bond Agreement. Pursuant to I.C. 35–33–8–3.2 and 35–33–8–4, the Hamilton County Clerk shall retain a portion of each cash bond posted in criminal cases as an administrative fee. The administrative fee shall not exceed ten percent (10%) of the monetary value of the cash bond or $50, whichever is less.

LACK OF IDENTIFICATION: Any person who cannot be positively identified at book-in shall be held **without bond** until the person is brought before the Court for a hearing to determine bond. This includes, but is not limited to, those individuals who refuse to cooperate in their identification by refusing to be fingerprinted, individuals who possess conflicting identification, and individuals whose identifying information cannot be verified.

24–HOUR HOLD: A person arrested for battery, stalking, invasion of privacy, or strangulation, shall not be allowed to post bond under this schedule until 24 hours after book-in.

BOND AMOUNTS ARE CUMULATIVE—EXCEPTIONS: If a person has been arrested for multiple charges, the bond amount shall be the total amount required for all charges, except for the following situations:

1. If a person has been arrested for multiple alcohol charges (operating while intoxicated, public intoxication, illegal consumption/transportation), only the highest class bond for one charge shall be imposed for all of the alcohol charges; and

2. If a person has been arrested for multiple misdemeanor charges, the total cumulative bond for all of the misdemeanors shall not exceed $5,000 ($10,000 for out-of-state residents).

BOND NOT AVAILABLE: This bond schedule shall not be used for any person arrested for a crime when it can be reasonably determined that the person was on probation, parole, bond or release on the person's own recognizance for another offense. In such case, the person shall be detained in custody until a Court establishes the bond.

CONDITIONS OF BOND: As conditions of bond or release on recognizance (O/R), **all persons posting a Bond** are subject to the following conditions: (a) they **shall appear** in Court at all times required by the Court; (b) they **shall not leave the State of Indiana** without the **prior written** consent of the Court; (c) they **shall not commit nor be arrested** for another criminal offense; (d) they shall keep their attorney and the Court advised in writing of any change of address within 24 hours of such change; and, (e) they shall comply with any other condition ordered by the Court. Pursuant to I.C. 35–33–8–3.2(a)(4) a person's release may also be conditioned upon refraining from any direct or indirect contact with the alleged victim of an offense or any other individual as ordered by the

Court. **Violation of any condition may result in the revocation of bond and the issuance of a re-arrest warrant.**

SUPERSEDES: This Bail Bond Schedule supersedes all previous Bail Bond Schedules ordered by the Circuit and Superior Courts of this County and the Carmel and Noblesville City Courts.

SO ORDERED this 1st day of January, 2012.

Original signed by the Honorables Felix, Nation, Pfleging, Hughes, Campbell, Sturtevant, Bardach, Poindexter, Caldwell, and Henke

Adopted effective July 1, 2000. Amended effective June 1, 2005; August 12, 2007; May 1, 2011; January 1, 2012; July 1, 2012.

HAMILTON COUNTY LOCAL FAMILY LAW RULES

Adopted Effective June 1, 2005

Including Amendments Received Through November 1, 2013

Research Notes

Annotations to the Hamilton County Local Family Law Rules are available in West's Annotated Indiana Code, *Title 34 Appendix.*

These rules may be searched electronically on Westlaw *in the* IN-RULES *database; updates to these rules may be found on* Westlaw *in* IN-RULESUPDATES. *For search tips and a summary of database content, consult the Westlaw Scope Screens for each database.*

LR29–FL00 Rule 401. Preliminary Orders

401.10 Preliminary Orders in dissolution of marriage cases shall be typewritten or prepared on the Preliminary Order forms provided by the Courts; however, the Court, at its option, may accept legibly handwritten Preliminary Orders.

Adopted effective June 1, 2005. Amended effective August 12, 2007.

LR29–FL00 Rule 402. Financial Declarations, Support Work Sheets, Visitation, and Children Cope with Divorce Workshop

402.10 Parties shall complete in full Indiana Child Support Obligation Worksheets (**Form FL00–402A**) and Financial Declarations (**Form FL00–402B**) on the forms adopted by the Court in all contested matters involving child support or disposition of assets. Parties must date and file these forms prior to any hearing or trial. Financial Declarations shall be exchanged by the parties and filed with the Court not less than three working days before any preliminary hearing and not less than ten working days before the final hearing. Child Support Worksheets shall be exchanged and filed with the Court on the hearing date. Child Support Worksheets must be attached to all proposed orders and decrees addressing child support.

402.20 If there are any assets or obligations not disposed of by written agreement between the parties, the litigants must prove the value of the assets and the amount of obligations at the hearing. Financial Declarations shall be considered as received in evidence subject to cross-examination. Direct examination, on matters in the Financial Declaration, should be confined to unusual factors which require explanation, or to corrections.

402.30 Prior to April 1, 2001, Hamilton County Circuit and Superior Courts had adopted Visitation Guidelines which are attached for information purposes in Appendix B. Effective March 1, 2013, the Indiana Supreme Court adopted Indiana Parenting Time Guidelines, which can be found at www.in.gov/judiciary/rules/parenting/index.html.

402.40 In the matters of child support and child support arrearages a CCS entry must be submitted to the Court in the following form:

"Court finds Petitioner's/Respondent's current Child Support obligation to be $ ___ per week/month as of ___ / ___ /20 ___, which modifies/affirms prior Child Support Order of _____. Petitioner's/Respondent's arrearage established in the amount of $ ___ as of _____ / ___ 20 ___. Additional payment of $ ___ per week/month toward arrearage."

402.50 The Circuit and Superior Courts of Hamilton County, find that it would be in the best interest of the minor child or children of the parties to encourage mediation and cooperation between divorcing parents prior to and after dissolution of their marriage. The Courts further find that a Mandatory Education Workshop will aid parents in post-separation parenting; aid development of healthy child/parent relationships in a post separation setting; be in the best interest of the minor child/children and; encourage agreements between the parties concerning child related matters.

a. Both of the parties in any cause of action for Dissolution of Marriage, in which there is a minor child/children under eighteen (18) years of age, attend a workshop entitled "Children Cope with Divorce" (COPE). Attendance shall be mandatory for all parties in a Dissolution of Marriage action that is filed on or after February 1, 1993, if there is minor child/children under eighteen (18) years of age.

b. The four-hour course shall be completed by both parties within Sixty (60) days of the filing of the Petition for Dissolution and prior to the Final Hearing. Parties are responsible for paying the cost of this program, with allowance for a waiver of the fee for indigence.

c. The parties in this cause of action are ordered to contact:

The Visiting Nurse Service, Inc.
4701 N. Keystone Avenue
Indianapolis, IN 46205
(317) 722–8201
1–800–248–6540

within 15 days of the filing of the Petition for Dissolution or the Receipt of Summons, whichever is sooner, to make an appointment to attend the workshop without further notice. Failure to complete the workshop can result in a party being ordered to appear and show cause why he/she should not be held in Contempt of Court and punished. If the parties cannot attend the COPE workshop, with the prior approval of the Court, they may use an alternative workshop.

402.60 The Sheriff of Hamilton County is Ordered to make due service of the Notice of Order on the Respondent when the Petition for Dissolution is served and make due return thereon.

Adopted effective June 1, 2005. Amended effective August 12, 2007; April 1, 2013.

LR29–FL00 Rule 403. Title IV–D Commissioner/Court

These local rules are adopted by the Hamilton County Circuit and Superior Courts to govern the practice and procedures in the Title IV–D Commissioner/Court, funded by the use of IV–D Incentive Funds.

403.10 Organization of Title IV–D Child Support Commissioner/Court. Pursuant to I.C. 31–25–4–15, the Judges of the Circuit and Superior Courts hereby establish a Title IV–D Commissioner/Court to establish and enforce paternity and child support orders under federal and state law.

403.10.1 Assignment of Commissioner to IV–D Court. The Judges of the Circuit and Superior Courts shall jointly appoint a commissioner to the IV–D Court. A commissioner so appointed shall be designated as a IV–D Commissioner.

403.10.2 Responsibilities of IV–D Commissioner. A IV–D Commissioner jointly appointed by the Judges and assigned to the IV–D Court pursuant to 403.10.1 has the authority to preside over, make findings of fact and recommendations for the approval of the Judges of the Circuit and Superior Courts in actions arising under Title IV–D of the Social Security Act. In addition, the IV–D Commissioner has the authority to provide such assistance as may be required in making these findings of fact and recommendations.

403.01.3[1] Temporary Absence of IV–D Commissioner. During the temporary absence of the duly appointed IV–D Commissioner, any sitting judicial officer of the Hamilton County Circuit and Superior Courts may hear and make recommendations upon Title IV–D matters.

403.10.4 Supervision of the IV–D Commissioner/Court. The Title IV–D Commissioner/Court shall be operated under the auspices and supervision of the Judges of the Hamilton County Circuit and Superior Courts.

403.20 Child Support Issues arising out of Legal Separation Decree or Dissolution of Marriage Provisional Orders

403.20.1 Pending Child Support Orders Arising from Legal Separation or Provisional Orders. All IV–D child support issues arising out of a Legal Separation Decree or out of a provisional order in a Dissolution of Marriage proceeding will NOT be assigned to the IV–D Commissioner/Court.

403.20.2 Arrearages from Child Support Orders Arising from Legal Separation or Provisional Orders. Once a Legal Separation Decree expires by order or operation of law or once a Dissolution of Marriage Decree is granted, arrearage issues arising out of the provisional order or the Legal Separation Decree may then be assigned to the IV–D Commissioner/Court by written ORDER OF ASSIGNMENT issued by the Judge of the Circuit or Superior Court upon a written finding that there is a IV–D support issue to be resolved.

403.30 IV–D Child Support Issues arising out of Dissolution Decrees or Post–Dissolution Orders. All IV–D child support issues arising out of a Dissolution Decree or a Post–Dissolution Order may be assigned to the IV–D Commissioner/Court by written ORDER OF ASSIGNMENT issued by the Judge of the Circuit or Superior Court upon a written finding that there is a IV–D support issue to be resolved or upon a finding that the only remaining matters involved in the case are properly within the jurisdiction of the IV–D judicial officer.

403.40 IV–D Child Support Issues arising out of Paternity Actions. All IV–D child support issues arising out of a Paternity Action or post- paternity proceedings may be assigned to the IV–D Commissioner/Court by written ORDER OF ASSIGNMENT issued by the Judge of the Circuit or Superior Court.

403.50 Procedure for Assignment of IV–D Matters to IV–D Commissioner/Court. Once a Judge of the Circuit or Superior Court has assigned a case involving IV–D issues to the IV–D Commissioner/Court for the resolution of IV–D issues, the following procedure will control:

(1) Cases may be considered for assignment at the oral or written request of any party or *sua sponte* by the assigning Judge.

(2) The Judge may issue a written ORDER OF ASSIGNMENT upon a finding that a IV–D support issue needs to be resolved or upon a finding that the only remaining matters involved in the case are properly within the jurisdiction of the IV–D Commissioner/Court. The ORDER OF ASSIGNMENT will be entered onto the original chronological case summary (CCS) or docket sheet.

(3) A copy of that ORDER OF ASSIGNMENT, a copy of the CCS, and copies of any relevant pleadings including but not limited to the initial pleadings on any pending IV–D matters and all orders entered regarding any previous IV–D matter shall be compiled by the clerk of the court of origin upon request of the Child Support Division of the Prosecutor's Office.

(4) The ORDER OF ASSIGNMENT will be served on all parties by the Child Support Division of the Prosecutor's Office. If a pending issue requires an immediate hearing, the Child Support Division shall also be responsible for coordinating the hearing date and time and notifying all parties.

(5) All non-IV-D matters that arise following an assignment to the IV–D Commissioner/Court shall be filed with the originating Circuit or Superior Court. Assigned IV–D issues may be recalled by the assigning judge at any time and the IV–D Commissioner/Court shall send back to the assigning judge any assigned issues that require the consideration of non-IV-D matters.

(6) All findings and recommendations of the IV–D Commissioner/Court shall become orders upon approval and adoption by the originating Judge.

(7) A transfer, assignment, or recall of cases shall be done by separate order of the sending or recalling judicial officer.

(8) Procedure for Objection to Assignment: Assignment to the Title IV–D Commissioner/Court is within the sole discretion of the regularly presiding judge to whom the case has been originally assigned. A change of venue from the regularly presiding judge may be made under applicable Indiana Trial Rules or statutes. An objection to assignment to the Title IV–D Commissioner/Court shall be made to the regularly presiding judge and is within his or her discretion to grant or deny.

Adopted Sept. 1, 2011, effective Jan. 1, 2012.

1 So in original. Probably should be "403.10.3".

Appendix B. Hamilton County Visitation Guidelines

APPENDIX B

TO LR29–FL–402.40

HAMILTON COUNTY VISITATION GUIDELINES

It is usually in the child's best interest that each parent has frequent, meaningful and continuing contact with the child. A visitation agreement made by both parents is preferred to a court imposed solution. However, if the parents are unable to agree on visitation, the following guidelines should be used in most cases. In situations where the non-custodial parent may not have had ongoing contact with the children, initial visitation may be shorter. Further, these provisions may not apply to very young children or situations where geographical distances between parents make compliance impossible. The parents, in exercising visitation, should be flexible enough to adapt to the circumstances, the child's age, ongoing activities and any religious holidays not set out below. The main goal of both parents should be to encourage and facilitate peaceful and frequent visitation of the children with the non-custodial parent.

If the parents do not agree otherwise, the following shall be considered the **MINIMUM** visitation to which the non-custodial parent shall be entitled.

A. VISITATION SCHEDULE WHEN ONE PARENT HAS SOLE CUSTODY OR PRIMARY PHYSICAL CUSTODY AND PARENTS RESIDE NO MORE THAN 150 MILES APART:

Weekend. Alternating weekends from 6:00 p.m. on Friday until 6:00 p.m. on Sunday (the starting and ending times may change to fit the parents' schedules).

Holidays. The non-custodial parent shall be entitled to holiday visitation as follows:

(1) In years ending in an odd number:

(a) New Year's Day from 6:00 p.m. December 31 to 8:00 p.m. January 1

(b) Memorial Day weekend from Friday at 6:00 p.m. until Monday at 8:00 p.m.

(c) Labor Day weekend from Friday at 6:00 p.m. until Monday at 8:00 p.m.

(d) Christmas Eve from 6:00 p.m. until noon Christmas Day

(e) Evening before child's birthday from 6:00 p.m. until 9:00 p.m.

(2) In years ending in an even number:

(a) Easter Sunday weekend from Friday at 6:00 p.m. until Sunday at 8:00 p. m.

(b) July 4 from 6:00 p.m. July 3 until 8:00 p.m. July 4

(c) Thanksgiving from 6:00 p.m. Wednesday until 8:00 p.m. Thursday

(d) Christmas Day from noon until 9:00 p.m.

(e) Day of child's birthday from 6:00 p.m. until 9:00 p.m.

(3) It is recognized by the Court that other days may be significant to families for religious reasons. If so, the Court recommends visitation days be allowed each parent based on an alternating schedule. If alternating visitation days cannot be agreed to by both parents, the issue may be addressed by the Court.

Conflicts between Regular Weekend, Holiday, and Extended Summer Visitation. When there is a conflict between a holiday weekend and the regular weekend visitation, the holiday takes precedence. Thus, if the non-custodial parent misses a regular weekend because it is the custodial parent's holiday, the regular alternating visitation schedule will resume following the holiday. If the non-custodial parent receives two consecutive weekends because of a holiday, the child will spend the following weekend with the custodial parent. When there is a conflict between holiday visitation and extended summer visitation, the holiday visitation takes precedence. When there is a conflict between regular weekend visitation and extended summer visitation, extended summer visitation takes precedence.

Mother's Day/Father's Day. Children shall be with their mother each Mother's Day and with their father each Father's Day, from 9:00 a.m. to 8:00 p.m..

Extended Visitation (Children Under 5). Up to three non-consecutive weeks during the year, the choice of the number of weeks to be determined by the non-custodial parent. At least 30 days notice of the intent to use a week shall be given. A week shall begin Friday at 6:00 p.m. and end Sunday of the following week at 8:00 p.m.

Extended Visitation (Children Over 5). One–half of the school summer vacation. At the option of the non-custodial parent, the time may either be consecutive or may be split into two segments. If the children attend summer school and it is impossible for the non-custodial parent to otherwise schedule the visitation that parent may elect to take that period when the children are in summer school (and be responsible for their attendance and transportation). Notice must be given by the non-custodial parent, in writing, on or before April 15 of each year. During periods of extended summer visitation, the non-visiting parent shall be entitled to alternating weekend visitation. However, both the custodial parent and the non-custodial parent, upon 30 days written notice to the other parent, shall be entitled to one period of two weeks in duration when they may, at their option, elect to take the child on an extended vacation; and the other parent shall not be entitled to alternating weekend visitation during said period.

B. VISITATION WHEN THERE IS SOLE CUSTODY OR PRIMARY PHYSICAL CUSTODY AND PARENTS RESIDE MORE THAN 150 MILES APART:

Children Under 5. Up to six non-consecutive, two-week segments annually, each separated by at least six weeks. This visitation is in lieu of alternating weekend and holiday visitation.

Children Over 5. All but three weeks of the school summer vacation, and on an alternating basis, the school winter vacation and spring break. This visita-tion is in lieu of alternating weekend and holiday visitation.

Notice. When the children are under five years of age, the non-custodial parent shall give at least 30 days of notice of each segment sought, while, when the children are over five, at least 60 days notice shall be given.

C. GENERAL RULES APPLICABLE TO ALL VISITATION:

The non-custodial parent shall give a minimum of three days notice of intent not to exercise all or part of a scheduled visitation.

Parents shall, at all times, keep each other advised of their home and work addresses and telephone numbers. So far as possible, all communication concerning the children shall be conducted between the parents in person or by telephoning at their residences (and not at their places of employment).

Each parent shall allow liberal but reasonable telephone and mail privileges with the children.

The custodial parent shall provide copies of all school and medical reports within 10 days of their receipt and shall notify the other parent immediately in the event of a medical emergency. The custodial parent shall inform the non-custodial parent of school, extra curricular, and/or social functions permitting parental participation within 24 hours of notification of such function.

Parents shall, at all times, avoid speaking negatively about each other and should firmly discourage such conduct by relatives or friends. Each parent should encourage the children to respect the other parent. The basic rules of conduct and discipline established by the custodial parent should be the baseline standard for both parents, and consistently enforced by both, so that the children do not receive mixed signals.

Parents are encouraged to have their children maintain ties with both the maternal and paternal relatives. In most cases, the children will visit with the paternal relatives during times the children are with their father and with the maternal relatives when with their mother.

Neither visitation nor child support is to be withheld due to either parent's failure to comply with a court order.

If the parties mutually agree to change any visitation schedule ordered by the Court to obligate themselves to a different visitation schedule, they shall petition the Court to approve and order that change. In the event that the parties do not obtain a court order, the Court shall not be bound to enforce any alleged agreement of the parties whether the agreement be verbal or written.

SO ORDERED this 1st day of January, 1997.

Original signed by the Honorables Proffitt, Nation, Barr, Hughes, Campbell, and Sturtevant

Adopted effective Jan. 1, 1997. Amended effective June 1, 2005. Amended effective August 12, 2007.

HAMILTON COUNTY LOCAL JURY RULES

**Adopted as General Rules Effective July 1, 2000,
and as Jury Rules Effective June 1, 2005**

Including Amendments Received Through November 1, 2013

Research Notes

Annotations to the Hamilton County Local Jury Rules are available in West's Annotated Indiana Code, Title 34 Appendix.

These rules may be searched electronically on Westlaw in the IN-RULES database; updates to these rules may be found on Westlaw in IN-RULESUPDATES. For search tips and a summary of database content, consult the Westlaw Scope Screens for each database.

LR29–JR04 Rule 501. Summoning Jurors

501.10 A two-tier notice for summoning jurors will be used. The jury qualification form and notice will be the first tier and summoning the prospective juror at least one week before service will be the second tier.

Adopted as General Rule 121, effective July 1, 2000. Renumbered as Jury Rule 501 and amended effective June 1, 2005. Amended effective August 12, 2007.

HAMILTON COUNTY LOCAL TRIAL DE NOVO RULES

Adopted as Criminal Rules Effective July 1, 2000, and as Trial De Novo Rules Effective June 1, 2005

Including Amendments Received Through November 1, 2013

Research Notes

Annotations to the Hamilton County Local Trial De Novo Rules are available in West's Annotated Indiana Code, *Title 34 Appendix.*

These rules may be searched electronically on Westlaw *in the* IN-RULES *database; updates to these rules may be found on* Westlaw *in* IN-RULESUPDATES. *For search tips and a summary of database content, consult the Westlaw Scope Screens for each database.*

LR29–DN00 Rule 601.   Rules for Trial De Novo

601.10   This rule is adopted to implement the Supreme Court Rules of procedure regarding trial de novo requests from city and town courts. The application of this rule shall be coextensive with those rules.

Adopted as Criminal Rule 203, effective July 1, 2000. Renumbered as Trial De Novo Rule 601 and amended effective June 1, 2005. Amended effective August 12, 2007.

LR29–DN01 Rule 602.   Rules for Trial De Novo Following Civil Judgments

602.10   Supreme Court Trial De Novo Rule 1 for following civil judgments in city and town courts is incorporated by reference.

602.20   Bond or Other Undertaking:

a.   The party filing the request for trial de novo shall file with the Clerk of the Court a surety bond or cash deposit in accordance with Supreme Court Rule 1(C)(1). The bond or cash deposit required by Supreme Court Rule 1(C)(1) shall be in the amount of the judgment entered in the city or town court, plus an amount equaling eight percent (8%) of the total judgment as an allowance for interest. In any case where attorney fees have been awarded as part of the total judgment, the amount of bond shall be increased by 25 percent (25%) of the total judgment as an allowance for additional attorney fees. This bond, however, shall not exceed the jurisdictional limit of the city or town court from which the appeal is taken.

b.   If unable to afford a surety bond or cash deposit, the party filing the request may instead file an affidavit of indigence and personal undertaking in accordance with Supreme Court Rule 1(C)(2) on a form prescribed by the Court **(Form DN01/02–602/03).**

602.30   Filing and Court Assignment:

a.   The Clerk shall not accept for filing or file a request for trial de novo unless it meets the requirement of Supreme Court Rule 1(B)(4). Further, the Clerk shall not accept or file a request for trial de novo supported by an affidavit of indigence and personal undertaking unless the affidavit and personal undertaking are on the form provided by the Courts. If a request for trial de novo supported by an affidavit of indigence and personal undertaking is accepted for filing, it may be ordered stricken from the record if the Court in which it is filed determines that the party filing the request is able to afford to post a surety bond or cash deposit, and the party fails to post the surety bond or cash deposit required within the time set by the Court.

b.   The Clerk shall docket the request for trial de novo and the copies of the complaint and any responsive pleadings as a small claims action on the small claims docket of either Superior Court No. 4, Superior Court No. 5, or Superior Court No. 6 unless the request for trial de novo demands that the trial be by jury, in which case the assignment may be to a Circuit or any Superior Court in the county.

Adopted as Criminal Rule 203, effective July 1, 2000. Renumbered as Trial De Novo Rule 602 and amended effective June 1, 2005. Amended effective August 12, 2007; January 1, 2012.

LR29–DN02 Rule 603.   Rules for Trial De Novo Following Judgments for Infractions or Ordinance Violations

603.10   Supreme Court Trial De Novo Rule 2 for infraction or ordinance violation judgments in city or town courts is incorporated by reference.

603.20 Bond or Other Undertaking:

a. The party filing request for trial de novo shall file with the Clerk of the Court a surety or cash deposit in accordance with Supreme Court Rule 2(D)(1).

b. The bond required by Supreme Court Rule 2(D)(1) shall secure the State or municipality's claims, interest, and court costs, undertaking both the litigation of the trial de novo to a final judgment and payment of any judgment entered against a party filing the request by the trial de novo court.

c. The bond shall be in an amount as follows:

"C" infraction and traffic ordinance violations	500.00;
"B" infraction	$1,000.00;
"A" infraction and non-traffic ordinance violations plus the statutory costs in the trial de novo court.	$1,500.00;

d. If unable to afford a surety bond or cash deposit, the party filing the request may instead file an affidavit of indigence and personal undertaking in accordance with Supreme Court Rule 2(D)(2) on the form prescribed by the Court (**Form DN01/02–602/03).**

603.30 Filing and Court Assignment:

a. The Clerk shall not accept for filing nor file any request for trial de novo unless it meets the requirement of Supreme Court Rule 2(B). Further, the Clerk shall not accept or file a request for trial de novo supported by an affidavit of indigence and personal undertaking unless the affidavit and personal undertaking are on the form provided by the Courts. If a request for trial de novo supported by an affidavit of indigence and personal undertaking is accepted for filing, it may be ordered struck from the record if the Court in which it is filed determines that the party filing the request is able to afford to post a surety bond or cash deposit, and the party fails to post the surety bond or cash deposit required within the time set by the Court.

b. The Clerk shall docket and assign the request for trial de novo to the traffic division of either Superior Court No. 4, Superior Court No. 5, or Superior Court No. 6 as an infraction or ordinance violation proceeding.

603.40 Notice to Prosecutor or Municipal Counsel of Trial De Novo:

a. Promptly after the request for trial de novo is filed and assigned to the appropriate court, the Clerk shall send notice of the request to the prosecuting attorney or the municipal counsel.

b. Upon receiving the notice of request, the Prosecutor or the municipal counsel is ordered to file, within fifteen (15) days, a duplicate infraction or ordinance complaint and summons alleging the infraction or ordinance violation as originally filed

with the city or town court, together with any amended complaint alleging additional or amended counts also filed with the city or town court.

c. In the discretion of the prosecuting attorney or municipal counsel, and in lieu of filing such duplicate infraction or ordinance complaint and summons, the prosecuting attorney or the municipal counsel shall file with the Court a notice that no proceeding will be filed, together with a proposed order of dismissal including that the Clerk shall refund to the defendant the entire amount of any payment received from the city or town court. The order of dismissal shall also include a release of the surety bond, cash deposit, or personal undertaking.

Adopted as Criminal Rule 203, effective July 1, 2000. Renumbered as Trial De Novo Rule 603 and amended effective June 1, 2005. Amended effective August 12, 2007; January 1, 2012.

LR29–DN03 Rule 604. Rules for Trial De Novo Following Judgments Misdemeanor Trial in City or Town Court

604.10 Supreme Court Trial De Novo Rule 3 for misdemeanor cases is incorporated by reference.

604.20 DEMAND: The written request for trial de novo must comply with Supreme Court Rule 3(B), but, in addition, must also contain the offense(s) of which the defendant was convicted in the city or town court to enable the Clerk to assign the request for trial de novo to the appropriate court pursuant to the Hamilton County Criminal Random Filing Rule.

604.30 FILING AND COURT ASSIGNMENT:

a. The Clerk of the Courts shall docket and assign the request for trial de novo as a misdemeanor in the appropriate Superior Court in accordance with the Hamilton County Criminal Random Filing Rule (LR29–CR00–301) if the request is sufficient to make such an assignment. If the request contains insufficient information to make such assignment, it may be accepted for filing conditioned upon the defendant providing, within ten (10) days, the information necessary to complete the assignment. If the defendant fails to provide this information within the time specified, then the request for trial de novo shall be stricken as un-assignable.

b. The Court to which the request is assigned has full jurisdiction of the case and of the person of the defendant from the time the request for trial de novo is filed and assigned by the Clerk.

604.40 BAIL OR INCARCERATION:

a. Stay of City or Town Court Judgment and Appearance Bond. At the time the request for trial de novo is filed, the defendant may also file with the Clerk a surety bond or cash deposit conditioned on appearance for trial and sentencing as required by applicable statutes on bail in criminal prosecution and in accordance **with the trial de novo bail schedule in Appendix C.** Filing of the bond or undertaking stays the judgment of the city or town court, and during the period of the stay the defendant shall not be subject to incarceration or probation orders of the city or town court. Any defendant who is incarcerated pursuant to the judgment of the city or town court shall be released upon the posting of this bond or cash deposit. If the defendant does not file the surety bond or cash deposit, the judgment of the city or town court shall not be stayed, and the defendant will remain incarcerated or subject to probation orders of the city or town court until the stay imposed under subsection (F)(1) of Supreme Court Rule 3 takes effect. Even if the defendant is not seeking a stay, the posting of such a bond will serve as an appearance bond for the defendant. If such surety bond or cash deposit is posted, then a summons shall be issued to the defendant in accordance with IC 35–33–4–1, in lieu of any warrant that the State may request pursuant to IC 35–33–2–1.

b. The city or town court may transfer any *cash* bond previously posted in the city or town court to the Clerk of the Court to be applied against the trial de novo bond. In addition, the trial de novo court may accept any *surety* bond previously posted in the city or town court to be applied against the trial de novo bond, but only if the trial de novo court receives written consent from the surety bondsman.

604.50 Notice to the Prosecuting Attorney:

a. Promptly after the request for trial de novo is filed and assigned to the appropriate court, the Clerk shall send notice of the request to the prosecuting attorney.

b. Upon receiving the notice of the request, the Prosecutor is ordered to file within fifteen (15) days a duplicate charging instrument charging the offense or offenses as originally filed with the city or town court together with any additional charging instrument charging additional or amended counts also filed with the city or town court.

c. In the prosecuting attorney's discretion, and in lieu of filing such charging instrument, the State shall file with the Court a notice that no proceeding will be filed, together with a proposed Order of Dismissal, including that the Clerk shall refund to the defendant the entire amount of any payment received from the city or town court.

d. Upon the filing of the charging instrument, the Court to which the request for trial de novo has been assigned, shall proceed in accordance with IC 35–33–2–1, to issue a warrant for the arrest of the defendant, or in accordance with IC 35–33–4–1, to issue a summons for the defendant to appear. If the defendant has posted a surety bond or cash deposit in accordance with paragraphs 604.40(a) or (b) above, then the Court shall issue a summons in lieu of a warrant.

604.60 Notice to City or Town Court:

a. Upon the filing of a request for trial de novo, the Clerk shall promptly send notice of the filing of the request to the city or town court from which the trial de novo was taken.

b. The Clerk shall hold any fine or payment received from the city or town court pending the outcome of the trial de novo and shall apply the payment to any judgment for fine or costs imposed by the de novo court following the trial de novo, or to any order for probation users' fees or recoupment of trial expenses otherwise authorized by law and ordered by the de novo court. If any amount of the original fine payment remains after application to judgments or orders imposed by the trial de novo court, the Clerk shall refund the balance to the defendant.

604.70 Procedure When Plea of Guilty was Entered in City or Town Court: If the defendant entered a plea of guilty in the city or town court, the procedure to be followed shall be in accordance with Supreme Court Trial De Novo Rule 3(G).

604.80 Procedure When Plea of Not Guilty is Entered in City or Town Court: If the defendant entered a plea of not guilty in the city or town court, the procedure to be followed shall be in accordance with Supreme Court Trial De Novo Rule 3(H).

Adopted as Criminal Rule 203, effective July 1, 2000. Renumbered as Trial De Novo Rule 604 and amended effective June 1, 2005. Amended effective August 12, 2007.

Appendix C. Trial De Novo Bail Schedule for Misdemeanor Offenses

APPENDIX C
TO LR29–DN03–604.40

TRIAL *DE NOVO* BAIL SCHEDULE
FOR MISDEMEANOR OFFENSES

The bond required by LR29–DN03–604.40 shall be posted by cash deposit or surety bond and shall be in accordance with the following schedule:

Class A Misdemeanor	$5,000.00
Class B Misdemeanor	$3,000.00
Class C Misdemeanor	$2,000.00

However, the following exceptions shall apply to the above listed schedule:

Operating with .10% Blood Alcohol Content (Class C Misdemeanor)	$5,000.00
Contributing to the Delinquency of a Minor (Class A Misdemeanor)	$2,000.00
Reckless Driving (No Property or Personal Injury) (Class B Misdemeanor)	$2, 000.00
Reckless Driving (Property Damage or Personal Injury) (Class B Misdemeanor)	$5,000.00

If the request for trial *de novo* is on a finding of violation of probation, then bond shall be set as follows:

(a)   If the defendant is on probation for a Class A Misdemeanor $7,500.00

(b)   If the defendant is on probation for a Class B or C Misdemeanor $5, 000.00

If the request for trial *de novo* involves multiple charges/convictions or where the defendant is on probation on multiple convictions, the bond applied shall be the total amount required for all offenses.

All bail bonds posted by the defendants are subject to the following conditions:

(a) Defendant shall appear in court at all times required by the Court;

(b) Defendant shall not leave the state of Indiana without the prior written consent of the Court.

(c) Defendant shall not commit or be arrested for another criminal offense;

(d) Defendant shall keep his/her attorney and the Court advised in writing of any change of address within twenty-four (24) hours of such change;

(e) In appropriate cases the defendant may be required to refrain from any direct or indirect contact with an alleged victim of an offense or other individual as ordered by the Court pursuant to IC 38–33–8–3.1(a)(4).

A violation of any condition may result in revocation of bond and issuance of re-arrest warrant.

Originals signed by The Honorables Proffitt, Nation, Barr, Campbell and Sturtevant

Adopted as Criminal Appendix B, effective July 1, 2000. Renumbered as Trial De Novo Appendix C and amended effective June 1, 2005. Amended effective August 12, 2007.

HAMILTON COUNTY LOCAL PROBATE RULES

Adopted Effective July 1, 2000

Including Amendments Received Through November 1, 2013

Research Notes

Annotations to the Hamilton County Local Probate Rules are available in West's Annotated Indiana Code, Title 34 Appendix.

These rules may be searched electronically on Westlaw in the IN-RULES database; updates to these rules may be found on Westlaw in IN-RULESUPDATES. For search tips and a summary of database content, consult the Westlaw Scope Screens for each database.

LR29–PR00 Rule 701.   Notice

701.10   Whenever notice by publication and/or written notice by U.S. Mail is required to be given, the attorney shall prepare such notice and shall ensure that such notice is properly published and/or served by certified mail, return receipt requested. In all respects, the notice shall comply with all statutory requirements. It shall be the attorney's responsibility to ascertain and provide adequate proof thereof regarding whether notice was properly served prior to bringing a matter to the Court.

701.20   Copies of petitions or motions shall be sent with all notices where the hearing involved arises from the matters contained in the petition or motion.

701.30   Whenever any estate or guardianship account (including a final account in a supervised estate) is set for hearing, copies of the account must be served with the notice of hearing.

701.40   Notice of the opening of an estate shall be sent by First Class United States Mail to all reasonably ascertainable creditors; however, the use of "cer-tified mail, return receipt requested," to serve such notice is recommended.

701.50   Notice of the hearing to be held on a Petition to determine an estate insolvent shall be served on all interested parties, including the local representative of the Inheritance Tax Division of the Indiana Department of Revenue.

Adopted as Rule 301, effective July 1, 2000. Renumbered as Rule 701 and amended effective June 1, 2005. Amended effective August 12, 2007.

LR29–PR00 Rule 702.   Filing of Pleadings

702.10   When pleadings are filed by mail or left with the Court for filing, a self-addressed, stamped envelope shall be included for return of documents to the attorney.

702.20   If petitions or motions are filed by electronic facsimile transmission, then such filing must conform with the requirements set forth in the trial rules and LR29–AR–103.

702.30   All parties are required to prepare orders for all proceedings except when expressly directed otherwise by the Court.

702.40   Every inventory and accounting filed in an estate or guardianship will be signed and verified by the fiduciary and signed by the attorney for the fiduciary.

702.50   All pleadings filed shall contain the parties' name, address and telephone number and/or the parties' attorney's name, address, telephone number and registration number.

702.60   The initial petition to open an estate or guardianship shall contain the name, address, social security number (in compliance with Indiana Administrative Rule 9) and telephone number of the personal representative or guardian, if a person.

702.70   The Instructions to the Personal Representative or Guardian, executed by the fiduciary, must be filed with the Court at the time letters are ordered issued in the proceeding (**Forms PR00–1, PR00–2, PR00–3, PR00–4**)

702.80 The affidavit of compliance with the notice provisions directed to creditors in an estate proceeding shall be timely filed with the Clerk of the Court.

702.90 *ASSIGNMENT OF MH PROBATE CASE NUMBERS*:

a. The Clerk shall assign cause numbers for new filings of all MH case types to Hamilton Superior Court No. 1 and Hamilton Superior Court No. 3.

b. The Clerk shall equally assign such new filings to Superior Court No. 1 and Superior Court No. 3 or other method as the judges of said courts shall agree.

702.100   Assignment of ES/EU, GU, and TR Probate Case Numbers: As requested by the parties, or directed by the judges, the Clerk shall assign cause numbers for new filings of ES/EU, GU, and TR case types to either Hamilton Superior Court No. 1 and/or Hamilton Superior Court No. 3.

Adopted as Rule 302, effective July 1, 2000. Renumbered as Rule 702 and amended effective June 1, 2005. Amended effective August 12, 2007.

LR29–PR00 Rule 703.   Attendance of Proposed Fiduciaries

703.10 All proposed personal representatives and guardians who are residents of Indiana shall appear before the Court to qualify.

703.20 Nonresident personal representatives and guardians shall either appear or submit an affidavit describing their education, employment, and lack of felony convictions.

703.30 Such personal representative or guardian is under a continuing order of the Court to personally advise the Court and the attorney or record in writing as to any change of any required information such as name, address, social security number, or telephone number.

Adopted as Rule 303, effective July 1, 2000. Renumbered as Rule 703 and amended effective June 1, 2005. Amended effective August 12, 2007.

LR29–PR00 Rule 704.   Representation of Fiduciaries by Counsel

704.10 No personal representative or guardian of an estate may proceed without counsel, without court approval.

Adopted as Rule 304, effective July 1, 2000. Renumbered as Rule 704 and amended effective June 1, 2005. Amended effective August 12, 2007.

LR29–PR00 Rule 705.   Bond

705.10 In every estate and guardianship, the fiduciary, prior to the issuance of letters, shall file a corporate surety bond in an amount not less than the value of the personal property to be administered, plus the probable value of annual rents and profits of all property of the estate or in such amount as shall be set by the Court, except as hereafter provided:

a. Where, under the terms of the Will, the testator expresses an intention that the bond be waived, the Court shall set a bond adequate to protect creditors, tax authorities, and devises.

b. Where the fiduciary is an heir or legatee of the estate, the bond may be reduced by said fiduciary's share of the estate, or the value of real estate, or other assets that cannot be transferred or accessed without court approval or order. The Court shall have the right to review the amount of bond if the Court should grant access to such property or asset.

c. Where the heirs or legatees have filed a written request that the fiduciary serve without bond, the Court may set bond in an amount adequate to protect the rights of the creditors and tax authorities only.

d. In an unsupervised estate, bond may be set at the discretion of the Court.

e. No bond shall be required in any supervised estate or guardianship in which corporate banking fiduciary qualified by law to serve as such is either the fiduciary or one of several co-fiduciaries.

705.20 In lieu of a bond as required by LR29–PR00–705.10, the Court, upon the fiduciary's request, may restrict transfer of all or part of the estate or guardianship liquid assets by placing those assets in a federally-insured financial institution or in a court approved investment with the following restriction placed on the face of the account or in the investment document:

"NO PRINCIPAL OR INTEREST SHALL BE WITHDRAWN WITHOUT WRITTEN ORDER OF _____ COURT OF _____, INDIANA."

The fiduciary shall thereafter file with the Court within ten (10) days of the order authorizing the creation of the account or investment, a certification by an officer of the institution at which the account or investment has been created, affirming that the account or investment is restricted as required by the Court order and is in compliance with this rule (**Form PR00–5**).

705.30 All petitions to open an estate or guardianship shall set forth the probable value of the personal property plus the estimated annual rents and profits to be derived from the property in the estate or guardianship.

705.40 The name and address of the insurance agency providing the corporate surety shall be typed or printed on all corporate bonds in any estate or guardianship.

Adopted as Rule 305, effective July 1, 2000. Renumbered as Rule 705 and amended effective June 1, 2005. Amended effective August 12, 2007.

LR29–PR00 Rule 706. Inventory

706.10 An inventory shall be filed by the fiduciary in estates and guardianships as follows: Supervised estates, within sixty (60) days; guardianships, within ninety (90) days for permanent guardians and within thirty (30) days for temporary guardians. All times relate to the date of appointment of the fiduciary.

706.20 In the event a partial inventory is filed, all subsequent inventories must contain a recapitulation of prior inventories.

706.30 In the event that the personal representative should request that an inventory be sealed, the Court may, in its sole discretion, seal such inventory. If an inventory is sealed, it shall be maintained in the court reporter's evidence file in the Court in which such estate is filed.

Adopted as Rule 306, effective July 1, 2000. Renumbered as Rule 706 and amended effective June 1, 2005. Amended effective August 12, 2007.

LR29–PR00 Rule 707. Real Estate

707.10 In all supervised estates and guardianships in which real estate is to be sold, a written professional appraisal shall be filed with the Court at the time of filing the Petition for Sale, unless such appraisal was filed with the inventory. Such written appraisal shall include as a minimum the following elements:

a. A brief description of the property interest being appraised, including the full and legal description thereof.

b. Purpose or objective of the appraisal.

c. Date for which fair market value is determined.

d. Data and reasoning supporting the fair market value.

e. Fair market value determined.

f. Statement of assumptions and special or limiting conditions.

g. Certification of disinterest in real estate.

h. Signature of the appraiser.

707.20 All such appraisals required by LR29–PR00–707.10 shall be made within one year of the date of the Petition for Sale.

707.30 All deeds submitted to the Court for approval in either estate or guardianship proceedings shall be signed by the fiduciary and the signature notarized prior to its submission. All such deeds shall be submitted with the Report of Sale of Real Estate or at the time of the hearing on the Final Account. Copies of such deeds shall be submitted with the Report of Sale of Real Estate or at the time of the hearing on the Final Account. Copies of such deeds shall be filed with the Court for its records.

707.40 Whenever a Final Decree reflects that real estate has vested in heirs or beneficiaries, the Decree shall be recorded with the County Recorder of the County where any such real estate is located and evidence of said recording shall be provided to the Court with the Supplemental Report.

707.50 No Personal Representative's Deed shall be approved in unsupervised estates.

Adopted as Rule 307, effective July 1, 2000. Renumbered as Rule 707 and amended effective June 1, 2005. Amended effective August 12, 2007.

LR29–PR00 Rule 708. Sale of Assets

708.10 In all supervised estates and guardianships, no Petition to Sell Personal Property shall be granted unless a written appraisal prepared by a person competent to appraise such property and setting forth the fair market value thereof, is filed with the Court at the time of the filing of the Petition to Sell, unless such appraisal was filed with the inventory. This rule shall not apply to personal property which is sold at public auction.

708.20 All appraisals required by LR29–PR00–707.10 shall be made within one year of the date of the Petition to Sell.

708.30 No written appraisal shall be required for the sale of assets which are traded in a market and the value of which is readily ascertainable. Such assets include, but are not limited to, stocks, bonds, mutual funds, commodities, and precious metals.

Adopted as Rule 308, effective July 1, 2000. Renumbered as Rule 708 and amended effective June 1, 2005. Amended effective August 12, 2007.

LR29–PR00 Rule 709. Claims

709.10 Three (3) months and fifteen (15) days after the date of the first published notice to creditors, the fiduciary, or the fiduciary's attorney, shall examine the Claim Docket and shall allow or disallow each claim filed against the estate.

Adopted as Rule 309, effective July 1, 2000. Renumbered as Rule 709 and amended effective June 1, 2005. Amended effective August 12, 2007.

LR29–PR00 Rule 710. Accounting

710.10 Whenever an estate cannot be closed within one (1) year, the personal representative shall:

a. File an intermediate account with the Court within thirty days (30) after the expiration of one (1) year and each succeeding year thereafter. The accounting shall comply with the provisions of IC 29–1–16–4 and 29–1–16–6 and:

(1) Shall state facts showing why the estate cannot be closed and an estimated date of closing.

(2) Shall propose partial distribution of the estate to the extent that partial distribution can be made without prejudice to the distributees and claimants; or

b. File a statement with the Court stating the reasons why the estate has not been closed. In addition, the Court reserves the power to require the personal representative to comply with the accounting provisions of sub-part (a) above.

710.20 All guardianship accountings shall contain a certification of an officer of any financial institution in which guardianship assets are held, verifying the account balance (**Form PR00–5**).

710.30 All social security or Medicare benefits received on behalf of an incapacitated person shall be included and accounted for in the guardianship accounting unless court approval has been previously granted to allow said funds to be paid directly to a residential or health care facility, or because of the amount of such funds, the Court finds that such funds can only be used by the guardian or designated person for the benefit of use of such incapacitated person.

710.40 In all supervised estate and guardianship accountings, vouchers or canceled checks for the expenditures claimed shall be filed with the accounting. No affidavits in lieu of vouchers or canceled checks will be accepted from individual fiduciaries, unless prior written approval is granted by the Court (the Court may set forth any and all additional conditions and/or extra ordinary circumstances needed for such approval). An affidavit in lieu of vouchers or canceled checks may be accepted from a state or federally chartered financial institution who serves as a fiduciary, provided the financial institution retains the vouchers or canceled checks on file or by electronic recording device and makes same available to interested parties upon court order. The Court may require such institution to provide a certification from its Internal Audit Department verifying the accuracy of the accounting.

710.50 In all supervised estate and guardianship accountings, a notation shall be placed by each expenditure indicating the reason for or nature of the expenditure unless the payee name indicates the nature of the expenditure.

EXAMPLE: Bogota Drugs—Toiletries for incapacitated person

Dr. John Jones

Sam Smith—Repair roof of home at 162 Maple Street, Any Town, Indiana

Tender Care Nursing Home

710.55 All accountings to the Court shall contain an itemized statement of the assets on hand.

710.60 Receipts or canceled checks for all final distributions shall be filed either in the final report, or a supplemental report, before discharge will be granted by the Court.

710.65 All accountings shall follow the prescribed statutory format. Informal, handwritten, or transactional accountings will not be accepted, except as permitted by LR29–PR00–714.

710.70 All court costs shall be paid and all claims satisfied and released before the hearing on the Final Account and a Clerk's Certification thereof (**Form PR00–6**) shall be filed with the Court before such Final Account shall be approved.

710.75 The Federal Estate Tax Closing letter and the Indiana Inheritance Tax Closing letter (or the countersigned receipt) or a photocopy thereof, showing payment of all Federal Estate and/or Indiana Inheritance Tax liability in the estate, executed by the Internal Revenue Service or the Indiana Department of State Revenue, shall be attached to the Final Accounting at the time of filing, unless the Court has given prior written approval to attach such letter to the Final Report, after filing but prior to the hearing on the Final Accounting.

710.80 When an individual has been appointed to handle the financial affairs of a protected person, an accounting shall be filed within thirty (30) days after the first anniversary of the date the guardianship letters were issued. Thereafter, unless a contrary order is issued by the Court, all accountings shall be filed biennially.

Adopted as Rule 310, effective July 1, 2000. Renumbered as Rule 710 and amended effective June 1, 2005. Amended effective August 12, 2007; January 1, 2012.

LR29–PR00 Rule 711.   Fees of Attorneys and Fiduciary

711.10 No fees for fiduciaries or attorneys shall be paid out of any supervised estate or guardianship without prior written order of the Court.

711.20 All orders for fees in estates shall provide that said fees are to be paid only after approval of the Final Accounting except the Court may in its sole discretion, if all paperwork has been properly filed, award partial attorney or fiduciary fees when the Indiana Inheritance Schedule is filed or the Federal Estate Tax Return is filed.

711.30 A guardian or guardian's attorney may petition for fees at the time of filing an inventory. Other than as provided hereafter, no further petition for fees may be filed until a biennial, annual, or final accounting has been filed. When unusual items of substantial work occur during the proceedings, the Court may consider a petition to allow fees for such services.

711.40 No attorney or fiduciary fees will be determined and authorized for payment by the Court in any unsupervised administration of a decedent's estate.

711.50 Where contracts for legal services have been entered into prior or subsequent to the opening of an estate or guardianship, the Court reserves the right to approve or disapprove the fee contracts consistent with this court's fee guidelines.

711.60 All petitions for fees for the attorney and/or fiduciary shall conform to the guidelines for fees enumerated in 711.70 below and shall specifically set forth all services performed in detail as well as the amount of the fee requested and how it has been calculated.

711.70 Pursuant to relevant statute, if a testator does not provide for compensation of the personal representative and/or the attorney performing services for the estate, the Court may award "just and reasonable" fees. In determining a "just and reasonable" amount of fees, the Court may consider several factors, including: the labor performed, the nature of the estate, difficulties in recovering assets or locating devises, and the peculiar qualifications of the administrator and/or attorney. Additionally, for attorneys, the Court may consider the guidelines for determining legal fees as set forth in Rule 1.5 of the Indiana Rules of Professional Conduct. In all fee determinations, the key factor considered by the Court will be that the fees are reasonably commensurate to the time and work involved.

711.80 Unjustified delays in carrying out duties by the fiduciary and/or attorney will result in a reduction of fees.

711.90 Attorney fees for representing a minor in settlement of a claim for personal injuries are subject to court approval. If the entire attorney fee is to be paid at the same time a structured settlement is approved, the amount of the fee must be based on the present value of the settlement.

Adopted as Rule 311, effective July 1, 2000. Renumbered as Rule 711 and amended effective June 1, 2005. Amended effective August 12, 2007; Aug. 1, 2011.

LR29–PR00 Rule 712. Unsupervised Administration

712.10 No petition for administration without court supervision shall be granted unless the consent requirement of IC 29–1–7.5–2(a) is fulfilled.

712.20 All court costs shall be paid and all claims satisfied and released on or before the date of the filing of the Closing Statement and a Clerk's Certification thereof (see attached form) shall be filed with the Court at the time such Closing Statement is filed with the Court.

712.30 Every Closing Statement shall comply with LR29–PR00–710.10 (**Form PR00–6**).

712.40 The Court will not enter an order approving the Closing Statement since such estate is closed by operation of law.

Adopted as Rule 312, effective July 1, 2000. Renumbered as Rule 712 and amended effective June 1, 2005. Amended effective August 12, 2007.

LR29–PR00 Rule 713. Miscellaneous

713.10 If the Court determines that no Inheritance Tax Schedule is required to be filed, a copy of the Court's order shall be served on the local representative of the Inheritance Tax Division of the Indiana Department of Revenue.

713.20 The Court may adapt procedures by standing order to effectuate the implementation of these rules, and may deviate from these rules when justice requires, but only upon showing of severe prejudice or hardship.

Adopted as Rule 313, effective July 1, 2000. Renumbered as Rule 713 and amended effective June 1, 2005. Amended effective August 12, 2007.

LR29–PR00 Rule 714. Guardianships

714.10 In all guardianship matters seeking to declare an adult incapacitated for any reason, the incapacitated person shall be present at the hearing or sufficient evidence shall be presented showing that the incapacitated person is unable to appear. The Court may at any time appoint a guardian ad litem to investigate and protect the best interest of the incapacitated person (**Forms PR00–8, PR00–9**).

714.20 In all guardianship matters seeking to declare an adult incapacitated for any reason, a Physician's Report by the doctor treating the alleged incapacitated person or such additional evidence as the Court shall require, shall be presented to the Court at the time the petition is filed or on the hearing date. No determination will be made without a supporting medical report or testimony (**Form PR00–10**).

714.30 Pursuant to IC 29–3–3–4(a) no guardian of an adult shall be appointed or protective order entered without notice except upon verified allegations that delay may result in immediate and irreparable injury to the person or loss or damage to the property.

714.40 In every petition for the appointment of a guardian of the person of a minor child, the following information shall be given:

  a. The child's present address.

  b. The places where the child has lived within the past two years and the names and present addresses of persons with whom the child has lived during that period.

  c. General information concerning school, health, etc.

  d. Whether, to petitioner's knowledge, any other litigation is pending concerning the custody of the child in this or any other state.

  e. Whether, to petitioner's knowledge, any person not a party to the guardianship proceeding has physical custody of the child or claims to have custody or visitation rights with respect to the child.

714.50 Current reports filed by a guardian of the person shall state the present residence of the incapacitated person and his or her general welfare. If the incapacitated person is an adult, a report of a treating physician shall be filed with the current report, verifying that the incapacity of the person remains unchanged since the date the guardianship was established or the date of the last current report and that the living arrangements for the incapacitated person are appropriate (**Forms PR00–10, PR00–11, PR00–12**).

714.60 Nothing herein shall be deemed as amending, superseding or altering the Probate Rules and Regulations promulgated by the Veteran's Administration of the United States of America, and every fiduciary and attorney shall comply with same, if applicable.

714.70 Other than for routine matters, the guardian shall obtain court approval prior to taking any action on any financial matter pertaining to carrying out the guardian's duties and responsibilities for the protected person.

Adopted as Rule 314, effective July 1, 2000. Renumbered as Rule 714 and amended effective June 1, 2005. Amended effective August 12, 2007.

LR29–PR00 Rule 715. Waiver of Notice of Inheritance Tax Appraisal

715.10 Waivers of notice of the time and place of the appraisal of each property interest of a decedent for inheritance tax purposes and of the hearing on the appraisal report shall be filed on or before the date upon which the inheritance tax return is filed.

715.20 Such waivers of notice shall be signed by each person known to have an interest in the property interests to be appraised and by any person designated by the Court. A waiver filed by an entity other than an individual shall state the capacity of the person who has signed for such entity.

715.30 A waiver signed by an attorney or another person on behalf of a person who is entitled to notice under IC 6–4.1–5–3 and IC 6–4.1–5–9 shall include a copy of the power of attorney, letters of guardianship or other authority for the signer to act on behalf of such person. In the event that the interested person is a minor, the waiver shall include a statement of the relationship of the signer to the minor.

715.40 In the event that a waiver is not filed for each interested person, the personal representative shall, at the time of filing the inheritance tax return, provide notice of the time and place of the appraisal to each interested person who has not filed a waiver. Upon the filing of the appraiser's report, the personal representative shall provide notice of the time and place of the hearing on the report to all persons known to be interested in the resident decedent's estate, including the Department of State Revenue.

Adopted as Rule 315, effective July 1, 2000. Renumbered as Rule 715 and amended effective June 1, 2005. Amended effective August 12, 2007.

LR29–PR00 Rule 716. Minors' Settlements

716.10 This rule shall govern requests for approval of settlements for minors (pursuant to IC 29–3–9 and/or IC 29–3–4) and guardianships for minors, if such settlements are approved by the Court.

716.20 A hearing shall be set at the request of counsel in which testimony or evidence is presented so as to fully and independently satisfy the Court that the requested settlement fully protects the minor's rights and interests. The Court may at any time appoint a guardian ad litem to protect the best interest of the minor and investigate such settlement **(Forms PR00–8, PR00–13)**.

716.30 In all settlement proceedings, whether wrongful death, minor's settlement or incapacitated person's settlement, the personal representative, one custodial parent or the guardian must be present at the time the settlement is presented to the Court for approval. The Court retains the right to require the presence of the minor or incapacitated person at such times.

716.40 If the Court should grant such settlement and a guardianship is needed, then the appointment of a guardian will be determined as set forth by statute and by these rules.

716.50 Once a guardian is appointed, then such guardian shall post bond pursuant to LR29–PR00–305.10, unless, in lieu of a bond, a fiduciary places all funds or assets in a restricted account at a federally-insured financial institution or in a court approved investment, designating that no principle or interest may be withdrawn without a written order of the Court, and with the following restriction placed on the face of the account or in the investment document **(Forms PR00–5, PR00–14)**:

"NO PRINCIPAL OR INTEREST SHALL BE WITHDRAWN WITHOUT WRITTEN ORDER OF _____ COURT OF _____, INDIANA."

The fiduciary shall file the following with the Court:

a. Prior to issuance of letters, the fiduciary's attorney shall execute an Attorney's Undertaking for such assets **(Form PR00–15)**.

b. Within ten (10) days of the order authorizing the creation of the account or investment, a certification by an officer of the institution at which the account or investment has been created, affirming that the account or investment is restricted as required by Court order and is in compliance with this rule.

716.60 No surety bond or restricted account is required where a corporate fiduciary serves as a guardian of the estate.

716.70 The guardian shall be required to file an inventory pursuant to LR29–PR00–705 unless such guardian has deposited all funds in a restricted account.

716.80 When the guardian files an accounting pursuant to LR29–PR00–710, then such guardian shall be required to attach a copy of the most recent bank statement showing any and all transactions on such bank account **(Forms PR00–12, PR00–16)**.

716.90 Attorney fee awards must conform with LR29–PR00–711.

Adopted as Rule 316, effective July 1, 2000. Renumbered as Rule 716 and amended effective June 1, 2005. Amended effective August 12, 2007.

LR29–PR00 Rule 717. Wrongful Death Estates

717.10 All proposed wrongful death settlements must be approved by the Court, whether the estate is supervised, unsupervised, or a special administration for the sole purpose of prosecuting the wrongful death claim.

717.20 When an estate remains open one (1) year, the personal representative shall file a status report as to any wrongful death claims. If an action is pending, the report shall show the cause number and the Court.

717.30 When a judgment has been paid or a petition for approval of settlement is filed in any estate, a petition shall be filed showing the proposed distribution in accordance with IC 34–1–1–2. Such petition must set out the proposed distribution to the appropriate statutory damage distributes, such as:

a. Expenses of administration;

b. Providers of funeral and burial expenses;

c. Providers of medical expenses in connection with last illness of decedent;

d. Surviving spouse;

e. Dependent children; and

f. Dependent next of kin (if there is no surviving spouse or dependent children).

A proposed order shall be presented to the Court, ordering distribution in accordance with IC 34–1–1–2 and requiring that a final account as to the wrongful death proceeds be filed within thirty (30) days.

717.40 IC 34–1–1–8 does not provide for the opening of a minor's wrongful death estate.

Adopted as Rule 317, effective July 1, 2000. Renumbered as Rule 717 and amended effective June 1, 2005. Amended effective August 12, 2007.

LR29–PR00 Rule 718. Adoptions

718.10 Except for good cause shown, no final hearings in adoption proceedings shall take place until the adopting couple (or the birth parent and adoptive stepparent) have been married for at least one (1) year and the child has been in the home of the adoptive parent(s) for at least three (3) months.

718.20 A consent to adoption must be notarized.

Adopted as Rule 318, effective July 1, 2000. Renumbered as Rule 718 and amended effective June 1, 2005. Amended effective August 12, 2007.

HAMILTON COUNTY JUVENILE RULES

Adopted Effective June 1, 2005

Including Amendments Received Through November 1, 2013

Research Notes

Annotations to the Hamilton County Juvenile Rules are available in West's Annotated Indiana Code, *Title 34 Appendix.*

These rules may be searched electronically on Westlaw in the IN-RULES *database; updates to these rules may be found on Westlaw in* IN-RULESUPDATES. *For search tips and a summary of database content, consult the Westlaw Scope Screens for each database.*

LR29–JV00 Rule 801. Assignment of Juvenile Case Numbers

801.10 The Hamilton County Criminal Random Filing Rule (LR29–CR00–303) does not apply to juvenile cases. It is therefore necessary to establish assignment of Juvenile Delinquency and Juvenile Status Offense causes.

801.20 The Clerk of the Court shall assign cause numbers for new filings of all JS and JD case types to Hamilton Circuit Court and Hamilton Superior Court No. 1.

801.30 The Clerk shall file all cases involving juveniles with last names beginning with the letters A—L in Hamilton County Superior Court No. 1 and cases involving juveniles with last names beginning M–Z shall be filed in Hamilton Circuit Court.

801.40 The Clerk of the Court shall file all cases involving juvenile cases now filed in such court. Any cases involving new charges concerning a juvenile whose case is still pending disposition or is on probation supervision in Hamilton Superior Court No. 3 shall be filed by the Clerk in Hamilton Superior Court No. 3.

801.50 The designation of the Clerk concerning the proper court in which to file a cause shall take precedence over the designation of any other entity or individual, except upon specific order entered by the Judge of Hamilton Circuit Court, Hamilton Superior Court No. 1, or Hamilton Superior Court No. 3.

801.60 When a motion is filed requesting a joinder of juvenile cases because of such cases being related in subject matter or by individuals, the Court may, after finding probable cause, order such cases joined and the cases may be filed in one court regardless of the first initial of their name for the sake of judicial economy.

801.70 When a Judge disqualifies or recuses from a juvenile case, the Clerk shall reassign to another court pursuant to this rule. When the disqualification or recusal is by the Judge of the Hamilton Circuit Court, the Clerk shall reassign such case to the Hamilton Superior Court No. 1. Upon disqualification or recusal of Hamilton Superior Court No. 1, the Clerk shall reassign such case to the Hamilton Circuit Court.

801.80 In the event the above reassignment is not permitted and a subsequent reassignment is required, said case reassignment shall be achieved by obtaining a new court assignment from the remaining Hamilton County Courts using a random assignment procedure.

Adopted effective June 1, 2005. Amended effective August 12, 2007.

LR29–JV00 Rule 802. Access Confidential Juvenile Records

802.10 The Circuit and Superior Courts of Hamilton County find that in order to facilitate effective legal representation of juveniles, it is necessary that confidential juvenile records be made accessible as follows:

a. All persons permitted access pursuant to statute; and

b. Paralegals and employees of the juvenile's attorney of record may have access to such juvenile files if they are acting at the direction of and under the control of such attorney of record. Written documentation may be required by the clerk before such paralegal or employee may have access to such juvenile files.

Adopted effective June 1, 2005. Amended effective August 12, 2007.

HENDRICKS COUNTY LOCAL RULES

Adopted June 1, 2006, Effective January 1, 2007

Including Amendments Received Through November 1, 2013

Research Notes

These rules may be searched electronically on Westlaw *in the* IN-RULES*database; updates to these rules may be found on* Westlaw *in* IN-RULESUPDATES. *For search tips and a summary of database content, consult the Westlaw Scope Screens for each database.*

LR32–TR79 Rule 1. SPECIAL JUDGE SELECTION IN CIVIL CASES

1. Pursuant to T.R. 79(C), A judge shall disqualify and recuse whenever the judge, the judge's spouse, a person within the third degree of relationship to either of them, the spouse of such a person, or a person residing in the judge's household:

(1) is a party to the proceeding, or an officer, director or trustee of a party;

(2) is acting as a lawyer in the proceeding;

(3) is known by the judge to have an interest that could be substantially affected by the proceeding; or

(4) is associated with the pending litigation in such fashion as to require disqualification under the *Code of Judicial Conduct* or otherwise.

Upon disqualification or recusal under this section, a special judge shall be selected from a list of the current Circuit Court Judge, Superior Court Judges and Magistrates of the other county.

2. Pursuant to T.R. 79(D), within seven (7) days of the notation in the Chronological Case Summary of the order granting a change of judge or an order of disqualification, the parties may agree to an eligible special judge. The agreement of the parties shall be in writing and shall be filed in the court where the case is pending. Upon the filing of the agreement, the court shall enter an order appointing such individual as the special judge in the case and provide notice pursuant to Trial Rule 72(D) to the special judge and all parties. A judge appointed under this section shall have seven (7) days from the date of appointment to decide whether or not to accept the case and enter his or her decision. The filing of the acceptance vests jurisdiction in the special judge. An oath or additional evidence of acceptance of jurisdiction is not required.

3. Pursuant to T.R. 79 (H), the Clerk of Morgan County and the Clerk of Hendricks County shall maintain a separate list of all Circuit Court Judges, Superior Court Judges and Magistrates of Morgan County and Hendricks County to be used to randomly select a special judge in all cases in which the parties do not agree to a special judge, or a judge selected by the parties decides not to accept the case, as set out in this rule.

4. If the parties fail to agree to the selection of a special judge, the Clerk of the County in which the case is filed shall randomly select a special judge from the judges of that county and notify the Court, the selected special judge and the parties of the random selection.

5. If either of the counties of Morgan or Hendricks County do not have a sufficient number of regular sitting judges from which to select a judge from the county in which the case is filed, the Clerk of the County shall randomly select from a list of the current Circuit Court Judge, Superior Court Judges and Magistrates of the other county.

6. The sitting judge may forego the requirements set forth herein and certify immediately to the Indiana Supreme Court for the appointment of a special judge if the particular circumstances of a case warrant selection of a special judge by the Indiana Supreme Court.

Adopted June 1, 2006, effective Jan. 1, 2007. Amended effective Oct. 11, 2007; July 1, 2011; May 1, 2013.

LR32–CR2.2 Rule 2. ASSIGNMENT OF CRIMINAL CASES

LR32—CR2.2–2 Rule 1. Definitions

A. "**Week**" shall mean 12:01 a.m. Friday until 12:00 a.m. the following Friday.

B. The "**weekly rotation**" for assignment of criminal cases shall be:

1. **"Week 1"** means Hendricks Superior Court No. 1.

2. **"Week 2"** means Hendricks Superior Court No. 2.

3. **"Week 3"** means Hendricks Superior Court No. 3.

4. **"Week 4"** means Hendricks Superior Court No. 4.

5. **"Week 5"** means Hendricks Superior Court No. 5.

6. **"Week 6"** means Hendricks Circuit Court.

LR32—CR2.2–2 Rule 2. Criminal Case Assignment

A. General Rule.

1. Except as set forth below, all MRs, FAs, FBs, FCs, FDs, and CMs shall be assigned according to the weekly rotation as defined in LR32—CR2.2–2 Rule 1 by the date on which the offense alleged in the charging document (including grand jury indictments) occurred.

2. In the event of multiple offenses, the date on which the earliest offense alleged in the charging document occurred shall govern the assignment. Filing of multiple offenses shall comply with Administrative Rule 1(B) of the Indiana Rules of Court.

3. In the event a charging document does not set forth a date on which the alleged offense occurred, the case shall be assigned to a court of record in the county on a random basis.

4. The week beginning 12:01 am on Friday, January 3, 2014 shall be deemed Week 4.

B. IC Title 9 Cases.

1. All FAs, FBs, FCs, FDs, and CMs filed under IC Title 9 shall be assigned to Hendricks Superior Court No. 2, Hendricks Superior Court No. 3, Hendricks Superior Court No. 4, and Hendricks Superior Court No. 5 according to the weekly rotation.

2. All FAs, FBs, FCs, FDs, and CMs filed under IC Title 9 during Weeks 1 and 6 shall be assigned on a rotating basis to Hendricks Superior Court No. 2, Hendricks Superior Court No. 3, Hendricks Superior Court No. 4, and Hendricks Superior Court No. 5.

C. Domestic Violence Cases. All cases filed under IC 35–42–2–1.3 or IC 35–46–1–15.1 shall be assigned to Hendricks Superior Court No. 1.

D. Post Conviction Relief Petitions.

1. All PCs shall be assigned to the same court where the defendant was tried or pled guilty.

2. In the event the defendant was tried or pled guilty in another county, the PC shall be assigned according to the weekly rotation as defined in LR32—CR2.2–2 Rule 1.

E. Miscellaneous Criminal Cases. All MCs shall be assigned according to the weekly rotation as defined in LR32—CR2.2–2 Rule 1.

F. Infractions and Ordinance Violations.

1. Unless filed as additional charges in a felony or misdemeanor proceeding—in which case the infractions shall be resolved in conjunction with the felony or misdemeanor proceeding:

a. All IFs issued by the Danville Police Department shall be assigned to Hendricks Superior Court No. 5.

b. All other IFs shall be assigned to the appropriate Town Court.

2. All OVs shall be assigned to Hendricks Superior Court No. 5.

G. Town Courts.

1. Brownsburg Town Court

a. All cases filed under IC 35–43–5–5 shall be assigned to Brownsburg Town Court.

b. All CMs that occur within the limits of the town of Brownsburg shall be assigned to Brownsburg Town Court except cases filed under:

   i. IC 9–30–5–1,

   ii. IC 9–30–5–2,

   iii. IC 35–42–2–1.3, or

   iv. IC 35–46–1–15.1.

2. Plainfield Town Court

a. All CMs that occur within the limits of the town of Plainfield shall be assigned to Plainfield Town Court except cases filed under:

   i. IC 9–30–5–1,

   ii. IC 9–30–5–2,

   iii. IC 35–42–2–1.3, or

   iv. IC 35–46–1–15.1.

LR32—CR2.2–2 Rule 3. Re–Filings and Subsequent Filings

A. Subsequent to Dismissals. In the event the State of Indiana dismisses a case or charge, any subsequent re-filing of that case or charge against the defendant shall be assigned to the court from which the dismissal was taken.

B. Filing of Additional Charges. When additional charges are filed against a defendant subsequent to the assignment of the case, all such additional charges to be resolved in conjunction with the pending case shall be assigned to the court of initial assignment.

C. New Causes of Action.

1. When a new cause of action is filed against a defendant in a court of record in the county with an existing felony or misdemeanor proceeding in a Town Court, the existing cause(s) of action shall be assigned to the court of record administering the new cause of action.

2. When a new cause of action is filed against a defendant who is on probation or is a defendant in an existing felony or misdemeanor proceeding, the judge of the court in which the probation is being supervised or in which the existing cause of action is pending shall confer with the judge of the court where the new cause of action is filed in order to determine into which court to consolidate all proceedings.

3. If the judges in subsection (2) cannot agree upon which court to consolidate all proceedings, all proceedings in subsection (2) shall be returned to the Clerk for random assignment to a court of record in the county.

LR32—CR2.2–2 Rule 4. Reassignment

A. In the event a change of judge is granted, an order of disqualification or recusal has been entered, or it becomes necessary to assign another judge in any felony or misdemeanor proceeding, the case shall be returned to the Clerk for random assignment to another court of record in the county.

B. A judge, by appropriate order entered in the record of judgments and orders, may transfer and reassign any pending case to any other court of record in the county, subject to acceptance by the receiving court.

C. This rule does not limit the authority of the judges and magistrates of the courts of record in the county to preside over hearings or issue orders for one another in order to promote efficiency and provide for timely resolution of cases.

LR32—CR2.22 Rule 5. Appointment of Special Judge

A. In the event a local judge in unavailable to accept reassignment of a case pursuant to LR32—CR2.2–2 Rule 4, the case shall be returned to the Clerk for random assignment from a list of full-time judicial officers from contiguous counties and counties within the administrative district of the court and any senior judges assigned to the court who have agreed to serve as a special judge.

B. In the event that no judge under this local rule is available, or the judge presiding in a felony or misdemeanor case concludes that the unique circumstances presented in such proceeding require appointment by the Indiana Supreme Court of a special judge, the presiding judge may request the Indiana Supreme Court for such appointment.

Adopted June 1, 2006, effective Jan. 1, 2007. Amended effective Oct. 11, 2007; June 12, 2009, Jan. 1, 2010; Jan. 1, 2014.

LR32–AR1 Rule 3. PLAN FOR ALLOCATION OF JUDICIAL RESOURCES

LR32—AR1–3 Rule 1. Definitions

A. "**Week**" shall mean 12:01 a.m. Friday until 12:00 a.m. the following Friday.

B. The "**weekly rotation**" for assignment of cases shall be:

1. "**Week 1**" means Hendricks Superior Court No. 1.

2. "**Week 2**" means Hendricks Superior Court No. 2.

3. "**Week 3**" means Hendricks Superior Court No. 3.

4. "**Week 4**" means Hendricks Superior Court No. 4.

5. "**Week 5**" means Hendricks Superior Court No. 5.

6. "**Week 6**" means Hendricks Circuit Court.

LR32—AR1–3 Rule 2. Criminal Cases.
Criminal case assignment will operate as specified in LR32–CR2.2–2.

LR32—AR1–3 Rule 3. Juvenile Cases.
All JCs, JDs, JSs, JPs, JMs, and JTs shall be filed in Hendricks Circuit Court.

LR32—AR1–3 Rule 4. Remaining Civil Cases

A. Civil Plenary. PLs shall be filed in Hendricks Superior Court No. 2, Hendricks Superior Court No. 3, and Hendricks Superior Court No. 4 subject to the case type limits set forth in Appendix A.

B. Civil Tort.

1. CTs shall be filed in Hendricks Superior Court No. 3, Hendricks Superior Court No. 4, and Hendricks Superior Court No. 5 subject to the case type limits set forth in Appendix A.

2. When all courts have reached their limit for CTs, any additional CTs shall be filed in Hendricks Superior Court No. 3 and Hendricks Superior Court No. 4 on an alternating basis.

C. Civil Collection. CCs shall be filed in Hendricks Circuit Court, Hendricks Superior Court No. 1, Hendricks Superior Court No. 2, Hendricks Superior Court No. 3, Hendricks Superior Court No. 4, and Hendricks Superior Court No. 5 subject to the case type limits set forth in Appendix A.

D. Domestic Relations.

1. Except as set forth below, DRs shall be filed in Hendricks Circuit Court, Hendricks Superior Court No. 1, Hendricks Superior Court No. 2, Hendricks Superior Court No. 3, Hendricks Superior Court No. 4, and Hendricks Superior Court No. 5 subject to the case type limits set forth in Appendix A.

2. Unless a court has reached its limit for DRs—in which case the DR shall be filed in another court that has not reached its DR limit:

a. DRs involving the same parties as a pending PO shall be filed in the court presiding over the PO.

b. DRs involving the same parties for which an order of protection has been issued shall be filed in the court that issued the order of protection.

E. Miscellaneous. MIs shall be filed in Hendricks Superior Court No. 1, Hendricks Superior Court No. 2, Hendricks Superior Court No. 3, Hendricks Superior Court No. 4, and Hendricks Superior Court No. 5 subject to the case type limits set forth in Appendix A.

F. Mortgage Foreclosure. MFs shall be filed in Hendricks Circuit Court and Hendricks Superior Court No. 2 subject to the case type limits set forth in Appendix A.

G. Order of Protection.

1. Except as set forth below, all POs shall be assigned according to the weekly rotation as defined in AR1–3 Rule 1.

2. The week beginning 12:01 am on Friday, January 3, 2014 shall be deemed Week 4.

3. Unless a court has reached its limit for POs— in which case the PO shall be filed in another court that has not reached its PO limit:

    a. POs filed by a party to a pending DR shall be filed in the court presiding over the DR.

    b. POs filed by a party to a pending JP shall be filed in the court presiding over the JP.

    c. POs involving the same parties as a pending PO shall be filed in the court presiding over the pending PO.

H. Probate.

1. All ADs, MHs, and TRs shall be filed in Hendricks Superior Court No. 1.

2. All GUs shall be filed in Hendricks Superior Court No. 5.

3. ES, EUs, and EMs shall be filed in Hendricks Superior Court No. 1 and Hendricks Superior Court No. 5 subject to the case type limits set forth in Appendix A.

I. Small Claims. SCs shall be filed in Hendricks Superior Court No. 1, Hendricks Superior Court No. 2, Hendricks Superior Court No. 3, Hendricks Superior Court No. 4, and Hendricks Superior Court No. 5 subject to the case type limits set forth in Appendix A.

J. Reciprocal Support. All RSs shall be filed in Hendricks Circuit Court.

K. In the event a party in a civil case does not request to file in a particular court, the case shall be assigned on a random basis to a court that hears that case type, subject to the case type limits set forth in Appendix A.

LR32—AR1–3 Rule 5. Reassignment

A. When a court has reached its limit for a case type, no additional cases of that type shall be filed in that court until all other courts have reached their limit for that case type as set forth in Appendix A.

B. When a court has reached its limit for a case type, the Clerk shall notify all courts of this fact and post notice to this effect in the Clerk's Office.

C. Except where these rules provide otherwise, when all courts have reached their limit for a case type, any additional cases of that type shall be assigned on a rotating basis among the courts that hear that case type.

D. This rule does not limit the authority of the judges and magistrates of the courts of record in the county to preside over hearings or issue orders for one another in order to promote efficiency and provide for timely resolution of cases.

E. Cases transferred from one court to another shall not be included in the receiving court's limit for that case type as set forth in Appendix A.

LR32—AR1–3 Rule 6. Evaluation of Caseload. Changes necessary to ensure that the Hendricks County Courts remain in compliance with the Order for Development of Local Caseload Plans shall be developed and approved by a majority vote of the judicial officers.

Appendix A

Case Type	C01	D01	D02	D03	D04	D05
JC	ALL					
JD	ALL					
JS	ALL					
JP	ALL					
JM	ALL					
JT	ALL					
PL			45	45	46	
MF	100		735			
CC	712	200	200	200	200	200
CT				46	62	46
SC	0	694	695	695	695	695
DR	52	125	150	200	150	125
RS	ALL					
MH		ALL				
AD		ALL				
EU		193				192
GU						ALL
TR		ALL				
MI		58	59	59	59	59

Adopted June 1, 2006, effective Jan. 1, 2007. Amended effective Oct. 11, 2007; amended June 12, 2009, effective Jan. 1, 2010; Jan. 1, 2012; Jan. 1, 2014.

LR32–AR15 Rule 4. COURT REPORTER SERVICES

1. **Definitions.** The following definitions shall apply under this local rule.

    1.1. A **Court Reporter** is an employee at will, not an independent contractor, not self-employed subject to the control of the Judge and is specifically designated to perform the official court reporting services for the court including preparing a transcript of the record.

1.2. *Equipment* means all physical items owned by the court or other governmental entity and used by a court reporter in performing court reporting services. Equipments shall include, but not be limited to, telephones, computer hardware, software programs, disks, tapes, and any other device used for recording and storing, and transcribing electronic data.

1.3. *Work Space* means that portion of the court's facilities dedicated to each court reporter, including but not limited to actual space in the courtroom and any designated office space.

1.4. *Page* means the page unit of transcript which results when a recording is transcribed in the form required by Indiana Rule of Appellate Procedure 7.2.

1.5. *Recording* means the electronic, mechanical, stenographic or other recording made as required by Indiana Rule of Trial Procedure 74.

1.6. *Regular Hours Worked* means those hours which the court is regularly scheduled to work during any given work week. Depending on the particular court, these hours may vary from court to court within the county but remain the same for each work week.

1.7. *Gap hours worked* means those hours worked that are in excess of the regular hours worked but hours not in excess of forty (40) hours per work week.

1.8. *Overtime hours worked* means those hours worked in excess of forty (40) hours per work week.

1.9. *Work Week* means a seven (7) consecutive day week that consistently begins and ends on the same days throughout the year, i.e. Sunday through Saturday, Wednesday through Tuesday, Friday through Thursday.

1.10. *Court* means that particular court for which the court reporter performs services. Court may also mean all of the courts in Hendricks County.

1.11. *County indigent transcript* means a transcript that is paid for from county funds and is for the use on behalf of a litigant who has been declared indigent by a court.

1.12. *State indigent transcript* means a transcript that is paid for from state funds and is for the use on behalf of a litigant who has been declared indigent by a court.

1.13. *Private transcript* means a transcript, including but not limited to a deposition transcript that is paid for by a private party.

2. Salaries and Per Page Fees.

2.1. Court Reporters shall be paid for time spent working under the control, direction and direct supervision of their supervising court during any regular work hours, gap hours or overtime hours. The supervising court shall enter into a written agreement with the court reporter which outlines the manner in which the court reporter is to be compensated for gap and overtime hours, i.e. monetary compensation or compensatory time off regular work hours.

2.2. The maximum per page fee a court reporter may charge for the preparation of a county indigent transcript shall be $4.25. The court reporter shall submit a claim directly to the county for the preparation of any county indigent transcripts.

2.3. The maximum per page fee a court reporter may charge for the preparation of a state indigent transcript shall be $4.25.

2.4. The maximum per page fee a court reporter may charge for the preparation of a private transcript shall be $4.25.

2.5. A minimum transcript fee of $40.00 may be charged for any transcript.

2.6. Each court reporter shall report, at least on an annual basis, all transcript fees received for the preparation of county indigent, state indigent or private transcripts to the Indiana Supreme Court Division of State Court Administration. The reporting shall be made on forms prescribed by the Division of State Court Administration.

2.7. Court reporters may charge an additional hourly labor charge for time spent binding the transcripts and copying the exhibits and binding the exhibits. This labor charge shall be equivalent to the court reporter's hourly compensation rate.

2.8. Court reporters may charge a supply charge as follows:

(1)	Paper	$.05 per sheet
(2)	Binders	$1.00 per binder
(3)	Computer disk	$.40 per disk
(4)	Diskette Pocket	$.70 each
(5)	Diskette Cases	$1.20 each

3. Appellate Transcripts.

3.1. Court reporters may charge up to an additional $.50 per page for transcripts prepared in accordance with the Indiana Rules of Appellate Procedure.

4. Private Practice.

4.1. If a court reporter elects to engage in private practice through the recording of a deposition and/or preparing of a deposition transcript, and the court reporter desires to utilize the court's equipment, work space and supplies, and the court agrees to the use of the court equipments for such purpose, the court and the court reporter shall enter into a written agreement which must, at a minimum, designate the following:

(1) The reasonable market rate for the use of equipment, work space and supplies:

(2) The method by which record are to be kept for the use of equipment, work space and supplies and

(3) The method by which the court reporter is to reimburse the court for the use of the equipment, work space and supplies.

4.2. If a court reporter elects to engage in private practice through the recording of a deposition and/or preparing of a deposition transcript, all such private practice work shall be conducted outside of regular working hours.

Adopted June 1, 2006, effective Jan. 1, 2007. Amended effective Oct. 11, 2007.

LR32–AR00 Rule 5. HENDRICKS COUNTY SUPERIOR COURTS ALCOHOL AND DRUG SERVICES PROGRAM FEE

1. The Hendricks Superior Courts have established a court operated Alcohol and Drug Services Program pursuant to I.C. § 12–23–14 administered through the Hendricks Superior Courts Probation Department.

2. In any criminal case where substance is alleged to have been a contributing factor, the person convicted shall be ordered to pay a Substance Abuse Fee of $100.00. This fee includes substance abuse assessment, client intake and orientation, referral to treatment if required, transfer to another jurisdiction if required, substance abuse education if required, client monitoring, urine screening, case management and compliance monitoring until discharge.

3. The Substance Abuse Fee may be waived if the person is actively involved in a substance abuse treatment program at the time of sentencing or successfully completed a substance abuse treatment program as a result of the charge for which the person is currently being sentenced.

Adopted effective Oct. 11, 2007. Amended effective Dec. 1, 2012; May 1, 2013.

LR32–AR00 Rule 6. HENDRICKS SOUNTY SUPERIOR COURT NO. 4 DRUG COURT FEES

1. The Hendricks Superior Court No. 4 has established a drug court pursuant to I.C.§ 33–23–16 and the Problem Solving Court Rules.

2. Participants admitted to the Hendricks Superior Court No. 4 Drug Court shall be assessed a problem-solving court administration fee of $100.00 for initial problem-solving court services upon admission into the program.

3. Participants admitted to the Hendricks Superior Court No. 4 Drug Court shall be assessed a monthly user fee of $50.00 beginning with the second month of participation and for each month thereafter for the duration of their participation in the program.

4. Participants admitted to the Hendricks Superior Court No. Drug Court shall be responsible for all chemical testing fees. Participants shall be responsible for $5.00 per urine drug screen at the time of testing. Participants shall be responsible for the cost of any confirmatory test.

5. Participants may be assessed a fee for services received as a result of referrals made by the Court, including mental health services, health services and monitoring services. Fees for those services are payable to the entity providing the service.

LR32–AR00 Rule 7. HENDRICKS COUNTY PROBATION THEFT CLASS FEE

1. The Hendricks County Courts have established a Theft Class pursuant to I.C. § 35–38–2–2.3(4) administered through the Hendricks County Probation Department.

2. In criminal cases involving some form of Theft, where the offender is Court ordered to attend a Theft Class, or as part of a Diversion Program through the Prosecutor's Office is required to attend a Theft Class as part of the agreement, the person shall be ordered to pay a Theft Class Fee of $75.00. This fee includes services being provided for a cognitive based eight (8) hour education class, the cost of the workbook and all other materials necessary for successful completion of the Class.

3. The Theft Class Fee may be waived by the Judge at the time of sentencing, or at other supplemental hearings.

4. The Theft Class Fee should be deposited into the Adult User Fee Fund.

Adopted effective May 1, 2013.

LR32–JR04 Rule 8.[1] SUMMONING JURORS

1.[2] A two-tier notice for summoning jurors will be use. The jury qualification form and notice will be the first tier and summoning the prospective juror at least one (1) week before service will be the second tier.

Formerly LR32–JR04 Rule 7, adopted Oct. 22, 2007, effective Dec. 30, 2007. Renumbered as LR32–JR04 Rule 8 effective May 1, 2013.

[1] There are two "Rule 8" headings in original data.

[2] There is no subdivision 2 in original.

LR32–CR–00 Rule 8.[1] HENDRICKS COUNTY BAIL BOND SCHEDULE

Hendricks Circuit, Superior No. 1, 2, 3, 4, and 5 Courts

The following Bail Bond Schedule is effective February 1, 2013, and supersedes all prior schedules.

THE CASH BOND PROVISIONS DO NOT APPLY TO CASES TO BE FILED IN THE HENDRICKS CIRCUIT COURT IF THERE IS A SURETY BOND PROVISION IN THIS ORDER.

The Surety Bond for Class D Felonies shall not apply to the Superior Courts.

OFFENSE/CLASS	Surety Bond	Cash Bond
Murder	No Bond	No Bond
Resisting Law Enforcement	$100,000	NONE

(until the initial hearing or 24 hours after the arrest of the defendant. At such time, the bond shall be that applicable to the regular bond schedule for that level of offense.)

OFFENSE/CLASS	Surety Bond	Cash Bond
Class A felony	$100,000 None	
Class B felony	$ 50,000	$7,500
Class C felony	$ 25,000	$3,500
Habitual Offender	$ 30,000	$5,000

INDIANA RESIDENTS

OFFENSE/CLASS	Surety Bond	Cash Bond
Class D felony	$5,000.00 (Circuit only)	$ 500
Class A misdemeanor		$ 300
Class B misdemeanor		$ 300
Class C misdemeanor		$ 300
I.C. 9–30–5		$ 500
(OWI and related offenses)		

OUT–OF–STATE RESIDENTS

OFFENSE/CLASS	Surety Bond	Cash Bond
Class D felony	$ 15,000	$1,000
Class A misdemeanor	$ 5,000	$ 500
Class B misdemeanor	$ 3,000	$ 500
Class C misdemeanor	$ 2,000	$ 500

IDENTIFICATION CASES

Any person who cannot be positively identified at book-in shall be held without bond until the person is brought before the Court for a hearing to determine bond. This includes, but is not limited to, those individuals who refuse to cooperate in their identification by refusing to be fingerprinted, individuals who possess conflicting identification, and individuals whose identifying information cannot be verified.

PERSONS CHARGED WITH A CRIME OF DRIVING WHILE SUSPENDED or NO VALID LICENSE

After being processed by the Hendricks County Sheriff and completing the "Promise to Appear" form, defendants who have been arrested for Driving While Suspended (I.C. 9–24–19–2, 9–24–19–3) or No Valid License (I.C.9–24–18–1) shall be released without having to post a bond. The Sheriff shall provide such persons with an Initial Court Hearing date as if the person posted a bond.

PERSONS CHARGED WITH A CRIME OF DOMESTIC VIOLENCE

A person charged with a crime of domestic violence as defined in I.C. 35–41–1–6.3 shall be kept in custody and not released on bail for at least eight (8) hours from the time of arrest pursuant to I.C. 35–33–1–1.7 and I.C. 35–33–8–6.5.

SEXUALLY VIOLENT PREDATOR DEFENDANTS

Pursuant to I.C. 35–33–8–3.5, a person who is a sexually violent predator under I.C. 35–38–1–7.5, and who is arrested or charged with the commission of an offense that would classify the person as a sex or violent offender as defined in I.C. 11–8–8–5 shall not be admitted to bail until a court has conducted a bail hearing in open court.

PERSONS CHARGED WITH CHILD MOLESTING OR CHILD SOLICITATION

Pursuant to I.C. 35–33–8–3.5, a person charged with Child Molesting or Child Solicitation shall not be admitted to bail until the court has conducted a bail hearing in open court.

OTHER CONDITIONS OF BOND

All appearance bonds posted by defendants are subject to the following conditions: a) the defendant shall appear in court at all times required by the Court; b) the defendant shall not leave the State of Indiana without the prior written approval of the Court; c) the defendant shall not commit or be arrested for another criminal offense; d) the defendant shall make contact and schedule an appointment with court appointed counsel immediately upon posting bond and keep all appointments; e) the defendant shall keep his or her attorney and the Court advised in writing of any change of address within twenty-four (24) hours of such change; f) any other condition of bond ordered by the Court; g) pursuant to I.C. 35–33–8–3.29a)(4), a defendant's release may also be conditioned upon refraining from any direct or indirect contact with the alleged victim of an offense or other individual so ordered by the Court. Violation of any condition of bond may result in the Court revoking the defendant's release on bond and the issuance of a warrant for re-arrest.

Pre-trial Motions for Bond Reduction shall be presented to the Court in writing and proper notice of the hearing scheduled thereon shall be given to the Prosecuting Attorney.

All property bonds shall be granted only after notice is sent to the Prosecuting Attorney and a hearing is set to determine whether such bonds are proper.

This bond schedule shall be followed by the Circuit, Superior No. 1, 2, 3, 4, and 5 Courts of this County and by the Clerk of said Courts in the setting of bond on warrants issued on criminal information or indictments, except multiple-count information or where justice demands a lesser or greater amount.

This bond schedule shall apply to the highest charge pending against a person if multiple charges are or may be filed. If the listed bond amount is inappropriate under the circumstances, the Prosecuting attorney shall bring such circumstances to the attention of the Court by written motion.

This bond schedule shall not be applicable in the case of a person who has been arrested for a crime while on probation, parole, bond or released on own recognizance for another offense. In such case, the person may be detained for a maximum period of 15 calendar days, during which period the Prosecuting Attorney shall notify the appropriate parole or probation authority, and the Court shall determine the proper amount of bond, if any

CASH BONDS

All cash bonds shall be posted with the Hendricks County Clerk or the Hendricks County Sheriff only after the defendant signs a personal appearance bond.

IT IS ORDERED that effective this date and until further order of the Court, the Hendricks County Clerk is ORDERED to retain a portion of each cash bond posted in criminal cases as an administrative fee in all cases pending in the Circuit and Superior Courts. The administrative fee shall not exceed ten percent (10%) or the monetary value of the deposit or fifty dollars ($50.00) whichever is less.

Amended effective June 1, 2012; Feb. 1, 2013.

[1] There are two "Rule 8" headings in original data.

HOWARD COUNTY LOCAL RULES

Adopted July 14, 2006, Effective January 1, 2007

Including Amendments Received Through November 1, 2013

Research Notes

These rules may be searched electronically on Westlaw in the IN-RULES database; updates to these rules may be found on Westlaw in IN-RULESUPDATES. For search tips and a summary of database content, consult the Westlaw Scope Screens for each database.

LR34-AR81 Rule 1. SCOPE OF RULES

Pursuant to Trial Rule 81 of the Indiana Rules of Court, and except as otherwise provided, these rules govern the procedure and practice of the Circuit Court and the Superior Courts of Howard County.

These local rules shall be read and applied in a manner not inconsistent with the Indiana Rules of Trial Procedure.

Adopted July 14, 2006, effective Jan. 1, 2007.

LR34–AR1 Rule 2. ASSIGNMENT OF CASE FILINGS

A. Howard Circuit Court. All Juvenile Matters, Adoptions and other cases required by law to be field in the Circuit Court shall be filed in the Howard Circuit Court.

B. Howard Superior Courts II & IV. Mental Health Matters shall be filed in the Howard Superior Court II or the Howard Superior Court IV. The court of filing shall be determined by random selection, by the clerk.

C. Howard Superior Court III. Small Claims, Infractions, and Ordinance Violations shall be filed in the Howard Superior Court III. Howard Superior Court III shall also maintain a Plenary Docket for the purpose of accepting transfer cases. This shall include any civil case transferred from the other Howard County Courts or cases in which the Judge of Howard Superior Court III has been selected as a special judge pursuant to Section (J) of Trial Rule 79. All small claims which are transferred to the Plenary Docket as a result of a jury request or because a party seeks to pursue a claim that exceeds the jurisdictional amount allowed shall be transferred to the Plenary Docket of Howard Superior Court III.

D. Howard Superior Court I. Miscellaneous Matters (MI) shall be filed in Howard Superior Court I.

E. Other Civil Filings. All other civil cases shall be filed in the Howard Circuit Court, the Howard Superior Court II, or the Howard Superior Court IV. The court of filing shall be determined by random selection, by the Clerk, using a method which will result in thirty percent (30%) being filed in Circuit Court, and thirty-five percent (35%) being filed in Superior Court II, and thirty-five percent (35%) being filed in Superior Court IV.

Adopted July 14, 2006, effective Jan. 1, 2007. Amended effective Jan. 19, 2010; amended Sept. 8, 2010, effective Jan. 1, 2011.

LR34-TR76 Rule 3. TRANSFER OF ACTION

It may, from time to time, be expedient for the Judges of Howard Circuit Court and Superior Courts to transfer cases between those courts. This shall be done with the consent of the two judges involved in the transfers, pursuant to I.C. 35–5–20.1–21 and I.C. 35–5–20.1–22. If such transfer is consummated, the time for taking a change of venue from the Judge shall be extended for a period of ten (10) days from the service of notice of such transfer or until such period expires pursuant to T.R. 76 or other applicable law.

Adopted July 14, 2006, effective Jan. 1, 2007.

LR34-AR00 Rule 4. JUDGES SITTING IN EITHER COURT

It may, from time to time, be expedient for the Judges of Howard Circuit and Superior Courts to hear cases pending in another court.

The Judge of the Howard Circuit Court authorizes the Judges of the Howard Superior Courts to sit as Judge of the Howard Circuit Court, at any time, in any case.

The Judges of the Howard Superior Courts authorize the Judge of the Howard Circuit Court to sit as Judge of the Howard Superior Courts, at any time, in any case.

Adopted July 14, 2006, effective Jan. 1, 2007.

LR34-TR3.1 Rule 5. APPEARANCE AND WITHDRAWAL

A. APPEARANCE. An appearance by counsel, or by a party appearing without an attorney shall be made in writing and filed with either the Clerk or the Court. It shall be in compliance with the Indiana Supreme Court Rules. A copy must be served on other counsel or parties. The Clerk shall note the appearance on the Chronological Case Summary.

WITHDRAWAL: All withdrawals of appearance shall be in writing and by leave of Court. Permission to withdraw shall be given only after the withdrawing attorney has given his client ten (10) days written notice of his intention to withdraw and has filed a copy of the notice with the court, except in the following cases:

(1) when another attorney has already filed an appearance for the same party; or

(2) when the withdrawing attorney files a pleading indicating that he or she has been terminated from the case by the client; or

(3) when the appearance of an attorney is deemed withdrawn upon conclusion of an action or matter.

The court will not grant a request to withdraw an appearance unless the same has been filed with the court at least ten (10) days prior to trial date, except for good cause. A withdrawal of appearance when accompanied by the appearance of other counsel shall constitute a waiver of this requirement. All withdrawals of appearance shall comply fully with the provisions of Rules of Professional Conduct.

Adopted July 14, 2006, effective Jan. 1, 2007. Amended effective Jan. 19, 2010.

LR34-AR11 Rule 6. PREPARATION OF PLEADINGS, MOTIONS AND OTHER PAPERS

A. PRODUCTION. Pleading, motions, and other paper shall be on white paper. All pleadings, copies, motions, and documents filed with the court, with the exception of exhibits and existing wills, shall be prepared on 8.5″ × 11″ paper. The lines shall be double spaced except for quotations, which shall be indented and single spaced.

B. TITLES. Titles on all pleadings shall delineate each topic included in the pleading, e.g. where a pleading contains and Answer, a Motion to Strike or Dismiss, or a Jury Request, each shall be set forth in the title.

Adopted July 14, 2006, effective Jan. 1, 2007.

LR34-TR5 Rule 7. FILINGS

A. PLEADINGS. The entry of appearance and the filing of pleadings or other matters not requiring immediate Court action shall be filed with the Clerk. The Judge may, however, permit papers to be filed with the Court, in which event the filing date shall be noted thereon.

B. CHRONOLOGICAL CASE SUMMARY ENTRIES. Written pleadings presented for filing shall be accompanied by a proposed entry for the Chronological Case Summary. It shall contain the title and number of the case, the date, and exact entry to appear on the Chronological Case Summary. The proposed entry shall be signed by counsel.

C. COPIES TO SPECIAL JUDGES. When a Special Judge is selected, copies of all pleadings, motions, or briefs filed shall be mailed or delivered to the office of the Special Judge with certificate of forwarding same made a part of the original papers.

Adopted July 14, 2006, effective Jan. 1, 2007.

LR34–TR79 Rule 8. CHANGE OF JUDGE

Purpose of Rule: This rule is adopted to comply with the requirements of Trial Rule 79(H) of the Indiana Rules of Trial Procedure. It is intended to provide a means of selection of special judges insuring the effective use of all judicial resources within Administrative District 8, and includes each person eligible for appointment under Section (J) of Trial Rule 79.

Central Office Established: There is established a Central Office for keeping of records of appointment and selection of special judges for this District. The Central Office of this District shall be Howard Superior Court 4.

The Howard County Courts shall hereafter refer to the Central Office of this District whenever selection of a special judge is required under this rule. The particular Court shall accept from the Central Administrator the name of the individual to then be appointed as special judge.

The person serving as Administrator of the Central Office shall have the following responsibilities:

1. To maintain a list of persons qualified to serve as special judge under Section (J) of Trial Rule 79.

2. To take referrals from the several courts of this District, requesting appointment of a special judge.

3. To alternately and on a rotating basis appoint qualified judges from the list maintained for that purpose.

4. To notify the referring Court of the individual to be appointed under this Rule.

Rotation Schedule: The following shall be the rotation schedule used by the Central Administrator.

1. The Judge of Cass Superior Court I
2. The Judge of the Howard Superior Court III
3. The Judge of the Fulton Superior Court
4. The Judge of the Howard Superior Court II
5. The Judge of the Fulton Circuit Court
6. The Judge of the Howard Circuit Court
7. The Judge of the Miami Superior Court I
8. The Judge of the Howard Superior Court I
9. The Judge of the Cass Circuit Court
10. The Judge of the Miami Circuit Court
11. The Judge of the Cass Superior Court II
12. The Judge of the Howard Superior Court IV
13. The Judge of Miami Superior Court II

Administrative Fee: Each court participating under this Rule shall pay each year the sum of Fifty Dollars ($50.00) to the Central Administrator, payable directly to the Administrator by the 15th of September of each year.

Certification to Supreme Court: In cases in which no judge is eligible to serve as special judge in a particular case, or where the circumstances of a case require it, the Court shall certify those circumstances to the Supreme Court, and that Court shall make appointment.

Adopted July 14, 2006, effective Jan. 1, 2007; July 1, 2011.

LR34-AR00 Rule 9. PROPOSED ORDERS

Prior to entry by the court of Orders granting motions, applications or setting hearing dates, the moving party or applicant shall, unless the court directs otherwise, furnish the court with proposed Orders in the following matters:

1. Enlargement of Time
2. Continuance
3. Default Judgment
4. Compel Discovery
5. Dismissal
6. Appointment of Receiver
7. Appointment of Guardian

8. Restraining Order, Temporary or Permanent Injunction
9. Immediate Possession of Real Estate
10. Immediate Possession of Personal Property
11. Findings of Fact and Conclusions of Law
12. Foreclosure of a Mortgage or other Lien
13. Setting Hearing Dates
14. Such other Order, Judgments or Decrees as the Court may direct.

All proposed Orders left with the Clerk or Court shall be submitted in sufficient numbers so that distribution may be made to all affected parties.

Adopted July 14, 2006, effective Jan. 1, 2007.

LR34-TR73 Rule 10. MOTIONS

A. ORAL ARGUMENTS. The Court shall not hear oral arguments on motions unless required by the Indiana Rules of Procedure, requested by a party and allowed by the Court in its discretion, or at the request of the Court.

B. BRIEFS AND MEMORANDA REGARDING MOTIONS. If a party desires to file a brief and memorandum in support of any motion, such brief or memorandum shall accompany or be filed simultaneously with the motion, and a copy served on the adverse party. If the adverse party desires to file a brief or memorandum, the adverse party shall file it as ordered by the Court.

C. ENLARGEMENT OF TIME. An initial written motion for enlargement of time pursuant to Trial Rule 6(B)(1) to respond to a claim shall be automatically allowed for an additional 30 days from the date of filing by a written order of the Court except in matters denominated in the pleadings as emergency in nature. Any motion filed pursuant to this rule shall state the date when such response is due and the date to which time is enlarged. The motion must be filed on or before the original due date, or this rule is inapplicable.

Adopted July 14, 2006, effective Jan. 1, 2007.

LR34-TR53.5 Rule 11. CONTINUANCES

A motion for a continuance, unless made during the hearing of the cause, shall be for cause, in writing and verified. A motion for continuance shall be filed as soon after the cause for continuance is discovered by the moving party. The attorney's signature on a request for a continuance is considered a certification that the client has been notified of the request.

The motion shall contain a statement concerning notification to opposing counsel or to pro se party:

1. That other counsel/party has been contacted and has no objection.
2. That other counsel/party has been contacted and does object.

3. That other counsel/party has not been contacted after diligent effort.

Adopted July 14, 2006, effective Jan. 1, 2007.

LR34-TR47 Rule 12. VOIR DIRE

A. EXAMINATION OF PANEL AS A WHOLE BY COURT. Unless otherwise directed, the entire panel of prospective jurors shall be sworn by the court. The court may conduct its own voir dire examination of the entire panel with a view primarily of establishing a basis for challenge for cause.

B. JURY QUESTIONNAIRES. Jury questionnaires shall be on file with the Bailiff or Security Officer and copies shall be made available to counsel, but it shall be the responsibility of counsel to obtain such copies from the Bailiff or Security Officer, and to review the same before the voir dire begins.

C. SUPPLEMENTAL EXAMINATION BY COUNSEL. Following examination by the court, counsel shall be permitted to supplement the court's examination on subjects not expressly covered by the court or the jury questionnaires. Questions shall be, so far as possible, directed to the entire panel seated in the jury box. The side with the burden of proof shall proceed first with such examination and the opposing side will then proceed.

D. PEREMPTORY CHALLENGES. After each side has completed its supplementary examination, peremptory challenges must then be made. Such challenges will be made in writing and submitted to the court. After submission to the court, the court will then advise the prospective jurors so challenged.

E. PEREMPTORY CHALLENGES OF SAME JUROR. A peremptory challenge of the same juror by both sides shall count against the number of challenges for each side.

Adopted July 14, 2006, effective Jan. 1, 2007.

LR34-TR51 Rule 13. JURY INSTRUCTIONS

All requests for instructions tendered in accordance with Trial Rule 51 shall be in writing with citations on the Court's copy, to applicable authority. Reasonably anticipated final instructions shall be exchanged and filed with the Court as directed. Proposed preliminary instructions shall be exchanged and filed. The plaintiff in a civil matter shall prepare and exchange with opposing counsel a proposed preliminary instruction on the issues, which shall be included in the Pre–Trial Order. The Court shall, in the interest of justice, permit the tender of additional instructions during the trial on matters which could not have been reasonably anticipated in advance of trial. Such proposed instructions shall be no more than ten (10) in number from each party or in the case of multiple parties no more than fifteen (15) total.

Adopted July 14, 2006, effective Jan. 1, 2007.

LR34-TR16 Rule 14. PRE-TRIAL CONFERENCE

A. WHEN. There shall be a pre-trial conference in every civil case scheduled for jury trial. In other cases, upon motions of any party or upon motion of the Court, a pre-trial conference may be held.

B. CERTIFICATE OF READINESS. Any party may request that a pre-trial conference be held or that the cause be set for trial if no pre-trial conference is required by filing a Certificate of Readiness, certifying to the Court that the cause is at issue; that discovery is completed or that discovery will be completed by the time of the pre-trial conference; that the cause is ready to be assigned for pre-trial conference or that a pretrial conference should be waived and the matter assigned for trial. If any party should oppose any matter contained in the Certificate of Readiness, he shall, within 10 days following receipt of a copy of the Certificate of Readiness, file with the Court, with service to all counsel of record, his verified objections citing in particular why the cause is not ready for pre-trial conference and trial. The Court may summarily rule on any verified objections or, upon written request, set the matter for hearing. If no objections are filed within the time prescribed or allowed, the Court will set the cause for pre-trial conference. Following a pre-trial conference and entry of a pre-trial order in a cause, if required, the cause shall be placed on the Court's calendar for trial.

C. PRE-PRETRIAL CONFERENCE. At least 10 days prior to the date set for pre-trial conference, the attorneys for all parties shall meet and/or confer for the purposes set forth in Trial Rule 16(C).

D. PRE-TRIAL ORDER. Following the pre-trial conference, a pre-trial order shall be prepared, signed, and filed as directed by the Court at the pre-trial conference. When signed by the Court and entered of record, the pre-trial order shall control the course of trial, and the pleadings will be deemed merged therein.

Adopted July 14, 2006, effective Jan. 1, 2007.

LR34-TR40 Rule 15. TRIAL SETTINGS

Unless otherwise ordered by the court at the pre-trial conference, when more than one case is set for trial on a given date, the case set second shall be required to stand for trial if counsel is given five (5) days notice, excluding Saturday and Sunday, that the case first set will not be heard. Counsel for all other subsequent settings are required to communicate with each other and counsel for the first and second settings to determine priorities.

Counsel shall inform the court at least fourteen (14) days before the trial is scheduled to commence, excluding Saturday and Sunday, of the need to call a jury.

Adopted July 14, 2006, effective Jan. 1, 2007.

LR34-FL Rule 16.   DOMESTIC RELATIONS

A. WORKSHEET—CHILD SUPPORT OBLI-GATION. A copy of the worksheet provided in the Indiana Child Support Guidelines shall be submitted to the Court in each case in which the Court is asked to determine support, including cases in which agreed orders are submitted. A worksheet shall be signed by a party under penalties of perjury.

B. SCHEDULE OF ASSETS AND LIABILI-TIES. A schedule of assets and liabilities, together with copies of any and all inventories and appraisals, may be submitted to the Court prior to the beginning of a contested trial and copies served upon opposing counsel.

Adopted July 14, 2006, effective Jan. 1, 2007.

LR34-FL Rule 17.   PARENTING TIME

1. PARENTING TIME. It is the express preference of the Howard Circuit and Superior Courts that parenting time be defined simply as occurring "at all reasonable times and places". Such parenting time means that parties take into consideration the schedules and economic and geographic circumstances of each other as well as the schedules and activities of the children.

2. PARENTING TIME GUIDELINES. The Indiana Supreme Court has adopted Parenting Time Guidelines. These guidelines are designed for those situations when the parties are unable to resolve "parenting time" without having specific guidelines. Consequently, if the parties cannot agree on parenting time, the Parenting Time Guidelines will be adopted unless the Court orders otherwise.

Adopted July 14, 2006, effective Jan. 1, 2007.

LR34-TR16 Rule 18.   EXHIBITS

Exhibits shall be presented to the reporter for marking prior to the beginning of the trial or during recess, to ensure that the trial is not delayed for the marking of exhibits.

The exhibits of plaintiffs, petitioners, or any other party who initiates an action shall be marked numerically as 1, 2, 3 etc. The exhibits of defendants, respondents, or any other party who responds to an action initiated by another shall be marked alphabetically as A, B, C etc. Where alphabetically marked exhibits exceed the letters in the alphabet, exhibits shall then be marked as AA, BB, CC, etc.

After being marked for identification and offered in evidence, all exhibits and proposed exhibits shall be placed in the custody of the reporter, who is responsible for their safekeeping unless otherwise ordered by the trial judge.

After a case has been decided and no appeal has been taken, or after all appeals are completed, if there has been no request for the return of such items within 90 says of final judgment, they may be disposed of by the reporter as the Court may direct.

Copies of all documentary exhibits shall be provided as follows: one for the Court: one for each party and one for each Juror.

Adopted July 14, 2006, effective Jan. 1, 2007.

LR34-AR00 Rule 19.   DOCUMENTS, FILES AND DEPOSITIONS

A.[1] REMOVAL OF ORIGINAL PLEADINGS, PAPERS AND RECORDS. No person shall withdraw any original pleading, paper, or record from the custody of the clerk or other officer of the Court except after giving proper receipt.

Adopted July 14, 2006, effective Jan. 1, 2007.

[1] There is no Subd. B. in this rule.

LR34-AR00 Rule 20.   LIBRARY

The books and electronic devices in the law library shall be in the custody of the Judges of the Courts of Howard County. No person shall remove any book or electronic device from the law library until he signs out the same. Any item removed from the law library shall not be retained more than ten consecutive days.

Adopted July 14, 2006, effective Jan. 1, 2007.

LR34-AP9 Rule 21.   APPELLATE RECORD

When an appeal is initiated by the filing of a Notice of Appeal pursuant to Appellate Rule 9, and a transcript of all or any part of the evidence is sought for the record on appeal, counsel filing the Notice of Appeal shall deliver, contemporaneously and personally, a copy of the Notice of Appeal to the Court Reporter, advise the Court Reporter of the deadline for preparation of the records, and then make arrangements to pay the Court Reporter for preparation of the records.

Adopted July 14, 2006, effective Jan. 1, 2007.

LR34-AR00 Rule 22.   TRANSCRIPTS

Persons requesting transcripts shall make a deposit with the Court Reporter sufficient to cover the cost of the transcript at the time of the request unless other arrangements are made with the Court Reporter who is preparing the transcript.

Adopted July 14, 2006, effective Jan. 1, 2007.

LR34-AR00 Rule 23.   COURTROOM SECURITY

No person shall enter the courtroom or the court's chambers or environs in possession of a firearm or any type of knife, club, bomb, or explosive device or any other offensive weapon. This order does not apply to law enforcement officers in uniform or law enforcement officers in plain clothes, who publically display identification.

Violators will be found in contempt of court and punished according to applicable law.

Adopted July 14, 2006, effective Jan. 1, 2007.

LR34-AR12 Rule 24. FACSIMILE TRANSMISSIONS

A. FILING BY ELECTRONIC FACSIMILE TRANSMISSION. Howard Circuit and Superior Courts authorizes the filing of pleadings, motions and other papers by electronic facsimile transmission, provided:

(1) such matter does not exceed ten (10) pages, including the cover sheet;

(2) such matter does not require the payment of fees

(3) The sending party creates at the time of transmission a machine generated log for such transmission; and

(4) the original document and the transmission log are maintained by the sending party for the duration of the litigation.

B. TIME OF FILING. During normal, posted business hours, the time of filing shall be the time the duplicate document is produced in the office of the Court of Clerk of the Circuit and Superior Courts. Duplicate documents received at all other times shall be filed as of the next normal business day.

If the receiving FAX machine endorses its own time and date stamp upon the transmitted documents and the receiving machine produces a delivery receipt which is electronically created and transmitted to the sending party, the time of filing shall be the date and time recorded on the transmitted document by the receiving FAX machine.

C. COVER SHEET. Any document sent to the Clerk or Court by electronic facsimile transmission shall be accompanied by a cover sheet which states the title of the document, case number, number of pages, identify and voice telephone number of the sending party and instructions for filing. The cover sheet shall contain the instructions for filing. The cover sheet shall contain the signature of the attorney or party, pro se, authorizing the filing.

D. DESIGNATED TELEPHONE NUMBER. The designated telephone number to receive electronic facsimile are as follows:

Howard Circuit Court   (765) 456–2016

Howard Superior Court I   (765) 456–2327

Howard Superior Court II   (765) 456–2936

Howard Superior Court III   (765) 456–7003

Howard Superior Court IV   (765) 456–2901

Adopted July 14, 2006, effective Jan. 1, 2007.

LR34-AR15 Rule 25. COURT REPORTER

Section One. Definitions. The following definitions shall apply under this local rule:

(1) A *Court Reporter* is a person who is specifically designated by a court to perform the official court reporting services for the court including preparing a transcript of the record.

(2) *Equipment* means all physical items owned by the court or other governmental entity and used by a court reporter in performing court reporting services. Equipment shall include, but not be limited to telephones, computer hardware, software programs, disks, tapes, and any other device used for recording and storing, and transcribing electronic data.

(3) *Work Space* means that portion of the court's facilities dedicated to each court reporter including but not limited to actual space in the courtroom and any designated office space.

(4) *Page* means the page unit of transcript which results when a recording is transcribed in the form required by Indiana Rule of Appellate Procedure 28.

(5) *Recording* means the electronic, mechanical, stenographic or other recording made as required by Indiana Rule of Trial Procedure 74.

(6) *Regular hours worked* means those hours which the court is regularly scheduled to work during any given work week. Depending on the particular court, these hours may vary from court to court within the county but remain the same for each work week.

(7) *Gap hours worked* means those hours worked that are in excess of the regular hours worked not in excess of forty (40) hours per work week.

(8) *Overtime hours worked* means those hours worked that are in excess of the regular hours worked and are in excess of forty (40) hours per work week.

(9) *Work Week* means a seven (7) consecutive day week that consistently begins and ends on the same days throughout the year, e.g. Sunday through Saturday, Wednesday through Tuesday, or Friday through Thursday.

(10) *Court* means the particular court for which the court reporter performs services. Court may also mean all of the courts in Howard County.

(11) *County indigent transcript* means a transcript that is paid for from county funds and is for the use on behalf of a litigant who has been declared indigent by a court.

(12) *State indigent transcript* means a transcript that is paid for from state funds and is for the use on behalf of a litigant who has been declared indigent by a court.

(13) *Private transcript* means a transcript, including but not limited to a deposition transcript, that is paid for by a private party.

Section Two. Salaries and Per Page Fees.

(1) Court Reporters shall be paid an annual salary for time spent working under the control, direction

and direct supervision of their supervising court during any regular work hours, gap hours, or overtime hours. The supervising court shall enter into a written agreement with the court reporters which outlines the manner in which the court reporter is to be compensated for gap and overtime hours, i.e. Monetary compensation or compensatory time off regular work hours.

(2) The maximum per page fee a court reporter may charge for the preparation of a county indigent transcript shall be $4.00; the court reporter shall submit a claim directly to the county for the preparation of any county indigent transcript.

(3) The maximum per page fee a court reporter may charge for the preparation of a state indigent transcript shall be $4.00.

(4) The maximum per page fee a court reporter may charge for the preparation of a private transcript shall be $4.00.

(5) That preparation of all transcripts shall be done outside of the work space and after regular work hours.

(6) Each court reporter shall report, at least on an annual basis, all transcripts fees received for the preparation of either county indigent, state indigent or private transcripts to the Indian Supreme Court Division of State Court Administration. The reporting shall be made on forms prescribed by the division of State Court Administration.

(7) A minimum fee up to $35.00 may be charged by the court reporter per transcript.

(8) Index and Table of Contents pages should be charged by the court reporter at the per page rate being charged for the balance of the transcript.

(9) An additional labor charge of $5.00 to $10.00 may be charged for the time spent binding the transcript and exhibits depending on size.

(10) A reasonable charge for the office supplies required and utilized for the binding and electronic transmission of the transcript, pursuant to Indiana Rules of Appellate Procedure 28 and 29, is permissible; the costs for these supplies should be determined pursuant to a Schedule of Transcript Supplies which should be established and published annually by the judge or judges of the county.

Section Three. Private Practice.

(1) If a court reporter elects to engage in private practice through the recording of a deposition transcript, and the court reporter desires to utilize the court's equipment, work space and supplies, and the court agrees to the use of the court equipment for such purpose, the court and court reporter shall enter into a written agreement which must, at a minimum, designate the following:

(a) The reasonable market rate for the use of equipment, work space and supplies;

(b) The method by which records are to be kept for the use of equipment, work space and supplies, and;

(c) The method by which the court reporter is to reimburse the court for the use of the equipment, work space and supplies.

(2) If a court reporter elects to engage in private practice through the recording of a deposition and/or preparing of a deposition transcript, all such private practice work shall be conducted outside of regular working hours.

Adopted July 14, 2006, effective Jan. 1, 2007.

LR34-CR00 Rule 26. INITIAL HEARING

Any defendant held in custody by reason of warrant or civil attachment shall be brought before the court for initial hearing upon order of the court following the arrest. This rule shall not prohibit the release of any defendant on bond as per order of the court.

Adopted July 14, 2006, effective Jan. 1, 2007.

LR34-CR00 Rule 27. WITHDRAWAL OF APPEARANCE

In criminal cases, withdrawal of representation of a defendant will be in compliance with I.C. 35–36–8–2. It will be considered after a hearing is conducted in open court, on record, in the presence of the defendant, unless another attorney has entered an appearance for the defendant. Withdrawal of appearance may be allowed without compliance with the requirements of this rule, if the reason for withdrawal is the inability to locate and communicate with the defendant. In such event a warrant may be issued for the arrest of the defendant. Notice of withdrawal is required pursuant to LR34-TR3.1-5.

Adopted July 14, 2006, effective Jan. 1, 2007.

LR34-CR00 Rule 28. WARRANTLESS ARRESTS

Any defendant held in custody by reason of a warrantless arrest, shall be brought before a judge for probable cause determination within forty-eight (48) hours following arrest. The probable cause determination may be made either by hearing or by affidavit(s).

When the judge has authorized release on bond before probable cause determination, the Sheriff shall give notice to the defendant of a court appearance date on the Report of Bonding form with a copy delivered to the court and prosecutor.

After determination of probable cause, the prosecutor shall file appropriate charges with the court within forty-eight (48) hours.

Adopted July 14, 2006, effective Jan. 1, 2007.

LR34–CR2.2 Rule 29. FILING CRIMINAL CASES

A. **WEEKLY ROTATION:** Beginning January 2, 2006, weekly rotation will be as follows:

1.   Week # 1—Circuit Court

2. Week # 2—Superior Court II

3. Week # 3—Superior Court IV

Weekly rotation thereafter will be from 12:01 a.m. Monday until twelve o'clock midnight Sunday each week.

The Clerk shall maintain a projected calendar for one year in advance showing the weekly rotation and shall in retrospect project a calendar for the previous one year and beyond if necessary for weekly rotation.

The weekly rotation calendar shall be public and posted in the Clerk's office and in each court participating in the weekly rotation.

B. FILING FELONIES: The court in which criminal charges shall be filed, other than as hereafter provided, will be the court on weekly rotation on the day on which the offense alleged in the charging document occurred with the following guidelines:

1. Where multiple offenses are filed, the date of the earliest offense alleged in the charging document shall control the rotation date.

2. In other cases where the date of the case is ambiguous, or covers a period of time, or is not otherwise specifically alleged, the controlling date will be the date that the Prosecutor's Office logged in the original complaint, case, report, or other notification of the alleged offense. The Prosecutor shall maintain a system of logging in cases which shall be open for reasonable inspection by the courts and members of the Bar.

3. In cases where the charges are drawn under IC 35–48, the cases shall be filed in Superior Court I. In the event of multiple counts, with charges drawn under IC 35–48, and other criminal statutes, the case shall be filed in the court which would otherwise be proper for the highest charged class of felony. Provided, however, in cases where the highest felonies are of the same class, the cases shall be filed in Superior Court I.

4. In cases where the charges are drawn under IC 35–46–1–15.1, IC 35–42–2–1.3, or, if the victim is or was the spouse of the accused, is or was living as the spouse of the accused, or has a child in common with the accused, under IC 35–43–1–2, 35–43–2–1.5, 35–43–2–2, 35–45–2–1, 35–45–2–2, 35–45–2–5 or 35–45–10–5 (all hereinafter collectively referred to as "domestic or family violence"), the cases shall be filed in Superior Court I. In the event of multiple counts, with charges involving domestic or family violence and other criminal statutes, the case shall be filed in the court which would otherwise be proper for the highest charged class of felony. Provided, however, in cases where the highest felonies are of the same class, the cases shall be filed in Superior Court I.

5. In case where the accused has a previously filed and pending felony charge(s), and is charged with one or more subsequent felony charge(s), the

subsequent case shall be filed in the court in which the previously filed case is pending. If the previous charge(s) is no longer pending at the time the subsequent charge(s) is filed, the subsequent charge(s) shall be filed in the court as designated by the weekly rotation schedule in section A. The previous charge(s) will be considered pending if the State filed the charge(s) and the court has not entered a dismissal or judgment of conviction or acquittal of the pending charge(s)

C. SUPERIOR COURT III: This court will be the court in which misdemeanors, other than those referred to in B(3) or B(4) hereof, and Class D felonies involving the operation of a motor vehicle are filed, with the following qualifications:

1. A misdemeanor charge which is filed contemporaneous with a felony charge against the same individual will be filed in the court where the felony charge is filed.

2. Where a defendant has a pending misdemeanor charge and a subsequent felony charge is filed, the misdemeanor charge will remain in Superior Court III, or with the consent of the accused, the Prosecutor, and the Judge of the Superior Court III, may be transferred to the court having the felony case under Transfer of Action, Local Civil Rule 3.

D. CHANGE OF JUDGE: Where there has been a change of venue granted, the Clerk shall select the new court by random selection from the other four (4) Howard County Courts.

After selection, the cause may then be reassigned to the new court by transfer under Local Civil Rule 3.

E. TIME FOR OBJECTION: Any party may file a written objection to an alleged violation of this rule. Upon a finding that the charge(s) were improperly filed, the court where the charge(s) were originally filed shall transfer the charge(s) to the proper court without the necessity of obtaining consent from the receiving court. Any such objection shall be deemed waived unless filed on or before thirty (30) days after the Omnibus Date; however, upon a showing of good cause and in the interest of justice, the court may permit the filing of the objection any time before the commencement of trial.

Adopted July 14, 2006, effective Jan. 1, 2007. Amended effective June 1, 2009; Jan. 1, 2013.

LR34-CR00 Rule 30. BAIL SCHEDULE

A. AMOUNTS. The following amounts shall be the amounts set for bail bonds in those courts which authorize the use of the schedule, unless otherwise ordered by the Court:

CLASS OF OFFENSE	BAIL AMOUNT
A. Murder	None
B. Habitual Offender	$50,000.00

C. Class A Felony $75,000.00

D. Class B Felony $30,000.00

E. Class C Felony $15,000.00

F. Class D Felony $10,000.00

G. Class A Misdemeanor $8,000.00

H. Class B Misdemeanor $6,500.00

I. Class C Misdemeanor $5,000.00

EXCEPTIONS TO SCHEDULE

B. MULTIPLE CHARGES. If an arrest is made on more than one charge and there has been no prior judicial determination of bail, bail must be posted as to each charge. The amounts may be varied or determination stayed until court appearance by oral order of the judge, which order may be made by telephone.

C. RELEASE ON PROMISE TO APPEAR. The bail schedule shall not apply to cases in which a person may be released upon written promise to appear or the posting of other appropriate security including, but not limited to the following:

1. TRAFFIC OFFENSES. Pursuant to IC 9–4–1–131, a resident of Indiana charged with a **misdemeanor** regulating the use and operation of a motor vehicle other than one listed in IC 9-4-130.1 shall be released upon signing a promise to appear. The offenses excepted from this rule by IC 9–4–2–130.1 are as follows: (a) an offense causing or contributing to an accident involving injury or death to any person; (b) a violation of IC 9-11-2; and (c) failure to stop in the event of an accident causing death, personal injuries, or damage to property. Residents of states which are members of the nonresident violator agreement, IC 9–5–1.1–1 *et seq.*, shall be treated in the same manner as residents of Indiana. Resident of other states shall be required to provide security as provided in IC 9-4-1-131(b) or, failing to do so, they shall post bail in the amount provided above.

Any person refusing to sign a promise to appear shall post bond.

2. CONSERVATION OFFENSES. Pursuant to IC 14–2–9–3 case of violation of snowmobile and fish and game laws may be dealt with by summons rather than arrest.

D. INTOXICATED PERSONS. If any person is arrested or charged involving intoxication or use of drugs and, in the opinion of the Sheriff or his department, cannot safely be released because of such condition, that person shall be held until the Sheriff or his department determines that the person would not constitute a danger to himself or others. This provision is subject to the rule that all persons arrested

who remain in jail shall be brought into court no later than the next day court is in session.

E. ARREST IN CIVIL PROCESS. The bail schedule applies only to arrest on criminal charges. On civil arrests (body attachments), the bond applicable is the amount stated by the court on the Body Attachment. Such bail is to be accepted in cash, or, where applicable, by credit card. The court will consider the cash bail posed to be the property of the person arrested and subject to attachment.

F. TEN PERCENT CASH. In all cases, unless a specific order to the contrary is made by the court when setting bail, the person, if a resident of the State of Indiana, may post cash in the amount ten percent (10%) of the bail. The court approved bond form must be used. If ten percent (10%) is posted, the paid sum shall be returned to the payer at the close of the case with the following deductions:

(a) administrative fee as per statute;

(b) fine, fees, and costs;

(c) restitution ordered by the court;

(d) alcohol or drug program fees;

(e) reimbursement to the Howard County Public Defender Supplemental fund;

(f) costs of extradition;

(g) cost of housing in jail or other facility outside Howard County;

(h) Probation User fees.

Adopted July 14, 2006, effective Jan. 1, 2007. Amended effective Jan. 19, 2010.

LR34-SC00 Rule 31. SMALL CLAIMS RULE

In Small Claims cases, attorneys of record are responsible for providing a proposed Order on all matters submitted where an Order is appropriate. The proposed Order may be at the bottom of the document submitted.

Adopted July 14, 2006, effective Jan. 1, 2007.

LR34-SC9 Rule 32. CONTINUANCES IN SMALL CLAIMS CASES

Motions to Continue will normally be granted only if the request indicates the position of the adverse party in regard to the continuance.

Adopted July 14, 2006, effective Jan. 1, 2007.

LR34-SC8 Rule 33. SMALL CLAIMS HEARINGS

The first hearing date, as shown on the Notice of Claim, will generally be set for trial. If the Defendant fails to appear at this first setting, a default judgment may be requested.

Adopted July 14, 2006, effective Jan. 1, 2007.

LR34–AR00 Rule 34. DRUG COURT FEES

Those persons directed to participate in the Howard County Circuit Court Juvenile Drug Court Program or the Howard County Superior Court I Drug Court Program shall pay a program fee of fifty dollars

($50.00) per month, not to exceed five hundred dollar ($500.00). Any or all of said fee may be waived, by the respective Drug Court, in its sole discretion, as an "incentive award" for an individual participant.

Adopted May 28, 2008, effective June 29, 2008. Amended effective Jan. 15, 2013.

LR34-AR00 Rule 35. ALCOHOL AND DRUG SERVICES FEES

Those persons directed to participate in the Howard County Courts Alcohol and Drug Services program shall fees in accordance with the following schedule:

Whole program	$400.00
Transfer fee (to another county, no evaluation)	$ 50.00
Evaluation only	$100.00
Transfer in (no evaluation, Level I education)	$100.00
Instant Urine Drug Screen	$ 10.00
Laboratory Urine Drug Screen	$ 25.00
Confirmatory test of Instant UDS	$ 35.00

Adopted May 28, 2008, effective June 29, 2008.

LR34-TR32 Rule 36. DEPOSITIONS

A. Video Tape Depositions: A transcript of the video tape testimony shall be tendered to the Court when the deposition is offered into evidence. Any party may view a video taped deposition in the custody of the Court only upon order of the Court.

B. Depositions of Experts: All depositions of experts shall be admissible at trial unless objection to the admissibility be given in writing five (5) days prior to the taking of said deposition or within ten (10) days subsequent to notice of the deposition, whichever deadline occurs first. A copy of the notice shall be tendered to the reporter at the time of taking the deposition for inclusion with the deposition. In the absence of such written notification, the deposition of an expert may be admitted by stipulation. The presence of the expert within the limits of the subpoena area shall not be grounds, in and of itself, for the inadmissibility of the deposition at trial. Notwithstanding the above, either party may subpoena such expert for the trial.

C. Copy of Deposition: Any party or counsel to an action may obtain a copy of a deposition on file with the Clerk of the Court upon tender of a receipt showing payment to the deposing party of 50% of the cost of said deposition. In addition, the requesting party of counsel shall tender to the Clerk the present statutory rate per page for the copying service.

Adopted effective Jan. 19, 2010.

LR34-AR00 Rule 37. RE-ENTRY PROGRAM FEES

Those persons directed to participate in the Howard County Superior Court 1 Re-Entry Program shall pay Fees as follows:

1. For Supervision: Fees in accordance with the current In-Home Detention or CTP supervision fee schedule.

2. For Participating in the Program, Fifty dollars ($50.00) per month, not to exceed Five hundred Dollars ($500.00) covering program fees, including but not limited to:

    a. Offender assessment.

    b. Judicial involvement.

    c. Case management.

    d. Program evaluation.

3. For Confirmatory test of Instant UDS, thirty-five dollars ($35.00).

4. For services provided by affiliated treatment and service providers, in accordance with their respective fee schedules.

Any or all of said fees may be waived, by the Re-entry Program in its sole discretion, as an "incentive award" for an individual participant.

Adopted effective July 1, 2011. Amended effective Jan. 15, 2013.

JOHNSON COUNTY LOCAL RULES

Adopted Effective November, 2005

Including Amendments Received Through November 1, 2013

Research Notes

These rules may be searched electronically on Westlaw in the IN-RULES database; updates to these rules may be found on Westlaw in IN-RULESUPDATES. For search tips and a summary of database content, consult the Westlaw Scope Screens for each database.

SMALL CLAIMS RULES

LR41-SC01 Rule 001.   Scope

A. Scope. These rules shall govern the procedure and practice of the Small Claims Division, Johnson County Superior Court No. 2

B. Citation. These rules may be cited as LR41—SC ___—___. The small claims rules promulgated by the Indiana Supreme Court are hereinafter referred to as S.C. ___; and the Indiana Rules of Trial Procedure are hereinafter referred to as T.R. ___

Adopted effective Nov. 2005.

LR41-SC00 Rule 002.   General Practice

A. Conflict of rules. All proceedings in the Johnson County Superior Court No. 2 Court, Small Claims Division shall be governed by the Small Claim Rules promulgated from time to time by the Indiana Supreme Court, and the local rules set forth herein. In instances where these local rules conflict with the rules promulgated by the Indiana Supreme Court, the latter shall control.

B. Tender of completed documents and property costs. Parties or their attorneys are solely responsible to tender to the Court any documents desired to be filed in complete and correct form, together with proper costs, as determined by the Clerk. Neither the Court nor the Clerk will be responsible for delays or deadlines missed due to the tender of incomplete or incorrect documents, or improper costs.

C. Parties' current addresses. Notices from the Court will be sent to the parties at the most recent addresses contained in the Court's file. The parties are therefore solely responsible to maintain their current address in all files concerning them.

Adopted effective Nov. 2005.

LR41-SC00 Rule 003.   Forms

A. Court's forms. The Court shall from time to time and with the consultation of the Clerk, draft forms for use of litigants, the Clerk, and the Court in small claims actions.

B. No other forms. Originals or photocopies of the forms described in LR41-SC00-003(A) shall be acceptable for filing. Any other form or photocopy thereof presented to the Clerk shall be accepted for filing only if such form received prior approval of the Court and in such instance, blank forms identical to that submitted and approved shall be immediately provided to the Clerk and to the Court for future reference and comparison.

C. Form size. All forms and pleadings shall be prepared with white 8 1/2 × 11 inch paper.

Adopted effective Nov. 2005.

LR41-SC08 Rule 004.   Hearing Calendars

A. General procedure. Upon the filing of the notice of claim, the Johnson County Magistrate will initially schedule all cases, except actions involving possession of real estate or personal property; on the Magistrate's non contested calendar.

B. Magistrate's and judge's calendars. At the non contested hearing the parties are not expected to be prepared for trial on the merits. However, at the first scheduled contested hearing, all parties are expected to be prepared for trial on the merits. A parties failure to appear at any contested or non-contested hearing may result in a dismissal or default judgment.

C. Change of calendar. If the Plaintiff requests the first hearing be set for a contested hearing, said request should be noted on the notice of claim. If said request is granted, the matter will be set on the notice of claim for a contested hearing at which time evidence may be presented. If the Defendant notifies the Court of a dispute as to the claim and issues, or if a Counterclaim is asserted, the Court shall reschedule the matter for hearing on the Magistrate's contested hearing calendar.

Adopted effective Nov. 2005.

LR41-SC00 Rule 005. Change of Judge, Removal of Magistrate

A. Magistrate. The Johnson County Magistrate shall preside over all small claims matters and make recommendations to the Judge for final Order and Judgment.

B. General procedure for change of judge. A change of Judge shall be granted as provided by statute and by the Indiana Rules of Trial Procedure.

C. Striking. If a party fails to file a report of striking within fourteen (14) days, after a Change of Judge is granted, said party shall not be entitled to a change of judge, or shall be subject to the Court's arbitrary assignment of the case to one of the remaining judicial officers, as appropriate.

Adopted effective Nov. 2005.

LR41-SC09 Rule 006. Continuances

A. General rule. Except as provided in LR41-SC09-006(B) and (D) below each party to an action may be granted one (1) continuance with a showing of good cause. A continuance under this subsection shall not be granted within seventy two (72) hours of the trial, unless approved by a Judge or Magistrate. All motions for continuance must be made in person or by the party's attorney who has filed a written appearance on behalf of said party. The party or attorney obtaining the continuance shall notify any opposing party in a timely fashion and the motion must state whether the opposing party objects or not to than one continuance.

B. Possession of real estate of personal property.[1] No continuance will be granted to a Defendant where the action involves the issue of possession of real estate.

C. Agreed continuances. Any action may be continued by agreement of the parties and approval of the Judge or Magistrate.

D. Proceedings supplemental. No motion for continuance of a proceedings supplemental hearing will be granted, except by agreement of the parties, or

on good cause shown and upon approval by a Judge or Magistrate.

Adopted effective Nov. 2005.

[1] So in original.

LR41-SC10 Rule 007. Dismissal of Actions

A. Dismissal by plaintiff. Any claim may be dismissed by the Plaintiff at any time before judgment has been entered unless a counterclaim or motion for summary judgment has been filed by a Defendant.

B. Dismissal by stipulation. Any claim may be dismissed by filing a stipulation of dismissal signed by all parties to the claim

C. Dismissal by court. The cause or any pending pleadings in the cause may be dismissed with or without prejudice upon order of the Court, including by way of illustration and not of limitation, as follows:

1. the cause has not been reduced to judgment and where there has been no action on the case for a period of six (6) months; provided however, that no such cause shall be dismissed without notice; or
2. a proceedings supplemental pleading has been filed and there is no action on the day on which the proceedings supplemental is set for hearing.

Adopted effective Nov. 2005.

LR41-SC10 Rule 008. Judgment upon Failure of a Party to Appear

A. Prejudgment grace period. The Court shall permit each party a ten (10) minute grace period to appear for any prejudgment hearing setting, or for any other matter not pertaining to a proceedings supplemental hearing.

B. Judgment default of defendant and default affidavit. Upon the failure of a Defendant to appear at a non-contested hearing or at a contested hearing on the merits, the Plaintiff shall be entitled to a judgment against said Defendant after sworn testimony. In addition to any other applicable requirement of Indiana law, the Plaintiff or Plaintiff's attorney shall sign and file a completed "Affidavit for Judgment by Default" form, if Plaintiff is not available to testify.

C. Default of plaintiff. Upon the failure of a Plaintiff or Plaintiff's attorney to appear at the non-contested hearing or at a contested hearing, the cause shall be dismissed without prejudice and judgment shall be entered for the Defendant against the Plaintiff on any timely-filed counterclaim. Upon the failure of Plaintiff or Plaintiff's attorney to appear at the non-contested hearing or at a contested hearing in a subsequent cause based on the same facts as the cause earlier dismissed without prejudice, said subsequent cause shall be dismissed with prejudice and judgment shall be entered for the Defendant against the Plaintiff on any timely-filed counterclaim.

D. Setting aside default judgment. A default judgment may be set aside according to the procedures set forth in LR41-SC11-010(C) and T.R. 60(B). Forms for this purpose are available from the Court upon request.

E. Stay pending ruling on LR41-SC10-008(D). In any cause in which a motion to set aside default judgment has been filed, collection proceedings as to the judgment debtor filing the motion will not be stayed unless a motion to stay such proceedings is filed and granted pursuant to T.R. 62(B), and any required bond secured.

F. Default on proceedings supplemental. The Court shall permit party a fifteen (15) minute grace period to appear for any proceedings supplemental hearing. After the fifteen (15) minute grace period has elapsed a judgment creditor shall be entitled to apply for appropriate proceedings supplemental sanctions.

Adopted effective Nov. 2005.

LR41-SC00 Rule 009. Attorney Fees

Evidence required to support award. The amount of attorney fees awarded shall be with the sound discretion of the Court. No attorney fees shall be awarded unless:

A. provided for by written agreement(s) between the parties; or

B. according to applicable statute(s), trial rules or common law. Proof of such fees shall be in the form of sworn testimony from, or the affidavit of, the attorney(s) whose services are being proved.

Adopted effective Nov. 2005.

LR41-SC11 Rule 010. Judgments for Payment of Money

In general. Judgments for payment of money shall be enforceable according to the Indiana Rules of Trial Procedure and applicable statutes.

Adopted effective Nov. 2005.

LR41-SC16 Rule 011. Judgments for Possession of Real Estates or Personal Property

A. Bifurcated judgment and expedited hearing on possession. Judgments in actions involving the issue of the possession of real estate or personal property shall be bifurcated. The initial hearing on possession issues shall be set in an expedited setting on the Magistrate's calendar. A final judgment for possession of the real estate or personal property shall be entered at the initial hearing and a judgment for back rent and/or other damages, if any, shall be considered at a subsequent hearing.

B. Notice to tenant. Unless the landlord shall file the pleadings and bond set forth in I.C. 32–6–1.5–1, et. seq., or has an agreement with the tenant, notice to a tenant shall be ten (10) days as required by S.C. 2.

Adopted effective Nov. 2005.

LR41-SC11 Rule 012. Release of Judgment

A. Release of judgment. When any judgment has been fully paid and satisfied, including any interest and all costs, and the judgment creditor has received all said monies or they are available in the Clerk's office, said judgment creditor shall immediately release the judgment against the debtor by personally executing such release on the judgment records of the Clerk, or by causing such release to be filed with the Clerk.

B. Failure to release judgment. Upon a judgment creditor's failure to release a judgment fully paid and satisfied, the affected debtor may:

1. proceed to notify the judgment creditor and file suit for penalties as set forth in I.C. 32–8–1–2; or

2. move on the record of the cause in which the judgment was entered to have said judgment deemed satisfied pursuant to T.R. 13(M), upon which motion notice shall issue and a hearing shall be held by the Court.

Adopted effective Nov. 2005.

LR41-SC00 Rule 013. Proceedings Supplemental

A. General Procedure. Proceedings supplemental to execution shall be governed by T.R. 69(E) of the Indiana Rules of Trial Procedure and applicable statutes.

B. One Year Rule. Except by order of the Court for good cause shown, no proceedings supplemental may pend for more than six (6) months from the date of its filing, and no judgment creditor may file more than four (4) proceedings supplemental per year against any individual judgment debtor in a given cause. At the end of said (6) month period, any pending proceedings supplemental shall not be dismissed if good cause is shown.

C. Conduct Of Hearings. Unless the judgment creditor is represented by an attorney at the proceedings supplemental hearing, said hearing shall be conducted by the Court.

D. Proceedings Supplemental During Pendency Of Garnishment Order. If a garnishment order has been issued and payments are being received by the Clerk, but the judgment remains unsatisfied, additional proceedings supplemental directed to the judgment debtor or to an additional garnishee defendant may be filed only by order of the Court for good cause shown.

Adopted effective Nov. 2005.

LR41-SC00 Rule 014. Court Orders to Appear

A. General Use. Judgment creditors may request the Court to issue an order to appear (COTA) to judgment debtor(s) only when:

1. an active proceedings supplemental is pending against the judgment debtor;

2. the hearing date set for the COTA is within sixty (60) days of the date on which the COTA is issued and;

3. good cause exists for the COTA and is shown on the record at the time the COTA is requested.

B. Good Cause. "Good cause" under LR41-SC00-014(A)(3) shall include but not be limited to:

1. the judgment debtor failed to produce documents as previously ordered by the Court;

2. the judgment debtor has relocated with new address presently unknown

3. there is a reasonable certainty that the judgment debtor's financial status will substantially change within sixty (60) days.

4. payments on garnishment order have not started or have ceased for thirty (30) days.

C. COTA and Garnishment Orders. When a garnishment order has issued, and payments are being received by the Clerk, no pending COTA will be enforced, and no COTA will issue to the judgment debtor, except by order of the Court for good cause shown

D. Failure To Appear On COTA. Upon a judgment debtor's failure to appear on the date and time set by the COTA, the judgment creditor may request sanctions under LR41-SC00-15.

E. Agreements To Appear Without COTA. In any proceedings supplemental, the parties may agree to reset a hearing without use of a COTA. If after such agreement either party fails to appear at the reset hearing, no sanctions shall be available under LR41-SC00-015 for such failure to appear.

Adopted effective Nov. 2005.

LR41-SC00 Rule 015. Contempt / Rule to Show Cause / Body Attachment

A. Contempt. Upon failure of a judgment debtor or Garnishee-Defendant to appear as ordered for a scheduled hearing, or answer interrogatories, the judgment creditor may file a contempt citation as to said person. Said contempt citation must be filed within thirty (30) days of the failure to appear, or within thirty (30) days of the failure to answer interrogatories.

B. Body Attachment. Body attachment shall be requested and issued only when:

1. the judgment debtor or garnishee-defendant previously ordered to appear for scheduled hearing was personally served with an order to appear and failed to appear for the hearing at issue; and

2. the request for Body Attachment is made within thirty (30) days of the hearing at issue and

3. the judgment creditor properly completes and files all pleadings and forms from time to time required by the Court. Said pleadings and forms currently include for each judgment debtor;

a. one (1) request for Body Attachment with the necessary information for a warrant, including the judgment debtor's social security number and or date of birth and or physical description.

b. at least three (3) Writs of Attachment.

C. Procedure For Contacting Judgment Creditor When Attached Person Is In Custody And Unable To Post Bond. When the judgment creditor under LR41-SC00-015 requests the issuance of a Body Attachment, and as needed at any time thereafter, said creditor shall file with the Court any telephone numbers (not to exceed three (3)) at which the Court may notify the creditor of the attached person's appearance in custody. Upon such appearance in custody, the Court, to the best of its ability and consistent with the continued performance of its daily responsibilities, shall:

1. attempt to contact the creditor at the telephone numbers on file with the Court; and

2. thereby notify the creditor of a time later during the same Court business day which the attached person will be brought before the Court for questioning by said creditor.

3. If the Court is unable to contact the judgment creditor as set forth above after attempting to do so for a period of twenty-four (24) hours, the attached person shall be brought before the Court for questioning, given a new Court date to appear released without bond.

D. Expiration And Recall Of Body Attachment.

1. *Expiration.* Body Attachments expire one hundred and eighty (180) days after issuance

2. *Recall.* If during the pendency of a Body Attachment, the judgment creditor desires to recall said body attachment, said judgment creditor shall:

a. appear personally or by attorney and move on the record for recall of the Body Attachment; and

b. state on the record the reason for the desired recall; and

c. Upon recall of a Body Attachment, the judgment creditor must refile a COTA for any subsequent hearing.

Adopted effective Nov. 2005.

LR41—SC00 Rule 016. GARNISHMENT

A. General Procedure. All garnishment proceedings shall comply with T.R. 69 (E) and applicable statues [1].

B. Requirements for Garnishment Order to Issue. A garnishment order shall not issue with respect to a judgment debtor's wage or other property without:

1. an active proceedings supplemental as to the judgment debtor or waiver of notice by said judgment debtor;

2. service on the garnishee-defendant of the proceedings supplemental by

   a. certified mail, or refusal there

   b. Sheriff's service

   c. private process server; and

   d. return of answered interrogatories, other verification of employment by the garnishee-defendant, or failure to answer interrogatories after notice.

C. Voluntary Garnishments. In instances where a judgment debtor has entered a voluntary agreement with respect to garnishment of wages or other property, notwithstanding the terms of the agreement, no garnishment order shall issue unless:

1. an active proceeding supplemental is pending against the judgment debtor; and,

2. the judgment debtor personally appears, testifies as to his or her employment and wages.

D. Garnishments Upon Default of Agreement. In instances where a judgment debtor has entered a voluntary agreement for periodic payments to satisfy the judgment and has further consented to garnishment upon default, notwithstanding the terms of the agreement, no garnishment order shall issue unless:

1. an active proceeding supplemental is pending against the judgment debtor and the garnishee-defendant;

2. the judgment debtor's employment by said garnishee-defendant has been verified as set forth in LR41—SC00—016(A) and (B) on the record within six (6) months prior to the date on which judgment creditor requests issuance of the garnishment order; and

3. the judgment creditor represents on the record either orally or by written pleading the default of judgment debtor.

E. Release. Upon receipt by the judgment creditor or by the Clerk on the judgment creditor's behalf of monies sufficient to fully satisfy the judgment, any accrued interest and costs, the judgment creditor shall immediately prepare and obtain a court order releasing the applicable garnishment order and shall forward a copy to the garnishee-defendant(s).

Adopted effective Nov. 2005. Amended effective May 1, 2013.
1 So in original.

LR41-SC00 Rule 017. Post-judgment Order to Self Employed / Other Judgment Debtor(s)

A. General Procedure. Post-judgment order to self employed and other judgment debtors are available pursuant to T.R. 69(E) and I.C. 34–1–44–7 upon the filing of a verified motion for proceedings supplemental by the judgment creditor.

B. Hearing Before Judge Or Magistrate. All motions for a court order requiring the judgment debtor(s) to apply specified or unspecified property towards the satisfaction of the judgment pursuant to T.R. 69(E)(3) or I.C. 34–1–44–7 shall be set for hearing before a Judge or the Magistrate.

Adopted effective Nov. 2005.

LR41-SC00 Rule 018. Writs

A. General Procedure. Writs to enforce the Court's orders or in aid of its jurisdiction are generally available as set forth in T.R. 70(A) and Title 34 of the Indiana Code.

B. Writs Of Execution For Delivery Of Possession Of Real Estate. Except by order of the Court for good cause shown, no writ of execution for delivery of possession of real estate shall issue before one (1) calendar week has expired after entry of the underlying judgment by the Court.

Adopted effective Nov. 2005.

LR41-SC00 Rule 019. Bankruptcy

A.[1] Bankruptcy of Judgement Debtor. All Court action, including pending collection proceedings, will be stayed as to any judgment debtor:

1. who files with the Court in each relevant action one (1) copy of the bankruptcy court's notice of relief; or

2. whose attorney files with the Court in each relevant action a motion for stay reciting the prior filing of bankruptcy by the judgment debtor and resultant stay of all proceedings by the bankruptcy court, including the cause number and court of the bankruptcy.

Adopted effective Nov. 2005.
1 There is no Subd. B. in this rule.

BOND SCHEDULE

LR41-CR00 Rule 020. Scope of the Johnson County Court Bail Bond Schedule

A. The Johnson County Court Bail Bond Schedule shall apply to all persons charged with offenses in Johnson County, unless otherwise endorsed upon a warrant or ordered by the Circuit, Superior or City Courts of Johnson County.

B. The Johnson County Court Bail Bond Schedule does not apply to any juvenile detainees or offenders.

C. This bond schedule supersedes any general schedules relating to bail or bonds previously issued by the Johnson County Circuit, Superior, or City Courts.

Adopted effective Nov. 2005.

LR41-CR00 Rule 021. Effective Date

This order shall become effective the date of this Order, and shall remain in full force and effect until modified or amended by subsequent Order of the Johnson County Courts.

Adopted effective Nov. 2005.

LR41-CR00 Rule 022. Review

All bail bonds fixed pursuant to this standard schedule shall be subject to review by a judicial officer upon the written request or either party.

Adopted effective Nov. 2005.

LR41-CR00 Rule 023. Type

A. The bail bond amounts listed herein refer to cash or surety bonds only.

B. No ten percent (10%) cash bonds shall be permitted.

C. All cash bail bonds shall be considered a personal asset of the Defendant, and shall be held in trust by the Court Clerk to be applied towards payment of the Defendant's fines, court costs, restitution, judgments and / or other fees which may be assessed by the Courts during the course of the proceedings.

Adopted effective Nov. 2005.

LR41-CR00 Rule 024. Bond Schedule.

The standard minimum bail bond in criminal cases shall be set as follows:

OFFENSE	BOND AMOUNT
Murder	None.
Class A Felony.	$50,000.00
Class B Felony.	$20,000.00
Class C Felony.	$8,000.00
Class D Felony.	$3,000.00
Class A Misdemeanor.	$1,000.00
Class B Misdemeanor	$1,000.00
Class C Misdemeanor	$1,000.00

Adopted effective Nov. 2005.

LR41-CR00 Rule 025. Other Pending or Prior Charges

A. Probation / Parol. If the Defendant is presently out on bail or bond for a pending criminal charge, is on probation, or is on parole, the bail amount to be posted on the new charge shall be double the amount stated in the standard bail bond schedule.

B. Domestic Violence. In situations where the Defendant has been arrested for a Second Offense involving allegations of Domestic Violence, the Defendant shall be held without bond, until the appropriate bond amount is determined by a judicial officer at the Defendant's first court appearance. (This section applies only if the Defendant has been previously arrested for, or convicted of, an offense involving domestic violence.)

Adopted effective Nov. 2005.

LR41-CR00 Rule 026. Multiple Charges

If the Defendant is being arrested or detained for more than one (1) offense, then bail under this standard schedule shall be established as follows.

A. All Felony and A Misdemeanor offenses shall be the aggregate amount of the offenses charged. **Example:** If the Defendant is charged with the offenses of: Burglary as a Class C Felony; Theft as Class D Felony; and, Resisting Law Enforcement as a Class A Misdemeanor, the bail would be the total of: $8,000.00 + $3,000.00 + $1,000.00 = $12,000.00.

B. All Class B and C Misdemeanors shall be concurrent and grouped into one bond amount of $1,000.00. **Example:** If the Defendant is charged with offenses of: Resisting Law Enforcement as a Class A Misdemeanor; Public Intoxication as a Class B Misdemeanor; and, Battery as a Class B Misdemeanor, the bail would be the total of: $1,000.00 on the A Misdemeanor + $1,000.00 on the two B Misdemeanors = $2,000.00.

Adopted effective Nov. 2005.

LR41-CR00 Rule 027. Intoxicated Defendants

The Sheriff of Johnson County or his / her designee, shall have the express authority to detain a person under the influence of intoxicating beverages or drugs until such time as that person may be safely released without being a danger to himself / herself or others.

Adopted effective Nov. 2005.

RULES FOR COURT REPORTERS

LR41–AR15 Rule 028. SCOPE

These rules apply in the Johnson County Circuit Court; the Johnson County Circuit Court, Juvenile Division; Johnson Superior Court 1; Johnson Superior Court 2; Johnson Superior Court 3; and the Johnson County Magistrate Court.

Adopted effective Nov. 2005. Amended effective May 1, 2013.

LR41–AR15 Rule 029. DEFINITIONS

The following definitions shall apply under these local rules:

A. Additional documents means the documents required by Indiana Rules of Appellate Procedure 28(A) and 29 which are not actually a portion of the text of court proceedings, including, but not limited to, the Title Page, Covers, and Table(s) of Contents.

B. Certified means the process, required by the Indiana Rule of Appellate Procedure 28(B) (or Indiana Rule of Appellate Procedure 7.2, prior to its repeal) by which the Court Reporter states and/or affirms that the Transcript is correct.

C. County means Johnson County, Indiana.

D. County Indigent Transcript means a Transcript that is paid for from County funds and is for the use on behalf of a litigant who has been declared indigent by a Court.

E. Court means the particular Court for which the Court Reporter performs services. Court may also mean all of the Courts in Johnson County.

F. Court Reporter is a person who is specifically designated by the Court to perform the official Court reporting services for the Court, including preparing a Transcript of the record.

G. Equipment means all physical items owned by the Court or other governmental entity and used by a Court Reporter in performing Court reporting services. Equipment shall include, but not be limited to, telephones, computer hardware, software programs, disks, tapes, and any other device used for recording and storing, and transcribing electronic data.

H. Emergency means a circumstance or situation which creates a need for a Transcript to be prepared in less time than is allowed under the Indiana Rules of Appellate Procedure. **Emergency** does not include those circumstances which result in Insufficient Notice or Short Notice.

I. Gap Hours Worked means those hours worked that are in excess of the regular hours worked but hours not in excess of 40 hours per work week.

J. Insufficient notice means a request for Transcript preparation which does not contain sufficient information and which causes delay in either: 1) the estimations of time for, and cost of, Transcript preparation, or 2) the preparation of the Transcript. Failure to make satisfactory payment arrangements pursuant to Indiana Rule of Appellate Procedure 9(H) may also constitute **insufficient notice.**

K. Judge means the permanent, elected or appointed judicial officer who presides over the Court.

L. Overtime Hours means those hours worked in excess of 40 hours per work week.

M. Page means the page unit of a Transcript which results when a recording is transcribed in the form required by Indiana Rule of Appellate Procedure 28 (or, Indiana Rules of Appellate Procedure 7.2, prior to its repeal). **Page** shall also mean the page unit of the Additional Documents produced by the Court Reporter, in accordance with Indiana Appellate Rules 28 and 29.

N. Private Practice means the recording of a deposition and/or preparation of a deposition Transcript, which is unrelated to Court proceedings.

O. Private Transcript means a Transcript, including but not limited to a deposition Transcript that is paid for by a private party.

P. Recording means the electronic, mechanical, stenographic or other recording made as required by Indiana Rule of Trial Procedure 74.

Q. Regular Work Hours means those hours which the Court is regularly scheduled to work during any given work week. Depending on the particular Court, these hours may vary from Court to Court within the county but remain the same for each work week.

R. Short notice means a request for Transcript preparation which is made less than seven days from the date which the Transcript is needed, i.e. a witness' testimony during jury trial to be used in closing arguments.

S. State Indigent Transcript means a Transcript that is paid for from state funds and is for the use on behalf of a litigant who has been declared indigent by a Court.

T. Transcript means the text of a Court proceeding which is produced in written form pursuant to Indiana Rules of Appellate Procedure 11 and 28 (or, Indiana Rules of Appellate Procedure 7.1 or 7.2, prior to their repeal).

U. Work Space means that portion of the Court's facilities dedicated to each Court Reporter, including but not limited to actual space in the Courtroom and any designated office space.

V. Work Week means a 7 consecutive day week that consistently begins and ends on the same days throughout the year; i.e. Sunday through Saturday, Wednesday through Tuesday, Friday through Thursday.

Adopted effective Nov. 2005. Amended effective May 1, 2013.

LR41–AR15 Rule 030. COMPENSATION

A. Salary. Court Reporters shall be paid an annual salary for time spent working under the control, direction and direct supervision of their supervising Judge during any Regular Work Hours, Gap Hours Worked, or Overtime Hours. The supervising Judge shall enter into a written agreement with the Court Reporters which outlines the manner in which the Court Reporter is to be compensated for Gap and Overtime Hours; i.e. monetary compensation or compensatory time off regular work hours.

B. Charges for Transcript Preparation:

1. Unless otherwise noted in this rule, or otherwise provided by specific, written order of the Judge, the per page fee for the preparation of a Certified Transcript is $ 5.00.

2. The Court Report shall submit a claim directly to the County for the preparation of any County Indigent Transcripts.

3. At the Judge's discretion, a per page fee exceeding $ 5.00, but not more than$ 6.25, may be charged for the preparation of a Transcript in cases of Emergency, Insufficient Notice, or Short Notice.

4. The minimum fee of $35.00 shall be charged for any Transcript of New Whiteland Town Court proceedings which is less than ten (10) pages, if the Transcript preparation also requires the Court Reporter's time to locate the original recording media.

5. The per page fee a Court Reporter may charge for an Uncertified copy of a previously prepared Transcript shall be $1.00.

C. Charges in Addition to Transcript Preparation.

1. Preparation of the Additional Documents required by Indiana Rules of Appellate Procedure 28(A) and 29 shall be compensated at the standard per page fee of $ 5.00.

2. Binding of the Transcript, Additional Documents, and Exhibits as required by Indiana Rules of Appellate Procedure 28(A) and 29 shall be compensated at the Court Reporter's hourly rate of the annual court Salary, referenced in section 3(A), as determined by the Johnson County Auditor. Such work shall be accounted for and billed in fifteen (15) minute increments.

3. The Court Reporter shall charge for office supplies required and utilized for the binding and electronic transmission of the Transcript, pursuant to Indiana Rules of Appellate Procedure 28 and 29.

a. The costs for these supplies shall be determined pursuant to the Schedule of Transcript Supplies which shall be published annually by the Judges of Johnson County.

b. At the direction of the Judge, the necessary supplies for County Indigent Transcripts, may be provided by the Court.

D. Payment Arrangements.

1. Pursuant to Indiana Rule of Appellate Procedure 9(H), the party requesting a Transcript shall make satisfactory payment arrangements with the Court Reporter, prior to the commencement of the Transcript preparation.

2. A deposit of at least one half (2) of the estimated cost of the completed Transcript will be required by the Court Reporter before beginning any Transcript.

E. Annual Reporting.

1. Each Court Reporter shall report all Transcript fees received for the preparation of either County Indigent or Private Transcripts, at least annually.

2. This report shall be on forms prescribed by the Indiana Supreme Court Division of State Court Administration.

Adopted effective Nov. 2005. Amended effective May 1, 2013.

LR41–AR15 Rule 031. CHOICE TO ENGAGE IN PRIVATE PRACTICE

A. A Court Reporter may elect to engage in Private Practice.

B. With a written agreement with the Judge, a Court Reporter may utilize the Court's Equipment, Work Space and supplies.

C. The written agreement between the Judge and the Court Reporter shall, at a minimum, designate the following:

1. The reasonable market rate for the use of Equipment, Work Space and supplies;

2. The method by which records are to be kept for the use of Equipment, Work Space and supplies; and

3. The method by which the Court Reporter is to reimburse the Court for the use of the Equipment, Work Space and supplies.

4. If a Court Reporter elects to engage in Private Practice, all such Private Practice work shall be conducted outside of Regular Work Hours.

Adopted effective Nov. 2005. Amended effective May 1, 2013.

RULES REGARDING PLACEMENT OF JUVENILES FACING NON-JUVENILE CHARGES

LR41-CR00 Rule 032. Scope

A. In accordance with the Indiana Code and this Court's probate jurisdiction, this Court operates both a Juvenile Court Division and the Johnson County Juvenile Detention Center.

B. The purpose of the Johnson County Juvenile Detention Center is to provide a secure placement for juveniles who are facing an allegation of delinquency or a status offense or who have been adjudicated to be delinquent.

C. From time to time, a juvenile may be charged with a non-juvenile offense (criminal or otherwise) which is outside the jurisdiction of the Juvenile Court.

D. As a courtesy to the Johnson County Sheriff and to the other Johnson County Courts, juveniles charged with or arrested for non-juvenile offenses may be held in the Juvenile Detention Center, assuming such admission is in complete compliance with the mandates of this Order.

Adopted effective Nov. 2005.

LR41-CR00 Rule 033.   Specific Authorization

A juvenile charged with or arrested for a non-juvenile offense shall be not be held in the Johnson County Juvenile Detention Center without the specific authorization or approval of the Judge or the Juvenile Magistrate of the Johnson Circuit Court.

Adopted effective Nov. 2005.

LR41-CR00 Rule 034.   Standard Intake Procedures

Upon the grant of said authorization or approval, a juvenile charged with, or arrested for, a non-juvenile offense must first complete the standard intake proce-dures which are normal in the course of commitment to the Johnson County Jail

Adopted effective Nov. 2005.

LR41-CR00 Rule 035.   Bond Processing

Having completed the standard intake processing at the Johnson County Jail, said juvenile should be considered for bond pursuant to the Johnson County Bond Schedule, or any amendments thereto.

Adopted effective Nov. 2005.

LR41-CR00 Rule 036.   Detention Duration

The duration of such detention shall be at the sole discretion of the Judge or the Juvenile Magistrate of the Johnson Circuit Court.

Adopted effective Nov. 2005.

LR41-CR00 Rule 037.   Prior Authorization for Deviations from Procedures

Any exceptions to or deviations from the procedures set forth in this Order must be authorized, in advance, by either the Judge or the Juvenile Magistrate of the Johnson Circuit Court.

Adopted effective Nov. 2005.

RULES ON ACCESS AND RELEASE OF APPELLATE MATERIALS

LR41-TR77 Rule 038.   Scope

These rules are issued pursuant to Indiana Appellate Rule 12 and govern the release and / or access to materials filed with the Johnson County Clerk of Courts pursuant to any provision of the Indiana Appellate Rules.

Adopted effective Nov. 2005.

LR41-TR77 Rule 039.   Definitions

For the purposes of these rules, the following definitions apply:

A. *Clerk of Courts:* The Clerk of the Johnson Circuit and Superior Courts.

B. *Clerk's Office:* Any office or deputy of the Clerk of Courts.

C. *Exhibits:* Those original items or documents admitted into evidence during proceedings in the Johnson Circuit and Superior Courts which are bound and filed with the Clerk of Courts by a Court Reporter of the Johnson Circuit and Superior Courts pursuant to the Indiana Rules of Appellate Procedure.

D. *Transcript:* Any transcribed materials filed with the Clerk of Courts by a Court Reporter of the Johnson Circuit and Superior Courts pursuant to the Indiana Rules of Appellate Procedure.

Adopted effective Nov. 2005.

LR41-TR77 Rule 040.   Transcript

A. During their respective briefing period, any party may have may, upon request, be provided with a copy of the Transcript by the Clerk's Office.

B. An attorney of record, representing any party, may withdraw the **original** Transcript from the Clerk's Office by filing a completed Request for Release of Appellate Materials.

1. The attorney who withdraws the Transcript shall return it to the Clerk of Courts the date their brief is filed with the Court on Appeal.

2. Failure to timely return the Transcript may result in notice of the same being made to the Court on Appeal.

Adopted effective Nov. 2005.

LR41-TR77 Rule 041.   Exhibits

A. During their respective briefing period, any party may, upon request, be provided a copy of any Exhibit, by filing a completed Request for Release of Appellate Materials.

B. Release of any original Exhibit or Exhibits which cannot be duplicated, replaced, or recreated shall be made only upon written authorization from the trial court.

1. The party who withdraws any original Exhibit shall return it to the Clerk of Courts the date their brief is filed with the Court on Appeal.

2. Failure to timely return the original Exhibit may result in notice of the same being made to the Court on Appeal.

Adopted effective Nov. 2005.

RULES REGARDING INCARCERATION OF COMMUNITY CORRECTIONS DETAINEES

LR41-CR00 Rule 042. Scope

A. Community Corrections has put into place a 24 hour hold policy and that the Community Corrections Advisory Board has approved the same.

B. The Community Corrections policy contains a provision for 24 hour incarceration upon any allegation of consumption of alcohol violation for any participant in Work Release, Home Detention and Day Reporting.

C. It is in the interest of judicial economy and uniformity to issue an order authorizing a 24 hour incarceration for active participants in Work Release, Home Detention or Day Reporting who test positive for alcohol use.

D. That this policy shall be in addition to, and not be considered to the exclusion of any additional policies or sanctions which may be considered for the participants conduct.

Adopted effective Nov. 2005.

LR41-CR00 Rule 043. Twenty-four Hour Incarceration

Accordingly, the Court **NOW ORDERS** that, in absence of specific order by the Court: Community Corrections is authorized to present for 24 hour incarceration, any participant in Work Release, Home Detention or Day Reporting who test positive for alcohol use.

Adopted effective Nov. 2005.

FAMILY COURT RULES

Mission Statement

The purpose of the Juvenile and Family Court is to effectuate maximum utilization of services to Johnson County families who are involved in particularly complex litigation or multiple, simultaneously pending litigation through the coordination of pre-trial proceedings and service referral.

Adopted effective Nov. 2005.

LR41-FL00 Rule 044. Definitions

A. **Family Court:** is the Johnson Circuit Court or Johnson Circuit Court, Juvenile Division, before which cases involving a family or household are linked together for purposes of case coordination. The individual cases maintain their separate integrity and separate docket number, but may be given a common family court designation.

B. **Family Court Proceeding:** is comprised of the individual cases of the family or household(s) which have been assigned to Family Court.

Adopted effective Nov. 2005.

LR41-FL00 Rule 045. Scope

A. These rules apply exclusively to the Johnson County Family Court Pilot Project operated in the Johnson Circuit Court, Juvenile Division as the Johnson County Juvenile and Family Court.

B. Unless explicitly set out in these rules, these rules do not abrogate or modify the Johnson County Local Rules.

Adopted effective Nov. 2005.

LR41-FL00 Rule 046. Eligibility

A. Case types eligible to be heard in the Family Court include, but are not limited to: AD, DR, GU, JC, JD, JM, JS, JT, MH, PO, and RS.

B. Where family members are involved in two or more simultaneously active cases, of eligible case types, with pending issues, these cases will be moved to the Family Court.

C. Pursuant to the Johnson County Local Criminal Rules, LR41-CR2.2-048, charges of Nonsupport of a Dependent Child shall be assigned to the Johnson Circuit Court and heard in the Juvenile and Family Court by the Juvenile Magistrate as a Family Court proceeding. It shall be the duty of the Prosecuting Attorney to file the Family Court Identification Form with the Juvenile and Family Court.

D. A case, of an eligible case type, involving particularly complex family law issues may be moved to the Family Court if:

1. A written request is received in the Family Court.

2. Notice is provided to all parties.

3. Approval is granted by the Judge of the originating court.

4. Approval is granted by a Judge of the Family Court.

Adopted effective Nov. 2005.

LR41-FL00 Rule 047. Identification of Eligible Families

A. Any person aware of a family involved in multiple, simultaneously pending litigation may identify such a family to the Family Court.

(i). The preferred method of referral is use of the Identification Form [Attachment 1 [1]].

(ii). Telephonic referrals will be accepted.

B. Identification of a family who may be eligible for case transfer to the Family Court is an administrative procedure which does not address the merits of the cases involved and which grants no procedural or tactical advantage. All parties will be informed in writing of the result of the identification process.

Adopted effective Nov. 2005.

1 Not included here.

LR41-FL00 Rule 048. Assignment of Cases

A. The Local Rules governing the assignment of cases among the Circuit and Superior Courts are not affected by the implementation of the Family Court or these rules.

B. Cases shall be assigned among the Circuit and Superior Courts in accordance with the Johnson County Local Rules governing the same.

C. There are no original filings in the Family Court.

Adopted effective Nov. 2005.

LR41-FL00 Rule 049. Filing of Pleadings

A. Pleadings may be filed in either the office of the Clerk of Courts or the Family Court.

B. However, in order to avoid any administrative delays in processing, emergency pleadings should be filed in the Office of the Family Court.

Adopted effective Nov. 2005.

LR41-FL00 Rule 050. Jurisdiction

A. The Family Court may exercise jurisdiction over any case involving the family at the same time it exercises jurisdiction over a juvenile case (Child In Need of Services, Delinquency, Status, and Paternity) involving the family.

B. Cases heard in the Family Court, whether by transfer or designation, shall remain in the Juvenile and Family Court for any post-dispositional proceedings.

Adopted effective Nov. 2005.

LR41-FL00 Rule 051. Hearings

A. **Status Hearings.** Unless specified otherwise in writing, the first appearance in the Family Court shall be a status hearing.

B. **Concurrent Hearings.** The Family Court may, in the Court's discretion, set hearings on related cases to be heard concurrently, take evidence on the related cases at these hearings, and rule on the admissibility of evidence for each cause separately as needed to adequately preserve the record for appeal. This rule applies only when the cases are pending before the same judicial officer.

Adopted effective Nov. 2005.

LR41-FL00 Rule 055 [1]. Designation of Family Court Case and Change of Judge for Cause

A. Once a notice is sent to the parties that a case has been selected for the Family Court, no motion for a change of venue from the judge may be granted except to the extent permitted by Indiana Trial Rule 76.

B. Within ten (10) days after notice is sent that a case has been selected for Family Court, a party may object for cause to the Family Court designation.

C. A motion for change of venue from the judge in any matters arising in the Family Court proceeding or any future cases joined in the Family Court proceeding after the initial selection of cases, shall be granted only for cause.

D. If a special judge is appointed, all current and future cases in the Family Court proceeding may be assigned to the special judge.

Adopted effective Nov. 2005.

1 There are no Rules 52 to 54.

LR41-FL00 Rule 056. Judicial Notice and Access to Records

A. **Notice of Case Assignment.** Within a reasonable time after a case is assigned to Family Court, the court shall provide to all parties in the Family Court Proceeding a list of all cases that have been assigned to that Family Court Proceeding.

B. **Judicial Notice.** Any court having jurisdiction over a case assigned to Family Court may take judicial notice of any relevant orders or Chronological Case Summary (CCS) entry issued by any Indiana Circuit, Superior, County, or Probate Court.

C. **Copies.** If a court takes judicial notice of:

1. A court order, the court shall provide a copy of that court order; or,

2. A Chronological Case Summary (Hereinafter: CCS) or CCS entry(s), the court shall provide a copy of the entire CCS.

3. The Court shall provide copies of the order or CCS to the parties to the case at or before the time judicial notice is taken

D. Access to Records. Parties to a Family Court Proceeding shall have access to all cases within the Family Court Proceeding, with the exception of confidential cases or records to which they are not a party. Parties may seek access to the confidential cases or records in another case within the Family Court Pro-

ceeding in which they are not a party, by written petition based on relevancy and need. Confidential records shall retain their confidential status and the Family Court shall direct that confidential records not be included in the public record of the proceedings. *Adopted effective Nov. 2005.*

PLAN FOR ALLOCATION OF JUDICIAL RESOURCES

LR41—AR01 Rule 057. CRIMINAL CASES

Criminal case allocation among the courts of record will operate as specified in the Rules for Filing and Reassignment of Criminal Cases, LR41—CR2.2—086. *Adopted effective Nov. 2005. Amended effective Jan. 1, 2011; June 5, 2013.*

LR41—AR01 Rule 058. JUVENILE CASES

All Juvenile cases (JC, JD, JM, JP, JS, and JT) shall be filed in the Johnson Circuit Court.

A. CHINS and Terminations. Unless a written order indicates otherwise, Juvenile CHINS (JC) and Juvenile Termination (JT) cases shall be heard by the Judge of the Johnson Circuit Court.

B. Other Juvenile Cases. Unless a written order indicates otherwise, Juvenile Delinquency (JD), Juvenile Miscellaneous (JM), Juvenile Paternity (JP), and Juvenile Status (JS) cases shall be heard by the Juvenile and Family Court Magistrate.

Adopted effective Nov. 2005. Amended effective Jan. 1, 2011; June 5, 2013.

LR41—AR01 Rule 059. FAMILY COURT CASES

Unless otherwise indicated by a written order, all Family Court cases shall be heard by the Juvenile and Family Court Magistrate of the Johnson Circuit Court,

Adopted effective Nov. 2005. Amended effective Jan. 1, 2011; June 5, 2013.

LR41—AR01 Rule 060. REMAINING CIVIL CASES

A. Reciprocal Support. Reciprocal Support (RS) cases shall be filed in the Johnson Circuit Court and will beard by the Magistrate of the Juvenile and Family Court.

B. Probate. All Probate cases (AD, ES, EM, EU, GU, MH, and TR) shall be filed in the Johnson Superior Court No. 1.

C. Consumer Collection. All Consumer Collection (CC) cases shall be filed in the Johnson Superior Court No. 1.

D. Domestic Relations. Domestic Relations (DR) cases shall be filed in the Johnson Circuit Court and the Johnson Superior Court No. 2, on a random and even basis.

E. Civil Plenary. All Civil Plenary (PL) cases will be filed in the Johnson Superior Court No. 1.

F. Remaining Civil Cases. All remaining civil cases (CT, MF, and MI) shall be filed in the Johnson Superior Court No. 1 and the Johnson Superior Court No. 3, on a random and even basis.

G. Small Claims. Small Claims (SC) cases shall be filed in the Johnson Circuit Court, Johnson Superior Court No. 1, Johnson Superior Court No. 2, and Johnson Superior Court No. 3 on a random and even basis. Small Claims cases shall be heard by the Magistrate of the Johnson Circuit and Superior Courts.

H. Protection Order. Protection Order cases shall be filed in the Johnson Circuit Court, Johnson Superior Court No. 1, Johnson Superior Court No. 2, and Johnson Superior Court No. 3 on a random and even basis, unless involving the same parties as an existing Domestic Relations (DR) or Juvenile Paternity (JP) case.

1. Protection Order (PO) cases not associated with Dissolution (DR) or Juvenile Paternity (JP) cases shall be heard by the Magistrate of the Johnson Circuit and Superior Courts.

2. Protection Order (PO) cases associated with Domestic Relations (DR) or Juvenile Paternity (JP) cases shall be opened in the courts wherein such associated cases are pending.

Adopted effective Nov. 2005. Amended effective Jan. 1, 2011; June 5, 2013.

LR41—AR01 Rule 061. PROCEEDINGS SUPPLEMENTAL

A. Proceedings Supplemental in Small Claims (SC) cases shall be heard by the Magistrate of the Johnson Circuit and Superior Courts.

B. Proceedings Supplemental in all other cases shall be heard in the court supervising that case.

Adopted effective Nov. 2005. Amended effective Jan. 1, 2011; June 5, 2013.

LR41—AR01 Rule 062. EVALUATION OF WORKLOAD INFORMATION

A. Future review of the Caseload Allocation Plan shall be conducted in compliance with the Schedule for the same established pursuant to Administrative Rule 1.

B. The caseload evaluation shall factor in the disparate allocation of administrative duties among the judicial officers, as well as any special circumstances such as death penalty cases.

C. Special service by: 1) Johnson County judicial officers outside their own courts; or, 2) special, senior judges, or transfer Judges serving in the Johnson County Courts shall also be considered. Such service shall be calculated, in accordance with the Weighted Caseload Worksheet and criteria established by the Indiana Supreme Court Division of State Court Administration, to the nearest half day of service.

D. Pursuant to the evaluation of factors outlined in steps 1—3 above, changes necessary to ensure that the Johnson County Courts remain in compliance with the Order for Development of Local Caseload Plans shall be developed and approved by a majority vote of the judicial officers and shall become effective on June 1 of each year.

Adopted effective Nov. 2005. Amended effective Jan. 1, 2011; June 5, 2013.

RULES FOR APPOINTMENT OF SPECIAL JUDGES

LR41—TR79 Rule 063. APPOINTMENT OF SPECIAL JUDGES IN CIVIL CASES

Appointment of Special Judges in Civil Cases shall be conducted pursuant to Indiana Judicial Administrative District Rule DR17—TR79—00002.

Adopted effective June 14, 2004. Renumbered as Rule 63, and amended effective Nov. 2005. Amended effective July 14, 2011; May 1, 2013.

LR41—TR79 Rule 064.   RESERVED

LR41—TR79 Rule 065.   RESERVED

LR41—TR79 Rule 066.   RESERVED

LR41—TR79 Rule 067.   RESERVED

LR41—TR79 Rule 068.   RESERVED

LR41—TR79 Rule 069.   RESERVED

Addendum A. Coordinated Local Rule of The Counties Of: Boone, Hendricks, Morgan, Johnson, Shelby, Hancock, and Hamilton Enacted in Compliance With T.R. 79(h)

Pursuant to Order Amending Rules of Trial Procedure entered by the Supreme court of Indiana bearing a date of June 7, 1995, the undersigned Judges and Magistrates of the seven contiguous counties to Marion County, Indiana, do hereby adopt the following rule to establish procedures for the selection of special judges in civil cases:

1. This rule shall be subject to any previous standing orders for the appointment of judges which may be in effect or which may become effective subsequent to the entry of this rule, which standing orders may be entered by the Supreme Court of Indiana. Standing orders shall pre-empt this rule and shall take precedence over it.

2. This rule shall have a seven part addendum, on part for each of the contiguous counties to Marion County, which addendums are attached hereto and incorporated herein by reference.   *

3. Pursuant to T.R. 79, parties to a civil action may agree (with concurrence with the judge selected) to any particular special judge.

4. In the absence of an agreement as to a particular special judge, the parties, alternatively, may agree to have the regular sitting judge appoint a special judge from a list of local judges, magistrates or senior judges.

5. In the absence of an agreement as to a particular special judge or an agreement to have the regular sitting judge appoint a special judge, the regular sitting judge shall name a panel consisting, whenever possible, or (sic [of]) other judges or magistrates with the county where the civil action is situated. If the count (sic [county]) in question does not have a sufficient number of regular sitting judges or magistrate (sic [magistrates]), when (sic [then]) such county (sic [court]) shall name a panel including the available local judges or magistrates and judge or magistrate from a county immediately adjoining that county also contiguous to Marion County, but excluding Marion County.

6. Should none of the above methods produce a special judge, the regular sitting judge shall select (on a rotating basis) one of the judge (sic [judges]) or magistrates from a contiguous county to the county where the civil action is situated, which counties are also contiguous to Marion County, but excluding Marion County, all pursuant as to the specifics of each county to the addendums attached hereto and incorporated herein by reference.

7. In the event that no judicial officer within Administrative District 8 is eligible to serve as special judge, or the particular circumstance of the case warrants selection of a special judge by the Indiana Supreme Court, the judge of the court in which the case is pending shall certify the matter to the Indiana Supreme Court for appointment of a special judge.

Adopted effective June 14, 2004. Renumbered as Addendum A, and amended effective Nov. 2005.

* County addenda are excluded from this copy of the text of the rule.

JURY RULES

LR41-JR00 Rule 070. Definitions [1]

A. **"Court"** shall mean the Circuit, Superior, and City Courts in Johnson County.

B. **"Jury Administrator"** is a person so appointed to administer and manage the jury process in a court by the Judge of the Circuit, Superior, or City Courts in Johnson County, to the extent permitted by Indiana law.

C. **"Jury Pool"** is a list of no less than nine thousand five hundred (9500) names drawn annually by Jury Administrators from voter registration and supplemental records.

D. **"Notice of Jury Service"** is a written document which accompanies the Juror Qualification and Questionnaire Form and provides general information regarding the juror selection process of the Johnson County Courts.

E. **"Juror Qualification and Questionnaire Form"** is a written document which solicits information from prospective jurors regarding statutory qualifications and exemptions.

F. **"Summons"** is a written documents which notifies a prospective juror of the dates and details of their jury service.

G. **"Quarterly Venire List"** is a random sub-set of the Jury Pool which shall be requested from the Clerk of Courts by each Court's Jury Administrator. Unless otherwise directed by the presiding judge of each Court, the Quarterly Venire List shall be composed of five hundred (500) names.

Adopted effective Aug. 31, 2004. Renumbered as Rule 70, and amended effective Nov. 2005.

[1] There are two Rules 70 in the Johnson County Local Rules.

LR41-JR00 Rule 071. Effective Date

In compliance with the Indiana Jury Rules, these amended rules shall become effective immediately upon execution in order govern [1] juror selection proceedings on or after August 31, 2004.

Adopted effective Aug. 31, 2004. Renumbered as Rule 71, and amended effective Nov. 2005.

[1] So in original. Should probably read: "in order to govern".

LR41-JR01 Rule 072. Scope

The rules shall govern grand and petit jury assembly, selection, and the management of grand and petit juries in the Johnson County Courts.

Adopted effective Aug. 31, 2004. Renumbered as Rule 72, and amended effective Nov. 2005.

LR41-JR02 Rule 073. Initial Appointment of Jury Administrators

A. **Circuit and Superior Courts.** The following are hereby appointed to act as Jury Administrators, to administer the jury assembly process under the supervision of the Judges of the Johnson County Circuit and Superior Courts.

1. Two (2) Jury Commissioners as appointed by the Judge of the Johnson Circuit Court pursuant to the Indiana Code.

2. Assistant Court Reporter / Bailiff of the Johnson Circuit Court.

3. Assistant Court Reporter / Bailiff of the Johnson Superior Court 1.

4. Assistant Court Reporter / Bailiff of the Johnson Superior Court 2.

5. Assistant Court Reporter / Bailiff of the Johnson Superior Court 3.

6. First Deputy Clerk of Courts, Voter Registration.

B. **City Courts.** To the extent permitted by Indiana law, the Judges of the Greenwood City Court and the Franklin City Court may appoint such Jury Administrators for their courts as necessary.

Adopted effective Aug. 31, 2004. Renumbered as Rule 73, and amended effective Nov. 2005.

LR41-JR02 Rule 074. Additional of Modification of Appointments [1]

Appointments as Jury Administrator shall be updated or modified, from time to time, as deemed necessary by any Judge of the Johnson County Circuit and Superior Courts.

Adopted effective Aug. 31, 2004. Renumbered as Rule 74, and amended effective Nov. 2005.

[1] So in original.

LR41-JR02 Rule 075. Assembly of the Jury Pool

A. No later than November 25 of each calendar year, the Jury Pool shall be assembled for the next calendar year by randomly selecting names from the Johnson County Voter Registration Records and at least one of the following:

1. Records of property tax payers maintained by the Johnson County Treasurer;

2. Records of motor vehicle registrations from the Indiana Bureau of Motor Vehicles.

B. The determination of which record to be used in addition to Voter Registration Records shall be made by the Clerk of Courts.

Adopted effective Aug. 31, 2004. Renumbered as Rule 75, and amended effective Nov. 2005.

LR41-JR04 Rule 076.   Summoning Jurors

Jurors in the Johnson County Circuit and Superior Courts shall be summoned using a Two Tier Notice and Summons procedure.

A.   At least quarterly, and pursuant to the schedule set forth below, the Clerk of Courts shall randomly draw the Quarterly Venire List from the Jury Pool provide the same to each Court.

B.   The Quarterly Venire List from the Jury Pool shall be provided to each Court no later than December 1, March 1, June 1, and September 1 of each calendar year.

C.   The Jury Administrator assigned to each Court shall mail to potential jurors, or cause to be mailed, the Notice of Jury Service and Juror Qualification and Questionnaire Form no later than December 8, March 8, June 8, and September 8 of each calendar year.

D.   Not later than one (1) week before a jury panel for jury selection is needed, the Jury Administrator assigned to each Court shall mail, or cause to be mailed, the Summons of Jury Service which shall specify the specific dates for which the prospective juror shall remain on call for jury service.

Adopted effective Aug. 31, 2004.   Renumbered as Rule 76, and amended effective Nov. 2005.

LR41-JR00 Rule 077.   Assistance of Clerk of Courts

At the discretion of the presiding Judge, the Jury Administrator assigned to each Court may receive technical, administrative, or clerical assistance in summoning prospective jurors from the Office of the Johnson County Clerk of Courts. *See* I.C. 33–4–11–10 *and* I.C. 33–4–11–15.

Adopted effective Aug. 31, 2004.   Renumbered as Rule 77, and amended effective Nov. 2005.

LR41-JR05 Rule 078.   Criteria for Disqualification

Prospective jurors shall be found disqualified from jury service using that only that criteria which is expressly provided in the Indiana Code and / or the Indiana Jury Rules.

Adopted effective Aug. 31, 2004.   Renumbered as Rule 78, and amended effective Nov. 2005.

LR41-JR06 Rule 079.   Criteria for Exemption

Prospective jurors shall be exempted from jury service using only those exemptions expressly provided in the Indiana Code and / or the Indiana Jury Rules.

Adopted effective Aug. 31, 2004.   Renumbered as Rule 79, and amended effective Nov. 2005.

LR41-JR08 Rule 080.   Documentation of Disqualification, Exemption, or Deferral

Facts supporting disqualification, exemption, or deferral from jury service shall be provided to the Court, in writing, under oath or affirmation.

Adopted effective Aug. 31, 2004.   Renumbered as Rule 80, and amended effective Nov. 2005.

LR41-JR09 Rule 081.   Term of Jury Service.

A.   A person who appears for service as a juror in a jury serves until the conclusion of the first trial in which the juror is sworn, regardless of the length of the trial or its manner of disposition.

B.   A person who appears for service but is not selected and sworn as a juror completes the person's service when jury selection is completed.

C.   A person who either:

1.   Serves as a juror; or,

2.   Serves until the jury selection is completed, but is not chosen to serve as a juror;

may not be selected for another jury panel until all nonexempt persons in the Jury Pool for that year have been called for jury duty; provided, however, jurors who are called for jury service are eligible to serve in any court in Johnson County on the day summoned.

Adopted effective Aug. 31, 2004.   Renumbered as Rule 81, and amended effective Nov. 2005.

LR41-JR12 Rule 082.   Record Keeping

Records of the jury management in the Johnson County Courts shall be maintained, in written format, or electronic format, or both, by the Jury Administrator assigned to each individual Court.

A.   Such records shall include, but are not limited to: annual jury pool, periodic list, jurors qualified, exemptions granted, deferrals granted, jurors who served, and / or terms of service.

B.   The protocols for record keeping and retention established in each Court shall comply strictly with the standards established in the Indiana Code, Indiana Jury Rules, Indiana Administrative Rules, or otherwise provided by Indiana law.

Adopted effective Aug. 31, 2004.   Renumbered as Rule 82, and amended effective Nov. 2005.

LR41-JR10 Rule 083.   Juror Privacy

A.   Personal information relating to a juror or prospective juror not disclosed in open court is confidential, other than for the use of the parties and counsel.

B.   Upon request, copies of the Juror Qualification and Questionnaire Form may be made available to counsel on the date of trial.

1.   All copies of the Juror Qualification and Questionnaire form so provided shall be returned to the Court at the completion of the jury selection process.

2.   No photocopies or duplicates of the Juror Qualification and Questionnaires shall be made, without specific Court authorization.

C.   Each Court shall take steps to protect and maintain juror privacy and the confidentiality of juror information.

Adopted effective Aug. 31, 2004.   Renumbered as Rule 83, and amended effective Nov. 2005.

LR41–JR00 Rule 084.   Miscellaneous

All other proceedings involving the assembly, selection, and management of juries in the Johnson County Circuit and Superior Courts shall be conducted as set out fully in the Indiana Jury Rules.

Adopted effective Aug. 31, 2004. Renumbered as Rule 84, and amended effective Nov. 2005.

CRIMINAL RULES

LR41–CR2.2 Rule 085.   AUTHORITY AND SCOPE

These rules are hereby promulgated pursuant to the authority of the Indiana Criminal Rules. These rules shall govern the practice and procedure for the filing assignment of all felony and misdemeanor cases in the Johnson County Circuit and Superior Courts.

Adopted effective Nov. 2005. Amended effective May 1, 2013.

LR41–CR2.2 Rule 086.   RANDOM CASE ASSIGNMENT

A. Felonies.   In conjunction with the Amended Johnson County Plan for Allocation of Judicial Resources, and subject to the provisions of LR41–CR2.2–087 and LR41–CR2.2–88, all cases involving Felonies shall assigned on a random and equal basis among the Johnson Circuit Court, Johnson Superior Court No. 2, and Johnson Superior Court No. 3.

B. Misdemeanors, Infractions, and Ordinance Violations.   In conjunction with the Amended Johnson County Plan for Allocation of Judicial Resources, and subject to the provisions of LR41–CR2.2–086 and LR41–CR2.2–87, Misdemeanors (CM), Infraction (IF), and Ordinance Violation (OV) cases shall be assigned on a random basis among the Johnson Circuit Court, the Johnson Superior Court No. 1, the Johnson Superior Court No. 2, and the Johnson Superior Court No. 3.   The distribution between these courts shall be:

1.   One quarter (25%) of such cases shall be filed in the Johnson Circuit Court, the Johnson Superior Court No. 1, and the Johnson Superior Court No. 2 on an random and even basis;

2.   The remaining three-quarters (75%) of such cases shall be filed in the Johnson Superior Court No. 3;

3.   Infraction and Ordinance Violation cases shall be heard by the Magistrate of the Johnson County Circuit and Superior Courts; and,

4.   Criminal Misdemeanor cases filed in the Johnson Circuit Court, the Superior Court No, 1, and the Johnson Superior Court No. 2, shall be heard by the Magistrate of the Johnson County Circuit and Superior Courts.

C. Miscellaneous Criminal Cases.

1.   *Search Warrants.*   Miscellaneous Criminal cases opened for Search Warrants shall be assigned among the Johnson Circuit Court, Johnson Superior Court No. 1, Johnson Superior Court No. 2, and Johnson Superior Court No. 3 based upon the annual Judges' On–Call Schedule.

2.   *Grand Jury.*   Miscellaneous Criminal cases opened for Grand Jury proceedings shall be opened in the court of the supervising Judge, pursuant to Rule LR41–CR00–091.

3.   *General.*

a.   Miscellaneous Criminal cases opened for rights advisements shall be assigned among the Johnson Circuit Court, Johnson Superior Court No. 1, Johnson Superior Court No. 2, and Johnson Superior Court No. 3 on a random and even basis;

b.   Miscellaneous Criminal cases opened for rights advisements shall be heard by the Magistrate of the Johnson County Circuit and Superior Courts; and,

c.   Miscellaneous Criminal cases opened for probation transfers shall be assigned to the Johnson Circuit Court.

Adopted effective Nov. 2005. Amended effective Jan. 1, 2011; Feb. 27, 2012, effective retroactively to Jan. 1, 2012; May 1, 2013; June 5, 2013.

LR41–CR2.2 Rule 087.   Re–Filings and Subsequent Filings

A.   Subsequent to Dismissals.

1.   In the event the State of Indiana dismisses a case or charge, any subsequent case or charge filed against the named defendant shall be assigned to the Court from which the dismissal was taken.

2.   It shall be the duty of the Prosecuting Attorney to bring this fact to the attention of the Clerk's Office when charges are re-filed.

B.   New Causes of Action, Generally.

1.   Subject to the provision of subsection (c) below, in the event of the origination of a new cause of action against a defendant with an existing felony or misdemeanor proceeding, the new cause of action shall be assigned to the Court administering the existing cause(s) of action.

2.   It shall be the duty of the Prosecuting Attorney to bring this fact to the attention of the Clerk's Office when the new charges are filed.

C.   New Causes of Action, Probation Revocation.

1.   If the new felony or misdemeanor cause of action filed against a defendant is supported by the same facts upon which a petition revoke probation or direct commitment to a Community Corrections program could be based, the new cause of action

shall be assigned to the Circuit or Superior Court in which the related probation or commitment is being supervised.

2. It shall be the duty of the Prosecuting Attorney to bring this fact to the attention of the Clerk's Office when such new charges are filed.

Adopted effective Nov. 2005.

LR41–CR2.2 Rule 088. Non–Support of Dependants

Charges of Nonsupport of a Dependent Child shall be assigned to the Johnson Circuit Court and heard in the Juvenile and Family Court by the Juvenile Magistrate as a Family Court proceeding. It shall be the duty of the Prosecuting Attorney to file the Family Court Identification Form with the Juvenile and Family Court.

Adopted effective Nov. 2005.

LR41–CR2.2 Rule 089. REASSIGNMENT

A. Reassignment Pursuant to District Rule. In the event a change of Judge is granted, or it becomes necessary to assign another Judge in any felony or misdemeanor proceeding, the procedures of Indiana Judicial Administrative District Rule DR17–CR–00003 will be followed.

B. When Case is Transferred. If a Johnson County Judicial Officer is selected as Special Judge the case shall be transferred to the selected Johnson County Court.

C. Misdemeanors. Misdemeanors reassigned to the Johnson Circuit Court, Johnson Superior Court No. 1, or Johnson Superior Court No. 2 in this manner shall be heard by the Magistrate of the Johnson County Circuit and Superior Courts.

D. Not a Limitation on Transfers. This rule is not intended to limit the authority of the Judges to transfer cases between the Courts by agreement of the Judges.

Adopted effective Nov. 2005. Amended Feb. 27, 2012, effective retroactively to Jan. 1, 2012; May 1, 2013.

LR41–CR13 Rule 090. APPOINTMENT OF SPECIAL JUDGE

In the event that no local Judge is available to accept reassignment of a case pursuant to LR41–CR2.2–089, or the particular circumstance warrants selection of a special judge by the Indiana Supreme Court such case shall be certified to the Indiana Supreme Court for appointment of a Special Judge.

Adopted effective Nov. 2005. Amended effective May 1, 2013.

LR41–CR00 Rule 091. GRAND JURY SUPERVISION

A. The November 16, 2001 Standing Order Regarding Grand Jury Proceedings in the Johnson Circuit and Superior Courts is hereby **VACATED.**

B. Grand Jury supervision shall rotate among the Johnson Circuit Court, Johnson Superior Court No. 2, and Johnson Superior Court No. 3 in the following manner:

1. Requests for a Grand Jury filed between January 1 and April 30 shall be supervised by the Johnson Circuit Court.

2. Requests for a Grand Jury filed between May 1 and August 31 shall be supervised by the Johnson Superior Court No. 2.

3. Requests for a Grand Jury filed between September 1 and December 31 shall be supervised by the Johnson Superior Court No. 3.

C. The Court's Jury Administrator shall, at the time of the creation of the Quarterly Venire List pursuant to the Amended Local Rules Regarding Selection Of Procedures For Juror Selection, randomly draw the names of twelve (12) Grand Jurors to serve as such.

D. Any new criminal case filings which result from Grand Jury Proceedings shall be filed in the Court in which the Grand Jury Proceedings were held, as an exception to LR41–CR2.2–086.

Adopted effective Nov. 2005. Amended effective May 1, 2013.

LR41–CR2.2 Rule 092. EFFECTIVE DATE

Pursuant to T.R. 81(D), there is good cause to deviate from the schedule for approval of local rules. Subject to the approval of the Indiana Supreme Court, these amended rules shall become effective immediately.

Adopted effective Nov. 2005. Amended effective May 1, 2013.

DOMESTIC RELATIONS RULES

LR41-FL00 Rule 093. Authority

These rules are promulgated pursuant to the authority of the Indiana Rules of Trial Procedure, Trial Rule 81, and are intended to supplement those rules. These rules shall govern the practice and procedure in all Domestic Relations and Paternity cases in the Johnson County Circuit and Superior Courts.

Adopted effective Nov. 2005.

LR41-FL00 Rule 094. Temporary Restraining Orders

A. Domestic Violence. Parties wishing protection from domestic or family violence in Domestic Relations cases may petition the Court pursuant to Indiana Code 34-26-5.

B. Without Notice. A Temporary Restraining Order may be granted without written or oral notice to the adverse Party or his attorney only if:

1. it clearly appears from specific facts shown by affidavit or by the verified complaint that immediate and irreparable injury, loss, or damage will result to the applicant before the adverse Party or his attorney can be heard in opposition; and

2. the applicant's attorney certifies to the court in writing the efforts, if any, which have been made to give notice and the reasons supporting his claim that notice should not be required.

C. Subject to the provisions of Indiana Trial Rule 65(B) and (E), in an action for dissolution of marriage, legal separation, or child support, the Court may issue a Temporary Restraining Order, without hearing or security, if either Party files a verified petition alleging an injury would result to the moving Party if no immediate order were issued.

1. *Joint Order.* If the Court finds that an order shall be entered, the Court may enjoin both Parties from:

A. Transferring, encumbering, concealing, selling or otherwise disposing of any joint property of the Parties or asset of marriage without the written consent of the Parties or the permission of the Court; and / or

B. Removing any child of the Parties then residing in the State of Indiana from the State with the intent to deprive the Court of jurisdiction over such child without prior written consent of all Parties or the permission of the Court.

2. *Separate Petitions and Orders.*

a. A joint or mutual restraining or order of protection shall not be issued.

b. If both Parties allege injury, they shall do so by separate petitions. The Court shall review each petition separately and rule on each petition on its individual merits.

c. The moving Party shall provide the Court with the following information concerning the non-moving Party:

1. Name
2. Date Of Birth
3. Race
4. Gender
5. Height
6. Weight
7. Existence And Location Of Scars, Tattoos And/Or Other Identifiable Characteristics
8. Home Address
9. Home Telephone Number
10. Work Address
11. Work Contact Number
12. Work Schedule

d. In the event a Party seeks to enjoin the non-moving Party from abusing, harassing, disturbing the peace, committing a battery on the moving Party or any child or step-child of the Parties, or exclude the non-moving Party from the marital residence, and the Court determines that an order shall be issued, such order shall be addressed to one person.

D. Unless appropriate under Indiana Code 34-26-5, the Court will not issue a custody order *ex parte* under any circumstances. Priority will be given to hear emergency matters, if necessary.

Adopted effective Nov. 2005.

LR41-FL00 Rule 095.   Financial Declarations

A. In any contested final hearing or any modification hearing involving child custody, support, division of assets or debts, the Parties will file an updated financial declaration accompanied with wage records and tax returns within five (5) days of trial.

B. If the matter is set for a preliminary hearing, the financial declaration must be filed no later than the day of the hearing.

Adopted effective Nov. 2005.

LR41-FL00 Rule 096.   Child Support Worksheets

In all matters regarding child support issues, the Parties shall, on or before the date of the hearing:

A. file a Child Support Obligation Worksheet, including, when appropriate, the Post-Secondary Education Worksheet and / or a Parenting Time Credit Worksheet; and

B. supporting documentation to establish proof of current income and income earned during the prior tax year.

Adopted effective Nov. 2005.

LR41-FL00 Rule 097.   Sanctions

Failure to comply with LR41-FL00-095 or LR41-FL00-096 herein subjects any person in non-compliance to sanctions as the Court may deem appropriate or remedial including but not limited to exclusion of evidence, attorney fees, or continuance.

Adopted effective Nov. 2005.

LR41-FL00 Rule 098.   Child Support

When Parties contend deviation from the Child Support Rules and Guidelines is appropriate, they shall indicate the reasons for deviation on the worksheet or in an attachment.

Adopted effective Nov. 2005.

LR41-FL00 Rule 099.   Parenting Time Guidelines

A. **General Rule.** In cases where the final decree or order is entered on or after March 31, 2001, the Johnson County Circuit and Superior Courts will use the Indiana Parenting Time Guidelines.

B. Previously issued orders. Orders issued pursuant to, or incorporating by reference, earlier versions of the Johnson County Visitation Guidelines will continue to be interpreted and enforced pursuant to those guidelines until modified, in writing, by the issuing court.

Adopted effective Nov. 2005.

LR41—FL00 Rule 100. MEDIATION

A. General Rule. Mediation shall be required on all Petitions for Dissolution of Marriage, Petitions to Establish Paternity, and Petitions to Modify without regard to the anticipated length of trial.

B. Contempt Proceedings. Mediation shall be required on Contempt Proceedings (i.e., Petitions for Order to Show Cause, etc.) that will take longer than one (1) hour to try.

B.[1] Scope. This Rule shall not apply to those issues in which the State of Indiana represents a Party.

Adopted effective Nov. 2005. Amended effective May 1, 2013.

 [1] So in original.

LR41-FL00 Rule 101. Hearings

Either Party will notify the Court in a praecipe for final hearing, and update that notice two (2) days prior to trial, of the anticipated length of the case so that the Court can determine whether to remove alternative choice settings.

Adopted effective Nov. 2005.

LR41-FL00 Rule 102. Physical Custody

A. Separate Praecipe. In an original action, whenever the temporary physical custody of a child or children is at issue between the parents, and if it is anticipated that more than twenty (20) minutes will be required for the presentation of evidence on the issue, the Party requesting more than twenty (20) minutes of the court's time shall petition separately therefore.

1. In such petition, the moving Party shall estimate the amount of time needed for the presentation of evidence on the issue of temporary physical custody, and shall also designate other issues known or likely to exist, including those pertaining to spousal maintenance, support, temporary possession of the marital residence, restraining or protective orders, and conditions or restrictions on parenting time access.

2. Any such petition shall be filed as soon as practicable after the issue is known to exist, and in any event, not less than three (3) days prior to a previously established hearing date concerning preliminary or provisional orders. The moving Party shall submit an order establishing a new hearing date, and the court may, in its discretion, continue the scheduled hearing date to a date on which all pending issues may be heard and determined.

3. Financial Declarations. Financial Declarations and supporting documentation of income and earnings shall be filed and exchanged not less than twenty-four (24) hours prior to the scheduled hearing date, the provision of LR41-FL00-095 notwithstanding. Failure by a Party to comply with any provisions of this rule may result in LR41-FL00-097 sanctions, or any other sanctions deemed reasonable by the court, including the exclusion of evidence offered on behalf of the offending Party.

4. Nothing in this rule shall limit the court in its regulation of the manner and order of proof, or in the conduct of the proceedings.

5. Preliminary Hearing Transcript. If permanent physical custody of a child or children is at issue at the time of the final hearing, upon request by either Party or by the court sua sponte, the Official Court Reporter shall prepare and certify a transcript of the preliminary hearing.

 a. Any request for a transcript pursuant to this rule shall be made pursuant to the Local Rules on Court Reporters (LR41-AR15-028 *through* LR41-AR15-031), not less than thirty (30) days prior to the final hearing.

 b. Copies of the transcript shall be provided to the Parties, who shall divide equally the cost of such transcription, subject to reallocation by the court at the time of the final hearing.

 c. The Indiana Rules of Evidence shall govern the use or admissibility of the transcript at the time of the final hearing.

6. The provisions of this rule do not preclude the right to seek an emergency hearing upon appropriate grounds or under warranting circumstances.

Adopted effective Nov. 2005.

LR41-FL00 Rule 103. Continuances

All motions for continuance must be filed at least three (3) days before trial. The motion must state the opposing Party has been notified (or a good faith attempt at notification has been made) and must state whether the opposing Party objects if known. A motion for continuance filed less than (3) days prior to trial must allege extenuating circumstances as to why the continuance is not filed timely and will be considered on a case by case basis.

Adopted effective Nov. 2005.

LR41-FL00 Rule 104. Summary Adjudication

The Courts prefer, if possible, the summary presentation and adjudication of preliminary hearings, contempt hearings and compliance hearings.

Adopted effective Nov. 2005.

LR41-FL00 Rule 105. Termination of Representative Capacity

A. Upon entry of a final dispositional order or an order of modification of any custody, parenting time and/or child support order, the representative capacity of all attorneys appearing on behalf of any Party shall be deemed terminated upon:

1. An order of withdrawal granted by the presiding Court;

2. The expiration of time within which an appeal of such Order may be preserved or perfected pursuant to the Indiana Rules of Trial Procedure and/or the Indiana Rules of Appellate Procedure; or,

3. The conclusion of any appeal of such Order commenced pursuant to Indiana Rules of Trial Procedure and/or the Indiana Rules of Appellate Procedure.

B. The service of any post dissolution pleadings upon any Party not represented by counsel pursuant to paragraph A above, shall be made upon that person pursuant to the Indiana Rules of Trial Procedure.

C. Any copy served upon original counsel will be deemed to be a matter of professional courtesy only, without substantive legal effect.

D. Any withdrawal or appearance shall include the last known address of the Party.

Adopted effective Nov. 2005.

LR41-FL00 Rule 106. "Families in Transition" Program

A. **When Required for Parents.** Parties in all Dissolution and Legal Separation cases must immedi-

ately enroll in and complete the Families in Transition program if there are children from the marriage under the age of sixteen (16) years of age.

B. **When Required for Children.** As of the date of the filing of the Petition for Dissolution or Legal Separation if there are children of the marriage between the ages of eight (8) and sixteen (16) years old, the children must enroll in and complete the program with their custodial parent(s).

C. **Waiver.** The Court shall consider a written waiver under this Rule, in extraordinary circumstances, on a case by case basis.

D. **Submission of Proposed Order.** Pursuant to this rule, the Petitioner must submit the following Order, with all information provided therein, at the time the Petition for Dissolution or Legal Separation is filed and the a Court will send a copy of the Order to the Johnson County Youth Connection, and the attorneys (or Parties if they are unrepresented). It is the duty of the attorney to provide a copy of the Order to the Parties.

E. **Other Programs.** The Court may consider allowing the use of other similar programs outside of Johnson County and/or the State of Indiana upon proper application.

Adopted effective Nov. 2005.

PROBATE RULES

LR41-PR00 Rule 107. Scope

These Amended Johnson County Probate Rules shall apply in all probate matters filed in the Circuit and Superior Courts in Johnson County, Indiana.

Adopted effective Nov. 2005.

LR41-PR00 Rule 108. Accountings Reports and Procedures

A. **Documentation of Disbursements.** In all Supervised Estates and Guardianship accounts, affidavits in lieu of Ability to occasionally work weekend, evening, and/or extended hours, and occasionally travel out of town, sometimes overnight.

B. The Personal Representative or Guardian shall procure and maintain receipts or proof of payment and make such receipts or proof of payment available to interested persons upon Court Order.

C. **Public or Pension Benefits.** All Social Security, Medicare, pension benefits, or other benefits, including IRS distributions, received on behalf of an incapacitated person or minor shall be included and accounted for in the Guardianship accounting, unless Court approval has been previously granted to allow said funds to be paid directly to a residential or health care facility.

D. **Disbursements to the Fiduciary.**

1. In Supervised Estates, disbursements by the Personal Representative to herself / himself shall be made only with complete documentation and / or original receipts which document the date, amount, and reason for the disbursement.

2. In Guardianships, the Guardian shall make no disbursement to herself / himself without prior Court order. A Guardian may petition the Court for authorization to disburse Guardianship funds to herself / himself by regular and periodic advances, if:

a. the Guardian is providing care to the incapacitated person and is allocating a portion of the Guardian's regular periodic expenses for the incapacitated person's care; and,

b. the Guardian's written request is supported by itemization of the past regular periodic expenses incurred and the proposed allocation of the expenses between the Guardian and the incapacitated person.

E. **Accounting Schedule Formats.** Accountings in Supervised Estates and in Guardianships shall be presented in the following schedules and format and in accordance with the Indiana Code. Informal, handwritten or transactional accountings will not be accepted.

1. Schedule 1: All Property Chargeable to the Personal Representative or Guardian.

a. The property held by the Personal Representative or Guardian may be established by reference to the Personal Representative's or Guardian's Inventory or most recent Accounting.

b. Additional property chargeable to the Personal Representative or Guardian during the period of the accounting shall be identified as follows as to each new item of property:

1. a description of the property;

2. an amount received or value of the property;

3. the income from principal shall include the property from which the income was received.

c. A report of change in the property held, such as a change in investment, shall include the following:

1. the description of the property sold, changed or lost;

2. any gain or loss resulting from the transaction;

3. the description of the property received, purchased or obtained.

2. Schedule 2: Payments, Charges, Losses and Distributions.

Each disbursement shall be reported, including the following information:

a. the payee;

b. check number or other identifying number on the instrument;

c. the amount disbursed; and,

d. the description of the reason for the disbursement sufficient to substantiate the reason for the disbursement as part of the administration of the Estate or Guardianship or the support of the incapacitated person or minor, if the reason for disbursement is not apparent from the description of the payee.

3. Schedule 3: Property at the End of the Period of Accounting.

a. The property held by the Personal Representative or Guardian at the end of the period of account shall be identified as follows:

1. an itemization of the property held by a description of property, asset or investment;

2. the value of the property, asset or investment as of the date of the end of the accounting period;

3. the basis for valuation of the property, asset, or investment, unless previously provided in the Inventory;

4. the market valuation at the end of the period of accounting if the intangible personal property is subject to market fluctuation.

b. The proposed distributions in Supervised Estates shall specifically set forth the payee and the property to be distributed.

c. In testate administration, the proposed distribution shall refer to the provision of the Will that authorizes the proposed distribution.

d. In intestate succession, the account shall include an heirship affidavit.

e. Administration Longer than One Year. Whenever a Supervised Estate cannot be closed within twelve (12) months, an intermediate report of account shall be filed with the Court within thirty (30) days after the expiration of the year and any succeeding year thereafter. Such report of accounting shall comply with the provisions of the Indiana Code and shall also include the following:

1. all facts showing why the Estate cannot be closed and an estimated date of closing.

2. a proposal for partial distribution of the Estate to the extent that partial distribution can be made without prejudice to distributees and claimants.

f. Tax Forms. The Federal Estate Tax Closing Letter and the Indiana Inheritance Tax Closing Letter (or the counter-signed receipt) or an electronic reproduction, showing payment of all Federal Estate and/or Indiana Inheritance Tax liability in the Estate, executed by the Internal Revenue Service or the Indiana Department of Revenue, shall be attached to the Final Report.

Adopted effective Nov. 2005.

LR41-PR00 Rule 109.   Adoption.

A.   Scheduling of Hearings. No hearing on a Petition for Adoption will be scheduled until all reports, affidavits, and consents required by the Indiana Code are on file with the Court.

B.   Scheduling of Final Hearing — Proof of Stability. No final hearings in Adoption proceedings shall be scheduled without a written offer of proof of stability in the adoptive placement. Indications of such stability may include, but are not limited to:

1. Placement of the child in the home of the adoptive parent(s) for at least three (3) months; or,

2. Length of marriage of the adoptive parents.

Adopted effective Nov. 2005.

LR41-PR00 Rule 110.   Appointment of a Fiduciary.

A.   Petition Contents. Request for appointment as Personal Representative or Guardian shall be made by verified application for appointment containing information as to the Petitioner's qualification to serve as Personal Representative or Guardian. The following information regarding the Petitioner is deemed relevant to the Petitioner's qualification to serve as Personal Representative or Guardian:

1. address;
2. educational background;
3. current employment;
4. any prior experience in financial management, including investments and checkbook management;
5. any prior felony convictions;.
6. a statement that the Petitioner has attained the age of majority and is not incapacitated for a reason other than physical illness, impairment, or infirmity; and,
7. a statement that

    a. the counsel for the Petitioner has been provided with the Petitioner's Social Security Number and Date of Birth; and,

    b. authorizes the release of the same to the Court in the event of breach of any legal or Fiduciary duty.

B. Petition Form. The Verified Application for Appointment of Personal Representative or Guardian shall be substantially in the form of Johnson County Probate Form 1. In lieu of Johnson County Probate Form 1, the information may be included in the Petition to Open Estate.

C. Appearance Not Required. A Petitioner need not appear before the Court to qualify as Personal Representative.

Adopted effective Nov. 2005.

LR41-PR00 Rule 111. Address Changes of Fiduciary

A Personal Representative or Guardian who changes address shall advise the Court in writing of the new address within thirty (30) days of the change.

Adopted effective Nov. 2005.

LR41-PR00 Rule 112. Bond and Alternatives Thereto

A. When Bond Not Required. Subject to the discretion of the Court and to the requirements of the Indiana Code, bond shall not be required if:

1. the Decedent's Will requests that a domiciliary Personal Representative be permitted to serve without bond;
2. all beneficiaries or heirs consent to a domiciliary Personal Representative serving without bond; or,
3. the Fiduciary serving in a Supervised Estate or Guardianship is a corporate banking Fiduciary which is legally qualified to so serve.

B. Alternative to Bond. In lieu of a bond otherwise required by law or by the Court, a Fiduciary may restrict transfer of all or part of the liquid assets of an Estate or Guardianship by placing those assets in a federally-insured financial institution with the follow-

ing restriction placed on the face of the account or document:

NO PRINCIPAL OR INTEREST SHALL BE WITHDRAWN WITHOUT WRITTEN ORDER OF THE JOHNSON CIRCUIT OR SUPERIOR COURT.

A certification, by an officer of the financial institution at which the account has been created, which states that the account is restricted as required by the Court and that the financial institution will honor the restriction, shall be filed with the Court within ten (10) days of the Order authorizing a restricted account. An acceptance of the terms of the restriction by the Fiduciary shall also be filed with the Court. The certification shall be substantially in accordance with the form of Johnson County Probate Form 2.

Adopted effective Nov. 2005.

LR41-PR00 Rule 113. Claims

Form. Claims shall be filed on forms substantially in accordance with Johnson County Probate Form 3.

Adopted effective Nov. 2005.

LR41-PR00 Rule 114. Effective Date

These rules shall become effective in all probate matters upon execution by the judge(s) exercising probate jurisdiction in Johnson County, Indiana.

Adopted effective Nov. 2005.

LR41-PR00 Rule 115. Fees

A. Fee schedules established. Fee schedules for attorneys and fiduciaries in probate matters shall be approved and implemented on an annual basis in compliance with the remaining provisions in this rule. *See* Appendix I.

B. Objectives for Fee Schedules. These Guidelines for Fees in Estates were developed by the Probate Committee of the Johnson County Bar Association, which are herein adopted by the Court. These Guidelines are intended to achieve the following objectives:

1. establish uniformity throughout the County in determining a fair and reasonable fee for Supervised Estates;
2. provide a guideline to assist the Court in determining fair and reasonable fees;
3. furnish guidelines to attorneys so they can discuss fees that may be reasonably incurred with their clients at the onset of administration; and,
4. assist the legal profession to arrive at a fair and reasonable fee for Estate work.

C. Use of Schedule. The schedule is NOT a minimum fee schedule, but a suggested maximum fee schedule. Every attorney and Personal Representative has an obligation to request a fee which is fair and reasonable for the work performed, taking into account Indiana Rules of Professional Conduct. In an uncomplicated Estate, fees should be less than the maximum fees listed in this schedule, and fees should always bear a reasonable relationship to the services rendered.

D. Guidelines for Fees in Estates.

1. While these Guidelines are recommended, they are neither mandatory nor binding on attorneys or the Court.

2. The guiding criteria to be considered when setting a fee include, but are not limited to, the following:

    a. the time and labor required, the novelty, complexity, or difficulty of the questions involved, the skill required to perform the services properly, and shall include a determination as to how much of the attorney's time was devoted to legal matters and how much of it was devoted to ministerial functions;

    b. the nature and extent of the responsibilities assumed by the attorney and the results obtained, and shall include the considerations of the identity of the Personal Representative and the character of the probate and non-probate transferred assets;

    c. the sufficiency of assets properly available to pay for legal services, and shall consider whether the attorney's duties are expanded by the existence of non-probate assets because of their inclusion for tax purposes, both federal and state; and,

    d. the timeliness with which the necessary services are performed consistent with statutory requirements, the Court's rules of procedure and the Rules of Professional Conduct applicable thereto.

3. In considering all of these criteria, all attorneys are expected to discuss with their client(s) their fee, and that of the Personal Representative, at the time they are retained in Probate matters.

4. In the event of a dispute of fees requested, the Court will consider records of time spent and / or work performed by the Attorney and Fiduciary.

E. Payment from Estate or Guardianship. No fees for Fiduciaries or attorneys, except corporate transactional fees, shall be paid out of any Supervised Estate or Guardianship without prior written order of the Court.

Adopted effective Nov. 2005.

LR41-PR00 Rule 116. Filing of Pleadings

A. Self-addressed Envelopes Required.

1. Subject to the subsection C below, all original pleadings filed with the Court shall be accompanied by self-addressed, stamped envelopes.

2. All proposed orders shall be accompanied with self-addressed, stamped envelopes for return, and, if necessary, for distribution to parties or beneficiaries.

3. Failure to provide self-addressed, stamped envelopes will result in the return of file-stamped copies via Courthouse Mail Box. If an attorney or Fiduciary does not have a Courthouse Mail Box, file stamped copies will be held at the Court until collected.

B. Preferred Filing Method. Pleadings, including Inventories, Inheritance Tax Schedules, Reports and Accountings, shall be filed in accordance with Trial Rule 5(F).

1. After a case is opened, filing directly with the Court under Trial Rule 5(F)(5) is preferred.

2. If the Court Office is closed, pleadings should be filed with the Clerk of the Court.

C. Proposed Orders Required.

1. A moving party shall provide proposed orders for rulings. Proposed Orders on contested hearings should be submitted in electronic format.

2. Proposed Letters Testamentary, Letters of Administration or Letters of Guardianship shall be filed with the Petition for Appointment.

3. Exceptions from this general rule shall be granted for Orders on Determination of Inheritance Tax or as expressly directed by the Court.

D. Attorney Contact Information. All pleadings filed shall contain the attorney's name, attorney number, office address and telephone number.

Adopted effective Nov. 2005.

LR41-PR00 Rule 117. Guardianships

A. Guardianship of an Incapacitated Adult. In all Guardianship matters seeking to declare an adult incapacitated, the Petitioner may submit with the petition any supporting documents.

1. Supporting documents may include physician reports, medical records, statements of qualified witnesses, photographs, police information, etc.

2. The admissibility of documents submitted with the Petition at hearing shall be subject to the Indiana Rules of Evidence.

3. If a Physician's Report is submitted, the Physician's Report shall substantially comply with Johnson County Probate Form No. 4.

B. Guardianship of a Minor. In every petition for the appointment of a Guardian of the person of a minor child, the following information shall be given:

1. the child's present address and the name(s) of the person(s) with whom the child resides;

2. the location(s) at which the child has lived within the past two years and the names and present addresses of the person(s) with whom the child has lived during that period, if different from the present information;

3. whether, to Petitioner's knowledge, any other litigation is pending concerning the custody of the child in this or any other state;

4. whether, to Petitioner's knowledge, any person not a party to the Guardianship proceeding has physical custody of the child or claims to have custody or visitation rights with respect to the child; and,

5. whether, to Petitioner's knowledge, any other Court has issued a custody order.

C. Veterans' Administration Rules and Regulations. Nothing herein shall be deemed as amending, superseding or altering the Probate Rules and Regulations promulgated by the United States Department of Veterans' Affairs, and every Fiduciary and attorney shall comply with same, where applicable.

Adopted effective Nov. 2005.

LR41-PR00 Rule 118. Inheritance Tax

All pleadings pertaining to the assessment or determination of the Indiana Inheritance Tax, including a Petition for Determination of No Tax Due, and any orders thereon shall be served upon the County Assessor.

Adopted effective Nov. 2005.

LR41-PR00 Rule 119. Instructions to Personal Representatives and Guardians

A. Instructions Required Prior to Appointment. The Instructions to the Personal Representative or Guardian, executed by the Fiduciary, must be filed with the Court prior to Court appointment and the issuance of letters.

B. Forms.

1. The preferred form for Instructions to the Personal Representative in Supervised Estates is set forth in Johnson County Probate Form 5.

2. The preferred form for Instructions to the Personal Representative in Unsupervised Estates is set forth in Johnson County Probate Form 6.

3. The preferred form for Instructions to the Guardian is set forth in Johnson County Probate Form 7.

Adopted effective Nov. 2005.

LR41-PR00 Rule 120. Inventory

A. Partial Inventories. Each partial inventory shall be denominated as a partial inventory.

B. Supervised Estates. In Supervised Estates, any written appraisals or evidence of value obtained to comply with the Indiana Code shall be attached as Exhibits to the Inventory or Inventories filed with the Court.

C. Unsupervised Estates. In Unsupervised Estates, the Personal Representative shall file a verified written certification with the Court within two (2) months of Court appointment that the Inventory required under the Indiana Code has been prepared and is available to a distributee who requests a copy.

Adopted effective Nov. 2005.

LR41-PR00 Rule 121. Interpretation

A. These rules are intended to supplement the provisions of the Indiana Probate Code.

B. Unless reference is made by Probate Rule to a specific form of probate proceeding, the Johnson County Probate Rules shall be generally applicable to all forms of probate proceedings.

C. Any provision of these rules which is not also required by law may be waived by the Court for good cause shown following a written request.

Adopted effective Nov. 2005.

LR41-PR00 Rule 122. Minors Settlements

A. Guardian ad Litem. In accordance with the Indiana Code, a Guardian *ad litem* may be appointed to protect the best interest of the minor and investigate the proposed settlement.

B. Evidentiary Hearing. At least one (1) evidentiary hearing shall be held in order to fully and independently satisfy the Court that the requested settlement fully protects the minor's rights and interests.

C. Minors Consent to Settlement. If the minor is at least fourteen (14) years of age, the proposed settlement shall be accompanied by a written consent to settlement by the minor.

D. Attendance at Hearings.

1. The custodial parent and / or the Guardian must be present at the evidentiary hearing.

2. A minor who is at least the age of fourteen (14) years shall attend the hearing.

3. Minors younger than fourteen (14) years of age may be required to appear at hearing.

4. Unless written consent is provided to the Court, notice of hearing shall be provided to a non-custodial parent.

E. Limited Settlements or Administration.

1. If the funds originating from a minor's settlement are less than the amount requiring establishment of Guardianship under the Indiana Code or if a Guardian of a minor's Estate is appointed for the limited purpose of administration of the minor's settlement, the Court will accept deposit of the minor's settlement in a restricted account at a federally insured financial institution or in a Court approved investment in lieu of any other requirement for inventory and accounting subject to affirmation on biennial account that the funds remain on deposit.

2. Any such restricted account must provide that no principal or interest may be withdrawn from the account without a written order of the Court, and with the following restriction placed on the face of the account or in the investment document:

NO PRINCIPAL OR INTEREST SHALL BE WITHDRAWN WITHOUT WRITTEN ORDER OF THE JOHNSON CIRCUIT OR SUPERIOR COURT

F. Certification. Within ten (10) days of an Order authorizing the creation of the account or investment, a certificate by an officer of the institution at which the account or investment is restricted as required by Court order and is in compliance with this rule. The Guardian and the financial institution shall both promptly notify the Court in the event that any principal or interest is withdrawn from the account without Court authorization.

G. Application of Guardianship Law. Minors Settlements shall otherwise be subject to the requirements for Guardianship, including the filing of inventory and accounting in Guardianships.

H. Attorney Fees. Attorney fees for representing a minor in settlement of a claim for personal injuries are subject to Court approval. If the entire attorney fee is to be paid at the same time a structured settlement is approved, the amount of the fee must be based on the present value of the settlement.

Adopted effective Nov. 2005.

LR41-PR00 Rule 123.   Notices

A. List of Notice Recipients. In each Estate, the Personal Representative shall prepare a List of Notice Recipients (Clerk's Certificate of Mailing).

1. The List of Notice Recipients shall include the names and addresses of all heirs, devisees, legatees, creditors, and organizations entitled to Notice of Administration.

2. The List of Notice Recipients of Notice of Administration shall be provided to the Clerk.

B. Notices of Administration.

1. The Personal Representative shall provide to the Clerk;

    A. a copy of the Notice of Administration for each person included in the List of Notice Recipients; and,

    B. a Clerk's Certificate of Mailing.

2. Following the issuance of the Notice of Administration, the Clerk of the Court shall execute and file the Certificate of Mailing Notice.

C.[1] Forms and Copies of Notice. Whenever notice by publication and / or written notice by U.S. Mail is required to be given, the party responsible for providing notice shall prepare such notice and submit it to the Clerk for service.

1. The notifying party shall provide the number of copies of the notice to be served sufficient to serve all persons to be so notified.

2. The notifying party shall provide a Clerk's Certificate of Mailing, to be executed by the Clerk, with all notices issued by United States Mail.

3. Notice shall issue by the Clerk as provided by Indiana Code or Indiana Trial Rules.

4. The form of the notice provided shall comply with all statutory requirements. It is the notifying party's responsibility to adequately document perfection of notice prior to seeking Court action on any matter.

C.[1] Notice of Hearings. If a hearing is scheduled on a particular matter, for which notice is statutorily required, a copy of the relevant petition or motion shall be served with the notice of hearing. In a hearing on an account in an Estate or Guardianship, a copy of the account must be served with the notice of hearing.

Adopted effective Nov. 2005.

1 There are two Subds. C. in this rule.

LR41-PR00 Rule 124.   Sale or Transfer of Real Property

A. Documentation of Value. In all Supervised Estates and Guardianships in which real property is to be sold, a written appraisal or market analysis by a qualified real estate professional shall be filed with the Petition for Sale, unless such document was previously filed with the Inventory. Such written appraisal or market analysis shall include, at a minimum, the following information:

1. a brief description of the property interest being appraised or valued, including the full legal description thereof;

2. purpose or objective of the appraisal or valuation;

3. date for which Fair Market Value is determined;

4. if valuation is established through the comparable method of valuation, identification of the comparable sales used to value the subject property as well as identification of all adjustments made to the comparable sale to determine the fair market value of the subject property;

5. if valuation is established through another method of valuation, all data and reasoning that supports the Fair Market Value;

6. the Fair Market Value determined;

7. a statement of assumption and special or limiting conditions;

8. the qualification and background of the real estate professional;

9. certification of disinterest in the real property;

10. signature of appraiser / analyst.

B. Limitations Period for Valuation. The appraisal or market analysis shall be made within one (1) year of the date of the Petition for Sale.

C. Deeds. All deeds submitted to the Court for approval, shall be signed by the Fiduciary and the signature notarized prior to its submission.

1. All such deeds shall be submitted with either the Petition to Sell Real Estate or the Report of Sale of Real Estate or at the time of the hearing on the Final Account.

2. Whenever a Final Decree reflects that real estate is vesting in the heirs or beneficiaries of the Estate, the Decree shall be recorded with the County Recorder of the County where any such real Estate is located, and evidence of said recording shall be provided to the Court with the Supplemental Report.

Adopted effective Nov. 2005.

LR41-PR00 Rule 125.   Sale of Personal Property.

A. Documentation of Value. In all Supervised Estates and Guardianships in which personal property is to be sold, a written basis for valuation shall be filed with the Court with the Petition for Sale, unless such document was previously filed with the Inventory. The written basis for valuation shall include the following information:

1. brief description of the property to be sold;

2. the date and basis of valuation;

3. the qualifications of the person providing the valuation or the authoritative nature of the source from which the valuation was obtained, including authoritative sources accessed by electronic media;

4. factors which would affect the value of the subject property.

B. Limitations Period for Valuation. Written basis for valuation shall be made within one (1) year of the date of the Petition for Sale.

C. Written Valuation Not Required. No written valuation shall be required for the sale of assets which are publicly traded or sold at public auction.

Adopted effective Nov. 2005.

LR41-PR00 Rule 126.   Supplemental Report

A supplemental report filed pursuant to the Indiana Code, the Indiana Trial Rules, or Court Order shall be filed within ninety (90) days after entry of the Order Approving Account. If any supplemental report cannot be filed in a timely manner, the Fiduciary shall file a written explanation.

Adopted effective Nov. 2005.

LR41-PR00 Rule 127.   Trusts

A. Any Petition to Docket Trust shall be served upon the Trustee.

B. The Trustee shall promptly file with the Court written notice of the name and address of each beneficiary known to the Trustee.

C. All additional pleadings and any notice of hearing shall be served upon all beneficiaries of the trust, whether the nature of the interest is present, future, vested, or contingent.

Adopted effective Nov. 2005.

LR41-PR00 Rule 128.   Title And Citation

These Rules shall be known as the Johnson County Probate Rules and shall be cited as Johnson County Probate Rules, LR41-PO00-107 *through* LR41-PO00-129 [1].

Adopted effective Nov. 2005.

[1] So in original. Should probably read: "LR41-PR00-107 through LR41-PR00-130".

LR41-PR00 Rule 129.   Unsupervised Administration

A. Tax Documentation. Proof of payment of all required federal and state taxes shall be attached to the Closing Statement. Such proof shall be documented by either the Federal Estate Tax Closing Letter and the Indiana Inheritance Tax Closing Letter (or the counter-signed receipt) or photocopies thereof.

B. Conversion to Supervised Administration. In an Unsupervised Estate, if the jurisdiction of the Court is invoked for any matter other than the judicial functions which are standard for unsupervised administration (i.e., opening the Estate, determining any inheritance tax due, and accepting the Closing Statement), the administration shall become a Supervised administration for all purposes. In that event, the Fiduciary and attorney shall give notice of such administration to all heirs, legatees, devisees, and other interested persons.

Adopted effective Nov. 2005.

LR41-PR00 Rule 130.   Wrongful Death Estates

A. Court Approval of Settlements Required. All proposed wrongful death settlements must be approved by the Court, regardless of the type of estate administration.

B. Administration Longer than One Year. If an Estate remains open in excess of one (1) year, the Personal Representative shall file a status report as to any wrongful death claims.

1. If an action to prosecute a civil wrongful death action is pending, the report shall show the case number, the Court in which the action is pending and the date of any current settings of the case.

2. A report shall be filed annually thereafter, on the anniversary date of the Personal Representative's appointment, until the Estate is closed.

C. Petition Approving Distribution. When a judgment has been paid or a petition for approval of settlement is filed in any Estate, a petition for approval of distribution shall be filed indicating the proposed distribution in accordance with the Indiana Code.

1. Such petition must set out the proposed distribution to the appropriate statutory damage distributees, such as:

    a. expenses of administration;

    b. providers of funeral and burial expenses;

    c. providers of medical expenses in connection with last illness of Decedent;

    d. surviving spouse;

    e. dependent children;

    f. dependent next of kin (if there is no surviving spouse or dependent children).

2. A proposed order shall be presented to the Court, ordering distribution in accordance with the Indiana Code and requiring the filing of a supplemental report of distribution of the wrongful death proceeds.

Adopted effective Nov. 2005.

APPENDICES

Appendix I. Fee Schedule (2005)

I. Attorney's Fees

A. Administration. Gross Estate services are considered to normally include: Opening of the Estate, qualifying the Personal Representative, preparing and filing the Inventory, paying claims, collecting assets, preparing and filing non-extraordinary petitions, preparing and filing the Inheritance Tax Schedule, obtaining the Court Order thereon and paying the taxes, preparing and filing the Final Report and schedules, obtaining Order approving same, distributing assets, obtaining discharge of the Personal Representative, and preparing and serving all notices on interested parties and readily ascertainable creditors throughout the proceedings.

This list shall not be considered to be exclusive:

Gross Estate Value:	Maximum Fee %:
Up to $100,000.00	6%
Next $200,000.00	4%
Next $700,000.00	3%
Excess over $1,000,000.00	1%

B. Miscellaneous. Other non Probate: Probate Will only: Small Estate settlement procedure: Inheritance Tax Schedule: Federal Estate Tax Return: etc. may be addressed on an hourly basis if not included in I above by considering the time involved, service rendered, attorney's expertise and other considerations as set forth by the Code of Professional Conduct.

C. Wrongful Death Administration.

Work Performed:	Maximum Fee %:
Settlement prior to filing.	25%
Settlement after filing but before trial.	33 1/3%
Trial.	40%
Appeal, or extra work.	50%

D. General. Unless the entire Estate is handled on an hourly basis, fees will be paid for hourly services only as set forth above or approved by the Court.

E. Unsupervised Estates. Due to the general lack of judicial involvement therein, the Court will not rule on fee requests or order fee awards in Unsupervised Estates.

II. Personal Representative's Fees

A. Professional Personal Representatives.

1. A professional Personal Representative is hereby defined as a person or corporation which regularly acts as a Personal Representative and has expertise in such matters.

2. A professional Personal Representative's applicable reasonable rate will be reviewed in light of <u>all</u> prevailing circumstances.

B. Non-Professional Personal Representatives. Fees for non-professional Personal Representatives shall normally be within the range from one-half (2) of attorney fees not to exceed the maximum attorney's fees allowed under this schedule.

C. Attorneys as Personal Representatives. When the attorney also serves as the Personal Representative, an additional amount not in excess of one-third (1/3) of the attorney may be allowed, provided:

a. additional services have been performed which are normally done by the Personal Representative; and

b. the assets of the Estate warrant the allowance of additional fees.

III. Limitation on Fees

In all instances, the combined total of the fees allowed to the Personal Representative and attorney for the administration of an Estate should not exceed twelve percent (12%) of the Decedent's gross Estate.

NOTE: THIS FEE SCHEDULE IS ONLY A GUIDELINE AND WILL BE CONSIDERED UNLESS THERE IS EVIDENCE PRESENTED TO CONVINCE THE COURT TO DEVIATE FROM THE FEE SCHEDULE.

Adopted effective Nov. 2005.

Appendix II.   2005 Table of Statutes
APPENDIX II

2005 Table of Statutes

Rule	Statutory Citation
LR41 - PR00 - 108	I.C. 29-1-16-4, I.C. 29-1-16-6
LR41 - PR00 - 109	I.C. 31-19-11-1
LR41 - PR00 - 110	I.C. 29-1-10-1
LR41 - PR00 - 112	I.C. 29-1-10-1, I.C. 29-1-11-1
LR41 - PR00 - 113	I.C. 34-9-1-1
LR41 - PR00 - 115	I.C. 29-1-1-9, I.C. 29-1-1-20
LR41 - PR00 - 120	I.C. 29-1-12-1, I.C. 29-1-7.5-3.2
LR41 - PR00 - 121	I.C. 29-3-3-2
LR41 - PR00 - 122	I.C. 29-1-7-7, I.C. 29-1-7.5-1.5
LR41 - PR00 - 126	I.C. 29-1-17-13
LR41 - PR00 - 130	I.C. 29-1-10-17, 34-23-11-1, *et.seq.*

Adopted effective Nov. 2005.

FORMS

Form 1. Johnson County General Pleading Form

Johnson County General Pleading Form 1

STATE OF INDIANA	)	IN THE JOHNSON _____ COURT
	) SS:	
COUNTY OF JOHNSON	)	41 ____—____—CC—____
	)	
PLAINTIFF NAME,	)	
v.	)	
DEFENDANT NAME.	)	

NOTICE REGARDING SUMMARY JUDGMENT MOTION

READ THIS NOTICE AND THE ENCLOSED PAPERS—
A MOTION FOR SUMMARY JUDGMENT HAS BEEN FILED AND,
IF UNOPPOSED, THIS MOTION MAY RESULT IN JUDGMENT BEING ENTERED AGAINST YOU WITHOUT
A HEARING OR TRIAL.

The Courts of Johnson County, Indiana require that this notice be sent to you about the motion for summary judgment that was filed by the opposing party. This notice does not contain legal advice, but does provide important information about your legal options. Please read it carefully.

The opposing party has filed a motion for summary judgment pursuant to Indiana Trial Rule 56(C). The motion alleges that the facts are not in dispute and the Court can rule as a matter of law. The motion asks the Court to enter judgment in favor of the opposing party without a trial.

As you are not represented by counsel, you are hereby advised of your obligation to respond to the summary judgment motion. Your previous answer, denial or even counterclaim in response to the original complaint is not sufficient to defend a motion for summary judgment. Unless you submit your own affidavits (or other documentary evidence) or a response that specifically identifies information within the existing court records that contradict the factual assertions of the evidence designated in the motion for summary judgment and supporting materials, any factual assertions in our motion and supporting documentation will be accepted by the Court as true. In essence, your failure to respond to the pending motion for summary judgment would be equivalent to failing to present any evidence in your favor at a trial.

If you wish to file a response to the motion, the Court must receive your response within thirty-three (33) days after your opponent's motion was mailed to you. Failure to meet this time frame will result in the Court being unable to consider your response or any attachments thereto.

Either party may request a court hearing on the summary judgment motion. A written request for a hearing must be received by the Court no later than ten (10) days after the response was filed or is due. The hearing will not be a trial, and neither party will be able to present evidence at the hearing. However, either party may make legal argument and refer to the evidence designated with the summary judgment motion or with any response. If no request for a hearing is filed with the Court, the Court may decide the motion without a hearing based on the affidavits and documents filed by the parties.

Any response or request for hearing must be served (or mailed) on the attorney for the opposing party. A response (or other pleading) filed with the Court must include a statement that you have complied with this requirement. Your statement may be in the following form: "I delivered a copy of this response to (Attorney Name) by United States Mail on this __ day of _____, 20 _____."

As with any legal matter, you may wish to consult with and/or retain an attorney to represent you in this lawsuit and to assist you in responding to our motion for summary judgment.

[If appropriate under the Federal Fair Debt Collection Act, the following identifying information should be included:

Notice:

Notice Provided by:

Attorney Name, Law Firm (if any), Address, Telephone Number

Our Law Firm is a debt collector. This Notice is provided as part of an attempt to collect a debt, and any information obtained by us will be used for that purpose. As we represent an opposing party, we cannot provide you with legal advice.]

Adopted effective Nov. 2005. Amended effective May 1, 2013.

Form 2.   Certification of Restriction on Account of Financial Institution

JOHNSON COUNTY PROBATE FORM 2

IN THE JOHNSON _____ COURT _____

CASE NO. 41 ___–___–___–___

CERTIFICATION OF RESTRICTION ON ACCOUNT BY FINANCIAL INSTITUTION

The undersigned hereby certifies that he or she is an officer or employee of the financial institution hereinafter designated and further certifies that the following account has been opened:

Type of Account: _____

Account Number: _____

Amount Deposited: _____

Owner per signature card or document of title: _____

The undersigned further certifies that the terms of such account include a restriction that withdrawal of principal or interest may be made only on written order of the Johnson Superior Court.

I affirm under the penalties of perjury that the foregoing declaration is true.

Dated: ___/___/_____   _____
                                                    Financial Institution

_____   _____
            Signature   Printed Name and Title

Adopted effective Nov. 2005.

Form 3.   Claim Against Estate

JOHNSON COUNTY PROBATE FORM 3

STATE OF INDIANA	)	IN THE JOHNSON _____ COURT
	) SS:	
COUNTY OF JOHNSON	)	CASE NO. 41 ___–___–___–___

IN RE: THE ESTATE OF:

_____, DECEASED.

Claim Against Estate, Number: __

To the Personal Representative of the above listed Estate:

The Claimant, _____ *(name of person making claim)* personally appeared before the verifying witness identified below, and was duly sworn, hereby files this claim against the above-captioned estate. This claim is for a total of *(amount)*: $_____ and is owed for the following reasons:

_____

_____.

In addition to this claim, there ☐ are ☐ are not other cases involving the claimant and the Decedent. Case Numbers for related cases: _____.

I HEREBY AFFIRM THAT the claimed amount was calculated after the application of all credits, set-off, and deductions to which the Estate of the Decedent is entitled and that claim is justly due and wholly unpaid, to the best of my knowledge and belief.

_____　　　_____
　　　　　Signature　　　　　　　　　　Printed Name

Address:　　_____

　　　　　　_____

Subscribed and sworn to before me, this ___ day of _____, 20___.

_____　　　_____
Signature　　　　　　　　　　　　**Printed Name**

Adopted effective Nov. 2005.

Form 4.　Physician's Report

JOHNSON COUNTY PROBATE FORM 4

STATE OF INDIANA　　　　　)　　　IN　THE　JOHNSON　_____　COURT

　　　　　　　　　　　　　　　) SS:

COUNTY OF JOHNSON　　　)　　　CASE NO. 41 ___–__–__–__

IN THE MATTER OF THE GUARDIANSHIP　　　)
　　　OF: _____　　)

PHYSICIAN'S REPORT

Dr. _____, a physician licensed to practice medicine in all its branches in the State of Indiana, submits the following Report on _____, the alleged incapacitated person, based on an examination of said person conducted within the last three (3) months, on the ___ day of _____, 20___.

1.　The nature and type of the incapacitated person's disability is: _____

_____

_____

2.　The incapacitated person's mental and physical condition, and, when appropriate, their educational condition, adaptive behavior and social skills are: _____

_____

_____

3.　In my opinion, the incapacitated person is ☐ totally or ☐ only partially incapable of making personal and financial decisions.

A.　　The kinds of decisions which the incapacitated person can and cannot make are:

_____

_____

_____

B.   The facts and/or reasons supporting this opinion are: _____

_____

_____

_____

4. In my opinion, the most appropriate living arrangement for the incapacitated person, is:

_____

_____

A.   The most appropriate treatment or rehabilitation plan for the incapacitated person is: _____

_____

_____

B.   The facts and / or reasons supporting this opinion are: _____

_____

_____

5. The incapacitated person ☐ can ☐ cannot appear in Court without injury to his/her health.

Where applicable: the medical reasons the incapacitated person cannot appear in Court are: _____

_____

_____

        I/We affirm under the penalties of perjury that the foregoing representations are true.

Physician:
Name: _____   Signature: _____
Address: _____
City/State/Zip _____   _____   _____
Telephone: (___) ___–_____
Other Evaluation Professionals:
Name: _____   Signature: _____
Profession: _____   Telephone: (___) ___–_____
Address: _____
City/State/Zip _____   _____   _____
Name: _____   Signature: _____
Profession: _____   Telephone: (___) ___–_____
Address: _____
City/State/Zip _____   _____   _____

Adopted effective Nov. 2005.

Form 5. Instructions to the Personal Representative of a Supervised Estate
JOHNSON COUNTY PROBATE FORM 5

STATE OF INDIANA   )   IN THE JOHNSON _____ COURT
) SS:
COUNTY OF JOHNSON   )   CASE NO. 41 ___–___–___–___

IN RE:
THE ESTATE OF:
_____, DECEASED.

**INSTRUCTIONS TO THE PERSONAL REPRESENTATIVE
OF A SUPERVISED ESTATE**

You have been appointed by this Court as Personal Representative of this estate. It is important that you fully realize your duties and responsibilities. <u>Please read</u>

carefully, date and sign one copy of this form and submit it to the Court. Keep one copy for your records. Listed below are some of these duties but not all of them.

As Personal Representative, you are required by Indiana law to:

1. Locate, collect, and maintain all property owned by the Decedent. Keep motor vehicles and real estate insured and protected.

2. Have your attorney file in this Court an inventory describing all property belonging to the estate, with date of death values, not later than two (2) months after your appointment.

3. Open a separate checking account in your name as Personal Representative for the estate of (the Decedent): and NEVER CO-MINGLE your funds or anyone else's funds with this account. Always make estate expenditures by check and retain the canceled checks. Make sure that the bank is willing to return canceled checks to you. Obtain a federal I.D. number for the checking account. Do not use your Social Security number or the Decedent's Social Security number.

4. Ascertain all debts that the Decedent owed. Look through Decedent's tax returns and other papers. Talk to anyone who knew Decedent's business. Consult your attorney as to payment of debts, costs of administration, bond premiums, and funeral bills. Some debts may be unenforceable. Some may have priority over others. DO NOT MAKE any distribution to an heir or devisee without prior consent from your attorney. Always obtain receipts for all distributions made. NEVER borrow estate property or put it to your own personal use.

5. Immediately fill out a change of address at the post office to have the Decedent's mail forwarded to you.

6. Prepare and file income tax returns for the tax year in which the Decedent died and any returns for prior years if needed. Timely prepare and file any estate, inheritance, or fiduciary tax returns and pay taxes as they come due.

7. Have your attorney file your final accounting, consisting of three (3) schedules, after the administration of the estate has been completed. The first schedule must include all assets listed on the inventory and any income and additional assets obtained during administration. The second schedule must be an itemized list of expenditures, supported by attached canceled checks. The third schedule must be a recapitulation, indicating the remaining estate property after subtracting expenditures. A proposed distribution of this remaining estate property to the heirs or devisees must be included. This accounting must be furnished to all interested parties, including heirs.

8. After the court approves your final account, make distribution to the proper people and file a supplemental report with the court, attaching receipts.

9. Notify the Court and your attorney of any change in your address or telephone number.

10. Never pay yourself or your attorney any fees without a prior Court Order. Keep a record of the time you spend working on the estate. You are entitled to a reasonable fee, unless you waive a fee. Time records will help the Court determine your fee.

11. Always contact your attorney for advice if you are unsure as to any act as Personal Representative. Have your attorney counsel you in relation to the estate and explain anything that you do not fully understand.

12. Do not sell an estate asset without prior court order unless the will, in very specific terms authorizes sale without court order. Consult your attorney about this.

You, as Personal Representative, are ultimately responsible to see that the estate is properly and promptly administered, and you are personally liable for incorrect distribution, payments, or acts, as well as any unpaid taxes or costs of administration.

I authorize my attorney to disclose to the Court any information relating to his or her representation of me as Personal Representative even if such information would be otherwise confidential.

I acknowledge that I have carefully and completely read the above instructions and received a copy for my records. I agree to properly carry out my duties.

Dated this ___ day of _____, 20___.

_____   _____
Signature, Personal Representative   Signature, Personal Representative

_____   _____
Printed Name, Personal Representative   Printed Name, Personal Representative

Adopted effective Nov. 2005.

Form 6. Instructions to the Personal Representative of a Unsupervised Estate

JOHNSON COUNTY PROBATE FORM 6

STATE OF INDIANA   )   IN THE JOHNSON _____ COURT
) SS:
COUNTY OF JOHNSON   )   CASE NO. 41 ___–___–___–___

IN RE:

THE ESTATE OF:

_____, DECEASED.

INSTRUCTIONS TO THE PERSONAL REPRESENTATIVE
OF AN UNSUPERVISED ESTATE

You have been appointed by this Court as Personal Representative of this estate. It is important that you fully realize your duties and responsibilities. *Please read carefully, date and sign one copy of this form and submit it to the Court. Keep one copy for your records.* Listed below are some of these duties but not all of them.

As Personal Representative, you are required by Indiana law to:

1. Locate, collect, and maintain all property owned by the Decedent. Keep motor vehicles and real estate insured and protected.

2. Prepare an inventory describing all property belonging to the estate, with date of death values, not later than two (2) months after your appointment, and file a certification with the Court that is prepared and available to heirs and distributees.

3. Open a separate checking account in your name as Personal Representative for the Estate of (name of the Decedent): and NEVER CO-MINGLE your funds or anyone else's funds with this account. Always make estate expenditures by check and retain the canceled checks. Make sure that the bank is willing to return canceled checks to you. Obtain a federal I.D. number for the checking account. Do not use your Social Security number or the Decedent's Social Security number.

4. Ascertain all debts that the Decedent owed. Look through Decedent's tax returns and other papers. Talk to anyone who knew Decedent's business. Consult your attorney as to payment of debts, costs of administration, bond premiums, and funeral bills. Some debts may be unenforceable. Some may have priority over others. DO NOT MAKE any distribution to an heir or devisee without prior consent from your attorney. Always obtain receipts for all distributions made. NEVER borrow estate property or put it to your own personal use.

5. Immediately fill out a change of address at the post office to have the Decedent's mail forwarded to you.

6. Prepare and file income tax returns for the tax year in which the Decedent died and any returns for prior years if needed. Timely prepare and file any estate, inheritance, or fiduciary tax returns and pay taxes as they come due.

7. After you fully complete the estate administration, you must file a closing statement with the Court verifying that all proper claims, expenses & taxes have been paid, all assets have been properly distributed, and a copy of the closing statement has been sent to all distributees. In addition, you must furnish a written

statement to all distributees fully accounting for all assets, expenses and distributions made to the heirs.

8. Notify the Court and your attorney of any change in your address or telephone number.

9. Keep a record of the time you spend working on the estate. You are entitled to a reasonable fee, unless you waive a fee.

10. Always contact your attorney for advice if you are unsure as to any act as Personal Representative. Have your attorney counsel you in relation to the estate and explain anything that you do not fully understand.

You, as Personal Representative, are ultimately responsible to see that the estate is properly and promptly administered, and you are personally liable for incorrect distribution, payments, or acts, as well as any unpaid taxes or costs of administration.

I acknowledge that I have carefully and completely read the above instructions and received a copy for my records. I agree to properly carry out my duties.

Dated this ___ day of _____, 20___.

_____   _____
Signature, Personal Representative   Signature, Personal Representative

_____   _____
Print, Personal Representative   Print, Personal Representative

Adopted effective Nov. 2005.

Form 7. Instructions to Guardian of Estate

JOHNSON COUNTY PROBATE FORM 7

STATE OF INDIANA   )   IN THE JOHNSON _____ COURT ___
) SS:
COUNTY OF JOHNSON   )   CASE NO. 41 ___–___–___–___

IN THE MATTER OF THE GUARDIANSHIP   )
OF: _____   )

INSTRUCTIONS TO GUARDIAN OF ESTATE

You have been appointed the Guardian of an individual, who is unable to care for his or her own affairs. Listed below are some of your duties, but not all of them. Please read carefully, date and sign one copy of this form and submit it to the Court. Keep one copy for your records. Though your attorney will file all papers with the Court, the ultimate responsibility to see that all accounts and other documents are accurately prepared and filed, rests with you.

As Guardian you are required to:

1. Locate, collect, and maintain all property owned by the protected person. Keep motor vehicles and real estate insured and protected.

2. Have your attorney file with the Court, within ninety (90) days after your appointment, a verified inventory and appraisal of all of the property belonging to the protected person, with values as of the date you were appointed. You must provide a copy of the inventory to the protected person (if over fourteen (14) years of age) and to certain other persons as set out in Indiana Code 29–3–9–5.

3. Have your attorney file with the court a verified current account of all the income and expenditures of the Guardianship every two (2) years after your appointment, consisting of three schedules. The first schedule must include all assets listed on the inventory or on the last current account. The second schedule must be an itemized list of expenditures, supported by attached canceled checks. The third schedule must be a recapitulation indicating the remaining property after subtracting expenditures.

4. Pay bond premiums as they become due.

5. File and pay taxes on the protected person's income and assets.

6. Have your attorney file a final accounting with the Court upon the termination of the Guardianship, whether due to the death of the protected person, or for any other reason.

7. Keep all of the assets for the protected person separate from your own. Guardianship funds should never be co-mingled with personal funds. Unauthorized use of Guardianship funds will result in personal liability.

8. Open a Guardianship checking account in your name as Guardian of (the protected person). This account shall be used for all payments or disbursements on behalf of the protected person. The account should be in the protected person's Social Security number, not yours. It should not be a joint account. Make sure that the bank is willing to return canceled checks to you.

9. Real estate, automobiles and other accounts and investments should be held in the name of the protected person.

10. Obtain approval from the court to use Guardianship assets, other than for normal bills.

11. Do not self deal. Do not buy anything from or sell anything to the protected person. Do not borrow anything from the protected person.

12. If applicable, timely qualify the protected person for Medicaid or other public assistance.

13. It is the duty of the Guardian to protect and preserve the protected person's property, to account for the use of the property faithfully, and to perform all the duties required by law of a Guardian.

14. The Guardian has the same duties and responsibilities concerning the protected person whether or not the protected person is a relative of the Guardian.

15. If any questions arise during the Guardianship, immediately consult with your attorney.

I authorize my attorney to disclose to the court any information relating to his or her representation of me as Guardian even if such information would be otherwise confidential.

I acknowledge that I have carefully and completely read the above instructions and received a copy for my records. I agree to properly carry out my duties.

Dated this ___ day of _____, 20___.

_____   _____
Signature, Guardian   Signature, Guardian

_____   _____
Print, Guardian   Print, Guardian

Adopted effective Nov. 2005.

RULES FOR FILING OF PLEADINGS

LR41-TR5 Rule 131. Courthouse Mail

A. Courthouse Mail Established. There is established a Courthouse Mail System for the Johnson County Circuit and Superior Courts, which is maintained by the Clerk of Courts.

B. Box Assignment. Subject to availability, attorneys having their principle place of business in Johnson County may have assigned to them a specific mail box in the Clerk's Office.

C. Service by Delivery. Delivery of a pleading or notice to an attorney's Courthouse mailbox constitutes service pursuant to the provisions of Indiana Trial Rule 5(B)(1)(d).

Adopted effective Jan. 1, 2005. Renumbered as Rule 131, and amended effective Nov. 2005.

LR41-TR5 Rule 132.　Certification of Compliance with Indiana Trial Rule 5(G) and Administrative Rule 9(G)

A.　Certification of Compliance Required.　All pleadings filed by a party shall contain a verification certifying that the pleading complies with the filing requirements of Indiana Trial Rule 5(G) applicable to information excluded from public access under Indiana Administrative Rule 9(G).

B.　Content of Certification.　A certification in substantially the following language shall be sufficient:

I / we hereby certify that the foregoing document complies with the requirements of Trial Rule 5(G) with regard to information excluded form the public record by Administrative Rule 9(G).

Adopted effective Jan. 1, 2005. Renumbered as Rule 132, and amended effective Nov. 2005.

LR41-TR5 Rule 133.　Nonconforming Pleadings

A.　Nonconforming Pleadings Impounded.　Any pleading filed by a party which does not comply with Trial Rule 5(G) and Administrative Rule 9(G) will be deemed filed with the Court but is subject to being impounded by the Court.

B.　Time for Amendment.　If a pleading is impounded, the Court will order the filing party to amend the pleading to conform with Trial Rule 5(G) by a date certain.

C.　Time for Responsive Pleadings Extended.　Subject to the filing of an amendment of the impounded pleading, the time of filing for any pleading responsive to the nonconforming pleading shall be extended for an equal period.

D.　Striking of Nonconforming Pleading.　Failure of a party to amend any impounded pleading may result in the pleading being stricken.

Adopted effective Jan. 1, 2005. Renumbered as Rule 133, and amended effective Nov. 2005.

LR41-TR81 Rule 134.　Effective Date

These rules become effective January 1, 2005.

Adopted effective Jan. 1, 2005. Renumbered as Rule 134, and amended effective Nov. 2005.

COURTHOUSE SECURITY RULES

LR41-AD00 Rule 135.　Weapons

A.　In coordination with relevant local ordinance, weapons, including, but not limited to guns and knives, may not be brought into any building in which proceedings of the Johnson Circuit and Superior Courts are regularly held.

B.　Law enforcement officers, including authorized agents of the Prosecuting Attorney, which are so identified, are exempted from this rule; providing that in the Juvenile Detention Center, law enforcement officers may be requested to store their weapons in the secure storage area provided for the same.

Adopted effective Jan. 30, 2008.

LR41-AD00 Rule 136.　Security Cameras

A.　Installation.　Each Judge may, in keeping with professional judicial standards, individually authorize the placement of surveillance cameras, by such vendor as may be selected by the Johnson County Sheriff, within the buildings in which proceedings of the Johnson Circuit and Superior Courts are regularly held.

B.　Recordings.　No audio recordings shall be made from the security cameras installed pursuant to the authority granted above. Only public areas, within which there is no expectation of privacy, shall be visible from such cameras.

C.　Ownership.　Such cameras, recordings made therefrom, and all accessories thereto shall remain the property of the Johnson Circuit and Superior Courts.

D.　Monitoring.　Monitoring of the broadcast from the surveillance cameras shall be conducted by the Courts' designated agents.

E.　Retention.　Recordings made from the surveillance cameras shall be retained for such period as designated within the discretion of the Courts.

F.　Use of Recordings.　No recordings made from these surveillance cameras shall be used for any purpose without notice to and advance written permission from a judicial officer.

Adopted effective Jan. 30, 2008.

LR41-AD00 Rule 137.　Non–judicial Use of Courtrooms

Use of any courtroom or hearing room for ceremonial, meeting, or other non-judicial purpose shall be permitted only with the advance permission of the presiding Judicial Officer.

Adopted effective Jan. 30, 2008.

LR41-AD00 Rule 138.　Effective Date

A.　Good cause has been found for deviation from the schedule for publishing local rules established by the Division of State Court Administration.

B.　These rules shall take effect thirty (30) days from the entry of this Order [December 21, 2006], following the notice procedure required by T.R. 81(D).

Adopted effective Jan. 30, 2008.

ALCOHOL AND DRUG SERVICES
PROGRAM RULES

LR41-AD00 Rule 139.   Program Implementation

Pursuant to Ind. Code 12–7–2–12, Johnson County has established a program entitled the Johnson County Alcohol and Drug Services Program, and the same has been approved to continue operating pursuant to Johnson County Ordinance No. 2001–6 as recorded in the Ordinances of Johnson County.

Adopted effective Jan. 30, 2008.

LR41-AD00 Rule 140.   Payment of Fee Required

For the continued operation of said program, and pursuant to Title 12 of the Indiana Code, it is mandatory that each person referred to the program from the courts of Johnson County and any other county pay a fee for said services.

Adopted effective Jan. 30, 2008.

LR41-AD00 Rule 141.   Fee Schedule

The following fee assessments are now ordered to be paid by all participants:

a.   Prior to July 1, 2001, said fee is $75.00.

b.   Effective July 1, 2001, said fee is $150.00.

c.   Effective January 1, 2002, said fee is $200.00.

d.   Effective January 1, 2003, said fee is $300.00.

Adopted effective Jan. 30, 2008.

LR41-AD00 Rule 142.   Periodic Review

It is necessary for the fee for the program to be evaluated on a regular basis and these rules may be amended as necessary.

Adopted effective Jan. 30, 2008.

LR41-AD00 Rule 143.   Effective Date

These rules became effective on January 4, 2002.

Adopted effective Jan. 30, 2008.

CIVIL MOTIONS PRACTICE RULES

LR41-AR00 Rule 144.   APPLICABILITY AND CITATION OF RULES

A.   Scope.   The following rules shall apply to all cases filed on the plenary dockets in the Johnson Circuit and Superior Courts, and shall not apply to Small Claim, Juvenile, Criminal, or Domestic Relations cases.

B.   Citation.   These rules may be cited as LR41-

Adopted effective May 1, 2013.

LR41-TR3.1 Rule 145.   LEAVE TO WITHDRAW APPEARANCE

A.   Motion to Withdraw.   All withdrawals of an appearance must be made in the form of a motion filed with the Court.

B.   Form of Motion.   Motions for leave to withdraw appearance must indicate the client's current mailing address in the Certificate of Service and Proposed Order.

C.   Client Notification.   An attorney must give the attorney's client ten (10) days written notice of the attorney's intention to withdraw unless:

(1) another attorney has filed an appearance for the same party; or

(2) the withdrawing attorney indicates in the motion that he or she has been terminated by the client.   Failure to conform to this rule may result in the denial of the motion to withdraw as counsel.

D.   Contents of Client Letter.

1.   The letter of withdrawal shall explain to the client that failure to secure the assistance of new counsel may result in dismissal of the client's case or a default judgment may be entered against the client, whichever is appropriate.

2.   The letter of withdrawal shall clearly indicate any pending motions, response dates, hearing dates, scheduling orders, or trial dates.

Adopted effective May 1, 2013.

LR41–TR4 Rule 146.   SUMMONS

A.   Form of Summons.   In addition to the information required under Trial Rule 4(C), the form of the Summons must include the following information:

(1) The Answer or response of the Defending or Responding Party must be in writing, signed by the party, and filed with the Court within the time period allowed for a response.

(2) The response must dispute the allegations of the Complaint or Petition by including the Defending or Responding Party's response(s) or defense(s) to each claim contained within the Plaintiff's or Moving Party's Complaint in short and plain terms.

(3) If a response is required and does not deny the allegations of the Complaint or Petition, the allegations in the Complaint or are admitted, and the moving party will be entitled to the relief requested.

(4) Responses are not required in Domestic Relations cases.

B. Material Submitted with Summons. At the time of submission of the Summons, the party shall also submit such material to assist the Clerk in causing service to be affected, along with a stamped, return envelope to the Clerk for the return of service. If service by certified mail, registered mail, express mail, or via third-party commercial carrier is requested, the party shall submit any forms or materials required by the United States Postal Service or the Clerk's third party commercial carrier. If service is requested by the Johnson County Sheriff, the party shall submit the fee(s) required. If service is required by a Sheriff from another County, the party shall submit an envelope addressed to the sheriff along with all such fees required for service by the sheriff.

Adopted effective May 1, 2013.

LR41–TR5 Rule 147. GENERAL PROVISIONS REGARDING FILING OF PLEADINGS, MOTIONS, AND OTHER PAPERS

A. Appearance & Signature Required for Filing. No pleading, motion, or other paper specified in Indiana Trial Rule 5, will be accepted for filing unless such pleading, motion, or other paper has been signed in accordance with Indiana Trial Rule 11 by the attorney of record or a self-represented party. If it is later discovered that a nonconforming pleading or motion has inadvertently been filed the pleading, motion, or paper may be stricken from the record.

B. Supporting Briefs & Memoranda.

1. If a party desires to file a brief or memorandum in support of a motion, such brief or memorandum must be filed with the motion.

2. A supporting brief or memorandum shall be filed with all motions filed under Trial Rules 12 and Trial Rule 56.

3. Unless accompanied by a Motion for Leave to File a Brief in Excess of Page Limits, Memoranda in support of or in opposition to motions filed under Trial 12 or Trial Rule 56 shall not exceed fifteen (15) pages in length and any reply or surreply briefs thereon shall not exceed eight (8) pages in length.

C. Responses & Memoranda.

1. Responses shall be filed within ten (10) days following the date the motion was filed.

2. Unless otherwise ordered, responses and supporting memoranda to motions filed under Trial Rule 12 and Trial Rule 56 shall be filed thirty (30) days following the date the motion was filed.

3. The Court may consider those Motions identified in paragraph (E) without a response.

D. Replies. Replies are only permitted pursuant to advance Court approval. Petition to file the reply, accompanied by the tendered proposed reply, must be filed within seven (7) days of the response.

E. Motions Subject To Consideration Without Response. The Court may consider motions of routine and procedural nature without necessity of a response. Such motions include, those for enlargement of time, for continuance, to withdraw appearance, to dismiss or to withdraw motion by the moving party, for entry of an Order setting hearing, amend pleadings, compel discovery, for default judgment, and other matters of a routine, non-adversarial nature without necessity of a response.

F. Hearing. Except as provided by rule or statute, motions will be subject to consideration by the Court without hearing. A praecipe for hearing shall be included in a separate rhetorical paragraph within the motion or shall be filed in a separate written motion no later than five (5) days after the response.

G. Tender of Proposed Orders.

1. All motions seeking an order of the Court shall be accompanied by a sufficient number of proposed orders to ensure copies for two (2) copies for the Court and sufficient additional copies for service, if necessary.

2. The party shall also submit stamped, addressed envelopes addressed to all parties, agencies, and third parties involved in the case.

3. Proposed Orders shall include a full distribution list of attorneys, parties, agencies, and third parties involved in the case, including names and addresses, to whom the orders should be sent.

4. Failure to comply with these procedures may delay official processing of proposed orders.

H. Proposed Orders In Contested Hearing.

1. Unless the Court establishes a different period of time, each party in a contested hearing shall submit proposed Orders to the Court for consideration within ten (10) days of the close of evidence in any contested hearing or trial.

2. The Orders shall be provided in both paper and modifiable electronic format.

I. Preparation of Orders. If the Court assigns the preparation of an Order to a party, the party shall prepare and submit the proposed Order to the Court within ten (10) days of the date on which the Court assigns preparation of the Order, unless the Court establishes a different period of time. The party shall submit a copy of the proposed Order to an opposing party for review prior to submission to the Court and include a certification to the Court that a copy has been provided to an opposing party.

J. Providing Digital Copies to Court.

1. This provision applies only to proposed order and / or other documents required by these rules to be provided to the Court in electronic format.

2. Proposed orders in modifiable electronic format shall be provided on Compact Disc, Digital Video Disc, flash drive, or by the Court's specific Proposed Order electronic mail address.

3. The following electronic mail addresses constitute the exclusive list for the purposes of providing digital copies to the Court.

    A. C01ElectronicCopy@co.johnson.in.us

    B. D01ElectronicCopy@co.johnson.in.us

    C. D02ElectronicCopy@co.johnson.in.us

    D. D03ElectronicCopy@co.johnson.in.us

    E. MagistrateElectronicCopy@co.johnson.in.us

    F. JuvenileElectronicCopy@co.johnson.in.us

4. Messages sent to the staff address do not satisfy this requirement.

5. Identifying Submission.

1. Electronic mail messages providing proposed orders through the Court's specific Proposed Order electronic mail address shall include the Case Name and Case Number in the Subject Line.

2. Electronic mail messages related to filings made within five (5) days of a hearing shall include the hearing date and time in the Subject Line and the Case Name and Number in the body of the message.

Adopted effective May 1, 2013.

LR41–TR5 Rule 148. SPECIAL PROVISIONS REGARDING FILING OF PLEADINGS, MOTIONS, AND OTHER PAPERS

A. Special Judge. When a special judge is selected, a copy of all pending pleadings, motions, and other papers must be mailed or delivered to the office of the special judge by the party who sought the change of venue from the judge. The copies shall be provided with a certificate of forwarding attached, a copy of which shall be made a part of the case file. Any proposed orders must be forwarded to the special judge as well.

B. Filing by Mail. When pleadings, motions, or other papers filed via mail or third party commercial carrier, the filing attorney or party must include a self-addressed, stamped envelope for the return of file-stamped documents to the attorney or party. Unless an addressed envelope is provided, file-stamped copies will not returned by any method other than Courthouse Mail.

C. Filing by Facsimile Transmission. Pleadings, motions, or other papers may not be filed by facsimile transmission.

D. Case Numbers. Except for the initial pleading (Complaint, etc.), no pleading or motion should be filed unless it has a Case Number placed prominently on the face thereof.

E. Documents Filed Which Affect Hearings. Any document filed pursuant to Indiana Trial Rule 5(F)(3) within five (5) days of a scheduled hearing which is relevant to, pertains to, or involves the subject matter of the hearing should also be provided to the Court through electronic mail, as set forth above in LR41–TR5–147(J).

Adopted effective May 1, 2013.

LR41–TR Rule 149. FILINGS REQUIRING IMMEDIATE ACTION

If a motion, pleading, or paper requires immediate action, the moving party shall bring the emergency nature of the filing to the Court's attention. The mere inclusion of the word "Emergency" in the caption is insufficient.

Adopted effective May 1, 2013.

LR41–TR10 Rule 150. GENERAL RULES FOR THE FORMAT OF PLEADINGS, MOTIONS, & OTHER PAPERS

A. Paper Size, Line Spacing, and Margins. All pleadings, motions, and other papers filed with the Court by attorneys shall follow the format requirements of Indiana Appellate Rule 43(B)—(G).

B. File Stamp Space. All pleadings, motions, and papers filed should allow sufficient blank space to the right of the case title to allow space for the file mark without covering the caption or case number. The space shall be a minimum of three (3) inches in width and two and one-half (2 ½) inches in height.

C. Citation. Citations to cases, statutes, or other authority should follow that provided in Indiana Appellate Rule 22 and the Uniform System of Citation (Bluebook) and should provide specific pinpoint page citations.

D. Binding. All pleadings, motions, and other papers filed with the Court shall be stapled or otherwise bound in the upper left-hand corner so that the pages appear in numerical order.

E. Non–Conforming Pleadings. Pleadings, motions, and other papers that do not comply with the foregoing provisions may either be accepted by the Court or returned to the filing party for compliance

Adopted effective May 1, 2013.

LR41–TR10 Rule 151. SPECIAL RULES FOR THE FORMAT OF PLEADINGS WITH SPECIAL JUDGE PRESIDING

If the case is before a special judge, all pleadings, motions, and other papers shall contain the following to the right of the case title: "BEFORE SPECIAL JUDGE _____."

Adopted effective May 1, 2013.

LR41–TR40 Rule 152. ASSIGNING CASES FOR TRIAL

A. A case shall be assigned for trial and placed upon the trial calendar by the Court upon written request of a party and notice to all other parties. Except in Small Claims, such request must:

1. contain the type of trial or hearing requested (e.g. jury trial, bench trial);

2. contain a good-faith estimate of the time needed for the trial or hearing;

3. state when it is expected that all parties will be prepared for trial; and

4. reasonably anticipated dates on which the attorney or party is not available.

B. In all cases in which trial is expected to exceed one (1) day, the Court will first conduct a scheduling conference and conference under Trial Rule 16, prior to setting a case for trial.

Adopted effective May 1, 2013.

LR41–TR40 Rule 153. SETTLEMENT AND REMOVING THE CASE FROM THE DOCKET

Counsel for the parties shall be responsible for notifying the appropriate Court immediately upon settlement of a case so that the docket can be cleared and a new case set therein. The appropriate agreed entry, agreed judgment or motion to dismiss shall be filed.

Adopted effective May 1, 2013.

LR41–TR53.5 Rule 154. GENERAL REQUIREMENTS FOR MOTIONS FOR A CONTINUANCE

A. **Scheduling Conflicts.** When counsel for a party requests a continuance because he or she has a conflicting trial scheduled in another court, the motion for a continuance must be filed within twenty-one (21) days after the case in this Court is set for trial or hearing. The motion must also state the name and case number of the other case, as well as the date that the other court set the conflicting case for trial. Failure to timely file may result in a denial of the motion for a continuance.

B. **Time.** With the exception of an emergency, a motion for a continuance must be filed:

1. at least seven (7) days before the court trial or hearing to which the motion pertains, or

2. at least 10 (10) days before the jury trial to which the motion pertains; or

3. as controlled by a pretrial conference order.

C. **Information in Motion.** Motions for a continuance shall contain the following information:

1. The date and time of the hearing or trial for which a continuance is being sought;

2. The reason for the continuance;

3. A good-faith estimate of the time needed for such hearing or trial when rescheduled;

4. The date and time the opposing counsel or opposing party was notified that the party would be seeking a continuance;

5. Whether opposing counsel or opposing party agrees with or objects to the request; and

6. Proposed date(s)s and time(s) on which the parties would be available for the rescheduled hearing or trial

D. **Resetting Hearings and Trials—Civil Plenary (PL) Cases.** In Civil Plenary (CP / PL) cases, for the purpose of determining a date on which a rescheduled hearing or trial may be reset, the moving party shall contact the assistant court reporter who is responsible for the specific case type and shall determine dates and times on which the Court is available to hearing the matter. The party shall then determine the availability of the opposing party or parties.

E. **Scope.** This provisions of this rule apply regardless of whether the parties are self-represented or are represented by counsel.

Adopted effective May 1, 2013.

LR41–TR56 Rule 155. NOTICE AT TIME OF FILING MOTION FOR SUMMARY JUDGMENT IN CIVIL COLLECTION CASES

In all Civil Collection (CC) cases, the moving party shall submit a Notice to the opposing party in a form substantially similar to Johnson County General Pleading Form 1 at the time of filing of a Motion for Summary Judgment against a self-represented party,

Adopted effective May 1, 2013.

LR41–TR76 Rule 156. TRANSFER OR CONSOLIDATION OF CASES

Aside from those matters which are transferred or consolidated under the Family Court Rules, requests to transfer cases to the Johnson Circuit or Superior Court shall be made in writing, accompanied by written order for the signature of the forwarding Court. No transfer or consolidation shall be approved, unless such order is consented to in writing by the Judge of the receiving Court.

Adopted effective May 1, 2013.

LR41–TR77 Rule 157. COSTS FOR OBTAINING COPIES OF ANY PLEADING, ORDER, OR RECORDING

A. **Pleadings and Orders.** On the request of any person, the Clerk of the Court shall make copies of any non-confidential pleading or order at the expense of the person making the request, pursuant to the Clerk's fee schedule. Only parties are entitled to copies to papers or cases deemed Not for Public Access or Confidential.

B. **Recordings.** Audio recordings of hearings are not subject to release.

C. Payment in Advance. All copy costs shall be paid in advance or at the time of receipt of the copied papers.

Adopted effective May 1, 2013.

LR41–TR77 Rule 158. REMOVAL OF ORIGINAL PLEADINGS, PAPERS, AND RECORDS

No person shall withdraw any original pleading, paper, or record from the custody of the Court or the Clerk of the Court except upon the order of the judge of the Court.

Adopted effective May 1, 2013.

LR41–TR79.1 Rule 159. REPLEADING UPON TRANSFER OF SMALL CLAIMS CASES TO PLENARY DOCKET

A. Issues. A Small Claim case which comes to the Johnson Circuit Court or Johnson Superior Courts from the Magistrate Court through transfer to the plenary docket shall be repled in its entirety by the filing a new Complaint and Answer(s) or responsive pleading in compliance with the Indiana Rules of Trial Procedure.

1. The new Complaint shall be filed within twenty (20) days of the date the case is docketed and filed in the Johnson Circuit Court or Johnson Superior Courts or as otherwise ordered by the said Court.

2. Failure to comply with this Rule may result in the Court not setting the case for trial until the case is repled or imposing sanctions which may include dismissal.

3. At the time of filing the repled Complaint, the Plaintiff shall also file a Summons. The Summons and repled Complaint shall be served on the opposing party as required by law.

B. Answer or Responsive Pleadings. The opposing party must file an Answer or responsive pleading to the repled Complaint as provided by the Indiana Rules of Trial Procedure.

C. Procedure and Evidence. Once transferred to the plenary docket of the Circuit or Superior Courts, the rules and informal procedures of Small Claims cases are not longer applicable to the matter. For that reason, any pleadings, motions, or other procedural matters which are filed after the new Complaint is filed will be governed by the Indiana Rules of Trial Procedure and the Indiana Rules of Evidence.

Adopted effective May 1, 2013.

LR41–TR00–TR Rule 160. RESPONSIBILITIES OF SELF–REPRESENTED LITIGANTS

A. Choice to Represent Yourself. Any person may choose to represent herself or himself in any civil case pending in the Johnson Circuit and Superior Courts. Such persons are known as "Self-represented Litigants."

B. Standards to Which You Will Be Held. Self-represented Litigants must present their case using the same procedural rules as do attorneys.

1. The Court cannot treat Self-represented Litigants differently than those represented by an attorney.

2. The Court and its staff cannot assist Self-represented Litigants in a way that would put the other party / parties at a disadvantage. The Court cannot talk to any litigants about the case without the other party being present.

3. The Court cannot teach Self–Represented Litigants the Indiana Rules of Evidence or the Indiana Rules of Trial Procedure because that would put the other party at a disadvantage.

4. Self-represented Litigants must follow the rules of evidence and trial procedure in the presentation of their claims and / or defenses and will generally be held to the same standards as are attorneys.

5. Self-represented Litigants must provide notice about all court hearings to all other parties.

6. Self-represented Litigants must provide copies of all papers or documents filed in the case to all other parties.

7. Self-represented Litigants are responsible for making certain that any witnesses they want to testify are notified of your hearing.

C. Correspondence to the Court.

1. Any letter filed with the Court must: contain the parties' names, the name of the court where the case is filed, and the case number on it.

2. You must provide a copy of any letter you file to the Court to all the other parties in the case.

3. In some circumstances, the Court cannot take action based upon a letter from a litigant.

D. Role of the Court.

1. The Court's job is to consider the testimony and evidence presented during any hearings to determine the facts of the case from any such testimony and evidence, and then to apply the law to those facts.

2. The Court may only consider testimony and evidence that is submitted and actually admitted into evidence according to the Indiana Rules of Evidence and the Indiana Rules of Trial Procedure.

Adopted effective May 1, 2013.

ADDITIONAL RULES

LR41–TR81 Rule 161. SCOPE OF LOCAL RULES OF THE JOHNSON CIRCUIT AND SUPERIOR COURTS

Unless otherwise noted by a specific provision, and absent specific court order, these rules apply to proceedings originating in or transferred to the Johnson Circuit and Superior Courts.

Adopted effective May 1, 2013.

LR41 CR00 Rule 162. PRIORITY OF FEE PAYMENT

A. Criminal Cases.

1. *Pre-trial Diversion.* In the absence of specific court order, the fees and costs ordered in Criminal Cases, when an Agreement to Withhold Prosecution has been filed, shall be collected and / or the payments applied in the following order of priority.

    a. Pre–Trial Diversion fee (I.C. 33–37–4–1 and 33–37–5–17)

    b. Alcohol and Drug Service fee (33–37–5–8)

2. In the absence of specific court order, the fees and costs ordered in Criminal Cases following conviction shall be collected and / or the payments applied in the following order of priority.

    a. Probation Administrative fee

    b. Probation User fee

    c. Alcohol and Drug Service fee (33–37–5–8)

    d. Supplemental Public Defender Fee or Public Defender Reimbursement* (I. C. 35–33–7–6)

    e. Court Costs (I.C. 33–37–4–1)

    f. Restitution (I.C. 35–50–5–3)

    g. Safe School fee (I.C. 33–37–5–18)

    h. Child Abuse Prevention fee (I.C. 33–37–5–12)

    i. Drug Interdiction fee (I.C. 33–37–5–9)

    j. Alcohol Countermeasures fee (I.C. 33–37–5–10)

    k. Domestic Violence fee (I.C. 33–37–5–13)

3. In the event that these specific fees, or any other court ordered fees, are not paid, the Court may enter judgment against the individual and may seek appropriate steps to collect the judgment owed.

B. Juvenile Cases.

1. In the absence of specific court order, the fees and costs ordered in Juvenile Cases following adjudication shall be collected and / or the payments applied in the following order of priority.

    a. Supplemental Public Defender Fee.

    b. Probation Administrative Fee

    c. Probation User Fee

    d. Community Corrections Programming Fees.

    e. Alcohol and Drug Service Fee.

    f. Restitution

    g. Public Defenders Fee

    h. Juvenile Detention Fees / Costs.

    i. Court Costs

2. In the event that these specific fees, or any other court ordered fees, are not paid, the Court may enter judgment against the individual, or the parent or guardian of a juvenile, and may seek appropriate steps to collect the judgment owed.

Adopted effective May 1, 2013.

LR41–AR7–00 Rule 163. EVIDENCE HANDLING, RETENTION AND DESTRUCTION

A. Preamble.

1. The retention and maintenance of exhibits shall proceed pursuant to these rules, unless the Court directs a longer retention period on its own motion or after motion by any party.

2. These procedures will become effective immediately and will be applied to any cases previously disposed which meet the criteria set forth fully below.

B. Provisions Applicable to All Cases.

1. The Court Reporter will photograph as many non-documentary or oversized exhibits as practical.

2. All Child Support Obligation Worksheets and Financial Declarations admitted into evidence shall be permanently archived with the case file.

3. After the lapse of time described below, the Court Reporter may dispose of the exhibits (i.e., diagrams, models, depositions, and documents) and / or trial material without further notice to the parties.

4. The Court Reporter shall retain the mechanical or electronic records or tapes, shorthand, stenographic, or electronic notes as provided in Indiana Administrative Rule 7.

5. The Court Reporter should maintain a log of retained evidence and scheduled disposition date and evidence should be held in a secure area.

6. Parties and Counsel are reminded of the requirements of Appellate Rule 29(B).

Non-documentary and Oversized Exhibits. Non-documentary and oversized exhibits shall not be sent to the Appellate level Court, but shall remain in the custody of the trial court or Administrative Agency during the appeal. Such exhibits shall be briefly identified in the Transcript where they were admitted into evidence. Photographs of any exhibit may be included in the volume of documentary exhibits. Under no circumstances should drugs, currency, or other dangerous or valuable items be included in appellate records.

7. At the time of removal, the party shall present a signed receipt to the Court Reporter, which shall be filed in the case.

8. If the exhibits are not removed within the time frame outlined fully below, the Court Reporter may dispose of the exhibits without notice.

C. Civil Cases.

1. *No Appeal.* All exhibits, including, but not limited to models, diagrams, documents, depositions, or other material admitted into evidence or pertaining to the case as exhibits shall be removed by the party offering them in evidence, except as otherwise ordered by the Court, 121 days after entry of a final, appealable order, unless an appeal is taken.

2. *Following Appeal.* If an appeal is taken, original exhibits shall be removed by the party offering them no less than 121 days after all appellate procedural options are resolved.

D. Post–Conviction Relief, Criminal Misdemeanors, Class D Felonies, and Class C Felonies.

1. *No Appeal.* All exhibits, including, but not limited to models, diagrams, documents, depositions, or other material admitted into evidence or pertaining to the case as exhibits shall be removed by the party offering them in evidence, except as otherwise ordered by the Court two (2) years after the entry of a final, appealable order, unless an appeal is taken.

2. *Following Appeal.* If an appeal is taken, all such exhibits shall be retained by the court reporter for one (1) year from termination of the appeal, retrial, or subsequent appeal and termination, whichever is later, unless an action challenging the conviction or sentence, or post-conviction action, is pending. If exhibits are not removed, the Court Reporter may dispose of all exhibits without notice.

E. Class B Felonies, Class A Felonies, and Murder.

1. *No Appeal.* All exhibits, including, but not limited to models, diagrams, documents, depositions, or other material admitted into evidence or pertaining to the case as exhibits shall be removed by the party offering them in evidence shall be removed by the parties offering them in evidence, except as otherwise ordered by the Court, five (5) years after the case is dismissed, the defendant found not guilty, or the defendant is sentenced, unless an appeal is taken.

2. *Following Appeal.* If an appeal is taken, all such exhibits shall be retained by the court reporter for five (5) years from termination of the appeal, retrial, or subsequent appeal and termination, whichever is later, unless an action challenging the conviction or sentence, or post-conviction action, is pending.

F. Biologically Contaminated Evidence.

1. A party who intends to offer biologically contaminated evidence must file a pretrial notice with the trial court and serve all the parties so that the Court can consider the issue and rule appropriately before trial.

2. A party can show contaminated evidence or pass photographs of it to jurors, but no such evidence, however contained, shall be handled or passed to jurors or sent to the Jury Room unless specifically ordered by the Court.

Adopted effective May 1, 2013.

KOSCIUSKO COUNTY LOCAL CRIMINAL RULES

Adopted Effective December 11, 2006

Including Amendments Received Through November 1, 2013

Research Notes

These rules may be searched electronically on Westlaw in the IN-RULES database; updates to these rules may be found on Westlaw in IN-RULESUPDATES. For search tips and a summary of database content, consult the Westlaw Scope Screens for each database.

LR43–CR Rule 00–1.   Criminal Discovery

In all criminal felony and misdemeanor cases, the reciprocal pretrial discovery shall be available to both the State of Indiana and the Defendant, without formal written request filed with, or Order issued by, the Court, as follows:

(A) State's Required Disclosure. The State shall disclose to the Defense the following material and information within its possession or control on or before thirty (30) days from the date of initial hearing of the Defendant:

(1) The names and last known addresses of persons whom the State may call as witnesses, together with their relevant written or recorded statements, memoranda containing substantially verbatim reports of their oral statements and a list of memoranda reporting or summarizing their oral statements.

(2) Any written or recorded statements and the substance of any oral statements made by the accused or by a codefendants, and a list of witnesses to the making and acknowledgment of such statements.

(3) A transcript of those portions of grand jury minutes containing testimony of persons whom the prosecuting attorney may call as witnesses at the hearing or trial, as designated by the defense after listening to the recording of the testimony.

(4) Any reports or statements of experts, made in connection with the particular case, including the results of physical or mental examinations and of scientific tests, experiments or comparisons.

(5) Any books, papers, documents, photographs or tangible objects which the prosecuting attorney intends to use in the hearing or trial or which were obtained from or belong to the accused.

(6) Any record of prior criminal convictions which may be used for impeachment of the persons whom the State intends to call as witnesses at the hearing or trial.

(7) Any evidence which tends to negate the guilt of the accused as to the offense charged or which would tend to mitigate the accused's punishment.

(8) Any Evidence Rule 404(b) evidence.

The State may comply with this Order (1) in any manner it and the Defense agree to, or (2) by notifying defense counsel that material and information, described in general terms, may be inspected, obtained, tested, copied, or photographed at specified reasonable times and places.

(B) Defendant's Required Disclosure. The Defense shall disclose to the State the following material and information within its possession or control on or before omnibus date.

(1) The names and addresses of persons whom the defendant may call as witnesses.

(2) Any books, papers, documents, photographs, or tangible objects which are intended to be used at a hearing or trial.

(3) Any medical or scientific reports relating to the defendant or defendant's evidence which may be used at a hearing or trial.

(4) Any defenses, procedural or substantive, which the defendant intends to make at a hearing or a trial.

(C) Objections to Discovery Order. Any objections to the discovery order must be filed within fourteen (14) days prior to omnibus date.

(D) Certificate of Compliance Required, Deadline. The State and the Defendant shall file with the Court Certificate of Compliance with the Order on or before pretrial conference.

(E) Continuing Discovery Required.

(1) Discovery is a continuing order through trial.

(2) No written motion is required except to compel discovery, for a protective order, or for an extension of time.

(F) Sanctions. Failure of either side to comply with this Order within fourteen (14) days before trial may result in exclusion of evidence at trial or other appropriate sanction.

Adopted effective Dec. 11, 2006. Amended effective April 10, 2012.

LR43–CR Rule 2.2–1. Initial Case Assignment

(A) Initial case assignments are as follows:

(1) *All D and C Felonies.* Thirty percent (30%) of D felonies shall be filed in the Kosciusko Circuit Court and should include any cases filed under Title 35, Article 48 (Controlled Substances).

Twenty percent (20%) of D felonies shall be filed in the Kosciusko Superior Court No. 1.

Ten percent (10%) of D felonies shall be filed in the Kosciusko Superior Court No. 2.

Forty percent (40%) of D felonies shall be filed in the Kosciusko Superior Court No. 3 and should include any cases involving felonies filed under Title 9 (Traffic) and I.C. 35–46–1–5 through and including I.C. 35–46–1–7.

Fifty percent (50%) of C felonies shall be filed in the Kosciusko Circuit Court and should include any cases filed under Title 35, Article 48 (Controlled Substances).

Thirty percent (30%) of C felonies shall be filed in the Kosciusko Superior Court No. 1.

Twenty percent (20%) of C felonies shall be filed in the Kosciusko Superior Court No. 3 and should include any cases filed under Title 9 (Traffic) and I.C. 35–46–1–5 through and including I.C. 35–46–1–7.

(2) *Felonies under Title 35–42–1 (Homicide) and I.C. 35–48 (Controlled Substances) cases.* All felonies filed under Title 35, Article 42, Chapter 1 (Homicide) and those filed under Title 35, Article 48 (Controlled Substances) shall be field [1] in the Kosciusko Circuit Court. (*Amended effective January 1, 2005*)

(3) *All other Felony cases.* All other felonies shall be assigned to the Kosciusko Superior Court No. 1 and Kosciusko Circuit Court on an alternating basis.

(4) *All Misdemeanor cases.* All misdemeanors shall be assigned to the Kosciusko Superior Court No. 2.

(5) *All I.C. 31–6–4 (Juvenile) cases.* All cases filed under Title 31, Article 6, Chapter 4 (Juvenile) of the Indiana Code shall be initially assigned to Kosciusko Superior Court No. 1. In the event a child is waived into adult court, the case shall be reassigned to the appropriate court in accordance with the proceeding provisions of this rule.

(6) *Combination of Felony and Misdemeanor cases.* In the event the case charges both felony and misdemeanor offenses, the case shall be considered a felony for the application of this rule.

(B) Transfer of Criminal Cases. The Judge in any Kosciusko Court, by appropriate order entered in the Record of Judgment and Orders, may transfer and reassign to any other court of record in the county with jurisdiction to hear the charged offense any pending cases subject to acceptance by the receiving court.

(C) Refiling and/or Subsequent Filings of Criminal Charges.

(1) *Dismissal and Subsequent Refiling of Charges.* In the event the State of Indiana dismisses a case, any subsequent case filed against such defendant within the next six months shall be assigned to the court from which the dismissal was taken.

(2) *Filing of Additional Charges.* In the event additional charges are filed against a criminal defendant subsequent to the assignment of the case, all such additional charges to be resolved in conjunction with the pending case shall be assigned to the court of initial assignment.

(D) Reassignment of Criminal Cases.

(1) *Kosciusko Circuit Court.* The following individuals have agreed to serve in the event it becomes necessary to reassign a criminal case in the Kosciusko Circuit Court:

  1. The Judge of the Kosciusko Superior Court No. 1

  2. The Judge of the Marshall Circuit Court

  3. The Judge of the Wabash Circuit Court

By order of adoption of these rules, the Indiana Supreme Court, pursuant to Indiana Code 33–24–6–10 temporarily transfers the above judges to the Kosciusko Circuit Court for the purpose of reassignment in criminal cases.

(2) *Kosciusko Superior Court 1.* The following individuals have agreed to serve in the event it becomes necessary to reassign a criminal case in the Kosciusko Superior Court No. 1:

  1. The Judge of the Kosciusko Circuit Court

  2. The Judge of the Marshall Circuit Court

  3. The Judge of the Wabash Circuit Court

By order of adoption of these rules, the Indiana Supreme Court, pursuant to Indiana Code 33–24–6–10 temporarily transfers the above judges to the Kosciusko Superior Court No. 1 for purpose of reassignment of criminal cases.

(3) *Kosciusko Superior Court 2.* The following individuals have agreed to serve in the event it becomes necessary to reassign a criminal case in the Kosciusko Superior Court No. 2:

  1. The Judge of the Kosciusko Circuit Court

  2. The Judge of the Kosciusko Superior Court No. 1

  3. The Judge of the Kosciusko Superior Court No. 3

By order of adoption of these rules, the Indiana Supreme Court, pursuant to Indiana Code 33–24–6–10 temporarily transfers the above judges to the Kosciusko Superior Court No. 2 for the purpose of reassignment of criminal cases.

(4) *Kosciusko Superior Court 3.* The following individuals have agreed to serve in the event it becomes necessary to reassign a criminal case in the Kosciusko Superior Court No. 3:

　　1. The Judge of the Kosciusko Superior Court No. 2

　　2. The Judge of the Kosciusko Circuit Court

　　3. The Judge of the Kosciusko Superior Court No. 1

By order of adoption of these rule [2], the Indiana Supreme Court, pursuant to Indiana Code 33–24–6–10 temporarily transfers the above judges to the Kosciusko Superior Court No. 3 for the purpose of reassignment of criminal cases.

(5) *Method of Reassignment of Cases.* In the event it becomes necessary to reassign a criminal case in the Kosciusko Circuit Court, Kosciusko Superior Court No. 1, Kosciusko Superior Court No. 2 or Kosciusko Superior Court No. 3, the cases will be reassigned in consecutive order to the above noted judges.

Adopted effective Dec. 11, 2006. Amended effective April 16, 2007; Jan. 1, 2008; Dec. 20, 2011, effective retroactively Jan. 1, 2011; effective April 10, 2012.

　[1] So in original. Should probably read "filed".

　[2] So in original.

LR43–CR Rule 13–1. Appointment of Special Judges

(A)[1] In the event no judge is available for assignment or reassignment of a felony or misdemeanor case, such case shall be certified to the Indiana Supreme Court for the appointment of a special judge. In the event the judge presiding in a felony or misdemeanor case concludes that the unique circumstances presented in such proceeding require appointment by the Indiana Supreme Court of a special judge, this presiding judge may request the Indiana, Supreme Court for such appointment.

Adopted effective Dec. 11, 2006. Amended effective April 10, 2012.

　[1] There is no Subd. (B) in this rule.

KOSCIUSKO COUNTY LOCAL CIVIL RULES

Adopted Effective December 11, 2006

Including Amendments Received Through November 1, 2013

Research Notes

These rules may be searched electronically on Westlaw in the IN-RULES database; updates to these rules may be found on Westlaw in IN-RULESUPDATES. For search tips and a summary of database content, consult the Westlaw Scope Screens for each database.

LR43–AR Rule 1.   CIVIL CASE ASSIGNMENT

A.   (1) All cases which have case classification code MH shall be filed in the Kosciusko Circuit Court.

(2) All cases which have case classification code JC, JD, JS, JP, JM and JT shall be filed in Kosciusko Superior Court No. 1.

(3) All cases which have case classification code PL, CT, RS, AD, AH, ES, EU, GU and TR may be filed in either Kosciusko Circuit Court or Kosciusko Superior Court No. 1; however, attorneys are strongly encouraged to file such cases on an alternating basis in Kosciusko Circuit and Kosciusko Superior Court No. 1.

(4) Seventy-five percent (75) of MI cases shall be filed in Kosciusko Superior Court No. 3, Twenty-five percent (25%) may be filed in either Kosciusko Circuit or Kosciusko Superior Court No. 1; however, attorneys are strongly encouraged to file such cases on an alternating basis in Kosciusko Circuit and Kosciusko Superior Court No. 1.

(5) All cases which have case classification code IF shall be filed in Kosciusko Superior Court No. 2.

(6) All cases which have case classification code OV, OE, PO (except PO cases where a JP case is in existence involving the same parties which shall then be filed in the court having the JP case), and SC shall be filed in Kosciusko Superior Court No. 3.

(7) One-fourth (1/4) of dissolution cases shall be filed in Kosciusko Superior Court No. 3.

(8) One-half (1/2) of dissolution cases shall be filed in Kosciusko Circuit Court.

(9) One-fourth (1/4) of dissolution cases shall be filed in Kosciusko Superior Court No. 1.

(10) Collection (CC) cases shall be filed in Kosciusko Superior Court No. 3 or Kosciusko Superior Court No. 2, with case assignment to be made by the Clerk in order that: three-fourths (3/4) are filed in Kosciusko Superior Court No. 3; one-fourth (1/4) are filed in Kosciusko Superior Court No. 2.

(11) Mortgage foreclosure cases shall be filed in Kosciusko Circuit Court and Kosciusko Superior Court No. 3 with case assignment to be made by the Clerk in order that: on-half (1/2) are filed in Kosciusko Circuit Court; and one-half (1/2) are filed in Kosciusko Superior Court No. 3.

B.   It may, from time to time, be expedient for the Judges of Kosciusko Circuit Court and Kosciusko Superior Courts to hear cases pending in the other Court.

(1) The judge of Kosciusko Circuit Court authorizes the Judge of Kosciusko Superior Court No. 1 to sit as Judge of Kosciusko Circuit Court, at any time, in any case.

(2) The judge of Kosciusko Superior Court No. 1 authorizes the Judge of Kosciusko Circuit Court to sit as Judge of Kosciusko Superior Court No. 1, at any time, in any case.

(3) The judge of Kosciusko Superior Court No. 2 authorizes the Judge of Kosciusko Superior Court No. 3 to sit as Judge of Kosciusko Superior Court No. 2, at any time, in any case.

(4) The judge of Kosciusko Superior Court No. 3 authorizes the Judge of Kosciusko Superior Court No. 2 to sit as Judge of Kosciusko Superior Court No. 3, at any time, in any case.

(5) Senior judge services shall be allocated to the various courts of Kosciusko County to enable the judges of Kosciusko County to have vacation, sick days and attendance at judicial seminars and to allow continuance of cases and court duties in the absence of the elected judge.

Adopted effective Dec. 11, 2006. Amended effective April 16, 2007; Jan. 1, 2008; Dec. 20, 2011, effective retroactive to Jan. 1, 2011.

LR43—AR Rule 2.   COURT REPORTER SERVICES

(A) Definitions.   The following definitions shall apply under this local rule:

(1) A Court Reporter is a person who is specifically designated by a court to perform the official court reporting services for the court including preparing a transcript of the record.

(2) Equipment means all physical items owned by the court or other governmental entity and used by a court reporter in performing court reporting services. Equipment shall include, but not be limited to, telephones, computer hardware, software programs, disks, tapes, and any other device used for recording and storing, and transcribing electronic data.

(3) Work space means that portion of the court's facilities dedicated to each court reporter, including but not limited to actual space in the courtroom and any designated office space.

(4) Page means the page unit of transcript which results when a recording is transcribed in the form required by Indiana Rule of Appellate Procedure 7.2.

(5) Recording means the electronic, mechanical, stenographic or other recording made as required by Indiana Rule of Trial Procedure 74.

(6) Regular hours worked means those hours which the court is regularly scheduled to work during any given work week. Depending on the particular court, these hours may vary from court to court within the county but remain the same for each work week.

(7) Gap hours worked means those hours worked that are in excess of the regular hours worked but hours not in excess of forty (40) hours per work week.

(8) Overtime hours worked means those hours worked in excess of forty (40) hours per work week.

(9) Work week means a seven (7) consecutive day week that consistently begins and ends on the same days throughout the year; i.e. Sunday through Saturday, Wednesday through Tuesday, Friday through Thursday.

(10) Court means the particular court for which the court reporter performs services. Court may also mean all of the courts in Kosciusko County.

(11) County indigent transcript means a transcript that is paid for from county funds and is for the use on behalf of a litigant who has been declared indigent by a court.

(12) State indigent transcript means a transcript that is paid for from state funds and is for the use on behalf of a litigant who has been declared indigent by a court.

(13) Private transcript means a transcript, including by not limited to a deposition transcript that is paid for by a private party.

(B) Salaries and Per Page Fees.

(1) Court Reporters shall be paid an annual salary for time spent working under the control, direction and direct supervision of their supervising court during any regular work hours, gap hours, or overtime hours. The supervising court shall enter into a written agreement with the court reporters which outlines the manner in which the court reporter is to be compensated for gap and overtime hours, i.e. monetary compensation or compensatory time off regular work hours.

(2) The maximum per page fee a court reporter may charge for the preparation of a county indigent transcript shall be $3.50 per page until further order of the Courts. The court reporter shall submit a claim directly to the county for the preparation of any county indigent transcripts.

(3) The maximum per page fee a court reporter may charge for the preparation of a state indigent transcript shall be $3.50 per page until further order of the Courts.

(4) The maximum per page fee a court reporter may charge for the preparation of a private transcript shall be $3.50 per page.

(5) The maximum per page fee a court reporter may charge for the preparation of an expedited transcript is $4.50 per page.

(6) A minimum fee up to $40.00 is permissible.

(7) An additional labor charge approximating the hourly rate based upon the court reporter's annual court compensation may be charged for the time spent binding the transcript and the exhibit binders depending on the size of the transcript.

(8) Each court reporter shall report, at least on an annual basis, all transcript fees received for the preparation of county indigent, state indigent or private transcripts to the Indiana Supreme Court Division of State Court Administration. The reporting shall be made on forms prescribed by the Division of State Court administration.

(C) Private Practice.

(1) If a court reporter elects to engage in private practice through the recording of a deposition and/or preparing of a deposition transcript, and the court reporter desires to utilize the court's equipment, work space and supplies, and the court agrees to the use of the court equipment for such purpose, the court and the court reporter shall enter into a written agreement which must, at a minimum, designate the following:

a) the reasonable market rate for the use of equipment, work space and supplies;

b) the method by which records are to be kept for the use of equipment, work space and supplies; and

c) the method by which the court reporter is to reimburse the court for the use of equipment, work space and supplies.

(2) If a court reporter elects to engage in private practice through the recording of a deposition and/or preparing of a deposition transcript, all such private practice work shall be conducted outside of regular working hours.

Adopted effective Dec. 11, 2006. Amended effective April 10, 2012; June 1, 2012.

LR43—AR Rule 3. COURT FILES

(A) Court files will not be removed from the Kosciusko County Justice Building without the express written consent of the Clerk of the Court and the giving of a receipt for such file if consent is given.

(B) Routine court filings shall be made in the Clerk's Office and left with the Clerk for delivery to the appropriate Court.

(C) Attorneys may direct filings with the Court; however, the Court file must be secured by the attorney from the Clerk's Office and a sign-out sheet signed by the attorney requesting the file for direct filing. After completing the direct filing, the file will either be left with the Court or in the case of probate filings, personally returned by the attorney to the Probate Clerk.

Adopted effective Dec. 11, 2006.

LR 43–AR Rule 4. KOSCIUSKO COUNTY ALCO- HOL AND DRUG PROGRAM FEES

The following fees will be assessed for participants in the Kosciusko County Alcohol and Drug Program (KCADP)

Full Program Fee:	$400.00
Transfer Fee:	$50.00
Referral Fee:	$100.00

Adopted effective April 16, 2007. Amended effective May 10, 2010; Dec. 3, 2012.

LR43–AR Rule 5. KOSCIUSKO COUNTY DRUG COURT FEES

Those persons directed to participate in the Kosciusko County Drug Court may be assessed in accordance with the following SCHEDULE OF FEES pursuant to the authority granted by Indiana Code 33–23–16–23:

1. A Drug Court administration fee of $100.00 per participant payable to the Kosciusko County Probation Department.

2. A Drug Court user fee of $50.00 per month for every month that an individual participant in Drug Court, payable to the Kosciusko County Probation Department.

3. A Drug Court drug testing fee of $20.00 payable to the Kosciusko County Probation Department.

4. A Drug Court transfer fee of $25.00 per participant per transfer, payable to the Kosciusko County Probation Department.

Adopted effective Oct. 1, 2013.

KOSCIUSKO COUNTY LOCAL TRIAL RULES

Adopted Effective December 11, 2006

Including Amendments Received Through November 1, 2013

Research Notes

These rules may be searched electronically on Westlaw *in the* IN-RULES *database; updates to these rules may be found on* Westlaw *in IN-RULESUPDATES. For search tips and a summary of database content, consult the Westlaw Scope Screens for each database.*

Rule
LR43–TR Rule 64.   Judicial Sales of Land

LR43–TR Rule 64.   Judicial Sales of Land

(A) In the case of any judicial sale of land, including without limitation mortgage and lien foreclosures, execution sales, sales by receivers, assignees for the benefit of creditors, guardians or trustees, or partition sale, the judgment creditor, person seeking the sale, or officer conducting the sale to procure a qualified title opinion or a title insurance policy from a title insurance company authorized to do business in Indiana with respect to the interest of the person whose land is being sold.

(1) The policy musts [1] be conditioned to cover the purchase price at the sale and may be given with any necessary exclusions.

(2) The opinion or policy shall run to all parties interested in the litigation and to any purchaser or purchasers at the sale.

(3) The opinion or policy or copy thereof shall be available for inspection in the court from which the sale is being conducted or in the office of the court officer conducting the sale at the first notice of sale and shall be made available for inspection at the sale.

(4) Expenses of the opinion or policy shall be taxed as costs like other expenses of the sale and paid fro [2] the first proceeds of the sale.

(5) The opinion or policy shall not cover defects arising in the conduct of the sale.

(B) The Court in its discretion may, in the proper case, on motion duly made grant relief from the strict requirements of this order.

Adopted effective Dec. 11, 2006.

[1] So in original. Should probably read "must".
[2] So in original. Should probably read "from".

KOSCIUSKO COUNTY LOCAL FAMILY LAW RULES

Adopted Effective December 11, 2006

Including Amendments Received Through November 1, 2013

Research Notes

These rules may be searched electronically on Westlaw *in the* IN-RULES *database; updates to these rules may be found on* Westlaw *in IN-RULESUPDATES. For search tips and a summary of database content, consult the Westlaw Scope Screens for each database.*

Rule
LR43—FL Rule 1. Child custody action

LR43—FL Rule 1. Child custody action

(A)[1] Each party, who is a parent of a minor child(ren) with the other party in a DR action, shall arrange with the Otis R. Bowen Center, Inc., for enrollment in and attendance at the **TransParenting Program** established between the Court and the Bowen Center. Each party shall pay the $40.00 enrollment fee for participation, and the action will not be scheduled for pretrial conference or final hearing until the Bowen Center certifies to the Court that each of the parties has completed the program.

Adopted effective Dec. 11, 2006.

1 There is no Subd. (B) in the original.

LAKE COUNTY RULES OF CIVIL PROCEDURE

Adopted Effective January 1, 1993

Including Amendments Received Through November 1, 2013

Research Notes

Annotations to the Lake County Rules of Civil Procedure are available in West's Annotated Indiana Code, *Title 34 Appendix.*

These rules may be searched electronically on Westlaw *in the* IN-RULES *database; updates to these rules may be found on Westlaw in* IN-RULESUPDATES. *For search tips and a summary of database content, consult the Westlaw Scope Screens for each database.*

LR 45–TR1 Rule 1.   SCOPE AND TITLE

A.   Scope.   These rules shall apply in the Lake Circuit Court and the Superior Court of Lake County, Civil Division and Juvenile Division.

B.   These rules shall also apply to all civil cases in the Superior Court, County Division that are not designated as SC, IF or OV. However, L.R. 45–T.R. 79 Rule 15, regarding the assignment of special judges, shall apply to small claims cases.

C.   Title.   These rules may be known as the Lake County Rules of Civil Procedure, and abbreviated as LR.

Adopted effective Jan. 1, 1993. Amended effective May 21, 1997; Dec. 5, 2006; Oct. 18, 2013.

LR 45–TR10 Rule 2. PREPARATION OF PLEADINGS, MOTIONS AND OTHER PAPERS

For the purpose of uniformity, convenience, clarity and durability, the following requirements shall be observed in the preparation of all pleadings, motions and other papers:

A.   Paper—Print, Quality and Binding.   All pleadings, motions, chronological case summary entry forms, orders, process and other papers shall be neatly and legibly printed, typewritten or mechanically reproduced, on one side only, on white opaque paper. To satisfy the recordkeeping requirements of Indiana Rules of Procedure, Trial Rule 77, the print shall be of sufficient density and clarity for preservation and reproduction of microfilming, optical disk or other secondary sources. For this reason, the use of non-letter-quality printers is discouraged.

Paper and ink shall be of such quality as to withstand the test of time. All documents shall be produced on acid-free, non-thermal paper. It is recommended that a minimum of 20–pound, 25% cotton paper product be used. Documents of multiple pages shall be submitted in bound or stapled fashion, and the binding or stapling shall be at the top only. Covers or backings shall not be used.

B.   Sanctions.   Whenever materials submitted fail to meet the foregoing standards, the Court may impose appropriate sanctions.

C.   Papers—Handwritten; Electronic Facsimile Transmission ("FAX").   Handwritten papers may be filed only if approved by the Court and a typewritten or printed true rendition thereof is filed within three (3) days thereafter and approved by the Court. Upon such approval, they shall be deemed and filed as the original, while the handwritten papers shall be retained therewith for evidentiary purposes.

Only when necessary on an emergency basis (i.e., when certified mail or other means of filing will not bring the document to the Judge's attention prior to the scheduled hearing or ruling), pleadings, motions and other papers may be filed by electronic facsimile transmission, or when specifically authorized by the Court.

D. Minute Sheets; Motion Blanks. Minute sheets and motion blanks shall no longer be used.

E. Special Judge Matters. The caption of all CCS Entry Forms, pleadings, motions, orders and other papers to be filed in a special judge case shall include in block text the words SPECIAL JUDGE and the name of the judge directly below the cause number on the caption.

Adopted effective Jan. 1, 1993. Amended effective Nov. 1, 1994; May 21, 1997; Dec. 5, 2006; Jan. 1, 2009.

LR 45–TR5 Rule 3.   FILING

A. Filing and Submission Only to the Clerk; Proof of Service; Sanctions. All papers presented for filing shall be submitted to the Clerk and not to the court. All papers submitted for filing shall be mailed or delivered to the Clerk's office at the courthouse in which the case is pending; provided however, for special judge matters where the special judge is a full-time judge or magistrate serving within Lake County, all papers submitted for filing shall be delivered or mailed to the Clerk's office at the courthouse where the special judge regularly serves. All pleadings, motions and other papers submitted for filing which are required to be served under Trial Rule 5(A) shall be filed no later than three (3) days after service and shall contain proof of service pursuant to Trial Rule 5(B)(2). If such papers are filed before service, proof of service thereof shall be filed no later than three (3) business days thereafter. Upon failure to comply with this rule, the Court may, on motion of any party or on its own motion, impose appropriate sanctions.

B. Separate Motions and Orders; Order by Chronological Case Summary Entry Form; Service. Proposed orders shall be prepared and filed separately from the pleadings, petitions, motions or other papers to which they have reference.

Orders, either routine in nature or uncontested including, for example, those setting or continuing a hearing, shall be effected by the chronological case summary entry only, which shall contain the concise substance of the order.

All orders shall be accompanied with sufficient copies and stamped, pre-addressed envelopes, so that copies may be mailed to all parties.

C. Chronological Case Summary (CCS) Entry Forms. All filings shall be accompanied by a Chronological Case Summary (CCS) Entry Form to define or identify the documents filed. The Form used should be substantially similar to Appendix A.

Adopted effective Jan. 1, 1993. Amended effective May 21, 1997; Dec. 5, 2006; Jan. 1, 2009; amended July 31, 2009, effective Jan. 1, 2010; Oct. 18, 2013.

LR 45–TR7 Rule 4.   MOTIONS

A. Briefs. All motions filed pursuant to Trial Rules 12 and 56 shall be accompanied by a separate supporting brief. An adverse party shall have thirty (30) days after service of the initial brief in which to serve and file an answer brief, and the moving party shall have ten (10) days after service of the answer brief in which to serve and file a reply brief. With regard to all other motions or matters submitted to the court, and so long as consistent with the Indiana Rules of Procedure, an adverse party wishing to respond shall do so within fifteen (15) days of service. The moving party shall have ten (10) days after service of the response within which to reply. Each motion shall be separate, while alternative motions filed together shall each be identified on the caption. Failure to file an answer brief or reply brief within the time prescribed shall be deemed a waiver of the right thereto and shall subject the motion to summary ruling.

B. Oral Arguments. The granting of a motion for oral argument, unless required by the Indiana Rules of Procedure, shall be wholly discretionary with the court.

Adopted effective Jan. 1, 1993. Amended effective Dec. 5, 2006.

LR 45–TR3.1 Rule 5.   APPEARANCE BY ATTORNEY

A. Initiating Party. At the time an action is commenced, an attorney representing the initiating party must:

(1) be a member in good standing of the Bar of the State of Indiana; and

(2) file with the Clerk of the Court an appearance form setting forth the printed name, address, attorney number, the name of the firm, if any, telephone number, FAX number and signature of any attorney representing the initiating party as applicable.

B. Responding Party. At the time the responding party or parties first appear in a case, if that party or parties are represented by an attorney, the attorney must:

(1) be a member in good standing of the Bar of the State of Indiana; and

(2) file with the Clerk of the Court an appearance form setting forth the printed name, address, attorney number, the name of the firm, if any, telephone number, FAX number and signature of any attorney representing the responding party as applicable.

C. Pro Hac Vice. A person not a member of the Bar of the State of Indiana shall not generally be permitted to practice in the Civil Division of the Lake County Court System. The Court in its discretion may permit such counsel to appear only for a specifically limited purpose and time. Counsel's Motion shall strictly comply with Admission and Discipline

Rule 3, and disclose such purpose, time, and all other cases in which the attorney or members of the firm have been permitted to appear in the State of Indiana.

D. Non–Resident Attorney. Whenever in its discretion the Court believes it would facilitate the conduct of litigation, the Court may require any attorney who is a member of the Bar of Indiana and who does not maintain an office in Indiana, to retain as local counsel a member of the Bar of Indiana who maintains a local office in Indiana. Notice served upon such local counsel shall constitute service upon all other counsel appearing of record for such party.

E. Withdrawal of Appearance. All withdrawals of appearance shall be in writing and by leave of Court. Permission to withdraw shall be given only after the withdrawing attorney has given a client ten (10) days' written notice of intention to withdraw. A copy of the notice of intention to withdraw shall be attached to the motion seeking leave to withdraw. This rule may be waived by the Court if withdrawal is at the written request of the client; accompanied by the appearance of successor counsel; or for other good cause. In any event, all withdrawals shall fully comply with the Rules of Professional Conduct, Rule 1.16.

F. Withdrawal Shall Not Effect Continuance. Withdrawal, in and of itself, shall not effect a continuance of any pending matter.

Adopted effective Jan. 1, 1993. Amended effective Nov. 1, 1994; Dec. 5, 2006.

LR 45–AR10 Rule 6

Consistent with the intent of Administrative Rule 10, neither the Case File, Chronological Case Summary nor contents of the Record of Judgments and Orders may be removed from the custody of the court or Clerk; provided, however, the Case File or Chronological Case Summary, upon proper receipt, may be entrusted to an attorney with whom the Clerk is familiar for delivery to the court.

No books may be removed from the judge's chambers or law libraries maintained in the respective courthouses or by the Lake County Central Law Library.

Adopted effective Jan. 1, 1993. Amended effective Dec. 5, 2006.

LR 45–TR53.5 Rule 7. CONTINUANCES—EXTENSIONS OF TIME TO ANSWER

A. Motion. A motion for continuance, unless made during the hearing of a matter, shall be for cause, in writing and verified, with a copy thereof timely served upon opposing counsel unless the court otherwise directs. A motion for continuance may be granted ex parte only if the movant's attorney certifies to the court in writing the efforts, if any, which have been made to give notice and the reasons supporting his claim that actual notice should not be required.

B. Time for Filing. A motion for continuance must be filed as soon as possible after the cause for continuance is discovered, and not later than ten (10) days before hearing or trial, unless the reason therefor is shown by affidavit to have occurred within that period.

C. By Agreement of Counsel. An agreement by counsel to continue the hearing of any pending matter shall be signed by both counsel and parties (or proof of written notice to the parties in lieu of their signatures), and filed at least ten (10) days before hearing or trial, or such shorter period as the court in its discretion may allow.

D. Automatic Extension for Answer. Provided it is timely filed, the mere entry of appearance by a party or counsel in response to a summons in an action that requires an answer shall effect an extension of thirty (30) days from the filing thereof within which to respond. This provision is inapplicable to actions in replevin and ejectment.

Adopted effective Jan. 1, 1993. Amended effective Dec. 5, 2006.

LR 45–TR26 Rule 8. DISCOVERY

A. Commencement and Extensions. In general, counsel are expected to begin discovery promptly and shall be granted extensions only upon a showing of diligence and good cause.

B. Interrogatories. Interrogatories shall be tailored specifically to the cause in which they are served and numbered consecutively to facilitate response. No party shall serve on any other party more than thirty (30) interrogatories or more than thirty (30) requests for admission (other than requests relating to the authenticity or genuineness of documents in the aggregate), including subparagraphs, without leave of court. Subparagraphs shall relate directly to the subject matter of the interrogatory or request for admission. Any party desiring to serve additional interrogatories or requests for admission shall file a written motion setting forth those proposed and the necessity therefor.

C. Attorney Conference. Strict compliance with Trial Rules 26 through 37 is required. The discovery process is intended to be largely self-actuating, with minimal court supervision. Therefore, the court will not rule on motions related to discovery disputes unless moving counsel represents that, after personal or telephonic conference in good faith effort to resolve differences, counsel are unable to reach accord. If counsel advises the court, by way of motion or response thereto, that opposing counsel has refused or delayed resolution of the discovery dispute, the court may, after hearing, impose appropriate sanctions.

Adopted effective Jan. 1, 1993. Amended effective Dec. 5, 2006.

LR 45–TR16 Rule 9.　PRE–TRIAL PROCEDURE

A.　Initial Status Conference. Upon motion of any party or the court, an initial status conference shall be scheduled and held within six (6) months of the filing of any Complaint in a civil plenary or civil tort case. Each party shall be represented at this conference by an attorney familiar with the case, who shall be prepared to discuss and enter into stipulations concerning:

(1) the exchange of lists of witnesses known to have knowledge of the facts supporting the pleadings. The parties thereafter shall be under a continuing obligation to advise opposing parties of other witnesses as they become known;

(2) the exchange of all documents, and any other evidence reasonably available, contemplated for use in support of the pleadings;

(3) a discovery schedule;

(4) the necessity for additional conferences in complex litigation; and

(5) the necessity for amendments to the pleadings and the filing or hearing of dispositive motions. Absent agreement, the court shall schedule the filing, briefing and hearing thereof.

B.　Case Management Order. At the conclusion of the initial status conference, the court shall enter a case management order setting forth:

(1) a time limit for completion of discovery;

(2) a time limit for joinder of additional parties and amendment of pleadings;

(3) a time limit for filing all pre-trial dispositive motions;

(4) the scheduling of a pre-trial conference; and

(5) any other matters which the parties or the court have seen fit to address.

C.　Mandatory Pre–Trial Conference. A pre-trial conference shall be held in every civil plenary and civil tort action, at which each party shall be represented by the attorney who will conduct the trial.

The parties shall exchange written lists of witnesses and photocopies of exhibits, together with contentions and statements of issues of fact and law, at least thirty (30) days prior to the pre-trial conference. Counsel for the plaintiff shall prepare a proposed pre-trial order, which shall be executed by counsel for all parties and filed not later than five (5) days prior to the pre-trial conference. The pre-trial stipulation shall set forth in the following sequence:

(1) the jurisdiction of the court;

(2) the pleadings raising the issues;

(3) a list of motions or other matters requiring action by the court;

(4) a concise statement of stipulated facts, with reservations, if any;

(5) a concise statement of issues of fact which remain to be litigated;

(6) a concise statement of issues of law which remain for determination by the court;

(7) the plaintiff's contentions;

(8) the defendant's contentions;

(9) the plaintiff's numbered list of trial exhibits;

(10) the defendant's numbered list of trial exhibits;

(11) the plaintiff's numbered list of trial witnesses, with addresses. Expert witnesses shall be so designated;

(12) the defendant's numbered list of trial witnesses, with addresses. Expert witnesses shall be so designated; and

(13) the estimated length of trial.

When, for any reason, the pre-trial stipulation is not executed by all counsel, each shall file not later than five (5) days prior to the pre-trial conference a written statement of the reason therefor accompanied with a proposed pre-trial stipulation.

D.　Pre–Trial Order. At the conclusion of the pre-trial conference, the court shall render a pre-trial order which, when entered, shall control the course of the trial and may not be amended except by order of the court to prevent manifest injustice.

E.　Memoranda of Law. Memoranda of law, addressing any unusual questions of law, shall be filed and served no later than seven (7) days prior to trial.

F.　Proposed Jury Instructions. Proposed preliminary and final jury instructions shall be filed and served no later than seven (7) days prior to trial. Instructions covering issues arising at trial which could not reasonably be anticipated may be submitted during the trial. Each instruction shall be accompanied by citations of authority.

G.　Sanctions. A failure of the parties or their attorneys to be prepared for the initial status conference, for the pre-trial conference, or to otherwise comply with this Rule, shall subject them to sanctions under Trial Rule 16(K).

Adopted effective Jan. 1, 1993. Amended effective Dec. 5, 2006.

LR 45–TR40 Rule 10.　TRIAL SETTINGS

Except for those set by the pre-trial order, all cases shall be set for trial by the court upon motion preceded by good faith effort of the parties to agree to the date thereof.

Adopted effective Jan. 1, 1993. Amended effective Dec. 5, 2006.

LR 45–TR6 Rule 11.　BRIEFS

Briefs, other than those addressed in Rules 4 and 9 hereof, shall be filed no later than two (2) calendar days preceding the hearing or trial to which directed.

Adopted effective Jan. 1, 1993. Amended effective Dec. 5, 2006.

LR 45–TR43 Rule 12. EXHIBITS

All exhibits offered or admitted into evidence shall be placed in the custody of the Court Reporter unless otherwise ordered. No earlier than three (3) years after the date of trial, they may be obtained by the parties offering them. A detailed receipt shall be left with the Court Reporter. No earlier than forty-two (42) months after the date of trial, the Court Reporter shall, upon order of the court, dispose of those exhibits unclaimed.

Adopted effective Jan. 1, 1993. Amended effective Dec. 5, 2006.

LR 45–TR63 Rule 13. COURTS

Whenever the presiding judge in any Room of the Civil Division of the Superior Court is absent or otherwise unavailable, and there is no judge pro tempore or temporary judge sitting in his stead, cases docketed in that Room may be submitted to any other judge of the Civil Division then available.

Adopted effective Jan. 1, 1993. Amended effective Dec. 5, 2006.

LR 45–TR75 Rule 14. EN BANC COURT

In the event the Civil Division is called upon to sit en banc, the following rules shall apply:

A. The judge of the court in which the action is filed shall serve as the presiding judge for all proceedings.

B. A majority of the Civil Division judges shall constitute a quorum sufficient to conduct en banc proceedings.

C. Oral arguments will not be heard on any matter without court approval.

D. In the event of an emergency, the presiding judge, or if the presiding judge is unavailable, any of the remaining judges, may hear and determine the matter until en banc action may be taken.

Adopted effective Jan. 1, 1993. Amended effective Dec. 5, 2006.

LR 45–TR79 Rule 15. APPOINTMENT OF SPECIAL JUDGE

A. If a motion for change of Judge is granted in a case or an order of disqualification is entered in a case, and a special judge is not appointed and qualified as provided in Trial Rule 79(D), (E) or (F), a special judge shall be appointed from the attached lists of eligible persons on a rotating basis.

B. Each eligible person shall have the option to be removed from or remain on the attached lists or, if omitted, the option to be added to said lists.

C. This rule shall have no application to the selection of a special judge in a Post Conviction Relief petition. The rules of Criminal Procedure and the Local Rules of the Lake Superior Court, Criminal Division, shall apply in said instance.

D. The lists of eligible persons shall be maintained in the office of the Lake Superior Court Administrator (Administrator). When it becomes necessary to select a special judge from said lists, the following procedure shall be followed:

1. The judge who submitted the panel from which the special judge did not accept the appointment shall immediately contact the Administrator for the name of the next available person. The Administrator shall provide a name from the attached lists on a rotating basis beginning with the first name on the list for the particular case category.

2. The selected person appointed to serve under this local rule must accept jurisdiction unless disqualified under circumstances set out in the Rules of Trial Procedure 79(H). The order of appointment by the regular judge shall constitute acceptance. An oath or additional evidence of acceptance is not required.

Case Designation–PL	Case Designation–MH
Judge Dywan	Judge Arredondo
Judge Davis	Judge Dywan
Judge Svetanoff	Judge Davis
Judge Pera	Judge Svetanoff
Judge Schneider	Judge Pera
Judge Hawkins	Judge Cantrell
Judge Cantrell	Judge Schneider
Magistrate Pagano	Judge Hawkins
Judge Tavitas	Magistrate Pagano
Magistrate Hill	
Magistrate Raduenz	

Case Designation—CT	Case Designation—PO
Judge Arredondo	Judge Davis
Judge Dywan	Judge Pera
Judge Davis	Judge Schneider
Judge Svetanoff	Judge Cantrell
Judge Pera	Judge Hawkins
Judge Schneider	Judge Tavitas
Judge Hawkins	Magistrate Hill
Judge Tavitas	Magistrate Raduenz
Magistrate Hill	Judge Villalpando
Magistrate Raduenz	Magistrate Pagano
Judge Cantrell	
Magistrate Pagano	

Case Designation–SC	Case Designation–EU/GU/TR
Judge Davis	Judge Schneider
Judge Hawkins	Judge Hawkins
Judge Cantrell	Judge Tavitas
Magistrate Pagano	Magistrate Hill
	Magistrate Raduenz
	Judge Pera

Case Designation—JP	Case Designation—MI
Judge Hawkins	Judge Dywan
Judge Tavitas	Judge Pera
	Judge Schneider

Judge Hawkins
Judge Tavitas
Magistrate Hill
Magistrate Raduenz
Judge Arredondo
Judge Cantrell
Magistrate Pagano

Case Designation—AD/AH	Case Designation—JD/JS/JM
Judge Schneider	Judge Hawkins
Judge Hawkins	Judge Tavitas
Judge Tavitas	Magistrate Pagano
Magistrate Raduenz	Judge Cantrell
Judge Pera	

Case Designation—DR	Case Designation—JC/JT
Judge Hawkins	Judge Tavitas
Judge Tavitas	
Magistrate Hill	
Magistrate Raduenz	

Case Designation–MF	Case Designation–CC
Judge Schneider	Judge Schneider
Judge Hawkins	Judge Hawkins
Judge Svetanoff	Judge Tavitas
Judge Davis	Magistrate Hill
Judge Pera	Judge Davis
Judge Dywan	Judge Pera
Judge Cantrell	Judge Dywan
Magistrate Pagano	Judge Arredondo
	Judge Villalpando
	Judge Cantrell
	Magistrate Pagano

CCS ENTRY FORM

LAKE SUPERIOR COURT   )
ROOM NUMBER THREE   )

CAUSE NO:

CAPTION:

The activity of the Court should be summarized as follows on the Chronological Case Summary (CCS):

ATTORNEY FOR: ATTORNEY FOR:
PETITIONER   RESPONDENT

* * * * * * * * * * * *
(TO BE DESIGNATED BY THE COURT)
THIS ENTRY FORM SHALL BE:
{ } PLACED IN CASE FILE
{ } DISCARD AFTER ENTRY ON THE CCS
{ } MAILED TO ALL COUNSEL BY: ___ COUNSEL ___
CLERK ___ COURT
{ } THERE IS NO ATTACHED ORDER; OR THE AT-
TACHED ORDER SHALL BE PLACED IN THE RJO:
{ } YES { } NO
DATE: _____   APPROVED: _____

Adopted effective Jan. 1, 1993. Amended effective Jan. 23, 1996; May 21, 1997; Jan. 27, 1999; Oct. 2, 2000; Oct. 4, 2005; Jan. 9, 2006; Sept. 29, 2006; Dec. 5, 2006; Jan. 1, 2009; Jan. 1, 2011; Oct. 4, 2012; Oct. 18, 2013.

LR 45–A.R.9 (G)(1) Rule 16.   CONFIDENTIAL IN-FORMATION AND SEALED DOCUMENTS

Pursuant to Trial Rule 81, the Superior Court of Lake County and the Lake Circuit Court hereby adopt this rule regarding the filing and retention of documents containing information which is excluded from public access under Administrative Rule 9 or which are governed by an order for the sealing of records.

A. Cases Subject to Rule for Electronic Filing and Service.

1. Documents containing information excluded from public access pursuant to Administrative Rule 9, or documents which are ordered to be filed under seal shall be filed electronically, pursuant to L.R.45–A.R.16–17(D)(9), whenever possible, along with a copy of the applicable order to seal the records, and the filer shall designate the documents as "Not for Public Access Pursuant to Administrative Rule 9(G)(1)" at the time of filing.

2. Documents containing information excluded from public access pursuant to Administrative Rule 9, or documents which are ordered to be filed under seal, which cannot be legibly scanned and filed electronically, shall be conventionally filed under seal and designated by the filer as "Not for Public Access Pursuant to Administrative Rule 9(G)(1)" at the time of filing. The unredacted version shall be filed on light green paper which is conspicuously marked "Not for Public Access"; and a redacted version, with confidential information deleted, shall be filed on white paper which shall be available for public access. The filer shall also electronically file a Notice of Manual Filing.

B. Cases Not Subject to Rule for Electronic Filing and Service.

Documents containing information excluded from public access pursuant to Administrative Rule 9, or documents which are ordered to be filed under seal, shall be conventionally filed under seal and designated by the filer as "Not for Public Access Pursuant to Administrative Rule 9(G)(1)" at the time of filing. The unredacted version shall be filed on light green paper which is conspicuously marked "Not for Public Access"; and a redacted version, with confidential information deleted, shall be filed on white paper which shall be available for public access.

C. The clerk shall maintain all sealed and "Not For Public Access" documents, whether in electronic or paper format, as required by Administrative Rule 9.

D. Attorneys or others who violate the rules regarding the filing of documents containing information excluded from public access shall, after a hearing, be subject to appropriate sanctions by the court having jurisdiction over the case in which the documents were filed in violation of the rules. Any person may petition the court with jurisdiction over the case for the imposition of sanctions, or the court may act *sua sponte*.

Adopted effective Jan. 1, 2011.

LR 45–A.R.16 Rule 17.   ELECTRONIC FILING AND SERVICE

Pursuant to Administrative Rule 16 and Trial Rule 77, the Superior Court of Lake County and the Lake Circuit Court, are authorized to establish practices and procedures for the filing, signing, verification and service of pleadings and papers, and sending notices, by electronic means. The judges and the clerk of the Superior Court of Lake County and the Lake Circuit Court have determined that an electronic filing system would advance efficiency in the Clerk's offices and the courts, and that members of the public and bar would be well served by such a system. Pursuant to Trial Rule 81 and Administrative Rule 16, the Superior Court of Lake County and Lake Circuit Court hereby adopt these rules establishing an electronic filing and service system in Lake County by using the Lake County Online Docket (LCOD) to file documents in the court's case management system, CourtView, and to serve the documents upon other persons in a case. The electronic filing and service system shall be designed, constructed, and maintained so as to function in compliance with Administrative Rules 6, 7, 9, and 16.

A.   Application. Unless otherwise ordered, these rules apply to all documents submitted for filing, no matter when the case was originally filed, according to the following schedule:

1.   For all cases in Case Type MF in the Circuit Court and all Rooms of the Civil Division commencing on February 1, 2010.

2.   For all cases in Case Type CC, PL, CT, MF, and MI in Rooms 2 and 3 of the County Division, in the Circuit Court and all Rooms of the Civil Division commencing July 16, 2012, and cases in Case Type CC commencing September 1, 2013 in County Division Room 4.

3.   Other case types and/or courts may be added to become subject to these electronic filing rules. Any additions will be made upon at least sixty (60) days advance notice which shall be published in the offices of the Clerk of the Circuit and Superior Courts and on the Lake County Online Docket.

B.   Official Record. The official record of the court for all documents filed under these rules is the electronic record maintained by the clerk. The clerk shall establish an electronic Record of Judgments and Orders as provided by Trial Rule 77(D).

C.   Registered Users. Attorneys admitted to practice before the Supreme Court of Indiana (including those admitted *pro hac vice*) may register as users of the LCOD. A *pro se* litigant may elect to register as a user for the limited purpose of utilizing the electronic filing and service features for purposes of

his or her case. Registrants will be issued a login and password upon fulfilling the registration requirements for the LCOD. *Pro se* registrants shall not knowingly permit or cause to permit their password to be used by anyone other than themselves. Attorney registrants shall not knowingly permit or cause to permit the password to be used by anyone other than an authorized agent of the registrant. Registered users will be assessed fees in accordance with the Schedule of Fees and Charges. Registered users are bound by the Registered User Agreement, which is posted on the LCOD, and registration also constitutes the following:

1.   The registrant's consent to receive service and/or notice electronically and a waiver of the right to receive service and/or notice by personal delivery or first class mail, including notice of the entry of an order or judgment under Trial Rule 72, except with regard to documents which are excluded from electronic filing, or service of a summons and complaint, or other legal process which is required by law to be served under Trial Rules 4—4.17.

2.   An affirmation that the registrant will endeavor to file all documents electronically.

3.   The registrant is responsible for all transactions under his or her password and is obligated to notify the Web Administrator if his or her password is compromised.

D.   Electronic Filing of Documents. Unless otherwise permitted by these rules or otherwise authorized by the judicial officer assigned to a particular case, all documents submitted for filing (including the original complaint, or equivalent pleading, and summons) shall be filed electronically with the clerk using the LCOD, no matter when the case was originally filed. The LCOD may be accessed via any Internet connection available to the registered user and at public access terminals located in the offices of the clerk. Attorneys who wish to be exempted from the requirement that they file electronically may file a Petition for Electronic Filing Exemption and an *Electronic Filing Technical Requirements Questionnaire*, which must be filed in each pending case to which these rules are applicable. The petition will be reviewed by the judicial officer assigned to that particular case and granted only upon a showing of good cause. The *Electronic Filing Technical Requirements Questionnaire* is appended hereto as Form 1.

1.   *Format.* Electronically filed documents must meet the same requirements of format as documents Aconventionally filed@ pursuant to L.R.45–T.R.10–2 or other applicable Local Rule(s).

2.   *Appearance.* Electronic filing of a Notice of Appearance shall act to establish the filing attorney as an attorney of record representing a designated party in a particular case.

3.   *Titles of Documents.* The person electronically filing a document will be responsible for desig-

nating a title for the document at the time it is filed. The LCOD will generate the appropriate entry onto the CCS to record the filing of the document.

4. *Chronological Case Summary Entry Forms (CCS Entry Forms).* Separate CCS Entry Forms shall not be submitted. The LCOD shall make an appropriate entry upon the CCS whenever any document is filed electronically.

5. *Citations and Hyperlinks.* Electronically filed documents may contain hyperlink references to an external document as a convenient mechanism for accessing material cited in the document. Filers wishing to insert hyperlinks into documents shall continue to use the traditional method of citation to authority in addition to the hyperlink provided. The hyperlink is merely a convenience to the court and the material referenced is extraneous to the file and not a part of the court's record.

6. *Attachments and Exhibits.* All documents which form part of a single submission and which are being filed at the same time and by the same filer may be electronically filed together under one document filing, e.g., the motion, supporting affidavits, memorandum in support, designation of evidence, exhibits.

Large documents which do not exist in an electronic format shall be scanned into .pdf format and filed electronically as separate attachments. A scanner is available in each clerk's office for use by the public and the bar in scanning and saving image files if needed.

7. *Filings Requiring Leave of Court.* In order to file a document which requires leave of court, such as an amended pleading or a document to be filed late, the proposed document shall be attached as an exhibit to a motion.

8. *Form Orders.* Proposed orders, which are submitted for the court's convenience under L.R.45–T.R.5–3 or other applicable Local Rule(s), shall be submitted as attachments to motions.

9. *Confidential Documents.* Documents containing information excluded from public access under Administrative Rule 9, or governed by an order for the sealing of records, which can be filed electronically shall be designated by the filer as "Not for Public Access Pursuant to Administrative Rule 9(G)(1)" at the time of filing on the LCOD. The LCOD shall permit only the Judge, the clerk, and attorneys or parties in a particular case to view the confidential documents in the case. Such confidential documents or information shall be served upon the parties in accordance with the applicable Indiana Rules of Court and local rules for filing and service. The Judge may permit additional persons to view the confidential documents in a case pursuant to Administrative Rule 9(I).

E. Conventional Filing of Documents. A conventionally filed document is one presented to the clerk or to a party in paper or other nonelectronic, tangible format. Unless specifically authorized by the court, only the following documents may be filed conventionally and not electronically:

1. *Exhibits And Other Documents That Cannot Be Converted To A Legible Electronic Form, Such as Videotapes, X–Rays, and Similar Materials.* Whenever possible, the filer is responsible for converting filings to an electronic form. If electronic filing is not possible, the filer shall electronically file a *Notice of Manual Filing* as a notation to be placed on the CCS that filings are being held in the clerk's office in paper. The filer shall serve the *Notice of Manual Filing* and the documents in accordance with the Indiana Rules of Civil Procedure and applicable Local Rule(s); and shall file a certificate of service. A *Notice of Manual Filing* form is appended hereto as Form 2; a *Certificate of Service* form is appended hereto as Form 3.

2. *Documents Delivered To The Clerk By Pro Se Litigants.* Documents filed by *pro se* litigants who have not elected to become registered users may be presented in the clerk's office for filing. Such documents shall then be converted to an image document by the clerk. The clerk shall thereupon electronically file and serve such documents upon each registered user of record in that case; and, the filer shall also conventionally serve these documents upon opposing attorneys or parties who are not registered users in accordance with the Indiana Rules of Civil Procedure and applicable Local Rule(s); and, shall also file a certificate of service. After completion of scanning and filing, the original paper documents shall remain in the custody of the *pro se* litigant who has not elected to become a registered user.

If the original documents cannot be scanned into a legible electronic document, then the originals shall be placed into the case file and a notation of that action shall be placed onto the CCS; and, the filer shall also conventionally serve these documents in accordance with the Indiana Rules of Civil Procedure and applicable Local Rule(s); and, shall also file a certificate of service.

3. *Documents Mailed To The Clerk By Pro Se Litigants.* Documents received by the clerk in the mail from *pro se* litigants who have not elected to become registered users shall be scanned and electronically filed by the clerk. The clerk shall thereupon serve such documents upon each registered user of record in that case; and, the filer shall also conventionally serve these documents in accordance with the Indiana Rules of Civil Procedure and applicable Local Rule(s); and, shall also file a certificate of service. After scanning, the originals shall be returned to the filer, if a return envelope is provided. If no return envelope is provided, the original documents shall be discarded.

If the original documents cannot be scanned into a legible electronic document, then the originals shall be placed into the case file and a notation of that action shall be placed onto the CCS. The filer shall also conventionally serve these documents in accordance with the Indiana Rules of Civil Procedure and applicable Local Rule(s); and, shall also file a certificate of service.

4. *Confidential Documents.* Documents containing information excluded from public access under Administrative Rule 9, or governed by an order for the sealing of records, which cannot be legibly scanned and filed electronically, shall be conventionally filed under seal and designated by the filer as "Not for Public Access Pursuant to Administrative Rule 9(G)(1). " Only the Judge, the clerk, and attorneys or parties in a particular case may view the confidential documents in the case. The Judge may permit additional persons to view the confidential documents in a case pursuant to Administrative Rule 9(I). Such confidential documents or information shall be served upon the parties in accordance with the applicable Indiana Rules of Court and local rules for filing and service of conventional documents.

5. *Notice of Manual Filing.* Parties making a conventional filing shall file electronically, in place of the conventionally filed document, a Notice of Manual Filing setting forth the reasons why the document could not be filed electronically. The conventionally filed documents must be presented to the clerk within 24 hours after the electronic submission of the Notice of Manual Filing. A paper copy of the electronically filed Notice of Manual Filing must accompany the component at the time of conventional filing.

6. *Titles of Documents.* The person conventionally filing a document will be responsible for designating a title for the document at the time it is filed.

7. *Chronological Case Summary Entry Forms (CCS Entry Forms).* Separate CCS Entry Forms shall not be submitted. The clerk shall make an appropriate entry upon the CCS whenever any document is filed conventionally.

F. Service of Documents.

1. *Service of Process.* A party may not electronically serve a summons or other process and complaint or equivalent pleading, but instead must perfect service according to Trial Rules 4 B 4.17.

a. Service by Sheriff. The copies of the complaint or equivalent pleading and summons or other process, or any other documents such as an order to appear, necessary for service by sheriff shall be printed by the office of the clerk. The copies of the complaint and summons, or other documents, shall be forwarded to the sheriff for service and return. The clerk shall scan and electronically file the return of service and the paper original may then be discarded.

b. Service by Certified Mail—Initial Summons for a Defendant. If a plaintiff does not request service by sheriff, the clerk will upon request electronically issue a summons for service by certified mail, and the initial summons to be served upon a defendant will be printed and served by certified mail by the clerk. The clerk shall scan and electronically file the return receipt or notice of unsuccessful service when received by return mail, and the paper original may then be discarded.

c. Service by Certified Mail—Additional Summons or Other Process after Initial Service. The clerk will electronically issue any additional summons or other process requested for service by certified mail or special process server, and the summons or other process will be printed and served by certified mail by the party or attorney requesting the documents to issue, or by the special process server appointed for that purpose. The party or attorney shall scan and electronically file the certificate of mailing and/or service, and the return receipt or notice of unsuccessful service when received by return mail, and retain the original documents.

2. *Service of Other Documents.* The LCOD will generate a Notice of Electronic Filing and Service when any document is filed and served. This notice will be emailed to each registered user of record in a case, and an electronic service event will be added to the work queue of each registered user of record in the case. The party filing the document should retain a paper or electronic copy of the Notice of Electronic Filing and Service. This notice represents proof of filing and service of the document on registered users of record in that case. The filer shall not be required to conventionally serve any document on any party receiving electronic service.

The filer shall also conventionally serve those parties not designated or able to receive electronic notice or service but who are nevertheless entitled to notice of said pleading or other document in accordance with the Indiana Rules of Civil Procedure and applicable Local Rule(s). In such cases, the filer shall also file a certificate of service, as appropriate.

G. Signatures.

1. *Signature of Registered User.* The electronic filing of a document which is required to be signed shall constitute the filer's representation under Trial Rule 11. Unless the electronically filed document has been scanned and shows the filer's original signature, the signature of the filer shall be indicated by As/Attorney's Name, or As/Party's Name as in the case of a *pro se* litigant, on the line where the signature would otherwise appear.

2. *Signatures on Jointly Signed or Filed, Verified or Other Documents.* In the case of a stipulation, agreed order, jointly signed motion or other document which needs to be signed by two (2) or more persons, or in the case of documents which must contain original signatures and which require verification or an unsworn declaration under rule or statute, the signatures may be indicated by either:

a. submitting a scanned copy of the originally signed document; or,

b. submitting the document with the use of As/Name in the signature block(s) where the original signature(s) appear(s) in the original document; provided, however, that the filer shall first obtain the physical signature of all persons necessary.

The filer shall retain the original executed document.

H. Orders and Judgments. All orders and judgments shall be entered or filed electronically by a judicial officer assigned to the case.

1. *Administrative Entries.* The judicial officer may direct the issuance of administrative entries which are routine in nature (e.g., setting or continuing dates) by way of a text entry upon the Chronological Case Summary (CCS). In such a case, the signature of the judicial officer is not required, no further document will issue and the CCS entry shall indicate that the court will issue no further written order.

2. *All Other Orders and Judgments.* In all other cases, unless the original document has been scanned and shows the signature(s) of the judicial officer(s), the signature(s) of the judicial officer(s) shall be indicated by As/Judicial Officer's Name on the line where the signature(s) would otherwise appear; and, shall carry the same weight and authority as a written order signed by the judicial officer(s). Judicial officers shall not knowingly permit or cause to permit their passwords to be used by anyone other than an agent authorized in writing by the judicial officer. Such written authorization, or a revocation of such authorization, shall be filed with the clerk. Whenever appropriate, the clerk shall place a hardcopy version of any designated order or judgment in the Court's Record of Judgments and Orders, pursuant to Trial Rule 77(D).

3. *Service.* The LCOD will generate a "Notice of Electronic Filing and Service" when any order is filed and served. This notice will be emailed to each registered user of record in a case, and an electronic service event will be added to the work queue of each registered user of record in the case. This notice represents proof of filing and service of the order on registered users of record in that case. All other parties or attorneys of record will be served with a hardcopy version by first class mail in accordance with the provisions of Trial Rule 72(D).

I. Time of Filing. Filing electronically does not alter any filing deadlines or any time computation pursuant to state or federal statutes, any Rules of the Indiana Supreme Court, including without limitation the Rules of Trial Procedure, the Rules of Appellate Procedure or the Administrative Rules, or applicable Local Rule(s). The office of the Lake County Clerk is open for electronic filing under these rules 24 hours a day. A document is deemed filed at the date and time it is received by the LCOD server. Filing must be completed before midnight local time in order to be considered filed that day. Lake County observes Central Time and electronic filers are strongly urged to file documents during hours when the LCOD help line is available, from 9:00 a.m. to 4:00 p.m. local time, although documents can be filed electronically 24 hours a day.

In the event of complete failure of the LCOD to accept documents from all electronic filers for a period of in excess of three (3) hours, as determined by the Web Administrator, any filing deadlines which expire on the date of such failure, in cases subject to electronic filing, shall be extended until 6:00 p.m. of the first day on which the court is open for business following the day the LCOD returns to operation. The date, time and duration of such complete failure, as well as the time and date of the return to operation, shall be posted on the LCOD as soon as possible.

J. Technical Failures. If a registered user is unable to file a document in a timely manner due to technical difficulties in the LCOD, the registered user must file a document with the court as soon as possible notifying the court of the inability to file the document. A sample document titled *Declaration that Party was Unable to File in a Timely Manner Due to Technical Difficulties* is attached hereto as Form 4. Delayed filings shall be rejected unless accompanied by the declaration attesting to the filer's failed attempts to file electronically at least two times, separated by at least one hour, after noon on each day of delay due to such technical failure.

K. Retention of Documents in Electronically Filed Cases. Registered users must retain signed copies of electronically filed documents until two (2) years after all time periods for appeals expire. Documents that are electronically filed and require original signatures other than that of the registered user must be maintained in paper form. On request of the court, the registered user must provide original documents for review.

Originals of documents filed electronically which require scanning (*e.g.* documents that contain signatures, such as affidavits) must be retained by the filer and made available, upon request, to the court and other parties for a period of two (2) years following the expiration of all time periods for appeals.

The clerk shall maintain all filed documents in accordance with the Administrative Rules 6 and 7 and all other applicable law.

L. Fees and Charges. The clerk shall collect all filing and electronic system fees due at the time of the commencement of a case or appearance in a case. Persons who have been determined by court order to be indigent in a case shall not be required to pay fees for electronic filing or service in that case. In the case of registered users, all fees due shall be collected via a credit card charge to each registered user's designated credit card at the time of filing.

Conventional copies and certified copies of documents may be purchased at the offices of the clerk during regular business hours and upon payment of the customary copying fees prescribed by law.

The fees so collected shall be collected, maintained, and accounted for pursuant to Lake County Ordinance and all existing procedures as approved by the Indiana State Board of Accounts.

M. Public Access to the LCOD. Remote access to documents filed through the LCOD via the Internet shall only be available to registered users. Other individuals shall have access only at terminals located in each of the offices of the clerk, during regular business hours.

Access to documents that are confidential as provided by Adm. R. 9 shall be restricted as required by that rule.

Adopted effective Jan. 1, 2011. Amended effective Oct. 4, 2012; Oct. 18, 2013.

APPENDIX A. CCS ENTRY FORM

CIRCUIT/SUPERIOR COURT OF LAKE COUNTY

Case No.:

Title of Case:

The activity of the Court should be summarized as follows on the Chronological Case Summary (CCS):

Attorney for Plaintiff: **Attorney for Defendant:**

_____

(TO BE DESIGNATED BY THE COURT)

This CCS Entry Form shall be:

( ) Placed in case file

( ) Discarded after entry on the CCS

( ) Mailed to all counsel by: ___ Counsel ___ Clerk ___ Court

( ) There is no attached Order; or

            The attached Order shall be placed in the RJO: ___ Yes ___ No

       Date: Approved: _____

Adopted effective May 29, 1997. Amended effective Dec. 5, 2006; Jan. 1, 2011.

FORM 1. ELECTRONIC FILING TECHNICAL REQUIREMENTS QUESTIONNAIRE

SUPERIOR COURT OF LAKE COUNTY AND LAKE CIRCUIT COURT
ELECTRONIC FILING TECHNICAL REQUIREMENTS QUESTIONNAIRE

1. Have you attended or would you be able to attend (in person or by phone) a free, 90–minute e-filing training session conducted by the Administrator?

    Yes ☐   No ☐

2. Does your office have at least one computer running on a Windows or Macintosh operating system?

    Yes ☐   No ☐

    Please indicate the operating system(s) installed on your computer(s): _____

    (For example, Windows 98, Windows XP, Windows Vista, Mac OS10, etc.)

3. Does your office have word processing software to create court- filed documents (e.g., Microsoft Word or Corel WordPerfect)?

    Yes ☐   No ☐

4. Does your office have Internet access via a 56K modem or faster?

    Yes ☐   No ☐

    If so, please indicate the type of Internet connection used in your office, dial-up or broadband. _____

5. Does your office have at least one e-mail account?

    Yes ☐   No ☐

6. Have you ever filed a Petition for E-filing Exemption in any other cases in the Lake Superior Court or Lake Circuit Court?

    Yes ☐   No ☐

    If so, please provide the case number(s):

    Case Number(s): _____

    Note: All questions above must be answered and attached to each Petition for E-filing Exemption before the Petition will be considered.

If you have any questions about these requirements, please contact the Lake County Online Docket Administrator at 219–755–3635.

Adopted effective Jan. 1, 2011.

FORM 2. NOTICE OF MANUAL FILING

STATE OF INDIANA   )

IN THE LAKE CIRCUIT/SUPERIOR COURT   )

COUNTY OF LAKE   ) SS:

_____,   )

Plaintiff(s),   )

v.   ) CASE NO. _____

)

_____,   )

Defendant(s).   )

NOTICE OF MANUAL FILING

_____ is in paper form only and is being maintained in the case file in the Clerk's Office.

_____

Attorney for (Plaintiff or Defendant) *or*

Name of *pro se* litigant

Address: _____

_____

_____

Date: _____

Adopted effective Jan. 1, 2011.

FORM 3.   CERTIFICATE OF SERVICE

STATE OF INDIANA   )

IN THE LAKE CIRCUIT/SUPERIOR COURT   )

COUNTY OF LAKE   ) SS:

_____,   )

Plaintiff(s),   )

v.   ) CASE NO. _____

)

_____,   )

Defendant(s).   )

CERTIFICATE OF SERVICE

I hereby certify that on ___(date)__ I

(a) electronically filed the foregoing document(s) with the Clerk of the Court using the Lake County Online Docket Electronic Filing System which sent notification of such filing to the following parties or attorneys who are registered for electronic filing and service in the case: _____, *or*

(b) I conventionally filed the foregoing document(s) with the Clerk of the Court. I hereby certify that I have mailed copies of the document(s)by United States Postal Service to the following parties or attorneys who are not registered for electronic filing in this case: _____.

Dated: _____   _____

Adopted effective Jan. 1, 2011.

FORM 4. DECLARATION THAT PARTY WAS UNABLE TO FILE IN A TIMELY MANNER

STATE OF INDIANA   )

IN THE LAKE CIRCUIT/SUPERIOR COURT   )

COUNTY OF LAKE   ) SS:

_____,   )

Plaintiff(s),   )

v.   ) CASE NO. _____

)

_____,   )

Defendant(s).   )

DECLARATION THAT PARTY WAS UNABLE
TO FILE IN A TIMELY MANNER

Please take notice that _____ was unable to file _____ in a timely manner due to technical difficulties. The deadline for filing the _____ was _____. The reason(s) that I was unable to file the _____ in a timely manner and the good faith efforts I made prior to the filing deadline to both file in a timely manner and to inform the Court and the other parties that I could not do so are set forth below.

[Statement of reasons and good faith efforts to file and to inform]

I declare under penalty of perjury that the foregoing is true and correct.

s/[Name of Password Registrant]

Name of Password Registrant

Address

City, State, Zip Code

Phone: XXX–XXX–XXXX

Fax: XXX–XXX–XXXX

E-mail: XXX@XXX.XXX

Adopted effective Jan. 1, 2011.

LAKE COUNTY ALTERNATIVE DISPUTE RESOLUTION RULES

Adopted Effective January 1, 1993

Including Amendments Received Through November 1, 2013

Research Notes

Annotations to the Lake County Alternative Dispute Resolution Rules are available in West's Annotated Indiana Code, *Title 34 Appendix.*

These rules may be searched electronically on Westlaw *in the* IN-RULES *database; updates to these rules may be found on* Westlaw *in* IN-RULESUPDATES. *For search tips and a summary of database content, consult the Westlaw Scope Screens for each database.*

LR 45–ADR2.2 Rule 1. APPLICATIONS AND LIST OF MEDIATORS

A. Any individual who fulfills the qualifications for mediator established by the Supreme Court of Indiana may submit an application to the circuit or any superior court to be placed upon the list of mediators. The application shall include the following information:

1. mediator's name, address and telephone number;

2. county of residence;

3. information about co-mediator if applicable;

4. type of cases which the mediator is competent to mediate;

5. any known limitations on referrals, such as disqualification because of marital relationship or employment, etc.;

6. statement of mediation training;

7. statement of professional background, including attorney number and date of admission to bar, and/or educational requirements for domestic mediation;

8. statement of use of effective conflicts-checking system;

9. such other information on background and mediation training relevant to the court's review of the application.

A sample form is provided as Appendix A.

B. The court shall review each application and determine the eligibility of the individual to be included on the list of mediators approved by the court.

1. The court administrator shall maintain a comprehensive list of all court-approved mediators for the county. A copy of the list of mediators shall be available to the public for inspection in the Office of the Clerk of Lake County.

2. The court administrator shall also maintain a comprehensive list of lawyers engaged in the practice of law in the county who are willing to serve as arbitrators. A copy of the list of arbitrators shall likewise be available to the public for inspection in the Office of the Clerk of Lake County.

Adopted as Rule A, effective Jan. 1, 1993. Renumbered as Rule 1, and amended effective Dec. 5, 2006.

LR 45–ADR2.7 Rule 2. CIVIL CASES

A. Definition. For the purposes of this rule, "alternative dispute resolution" and "ADR" shall mean mediation and/or mini-hearings. This rule does not affect the parties' rights to agree to arbitration as provided by the ADR Rules of the Supreme Court of Indiana.

B. Case Selection and Objections. The court may order the parties to mediation or mini-hearing upon the occurrence of any of the following:

1. Any party's written request for mediation or mini-hearing any time after the expiration of the fifteen (15) day period allowed for peremptory change of venue;

2. At any time following the filing of the claim for relief if all of the parties file a written stipulation therefor; or

3. More than ninety (90) days have elapsed since the initiation of the claim and the case has not been scheduled for a pretrial conference.

In determining whether a case is appropriate for a judicial referral to ADR, the court may consider such factors as:

(a) whether the case has been pending more than 180 days;

(b) whether a pretrial conference has been requested;

(c) whether the case is eligible for dismissal pursuant to TR 41(E);

(d) whether the case is set for trial.

C. Nothing in this rule shall be interpreted to constrain or otherwise limit the court from referring a case to ADR at such other time as the court deems appropriate.

D. Any party may object to an order for mediation or mini-hearing by filing a written objection specifying the grounds for the objection within fifteen (15) days of the date of the order referring the case to mediation or mini-hearing, as provided in ADR Rule 2.2. Any response to the objection must be filed within ten (10) days of the service of the objection.

E. Completion of Mediation. The mediator and the parties shall make a good faith effort to complete the mediation process within ninety (90) days from the date of the order to engage in ADR, unless specifically ordered otherwise. In the event mediation is not complete within that time, the mediator shall file a report with the court as to the current status of the mediation and the projected date of completion of the mediation.

If the mediation is complete, the mediator shall file the agreement and report as required by ADR Rule 2.7(E) within 15 days of completion of the mediation. However, if the parties agree, a party may file the agreement in place of the mediator. If a party is to file the agreement, that party shall be identified in the mediator's report.

F. Payment of the Mediator's Fees. Unless otherwise specifically set forth in the order referring the case to mediation, or unless otherwise agreed by the parties, the mediator's fees shall be paid in the following proportions:

one-third (1/3) by the plaintiff or plaintiffs;

one-third (1/3) by the defendant or defendants;

one-third (1/3) by the intervenor or third party.

In the case of multiple plaintiffs, defendants or intervenors, the mediator's fee shall be apportioned equally among the number of plaintiffs, defendants or intervenors, unless they shall agree otherwise.

G. Written Agreements. All agreements which resolve issues shall be reduced to writing and signed by all parties and their counsel, and shall be submitted to the court with the mediator's report, or as soon thereafter as is practicable.

H. Parties to Attend. In all non-family cases, the attorney(s) who will try the case and the parties shall attend the mediation conference. A corporate party shall send a corporate representative with full authority to settle the case. If insurance is involved in the matter, the insurance carrier shall send a company representative who has full and absolute authority to resolve the matter for an amount which is the lesser of the policy limits or the most recent demand of the adverse party.

Adopted as Rule B, effective Jan. 1, 1993. Amended effective Jan. 14, 2004; renumbered as Rule 1, and amended effective Dec. 5, 2006.

LR 45–ADR00 Rule 3. DOMESTIC RELATIONS CASES

A. Case Selection. In applying the Alternative Dispute Resolution Rules, mediation is the appropriate method of court-ordered dispute resolution in domestic relations cases.

B. Time for Filing Motions and Stipulations. Either party may file a motion for referral to mediation at any time during the pendency of the case, from the time of filing and thereafter until the final hearing. The parties may file a joint application for referral to mediation at any time during the pendency of the case.

1. In determining whether a case is appropriate for judicial referral to ADR, the court may consider such factors as:

. (a) whether the time for exchange of financial disclosure information has passed;

(b) when time for a contested hearing has been requested on the court's calendar;

(c) whether the case involves post-decree issues.

2. Nothing in this rule shall be interpreted to constrain or otherwise limit the court from referring a case to ADR at such other time as the court deems appropriate.

3. *Completion of Mediation.* The mediator and the parties shall make a good faith effort to complete the mediation process within sixty (60) days from the date of the order to engage in ADR. In the event that mediation is not complete within that time, the mediator shall file a report with the court as to the current status of the mediation and the projected date of completion of the mediation. If the mediation is complete, the mediator shall file the agreement and report as required by ADR Rule 2.7(E). However, if the parties so agree, a party may file the agreement separately, and that party shall be identified in the mediator's report.

The mediator's report shall also include the parties' agreement as to a date certain for filing their agreement.

4. *Payment of Mediator's Fees.* Unless otherwise specifically set forth in the order referring the case to mediation, or unless otherwise agreed by the parties prior to the mediation conference, the mediator's fees shall be paid in the following proportions:

one-half (1/2) by the petitioner;

one-half (1/2) by the respondent.

5. *Parties to Attend.* In domestic relations cases, the attendance of the parties' counsel is not required at every session. If counsel choose not to attend, they shall be given the opportunity to review and discuss any settlement proposal made at a mediation conference.

Adopted as Rule C, effective Jan. 1, 1993. Renumbered as Rule 3, and amended effective Dec. 5, 2006.

APPENDIX A.   MEDIATOR'S APPLICATION FOR CIVIL/DOMESTIC CASES

(strike one if necessary)

I, _____, hereby apply to be placed on the court's listing of mediators, and include the following information pursuant to ADR Rule 2.5:

1.   NAME AND ADDRESS.

Name: _____

Business address: _____

_____

Phone: _____

Resident of _____ County

2.   CO–MEDIATOR (check one).

This is not a joint application _____

This is a joint application _____

My co-mediator has also filed an application with the court, and his/her name is

_____

3.   TYPES OF CASES. In accordance with ADR Rule 2.3, I am applying to mediate the following types of cases:

CIVIL:

___ CONTRACT   ___ PROBATE
___ TORT   ___ PROPERTY
___ PROBATE   ___ OTHER (list)
___ all civil cases

DOMESTIC RELATIONS:

___ CHILD CUSTODY ONLY   ___ CHILD SUPPORT ONLY
___ PROPERTY DIVISION   ___ OTHER (list)
___ COMPLETE DIVORCE—NO CHILDREN
___ COMPLETE DIVORCE WITH CHILDREN

4.   LIMITATION ON REFERRALS I am unable to accept referrals pursuant to ADR Rule 2.5(A)(1) when one of the following attorneys is an attorney of record in the case, because I am employed by them OR related to them: _____.

5.   MEDIATION TRAINING I have completed the following total number of hours of mediation training:

CORE MEDIATION TRAINING I have attended a forty (40) hour minimum mediation training course certified as appropriate by the Indiana Commission for Continuing Legal Education.

Number of hours: _____

Dates of training: _____

Trainers: _____

Title of seminar: _____

Location of seminar: _____

Sponsor: _____

Such training was: _____ pre-certified by the commission; or _____ certified after the fact by the commission.

(Attach copy of certificate)

6.   PROFESSIONAL BACKGROUND:

CIVIL: I am an attorney in good standing in Indiana. I was admitted to the Indiana bar on _____, and my attorney number is _____.

DOMESTIC RELATIONS: I am an attorney in good standing in Indiana. I was admitted to the Indiana bar on _____, and my attorney number is _____.

AND/OR:

I have a bachelor's degree from the following accredited institution of higher learning:

degree earned: _____

Date conferred: ___ Major: ___ Other graduate degrees: _____

7.   CONFLICT–CHECKING SYSTEM I utilize an effective system to identify potential conflicts of interest, as required by ADR Rule 2.8.

8.   DOMESTIC MEDIATOR KNOWLEDGE REQUIREMENTS I have knowledge (or my mediation team has combined knowledge) of all of the following to the extent practicable, as required by ADR Rule 2.5(C)(2).   I personally have knowledge of the following:

___ Indiana judicial system

___ procedures used in domestic relations cases

___ community resources for client referral

___ stages of child development

___ clinical issues relating to children

___ the effects of divorce on children

___ family systems theory

9.   FEES

My fee or fee range for civil matters is _____.

_____

My fee or fee range for domestic matters is _____.

_____

Signature

_____

Date

(VERIFICATION)

Adopted effective Jan. 1, 1993.   Amended effective Dec. 5, 2006.

LAKE COUNTY LOCAL PROBATE RULES

Adopted Effective March 1, 1995

Including Amendments Received Through November 1, 2013

Research Notes

Annotations to the Lake County Local Probate Rules are available in West's Annotated Indiana Code, *Title 34 Appendix.*

These rules may be searched electronically on Westlaw *in the* IN-RULES *database; updates to these rules may be found on* Westlaw *in* IN-RULESUPDATES. *For search tips and a summary of database content, consult the Westlaw Scope Screens for each database.*

PROBATE FEE GUIDELINES AND RULES

INTRODUCTION

It is important that certain criteria be called to your attention as they pertain to Attorney and Personal Representative Fees.

The Attorney, and his or her Client, must consider these factors. The Court in making its determination as to the fees allowed will also consider the same.

The criteria to be considered include the following:

A. The time and labor required; the novelty, complexity, or difficulty of the questions involved; and, the skill required to perform the services properly;

This factor shall include a determination as to how much of the Attorney's time was devoted to legal matters and how much of it was devoted to ministerial functions.

B. The nature and extent of the responsibilities assumed by the Attorney and the results obtained;

Included herein are considerations such as the identity of the Personal Representative, and his/her level of expertise in administering an estate; the character of the probate assets; and the character of any non-probate assets transferred.

C. The sufficiency of assets properly available to pay for legal services;

Inherent herein is whether the Attorney's duties are expanded by the existence of non-probate assets because of their inclusion for tax purposes, both federal and state.

and

D. The timeliness with which the necessary services are performed consistent with statutory requirements, the Court's Rules of Procedure and the Rules of Professional Conduct applicable thereto.

In considering all of these factors, Attorneys are urged to discuss their fee and that of the Personal Representative or Guardian at the time they are retained in all Probate and Guardianship matters.

Adopted effective Jan. 1, 2009.

LAKE COUNTY RULES OF PROCEDURE APPLICABLE TO ESTATES

LR 45–PR00 Rule 1

All Probate rules and regulations promulgated by the Veterans Administration are hereby adopted as probate rules of the Court.

Adopted effective March 1, 1995. Amended effective Dec. 5, 2006.

LR 45–PR00 Rule 2

Probate matters must be transacted with the Probate Commissioner. Only emergency matters may be submitted to the presiding Judge. Telephone calls or visits to the Probate Commissioner's private office should be kept at a minimum.

Adopted effective March 1, 1995. Amended effective Dec. 5, 2006.

LR 45–PR00 Rule 3

Unless the Probate Clerk has sent the files to the Probate Commissioner, Attorneys must obtain files from the Probate Clerk prior to submitting any matter to the Probate Commissioner.

Adopted effective March 1, 1995. Amended effective Dec. 5, 2006; Jan. 1, 2009.

LR 45–PR00 Rule 4

All petitions, of any nature or kind, in all matters, must be executed and verified by the Personal Representative, the Trustee, or the Interested Party (Petitioner), and not by the Attorney.

Adopted effective March 1, 1995. Amended effective Dec. 5, 2006; Jan. 1, 2011.

LR 45–PR00 Rule 5

All Attorneys are required to prepare CCS Entry Forms showing each pleading filed, and setting forth all necessary matters for all proceedings.

Adopted effective March 1, 1995. Amended effective Dec. 5, 2006; Jan. 1, 2011.

LR 45–PR00 Rule 6

All Attorneys are required to prepare orders in a form approved by the Court (order per form or OPF) for all proceedings, except where expressly indicated to the contrary by the respective Probate Commissioner.

Adopted effective March 1, 1995. Amended effective Dec. 5, 2006; Jan. 1, 2009.

LR 45–PR00 Rule 7

Where matters are filed by mail, or left with the Court for filing, a self-addressed stamped envelope must be included for return of documents to the Attorney.

Adopted effective March 1, 1995. Amended effective Dec. 5, 2006.

LR 45–PR00 Rule 8

Routine matters, such as Inventories, Proofs of Publication, Inheritance Tax Returns, Affidavits of No Inheritance Tax Due, Closing Statements, and Final Reports, may be filed with the Probate Clerk for transmittal to the Probate Commissioner.

Adopted effective March 1, 1995. Amended effective Dec. 5, 2006; Jan. 1, 2009.

LR 45–PR00 Rule 9

Attorneys desiring to have the Court Reporter present for a hearing must make a written request for same ten (10) days in advance of the hearing. Hearings involving the Court Reporter shall be set subject to his or her availability.

Adopted effective March 1, 1995. Amended effective Dec. 5, 2006.

LR 45–PR00 Rule 10

Any contested matters scheduled for hearing on a probate day shall take precedence over unscheduled business; attorneys are encouraged to call the Court to find out when contested matters are routinely scheduled.

Adopted effective March 1, 1995. Amended effective Dec. 5, 2006; Jan. 1, 2009.

LR 45–PR00 Rule 11

The Attorney shall prepare any required notices and shall ensure that such notices are properly served in compliance with statutory requirements. The Attorney shall ascertain and provide adequate proof that notice was properly served prior to bringing a matter to the attention of the Probate Commissioner.

Adopted effective March 1, 1995. Amended effective Dec. 5, 2006; Jan. 1, 2009.

LR 45–PR00 Rule 12

Copies of petitions and accountings must be sent with all notices, where the hearing involved arises from the matters contained in the petition and/or accounting.

Adopted effective March 1, 1995. Amended effective Dec. 5, 2006.

LR 45–PR00 Rule 13

An inventory must be filed in all supervised estates within sixty (60) days after appointment of the Personal Representative. An inventory is not required to be filed in an unsupervised estate.

Adopted effective March 1, 1995. Amended effective Dec. 5, 2006; Amended effective Jan. 1, 2009.

LR 45–PR00 Rule 14

Attorneys must attend the hearings on current or final accounts on the date scheduled for such hearings. The Court may, in its discretion, require the attendance of the Personal Representative or Trustee at all such hearings.

Adopted effective March 1, 1995. Amended effective Dec. 5, 2006; Jan. 1, 2009.

LR 45–PR00 Rule 15

Unless otherwise ordered by the Court, all accountings to the Court shall be accompanied by an affidavit stating that receipts are available for disbursements contained in the accounting.

Adopted effective March 1, 1995. Amended effective Dec. 5, 2006; Jan. 1, 2009.

LR 45–PR00 Rule 16

Receipts for all final distributions must be filed with the final report or the supplemental report before discharge will be given by the Court.

Adopted effective March 1, 1995. Amended effective Dec. 5, 2006; Jan. 1, 2009.

LR 45–PR00 Rule 17

All accountings must follow the prescribed statutory format. Informal or handwritten accounting will not be accepted.

Adopted effective March 1, 1995. Amended effective Dec. 5, 2006; Jan. 1, 2009.

LR 45–PR00 Rule 18

The name and address of the Insurance Agency providing the corporate surety must be typed on all corporate bonds filed in any estate.

Adopted effective March 1, 1995. Amended effective Dec. 5, 2006; Jan. 1, 2009.

LR 45–PR00 Rule 19

In all contested matters, the Indiana Rules of Trial Procedure shall apply.

Adopted effective March 1, 1995. Amended effective Dec. 5, 2006; Jan. 1, 2009.

LR 45–PR00 Rule 20

In a supervised estate, any petition for the allowance of fees for the Attorney and/or the Personal Representative shall be set forth a description of the services performed and a calculation of the amount of the fee requested. At the time the petition is considered by the Court, the Attorney must be present. No fee request will be considered as a part of the final report or account in a supervised estate. A separate petition must be filed requesting such fee determination. No fee shall be paid without the prior approval of the Court. No Attorney or Personal Representative fees will be authorized for payment until the estate is substantially settled.

Adopted effective March 1, 1995. Amended effective Dec. 5, 2006; Jan. 1, 2009.

LR 45–PR00 Rule 21

Where contracts for legal services have been entered into prior or subsequent to the opening of, or conversion to, a supervised estate without prior Court approval, the Court reserves the right to approve or disapprove the fee contracts.

Adopted effective March 1, 1995. Amended effective Dec. 5, 2006; Jan. 1, 2009.

LR 45–PR00 Rule 22

Attorney and Personal Representative fees will not be determined or authorized for payment by the Court in an unsupervised estate.

Adopted effective March 1, 1995. Amended effective Dec. 5, 2006; Jan. 1, 2009.

LR 45–PR00 Rule 23

Unless otherwise stated in the decedent's Last Will and Testament, any Attorney or Personal Representative fees determined to be due by reason of non-probate assets shall be assessed against the recipients of the non-probate assets.

Adopted effective March 1, 1995. Amended effective Dec. 5, 2006; Jan. 1, 2009.

LR 45–PR00 Rule 24

All deeds submitted to the Court for approval must be signed by the Personal Representative and the signature notarized prior to its submission. Copies of such deeds must be filed for the Court records.

Adopted effective March 1, 1995. Amended effective Dec. 5, 2006; Jan. 1, 2009.

LR 45–PR00 Rule 25

In all wrongful death proceedings, the Personal Representative must be present at the time of the settlement, either partial and/or final, is presented to the Court for approval.

Adopted effective March 1, 1995. Amended effective Dec. 5, 2006; Jan. 1, 2009.

LR 45–PR00 Rule 26

All documents filed with the Court must comply with the requirements of Indiana Trial Rule 5(G) and Administrative Rule 9(G)(1).

Adopted effective March 1, 1995. Amended effective Dec. 5, 2006; Jan. 1, 2009.

LR 45–PR00 Rule 27

For good cause shown, the Court may waive any local procedural rule.

Adopted effective March 1, 1995. Amended effective Dec. 5, 2006.

LR 45–PR00 Rule 28

When required by law, all Wills must be admitted to Probate unless filed with the Clerk pursuant to Indiana Code 29–1–7–3.1, as amended.

Adopted as Probate Estate Rule 1, effective March 1, 1995. Renumbered as Probate Rule 28, and amended effective Dec. 5, 2006; Jan. 1, 2009.

LR 45–PR00 Rule 29

Bond procedures for Estates:

a. If the decedent's Will provides for no bond, the Court may honor the request unless otherwise required by statute;

b. If all heirs request no bond or a minimal bond, the Court may honor such request unless otherwise required by statute;

c. In all instances, upon petition by an interested person, the Court may require a bond to protect creditors, heirs, legatees, or devisees;

d. In all other situations, the Court will determine and set the amount of the bond and in no event shall it be less than that required to protect creditors and taxing authorities;

e. Personal surety must meet the requirements of Indiana Code 29–1–11–5;

f. No Attorney will be accepted as personal surety on any bond required to be filed in Court.

Adopted as Probate Estate Rule 2, effective March 1, 1995. Renumbered as Probate Rule 29, and amended effective Dec. 5, 2006; Jan. 1, 2009.

LR 45–PR00 Rule 30

Where an account with expenditures restricted by Court Order has been created, an acknowledgment of or acquiescence to the restriction by the financial institution involved must be filed by the Personal Representative's Attorney within ten (10) days of the Court Order creating such an account.

Adopted as Probate Estate Rule 3, effective March 1, 1995. Renumbered as Probate Rule 30, and amended effective Dec. 5, 2006; Jan. 1, 2009.

LR 45–PR00 Rule 31

Three (3) months and fifteen (15) days after the date of the first published notice to creditors, the Personal Representative, or the Personal Representative's Attorney, must allow or disallow each claim filed against the estate.

Adopted as Probate Estate Rule 4, effective March 1, 1995. Renumbered as Probate Rule 31, and amended effective Dec. 5, 2006; Jan. 1, 2009.

LR 45–PR00 Rule 32

If an estate cannot be closed, the Personal Representative must report the condition of the estate to the Court one (1) year after the date of the Personal Representative's appointment, and thereafter every year until the estate is fully administered.

Adopted as Probate Estate Rule 5, effective March 1, 1995. Renumbered as Probate Rule 32, and amended effective Dec. 5, 2006; Jan. 1, 2009.

LR 45–PR00 Rule 33

Inheritance Tax Returns, with all required attachments, must be filed in triplicate. Proposed Orders Determining Inheritance Tax Due must be filed in quadruplicate at the time of determination of the tax.

Adopted as Probate Estate Rule 6, effective March 1, 1995. Renumbered as Probate Rule 33, and amended effective Dec. 5, 2006; Jan. 1, 2009.

LR 45–PR00 Rule 34

The Federal Estate Tax closing letter and/or the countersigned receipt, or a photocopy thereof, showing payment of the Federal Estate and/or Indiana inheritance tax liability in the estate must be filed with the Final Report or the Supplemental Report.

Adopted as Probate Estate Rule 7, effective March 1, 1995. Renumbered as Probate Rule 34, and amended effective Dec. 5, 2006; Jan. 1, 2009.

LR 45–PR00 Rule 35

Proof of publication of all notices required to be published shall be filed with the Court by the Attorney for the estate. It is the Attorney's responsibility to ensure that publication was timely made, and proof thereof is properly filed with the Court.

Adopted as Probate Estate Rule 8, effective March 1, 1995. Renumbered as Probate Rule 35, and amended effective Dec. 5, 2006; Jan. 1, 2009.

LR 45–PR00 Rule 36

The Court shall have no involvement, other than for opening, closing and determining Indiana inheritance tax due in an unsupervised estate. If the jurisdiction of the Court is invoked for any other matter, the administration shall become a supervised administration from there on for all remaining matters.

Adopted as Probate Estate Rule 9, effective March 1, 1995. Renumbered as Probate Rule 36, and amended effective Dec. 5, 2006; Jan. 1, 2009.

LR 45–PR00 Rule 37

When a verified closing statement has been filed, an affidavit executed by the Personal Representative stating that no proceedings are pending shall be filed with the Court upon the expiration of the three (3) month statutory waiting period.

Adopted as Probate Estate Rule 10, effective March 1, 1995. Renumbered as Probate Rule 37, and amended effective Dec. 5, 2006; Jan. 1, 2009.

LR 45–PR00 Rule 38

If the Personal Representative has filed a claim in the estate, the claim may be allowed by the Court if all interested parties have consented. In the event the consents have not been obtained, a special administrator shall be appointed and a hearing on the claim will be held as prescribed by statute.

Adopted as Probate Estate Rule 11, effective March 1, 1995. Renumbered as Probate Rule 38, and amended effective Dec. 5, 2006; Jan. 1, 2009.

LAKE COUNTY RULES OF PROCEDURE APPLICABLE TO GUARDIANSHIPS

LR 45–PR00 Rule 39

All probate rules and regulations promulgated by the Veterans Administration are hereby adopted as probate rules of the Court.

Adopted as Probate Estate Rule 12, effective March 1, 1995. Renumbered as Probate Rule 39, and amended effective Dec. 5, 2006; Jan. 1, 2009.

LR 45–PR00 Rule 40

Guardianship matters must be transacted with the Probate Commissioner. Only emergency matters may be submitted to the presiding Judge. Telephone calls or visits to the Probate Commissioner's private office should be kept at a minimum.

Adopted as Probate Estate Rule 13, effective March 1, 1995. Renumbered as Probate Rule 40, and amended effective Dec. 5, 2006; Jan. 1, 2009.

LR 45–PR00 Rule 41

Unless the Probate Clerk has sent the files to the Probate Commissioner, attorneys must obtain files from the Probate Clerk prior to submitting any matter to the Probate Commissioner.

Adopted as Probate Estate Rule 14, effective March 1, 1995. Renumbered as Probate Rule 41, and amended effective Dec. 5, 2006; Jan. 1, 2009.

LR 45–PR00 Rule 42

All petitions, of any nature or kind, in all matters, must be executed and verified by the Guardian or the Interested Party (Petitioner), and not by the Attorney.

Adopted as Probate Estate Rule 15, effective March 1, 1995. Renumbered as Probate Rule 42, and amended effective Dec. 5, 2006; Jan. 1, 2009.

LR 45–PR00 Rule 43

All Attorneys are required to prepare CCS Entry Forms showing each pleading filed, and setting forth all necessary matters for all proceedings.

Adopted as Probate Estate Rule 16, effective March 1, 1995. Renumbered as Probate Rule 43, and amended effective Dec. 5, 2006; Jan. 1, 2009.

LR 45–PR00 Rule 44

All Attorneys are required to prepare orders in an form approved by the Court (order per form or OPF) for all proceedings, except where expressly indicated to the contrary by the respective Probate Commissioner.

Adopted as Probate Estate Rule 17, effective March 1, 1995. Renumbered as Probate Rule 44, and amended effective Dec. 5, 2006; Jan. 1, 2009.

LR 45–PR00 Rule 45

Where matters are filed by mail, or left with the Court for filing, a self-addressed stamped envelope must be included for return of documents to the Attorney.

Adopted as Probate Estate Rule 18, effective March 1, 1995. Renumbered as Probate Rule 45, and amended effective Dec. 5, 2006; Jan. 1, 2009.

LR 45–PR00 Rule 46

Routine matters, such a Bonds, Inventories, and Status Reports, may be filed with the Probate Clerk for transmittal to the Probate Commissioner.

Adopted as Probate Guardianship Rule 1, effective March 1, 1995. Renumbered as Probate Rule 46, and amended effective Dec. 5, 2006; Jan. 1, 2009.

LR 45–PR00 Rule 47

Attorneys desiring to have the Court Reporter present for a hearing must make a written request for same ten (10) days in advance of the hearing. Hearings involving the Court Reporter shall be set subject to his or her availability.

Adopted as Probate Guardianship Rule 2, effective March 1, 1995. Renumbered as Probate Rule 47, and amended effective Dec. 5, 2006; Jan. 1, 2009.

LR 45–PR00 Rule 48

Any contested matters scheduled for hearing on a probate day shall take precedence over unscheduled business; attorneys are encouraged to call the Court to find out when contested matters are routinely scheduled.

Adopted as Probate Guardianship Rule 3, effective March 1, 1995. Renumbered as Probate Rule 48, and amended effective Dec. 5, 2006; Jan. 1, 2009.

LR 45–PR00 Rule 49

The Attorney shall prepare any required notices and shall ensure that such notices are properly served in compliance with statutory requirements. The Attorney shall ascertain and provide adequate proof that notice was properly served prior to bringing a matter to the attention of the Probate Commissioner.

Adopted as Probate Guardianship Rule 4, effective March 1, 1995. Renumbered as Probate Rule 49, and amended effective Dec. 5, 2006; Jan. 1, 2009.

LR 45–PR00 Rule 50

Copies of petitions and accountings must be sent with all notices, where the hearing involved arises from the matters contained in the petition and/or accounting.

Adopted as Probate Guardianship Rule 5, effective March 1, 1995. Renumbered as Probate Rule 50, and amended effective Dec. 5, 2006; Jan. 1, 2009.

LR 45–PR00 Rule 51

Inventories must be filed in all temporary guardianships of the estate within thirty (30) days after appointment of the Guardian. For permanent guardianships of the estate, inventories must be filed within ninety (90) days after appointment of the Guardian.

Adopted as Probate Guardianship Rule 6, effective March 1, 1995. Renumbered as Probate Rule 51, and amended effective Dec. 5, 2006; Jan. 1, 2009.

LR 45–PR00 Rule 52

Attorneys must attend the hearing on current or final accounts on the date scheduled for such hearings. The Court may, in its discretion, require the attendance of the Guardian at all such hearings.

Adopted as Probate Guardianship Rule 7, effective March 1, 1995. Renumbered as Probate Rule 52, and amended effective Dec. 5, 2006; effective Jan. 1, 2009.

LR 45–PR00 Rule 53

Unless otherwise ordered by the Court, all accounting to the Court shall be accompanied by an affidavit stating that receipts are available for all disbursements contained in the accounting.

Adopted as Probate Guardianship Rule 8, effective March 1, 1995. Renumbered as Probate Rule 53, and amended effective Dec. 5, 2006; Jan. 1, 2009.

LR 45–PR00 Rule 54

Receipts for all final distributions must be filed with the final report or the supplemental report before discharge will be given by the Court.

Adopted as Probate Guardianship Rule 9, effective March 1, 1995. Renumbered as Probate Rule 54, and amended effective Dec. 5, 2006; Jan. 1, 2009.

LR 45–PR00 Rule 55

All accountings must follow the prescribed statutory format. Informal or handwritten accountings will not be accepted.

Adopted as Probate Guardianship Rule 10, effective March 1, 1995. Renumbered as Probate Rule 55, and amended effective Dec. 5, 2006; Jan. 1, 2009.

LR 45–PR00 Rule 56

The name and address of the Insurance Agency providing the corporate surety must be typed on all corporate bonds filed in any guardianship.

Adopted as Probate Guardianship Rule 11, effective March 1, 1995. Renumbered as Probate Rule 56, and amended effective Dec. 5, 2006; Jan. 1, 2009.

LR 45–PR00 Rule 57

In all contested matters, the Indiana Rules of Trial Procedure shall apply.

Adopted as Probate Guardianship Rule 57, Jan. 1, 2009.

LR 45–PR00 Rule 58

Any petition for the allowance of fees, for the Attorney and/or the Guardian shall set forth a description of the services performed and a calculation of the amount of the fee requested. At the time the petition is considered by the Court, the Attorney must be present. No fee request will be considered as a part of the final report or account in a guardianship proceeding. A separate petition must be filed requesting such fee determination. No fee shall be paid without prior approval of the Court.

Adopted as Probate Guardianship Rule 58, Jan. 1, 2009.

LR 45–PR00 Rule 59

Where contracts for legal services have been entered into prior or subsequent to the opening of a guardianship over the estate of an incapacitated individual without prior Court approval, or when a settlement has been reached and no Guardianship is required, the Court reserves the right to approve or disapprove the fee contracts.

Adopted as Probate Guardianship Rule 59, Jan. 1, 2009.

LR 45–PR00 Rule 60

Attorney and Guardian fees will not be determined or authorized for payment by the Court in guardianship proceedings over the person of the incapacitated individual.

Adopted as Probate Guardianship Rule 60, Jan. 1, 2009.

LR 45–PR00 Rule 61

All deeds submitted to the Court for approval must be signed by the Guardian and the signature notarized prior to its submission. Copies of such deeds must be filed for the Court records.

Adopted as Probate Guardianship Rule 61, Jan. 1, 2009.

LR 45–PR00 Rule 62

In all wrongful death proceedings, the Guardian must be present at the time the settlement, either partial and/or final, is presented to the Court for approval. The Court retains the right to require the presence of the minor, incapacitated person, or a Custodial parent at the time the settlement is presented to the Courts for approval.

Adopted as Probate Guardianship Rule 62, Jan. 1, 2009.

LR 45–PR00 Rule 63

All documents filed with the Court must comply with the requirements of Indiana Trial Rule 5(G) and Administrative Rule 9(G)(1).

Adopted as Probate Guardianship Rule 63, Jan. 1, 2009.

LR 45–PR00 Rule 64

For good cause shown, the Court may waive any local procedural rule.

Adopted as Probate Guardianship Rule 64, Jan. 1, 2009.

LR 45–PR00 Rule 65

In all guardianship matters pertaining to declaring an adult incapacitated for any reason, at a minimum, the Physician's Statement in a form acceptable to the Court, executed by the licensed physician treating the alleged incapacitated person, must be submitted at the time the petition is filed or on the hearing date. No determination will be made without the Physician's Statement and/or supporting medical testimony. (SEE ATTACHED FORM)

Adopted as Probate Guardianship Rule 65, Jan. 1, 2009.

LR 45–PR00 Rule 66

A bond shall be required equal to the sum of the full value of the personal property of the protected person and one year's estimated income from all assets in the Guardianship. Exceptions as provided by statute may be permitted, in the Court's discretion.

Adopted as Probate Guardianship Rule 66, Jan. 1, 2009.

LR 45–PR00 Rule 67

Where an account with expenditures restricted by Court order has been created, an acknowledgement of or acquiescence to the restriction by the financial institution involved must be filed by the guardian's Attorney within ten (10) days of the Court Order creating such an account. (SEE ATTACHED FORM)

Adopted as Probate Guardianship Rule 67, Jan. 1, 2009.

LR 45–PR00 Rule 68

Current reports filed by the Guardian must show the present whereabouts of the protected person and his/her general welfare.

Adopted as Probate Guardianship Rule 68, Jan. 1, 2009.

LR 45–PR00 Rule 69

All Guardian's accountings must contain a certification by an officer of a financial institution or the holding institution that the assets remaining in the guardianship which are in the charge, custody, or control of the holding institution, other than real estate, have been exhibited to said officer, and that they correspond with what is shown in the recapitulation section of the accounting. (SEE ATTACHED FORMS)

Adopted as Probate Guardianship Rule 69, Jan. 1, 2009.

LR 45–PR00 Rule 70

All benefits and payments, such as Social Security benefits received on behalf of a protected person, must be included and accounted for in the Guardian's accountings unless excluded by prior order of the Court.

Adopted as Probate Guardianship Rule 70, Jan. 1, 2009.

LR 45–PR00 Rule 71

Neither the Guardian nor the Attorney shall take or receive any fees until the amount thereof has been approved by the Court.

Adopted as Probate Guardianship Rule 71, Jan. 1, 2009.

LR 45–PR00 Rule 72

An order in a form approved by the Court (order per form or OPF) must be submitted at the time of the appointment of a Guardian, detailing the duties, responsibilities and powers of the Guardian. Any limitations on the duties, responsibilities and powers of the Guardian must be detailed on a separate schedule which shall be incorporated in or attached to the Letters of Guardianship.

Adopted as Probate Guardianship Rule 72, Jan. 1, 2009.

LR 45–PR00 Rule 73

In all instances in which the appointment of a Guardianship is contested, a Guardian Ad Litem shall be appointed unless waived by law, or by the Court in the Court's discretion, or if the alleged incapacitated person is represented by counsel.

Adopted as Probate Guardianship Rule 73, Jan. 1, 2009.

GUARDIANSHIP FORMS

FORM A. ACCOUNT VERIFICATION

ACCOUNT VERIFICATION

TO: _____

FROM: _____

Guardian's Name

RE: Guardianship of _____

In order to comply with the rules of the Probate Court, I am required to file a Certification of Account Balances. Please certify the balances and names on the accounts I have listed below, as of _____, 2 ___.

Dated: _____

Guardian: _____

Guardian's Name

FOR BANK USE ONLY:

I certify that on _____, 2 ___, on deposit in this institution to the the* last day of the period credit of the Guardian, the following covered by this accounting, there was balance:

NAME ON ACCOUNT	ACCOUNT NUMBER	BALANCE	DATE
_____	_____	_____	_____
_____	_____	_____	_____
_____	_____	_____	_____

Name and Address of Institution: Signature of Certifying Officer:

_____

_____   Signature

                                     Title

_____

                                     Date

Adopted as Guardianship Form A, effective March 1, 1995. Renumbered as Probate Form 20, and amended effective Dec. 5, 2006. Renumbered as Probate Form A, and amended effective Jan. 1, 2009.

FORM B. CERTIFICATE OF INVESTMENT

CERTIFICATE OF INVESTMENT

KIND OF SECURITY	INTEREST RATE	DATE OF ACQUISITION	FACE VALUE	GUARDIANSHIP VALUE

I certify that the securities listed as being the property of the Protected herein were exhibited to me by the Person and in the custody of the Guardian.

————————,

Guardian

————————————   ————————————————————
Date   Signature and Title of Certifying Officer

————————————————————

Name and Address of Institution

Adopted as Guardianship Form B, effective March 1, 1995. Renumbered as Probate Form 21, and amended effective Dec. 5, 2006. Renumbered as Probate Form B, and amended effective Jan. 1, 2009. Amended Jan. 1, 2011.

FORM C. PHYSICIAN'S REPORT

PHYSICIAN'S REPORT

————————, **a physician holding an unlimited license to practice medicine in the State of Indiana, submits the following report on** ————————, **'Patient', based upon examination of Patient.**

1. Set forth the dates of all examinations of the Patient within the last one (1) year from the date hereof.

——
——
——

2. In your opinion, based upon your examination and observation of the Patient, is the Patient incapacitated? If so, describe the nature and type of incapacity.

——
——
——

3. In your opinion, based upon your examination and observation of the Patient, how long has the Patient been incapacitated?

——
——
——

4. Describe the Patient's mental and physical condition; and if appropriate, describe the Patient's educational condition, adaptive behavior and social skills.

——
——
——

5. In your opinion, is the Patient totally or only partially incapable of making personal and financial decisions? And, if the latter, state the kinds of decisions which the Patient can and cannot make. Include the reason for this opinion.

——
——
——

6. In your opinion, what is the most appropriate living arrangement for the Patient? And, if applicable, describe the most appropriate treatment or rehabilitation plan. Include the reasons for your opinion.

_____

_____

_____

7. Can the Patient appear in Court without injury to his/her health? ___ Yes ___ No

If the answer is no, explain the medical reasons for your answer.

_____

_____

_____

8. If the Patient capable of consenting to the appointment of a Guardian? ___ Yes ___ No

9. Is the nature of the Patient's incapacity such that it prevents the Patient from making a knowing and voluntary Waiver of Notice? ___ Yes ___ No

10. In your opinion, is a Guardian needed to care for the Patient? ___ Yes ___ No

If a Guardian is needed, is one needed for personal or financial needs, or both?

___ Yes ___ No

I affirm, under the penalties of perjury, the above and foregoing is true and correct to the best of my knowledge and belief.

Signed: _____

Address: _____

_____

Telephone: _____

Dated: _____

If the description of the Patient's mental, physical and educational condition, adaptive behavior or social skills is based on evaluations by other professionals, please provide the names and addresses of all professionals who are able to provide additional evaluations. Evaluations on which the report is based should have been performed within three (3) months of the date of the filing of the Petition.

Names and addresses of other persons who performed evaluations upon which this report is based:

Name: _____

Address: _____

_____

Telephone: _____

Name: _____

Address: _____

_____

Telephone: _____

Adopted as Guardianship Form C, effective March 1, 1995. Renumbered as Probate Form 22, and amended effective Dec. 5, 2006. Renumbered as Probate Form C, and amended effective Jan. 1, 2009.

FORM D.   LAWYER'S UNDERTAKING AND OBLIGATION

LAWYER'S UNDERTAKING AND OBLIGATION

I, _____, having been appointed as Guardian or as the Person best suited to protect the Estate of _____, by the Superior Court of Lake County, sitting at _____, Indiana, hereby authorize my Attorney _____, to deposit all of the net guardianship assets, in the amount of $ ___, in a bank account or other interest bearing account in my name on behalf of the Protected Person, _____, with the restriction that withdrawal of principal or interest may be made ONLY on written order of the Court, or upon the Protected Person reaching the age of majority.

DATE: _____   _____

                                           Guardian of Protected Person

I, as an Officer of the Court and as Attorney for the above Guardianship, hereby assume and undertake personal responsibility to the above named Protected Person and to the Court to make the above designated restricted deposit and to deliver copies of the SIGNATURE CARD or CERTIFICATE evidencing the restricted deposit and the amount thereof to the Court with ten (10) days from the receipt of the funds, or to refund all of the funds to the Court immediately upon demand.

DATE: _____   _____

                                                       Attorney

Adopted effective Jan. 1, 2009.

FORM E.   CERTIFICATE OF ACCOUNT RESTRICTION CERTIFICATE OF RESTRICTION OF ACCOUNT IN COMPLIANCE WITH LAWYER'S UNDERTAKING

The undersigned hereby certifies that he/she is an Officer or employee of the below named financial institution and that the following account has been opened:

Type of Account: _____

Account Number: _____

Amount Deposited: _____

Owner per Signature Card or Document of Title: _____

The undersigned further certifies that a copy of the Order of the Superior Court of Lake County has been examined in full by us and that the terms of this account included a restriction that withdrawal of principal or interest may be made only on written order of the Superior Court of Lake County, or upon the Protected Person reaching the age of majority.

DATE: _____   _____

                                           Name of Financial Institution

                                           _____

                                           Signature

                                           _____

                                           Printed

Title

Adopted effective Jan. 1, 2009. Amended effective Jan. 1, 2011.

LAKE COUNTY RULES OF FAMILY LAW

Adopted Effective January 1, 1993

Including Amendments Received Through November 1, 2013

Research Notes

*Annotations to the Lake County Rules of Family Law are available in*West's Annotated Indiana Code, *Title 34 Appendix.*

These rules may be searched electronically on Westlaw *in the* IN-RULES *database; updates to these rules may be found on Westlaw in IN-RULESUPDATES. For search tips and a summary of database content, consult the Westlaw Scope Screens for each database.*

PREAMBLE

The Rules of Professional Conduct mandate that all lawyers conduct themselves honorably and remind lawyers that they have a special responsibility for the quality of justice. For lawyers who practice family law, that special responsibility for the quality of justice often occurs in an emotionally-charged arena with litigants who are angry, disappointed, hurt, hostile, betrayed, sad, fearful, shocked, and/or lost. When a case involves minor children, emotions run even higher.

Some statistics indicate that, every thirty-two seconds, a child in America witnesses his or her parents' divorce. Out of wedlock births to adults have increased exponentially. Research establishes that how parents conduct themselves during a domestic relations proceeding has a greater impact on their children than the proceeding itself. These local rules have been enacted to help effectuate a dignified and effective means of resolving all family law disputes, but especially those disputes involving minor children. While recognizing our adversarial system for resolving family law problems, these local rules mandate that attorneys not ignore but embrace their equally important roles as negotiators and advisors and their special responsibility for the quality of justice.

Adopted effective Jan. 1, 2009.

LR 45–FL00 Rule 1. SCOPE, CITATION AND DEFINITION, COOPERATIVE APPROACH AND LIBERAL CONSTRUCTION

A. Scope. These rules shall apply to family cases in the Lake Circuit Court and the Superior Court of Lake County, Civil and Juvenile Divisions.

B. Citation. These rules may be cited as the Lake County Rules of Family Law and abbreviated as F. L. R.

C. Definition. Family cases shall include all cases involving claims for or related to marital dissolution or separation, paternity, child custody, parenting time or visitation with a child, and support of a child or spouse.

Adopted effective Jan. 1, 1993. Amended effective Dec. 5, 2006; Jan. 1, 2009.

LR 45–FL00 Rule 2. STATEMENT OF POLICY AND PURPOSE

The Circuit and Superior Courts of Lake County are committed to a cooperative model for the handling of family cases by parents, attorneys, and judges. These rules shall be liberally construed and applied to serve the healthy and child-sensitive functioning of families. In all family cases with children, the goal will be protecting the best interests of those children.

Adopted effective Jan. 1, 1993. Amended effective Dec. 5, 2006; Jan. 1, 2009.

LR 45–FL00 Rule 3. GENERAL OBLIGATIONS OF COOPERATION OF ATTORNEYS AND PARTIES

A. Attorneys and parties in family cases are expected to act with the courts as co-problem solvers, not mere problem-reporters. Attorneys shall both inform and remind their clients about the judicial expectations of cooperation in family cases, assist their clients to understand and observe these standards, and encourage clients to participate in co-parenting classes, counseling, mediation, and other appropriate problem-solving processes.

B. In order to establish and maintain an atmosphere which fosters cooperative problem-solving, all parties and attorneys shall:

(1) explore resources which may reduce conflict, build cooperation and protect children;

(2) attempt reasonable cooperative measures before resorting to the court;

(3) avoid disrespectful language and behavior; and,

(4) avoid unnecessary motions or petitions, hearing and arguments.

Commentary

The Circuit and Superior Courts of Lake County recognize that conflict in family cases is destructive and often dangerous. Litigating family cases does not end or resolve the conflict; it heightens the conflict. The cooperative model for handling family cases is implemented in order to minimize such conflict and, instead, foster the healthy and child-sensitive functioning of families.

Actions taken in the earliest stages of parents' separation and other family crises, whether those actions are helpful or destructive, often define much of the future of the family case and the family; and, attorneys' language and conduct in these earliest days are often crucial to the future course of both the case and the future functioning of the family. Until the case is filed, the courts have no involvement and are powerless to help families at that point; however, at such early stages, attorneys can either set a tone of beneficial cooperation or of destructive conflict for the families they touch.

All too often in family cases the courtroom becomes an arena in which the parties are subjected to criticism, sometimes even ridicule or similar abuse. Such conduct will not be tolerated. Attorneys have an ethical obligation to refrain from abusive conduct and other offensive tactics; to treat all parties, witnesses and all others involved in the legal process with courtesy and respect; and, to refuse to participate in any effort to embarrass, delay or burden someone. The courts consider such conduct to be repugnant. So should the attorneys and all members of the family. Attorneys have an ethical obligation to consult with their client about the means to be employed and clients normally defer to the attorney's special knowledge and skill in such matters. These rules and comments require that when doing so, the attorney should educate the client about the substantial risk that conflict presents for members of the family and of the benefits and opportunities for resolution through the cooperative model. If the prospective client will not abide by such advice, the attorney can and should consider declining the engagement. If a client agrees to abide but later shows the inability to do so or otherwise refuses, the attorney may and should consider withdrawing. Family members who elect to pursue the path of conflict instead of cooperation are not acting in the best interests of the children; and, the courts **will** consider the decisions made by the parties in this regard as part of its evaluation of the children's best interests and in the allocation of attorney fees.

This cooperative model will require some fundamental changes in the local legal culture, including the manner in which attorneys approach family cases. While fundamental change does not occur overnight, it must be done and begin now. Attorneys must change their primary focus in family cases. Instead of the gathering of evidence or other "case building", the attorney's primary focus must be on defusing the underlying source(s) of conflict(s) by helping the family to find the ways to reach resolution of their issues by using means which are less destructive than litigation.

As part of the cooperative model the courts will expect all parties and attorneys to consistently observe:

(1) personal responsibility by acting on one's own opportunities to solve problems and improve circumstances rather than merely reporting on the alleged fault in others;

(2) cooperation by sensibly defining and pursuing the best interests of all family members;

(3) courtesy by constant observance of respectful language and behavior; and,

(4) focused attention on children's needs including an awareness that parent conflict is dangerous to children.

As part of their duty to work as co-problem-solvers with the court in all family cases, if safe to do so, attorneys should:

(1) speak with all clients, as early as possible and as often as necessary, about the advantages

and judicial expectations of safe cooperation in family cases;

(2) refer clients to all co-parenting classes, counseling, mediation, and other problem-solving processes that appear to counsel to be promising resources for their clients;

(3) work with other counsel to ensure safety in families where domestic violence has been, or reasonably could be, an issue;

(4) work with other counsel in all cases to reduce conflict, build cooperation, and protect children;

(5) avoid unnecessary motions and hearings; and

(6) use the least divisive processes in pursuing safety, fairness, cooperation, and the protection of the best interests of children, for example:

(a) using certified mail or acknowledgment of service instead of sheriff service of process if viable,

(b) encouraging restraint and safe cooperation between family members,

(c) avoiding unnecessary motions and arguments, and

(d) exhausting all viable cooperative measures before requesting custody evaluations or trial settings.

Before a case is filed, an attorney should:

(1) Assessment of Case and Safety Considerations. Counsel meeting with a person contemplating filing a family case should promptly assess whether the case can safely be handled cooperatively and without adversarial motions, hearings and other formal proceedings. Unless safety or exceptional circumstances make cooperation unreasonable, counsel should handle the case in ways that avoid court and maximize the parties' development of cooperative problem-solving.

(2) Cooperation between Counsel Before Initial Filings. Counsel representing persons wishing to initiate a family case should make reasonable efforts to determine if the other spouse, parent, or putative parent is represented or may be seeking representation. Unless doing so might create a danger or substantial prejudice to their client or it is otherwise unreasonable to do so, counsel should:

(a) consult and cooperate with each other before filing;

(b) attempt in good faith to find cooperative resolutions to provisional matters, including peaceful separation, so that unnecessary provisional filings and hearings can be avoided; and

(c) refer parents to resources such as co-parent education, co-parent counseling, marital counseling, and mediation that can help them build cooperation between them.

(3) Cooperation with Unrepresented Parties before Initial Filings. Unless doing so might create a danger or substantial prejudice to their client or it is otherwise unreasonable to do so, this same effort at consultation and cooperation should be made when counsel learns that the other spouse, parent, or putative parent is not intending to use legal representation. In such case, unless doing so might create a danger or substantial prejudice to

their client or it is otherwise unreasonable to do so, counsel or the client should (a) communicate directly with that other spouse, parent, or putative parent and (b) attempt to avoid provisional filings and hearings on matters that could be resolved by cooperative measures including discussion, co-parent education, counseling, and mediation.

C. Website. Parties and counsel should visit the court's website at www.LakeCountyKids.org for more information on the procedures in use in Lake County in support of the cooperative handling of family cases.

Adopted effective Jan. 1, 1993. Amended effective Dec. 5, 2006; Jan. 1, 2009; Oct. 18, 2013.

LR 45–FL00 Rule 4. INITIAL AND PROVISIONAL HEARINGS

Unless considerations of safety or other good cause make it unreasonable, before the date and time set for an initial or provisional hearing, counsel shall meet with each other (or any unrepresented party) in a good-faith attempt to resolve all matters.

Adopted effective Jan. 1, 1993. Amended effective Dec. 5, 2006; Jan. 1, 2009.

LR 45–FL00 Rule 5. MANDATORY WEBSITE WORK FOR PARENTS

A. Dissolution of Marriage. In all dissolution cases where the parties have any children together under the age of 18, both parties shall complete the work on www.UpToParents.org within 30 days of initial filing.

B. Legal Separation. In all separation cases where the parties have any children together under the age of 18, both parties shall complete the work on www.WhileWeHeal.org within 30 days of initial filing.

C. Paternity. In all paternity cases, both parents shall complete the work on www.ProudToParent.org within 30 days of the court's finding of paternity.

D. Following completion of the website work required by this rule, the parents shall merge or exchange their chosen Commitments from their website work.

Adopted effective Jan. 1, 1993. Amended effective Dec. 5, 2006; Jan. 1, 2009.

Commentary

The rule contemplates that, following completion of the website work required by this rule, the parents shall merge their chosen Commitments from their website work into a set of Agreed Commitments, review those Agreed Commitments before all hearings, and take copies of them to all hearings. If a hearing is held more than a year since the parents' completion of the website work, they shall redo the work, again merge their Commitments into a set of Agreed Commitments, and bring those Agreed Commitments to all hearings.

LR 45–FL00 Rule 6.   CO–PARENTING CLASS

A.   Dissolution of Marriage and Legal Separation. Mandatory Attendance. In all dissolution and separation cases where the parties have any children together under the age of 18, both parties shall complete a co-parenting class. The court may order both parties to attend additional co-parenting classes in post-decree matters. Information regarding the approved classes is available on the court's website at www.LakeCountyKids.org.

B.   Paternity. In all paternity cases the court may order the parties to attend and complete a co-parenting class.

Adopted effective Jan. 1, 1993. Amended effective Dec. 5, 2006; Jan. 1, 2009.

LR 45–FL00 Rule 7.   PROOF OF COMPLIANCE

A.   Dissolution of Marriage and Legal Separation. In order to monitor compliance, within 60 days of the initial filing of an action for dissolution or separation, each party shall file a verified certification of their completion of the mandatory website work as required under FLR. 5, above, and of any mandatory co-parenting class as required under FLR. 6, above, a sample form of which is attached hereto as Appendix "A".

B.   Paternity. In order to monitor compliance, within 45 days of the court's finding of paternity, each party shall file a verified certification of completion of the mandatory website work as required under FLR 5, above. A sample form is attached hereto as Appendix "B".

C. Any party failing to timely file such a certification may be subject to a hearing on such a failure.

Adopted effective Jan. 1, 1993. Amended effective Dec. 5, 2006; Jan. 1, 2009.

LR 45–FL00 Rule 8.   PARENTING PLAN PROPOSALS

A. The Indiana Parenting Time Guidelines provide useful outlines of the **minimum** time each parent should have with the children to maintain frequent, meaningful, and continuing contact with them. Any parenting time plan submitted by agreement that provides for less then the **minimum** time allowed under the Indiana Parenting Time Guidelines must contain a written explanation for deviating from those guidelines. Agreed parenting plans that exceed the **minimum** time allowed under the Guidelines will not require a written explanation.

B. Unless they have already executed an agreed parenting plan, the parties shall each prepare and exchange their written Parenting Plan Proposals utilizing the form which is attached hereto as Appendix "C". Parents, personally and with the help of counsel and all useful counseling, mediation and other problem-solving resources, shall continue to attempt to reach an agreed parenting plan. Parents shall bring their respective Parenting Plan Proposals to all hearings, mediation sessions, and settlement discussions.

Adopted effective Jan. 1, 1993. Amended effective Dec. 5, 2006; Jan. 1, 2009.

Commentary

A.   Children whose parents live apart have special needs above and beyond those of other children, including the need for frequent, meaningful, and continuing contact with both parents. The courts will expect separated and divorced parents, wherever safely possible, to work together to support children's best possible relationships with each parent.

B   To assist parents and their counsel in developing parenting plans that will meet the needs of these children, parents with children under the age of 18 or dependent children over the age of 18 should use all reasonable efforts, discussion, counseling, mediation, and other resources to promptly agree on a parenting plan to include the decision-making and living arrangements that will serve to nurture and protect their children as the years progress. If a parenting plan is agreed on and signed by the parents, it may be submitted to the court for its consideration as the order which will govern the parents' co-parenting unless changed by agreement or court order.

C.   Unless the parties have already entered in to a signed agreement resolving all such issues then, within 60 days of the initial filing of all actions for marital dissolution or separation, or any post-decree filing regarding the children, or the court's finding of paternity in all paternity cases, the parties shall each prepare and exchange their written Parenting Plan Proposals utilizing the form which is attached hereto as Appendix "C". Parents, personally and with the help of counsel and all useful counseling, mediation and other problem-solving resources, shall continue to attempt to reach an agreed parenting plan. If parents do not reach an agreed parenting plan, they shall bring their respective Parenting Plan Proposals to all hearings, mediation sessions, and settlement discussions.

*D.   The Indiana Parenting Time Guidelines provide useful outlines of the **minimum** time each parent should have with children to maintain frequent, meaningful, and continuing contact with them. It is the express preference of the Lake Circuit and Superior Courts that parenting plans, wherever safely possible, should:*

(1) help parents understand the important advantages of supporting each other's relationships with their children;

(2) exceed the Guideline minimums for each parent;

(3) fit the particular needs of the family; and,

(4) encourage parents' use of sensibility, flexibility, and reasonableness to allow for cooperative accommodations of special needs and circumstances in family activities.

E.   Whenever parents need resources to reduce conflict, build cooperation, preserve family relationships, or respond to the needs of their children, they and their attorneys (if any), should use all resources that could help them. Such resources include:

(1) redoing the website work from www.UpTo Parents.org, www.WhileWeHeal.org, or www.Proud ToParent.org;

(2) additional co-parenting classes, including re-attending the basic class or attending high-conflict classes;

(3) completing a new Parenting Plan Proposal;

(4) mediation;

(5) arbitration;

(6) a confidential therapeutic assessment of the parents to develop a set of recommendations for their improved interaction;

(7) individual, joint, family or child counseling;

(8) appointment of a parenting coordinator;

(9) appointment of a guardian ad litem for the children; and,

(10) any other measure that might protect children, reduce conflict, or build cooperation.

F. If parents nevertheless continue to have conflict and appear in court without an agreement about the resources they will use, the court may select the resources the parents will be ordered to use.

LR 45–FL00 Rule 9. PROTOCOLS AFTER INITIAL FILING

A. Duties Regarding Consultation. Except in emergencies or when it might create a danger or substantial prejudice or is otherwise unreasonable to do so, counsel and pro se parties shall make a reasonable attempt to have a personal or telephonic consultation to resolve any issue before filing or seeking any other relief through the court. Counsel and pro se parties contacted for a consultation shall make themselves reasonably available for consultation. The duty of consultation shall be continuing.

B. Substance of Consultation. In the consultation, counsel and pro se parties shall:

(1) attempt to resolve all matters at issue;

(2) confirm the parties' compliance with FLR 5, FLR 6, FLR 7 and FLR 8; and,

(3) discuss the resources they believe the parents could use to resolve current and future issues and to build cooperation, including any resources listed in Commentary E to FLR 8.

C. Cooperation Update—Mandatory. All motions and pleadings other than the initial filings shall include a statement confirming compliance with items (1) through (3), above, including the date of the required personal or telephonic consultation; or, shall recite the specific reasons for the lack of a consultation.

D. Parents shall review and bring a copy of their website Commitments, as required by FLR 5 and the current Parenting Plan Proposals, as required by FLR 8, to every hearing.

Adopted effective Jan. 1, 1993. Amended effective Dec. 5, 2006; Jan. 1, 2009.

Commentary

Counsel and pro se parties shall consult in advance of all court settings and exchange suggestions for the future course of the case that would serve the best interests of all family members.

During a Status Conference:

A. the attorneys and pro se parties will report on:

(1) the status of compliance with each of these rules by the parties and their attorneys; and,

(1) parent progress in reducing conflict, building cooperation, preserving family relationships, and responding to the needs of the children.

B where beneficial, the families will to be referred for any necessary help; and,

C. the court will consider the future course of the case.

LR 45–FL00 Rule 10. REQUIREMENTS BEFORE CUSTODY EVALUATIONS

All requests for custody evaluations must be (1) in writing (2) certify that both parties and their counsel, if any, have engaged in at least one good faith attempt to resolve the issues through the use of a settlement conference or mediation.

The court will not grant a request for or otherwise order a custody evaluation except following a Status Conference in the presence of both parties and their attorneys, if any, during which the court has been satisfied that:

A. both parties have completed the mandatory website work pursuant to FLR 6, above; and,

B. both parents have completed any required co-parenting class pursuant to FLR 7, above; and,

C. both parties have exchanged Parenting Plan Proposals pursuant to FLR 8, above; and,

D. both parties and their attorneys, if any, have engaged in at least one good faith attempt to resolve the issues through the use of a settlement conference or consultation pursuant to FLR 9, above; and,

E. the court has carefully considered and reviewed, with both parties and their attorneys, if any, the use of other resources including those listed in Commentary E to FLR 8.

Adopted effective Jan. 1, 2009.

Commentary

Custody evaluations are sometimes divisive and produce less, rather than more, cooperation between parents. As a result, custody evaluations will be reserved for cases where one or both parents lack the capacity to safely resolve the issues they face. No custody evaluation will be ordered or conducted unless reasonable cooperative measures have been attempted, such as coparenting education, counseling and mediation.

LR 45–FL00 Rule 11.   CASE CAPTIONING

Parties in dissolution, separation, and paternity cases shall not be captioned or designated as "petitioner", "respondent", "plaintiff", or "defendant". The parties shall be designated as "Mother", "Father", "Husband", or "Wife", "Former Husband", "Former Wife", and "Putative Father". All captions shall comply with applicable statutes and case law.

Adopted effective Jan. 1, 2009.

LR 45–FL00 Rule 12.   FORM OF SUMMONS

Parties in dissolution, separation, and paternity cases shall prepare and utilize forms of summons as set forth herein.

A.   Dissolution of Marriage and Legal Separation. In dissolution and separation cases, the appropriate summons shall be used and shall be substantially the same as the form(s) which attached hereto as Appendix "D", "D–1", "D–2", or "D–3".

B.   Paternity. In paternity cases, the summons shall be substantially the same as the form which is attached hereto as Appendix "E".

Adopted effective Jan. 1, 2009.

LR 45–FL00 Rule 13.   PREPARATION OF INFORMATION SHEET FOR FAMILY COURT PILOT PROJECT

Contemporaneously with the filing of any action for dissolution, separation, or paternity, the party filing the initial petition shall complete and furnish the Clerk with an Information Sheet which is substantially the same as the form which is attached hereto as Appendix "F". Because this form requires information which is excluded from the public access under Ind. Administrative Rule 9, this form shall be submitted on light green paper and conspicuously marked **"Not For Public Access"**.

Adopted effective Jan. 1, 2009.

LR 45–FL00 Rule 14.   JUDGES' NOTICE

Whenever the initial filing is prepared by an attorney, the attorney shall also prepare and provide the client and the Clerk with a sufficient number of copies of the appropriate the Judges' Notice as required herein. In cases filed by pro se parties, the Clerk shall provide the appropriate Judges' Notice. The Judges' Notice to Parents Going through Divorce is attached as Appendix "G" and Judges' Notice to Parents in Paternity Cases is attached as Appendix "H".

Adopted effective Jan. 1, 2009.

LR 45–FL00 Rule 15.   FINANCIAL DECLARATION FORM

A.   Requirement. In all relevant cases including dissolutions, separation, paternity, post-decree, or support proceedings and, irrespective of which court, each party shall prepare and exchange, within 60 days of initial filing for dissolution or separation or within 30 days of filing of any paternity or post-decree matters, the appropriate Financial Declaration Form (see Appendix "I" and "J"). These time limits may be extended or shortened by court order for good cause shown. In those cases where there is service, but no appearance by counsel, it is the responsibility of the initiating party to provide the other party with the appropriate blank Form and to notify that party of the duty to prepare and serve the same.

B.   Exceptions. The Form need not be exchanged if:

(1) the parties agree in writing within 60 days of the initial filing to waive exchange;

(2) the parties have executed a written agreement which settles all financial issues;

(3) the proceeding is merely at a provisional or emergency relief stage;

(4) the proceeding is one in which the service is by publication and there is no response; or,

(5) the proceeding is post-decree and concerns issues without financial implications.

Provided, however, when the proceeding is post-decree and concerns an arrearage, the alleged delinquent party shall complete the entire Form, while the support recipient need complete merely the portion thereof which requires specification of the basis of the arrearage calculation (with appropriate supporting documentation).

C.   Use at trial. The Forms are intended primarily as mandatory discovery though, subject to appropriate objection, they shall be admissible at the request of any party. Therefore, particularly in view of the presumptive nature of the Indiana Child Support Guidelines, direct examination on form data shall address only unusual factors which require explanation or corrections and shall not, particularly with respect to issues of support, be routinely permitted. For evidentiary purposes, the pages of the Form shall be deemed severable.

D.   Supporting documents. For the purposes of providing a full and complete verification of assets, liabilities, and values, each party shall attach to the form all information reasonably required and reasonably available. This shall include recent bills, wage and tax records, and bank, pension and year-end mortgage statements. Reasonably available means that material which may be obtained by letter accompanied with an authorization, but does not mean material that must be subpoenaed or is in the possession of the other party. Appraisals of real estate and pensions, or appraisals of personal property such as jewelry, antiques, or special collections (stamps, coins, or guns, for example) are not required. However, once an appraisal is obtained, it must be exchanged unless the appraisal was obtained in accordance with the provisions of Trial Rule 26(B) (4) (b) and is not expected to be utilized during trial. Moreover, the court may direct that an appraisal be obtained just as it may designate the appraiser.

E. Privacy—Sealing of Forms. Whenever the interest of privacy so requires, the court may, upon motion, direct the admitted Forms sealed until further order. However, such requests shall not be made as a matter of course.

When ordered sealed, the Court Reporter shall place the Forms in a flat manner in an envelope of sufficient size, seal the envelope, and affix a copy of the order. Forms may be withdrawn at the conclusion of the case on such terms as the court allows.

F. Financial Declaration Form as Mandatory Discovery. The exchange of Forms constitutes mandatory discovery. Thus, Indiana Rules of Procedure, Trial Rule 37 sanctions apply. Additionally, pursuant to Trial Rule 26(E) (2) and (3), the Form shall be supplemented if additional material becomes available. Further, any additional discovery, such as a motion to produce, interrogatories, or depositions of the parties shall not commence until the Forms are exchanged and, once exchanged, shall not seek information already obtained.

Adopted effective Jan. 1, 2009.

LR 45–FL00 Rule 16. INDIANA CHILD SUPPORT GUIDELINES

A. Worksheet Required. In all proceedings involving child support, each party shall file with any settlement or enter into evidence during any trial Indiana Child Support Guidelines Worksheets—one or more depending upon the facts. Further, the Worksheet(s) shall, when reasonably possible, be delivered to the other parent simultaneously with the Financial Declaration Form, but, in any event, within 10 days of receiving the other parent's Form. The Worksheets shall be promptly supplemented if any changes occur prior to resolution. All Worksheets shall be signed by the party(ies) submitting the Worksheet.

B. Support Settlement Agreements. If an agreement concerning support provides any deviation from the amount calculated under the Indiana Child Support Guidelines, the parents shall present the court with a written explanation justifying the deviation.

Adopted effective Jan. 1, 2009.

LR 45–FL00 Rule 17. PREPARATION OF ORDERS

A. Exchange. It shall be the duty of the parties' attorneys to prepare decrees and other orders as directed by the court. The attorney so directed is first to submit them to all other attorneys of record or to the unrepresented party to enable them to challenge any provision thereof before submission to the court for entry.

B. Additions. If the preparing attorney believes the other attorney or the other party, if the other party is proceeding pro se, is unreasonably withholding approval as to form, or if either believes the other is attempting to make additions not addressed by the court, either may submit a proposed form to the court and shall attach thereto a written explanation of the dispute. The other party shall have 7 days to respond before the court enters any order. The court may enter sanctions against a party who has unreasonably withheld approval or attempted to make additions not addressed by the court.

C. Signatures. The signature line for counsel or pro se litigant shall indicate Approved as to Form. Such signature indicates that the order correctly reflects the court's ruling. It does not necessarily signify that the signing party or attorney agrees with the ruling.

Adopted effective Jan. 1, 2009.

LR 45–FL00 Rule 18. SANCTIONS

If a party or counsel fails to timely prepare, exchange or file a Financial Declaration Form or Child Support Worksheet or to cooperate in providing information therefore in a timely manner, either is subject to sanctions under Trial Rule 37.

Adopted effective Jan. 1, 2009.

LR 45–FL00 Rule 19. ATTORNEY FEE REQUESTS

A. Affidavits. When attorney fees (except those sought provisionally) are requested from the opposing party, the requesting attorney shall submit an appropriate affidavit, which, if the affidavit comports with these rules, the court shall admit as an exhibit.

B. Content. The affidavit shall indicate the:

(1) requested fee and the basis thereof;

(2) amounts counsel has billed, contracted for, or been promised; and,

(3) amount counsel has received from all sources.

A copy of the written fee contract, if any, shall be attached to the affidavit and deemed a part thereof.

Opposing counsel may cross examine the requesting attorney as to any of the submitted material.

Adopted effective Jan. 1, 2009.

LR 45–FL00 Rule 20. AGREED MATTERS—SUBMISSION

No agreed matter shall be submitted unless accompanied with a signed agreement, and other appropriate documents, such as the decree, a wage withholding order, or a qualified domestic relations order. However, if the parties reach a settlement on the courthouse steps, then the court shall accept evidence of that settlement on the record, and enter the appropriate order upon preparation and filing by counsel within 21 days after submission, or such additional time as the court may allow.

Adopted effective Jan. 1, 2009.

LR 45–FL00 Rule 21. ORDERS EXCLUDING PARENT FROM THE RESIDENCE

In all instances where emergency or extraordinary relief is requested including, but not limited to, excluding a parent from the residence, the court shall require full compliance with the provisions of Trial Rules 65(B) and 65(E). In situations involving allegations of physical abuse, intimidation or stalking, relief may be sought by a separate filing for an Order of Protection.

Adopted effective Jan. 1, 2009.

APPENDICES

APPENDIX A. CERTIFICATION OF COMPLIANCE IN DISSOLUTION CASES

CAPTION

CERTIFICATION OF COMPLIANCE
IN DISSOLUTION CASES

The undersigned, as the (select: Mother or Father) in the within cause, does hereby certify that:

1. On (type date) I did complete the mandatory website work as required by FLR 5 and have attached hereto my certificate to confirm the same; and,

2. On (type date) I did complete the mandatory co-parenting class as required by FLR 6 and have attached hereto my certificate to confirm the same.

I affirm under the penalties for perjury that the foregoing representations are true.

Date: _____   _____

(Type name), (select: Mother or Father)

Adopted effective Jan. 1, 1993. Amended effective Dec. 5, 2006; Jan. 1, 2009; Jan. 1, 2011.

APPENDIX B. CERTIFICATION OF COMPLIANCE IN PATERNITY CASES

CAPTION

CERTIFICATION OF COMPLIANCE IN PATERNITY CASES

The undersigned, as the (select: Mother or Father) in the within cause, does hereby certify that:

On (type date) I did complete the mandatory website work as required by the FLR 5 and have attached hereto my certificate to confirm the same.

I affirm under the penalties for perjury that the foregoing representations are true.

Date: _____   _____

(Type name), (select: Mother or Father)

Adopted effective Jan. 1, 1993. Amended effective Jan. 20, 1998; Dec. 5, 2006; Jan. 1, 2009; Jan. 1, 2011.

APPENDIX C. PARENT'S AFFIRMATION

In Re The (select: Marriage/Paternity) of: _____

Cause No.: _____

(Select: Mother's/Father's) Parenting Plan Proposal

Parent's Affirmation

I hereby affirm, under the penalties for perjury, that **before** preparing this proposal I have:

1. carefully read the Indiana Parenting Time Guidelines, including the Preamble and General Rules and understand that they reflect the **minimum** parenting time; and,

2. completed all the work assignments for parents at (select: www.UpToParents.org/www.ProudToParent.org [delete paragraph # 3 in paternity cases]; and,

3. completed the co-parenting class required by the court.

Dated: _____, 20 _____.   _____

(Select: Mother/Father)

Terms of This Proposal

The following proposal for the parenting plan for our children was prepared and is submitted in compliance with the Lake County Rules of Family Law and is part of the effort of both parents to devise a parenting plan to include the decision making and living arrangements that will serve to nurture and protect our children as the years progress. As stated in the Lake County Rules of Family Law, the following proposal was prepared and is submitted as part of the effort to compromise and settle these and other issues which now exist between the parents and, as a result, unless all of the terms of the following proposal are accepted as shown by the signature of both parents on page four (4) hereof, the following proposal and all of its terms, constitute privileged communications which are inadmissible for any purposes.

1. As the parents, important decisions in our children's lives (such as place of residence, school selection and other educational decisions, healthcare and religious upbringing) will be made as follows:

_____

_____

_____

_____

2. The declared legal residence of our children for school and legal purposes will be:

_____

_____

_____

3. Due to the circumstances of the lives of the members of our family, including work schedules and the like, our parenting time schedule for our children to be with each of us will vary from the **minimum** set forth in the Indiana Parenting Guidelines, as follows:

Weekdays: _____

_____

_____

Weekends: _____

_____

Holidays and Special Days: _____

_____

Extended Parenting Time/Summer Vacation: _____

_____

_____

4. In the event of disagreement, we will speak to one another first to try to resolve any parenting issues. If we are unable to resolve all the issues, then we will utilize the following:

(Circle all that apply and add any additional ones.)

     A.   Redoing the (select: www.UpToParents.org/ www.ProudToParent.org) website work.

     B.   Additional co-parenting classes, including re-attending the basic class or attending high-conflict classes.

     C.   Mediation.

     D.   Arbitration.

     E.   Individual, joint, family, or child counseling.

     F.   Appointment of a parenting time coordinator (PTC) to work with us.

     G.   Appointment of a guardian ad litem (GAL) for our children.

     H.   Other (specify): _____

_____

_____

    5.   Other provisions of our parenting plan would be: _____

_____

_____

Dated: _____, 20 ___.

_____
(Select: Mother/Father)

_____
(attorney's name)

Indiana Attorney No.: _____

(firm name)

Attorney for (select: Mother/Father)

(address)

(phone number)

ACCEPTANCE

By our signatures, we, as the parents, we now agree to all of the terms set forth above as our Parenting Agreement and that this document is now admissible in to evidence in court.

_____	_____
(Select: Mother/Father)	(Select: Mother/Father)
Date: _____, 20 ___.	Date: _____, 20 ___.
_____	_____
(attorney's name)	(attorney's name)
Indiana Attorney No.: _____	Indiana Attorney No.: _____
(firm name)	(firm name)
Attorney for (select: Mother/Father)	Attorney for (select: Mother/Father)
(address)	(address)
(phone number)	(phone number)

As dedicated parents, we will do our best to:

Remember that our children's only job is to be children, not our messengers, spies, counselors, confidants, or carriers of our hurt.

Be sure to remember that our love for our children is greater than any issue we could have with each other.

Respect each other's parenting time while also being flexible, so the children's lives can be as normal as possible.

Educate our extended families and close friends that they need to make peace as well.

Pay special attention to keep our appointments and schedules with each other and calling promptly if any problems come up.

Adopted effective Jan. 1, 2009 Amended effective Jan. 1, 2011.

APPENDIX D. SUMMONS AND NOTICE OF HEARING IN PROCEEDINGS FOR DISSOLUTION OF MARRIAGE

STATE OF INDIANA   IN THE (Title, Address and
                                                                 Phone Number of Court)

                                    SS:

COUNTY OF LAKE

IN RE: THE MARRIAGE OF   Cause No.

(Name of Filing Party),

    (select: Mother, Wife, Father, Husband)

    and

(Name of Spouse),

    (select: Mother, Wife, Father, Husband)

SUMMONS
AND NOTICE OF HEARING
IN PROCEEDINGS FOR DISSOLUTION OF MARRIAGE

THE STATE OF INDIANA TO: (name of spouse being served)

                                        (address)

Your spouse has filed an action for dissolution of marriage in the Court stated above. A copy of the Petition (and, in some cases, other documents) together with a separate Notice from the Court which is printed on yellow paper are attached to or otherwise served with this Summons and contain important details regarding the nature of these proceedings. Local Rules in Lake County require that both you and your spouse complete certain, specific tasks and you should immediately and carefully review those requirements at the website established by the Court at: www.LakeCountyKids. org.

THIS IS YOUR OFFICIAL NOTICE that a hearing on Provisional Orders has been scheduled for   , 20 ___, at _____ ___ M. before this Court, in (room number) which is located on the (floor), at the address listed in the upper right hand corner of this Summons. If you wish to hire an attorney to represent you in this matter, it is advisable to do so before that date. If you do not appear for that hearing, a provisional order could be entered by default which could remain in effect until this action is concluded.

THIS IS YOUR OFFICIAL NOTICE that a final hearing has been scheduled for _____, 20 ___, at M. before this Court, in (room number) which is located on the (_____ floor), at the address listed in the upper right hand corner of this Summons.

If you do not file a written appearance with the Clerk and serve a copy on your spouse's attorney, you may not receive notice of any further proceedings in this action. If you do not make such an appearance, a final decree could be entered by default which grants the relief sought in your spouse's Petition after the expiration of sixty (60) days from the date of the filing of the Petition. You are not required to file any written Answer to respond to the Petition; however, certain grounds for dismissal must be asserted in a timely fashion or are waived; and, if you have a claim for relief against your spouse you may be required to assert such a claim in a written pleading which must be filed with the Clerk and served on your spouse's attorney.

The following manner of service of this SUMMONS is hereby designated:

Date:

(Name of attorney for Filing Party)   THOMAS R. PHILPOT

Indiana Attorney No: (insert)   CLERK, LAKE CIRCUIT/SUPERIOR COURTS

(firm name)

Attorney for (select: Mother, Wife, Father, Husband)

(address)   By: _____

                                     Deputy Clerk

(phone number)

PREPARATION DATA:

All summons are to be prepared in triplicate with the original of each to be placed in the Court file with two copies available for service.

If service is by certified mail a properly addressed envelope shall be provided for the party being served. Certified mail labels and return receipts must also be furnished for each mailing and the cause number must appear on each return receipt, which shall be returnable to the Clerk at the address of the Court.

CLERK'S CERTIFICATE OF MAILING

I hereby certify that on the ___ day of _____, 20 ___, I mailed a copy of this Summons and a copy of the Petition to the party being served, _____, by _____ mail, requesting a return receipt, at the address furnished by the filing party.

THOMAS R. PHILPOT
CLERK, LAKE CIRCUIT/SUPERIOR COURTS

Dated: _____, 20 ___.   BY: _____

                                       Deputy Clerk

RETURN ON SERVICE OF SUMMONS BY MAIL

I hereby certify that the attached return receipt was received by me showing that the Summons and a copy of the Petition mailed to the party being served, _____, was accepted by the party being served on the ___ day of _____, 20 ___.

       I hereby certify that the attached return receipt was received by me showing that the Summons and a copy of the Petition was returned not accepted on the ___ day of _____, 20 ___.

THOMAS R. PHILPOT
CLERK, LAKE CIRCUIT/SUPERIOR COURTS

Dated: _____, 20 ___.   BY: _____

                                       Deputy Clerk

RETURN OF SERVICE OF SUMMONS BY SHERIFF

I hereby certify that I have served the within Summons:

     1) By delivering on _____, 20 ___, a copy of this Summons and a copy of the Petition to each of the within named person(s).

     2) By leaving on _____, 20 ___, for each of the within named person(s) a copy of the Summons and a copy of the Petition at the respective dwelling house or usual place of abode, in _____, Indiana, with a person of suitable age and discretion residing within, whose usual duties or activities include prompt communication of such information to the person served, or by otherwise leaving such process thereat, and by mailing a copy of the Summons without the Petition to the said named person(s) at the address listed herein.

     3) This Summons came to hand this date, _____, 20 ___. The within named _____ was not found in my bailiwick this date, _____, 20 ___.

       ALL DONE IN LAKE COUNTY, INDIANA.

            ROY DOMINGUEZ
            SHERIFF OF LAKE COUNTY, INDIANA
            By: _____

SERVICE ACKNOWLEDGED

I hereby acknowledge that I received a copy of the within Summons and a copy of the Petition at _____ in _____, Indiana, on this date, _____, 20 ___.

_____
          Signature of Party Served

Adopted effective Jan. 1, 2009. Amended effective Jan. 1, 2011.

APPENDIX D–1. SUMMONS IN PROCEEDINGS FOR DISSOLUTION OF MARRIAGE

STATE OF INDIANA   IN THE (Title, Address and
                                            Phone Number of Court)
               SS:

COUNTY OF LAKE

IN RE: THE MARRIAGE OF   Cause No.

(Name of Filing Party),

     (select: Mother, Wife, Father, Husband)

     and

(Name of Spouse),

_____ (select: Mother, Wife, Father, Husband)

SUMMONS

IN PROCEEDINGS FOR DISSOLUTION OF MARRIAGE

THE STATE OF INDIANA TO: (name of spouse being served)

                          (address)

Your spouse has filed an action for dissolution of marriage in the Court stated above. A copy of the Petition (and, in some cases, other documents) together with a separate Notice from the Court which is printed on yellow paper are attached to or otherwise served with this Summons and contain important details regarding the nature of these proceedings. Local Rules in Lake County require that both you and your spouse complete certain, specific tasks and you should immediately and carefully review those requirements at the website established by the Court at: www.LakeCountyKids. org.

If you do not file a written appearance with the Clerk and serve a copy on your spouse's attorney, you may not receive notice of any further proceedings in this action. If you do not make such an appearance, a final decree could be entered by default which grants the relief sought in your spouse's Petition after the expiration of sixty (60) days from the date of the filing of the Petition. You are not required to file any written Answer to respond to the Petition; however, certain grounds for dismissal must be asserted in a timely fashion or are waived; and, if you have a claim for relief against your spouse you may be required to assert such a claim in a written pleading which must be filed with the Clerk and served on your spouse's attorney.

The following manner of service of this SUMMONS is hereby designated:

(select: Registered or certified mail, return receipt #

Sheriff of Lake County

Private service by:

Other (specify): _____'_____)

Date:

(Name of attorney for Filing Party)   THOMAS R. PHILPOT

Indiana Attorney No: (insert)   CLERK, LAKE CIRCUIT/SUPERIOR COURTS

(firm name)

(Attorney for (select: Mother, Wife, Father, Husband)

(address)   By:_____
                                                         Deputy Clerk

(phone number)

PREPARATION DATA:

All summons are to be prepared in triplicate with the original of each to be placed in the Court file with two copies available for service.

If service is by certified mail a properly addressed envelope shall be provided for the party being served. Certified mail labels and return receipts must also be furnished for each mailing and the cause number must appear on each return receipt, which shall be returnable to the Clerk at the address of the Court. (Form: DS 1/97)

Adopted effective Jan. 1, 2009. Amended effective Jan. 1, 2011.

APPENDIX D–2. SUMMONS AND NOTICE OF HEARING IN PROCEEDINGS FOR DISSOLUTION OF MARRIAGE

STATE OF INDIANA   IN THE (Title, Address and
                                           Phone Number of Court)

SS:

COUNTY OF LAKE

IN RE: THE MARRIAGE OF   Cause No.

(Name of Filing Party),

    (select: Mother, Wife, Father, Husband)

    and

(Name of Spouse),

    (select: Mother, Wife, Father, Husband)

347

SUMMONS
AND NOTICE OF HEARING
IN PROCEEDINGS FOR DISSOLUTION OF MARRIAGE

THE STATE OF INDIANA TO: (name of spouse being served)

                              (address)

Your spouse has filed an action for dissolution of marriage in the Court stated above. A copy of the Petition (and, in some cases, other documents) together with a separate Notice from the Court which is printed on yellow paper are attached to or otherwise served with this Summons and contain important details regarding the nature of these proceedings. Local Rules in Lake County require that both you and your spouse complete certain, specific tasks and you should immediately and carefully review those requirements at the website established by the Court at: www.LakeCountyKids. org.

THIS IS YOUR OFFICIAL NOTICE that a hearing on Provisional Orders has been scheduled for _____, 20 ___, at _____ ___ M. before this Court, in (room number) which is located on the (_____ floor), at the address listed in the upper right hand corner of this Summons. If you wish to hire an attorney to represent you in this matter, it is advisable to do so before that date. If you do not appear for that hearing, a provisional order could be entered by default which could remain in effect until this action is concluded.

If you do not file a written appearance with the Clerk and serve a copy on your spouse's attorney, you may not receive notice of any further proceedings in this action. If you do not make such an appearance, a final decree could be entered by default which grants the relief sought in your spouse's Petition after the expiration of sixty (60) days from the date of the filing of the Petition. You are not required to file any written Answer to respond to the Petition; however, certain grounds for dismissal must be asserted in a timely fashion or are waived; and, if you have a claim for relief against your spouse you may be required to assert such a claim in a written pleading which must be filed with the Clerk and served on your spouse's attorney.

The following manner of service of this SUMMONS is hereby designated:

     Date:

(Name of attorney for Filing Party)   THOMAS R. PHILPOT

Indiana Attorney No: (insert)   CLERK, LAKE CIRCUIT/SUPERIOR COURTS

(firm name)

Attorney for (select: Mother, Wife, Father, Husband)

(address)   By:_____
                                 Deputy Clerk

(phone number)

     PREPARATION DATA:

All summons are to be prepared in triplicate with the original of each to be placed in the Court file with two copies available for service.

If service is by certified mail a properly addressed envelope shall be provided for the party being served. Certified mail labels and return receipts must also be furnished for each mailing and the cause number must appear on each return receipt, which shall be returnable to the Clerk at the address of the Court.

Adopted effective Jan. 1, 2009. Amended effective Jan. 1, 2011.

APPENDIX D–3. SUMMONS AND NOTICE OF HEARING IN PROCEEDINGS FOR DISSOLUTION OF MARRIAGE

STATE OF INDIANA   IN THE (Title, Address and
                               Phone Number of Court)
          SS:

COUNTY OF LAKE

IN RE: THE MARRIAGE OF   Cause No.

(Name of Filing Party),

    (select: Mother, Wife, Father, Husband)

    and

(Name of Spouse),

    (select: Mother, Wife, Father, Husband)

SUMMONS AND NOTICE OF HEARING IN PROCEEDINGS
FOR DISSOLUTION OF MARRIAGE

THE STATE OF INDIANA TO: (name of spouse being served)

           (address)

Your spouse has filed an action for dissolution of marriage in the Court stated above. A copy of the Petition (and, in some cases, other documents) together with a separate Notice from the Court which is printed on yellow paper are attached to or otherwise served with this Summons and contain important details regarding the nature of these proceedings. Local Rules in Lake County require that both you and your spouse complete certain, specific tasks and you should immediately and carefully review those requirements at the website established by the Court at: www.LakeCountyKids. org.

THIS IS YOUR OFFICIAL NOTICE that a final hearing has been scheduled for _____, 20 ___, at M. before this Court, in (room number) which is located on the (_____ floor), at the address listed in the upper right hand corner of this Summons.

If you do not file a written appearance with the Clerk and serve a copy on your spouse's attorney, you may not receive notice of any further proceedings in this action. If you do not make such an appearance, a final decree could be entered by default which grants the relief sought in your spouse's Petition after the expiration of sixty (60) days from the date of the filing of the Petition. You are not required to file any written Answer to respond to the Petition; however, certain grounds for dismissal must be asserted in a timely fashion or are waived; and, if you have a claim for relief against your spouse you may be required to assert such a claim in a written pleading which must be filed with the Clerk and served on your spouse's attorney.

The following manner of service of this SUMMONS is hereby designated:

    (select: Registered or certified mail, return receipt #

        Sheriff of Lake County

        Private service by:

        Other (specify): _____)

Date:

(Name of attorney for Filing Party)   THOMAS R. PHILPOT

Indiana Attorney No: (insert)   CLERK, LAKE CIRCUIT/SUPERIOR COURTS

(firm name)

Attorney for (select: Mother, Wife, Father, Husband)

(address)   By:_____
                             Deputy Clerk

(phone number)

PREPARATION DATA:

All summons are to be prepared in triplicate with the original of each to be placed in the Court file with two copies available for service.

If service is by certified mail a properly addressed envelope shall be provided for the party being served. Certified mail labels and return receipts must also be furnished for each mailing and the cause number must appear on each return receipt, which shall be returnable to the Clerk at the address of the Court. (Form: DS 1/97)

CLERK'S CERTIFICATE OF MAILING

I hereby certify that on the ___ day of _____, 20 ___, I mailed a copy of this Summons and a copy of the Petition to the party being served, _____, by _____ mail, requesting a return receipt, at the address furnished by the filing party.

THOMAS R. PHILPOT
CLERK, LAKE CIRCUIT/SUPERIOR COURTS

Dated: _____, 20 ___.   BY:_____

Deputy Clerk

RETURN ON SERVICE OF SUMMONS BY MAIL

I hereby certify that the attached return receipt was received by me showing that the Summons and a copy of the Petition mailed to the party being served, _____, was accepted by the party being served on the ___ day of _____, 20 ___.

I hereby certify that the attached return receipt was received by me showing that the Summons and a copy of the Petition was returned not accepted on the ___ day of _____, 20 ___.

THOMAS R. PHILPOT
CLERK, LAKE CIRCUIT/SUPERIOR COURTS

Dated: _____, 20 ___.   BY:_____

Deputy Clerk

RETURN OF SERVICE OF SUMMONS BY SHERIFF

I hereby certify that I have served the within Summons:

1) By delivering on _____, 20 ___, a copy of this Summons and a copy of the Petition to each of the within named person(s).

2) By leaving on _____, 20 ___, for each of the within named person(s) a copy of the Summons and a copy of the Petition at the respective dwelling house or usual place of abode, in _____, Indiana, with a person of suitable age and discretion residing within, whose usual duties or activities include prompt communication of such information to the person served, or by otherwise leaving such process thereat, and by mailing a copy of the Summons without the Petition to the said named person(s) at the address listed herein.

3) This Summons came to hand this date, _____, 20 ___. The within named _____ was not found in my bailiwick this date, _____, 20 ___.

ALL DONE IN LAKE COUNTY, INDIANA.

ROY DOMINGUEZ
SHERIFF OF LAKE COUNTY, INDIANA

By: _____

SERVICE ACKNOWLEDGED

I hereby acknowledge that I received a copy of the within Summons and a copy of the Petition at _____ in _____, Indiana, on this date, _____, 20 ___.

_____
Signature of Party Served

Adopted effective Jan. 1, 2009. Amended effective Jan. 1, 2011.

APPENDIX E. SUMMONS AND NOTICE OF INITIAL HEARING IN A PATERNITY CASE

STATE OF INDIANA   IN THE SUPERIOR COURT OF LAKE
COUNTY

                                               JUVENILE DIVISION, 3000 West 93rd Avenue,

COUNTY OF LAKE   Crown Point, Indiana 46307 (219) 660–6900

IN THE MATTER OF THE PATERNITY OF: CAUSE NO. 45D06–0107–JP–0000

KIRBY UPRIGHT

Male Born 1/1/2007

HOOVER ORECK,

        Putative Father,

and

DYSON UPRIGHT,

        Mother

KIRBY UPRIGHT b/n/f HOOVER ORECK

SUMMONS
AND NOTICE OF INITIAL HEARING IN A PATERNITY CASE

THE STATE OF INDIANA TO: Dyson Upright

                                            1234 Electrolux Lane

                                            Berber, IN 46000

A paternity action has been filed in the Court stated above. A copy of the Petition (and, in come cases, other documents) together with a separate Notice from the Court which is printed on yellow paper are attached to or otherwise served with this Summons and contain important details regarding the nature of these proceedings. Local Rules in Lake County require that both parties to this case complete certain specific tasks. You should immediately and carefully review those requirements at the website established by the Court at: www.Lake CountyKids.org.

THIS IS YOUR OFFICIAL NOTICE that an Initial Hearing to Establish Paternity is scheduled for **the ___ day of _____, 20 ___, at ___ o'clock ___.m.** at the address listed in the upper right hand corner of this Summons. If you wish to hire an attorney to represent you in this matter, it is advisable to do so before that date. **If you do not appear for that hearing, a final order could be entered by default determining paternity, custody, parenting time and child support.**

If you do not file a written appearance with the Clerk and serve a copy on the attorney whose name and address is set forth at the bottom of this page, you may not receive notice of any further proceedings in this action. You are not required to file any written Answer to respond to the Petition; however, certain grounds for dismissal must be asserted in a timely fashion or are waived; and, if you have a claim for relief against the person who filed the Petition, you may be required to assert such a claim in a written pleading which must be filed with the Clerk and served upon the attorney whose name and address is set forth at the bottom of this page.

The following manner of service is designated: **Sheriff (or CMRRR, or Private Server etc.)**

    Date: THOMAS R. PHILPOT

    F.Q. Cannister, #000–45   CLERK, SUPERIOR COURT OF LAKE
                                                            COUNTY

    Attorney for Putative Father   By: _____

    789 Suction Lane   Deputy Clerk

Vacuum, IN 46000

219.000.0000

CLERK'S CERTIFICATE OF MAILING

I hereby certify that on the ___ day of _____, 20 ___, I mailed a copy of this Summons and a copy of the Petition to the party being served, _____, by _____ mail, requesting a return receipt, at the address furnished by the filing party.

THOMAS R. PHILPOT
CLERK, LAKE CIRCUIT/SUPERIOR COURTS

Dated: _____, 20 ___.   BY:_____

Deputy Clerk

RETURN ON SERVICE OF SUMMONS BY MAIL

I hereby certify that the attached return receipt was received by me showing that the Summons and a copy of the Petition mailed to the party being served, _____, was accepted by the party being served on the _____ day of _____, 20 ___.

I hereby certify that the attached return receipt was received by me showing that the Summons and a copy of the Petition was returned not accepted on the ___ day of _____, 20 ___.

THOMAS R. PHILPOT
CLERK, LAKE CIRCUIT/SUPERIOR COURTS

Dated: _____, 20 ___.   BY:_____

Deputy Clerk

RETURN OF SERVICE OF SUMMONS BY SHERIFF

I hereby certify that I have served the within Summons:

1. By delivering on _____, 20 ___, a copy of this Summons and a copy of the Petition to each of the within named person(s).

2. By leaving on _____, 20 ___, for each of the within named person(s) a copy of the Summons and a copy of the Petition at the respective dwelling house or usual place of abode, in _____, Indiana, with a person of suitable age and discretion residing within, whose usual duties or activities include prompt communication of such information to the person served, or by otherwise leaving such process thereat, and by mailing a copy of the Summons without the Petition to the said named person(s) at the address listed herein.

3. This Summons came to hand this date, _____, 20 ___. The within named _____ was not found in my bailiwick this date, _____, 20 ___.

ALL DONE IN LAKE COUNTY, INDIANA.

ROY DOMINGUEZ
SHERIFF OF LAKE COUNTY, INDIANA

By: _____

SERVICE ACKNOWLEDGED

I hereby acknowledge that I received a copy of the within Summons and a copy of the Petition at _____ in, Indiana, on this date, _____, 20 ___.

_____
Signature of Party Served

Adopted effective Jan. 1, 2009. Amended effective Jan. 1, 2011.

APPENDIX F. INFORMATION SHEET FOR FAMILY COURT PILOT PROJECT

NOT FOR PUBLIC ACCESS

Cause No. _____

_____

Petitioner

_____

Respondent

INFORMATION SHEET
FOR FAMILY COURT PILOT PROJECT

This form is required to be completed in full and filed with the Clerk's Office with all new petitions filed for dissolution of marriage, legal separation and determination of paternity. The information on this form will be used to identify families who have more than one cause of action pending in the Lake County Court system, and to aid the Courts in tracking the progress of these matters.

Full Name	Soc. Sec. Number	Date of Birth	Sex (M/F)
Petitioner:			
Respondent:			

Names of all children of the parties:

Full Name	Soc. Sec. Number	Date of Birth	Sex (M/F)

Names of all other persons residing in the parties' household:

Full Name	Soc. Sec. Number	Relationship	Date of Birth	S ex (M/F)

Please list all other court cases in which the parties, their children or any members of their household are involved in any capacity.   Include all cases, including Juvenile, Probate, Criminal, Civil, Domestic Relations, Protective Orders, Small Claims and Traffic.

Title of case: Name and location of court:

Type of case: Cause Number:

Title of case: Name and location of court:

Type of case: Cause Number:

Title of case: Name and location of court:

Type of case: Cause Number:

Use additional sheets if necessary to supply complete information.

Adopted effective Jan. 1, 2009. Amended effective Jan. 1, 2011.

APPENDIX G. JUDGES' NOTICE TO PARENTS GOING THROUGH DIVORCE

JUDGES' NOTICE TO PARENTS GOING THROUGH DIVORCE

We, the Judges and Magistrates of Lake County, share the following information so that you will know of our commitment to the best interests of children. *Please read this information carefully, as we expect you and all other persons involved in your case to be partners in serving those best interests.*

1. As soon as possible, visit www.LakeCountyKids.org to learn about the Courts' expectations and to read the Lake County Rules of Family Law for important information about how divorce cases will be handled to:

- ensure safety;
- reduce conflict;
- build cooperation; and,
- protect the best interests of all family members, especially all children.

2.   If there will be no attorneys in your case, see the "Cases Without Attorneys" link on Courts' website, www. LakeCountyKids.org, for special work required of you.

3.   If you and your spouse have any children under the age of 18, you **must** do the following within 30 days:

> a.   *Register for a co-parenting class.* You will find more information about the class and how to register at the link on the Courts' website, www.LakeCountyKids. org.
>
> b.   Complete the work on www.UpToParents.org, and take your completed work to your coparenting class, give a copy to your attorney, and bring it with you to all court appearances and other meetings.

4.   If you and your spouse have any children under the age of 18, you should attempt to establish your own plan for the decision making and living arrangements that will serve to nurture and protect your children. A plan which is worked out between the parents to fit the needs of their children and family is almost always the best. You should review the Indiana Parenting Time Guidelines at the link on the Courts' website, www.LakeCounty Kids.org. The Court considers those Guidelines to be the **minimum** parenting time for each parent to have frequent, meaningful, and continuing contact with their children. We recommend that you use the Parenting Plan Proposal/Worksheet which you will also find on the Courts' website, www.LakeCountyKids.org.

5.   You and your spouse must complete and exchange Financial Declaration Forms with all required attachments. You will find this Form at the link on the Courts' website, www.LakeCountyKids.org.

Adopted effective Jan. 1, 2009. Amended effective Jan. 1, 2011.

APPENDIX H. JUDGES' NOTICE TO PARENTS IN PATERNITY CASES

JUDGES' NOTICE TO PARENTS IN PATERNITY CASES

We, the Judges and Magistrates of Lake County, share the following information so that you will know of our commitment to the best interests of children. *Please read this information carefully, as we expect you and all other persons involved in your case to be partners in serving those best interests.*

> 1.   **If either of you question whether or not the man named as the father in this case is the father,** the Court will order genetic testing at the initial hearing to establish paternity. If the man named as father is found not to be the father by genetic testing, the case will be dismissed.
>
> 2.   **If paternity is established,** whether by agreement or otherwise, or following genetic testing, the Local Rules of the Circuit and Superior Court of Lake County, Indiana, require you to do the following:
>
> A.   **Complete the work on www.ProudToParent.org** and furnish the Court with a certification that you have done so.
>
> B.   **Complete and exchange Financial Declaration Forms with all required attachments.** You will find this form at the link on the Court's website, www. LakeCountyKids.org.
>
> C.
>
> 3.   **In addition, if paternity is established,** whether by agreement or otherwise, or following genetic testing, you will be expected to do the following:
>
> A.   **Devise a Parenting Plan for your children.** A Parenting Plan consists of the decision making and living and financial arrangements that will serve to nurture and protect your children as the years progress. A plan which is worked out between the parents to fit the needs of their children and family is almost always best. You should review the Indiana Parenting Time Guidelines at the link on the Court's website, www.LakeCountyKids.org. The Court considers those Guidelines to be the **minimum** parenting time for each parent to have frequent, meaningful, and continuing contact with their children. We recommend that you use the Parenting Plan Proposal/Worksheet which you will also find on the Court's website, www.LakeCountyKids.org. If you fail to devise a successful Parenting Plan for your children, this Court may require you to attend and complete, at your own expense, a coparenting class.

    B. If there will be no attorneys in your case, read the "Cases Without Attorneys" link on the Court's website, www.LakeCountyKids.org, for special work required of you.

    C. Read the Lake County Rules of Family Law and the Indiana Parenting Time Guidelines which are available on the Court's website, www.LakeCounty Kids.org, for additional important information on the Court's expectation that everyone involved in your case will be a partner in:

- **ensuring safety;**
- **reducing conflict;**
- **building cooperation; and,**
- **protecting the best interests of all family members, especially all children.**

Adopted effective Jan. 1, 2009. Amended effective Jan. 1, 2011.

APPENDIX I. DISSOLUTION OF MARRIAGE: FINANCIAL DECLARATION FORM

DISSOLUTION OF MARRIAGE: FINANCIAL DECLARATION FORM
STATE OF INDIANA: CIRCUIT AND SUPERIOR COURTS OF LAKE COUNTY

IN RE THE MARRIAGE OF:

                                                   Cause No. _____

_____

(select: Mother, Wife, Father, Husband)
and

_____

(select: Mother, Wife, Father, Husband)
FINANCIAL DECLARATION OF: _____

This declaration is considered mandatory discovery and must be exchanged between the parties within 60 days of the initial filing of the Dissolution of Marriage. Parties not represented by counsel are required to comply with these practices. Failure by either party to complete and exchange this form as required will authorize the court to impose sanctions set forth in Rule 6 of the Lake County Rules of Family Law. If appraisals or verifications are not available within 60 days the from must be exchanged within 60 days with a notation that appraisals or verifications are being obtained and then the Declaration shall be supplemented within 30 days thereafter.

Husband: _____   Wife: _____

Address: _____   Address: _____

_____   _____

Soc. Sec. No.: _____   Soc. Sec. No.: _____

Badge/Payroll No.: _____   Badge/Payroll No.: _____

Occupation: _____   Occupation: _____

Employer: _____   Employer: _____

Date started this employment: _____   Date started this employment: _____

Birth Date: _____   Birth Date: _____

Date of Marriage: _____

Date of Physical Separation: _____

Date of Filing: _____

List Names, dates of birth, and social security numbers of all children of this relationship, whether by birth or adoption:

_____   _____

_____   _____

_____   _____

List Names and dates of birth of any other children living at the residence of the person responding (identify if these are children of the responding party) and for each such person indicate the amount of support, if any, that is received:

_____   _____

_____   _____

_____   _____

Part I INCOME AND EXPENSES STATEMENT

Attach COMPLETE copies of your Federal Income Tax Returns for the last three taxable years including all W2's and 1099's. Also attach proof of all wages earned in the present year up to the date of your response. If current wage statement shows year to date wages and itemized deductions this is sufficient. If current wage statement does not indicate year to date earnings and deductions attach the 8 most recent pay stubs.

Person Responding

    A. Gross yearly income from Salary and Wages, including commissions, bonuses, allowances and overtime received in _____ most recent year.

    Average gross pay per pay period (indicate whether you are _____ paid weekly each 2 weeks or twice per month)

B. Gross Monthly Income from Other Sources[1]

List and explain in detail any Rents received, Dividend income, or Pension, Retirement, Social Security, Disability and/or Unemployment Insurance benefits—or any other source including Public assistance, food stamps, and child support received for any child not born of the parties of this marriage.

_____

C. SELECTED LIVING EXPENSES: List names and relations of each member of the household of the Responding party whose expenses are included.

_____   _____

_____   _____

_____   _____

For each expense attach verification of payment even if it is not specifically requested on this form—please note that Indiana uses an Income Shares model for determining support and thus in most cases the expenses that a party has or does not have are not relevant in determining support under the Indiana Support Guidelines. **However if** you claim your expenses justify a deviation from the support guidelines attach a detailed list of expenses together with verification of same.

    Person Responding

    Rent or Mortgage payments (residence)   _____

    Real Property Taxes (residence) if not included in mortgage payment   _____

Real Property Insurance (residence) if not included in mortgage payment   _____

Cost of all Medical Insurance—specify time period—Attach verification of payment if not on pay stub   _____

Cost of only that medical insurance that is related to the children of this action—specify time period—attach verification from employer or insurance company   _____

Child care costs—to permit work—specify time period (per day, week, month)—attach verification   _____

Pre–School Costs (specify time period week, semester or year)   _____

School Tuition—per semester (Grade or High School)   _____

Book Costs—per semester (Grade or High School)   _____

For Post High School Attach separate list with explanation of loans and scholarships and grants   _____

Child support paid for children other than those involved in this case—attach proof of payment   _____

D. IN ALL CASES INVOLVING CHILD SUPPORT: Prepare and attach any Indiana Child Support Guideline Worksheet (with documentation verifying your income); or, supplement with such a Worksheet within ten (10) days of the exchange of this Form.

Further, if there exists a parenting plan or pattern then state the number of overnights the non-custodial parent will have the child during the year.

The yearly number of overnights is _____

E. POST HIGH SCHOOL EDUCATION EXPENSE

If any of the children subject to this case are attending post high school classes, or will attend within the next six months list the following information for each such student. **Further attach to this financial affidavit any documentation you have in support of these answers.**

Name of Student _____

Name of School _____

Cost of School per year—If applicable, include room and board _____

Identify all student financial aid including grants, scholarships, and loans and for each indicate what it is and how much will be received: _____

Note in those cases where it is appropriate parties may want to engage in additional discovery concerning assets that might be applied to education such as IRA's, 401 K's etc. Note further that withdrawals from IRA's for educational expenses do not suffer a 10% penalty (IRC code sec 72 (t) 2 (e).

F. Debts and Obligations: (Include credit union) attach additional sheets as needed. Indicate any special circumstances, i.e., premarital debts, debts in arrears on the date of physical separation, or date of filing and the amount or number of payments in arrears.

ATTACH A COPY OF THE MOST RECENT STATEMENT FOR EACH LISTED DEBT

Creditor's Name & Persons on Account	Balance	Monthly Payment

PART II NET WORTH—ATTACH ALL AVAILABLE DOCUMENTATION TO VERIFY VALUES—

List all property owned either individually or jointly. Indication who holds or how the title is held: (H) Husband, (W) Wife, or (J) Jointly or other appropriate indication. WHERE SPACE IS INSUFFICIENT FOR COMPLETE INFORMATION OR LISTING PLEASE ATTACH SEPARATE PAGE.

A. Household Furnishings: (Value of Furniture, Appliances, and Equipment, as a whole—You need not itemize—indicate whether you use replacement cost or a garage sale value)

B. Automobiles, Boats, Snowmobiles, Motorcycles, Etc.:

Year—Make & Present Value	Titled Owner	Balance Owed

C. Cash and Deposit Accounts: (including **ALL** banks, savings and loan associations, credit unions, thrift plans, mutual funds, certificate of deposit, savings and/or checking accounts, IRA's and annuities). **This also includes listing the contents of any safety deposit boxes.** Use additional page if necessary.

Name of Institution & Type of Account	" Owners"	Account No.	Balance

_____

_____

_____

_____

_____

D.   Securities: (Stocks, Bonds, Etc)—use additional page if necessary

Company Name	"Owner"	Shares	Value

E.   Real Estate: (attach separate sheet with the following information for each separate piece of real estate).

Address: _____   Type of Property: _____

_____   Date of Acquisition: _____

Original Cost: _____   Present Value: _____

Basis for Valuation: _____

(Attach appraisal if obtained)

1st MORTGAGE BALANCE AS OF DATE OF ANSWER: _____
Other liens (amount and type): _____
Monthly payment on each mortgage: 1st: _____ 2nd: _____

To whom paid: _____
Taxes (if not included in Mtg. payment): _____
Insurance (if not included in Mtg. payment): _____
Special Assessments (including utility or condo assessments): _____
Identify Individual contributions to the real estate (for example, inheritance, pre-marital assets, personal loans, etc.): _____
_____
_____

F.   Retirement Plans: List monthly amount you would be entitled to at earliest retirement date (indicating that date) if you stopped work today. Your response should indicate date of valuation. Further, if it is a defined interest plan list present amount in plan and date of valuation.

Also, identify whose plan it is and list both the name and the address of administrator of plan—indicate whether plan is vested—if not vested, indicate when it will vest: _____

_____

Attach documents from each plan verifying information. If not yet received, attach a copy of your written request to the plan(s).

G.   Life Insurance: Give name of insured, beneficiary, company issuing, policy #, type of insurance (term, whole life, group), face value, cash value and any loans against—include plans provided by employer: _____

H. **Business or Professional Interests:** Indicate name, share, type of business, value less indebtedness, etc.:

I. **Other Assets:** (this includes coin, stamp or gun collections or other items of unusual value). Use additional pages as needed: _____

PART III VERIFICATION

I declare, under the penalty of perjury, that the foregoing, including any valuations and attachments, is true and correct and that I have made a complete and absolute disclosure of all of my assets and liabilities. Furthermore, I understand that if, in the future, it is proven to this court that I have intentionally failed to disclosure any asset or liability, I may lose the asset and may be required to pay the liability. Finally, I acknowledge that sanctions may be imposed against me, including reasonable attorney's fees and expenses incurred in the investigation, preparation and prosecution of any claim or action that proves my failure to disclose income, assets or liabilities.

DATE: _____   _____

PARTY'S SIGNATURE

PART IV ATTORNEY'S CERTIFICATION

I have reviewed with my client the foregoing information, including any valuations and attachments, and sign this certificate consistent with my obligation under Trial Rule 11 of the Indiana Rules of Procedure.

DATE: _____

_____
(attorney's name)

Indiana Attorney No.: _____

(firm name)

Attorney for (select: Mother/Father)

(address)

(phone number)

Adopted effective Jan. 1, 2009. Amended effective Jan. 1, 2011.

APPENDIX J. PATERNITY & POST DECREE: FINANCIAL DECLARATION FORM

PATERNITY & POST DECREE: FINANCIAL DECLARATION FORM STATE OF INDIANA: CIRCUIT AND SUPERIOR COURTS OF LAKE COUNTY

IN RE THE MARRIAGE OF: Cause No. _____

_____
(select: Mother, Wife, Father, Husband)
and

_____
(select: Mother, Wife, Father, Husband)

FINANCIAL DECLARATION OF: _____

This declaration is considered mandatory discovery and must be exchanged between the parties within 30 days of the filing of any paternity case or any post decree matter. Parties not represented by counsel are required to comply with these practices. Failure by either party to complete and exchange this form as required will authorize the court to impose the sanctions set forth in Rule 6 of the Lake County Rules of Family Law, these include costs and attorney fees.

Father: _____   Mother: _____

Address: _____   Address: _____

_____   _____

Soc. Sec. No.: _____ Soc. Sec. No.: _____

Badge/Payroll No.: _____ Badge/Payroll No.: _____

Occupation: _____   Occupation: _____

Employer: _____   Employer: _____

Date stated this employment: _____ Date started this employment: _____

Birth Date: _____   Birth Date: _____

List the following Dates as Applicable:
Date of Dissolution: _____ Date of most recent support order: _____
Date of Filing of this paternity action: _____
Date of Filing of this post decree action: _____
List Names, dates of birth, and social security numbers of all children of this relationship, whether by birth or adoption:

_____   _____

_____   _____

_____   _____

List Names and dates of birth of any other children living at the residence of the person responding (identify if these are children of the responding party) and for each such person indicate the amount of support, if any, that is received:

_____   _____

_____   _____

_____   _____

Part I. INCOME AND EXPENSES STATEMENT

Attach COMPLETE copies of your Federal Income Tax Returns for the last three taxable years including all W2's and 1099's. Also attach proof of all wages earned in the present year up to the date of your response. If current wage statement shows year to date wages and itemized deductions this is sufficient. If current wage statement does not indicate year to date earnings and deductions attach the 8 most recent pay stubs.

Person Responding
A. **Gross yearly income from Salary and Wages,**
including commissions, bonuses, allowances and
overtime received in most recent year.   _____

Average gross pay per pay period (indicate whether
you are paid weekly each 2 weeks or twice per
month)   _____

B. **Gross Monthly Income from Other Sources**[2]

List and explain in detail any Rents received, Dividend income, or Pension, Retirement, Social Security, Disability and/or Unemployment Insurance benefits—or any other source including Public assistance, food stamps, and child support received for any child not born of the parties of this marriage.

_____

_____

_____

C. **Selected Living Expenses:** List names and relations of each member of the household of the Responding party whose expenses are included.

_____   _____

_____   _____

_____   _____

For each expense attach verification of payment even if it is not specifically requested on this form -please note that Indiana uses an Income Shares model for determining support and thus in most cases the expenses that a party has or does not have are not relevant in determining support under the Indiana Support Guidelines. However if you claim your expenses justify a deviation from the support guidelines attach a detailed list of expenses together with verification of same. Person Responding Rent or Mortgage payments (residence)   _____

Real Property Taxes (residence) if not included in mortgage payment   _____

Real Property Insurance (residence) if not included in mortgage payment   _____

Cost of all Medical Insurance—specify time period—Attach verification of payment if not on pay stub   _____

Cost of only that medical insurance that is related to the children of this action—specify time period—attach verification from employer or insurance company   _____

Child care costs—to permit work—specify time period (per day, week, month)—attach verification   _____

Pre–School Costs (specify time period week, semester or year)   _____

School Tuition—per semester (Grade or High School)   _____

Book Costs—per semester (Grade or High School)   _____

For Post High School Attach separate list with explanation of loans and scholarships and grants

Child support paid for children other than those involved in this case—attach proof of payment   _____

D. **In All Cases Involving Child Support**: Prepare and attach any Indiana Child Support Guideline Worksheet (with documentation verifying your income); or, supplement with such a Worksheet within ten (10) days of the exchange of this Form.

Further, if there exists a parenting plan or pattern then state the number of overnights the non-custodial parent will have the child during the year.

The yearly number of overnights is _____

PART II ARREARAGE COMPUTATION

If case involves a claim of a support or other arrearage, attach all records or other exhibits regarding payment history and compute the arrearage as of the date of the filing of the petition or motion which raises that issue. Explain in detail how arrearage is calculated.

_____

_____

PART III POST HIGH SCHOOL EDUCATION EXPENSE

If any of the children subject to this case are attending post high school classes, or will attend within the next six months list the following information for each such student. Further attach to this financial affidavit any documentation you have in support of these answers.

Name of Student _____

Name of School _____

Cost of School per year—If applicable, include room and board _____

Identify all student financial aid including grants, scholarships, and loans and for each indicate what it is and how much will be received:

_____

_____

_____

_____

Note in those cases where it is appropriate parties may want to engage in additional discovery concerning assets that might be applied to education such as IRA's, 401 K's etc. Note further that withdrawals from IRA's for educational expenses do not suffer a 10% penalty (IRC code sec 72 (t) 2 (e).

PART IV VERIFICATION

I declare, under the penalty of perjury, that the foregoing is true and correct and that I have made a complete and absolute disclosure of all of my income and expenses as asked. I acknowledge that sanctions may be imposed against me, including reasonable attorney's fees and expenses incurred in the investigation, preparation and prosecution of any claim or action that proves my failure to disclose income or liabilities.

      DATE: _____   _____

                                 PARTY'S SIGNATURE

PART V ATTORNEY'S CERTIFICATION

I have reviewed with my client the foregoing information, including any valuations and attachments, and sign this certificate consistent with my obligation under Trial Rule 11 of the Indiana Rules of Procedure.

      DATE: _____   _____

      (attorney's name)

      Indiana Attorney No.: _____
      (firm name)

      Attorney for (select: Mother/Father)
      (address)

      (phone number)

Adopted effective Jan. 1, 2009. Amended effective Jan. 1, 2011.

LAKE COUNTY CRIMINAL CASE ASSIGNMENTS

Adopted as Local Rule for the Assignment of Criminal Cases, Effective April 28, 1995; as Lake County Criminal Rules, Effective December 5, 2006; and as Lake County Criminal Case Assignments, Effective January 1, 2011.

Including Amendments Received Through November 1, 2013

Research Notes

Annotations to the Lake County Criminal Case Assignments are available in West's Annotated Indiana Code, *Title 34 Appendix.*

These rules may be searched electronically on Westlaw *in the* IN-RULES *database; updates to these rules may be found on* Westlaw *in* IN-RULESUPDATES. *For search tips and a summary of database content, consult the Westlaw Scope Screens for each database.*

Rule
LR45–CR2.2 Rule 1.   Local Rule for the Assignment of Criminal Cases in Lake County

LR 45–CR2.2 Rule 1. LOCAL RULE FOR THE ASSIGNMENT OF CRIMINAL CASES IN LAKE COUNTY

All misdemeanors and felonies not' filed by the prosecuting attorney in the city or town courts of the circuit shall be filed, assigned, and reassigned only in accordance with this rule.

A. Filing.

1. Except as otherwise provided, unless the prosecuting attorney elects to file a misdemeanor charge in a city or town court, all misdemeanors shall be filed in the county division of the superior court.

2. All murder, Class A, B and C felonies shall be filed in the criminal division.

3. Except as otherwise provided, the prosecuting attorney may file a Class D felony in either the county or criminal division.

4. If a defendant who is being charged with a Class D felony is on probation to the county division, has other charges pending in the county division, or has previously been sentenced in the county division for an offense, then the Class D felony shall be filed in the county division.

5. If a defendant who is being charged with a Class D felony is on probation to the criminal division, has other charges pending in the criminal division, or has previously been sentenced in the criminal division for an offense, then the Class D felony shall be filed in the criminal division.

6. Notwithstanding the filing requirements above, all charges involving multiple offenses or defendants shall be filed in the same division as one another if the charges arise from:

a. a single act;

b. a series of acts connected together or constituting parts of a single scheme or plan;

c. a conspiracy; or,

d. a number of offenses so closely connected in respect to time, place, and occasion that it would be difficult to separate proof of one offense from proof of the others.

7. Except as otherwise provided, and whenever possible, charges which have previously been filed and dismissed may only be refiled in the same division. This includes all charges arising out of the same offense report, arrest report, or set of operative facts.

B. Assignment.

1. Charges shall be assigned within a division according to the following rules, which are listed in order of precedence:

a. Charges involving multiple offenses or defendants shall be assigned to the same judge if the charges arise from:

(1) a single act;

(2) a series of acts connected together or constituting parts of a single scheme or plan;

(3) a conspiracy; or,

(4) a number of offenses so closely connected in respect to time, place, and occasion that it would be difficult to separate proof of one offense from proof of the others.

b. Charges filed against defendant who has other charges pending shall be assigned to the judge handling the pending charges.

c. Charges filed against a defendant who has previously been sentenced by a judge shall be assigned to that same judge. If the defendant has previously been sentenced by more than one judge of the division, then the case shall be assigned to the judge who still has jurisdiction over the defendant through probation, if applicable, or else to the judge who sentenced the defendant most recently.

d. Charges against a defendant who has previously been a defendant in the division shall be assigned to the same room of the division.

e. If more than one defendant in a new case has other charges pending before separate judges within the same division, the new case shall be assigned to the judge with the greater number of cases pending against all codefendants in the case. If the number of such pending cases is equal for two or more judges, then the case shall either be randomly assigned to one of those judges or else be assigned to the judge whose cases are closer to disposition at the time of the new filing.

f. Charges filed in the county division involving violations of IC 35–48 shall be assigned to Room 2 of that division if the defendant is a resident of the city of Gary or the offense is alleged to have occurred in Gary.

g. All other cases shall be randomly assigned so that the assignment of all criminal cases to judges within a division is kept relatively equal.

2. Charges which have been dismissed and refiled shall be assigned to the same judge who had jurisdiction of the charges when they were dismissed. This includes all charges arising out of the same offense report, arrest report, or set of operative facts.

C. Reassignment. If a motion for change of judge is granted in a case or an order of disqualification or recusal is entered in the case, then the case shall be reassigned to another judge of the same division following the rules of precedence set forth above.

D. Transfer. This rule shall not prohibit the court from transferring a case from one judge to another or from one division to another in accordance with statute. This rule shall also not be understood to encourage or permit the transfer of a case merely on the agreement of the prosecution and defense.

Caseload Allocation Rule	**LR 45–AR1–01**
Priority of Bond Schedule	**LR 45–AR 00–02**
Alcohol and Drug Services Program Fees	**LR 45–AR 00–03**
Court Reporter Services	**LR 45–AR 15–04**

Adopted as Local Rule for the Assignment of Criminal Cases, effective April 28, 1995. Amended effective Jan. 16, 1997; renumbered as Criminal Rule 1, and amended effective Dec. 5, 2006; Jan. 1, 2011; Oct. 18, 2013.

LAKE COUNTY ADMINISTRATIVE RULES

Adopted effective January 1, 2009

Including Amendments Received Through November 1, 2013

Research Notes

Annotations to the Lake County Administrative Rules are available in West's Annotated Indiana Code, Title 34 Appendix.

These rules may be searched electronically on Westlaw in the IN-RULES database; updates to these rules may be found on Westlaw in IN-RULESUPDATES. For search tips and a summary of database content, consult the Westlaw Scope Screens for each database.

Rule

LR45–AR1 Rule 01. CASELOAD ALLOCATION RULE

Pursuant to TR81(a), the Lake Circuit/Superior Court adopts this Rule governing the assignment of cases as required by and in accordance with AR 1(E). This rule shall be effective January 1, 2013.

I. Judicial Reallocation. To comply with the requirement that the utilization variances between all courts of record in Lake County not exceed forty (40) percentage points, the Court adopted the modifications set forth in Table 1 for the 2011 Caseload Plan. This plan will remain in place for the 2013 Caseload Plan.

TABLE 1

COURT	JUDICIAL OFFICERS ASSIGNED UNDER 2011 PLAN
Criminal Division 1 G01	1.5
Criminal Division 2 G02	1.5
Criminal Division 3 G03	1.5
Criminal Division 4 G04	1.5
Circuit Court C01	3.4
Civil Division 1 D01	1.2
Civil Division 2 D02	1.2
Civil Division 3 D03	3
Civil Division 4 D04	1.2
Civil Division 5 D05	1
Civil Division 6 D10	1
Civil Division 7 D11	1
Juvenile Court D06	7.5
County Division 1 D07	2
County Division 2 D08	2.3
County Division 3 D09	2.4
County Division 4 D12	1.3

III. Civil and County Division Case Filing. Notwithstanding the enactment of the following statutes, IC 33–28–1–2, IC 33–29–1–1.5, IC 33–29–1.5–2 and IC 33–31–1–9, all of which address jurisdictional issues, the Lake Circuit and Superior Court adopts the following assignment schedule to maintain the efficient administration of justice and to ensure an even distribution of judicial workload among the courts of record in the County of Lake, pursuant to AR1(E).

The following case types shall be filed as follows:

1. Random filing of PL, CT, MF, and MI cases in the Circuit Court and the Civil Division, Rooms 1, 2, 4, 5, 6 and 7.

2. Random filing of CC and PO cases in the Circuit/Civil Division Courts by court location.

3. The equal distribution amongst the Civil Division of quiet title cases, previously filed exclusively in the Circuit, will allow the Court to meet the .40 objective detailed in AR1(E)(2).

4. With respect to PO cases in Crown Point and Gary, the Circuit Court and Civil Division, Room 3, hear all cases where there is a pending or concluded DR case in those courts involving the same parties. All other PO cases are randomly filed between the Circuit Court and Civil Division Courts at each location.

5. The Superior Court will also continue the practice of assigning CT and PL cases equally amongst the members of the Superior Court, pursuant to the court order of May 7, 2010.

6. Random filing of FD cases will also continue between the 4 Criminal Division and 4 County Division Courts with the Court maintaining sole discretion over the filing of FD cases in the Superior Court.

7. The filing of IF and OV cases are addressed in LR45–C.R.2.2–1

8. There shall be no random filing of civil cases in the County Division.

9. The County Division shall have exclusive original jurisdiction of all Small Claims Cases, and appeals and/or Trials De Novo of civil cases from City or Town Courts and shall maintain a Plenary Docket, with limited jurisdiction as more fully described below:

  1. A. The Plenary Docket is limited to cases designated as PL, CT, CC, PO and MI.

  2. B. Damages for any case filed on the Plenary Docket shall be capped at $10,000.00 (ten-thousand dollars).

  C. The term "damages" shall include attorney fees, but excludes court costs, post judgment interest and any sanctions that a court may impose.

  D. No case seeking equitable relief shall be filed on the Plenary Docket, with the following exceptions:

    a Orders directing the Bureau of Motor Vehicles to issue car titles, car registrations and driver's licenses

    b Evictions,

    c Replevins, provided the value of the property at issue does not exceed $10,000.00,

    d Civil proceedings against property related to criminal activities, provided the value of the property does not exceed $10,000.00,

    e This rule shall not be construed as limiting the powers of the County Division Courts with respect to collecting judgments, punishing contempts or enforcing its orders.

  E. These rules should not be construed to exclude a County Division Judicial Officer from adjudicating a case, via transfer or special judge assignment, that would otherwise exceed the jurisdictional parameters set forth for the County Division Courts.

  F. By filing suit on the Plenary Docket or by filing a counterclaim or cross claim, a party waives any right to relief that is beyond the County Division's jurisdictional parameters. However, if a party can establish that the claim was mandatory or that due diligence would not have disclosed the need to request such relief prior to filing their suit, or that transfer is appropriate pursuant to T.R. 75(B), upon motion, the case shall be transferred to a court of general jurisdiction. Upon such transfer, the case shall no longer be constrained by the jurisdictional parameters laid out in this rule.

10. This rule shall apply to all cases pending in the County Division upon its adoption

IV. Case Movement.

County Division 1—D07 will receive **60%** of all IF cases filed in the Superior Court.

County Division 2—D08 will not have new IF cases filed.

County Division 3—D09 will receive **25%** of all IF cases filed in the Superior Court.

County Division 4—D12 will receive **15%** of all IF cases filed in the Superior Court.

To address the utilization disparities in the least intrusive manner, the 2013 Caseload Allocation plan focuses mainly on the movement of cases rather than judicial officers whenever possible. The 2011 Caseload Allocation plan returned all SC cases filed in Hammond to County Division 4. As such, these cases are no longer assigned to Civil Division 5 in Hammond.

The current filing pattern in the County Division, which calls for an additional 350 CM cases be filed in County Division 1, will be maintained.

To maintain parity and allowable utilization figures in the Civil Division of the Superior Court, additional PL and CT cases will be assigned, as needed, to Civil Division 4 and Civil Division 5 as part of the normal distribution of cases for equalization purposes. The majority of these cases would have normally been assigned to Civil Division 2, but given the large CC caseload in Civil Division 2 and the nature of batch filing CC cases, PL and CT cases will be reduced in that court, bringing the utilization figures in Civil Divisions 4 and 5 closer to the other courts in the Civil Division.

Finally, to close the gap and achieve the .40 variance threshold, the quiet title cases that had been exclusively filed in the Circuit Court, will be equally distributed amongst the 8 Civil Courts. In 2011, there were 74 such cases filed. By equally dividing the quiet title PL caseload, the gap between the court with the highest utilization figure, Circuit Court, would drop from 1.33 to 1.30 and the court with the lowest utilization figure, Civil Division Room 5, would rise from .88 to .90, thus meeting the requirements set forth in AR1(E)(2). The projected 2013 utilization figures for the Lake Superior and Circuit Courts are portrayed below in Table 3. The Courts with the highest utilization figure under this plan will be the Circuit Court, with projected utilization figures of 1.30. The Court with the lowest projected utilization figure is Civil Division 5 at .90. This .40 difference again meets the requirements of Administrative Rule 1(E).

TABLE 3

COURT	CURRENT 2011 UTILIZATION	2013 PROJECTED UTILIZATION
Criminal Division 1 G01	1.11	1.11
Criminal Division 2 G02	1.06	1.06
Criminal Division 3 G03	1.09	1.09
Criminal Division 4 G04	1.08	1.08
Circuit Court C01	1.33	1.30
Civil Division 1 D01	.89	.90
Civil Division 2 D02	1.09	1.10
Civil Division 3 D03	1.01	1.10
Civil Division 4 D04	.89	.90
Civil Division 5 D05	.88	.90
Civil Division 6 D10	.91	.92
Civil Division 7 D11	.91	.92
Juvenile Court D06	1.17	1.17
County Division 1 D07	1.15	1.15
County Division 2 D08	1.21	1.21
County Division 3 D09	1.10	1.10
County Division 4 D12	1.23	1.23
	CURRENT UTILIZATION DIFFERENCE .45	PROJECTED. UTILIZATION DIFFERENCE .40

Adopted effective Jan. 1, 2009. Amended effective Jan. 1, 2011; Jan. 1, 2013.

LR 45–AR00 Rule 02. PRIORITY OF BOND SCHEDULE

The Clerk of the Circuit Court, at the time of disposition, in all cases in which fees are owed and there is a cash bond, before bond is released to defendant, or to the attorney pursuant to bond assignment, shall deduct and collect fees from the cash bond in the subsequent manner:

1st   Restitution when ordered;

2nd   LADOS Full Program Fee/ LADOS Monitoring Referral Fee/ LADOS Transfer Fee/LADOS Education Only Fee/ LADOS Evaluation Only Fee. The Clerk of the Circuit Court, is ordered to deposit all funds collected for said LADOS Division 1 Program into the Lake Superior Court, County Division Room 1 (**LADOS Division 1**) **User Fee Fund 217**. The Clerk of the Circuit Court, is ordered to deposit all funds collected for said LADOS Division 2 Program into the Lake Superior Court, County Division Room 2 (**LADOS Division 2**) **User Fee Fund 218**;

3rd   Administration Probation Fee pursuant to statute;

4th   All Probation User Fees pursuant to statute;

5th   Countermeasure and/or any other fee;

6th   Court Costs

Adopted effective Oct. 18, 2013.

LR 45–AR00 Rule 03. ALCOHOL AND DRUG SERVICES PROGRAM FEES

1. Full Program Fee: Includes Intake, Objective Testing, Substance Abuse Assessment, Case Management, placement in Level 2 (10) Hour or Level 3 (20) Hour Prime for Life Education, and/or may also include referral to a certified substance abuse, or mental health agency, case management, ancillary services, and compliance monitoring until program discharge.

Full Program Fee: $ 400.00

2. Substance Abuse Assessment Only Fee: Includes Intake, Objective Testing and Client Interview, development of Independent Service Contract and referral recommendations supported by the evidence and findings of the assessment.

Substance Abuse Assessment Only Fee: $ 150.00

3. Substance Abuse Education Only Fee: Includes placement in the Prime for Life Level 2 (10) hour or Level (3) 20 hour education component, workbook, case management and compliance monitoring until course completion and/or discharge.

Substance Abuse Education Only Fee: $ 300.00

4. Referral Monitor Fee: Includes Intake, referral to a certified substance abuse treatment facility, mental health agency, or inpatient substance abuse treatment facility, case management, ancillary services and compliance monitoring until discharge.

Transfer Monitor Fee: **$ 200.00**

5. Transfer Fee: Includes Intake, case management, and case transfer to a State Certified Court Administered Alcohol and Drug Service Program.

Transfer Fee: **$ 100.00**

Adopted effective Oct. 18, 2013.

LR 45–AR 15 Rule 04.   COURT REPORTER SERVICES

The following rule for the provision of court reporter services in the Civil, County, Criminal and Juvenile Divisions of the Circuit and Superior Courts of Lake County is hereby adopted.

I. Definitions.

A. A *court reporter* is a person who is designated by a court, division or room to perform court reporting services, including the preparation of transcripts.

B. *Equipment* means all physical property owned by the court or other government entity and used by a court reporter in providing court reporting services. Equipment shall include, but not be limited to, telephones, photocopiers, computer hardware and software, disks, tapes, and any other device for recording, storing, and transcribing electronic data.

C. *Work space* means those portions of court facilities used by a court reporter while providing court reporting services.

D. *Page* means the page unit of a transcript prepared in accordance with the Indiana Rules of Appellate Procedure.

E. *Recording* includes any electronic, mechanical, stenographic or other recording of a proceeding.

F. *Regular hours worked* means the hours that a court, division or room is officially open each work week.

G. *Gap hours worked* means those hours worked in excess of the regular hours worked, but not hours in excess of forty hours per work week.

H. *Overtime hours worked* means those hours worked in excess of forty hours per work week.

I. A *work week* means Sunday through Saturday.

J. *Court* means the Circuit and/or Superior Courts of Lake County, including all civil, county, criminal and juvenile divisions.

K. *Division* means the civil, county, criminal or juvenile division of the court.

L. *Room* means an individual courtroom of a division of the court.

M. *Transcript* means the original of the transcription of a proceeding. Under the rules of trial, criminal and appellate procedure, the original is usually filed with the clerk of the court.

Deposition transcript means the original and one copy of the transcription of a proceeding. The original and one copy is provided to the requesting party.

N. An *expedited transcript* is a transcript which is required to be delivered to a requesting party within fifteen (15) calendar days.

O. A *daily transcript* is a transcript which is required to be delivered to a requesting party within twenty-four (24) hours.

P. An *hourly transcript* is a transcript which is required to be delivered to a requesting party within the same day.

Q. *County indigent transcript* means a transcript that is paid for from county funds.

R. *State indigent transcript* means a transcript paid for from state funds.

S. *Private transcript* means a transcript, including but not limited to a deposition transcript that is paid for from funds other than county or state funds.

T. *Independent transcript* means a transcript that is prepared by a *contract transcriber*.

U. In a court, division or room currently without a court reporter on its payroll or assigned for the court's use, whose duties include the preparation of transcripts, a *contract transcriber* is a person not on a court's payroll, but who is designated by a court, division or room, pursuant to a memorandum of understanding consistent with the requirements of Administrative Rule 15, to prepare transcripts and who is prohibited from using court or county equipment, work space or supplies.

II. Compensation.

A. A court reporter shall be paid an annual salary for time spent working under the control, direction and direct supervision of the court, a division or a room during any regular work hours, gap hours or overtime hours. A written agreement consistent with the personnel policies of the court reporter's division which outlines the manner in which the court reporter is to be compensated for gap hours and overtime hours worked shall be entered into between a court reporter and the court, division or courtroom for which the court reporter provides services.

B. The fee that a court reporter or contract transcriber may charge for the preparation of a county indigent transcript four dollars ($4.00) per page.

C. A claim for the preparation of a county indigent transcript shall be submitted directly to the county.

D. The fee that a court reporter or contract transcriber may charge for the preparation of a state indigent transcript four dollars ($4.00) per page.

E. The fee that a court reporter or contract transcriber may charge for the preparation of an indigent deposition transcript is four dollars ($4.00) per page.

The fee that a court reporter or contract transcriber may charge for the preparation of a private deposition transcript is four dollars and twenty-five cents ($4.25) per page.

F. The fee that a court reporter or contract transcriber may charge for the preparation of all other private transcripts is four dollars and fifty cents ($4.50) per page, with a minimum fee of forty dollars ($40.00).

G. The fee that a court reporter or contract transcriber may charge for an additional copy of a transcript two dollars ($2.00) per page.

H. A court reporter or contract transcriber may charge up to an additional one dollar ($1.00) per page for an expedited county transcript.

I. A court reporter or contract transcriber may charge up to an additional one dollar and fifty cents ($1.50) per page for an expedited private transcript.

J. A court reporter or contract transcriber may charge up to an additional two dollars and fifty cents ($2.50) per page for a daily transcript.

K. A court reporter or contract transcriber may charge up to an additional three dollars and fifty cents ($3.50) per page for an hourly transcript.

L. A court reporter or contract transcriber may charge up to an additional one dollar and 25 cents ($1.25) per page for a private transcript consisting primarily of technical testimony.

M. A court reporter or contract transcriber may charge up to an additional one dollar ($1.00) per keyword index page for a private or indigent transcript with a keyword index.

N. A court reporter or contract transcriber may charge up to an additional twenty-five cents ($0.25) per page for a private or indigent transcript which is printed in a condensed format.

O. A court reporter or contract transcriber may charge thirty cents ($0.30) per page for photocopying of exhibits for private transcripts.

P. A court reporter or contract transcriber may charge an additional labor charge approximating an hourly rate based upon the court reporter's annual court compensation or contract transcriber's hourly rate of pay for the time spent binding the transcript and the exhibits pursuant to Indiana Rules of Appellate Procedure 28 and 29.

Q. A court reporter or contract transcriber shall be reimbursed for the cost of office supplies required and utilized for the binding and electronic transmission of the transcript, pursuant to Indiana Rules of Appellate Procedure 28 and 29, as itemized in the "Schedule of Supplies".

R. The county shall provide supplies for the preparation of notices of filing private transcripts and motions for extension.

S. At least once each year a court reporter shall report all transcript fees received to the Indiana Supreme Court, Division of State Court Administration.

III. Private Practice.

A. If a court reporter elects to engage in private practice through the recording of a deposition or preparing of a deposition transcript and the court reporter desires to use the court's equipment, work space or supplies, the court reporter shall enter into a written agreement which must, at a minimum, designate the following:

   1. the reasonable market rate for the use of the equipment, work space and supplies;

   2. the method by which records are to be kept for the use of equipment, work space and supplies; and,

   3. the method by which the court reporter is to reimburse the court for the use of equipment, work space and supplies.

B. If the court reporter elects to engage in private practice through the recording of a deposition or preparing of a deposition transcript, all such private practice shall be conducted outside of regular working hours.

Adopted effective Oct. 18, 2013.

MADISON COUNTY LOCAL RULES OF COURT

Adopted May 17, 2006, Effective January 1, 2007

Including Amendments Received Through November 1, 2013

Research Notes

Annotations to the Madison County Local Rules of Court are available in West's Annotated Indiana Code, *Title 34 Appendix.*

These rules may be searched electronically on Westlaw *in the* IN-RULES *database; updates to these rules may be found on* Westlaw *in* IN-RULESUPDATES. *For search tips and a summary of database content, consult the Westlaw Scope Screens for each database.*

ADMINISTRATIVE RULES

LR48–AR00 Rule 01.   COURT CLOSINGS

When the County Commissioners close the Government Center due to inclement weather or other reason, all Court Offices shall be closed unless specifically otherwise ordered by the presiding Judge.

Adopted as Unified Court Rule 34, effective June 17, 1996. Amended effective June 30, 1999; renumbered as Unified Court Rule 33 and amended effective Jan. 17, 2002; amended and renumbered as Local Rule 01, May 17, 2006, effective January 1, 2007; amended effective Sept. 30, 2011; effective Jan. 1, 2012.

LR48–AR00 Rule 02.   DIVISIONS OF THE MADISON CIRCUIT COURT

The Madison Circuit Court shall consist of divisions of the court and shall be known as Madison Circuit Court No. 1 (f/k/a the Madison Circuit Court); Madison Circuit Court No. 2 (f/k/a Madison Superior Court 2); Madison Circuit Court No. 3 (f/k/a Madison Superior Court No. 3); Madison Circuit Court No. 4 (f/k/a Madison Superior Court 4); Madison Circuit Court No. 5 (f/k/a Madison Superior Court 5); Madison Circuit Court No. 6 (f/k/a Madison Superior Court 1).

Adopted as Unified Rule 1, effective June 17, 1996. Amended effective June 30, 1999; amended effective Jan. 17, 2002; amended and renumbered as Local Rule 02, May 17, 2006, effective Jan. 1, 2007; amended effective Jan. 1, 2009; amended Sept. 29, 2009, effective Nov. 9, 2009; amended effective Sept. 30, 2011; effective Jan. 1, 2012.

LR48–AR00 Rule 03.   ADMINISTRATION OF THE MADISON CIRCUIT COURT AND SELECTION OF A CHIEF JUDGE

A.   To efficiently administer the Court, all divisions shall utilize a common budget, public defender services, probation services, and share other resources as deemed necessary. The Judges of the divisions shall comprise the administrative board of the Court.

B.   There shall be a Chief Judge of the Court who shall automatically be selected on the following rotation schedule:

Presiding Judge of Circuit Court 6 (beginning 1/1/98)

Presiding Judge of Circuit Court 4

Presiding Judge of Circuit Court 2

Presiding Judge of Circuit Court 5

Presiding Judge of Circuit Court 3

Presiding Judge of Circuit Court 1

Thereafter, the Chief Judge shall continue to be selected and serve pursuant to this schedule. The term of the Chief Judge shall be one year, beginning January 1 and ending on December 31 of year of service. In the event a designated Chief Judge is unavailable to serve as Chief Judge, the previous year's Chief Judge will assume Chief Judge duties if

the vacancy occurs before June 30. If the vacancy occurs subsequent to June 30, the Chief Judge for the subsequent year shall assume the duties of Chief Judge.

C.   Each Division of the Court shall maintain its own chronological case summary (CCS), record of judgment and orders (RJO), and calendar.

D.   The staff of each Court shall report to the presiding Judge of that Court and shall not be considered an employee of any other Court.

E.   All actions affecting the six Courts shall require the consent of a majority of the Unified Court Judges.

Adopted as Unified Rule 2, effective June 17, 1996. Amended effective Feb. 4, 1999; amended effective Jan. 17, 2002; amended and renumbered as Local Rule 03, May 17, 2006, effective Jan. 1, 2007; amended effective Jan. 1, 2009; amended Sept. 29, 2009, effective Nov. 9, 2009; amended effective Sept. 30, 2011; effective Jan. 1, 2012.

LR48–AR00 Rule 04.   COURT ADMINISTRATOR

A.   The Presiding Judges of the Court shall appoint a Director of Court Administration who shall have such duties and responsibilities as are assigned by said Judges.

B.   The presiding Judges shall appoint other Directors and Administrators as may be necessary to carry on the business of the Court. Employees of the various divisions shall be selected by said Directors with the advice and consent of the Judges.

Adopted as Unified Rule 6, effective June 17, 1996. Amended effective June 30, 1999; amended effective Jan. 17, 2002; amended and renumbered as Local Rule 04, May 17, 2006, effective Jan. 1, 2007; amended effective Sept. 30, 2011; effective Jan. 1, 2012.

LR48–AR00 Rule 05.   JURISDICTION OF DIVISIONS

A.   Dockets for each division of the Court shall be assigned as follows:

Civil dockets	Divisions 1, 2, 3, 4, 5, and 6.
Criminal dockets	Divisions 1, 3, 4, 5, and 6.
Probate dockets	Divisions 1, 3, and 6.
Juvenile dockets	Divisions 2 and 1.

C.[1]   Civil cases may be filed in any appropriate division in accordance with the caseload plan for Madison County (see LR48–AR00–07). Division selection in criminal cases will be effectuated randomly by the Clerk of the Court, in accordance with LR48–CR2.2–13.

D.   Requests for Trial De Novo filed in a Circuit Court shall automatically be transferred by the Madison County Clerk to the Madison Circuit Court, in the same manner as criminal cases are assigned, that is to say, by random selection.

Adopted as Unified Rule 3a, effective June 17, 1996. Amended effective June 30, 1999; renumbered as Unified Rule 3 and amended effective Jan. 17, 2002; amended and renumbered as Local Rule 05, May 17, 2006, effective Jan. 1, 2007; amended effective Jan. 1, 2009; amended Sept. 29, 2009, effective Nov. 9, 2009; amended effective Sept. 30, 2011; effective Jan. 1, 2012.

1 So in original. There is no subdivision B.

LR48–AR00 Rule 06. WHEN OTHER JUDGES PRESIDE

Whenever the Judge who presides in any Court is absent or cannot, for any reason, hear any cause pending in such Court or issue any emergency order in connection therewith, any other Judge of a Court may preside in such division, and for such purpose shall be considered to be the Judge of that Court to transact business therein.

Adopted as Unified Rule 10, effective June 17, 1996. Amended effective June 30, 1999; amended effective Jan. 17, 2002; amended and renumbered as Local Rule 06, May 17, 2006, effective Jan. 1, 2007; amended Sept. 29, 2009, effective Nov. 9, 2009; amended effective Sept. 30, 2011; effective Jan. 1, 2012.

LR48–AR00 Rule 07.   CASELOAD PLAN

A. In compliance with Administrative Rule 1(E), the following chart reflects the directed jurisdictional caseload allocation for the Madison Circuit Court. No part of this rule shall prohibit the transfer of individual cases to promote efficiency, fair distribution, or the timely resolution of cases.

CASELOAD ALLOCATION						
Case Type	Circuit 1	Circuit 2	Circuit 3	Circuit 4	Circuit 5	Circuit 6
MR			33.3%	33.3%		33.3%
FA			33.3%	33.3%		33.3%
FB			33.3%	33.3%		33.3%
FC			33.3%	33.3%		
FD	50%				50%	
CM	50%				50%	
MC						
PL						
MF	33.3%		33.3%			33.3%
CC	Over $3,000		Over $3,000	Under $3,000		Over $3,000
CT						
SC				50%	50%	
DR						
DR (Pro se)	33.3%		33.3%			33.3%
RS						
MH	100%					
AD						
ES/EU						
GU						
TR						
PO			50%		25%	25%
MI	20%		20%	20%	20%	20%
MI (IV-D)	33.3%		33.3%			33.3%
OV						
JC		100%				
JD		100%				
JS		100%				
JP		100%				
JM		100%				
JT		100%				

Adopted as Unified Rule 41, effective Jan. 17, 2002. Amended and renumbered as Local Rule 07, May 17, 2006, effective Jan. 1, 2007; amended effective Jan. 1, 2009; amended Sept. 29, 2009, effective Nov. 9, 2009; March 7, 2011, effective Jan. 1, 2011; amended effective Sept. 30, 2011; Jan. 1, 2012; March 1, 2013.

LR48–AR15 Rule 08. COURT REPORTER SERVICES

A. Definitions. The following definitions shall apply under this local rule:

1. *Court Reporter*: a person who is specifically designated by a court to perform the official court reporting services for the court, including preparing a transcript of the record.

2. *Equipment*: all physical items owned by the court or other governmental entity and used by a court reporter in performing court reporting services. Equipment shall include, but not be limited to, telephones, computer hardware, software programs, disks, tapes, and any other device used for recording, storing, and transcribing electronic data.

3. *Work space*: that portion of the court's facilities dedicated to each court reporter, including but not limited to actual space in the courtroom and any designated office space.

4. *Page*: the page unit of transcript which results when a recording is transcribed in the form required by Indiana Rule of Appellate Procedure VII B.

5. *Recording*: the electronic, mechanical, stenographic, or other recording made as required by Indiana Rule of Trial Procedure 74.

6. *Regular hours worked*: those hours which the court is regularly scheduled to work during any given work week.

7. *Overtime hours worked*: those hours worked in excess of forty (40) hours per work week.

8. *Work week:* means a seven (7) consecutive day week that consistently begins and ends on the same day throughout the year.

9. *County indigent transcript*: a transcript that is paid for from county funds and is for the use on behalf of a litigant who has been declared indigent by a court.

10. *State Indigent transcript*: a transcript that is paid for from state funds and is for the use on behalf of a litigant who has been declared indigent by a court.

11. *Expedited transcript:* a transcript that is required to be completed in three days or less.

B. Salaries and Per Page Fees.

1. Court Reporters shall be paid an annual salary for time spent working under the control, direction, and direct supervision of their supervising Judge during regular work hours or overtime hours. The supervising Judge shall enter into a written agreement with the court reporter which outlines the manner in which the court reporter is to be compensated for overtime hours.

2. The maximum per page fee a court reporter may charge for the preparation of a non-expedited transcript shall be $4.00 per page. However, the Court may authorize up to $5.00 per page for expedited transcripts.

3. A minimum fee up to $35.00 per transcript is permissible.

4. Index and Table of Contents pages should be charged at the per page rate being charged for the rest of the transcript.

5. An additional labor charge equal to the court reporter hourly court salary will be charged for the time spent binding the transcript and the exhibit binders.

6. A Court Reporter shall not be compensated for transcripts prepared during regular working hours. Private transcripts shall not be prepared during regular working hours.

7. A reasonable charge for the office supplies required and utilized for the binding and electronic transmission of the Transcript, pursuant to Indiana Rules of Appellate Procedure 28 and 29, is permissible. The costs for these supplies should be determined pursuant to a Schedule of Transcript Supplies which should be established and published annually by the Judges of the county.

8. At separation of employment, the court reporter forfeits all future claim to income derived from requested copies of previously typed transcripts.

9. Upon payment for an indigent transcript, the court reporter shall transfer the original floppy disk (or other electronic media) containing the fully transcribed record to the custody of the court.

C. Private Practice.

1. If a court reporter elects to engage in private practice through the recording of a deposition and/or preparing of a deposition transcript, and the court reporter desires to utilize the court's equipment, workspace, and supplies, and the court agrees to the use of the court equipment for such purposes, the court and the court reporter shall enter into a written agreement which must, at a minimum, designate the following:

   a. The reasonable market rate for the use of equipment, work space and supplies;

   b. The method by which records are to be kept for the use of equipment, work space and supplies, and

c. The method by which the court reporter is to reimburse the court for the use of the equipment, work space and supplies.

2. If a court reporter elects to engage in private practice through the recording of a deposition and/or preparing of a deposition transcript, all such private practice work shall be conducted outside of regular working hours.

D. Relevant Indiana Statutes and Trial Rules. Pertinent Indiana Statutes and Indiana Rules of Court regarding the Unified Court policy regarding the transcription of court proceedings are as followings:

I.C. 33–5–33.1–8, Appointment of personnel. The court may appoint court reporters to transact the business of the court. The persons so appointed shall perform such duties as prescribed by the court.

I.C. 33–15–23–1, Appointment and duties of official reporters. The The [1] Judges of each division of the Circuit Court shall appoint an official reporter.

I.C. 33–15–23–5, Transcript of proceedings. Whenever . . . such reporter shall be requested to do so (they) shall furnish to either party a transcript of all or any part of said proceedings required by (them) to be taken, . . . and it shall be (their) duty to furnish the same in . . . typewriting . . . and shall certify that it contains all the evidence given in the cause.

Trial Rule 74 (A), Court reports. The Judge may authorize or direct the court reporter or *any other responsible, competent person, in his discretion, to make a transcription from* such recordings, and the same shall be certified by the person making said transcription.

E. Court Transcription Policy.

1. Any person who is a court reporter or any other responsible person directed to prepare certified transcripts of court proceedings shall be administered a court reporter's oath before said person is entitled to prepare certified transcripts of proceedings.

2. Only Court employees are authorized to make certified transcriptions from recordings for the purpose of facilitating and expediting the trial of causes and appeals.

3. The court reporter or other designated person causing a matter to be recorded shall have the first right of refusal to prepare any necessary certified transcriptions from said recording.

a. If the person with the first right of refusal to prepare a certified transcript declines to prepare said transcript, then other competent persons in the court of said recording's origination shall have, on a rotating basis, the next right of refusal to prepare said certified transcript.

b. If no person in the originating court exercises their option to prepare said certified tran-

script, then the person who caused the matter to be recorded shall select from a list maintained by Court Administration another responsible and competent person employed by the Court to prepare said certified transcript.

4. Court Administration shall be notified by transcript preparers of the beginning and completion of transcripts.

5. The person who prepares the certified transcript from recordings shall be the person who certifies the transcript as being complete and accurate.

6. All court reporters must use the same invoice for submission of payment (format on file in court administration).

7. The invoice must be accompanied by a copy of the transcript (to verify page numbers) and the minute entry approving the transcript.

8. The transcript shall be certified by the Court Administrator and signed by the judge of the court of origination unless the originating judge does not require the transcript to be first approved.

9. The payroll administrator will make a docket entry indicating the court reporter, number of pages, per page price, and total amount due once the invoice is submitted to Court Administration.

Adopted as Unified Rule 42, effective June 17, 1996. Amended effective June 30, 1999; renumbered as Unified Rule 40 and amended effective Jan. 17, 2002; amended and renumbered as Local Rule 08, May 17, 2006, effective Jan. 1, 2007; amended effective Sept. 30, 2011; effective Jan. 1, 2012.

[1] So in original.

LR48–AR10 Rule 09. PLEADING REQUIREMENTS

A. Filings shall comply fully with the provisions of Trial Rule 77 and Administrative Rule 9 regarding confidentiality.

Commentary: It is not the intention of this rule for all pleadings to be copied to green paper prior to filing. Only confidential information should be listed separately on green paper at filing. A recommended form that conforms with Administrative Rule 9 requirements is on file in Court Administration.

B. Number of Copies. Parties shall provide the Court with a sufficient number of pleadings and proposed orders as provided by Exhibit A, attached and made a part hereof. Failure to provide sufficient copies will result in a Chronological Case Summary entry being made showing pleadings filed but with no action taken nor distribution made. When pleadings or proposed orders are filed by mail or left with the court for filing, a self-addressed, stamped envelope shall be included for return of documents to the attorney.

C. Signature on Pleadings. All pleadings to be signed by an attorney shall contain an original written signature of the attorney, printed name, attorney number, firm name (if applicable), mailing address, telephone number, and a designation of the party for whom the attorney appears.

D. Distribution Lists. All documents for which distribution is requested shall include a distribution list at the end of document. Distribution may not be made to parties not included on the distribution list.

E. Certificates of Service. Certificates of Service which are required by the trial rules shall set out with specificity the names of the lawyers or litigants who have been served. The generic and generalized language "served upon counsel of record" shall not be acceptable compliance with the trial rule.

F. Two–Sided Pleadings. Two-sided pleadings, motions, orders or decrees will not be accepted with the exception of court-approved forms relating to small claims matters.

G. Caption Requirement. In any matter being heard by special judge, magistrate, senior judge, or other judicial officer who is not the regular judge, the judicial officer's name shall appear in the caption, and below the cause number as follows:

"Before Hon. _____"
(Title—Special Judge, etc . . .)

H. Adequate Notice to Court. A copy of any pleading or motion filed less than five days before a scheduled hearing shall be served personally upon the presiding Judge of the case.

Adopted as Unified Rules 12G, 32, 33, 36, 37, and 39, effective June 17, 1996. Amended effective June 30, 1999; renumbered as Unified Rules 31, 32, 35, 36, and 38 and amended effective Jan. 17, 2002; amended and renumbered as Local Rule 09, May 17, 2006, effective Jan. 1, 2007; amended effective Sept. 30, 2011; effective Jan. 1, 2012.

LR48–AR00 Rule 10.   BENCH TRIAL AND MEDI-ATION

All bench trials expected to last a full day or more shall be referred to mediation unless for good cause shown.

Adopted May 17, 2006, effective Jan. 1, 2007. Amended effective Sept. 30, 2011; effective Jan. 1, 2012.

LR48–AR00   Rule 11. USE OF REGULAR JUDGE'S MECHANICALLY STAMPED SIG-NATURE

A. The regular Judge's mechanically stamped signature may be utilized by Court staff and appointed judicial officers designated by the regular judge.

B. Such use shall include, but not be limited to: Notices of Hearing, Orders to Appear, Travel permits when approved by a probation officer, Orders for continuance of proceedings, and other Administrative Orders, following the Judge's oral or dictated directive to do so. Court staff or appointed judicial officers utilizing a mechanically stamped signature must place

their initials next to the stamped signature on the original document.

C. Such use shall include the countersignature of the regular Judge, required on any action taken by a Magistrate, regular Court Commissioner, IV–D Commissioner or Referee, providing the original signature of the Magistrate, regular Court Commissioner, IV–D Commissioner or Referee appears on the original of the instrument or document.

D. The Senior Court Reporter of each Court shall maintain a list of those staff members and appointed judicial officers having use of a mechanically stamped signature device.

Adopted May 17, 2006, effective Jan. 1, 2007. Amended effective Sept. 30, 2011; effective Jan. 1, 2012.

LR48–AR00 Rule 12.   TIMEKEEPING AND COM-PENSATION POLICIES AND PROCEDURES

The Courts of Madison County shall adhere to and follow the "Ordinance #2001–BC–0–14" adopted by the Madison County Board of Commissioners on October 16, 2001 regarding timekeeping and compensation policies and procedures to the extent that this, or any other county personnel policies or procedures, are not inconsistent with any specific rules adopted by the Judiciary.

Adopted as Unified Rule 42, effective Jan. 17, 2002. Amended and renumbered as Local Rule 12, May 17, 2006, effective Jan. 1, 2007; amended effective Sept. 30, 2011; effective Jan. 1, 2012.

LR48—AR7 Rule 12.5.   EVIDENCE HANDLING, RETENTION AND DISPOSITION

A. Preamble. In all cases, the court shall proceed pursuant to these Rules unless the court directs a longer retention period after motion by any party or on its own motion.

B. Retention Periods for Evidence introduced in Civil Proceedings.

1. *Civil Cases, Including Adoption, Paternity, and Juvenile Proceedings.* All models, diagrams, documents, or material admitted in evidence or pertaining to the case placed in the custody of the court reporter as exhibits, shall be taken away by the parties offering them in evidence, except as otherwise ordered by the court, four (4) months after the case is decided unless an appeal is taken. If an appeal is taken, all such exhibits shall be retained by the court reporter for two (2) years from termination of the appeal, retrial, or subsequent appeal and termination, whichever is later. Exceptions to this rule are the following case types: GU, JP, MI, and DR. For those case types, all models, diagrams, documents, or material admitted in evidence or pertaining to the case placed in the custody of the Court Reporter shall be taken away by the parties offering them in evidence 10 years after the case is decided.

The Court reporter shall retain the mechanical or electronic records or tapes, shorthand or stenographic notes as provided in Administrative Rule 7.

C. Retention Periods for Evidence Introduced in Criminal Misdemeanor, Class D and Class C Felonies and Attempts.

1. All models, diagrams, documents, or material admitted in evidence or pertaining to the case placed in the custody of the court reporter as exhibits shall be taken away by the parties offering them in evidence except as otherwise ordered by the court, three (3) years after the case is dismissed, the defendant found not guilty, or the defendant is sentenced, unless an appeal is taken. If an appeal is taken, all such exhibits shall be retained by the court reporter for three (3) years from termination of the appeal, retrial, or subsequent appeal and termination, whichever is later, unless an action challenging the conviction or sentence, or post conviction action, is pending.

The Court reporter shall retain the mechanical or electronic records or tapes, shorthand or stenographic notes as provided in Administrative Rule 7.

D) Retention Periods for Evidence Introduced in Criminal Class B and A Felonies and Murder Attempts.

1. All models, diagrams, documents, or material admitted in evidence or pertaining to the case placed in the custody of the court reporter as exhibits shall be taken away by the parties offering them in evidence, except as otherwise ordered by the court, twenty (20) years after the case is dismissed, the defendant found not guilty, or the defendant is sentenced, unless an appeal is taken. If an appeal is taken, all such exhibits shall be retained by the court reporter for twenty (20) years from termination of the appeal, retrial, or subsequent appeal and termination, whichever is later, unless an action challenging the conviction or sentence, or post conviction action, is pending.

The court reporter shall retain the mechanical or electronic records or tapes, shorthand or stenographic notes as provided in Administrative Rule 7.

E. Non–documentary and Oversized Exhibits. Non-documentary and oversized exhibits shall not be sent to the Appellate level Court, but shall remain in the custody of the trial court or Administrative Agency during the appeal. Such exhibits shall be briefly identified in the Transcript where they were admitted into evidence. Photographs of any exhibit may be included in the volume of documentary exhibits.

1. Drugs, currency, or other dangerous or valuable items shall not be included in appellate records.

F. Notification and Disposition. In all cases, the court shall provide actual notice, by mail or through the Madison County Courthouse mailbox system, to all attorneys of record and to parties only if unrepresented by counsel, that the evidence will be destroyed by a date certain if not retrieved before that date. Counsel and parties have the duty to keep the court informed of their current addresses and notice to the last current address shall be sufficient. Court reporters should maintain a log of retained evidence and scheduled disposition date and evidence should be held in a secure area. At the time of removal, the party receiving and removing the evidence shall give a detailed receipt to the court reporter, and the receipt will be made part of the court file.

1. In all cases, the Court, or the Sheriff on the Court's order, should dispose of evidence that is not retaken after notice. The Sheriff should be ordered to destroy evidence if its possession is illegal, or if it has negligible value. The Sheriff should auction evidence of some value with proceeds going to the county general fund. These Rules and their retention periods will take precedence over inconsistent language in statutes. I.C. 35–33–5–5(c)(2).

G. Biologically Contaminated Evidence. A party who offers biologically contaminated evidence must file a pretrial notice with the trial court and serve all the parties so that the court can consider the issue and rule appropriately before trial. A party can show contaminated evidence or pass photographs of it to jurors, but no such evidence, however contained, shall be handled or passed to jurors or sent to the Jury Room unless specifically ordered by the Court.

H. Rationale on Destruction and Disposal of Evidence. There are two goals in the destruction or disposal of stored evidence. The first is that nothing of a confidential nature be compromised, and second, that storage space is created.

The following are suggested methods of disposal of such items in the absence of any statutory provision:

a) Paper: shredding or burning.

b) Drugs: to Sheriff for disposal.

c) Guns: to Sheriff for auction or destruction.

d) Plastic, glass, stone or stone-like objects, wood: to County Dump.

e) Money: per statute

f) Jewelry or other valuables: Notify owner to retrieve or sale at Sheriff's auction.

g) For any other material: The regular judge shall make written instructions for disposal.

h) For any of the above, or for any item not mentioned, the regular Judge may give written instructions for disposal.

Adopted effective Jan. 1, 2013.

CRIMINAL RULES

LR48–CR2.2 Rule 13. CRIMINAL DOCKETS (ASSIGNMENT)

SECTION I.

All felonies and misdemeanors filed in the Madison Circuit Court shall be assigned and docketed in accordance with this Rule.

Charges shall be filed and assigned pursuant to Section II, if applicable. If Section II is not applicable, charges shall be filed and assigned in accordance with Section III.

Cases with multiple defendants or with co-defendants shall be considered one case for filing purposes and shall be assigned to a single court, although each defendant may be given a separate cause number.

SECTION II.

If jurisdiction exists in said Court, new felony and misdemeanor charges shall be filed in the Court where other charges are pending against the defendant or where the defendant is on probation or otherwise under supervision.

SECTION III.

Capital cases, life without parole cases, Murder cases, Class A felonies, Class B felonies and Class C felonies shall be randomly filed in Circuit Court 3, Circuit Court 4, and Circuit Court 6. Class D felonies and misdemeanors shall be randomly filed in Circuit Court 1 (50%) and Circuit Court 5 (50%).

SECTION IV.

When a case requires a change of Judge, the Clerk shall randomly select a new Judge from the remaining judges exercising comparable jurisdiction. The Clerk shall so notify the new Judge of the appointment as Special Judge. If a selected Special Judge is unable to accept jurisdiction due to conflict of interest, or the Special Judge is later disqualified, the Clerk shall select a successor Special Judge at random from the remaining Judges of the Circuit Court exercising criminal jurisdiction.

Adopted as Unified Rule 3b, effective June 17, 1996. Amended effective June 30, 1999. Renumbered as Unified Rule 4 and amended effective Jan. 17, 2002. Amended and renumbered as Local Rule 13, May 17, 2006, effective Jan. 1, 2007. Amended effective Jan. 1, 2009; amended Sept. 29, 2009, effective Nov. 9, 2009; amended effective Sept. 30, 2011; Jan. 1, 2012; March 1, 2013.

LR48–CR2.2 Rule 13.5. PROBLEM SOLVING COURTS

Effective January 1, 2012, the Madison Circuit Court shall establish and administer a single Problem Solving Court with a single presiding judge. The single Problem Solving Court replaces the current Mental Health Court, Drug Court, and Re–Entry Court and shall continue to operate under guidelines and certifications of the Indiana Supreme Court through the agency of the Indiana Judicial Center. Policies, Procedures and Personnel for the Problem Solving Court shall be subject to supervision by the presiding judge of the Problem Solving Court, subject to advice and approval by a majority of the Circuit Court judges.

The presiding judge appointment shall be for a period of three (3) years and rotate among the judges with criminal court jurisdiction. The first presiding judge shall be the judge shall be the judge of Circuit Court, Division 4. Thereafter, the appointments shall continue on the following schedule: Circuit Court, Division 1; Circuit Court, Division 5; Circuit Court, Division 6; and Circuit Court, Division 3. Should any judge decline an appointment, the next judge on the schedule shall be appointed to serve. If a presiding judge resigns or is unable to continue for any reason, a majority of the Circuit Court judges will select one of their colleagues to fill the unexpired term.

The Circuit Court may also establish and administer additional Problem Solving Courts, such as Family Court and Teen Court, as the need arises. The presiding Juvenile Judge shall establish rules for the operation of said courts and shall be the presiding Judge subject to the approval of the majority of the Judges.

The following fees are assessed to participants of Problem Solving Courts:

Drug Court: Monthly Court User Fee of $40.00

Mental Health Court: Monthly Court User Fee of $40.00

Re-entry Court: Monthly Court User Fee of $40.00

Court User Fees are due the 10th of each new month.

Drug Court participants who are in Phase 4 do not accrue a Court User Fee.

Adopted Sept. 29, 2009, effective Nov. 9, 2009. Amended effective Sept. 30, 2011; Jan. 1, 2012; March 1, 2013.

LR48–CR00 Rule 14. FELONY BOND SCHEDULE

A. Unless otherwise ordered by a court, bail on felony charges shall be as follows:

Felony Class	Amount
Murder (35–42–1–1)	Non-bondable
A Felony	$35,000.00
B Felony	$20,000.00
C Felony	$10,000.00
D Felony	$ 5,000.00

Misdemeanors	Amount
All Classes	$3,000.00 maximum

B. If Defendant's residence (or usual place of abode) is within the State of Indiana, but outside Madison or its contiguous Counties, bond shall be doubled.

C. If Defendant's residence (or usual place of abode) is outside the State of Indiana, bond shall be tripled.

D. If defendant, at the time of arrest, is on parole or probation, or is free on bail awaiting trial on other charges, he shall not be admitted to bail per this schedule, but shall be brought before a judge or magistrate of the County on the next regular day of Court who shall set bail or order other disposition. (The presiding judge, if available, of the Division in which charges have been filed shall determine bail.)

E. A detainee-defendant who posts bond pursuant to the Felony Bond Schedule for crimes listed as "offenses against the person" under IC 35–42 shall be subject to a No Contact Order in favor of the alleged victim.

F. A detainee-defendant arrested for felony battery or invasion of privacy shall not be afforded access to the felony bond schedule. The defendant shall be held pending review and bond setting by a judicial officer.

Adopted May 17, 2006, effective Jan. 1, 2007; amended effective Jan. 1, 2009; amended effective Sept. 30, 2011. Amended effective Jan. 1, 2012.

JURY RULES

LR48–JR02 Rule 15. APPOINTMENT OF JURY ADMINISTRATOR

Pursuant to Indiana Jury Rules, the position of Circuit Court Jury Administrator is created and shall be selected by majority vote of the Court Judges, who shall assign to said administrator such duties as they may designate from time to time, together with those prescribed by the Indiana Jury Rules.

Adopted May 17, 2006, effective Jan. 1, 2007. Amended effective Sept. 30, 2011; effective Jan. 1, 2012.

LR48–JR04 Rule 16.   JURY PANELS

The panel of potential jurors shall be derived from the Madison County portion of the Statewide Master Jury List reflecting the combined records of Bureau of Motor Vehicles and Department of Revenue or such additional records as may be designated.

Adopted as Unified Rule 8, effective June 17, 1996. Amended effective June 30, 1999; amended effective Jan. 17, 2002; amended and renumbered as Local Rule 16, May 17, 2006, effective Jan. 1, 2007; amended effective Sept. 30, 2011; effective Jan. 1, 2012.

FAMILY LAW RULES

LR48–FL00 Rule 17. FINANCIAL DECLARATIONS/SUPPORT WORK SHEETS

Financial Declarations on forms adopted by the Court and Indiana Child Support work-sheets shall be completed in full, dated and filed prior to trial in all contested matters involving child support or disposition of assets. Financial Declarations, with current pay stub attached, shall be filed with the Court two (2) days before any preliminary or final hearing. Child support worksheets shall be filed with the Court on the hearing date. Absent objection, the financial declaration shall be considered as received in evidence subject to cross-examination. Direct examination on matters in the financial declaration shall be confined to unusual items or factors requiring explanation or correction.

Adopted as Unified Rule 15, effective June 17, 1996. Amended effective June 30, 1999; amended effective Jan. 17, 2002; amended and renumbered as Local Rule 17, May 17, 2006, effective Jan. 1, 2007; amended effective Sept. 30, 2011; effective Jan. 1, 2012.

LR48–AR00 Rule 18. CHILDREN AND DISSOLUTION PROCEEDINGS

A. In all dissolution and separation actions where there are minor children of the marriage, the Petitioner and Respondent shall separately attend a dissolution education workshop approved by the court. Seminars must be completed within thirty (30) days after a petition for separation or dissolution is filed.

B. Children over the age of 6 and under the age of 17 shall attend the court approved dissolution education program for minor children.

C. Seminar scheduling shall be arranged with the Office of Court Administration (phone 641–9503), Room 417, Courthouse, Anderson, Indiana. Each party shall pay a fee of twenty five dollars ($25.00) for the dissolution education seminar. The parties shall equally divide the cost of ten dollars ($10.00) per child (not to exceed twenty dollars ($20.00) per family) for the dissolution education seminar for children. Seminar fees may be deferred upon a showing of indigence. The Clerk shall maintain a trust account for the collection of these fees and said fees shall be disbursed by Court order.

D.   The Clerk shall bring this rule to the attention of all dissolution and separation petitioners and shall collect the petitioner's fee at the time of filing. The respondent's fee is due at the time of scheduling. The Clerk shall cause a copy of the rule to accompany the summons for service upon respondents.

E.   Failure to comply with this rule may be considered civil contempt, and may delay the issuance of a final decree.

F.   Upon its own motion or upon the motion of a party, the Court may require compliance in all cases involving the custody of children or in re-docketed cases.

Adopted as Unified Rule 41, effective June 17, 1996. Amended effective June 30, 1999; renumbered as Unified Rule 39, and amended effective Jan. 17, 2002; amended and renumbered as Local Rule 18, May 17, 2006, effective Jan. 1, 2007; amended effective Sept. 30, 2011; effective Jan. 1, 2012.

TRIAL RULES

LR48–TR53 Rule 19.   OFFICE STAFF, REFEREES, MASTER COMMISSIONERS, SENIOR JUDGES, AND MAGISTRATE

A.   Each presiding Judge shall appoint appropriate office staff pursuant to statute. If a Judge shall appoint a Commissioner, Referee or Master Commissioner, then said Judge shall define said responsibility of said appointee. A Commissioner, Referee or Master Commissioner shall not have jurisdiction over or be allowed to conduct hearings of any type in matters filed in divisions of the Court in which they are not employed.

COURT COMMISSIONERS

B.   Preliminary matters may be scheduled on a Commissioner's calendar. There shall be no automatic right to have preliminary matters set on the calendar of the presiding Judge or removed from the Commissioner's calendar to the Judge's calendar.

SENIOR JUDGES

C.   Senior Judges who are assigned to a court shall serve the court as deemed appropriate by the Court's presiding Judge. Said service may include assignment to specific cases, to specialized cases or to all cases placed on the Senior Judge's calendar (See also Supreme Court Administrative Rule 5).

MAGISTRATE

D.   Pursuant to I.C. 33–23–5, the Judges of the Madison Circuit Court shall appoint a full-time, state-paid Magistrate and assign to said Magistrate such duties as they may designate from time to time.

Adopted as Unified Rules 5, 7, 19, and 20, effective June 17, 1996, and as Unified Rule 19, effective Jan. 17, 2002. Amended effective June 30, 1999; renumbered as Unified Rule 20, and amended effective Jan. 17, 2002; amended and renumbered as Local Rule 19, May 17, 2006, effective Jan. 1, 2007; amended effective Jan. 1, 2009; amended Sept. 29, 2009, effective Nov. 9, 2009; amended effective Sept. 30, 2011; effective Jan. 1, 2012.

LR48–TR79 Rule 20.   SPECIAL JUDGE SELECTION IN CIVIL AND JUVENILE CASES

A.   A copy of each pleading or each paper filed with the Court after a Special Judge has qualified shall be mailed or delivered by counsel to the office of that Special Judge with service to that Special Judge indicated on the certificate of service.

B.   Pursuant to Trial Rule 79, should all remedies listed under 79 (D), (E), and (F) fail to produce a special judge then the appointment of an eligible special judge shall be made pursuant to local rule, as follows, in accordance with 79 (H)

C.   The Madison County Clerk, on a rotating basis in consecutive order, shall appoint the eligible judge in Madison County as follows:

For all domestic relations or paternity cases:
Presiding Judge of Circuit Court 1
Presiding Judges of Circuit Court 2 and 4
Presiding Judge Circuit Court 3
Presiding Judge of Circuit Court 6

For all other case types:
Presiding Judge of the Circuit Court 1
Presiding Judge of Circuit Court 2
Presiding Judge of Circuit Court 3
Presiding Judge of Circuit Court 4
Presiding Judge of Circuit Court 5
Presiding Judge of Circuit Court 6

C.   Should none of the above referenced judges accept jurisdiction due to disqualification pursuant to the Code of Judicial Conduct, ineligibility for service under this rule Trial Rule 79 or excused from service by the Indiana Supreme Court, then the appointment shall be made at random by the Clerk from eligible Judges within Administrative District 14 (Grant County Circuit Court, Grant County Superior Court Divisions 1, 2, 3.

D.   In the event that no judicial officer within Administrative District 14 is eligible to serve as special judge or the particular circumstances of the case warrant selection of a special judge by the Indiana Supreme Court, the judge of the court in which the case is pending shall certify the matter to the Indiana Supreme Court for appointment of a special judge.

Adopted as Unified Rules 18a and 18b, effective June 17, 1996. Amended effective June 30, 1999; renumbered as Unified Rule 18, and amended effective Jan. 17, 2002; amended and renumbered as Local Rule 20, May 17, 2006, effective Jan. 1, 2007; amended effective Jan. 1, 2009; July 1, 2011; amended effective Sept. 30, 2011; effective Jan. 1, 2012.

LR48–TR06 Rule 21. AUTOMATIC ENLARGEMENT OF TIME

An initial written motion for enlargement of time, pursuant to Trial Rule 6(B)(1), to respond to a claim shall be automatically allowed for an additional thirty (30) days from the original due date without written order of the Court. Any motion filed pursuant to this rule shall state the date when such response is due and the date to which time is enlarged. Said motion must be filed on or before the original due date or this rule shall not apply. No proposed order should be submitted. An enlargement in excess of thirty (30) days will be permitted by the Court only upon a showing of necessity. This rule does not apply to matters on the small claims docket.

Adopted as Unified Rule 11, effective June 17, 1996. Amended effective June 30, 1999; amended effective Jan. 17, 2002; amended and renumbered as Local Rule 21, May 17, 2006, effective Jan. 1, 2007; amended effective Jan. 1, 2009; effective Sept. 30, 2011; effective Jan. 1, 2012.

LR48–TR53 Rule 22. CONTINUANCES

A. Unless made in open Court, motions for continuance shall be in writing and shall include the following information:

1. The date and time of the hearing or trial for which a continuance is being sought.

2. The date and time opposing counsel (or pro se opponent) was advised that a continuance would be requested.

3. Whether opposing counsel (or party) agrees with or objects to said request.

4. The reason a continuance is necessary and an estimate of the amount of time needed to elapse before the matter can be rescheduled.

5. A good-faith estimate of the time needed for such hearing or trial if rescheduled.

6. A proposed date and time available on the Court's calendar if all parties agree upon a new hearing date.

7. If the continuance is requested because of conflicts on counsel's trial calendar: the conflicting cause caption, cause number, current status of the conflicting cause, and the date said conflicting cause was set for hearing.

B. No motions for continuance will be considered unless filed at least five (5) days before a bench trial or hearing, unless good cause is shown, and at least ten (10) days before a jury trial, unless good cause is shown. No case shall be continued or removed from the trial calendar without approval of the court.

C. The continuance of a preliminary hearing is not favored and will NOT be granted when requested less than five (5) days before the hearing. A motion for change of venue from the Judge or county shall NOT cause a preliminary motion hearing to be continued where immediate or emergency relief may be required.

D. All motions for continuances shall be accompanied by a proposed order containing a space for the Court to set a new date for the hearing or trial, or at the Court's election, directing the parties to contact the bailiff for a new trial date.

E. When an attorney enters an appearance, it is the attorney's responsibility to review the file and become aware of all previously scheduled hearing dates. Entry of an appearance just prior to a hearing will not necessarily constitute a reason for a continuance.

F. Unless otherwise indicated in the motion, a signature by an attorney on the request for continuance is certification by that attorney that their client has been notified of the request and of the reason for which the continuance is sought. If the client was not notified, the attorney shall state the specific reason(s) notice could not be given, and that the client will not be prejudiced by the continuance.

Adopted as Unified Rule 12, effective June 17, 1996. Amended effective June 30, 1999; amended effective Jan. 17, 2002; amended and renumbered as Local Rule 22, May 17, 2006, effective Jan. 1, 2007; amended effective Jan. 1, 2009; amended effective Sept. 30, 2011; effective Jan. 1, 2012.

LR48–TR26 Rule 23. DISCOVERY TIME LIMITS

A. Discovery shall not be permitted in small claims actions, except by leave of Court.

B. In all other cases, discovery shall be completed within six months after the case is at issue, unless otherwise ordered by the Court. For good cause shown, time may be extended for completion of discovery.

C. Pursuant to Indiana Rules of Court, routine discovery shall not be accepted for filing except by leave of Court. However, the Court will accept for filing a one-page Notice of Service of Discovery or Notice of Compliance.

Adopted as Unified Rule 13, effective June 17, 1996. Amended effective June 30, 1999; amended effective Jan. 17, 2002; amended and renumbered as Local Rule 23, May 17, 2006, effective Jan. 1, 2007; amended effective Sept. 30, 2011; effective Jan. 1, 2012.

LR48–TR33 Rule 24. LIMITATION ON INTERROGATORIES

Interrogatories shall be limited to a total of fifty (50), including subparts, and be used solely for the purpose of discovery and shall NOT be used as a substitute for the taking of a deposition. For good cause shown, additional interrogatories may be permitted.

Adopted as Unified Rule 14, effective June 17, 1996. Amended effective June 30, 1999; amended effective Jan. 17, 2002; amended and renumbered as Local Rule 24, May 17, 2006, effective Jan. 1, 2007; amended effective Sept. 30, 2011; effective Jan. 1, 2012.

LR48–TR73 Rule 25.   EX PARTE MATTERS

A.   All motions for which an ex parte order is requested or anticipated shall be filed with an appropriate proposed order for signature by the Court. No ex parte motion shall be considered unless the motion is verified by the petitioner. Unless waived by the Court, there shall be a recorded evidentiary hearing showing corroboration of the motion's allegations.

B.   An ex parte order shall not be signed unless opposing counsel or the opposing party(s) have been notified, or unless an affidavit has been filed from petitioner's attorney which indicates attempts to notify opposing counsel or opposing party(s), or reasons supporting the claim that notice should not be required. See *Matter of Anonymous* 729 E.2d 566 (Ind.2000)

C.   This rule shall not be triggered by ex parte matters that are merely procedural (e.g., compelling discovery, extensions of time, orders to appear). Further, a domestic relations mutual restraining order sought at the time a dissolution action is filed, which order prohibits harassment, violence, and dissipation of assets or which continues the status quo pending hearing, shall not trigger the requirement of this rule.

D.   No ex parte relief shall be granted unless specific facts are presented, either at a hearing or by affidavit, that immediate and irreparable injury or loss or damage will result before an adverse party may be heard in opposition.

E.   No ex parte protective order (PO) shall cancel or restrict an existing Order on child visitation or custody issued by a Court of competent jurisdiction unless the protective order specifically and clearly so directs and references the existing Order by cause number.

F.   If ex parte relief is granted, a hearing shall be set and held within 10 days of the granting of such ex parte relief, and the adverse party shall be notified of said hearing. By seeking ex parte relief, a party waives any objection to said hearing being assigned to any available judicial officer.

Adopted as Unified Rule 16, effective June 17, 1996. Amended effective June 30, 1999; amended effective Jan. 17, 2002; amended and renumbered as Local Rule 25, May 17, 2006, effective Jan. 1, 2007; amended effective Sept. 30, 2011; effective Jan. 1, 2012.

LR48–TR3.1 Rule 26.   ENTRY AND WITHDRAWAL OF APPEARANCE

A.   Upon entering a cause, an attorney or law firm shall file a notice of appearance with the Court. In addition to the firm name, address, and phone number, said appearance shall include the individual name and attorney number of the lawyer who is to be identified on the Chronological Case Summary as principal counsel for purposes of notice or other Court Communication.

B.   An attorney's appearance for a party will be withdrawn upon the filing of a motion, if:

1.   Another attorney simultaneously appears for the party;

2.   The attorney provides satisfactory evidence that the party has discharged the attorney; or

3.   The party acquiesces to the withdrawal.

C.   In all other circumstances, an attorney seeking permission to withdraw an appearance shall file a written motion stating justification for the withdrawal. The attorney shall give the party 21 days' written notice of the attorney's intention to seek permission to withdraw. This notice shall (1) inform the party that failure to secure new counsel may result in dismissal of the party's case or in entry of a judgment or ruling against the party, (2) set forth the date of any scheduled hearing or trial, and (3) include any other pertinent information.

D.   Except for good cause shown, a withdrawal of appearance shall not be granted within 5 days of trial commencement.

Adopted as Unified Rule 21, effective June 17, 1996. Amended effective June 30, 1999; renumbered as Unified Rule 22, and amended effective Jan. 17, 2002; amended and renumbered as Local Rule 26, May 17, 2006, effective Jan. 1, 2007; amended effective Sept. 30, 2011; effective Jan. 1, 2012.

LR48–TR40 Rule 27.   TRIAL AND PROVISIONAL HEARING SETTINGS

A.   Causes shall be calendared in consultation with opposing counsel and the Court. In the event counsel are unable to agree upon a trial setting, the moving party may file a motion for trial setting with the Court. A proposed CCS entry shall be submitted by moving counsel, or party, confirming the hearing date, time, and hearing officer.

B.   All motions for trial setting shall include:

1.   a statement indicating whether the matter is to be tried by jury or by the Court;

2.   a statement indicating the estimated time required for trial;

3.   a statement indicating efforts to set the cause by agreement have been unsuccessful.

C.   Except by special leave of Court, provisional hearings shall be scheduled not less than fifteen (15) days after the filing of the motion.

D.   Service   of   Process—Re-Docketed   Cases. Whenever a domestic relations case or similar case (DR, JP, GU, or MI) is re-docketed after more than 8 months of inactivity, the party initiating the re-docketed activity (such as a Petition to Modify) shall promptly serve new process or a notice of hearing upon responding parties in accordance with TR 4.

Adopted as Unified Rule 22, effective June 17, 1996. Amended effective June 30, 1999; renumbered as Unified Rule 23, and amended effective Jan. 17, 2002; amended and renumbered as Local Rule 27, May 17, 2006, effective Jan. 1, 2007; amended Sept. 29, 2009, effective Nov. 9, 2009; amended effective Sept. 30, 2011; effective Jan. 1, 2012.

LR48–TR05 Rule 28.   TITLE IV–D

All pleadings, motions and other documents related to Title IV–D proceedings shall be filed with the Clerk of the Court, regardless of the Court of origin, and then taken to the Court Administrator's office. When the Title IV–D Prosecutor's Office intervenes in an existing cause of action, the Office shall file a written appearance with a Title IV–D Court Reporter.

Adopted as Unified Rule 25, effective June 17, 1996. Amended effective June 30, 1999; renumbered as Unified Rule 24, and amended effective Jan. 17, 2002; amended and renumbered as Local Rule 28, May 17, 2006, effective Jan. 1, 2007; amended effective Sept. 30, 2011; effective Jan. 1, 2012.

LR48–TR64 Rule 29.   WRITS OF BODY ATTACH-MENT

A.   Requests for Body Attachments. An application for a writ of body attachment must be sworn or verified and include the following:

1.   An allegation that the target of the body attachment failed to appear at a hearing to show cause why the target should not be held in contempt for failure to appear at a prior hearing,

2.   An allegation that the target of the body attachment received service of the order to show cause, including the date and manner of service,

3.   The amount of the judgment still owing at the time the body attachment is requested, and

4.   Only if service of the order to appear at the show cause hearing was not by personal service, and the service address was neither an address where the party has previously received good service in this case nor an address provided to the Court by the party, an allegation explaining how the service address is known to be the party's actual address.

The party seeking the body attachment must also complete a civil warrant information sheet on forms provided by the Clerk before a Writ of Body Attachment can be issued.

B.   Expiration of Writs of Body Attachment. A writ of body attachment expires 180 days after its issuance. An expired writ may be reissued upon written request referencing and reaffirming the allegations contained in the original request, accompanied by an updated warrant information sheet.

C.   Proceedings Supplemental Stop While Body Attachment Outstanding. After the issuance of a body attachment for a party against whom a judgment has been rendered, no further hearings or other collection proceedings shall be scheduled for that party, nor shall any order garnishing wages issue until such time as the writ of body attachment is withdrawn, executed, or expires. This rule shall not prevent either attachments of the party's assets or third-party discovery related to the party's income or assets.

Adopted as Unified Rule 26, effective June 17, 1996. Amended effective June 30, 1999; renumbered as Unified Rule 25, and amended effective Jan. 17, 2002; amended and renumbered as Local Rule 29, May 17, 2006, effective Jan. 1, 2007; amended Sept. 29, 2009, effective Nov. 9, 2009; amended effective Sept. 30, 2011; effective Jan. 1, 2012.

LR48–TR10 Rule 30. PRO SE LITIGANTS (FORM OF PLEADING)

No pleading, motion, or proposed CCS entry, shall be accepted for filing from a pro se party unless the litigant's current address and phone number and the current address and phone number of the opposing party appear on the pleading.

Adopted as Unified Rule 27, effective June 17, 1996. Amended effective June 30, 1999; renumbered as Unified Rule 26, and amended effective Jan. 17, 2002; amended and renumbered as Local Rule 30, May 17, 2006, effective Jan. 1, 2007; amended effective Sept. 30, 2011; effective Jan. 1, 2012.

LR48–TR10   Rule   31. ORDERS/DECREES (FORM OF)

A.   The second and subsequent pages of all proposed orders shall contain an abbreviated case caption including the complete cause number.

B.   Proposed orders and decrees shall be legible, dignified and appropriate to the cause. Mimeographed or printed orders will be accepted for filing only if legible, clearly understandable, and void of strike overs and erasures. The appropriate Judge's name shall be placed under the appropriate signature line. The name of the person preparing the document shall appear on the order or decree. In the event an order or decree is submitted for approval of the court, the name of the preparer shall not appear on the order or decree.

C.   A proposed judgment or decree shall not be filed until such time the Court may grant the judgment or decree. Proposed divorce decrees shall not be submitted at the time the petition for dissolution is filed nor shall adoption decrees, garnishment orders, summary judgments or similar orders be submitted to the Court to be held in the Clerk's file for later use.

D.   Whenever the Court directs counsel to submit proposed findings and conclusions, or a proposed decree or memorandum order, in addition to filing a hard copy of said submission to the clerk, counsel shall submit a copy of said submission directly to the Court on floppy disk (or other approved electronic media) in Microsoft Word format, or as an email attachment in Word format to the court reporter of the Court.

E.   Proposed judgments or decrees submitted to the Court must be accompanied by a proposed CCS entry of six lines or less.

DECREES AND ORDERS SIGNED BY NON–REGULAR JUDGES

F. All proposed orders or decrees filed by counsel following a hearing before the Magistrate, Commissioner, or Referee shall include the following language:

"This matter comes before the Magistrate/Commissioner, etc ... (name) for hearing ..." At the end of the decree or order, the following language should appear, followed by a line for the Magistrate/Commissioner's, etc ... signature "Recommended for Approval". The following entry should appear after the Hearing Officer's signature: "COMES NOW THE COURT AND ENTERS JUDGMENT ON THE COMMISSIONER'S FINDINGS AND RECOMMENDATIONS."

/s/ _____
Judge

Commentary: This rule does not apply to Senior Judges, Temporary Judges, or Pro tems.

G. Notwithstanding the above, timely objections filed pursuant to Trial Rule 53(E)(2) will be given due consideration by the presiding Judge.

H. All Judgments or Decrees for the foreclosure of a Real Estate Mortgage shall provide (and if inadvertently omitted therefrom shall be deemed to provide) as follows:

1. Counsel for the Mortgagee shall submit a form of Sheriff's Deed, with appropriate blanks for the name and address (for purpose of real estate tax billings) of the Purchaser to be filled in by the Sheriff (or his or her Deputy) immediately after the sale;

2. That the Sheriff shall include as part of the costs of the Sale the recording and transfer fees for the recording of the Sheriff's Deed.

3. That the Sheriff shall cause the Sheriff's Deed to be promptly recorded after the completion of the Sheriff's Sale.

4. A copy of the Sheriff's return and the Sheriff's Deed shall be provided to the respective court's filing clerk for filing in the Court's case file.

Adopted as Unified Rules 20, 28, 29, and 30, effective June 17, 1996. Amended effective June 30, 1999; renumbered as Unified Rules 21, 27, 28, and 29, and amended effective Jan. 17, 2002; amended and renumbered as Local Rule 31, May 17, 2006, effective Jan. 1, 200; amended effective Sept. 30, 2011. Amended effective Jan. 1, 2012.

LR48–TR 5(G) Rule 32. FAX FILING

A. A lawsuit or other original action may not be initiated by FAX. However, the Madison County Clerk shall accept subsequent pleadings, not exceeding ten (10) pages (including a cover page), during regular business hours and shall promptly file stamp and transmit said documents to the designated Court. The Clerk may assess a reasonable fee for accepting and processing FAX filings.

B. Upon receipt of the FAX, the Court shall show the pleading filed. The original pleading and sufficient copies to effectuate distribution shall be mailed to the Court. The original pleading shall include a cover sheet or letter advising the Court that the attached documents are the originals of pleadings previously filed with the Court by FAX transmission.

C. Any pleadings faxed to the Court shall be contemporaneously faxed, or otherwise promptly delivered, to the opposing party. The certificate of service shall stipulate the method of notification.

Adopted as Unified Rule 35, effective June 17, 1996. Amended effective June 30, 1999; renumbered as Unified Rule 34, and amended effective Jan. 17, 2002; amended and renumbered as Local Rule 32, May 17, 2006, effective Jan. 1, 2007; amended effective Jan. 1, 2009; amended effective Sept. 30, 2011; effective Jan. 1, 2012.

LR48–TR16 Rule 33. PRE–TRIAL CONFERENCE

A. All trials which are scheduled for a full day or more on the trial calendar shall be docketed by counsel for pre-trial conference before the Court at least ten (10) days before the date of trial. Counsel should review the requirements of Trial Rule 16 in anticipation of the pre-trial conference.

B. In small claim matters, all cases, except suits for possession of real estate, shall first be set for an informal trial where issues may be identified for purposes of a later formal trial, or where evidence may be heard and the case decided.

Adopted as Unified Rule 17, effective June 17, 1996. Amended effective June 30, 1999; amended effective Jan. 17, 2002; amended and renumbered as Local Rule 33, May 17, 2006, effective Jan. 1, 2007; amended effective Sept. 30, 2011; effective Jan. 1, 2012.

LR48–TR45 Rule 34. SUBPOENAS AND NOTICE OF HEARING

A. Except in an emergency, a subpoena or notice of hearing will not be served by the Bailiff unless the same has been filed four (4) working days prior to a scheduled hearing. All subpoenas shall state a time and date calculated to minimize unnecessary delay and inconvenience to prospective witnesses.

B. A copy of every subpoena issued by any party shall be promptly filed with the Court and noted on the Chronological Case Summary. The Clerk shall maintain a copy of the subpoena in the permanent case file.

C. The failure to notify a subpoenaed witness that a cause has been continued or settled may result in an assessment of mileage and costs against counsel responsible for the failure.

Adopted as Unified Rule 31, effective June 17, 1996. Amended effective June 30, 1999; renumbered as Unified Rule 30, and amended effective Jan. 17, 2002; amended and renumbered as Local Rule 34, May 17, 2006, effective Jan. 1, 2007; amended effective Sept. 30, 2011; effective Jan. 1, 2012.

LR48–TR05 Rule 35. SERVICE ON ATTORNEY (CHRONOLOGICAL CASE SUMMARY)

Copies of a Chronological Case Summary deposited in the Court mail box in respective attorneys' slots shall be considered notice of said Chronological Case Summary entries. Attorneys may use said mail boxes to facilitate "certificate of service" and in such case shall indicate on the served document that service was so effected.

> *Commentary: Service to opposing counsel by assigned court mailboxes is appropriate only in fresh cases. If cases have become stale, then traditional efforts at service should be employed.*

Adopted as Unified Rule 9, effective June 17, 1996. Amended effective June 30, 1999; amended effective Jan. 17, 2002; amended and renumbered as Local Rule 35, May 17, 2006, effective Jan. 1, 2007; amended effective Sept. 30, 2011; effective Jan. 1, 2012.

LR48–TR3.1 Rule 35.5. DUTY TO UPDATE SERVICE ADDRESS

After a party has initiated a lawsuit, been served process, intervened or otherwise appeared as a party to an action, that party has an ongoing obligation to keep the Court and other parties advised of any change in that party's residential address or other address provided by law as appropriate for service of process. This obligation continues until such time as that party is dismissed from the action, the litigation is concluded without a judgment against that party, or until any judgment entered against the party is satisfied or released.

Adopted Sept. 29, 2009, effective Nov. 9, 2009. Amended effective Sept. 30, 2011; effective Jan. 1, 2012.

LR48–TR4.11 Rule 36. REQUIREMENTS FOR SERVICE BY CERTIFIED MAIL

For service by certified mail, the attorney, or litigant pro se, shall provide a typed certified mail card and envelope for each litigant.

Adopted as Unified Rule 9, effective June 17, 1996. Amended effective June 30, 1999; amended effective Jan. 17, 2002; amended and renumbered as Local Rule 36, May 17, 2006, effective Jan. 1, 2007; amended effective Sept. 30, 2011; effective Jan. 1, 2012.

LR48–TR41 Rule 37. DELINQUENT LISTS

A. Any civil case pending for more than six months may be placed upon a delinquent list pursuant to Trial Rule 41(E). Any case so listed may, after 45 days, be dismissed at the cost of the filing party, except for good cause shown. Any case so dismissed may be deemed dismissed with prejudice as to all parties, unless otherwise ordered.

B. Any probate matter in which no filing has been made for more than one year may be placed upon a delinquent list. If no significant action is taken within 45 days thereafter, the Court may require the personal representative, and/or counsel to show cause why the Court should not impose an appropriate sanction.

C. Guardianships shall not be placed upon a delinquent list within two years after the issuance of letters of guardianship, the filing of an inventory, or the filing of a current account.

Adopted May 17, 2006, effective Jan. 1, 2007. Amended effective Sept. 30, 2011; effective Jan. 1, 2012.

LR48–TR67 Rule 38. POST–JUDGMENT INTEREST

PAYMENT OF MONEY JUDGMENTS

(a) If the court orders a judgment debtor to make all payments through the Clerk's office and the judgment creditor does not in fact accept any payments toward a money judgment directly from the payor, then post-judgment interest will be automatically calculated by the Clerk's office and added to the amount due under the judgment without further action by the judgment creditor.

(b) If a judgment creditor accepts payments in satisfaction of a money judgment directly from the payor, as opposed to payment being made through the Clerk's office, then post-judgment interest shall not be amended to existing judgments or otherwise added to the calculated amount due until such time as the original judgment amount and costs have been paid and the judgment creditor then submits to the Clerk a statement of post-judgment interest due.

Adopted Sept. 29, 2009, effective Nov. 9, 2009. Amended effective Jan. 1, 2011; amended effective Sept. 30, 2011; effective Jan. 1, 2012.

EXHIBIT A. GUIDELINES FOR SUBMITTING COURT PLEADINGS

THESE COPIES ARE REQUIRED FOR THE COURT AND CLERKS OFFICE ONLY.
IF ANY COPIES ARE TO BE RETURNED TO THE ATTORNEY OR ATTORNEYS OFFICE
THEN ADDITIONAL COPIES ARE TO BE SUBMITTED.

ADOPTIONS:

1. MEDICAL HISTORY (FOR EACH CHILD)

ORIGINAL + 2

2. THREE PART ADOPTION FORM (PER EACH CHILD)

3. PETITION (SEND ADDITIONAL COPIES IF ATTORNEY NEEDS ANY BACK)

ORIGINAL + 3

4. CONSENTS (SEND ADDITIONAL COPIES IF ATTORNEY NEEDS ANY BACK)

ORIGINAL + 3

5. APPEARANCE (SEND ADDITIONAL COPIES IF ATTORNEY NEEDS ANY BACK)

ORIGINAL + 3

6. DECREE OF ADOPTION (SEND ADDITIONAL COPIES IF ATTORNEY NEEDS ANY BACK)

ORIGINAL + 3

CITATION:

1. CITATION ONLY TO BE SERVED PERSONAL SERVICE

ORIGINAL + 3

2. CITATION ONLY TO BE SENT CERTIFIED MAIL

ORIGINAL + 2—GREEN CARD AND ENVELOPE ARE TO BE PROVIDED BY THE ATTORNEYS OFFICE.

COMPLAINT:

1. PERSONAL SERVICE (PER DEFENDANT)

ORIGINAL + 2

2. CERTIFIED MAIL (PER DEFENDANT)

ORIGINAL + 1

GREEN CARD AND ENVELOPE TO BE PROVIDED BY THE ATTORNEYS OFFICE

DECREES:

1. ORIGINAL + 1 (FOR ORDER BOOK AND THE FILE)

IF DISTRIBUTION IS TO BE MADE BY THE CLERK TO THE PARTIES BY REGULAR MAIL 2 ADDITIONAL COPIES AND ADDRESSED ENVELOPES ARE TO BE PROVIDED BY THE ATTORNEYS OFFICE. (IF ATTORNEY NEEDS COPY SEND EXTRA)

THESE COPIES ARE REQUIRED FOR THE COURT AND CLERK'S OFFICE ONLY.
IF ANY COPIES ARE TO BE RETURNED TO THE ATTORNEY OR ATTORNEY'S OFFICE THEN ADDITIONAL COPIES ARE TO BE SUBMITTED.

FINAL ORDERS:

1. ORIGINAL + 4

INCOME WITHHOLDING OR WAGE ASSIGNMENTS:

1. ORIGINAL + 4

MENTAL HEALTH PETITIONS:

1. ORIGINAL + 4

NOTICE OF HEARING:

1. ORIGINAL + 3 (FOR EACH DEFENDANT) PERSONAL SERVICE

2. ORIGINAL + 2 (FOR EACH DEFENDANT) CERTIFIED MAIL GREEN CARD AND ENVELOPES TO BE PROVIDED.

ORDER TO APPEAR:

1. ORIGINAL + 4 (FOR EACH DEFENDANT) PERSONAL SERVICE

2. ORIGINAL + 2 (FOR EACH DEFENDANT) CERTIFIED MAIL GREEN CARD AND ENVELOPES TO BE PROVIDED.

PETITION TO MODIFY:

1. ORIGINAL + 2

PETITION FOR DISSOLUTION:

1. ORIGINAL + 2

QDRO:

1. ORIGINAL + 3 GREEN CARD AND ENVELOPE (PER ONE EMPLOYER)

THESE COPIES ARE REQUIRED FOR THE COURT AND CLERK'S OFFICE ONLY.
IF ANY COPIES ARE TO BE RETURNED TO THE ATTORNEY OR ATTORNEY'S OFFICE THEN ADDITIONAL COPIES ARE TO BE SUBMITTED.

MOTION FOR SUMMARY JUDGMENT:

1. ORIGINAL + 3 (PER DEFENDANT OR GARNISHMENT DEFENDANT)

IF YOU HAVE A SUMMONS, CITATION, SUBPOENA, NOTICE OF HEARING, OR AN ORDER TO APPEAR, AND OTHER PAPERWORK THAT NEEDS TO GO WITH IT. (EX: PETITION, MOTIONS, ETC.) AND IT IS TO GO PERSONAL SERVICE. WE NEED 4 OF THE SUMMONS, ETC., AND 3 OF EVERYTHING ELSE PER PERSON. IF ITS TO GO CERTIFIED MAIL, THE ATTORNEY NEEDS TO PROVIDE THE GREEN CARD AND ENVELOPE PER PERSON.

ORDERS AND JUDGMENTS:

1. ORIGINAL + 4. IF REGULAR MAIL, PROVIDE ENVELOPE. IF CERTIFIED MAIL, PROVIDE GREEN CARD AND ENVELOPE. (PER PERSON)

PROCEEDINGS SUPPLEMENTAL:

1. ORIGINAL + 4 PER DEFENDANT

ORDERS:

IF TO GO CERTIFIED MAIL, PROVIDE GREEN CARD AND ENVEL1.

ORIGINAL + 4 PER DEFENDANT OPE.

PROPERTY SETTLEMENT:

1. ORIGINAL + 1

(IF THIS NEEDS SENT TO EITHER PARTY YOU WILL NEED TO PROVIDE EXTRA COPIES. REGULAR MAIL 1 COPY PER DEFENDANT AND ENVELOPE. CERTIFIED MAIL 2 PER DEFENDANT, GREEN CARD AND ENVELOPE.)

RESTRAINING ORDERS AND PROTECTIVE ORDERS:

1. WITH ALL PROTECTIVE ORDERS AND RESTRAINING ORDERS (TEMPORARY OR PERMANENT) NEED 3 COVER SHEETS TO GO TO THE POLICE DEPARTMENTS.

2. ORIGINAL + 9 (THIS INCLUDES 1 COPY TO BE GIVEN TO BOTH ATTORNEYS)

THESE COPIES ARE REQUIRED FOR THE COURTS AND CLERKS OFFICE ONLY.

IF ANY COPIES ARE TO BE RETURNED TO THE ATTORNEY OR ATTORNEYS OFFICE THEN ADDITIONAL COPIES ARE TO BE SUBMITTED.

RECIPROCAL SUPPORT:

1. ORIGINAL + 5

SUBPOENAS:

1. ORIGINAL + 3 (PERSONAL SERVICE)

2. ORIGINAL + 3 (CERTIFIED MAIL, GREEN CARD AND ENVELOPE)

SUMMONS:

1. ORIGINAL + 3 (PERSONAL SERVICE)

2. ORIGINAL + 2 (CERTIFIED MAIL, GREEN CARD AND ENVELOPE)

TORT CLAIM:

1. ORIGINAL + 2 PER DEFENDANT (PERSONAL SERVICE)

2. ORIGINAL + 1 PER DEFENDANT (CERTIFIED MAIL, GREEN CARD AND ENVELOPE)

PATERNITY ORDERS:

1. ORIGINAL + 6

2. VOLUNTARY PETITION–ORIGINAL ONLY

3. INVOLUNTARY PETITION–ORIGINAL + 2

4. SUMMONS–ORIGINAL + 2

THESE COPIES ARE REQUIRED FOR THE COURT AND CLERK'S OFFICE ONLY.

IF ANY COPIES ARE TO BE RETURNED TO THE ATTORNEY OR ATTORNEY'S OFFICE THEN ADDITIONAL COPIES ARE TO BE SUBMITTED.

PROBATE

ESTATES:

1. ORIGINALS OF EVERYTHING

TWO ORDERS FOR OFFICE + COPIES OF ORDERS FOR FILES

2. NOTICES TO HEIRS WITH ENVELOPES

NEED ORIGINAL PETITIONER, OATH, WAIVERS, NOTICES, CERTIFICATE OF CLERK, ETC.

SUBMIT TWO ADDITIONAL COPIES OF ORDER (FOR FILE)

SUBMIT NOTICE (FOR THE NEWSPAPER)

GUARDIANSHIP & TRUSTS:

1. ORIGINALS OF EVERYTHING

TWO ORDERS FOR OFFICE + COPIES OF ORDERS FOR FILES

2. PERSONAL SERVICE

TWO COPIES

3. NEED ORIGINAL PETITION, CONSENTS, OATH, WAIVER, ETC.

SUBMIT TWO ADDITIONAL COPIES OF ORDER (FOR FILE)

4. CERTIFIED MAIL AND NOTICE OF HEARING

TWO COPIES + GREEN CARD ADDRESSED

INHERITANCE TAX SCHEDULE:

1. ORIGINAL + 2

INVENTORY:

1. ORIGINAL ONLY

FINAL ACCOUNTING:

1. ORIGINAL ONLY

2. NEED ORIGINAL PETITION, WAIVERS, CERTIFICATE OF CLERK, ETC.

SUBMIT TWO ADDITIONAL COPIES OF ORDER (FOR FILE).

NOTICES TO HEIRS WITH ENVELOPES

CLAIMS:

1. ORIGINAL + 2

ONE FILE MARKED COPY WILL BE RETURNED.

ONE COPY WILL BE SENT TO ATTORNEY OF RECORD, AND ORIGINAL WILL BE KEPT ON FILE.

COMMENTS:

PLEASE USE SHORT FORMS. IF YOU DO NOT HAVE THESE FORMS, OBTAIN THEM FROM THE PROBATE OFFICE. PETITIONS AND ORDERS SHALL BE SUBMITTED ON SEPARATE PAGES.

Adopted as App. A, effective June 17, 1996. Amended effective June 30, 1999; amended effective Jan. 17, 2002; amended and renumbered as Exhibit A, May 17, 2006, effective Jan. 1, 2007; amended effective Sept. 30, 2011. Adopted effective Jan. 1, 2012.

PROBATE RULES

LR48–PR00 Rule 38.5.   NOTICE

Section I Whenever notice by publication and/or written notice by U.S. Mail is required to be given, the attorney shall prepare such notice and shall ensure that such notice is properly published and/or

served by mail. In all respects, the notice shall comply with all statutory requirements. It shall be the attorney's responsibility to ascertain and provide adequate proof thereof regarding whether notice was properly served prior to bringing a matter to the Court.

Section II Copies of petitions or motions shall be sent with all notices where the hearing involved arises from the matters contained in the petition or motion.

Section III Whenever any estate or guardianship account (including a final account in a supervised estate) is set for hearing, copies of the account must be served with the notice of hearing.

Section IV Notice of the opening of an estate shall be sent by First Class United States Mail to all reasonably ascertainable creditors; however, the use of "certified mail, return receipt requested," to serve such notice is recommended.

Section V Notice of the hearing to be held on a Petition to determine an estate insolvent may be served on all interested parties, at the discretion of the Court.

Adopted Sept. 29, 2009, effective Nov. 9, 2009. Amended effective Sept. 30, 2011; effective Jan. 1, 2012.

LR48–PR00 Rule 39.   FILING OF PLEADINGS

Section I When pleadings are filed by mail or left with the Court for filing, a self-addressed, stamped envelope shall be included for return of documents to the attorney, unless Courthouse mail is available.

Section II All parties are required to prepare orders for all proceedings except when expressly directed otherwise by the Court.

Section III Upon the opening of an estate or guardianship, the Clerk shall provide a copy of the Court's instructions to all personal representatives and guardians.

Section IV The Instructions to the Personal Representative or Guardian, executed by the fiduciary, must be filed with the Court within 10 days of the issuance of the Letters.

Section V The affidavit of compliance with the notice provisions directed to creditors in an estate proceeding shall be timely filed with the Clerk of the Court.

Adopted Sept. 29, 2009, effective Nov. 9, 2009. Amended effective Sept. 30, 2011; effective Jan. 1, 2012.

LR48–PR00 Rule 40. ATTENDANCE OF PROPOSED FIDUCIARIES

Section I All proposed Pro Se personal representatives and guardians who are residents of Indiana shall appear before the Court to qualify.

Section II All personal representatives or guardians are under a continuing order of the Court to personally advise the Court and the attorney of record, in writing, as to any change of any required information such as name, address, or telephone number.

Adopted Sept. 29, 2009, effective Nov. 9, 2009. Amended effective Sept. 30, 2011; effective Jan. 1, 2012.

LR48–PR00 Rule 41. REPRESENTATION OF FIDUCIARIES BY COUNSEL

Section I No personal representative or guardian of an estate may proceed without counsel, without court approval.

Adopted Sept. 29, 1009, effective Nov. 9, 2009. Amended effective Sept. 30, 2011; effective Jan. 1, 2012.

LR48–PR00 Rule 42.   BOND

Section I If a bond is required in an estate or guardianship, the fiduciary, prior to the issuance of letters, shall file a corporate surety bond in an amount determined by the Court after considering the following factors: (a) the value of the personal property to be administered; (b) the probable value of annual rents and profits of all property of the estate; (c) the rights of creditors, taxing authorities and devises.

Section II No bond shall be required in any supervised estate or guardianship in which a corporate banking fiduciary qualified by law to serve as such is either the fiduciary or one of several co-fiduciaries.

Section III In lieu of a bond, and upon the fiduciary's request, the Court may restrict transfer of all or part of the estate or guardianship liquid assets by placing those assets in a federally insured financial institution or in a court approved investment with the following restriction placed on the face of the account or in the investment document:

"NO PRINCIPAL OR INTEREST SHALL BE WITHDRAWN WITHOUT WRITTEN ORDER OF _____ COURT OF _____, INDIANA."

The fiduciary shall thereafter file with the Court, within ten (10) days of the order authorizing the creation of the account or investment, a certification by an officer of the institution at which the account or investment has been created, affirming that the account or investment is restricted as required by the Court order and is in compliance with this rule.

Section IV All petitions to open an estate or guardianship shall set forth the probable value of the personal property plus the estimated annual rents and profits to be derived from the property in the estate or guardianship.

Section V The name and address of the insurance agency providing the corporate surety shall be typed or printed on all corporate bonds in any estate or guardianship.

Adopted Sept. 29, 2009, effective Nov. 9, 2009. Amended effective Sept. 30, 2011; effective Jan. 1, 2012.

LR48–PR00 Rule 43.   INVENTORY

Section I An inventory shall be filed by the fiduciary in estates and guardianships as follows: Supervised estates, within sixty (60) days; guardianships, within ninety (90) days for permanent guardians and within thirty (30) days for temporary guardians. All times relate to the date of appointment of the fiducia-ry.

Section II In the event a partial inventory is filed, all subsequent inventories must contain a recapitulation of prior inventories.

Section III In the event that the personal representative should request that an inventory be sealed, the Court may, in its sole discretion, seal such inventory. If an inventory is sealed, it shall be maintained in the court reporter's evidence file in the Court in which such estate is filed.

Adopted Sept. 29, 2009, effective Nov. 9, 2009. Amended effective Sept. 30, 2011; effective Jan. 1, 2012.

LR48–PR00 Rule 44. REAL ESTATE

Section I In all supervised estates and guardianships in which real estate is to be sold, if required by the Court, a written professional appraisal shall be filed with the Court at the time of filing the Petition for Sale, unless such appraisal was filed with the inventory. Such written appraisal shall include as a minimum the following elements:

a. A brief description of the property interest being appraised, including the full and legal description thereof.

b. Purpose or objective of the appraisal.

c. Date for which fair market value is determined.

d. Data and reasoning supporting the fair market value.

e. Fair market value determined.

f. Statement of assumptions and special or limiting conditions.

g. Certification of disinterest in real estate.

h. Signature of the appraiser.

Section II All such appraisals if required by the Court shall be made within one year of the date of the Petition for Sale.

Section III All deeds submitted to the Court for approval in either estate or guardianship proceedings shall be signed by the fiduciary and the signature notarized prior to its submission.

Adopted Sept. 29, 2009, effective Nov. 9, 2009. Amended effective Sept. 30, 2011; effective Jan. 1, 2012.

LR48–PR00 Rule 45. SALE OF ASSETS

Section I In all supervised estates and guardianships, no Petition to Sell Personal Property shall be granted unless a written appraisal prepared by a person competent to appraise such property and setting forth the fair market value thereof, is filed with the Court at the time of the filing of the Petition to Sell, unless such appraisal was filed with the inventory. This rule shall not apply to personal property which is sold at public auction.

Section II All appraisals required by the Court shall be made within one year of the date of the Petition to Sell.

Section III No written appraisal shall be required for the sale of assets which are traded in a market and the value of which is readily ascertainable. Such assets include, but are not limited to, stocks, bonds, mutual funds, commodities, and precious metals.

Adopted Sept. 29, 2009, effective Nov. 9, 2009. Amended effective Sept. 30, 2011; effective Jan. 1, 2012.

LR48–PR00 Rule 46. ACCOUNTING

Section I All social security or Medicare benefits received on behalf of an incapacitated person shall be included and accounted for in the guardianship accounting unless court approval has been previously granted to allow said funds to be paid directly to a residential or health care facility, or because of the amount of such funds, the Court finds that such funds can only be used by the guardian or designated person for the benefit of, or use by, such incapacitated person.

Section II In all supervised estate and guardianship accountings, a notation shall be placed by each expenditure indicating the reason for or nature of the expenditure unless the payee name indicates the nature of the expenditure.

Section III All court costs shall be paid and all claims satisfied and released before the hearing on the Final Account.

Adopted Sept. 29, 2009, effective Nov. 9, 2009. Amended effective Sept. 30, 2011; effective Jan. 1, 2012.

LR48–PR00 Rule 47. FEES OF ATTORNEY AND FIDUCIARY

Section I No fees for fiduciaries or attorneys shall be paid out of any supervised estate or guardianship without prior written order of the Court.

Section II All orders for fees in estates shall provide that said fees are to be paid only after approval of the Final Accounting except as otherwise ordered by the Court.

Section III A guardian or guardian's attorney may petition for fees at the time of filing an inventory, or, as otherwise provided by the Court.

Section IV No attorney or fiduciary fees will be determined and authorized for payment by the Court in any unsupervised administration of a decedent's estate.

Section V Where contracts for legal services have been entered into prior or subsequent to the opening of an estate or guardianship, the awarding of such fees shall require the approval of the Court.

Section VI All petitions for fees for the attorney and/or fiduciary shall conform to the fee guidelines set forth by this Court.

Section VII Unjustified delays in carrying out duties by the fiduciary and/or attorney may result in a reduction of fees.

Section VIII Attorney fees for representing a minor in settlement of a claim for personal injuries are subject to court approval. If the entire attorney fee is to be paid at the same time a structured settlement is approved, the amount of the fee must be based on the present value of the settlement.

Section IX MAXIMUM FEE GUIDELINES FOR SUPERVISED ESTATES

Principles Applicable to Fee Determinations

Although fee guidelines have been promulgated by the court for probate matters, it is important that your attention be directed to certain criteria as they pertain to these Guidelines.

The existence of the Guidelines does not assure that all fees allowed by the court will adhere to them. Other factors must be considered by the attorney and his, or her, client. The same factors will also be considered by the court in making its final determination.

The criteria to be considered include the following:

A. The time and labor required, the novelty, complexity, or difficulty of the questions involved, the skill required to perform the services properly, and shall include a determination as to how much of the attorney's time was devoted to legal matters and how much of it was devoted to ministerial functions;

B. The nature and extent of the responsibilities assumed by the attorney and the results obtained, and shall include the considerations of the identity of the personal representative and the character of the probate and non-probate transferred assets;

C. The sufficiency of assets properly available to pay for legal services, and shall consider whether the attorney's duties are expanded by the existence of non-probate assets because of their inclusion for tax purposes, both federal and state;

D. The timeliness with which the necessary services are performed consistent with statutory requirements, the Court's rules of procedure and the Rules of Professional Conduct applicable thereto.

In considering all of these factors, attorneys are urged to discuss their fee and that of the personal representative at the time they are retained in all probate matters.

PERSONAL REPRESENTATIVE FEES

I. PROFESSIONAL

Their applicable reasonable rate shall be reviewed in light of all prevailing circumstances.

II. NON–PROFESSIONAL

An amount not in excess of one-half (1/2) of the attorney's fees.

III. ATTORNEY

When the attorney also serves as the personal representative, an additional amount not in excess of one-half (1/2) of the attorney fee may be allowed.

Adopted Sept. 29, 2009, effective Nov. 9, 2009. Amended effective Sept. 30, 2011; effective Jan. 1, 2012.

LR48–PR00 Rule 48. UNSUPERVISED ADMINISTRATION

Section I All court costs shall be paid and all claims satisfied and released on or before the date of the filing of the Closing Statement.

Section II An order approving the Closing Statement shall be required.

Adopted Sept. 29, 2009, effective Nov. 9, 2009. Amended effective Sept. 30, 2011; effective Jan. 1, 2012.

LR48–PR00 Rule 49. GUARDIANSHIPS

Section I In all guardianship matters seeking to declare an adult incapacitated for any reason, the incapacitated person shall be present at the hearing or sufficient evidence shall be presented showing that the incapacitated person is unable to appear. The Court may at any time appoint a guardian ad litem to investigate and protect the best interest of the incapacitated person.

Section II In all guardianship matters seeking to declare an adult incapacitated for any reason, a Physician's Report by the doctor treating the alleged incapacitated person or such additional evidence as the Court shall require, shall be presented to the Court at the time the petition is filed or on the hearing date. No determination will be made without a supporting medical report or testimony.

Section III In every petition for the appointment of a guardian of the person of a minor child, the following information shall be given, in addition to the statutory requirement, if known to the petitioner:

a. The places where the child has lived within the past two years and the names and present addresses of persons with whom the child has lived during that period.

b. General information concerning school, health, etc.

c. Whether any other litigation is pending concerning the custody of the child in this or any other state.

d. Whether any person not a party to the guardianship proceeding has physical custody of the child or claims to have custody or visitation rights with respect to the child.

Section IV Nothing herein shall be deemed as amending, superseding or altering the Probate Rules and Regulations promulgated by the Veteran's Administration of the United States of America, and every fiduciary and attorney shall comply with same, if applicable.

Adopted Sept. 29, 2009, effective Nov. 9, 2009. Amended effective Sept. 30, 2011; effective Jan. 1, 2012.

LR48–PR00 Rule 50.   MINORS' SETTLEMENTS

Section I   This rule shall govern requests for approval of settlements for minors (pursuant to IC 29–3–9 and/or IC 29–3–4) and guardianships for minors, if such settlements are approved by the Court.

Section II   A hearing shall be set at the request of counsel in which testimony or evidence is presented so as to fully and independently satisfy the Court that the requested settlement fully protects the minor's rights and interests.   The Court may at any time appoint a guardian ad litem to protect the best interest of the minor and investigate such settlement.

Section III   Once a guardian is appointed, then such guardian shall post bond, unless, in lieu of a bond, a fiduciary places all funds or assets in a restricted account at a federally-insured financial institution or in a court approved investment, designating that no principle or interest may be withdrawn without a written order of the Court, and with the following restriction placed on the face of the account or in the investment document:

"NO PRINCIPAL OR INTEREST SHALL BE WITHDRAWN WITHOUT WRITTEN ORDER OF _____ COURT OF _____, INDIANA."

The fiduciary shall file the following with the Court:

a.   Prior to issuance of letters, the fiduciary's attorney shall execute an Attorney's Undertaking for such assets.

Section IV   No surety bond or restricted account is required where a corporate fiduciary serves as a guardian of the estate.

Adopted Sept. 29, 2009, effective Nov. 9, 2009. Amended effective Sept. 30, 2011; effective Jan. 1, 2012.

LR48–PR00 Rule 51.   WRONGFUL DEATH ESTATES

Section I[1]   All proposed wrongful death settlements must be approved by the Court, whether the estate is supervised, unsupervised, or a special administration for the sole purpose of prosecuting the wrongful death claim.

Adopted Sept. 29, 2009, effective Nov. 9, 2009. Amended effective Sept. 30, 2011; effective Jan. 1, 2012.

1 There is no Section II in original.

LR48–PR00 Rule 52.   MAGISTRATE

Section I[1]   The Madison County Magistrate shall have and exercise all powers and authority in probate matters which are granted to Probate Commissioners by State Statute, Local Rule, or, as ordered by a regular Judge.

Adopted Sept. 29, 2009, effective Nov. 9, 2009. Amended effective Sept. 30, 2011; effective Jan. 1, 2012.

1 There is no Section II in original.

MARION CIRCUIT AND SUPERIOR COURT CIVIL DIVISION RULES

Amended Effective October 2, 2006

Including Amendments Received Through November 1, 2013

Research Notes

Annotations to the Marion Circuit and Superior Court Civil Rules are available in West's Annotated Indiana Code, *Title 34 Appendix.*

These rules may be searched electronically on Westlaw *in the* IN-RULES *database; updates to these rules may be found on* Westlaw *in* IN-RULESUPDATES. *For search tips and a summary of database content, consult the Westlaw Scope Screens for each database.*

LR49–TR3 Rule 200. RANDOM FILING OF CIVIL CASES

A. All civil cases filed with the Marion County Clerk's Office designated by statute or rule as being required to be filed in certain named Courts shall be so assigned.

B. Cases involving a petition for a restricted driving permit under I. C. 9–24–15–2 shall be filed in the Marion County Circuit Court; and all other petitions filed pursuant to I.C. 9–24–15–4(a)(1), (2) or (3) may, at the discretion of the Judge of the court in which the petition was filed, be transferred as soon as possible to the Marion County Circuit Court.

C. Civil Plenary (PL), Mortgage Foreclosure (MF), Civil Collections (CC), Civil Torts (CT), and Domestic Relations (DR) cases shall be allocated at follows:

1. *Civil Plenary (CP/PL) Cases.*

   a. 1% shall be randomly filed in Circuit Court, and

   b. 99% shall be filed in Superior Court, divided randomly and evenly among the judges of the Civil Division (49D01, 49D02, 49D03, 49D04, D9D05, 49D06, 49D07, 49D10, 49D11, 49D12, 49D13, and 49D14).

2. *Mortgage Foreclosure (MF) Cases.*

   a. 5% shall be randomly filed in Circuit Court, and

b. 95% shall be filed in Superior Court, divided randomly and evenly among the judges of the Civil Division (49D01, 49D02, 49D03, 49D04, D9D05, 49D06, 49D07, 49D10, 49D11, 49D12, 49D13, and 49D14).

3. *Civil Collections (CC) Cases.*

a. 1% shall be randomly filed in Circuit Court, and

b. 99% shall be filed in Superior Court, divided randomly and evenly among the judges of the Civil Division (49D01, 49D02, 49D03, 49D04, D9D05, 49D06, 49D07, 49D10, 49D11, 49D12, 49D13, and 49D14).

4. *Civil Torts (CT) and Domestic Relations (DR) Cases.* Shall be assigned in the proportion of 100% in Superior Court, divided randomly and evenly among the judges of the Civil Division (49D01, 49D02, 49D03, 49D04, D9D05, 49D06, 49D07, 49D10, 49D11, 49D12, 49D13, and 49D14).

D. Marion Superior Court F12 (Environmental Court) shall be assigned the following cases:

1. Any civil case where the environment is involved as the lead issue or where a decision of an environmental administrative agency is being appealed;

2. Any civil action that includes a count based upon or involving Indiana Code Title 13/ Environment or Title 14/ Natural and Cultural Resources;

3. Any civil action requiring judicial review from final agency action involving an environmental matter;

4. Department of Revenue UST and solid waste fee tax warrants;

5. Common law theories of recovery such as toxic torts, property contamination cases alleging nuisance, trespass, negligence and environmental cleanup and contribution actions;

6. Open Door and Public Record suits or appeals related to IDEM, DNR, ISHD, State Fire Marshall or the Fire Prevention and Building Safety Commission; and

7. Contract or other disputes involving a substantive environmental issue.

E. Civil cases involving judicial review of a zoning decision pursuant to IC 36–7–4–1601 et seq. shall be filed in Marion Superior Court, Civil 7 (D07).

F. Civil cases requiring judicial review of a final State Agency decision under Article 21.5 of the Indiana Administrative Orders and Procedures Act (I.C. 4–21.5 et seq.) shall be randomly assigned.

All civil cases other than those listed above filed with the Marion County Clerk's Office for the Marion Superior Court shall be assigned to an individual courtroom on a random basis. The process for the random assignment shall be done through the Court and Clerk's automated case management system.

Adopted as Civil Division Rule 3, Feb. 6, 2005, effective March 15, 2006. Renumbered as Civil Rule 200, and amended effective Oct. 2, 2006. Amended Sept. 8, 2008, effective Oct. 7, 2008; Jan. 1, 2012.

LR49–TR3.1 Rule 201. WITHDRAWAL OF APPEARANCE

All withdrawals of appearances shall be in writing and by leave of Court. Permission to withdraw shall be given only after the withdrawing attorney has given his client ten days written notice of his intention to withdraw, has filed a copy of such with the Court; and has provided the Court with the party's last known address; or upon a simultaneous entering of appearance by new counsel for said client. The letter of withdrawal shall explain to the client that failure to secure new counsel may result in dismissal of the client's case or a default judgment may be entered against him, whichever is appropriate, and other pertinent information such as trial setting date or any other hearing date. The Court will not grant a request for withdrawal of appearance unless the same has been filed with the Court at least ten days prior to trial date, except for good cause shown.

Adopted as Civil Division Rule 3.2, Jan. 19, 1999, effective Mar. 1, 1999. Renumbered as Civil Rule 201, and amended effective Oct. 2, 2006. Amended effective Mar. 5, 2009.

LR49–TR4.12 Rule 202. ATTACHMENT: SERVICE BY SHERIFF

A. Attachment–Duties of Sheriff. Unless otherwise directed by the Judge, when a body attachment is signed by the Judge and taken to the Civil Sheriff's Office, the Civil Sheriff's Office will issue a letter to the party concerned requesting that he appear voluntarily at said office. If no response is made to this letter by the judgment defendant within 30 days, the Civil Sheriff shall then execute said body attachment and bring the defendant into court during court hours.

If the Civil Sheriff is not successful in attaching the individual in question after 60 more days, a total of 90 days, he shall return the attachment to the appropriate court with a return that service cannot be made.

The plaintiff's attorney will be duly informed of the return of the attachment and he may then proceed to request that the Court place a bond upon the judgment defendant; such a bond may be fixed within the discretion of the Court if the Court finds that the defendant has actual knowledge of the attachment, is deliberately evading process of service, or such other matters as may convince the Court that a bond would be desirable under the circumstances and in the situation involved. If a new attachment is issued with bond fixed thereon, the Sheriff's Office will once again make an attempt to pick up the judgment defendant at the address indicated, and if picked up outside of court hours, he will be taken to the jail and required to post the amount of bond indicated to guarantee his appearance in court. Upon posting of the bond, he will be released with the admonition to appear in the appropriate court on the next court day during court hours. If, in an additional 30 days, the Sheriff is again unable to obtain good service on the judgment defendant, the attachment will be returned to the appropriate court for disposition.

B. Attachments–Hearings. When a judgment defendant has been brought into court on a body attachment, a hearing will be conducted at the earliest convenience of the Court. Counsel for the plaintiff will respond to the telephone request by court personnel to appear at the hearing forthwith, and counsel will have deemed to consent to such notice to appear by requesting a body attachment. The hearing requires the presence of the attorney of record, and clerical or secretarial personnel shall not appear to interrogate the attached judgment defendant. Failure to respond promptly to such request may result in the discharge of the attached defendant or other appropriate measures by the Court.

Adopted as Civil Division Rule 4.12, Jan. 19, 1999, effective Mar. 1, 1999. Renumbered as Civil Rule 202, and amended effective Oct. 2, 2006. Amended effective Mar. 5, 2009.

LR49–TR5 Rule 203. REQUIREMENTS FOR MOTIONS

A. Notice. When a motion requires notice, the serving of the copy of the motion upon the other parties in the cause shall constitute notice of filing. If the motion requires a hearing or oral argument, the Court shall set the time and place of hearing or argument on the motion. Except for initial motions made pursuant to subsection D herein, all motions filed with the court shall include a brief statement indicating whether opposing party(ies) object to or approve of the granting of said motion.

B. Response. If the statement regarding the position of the opposing party(ies) required under subsection A herein indicates that objection to the granting of said motion may ensue, said objecting a party shall have 15 days from the date of filing to file a response to said motion.

C. Oral Arguments on Motions and Other Pleadings. When an oral argument is requested, the request shall be by separate instrument and filed with the pleading to be argued. Any such oral argument requested may be heard at the discretion of the Court, except for motions for summary judgment which shall be set for hearing upon request of any party.

D. Enlargement of Time. Initial written motion for enlargement of time pursuant to Rule TR 6(B)(1) to respond to a claim shall be automatically allowed for an additional 30 days from the original due date without a written order of the Court. Any motion filed pursuant to this rule shall state the date when such a response is due and the date to which time is enlarged. The motion must be filed on or before the original due date or this rule shall be inapplicable. All subsequent Motions shall be so designated and will be granted only for good cause shown.

E. Tender of Orders. All motions seeking an order of the Court shall be accompanied by a sufficient number of orders to be executed by the Court in granting said motion. In addition to the orders, the notice shall be accompanied by stamped, addressed envelopes to all parties of record.

Adopted as Civil Division Rule 5.1, Jan. 19, 1999, effective Mar. 1, 1999. Amended effective Mar. 7, 2005. Renumbered as Civil Rule 203, and amended effective Oct. 2, 2006. Amended effective Mar. 5, 2009.

LR49–TR8 Rule 204. PREPARATION OF PLEADINGS, MOTIONS AND OTHER PAPERS

All pleadings, motions and other papers shall be prepared in accordance with the provisions of the Indiana Rules of Procedure. For the purpose of uniformity and convenience, the following requirements shall also be observed.

A. Production. Pleadings, motions and other papers may be either printed or typewritten on white opaque paper of at least 16 pound weight, 8–½ inches wide and 11 inches in length. All copies shall likewise be on white paper of sufficient strength and durability to resist normal wear and tear. If typewritten, the lines shall be double spaced, except for quotations, which shall be indented and single spaced. Script type shall not be used.

B. Caption. Every pleading shall contain a caption setting forth the name of the Court, the Division and Room Number, the title of the action and the file number.

C. Titles. Titles on all pleadings shall delineate each topic included in the pleading e.g. where a pleading contains an Answer, a Motion to Strike or Dismiss, or a Jury Request each shall be set forth in the title.

D. Margins and Binding. Margins shall be one inch. Binding or stapling shall be at the top and at no other place. Covers or backing shall not be used.

E. Signature. All pleadings and motions shall contain the original or authorized signature of the attorney, the name of the attorney in typed or printed form, the name of the law firm if a member of a firm, the attorney's address, identification number, e-mail address, telephone number, fax number, and the designation as to the party for whom he appears. The following form is recommended:

John Doe
Attorney Identification Number
DOE, ROWE, and SMITH
Suite 35 Blackacre Building
Indianapolis, Indiana 46204
John.doe@DRSlaw.com
939–3000 Fax: 233–1744

Attorney for Defendant
(Name)

Adopted as Civil Division Rule 8.1, Jan. 19, 1999, effective Mar. 1, 1999. Renumbered as Civil Rule 204, and amended effective Oct. 2, 2006. Amended effective Mar. 5, 2009.

LR49–TR5 Rule 205. FILING OF PLEADINGS, MOTIONS AND OTHER PAPERS

A. Room Clerk. All pleadings, petitions and motions are filed with the Clerk designated by the Court at any time during office hours established by the Clerk and the Court. All orders submitted to the Court shall be in sufficient number and shall be accompanied by postage paid envelopes addressed to each party or counsel of record.

B. Facsimile. Facsimile filing is discouraged, but permitted in the Marion Circuit and Marion Superior Court. All documents filed by facsimile shall also be filed in hard copy within seven days of the facsimile filing, along with proposed orders and stamped addressed envelopes, as required by LR49–TR5–203 (E). **To avoid duplicate filings, the hard copies of the facsimile filing shall indicate in bold letters that the pleading was previously filed by facsimile transmission.** Proof of transmission by facsimile, including certificate of service and manner of service, shall be the responsibility of the filing party. If the filing requires immediate attention of the Judge, it shall be so indicated in bold letters in an accompanying transmittal memorandum. Legibility of documents and timeliness of filing is the responsibility of the sender.

C. Counsel to Furnish Pleadings to Special Judge. When a Special Judge who is not a Marion County Judge is selected, all parties or attorneys shall furnish such Judge with copies of all filings prior to the qualification of such Special Judge. Thereafter, copies of all filings shall be delivered in person, by mail or by facsimile to the office of the Special Judge with certificate of forwarding same made a part of the filing.

D. Number. Counsel shall file with the court an original and one copy of all briefs, and memoranda of law filed in support of a motion.

E. Appearance Form. Pursuant to Trial Rule 3.1(A), an appearance form shall be filed by the initiating party at the time an action commenced. If the action is appropriate for filing and disposition in Marion Superior Court, Environmental Division, per Order of the Executive Committee of the Marion Superior Court, then the initiating party shall indicate such on the appearance form.

Adopted as Civil Division Rule 8.2, Jan. 19, 1999, effective March 1, 1999. Amended effective May 21, 2001; renumbered as Civil Rule 205, and amended effective Oct. 2, 2006; Jan. 1, 2008.

LR49–TR11 Rule 206. SIGNING AND VERIFICATION OF PLEADINGS, MOTIONS AND OTHER PAPERS–SERVICE ON OPPOSING PARTY

In all cases where any pleading or other document is required to be served upon opposing counsel, proof of such service may be made either by:

(1) a certificate of service signed by counsel of record for the serving party and the certificate shall specify by name and address all counsel upon whom the pleading or document was served or

(2) an acknowledgment of service signed by the party served or counsel of record.

Adopted as Civil Division Rule 11.1, Jan. 19, 1999, effective March 1, 1999. Renumbered as Civil Rule 206, and amended effective Oct. 2, 2006; Jan. 1, 2008.

LR49–TR16 Rule 207. CASE MANAGEMENT

A. Case Management Conference. Plaintiff shall arrange a meeting of all parties within 90 days after the filing of a complaint for the following purposes:

1. *List of Witnesses.* Exchange lists of witnesses known to have knowledge of the facts supporting the pleadings. The parties shall thereafter be under a continuing obligation to advise opposing parties of other witnesses as they become known.

2. *Documents.* Exchange all documents which are contemplated to be used in support of the pleadings. Documents later shown to have been reasonably available to a party and not exchanged may be subject to exclusion at time of trial.

3. *Other Evidence.* Exchange any other evidence reasonably available to obviate the filing of unnecessary discovery motions.

4. *Settlement.* Discuss settlement of the action.

5. *Discovery Schedule.* Agree upon a preliminary schedule for all discovery.

6. *Complicated Case.* Discuss whether the action is sufficiently complicated so that additional conferences may be required.

B. Case Management Order. Within ten (10) days after meeting those attending are to file a joint Case Management Order setting forth:

1. the likelihood of mediation and settlement;

2. a detailed schedule of discovery for each party;

3. a limitation on the time to join additional parties and to amend the pleadings;

4. a limitation on the time to file all pre-trial motions;

5. any other matters which the parties want to address;

6. a preliminary estimate of the time required for trial; and

7. the date by which the parties expect the matter to be ready for trial.

Adopted as Civil Division Rule 16.1, Jan. 19, 1999, effective Mar. 1, 1999. Renumbered as Civil Rule 207, and amended effective Oct. 2, 2006. Amended effective Mar. 5, 2009.

LR49–TR16 Rule 208. PRE–TRIAL CONFERENCE

A. Pre-trial Conference Mandatory. A pre-trial conference shall be held in every civil jury action. Each party shall be represented at the pre-trial conference by the attorney who will conduct the trial.

B. Pre-trial Stipulation Must Be Filed. Counsel for the plaintiff shall see that a pre-trial stipulation is prepared, executed by counsel for all parties, and filed with the Court no later than five days prior to the pre-trial conference. The pre-trial stipulation shall contain the following statements in separate numbered paragraphs as indicated:

1. the nature of the action.

2. the basis of jurisdiction.

3. the pleadings raising the issues.

4. a list of all motions or other matters requiring action by the Court.

5. a concise statement of stipulated facts, with reservations, if any.

6. a statement of issues of fact which remain to be litigated at trial.

7. a concise statement of issues of law on which there is agreement.

8. a concise statement of issues of law which remain for determination by the Court.

9. each party's numbered list of trial exhibits, other than impeachment exhibits, with objections, if any, to each exhibit. The list of exhibits shall be on separate schedules attached to the stipulation.

10. each party's numbered list of trial witnesses, with their addresses. Impeachment witnesses need not be listed. Expert witnesses shall be so designated.

11. estimated trial time.

C. Unilateral Filing of Pre-trial Stipulation Where Counsel Do Not Agree. If for any reason the pre-trial stipulation is not executed by all counsel, each counsel shall file a proposed pre-trial stipulation not later than five days prior to the pre-trial conference with a statement why no agreement was reached.

D. Memoranda of Law. Counsel shall file memoranda treating any unusual questions of law involved in the trial no later than five days prior to the pre-trial conference.

E. Proposed Jury Instructions. Seven days prior to trial, counsel shall submit proposed jury instructions to the Court, with copies to all other counsel. Instructions covering matters occurring at the trial which could not reasonably be anticipated may be substituted at the conclusion of the testimony. Each instruction shall be accompanied by citations of authority.

F. Objections to Proposed Jury Instructions. Written objections to proposed jury instructions shall be submitted to the Court on or before the first day of trial. Written objections shall be numbered and shall specify distinctly the objectionable matter in the proposed instruction. Each objection shall be accompanied by citations of authority.

Adopted as Civil Division Rule 16.2, Jan. 19, 1999, effective Mar. 1, 1999. Renumbered as Civil Rule 208, and amended effective Oct. 2, 2006. Amended effective Mar. 5, 2009.

LR49–ADR2 Rule 209. ALTERNATIVE DISPUTE RESOLUTION—MEDIATION PROCEDURE

A. Case selection shall be governed by A.D.R. Rule 2.2.

B. Mediator selection shall be governed by A.D.R. Rule 2.4. Mediators approved by the Indiana Supreme Court Commission for Continuing Legal Education shall be entered into the Court's computer system. If the parties are unable to select a mediator by agreement pursuant to A.D.R. Rule 2.4, the Court will generate a list of three mediators by random selection through the computer.

C. The parties shall have ten days to strike from the panel of mediators named by the Court. The party that initiated the cause of action shall strike first. If the parties fail to strike within ten days, the Court shall select a mediator. Upon selection of the mediator, counsel for the party that initiated the litigation shall submit a proposed order appointing the mediator selected in the case.

D. During the entire mediation process, the lawsuit shall remain on the Court's docket.

E. Absent an agreement by the parties or unless otherwise ordered by the Court the fees and expenses associated with the mediation shall be shared equally by the parties unless good cause can be shown by a party why an equal division of the fees should not be ordered. In the case of team mediation, the fee is to be split between the mediators as the co-mediators are to be treated as a unit.

F. The mediator and the parties shall make a good faith effort to complete the mediation process within sixty (60) days from the date of the Order to engage in mediation. In the event that the mediation process is not completed within this time, the mediator shall file a status report with the Court setting forth the projected date of completion.

G. Within 24 hours prior to the scheduled mediation conference or such other time as the mediator declares, the parties shall submit to the mediator a Confidential Mediation Statement. Such statement shall include, without limitation, a brief recitation of: (a) the facts relevant to the dispute; (b) the amount in controversy or other relief requested; (c) the progress of the litigation to date; (d) the status of negotiations; and (e) the factors, including factual and legal contentions as to both liability and damages, which have been considered or relied upon in arriving at the current settlement posture.

H. All parties, attorneys with settlement authority, representatives with settlement authority, and other necessary individuals shall be present at each mediation conference to facilitate settlement of a dispute unless excused by the court or by stipulation of the parties.

I. After the conclusion of the mediation, the mediator will have fifteen days to prepare and send his or her bill to the parties. The parties shall have 15 days thereafter to pay the mediator. If the mediator's bill is not paid within 30 days after the close of mediation, the mediator may file a bill with the Court and it shall be reduced to judgment unless objected to by one of the parties within ten days after the filing of the bill with the Court.

Mandatory Mediation

A. Civil Jury Trials. All cases where a timely demand for jury trial is made, mediation pursuant to A.D.R. Rule 2 and subsection A herein is mandatory. Mediation is to be completed 60 days prior to trial, unless the mediation referral is vacated for good cause shown. Objections to mediation may be made within 15 days of the completion of the case management conference required by Rule 16.1(A).

B. Post–Decree Domestic Litigation. Parties must submit post-decree child related issues to mediation prior to presenting such issues to the Court for hearing, unless this rule is waived for good cause shown.

C. Pro Bono Mediation Services. All mediators maintained on the Court's approved Civil and Domestic Mediation list shall, upon request from any Judge of this Court, serve as a pro bono mediator for at least one (1) case per calendar year.

D. Any litigant affected by this mandatory mediation order may qualify for pro bono mediation services upon good cause shown, pursuant to criteria established by the Presiding Judges of the Court.

Adopted as Civil Division Rule 16.3, Jan. 19, 1999, effective March 1, 1999. Amended effective July 12, 2004. Renumbered as Civil Rule 209, and amended effective Oct. 2, 2006. Amended effective Jan. 1, 2008.

LR49–ADR3 Rule 210. ALTERNATIVE DISPUTE RESOLUTION—ARBITRATION PROCEDURE

A. Arbitration procedures shall be governed by A.D.R. Rule 3.

B. Attorneys wishing to serve as arbitrators in the Marion Circuit or Superior Court shall file written notice with the Marion Superior Court Administrator indicating a desire to serve as an arbitrator for cases in Marion County.

Adopted as Civil Division Rule 16.3, Jan. 19, 1999, effective March 1, 1999. Amended effective July 12, 2004; renumbered as Civil Rule 210, and amended effective Oct. 2, 2006; Jan. 1, 2008.

LR49–ARD1 Rule 211. GENERAL PROVISIONS

A. These rules are designed to clarify and supplement the Rules for Alternative Dispute Resolution promulgated by the Indiana Supreme Court on January 1, 1992, as amended from time to time. The rules promulgated by the Indiana Supreme Court shall be followed in every way by the parties and shall govern the various forms of Alternative Dispute Resolution stated therein.

B. The failure to comply any with any Court Order regarding Alternative Dispute Resolution may result in appropriate sanctions being levied by the Court.

Adopted as Civil Division Rule 16.3, Jan. 19, 1999, effective March 1, 1999. Amended effective July 12, 2004; renumbered as Civil Rule 211, and amended effective Oct. 2, 2006; Jan. 1, 2008.

LR49–TR32 Rule 212. VIDEO TAPE DEPOSITIONS

All video tape depositions filed with the Court shall be accompanied by a transcript of the testimony.

Adopted as Civil Division Rule 32.1, Jan. 19, 1999, effective March 1, 1999. Renumbered as Civil Rule 211, and amended effective Oct. 2, 2006.

LR49–TR33 Rule 213. INTERROGATORIES

A. Number Limited. Interrogatories shall be limited to a total of 25 including subparts and shall be used solely for the purpose of discovery and shall not be used as a substitute for the taking of a deposition. For good cause shown and upon leave of Court additional interrogatories may be propounded.

B. Answers and Objections. Answers or objections to interrogatories under Rule TR 31 or 33 shall set forth in full the interrogatories being answered or objected to immediately preceding the answer or objection.

C. Duplicated Forms. No duplicated forms containing interrogatories shall be filed or served upon a party unless all interrogatories on such forms are consecutively numbered and applicable to the cause in which the same are filed and served.

Adopted as Civil Division Rule 33.1, Jan. 19, 1999, effective Mar. 1, 1999. Renumbered as Civil Rule 213, and amended effective Oct. 2, 2006. Amended effective Mar. 5, 2009.

LR49–TR40 Rule 214. SETTING CASES FOR TRIAL

A. Setting Cases for Trial. Litigants desiring their cause of action to be set for trial shall file a written Praecipe for Trial which indicates whether a jury or court trial is requested. No trial date will be set unless a Case Management Order pursuant to Rule 16.1(B) has been filed. The Praecipe shall state the number of days needed to try the case.

B. Notice in Dissolution and Paternity Matters. In all dissolution or paternity matters, the Moving party or their counsel shall give notice of the time and place of the hearing or trial by subpoena, notice of hearing or letter, served upon the adverse party at least seven days prior to the trial date and file a copy of said notice with the Court on or prior to the trial date.

Adopted as Civil Division Rule 39.1, Jan. 19, 1999, effective Mar. 1, 1999. Renumbered as Civil Rule 214, and amended effective Oct. 2, 2006. Amended effective Mar. 5, 2009.

LR49–TR53.5 Rule 215. MOTIONS FOR CONTINUANCE

Motions for Continuance are discouraged. Neither side is entitled to an automatic continuance as a matter of right.

A. Motion. A Motion for Continuance, unless made during the hearing of the cause, shall be in writing, state whether opposing counsel objects to the motion and whether prior continuances have been requested by the moving party. The Court may require any written Motion for Continuance to be signed by the party requesting the continuance.

B. Time for Filing. Motions for Continuance must be filed as soon after the cause for continuance or delay is discovered by the party seeking same, and no later than seven days before the date assigned for trial, unless the reason therefor is shown by affidavit to have occurred within the seven day period.

C. Title of Motion. A Motion for Continuance, whether it is plaintiff's or defendant's motion, shall denominate whether it is the First, Second, Third, etc. Motion for Continuance filed by plaintiff or defendant.

D. Dispositive Motions. The filing of a dispositive motion shall not constitute good cause for a Motion for Continuance of a trial if the time requirements governing such motion will not allow for the resolution of the motion prior to the date of trial.

Adopted as Civil Division Rule 53.5, Jan. 19, 1999, effective Mar. 1, 1999. Renumbered as Civil Rule 211, and amended effective Oct. 2, 2006. Amended effective Mar. 5, 2009.

LR49–TR55 Rule 216. AFFIDAVIT OF DEBT/ATTORNEY FEES IN DEFAULT JUDGMENTS

On all default judgments relating to commercial cases plaintiff or his counsel must submit an affidavit of debt signed by the plaintiff and an affidavit in support of attorney fees requested by counsel, signed by plaintiff's counsel. The affidavit for attorney fees shall set forth the number of hours spent on the case and the hourly charge.

Adopted as Civil Division Rule 55.1, Jan. 19, 1999, effective Mar. 1, 1999. Renumbered as Civil Rule 216, and amended effective Oct. 2, 2006. Amended effective Mar. 5, 2009.

LR49–TR58 Rule 217. DUTIES OF ATTORNEYS ON ENTRIES OF JUDGMENTS

A. Attorneys to Prepare Documents Requiring Court's Signature. It shall be the duty of attorneys to prepare decrees of all final judgments and of such interlocutory and other orders as may be required by the Court, including Pre-Trial Orders, Findings of Fact and Conclusions of Law.

B. Decrees and Entries Prepared by One Attorney to Be Submitted to Other Attorneys Interested in Cause. Where there are several attorneys interested in a decree, order, entry or judgment to be entered in a cause and one or more of them desires such document entered, he or they, shall submit such document to the other attorneys who may be interested in the cause, and obtain an endorsement thereon of "Inspected", provided that this rule shall not apply when the attorneys of all parties are in court when the judgment or decree is proffered.

C. Obligation to Keep Themselves Informed of Case Status. Counsel and parties to a suit should keep themselves informed of all steps taken in all matters pending before the Court, and are bound by the Court's actions, including but not limited to rulings, notice of trial date settings, and current position of cases on jury trial calendar, all without special or additional oral or written notice by the Court.

D. Duty of Attorney to State Time Required for Hearing. It is the duty of counsel to determine the amount of time required by both sides for the hearing. No hearing will be scheduled until such time is stated, and it will be limited to the time requested.

Adopted as Civil Division Rule 58.1, Jan. 19, 1999, effective March 1, 1999. Renumbered as Civil Rule 217, and amended effective Oct. 2, 2006.

LR49–TR59 Rule 218. SERVICE UPON JUDICIAL OFFICERS

In addition to serving the judge with a separate copy of motion to correct error pursuant to Ind. Trial Rule 59(C), parties filing motion to correct errors shall also serve the Magistrate or Commissioner with a copy of the motion to correct error if a Magistrate or Commissioner recommended and signed the final judgment or appealable final order at issue. Non-compliance with this Rule shall not be grounds for forfeiture of any post-trial, post-judgment or appellate rights.

Adopted as Civil Division Rule 59.1, Jan. 19, 1999, effective Mar. 1, 1999. Renumbered as Civil Rule 218, and amended effective Oct. 2, 2006. Amended effective Mar. 5, 2009.

LR49–TR63 Rule 219. WHEN OTHER JUDGES TO PRESIDE

Whenever the Judge who presides in the Marion Circuit or Superior Court is absent or cannot, for any reason, hear any cause pending in such court, or issue any emergency orders in connection herewith, any other Judge of such Marion Circuit or Superior Court may preside in that court.

Adopted as Civil Division Rule 63.1, Jan. 19, 1999, effective March 1, 1999. Renumbered as Civil Rule 219, and amended effective Oct. 2, 2006.

LR49–TR00 Rule 220.   EXHIBITS

All models, diagrams, documents, depositions, or material placed in the custody of the Court Reporter as exhibits shall be removed by the parties offering them in evidence, except as otherwise ordered by the Court, four months after the case is decided unless an appeal is taken. At the time of removal, a detailed receipt shall be given to the Court Reporter and filed with the cause. If not removed after four months, the Court Reporter may dispose of them without notice.

Adopted as Civil Division Rule 74.1, Jan. 19, 1999, effective Mar. 1, 1999. Renumbered as Civil Rule 220, and amended effective Oct. 2, 2006. Amended effective Mar. 5, 2009.

LR49–TR76 Rule 221.   TRANSFER OR CONSOLI-DATION OF CASES

No case filed in the Circuit Court or the Marion Superior Court, Civil Division, may be transferred or consolidated to another room or court except upon written motion accompanied by written order for the signature of the forwarding Court. The order shall not be approved and signed by the forwarding Judge unless such order is consented to in writing by the Judge of the receiving Court.

Adopted as Civil Division Rule 76.1, Jan. 19, 1999, effective March 1, 1999. Renumbered as Civil Rule 221, and amended effective Oct. 2, 2006.

LR49–TR76 Rule 222.   TRANSFER OF CASES ASSIGNED TO THE MARION COUNTY FAMILY COURT PROJECT

This Rule applies only in the following situations: (1) a child who is the subject of a Child in Need of Services or a Delinquency case is also the subject of a divorce, paternity or guardianship case in which there is a pending or continuing custody, visitation and/or child support order, and (2) these multiple cases have been assigned to the Marion County Family Court Project. The purpose of the rule is to allow the transfer of cases involving the same child or children to the same judge for a temporary period of time. The rule will help to ensure that multiple cases involving the same child will have consistent orders regarding custody, visitation, care, and child support, and multiple hearings and re-hearings will not occur before different judges regarding the same issues.

When consistent with the best interest of the child, the lead Family Court Project Judge may issue an order transferring any of the cases specifically assigned to the Marion County Family Court Project to the Marion Circuit Court or to any Marion Superior Court, Juvenile or Civil Division. The Order of Family Court Assignment shall include the Order of Case Transfer and the order shall state to what court and

division the cases have been transferred. The transferred cases will not be consolidated. The court receiving the cases shall have jurisdiction in those cases. Each case will retain its own original docket number and separate Chronological Case Summary.

The lead Family Court Judge shall transfer back to the court of origin any case or cases when the lead judge determines that the purpose of the family court assignment has been completed. The supervising judge shall issue an order "Closing the Family Court Assignment and Transferring Case/s back to the Court of Origin."

A transfer for family court purposes shall not constitute a transfer for purposes of the Quarterly Status Report.

Adopted as Civil Division Rule 76.2, effective July 3, 2003. Renumbered as Civil Rule 222, and amended effective Oct. 2, 2006.

LR49–TR79 Rule 223.   INITIAL REQUEST FOR CHANGE OF JUDGE

Upon a timely filed motion for a change of judge under Indiana Trial Rule 79, the court shall grant the motion. Within seven (7) days of the notation of the motion in the Chronological Case Summary, the parties may agree upon an eligible special judge.

Adopted as Civil Division Rule 79.1, Jan. 19, 1999, effective Mar. 1, 1999. Amended Feb. 24, 1999, effective Mar. 1, 1999; amended effective May 21, 2001. Renumbered as Civil Rule 223, and amended effective Oct. 2, 2006. Amended effective Mar. 5, 2009; Aug. 12, 2013.

LR49–TR79   Rule   224.   APPOINTMENT   BY CLERK

Upon the parties not reaching an agreement or the agreed upon judge not accepting the case under Local Rule 225, the appointment of an eligible special judge shall be made by means of the Marion County Clerk selecting a name of the next judge from lists of judges from Marion County maintained by the Clerk. A separate list shall be kept for domestic and juvenile cases.

All judges of the Marion Circuit and Superior Court Civil Division are eligible persons under this rule except as follows: the judge of the Marion Circuit Court shall not be named on the list for domestic relation cases; the judges of the Juvenile Division and the Environmental Division shall not be named on any list; and the judge of the Probate Division shall be named only on the lists for domestic relations and juvenile cases.

Should the next judge on the list be disqualified pursuant to the *Code of Judicial Conduct*, ineligible for service under this rule, or excused from service by the Indiana Supreme Court, the clerk shall continue down the list until all judges on the list have been exhausted. Upon exhaustion of the list, the judge from whom the change of judge was taken, or who is ineligible or disqualified, shall certify the case to the

Indiana Supreme Court for the appointment of a special judge by the Court. Further, the judge may certify a case directly to the Indiana Supreme Court where the particular circumstances of the case warrant selection by the Court without reference to the clerk for selection from a list.

Adopted as Civil Division Rule 79.2, Jan. 19, 1999, effective March 1, 1999. Amended Feb. 24, 1999, effective March 1, 1999. Renumbered as Civil Rule 224, and amended effective Oct. 2, 2006. Amended effective Aug. 12, 2013.

LR49–79 Rule 225.   ACCEPTANCE

A judge appointed to serve as special judge under this Local Rule must accept jurisdiction in the case unless the appointed special judge is disqualified pursuant to the *Code of Judicial Conduct*, ineligible for service under this rule, or must be excused from service by the Indiana Supreme Court. The order of appointment under this Local Rule shall constitute acceptance. An oath or additional evidence of acceptance of jurisdiction is not required.

Adopted as Civil Division Rule 79.3, Jan. 19, 1999, effective March 1, 1999. Renumbered as Civil Rule 225, and amended effective Oct. 2, 2006. Amended effective Aug. 12, 2013.

LR49–TR79 Rule 226.   CERTIFICATION TO THE SUPREME COURT

The Presiding Judge of the Marion Circuit and Superior Courts or any judge in whose court a case is filed shall certify to the Indiana Supreme Court all cases in which no judge is eligible to serve as special judge or the particular circumstances of a case warrants selection of a special judge by the Supreme Court under Ind. Trial Rule 79(H)(3).

Adopted as Civil Division Rule 79.4, Jan. 19, 1999, effective March 1, 1999. Renumbered as Civil Rule 226, and amended effective Oct. 2, 2006; Jan. 1, 2008.

LR49–TR79.1 Rule 227.   SPECIAL JUDGE SELECTION PROCESS UNDER LOCAL RULE 79. 2

In the event a special judge does not accept the case under Ind. Trial Rule 79 (D) or (F) or a judge disqualifies or recuses under T.R 79(C) the case file shall be brought to a Superior Court Clerk supervisor in the Marion County Clerk's Office. The supervisor shall utilize a file of index cards on each of which is printed the name of a judge eligible for selection. The supervisor shall select the top card, or the first judge in line for assignment as the special judge in the case. The selected care shall then be returned to the back of the file. In this way, the assignment is always random and no judge is selected on consecutive occasions. Judges eligible for selection under this Local Rule shall be those elected judges serving in the Civil Division of the Superior Court.

A Judge appointed to serve as special judge under this Local Rule must accept jurisdiction in the case unless the appointed special judge is disqualified pursuant to the Code of Judicial Conduct, ineligible for service under this rule or must be excused from service by the Indiana Supreme Court. The order of appointment under this Local Rule shall constitute acceptance. An oath or additional Evidence of acceptance of jurisdiction is not required.

Adopted as Civil Division Rule 81.1, Jan. 19, 1999, effective March 1, 1999. Renumbered as Civil Rule 227, and amended effective Oct. 2, 2006; Jan. 1, 2008.

LR49–TR79.1   Rule   228.   MARION   COUNTY SMALL CLAIMS COURT CASES

A.   Issues.   A cause of action which comes to the Marion Superior Court from the Small Claims Courts of Marion County for either jury trial or appeal shall be repled[1] in its entirety commencing with the plaintiff below filing a new Complaint in compliance with the Indiana Rules of Trial Procedure. The new Complaint shall be filed within 20 days of the date the case is docketed and filed in the Marion Superior Court or as otherwise ordered by the Court. Failure to comply with this Rule shall result in the Court imposing sanctions which may include dismissal or default where appropriate.

B.   Procedure and Evidence.   Any pleadings, motions or other procedural matters which are filed after the filing of the Complaint in the Marion Circuit and Superior Court will be governed by the Indiana Rules of Trial Procedure and the Marion Circuit and Superior Court Rules. Evidentiary questions will be ruled on in the same manner as any other cases originally filed in the Marion Circuit and Superior Court.

C.   Appeals From Marion County Small Claims Courts.   The following rules shall govern all appeals from the Marion County Small Claims Courts to the Marion Superior Court.

(1) Any party may appeal from the judgment of the Marion County Small Claims Court to the Marion Superior Court, within 60 days from its entry; and when there are two or more plaintiffs or defendants, one or more of such plaintiffs or defendants may appeal without joining the others in such appeal or plaintiff may add new parties at the time he repleads his Complaint in accordance with the Indiana Rules of Trial Procedure.

(2) The Small Claims Court Judge shall certify a completed transcript of all the proceedings had before said Judge and transmit the same, together with all other papers in the cause, to the Marion County Clerk, within 20 days.

(3) Appeals may be authorized by the Marion Superior Court after the expiration of Sixty (60) days, when the party seeking the appeal has been prevented from taking the same by circumstances not under his control.

Adopted as Civil Division Rule 81.1, Jan. 19, 1999, effective March 1, 1999. Renumbered as Civil Rule 227, and amended effective Oct. 2, 2006. Renumbered as Civil Rule 228, and amended effective Jan. 1, 2008. Amended effective Jan. 1, 2012.

[1] So in original.

LR49–TR81 Rule 229. MARION COUNTY LAW LIBRARY

A. Taking Books From the Library. No book, periodical, manuscript or other paper or equipment belonging to the Marion County Law Library, located in the City–County Building, Indianapolis, Indiana, shall be removed therefrom by any person other than a judge of any of the courts located in the City–County Building, without the written consent of one of said judges. Said consent shall be addressed to the Librarian of the Marion County Law Library. Any book or periodical removed from the Library, as aforesaid, may be used only in the City–County Building and must not be taken therefrom.

B. Sign–Out Procedure. Any person having authority to remove law books from the Library, as aforesaid, shall sign out for same, giving borrower's name, date of withdrawal and place where book will be used. The borrower shall be held personally responsible for the return of said books to the Marion County Law Library on the same day of their withdrawal. In case the Library is closed said books shall be left with the bailiff of the court where the books were used.

Adopted as Civil Division Rule 81.2, Jan. 19, 1999, effective March 1, 1999. Renumbered as Civil Rule 228, and amended effective Oct. 2, 2006. Renumbered as Civil Rule 229, and amended effective Jan. 1, 2008.

LR49–81 Rule 230. JOINT SESSION OF CIRCUIT AND MARION SUPERIOR COURTS

The Judges of the Marion Circuit and Superior Courts may meet in joint session to consider matters of mutual interest.

Adopted as Civil Division Rule 81.3, Jan. 19, 1999, effective March 1, 1999. Renumbered as Civil Rule 229, and amended effective Oct. 2, 2006. Renumbered as Civil Rule 230, and amended effective Jan. 1, 2008.

LR49–TR85 Rule 231. MANDATORY SETTLEMENT CONFERENCES IN MORTGAGE

1. Findings.

A. In order to avoid confusion as to rights and procedures concerning settlement agreements in residential mortgage foreclosures, the Marion Circuit and Superior Courts find that LR 231 should be amended.

B. The Courts further find that prohibiting the filing of dispositive motions until settlement discussions have been completed is necessary for the full utilization of the Foreclosure Prevention Agreements for Residential Mortgages Act IN Code 32–30–10.5–1 et seq. (Act), conservation of judicial resources and avoidance of unnecessary legal expenses.

C. The Courts find that this Rule will promote the purposes of the Act as set forth at IN Code 32–30–10.5–1.

2. Upon the filing of a foreclosure action covered by the Act, the plaintiff may not file a Motion of Default Judgment or for Summary Judgment against the debtor until the expiration of the time for requesting a settlement conference; or in the event of a timely request for a settlement conference; until the creditor files a notice with the Court as required by either section 10 (e) or 10 (f) of the Act, provided that the creditor may file such motions if the settlement conference is not scheduled or is vacated by the court pursuant to section 9 (b) of the Act.

3. Upon the debtor's request for a settlement conference, the Court will automatically enlarge debtor's time to file a responsive pleading until twenty (20) days after the creditor files a notice as required by either section 10 (e) or (f). In the event that the court vacates the settlement conference pursuant to section 9(b) of the Act, the period of enlargement will be modified to twenty (20) days after the date the conference was vacated.

4. This rule shall be applied prospectively to actions filed after October 5, 2009.

Adopted Jan. 22, 2009, effective Feb. 23, 2009. Amended effective Mar. 5, 2009. Amended effective Oct. 5, 2009; Jan. 8, 2010.

Appendix A. MARION SUPERIOR COURT COMMITMENT TO RESPECT AND CIVILITY

I will maintain the highest level of professional integrity and personal courtesy in all dealings with parties, counsel, witnesses and courts.

I will advise clients that I am bound by the responsibilities and restrictions set forth in the Rules of Professional Conduct in all matters relating to the handling of their cases.

I will pursue the advancement of clients' legitimate objectives, but I will not participate in litigation based upon vengeance or other inappropriate emotions.

I will use legal procedures for the fullest benefit of clients without misusing or abusing the legal process.

I will not intentionally speak or act in an abrasive, hostile, offensive or acrimonious manner toward parties, counsel or courts.

I will not knowingly misstate, mischaracterize or fail to disclose relevant facts or legal authority.

I will familiarize myself with and comply with all requirements of the common law, the trial rules, the local rules, and the court policy and procedure.

I will endeavor to have clients fully disclose assets and liabilities, informally exchange information and confer with opposing counsel to discuss settlement, stipulate undisputed matters, and identify issues prior to scheduled hearings.

I will strive to reach agreements on procedural and preliminary matters consistent with clients' legitimate objectives.

I will honor promises and commitments in an effort to raise the level of professionalism and civility.

I will, whenever possible, encourage clients to reach amicable settlement of all issues after careful review of statutes and reasonable consideration of the risks, costs, delay and emotional trauma of trial.

I will not seek judicial intervention in matters that can be resolved through cooperation and communication between counsel and parties.

I will not resort to ex parte proceedings in the absence of extreme emergency, as the interests of justice and fair play mandate notice to the opposing party.

I will not abuse time limitations set by courts, will be punctual and prepared for all court appearances and I will notify the court promptly when a case has been settled or must be continued.

I will prepare clients and witnesses for court appearances and advise them of the conduct required of them in order to promote the prompt and efficient administration of justice and to avoid conduct that brings disorder, disruption and disrespect upon the courts.

_____   _____
Date   Signature

Adopted effective Jan. 1, 2008.

Appendix B. APPEARANCE FORM

IN THE MARION SUPERIOR COURT

APPEARANCE FORM

Initiating / Responding Party / Intervening Party

(Caption)   )   Cause No. _____
)   *(To be supplied by Clerk when case is filed.)*
)

☐ Check if *Pro Se*

1. _____

    Name of party

2. Attorney information (as applicable for service of process): (**Pro Se litigants must complete this**)

    Name: _____ Atty. Number: _____
    Address: _____ Phone: _____
    _____ FAX: _____
    _____ Email Address: _____

3. Will accept Fax service: Yes _____ No _____

4. Are there now or have there been within the last twelve months pending related cases?
    Yes _____ No _____ If yes, list case and cause number below:

    If the caption has a name other than that of the parties, please explain.

    Caption _____Cause No. _____

    Status _____

    Caption _____Cause No. _____

    Status _____

    Caption _____Cause No. _____

    Status _____

5. Additional information required by state or local rule:
    _____
    _____
    _____

6. This appearance form has been served on all parties and/or counsel.

7. I have reviewed and discussed the **Commitment to Respect and Civility** with my client and agree to aspire to its goals.

                              _____
                              Attorney or Pro Se Signature

                              _____
                              Printed

    Pursuant to Trial Rule 3.1, this form shall be filed upon the first appearance in the case. In emergencies, the requested information shall be supplied when it becomes available. Parties shall advise the court of change in information previously provided to the court. The Division of State Court Administration has approved this format.
    PURSUANT TO TRIAL RULE 3.1(E), THIS APPEARANCE FORM SHALL BE UPDATED PROMPTLY SHOULD THERE BE ANY CHANGE IN OR

SUPPLEMENT TO THE INFORMATION PREVIOUSLY SUPPLIED TO THE COURT

Adopted effective Jan. 1, 2008.

Appendix C. NOTICE AND ORDER FOR SETTLEMENT CONFERENCE

STATE OF INDIANA)
) SS:
COUNTY OF MARION)

IN THE MARION SUPERIOR COURT
CIVIL DIVISION, ROOM _____
CAUSE NO. _____

_____)
)
_____)
)
    Plaintiff(s),)
)
VS.)
)
_____)
)
_____)
)
    Defendant(s).)

NOTICE AND ORDER FOR SETTLEMENT CONFERENCE

This matter, having come before the Court on Plaintiff's Complaint for Decree of Foreclosure, and the Court, being duly advised in the premises, now finds that it is appropriate to schedule this matter for a settlement conference.

IT IS THEREFORE ORDERED BY THE COURT:

1. That this matter is scheduled for a settlement conference to be held on the _____ day of _____, 2009 at _____ a.m./p.m. Defendant(s), _____, is/are to appear in this Court, in person and, if represented by counsel, with said counsel. Plaintiff(s) _____ is/are to appear, by counsel and by an authorized officer of Plaintiff(s), either in person or by telephone on the above-referenced date and time. If Plaintiff(s) elects to be available by telephone only, Plaintiff(s) shall call the Court at the appropriate time and at the following telephone number: (317) _____. The Defendant(s) shall execute the enclosed Confirmation of Attendance form and return said confirmation to the Court office within fifteen (15) days following receipt of this Notice. **Failure to execute the Confirmation of Attendance within fifteen (15) days will result in cancellation of the settlement conference**. If the parties choose to conduct the Settlement Conference at an alternate location, date and time, Plaintiff's counsel is to notify the Court in writing.

2. To adequately assess the loss mitigation options available, the homeowner or primary borrower shall mail copies of the following documents to the Court and to the lender's attorney at least 7 days prior to the settlement conference.

    (a) two (2) most recent pay stubs;

    (b) two (2) most recent bank statements;

    (c) two (2) most recent tax returns;

    (d) a worksheet containing the Defendant(s) monthly expenditures (sample attached).

    (e) **Financial documents must be provided to Plaintiff's attorney seven (7) days prior to the settlement conference**.

3. During the course of the settlement conference, Plaintiff(s), by counsel, and through the corporate representative, shall convey and explain, as necessary, any

and all loss mitigation options which may be available to the Defendant(s). Those options may include one or more of the following:

(a) <u>Repayment Plan</u>: The amount past due on your loan would be spread out over a certain time period.

(b) <u>Modification</u>: A loan modification is a written agreement between you and the lender that permanently changes the terms of the loan.

(c) <u>Deed in Lieu of Foreclosure</u>: You would transfer ownership of your home to the lender. You would be given a short period of time to move from your home. You would receive a full release of your debt, or a substantial reduction of the debt.

(d) <u>Reinstatement of Your Loan</u>: You would pay the total amount past due in one lump sum

(e) <u>Sell Your Property</u>: This means that your property would be sold by you prior to the foreclosure. Approval is required if your sale does not pay off your lender in full.

4. The settlement conference shall be an informal process. No evidence will be taken at the settlement conference nor any findings be made as to the allegations of Plaintiff's Complaint or any responses thereto filed by or on behalf of the Defendant(s). The parties hereto shall be prepared to negotiate, in good faith, an amicable resolution of the pending matter and shall have the authority to enter into a binding agreement at the conclusion of the settlement conference.

SO ORDERED this _____ day of _____, 2009.

_____
JUDGE, MARION SUPERIOR COURT

DISTRIBUTION:
Attorney(s) of Record
Defendant(s)

Adopted effective Mar. 5, 2009.

Appendix D. BORROWER FINANCIAL INFORMATION

Borrower Financial Information

Borrower Financial Information

BORROWER		CO–BORROWER	
BORROWER'S NAME		CO–BORROWER'S NAME	
SOCIAL SECURITY NUMBER	DATE OF BIRTH	SOCIAL SECURITY NUMBER	DATE OF BIRTH
HOME PHONE NUMBER WITH AREA CODE	(Best Number to reach borrower)	HOME PHONE NUMBER WITH AREA CODE	(Best Number to reach borrower)
WORK PHONE NUMBER WITH AREA CODE	(BEST TIME TO CALL)	WORK PHONE NUMBER WITH AREA CODE	(BEST TIME TO CALL)
CELL PHONE NUMBER WITH AREA CODE	(BEST TIME TO CALL)	CELL PHONE NUMBER WITH AREA CODE	(BEST TIME TO CALL)
MAILING ADDRESS (If different from property address)			
PROPERTY ADDRESS			EMAIL ADDRESS
Number of Dependants: Do you occupy the property? Yes ☐ No ☐		Is it a Rental? Yes ☐ No ☐ Is it leased? Yes ☐ No ☐ If you have a lease agreement, please provide a copy.	
Is this a mobile home? Yes ☐ No ☐			
Is the property listed for sale? Yes ☐ No ☐ If yes, please provide a copy of the listing agreement.		Agent's Name: Agent's Phone Number:	
Have you contacted a credit-counseling agency for help? Yes ☐ No ☐		Counselor's Name:	

If yes, please provide a copy of the listing agreement.　　　Counselor's Phone Number:

Do you pay Real Estate Taxes outside of your mortgage?　Yes ☐　No ☐
If you pay it, please provide a copy of your tax statement.　Are the taxes current?　Yes ☐　No ☐

Have you filed for bankruptcy?　Yes ☐　No ☐　If yes:　Chapter 7 ☐　Chapter 13 ☐ Filing Date:
Has your bankruptcy been discharged?　Yes ☐　No ☐　If yes, please provide a copy of the discharge paper.

INVOLUNTARY INABILITY TO PAY

I (We), _____, am/are requesting that the Federal Home Loan Mortgage Corporation

(Freddie Mac) review my/our financial situation to determine if I/we qualify for a workout option.

I am having difficulty making my monthly payment because of financial difficulties created by *(Please check all that apply)*:

☐ Abandonment of Property	☐ Excessive Obligations	☐ Military Service　　Other
☐ Business Failure	☐ Fraud	☐ Payment Adjustment
☐ Casualty Loss	☐ Illness in Family	☐ Payment Dispute
☐ Curtailment of Income	☐ Illness of Mortgagor	☐ Property Problems
☐ Death in Family	☐ Inability to Rent Property	☐ Title Problems
☐ Death of Mortgagor	☐ Incarceration	☐ Transferring Property
☐ Distant Employment Transfer	☐ Marital Difficulties	☐ Unemployment

I believe that my situation is:　☐ Short term (under 6 months)　　☐ Long term (over 6 months)　　Permanent

I want to:　　　☐ Keep my house　　　☐ Sell my house

Please provide a detailed explanation of the hardship on a separate sheet of paper.

If there are additional Liens/Mortgages or Judgments on this property, please name the person(s), company or firm and their respective telephone numbers.

	$	
Lien Holder's Name	Balance / Interest Rate	Phone Number (WITH AREA CODE)
	$	
Lien Holder's Name	Balance / Interest Rate	Phone Number (WITH AREA CODE)

Borrower's Signature	Date	Co–Borrower's Signature	Date

EMPLOYMENT (see paystubs, if attached)

BORROWER—EMPLOYER'S ADDRESS & PHONE #	HOW LONG?	CO–BORROWER—EMPLOYER'S ADDRESS & PHONE #	HOW LONG?

Monthly Income—Borrower		Monthly Income—Co–Borrower	
Wages	$	Wages	$
Unemployment Income	$	Unemployment Income	$
Child Support / Alimony	$	Child Support / Alimony	$
Disability Income	$	Disability Income	$
Rents Received	$	Rents Received	$
Other	$	Other	$
Less: Federal and State Tax, FICA	$	Less: Federal and State Tax, FICA	$
Less: Other Deductions (401K, etc.)	$	Less: Other Deductions (401K, etc.)	$
Commissions, bonus and self-employed income	$	Commissions, bonus and self-employed income	$

* * * * *ALL INCOME NEEDS TO BE DOCUMENTED* * * * *
Paystub must be most recent date with year to date information.

Total (Net income)	$	Total (Net income)	$

Monthly Expenses		Assets	
Other Mortgages / Liens	$	Type	Estimated Value
Auto Loan(s)	$	Checking Account(s)	$
Auto Expenses / Insurance	$	Saving /Money Market	$
Credit Cards / Installment Loan(s) (total minimum payment for both per month)	$	Stocks / Bonds / CDs	$
Health Insurance (not withheld from pay)	$	IRA / Keogh Accounts	$
Medical (Co-pays and Rx)	$	401k/! ESPO Accounts	$
Child Care / Support / Alimony	$	Home	$
Food / Spending Money	$	Other Real Estate　#	$
Water / Sewer / Utilities / Phone	$	Cars　　#	$
HOA/Condo Fees/Property Maintenance	$	Life Insurance (Whole Life not Term)	$
Life Insurance Payments (not withheld from pay)	$	Other	$
Total	$	Total	$

"I agree as follows: My lender may discuss, obtain and share information about my mortgage and personal financial situation with third parties such as purchasers, real estate brokers, insurers, financial institutions, creditors and credit bureaus. Discussions and negotiations of a possible foreclosure alternative will not constitute a waiver of or defense to my lender's right to commence or continue any foreclosure or other collection action, and an alternative to foreclosure will be provided only if an agreement has been approved in writing by my lender. The information herein is an accurate statement of my financial status."

Submitted this _____ day of _____, 20 _____

By_____
     Signature of Borrower

By_____
     Signature of Co–Borrower

Before mailing, make sure you have signed and dated the form and attached appropriate documentation.

Adopted effective Mar. 5, 2009.

Appendix E.   DEFENDANT(S) CONFIRMATION OF ATTENDANCE AT SETTLEMENT CONFERENCE

STATE OF INDIANA	)	IN THE MARION SUPERIOR COURT
	) SS:	CIVIL DIVISION, ROOM _____
COUNTY OF MARION	)	CAUSE NO. _____

Plaintiff(s),   )

VS.   )
)
)
)
)
Defendant(s).   )

DEFENDANT(S) CONFIRMATION OF ATTENDANCE AT SETTLEMENT CONFERENCE

The Defendant(s), _____ in the above-captioned cause, confirm that they _____ will _____ will not be attending _____ in person or _____ by telephone, the Settlement Conference scheduled to take place in this Court on the _____ day of _____, 2009 at _____ a.m./p.m.

This Confirmation is to be filed with the Court within fifteen (15) days of receiving the Notice and Order for Settlement Conference from this Court.

If the Defendant(s) will not be attending the Settlement Conference, please state the reason: _____

_____

Dated: _____

Signature of Defendant(s):

_____

_____

** Please return this Confirmation of Attendance in person or by mail to: Marion County Superior Court, 200 E. Washington St., Room _____, Indianapolis, IN 46204

Adopted effective Mar. 5, 2009.

MARION COUNTY CIRCUIT MASS TORT LITIGATION RULES

Adopted Effective January 1, 2008

Including Amendments Received Through November 1, 2013

Research Notes

Annotations to the Marion Mass Tort Litigation Rules are available in West's Annotated Indiana Code, Title 34 Appendix.

These rules may be searched electronically on Westlaw in the IN-RULES *database; updates to these rules may be found on Westlaw in* IN-RULESUPDATES. *For search tips and a summary of database content, consult the Westlaw Scope Screens for each database.*

LR49–TR3 Rule 600. CAUSE NUMBER ASSIGNMENT, CASE INITIATION, SERVICE AND RULE APPLICATION

A. Application of Rules. These Rules apply to all filings on the Marion County Mass Tort Litigation Docket. The Mass Tort Litigation Docket consists of those cases assigned to the docket by the Executive Committee of the Marion Superior Court. File & Serve is the exclusive method of filing and service for cases assigned to the mass tort litigation docket. These Rules are to be construed together with the Indiana Rules of Court and the Marion County Civil Court Local Rules. When two or more of these Rules apply to a given situation, the more docket-specific or document-specific provision shall control. "Court" as used herein, shall mean the Court to which the mass tort docket has been assigned.

B. Cause Number Assignment and Case Initiation. Prior to filing a complaint on a Marion County Mass Tort Litigation Docket, the party shall obtain from the Court a cause number, pursuant to Ind. Admin. Rule 8, with an additional three-digit suffix number. In addition to the requirements of Ind. Trial Rule 3, Plaintiffs shall initiate the case on File & Serve as soon as reasonably possible after obtaining a cause number. Plaintiff's counsel must post an appearance at the time of initiation, along with the complaint.

C. Citation to Cause Number. Parties may cite to the cause number by the full 20 digit cause number or the shortened cause number in the following format: [Uniform Case Number] + ["-"] + [assigned suffix number]. The "Uniform Case Number" is equivalent to the first two characters referenced in Admin. R. 8(B)(2), with the exception that the numbers do not reference the actual year the case was filed, but rather the numbers reference reserved cause numbers for consistent cause numbering.

D. Service. Posting a complaint on File & Serve does not constitute service of process on any defendant. In addition to providing the clerk necessary copies of the complaint and summons, the serving party shall provide the clerk with sufficient copies of the notice provided in Rule 602. File & Serve is the "alternative method of notice," to all parties of all documents in cases assigned to the Marion County Mass Tort Litigation docket.

E. Duty of plaintiffs to provide proof of service. If a party serves process on an individual or an organization, the party shall provide the Court's filing clerk with original proof of service within 10 days of receipt. When perfecting service by registered or certified mail, the party shall provide the original return receipt card to the Court's filing clerk within 10 days of the return of service.

Adopted effective Jan. 1, 2008. Amended effective Feb. 25, 2008; Jan. 1, 2011.

LR49–TR3.1 Rule 601. APPEARANCES

A. Form for Appearances. The attached form is adopted as the exclusive Appearance Form for Attorneys admitted to the Indiana Bar for the Marion County Mass Tort Litigation Docket. An appearance must be completed, signed, filed and served before the first document filed and posted by the signing attorney.

B. Titling. A single attorney appearance shall be filed on File & Serve with the title on the document and on the docket in the following format: ["Attorney"] + [Name, Attorney number, Email address,] + ["Appearing on Behalf of"] + [Party type] + [Party name]. For example: "Attorney John H. Doe, #11111–49, j.doe@firm.com, Appearing on behalf of ABC Company, Inc." Where multiple attorneys use a single form for the same party, the above information shall be provided for each individual attorney. For example: "Attorneys John H. Doe, #11111–49, j.doe@firm.com and Jane M. Doe, 22222–49, j.doe@firm.com, Appearing on behalf of ABC Company, Inc." If several attorneys share a designated email address, that email address may be placed at the end of the named attorneys rather than throughout the title.

C. Substitutions. Where a party serves a Substitution of Appearance to reflect a change of counsel of record, the following format must be used: [Party type] + [Party name] + ["Notice of Substitution of Counsel"] + [New attorney name, New attorney's number, New attorney's email] + [For] + [Former attorney name, Former attorney number, Former attorney's email]. Example: "Defendant ABC Company, Inc.'s Notice of Substitution of Counsel John Doe, 11111–49, j.doe@firm.com, for Attorney Sam Smith, 22222–49, s.smith@firm.com."

For substitution appearances, counsel shall file with the Court both the notice of substitution and the new attorney's appearance form for each affected case. The appearance may be filed as a supporting document to the main document, Notice of Substitution.

D. Pro hac vice Attorneys. Out of state attorneys who have sought and received limited admission shall use the same appearance form as attorneys regularly admitted to practice law in Indiana after the attorney has received a temporary license number and the Court has granted the petition for limited admission in that case.

E. Withdrawal of Appearances. A motion for withdrawal of an appearance where new counsel has not appeared must include a letter to the client that was mailed at least 10 days prior to the filing of the motion and certify the last known address and telephone number of the party, pursuant to T.R. 3.1(E). The letter of withdrawal shall explain to the client that failure to secure new counsel may result in dismissal of the client's case or a default judgment entered against him and shall contain other pertinent information such as hearing dates.

If a plaintiff is the moving party, the motion shall be accompanied by a proposed order that both grants the motion for withdrawal and sets a T.R. 41(E) hearing for a date and time to be indicated on the attached Information/Comments page. The Relief Requested paragraph shall state, "It is therefore ORDERED that the motion for withdrawal of appearance is GRANTED, and Plaintiff shall appear for a hearing at the date and time indicated on the attached Information/Comments page or

Plaintiff's case may be dismissed with prejudice." Counsel who moved for the withdrawal shall mail the order setting the T.R. 41(E) hearing to the plaintiff within five days of the date of the service of the Order. The distribution list shall indicate that the Order will be mailed to the plaintiff and was distributed electronically.

IN THE MARION SUPERIOR COURT

		Case Number: 49D02–9901–MI–0001– _____
IN RE MASS TORT LITIGATION	)	Case Number: 49D02–9801–MI–0001– _____
MARION COUNTY	)	Case Number: 49D02–9601–MI–0001– _____
SUPERIOR COURT ROOM 2	)	Case Number: 49D02–9501–MI–0001– _____

["Attorney"] + [Name, Attorney Number, E-mail address] + [Appearing on Behalf of"] [Party Type] + [Party Name]

Party Classification: Initiating _____   Responding _____   Intervening _____

1.   The undersigned attorney and all attorneys listed on this form now appear in this case for the following party member(s):
_____

2.   Applicable attorney information for service as required by Trial Rule 5(B)(2) and for case information as required by Trial Rules 3.1 and 77(B) is as follows:
Name: _____   Atty. Number: _____
Address: _____   Phone: _____
FAX: _____
Computer Address: _____

[Please add additional lines for each attorney appearing and provide their attorney number and computer address]

3. I will accept service by FAX at the above noted number: Yes _____ No ✓

4. I have reviewed and discussed the **Commitment to Respect and Civility** with my client and agree to aspire to its goals.

5.   This form has been filed and served on all other parties in the above referenced case via File & Serve. The attached Certificate of Service must be completed, pursuant to LR49–TR5–MTL–2(L).

CERTIFICATE OF SERVICE

I hereby certify that a copy of the foregoing was electronically served on all counsel of record on the date shown on the service stamp on the first page of this document, by using File & Serve.

[Signature]

Adopted effective Jan. 1, 2008. Amended affective Feb. 25, 2008; Jan. 1, 2011.

LR49–TR4 Rule 602.   FILE & SERVE INITIAL NOTICE SHEET

The following Notice shall be served with each Summons and Complaint in all cases assigned to the Marion County Mass Tort Litigation Docket:

********** NOTICE **********

DOCKET ASSIGNMENT: The enclosed Complaint has been filed in Marion Superior Court, Civil Division, in the State of Indiana and has been assigned to the Mass Tort Litigation Docket. Therefore, several Local Rules, including required Electronic Service procedures, govern the case. You are directed to provide this sheet to any counsel you retain for the defense of this case.

ELECTRONIC SERVICE: All service required by Ind. Trial Rule 5 and other required documents shall be served exclusively using File & Serve as authorized by Local Rules. File & Serve is an electronic, web-based service system. Counsel must contact the File & Serve vendor to establish an administrator who will register and receive user names and passwords for appearing counsel and their staff. All counsel must have Internet connectivity and an e-mail account. A File & Serve user name and password is required to serve any pleadings or other documents in this case, as well as receive electronic notice of documents served in the case. To sign up for File & Serve, contact Customer Service at 888.529.7587.

LOCAL RULES: The Marion County Local Rules governing the Marion County Mass Tort Litigation Docket are available on the Indiana Judicial Website, in the Marion County Clerk's Office, and through File & Serve after counsel obtains a user name and password. The File & Serve vendor will provide all technical information and instructions necessary to use File & Serve and will identify those Local Rules applicable to Marion County Mass Tort Litigation

Docket. The Local Rules have been adopted pursuant to T.R. 81 and compliance is mandatory.

COURT CONTACT: Contact the Marion County Clerk's Office at 317.327.4740 for the Court contact information for the Court in which your case was filed. *Adopted effective Jan. 1, 2008. Amended effective Feb. 25, 2008.*

LR49–TR5 Rule 603. FILE & SERVE PROCEDURE AND ACCESS

A. Electronic Filing and Service.

1. Electronic filing is the electronic transmission of documents to the Court, and from the Court, for the purposes of filing.

2. Electronic service is the electronic transmission of documents to a party, attorney or representative under these rules.

3. All documents filed with the Court must be served on all counsel of record. This subsection does not apply to Trial Briefs, which are addressed separately in Local Rule 711, or to submissions for *in camera* review.

4. File & Serve is authorized as the exclusive means for filing or serving all documents to be filed or served pursuant to T.R. 5 and other Rules in cases assigned to the Marion County Mass Tort litigation docket. All references to "document" in this Rule shall include any exhibits or attachments to a document. Document formats and types are defined in Rules 604 and 605.

B. Documents Filed Under Seal. Documents filed under seal ("sealed documents") may not be efiled and shall be filed conventionally as required by the trial rules. A notice entitled "Notice of Filing of Sealed Document(s)" shall be served via File & Serve. This notice shall reference the date the sealed documents were independently served and filed and the means of service.

C. Posting of Documents. All documents posted on File & Serve must be served on all counsel of record, and it is not permissible to deselect any counsel from the service list on File & Serve.

A copy of each document filed or served in this litigation shall be sent to File & Serve by one of the following methods: (1) electronic transfer via the Internet ("uploaded documents") or (2) facsimile transmission. Uploaded documents may be submitted in WordPerfect, Microsoft Word, .pdf, .tif, .bmp, .jpg, .gif, or .hfd format. File & Serve will convert all documents into .pdf format and will make them available to system users on an internet website maintained by File & Serve ("Website"). Timing for posting to the Website is as follows:

1. Electronic documents will be posted immediately upon submission by counsel and receipt by File & Serve (documents are converted to .pdf prior to submission as efiled or eserved documents).

2. Faxed documents will be converted to .pdf by File & Serve. Users will receive an e-mail notification once their document is converted. Users must then finalize transmission of the document on File & Serve. The document is not served until the transmission step is completed.

D. Service Stamp and Time of Filing and Service. Any posted document shall be deemed filed and served as of the date and time indicated on the File & Serve service stamp, located on the first page of every posted document. The "service stamp" contains the date, time and Transaction ID Number (TID) of the document and appears in the upper right-hand corner of the first page of all documents transmitted to File & Serve. For purposes of this rule, "transmitted" or "transmission" is defined as .pdf-converted documents submitted to File & Serve for posting. The provisions of T.R. 6(E) allowing for additional time after service by mail shall not apply to extend deadlines.

E. Linking. File & Serve shall organize the documents through a chronological index, which will indicate whether that document is linked to others. If the document being served is in response or in addition to another document(s) served on the system, it must be "linked" to that document, as explained in the online rules for the File & Serve system. A document may be linked to multiple other documents, but only within the same case. Failure to properly link a document may result in omitted consideration of a submission.

F. Signature on Documents Filed or Served Electronically.

1. The LexisNexis File & Serve log-in and password required to submit documents to the File & Serve system serve in part as the Filing User's signature on all electronic documents filed with the Court. They also serve as a signature for purposes of the Indiana Rules of Trial Procedure, including T.R. 11, the Local Rules of this Court and any other purpose for which an attorney's signature is required in connection with proceedings before the Court.

2. All filings must contain either a traditional, scanned signature that attests to the verification or the individual name of the attorney who is authorizing the filing and/or service of the document preceded by an "/s/" typed on the signature line where the attorney's handwritten signature would otherwise appear. Reference to "one of the attorneys" is not proper and may result in summary denial or striking of the filing.

3. Electronically filed documents must include a signature block above the certificate of service (except on appearances) that includes the signature (described above), name, party for whom appearing, attorney number, firm, address, telephone number, and e-mail address of the authorizing attorney or the designated e-mail address for the attorney's firm.

G. Notification of Submissions. Each registered File & Serve user will be provided with an electronic "mailbox" on the Website. Within one hour of posting the document to the system, File & Serve will send a document hyperlink to the mailboxes of all relevant registered users. Sending such a hyperlink to the recipient's mailbox shall constitute service of the document pursuant to T.R. 5, T.R. 72(D) and Rule 600(D), and File & Serve and the parties will have no further duty to notify recipients of postings. "Relevant registered users" refers to counsel who have filed their appearances in the case and staff members within the same firm to whom notice is forwarded through File & Serve. Notice is not forwarded to staff or attorneys outside the Appearing Attorneys' firms.

Only those registered users who have properly served appearances in the case by the time a document was transmitted will receive notice that the document was posted. Counsel who appear in a case have a duty to review and appropriately respond to documents served in a case prior to the counsel's appearance. Knowledge of the contents of documents posted prior to a user's appearance in the case will be imputed to a user who appears in the case, regardless of when the user does appear.

H. User Access to File & Serve. Only registered users may post documents on the case dockets or receive notice of document postings. National counsel who has not filed an appearance must either rely on their local counsel to send those copies or become part of the service list by filing an appearance or petition for temporary admission. In order to file documents on the system, the registered user must also be an attorney admitted to the Indiana Bar. Attorneys admitted *pro hac vice* may sign documents, but Local Counsel must also sign and post the document on the system. Non-filed documents are exempt from the Local Counsel posting rule.

I. Public Access. Public access to the system is provided through use of the Court's Public Access Terminal to view selected documents pursuant to Admin. Rule 9. Members of the public may schedule an appointment to view selected dockets on File & Serve by scheduling an appointment with the Court.

Adopted effective Jan. 1, 2008. Amended effective Feb. 25, 2008; Jan. 1, 2011.

LR49–TR5 Rule 604. DOCUMENT FORMATTING AND SUBMISSION

A. Service Stamp. The first page of all documents will receive a service stamp upon submission and acceptance with the date, time and Transaction ID Number (TID).

B. Top margin. All filed documents must have a two-inch top margin on the first page.

C. Depositions. Publication of depositions, pursuant to T.R. 5(E)(5), shall be made, without Motion, on the Deposition Docket (98–000) only.

D. Captioning. With the exception of the captions for the Complaint, documents filed with the Court and served on File & Serve may be captioned, using the shortened cause number defined in Rule 600(C) in the following format:

```
STATE OF INDIANA        )   MARION SUPERIOR
                        )   COURT TWO
                        )   MASS TORT LITIGATION
                        )   DOCKET
COUNTY OF MARION        )   ["Asbestos," "Silica,"
                        )   "Coal Tar Pitch"] Section

CARL CLAIMANT AND CARRIE CLAIMANT,   )    [95–002]
Plaintiffs.                          )
```

E. Proposed Order Format. All motions must be accompanied by a separate Proposed Order, posted as a supporting document with Document Type "Proposed Order," when submitted to File & Serve. The Order shall be in the following format:

1. *Margin.* There shall be a margin of two inches on top of the first page of the Proposed Order.

2. *Caption.* The document may be captioned as described in subdivision D above.

3. *Title.* The Title of the Proposed Order shall not presume the Court's Ruling. Proposed orders served on File & Serve shall be titled in the following format: [Proposed order on] + [Party type] + [Party name] + [Title of judicial review document]. An example is "Proposed Order on Defendant ABC Corporation's Motion for Enlargement of Time to File Preliminary Exhibit List."

4. *Text of Order.*

a. Introduction. The Proposed Order shall initially state that the moving party filed a Motion, followed by the exact title of the Motion as well as any supporting document titles, and that the Court is duly advised in the premises. No further reference to the Motion is necessary and use of the notation "H.I." or other incorporation language is improper. Example: "Plaintiff John Doe filed his Motion for Enlargement of Time to File Final Exhibit List, and the Court is duly advised on the premises."

b. Ruling. The second paragraph of the Proposed Order shall state: "The Court rules as indicated herein, and on the attached Information/Comments Page," as described in subdivision (F)(2) below.

c. Relief Requested. The third paragraph of the Proposed Order shall state "IT IS THEREFORE ORDERED ["ADJUDGED AND DECREED" if the Ruling is final and appealable] [Relief requested in Motion]." In the event that the Court ruling is "Ruling with Comments," the relief requested paragraph on the proposed order shall have no weight and shall not form a part of the ruling unless expressly adopted in the Court's comments.

    d. _Signature._ No provision shall be made for Judicial signing or dating the Order.

    e. _Distribution._ The distribution information provided on the Proposed Order shall state "DISTRIBUTION via Electronic Service."

F. Official Order Format. A complete Order issued on the Marion County Mass Tort Litigation Docket shall be in the format of one of the following: (1) A file stamped, signed Order in the standard Order format; or (2) An Order including the text and format referenced in subdivision E, along with the Court's electronic Ruling Overlay in the upper margin and the Court's attached Information/Comments Page.

    1. _Ruling Overlay._ The Court's electronic Ruling Overlay shall be superimposed on the Proposed Order and shall include the State Seal, the Judge's signature, and the ruling language.

    2. _Information/Comments Page._ Every Order shall include an additional page including pertinent information and comments regarding the ruling indicated in the Ruling Overlay. Such information provided includes the Court, the Cause Number and case name, the Original Proposed Order Transaction ID Number (TID), the current date and the Judge's signature, as well as comments, if any, necessary to the ruling.

G. Previously Served Documents. Any document already posted using File & Serve should not be attached to new documents or resubmitted to File & Serve. Reference shall be made to the File & Serve TID, the Document Title, the cause number, and the date submitted. Users shall link to the document if on the same docket.

H. Certificate of Service. All filed documents must include a Certificate of Service referencing the service stamp and the manner of service. The Certificate of Service shall be in the following format:

CERTIFICATE OF SERVICE

The undersigned attorney certifies that the foregoing was electronically served on all counsel of record on the date shown on the service stamp on the first page of this document, by using File & Serve.

"Electronically served" shall mean the methods described in Rule 603. The document, before the Certificate of Service, must include the filing attorney's name, party for whom appearing, attorney number, firm, address, telephone number, and e-mail address of the authorizing attorney or the designated e-mail address for the attorney's firm.

I. Exhibits. To prevent the file stamp from obscuring information on an exhibit, a cover page shall be filed with exhibits. The cover page shall contain a two-inch top margin and only succinctly identify the exhibit to which it is attached. Exhibits must be marked in such a way, e.g., Bates stamped, to allow for easy reference and specific designation.

J. Rules for Titling Documents. Documents filed or served via File & Serve shall comply with the following title requirements to facilitate searching and generating reports and to comply with T.R. 77(B):

    1. _Filings, excluding Appearances and Proposed Orders._ Documents filed with the Court shall be titled on File & Serve in the following format: [Party Type] + [Name of Party] + [Title of Document] + [Title of document to which the new document relates or responds, if applicable] + [Basis therefore]. The following are examples of how to title documents:

    a. Plaintiff John Doe's Complaint;

    b. Defendant XYZ Corporation's Motion to Dismiss Plaintiffs' Complaint on the basis of the Statute of Limitations;

    c. Plaintiffs John Doe's and Jane Doe's Response in Opposition to Defendant XYZ Corporation's Motion to Dismiss on the Basis of the Statute of Limitations.

    d. Plaintiff John Doe's Exhibit A to Designation of Evidence to collective Response to Defendants' Motion for Summary judgment.

    e. Deposition of Phil Physician, January 1, 2005, Vol. 2.

    f. Defendant XYZ Corporation's Response to Plaintiff's Supplemental Interrogatories.

    2. _Letters or Notices._ Letters or other document forms served on File & Serve shall be titled in the following format: ["Letter" or Other Document Form] + "From" + [Name of Sending Party] + "to" + [Name of Recipient Party] + [Subject Matter]. The following are examples of how to title these documents:

    a. Letter from XYZ Corporation to Plaintiffs Concerning Case Management Order Conference Schedule

    b. Notice From XYZ Corporation to All Counsel of Record of John Doe's Availability for Deposition

    3. _Cancellations._ Documents intended to cancel previously scheduled events must use the document type "CANCELLATION" and be titled on File & Serve in the following format: ["CANCELLATION:"] + [Party Type] + [Party Name] + [Description of Canceled Event]. Example: "CANCELLATION: Defendant ABC Company, Inc.'s Notice of Canceling John Doe's Deposition scheduled for January 1, 2012."

    4. _Verified documents._ All documents required to be verified by statute, Ind. Trial Rules, or any

Local Rule shall include the word "Verified" in the title of the document.

Adopted effective Jan. 1, 2008. Amended effective Feb. 25, 2008; Jan. 1, 2011.

LR49–TR5 Rule 605.   DOCUMENT TYPES

A. "Document Type" Selection. When users submit documents to File & Serve, the user must specify the "Document Type" for each document from the menu of approved document categories. An asterisk (*) accompanies the document types that are referred for judicial review, and only those documents will receive judicial review.

B. Extra Documents. CCS entries are not permitted. Cover or transmittal letters shall not be served with documents submitted for filing.

C. Main and Supporting Documents. Each distinct document should be prepared and uploaded to File & Serve separately, as a main or supporting document. "Main" is the default setting for the first document uploaded on File & Serve in each transaction. "Supporting" documents may be uploaded, but are restricted to only those documents that relate to the main document uploaded in the transaction. File & Serve does not restrict the number of supporting documents.

For example, when filing a Motion for Summary Judgment, Designation of Evidence, Brief in Support, Exhibits and Proposed Order, each document type should be uploaded separately and properly titled. The motion for summary judgment is the main document and all others are supporting documents.

Adopted effective Jan. 1, 2008. Amended effective Feb. 25, 2008; Jan. 1, 2011.

LR49–TR5 Rule 606.   FILE & SERVE ERRORS

A. Resubmission. If a document that comprises part of a transaction filed on File & Serve contains errors in violation of these Local Rules, the entire transaction will be rejected by the filing clerk, and the entire transaction must be re-filed. Questions regarding reasons for rejection of a transaction may be directed to the Court's special master.

B. Relation Back. A document that has been resubmitted after being rejected for violations of these Local Rules will relate back to the time of the first attempted filing and be deemed filed as of the time of the first attempted filing provided that the violations were corrected and the document is resubmitted within two business days of the notice of rejection. Any time limit triggered by any resubmitted document does not begin until the day after the filing of the document.

C. Penalties. The Court may impose penalties, including striking documents, if firms or attorneys commit repeated or egregious violations of these Local Rules.

D. Tombstoning.

1. *Definition and application.* "Tombstoning" is the procedure by which all documents within a transaction are removed from the docket. This procedure is only to protect privileged or confidential information and is not for removal of merely incorrectly filed documents. A record of the transaction will remain in a user's mailbox, but the document will no longer be able to be viewed.

2. *Procedure.* In the event that privileged or confidential information is inadvertently posted on File & Serve, counsel shall contact the Court immediately to request that the document be tombstoned. After counsel has contacted the Court to initiate the tombstoning procedure, counsel must submit within two days a Verified Motion to Tombstone Documents, a proposed order, and any substitution documents.

a. Verified Motion to Tombstone Documents. This motion shall contain the document's TID number, date submitted, the cause number/case name, and the basis for claiming privilege and/or confidentiality. The verified motion shall explain how the error occurred and must be signed by the submitting/authorizing attorney. Any documents that the party wishes to substitute for the tombstoned document must be attached to the verified motion and contain the word "Substituted" in their title.

b. Proposed Order. The proposed order shall be titled, "Order Tombstoning [original document title] [(TID Number)]." If the party wishes to substitute documents for the tombstoned document, the proposed order must specifically refer to the documents and state, "By this Order, TID Number [TID number] and its Supporting Document(s) are removed from the docket of the above-captioned matter and the Court substitutes the document(s) *nunc pro tunc.*"

Adopted effective Jan. 1, 2008. Amended effective Feb. 25, 2008; Jan. 1, 2011.

LR49–TR5 Rule 607.   CONTACTING THE COURT

E-mail is the preferred method by which counsel should communicate with the Court regarding all Mass Tort Local Rules substantive language and requirements. All questions regarding technological procedure should be directed to File & Serve Technical Support.

When sending e-mail to the Court regarding specific items submitted to File & Serve, provide the following information:

A.   Cause number/case name;

B.   Date document submitted;

C.   Transaction ID Number (TID); and

D.   Title.

If a party files a motion or any other document that requires prompt Court review, the party shall e-mail the Court at masstortsmaster@indy.gov and provide notice of the filing.

Adopted effective Jan. 1, 2008. Amended effective Feb. 25, 2008; Jan. 1, 2011.

LR49–TR5 Rule 608.   MOTION PRACTICE

A.   Motions for Enlargement of Time.

All motions for enlargement of time must be verified and demonstrate good cause.

(1) *Plaintiffs.*   Plaintiffs shall not seek consent of opposing counsel before filing a motion for enlargement of time, but shall file a motion for enlargement of time. Defendants shall have five days, including days when the Court is not open, after the filing of plaintiffs' motion to file an objection.

(2) *Defendants.*   Defendants shall determine whether opposing counsel objects to a motion for enlargement before filing. The motion shall specify which opposing counsel was contacted and whether opposing counsel objected to the motion.

(a) Plaintiff cannot be reached. If opposing counsel cannot be reached, the motion shall specify the efforts made to contact opposing counsel.

(b) Plaintiff objects. If opposing counsel does object to the motion, the motion shall so state and demonstrate good cause for the enlargement in a verified motion.

(c) Plaintiff does not object. If opposing counsel does not object, only a "Notice of Agreed Enlargement of Time" needs to be filed and the name of the counsel consenting to the enlargement shall be specified. Such notice shall not include a proposed order.

(d) Contents of all motions for enlargement. The contents of a motion for enlargement of time or notice of agreed enlargement of time shall include

(1) Whether the case is currently set for trial, and, if so, when.

(2) The filing to be submitted, the time period that is sought to be extended, and the time period that triggered it.

(3) The specific due date requested.

Any motion not satisfying these requirements may be summarily denied.

B.   Time for Response to All Motions.   Notwithstanding LR49–TR5–203, any party objecting to a motion shall have 10 days from the date of filing to file a response, except as otherwise provided by Mass Tort Local Rule or Court order. The party filing the motion or any other interested party in the case may file a reply thereto within seven days of the responsive filing. The Court will not await a response before ruling on the following motions: defendants' motions to enlarge time, to file an oversize brief, or to withdraw an appearance.

C.   Joinder in Motions.   Any party wishing to join in a filed motion shall file a notice of joinder within seven days of the filing of the motion.

D.   Multiple case service.   Multiple case service document types are restricted to Appearances, Notices of Substitution of Counsel, Notices of Withdrawal of Counsel, Notices of Deposition, Notices of No Objection to Motion for Summary Judgment, Notices of Dismissal, Notices of Agreed Enlargement of Time, Notice of Naming a Nonparty, and Notices of Bankruptcy. Leave of Court is required to file any other document, including a motion and a proposed order, by multiple case service. A document may contain multiple captions before the title of the document, but unless it falls within the previous categories of documents approved for multiple case service or a party has received leave of Court, it must be transmitted in separate transactions for each case to which it applies.

Adopted effective Jan. 1, 2008. Amended effective Feb. 25, 2008; Jan. 1, 2011.

LR49–TR5 Rule 609.   MASTER DOCKET

Each section of the Marion County Mass Tort Litigation Docket has a Master Docket for serving items of general applicability such as Trial Calendars, Case Management Order proposals and Case Management Orders, Notices of Depositions if not case specific, Agenda Items, Committee Reports, Requests for Local Rules or amendments, Master Pleadings, Master Discovery and similar documents. Case Management Order proposals and Case Management Orders for trial settings shall be served on the Master Docket. Parties must first obtain leave of Court before filing any other documents on the Master Docket.

Adopted effective Jan. 1, 2008. Amended effective Feb. 25, 2008; Jan. 1, 2011.

LR49–TR8(C) Rule 610.   NONPARTY PRACTICE

When a party identifies a nonparty through written notice or pleading, that identification sufficiently amends the Answers of all parties by interlineation, regardless of whether the party first naming the nonparty is subsequently dismissed from the case.

Adopted effective Jan. 1, 2008. Amended effective Feb. 25, 2008.

LR49–TR12(B)(6) Rule 611.   GRANT OF TRIAL RULE 12 MOTIONS

A party shall have 30 days following the grant of a T.R. 12(B) motion within which to replead. All Proposed Orders for motions to dismiss must indicate the 30–day repleading period. Also, Proposed Orders for motions to dismiss must specify that the motion is granted "without prejudice" in the Relief Requested paragraph. An example is: "IT IS THEREFORE ORDERED that Defendant XYZ Corp.'s Motion to Dismiss Plaintiffs' Complaint on the basis of the Statute of Limitations is GRANTED without prejudice. Plaintiffs have thirty (30) days within which to replead their claims against Defendant XYZ Corporation." If Plaintiff fails to replead, parties may move for entry of final judgment.

Adopted effective Jan. 1, 2008. Amended effective Feb. 25, 2008; Jan. 1, 2011.

LR49–TR26 Rule 612. DISCOVERY

A. Joint Defense Privilege. All communications, in any form whether oral, written, or transcribed by any means, among defense counsel in the Marion County Mass Tort Litigation cases are hereby deemed privileged. Plaintiffs and their attorneys are prohibited from discovering such information in such filed cases.

B. Certificate of T.R. 26(F) Compliance. Parties must certify in detail in a motion to compel the efforts that the moving party has taken to informally resolve any discovery dispute. The statement of efforts shall include the dates, time, place, TID numbers of relevant correspondence, other methods of communication, and the names of all participating attorneys and parties. Failure to include a verified T.R. 26(F) certification may result in summary denial of a motion to compel.

C. Effect of Trial Rule 12 and Rule 706 motions. The filing of a motion under T.R. 12 or Rule 706 tolls pending discovery deadlines.

D. No Local Limits. The limitation on the number of interrogatories and requests for production in the Marion County Local Rules shall not apply.

Adopted effective Jan. 1, 2008. Amended effective Feb. 25, 2008.

LR49–TR41 Rule 613. PLAINTIFFS' DISMISSALS

A. Dismissal of Defendants. When plaintiff has resolved the claims with all the defendants named or no longer wishes to pursue claims against the remaining defendants, plaintiff shall file, "Plaintiff's Motion to Dismiss Remaining Defendants," together with a proposed order dismissing with or without prejudice all remaining defendants who have not settled for consideration. The filing of this motion does not divest this Court of jurisdiction with regard to enforcement of settlements or other agreements. After an order dismissing all defendants has been entered, the Court may administratively designate the case as closed. For cases dismissed without prejudice, defendants may file motions for entry of final judgment beginning two years after the dismissal.

B. Final Dismissal. When the plaintiff has filed the final signed Stipulation of Dismissal and there remains no further need for enforcement jurisdiction, the plaintiff shall file a "Notice of Final Dismissal of Pending Claims." The filing of this Notice closes the case statistically and completely divests this Court of jurisdiction over the matter.

Adopted effective Jan. 1, 2008. Amended effective Feb. 25, 2008; Jan. 1, 2011.

LR49–TR56 Rule 614. MOTIONS FOR SUMMARY JUDGMENT

A. Party Filing Motion for Summary Judgment. A party filing a motion for summary judgment shall:

1. File a motion, supporting brief, and designation of any evidence upon which the party relies.

2. The designation of evidence may be made in the motion or by a separate document, and shall contain specific and appropriate citations to discovery responses, depositions, affidavits, and other admissible evidence either already in the record or attached as an exhibit to the designation or brief.

3. The supporting brief must include a separate section labeled "Statement of Undisputed Material Facts" listing, in separately numbered paragraphs, the individual undisputed facts that are potentially determinative of the motion as to which the moving party contends there is no genuine issue that contain specific and appropriate citations to admissible evidence already in the record or attached as an exhibit to the brief. The Statement of Undisputed Material Facts should not contain mere background facts which put the case in perspective or the party's argument which should be in the argument portion of the brief.

4. The movant may not incorporate by reference any designation of evidence or statement of undisputed material fact contained in another section or part of the supporting brief.

5. The moving party must also submit to the Court a proposed order on its motion for summary judgment.

B. Party Responding to Motion for Summary Judgment.

1. No later than 30 days after service of the motion, a party opposing the motion shall file:

    a. a response brief, and;

    b. a designation of evidence that is specific and separate as to each movant and that designates evidence that the respondent asserts creates a disputed fact or a genuine issue. Respondents' designation shall contain specific and appropriate citations to discovery responses, depositions, affidavits, and other admissible evidence either already in the record or attached as an exhibit to the designation or brief.

2. The response brief shall contain a separate section labeled "Statement of Material Facts in Dispute and Genuine Issues," which shall contain a separate subsection as to each movant, listing in separately numbered paragraphs, the individual disputed facts and/or genuine issues as to that movant.

Each subsection shall contain at least one of the following two separate parts:

(a) the disputed material facts which preclude summary judgment; and/or

(b) the material facts which are not in dispute, but which respondent asserts create a genuine issue and preclude summary judgment.

3. The asserted material facts and genuine issues shall be supported by specific and appropriate citations to discovery responses, depositions, affidavits, and other admissible evidence either already in the record or attached as an exhibit to the brief.

4. The non-movant's Statement of Material Facts in Dispute and Genuine Issues should not contain mere background facts which put the case in perspective or the party's argument which should be in the argument portion of the brief.

5. The response brief shall contain a separate argument section as to each movant, unless the entire argument is identical as to each movant.

6. The respondent may not incorporate by reference any designation of evidence, statement of material fact in dispute, or genuine issue contained in another section or part of the response brief or "Statement of Material Facts in Dispute and Genuine Issues".

7. Citation to documents previously served on File & Serve shall be by document name, date document was served on File & Serve, and TID number, and if possible, page and line, paragraph number or similar specific reference.

C. Reply Brief. A party filing a motion for summary judgment may file a reply brief no later than 10 days after service of the opposing party's submissions.

D. Surreply. If, in reply, the moving party relies upon evidence not previously cited or objects to the admissibility of the non-moving party's evidence, the non-moving party may file a surreply brief limited to such new evidence and objections, no later than five days after service of the reply brief.

E. Page limits. Memoranda in support of or in opposition to motions for summary judgment shall not exceed 15 pages in length and reply briefs and surreply briefs shall not exceed eight pages in length, unless accompanied by a Motion for Leave to File a Brief in Excess of Page Limits, along with an email alerting the Court to the pending motion.

F. Designated Documents. With respect to documents designated in support of or in opposition to motions for summary judgment:

1. Counsel shall attach as supporting documents to the motion any designated documents not previously uploaded onto File & Serve, other than deposition transcripts.

2. Counsel shall upload any deposition transcripts, not previously uploaded on File & Serve, but relied upon for purposes of summary judgment,

in their entirety on the Deposition Docket, as provided in Rule 604(C).

3. Counsel need not upload copies of designated documents already posted on File & Serve unless they have been altered and such alteration is relevant to the designation.

4. Counsel need not attach as an exhibit any designated document already posted on File & Serve, but rather, citation to the document as described above shall be sufficient.

5. "Specific and appropriate citations" throughout this Rule shall mean case name and shortened cause number, document title, date document was served on File & Serve, TID number, and if possible, page and line, paragraph number or similar specific reference.

G. Hearings. Pursuant to Rule 711(I)(5), the Court schedules summary judgment hearings for each trial setting between 110–90 days prior to trial. This scheduled hearing will be vacated, unless a party files a request for hearing in accordance with Ind. T.R. 56(C) at least 10 days before the scheduled summary judgment hearing date. The request for hearing shall be made in a separate document from any other filing, but it may be submitted as a main or supporting document. The document type shall be "Request for Hearing," and the request shall be titled,

[Party type] [Party name]'s Request for Hearing on [(party name)'s or "Its"] Motion for Summary Judgment for the [month] [year] Summary Judgment Settings.

H. Outlines. At the time of the hearing, counsel must provide three copies of an outline summarizing the brief submitted to the Court in support of or opposing the motion for summary judgment. Two three-hole punched copies must be provided to the Court and opposing counsel shall receive one.

Adopted eff. Jan. 1, 2008. Amended effective Feb. 25, 2008; Jan. 1, 2011.

LR49–TR73 Rule 615. COURT HEARINGS

A. Status Conferences and Motion Days.

1. *Agenda Item Proposals.* Any party that wishes to address any pending motion or general issue at status conferences or on motion days must submit a written notice containing proposed agenda items. Proposed agendas must be filed on the Master Docket no less than 10 days prior to the scheduled motion days or status conference. Parties must describe proposed agenda items with particularity, including the cases, dates, titles, and File & Serve TID numbers for all written submissions relating to each item proposed in the agenda.

2. *Motions Must be Fully Briefed.* Only motions that are fully briefed and at issue at least seven days before the hearing will be considered by the Court.

3. *Failure to Submit Items.* If no proposed agendas are submitted to the Court by the aforementioned deadline, the motions day or status conference may be vacated.

B. Hearings Calendared by the Court.

1. All hearings scheduled by the Court will be posted on the File & Serve calendar. Parties may access the calendar from the File & Serve home page, search under Marion County Court, and input the desired search criteria. A search must include the relevant dates.

2. Court hearings will be marked as "tentative", "confirmed" or "cancelled". The Court does not send out notice when a hearing's status is changed. It is the responsibility of the parties to confirm a hearing's status by checking the Court's calendar.

Adopted effective Jan. 1, 2008. Amended effective Feb. 25, 2008; Jan. 1, 2011.

LR49–AD3 Rule 616. CONDUCT OF ATTORNEYS *PRO HAC VICE*

Local Counsel must appear on behalf of his client when an attorney admitted *pro hac vice* plans to participate at a hearing or trial. Trial counsel admitted *pro hac vice* and Local Counsel are required to attend any Final Pre–Trial Conferences scheduled for cases to which they have been admitted, unless the trial counsel admitted *pro hac vice* has received leave of Court not to attend the final pre-trial conference.

Adopted effective Jan. 1, 2008. Amended effective Feb. 25, 2008.

LR49–TR01–ASB Rule 700. SCOPE OF MARION COUNTY MASS TORT ASBESTOS LITIGATION DOCKET AND LOCAL RULES

Pursuant to the Order of the Marion Superior Court Executive Committee and this Rule, the Marion County Clerk of the Courts is directed to file all asbestos-related personal injury, wrongful death, or survival action cases in Marion Superior Court Two, Civil Division, creating the Marion County Mass Tort Asbestos Litigation Docket. The cause numbers assigned to these cases shall begin with 49D02–["95," "96," or "98"]01–MI–0001 followed by a numeric suffix. On File & Serve, the cases will be identified in the division field as "Asbestos."

Any Local Rule in the 700 Series shall apply to the asbestos division only. The Mass Tort Litigation Rules, Series 600 *et seq.*, govern litigation in the asbestos personal injury division.

The Master Docket for the Asbestos Division is 49D02–9501–MI–00001–000 (95–000).

E-mail is the preferred method by which counsel should contact the Court. The Court may be contacted at masstortsmaster@indy.gov

Adopted effective Jan. 1, 2008. Amended effective Feb. 25, 2008; Jan. 1, 2011.

LR49–TR8 Rule 701. MASTER COMPLAINTS

A. All plaintiffs' counsel who intend to file cases under the Master Docket shall file Master Complaints that shall set forth all allegations required by statute and case law for a personal injury lawsuit alleging exposure to asbestos.

B. There shall be a master complaint form filed for each form of filing anticipated by counsel (e.g., single plaintiff, married plaintiff, and deceased plaintiff).

C. Master Complaints shall be identified as "[Firm Name]'s [Single/Married/Deceased] Plaintiff Master [A/B/C] Complaint." The Firm Name may be shortened for ease of application.

D. Plaintiffs' counsel shall file their Master Complaints under the Master Docket and they shall be available for use and incorporation into new case filings by referencing the TID number.

E. In the event of a change in the name of the Plaintiffs' counsel's firm, Plaintiffs' counsel shall re-file each form of Master Complaint on the Master Docket, making sure that each Master Complaint contains the firm's proper and current name.

Adopted effective Jan. 1, 2008. Amended affective Feb. 25, 2008; Jan. 1, 2011.

LR49–TR8 Rule 702. CASE–SPECIFIC COMPLAINTS

At the time a specific Plaintiff's case is filed, the content of the case-specific Complaint shall include the following:

  a. Plaintiff's full name;

  b. Defendants' identities and the capacity in which the Defendant is being sued (e.g., product manufacturer);

  c. Statement that jurisdiction and venue are proper;

  d. The asbestos-related disease allegedly suffered by the plaintiff or plaintiff's decedent;

  e. Date of diagnosis of the alleged asbestos-related disease;

  f. Date of death of the plaintiff's decedent, if applicable;

  g. Decedent's alleged cause of death, if applicable;

  h. Statement indicating which Master Complaint plaintiff's counsel incorporates; and,

  i. Any other specific information required by law or the case.

Adopted effective Jan. 1, 2008. Amended effective Feb. 25, 2008.

LR49–TR8 Rule 703. RESPONSIVE PLEADINGS/ANSWERS

A. Time for Filing. The obligation of defendants to respond to a Plaintiff's Complaint is not triggered until 30 days after Plaintiff serves a Verified Initial Disclosure Statement or 30 days after the defendant is served with summons in the case, whichever time is later. No T.R. 12 motions or other responsive pleadings may be filed until the time for Plaintiff to file his VIDS has expired. LR49–TR5 Rule 203(D) shall not apply in Asbestos Section cases.

B. Master Answers. Defendants may file Master Answers in response to Master Complaints. Any Master Answers shall be identified as "Defendant [Party Name]'s Master Answer to [Firm Name]'s [Single/Married/Deceased] Plaintiff Master [A/B/C] Complaint." If a defendant has filed a Master Answer, the defendant's case-specific answer shall refer to the defendant's applicable Master Answer by TID number, if any, and may add any additional responses or defenses.

C. Additional Defendants. In cases where the plaintiff has been granted leave only to join additional defendants, the plaintiff shall limit the amendments to allegations pertaining to the new defendants. The original defendants need not respond to the amended complaint, and the filing of the amended complaint only to join additional defendants does not toll or vacate any existing deadlines under these rules as to the original defendants.

D. Denial of Trial Rule 12 and Rule 706 Motions. A defendant shall not be required to file an Answer while it has a T.R. 12 or Rule 706 motion pending, but rather shall file its Answer no later than 10 days after denial of its T.R. 12 or Rule 706 motion, if applicable.

Adopted effective Jan. 1, 2008. Amended effective Feb. 25, 2008; Jan. 1, 2011.

LR49–TR12 Rule 704. VERIFIED INITIAL DISCLOSURE STATEMENTS (VIDS)

A. Verified Initial Disclosure Statements.

1. Verified Initial Disclosure Statements ("VIDS") shall be signed under oath.

2. Plaintiff's VIDS shall be considered part of the Complaint and constitute a pleading pursuant to the Trial Rules.

3. Any party's VIDS may be used in all pre-trial proceedings and at trial consistent with the Indiana Rules of Trial Procedure and Indiana Rules of Evidence.

B. Timing.

1. In an exigent case, a plaintiff shall file and serve the VIDS no later than 30 days after filing the Motion for Expedited Trial Setting in accordance with Rule 711(G).

2. In a non-exigent case, a plaintiff shall file and serve the VIDS no later than 90 days after filing the Complaint.

3. A plaintiff will not be required to respond to any discovery, including interrogatories, requests

for productions, requests for admissions, or deposition requests propounded by defendants until after plaintiff has filed his VIDS, except for good cause shown by defendants, or as allowed by Rule 709.

Adopted effective Jan. 1, 2008. Amended effective Feb. 25, 2008; Jan. 1, 2011.

LR49–TR12 Rule 705. PLAINTIFFS' VIDS: CONTENT

Each plaintiff shall file a separate Verified Initial Disclosure Statement (VIDS) that shall contain the following information correlated for each alleged exposure:

1. "Who":

(a) The identity of the Plaintiff/Worker, including his or her full name, all other names by which he or she has been known, his or her trade or craft, current or last address, and, if applicable, place and date of death. The SSN and birth date shall be verified and mailed under separate cover to Sims & Associates, Inc. Plaintiff shall state in his VIDS that he has transmitted this information to Sims & Assoc., Inc., and Sims & Assoc. shall release this information upon request to defense counsel who appear in the case.

(b) The identity of the Plaintiff/Worker's employer at the time of each and every exposure to asbestos, or period of exposure to asbestos, setting forth the name and last known address for each employer, as well as the beginning and ending dates for each employment (e.g., "for the alleged exposure of April 14–18, 1956: ABC General Contractors, 1234 Main Street, Connersville, Indiana 46703, Employed from November 1, 1952 to July 15, 1961. ").

(c) The identities of those working with the products of asbestos-containing materials as described in 2, below, at the time of each such alleged exposure. State the identity of these persons, their trade, and their employer(s) (e.g., "Joe Smith, insulator, employee of XYZ Corporation.").

2. "What": The name or type of the asbestos-containing product or item the Plaintiff/Worker used or to which he or she was allegedly exposed, stating the manufacturer's company name (e.g., "Allbrand 85% magnesia pipe covering"), being as particular as possible. If Plaintiff cannot remember the name of the product he alleges he used or to which he alleges he was exposed, he shall provide a detailed description of the product.

3. "When": The dates during which the Plaintiff/Worker was allegedly exposed to asbestos at each jobsite, setting forth the beginning and ending dates for each exposure period, including date, month and year.

4. "Where": The location of each alleged exposure to asbestos, setting forth the address of the premises as well as the specific area on each premises where the claimed exposure occurred (e.g., "boiler room #3 of Generic plant on East Ohio Street in Indianapolis"), and;

5. "How": The circumstances of the alleged exposure to asbestos, including a description of what the Plaintiff/Worker was doing on the premises, and what, if anything, was occurring in the specific area on each premises where and when the claimed exposure occurred, including a description of work performed by both the Plaintiff/Worker at that time and by any third-party working with asbestos or asbestos-containing materials.

6. Foreign law. Plaintiff shall reference all foreign law plaintiff alleges applies in the case, if any, and the specific defendants to which plaintiff alleges the foreign law applies.

If Plaintiff is not able to provide the information provided above, Plaintiff shall specify the unsuccessful efforts to obtain the information and a date when the information will be provided to defendants.

Adopted effective Jan. 1, 2008. Amended effective Feb. 25, 2008; Jan. 1, 2011.

LR49–TR12 Rule 706. DISPOSITIVE MOTIONS BASED ON PLAINTIFFS' VIDS

Trial Rule 12 motions in a non-exigent case must be filed within 30 days of the filing of VIDS or, in a previously stayed case, within 30 days of the Court issuing a provisional order setting the case for trial (POST), whichever is later. Plaintiff's response to any motion to dismiss will be due 30 days after the motion was filed. Any reply shall be filed within 10 days after the response is filed. In an exigent case, a defendant must file a dispositive motion or motion for more definite statement based on the pleadings within 15 days of the filing of such VIDS, a response is due within 10 days, and any reply is due within five days.

Adopted effective Jan. 1, 2008. Amended effective Feb. 25, 2008; Jan. 1, 2011.

LR49–TR26 Rule 707. PLAINTIFF'S DISCOVERY PROPOUNDED TO DEFENDANTS

A. Service. A plaintiff may serve upon any defendant a Master Set of Interrogatories and Production Requests tailored appropriately to the type of defendant being served. Plaintiff may serve the Master Set of Interrogatories and/or Production Requests by letter, which must specifically reference the File & Serve TID number assigned to the document containing the discovery requests being served. A single service letter to all defendants may be served and applies to all defendants, regardless of time of filing their appearance. If plaintiff serves all defendants by letter prior to the appearance of a defendant, the discovery shall be deemed served on the defendant.

B. Time for responding. In a non-exigent case, defendants shall respond to Plaintiff's Master Set of Interrogatories and Production Requests or any other discovery within 120 days after the date of service or the filing of an Answer, whichever is later. In an

exigent case, defendants shall respond to Plaintiff's Master Set of Interrogatories and Production Requests or any other discovery within 60 days after the date that the Motion for Expedited Trial was filed, the date of service of the discovery, or the filing of its Answer, whichever is later. A defendant will not be required to respond to any discovery until after the defendant has filed its Answer, except for good cause shown by plaintiff.

C. Master Responses. Defendants may file a Master Set of Answers to Plaintiffs' Master Set of Interrogatories and Production Requests on the Master Docket and incorporate those answers into responses to discovery requests in individual cases.

D. Case-specific Discovery. Plaintiffs may serve case-specific discovery that is not duplicative of any master discovery.

Adopted effective Jan. 1, 2008. Amended effective Feb. 25, 2008; Jan. 1, 2011.

LR49–TR26 Rule 708. DEFENDANTS' DISCOVERY PROPOUNDED TO PLAINTIFFS

A. Time for response. In a non-exigent case, a plaintiff shall respond to Defendants' Master Set of Interrogatories and Requests for Production or any other discovery no later than 120 days after the VIDS was filed or the service of the discovery, whichever is later. In an exigent case, a plaintiff shall respond to Defendants' Master Set of Interrogatories and Requests for Production in accordance with Rule 711 (G). A plaintiff in an exigent case shall respond to any other discovery no later than 30 days after the date the Motion for Expedited Trial Setting was filed, the filing of the VIDS, or service of the discovery, whichever is later. Defendants may serve Master Discovery by letter, which must specifically reference the TID number assigned to the document containing the discovery requests being served.

B. Case-specific discovery. Individual defendants may serve additional written discovery in individual cases that is not duplicative of the Master Set of Interrogatories and Requests for Production or of other defendants' case-specific discovery in the individual case.

C. Effect of Service. Defendants shall not serve duplicative discovery. All Master Interrogatories or Master Requests for Production of Documents served by one defendant in a particular case shall be deemed to have been served on behalf of all defendants, and any defendant may rely on a plaintiff's answers or responses to the Master Discovery regardless of whether that defendant actually served the Master Discovery or when the defendant appeared in the case. Likewise, any defendant may seek to compel responses or otherwise enforce Master Discovery Requests.

Any other discovery served by one defendant in a particular case shall be deemed to have been served on behalf of all defendants who file a notice of joinder in the discovery within 10 days of the service of the discovery on Plaintiff. Any defendant who joins in the discovery may rely on a plaintiff's answers or responses to discovery regardless of which defendant actually served the written discovery or when the defendant appears in the case. Accordingly, any defendant who filed a joinder may seek to compel responses or otherwise enforce the case specific discovery requests.

D. Required Medical Information. Within 30 days of filing the VIDS, a plaintiff shall serve on defendants:

1. A description or name of all illnesses or injuries from which the Plaintiff/Worker allegedly suffers as a result of exposure to asbestos;

2. The date each such illness or injury was diagnosed;

3. The name and address of each person who made such diagnosis;

4. A list of all symptoms experienced by Plaintiff/Worker which were allegedly asbestos-related, including a description of each symptom;

5. If Plaintiff/Worker smokes or has smoked tobacco, the quantity and duration of tobacco usage during his or her lifetime, and the brand name of the products or a description of the items used; and,

6. A list of all health care providers who have treated Plaintiff/Worker for each illness or injury allegedly caused by exposure to asbestos or any other airborne contaminants along with their current or last known addresses.

7. Any medical or employment records of the plaintiff in the possession of Plaintiff or his counsel.

E. Required Records or Materials. A plaintiff shall provide to Sims & Associates copies of the following documents if in plaintiff's or his counsel's possession, or signed and dated authorizations to obtain the same:

1. Plaintiff/Worker's medical and hospital records, and diagnosing and treating physician's records in the possession of the plaintiff, plaintiff's counsel or their agents, including any written reports relating to any alleged diagnosis or alleged confirmation of any diagnosis of an asbestos-related disease or disease process or any other disease allegedly caused by airborne contaminants;

2. Pension records and all related information;

3. Social Security Administration Work Histories (Form SSA–7050);

4. X-ray films, CT scans, and/or pathologies which are in the possession of the plaintiff, plaintiff's counsel and/or their agents, or in the alternative, specifically identify the person or entity in possession of these materials;

5. Federal Income Tax Returns (Form 1040 or 1040A for the prior seven years, or in the case of a decedent, for the seven years preceding his or her death);

6. Any and all forms, claims, or other documents submitted to any trust or other entity on plaintiff's behalf related to any injury plaintiff claims is a result of alleged asbestos exposure.

7. Any and all documents generated by any health and/or disease screening in which the plaintiff participated;

8. A list of all previous lawsuits in which the plaintiff was involved, identifying them by name, location, cause number, filing date, and current status.

9. Signed and undated releases, compliant with the Health Insurance Portability and Accountability Act, authorizing such Defendants' designee to obtain complete copies of Plaintiff/Worker's:

(a) medical, hospital and other health care records;

(b) radiology and/or pathology materials, which shall be addressed individually to the "Department of Radiology" and the "Department of Pathology;"

(c) employment records;

(d) pension records and information;

(e) Social Security Administration work histories (Form SSA–7050);

(f) federal income tax returns (Form 1040 or 1040A) for the prior seven (7) years, or in the case of a decedent, for the seven years preceding his or her death;

(g) forms, claims, or other documents submitted to any trust or other entity on plaintiff's behalf related to any injury plaintiff claims is a result of alleged asbestos exposure; and,

(h) records of any screenings in which Plaintiff participated.

10. A list of all health care providers who have treated Plaintiff/Worker within the last 20 years.

11. Medicare Form A–1 (HICN request) and Medicare Form A–2 (Authorization to Release Information).

The time limit for providing this information to Sims & Associates is within 30 days of filing the VIDS in non-exigent cases, and within 15 days of filing the VIDS in exigent cases.

F. Standing to Compel Releases. Any defendant shall have the right to petition the Court for an Order to compel the plaintiff to provide a signed release if more than 30 days have passed from the time plaintiff was provided a release to be signed, provided that the defendant has complied with Rule 612(B).

G. Requirements to Produce. Failure to provide the materials or authorizations set forth in this Rule after an entry of an Order compelling the same may be grounds for dismissal. All records described in Subdivisions (D) and (E) shall be produced within the time period allotted regardless of the stayed status of any individual case.

Adopted effective Jan. 1, 2008. Amended effective Feb. 25, 2008; Jan. 1, 2011.

LR49–TR30 Rule 709. DEPOSITIONS DE BENE ESSE

A. If counsel for the plaintiff has a good faith belief that the health and medical condition of their client or a witness requires that a videotaped deposition de bene esse be taken of such witness, they shall provide to defendants not less than 20 days prior to the date set for such deposition, the following information:

1. written notice of their intent to take such a deposition to all defendants (to their counsel if counsel have appeared for such defendant(s), or to any defendant's appropriate person for receipt of service of process if no counsel has yet appeared for that defendant). Such Notice of Deposition shall be in writing, delivered by facsimile together with hard copy by mail, or by hard copy hand-delivered to counsel for such defendant (if there is one), or by electronic mail (or similar computer assisted electronic means), but if and only if such defendant has previously agreed to such service; and,

2. copies of the following documents:

(a) a copy of the Verified Initial Disclosure Statement;

(b) any and all medical and hospital records and reports in the possession of such plaintiffs' counsel (except that these are to be delivered to Sims & Associates);

(c) signed and undated authorizations for the release of all medical and hospital records (except that these are to be delivered to Sims & Associates);

(d) Plaintiff's Social Security Administration Work History (Form SSA–7050); and,

(e) Answers to Defendants' Master Set of Interrogatories and Requests for Production.

B. The de bene esse deposition shall not occur less than 60 days from the date the Complaint is filed, other than by leave of Court for good cause shown.

C. Prior to the taking of the witness' deposition de bene esse as noticed above, the non-noticing party shall have the right to take a discovery deposition of such witness, notwithstanding Rule 704(B).

D. The de bene esse deposition shall occur no less than seven days after the completion of the discovery deposition, except as by agreement of all parties or by order of the Court.

E. In extraordinary circumstances, counsel may conduct the evidentiary deposition de bene esse, without the non-noticing party first taking a discovery

deposition, if the noticing party's counsel can establish to the satisfaction of the non-noticing parties (or, if necessary, the Court) a necessity for doing so. The non-noticing party shall have the right to conduct cross examination immediately following the conclusion of the direct examination in the deposition de bene esse, which shall continue day-to-day until completed, as the witness's health permits.

Adopted effective Jan. 1, 2008. Amended effective Feb. 25, 2008; Jan. 1, 2011.

LR49–TR30 Rule 710. DEPOSITIONS

A. **Attendance by defendant.** A defendant shall not be required to attend depositions of product identification and exposure witnesses identified by plaintiff, unless plaintiff, in good faith, has identified, along with the notice of deposition or on the plaintiffs' Witness List, that this witness will testify regarding a product manufactured, distributed by, or attributed to, that particular defendant; an alleged exposure upon a premises owned by or in the control of that particular defendant; or an alleged exposure caused by work performed by that particular defendant.

B. **Use of testimony.** If a witness submits an affidavit, testifies in his or her deposition, or testifies at trial about a product or job site which was not identified with the notice of deposition or on the plaintiff's Witness List, plaintiff shall be prohibited from introducing that testimony at trial, using that testimony in opposition to a motion for summary judgment or using that testimony in any other manner against the defendant who did not receive proper notice. Plaintiff may be allowed to utilize such testimony, however, upon giving those defendants, who were only identified by such witness subsequent to the issuance of the original notice of deposition, proper notice and a chance to re-depose this witness as to issues regarding their products, job sites, or work at issue.

C. **Video Depositions.** Any party may videotape a deposition taken in a case subject to these Local Rules after providing advanced written pursuant to Ind. R. Trial P. 30(B)(4). Any party or parties who videotape a deposition must videotape the entire deposition and be responsible for the expense related to the videotaping.

Adopted effective Jan. 1, 2008. Amended effective Feb. 25, 2008; Jan. 1, 2011.

LR49–TR40 Rule 711. TRIAL SETTINGS

A. Nothing in this rule shall limit the Court's ability to place actions upon the trial calendar in such a manner as the Court determines will expedite trials. The Court will set six trial settings per calendar year for the asbestos cases pending on the Marion County Mass Tort Litigation Docket.

B. Plaintiffs' firms are generally assigned no more than three trial settings per year.

C. Once a particular trial setting has been established, the parties may not seek to add, remove, or alter the order of cases absent a written, verified showing of extraordinary circumstances.

D. The Court shall set the number of cases for each trial setting.

E. Provisional Order Setting Trial. No less than 18 months prior to a trial date, the Court shall issue a Provisional Order Setting Trial (POST) tentatively scheduling cases for trial pursuant to the trial setting criteria in Rule 713.

1. The POST shall list:

(a) first and second-choice settings, consisting of two exigent cases, if any, and if not, two (2) slots tentatively reserved for exigent cases;

(b) the remainder of the settings shall consist of non-exigent cases in First in, First out ("FIFO") order.

2. All non-exigent cases are only tentatively set for trial, and are subject to displacement by cases that are rolled over from the previous trial setting for the same plaintiffs' counsel.

3. This POST is intended to allow the parties to begin preparing the tentatively scheduled cases for trial and alleviate the burden the parties bear in litigating entire cases in very short time frames.

F. Final Order Setting Trial. No less than five months prior to a trial date, the Court shall issue a proposed Final Order Setting Trial (FOST) for that trial date which confirms the cases set for trial pursuant to the trial setting criteria in Rule 713.

1. The FOST will:

a. Identify the rollover case(s) from the previous trial setting for that same plaintiffs' counsel;

b. Confirm any exigent case(s); and,

c. Vacate any previously scheduled case(s) for trial that is/are displaced by any rollover case(s).

G. Exigent Case. In the event that a case is granted exigent status pursuant to Rule 712 and set for trial less than 18 months prior to its scheduled trial date, certain Case Management Deadlines provided in these Rules are modified:

1. Plaintiff's VIDS, Plaintiff's Responses to Master Discovery, and Plaintiff's Preliminary Fact Witness List shall be filed and/or served no later than 30 days after the Motion for Expedited Treatment is filed, or 480 days before trial, whichever is later;

2. Plaintiff's Statement of Special Damages shall be filed no later than 30 days after the Motion for Expedited Treatment is filed, or 270 days before trial, whichever is later;

3. Defendants' Preliminary Fact Witness Lists shall be filed no later than 30 days after the filing of Plaintiff's Preliminary Fact Witness List, or 420 days before trial, whichever is later;

4. This section modifies only those due dates specified herein. The deadlines established in section (I), below, control the remaining deadlines.

H. Stayed Cases.

1. *Definition and Designation of Stayed Cases.* A "stayed case" is one that is currently not set for trial or one that is not exigent under Rule 712. The stayed case designation shall be lifted automatically when the case is reached in FIFO order and set on a POST or FOST.

2. *Effect of Stayed Status.* In a stayed case, Plaintiffs must file their pleadings, appearances, and gather the information required in Rules 708(D) and 708(E). Any party may file a Rule 714 initial motion for summary judgment in a stayed case and the response times are those specified in Rule 714. No other formal activity is required in a stayed case. Other filings are permitted, but the response time shall not begin until the case is set on a POST or FOST.

I. Case Management Orders. Except as otherwise provided in Section (G), above, all cases shall be governed by the Case Management Order, provided herein:

STATE OF INDIANA	)	MARION SUPERIOR COURT TWO
	)	MASS TORT LITIGATION
COUNTY OF MARION	)	ASBESTOS DIVISION

IN RE: [month] [year] Trial Setting   Master Docket, 95–000
[CASE NAMES]   [CAUSE NO.'S]

CASE MANAGEMENT ORDER

Pursuant to Rule 711, the Court hereby enters the following Case Management Order to govern cases included in the POST.

The deadlines established in this Order shall supersede all prior deadlines. Except where specifically noted below, nothing in this order shall be read to require a party to re-file or re-serve any materials, except for Requests for Hearings on motions for summary judgment.

1. Disclosure Statements. Within 30 days after the Court issues the Provisional Order Setting Trial ("POST"), Plaintiffs shall file their Verified Initial Disclosure Statements ("VIDS"). To the extent that Plaintiffs have previously filed VIDS, Plaintiffs shall also by this date review them and supplement them to the extent necessary to comply with the Rules.

2. Statement of Special Damages and Settled Parties.

A. Two hundred seventy (270) days before trial, Plaintiffs shall file their statement of special damages and their list of settled Defendants.

B. Plaintiffs shall have a continuing obligation to update this list of settled Defendants and shall provide a complete list to opposing counsel and the Court at the Final Pre–Trial Conference, at which time counsel for the Defense may orally amend their Answer and the record to add any Defendants recently dismissed from the case as non-parties.

3. Written Discovery.

A. Written discovery shall be served and answered pursuant to Local Rules.

B. No party shall serve written discovery any later than 90 days before trial.

4. Witnesses.

A. Within 60 days after the Court issues the POST, Plaintiffs shall file their Preliminary Fact Witness Lists identifying all witnesses from whom Plaintiffs may offer testimony at trial or in connection with dispositive motions. Plaintiffs' counsel shall accept service of subpoenas on behalf of all Plaintiffs' fact witnesses and/or produce those witnesses for deposition, unless Plaintiffs' counsel notifies Defendants otherwise. Except by agreement of all parties or by order of the Court for good cause shown, Plaintiff must produce for deposition by Defendants all of Plaintiff's fact witnesses upon whom Plaintiff will rely for purposes of summary judgment no later than 210 days before trial.

B. At least seven days prior to the scheduled deposition of a Plaintiff, co-worker, or other identification witness, Plaintiff shall serve Defendants with a notice containing the names of each Plaintiff for whom the witness will be called to testify and against which Defendants the witness is offered. These witnesses shall be produced for deposition by Plaintiff's counsel without subpoena upon reasonable notice by Defendants. Plaintiff will be prohibited from relying on or using at summary judgment or trial any evidence from any witness who fails to appear for a deposition as noticed, without good cause.

C. Four hundred twenty (420) days before trial, or 30 days after Plaintiffs' file their Preliminary Fact Witness Lists, whichever is later, Defendants shall file their Preliminary Fact Witness Lists identifying all witnesses from whom Defendants may offer testimony at trial or in connection with dispositive motions.

D. One hundred eighty (180) days before trial, Plaintiffs shall file their Expert Witness Lists identifying those expert witnesses from whom Plaintiffs may offer testimony at trial or in connection with any dispositive motions. Plaintiffs shall also by this date serve copies of any expert reports prepared in connection with these cases, if any, and reliance materials. Plaintiffs shall also by this date provide available deposition dates and locations for all of their testifying experts. Pursuant to T.R. 26(B)(4)(c), the parties seeking expert discovery shall pay the expert's reasonable fee for deposition testimony.

E. One hundred twenty (120) days before trial, or 30 days after Plaintiffs file their Expert Witness Lists, whichever is later, Defendants shall file their Expert Witness Lists identifying those expert witnesses from whom Defendants may offer testimony at trial or in connection with any dispositive motions. Defendants shall also by this date serve copies of any expert reports prepared in connection with these cases, if any, and reliance materials. Defendants shall also by this date provide available deposition dates and locations for all of their testifying experts. Pursuant to T.R. 26(B)(4)(c), the parties seeking expert discovery shall pay the expert's reasonable fee for deposition testimony.

F. One hundred twenty (120) days before trial, Plaintiffs shall file their Final Witness and Exhibit Lists. The lists shall contain only those witnesses and exhibits Plaintiffs actually intend to call to testify or to introduce at trial.

G. Sixty (60) days before trial, or 60 days after Plaintiffs file their Final Witness and Exhibit Lists, Defendants shall file their Final Witness and Exhibit Lists. The lists shall contain only those witnesses and exhibits Defendants actually intend to call to testify or to introduce at trial.

H. Thirty (30) days before trial, the parties shall have made available for deposition all witnesses and all experts they have retained to testify. The parties shall cooperate in the scheduling of depositions and shall complete all deposition discovery by that date, unless otherwise agreed by all parties or by order of Court with good cause shown.

I. All parties are under a continuing obligation to review, amend and supplement witness lists to identify those witnesses the party believes will actually testify.

5. Motions.

A. Motions for summary judgment shall be filed at least 150 days before trial and comply with Rule 614. Responses, replies and surreplies shall be filed as set forth in T.R. 56 and in Rule 614. Hearings on motions for summary judgment will be scheduled for any party requesting a hearing, pursuant to T.R. 56 and Rule 614.

B. Hearings on motions for summary judgment will be set at least 90 days before trial or on such other dates as the Court may schedule for particular motions for any party tendering notice as required by T.R. 56. The Court will provide counsel with a schedule setting forth the order of arguments and time limits. The parties are encouraged to file written waivers of these oral arguments.

C. All responses and/or objections to motions, with the exception of motions for summary judgment and motions to dismiss, served by one Defendant shall be deemed joined by all other Defendants, without the filing of any joinders.

D. Parties must contact the Court to request a hearing on any motion.

6. Trial Preparation.

A. Not later than 21 days before the trial date, the parties shall make each of the exhibits described in their Final Exhibit Lists available for inspection and copying. Nothing in this Order is intended to limit any party's right to copy or inspect trial exhibits earlier through discovery requests.

B. Not later than 14 days prior to the trial date, each party shall file:

1) Any stipulations of fact;

2) A list of depositions intended to be used in the party's case-in-chief that includes page and line numbers that will be read;

3) Any motions in limine. All motions in limine must divide the subjects into categories and include legal authority for each point. Motions in limine which simply list subjects without proper briefing ad legal authority will not be considered; and

4) A trial brief succinctly addressing the following matters: (a) contested issues of fact; (b) contested issues of law and supporting authority; (c) a summary of motions in limine and anticipated evidentiary disputes; (d) a list of witnesses counsel intends to call at trial. The trial brief shall be delivered to the Court and shall not be served on other parties or filed using File & Serve. Each party shall present two copies of the trial brief to the Court which the Clerk shall stamp as "RECEIVED."

C. Not later than seven days before trial, each party shall file:

1) Objections and counter-designations to depositions;

2) Objections or responses to motions in limine; and

3) Any proposed preliminary jury instructions to be read to the jury prior to opening statements, and an agreed preliminary issue instruction. The issue instruction shall also be provided to the Court via email to masstortsmaster@indy.gov in "word" processing format. If the parties cannot agree to a preliminary issue instruction, the proposed instructions must be provided to the Court in both hard copy and electronic format along with a summary of any areas of disagreement.

D. Nothing in this Order is intended to prohibit the parties from raising matters related to these cases during other conferences scheduled on the Court's Mass Tort Litigation dockets. The parties shall submit proposed agendas which comply with Rule 615 and list specifically those matters which require attention. If no agendas are received or if all parties represent that the status conference is unnecessary, the Court may vacate that conference from the Court's calendar.

E. The Court shall conduct a final pre-trial conference to be scheduled. All trial counsel who will participate in the trial shall attend the final pre-trial conference.

F. The Court will announce during the Defense Case-in-Chief the deadline for the Final Proposed Jury Instructions, as well as the number of proposed non-pattern instructions permitted per side. Counsel shall submit two copies of ALL proposed instructions (pattern and non-pattern), in three-ring binders, with numerical dividers; providing the instruction with the appropriate given/modified/refused/withdrawn provisions, followed by copies of the legal support for the proposed instructions. Counsel shall also provide proposed pattern instructions separated from the non-pattern instructions with the appropriate given/modified/refused/withdrawn provisions. The disks or email copies of the proposed instructions shall not have the citation that was provided on the hard copy (to reduce the amount of editing required during compilation for the instructions). Because the Court will require the Defendants to act in concert with regard to chargeable instructions, Defendants should collaborate when compiling the three-ring binder submission of proposed instructions.

Adopted effective Jan. 1, 2008. Amended effective Feb. 25, 2008; Jan. 1, 2011.

LR49–TR40 Rule 712. EXIGENT CASES AND EXPEDITED TRIAL SETTINGS

A. Exigent Cases.

1. "Exigent Case" shall mean the allegedly injured plaintiff has been diagnosed with malignant mesothelioma, any other asbestos-related Stage IV cancer, or can show other compelling circumstances that justifies deviating from the strong presumption that all cases shall be handled in FIFO Order.

2. Any case that does not meet the definition of an "exigent case" shall be a non-exigent case. If the plaintiff in an exigent case dies before the deadline to file summary judgment motions and the Court grants a party's motion to remove the case from an expedited trial setting, the case will no longer be considered exigent for purposes of establishing deadlines and trial settings.

3. To obtain exigent status and an expedited trial setting, a plaintiff must:

(a) File with the Court a Motion for Expedited Trial Setting showing good cause why the plaintiff should be afforded the preferential treatment; and,

(b) Attach to the Motion for Expedited Trial Setting an affidavit from a qualified physician speaking to the deteriorating health of the plaintiff and indicating that the plaintiff meets the definition of exigent. The qualified physician's affidavit must unequivocally state that the physician has read the Court's definition of an "exigent case" and that to a reasonable degree of medical certainty, the plaintiff meets the Court's definition. In the event that Plaintiff seeks exigent status on a basis other than the Plaintiff's serious medical condition, Plaintiff shall attach a detailed affidavit that demonstrates facts supporting the need for an expedited trial date.

4. Following a Motion to Expedite Trial, the case shall proceed as if exigent pending the Court's ruling on that Request

5. Plaintiff shall make all reasonable attempts to make the affiant available for deposition within thirty (30) days of the filing of such affidavit. A deposition of the affiant for the purposes of challenging the exigent status will be limited solely to the facts and circumstances surrounding the determination that Plaintiff qualifies for exigent status.

6. Defendant(s) shall file any objection to Plaintiff's request for an exigent trial setting on or before 60 days after the date of the Motion for Expedited Trial Setting was filed, or within 30 days of service upon that Defendant, whichever is later.

7. An exigent case shall remain exigent and receive expedited treatment only so long as:

(a) the Plaintiff remains living; or,

(b) the parties and the Court have invested substantial amounts of time and effort in preparing the case for trial, for example, if the deadline for filing motions for summary judgment has passed, then in the interest of judicial economy the case should continue to receive expedited treatment and remain in place on the upcoming trial calendar.

8. A case that has been granted exigent status will not be scheduled for an expedited trial setting less than eight months after the date on which plaintiff filed their request for the exigent status and expedited trial setting.

9. This Rule is only for the purposes of determining trial setting priority, and designation of a case as "exigent" shall not constitute evidence that the plaintiff's injuries were caused by or related to asbestos.

Adopted effective Jan. 1, 2008. Amended effective Feb. 25, 2008; Jan. 1, 2011.

LR49–TR40 Rule 713. TRIAL SETTING CRITERIA

A. Asbestos cases pending on the Marion County Mass Tort Litigation Docket shall be set for trial pursuant to the following criteria, absent a written, verified showing of good cause:

1. Any case identified by the Court as an "exigent case" may receive a priority setting and expedited trial date, in comparison with non-exigent cases.

2. No more than two "exigent cases", as that term is defined in Rule 712, will be scheduled for trial in any single trial setting.

3. Non-exigent cases will fill the remaining slots in a particular trial setting using cause number order, beginning with a particular plaintiffs' firm's oldest pending cases and moving forward according to cause number.

B. In the event that one or more cases set in any particular trial setting is not tried, settled, dismissed or otherwise resolved:

1. The case shall roll over and displace the settings in that firm's next trial setting.

2. Cases rolled over will be set for trial behind only exigent cases assigned to that trial setting by the Court.

3. Cases that are rolled over will be assigned to that firm's next trial setting in the same order as originally scheduled for trial.

4. Any vacancies remaining in the new trial setting shall be filled according to the trial setting criteria in section A of this Rule.

5. Cases displaced by the cases rolled over from the previous trial setting then become first choice settings in that firm's very next trial setting in the order that they were originally set for trial, behind any exigent cases set for that day.

6. Any vacancies remaining in that trial setting shall be filled according to trial setting criteria in section A of this Rule.

7. For good cause the Court may make exception to the limit of eight cases set in a trial setting.

8. In the event that one exigent case rolls over from the previous trial setting and two exigent cases are set for the next trial setting, no exigent case will be displaced, but all of the non-exigent cases will roll over to the next trial setting.

C. Cases will be released from a trial setting by the Court as follows:

1. Four weeks before the first scheduled day of trial, the seventh and eighth choice settings shall be released from the trial setting and roll over to the Plaintiff firm's next trial setting.

2. Two weeks from the first scheduled day of trial, cases that are not first, second, or third choices in the trial setting shall be released from the trial setting and roll over to the plaintiffs' firm's next trial setting.

3. At Noon on the day before trial is set to begin, all cases but the first choice in the trial setting shall be released from the trial setting and roll over to the plaintiffs' firm's next trial setting.

D. Once cases are assigned to a particular trial setting by the Court, the trial setting will not be altered or modified without good cause shown, other than to accommodate cases rolling over from previous trial settings, as described above.

E. A motion to continue trial may be made only by a written and verified motion pursuant to T.R. 53.5, and will be granted only upon a showing of exceptional circumstances.

F. If a motion to continue trial is granted:

1. The case(s) affected by the motion to continue shall roll over to the plaintiffs' firm's next trial setting immediately upon entry of the Court's order granting the motion; and,

2. The case(s) affected shall roll over to the plaintiffs' firm's next trial setting in the same order as previously set, in accordance with the provisions of this Rule.

3. All existing Case Management Order deadlines for that case are vacated.

Adopted effective Jan. 1, 2008. Amended effective Feb. 25, 2008; Jan. 1, 2011.

LR49–TR56 Rule 714. INITIAL SUMMARY JUDGMENT MOTION DOCKET

A. Application. This Rule shall apply to any summary judgment motion that is filed in a stayed case. Summary judgment motions filed pursuant to this Rule shall be termed "initial summary judgment motions." Only summary judgment motions that raise issues for which no significant discovery is deemed necessary for the preparation and filing of the motion may be filed as an initial summary judgment motion. Examples of such issues would be the product liability or construction statute of repose bars.

B. Title and Proposed Orders. The title of an initial summary judgment motion shall include the word "Initial." In addition to the requirements of Rule 614, parties moving for summary judgment pursuant to this Rule shall submit two proposed orders as supporting documents: one that sets a hearing date and time for the motion to be indicated on the attached Information/Comments page, and a second proposed order that grants the initial summary judgment motion. The proposed orders shall not be final or appealable. Motions that are submitted without both proposed orders will be rejected.

C. Procedure. A party may file an initial summary judgment motion at any time. The time for responding to an initial summary judgment motion is continued to such time as the Court orders that the initial summary judgment motion is set for a hearing date. A party shall have 30 days after an initial summary judgment motion is set for a hearing date to file a response. The party that filed the initial summary judgment motion shall have 10 days to file a reply. Documents on which a party relies in moving or responding to an initial summary judgment motion shall be attached as supporting documents to the motion or response. The requirements of Rule 614 shall apply to procedure and to the format and the content of filings to the extent not inconsistent with this Rule.

A Plaintiff who responds to the initial summary judgment motion by asserting that Plaintiff does not yet have sufficient information to file a substantive response to the initial summary judgment motion must comply with T.R. 56(F) and file a responding affidavit, request for case management conference and proposed order.

D. Requests for Hearing. If a plaintiff does not file a response to an initial summary judgment motion and request a hearing, the plaintiff must file a separate Request for Hearing that complies with Rule 614(G). Any defendant that desires a hearing on its initial motion for summary judgment shall file a Request for Hearing that complies with Rule 614(G). If no request for hearing is filed for the hearing date set in the order setting the initial summary judgment motions for hearing, the Court may vacate the hearing.

Adopted effective Jan. 1, 2008. Amended effective Feb. 25, 2008; Jan. 1, 2011.

LR49–TR01 Rule 800. SCOPE OF MARION COUNTY MASS TORT SILICA LITIGATION DOCKET AND LOCAL RULES

Pursuant to the Marion Superior Court Executive Committee and this Rule, the Marion County Clerk of the Courts is directed to file all Silica and Mixed–Dust related personal injury cases in Marion Superior Court Two, Civil Division, creating the Marion County Mass Tort Silica and Mixed–Dust Litigation Docket ("Silica Division"). The cause numbers assigned to these cases shall begin with 49D02–["95," "96," or "98"]01–MI–0001 followed by a numeric suffix.

Any Local Rule in the 800 Series shall apply to the Silica and Mixed–Dust personal injury division only. The Mass Tort Litigation Rules, Subset 600 *et seq.,* govern litigation in the Silica Division.

The Master Docket for the Silica Division is 49D02–9601–MI–00001–000 (96–000). Master Docket filings for the Silica Division submitted prior to June 1, 2007, may be found on the Master Docket for the Asbestos Division, 49D02–9501–MI–00001–000 (95–000). Counsel who appear in a Silica Division case are ordered to link themselves to the Silica Master Docket. Users may contact Sims & Associates at 765.483.9528, for assistance.

E-mail is the preferred method by which counsel should contact the Court. The Court contact is the Special Master for Mass Tort Litigation at masstorts master@indy.gov

Adopted effective Jan. 1, 2008. Amended effective Feb. 25, 2008; Jan. 1, 2011.

LR49–TR01 Rule 900. SCOPE OF MARION COUNTY MASS TORT COAL TAR PITCH LITIGATION DOCKET AND LOCAL RULES

Pursuant to Order of the Marion Superior Court Executive Committee and this Rule, the Marion County Clerk of the Courts is directed to file all Coal Tar Pitch related personal injury cases in Marion Superior Court Two, creating the Marion County Mass Tort Coal Tar Pitch Litigation Docket ("CTP Division"). The cause numbers assigned to these cases shall begin with 49D02–9901–MI–00001, followed by a numeric suffix.

Any Local Rule in the 900 Series shall apply to the Coal Tar Pitch personal injury division only. The Mass Tort Litigation Rules, Subset 600 *et seq.*, govern litigation in the CTP division.

The Master Docket for the CTP Division is 49D02–9901–MI00001–000 (99–000). Counsel who appears in a CTP Division case is ordered to link themselves to the CTP Master Docket. Users may contact Sims & Associates at 765.483.9528, for assistance.

E-mail is the preferred method by which counsel should contact the Court. The Court contact is Special Master for Mass Tort Litigation at masstorts master@indy.gov

Adopted effective Jan. 1, 2008. Amended effective Feb. 25, 2008; Jan. 1, 2011.

MARION CIRCUIT AND SUPERIOR COURT FAMILY LAW RULES

Amended Effective October 2, 2006

Including Amendments Received Through November 1, 2013

Research Notes

Annotations to the Marion Circuit and Superior Court Family Law Rules are available in West's *Annotated Indiana Code, Title 34 Appendix.*

These rules may be searched electronically on Westlaw *in the* IN-RULES *database; updates to these rules may be found on* Westlaw *in* IN-RULESUPDATES. *For search tips and a summary of database content, consult the Westlaw Scope Screens for each database.*

LR49–FR00 Rule 500. FAMILY LAW COMMITMENT TO RESPECT AND CIVILITY

PREAMBLE

The Members of the Family Law Section of the Indianapolis Bar Association, recognizing the high degree of conflict and the volatile nature of domestic disputes, their impact on children and the need for direction in balancing the duty to represent the client with the obligation to rational, peaceful and efficient administration of justice, now make this pledge to promote the highest degree of respect and civility in conduct with parties, attorneys and courts.

GUIDELINES

I will maintain the highest level of professional integrity and personal courtesy in all dealings with parties, counsel, witnesses and courts.

I will advise clients that I am bound by the responsibilities and restrictions set forth in the Rules of Professional Conduct in all matters relating to the handling of their cases.

I will pursue the advancement of clients' legitimate objectives, but I will not participate in litigation based upon vengeance or other inappropriate emotions.

I will use legal procedures for the fullest benefit of clients without misusing or abusing the legal process.

I will not intentionally speak or act in an abrasive, hostile, offensive or acrimonious manner toward parties, counsel or courts.

I will not knowingly misstate, mischaracterize or fail to disclose relevant facts or legal authority.

I will familiarize myself with and comply with all requirements of the common law, the trial rules, the local rules, and the court policy and procedure.

I will endeavor to have clients fully disclose assets and liabilities, informally exchange information and confer with opposing counsel to discuss settlement, stipulate undisputed matters, and identify issues prior to scheduled hearings.

I will strive to reach agreements on procedural and preliminary matters consistent with clients' legitimate objectives.

I will honor promises and commitments in an effort to raise the level of professionalism and civility in domestic matters.

I will advise clients of the legal standards by which courts decide family law issues including the rebuttable presumption of an equal division of the marital estate and application of the best interest standard when determining custody of the children.

I will, whenever possible, encourage clients to reach amicable settlement of all issues after careful review of statutes and reasonable consideration of the risks, costs, delay and emotional trauma of trial.

I will not seek judicial intervention in matters that can be resolved through cooperation and communication between counsel and parties.

I will not resort to ex parte proceedings in the absence of extreme emergency, as the interests of justice and fair play mandate notice to the opposing party.

I will not abuse time limitations set by courts, will be punctual and prepared for all court appearances and I will notify the court promptly when a case has been settled or must be continued.

I will prepare clients and witnesses for court appearances and advise them of the conduct required of them in order to promote the prompt and efficient administration of justice and to avoid conduct that brings disorder, disruption and disrespect upon the courts.

Adopted as Preamble and Guidelines, effective Feb. 4, 2002. Renumbered as Rule 500, and amended effective Oct. 2, 2006; Jan. 1, 2008.

LR49–FR00 Rule 501.　TITLE AND SCOPE

A. Title. These Rules shall be known as the Marion Circuit and Superior Court Family Law Rules.

B. Scope. These Rules are in addition to the Marion Circuit and Superior Court Civil Division Rules. In the event of a conflict between the Civil Division and Family Law Rules, these Rules shall control. The Indiana Trial Rules and Indiana Rules of Evidence also apply in all family law matters.

Adopted as Rule 1, Jan. 10, 2000, effective March 1, 2000. Amended Feb. 4, 2002, effective March 1, 2002; renumbered as Rule 501, and amended effective Oct. 2, 2006.

LR49–FR00 Rule 502.　ADMINISTRATIVE PROCEDURES

A. Provisional Orders. A request for provisional orders may be made a part of the petition for dissolution of marriage, legal separation or paternity, in which case the petition shall be titled "Petition for Dissolution of Marriage [Legal Separation] [Paternity] and for Provisional Orders".

B. Time Required. In all contested family law matters, the moving party shall advise the court of the time required for hearing and contested issues to be considered in the text of a petition or praecipe for hearing. Parties should petition for time necessary for hearing with the expectation that each side will be allotted one-half of the total time allocated. The court normally allows 15 minutes for preliminary hearings and contempt petitions.

C. Summary Presentation. By agreement of the parties, all issues and evidence relevant to a domestic relations case may be presented in summary fashion by counsel.

D. Copies Required. The parties shall submit sufficient copies of the Final Decree and Property Settlement for the court to retain an original and two copies of each and provide copies to all parties or counsel of record.

E. Bench Warrant. In order to obtain a bench warrant from the court, a party must have personal service on the adverse party and complete a bench warrant information sheet. The court may issue a bench warrant on copy service with sworn testimony confirming actual notice to the adverse party.

F. Summons and Appearance. In all family law matters, the petitioner shall use the form of summons and appearance form set forth in Appendix A and shall attach the Verified Financial Declaration Form. Only the last 4 digits of a social security number should appear on the appearance form.

G. Verification. Verification language where required shall be in the form as stated in Indiana Trial Rule 11(B): I affirm, under the penalties for perjury, that the foregoing representations are true.

H. Mandatory Mediation. Parties must submit all contested final hearing issues requiring two hours or more of court time and all non-contempt post-decree child related issues to mediation prior to presenting the issues to the court for hearing, unless this rule is waived for good cause shown after written request by a party. The court may in its discretion assign matters to mediation at any stage of the proceeding.

I. Negotiations. Parties and counsel shall exchange documents, negotiate pending issues prior to scheduled hearing time and report to the Court.

Adopted as Rule 2, Jan. 10, 2000, effective March 1, 2000. Amended Feb. 4, 2002, effective March 1, 2002; renumbered as Rule 502, and amended effective Oct. 2, 2006; Jan. 1, 2008.

LR49–FR00 Rule 503.　NOTICE AND SPECIAL DISCLOSURE REQUIREMENTS

A. Notice. In all relevant family law matters, the moving party shall give notice of the time, place of the hearing or trial and that matters may be heard and determined in a party's absence, by summons, subpoena, order to appear, notice of hearing, served upon the adverse party at least seven days prior to the hearing or trial and file a copy of the notice with the Court. Proof of service by certified mail or sheriff is generally required.

B. Other Pending Legal Proceedings. In all family matters, the moving party shall provide the court with written notice of all other pending legal proceedings in which either party is involved. The written notice shall include the cause number, name and location of the court, names of parties involved and nature of the legal proceeding, per the appearance form in Appendix A.

C. *Ex Parte* Proceedings. The Court in its discretion shall decline to issue an order on any *ex parte* petition for emergency relief absent a showing the moving party has complied with Trial Rule 65 and Indiana case law.

D. Children Cope with Divorce. Prior to a final hearing in a dissolution involving minor children or paternity proceeding, the parties shall attend and ensure that the court is provided with written certification that the parties have completed a Children Cope with Divorce Program, or similar type program approved by the Court, unless waived by the Court.

E. Child Support Account Information Form. In all family law matters, the parties shall use the Child Support Account Information Form set forth in Appendix B. Anytime the court signs an order creating, modifying or terminating a child support obligation, the parties shall complete and submit a Child Support Account Information Form to the Clerk of the Marion Circuit and Superior Courts.

Adopted as Rule 3, Jan. 10, 2000, effective March 1, 2000. Amended Feb. 4, 2002, effective March 1, 2002; renumbered as Rule 503, and amended effective Oct. 2, 2006; amended May 7, 2007.

LR49–FR00 Rule 504. FINANCIAL DECLARATION FORM

A. Requirement. In all family law matters, the initiating party shall complete, serve and file a Financial Declaration Form within 30 days of filing a Petition for Dissolution of Marriage, Legal Separation or to Establish Paternity or a Petition for Modification of Child Support or at least seven days prior to any hearing, whichever is sooner. A blank form shall be served upon the responding party with the summons or order to appear instructing the respondent to complete, serve and file the form within 30 days of receipt or at least seven days prior to any hearing, whichever is sooner. Failure by any party to submit the Verified Financial Declaration Form as required shall preclude him or her from presenting evidence as to those matters contained in the Verified Financial Declaration Form, except for good cause shown. These time limits may be amended by court order for good cause shown.

B. Exceptions. The Financial Declaration Form need not be exchanged if:

1. The parties have obtained leave of court; or

2. The parties have a signed agreement;

3. The proceeding is one in which the service is by publication and there is no response;

4. The proceeding is post-decree and concerns issues without financial implications. Provided, however, when the proceeding is post-decree and concerns only a child support arrearage, the alleged delinquent party shall complete the entire Form, while the support recipient need complete merely that portion thereof which requires specification of the basis of the arrearage calculation.

C. Admissibility. Subject to specific evidentiary challenges, the Financial Declaration shall be admissible into evidence upon filing.

D. Supporting Documents. For the purpose of providing a full and complete verification of income, assets, liabilities and values, each party shall attach to the Financial Declaration Form all information reasonably required and reasonably available. At the minimum this shall include current wage records, income tax returns and supporting documentation. "Reasonably available" means that material which may be obtained by letter accompanied with an authorization, but does not mean material that must be subpoenaed or is in the possession of the other party. The court may require either party to supplement the Financial Declaration Form with appraisals, bank records, and other supporting documentation. Such supporting documentation shall not be attached to the Financial Declaration filed with the court, or, if attached, shall have all information redacted as necessary to comply with Indiana Trial Rule 5 (G). Supporting documentation, if relevant, may be admitted into evidence at a hearing as an exhibit subject to the Rules of Evidence.

E. Financial Declaration Forms—Mandatory Discovery. The exchange of Financial Declaration Forms constitutes mandatory discovery and Indiana Trial Rule 37 sanctions apply. The Forms shall be supplemented if additional material becomes available pursuant to Indiana Trial Rule 26(E)(2).

Adopted as Rule 4, Jan. 10, 2000, effective March 1, 2000. Amended Feb. 4, 2002, effective March 1, 2002; Sept. 20, 2004, effective Jan. 1, 2005; renumbered as Rule 504, and amended effective Oct. 2, 2006; Jan. 1, 2008.

LR49–FR00 Rule 505. CHILD SUPPORT GUIDELINES

A. Child Support Worksheet Required. In all proceedings involving child support or educational expenses, a Child Support Worksheet shall be provided with any settlement agreement, final decree, or at the time of any hearing or trial.

B. Deviation from the Child Support Guidelines. If an agreement concerning child support provides any deviation from the Child Support Guidelines, the parties shall provide the court a written explanation for the deviation.

C. Income Withholding Order Required. In all proceedings involving child support, absent other court order, an Income Withholding Order providing for payment through the state collection agency, shall be submitted with any settlement agreement, final decree, or modification.

Adopted as Rule 5, Jan. 10, 2000, effective March 1, 2000. Amended Feb. 4, 2002, effective March 1, 2002; renumbered as Rule 505, and amended effective Oct. 2, 2006; effective Jan. 1, 2012.

LR49–FR00 Rule 506. SUBMISSION OF AGREED MATTERS

A. Written Agreement Required. No agreed matter shall be submitted unless accompanied with a signed agreement and other appropriate documents such as a Decree. However, if the parties reach a settlement just prior to hearing or trial and there is insufficient time for the attorneys to prepare a type-written agreement, then the court may accept evidence of that settlement in handwritten form and on the record. If the agreement is entered orally on the record, counsel shall submit an order setting forth the agreement for approval by the court within ten (10) days or such additional time as the court may allow.

B. Petition for Modification Required. A verified Petition for Modification shall be included with any Agreed Entry pursuant to Indiana Trial Rule 7(B).

Adopted as Rule 6, Jan. 10, 2000, effective March 1, 2000. Amended Feb. 4, 2002, effective March 1, 2002; renumbered as Rule 506, and amended effective Oct. 2, 2006.

LR49–FR00 Rule 507. TEMPORARY RESTRAINING ORDERS

Subject to the provisions of Indiana Trial Rule 65 and Indiana case law, in all family law matters, the court may issue a Temporary Restraining Order without hearing or security, if either party files a verified petition with specific allegations that irreparable harm or injury would result to the moving party if no immediate order were issued, or as otherwise as delineated in this Rule.

A. Joint Order. If the court finds that an order shall be entered, the court may enjoin both parties from:

1. Transferring, encumbering, concealing, selling or otherwise disposing of any joint property of the parties or asset of the marriage without the written consent of parties or the permission of the court;

2. Removing any child of the parties then residing in the State of Indiana from the State with the intent to deprive the court of jurisdiction over such child without the prior written consent of all parties or the permission of the court.

B. Separate Order Required. In the event a party seeks to enjoin the non-moving party from abusing, harassing or disturbing the peace, of the moving party or any child or step-child of the parties, or exclude the non-moving party from the marital residence, the petition must allege specific facts indicating more than a generalized fear of an adverse action; contain evidence of actual or threatened physical or emotional abuse sufficient to find a risk of imminent danger; in the case of an eviction or custody request also show that the moving party is physically available to testify unless there is a showing of exceptional circumstances; and in all cases for restraining order, certify to the court the reasons supporting the claim that notice cannot be given. A joint or mutual restraining or protective order shall not be issued. If both parties allege injury, they shall do so by separate petitions. The court shall review each petition separately and rule on each with separate orders.

C. Confidential Form. The moving party shall provide the court with a completed Confidential Form concerning the non-moving party.

D. Notice of Termination. When a court issues a Temporary Restraining Order under Indiana Code § 31–15–4–3 and a protective order exists for the parties under Indiana Code § 34-26-2 et seq., a Notice of Termination of the protective order shall be completed pursuant to Indiana Code § 34-26-2-13. A Notice of Termination shall be completed when a Temporary Restraining Order is dissolved by the entry of a decree or court order.

E. Notice of Extension or Modification. When a Temporary Restraining Order is extended or modified by the entry of a decree or court order, a Notice of Extension or Modification shall be completed.

F. Protective Orders. When a court has issued a protective order prior to the filing of a Petition for Dissolution or initiation of a paternity proceeding, and a dissolution or paternity proceeding is later filed, pursuant to Ind. Code § 34-26-5-6(4), the court that issued the protective order may, on it own motion, or upon petition and order, transfer the protective order file to the court handling the dissolution or paternity case. If there is a pending family law matter, the court where the family law cause is pending shall hear the emergency protective order request, unless otherwise impractical. The Clerk shall file a new protective order proceeding in the court where the family law case is pending. An emergency request relating to a previously disposed cause involving a family with children or paternity shall be filed in the court where the case originated.

Adopted as Rule 7, Jan. 10, 2000, effective March 1, 2000. Amended Feb. 4, 2002, effective March 1, 2002; Sept. 20, 2004, effective Jan. 1, 2005; renumbered as Rule 507, and amended effective Oct. 2, 2006; Jan. 1, 2008.

LR49–FR00 Rule 508. CHILD CUSTODY AND VISITATION: REFERRALS FOR INVESTIGATION AND REPORT

On motion of either party with the approval of the court, or on the court's own motion, contested matters involving child custody and parenting time shall be referred to the Domestic Relations Counseling Bureau or to other sources for investigation and submission of a report to the court.

A. Domestic Relations Counseling Bureau. The DRCB shall conduct an investigation and report to the court on all contested matters referred to its attention, including written notice to the court when the evaluation has been conducted and the anticipated date a report will be submitted. In addition, the Bureau shall file a written report to the court if an investigation or evaluation is not conducted and the reason it was not completed.

B. Scope. This Rule shall apply to disputes involving child custody or parenting time that may exist either before or after the entry of a Final Decree of Dissolution of Marriage or an Entry of Paternity. The parties to contested matters shall meet and cooperate with the Domestic Relations Counseling Bureau as required.

C. Continuance. It shall be grounds for a continuance that a court ordered custody/parenting time evaluation or report has not been submitted to the court within seven days prior to the hearing date.

D. Admissibility. A court ordered custody/parenting time evaluation or report shall be admissible into evidence on the motion of either party without the evaluator needing to be present at the hearing. No part of this Rule is intended to supplant the right of either party to compel the attendance of the evaluator or other witnesses as set out in Indiana Trial Rule 45.

E. Release of Custody/Parenting Time Evaluation or Report. Upon written request, a court ordered custody/parenting time evaluation or report that was submitted only to the Court may be released to all parties.

F. Physical and Mental Examinations. In all contested family law matters involving child custody or parenting time, the provisions of Indiana Trial Rule 35 providing for physical or mental examinations by a physician shall be extended to include examinations and evaluations by a psychologist, therapist or other qualified evaluator upon order of the court.

G. Non disclosure of Report. Regardless of whether or not the evaluation/report was court-ordered, was conducted by the DRCB, or was a private evaluation, the content of the evaluation/report shall not be discussed with or in the presence of any minor child of the parties. Violation of this rule may result in a contempt of court proceeding. This provision regarding contempt applies even if the information is not provided to the minor child directly by the party, if the party has allowed, directly or indirectly, any other individual to have access to the evaluation/report, and that individual then discusses the matter with the child.

Adopted as Rule 9, Jan. 10, 2000, effective March 1, 2000. Amended Feb. 4, 2002, effective March 1, 2002; amended effective Dec. 2003; renumbered as Rule 509, and amended effective Oct. 2, 2006; renumbered as Rule 508, and amended effective Jan. 1, 2008.

LR49–FR00 Rule 509. ATTORNEY FEES

A. Preliminary Attorney Fees. Attorney fees may be awarded based on evidence presented by affidavit or oral testimony at a preliminary hearing. Affidavits shall be admissible subject to cross-examination. The following factors may be considered:

1. The number and the complexity of the issues;

2. The nature and extent of discovery;

3. The time reasonably necessary for the preparation and conduct of contested hearings;

4. The attorney's hourly rate; and

5. The amount counsel has received from all sources.

B. Preliminary Appraisal and Accountant Fees. Appraisal or accounting fees may be awarded based on evidence presented by affidavit or oral testimony at a preliminary hearing. The following factors may be considered:

1. An itemized list of property to be appraised or valued; and

2. An estimate of the cost of the appraisals and the retainer required

C. Contempt Citation Attorney Fees. There shall be a rebuttable presumption that attorney fees will be awarded to the prevailing party in all matters involving a contempt citation. An attorney may submit the requested fee by affidavit or oral testimony, which may be accompanied by an itemized statement.

Adopted as Rule 10, Jan. 10, 2000, effective March 1, 2000. Amended Feb. 4, 2002, effective March 1, 2002; renumbered as Rule 510, and amended effective Oct. 2, 2006; renumbered as Rule 509, and amended effective Jan. 1, 2008.

LR49–FR00 Rule 510. PARENTING TIME ORDERS

A. Reasonable Parenting Time. Except for specific deviations as approved by the Court, the phrase "reasonable parenting time" shall be presumed to be those rights and obligations provided for in the Indiana Parenting Time Guidelines, including the commentary, in effect at the time of the court-approved agreement or order, unless the agreement or order provides that parenting time shall be according to the guidelines as amended from time to time.

B. Reasonable Visitation. For cases involving visitation orders entered prior to March 31, 2001, and not modified thereafter, unless otherwise defined by court-approved agreement or order, the phrase "reasonable visitation" shall be defined as those rights and obligations provided for in the Marion County Visitation Guidelines, in their entirety, including the commentary, in effect at the time of the court-approved agreement or order, unless the agreement or order provides that visitation shall be according to the Guidelines as amended from time to time.

C. Acknowledgment. If the parties acknowledge in writing that they have received a copy of the Indian Parenting Time Guidelines and adopt the Guidelines as written or otherwise explain any deviation from the Guidelines in a settlement agreement or final decree, it will not be necessary that a copy of the Guidelines be attached to the agreement or decree.

Adopted as Rule 11, Jan. 10, 2000, effective March 1, 2000. Amended Feb. 5, 2001, effective March 31, 2001; Feb. 4, 2002; effective March 1, 2002; renumbered as Rule 511, and amended effective Oct. 2, 2006; renumbered as Rule 510, and amended effective Jan. 1, 2008.

LR49–FR00 Rule 511. CASE MANAGEMENT CONFERENCES

A case management conference shall be held in every contested family law matter requiring one day or more of trial time, or as ordered by the Court. Marion Circuit and Superior Court Civil Division Rule 16.1 shall apply in all respects. In addition, the case management order shall set forth stipulated and contested issues to be considered. The joint case management order shall be submitted at least 60 days prior to the hearing, unless an extension is granted after request by the parties. If there is no case management order timely filed, the hearing may be vacated by the Court

Adopted as Rule 12, Jan. 10, 2000, effective March 1, 2000. Amended Feb. 4, 2002, effective March 1, 2002; renumbered as Rule 512, and amended effective Oct. 2, 2006; renumbered as Rule 511, and amended effective Jan. 1, 2008.

LR49–FR00 Rule 512. TERMINATION OF REPRESENTATIVE CAPACITY

A. Upon the entry of a Final Decree of Dissolution of Marriage, Legal Separation or Paternity Judgment or a permanent modification of any custody, support or parenting time order, or the expiration of the appeal time thereon, all attorneys shall terminate their representative capacity by filing a Motion to Withdraw pursuant to Marion County Local Rule 2.

B. Service of process of any post dissolution or paternity decree pleadings shall be made upon the party pursuant to Indiana Rules of Trial Procedure.

C. Any copy served upon prior counsel who has properly withdrawn in compliance with this Rule, shall be deemed to be a matter of professional courtesy only.

D. Counsel for both initiating and responding parties shall be required to file a new appearance in any post dissolution or paternity decree action.

Adopted as Rule 14, Jan. 10, 2000, effective March 1, 2000. Amended and renumbered as Rule 13, Feb. 4, 2002, effective March 1, 2002; Sept. 20, 2004, effective Jan. 1, 2005; renumbered as Rule 513, and amended effective Oct. 2, 2006; renumbered as Rule 512, and amended effective Jan. 1, 2008.

APPENDICES

Appendix A. SUMMONS AND APPEARANCE FORMS

SUMMONS

IN THE MARION CIRCUIT AND SUPERIOR COURTS

IN RE: THE MARRIAGE OF

_____

                     Petitioner

and   CAUSE NO. _____

_____

                     Respondent

TO RESPONDENT: (Name)   _____

                         (Address) _____

                                     _____

You are hereby notified that you have been sued by the Petitioner for (Dissolution of Marriage) (Legal Separation) (Paternity) (Child Support) in the court indicated above.

You must complete the attached Financial Declaration Form and file it with the court within ten (10) days after receipt of this summons.

If this summons is accompanied by an Order to Appear, you must appear in court on the date and time stated in the Order to Appear. If you do not appear, evidence may be heard in your absence and a determination made by the court. If a Temporary Restraining Order is attached, it is effective immediately upon your receipt or knowledge of the Order.

If you wish to retain an attorney to represent you in this matter, it is advisable to do so before the date stated in the Order to Appear. If you take no action in this case after receipt of this summons, the court can grant a Dissolution of Marriage (Legal Separation) or make a determination regarding any of the following: paternity, child custody, child support, maintenance, visitation, property division (real or personal) and any other distribution of assets and allocation of debts.

Dated: _____   _____

                                      Clerk, Marion County

The following manner of Service of Summons is designated:

☐ Registered or Certified Mail
☐ Service on Individual
☐ Service at place of employment, to wit: _____
☐ Private Service

_____   _____

Attorney for Petitioner   Address

                                     _____

                                     Telephone

SHERIFF'S RETURN OF SERVICE OF SUMMONS

I hereby certify that I have served this summons on the ___ day of _____ ___:

(1) By delivering a copy of the Summons and a copy of the complaint to the defendant, _____.

(2) By leaving a copy of the Summons and a copy of the complaint at _____ which is the dwelling place or usual place of abode of and by mailing a copy of said summons to said defendant at the above address.

(3) Other Service or Remarks: _____

_____

Sheriff's Costs _____   Sheriff _____

                                           By: _____
                                                      Deputy

CLERK'S CERTIFICATE OF MAILING

I hereby certify that on the _____ day of _____, _____, I mailed a copy of this Summons and a copy of the complaint to the defendant, _____, by _____ mail, requesting a return receipt, at the address furnished by the plaintiff.

Dated: _____

                                           _____
                                           Clerk, Marion County

                                           By: _____
                                                      Deputy

RETURN ON SERVICE OF SUMMONS BY MAIL

I hereby certify that the attached receipt was received by me showing that the Summons and a copy of the complaint mailed to defendant _____ was accepted by the defendant on the _____ day of _____, _____.

I hereby certify that the attached return receipt was received by me showing that the Summons and a copy of the complaint was returned not accepted on the _____ day of _____, _____.

I hereby certify that the attached return receipt was received by me showing that the Summons and a copy of the complaint mailed to defendant _____ was accepted by _____ on behalf of the defendant on the _____ day of _____, _____.

Dated: _____

                                           _____
                                           Clerk, Marion County

                                           By: _____
                                                      Deputy

IN THE MARION SUPERIOR COURT
DOMESTIC RELATIONS
APPEARANCE FORM

Initiating / Responding Party

(Caption)   )   Cause No. _____
)   *(To be supplied by Clerk when case is filed.)*
)

☐ Check if *Pro Se*   **NOTE: This form is not required for pro se protective orders.**

1. _____ Name of party (must include date of birth and social security number in **DR, PO, GU** cases)

2. Attorney information (as applicable for service of process): **(Pro Se litigants must complete this section)**

   Name: _____   Atty. Number: _____
   Address: _____   Phone: _____
   _____   FAX: _____
   _____   Computer Address: _____

3. Case Type requested: _____

440

4. Will accept Fax service: Yes _____ No _____

5. For all occupants of the residence as well as any child/ren of either the petitioner or the respondent, supply the names, dates of birth and social security numbers.

Name: _____ D.O.B. ____ _____ SSN# _____

Name: _____ D.O.B. ____ _____ SSN# _____

Name: _____ D.O.B. ____ _____ SSN# _____

Name: _____ D.O.B. ____ _____ SSN# _____

6. Are there now or have there been within the last twelve months pending related cases?
Yes _____ No _____ If yes, list case and cause number below:

(The Court has determined that the following types of matters constitute cases that are related when a named party, family or household member(s) have matters pending of the following types: **CM, or DF filings involving domestic violence, family violence and/or substance abuse charges and all cases of the following types: JM, JS, JP, JT, JD, JC, DR, GU, MH, AD and PO)**
If the caption has a name other than that of the petitioner, please describe the relationship.

Caption _____ Cause No. _____
Relationship _____

Caption _____ Cause No. _____
Relationship _____

Caption _____ Cause No. _____
Relationship _____

Caption _____ Cause No. _____
Relationship _____

7. Additional information required by state or local rule:
_____

_____

_____

_____
Attorney at Law
Attorney Information

Authority: Pursuant to Trial Rule 3.1, this form shall be filed upon the first appearance in the case. In emergencies, the requested information shall be supplied when it becomes available. Parties shall advise the court of change in information previously provided to the court. The Division of State Court Administration has approved this format. Use additional continuation pages if needed.

**PURSUANT TO TRIAL RULE 3.1(E), THIS APPEARANCE FORM SHALL BE UPDATED
PROMPTLY SHOULD THERE BE
ANY CHANGE IN OR SUPPLEMENT TO THE INFORMATION PREVIOUS-
LY SUPPLIED TO THE COURT
APPEARANCE FORM (DR)**

Continuation Page

Cause Number _____

Continuation of item 1 (Names, addresses and phone numbers of additional parties):

Name: _____   Phone: (   ) _____
Address: _____

_____

Name: _____   Phone: (   ) _____
Address: _____

_____

Name: _____   Phone: (   ) _____
Address: _____

_____

Continuation of item 2 (Attorney information, as applicable for service of process)

Name: _____   Atty. Number: _____
Address: _____   Phone: _____
_____   FAX: _____
_____   Computer Address: _____

Name: _____   Atty. Number: _____
Address: _____   Phone: _____
_____   FAX: _____
_____   Computer Address: _____

Continuation of item 5 (Social Security numbers of additional children or occupants of residence):

Name: _____ D.O.B. ___ _____ SSN# _____
Name: _____ D.O.B. ___ _____ SSN# _____
Name: _____ D.O.B. ___ _____ SSN# _____
Name: _____ D.O.B. ___ _____ SSN# _____

Adopted Jan. 10, 2000, effective March 1, 2000. Amended Feb. 4, 2002, effective March 1, 2002; amended effective Oct. 2, 2006.

Appendix B.   CHILD SUPPORT INFORMATION FORM

**Clerk of the Marion Circuit and Superior Courts
Child Support Account Information**

Submitted by: _____   Date Submitted: ___ / ___ / ___

Cause Number: _____   Effective Date: ___ / ___ / ___

Child Support Account #: _____   ρ Original ρ Modification ρ Termination

Non–Custodial Parent / Person (Payor):
Name: _____   ρ Male ρ Female
Address: _____   S.S.N ____–____–_____
_____   D.O.B ___ / ___ / _____

City: _____   Phone (_____) _____ – _____
State/ZIP: _____   Ethnic Group: _____
                                     Attorney: _____

Payments will be made through: ρ Employer ρ Electronic Funds Transfer ρ Mail /
In Person
Comments: _____ .

Custodial Parent / Person (Payee):

Name: _____   ρ Male ρ Female
Address: _____   S.S.N _____ – _____ – _____
         _____   D.O.B _____ / _____ / _____
City: _____   Phone (_____) _____ – _____
State/ZIP: _____   Ethnic Group: _____
                                     Attorney: _____

Recipient will receive payments through: ρ Electronic Funds Transfer ρ Check
(mailed to address above)
Comments: _____ .

Obligation Information

Current Payment: $_____   Attorney's Fees: $_____   Medical Support:$_____
Arrearage Payment: $_____   Spousal Support: $_____   Blood Test: $_____
Delinquency Payment: $_____   Clerk Fee: $_____   Other (specify): $_____

Frequency: ρ Weekly ρ Bi–Weekly ρ Semi–Monthly ρ Monthly ρ Lump Sum

Dependent Information Name(s) of Child(ren)	Date of Birth	Social Security Number	Sex	Relationship
_____	____/____/____	_____–____–_____	___	_____
_____	____/____/____	_____–____–_____	___	_____
_____	____/____/____	_____–____–_____	___	_____
_____	____/____/____	_____–____–_____	___	_____
_____	____/____/____	_____–____–_____	___	_____

Use the reverse side to note any additional information.

Adopted Jan. 10, 2000, effective March 1, 2000. Amended Feb. 4, 2002, effective March 1, 2002; amended effective Oct. 2, 2006.

MARION SUPERIOR COURT PROBATE RULES

Amended Effective October 2, 2006

Including Amendments Received Through November 1, 2013

Research Notes

Annotations to the Marion Superior Court Probate Rules are available in West's Annotated Indiana Code, Title 34 Appendix.

These rules may be searched electronically on Westlaw in the IN-RULES database; updates to these rules may be found on Westlaw in IN-RULESUPDATES. For search tips and a summary of database content, consult the Westlaw Scope Screens for each database.

LR49–PR00 Rule 400. TITLE, AUTHORITY, PURPOSE, SCOPE, APPLICATION AND ADDITIONAL RULES

400.1 Title. These rules shall be known as the "Marion Superior Court Probate Rules" ("Rules") and may be cited as "MSCPR" followed by the Rule number.

400.2 Authority. These Rules are adopted pursuant to the authority granted by I.C. 29–1–1–7 and are intended to supplement the provisions of the Indiana Probate Code and the Indiana Trust Code.

400.3 Purpose. The purpose of these Rules and the MSCPR forms referenced herein is to facilitate the timely, orderly and uniform resolution of probate matters by providing guidance as well as emphasizing certain applicable Indiana statutory requirements.

400.4 Scope. These Rules shall be considered as standing Orders of the Marion Superior Court, Probate Division ("Court") applicable in all probate matters filed in the Marion Circuit and Superior Courts, and compliance is required without further written Order of the Court.

400.5 Application of Rules of Procedure. As supplemented by these Rules and except as otherwise provided in the Probate Code or other applicable rule of law, the Indiana Rules of Trial Procedure shall apply to trial procedures in any probate matter.

400.6 Application of Local Rules. These Rules are in addition to and are not intended to replace the Marion Circuit and Superior Court Civil Rules, which rules shall apply to probate proceedings. In the event of a conflict in a probate matter, the Marion Superior Court Probate Rules shall apply.

400.7 Adoption of Additional Rules. If in any proceeding before the Court, a situation arises which is not provided for by these Rules or by any statute or rule of procedure, the Court may formulate and declare a rule of procedure for that particular case.

400.8   Effect of Amendments to Statutes. If an Indiana statute applicable to decedents' estates, guardianships, protective proceedings, or adoptions is amended or adopted by the Indiana General Assembly after the adoption of these Rules and if that new or amended statute is in conflict with these Rules, these Rules must be treated as amended to the extent necessary to make them consistent with that new or amended statute.

Adopted as County Probate Rule 1, effective Feb. 1, 1995. Renumbered as Superior Court Probate Rule 400, and amended effective Oct. 2, 2006; amended effective Jan. 1, 2012.

LR49–PR00 Rule 401. PLEADINGS AND OR-DERS

401.1   Petition and Application for Appointment of Fiduciary. In addition to the requirements under I.C. §§ 29–1–7–5 and 29–3–5–1, all Petitions for appointment of a personal representative or guardian shall set forth minimally all the provisions in **MSCPR Form 401.1**. Additionally, if a proposed personal representative or proposed guardian (including a proposed co-fiduciary) is a non-resident of Indiana, the Petitioner shall also file an application form (**MSCPR Form 401.1–A or 401.1–B**) for his or her appointment, containing information as to the proposed non-resident fiduciary's qualification to serve as such fiduciary. The application shall include the following information regarding the proposed fiduciary's qualifications to serve:

1.   current residence address if an individual and business address if a corporate fiduciary;

2.   educational background;

3.   the proposed fiduciary's current employment or a statement that he or she is retired or is a homemaker or stay-at-home spouse or partner;

4.   all prior experience in financial management, including investments and checkbook management;

5.   a statement of the proposed fiduciary's prior felony convictions, if any;

6.   a statement that the Petitioner has attained the age of majority and is not incapable of performing the required fiduciary duties by reason of physical or mental illness, impairment, or infirmity.

7.   a statement providing the name, office address, attorney number, telephone number, fax number and email address of the attorney for the proposed fiduciary.

8.   a statement that:

a.   the attorney for the proposed fiduciary has been provided with the proposed fiduciary's Social Security Number and Date of Birth; and,

b.   authorizes the attorney to release the same to the Court in the event of breach of any legal or fiduciary duty.

9.   As required by I.C. 29–1–10–1, if the proposed fiduciary is a nonresident individual or a corporate fiduciary, the petition must also include the following:

a.   a statement that the proposed fiduciary accepts the appointment as fiduciary;

b.   a statement providing the name, address and telephone number of the resident agent appointed by the proposed fiduciary to accept service of process, notices, and other documents in the fiduciary proceeding;

c.   a statement that the Petitioner has agreed to submit personally to the jurisdiction of the Court in any proceeding that relates to the estate of the decedent or protected person.

10.   **MSCPR Form 401.1–A** must be completed and filed with the Court upon the filing of a Petition for appointment of a proposed personal representative or co-personal representative who is a non-resident individual. No substitute form will be accepted by the Court.

11.   **MSCPR Form 401.1–B** must be completed and filed with the Court upon the filing of a Petition for appointment of a proposed guardian or co-guardian who is a non-resident individual. No substitute form will be accepted by the Court.

401.2   Original Will or Affidavit Required. All petitions to probate a Will with administration or to Spread the Will of Record must be accompanied by the original Will. In the event that only a copy of the Will can be located, the copy of the Will and Proof of Lost Will and Affidavit, substantially in accordance with MSCPR Form 401.2, must accompany the petition.

401.3   Petitions Required. All requests for relief or action by the Court shall be made by the appropriate written petition filed with the Court.

401.4   Citation to Authority. All petitions requesting relief or action by the Court should, where applicable, contain reference to the appropriate statute or rule authorizing such relief or action.

401.5   Requirement of Verification. All motions, petitions, inventories and accounts in estates or guardianships shall be notarized or verified with the statement, "I verify under the penalties for perjury that the above statements are true."

401.6   Attorney Contact Information. All pleadings, motions, inventories and accounts in estates and guardianships shall contain the name, attorney number, office address, telephone number, fax number and email address of the attorney for the fiduciary.

401.7   Proposed Orders Required. A moving party shall provide proposed orders for rulings. Proposed Letters Testamentary, Letters of Administration or Letters of Guardianship shall be filed with the Petition for Appointment.

401.8 Self-addressed Envelopes Required. All proposed orders shall be accompanied with self-addressed, stamped envelopes for return, and, if necessary, for distribution to parties or beneficiaries, and creditors.

Adopted as County Probate Rule 2.1, effective Feb. 1, 1995. Renumbered as Superior Court Probate Rule 401, and amended effective Oct. 2, 2006; amended effective Jan. 1, 2012.

LR49–PR00 Rule 402. REPRESENTATION OF FIDUCIARIES BY ATTORNEY

402.1 Representation Required. Every personal representative and guardian of an estate must be represented at all times by an attorney of record.

402.2 Fee Agreement. It is strongly recommended by the Court that a written contract for legal services be entered into by the personal representative or guardian and his or her legal counsel. If a disagreement arises with regard to attorneys' fees, the Court will consider the written contract as evidence of the fee agreement between the parties. All fiduciaries in supervised estates and guardianships should be informed by counsel that fees to the attorney and fiduciary are subject to final court approval prior to payment.

402.3 Supervision and Guidance. An attorney for a fiduciary is required to reasonably supervise and guide the actions of the fiduciary unless and until said attorney is permitted by order of the Court to withdraw from representation of the fiduciary.

402.4 Attorney Notice of Possible Non–Compliance. An attorney for a fiduciary is required to notify the Court in the event the fiduciary is improperly performing his or her fiduciary duties to the protected person, creditors and beneficiaries of the estate. The notice and required proposed Order shall be substantially in accordance with the form of **MSCPR Form 402.4.** By the required signing of the Court's Instructions as provided in MSCPR 412, the fiduciary shall be deemed to have given his or her informed consent to waive the attorney-client privilege as to the filing of the notice and no other Order of the Court regarding such waiver shall be required or issued by the Court. Upon receipt of the notice, the Court will set the matter for hearing and require the fiduciary to personally appear and account to the Court for all actions taken or not taken by the fiduciary. At the hearing, the attorney shall not be required to testify as to the actions of the fiduciary unless the attorney believes that the fiduciary has committed perjury. In the occurrence of such event, the Court deems that Rule 1.6 (b) of the Indiana Rules of Professional Conduct requires the attorney to testify as the Court directs.

402.5 Fiduciary Notice of Possible Non–Compliance. A fiduciary is required to notify the Court in writing in the event the attorney for the fiduciary is not timely performing or improperly performing his or her duties to reasonably supervise and guide the actions of the fiduciary. Upon receipt of the notice, the Court will set the matter for hearing and require the attorney for the fiduciary to personally appear and account to the Court for all actions taken or not taken by the attorney. The Court reserves the right to require the attorney to undertake certain actions and to take the performance of the attorney on behalf of the estate into consideration in ruling upon any request by the attorney for fees and expenses.

402.6 Liability Unaltered. Nothing stated in these Rules shall be considered as altering the liability imposed on the personal representative by I.C. 29–1–16–1.

Adopted as County Probate Rule 2.2, effective Feb. 1, 1995. Renumbered as Superior Court Probate Rule 402, and amended effective Oct. 2, 2006; amended effective Jan. 1, 2012.

LR49–PR00 Rule 403. ATTENDANCE OF PROPOSED FIDUCIARIES

403.1 Except as otherwise permitted under MSCPR 403.2, all proposed personal representatives and guardians shall appear before the Court to qualify.

403.2 In extraordinary circumstances, and provided that the Petition for appointment of a non-Indiana resident as personal representative or guardian is accompanied by an application containing all the information required by paragraphs 10 or 11 of MSCPR 401.1, the Court, in its sole discretion, may waive the requirement in the preceding MSCPR 403.1 if the non-Indiana resident who is the proposed fiduciary is temporarily unable to appear in person when the Petition is filed, and if counsel for the Petitioner personally appears before the Court on behalf of the proposed fiduciary.

Adopted as County Probate Rule 3, effective Feb. 1, 1995. Renumbered as Superior Court Probate Rule 403, and amended effective Oct. 2, 2006; amended effective Jan. 1, 2012.

LR49–PR00 Rule 404. CHANGE IN ADDRESS OR INFORMATION

A personal representative or guardian who changes address shall immediately advise the Court and his or her counsel of the new address. A personal representative or guardian is under a continuing order of the Court to personally advise the Court and the attorney of record in writing as to any change in the information provided in compliance with MSCPR 401.

Adopted as County Probate Rule 4, effective Feb. 1, 1995. Renumbered as Superior Court Probate Rule 404, and amended effective Oct. 2, 2006; amended effective Jan. 1, 2012.

LR49–PR00 Rule 405. NOTICE

405.1 Whenever notice of any hearing or trial is given, it is the responsibility of the moving party to submit proof of service.

405.2 Copies of the subject motion or petition must be served with all notices of hearing.

405.3 Whenever any estate or guardianship account (including a final account in a supervised estate) is set for hearing, copies of the account must be served with notice of hearing.

Adopted as County Probate Rule 5, effective Feb. 1, 1995. Renumbered as Superior Court Probate Rule 405, and amended effective Oct. 2, 2006; amended effective Jan. 1, 2012.

LR49–PR00 Rule 406. UNSUPERVISED ADMINISTRATION OF DECEDENTS' ESTATES

406.1 Statutory Requirements. A Petition for administration of a decedent's estate without court supervision, filed in compliance with MSCPR 401 and accompanied (where applicable) by an Application under paragraphs 10 or 11 of MSCPR 401.1, may be granted if the requirements of I.C. §§ 29–1–7.5–2(a) or 29–1–7.5–2(b) are satisfied. Once a petition for administration without court supervision has been granted pursuant to such statute, a personal representative's authority shall not be subject to any requirement of Court approval or confirmation or be open to collateral attack on account of any defect or irregularity in the proceedings resulting in issuance of the order of no supervision.

406.2 Supervised Estate Required—Minor Children. Notwithstanding a provision in a Will specifically authorizing unsupervised administration, if there are minor distributees, the Court may order supervised administration or in the alternative may appoint a guardian *ad litem* to represent the interests of the minor distributees.

406.3 Instructions to Personal Representatives. *See* MSCPR 412.3.

406.4 Surety Bond. *See* MSCPR 407.1.

406.5 Inventory. In all unsupervised estates, the personal representative shall, within two (2) months of appointment either:

A. file an inventory conforming with the requirements of I.C. § 29–1–7.5–3.2 (b) and forthwith serve a copy of the inventory on all known heirs, beneficiaries or distributees, or,

B. file a verified certification that an inventory conforming with the requirements of I.C. § 29–1–7.5–3.2 has been prepared, that it is available to be furnished to distributees on request and that notice of preparation of the inventory and its availability has been forthwith served on all known heirs, beneficiaries or distributees.

406.6 Orders and Matters Considered in Unsupervised Estates. In the administration of an unsupervised estate, the Court's involvement shall in most cases be limited to the opening and closing of the estate and the determination of Indiana inheritance tax due. Unless revocation of unsupervised administration occurs pursuant to the provisions of MSCPR 406.8, invocation of the Court's jurisdiction on any other matter presented for its determination shall not convert the estate to supervised administration.

406.7 Orders and Sales of Property. In unsupervised estates, the Court will not issue an order approving closing statements or an order discharging the fiduciary. The sale of personal property or real estate in unsupervised estate administration may be accomplished without approval of the Court.

406.8 Revocation of Unsupervised Administration. Pursuant to I.C. § 29–1–7.5–2 (d), the Court may, on its own motion or the motion of an interested person, revoke an order of unsupervised administration and require an administration on terms and conditions which the Court specifies, if the Court finds that such a revocation is in the best interests of the estate, creditors, taxing authorities, heirs, legatees, or devisees. If the estate is converted to a supervised estate, the unsupervised cause number originally assigned to the estate shall remain the same.

406.10 [1] Time for Closing. *See* MSCPR 415.4.

406.11 Costs and Claims Paid. All Court costs shall be paid and all claims satisfied and released on or before the date of the filing of the closing statement.

406.12 Insolvent Estates. An insolvent unsupervised estate may be closed as an unsupervised estate or may, upon the petition of the personal representative or any interested person, be converted to a supervised estate and closed as such.

Adopted as County Probate Rule 6, effective Feb. 1, 1995. Renumbered as Superior Court Probate Rule 406, and amended effective Oct. 2, 2006; amended effective Jan. 1, 2012.

[1] 406.9 omitted in original.

LR49–PR00 Rule 407. BONDS IN ESTATES AND WILL CONTESTS

407.1 Except as hereinafter provided, in every unsupervised and supervised estate the personal representative shall file a corporate surety bond in an amount determined by the Court to be adequate to protect distributees, creditors and taxing authorities.

407.2 Except as provided in MSCPR 407.7, no surety bond is required where a corporate banking fiduciary qualified by law to serve as such is either the fiduciary or one of several co-fiduciaries.

407.3 No surety bond is required in a solvent estate where the decedent's spouse serves as personal representative and is the sole distributee.

407.4 Where a Will provides that bond be dispensed with, the Court shall nonetheless fix a bond in an amount adequate to protect creditors and taxing authorities.

407.5 Where the personal representative is a distributee, the bond may be reduced by the personal representative's estimated net distributive share, but the Court will fix a bond adequate to protect other distributees (if any), creditors and taxing authorities.

407.6 Where all distributees consent in writing that the personal representative serve without bond, the Court will nonetheless determine whether to require a bond in an amount adequate to protect creditors and taxing authorities.

407.7 As required by I.C. § 29–1–10–1, if the petitioner is a nonresident individual or corporate fiduciary, or if an appointed fiduciary becomes a nonresident of Indiana, the petitioner must file a bond in an amount: (A) not less than: (i) the probable value of the estate's personal property; plus (ii) the estimated rents and profits to be derived from the property in the estate during the probate period; and (B) not greater than the probable gross value of the estate.

407.8 Bond in Will Contests. Upon the initiation of a Will Contest, the plaintiff(s) must file a bond conditioned for the due prosecution of the proceedings and for the payment of all costs if in the proceedings judgment is rendered against the plaintiff. Since in Indiana, "costs" is a term of art with specific legal meaning including only filing fees and statutory witness fees and since I.C. § 33–37–10–3 provides that witness fees are five dollars ($5.00) per day, unless circumstances presented to the Court dictate otherwise, plaintiffs will be required to deposit with the Clerk of the Court the sum of five hundred dollars ($500) as the required bond, or, alternatively, may file a corporate surety bond in the amount of five hundred dollars ($500).

Adopted as County Probate Rule 7, effective Feb. 1, 1995. Renumbered as Superior Court Probate Rule 407, and amended effective Oct. 2, 2006; amended effective Jan. 1, 2012.

LR49–PR00 Rule 408.   INVENTORY IN ESTATES

408.1 In all supervised estates, the personal representative shall file an inventory conforming to the requirements of IC § 29–1–12–1 within two (2) months of appointment and shall forthwith serve a copy of the inventory on all known heirs, beneficiaries or distributees.

408.2 In all unsupervised estates, the personal representative shall comply with MSCPR 406.5.

408.3 Inventory Sealed. Upon application by the personal representative and after a hearing upon notice to interested persons, the Court may, in its sole discretion, order an inventory, or any supplement or amendment to it, to be sealed. If so ordered, it may not be opened without an order of the Court, after notice to the personal representative and an opportunity for hearing. In the event a supplement or an amendment to an inventory is filed, all such subsequent inventories must contain a recapitulation of prior inventories.

Adopted as County Probate Rule 8, effective Feb. 1, 1995. Renumbered as Superior Court Probate Rule 408, and amended effective Oct. 2, 2006; amended effective Jan. 1, 2012.

LR49–PR00 Rule 409.   BONDS IN GUARDIANSHIPS

409.1 Except as otherwise determined by the Court, in every guardianship, the guardian shall post a corporate surety bond in an amount determined by the Court to be adequate to protect the assets of the protected person.

409.2 Subject to the discretion of the Court, the guardian shall not be required to post a surety bond if:

(a) a resident corporate banking fiduciary qualified by law to serve as such is either the fiduciary or one of several co-fiduciaries, or,

(b) the Court determines that the guardianship assets are of such insufficient amount as to not justify the cost of the bond.

409.3 Subject to the discretion of the Court, in lieu of a bond otherwise required by law or by the Court, a Guardian may restrict transfer of all or part of the liquid assets of a Guardianship by placing those assets in a federally-insured financial institution or in a brokerage account (or any combination of the two) with the following restriction placed on the face of each account or document creating or evidencing the account:

NO PRINCIPAL OR INTEREST SHALL BE WITHDRAWN WITHOUT WRITTEN ORDER OF THE MARION SUPERIOR COURT, PROBATE DIVISION.

409.4 At the time the Court authorizes the creation of the account in lieu of a bond, the fiduciary and his or her attorney shall execute the Court's attorney's undertaking making the attorney personally responsible for the deposit of the funds in a restricted account. The attorney's undertaking shall be substantially in accordance with the form of **MSCPR Form 409.4**.

409.5. Within thirty (30) days after an Order authorizing the creation of the account or investment, a certificate by an officer of the institution at which the account or investment has been created shall be filed with the Court which affirms that the account or investment is restricted as required by Court order. The certification shall be substantially in accordance with the form of **MSCPR Form 409.5**.

409.6 The guardian and the financial institution shall both promptly notify the Court in writing in the event that any principal or interest is withdrawn from the account without Court authorization.

Adopted as County Probate Rule 9, effective Feb. 1, 1995. Renumbered as Superior Court Probate Rule 409, and amended effective Oct. 2, 2006; amended effective Jan. 1, 2012.

LR49–PR00 Rule 410. INVENTORY IN GUARD-IANSHIPS

410.1 Inventory. An inventory and appraisement shall be prepared by the guardian and filed with the Court within ninety (90) days after appointment as permanent guardian or within thirty (30) days after appointment of temporary guardian.

410.2 Petitions to Sever Jointly Owned Property. If a guardian seeks under I.C. § 29–3–8–6.5 to sever title to title to property jointly owned by the protected person and another, the guardian shall file a petition with the Court, with notice to all co-owners of the jointly held property interest. The Court may approve any petition under this MSCPR 410.2 without a hearing, and upon a showing by the guardian that the total value of the jointly-titled property to be severed is nominal or is *de minimis* in comparison to the time and cost of a petition or providing notice to all co-owners, the Court may waive the requirements of the preceding sentence regarding an advance petition or notice to co-owners or both.

410.3 Inventory Sealed. Upon application by the guardian and after a hearing upon notice to all interested persons, the Court may, in its sole discretion, order an inventory, or any supplement or amendment to it, to be sealed. If so ordered, it may not be opened without an order of the Court, after notice to the guardian and an opportunity for hearing. In the event a supplement or an amendment to an inventory is filed, all such subsequent inventories must contain a recapitulation of prior inventories.

Adopted as County Probate Rule 10, effective Feb. 1, 1995. Renumbered as Superior Court Probate Rule 410, and amended effective Oct. 2, 2006; amended effective Jan. 1, 2012.

LR49–PR00 Rule 411. ACCOUNTINGS PROCE-DURES AND REPORTS

411.1 Statutory Format for Accountings. In any guardianship or supervised estate, the personal representative or the guardian of the property must file each accounting in the three-schedule format required by I.C. § 29–1–16–4. Informal, handwritten or transactional accountings will not be accepted. Each disbursement (expenditure or distribution) must appear as a separate line item and must include the following information:

(a) Date of the disbursement;

(b) Check number or other identifying number for the method of payment used;

(c) The payee's name;

(d) The amount of the disbursement; and

(e) If the purpose or reason for the disbursement is not apparent from the information presented under (a) through (d), a brief description of the purpose or reason that is sufficient to show that the disbursement was made in the course of the proper administration of the estate or (in a guardianship) was made for the support or benefit of the incapacitated person or minor.

The following example of a disbursement line item contains sufficient detail to comply with this MSCPR 411.1:

01–27–2011 ck 205 Brown and Smith CPAs Decedent's 2011 Form 1040 prep. 800.00

An Indiana inheritance tax exemption affidavit described in I.C. § 6–4.1–4.0.5 is not required to be filed with the Court, but the Court will accept a copy of such an exemption affidavit as a supplement to an estate accounting under this Rule, provided that the filer complies with Administrative Rule 9(G) by redacting the decedent's social security number and any full account numbers from the copy filed.

411.2 Satisfying "Voucher" Requirement. I.C. § 29–1–16–4 requires a fiduciary to file "receipts for disbursements of assets," or "vouchers," and authorizes the Court to permit other methods of substantiating the amounts and purposes of disbursements. Only a corporate fiduciary (bank or trust company) may submit an affidavit confirming that all disbursements have been made as reported in the accounting, instead of filing receipts or vouchers. In order to satisfy the receipt or voucher requirement, a fiduciary who is an individual must file, with each accounting, one of the following types of proof for each disbursement reported in that accounting:

(a) A copy of the front of a canceled (paid) check;

(b) A digital image of the check as paid by the financial institution holding the estate's account, reproduced from the institution's records or from a periodic account statement;

(c) For distributions, a receipt signed by the distributee, confirming the payee's identity and the amount and approximate date of the distribution;

(d) For disbursements (other than distributions) to third-party creditors or providers of goods and services, a receipt signed by the payee or its authorized agent, bearing the payee's name and business address, and stating the amount, the purpose, and the date of the disbursement;

(e) For electronic fund transfers, wire transfers, or debit card transactions, a copy of the digital or paper record confirming the payee's identity and the date and amount of the disbursement; or

(f) In the court's discretion, other satisfactory proof showing the identity of the payee and the date and amount of the disbursement.

Documents described in (a), (b), (c), or (e) are prima facie evidence of payment.

411.3 Reimbursements to the Personal Representative. If the personal representative of a supervised or unsupervised estate uses his or her personal funds to pay funeral and burial or cremation expenses or administration expenses after the decedent's death, then without the approval of the Court or the advance consent of the distributees, that personal representative may reimburse himself or herself with estate funds for:

(a) Funeral, burial or cremation expenses paid by the personal representative out of personal funds and reimbursed out of estate funds within the statutory period under I.C. § 29-1-14-1(a) for filing creditor claims, and

(b) Administration expenses paid by the personal representative out of personal funds and reimbursed out of estate funds at any time before administration is concluded,

provided that the personal representative fully and accurately document the payment of and reimbursement for each such expenditure in the accounting filed or issued under I.C. 29-1-16 or 29-1-7.5-4(a)(6). All reimbursements permitted under the preceding sentence remain subject to objection by distributees and other persons whose interests are affected and subject to the approval or disapproval of the Court. This MSCPR 411.3 does not apply to claims by the personal representative against the decedent that arose before the decedent's death, and which are governed by I.C. §§ 29-1-14-2 and 29-1-14-17 and MSCPR 414.3.

411.4 Disbursements to the Guardian. In guardianships and without the advance approval of the Court, the guardian may reimburse himself or herself out of guardianship for all reasonable expenditures made from the guardian's personal funds for the benefit of the minor or protected person or for the preservation of guardianship property, *provided* that the guardian fully and accurately documents the original payment of and the reimbursement for each such expenditure in the guardian's next accounting. All reimbursements permitted under this MSCPR 411.4 remain subject to the later approval or disapproval of the Court.

411.5 Accountings in Guardianships. Within thirty (30) days after the second anniversary of his or her appointment as guardian of the property of a minor or incapacitated adult, and every two years thereafter, the guardian must file with the Court a verified accounting that complies with MSCPR 411.1 and 411.2, except that a guardian need not file bank account statements as support for an accounting other than a final accounting unless ordered to do so by the Court. Nothing in these Rules or in the guardianship statutes prohibits a guardian of the property from filing and seeking approval of accountings and allowances of guardian compensation and attorney fees on an annual basis, or at a time other than an anniversary date because of some change in the health, needs, or circumstances of the minor or incapacitated adult.

411.6 Public or Pension Benefits. If a guardian receives Social Security benefits, public benefits (such as food stamps, SSI, etc.), pension distributions, or annuity or IRA distributions on behalf of the incapacitated person or minor, the guardian must account fully for each such benefit or distribution so received, unless (a) the Court determines that the incapacitated person's incapacity is limited enough to permit him or her to live with some independence and less supervision (consistent with I.C. § 29-3-8-3(4)) and to have direct access to some funds from Social Security, public benefits, other distributions, or wages from supervised employment, or (b) the Court has previously granted approval to allow such benefits or distributions to be paid to a residential or health care facility that has physical custody of the minor or incapacitated person.

411.7 After Acquired Assets. Unless an amended inventory is filed, estate or guardianship assets acquired or discovered after the filing of the inventory or most recent previous accounting must be identified by the following information in the next accounting filed, as to each new item of income or principal: (a) a description of the property; (b) the amount received or the value of the property; (c) the approximate date of receipt; and (d) if the property received is classifiable as income, identification of the asset (e.g., shares of stock or a specific mutual fund) that was the source of the income.

411.8 Sales or Changes in Asset Value. If a sale, exchange, redemption, change in investment, or increase or loss in market value (capital change) occurs with respect to a guardianship or estate asset, the fiduciary must include the following information in the accounting: (a) the description of the asset sold, redeemed, exchanged, or lost, or with respect to which the market value changed; (b) the last value previously reported for the asset in the inventory or previous accounting; (c) the amount of gain, loss, or change of value; and (d) if a sale, exchange or redemption occurred, the date of the transaction and a description of the sales proceeds or other property received in the transaction. The fiduciary may report all such capital changes in a separate section of the accounting.

411.9 After Accrued Expenses. Expenses accrued after the filing of the inventory or most recent accounting shall be accounted for in an amended inventory or the next accounting pursuant to MSCPR 411.1.

411.10 Property at the End of an Accounting Period. When a personal representative or guardian files an accounting under MSCPR 411.1 or MSCPR 411.5, he or she must include, in the last schedule of the accounting, the following information with respect to the money or property that is on hand in the estate or the guardianship estate as of the ending date of the accounting period: (a) a description of each asset or investment, such as the name and partial account number of each account held with a financial institution, securities broker, or mutual fund; (b) the value or closing balance of each such asset or investment as of the ending date (market values as of the last statement date are sufficient for publicly-traded investments); and (c) for real property or tangible personal property, the cost basis or inventory value of such property, as most recently revised (if at all) in a schedule of capital changes under MSCPR 411.9. With each accounting, the personal representative or guardian must file copies of pages from bank account statements, brokerage or mutual fund statements, etc. for the months in which the beginning and ending dates of the accounting period fall, in order to confirm that the beginning and ending asset balances for the estate or guardianship estate agree with the opening and closing total mounts shown in the accounting.

411.11   Sale or Transfer of Real Property

A. *Documentation of Value.* In all supervised estates and guardianships in which real property is to be sold, a written appraisal or market analysis by a qualified real estate professional shall be filed with the Petition for Sale, unless such document was previously filed with the Inventory. Such written appraisal or market analysis shall include the following information: (a) a brief description of the property interest being appraised or valued, including the full legal description thereof; (b) purpose or objective of the appraisal or valuation; (c) date for which Fair Market Value is determined; (d) if valuation is established through the comparable method of valuation, identification of the comparable sales used to value the subject property as well as identification of all adjustments made to the comparable sale to determine the fair market value of the subject property; (e) if valuation is established through another method of valuation, all data and reasoning that supports the Fair Market Value; (f) the Fair Market Value determined; (g) a statement of assumption and special or limiting conditions; (h) the qualification and background of the real estate professional; (i) certification of disinterest in the real property; (j) signature of the real estate professional.

B. *Limitations Period for Valuation.* The appraisal or market analysis shall be made within one (1) year of the date of the Petition for Sale.

C. *Deeds.* The Court does not approve the form of deeds for the sale of real property in an estate or guardianship.

D. *Will Contains Specific Power to Sell.* If the decedent's probated Will expressly gives the personal representative the specific power to sell "property of the estate" or "real property" "without order of court," "without court approval or supervision," or in words with substantially the same effect, the personal representative of a supervised estate

need not comply with the petition and appraisal or valuation requirements of this MSCPR 411.11.

411.12   Sale of Personal Property.

A. *Documentation of Value.* In all supervised estates and guardianships in which personal property is to be sold, a written basis for valuation shall be filed with the Court with the Petition for Sale, unless such document was previously filed with the Inventory. The written basis for valuation shall include the following information: (a) brief description of the property to be sold; (b) the date and basis of valuation; (c) the qualifications of the person providing the valuation or the authoritative nature of the source from which the valuation was obtained, including authoritative sources accessed by electronic media; (d) factors which would affect the value of the subject property.

B. *Limitations Period for Valuation.* Written basis for valuation shall be made within one (1) year of the date of the Petition for Sale.

C. *Written Valuation Not Required.* No written appraisal shall be required for the sale of assets which are traded in a market and the value of which is readily ascertainable. Such assets include, but are not limited to, stocks, bonds, mutual funds, commodities, precious metals and items sold at public auction. In addition, upon a showing that non-publicly-traded personal property has a value that is small in comparison to the cost of obtaining a written appraisal, the Court may waive the appraisal requirement under this MSCPR 411.2.

D. *Will Contains Specific Power to Sell.* If the decedent's probated Will expressly gives the personal representative the specific power to sell "property of the estate" or "personal property" "without order of court," "without court approval or supervision," or in words with substantially the same effect, the personal representative of a supervised estate need not comply with the petition and appraisal or valuation requirements of this MSCPR 411.12.

411.13   Guardian's Current Reports. Current reports filed by a guardian of the person shall state the present residence of the incapacitated person and a statement of the incapacitated person's current condition and general welfare. If the incapacitated person is an adult, a report of a treating physician shall be filed with the current report verifying that the incapacity of the person remains unchanged since the date the guardianship was established or the date of the last current report.

411.14   Guardian's Bond. If a Guardian's bond is required, the guardian shall submit to the Court proof of payment of current premiums due on said bond. Failure to comply with this section may result in removal of the guardian.

411.15   Transfer Tax Closing Letters. When a Final Report (Closing Statement) is filed in an unsupervised estate or when a Supplemental Report of Distribution is filed in a supervised estate, the personal representative must attach copies of the following documents to the Court's original copy of the Report:

(a) The federal estate tax closing letter, if any;

(b) The Indiana inheritance tax closing letter (unless the Report recites that an inheritance tax exemption affidavit has been filed or recorded under I.C. § 6–4.1–4–0.5); and

(c) The Treasurer's official receipt showing full payment of the Indiana inheritance tax and estate tax (if any) that was due.

The personal representative must block out the decedent's social security number on the copies that are attached to or filed with the Report under this MSCPR 411.5. The personal representative may (but is not required to) file the copies of any or all of the documents described in (a), (b), and (c) on light green paper, consistent with Admin. Rule 9(G) and Trial Rule 5(G).

411.16 Petitions to Determine No Inheritance Tax Due. In a petition under I.C. § 6–4.1–5–7 to request an order determining that no Indiana inheritance tax is due, the personal representative or trustee who files the petition must state sufficient information to show that no transferee (distributee or beneficiary) has received or will receive assets with a total value exceeding his or her inheritance tax exemption. Such required information includes but is not limited to a statement of the total value of the decedent's property transfers that would be reported on an inheritance tax return if one were filed. A copy of an inheritance tax exemption affidavit described in I.C. § 6–4.1–4–0.5 may be filed with the Court, provided that the decedent's social security number is redacted from the affidavit, and the filer of a petition under I.C. § 6–4.1–5–7 may cite and rely on that filed affidavit. If the petition (and any attached or accompanying documents) contain information sufficient to show that no inheritance tax is or will be due, then in the absence of any objection by interested persons, the Court will enter an order under I.C. § 6–4.1–5–8 without holding a hearing.

Adopted as County Probate Rule 11, effective Feb. 1, 1995. Renumbered as Superior Court Probate Rule 411, and amended effective Oct. 2, 2006; amended effective Jan. 1, 2012.

LR49–PR00 Rule 412. INSTRUCTIONS TO FIDUCIARIES

412.1 Instructions to Guardians. The Court's Instructions to the guardian, executed by the guardian and his or her attorney, must be filed with the Court prior to Court appointment and the issuance of letters. These Instructions are to be considered as direct Orders of the Court. Instructions to Guardian **MSCPR Form 412.0** (when the guardianship will be of the person only) or **MSCPR Form 412.1** (when the guardianship will apply to the minor's or incapacitated

adult's property) must be completed and filed with the Court. No substitute form will be accepted by the Court.

412.2 Instructions to Personal Representatives of Supervised Estates. The Court's Instructions to the personal representative of a supervised estate, executed by the personal representative and his or her attorney, must be filed with the Court prior to Court appointment and the issuance of letters. These Instructions are to be considered as direct Orders of the Court. Instructions to Personal Representatives of Supervised Estates **MSCPR Form 412.2** must be completed and filed with the Court. No substitute form will be accepted by the Court.

412.3 Instructions to Personal Representatives of Unsupervised Estates. The Court's Instructions to the personal representative of an unsupervised estate, executed by the personal representative and his or her attorney, must be filed with the Court prior to Court appointment and the issuance of letters. These Instructions are to be considered as direct Orders of the Court. Instructions to Personal Representatives of Supervised Estates **MSCPR Form 412.3** must be completed and filed with the Court. No substitute form will be accepted by the Court.

Adopted as County Probate Rule 12, effective Feb. 1, 1995. Renumbered as Superior Court Probate Rule 412, and amended effective Oct. 2, 2006; Jan. 1, 2008; Jan. 1, 2012.

LR49–PR00 Rule 413. GUARDIANSHIPS

413.1 Petitions Not Accepted. No Petition for Guardianship over the person of a minor will be accepted by the Court if:

1. There is a current custody order in effect resulting from a dissolution decree;

2. There is a current custody order in effect resulting from any paternity proceeding;

3. There is a current custody order in effect resulting from a custody proceeding filed by a non-parent;

4. There are dissolution of marriage or paternity or non-parent custody proceedings currently pending; or

5. The child is involved in an open Child in Need of Services proceeding under IC 31–34.

With respect to any of the situations described above, Petitions for guardianship of the estate (property) of a minor will continue to be accepted.

413.2 Presence of Incapacitated Person. In all guardianship or protective proceedings seeking to declare an adult incapacitated, either the person alleged to be incapacitated shall be present at the hearing, or the petitioner shall present sufficient medical evidence to establish that a court appearance would result in injury to the person's health or safety. An opinion that the person would have difficulty in understanding the procedure or might say something inappropriate is not sufficient reason alone for absence.

413.3 Physician's Report. In all guardianship proceedings seeking to declare an adult incapacitated, a Physician's Report by the doctor treating the alleged incapacitated person, or such additional evidence as the Court may require, shall be presented to the Court at the time the petition is filed or on the date of the hearing. The Physician's Report shall substantially comply with **MSCPR Form 413.3**. No determination will be made without a supporting medical report or testimony at hearing. In the event the guardianship proceeding is contested, the Physician's Report shall be considered as hearsay unless the parties stipulate to its admissibility.

413.4 Notice. Consistent with I.C. § 29–3–3–4(a) and (b), no guardian of an adult shall be appointed or protective order entered without notice to the alleged incapacitated person or to his duly appointed attorney-in-fact (if known), except upon verified allegations that delay may result in immediate and irreparable injury to the alleged incapacitated person or loss or damage to property. The petitioner shall certify to the Court in writing the efforts, if any, that have been made to give notice and the reasons supporting the petitioner's claim that advance notice should not be required.

413.5 Appointment of Guardian *Ad Litem* or Attorney. The Court may in its discretion determine that the alleged incapacitated person should have a guardian *ad litem* or attorney appointed to represent his or her interests, and the hearing for appointment of a guardian for the alleged incapacitated person may be continued by the Court for that purpose. A guardian *ad litem* will be paid reasonable compensation, considering the needs of the alleged incompetent person, the nature and relative difficulty of the services provided, local custom, the availability or limitations of resources of the alleged incompetent person's estate, and, in the discretion of the Court, any other considerations deemed relevant under the circumstances of the case.

413.6 Petition for Guardianship of A Minor. In every petition for the appointment of a guardian of the person of a minor child, in addition to the statements required by I.C. § 29–3–5–1(a) and MSCPR 401.1, the following information shall also be contained in the petition:

1. The present address of the child.

2. The places where the child has resided during the past two years, and the names and present addresses of the persons with whom the child has lived during that period. If such information is not available, the petition should state the reason for such unavailability.

3. Whether, to petitioner's knowledge, any other litigation is pending in this state or in any other state concerning the custody of the child.

4. Whether, to petitioner's knowledge, any person not a party to the guardianship proceeding has physical custody of the child or claims to have custody or visitation rights with respect to the child.

The Court may, in its discretion, initiate such further investigation, and obtain a report by the Indiana Department of Child Services, pursuant to I.C. § 29–3–9–11.

413.7 Hearings. Hearing shall be held by the Court on any petition seeking guardianship over an adult alleged to be an incapacitated person. The court reserves the right to require and to hold a hearing on any petition seeking a guardianship over a child's person or property, but the Court may waive the necessity for a hearing based on all the material facts and circumstances, including but not limited to a showing that all interested persons entitled to notice under I.C. § 29–3–6–1 have given written waivers notice of a hearing or the necessity for a hearing.

413.8 Restricted Accounts.

1. In guardianships over the estate of a minor, unless otherwise authorized by the Court, funds shall be placed in a restricted account designating that no principal or interest may be withdrawn without written order of the Court.

2. Prior to the issuance of letters in a guardianship over a minor's estate or the compromise of a minor's claim, the guardian and attorney shall execute the Court's attorney's undertaking making the attorney personally responsible for the deposit of the funds in a restricted account. The attorney's undertaking in a guardianship shall be substantially in accordance with the form of **MSCPR Form 409.4**. With respect to compromise of a minor's claim, *see* MSCPR 418.6 and **MSCPR Form 418.6(A)**.

3. Within thirty (30) days after the Order authorizing the creation of the account, a certification by a financial institution that a properly restricted account has been created in accordance with this MSCPR 413.8 shall be filed. The certification shall be substantially in accordance with the form of **MSCPR Form 409.5**.

4. The guardian and the financial institution shall both promptly notify the Court in writing in the event that any principal or interest is withdrawn from the account without Court authorization.

413.9 Power of Attorney. An appointment of a guardian over an estate shall not operate to terminate a power of attorney, unless the power of attorney instrument provides for termination upon the incapacity of the principal. A guardian shall not have power over property or health decisions that are subject to a valid power of attorney, and cannot revoke or amend a power of attorney on behalf of a principal. A guardian seeking to revoke a valid power of attorney must obtain Court approval which can be granted only after hearing and notice to the attorney in fact.

413.10 Rules of the Veteran's Administration. Nothing contained in these rules shall amend or supersede the Probate Rules and Regulations promulgated by the Veteran's Administration of the United States, and every guardian appointed by the Court or the attorney for such guardian shall comply with those Rules and Regulations, if applicable.

Adopted as County Probate Rule 13, effective Feb. 1, 1995. Renumbered as Superior Court Probate Rule 413, and amended effective Oct. 2, 2006; amended effective Jan. 1, 2012.

LR49–PR00 Rule 414. CLAIMS AGAINST ESTATES

414.1 Except as hereinafter supplemented, all claims filed against an estate shall comply with and be governed by the provisions of I.C. 29–1–14.

414.2 If a claim is disallowed or neither allowed or disallowed by the personal representative within three (3) months and fifteen (15) days after the date of first published notice to creditors, the claimant shall pay to the Clerk of the Court the fee for filing a new cause of action and the claim will be assigned a new cause number in the Court and tried pursuant to the Indiana Rules of Trial Procedure. Failure of the claimant to pay the filing fee subjects the claim to dismissal pursuant to T.R. 41. Marion County Local Probate Rules Amended Effective January 1, 2012 April 1, 2011 Page 19 of 23

414.3 Personal Representative Claim. Pursuant to I.C. § 29–1–14–17, if a personal representative files a claim against the estate which the personal representative represents accrued before the death of the decedent, with the affidavit of the claimant attached, the claim shall not be acted upon by the personal representative unless all interested persons who would be affected by the allowance of the claim consent in writing to it. If the personal representative determines, either before or after filing the claim, that all interested persons do not consent to the allowance and payment of the claim, the personal representative shall promptly report that fact to the Court and shall ask the Court to appoint a special personal representative, who shall then represent the estate with respect to that claim. Failure to comply with this MSCPR 414.3 shall be grounds for automatic dismissal of the claim with prejudice.

Adopted as County Probate Rule 14, effective Feb. 1, 1995. Renumbered as Superior Court Probate Rule 414, and amended effective Oct. 2, 2006; amended effective Jan. 1, 2012.

LR49–PR00 Rule 415. TIME FOR CLOSING ESTATES

415.1 Personal representatives shall comply with I.C. § 29–1–16–2, which provides as follows: "Every personal representative shall close the estate as promptly as possible. Unless for good cause shown, the time for filing the final account in the estate shall not exceed one (1) year from the appointment of a personal representative."

415.2 Good cause for not closing a supervised estate within one (1) year may be shown by filing an intermediate account within thirty (30) days after the expiration of one (1) year. Such accounting shall comply with the provision of I.C. §§ 29–1–16–4 and I.C. 29–1–16–6.

415.3 The intermediate account shall be accompanied by the personal representative's Petition for Extension of Time which shall include the following: (a) a statement of facts showing why the estate cannot be closed; (b) estimated date of closing; (c) a proposal for partial distribution of the estate to the extent that partial distribution can be made without prejudice to distributees and claimants.

415.4 A closing statement shall be filed within one (1) year after opening an unsupervised estate. In the event the estate cannot be closed within that time period, the personal representative shall file a Petition for Extension of Time which shall include the following: (a) a statement of facts showing why the estate cannot be closed; (b) estimated date of closing; (c) a proposal for partial distribution of the estate to the extent that partial distribution can be made without prejudice to distributees and claimants.

415.5 Failure to close within one (1) year or show cause why estate cannot be closed may be grounds for removal of the personal representative, pursuant to I.C. § 29–1–10–6, and for reduction or forfeiture of personal representative fees and attorney fees.

Adopted as County Probate Rule 15, effective Feb. 1, 1995. Renumbered as Superior Court Probate Rule 415, and amended effective Oct. 2, 2006; amended effective Jan. 1, 2012.

LR49–PR00 Rule 416. WRONGFUL DEATH ESTATES

416.1 All proposed wrongful death settlements must be approved by the Court, whether the estate is supervised, unsupervised, or a special administration for the sole purpose of prosecuting the wrongful death claim.

416.2 When an estate remains open one (1) year, the personal representative shall file a Petition for Extension of Time which shall include the following: (a) a statement of facts showing why the estate cannot be closed; (b) estimated date of closing; (c) if an action is pending, the cause number and the court.

416.3 When a judgment has been paid or a petition for approval of settlement is filed in any estate, a petition shall be filed showing proposed distribution, in accordance with I.C. §§ 34–23–1–1, 34–23–1–2 and 34–23–2–1. Such petition must set out the proposed distribution to the appropriate statutory damage distributees, such as:

1. Expenses of administration;

2. Providers of funeral and burial expenses;

3. Providers of medical expenses in connection with last illness of decedent;

4. Surviving spouse;

5. Dependent children;

6. Dependent next of kin (if there is no surviving spouse or dependent children).

A proposed order shall be presented to the Court, ordering distribution in accordance with the above cited statutory provisions and requiring that a final account as to the wrongful death proceeds be filed within thirty (30) days.

Adopted as County Probate Rule 16, effective Feb. 1, 1995. Renumbered as Superior Court Probate Rule 416, and amended effective Oct. 2, 2006; amended effective Jan. 1, 2012.

LR49–PR00 Rule 417. ADOPTIONS

417.1 Final Hearings. Except for good cause shown, no final hearings in adoption proceedings shall take place until the adopting couple (including birth parent and adopting stepparent, cohabitating couples, and same sex couples) has been married or cohabitated for at least one (1) year.

Adopted effective Jan. 1, 2012.

LR49–PR00 Rule 418. MINOR'S SETTLEMENTS

418.1 Guardian Ad Litem. In accordance with the Indiana Code, a guardian *ad litem* may be appointed to protect the best interest of the minor and investigate the proposed settlement.

418.2 Evidentiary Hearing. The Court will hold a hearing on a proposed settlement of a minor's claim if a hearing is requested by the petitioner, by the guardian ad litem (if any), or by any other interested person, and the Court may schedule and hold an evidentiary hearing on its own motion after receiving and reviewing the Petition and the terms of the proposed settlement, in order to satisfy the Court that the requested settlement fully protects the minor's rights and interests. Unless the preceding sentence applies, the Court will normally consider and rule upon proposed minor's settlements in chambers and without an evidentiary hearing.

418.3 Minor's Consent to Settlement. If the minor is at least fourteen (14) years of age, the proposed settlement shall be accompanied by a written consent to settlement by the minor.

418.4 Attendance at Hearings. If an evidentiary hearing is ordered under MSCPR 418.2, the following persons must be present at the hearing: (a) the custodial parent or the guardian; (b) a minor who is at least the age of fourteen (14) years; and (c) at the discretion of the Court, minors younger than fourteen (14) years of age. Further, unless a written waiver and consent is provided to the Court, a non-custodial parent of the minor has the right to attend the hearing and must be provided with notice of the hearing.

418.5 Limited Settlements or Administration.

1. If the funds originating from a minor's settlement are less than the amount requiring establishment of guardianship under the Indiana Code or if a guardian of a minor's estate is appointed for the limited purpose of administration of the minor's settlement, the Court will accept the deposit of the minor's settlement in a restricted account at a federally insured financial institution or in another Court-approved investment in lieu of any other requirement for inventory and accounting, subject to affirmation in each biennial accounting that the funds remain on deposit.

2. The sole beneficiary named on the account so created must be "The Guardianship (or Guardianship Estate) of _____" [name of minor].

3. Any such restricted account must provide that no principal or interest may be withdrawn from the account without a written order of the Court, and with the following restriction placed on the face of the account or in the investment document:

NO PRINCIPAL OR INTEREST SHALL BE WITHDRAWN WITHOUT WRITTEN ORDER OF THE MARION SUPERIOR COURT, PROBATE DIVISION

418.6 Attorney's Undertaking and Certification.

1. At the time the settlement is approved by the Court, the fiduciary and his or her attorney shall execute the Court's attorney's undertaking making the attorney personally responsible for the deposit of the funds in a restricted account. The attorney's undertaking shall be substantially in accordance with the form of **MSCPR Form 418.6 (A)**.

2. Within thirty (30) days after an Order authorizing the creation of the account or investment, a certificate by an officer of the institution at which the account or investment has been created shall be filed with the Court which affirms that the account or investment is restricted as required by Court order and is in compliance with this MSCPR 418.6. The certification shall be substantially in accordance with the form of **MSCPR Form 418.6 (B)**.

3. The fiduciary and the financial institution shall both promptly notify the Court in writing in the event that any principal or interest is withdrawn from the account without Court authorization.

418.7 Application of Guardianship Law. Minors' settlements shall otherwise be subject to the requirements for guardianship, including the filing of inventory and accounting in guardianships.

418.8 Attorney Fees. Attorney fees for representing a minor in settlement of a claim for personal injuries are subject to Court approval. If the entire attorney fee is to be paid at the same time a structured settlement is approved, the amount of the fee must be based on the present value of the settlement.

Adopted effective Jan. 1, 2012.

LR49–PR00 Rule 419. TRUSTS

419.1 A Petition to Docket Trust shall be forthwith served upon the current Trustee of the trust, and the Petitioner shall certify that such service has been made.

419.2 All challenges to a trust shall be filed in the cause in which the trust is docketed.

419.3 No later than fifteen (15) days after receipt of the Petition to Docket Trust, the Trustee shall file with the Court written notice of the name and address of each beneficiary of the trust known to the Trustee and shall serve the Petitioner with the notice at that same time.

419.4 All additional pleadings and any notice of hearing shall be served upon all beneficiaries of the trust, whether the nature of the interest is present, future, vested, or contingent, unless such beneficiaries have signed in advance a proper written waiver of service waiver of hearing notice or a consent to the relief requested.

Adopted effective Jan. 1, 2012.

LR49–PR00 Rule 420. FEES IN SUPERVISED ESTATES AND GUARDIANSHIPS

420.1 No fees for personal representatives, guardians or attorneys shall be paid from the assets of any guardianship or supervised estate without prior written order of the Court. In guardianships and supervised estates, fees deposited with an attorney as advancement against future fees, sometimes known as a retainer, are not to be paid from the estate of the protected person or deceased person without prior Court approval.

420.2 Fees shall be in the amount determined by the Court to be reasonable, irrespective of whether a fee agreement requires payment from estate assets of fees in excess of that amount.

420.3 A petition for fees must be signed or approved in writing by the personal representative or guardian.

420.4 Partial fees in a supervised estate may be requested when:

    1. An intermediate accounting has been approved, or

    2. The Court finds upon petition that a tax advantage will result from payment of partial fees.

420.5 In all other cases, payment of fees in supervised estates shall be authorized as follows:

    1. One-half upon the filing of an inheritance tax return or upon a Court determination of no taxes due: and

    2. The remaining one-half upon approval of the final account.

420.6 A guardian or guardian's attorney may petition for fees at the time of filing an inventory. Other than as provided hereafter, no further petition for fees may be filed until a biennial, annual, or final accounting has been filed. When unusual circumstances require substantial work in a guardianship, the Court may award fees prior to the approval of an account.

420.7 All petitions for fees for personal representatives, guardians or attorneys shall specifically set forth all services performed in detail as well as the amount of the fee requested and how it has been calculated.

420.8 Unjustified delays in carrying out duties by the personal representative, guardian or attorney will result in a reduction of fees.

420.9 The Court has no jurisdiction to rule on fee petitions when there is a guardianship over the person only.

Adopted effective Jan. 1, 2012.

Marion County Probate Form 401.1–A.   Application for Appointment of Personal Representative
(for proposed personal representative who is a non-resident of Indiana)

STATE OF INDIANA   )   IN THE MARION SUPERIOR COURT
) SS: PROBATE DIVISION
COUNTY OF MARION   )   CAUSE NO: 49D08 _____

IN THE MATTER OF THE   )
UNSUPERVISED / SUPERVISED   )   *[choose one]*
ESTATE OF _____   )

APPLICATION FOR APPOINTMENT OF PERSONAL REPRESENTATIVE

[If there are Co–Personal Representatives, then complete
one form for each personal representative]

CONTACT INFORMATION:
Name of Petitioner: _____

Address of Petitioner: _____
[Including street
number, city, zip]   _____

Home Phone Number: _____

Cell Phone Number: _____

E–Mail: _____

EDUCATIONAL BACKGROUND:
Do you have a High School Education?   Yes _____   No _____

If you do not have a High School
Education, do you have a GDI?   Yes _____   No _____

Do you have a college education?   Yes _____   No _____

If so, please list college, number of years attended, and the year you obtained a
degree, and the type of degree you obtained.

_____
_____
_____

Do you have a post graduate or
professional degree   Yes _____   No _____

If so, please identify educational institution, the year you obtained that degree, and
the degree you obtained.

_____
_____

EMPLOYMENT:

Name of Employer: _____

Address of Employer: _____

Length of Employment: _____

If you are not currently employed, please state whether you are retired, or a
homemaker, or a surviving spouse or surviving partner of the deceased person, and

please describe your most occupation or work experience before your retirement or before you stopped working outside your home.

_____
_____

FINANCIAL EXPERTISE:

Please list all prior experience in financial management, including investments and checkbook management:

_____
_____
_____

FELONY CONVICTIONS:

Do you have any prior felony convictions   Yes _____   No _____

If so, list date of conviction and type of felony.

_____
_____

AFFIRMATIONS OF PETITIONER:

   As Petitioner requesting my appointment as Personal Representative of the Estate of _____, I hereby state as follows:

   1.   That I have a attained 18 years of age and I am not incapacitated in any manner that would interfere with my administration of the decedent's estate.

   2.   That my attorney is _____ with offices located at ____

_____

That my attorney's Phone Number is: _____
That my attorney's Fax Number is: _____
That my attorney's E–Mail address is: _____

   3.   That I have provided my attorney with my Social Security Number and the date of my birth.

   4.   That I accept my appointment as fiduciary.

   5.   That I agree to submit personally to the Jurisdiction of this Court in any proceeding that relates to the estate of the decedent.

AFFIRMATION AND VERIFICATION:

   I affirm under the Penalties of perjury that the foregoing information is true and correct. That as a condition of my appointment as fiduciary in this matter, I hereby waive the privilege associated with this information and authorize my attorney to disclose this information to the Court, upon Court order, in the event of my failure to render an account as required by law or other determination of a breach of my fiduciary duty.

Dated: This _____ day of _____, 20 _____.

                                        _____
                                             Signature of Petitioner

Adopted effective Jan. 1, 2012.

Marion County Probate Form 401.1–B.   Application for Appointment of Guardian (*for proposed guardian who is a nonresident of Indiana*)

STATE OF INDIANA   )   IN THE MARION SUPERIOR COURT
) SS: PROBATE DIVISION
COUNTY OF MARION   )   CAUSE NO: 49D08 _____

IN THE MATTER OF THE GUARDIANSHIP   )
OF THE _____ OF _____   )

APPLICATION FOR APPOINTMENT OF GUARDIAN

[If there are Co–Guardians, then complete one form for each Co–Guardian]

CONTACT INFORMATION:

Name of Petitioner: _____

Address of Petitioner: _____
[Including street
number, city, zip] _____

Home Phone Number: _____

Cell Phone Number: _____

E–Mail: _____

EDUCATIONAL BACKGROUND:

Do you have a High School Education?   Yes _____   No _____

If you do not have a High School
Education, do you have a GDI?   Yes _____   No _____

Do you have a college education?   Yes _____   No _____

If so, please list college, number of years attended, and the year you obtained a
degree, and the type of degree you obtained.

_____
_____
_____

Do you have a post graduate or
professional degree   Yes _____   No _____

If so, please identify educational institution, the year you obtained that degree, and
the degree you obtained.

_____
_____

EMPLOYMENT:

Name of Employer: _____

Address of Employer: _____

Length of Employment: _____

If you are not currently employed, please state whether you are retired, or a
homemaker, or a surviving spouse or surviving partner of the deceased person, and
please describe your most occupation or work experience before your retirement or
before you stopped working outside your home.

_____
_____

FINANCIAL EXPERTISE:

Please list all prior experience in financial management, including investments and
checkbook management:

_____
_____
_____

FELONY CONVICTIONS:

Do you have any prior felony convictions   Yes _____   No _____

If so, list date of conviction and type of felony.

_____
_____

AFFIRMATIONS OF PETITIONER:
   As Petitioner requesting my appointment as Guardian of the Estate of
_____, I hereby state as follows:
   1.   That I have a attained 18 years of age and I am not incapacitated in any manner that would interfere with my administration of the estate (property) of the minor or incapacitated adult.
   2.   That my attorney is _____ _____, with offices located at _____
That my attorney's Phone Number is: _____
That my attorney's Fax Number is: _____
That my attorney's E–Mail address is: _____

   3.   That I have provided my attorney with my Social Security Number and the date of my birth.
   4.   That I accept my appointment as fiduciary.
   5.   That I agree to submit personally to the Jurisdiction of this Court in any proceeding that relates to the estate of the minor or incapacitated adult.
AFFIRMATION AND VERIFICATION:
   I affirm under the Penalties of perjury that the foregoing information is true and correct. That as a condition of my appointment as fiduciary in this matter, I hereby waive the privilege associated with this information and authorize my attorney to disclose this information to the Court, upon Court order, in the event of my failure to render an account as required by law or other determination of a breach of my fiduciary duty.
   Dated: This __ day of _____, 20 __.

                              _____
                              Signature of Petitioner

Adopted effective Jan. 1, 2012.

Marion County Probate Form 401.1.   Petition to Appoint Personal Representative
STATE OF INDIANA   )   IN THE MARION SUPERIOR COURT
) SS: PROBATE DIVISION
COUNTY OF MARION   )   CAUSE NO. 49D08 _____

IN THE MATTER OF THE   )
UNSUPERVISED / SUPERVISED   )   *[choose one]*
ESTATE OF _____   )

PETITION TO APPOINT PERSONAL REPRESENTATIVE,
FOR PROBATE OF WILL, AND FOR ISSUANCE OF LETTERS

   Comes now _____, the Petitioner, [*delete or modify the next clause depending on whether the Petitioner is appearing in person in Court or whether he or she is a non-resident whose attorney is appearing alone*] in person and by counsel / by counsel, and respectfully request the Court to appoint h___ as Personal Representative of the Estate of _____, deceased, and in support thereof, states the following:
   1.   _____ ("the Decedent"), a ___ ___ married ___ male, age ___, having been born on _____, died testate on _____, while domiciled at _____ _____ in Marion County, Indiana.
   2.   On _____, Decedent properly executed h ___ Last Will and Testament by executing an acknowledgment of said will and verification of its execution by _____ and _____, witnesses thereto. **The original of said Last Will is attached hereto or submitted with this Petition.**
   3.   The Petitioner herein, _____, is a person qualified to serve as Personal Representative of the Estate of the Decedent in that: In Item ___ of h ___ Will, the Decedent nominated _____ to serve as her personal representative and as hereinafter set forth and in the accompanying Application, is otherwise suitable qualified to serve as a fiduciary.
   4.   The Petitioner's current residence address [*if an individual*] business address [*if a corporate fiduciary*] is as follows: _____

5.   The Petitioner is at least eighteen (18) years old and is not incapacitated by mental or physical health impairment, or infirmity, in any manner which would interfere with the ability to serve as a fiduciary.

6.   The name, office address, attorney number, telephone number, fax number and e-mail address of the attorney for the Petitioner are as follows:

7.   [*As required by I.C. § 29–1–10–1, if the Petitioner is a nonresident individual or corporate fiduciary, the petition must also include the following*:

   a.   a statement that the Petitioner accepts the appointment as fiduciary;

   b.   a statement providing the name, address and telephone number of the resident agent appointed by the Petitioner to accept service of process, notices, and other documents in the fiduciary proceeding;

   c.   a statement that the Petitioner has agreed to submit personally to the jurisdiction of the Court in any proceeding that relates to the estate of the decedent or protected person.]

8.   The name, residence address, and relationship to the Decedent of each person entitled to receive a devise, bequest, or distributive share from the Decedent's estate are as follows: [*insert list or table*]

9.   To the Petitioner's best knowledge, the Decedent's estate is believed to be solvent and to consist of the following assets with the following approximate market value:

   A.   Real Property: $ _____
   B.   Motor Vehicles: _____
   C.   Household Goods: _____
   D.   Other Tangible Personal Property: _____
   E.   Intangible Personal Property: _____

10.   That the names and addresses of Decedent's known creditors are as follows:

11.   [*Delete if not* applicable] Item ___ of the Decedent's Last Will specifically authorizes the administration of h ___ estate to be unsupervised.

12.   [*Alternative to* ¶ 11] As shown by the attached signed consents, all persons who are named beneficiaries in the Decedent's Last Will consent to the Court opening the estate under unsupervised administration; consent to _____ being appointed as personal representative of the estate; and consent that the Court should require no bond, or a minimum bond, to secure h ___ performance as personal representative.

WHEREFORE, the Petitioner prays the Court for an order appointing ___ as Personal Representative of the Estate of ___, decedent, directing Letters [*Testamentary / of Administration*] be issued upon the taking of an oath, and that said Petitioner be authorized to proceed with the unsupervised administration of the decedent's estate; that bond not be required but if it is so required it be established in the minimum amount; and for all other relief which is proper in the premises.

I _____ hereby affirm under the penalties for perjury that the statements in this Petition are true and correct.

           _____ [*signature*]
           _____ [*printed name*], Petitioner

           _____ [*attorney signature*]
           Printed name of Attorney and Atty. I.D. number
           Law firm name [*if any*]
           Attorney's mailing address
           Attorney's telephone number
           Attorney's fax number and e-mail address

Adopted effective Jan. 1, 2012.

Marion County Probate Form 401.2.   Proof of Lost Will and Affidavit

STATE OF INDIANA	)	IN THE MARION SUPERIOR COURT
	) SS:	PROBATE DIVISION
COUNTY OF MARION	)	CAUSE NO. 49D08 _____

IN THE MATTER OF:	)	
	)	
THE ESTATE OF _____	)	CAUSE NO. 49D08 _____

PROOF OF LOST WILL AND AFFIDAVIT REGARDING
WHETHER ORIGINAL WILL DESTROYED WITH INTENT TO REVOKE

The undersigned hereby alleges and represents as follows:

1.   Affiant is acquainted with the affairs of the above- entitled Decedent.

2.   While Affiant has not located Decedent's original Last Will and Testament, Affiant believes that the copy submitted for probate herewith is a true and accurate copy of Decedent's said Will as executed.

3.   Decedent gave no indication to Affiant or anyone else, to Affiant's knowledge of any intention to revoke said Will.

4.   Affiant believes that Decedent did not destroy said original Will with the intent to revoke.

Further Affiant sayeth* not.

I affirm under penalties of perjury that the foregoing representations are true.

_____
Affiant

Attorney for Personal Representative

* So in original.

Adopted effective Jan. 1, 2012.

Marion County Probate Form 402.2.   Suggested Form of Attorney Fee Agreement

The following suggested form of engagement letter does not necessarily address all issues (regarding the scope of the attorney's work, the attorney-client relationship with the fiduciary, or the determination, billing and payment of the attorney's fee) that should be addressed with respect to a particular estate or guardianship.

Date

Petitioner	Co–Petitioner (if any)
Address	Address

RE: Estate of _____

Dear _____:

I am pleased that you have chosen me and my law firm to represent your interests with respect to the matters involving the estate of _____ (deceased) (protected person).   Under the Indiana Rules of Professional Conduct, it is advisable that we confirm in writing the terms and conditions under which this law firm will provide services to you so that both we and you can concentrate on the provision of the services you require.

You have agreed to pay for the legal services provided by me at the rate of $ _____ an hour.   From time to time, it may be necessary to also utilize the services of other professional members of the firm in order to properly provide appropriate representation for you.   Our fees for legal services will be billed on an hourly basis according to the billing rates charged by each attorney or paralegal of our firm.   These rates currently range from $ _____ per hour for beginning associates to $ _____ per hour for more senior associates and to $ _____ per hour for partners.   Paralegal time is charged at $ _____ per hour.   These billing rates are subject to adjustment at the beginning of a calendar year.

In matters involving supervised probate estates and guardianship estates, the Court will determine the amount of attorneys' fees, expenses and fees to you and our firm that it will permit the estate to pay as costs of administration.   In the event the Court authorizes fees in an amount less than you agree to in this agreement, you (agree) (do not agree) to personally pay the difference.   Almost always, the fees and expenses we collect are in the amount authorized by the Court but given unforeseen circumstances that may apply to this case, I cannot make that commitment at the outset.

Our fees are not contingent in any way upon the outcome of your case, but will reflect the uniqueness, complexity and the difficulty of obtaining the resolution of the matters at issue. Due to the many variables which affect the time needed to provide the services you have requested, I am unable to provide you with an estimate of your total fees.

I have requested advancement against attorney fees and expenses of _____ ($). In the event of a supervised estate or guardianship, this advancement and all future advancements, if any, may not be paid from the assets of the estate without order of the Court. That amount will be placed into my trust account for your credit towards payment of the future fees and expenses of this law firm. You agree to keep that amount current in my trust account so that I will always have money in the trust account to pay on your behalf the attorney fees and expenses as they are incurred.

The following are firm billing policies which you should know. We will provide you with invoices on a monthly basis. The invoices will describe our services and itemize our expenses in accordance with our standard firm policies. These invoices reflect attorney services rendered during the month, the incurrence of litigation expenses and the current balance of your amount in our trust account. If the statement reflects an amount due you are expected to pay the amount upon receipt of the bill and replenish the retainer as set forth above. The bill for services rendered represents our time devoted to your case and our expenditures made on your behalf during the preceding month. Therefore, the services and costs may have been rendered up to thirty days or more prior to your receipt of the bill. Expenses which you agree to pay include such items as: _____.
If we anticipate that certain major expenses will be incurred, we may request that you pay these expenses directly in advance of when they are incurred.

Payment of each invoice is due upon receipt. Subject to any limitations imposed by the Indiana Rules of Professional Conduct, our firm will be entitled to cease work on any aspect of this representation if any invoices are not paid within thirty (30) days after the invoice is mailed. If any attorney fees or expenses remain unpaid by the time the bills are prepared for the following month, we reserve the right to assess a one percent late fee on all unpaid balances. If we are required to resort to collection proceedings to recover any amounts from you, we will also be entitled to recover all costs incurred concerning such collection proceedings including reasonable attorneys' fees incurred either by us or separate counsel.

You shall have the right at any time to terminate our services and representation upon written notice to the firm. Such termination shall not, however, relieve you of the obligation to pay for all services rendered and costs or expenses incurred on your behalf prior to the date of such termination. As permitted by law, we reserve the right to retain your files until all invoices have been paid in full.

We reserve the right to ask the Court's permission to withdraw from your representation if, among other things, you fail to honor the terms of this engagement letter, you fail to cooperate or follow our advice on a material matter, or any fact or circumstances would, in our view, render our continuing representation unlawful or unethical. If we elect to withdraw from your representation, you agree to take all steps necessary to free us of any obligation to perform further, including the execution of any documents reasonably necessary to complete our withdrawal, and we will be entitled to be paid for all services rendered and costs and expenses incurred on your behalf through the date of withdrawal.

During the course of our representation of you, I encourage you to call to discuss any questions or concerns that you may have. I have found that communication is the best means available for avoiding misunderstanding or undue anxiety regarding a pending case. You will find that I may not always be available to speak with you over the telephone. Commitments to other clients, regularly scheduled court appearances, depositions and other responsibilities both within and outside my office sometimes precludes my availability to speak with a client when such calls are received. I have given you all of my telephone numbers and want you to feel free to try to reach me after normal business hours.

By signing this letter, you agree with the terms of this engagement letter. I have enclosed an additional original of this letter for your signature. Please sign in the appropriate space and return it to me in the enclosed self-addressed, stamped envelope.

Again, I welcome the opportunity to represent you in this case. Please keep a copy of this letter for your files.

Sincerely,
LAW FIRM
Attorney

The undersigned acknowledges that she and he have read this letter and agree to all of the terms set forth herein.

_____   _____
Date   Name

_____   _____
Date   Name

Adopted effective Jan. 1, 2012.

Marion County Probate Form 402.4. Notice to Court and Order Setting Hearing

STATE OF INDIANA   )   IN THE MARION SUPERIOR COURT
) SS: PROBATE DIVISION
COUNTY OF MARION   )   CAUSE NO. 49D08 _____

IN THE MATTER OF THE   )
)
THE ESTATE/GUARDIANSHIP OF   )
)
_____   )

NOTICE OF POSSIBLE NON–COMPLIANCE

Comes now _____, attorney for _____ [fiduciary] heretofore appointed as [guardian / personal representative] on _____ by the Court to serve in such capacity, and, pursuant to MCPR 402.4, hereby notifies the Court that __ he is concerned that said fiduciary is not timely performing or improperly performing h ___ fiduciary duties to the [protected person or creditors and beneficiaries of the estate].

Wherefore, the Court is requested to set the matter for hearing and require the fiduciary to personally appear and account to the Court for all actions taken or not taken by the fiduciary.

Respectfully submitted,

LAW FIRM
Attorneys for the Fiduciary

_____
Attorney, # _____

Attorney Contact Information

CERTIFICATE OF SERVICE

The undersigned hereby certifies that a copy of the foregoing was served upon the following by first class, United States mail, postage prepaid, this _____ day of _____, 2 _____:

Fiduciary
Address

Beneficiary
Address

Creditor
Address

_____

Attorney

STATE OF INDIANA	)	IN THE MARION SUPERIOR COURT
	) SS:	PROBATE DIVISION
COUNTY OF MARION	)	CAUSE NO. 49D08 _____

IN THE MATTER OF THE   )
)
THE ESTATE/GUARDIANSHIP OF   )
)
_____   )

ORDER TO APPEAR FOR COMPLIANCE HEARING

This matter came before the Court on a Notice of Possible Non–Compliance filed by the attorney for the personal representative/guardian heretofore appointed to serve by the Court in this cause.

AND THE COURT being duly advised in the premises, hereby issues an Order that the personal representative/guardian _____ and their counsel _____ shall appear in this Court on the ___ day of _____, 20 ___, at _____ o'clock ___.m. to report to the Court on the actions of the personal representative/guardian in this matter.

The Clerk is hereby directed to mail a copy of this Order to the personal representative/guardian, their attorney, the protected person and all heirs/beneficiaries and creditors.

ALL OF WHICH IS ORDERED this ___ day of _____, 20 ___.

_____
Gerald S. Zore, Judge, Marion Superior Court
Probate Division

SERVE PERSONAL REPRESENTATIVE/GUARDIAN AT:
_____
_____
_____

SERVE ATTORNEY FOR PERSONAL REPRESENTATIVE/GUARDIAN AT:
_____
_____
_____

SERVE PROTECTED PERSON/HEIR/BENEFICIARY AT:
_____
_____
_____

SERVE CREDITOR AT:
_____
_____

Adopted effective Jan. 1, 2012.

Marion County Probate Form 409.4.   Attorney's Undertaking in Guardianship

STATE OF INDIANA	)	IN THE MARION SUPERIOR COURT
	) SS:	PROBATE DIVISION
COUNTY OF MARION	)	CAUSE NO. 49D08 _____

IN THE MATTER OF:)
)
THE GUARDIANSHIP OF   )
)
_____   )

DATE OF BIRTH _____

ATTORNEY'S UNDERTAKING AND OBLIGATION IN GUARDIANSHIP

I, the undersigned guardian, having been appointed by the Probate Court of Marion County on this date, hereby authorize attorney, _____, to deposit all of the next guardianship assets, in the amount of $_____, in a bank account or brokerage account in my name as guardian with the restriction that withdrawal of principal or income may be made **ONLY** on written order of this Court.

Date: _____   _____
                                                    Guardian

                                          _____
                                                    Co–Guardian

I, the undersigned, as an officer of this Court, hereby assume and undertake personal responsibility to the above-named incapacitated person and to the Court to make the restricted deposit designated above and to deliver a copy of the **Depository Institution's Acceptance Of Restrictions On Guardianship Account** in accordance with **Marion County Probate Form 413.8 (A)** evidencing such restricted deposit to the Court within thirty (30) days from date or to refund all of said funds to the Court forthwith upon demand.

Date: _____   _____
                                                        Attorney

Adopted effective Jan. 1, 2012.

Marion County Probate Form 409.5.   Acceptance of Restrictions on Guardianship Account

STATE OF INDIANA	)	IN THE MARION SUPERIOR COURT
	) SS:	PROBATE DIVISION
COUNTY OF MARION	)	CAUSE No. 49D08 _____

IN THE MATTER OF:)
THE ESTATE/GUARDIANSHIP OF   )
_____   )

DEPOSITORY INSTITUTION'S ACCEPTANCE OF RESTRICTIONS ON GUARDIANSHIP ACCOUNT

The undersigned hereby certifies that he or she is an authorized officer or employee of a financial institution or brokerage firm ("Undersigned Institution") whose name appears below and further certifies that the following account has been opened:

Type of account: _____

Account number: _____

Amount deposited: _____

Account opened in name of: _____

Authorized signer on account: _____

The Undersigned Institution further certifies and agrees that:

467

1. The terms of such account include a restriction that **withdrawal of principal or interest may be made only on written order of the Marion Superior Court, Probate Division** and that the Undersigned Institution agrees to comply with said restriction and to retain a copy of the court's order restricting the account.

2. No funds shall be released by the Undersigned Institution unless a certified order is tendered to the Undersigned Institution, bearing the signature of the Judge of the Court and the seal of the Marion Superior Court 8, Probate Division.

3. If the Undersigned Institution is uncertain as to whether funds should be released, it shall telephone the Probate Court at (317) 327–5063 with its request for instructions.

4. If a fiduciary attempts to withdraw funds without a certified court order, the Undersigned Institution shall promptly notify the Court in writing as to the fiduciary's attempt to withdraw funds without a certified court order.

Date: _____   _____
                                             (Name of Financial Institution)

                                             _____
                                             (Signature)

                                             _____
                                             (Printed)

Adopted effective Jan. 1, 2012.

Marion County Probate Form 412.0. Instructions to Guardian of the Person with Sample Annual Report

MARION SUPERIOR COURT—PROBATE DIVISION

GUARDIANSHIP OF _____

CAUSE NUMBER _____

COURT'S INSTRUCTIONS TO GUARDIAN OF THE PERSON

Please read carefully before you date and sign. One copy of this form must be filed with the Court before your appointment as guardian is confirmed by the Court. Keep a copy for your records.

You have been appointed as the guardian of an individual who is unable to care for his or her own personal affairs. It is important that you fully realize your duties and responsibilities. Listed below are some of your duties.

You should be represented at all times by an attorney of record. Your attorney is required to notify the Court if you are not properly performing your duties to the protected person. By signing these Instructions you agree that the filing of that notice does not violate the attorney-client privilege. If the Court receives such notice it will set the matter for hearing and require you to personally appear and account to the Court for all actions taken or not taken by you as guardian.

The Instructions which follow are to be considered by you as Orders of the Court which require you to perform as directed. The Court appreciates your efforts on behalf of the protected person.

Gerald S. Zore,

Judge, Marion Superior Court

Probate Division

As Guardian of the person, you have the following duties and authority:

1. You must be or become sufficiently acquainted with the protected person and maintain sufficient contact with the protected person to know his or her capabilities, disabilities, limitations, needs, opportunities, and physical and mental health.

2. You are responsible to make sure the protected person has an adequate place to live that is appropriate for the protected person's needs. You can decide where the protected person will live. You must obtain approval of the Court before you move the protected person to another residence or health facility that is more than fifty miles away.

3. You are responsible to make sure that the protected person receives needed and appropriate medical care. You can consent to medical or other professional care and treatment for the protected person's health and welfare. You can consent to the protected person's admission to a health care facility.

4. You shall, to the extent possible, encourage and promote the self-reliance and independence of the protected person.

5. You can, to the extent that the protected person is able, delegate to the protected person certain responsibilities for decisions affecting the protected person's well-being.

6. You or your attorney must notify the Court if your address changes.

7. You must file a report with the Court at least every two years. The report must state the present residence of the protected person and a statement of the protected person's current condition and general welfare. A sample report form is attached. Failure to file the report may result in your removal as guardian.

I authorize my attorney to notify the Court in the event that he or she has reason to believe that I am not timely performing or am improperly performing my duties to the protected person even if such information would be otherwise confidential.

I acknowledge that I have carefully and completely read the above instructions and received a copy for my records. I agree to properly carry out my duties.

Dated this _____ day of _____, 20 ___.

_____   _____
Signature, Guardian   Signature, Guardian

_____   _____
Print, Guardian   Print, Guardian

I acknowledge that I have carefully and completely discussed the above instructions with my client before this form was signed and believe that he or she is fully aware of and capable of performing the duties required of a guardian of the estate.

_____   _____
Signature, Attorney   Signature, Attorney

_____   _____
Print, Attorney   Print, Attorney

MARION SUPERIOR COURT—PROBATE DIVISION

GUARDIANSHIP OF _____

CAUSE NUMBER _____

REPORT OF GUARDIAN OF PERSON

The undersigned, _____, as guardian of the person of _____ [*name of protected person*], respectfully reports:

1. List the protected person's current address: _____

2. What type of residence is this? [*House, apartment, nursing home, etc.*] ____

3. What is the protected person's current condition and health? _____
_____

4. When did you, the Guardian, last personally see the protected person? ____
_____

5. Does the guardianship of the person of the protected person need to remain in effect? _____ If not, why not? _____

I affirm, under the penalties of perjury, that the above statements are true.

Dated: _____   _____
                                        Signature of Guardian

                                        _____
                                        Printed Name of Guardian

                                        _____
                                        Guardian's Address

                                        _____
                                        _____
                                        Guardian's Telephone Number

Adopted effective Jan. 1, 2012.

Marion County Probate Form 412.1. Instructions to Guardian of Estate

MARION SUPERIOR COURT—PROBATE DIVISION

GUARDIANSHIP OF _____
CAUSE NUMBER _____

COURT'S INSTRUCTIONS TO GUARDIAN OF ESTATE

Please read carefully before you date and sign. One copy of this form must be filed with the Court before your appointment as guardian is confirmed by the Court. Keep one copy for your records.

Introduction:

You have been appointed as the guardian of an individual who is unable to care for his or her own financial affairs. It is important that you fully realize your duties and responsibilities. Listed below are some of your duties, but not all of them.

You must be represented at all times by an attorney of record. Your attorney is required to reasonably supervise and guide your actions as guardian unless and until that attorney is permitted by order of the Court to withdraw from representing you.

Your attorney is required to notify the Court in the event that you are not timely performing or improperly performing your fiduciary duties to the protected person, and by signing these Instructions you agree that the filing of that notice does not violate the attorney-client privilege. If the Court receives such notice, it will set the matter for hearing and will require you to personally appear and account to the Court for all actions taken or not taken by you as guardian. You are required to notify the Court in writing in the event that your attorney is not timely performing or improperly performing his or her duties to reasonably supervise and guide your actions as guardian. Upon receipt of the notice, the Court will set the matter for hearing and require you and your attorney to personally appear and account to the Court for all actions taken or not taken by the attorney.

The Instructions which follow are to be considered by you as Orders of the Court which require you to perform as directed. Although your attorney will file all papers with the Court, the ultimate responsibility to see that all accounts and other documents are accurately prepared and filed, rests with you and you can be found personally liable should you not properly perform.

The Court appreciates your efforts on behalf of the protected person.

Gerald S. Zore,

Judge, Marion Superior Court

Probate Division

As Guardian you are required to:

470

1. Locate, collect and maintain all property owned by the protected person. Keep motor vehicles and real estate insured and protected.

2. Have your attorney file with the Court, within ninety (90) days after your appointment, a verified inventory and appraisal of all the property belonging to the protected person, with values as of the date you were appointed. You must provide a copy of the inventory to the protected person (if over fourteen (14) years of age) and to certain other persons as set out in Indiana Code § 29–3–9–5.

3. Have your attorney file with the Court a verified current account of all the income and expenditures of the guardianship every two (2) years after your appointment, consisting of three schedules. The first schedule must include all assets listed on the inventory or on the last current account along with any additions or adjustments to the inventory. The second schedule must be an itemized list of expenditures, supported by attached cancelled checks or facsimiles of paid checks as evidence of payment. The third schedule must be a recapitulation indicating the remaining property after subtracting expenditures.

4. Pay bond premiums as they become due.

5. File and pay taxes on the protected person's income and assets.

6. Have your attorney file a final accounting with the Court upon the termination of the guardianship, whether due to the death of the protected person, or for any other reason.

7. Keep all of the assets of the protected person separate from your own. Guardianship funds should **never be co-mingled** with personal funds. Unauthorized use of the guardianship funds will result in personal liability.

8. Open a guardianship checking account in your name "as guardian of (**the protected person**)" This account **shall** be used for all payments or disbursements on behalf of the protected person. The account should be in the protected person's Social Security number, not yours. It cannot be a joint account. Make sure that the financial institution you are utilizing will provide you with cancelled checks or images of paid checks and evidence of payments made from the account.

9. Real estate, automobiles and other accounts and investments should be held in the name of the protected person.

10. All investment accounts and other bank account holdings should be retitled as follows: "John Smith Guardianship, Mary Jones Guardian."

11. Obtain approval from the Court to use guardianship assets, other than for normal bills.

12. Do not self-deal. Do not buy anything from or sell anything to the protected person. Do not borrow anything from the protected person.

13. If applicable, timely qualify the protected person for Medicaid or other public assistance.

14. It is the duty of the guardian to protect and preserve the protected person's property, to account for the use of the property faithfully, and to perform all the duties required by law of a guardian.

15. The guardian has the same duties and responsibilities concerning the protected person whether or not the protected person is a relative of the guardian.

16. **NEVER** pay attorney fees or compensation to yourself from assets of the guardianship without first obtaining the advance written approval of the Court.

17. If any questions arise during the guardianship, immediately consult with your attorney.

I authorize my attorney to notify the Court in the event that he or she has reason to believe that I am not timely performing or improperly performing my fiduciary duties to the protected person even if such information would be otherwise confidential.

I acknowledge that I have carefully and completely read the above instructions and received a copy for my records. I agree to properly carry out my duties.

Dated this _____ day of _____, 20 ___.

_____　　_____
Signature, Guardian　　　　　　　　　Signature, Guardian

_____　　_____
Print, Guardian　　　　　　　　　　Print, Guardian

I acknowledge that I have carefully and completely discussed the above instructions with my client before this form was signed and believe that he or she is fully aware of and capable of performing the duties required of a guardian of the estate.

_____　　_____
Signature, Attorney　　　　　　　　　Signature, Attorney

_____　　_____
Print, Attorney　　　　　　　　　　Print, Attorney

Adopted effective Jan. 1, 2012.

Marion County Probate Form 412.2.　Instructions to Personal Representative of Supervised Estate

MARION SUPERIOR COURT—PROBATE DIVISION

SUPERVISED ESTATE OF _____

CAUSE NUMBER _____

COURT'S INSTRUCTIONS TO PERSONAL REPRESENTATIVE OF SUPERVISED ESTATE

Please read carefully before you date and sign. One copy of this form must be filed with the Court before your appointment as personal representative is confirmed by the Court. Keep one copy for your records.

Introduction:

You have been appointed as the personal representative of the estate of a deceased person. By your appointment, the Court has placed in you the highest trust that you will perform your duties in the best interests of all beneficiaries and creditors of the estate. It is important that you fully realize your duties and responsibilities. Listed below are some, but not all of them.

You must be represented at all times by an attorney of record. Your attorney is required to reasonably supervise and guide your actions as personal representative unless and until that attorney is permitted by order of the Court to withdraw from representing you.

Your attorney is required to notify the Court in the event that you are not timely performing or improperly performing your fiduciary duties to the beneficiaries and creditors of the estate and by signing these Instructions, you agree that the filing of that notice does not violate the attorney-client privilege. If the Court receives such notice, it will set the matter for hearing and require you to personally appear and account to the Court for all actions taken or not taken by you as personal representative. You are required to notify the Court in writing in the event that your attorney is not timely performing or improperly performing his or her duties to reasonably supervise and guide your actions as personal representative. Upon receipt of the notice, the Court will set the matter for hearing and require you and your attorney to personally appear and account to the Court for all actions taken or not taken by the attorney.

The Instructions which follow are to be considered by you as Orders of the Court which require you to perform as directed. Although your attorney will file all papers with the Court, you, as personal representative, are ultimately responsible to see that the estate is properly and promptly administered, and you are personally liable for incorrect distributions, payments, or acts, as well as any unpaid taxes or costs of administration. The Court appreciates your efforts on behalf of the estate.

Gerald S. Zore

Judge, Marion Superior Court

Probate Division

<u>As Personal Representative, you are required to:</u>

1. Locate, collect and maintain all property owned by the decedent.

2. Keep motor vehicles and real estate insured and protected.

3. Immediately fill out a change of address at the post office to have the decedent's mail forwarded to you.

4. No later than two (2) months after your appointment, have your attorney file in this Court an inventory describing all property belonging to the estate, with date of death values, and forthwith serve a copy of the inventory on all known heirs, beneficiaries or distributees of the estate.

5. **Estate Checking Account.**

    A. Open a separate checking account in your name "as personal representative for the estate of (the decedent)." Obtain a federal tax I.D. number for the checking account. Do not use your Social Security number or decedent's Social Security number.

    B. **DO NOT** put any of your funds or anyone else's funds in this account.

    C. Always pay for estate expenses by checks from this account. Do not pay any expenses with cash.

    D. Make sure that the bank is willing to return cancelled checks or electronic versions of the checks to you.

    E. Keep records of all deposits including the identity of the person or entity paying the money into the estate.

6. Determine all debts that the decedent owed. Look through decedent's tax returns and other papers. Talk to anyone who knew decedent's business. Consult your attorney as to payment of debts, costs of administration, bond premiums, and funeral bills. Some debts may be unenforceable. Some may have priority over others.

7. Have your attorney provide written notice of the administration of the estate to all known creditors of the estate.

8. If the decedent owned a business or was involved in contracts which were not yet fully performed, have your attorney obtain directions from the Court as to those matters.

9. **DO NOT MAKE** any distribution of personal property or real estate to an heir or devisee without prior Court order.

10. **NEVER** borrow estate property or put it to your own personal use.

11. Prepare and file income tax returns for the tax year in which the decedent died and any returns for prior years if needed. Timely prepare and file any estate, inheritance or fiduciary tax returns and pay taxes as they come due.

12. **Accounting.** Indiana law requires the estate to be closed within one (1) year of your appointment as personal representative. Before the estate can be closed, you must file with the Court a final accounting of your actions as personal representative.

    A. Have your attorney file your final accounting, consisting of three (3) schedules, after the administration of the estate has been completed.

    B. The first schedule must include all assets listed on the inventory, any income and additional assets obtained during administration, and any adjustments to the inventory.

    C. The second schedule must be an itemized list of expenditures. Documentation for each expense shall include: (a) the payee; (b) check number or other identifying number on the instrument; (c) the amount disbursed; and, (d) if the reason for disbursement is not apparent from the description of the payee, a description of the reason for the disbursement sufficient to substantiate the reason for the disbursement as part of the administration of the estate. Cancelled checks or facsimile copies of paid checks for each expenditure must be attached as evidence of payment.

D. The third schedule must be a recapitulation indicating the remaining estate property after subtracting expenditures. A proposed distribution must be furnished to all interested parties, including heirs.

13. After the Court approves your final account, make distribution to the proper people and file a supplemental report with the Court, attaching receipts.

14. Notify the Court and your attorney of any change in your address or telephone number.

15. **NEVER** pay yourself or your attorney any fees from assets of the estate without a prior Court Order, unless your attorney confirms to you that the law or local court rules allow you to reimburse yourself from estate assets for necessary expenses that you previously paid with your personal funds.

16. Keep a record of the time you spend working on the estate. You are entitled to a reasonable fee, unless you waive a fee. Time records will help the Court determine your fee.

17. Always contact your attorney for advice if you are unsure as to any act as personal representative. Have your attorney counsel you in relation to the estate and explain anything that you do not fully understand.

18. Do not sell an estate asset without prior Court Order unless the Will, in very specific terms, authorizes sale without court order. Consult your attorney about this.

I authorize my attorney to notify the Court in the event that he or she has reason to believe that I am not timely performing or improperly performing my fiduciary duties to the beneficiaries and creditors of the estate even if such information would be otherwise confidential.

I acknowledge that I have carefully and completely read the above instructions and received a copy for my records. I agree to properly carry out my duties.

Dated this _____ day of _____, 20 _____.

_____   _____
Signature,   Signature,
Personal Representative   Personal Representative

_____   _____
Print,   Print,
Personal Representative   Personal Representative

I acknowledge that I have carefully and completely discussed the above instructions with my client before this form was signed and believe that he or she is fully aware of and capable of performing the duties required of a personal representative of a supervised estate.

_____   _____
Signature, Attorney   Signature, Attorney

_____   _____
Print, Attorney   Print, Attorney

Adopted effective Jan. 1, 2012.

Marion County Probate Form 412.3. Instructions to Personal Representative of Unsupervised Estate

MARION SUPERIOR COURT—PROBATE DIVISION

SUPERVISED ESTATE OF _____

CAUSE NUMBER _____

COURT'S INSTRUCTIONS TO PERSONAL REPRESENTATIVE
OF UNSUPERVISED ESTATE

Please read carefully before you date and sign. One copy of this form must be filed with the Court before your appointment as personal representative is confirmed by the Court. Keep one copy for your records.

Introduction:

You have been appointed as the personal representative of the estate of a deceased person. By your appointment, the Court has placed in you the highest trust that you will perform your duties in the best interests of all beneficiaries and creditors of the estate. It is important that you fully realize your duties and responsibilities. Listed below are some, but not all of them.

You must be represented at all times by an attorney of record approved to so act by written order of the Court. Your attorney is required to reasonably supervise and guide your actions as personal representative unless and until that attorney is permitted by order of the Court to withdraw from representing you.

Your attorney is required to notify the Court in the event that you are not timely performing or improperly performing your fiduciary duties to the beneficiaries and creditors of the estate and by signing these Instructions you agree that the filing of that notice does not violate the attorney-client privilege. If the Court receives such notice it will set the matter for hearing and require you to personally appear and account to the Court for all actions taken or not taken by you as personal representative. You are required to notify the Court in writing in the event that your attorney is not timely performing or improperly performing their duties to reasonably supervise and guide your actions as personal representative. Upon receipt of the notice, the Court will set the matter for hearing and require you and your attorney to personally appear and account to the Court for all actions taken or not taken by the attorney.

The Instructions which follow are to be considered by you as Orders of the Court which require you to perform as directed. Although your attorney will file all papers with the Court, you, as personal representative, are ultimately responsible to see that the estate is properly and promptly administered, and you are personally liable for incorrect distributions, payments, or acts, as well as any unpaid taxes or costs of administration.

The Court appreciates your efforts on behalf of the estate.

Gerald S. Zore

Judge, Marion Superior Court

Probate Division

As personal representative, you are required to:

1. Locate, collect and maintain all property owned by the decedent.

2. Keep motor vehicles and real estate insured and protected.

3. Immediately fill out a change of address at the post office to have the decedent's mail forwarded to you.

4. Within two (2) months of your appointment you must either:

    A. file with the Court an inventory conforming with the requirements of I.C. 29–1–7.5–3.2 (b) and forthwith serve a copy of the inventory on all known heirs, beneficiaries or distributees of the estate, or,

    B. file with the Court a verified certification that an inventory conforming with the requirements of I.C. 29–1–7.5–3.2 has been prepared, that it is available to be furnished to distributees on request and that notice of preparation of the inventory and its availability has been forthwith served on all known heirs, beneficiaries or distributees.

5. **Estate Checking Account.**

A. Open a separate checking account in your name "as personal representative for the estate of (the decedent)." Obtain a federal tax I.D. number for the checking account. Do not use your Social Security number or decedent's Social Security number.

B. DO NOT put any of your funds or anyone else's funds in this account.

C. Always pay for estate expenses by checks from this account. DO NOT pay any expenses with cash.

D. Make sure that the bank is willing to return cancelled checks or electronic copies or digital images of the paid checks to you.

E. Keep records of all deposits, including the identity of each person or entity paying the money into the estate.

6. Determine all debts that the decedent owed. Look through decedent's tax returns and other papers. Talk to anyone who knew decedent's business. Consult your attorney as to payment of debts, costs of administration, bond premiums, and funeral bills. Some debts may be unenforceable. Some may have priority over others.

7. Have your attorney provide written notice of the administration of the estate to all known creditors of the estate.

8. **NEVER** borrow estate property or put it to your own personal use.

9. DO NOT distribute any estate assets until assets (including personal property) are appraised, and consult with your attorney prior to making any distribution.

10. Prepare and file income tax returns for the tax year in which the decedent died and any returns for prior years if needed. Timely prepare and file any estate, inheritance or fiduciary tax returns and pay taxes as they come due.

11. After you fully complete the estate administration, you must file a closing statement with the Court verifying that all proper claims, expenses and taxes have been paid, that all assets have been properly distributed, and that a copy of the closing statement has been sent to all distributes, fully accounting for all assets, expenses and distributions made to the heirs.

12. Notify the Court and your attorney of any change in your address or telephone number.

13. Keep a record of the time you spend working on the estate. You are entitled to a reasonable fee, unless you waive a fee. Time records will help the Court determine your fee.

14. Always contact your attorney for advice if you are unsure as to any act as personal representative. Have your attorney counsel you in relation to the estate and explain anything that you do not fully understand.

I authorize my attorney to notify the Court in the event that he or she has reason to believe that I am not timely performing or improperly performing my fiduciary duties to the beneficiaries and creditors of the estate even if such information would be otherwise confidential.

I acknowledge that I have carefully and completely read the above instructions and received a copy for my records. I agree to properly carry out my duties.

Dated this _____ day of _____, 20 ___.

_____   _____
Signature,   Signature,
Personal Representative   Personal Representative

_____   _____
Print,   Print,
Personal Representative   Personal Representative

I acknowledge that I have carefully and completely discussed the above instructions with my client before this form was signed and believe that he or she is fully aware of and capable of performing the duties required of a personal representative of a supervised estate.

_____   _____
Signature, Attorney   Signature, Attorney

_____   _____
Print, Attorney   Print, Attorney

Adopted effective Jan. 1, 2012.

Marion County Probate Form 413.3. Physician's Report

STATE OF INDIANA   )   IN THE MARION SUPERIOR COURT
) SS: PROBATE DIVISION
COUNTY OF MARION   )   CAUSE NO. 49D08 _____

IN THE MATTER OF THE   )
)
THE GUARDIANSHIP OF   )
)
_____   )

PHYSICIAN'S REPORT

Dr. _____, a physician licensed to practice medicine in all its branches in the State of Indiana, submits the following Report on _____, the alleged incapacitated person ("Person") named above, based on an examination of said person conducted within the last three (3) months, on the ___ day of _____, 20 ___.

1.   The nature and type of the Person's disability or other incapacity is:
_____
_____
_____

2.   The Person's mental and physical condition, and, when appropriate, their educational condition, adaptive behavior and social skills are:
_____
_____

3.   In my opinion, the Person is [ ] totally or [ ] only partially incapable of making personal and financial decisions.
    A.   The kinds of decisions which the Person can and cannot make are:
_____
_____
_____

    B.   The facts and/or reasons supporting this opinion are:
_____
_____
_____
_____

4.   In my opinion, the most appropriate living arrangement for the Person is:
_____
_____

    A.   The most appropriate treatment or rehabilitation plan for the Person is:
_____
_____

    B.   The facts and / or reasons supporting this opinion are:
_____
_____

5. The Person [ ] can [ ] cannot appear in Court without creating a threat to his or her health or safety.

Explain the specific risk to the Person's health or safety if he or she appears in Court.

_____

_____

_____

The report must be signed by a physician. If the description of the Person's mental, physical and educational condition, adaptive behavior or social skills is based on evaluations by other professionals, all professionals preparing or contributing evaluations must sign the report. Evaluations on which the report is based must been performed within three (3) months of the date of the filing of the petition.

I/We affirm under the penalties of perjury that the foregoing representations are true.

Physician:

Name: _____   Signature: _____

_____

Street Address: _____
City: _____ State: _____ Zip: _____ Phone: _____

Other professionals who performed evaluations upon which this report is based:
Name: _____   Signature: _____

Profession: _____
Street Address: _____
City: _____ State: _____ Zip: _____ Phone: _____

Name: _____   Signature: _____

Profession: _____
Street Address: _____
City: _____ State: _____ Zip: _____ Phone: _____

Name: _____   Signature: _____

Profession: _____
Street Address: _____
City: _____ State: _____ Zip: _____ Phone: _____

Adopted effective Jan. 1, 2012.

Marion County Probate Form 413.4.   Attorney's Affidavit Regarding Notice

STATE OF INDIANA   )   IN THE MARION SUPERIOR COURT
) SS: PROBATE DIVISION
COUNTY OF MARION   )   CAUSE NO. 49D08 _____

IN THE MATTER OF:)
)
THE GUARDIANSHIP OF   )
)
_____   )

ATTORNEY'S AFFIDAVIT CERTIFYING COMPLIANCE
WITH REQUIREMENTS FOR NOTICE REGARDING TEMPORARY GUARD-
IANSHIP PETITION

Comes now _____, as attorney for the petitioner in this proceeding, and being first duly sworn, certifies the following facts under I.C. § 29–3–3–4(b):

1. Before the filing of the petition for appointment of a temporary guardian in this proceeding, the undersigned attorney has made the following efforts to give notice to the alleged incapacitated person or minor named above or to his or her attorney, and to all other interested persons described in I.C. § 29–3–6–1(a)(3) or (a)(4), as applicable:

_____
_____
_____
_____

2. The reasons why advance notice cannot or should not be given to one or more interested persons are as follows:

_____
_____
_____

I certify, under the penalties for perjury, that the foregoing statements are true and accurate to the best of my knowledge.

_____
Signature of Attorney for Petitioner

_____
Printed Name of Attorney for Petitioner

NOTE: The purpose of this form is to comply with requirements stated in *In Re Anonymous*, 729 N.E.2d 566 (Ind. 2000) and *In the Matter of Anonymous*, 786 N.E.2d 1185 (Ind. 2003), as well as Trial Rule 65(B) and the Rules and Canons prohibiting improper *ex parte* contacts with the Court. *See also* subsection (b) of I.C. § 29–3–3–4 as added by P.L. 178–2011, section 3.

Adopted effective Jan. 1, 2012.

Marion County Probate Form 418.6(A). Attorney's Undertaking in Minor's Settlement

STATE OF INDIANA   )   IN THE MARION SUPERIOR COURT
) SS: PROBATE DIVISION
COUNTY OF MARION   )   CAUSE NO. 49D08 _____

IN THE MATTER OF:)
)
THE MINOR'S SETTLEMENT OF)
)
_____)

ATTORNEY'S UNDERTAKING AND OBLIGATION
REGARDING MINOR'S SETTLEMENT AND
BANK OR BROKERAGE ACCOUNT

I, the undersigned parent of the above-named minor, hereby authorize attorney _____, to deposit all of the net settlement funds, in the amount of $ _____, in a bank account or brokerage account in the minor's sole name with the restriction that withdrawal of principal or interest may be made **ONLY** on written order of this Court.

Date: _____   _____

                                Parent

I, the undersigned, as an officer of this Court, hereby assume and undertake personal responsibility to the above-named minor and to the Court to make the restricted deposit designated above and to deliver a copy of the **Depository Institution's Acceptance Of Restrictions On Minor's Settlement Account** in accordance with **Marion County Probate Form 418.6(B)** evidencing such restricted deposit to the Court within thirty (30) days from date or to refund all of said funds to the Court forthwith upon demand.

Date: _____   _____
                                               Attorney

Adopted effective Jan. 1, 2012.

Marion County Probate Form 418.6(B).   Acceptance of Restrictions on Minor's Settlement Account

STATE OF INDIANA	)	IN THE MARION SUPERIOR COURT
	) SS:	PROBATE DIVISION
COUNTY OF MARION	)	CAUSE NO. 49D08 _____

IN THE MATTER OF:)
THE MINOR'S SETTLEMENT OF   )
_____   )

DEPOSITORY INSTITUTION'S ACCEPTANCE OF RESTRICTIONS ON MINOR'S SETTLEMENT ACCOUNT

The undersigned hereby certifies that he or she is an authorized officer or employee of the financial institution or brokerage firm ("Undersigned Institution") whose name appears below and further certifies that the following account has been opened:

Type of account: _____
Account number: _____
Amount deposited: _____
Account opened in name of: _____
Name of Account Beneficiary: _____

The Undersigned Institution further certifies and agrees that:

1. The terms of such account include a restriction that **withdrawal of principal or interest may be made only on written order of the Marion Superior Court, Probate Division; that the Undersigned Institution retain a copy of the Court's Order restricting account;** and that the financial institution or brokerage firm agrees to comply with said restriction.

2. **Funds shall not be released** by the Undersigned Institution unless a certified order is tendered to the financial institution or brokerage firm bearing the signature of the Judge of the Court and the seal of the Marion Superior Court 8, Probate Division.

3. If the Undersigned Institution is uncertain as to whether funds should be released, it shall telephone the Probate Court at (317) 327–5063 with its request for instructions.

4. If a fiduciary attempts to withdraw funds without a certified court order, the Undersigned Institution shall promptly notify the Court in writing as to the fiduciary's attempt to withdraw funds without a certified court order.

Date: _____   _____
                                               (Name of Financial Institution)

                                          _____
                                               (Signature)

                                          _____
                                               (Printed Name and Title of Authorized Signer)

Adopted effective Jan. 1, 2012.

Marion County Probate Form 421.1.   Affidavit for Transfer of Assets without Administration

NOTE: This affidavit need not be filed with the Court unless the person signing the affidavit wants to request a Court order under I.C. 29–1–8–4.5. If

this affidavit is not filed with the Court, omit the text "In the Marion Superior Court, Probate Division" and the Cause number from the caption below.

STATE OF INDIANA	)	IN THE MARION SUPERIOR COURT
	) SS:	PROBATE DIVISION
COUNTY OF MARION	)	CAUSE NO. 49D08 _____

IN THE MATTER OF:)
)
THE ESTATE OF _____   )

AFFIDAVIT FOR TRANSFER OF ASSETS WITHOUT ADMINISTRATION

The undersigned, being duly sworn, states that:

1. The above decedent died on the ___ of _____, 20 ___, (testate) (intestate) while domiciled in Marion County, Indiana.

2. No petition for the appointment of a personal representative of the decedent's estate is pending or has been granted in any jurisdiction.

3. At least forty-five (45) days have elapsed since the death of said decedent.

4. The value of the gross probate estate of the decedent, wherever located, less liens and encumbrances, does not exceed $50,000.00.

5. The person or persons set forth in paragraph 6 below are entitled to the property as set forth after their names, by reason of:

   A. Being a beneficiary under the Will of the decedent, which was admitted to probate without administration in the Marion Superior Court 8, Probate Division, under Cause No. _____ in Marion County, Indiana, as recorded in the office of the Clerk of the Court on the ___ day of _____, 20 ___, **a copy of which probated Will is attached as Exhibit "A".**

   B. Being the surviving spouse, dependent child or children of the decedent.

   C. Other reasons: _____
   _____.

6. The following person or persons are entitled to receive, without Administration, the following listed property from the person, firm or Corporation shown after the property, subject to liens and encumbrances:

Name and Address of Person Entitled to Property	Share of the Property the Person is Entitled to	Description of the Property	Lien or Encumbrance (if any)	Name and Address of Person or Entity Holding the Property
_____	_____	_____	_____	_____
_____	_____	_____	_____	_____

7. The undersigned affiant, as claimant, has notified each person identified in the previous Paragraph of the claimant's intention to present an affidavit pursuant to IC 29–1–8–1.

8. The undersigned affiant, as claimant, is entitled to payment or delivery of the property on behalf of each person identified in this affidavit.

9. This affidavit is made for the purpose of inducing the above-named holder(s) of the decedent's above-described property to turn the property over to the persons indicated in Paragraph 7 or to the undersigned affiant on behalf of such persons, as provided by law. (See I.C. §§ 29–1–8–1 and 29–1–8–2)

I affirm under the penalties for perjury that the foregoing representations are true.

Date: _____   _____
                                           Signature of Affiant

Printed Name of Affiant

Affiant's Address

Affiant's Telephone Number

Adopted effective Jan. 1, 2012.

MARION SUPERIOR COURT CRIMINAL RULES

Amended Effective October 2, 2006

Including Amendments Received Through November 1, 2013

Research Notes

Annotations to the Marion Superior Court Criminal Rules are available in West's Annotated Indiana Code, Title 34 Appendix.

These rules may be searched electronically on Westlaw in the IN-RULES database; updates to these rules may be found on Westlaw in IN-RULESUPDATES. For search tips and a summary of database content, consult the Westlaw Scope Screens for each database.

LR49–CR2.2 Rule 100. RANDOM ASSIGNMENT OF CRIMINAL CASES

(a) All criminal cases filed in Marion County in the Superior Courts shall be assigned to an individual courtroom on a random basis. The random assignment rule for criminal cases does not apply to certain cases designated by the Court and Prosecutor as belonging in the:

- domestic violence courts; or
- protection order court; or
- major felony and class D felony drug court; or
- community court; or
- traffic court; or
- mental health court or
- those cases involved in LR49–CR2.3–101 Case Consolidation.

This rule strives for the equalization of caseload among all of the individual courtrooms.

(b) All hearings for Major Felony cases will be conducted in the Major Felony Court. Any new filing for a major felony case shall be randomly assigned to one of the multiple courtrooms designated as Major Felony Courts (G01, G02, G03, G04, G05, and G06) with the exception of a major felony drug offense case and a major felony handgun case which shall be assigned to court G20.

(c) Initial hearings for all Class D Felony Cases that are the result of a custodial arrest where the defendant is still in custody shall be conducted in the Initial Hearing Court (F11). These cases shall be subsequently assigned on a random basis to one of the multiple courtrooms designated as Class D Felony Courts (F09, F15, F18, F24 and F25). The random assignment rule for criminal cases does not apply to D felony cases involving allegations of domestic violence or to Class D felony cases designated as drug court cases. Cases involving an allegation of domestic violence shall be randomly assigned to either of the domestic violence courts (G16 and G17). Class D felony drug cases shall be assigned to the D felony drug court (G14).

(d) Initial hearings for cases involving Misdemeanor Cases that are a result of a custodial arrest where the defendant is still in custody shall be conducted in the Initial Hearing Court, Court 11. These cases shall be assigned on a random basis to one of the multiple courtrooms designated as Misdemeanor Courts (F07, F08, F10 and F19). Misdemeanor cases involving allegations of domestic violence shall be randomly assigned to either of the domestic violence courts (G16 and G17). Misdemeanors involving allegations of violations of traffic laws, with the exception of Operating a Vehicle While Intoxicated, shall be assigned to the Traffic Court (F13). Misdemeanors where the alleged offense occurred within the boundaries of the Community Court Project shall be assigned to the Community Court (F12). If the judge, defense counsel or prosecutor believe the defendant may have a mental illness and/or mental disability, the judge, defense counsel or prosecutor may apply to the PAIR Roundtable for evaluation. If, after evaluation, the PAIR Roundtable finds the defendant is PAIR eligible, the case shall be transferred to the designated mental health court. In the event the defendant fails the PAIR program, the case shall be returned to the originating court for adjudication.

(e) In the event that a defendant has a Misdemeanor or D Felony Domestic Violence case, and that case is amended to include a class C Felony charge, that case shall stay in the Domestic Violence Court to which is was originally assigned.

Adopted as Criminal Division Rule 1, effective April 8, 1996. Amended effective July 27, 1999; Oct. 16, 2000, effective April 1, 2000; amended effective April 2, 2001; June 2, 2003, effective July 1, 2003; December 28, 2004, effective March 1, 2005; renumbered as Criminal Rule 100, and amended effective Oct. 2, 2006; amended effective Jan. 1, 2008; June 30, 2008, effective Aug. 1, 2008; amended effective May 15, 2009; Sept. 8, 2010, effective Jan. 1, 2009; Jan. 1, 2012; April 1, 2013)

LR49–CR2.3 Rule 101.   CASE CONSOLIDATION

It shall be the policy of the Marion Superior Court, that wherever possible consistent with good case management principles, cases involving the same defendant shall be consolidated into one court for resolution of all of the pending cases.

(a) Murder, A, B and C Felony Cases (hereinafter "Major Felony case"). Any subsequently filed Major Felony case shall be assigned and/or transferred to the Court where the defendant's oldest Major Felony case is pending.

Any subsequently filed D Felony or Misdemeanor Case shall be assigned and/or transferred to the Court where the defendant's oldest Major Felony case is pending.

In the event the defendant has an open D Felony or Misdemeanor case pending in any criminal court and is subsequently charged with a Major Felony case, the pending D Felony or Misdemeanor case shall be transferred to the Major Felony Court.

In the event the defendant has an open probation case and/or open community corrections violation pending in any criminal court and is subsequently charged with a Major Felony case, the probation case and/or open community corrections violation shall be transferred to the Major Felony Court, unless the probation case and/or open community corrections violation can be resolved without the resolution of the new Major Felony case.

"Pending" as defined herein means any existing Major Felony, D Felony or Misdemeanor case which is in pre-disposition status.

No classification of cases is exempt from consolidation under this sub-paragraph.

(b) D Felony Cases. Any subsequently filed Misdemeanor or Class D Felony case shall be assigned and/or transferred to the Court where the defendant's oldest existing Class D Felony case is pending.

In the event the defendant has an open Misdemeanor case in any criminal court and is subsequently charged with a D Felony case, the Misdemeanor case shall be transferred to the D Felony Court.

In the event the defendant has an open probation case and/or open community corrections violation pending in any D Felony or Misdemeanor Court and is subsequently charged with a D Felony case, the probation case and/or open community corrections violation shall be transferred to the D Felony Court where the new case has been filed, unless the probation case and/or open community corrections violation can be resolved without the resolution of the new D Felony case.

"Pending" as defined herein means any existing Class D Felony or Misdemeanor case which is in pre-disposition status.

This rule shall not apply to Domestic Violence cases, cases assigned to Domestic Violence Courtrooms 16 and 17 or cases that are linked with a co-defendant. However, if one of the co-defendants is accepted into the PAIR program, the accepted defendant may be severed and transferred to the designated Mental Health Court without the non-accepted co–defendant(s) case(s).

(c) Misdemeanor Cases. Subject to the provisions of paragraphs (a) and (b) above, any subsequent Misdemeanor case filed against a defendant shall be assigned and/or transferred to the Court where the defendant's oldest existing Misdemeanor case is pending with the exception that Court 13 (Traffic Court) shall not receive assignment or transfer of cases when Court 13 has the oldest pending case.

In the event the defendant has an open probation case pending in any Misdemeanor Court and is subsequently charged with a new Misdemeanor case, the probation case shall be transferred to the new Misdemeanor Court unless the probation case can be resolved without the resolution of the new Misdemeanor case.

Pending as defined herein means any existing Misdemeanor case which is in predisposition status.

This rule shall not apply to Domestic Violence cases, cases assigned to Domestic Violence Courtrooms 16 and 17, or cases that are linked with co-defendants. However, if one of the co-defendants is accepted into the PAIR program, the accepted defendant may be severed and transferred to the designated Mental Health Court without the non-accepted co–defendant(s) case(s).

(d) All Misdemeanor and D Felony cases in which the defendant has a mental illness and /or mental disability shall be transferred to mental health court, subject to the discretion of the Judge in that court and considering the recommendation of the originating judge, prosecutor, and/or defense counsel.

(e) Other Considerations. In the event that a case involves both felony and misdemeanor offenses, pursuant to Administrative Rule 1, the case shall be considered a Felony case for the application of this rule.

It shall be the responsibility of the Prosecutor's Office Screening Department to provide a listing of all pending cases with the case filing documents to ensure that all case transfers can be made consistent with this rule.

The judge of each room of the criminal division, by appropriate order entered of record may transfer and re-assign to any other room of the criminal division any cause pending in that room subject to acceptance by the receiving court. Further the Presiding Judge of the Criminal Division or the Executive Committee may order the transfer of cases from one court to another if the Presiding Judge or the Executive Committee finds that a transfer and reassignment of cases in necessary to provide for the speedy and fair administration of justice.

All cases received by the criminal division on change of venue from outside Marion County shall be assigned to a room within the division on a random basis by the same method used to assign cases of original jurisdiction in Marion County. When the State of Indiana dismisses a case and chooses to re-file that case, the case shall be re-filed in the court where the case was originally docketed. All pleadings, petitions and motions shall be filed with the Clerk designated by the court at any time during filing hours established by the Clerk and the court and shall be accompanied by a proposed order. All orders submitted to the court shall be in sufficient number and shall be accompanied by postage paid envelopes addressed to each party or counsel of record. Service of orders on the Marion County Prosecutor and the Marion County Public Defender Agency may be through mailbox service established in each courtroom.

Adopted as Criminal Division Rule 1, effective April 8, 1996. Amended effective July 27, 1999; Oct. 16, 2000, effective April 1, 2000; amended effective April 2, 2001; June 2, 2003, effective July 1, 2003; December 28, 2004, effective March 1, 2005; renumbered as Criminal Rule 101, and amended effective Oct. 2, 2006; amended effective Jan. 1, 2008; June 30, 2008, effective Aug. 1, 2008; Sept. 8, 2008, effective Oct. 7, 2008; amended effective May 15, 2009; Sept. 8, 2010, effective Jan. 1, 2009; Jan. 1, 2012; April 1, 2013)

LR49–CR23 Rule 102.   RECORDS

(a) The Clerk of the Marion County Circuit Court shall keep and maintain all records in accordance with Trial Rule 77. In addition the criminal division shall enter records of its proceedings and orders issued in the general division order book.

(b) The Clerk of the Marion Circuit Court shall also maintain a grand jury order book in which each impaneling court shall enter all records of proceedings and orders issued pertaining to the regular or special grand jury.

Adopted as Criminal Division Rule 2, effective April 8, 1996. Renumbered as Criminal Rule 102, and amended effective Oct. 2, 2006; Jan. 1, 2008.

LR49–CR00 Rule 103.   GRAND JURY

(a) The judges assigned to preside in the respective rooms of the criminal division with felony jurisdiction shall be in charge of selection, receiving and properly recording indictments and reports of the grand jury, as well as carrying out all other judicial functions relative to the grand jury during the respective quarters to which they have been assigned.

(b) Effective January 1, 1996, the grand jury shall be impaneled by the Judge of Criminal Division, Room I, for January, February, and March of 1996, as provided by law. Thereafter, the grand jury shall be impaneled in numerical sequence by quarters by each of the criminal courts designated to hear Class A, B, and C felonies. All indictments shall be returned to the impaneling court, who shall order the indictments filed pursuant to Rule 1.

Adopted as Criminal Division Rule 3, effective April 8, 1996. Renumbered as Criminal Rule 103, and amended effective Oct. 2, 2006.

LR49–CR00 Rule 104.   SPECIAL GRAND JURY

Special grand juries shall be impaneled pursuant to statute and all indictments returned ordered filed by the impaneling judge pursuant to Rule 1.

Adopted as Criminal Division Rule 4, effective April 8, 1996. Renumbered as Criminal Rule 104, and amended effective Oct. 2, 2006.

LR49–CR00 Rule 105.   TRIAL RULES

(a) The judges of the Criminal Division shall from time to time convene to adopt rules of procedure and such other business of court as they may deem necessary, proper and advisable, all subject to the ratification of the Marion Superior Court in a general meeting.

(b) The trial rules of procedure in each room of the criminal division shall be the same as provided for in the Indiana Rules of Trial Procedure and of Criminal Procedure as duly adopted by the Indiana Supreme Court, and as further provided by law.

Adopted as Criminal Division Rule 5, effective April 8, 1996. Renumbered as Criminal Rule 105, and amended effective Oct. 2, 2006.

LR49–CR2.1   Rule   106.   APPEARANCE   AND WITHDRAWAL OF COUNSEL

(a) Appearance of counsel in all cases shall be made without qualification and in writing in the form designated by Rules of the Indiana Supreme Court. Withdrawals shall be by permission of the court only, and upon written motion of the party wanting to withdraw, showing notification to the client. Upon entering an appearance, the attorney must become familiar with the Rules of the Criminal Division and rules of the court in which an appearance is entered.

(b) Pro Se Appearance. A defendant wanting to legally represent himself at trial must direct such request to the court, in clear and unequivocal terms, at least three days before date of trial. Otherwise, said request may be denied.

Adopted as Criminal Division Rule 6, effective April 8, 1996. Renumbered as Criminal Rule 106, and amended effective Oct. 2, 2006.

LR49–CR00 Rule 107. DISCOVERY

1. General.

(a) The court at initial hearing will automatically order the State to disclose and furnish all relevant items and information under this Rule to the defendant (s) within 20 days from the date of the initial hearing, subject to Constitutional limitations and protective orders, and the defendant (s) to provide the State with discovery within 45 days of the initial hearing.

(b) No written motion is required, except:

(1) To compel compliance under this Rule

(2) For additional discovery not covered under this Rule

(3) For a protective order

(4) For an extension of time

(c) All discovery shall be completed by the omnibus date unless extended for good cause shown.

(d) Although each side has a right to full discovery under this Rule, each side has a corresponding duty to seek out the discovery. Motions for original discovery and compliance with Indiana Rule of Evidence 404B are unnecessary and disfavored. Motions for specific discovery are permitted. Failure to file a Motion to Compel may result in the waiver of this right; failure to comply with providing discovery may result in sanctions, including the exclusion of evidence.

2. State Disclosure.

(a) The State shall disclose the following material and information within its possession or control:

(1) The names and last known addresses of persons whom the State intends to call as witnesses, with their relevant written or recorded statements. The State may refrain from providing a witness' address under this rule if the State in good faith believes the disclosure of the witness' address may jeopardize the safety of the witness or the witness' immediate family. If the State does not disclose the witness' address for the reason stated under this rule then the State shall make the witness available for deposition or interview by defense counsel upon reasonable notice.

Should there be a dispute among the parties concerning the disclosure of a witness' address, counsel shall meet and make a reasonable effort to resolve this dispute before seeking intervention from the court. The party seeking disclosure or a protective order under this rule shall include in the party's motion or request a statement showing that the attorney making the motion or request has made a reasonable effort to reach agreement with opposing counsel concerning the matter set forth in the motion or request. This statement shall recite in addition, the date, time and place of this effort to reach agreement, whether in person or by telephone and the names of all parties and attorneys participation therein. If an attorney for any party advises the court in writing that an opposing attorney has refused or delayed meeting and discussing the issue of witness address disclosure, the court may take such action as appropriate.

The Court may deny a discovery motion filed by a party who has failed to comply with the requirements of this subsection.

(2) Any written, oral or recorded statements made by the accused or by a co-defendant, and a list of witnesses to the making and acknowledgement of such statements.

(3) A transcript of those portions of grand jury minutes containing testimony of persons whom the prosecuting attorney intends to call as witnesses at the hearing or trial.

(4) Any reports or statements of experts, made in connection with the particular case, including results of physical or mental examinations and of scientific tests, experiments, or comparisons.

(5) Any books, papers, documents, photographs, or tangible objects that the prosecuting attorney intends to use in the hearing or trial or which were obtained from or belong to the accused.

(6) Any record of prior criminal convictions that may be used for impeachment of the persons whom the State intends to call as witnesses at the hearing or trial.

(7) All evidence required by Indiana Rules of Evidence 404(B), at least 30 days prior to trial, or within two weeks following the request for trial, whichever is later.

(b) The State shall disclose to defense counsel any material or information within its possession or control that tends to negate the guilt of the accused as to the offense charged or would tend to reduce the punishment therefore.

(c) The State may perform these obligations in any manner mutually agreeable to the prosecutor and defense counsel.

3. Defendant Disclosure.

(a) Defendant's counsel shall furnish the State with the following material and information within his/her possession or control.

(1) Any defense that he/she intends to make at a hearing or trial.

(2) The names and last know addresses of persons whom the defense intends to call as witnesses, with their relevant written or recorded statements and any record of prior criminal convictions known to him/her. The defense may refrain from providing a witness' address under this rule if the defense in good faith believes the disclosure of the witness' address may jeopardize the safety of the witness or the witness' immediate family. If the defense does not disclose the witness' address for the reason stated under this rule then the defense shall make the witness available for deposition or interview by counsel for the State upon reasonable notice. Should there be a dispute among the parties concerning the disclosure of a witness' address, counsel shall meet and make a reasonable effort to resolve this dispute before seeking intervention from the court. The party seeking disclosure or a protective order under this rule shall include in the party's motion or request a statement showing that the attorney making the motion or request has made a reasonable effort to reach agreement with opposing counsel concerning the matter set forth in the motion or request. This statement shall recite in addition, the date, time and place of this effort to reach agreement, whether in person or by telephone and the names of all parties and attorneys participation therein. If an attorney for any party advises the court in writing that an opposing attorney has refused or delayed meeting and discussing the issue of witness address disclosure, the court may take such action as is appropriate. The court may deny a discovery motion filed by a party who has failed to comply with the requirements of this subsection.

(3) Any books, papers, documents, photographs, or tangible objects he/she intends to use as evidence.

(4) Medical, scientific, or expert witness evaluations, statements, reports, or testimony that may be used at a hearing or trial.

(5) All Evidence required by Indiana Rules of Evidence 404(B), at least 30 days prior to trial, or within two weeks following the request for trial, whichever is later.

(b) After the formal charge has been filed, upon written motion by the State, the Court may require the accused, among other things, to:

(1) Appear in a line-up.

(2) Speak for identification by witnesses to an offense.

(3) Be fingerprinted.

(4) Pose for photographs not involving re-enactment of a scene.

(5) Try on articles of clothing.

(6) Allow the taking of specimens of material from under his/her fingernails.

(7) Allow the taking of samples of his/her blood, hair, and other materials of his/her body that involve no unreasonable intrusion.

(8) Provide a sample of his/her handwriting.

(9) Submit to a reasonable physical or medical inspection of he/her body.

Whenever the personal appearance of the accused is required for the foregoing purposes, reasonable notice of the time and place of such appearance shall be given by the State to the accused and his/her counsel, who shall have the right to be present. Provision may be made for appearances for such purposes in an order admitting the accused to bail or providing for his/her release.

4. **Additions, Limitations, and Protective Order.**

(a) *Discretionary Disclosures.* Upon a showing of materiality to the preparation of the defense, and if the request is reasonable, the court, in its discretion, may require disclosure to defense counsel of relevant material and information not covered by this Rule.

(b) *Denial of Disclosure.* The court may deny disclosure authorized by this Rule if it finds that there is a substantial risk to any person of physical harm, intimidation, bribery, economic reprisals, or unnecessary annoyance or embarrassment resulting from such disclosure to counsel.

(c) *Matters Not Subject to Disclosure.*

(1) Work product. Disclosure hereunder shall not be required of legal research or records, correspondence, reports or memoranda to the extent that they contain the opinions, theories, or conclusions of the State or members of its legal or investigative staffs, or of defense counsel or his/her staff.

(2) Informants. Disclosure of an informant's identity shall not be required where there is a paramount interest in non-disclosure and a failure to disclose will not infringe the Constitutional rights of the accused. Disclosure shall not be denied hereunder of the identity of witnesses to be produced at a hearing or trial.

(a) Either side may apply for a protective order for non-disclosure of requested discovery.

5. **Depositions.** Any sworn tape-recorded interview in which the prosecutor, the defense attorney and the witnesses are present shall be considered a deposition under the Indiana Trial Rules. Deputy prosecutors and public defenders shall cooperate in using such recorded statements instead of formal de-

positions under any circumstance that will expedite case preparation.

Adopted as Criminal Division Rule 7, effective April 8, 1996. Amended effective May 25, 1999; amended effective Nov. 3, 2003; renumbered as Criminal Rule 107, and amended effective Oct. 2, 2006; Jan. 1, 2008; May 15, 2009.

LR49–CR00 Rule 108. BAIL

I. SCOPE: This Provisional Bail Schedule shall apply to all defendants arrested outright in Marion County. This schedule shall not apply to those cases where a judicial officer already has issued a warrant with a predetermined bail.

II. GENERAL PROVISIONS

A. Bail amounts set pursuant to this schedule shall be based upon the lead charge brought against the defendant. No bail amount set pursuant to this schedule shall exceed $200,000. The bail clerk does not have discretion to alter provisional bail amounts. Bail amounts set pursuant to this schedule shall not be altered until such time as the assigned trial judge has the opportunity to conduct further review.

B. Arrestee Processing Center commissioners are responsible for reviewing the bail set by the bail clerk and may correct that amount pursuant to the schedule if a commissioner becomes aware of relevant information not considered when bail was first set. Arrestee Processing Center commissioners also may impose appropriate pre-trial release conditions.

III. MAJOR FELONY BAIL AMOUNTS:

A. General.

Murder	No Bail
Class A Felony	$50,000 Surety
Class B Felony	$20,000 Surety
Class C Felony	$7,500 Surety

B. Enhancements: The bail schedule amounts shall double for each of the following circumstances applying to the defendant:

1. The defendant is not a Marion County resident,

2. The crime alleged involves a deadly weapon or serious bodily injury,

3. The defendant has two or more alleged victims,

4. The defendant has two or more prior felony convictions,

5. The defendant has two or more failures to appear,

6. The defendant has ten or more prior arrests (not including public intoxication arrests). This category shall double for each additional 10 arrests a defendant has.

7. The defendant has been arrested for an offense while on probation, parole, bond or released on the person's own recognizance for another offense.

IV. CLASS D FELONY BAIL AMOUNTS:

A. General: Class D Felony—Own Recognizance (OR) up to $2,500 Surety, $2,500 10% PR, or $250 Cash Bond.

The bail clerk shall set bail for a Class D felony at $2,500 Surety. Arrestee Processing Center commissioners shall have the discretion to modify the bail within the range provided if deemed appropriate.

B. Enhancements. The bail schedule amounts shall double, up to a maximum of $5,000, for each of the following circumstances:

1. The defendant is not a Marion County resident,

2. The defendant has one or more failures to appear,

3. The defendant has one or more prior felony convictions,

4. The defendant is charged with one of the following Class D felonies:

- Battery (I.C. § 35–42–2–1)
- Criminal Confinement (I.C. § 35–42–3–3)
- Criminal Gang Activity (I.C. § 35–45–9–3)
- Criminal Recklessness (I.C. § 35–42–2–2—all sections)
- Escape (I.C. § 35–44–3–5)
- Intimidation (I.C. § 35–45–2–1)
- Pointing a Firearm (I.C. § 35–47–4–3)
- Residential Entry (I.C. § 35–43–2–1.5)
- Resisting Law Enforcement (I.C. § 35–44–3–3)
- Stalking (I.C. § 35–45–10–5)
- Strangulation (I.C. § 35–42–2–8)

V. MISDEMEANOR BAIL AMOUNTS:

Class A Misdemeanor	Own Recognizance up to $1,500 10% Cash
Class B Misdemeanor	Own Recognizance
Class B Misdemeanor (Battery)	Own Recognizance up to $1,500 10% Cash
Class C Misdemeanor	Own Recognizance

The bail clerk shall set bail for Class A misdemeanors and Class B misdemeanor battery cases at $1,500. If the new offense is a Class B or Class C misdemeanor and the defendant has been arrested for an offense while on probation, parole, bond, or released on the person's own recognizance for another offense, bail shall be set at $1,500 10% Cash. Arrestee Processing Center commissioners shall have the discretion to modify the bail within the ranges provided if deemed appropriate.

VI. SPECIAL CONSIDERATIONS

A. Domestic Violence Cases.

Class C Felony	$25,000 Surety
Class D Felony	$10,000 Surety plus
	$10,000 10% Cash
Class A Misdemeanor	$5,000 Surety plus
	$5,000 10% Cash

A person charged with a crime of domestic violence as defined in I.C. § 35–41–1–6.3 shall be kept in custody and not released on bail for at least eight (8) hours from the time of arrest pursuant to I.C. § 35–33–1–1.7 and I. C. § 35–33–8–6.5.

If a domestic violence charge is not the lead charge and this schedule would require a higher bail for the domestic violence charge standing alone, the bail clerk should set the bail as if the domestic violence charge were the lead charge.

B. Invasion of Privacy Cases.

Class D Felony	$10,000 Surety plus
	$10,000 10% Cash
Class A Misdemeanor	$5,000 Surety plus
	$5,000 10% Cash

If an invasion of privacy charge is not the lead charge and this schedule would require a higher bail for the invasion of privacy charge standing alone, the bail clerk should set the bail as if the invasion of privacy charge were the lead charge.

C. Operating Vehicle While Intoxicated (Misdemeanor) Cases. Bail shall be set at $1,500 10% Cash with a $1,000 increase for each prior conviction under I.C. § 9–30–5.

D. Court 13 Cases. A person arrested for or charged with a misdemeanor traffic offense and slated into Court 13 shall be released on the person's own recognizance.

E. Child Molesting, Child Solicitation, and Sexually Violent Predator Cases. No bail will be issued until the trial court has conducted a bail hearing for a person who is charged with Child Molesting (I.C. § 35–42–4–3) or Child Solicitation (I.C. § 35–42–4–6);

No bail will be issued until the trial court has conducted a bail hearing for a person who has been determined to be a sexually violent predator defendant as defined in I.C. § 35–33–8–3.5.

The Arrestee Processing Center commissioner shall set such cases for a bail hearing in the appropriate court no later than 48 hours after the person has been arrested or at the earliest possible setting if exigent circumstances prevent holding the hearing within 48 hours.

VIII REVIEW OF PROVISIONAL BAIL AMOUNT

Except for major felony courts, the trial court to which the defendant's case is assigned shall review the bail set:

A. within 5 days of the arrest of any defendant who has not yet made bail as set by the Arrestee

Processing Center commissioner or pursuant to the Provisional Bail Schedule; or,

B. within 5 days upon receipt of motion of the State or the defendant pursuant to I.C. § 35–33–8–5.

Adopted as Criminal Division Rule 8, effective April 8, 1996. Amended effective Dec. 5, 1997; Sept. 29, 1998; Oct. 6, 1999; June 23, 2000; July 1, 2001; renumbered as Criminal Rule 108, and amended effective Oct. 2, 2006; amended effective April 4, 2008; Mar. 10, 2010.

LR49–CR20 Rule 109. CONTINUANCES, INITIAL HEARINGS and REVIEW OF COUNSEL

(a) Felonies/misdemeanors: If a party desires to continue a setting in a felony or misdemeanor case, trial or otherwise, the party shall file a verified written motion stating in detail the reasons why the setting needs to be continued. The motion shall also include the type of hearing, opposing counsel's position, and suggested dates for the court. Such motion shall be filed at least five days (excluding Saturdays, Sundays and court holidays) before the setting that the party desires the court to continue unless the time has been modified by the judge presiding over the cause. A written order with sufficient copies for all parties shall accompany the motion. Until such motion is granted by the court, it shall be deemed denied.

(b) Misdemeanors: If a party files a motion for Waiver of Initial Hearing *and the only future court event is scheduled is an initial hearing, or if a party files a motion to add a new case event*, then the party shall include in the motion the type of future case event requested and shall provide suggested dates, per the Trial Court's scheduling guidelines. Such motion shall be filed at least five days (excluding Saturdays, Sundays, and court holidays) before the date on which the hearing is currently set, unless the time has been modified by the judge presiding over the cause. A written order with sufficient copies for all parties shall accompany the motion.

(c) When an attorney's appearance is filed *and the only future case event scheduled is Review of Counsel,* then the Review of Counsel hearing shall be converted to a Pre Trial Conference

(d) Infractions/ordinance violations: If a party desires to continue a setting in a case involving only infractions and/or ordinance violations, the party shall file a verified written motion stating in detail the reasons why the setting needs to be continued. Such motion shall be filed at least ten days (excluding Saturdays, Sundays, and court holidays) prior to the setting that the party desires the court to continue.

(e) No criminal court shall grant a continuance in excess of 14 calendar days for in-custody D felony and misdemeanor cases, or in excess of 30 calendar days for in-custody major felony cases, without good cause shown.

Adopted as Criminal Division Rule 9, effective April 8, 1996. Renumbered as Criminal Rule 109, and amended effective Oct. 2, 2006; Jan. 1, 2008; May 15, 2009; Aug. 8, 2011.

LR49–CR10.1 Rule 110. REQUEST FOR GUILTY PLEA HEARING

The court will set a guilty plea hearing only after an oral request on the record or a written pleading, i.e., a petition to enter plea of guilty or a plea agreement is filed.

Adopted as Criminal Division Rule 10, effective April 8, 1996. Renumbered as Criminal Rule 110, and amended effective Oct. 2, 2006.

LR49–TR4.1 Rule 111. SERVICE—LAW ENFORCEMENT

Service of a subpoena may be made upon a law enforcement officer, by delivering the subpoena to the officer's place of employment. A copy of the subpoena shall be left with the official in charge of the department. It shall be the duty of the official to immediately deliver the subpoena to the officer being served. Service in this manner shall be deemed service on the officer.

Adopted as Criminal Division Rule 11, effective April 8, 1996. Renumbered as Criminal Rule 111, and amended effective Oct. 2, 2006.

LR49–CR00 Rule 112. MANDATORY CONSECUTIVE SENTENCES

Where consecutive sentencing is mandated under Indiana Code 35–50–1–2(d), the sentence calling for more restrictive placement shall be served prior to any sentence for less restrictive placement. For purpose of this rule, the following placements are listed in order from most restrictive to least restrictive:

1. Incarceration at the Indiana Department of Corrections

2. Incarceration at the Marion County Jail

3. Incarceration at the Correctional Component (Jail Annex) of Marion County Community Corrections

4. Commitment to a Work Release Facility (VOA or Riverside)

5. Commitment to Home Detention with Electronic Monitoring

6. Commitment to Day Reporting

If the sentence calling for more restrictive sentencing is entered after the sentence for less restrictive sentencing, the Judge ordering less restrictive placement shall issue an amended abstract ordering such sentence to be served consecutive to the more restrictive placement. The amended abstract shall be issued no more than 10 days following notice that a more restrictive sentence has been entered.

Where terms of probation are mandated to run consecutively under Indiana Code 35–40–1–2(d), the term calling for the least restrictive conditions shall run consecutive to the term(s) calling for more restrictive conditions. The Marion Superior Probation Department shall make the determination as to which term of probation is most restrictive, and as to which term shall be served first.

The Chair of the Criminal Division is authorized to issue any orders necessary to enforce the provisions of this rule.

Adopted as Criminal Division Rule 12, effective May 25, 1999. Amended effective July 27, 1999; renumbered as Criminal Rule 112, and amended effective Oct. 2, 2006.

LR49–CR00 Rule 113. TRANSFER OF PRISONERS TO THE INDIANA DEPARTMENT OF CORRECTIONS

Unless otherwise ordered by the Court, any defendant sentenced for a felony offense, including Class D Felonies, shall be sentenced to the Indiana Department of Corrections.

In cases where a defendant has been sentenced to the Indiana Department of Corrections and has another case pending in Marion County, the Marion County Sheriff may not transfer the defendant to the Department of Corrections without first providing seven days notice to the Court with jurisdiction over the pending case. Either party may petition the Court to have a defendant or prisoner held in the Marion County Jail. The Court shall promptly notify counsel in the pending case of the defendant's proposed transfer to the Department of Corrections. After seven days, the defendant shall be transferred to the Department of Corrections unless the Court issues an Order for good cause shown to hold the defendant in the Marion county jail. The Marion County Sheriff's Department shall then notify the Court with jurisdiction over the defendant's pending case, that the defendant has been transferred to the Indiana Department of Corrections. Notification under this rule should be by facsimile or electronic mail.

Adopted as Criminal Division Rule 13, effective April 2, 2001. Renumbered as Criminal Rule 113, and amended effective Oct. 2, 2006.

LR49–CR00 Rule 114. CASE DISPOSITION GUIDELINES

Unless there is good cause shown, all criminal matters with a jailed defendant shall be tried, plead or dismissed as follows:

1. All misdemeanors within 45 days of initial hearing.

2. All class D felonies within 90 days of initial hearing.

3. All class C felonies within 120 days of initial hearing.

4. All class A and B felonies within 180 days of initial hearing.

5. Murder cases within 365 days of initial hearing.

The following deadlines shall apply to all cases filed in the Marion Superior Court after the effective date of this rule:

Initial Discovery is to be provided according within the following time frame:

C Felonies	20 days after initial hearing
A & B Felonies	20 days after initial hearing
Murder	30 days after initial hearing

State's Notice of Intended Witnesses and Exhibits is to be filed within the following time frame:

C Felonies	20 days after initial discovery
A & B Felonies	20 days after initial discovery
Murder	30 days after initial discovery

Defendant's Notice of Intended Witnesses and Exhibits is to be filed within the following time frame:

C Felonies	5 days after receipt of State's Notice of Witnesses
A & B Felonies	5 days after receipt of State's Notice of Witnesses
Murder	5 days after receipt of State's Notice of Witnesses

Depositions are to be scheduled within the following time frame:

C Felonies	30 days after receipt of Notice of Witnesses & Exhibits
A & B Felonies	45 days after receipt of Notice of Witnesses & Exhibits
Murder	60 days after receipt of Notice of Witnesses & Exhibits

Counsel seeking depositions are to confer with opposing counsel to determine dates that are mutually convenient to all counsel and the potential deponent. Motions (Substantive), for which deadlines are not otherwise established by statute or rule, including but not limited to Motions to Suppress, Requests for Hearings under the Protected Person Statute and IRE 702, are to be filed within the following time frame:

C Felonies	30 days after receipt of Notice of Witnesses & Exhibits
A & B Felonies	30 days after receipt of Notice of Witnesses & Exhibits
Murder	30 days after receipt of Notice of Witnesses & Exhibits

Final Witness & Exhibit List

C Felonies	15 days before any scheduled trial date
A & B Felonies	30 days before any scheduled trial date
Murder	30 days before any scheduled trial date

Motions in Limine

C Felonies	3 business days before final pre-trial conference
A & B Felonies	5 business days before final pre-trial conference
Murder	5 business days before final pre-trial conference

Objections/Responses to Motions in Limine

C Felonies	1 business day before final pre-trial conference
A & B Felonies	2 business days before final pre-trial conference
Murder	2 business days before final pre-trial conference

Proposed Preliminary Instructions

C Felonies	2 business days before trial date
A & B Felonies	2 business days before trial date
Murder	2 business days before trial date

Sanctions: Failure to comply with the provisions of this rule may result in sanction including exclusion of witnesses or exhibits, continuance of a trial charged to the party necessitating the continuance, issuance of an order compelling or prohibiting discovery, or any other remedy deemed appropriate by the court.

Adopted as Criminal Division Rule 14, effective July 23, 2002. Renumbered as Criminal Rule 114, and amended effective Oct. 2, 2006. Amended effective Mar. 10, 2010.

LR49–CR00 Rule 115.   FEES

A. In addition to costs as set by I.C 33–37–4–1 whenever an individual is placed on probation, or without placing a person on probation the following fees and costs shall be imposed under the Probation Court or Probation Order unless the sentencing Judge specifically modifies the Order. The fees and costs collected under the Court or Probation Order shall be applied in this order of priority.

Administrative fee
Probation User fee
Alcohol and Drug Service fee (33–37–5–8)
Court Costs (I.C 33–37–4–1)
Restitution (35–50–5–3)
Public Defender Reimbursement * (35–33–7–6)
Safe School fee (I.C. 33–37–5–18)
Child Abuse Prevention fee (I.C. 33–37–5–12)
Drug Interdiction fee (I.C. 33–37–5–9)
Alcohol Countermeasures fee (I.C. 33–37–5–10)
Domestic Violence fee (33–37–5–13)

(*Fee imposed only after judicial determination of ability to pay)

In the event that these specific fees, or any other court ordered fees, are not paid, the Court may enter judgment against the individual and may seek appropriate steps to collect the judgment owed.

B. Whenever a juvenile is placed on probation from Juvenile Court the following fees and costs shall be imposed under the appropriate Court Order unless the Judge presiding over the case specifically modifies the Order. The fees and costs collected under the Order shall be applied in this order of priority.

Probation User Fee
Restitution
Public Defenders Fee
Court Costs

In the event that these specific fees, or any other court ordered fees, are not paid, the Court may enter judgment against the individual and may seek appropriate steps to collect the judgment owed.

C. Whenever a person is ordered by any Judicial Officer of the Marion Superior Court to be tested by the Marion Superior Court Drug Testing Laboratory, an appropriate fee shall be paid at the time of testing. The Marion County Drug Lab shall collect said fee and all such fees shall be Probation Department funds. If a confirmatory test is requested by an individual, an appropriate fee shall be paid at the time of testing. The Judicial Officer ordering an individual for drug testing retains authority to determine that individual is indigent and order a waiver of the testing

D. All Marion County Courts certified as Problem–Solving Courts under I.C. 33–23–16 may assess costs pursuant to statute.

Adopted effective Oct. 2, 2006. Amended effective Jan. 1, 2008; amended June 30, 2008, effective Aug. 1, 2008; amended March 5, 2009, effective April 4, 2009; amended Oct. 5, 2011, effective Nov. 8, 2011.

MARION SUPERIOR COURT ADMINISTRATIVE RULES

Amended Effective October 2, 2006

Including Amendments Received Through November 1, 2013

Annotations to the Marion Superior Court Administrative Rules are available in West's Annotated Indiana Code, *Title 34 Appendix.*

These rules may be searched electronically on Westlaw *in the* IN-RULES *database; updates to these rules may be found on Westlaw in* IN-RULESUPDATES. *For search tips and a summary of database content, consult the Westlaw Scope Screens for each database.*

LR49–AR00 Rule 300.	Executive Committee
LR49–AR00 Rule 301.	Administrative Management
LR49–AR1(E) Rule 302[1].	Rules on Caseload Allocation
LR49–AR00 Rule 303.	Court Administrator
LR49–TR78 Rule 304.	Judicial Officers
LR49–AR00 Rule 305.	Budgetary Procedures
LR49–AR00 Rule 306.	Amendment of Administrative Rules
LR49–AR15 Rule 307.	Court Reporter Services
[1]LR49–AR00 Rule 308.	Purchases Made with Federal Grant Funds
LR49–AR00 Rule 309.	Ex Parte Communication in Problem Solving Courts
LR49–AR00 Rule 310.	Late Fees
LR49–AR16 Rule 311.	Electronic Filing

LR49–AR00 Rule 300. EXECUTIVE COMMITTEE

A. Creation. An Executive Committee comprised of four judges: one Presiding Judge and three Associate Presiding Judges, shall exercise the power of the Court. The Executive Committee shall be elected to a two-year term of office by a two-thirds (⅔) vote of the total number of judges sitting on the Court. No more than two members of the Executive Committee may be members of the same political party.

B. Qualifications. The candidates for the Executive Committee should possess management, administrative and leadership skills, and a capacity to work effectively with other branches of government.

C. Election.[1] The Court shall hold an election for the Executive Committee on the third Tuesday in January, 1997. The Court shall thereafter hold elections for the Executive Committee on the third Tuesday in January, every two years. Election shall be held by secret ballot.

1. *Statement of Candidacy.* Any qualified judge wishing to be a candidate for the Executive Committee must notify the Executive Committee in writing not less than 30 days prior to the election. The Executive Committee shall be responsible for adopting and distributing Statement of Candidacy forms. Nominations from the floor will not be accepted unless there are an insufficient number of qualified candidates on the date of the election.

2. *Election.* The election shall be held at a time and place to be announced by the Executive Committee. The Court Administrator shall serve as clerk of the election (hereinafter "Clerk"). The Clerk shall prepare ballots listing in alphabetical order the name and political party of each candidate for the Executive Committee. Each judge eligible to vote shall receive a ballot. Each judge shall vote in person or by absentee ballot for four candidates, no more than two of whom are members of the same political party. Any ballot, which is cast for more than four candidates or more than two candidates from the same party, shall be void and not counted.

A qualified judge may vote by absentee ballot on the form provided by the Executive Committee not less than three days prior to the election in the Court Administrator's office. **An absentee ballot is only valid for the first ballot.**

3. *Process.* The Executive Committee shall be elected in the following manner:

On the first ballot, each judge shall cast a ballot for four candidates no more than two of whom are members of the same political party.

On a second and subsequent ballot, each judge shall cast a ballot for the total number of vacancies remaining on the Executive Committee after the previous ballot but in no event shall the Executive Committee have more than two members of the same political party.

If, on the first ballot, four candidates receive a two-thirds (⅔) vote of the total number of judges sitting on the court, and no more than two are from the same political party they will comprise the Executive Committee.

If fewer than four judges receive a two-thirds (⅔) vote on the first ballot, then that judge or those judges receiving a two-thirds (⅔) vote, shall be members of the Executive Committee and other ballots shall be taken to fill the vacancy on the Executive Committee.

If a second ballot is required to complete the Executive Committee because fewer than four judges received a two-thirds (⅔) vote, all subsequent ballots shall be determined by a two-thirds (⅔) vote of those sitting judges voting in person at the time of the subsequent ballot.

If fewer than the candidates necessary to complete the Executive Committee receive a two-thirds (⅔) vote of those voting, then subsequent ballots shall be taken at which time the judge with the lowest number of votes on the previous ballot shall be dropped from the ballot and a vote taken until the Executive Committee is selected.

4. *Results.* The Clerk shall count the ballots and announce the vote totals. The ballots shall be retained by the Clerk for 60 days after the election and then destroyed.

5. *Term.* Members of the Executive Committee shall be elected to serve a two-year term and shall not be prohibited from serving additional terms.

6. *Presiding Judge.* The Presiding Judge of the Executive Committee shall be elected from the four members of the Executive Committee by a majority vote of the total number of judges present and voting. The remaining three members of the Executive Committee shall serve as Associate Presiding Judges.

7. *Executive Committee Vacancy.* Any vacancy created during the two-year term of the Executive Committee shall be filled in the following manner:

A vote to fill the position for the remainder of the term shall be taken within 30 days after the vacancy is created.

The Presiding Judge of the Executive Committee shall set a date for the election to fill the vacant position of the Executive Committee.

Any qualified judge wishing to be a candidate for the vacancy on the Executive Committee must notify the Executive Committee in writing not less than ten days prior to the election. A qualified judge shall be a judge from the same political party as the judge whose position on the Executive Committee is being filled.

The Court Administrator shall serve as the Clerk of the election, and shall prepare ballots listing in alphabetical order the name and political party of each candidate for the vacancy of the Executive Committee.

The election to fill a vacancy on the Executive Committee shall be filled by a vote as set out in LR49–AR00–300(C).

A judge who is elected to fill a vacancy shall serve the remainder of the term of the judge he or she is replacing.

If the vacancy is the position of Presiding Judge, when the vacancy is filled, a second ballot shall be taken with respect to the four judges comprising the Executive Committee, and the judge receiving the most votes shall become the Presiding Judge.

If the vacancy is not the position of Presiding Judge, the Presiding Judge shall continue to serve in that capacity until the end of his or her term.

If the vacancy that occurs is not the position of the Presiding Judge, the Presiding Judge shall set the date for the election and send notice to all superior court judges. The date of the election shall not be less than 30 days from the date when notice is issued.

If the vacancy that occurs is the position of Presiding Judge, the three Associate Presiding Judges shall determine the date of the election and shall serve notice in accordance with paragraph i.

Any qualified judge who wishes to run for a position on the Executive Committee shall send written notice to the Court Administrator not less than ten days prior to the scheduled election. Any notice received after the tenth day preceding the election shall be void and the judge's name shall not be added to the ballot. All notices shall be date stamped by the Court Administrator on the day received.

D. Authority. The Executive Committee is responsible for the operation and conduct of the Court. Each member of the Executive Committee shall have an equal vote in all matters pertaining to the operation of the Court. In the event of a tie, the Presiding Judge's vote shall be the tiebreaking vote. Beginning with the election of the Executive Committee in 2007, no Presiding Judge may be elected from the same political party as the Presiding Judge who served the previous term. Action may be taken upon a majority vote of the Executive Committee, except for the reassignment of a judge to a different courtroom which shall require a unanimous vote.

E. Duties. The Executive Committee shall have the following duties, which are subject to the review process as outlined in LR49–AR00–300(F):

1. Initiate policy concerning the Court's internal operations and its position on external matters affecting the Court;

2. Represent the Court in its relations with other agencies of government, the bar, the general public, the news media, and in ceremonial functions;

3. Counsel and assist other judges in the performance of their responsibilities in the administration of the Court;

4. Assign judges and judicial officers in the interest of speedy, economical and uniform disposition of cases;

5. Establish policies concerning such matters as personnel management, case flow management, and other areas of concern that effect the management of the Court.

6. Be responsible for the fiscal operations of the Court;

7. Appoint a magistrate under Ind. Code § 33–4–7;

8. Appoint the Court Administrator and the Chief Probation Officer; and other personnel necessary to maintain the efficient operation of the Court;

9. Review and take any action necessary concerning the performance of the Court Administrator and the Court Services Agency; and

10. Report all actions and proposed actions to the General Term through minutes or otherwise.

F. Review. With the exception of subsections (1) and (2) below, any judge affected by a decision of the Executive Committee may call for a vote to override the decision, at the first General Term Meeting following the decision. However, if there are fewer than ten days between the date of the decision and the next scheduled General Term Meeting, the vote shall be taken at the second meeting following the announcement of the decision. A decision of the Executive Committee may be overruled by a two-thirds (⅔) vote of the total number of judges sitting on the Court. A call to override a decision of the Executive Committee shall be filed in writing with the Presiding Judge with copy service to all judges sitting on the Marion Superior Court.

Re-assignment of Judges. Decisions of the Executive Committee, which re-assign a judge to a different courtroom or a substantially different type of caseload without the written consent of the affected judge, will not be effective until approved by a two-thirds (⅔) vote of the total number of judges sitting on the Court.

Staffing. Decisions of the Executive Committee, concerning staffing levels or transfer of staff employees for the Court without the written consent of the affected judge, will not be effective until approved by a two-thirds (⅔) vote of the total number of judges sitting on the Court.

G. Meetings. The Executive Committee shall meet regularly as it deems necessary. The Presiding Judge shall call and preside over meetings of the Executive Committee and other meetings of the Court.

H. Committees. The Executive Committee may establish such committees to be appointed by the

Presiding Judge, as may be useful to establish policy and to consult with the Executive Committee.

Adopted as Article III, effective Sept. 11, 2000. Amended effective Dec. 4, 2000; renumbered as Rule 300, and amended effective Oct. 2, 2006; amended effective Jan. 1, 2012.

LR49–AR00 Rule 301. ADMINISTRATIVE MANAGEMENT

A. The Executive Committee shall, by Rules of the Court, divide the work of the Court into various divisions, including but not limited to the following:

1. Civil Division;

2. Criminal Division;

3. Juvenile Division; and

4. Probate Division.

The Executive Committee shall appoint a chair for each division for a period of two years. The chairs of the divisions shall alternate between parties unless there is only one judge in a division.

B. The Executive Committee shall determine the assignment of judges following a general election as follows:

1. An incumbent judge shall be allowed the option of remaining in a particular division or room.

2. The expertise and abilities of the judge shall be given consideration.

3. Seniority shall be a primary consideration, but not the sole determinant factor. Seniority is defined as length of service as a judge on the Marion Superior or former Marion Municipal Courts

4. The desire of the particular judge regarding his or her assignment shall be given consideration.

5. The political balance of each division shall be considered along with the desire to maintain racial and gender diversity within each division. All appointments shall reflect the bipartisan composition of the Court, whenever possible.

6. Reassignment of a sitting judge to a different courtroom requires a unanimous vote of the Executive Committee.

C. The Executive Committee shall fill a vacancy on the Court in the following manner:

1. Any qualified judge wishing to be a candidate for the vacancy on the Court shall notify the Executive Committee in writing not more than ten days after the vacancy is created.

2. The Executive Committee may interview any qualified judge interested in reassignment to fill a vacancy

3. The Executive Committee shall consider the criteria used for assignment of judges following an election in determining who shall fill a vacancy.

4.   The Executive Committee shall fill the vacancy within 30 days after the vacancy is created or as soon as possible.

D.   The Executive Committee shall assign cases, offices and courtrooms for judges or reassignment of newly filed cases in the interests of the speedy, economical and uniform disposition of cases.

E.   Pursuant to LR49–AR00–300(G), the Executive Committee shall determine the number of hearing judges, commissioners, referees, bail commissioners, court reporters, probation officers, and other personnel required to efficiently serve the Court. The salaries of the personnel shall be fixed and paid as provided by law.

F.   The Executive Committee shall prepare and administer a budget for the Court so that the Court is provided with supplies and sufficient personnel. Each judge shall appoint the judge's bailiffs, clerks, court reporters and secretary.

G.   On the first Monday of each month, unless otherwise designated, the Presiding Judge of the Executive Committee shall preside over a General Term Meeting of the judges. A special order book shall be kept for the Court in which shall be entered all appropriate records, rules, orders and assignments of the Court.

1.   *Voting:* Judges may cast their votes in person or by written proxy at any duly constituted meeting of the Marion Superior Court. All votes shall be by voice vote unless any judge present shall request a written ballot. Proxies may only be given to another member of the court to be exercised as directed.

2.   *Special Meetings:* The presiding judge may call a special meeting upon proper notice given and shall call a special meeting at the request of at least three of the judges of the Marion Superior Court.

3.   *Notice:* Notice of any special meeting shall be given in writing to each judge at least 24 hours before such scheduled special meeting.

4.   *Quorum:* The presence of one-third (⅓) of the judges shall constitute a quorum for any meeting of the Marion Superior Court. Proxies shall be included in determining whether a quorum exists.

Adopted as Article IV, effective Sept. 11, 2000. Renumbered as Rule 301, and amended effective Oct. 2, 2006.

LR49–AR1(E) Rule 302[1].   RULES ON CASELOAD ALLOCATION

A.   Purpose.   Caseload allocations shall allow the judges of the Marion Superior Court to make thoughtful, timely, reasonable and just decisions.

B.   Procedure.   The Executive Committee shall at least annually:

1.   Review and assess literature on case flow management from any source with a view toward the improvement of the Court's case flow from filing to disposition;

2.   Review and consider suggestions made by members of the bar, the public and other interested parties; and

3.   Review and analyze the statistics or current workload and case flow within the Court.

a.   Civil cases shall be assigned in accordance with LR49–TR3–200 Random Filing of Civil Cases. Criminal cases shall be filed in accordance with LR49–CR 2.2–100 Random Assignment of Criminal Cases and LR49–CR 2.3–101 Case Consolidation.

b.   Allocate Judicial Officers where appropriate to keep within the weighted caseload requirements of no more than a .40 deviation between any two courts.

c.   Any change involving caseloads, whether it is type of case or number of cases, shall require a majority vote of the Executive Committee and is subject to review under LR49–AR00–300(F)(2).

d.   In deciding changes, the Executive Committee shall give due weight to the expertise and abilities of each judge, the stress associated with the types of cases and caseloads, and the goal of keeping each judge competent in the various areas of the law. Seniority shall be a consideration, but not the determinant factor for caseload allocation or courtroom assignment.

e.   As new judges are appointed or elected to the Court, the Executive Committee shall assign them to courtrooms using the same criteria.

C.   Implementation.   The Clerk of the Court shall maintain systems as required to implement orders of the Court relating to case allocation.

D.   Record Keeping.   All matters of statistics and case flow management shall be collected and maintained by personnel in the office of Marion County Court Administration. All judges and their staffs shall be responsible for the collection and preparation of these statistics in a form and manner directed by the Executive Committee.

Adopted as Article V, effective Sept. 11, 2000. Renumbered as Rule 302, and amended effective Oct. 2, 2006. Amended effective Jan. 11, 2008; effective March 29, 2010; Jan. 1, 2012.

1 See Supreme Court Order regarding Local Rules for Caseload Management issued on September 8, 2010.

LR49–AR00 Rule 303.   COURT ADMINISTRATOR

The Court Administrator shall have the following duties:

A.   Coordinate preparation of a budget for the Court.

B.   Supervise expenditures of the Court, including but not limited to the following:

1.   Jury meals, lodging and *per diem* expenses;

2. Witness fees;

3. Pauper transcripts;

4. Contractual legal services;

5. Contractual professional services;

6. Maintenance agreements; and

7. Any other claims designated by the judges of the Court.

C. Report expenditures of the Court not less than quarterly to the Executive Committee.

D. Hire administrative officers for the Court Services Agency, the Domestic Relations Counseling Bureau, the Jury Pool, the Marion County Law Library, and other personnel necessary to maintain the efficient operation of the Court.

E. Supervise the management of the Court Services Agency, Domestic Relations Counseling Bureau, the General Term Reporter, and the Marion County Law Library in accordance with rules and guidelines established by the Executive Committee.

F. Provide orientation and continuing education programs for judicial officers and other Court personnel.

G. Coordinate support services to handle purchasing and explore the advantages of group purchasing for the Court.

H. Coordinate the maximum utilization of available courtrooms.

I. Develop and implement uniform personnel classifications and guidelines to comply the Fair Labor Standards Act [1].

J. Review and analyze the statistics of the Court and file quarterly reports with the office of the State Court Administrator.

K. Any other duties established by the Executive Committee.

Adopted as Article VI, effective Sept. 11, 2000. Amended effective Dec. 4, 2000; renumbered as Rule 303, and amended effective Oct. 2, 2006.

[1] 29 U.S.C.A. §§ 201 to 209.

LR49–TR78 Rule 304. JUDICIAL OFFICERS

The Court may employ judicial officers, including magistrates and commissioners, to perform limited judicial functions under the authority of the Court and subject to judicial approval. The judge or judges to whom they are assigned may recommend commissioners.

A. Qualifications. Judicial officers shall be residents of Marion County in good standing as members of the Indiana bar, be admitted to practice of law at least five years, and possess any other qualifications required by statute or rule of court.

B. Duties. Judicial officers shall assist the Court by performing such functions as conducting preliminary and interlocutory hearings in criminal and civil cases, presiding over disputed discovery proceedings, receiving testimony as referees or masters, and hearing other causes and motions, all of which are subject to judicial approval.

C. Selection. The Executive Committee may advertise notice of prospective appointments of judicial officers publicly to encourage applications for consideration. Applicants may be interviewed with regard to their potential proficiency as judicial officers. The Executive Committee may appoint a screening committee to review the applicants and make recommendations on their qualifications.

Where the application is for a Commissioner, the judge or judges to whom they are assigned shall select the applicant to be appointed by the Executive Committee. If the judges are unable to agree, the applicant shall be selected and appointed by the Executive Committee.

Appointments shall require ratification by a majority vote by secret ballot of the total number of judges sitting on the Court. The Executive Committee shall make the appointments. All appointments shall reflect the bipartisan composition of the Court, whenever possible.

D. Term. Judicial officers shall serve at the discretion of the Executive Committee. The Executive Committee shall assign magistrates. Supervising judges may recommend termination of the employment of their commissioners. If both judges agree, employment shall be terminated. If one of the supervising judges does not agree, the Executive Committee shall determine the issue of continued employment.

E. Annual Evaluation. Magistrates and Commissioners shall be evaluated annually.

Adopted as Article VII, effective Sept. 11, 2000. Amended effective Dec. 4, 2000; renumbered as Rule 304, and amended effective Oct. 2, 2006.

LR49–AR00 Rule 305. BUDGETARY PROCEDURES

A. Budgets. The Executive Committee shall prepare and submit a unified budget for the Court to be funded upon approval of the City-County Council.

B. Annual Procedure. Each year the Executive Committee shall establish a schedule for the Court and its divisions to submit a proposed budget for budget preparation, review and submission by the Executive Committee with the goal of providing for the effective functioning of the Court, as follows:

1. Each judge and administrative officer shall submit written budget requests to the Court Administrator.

2. The Executive Committee shall meet to review the budget requests and may request further information from the judges and administrative officers or any other source.

3. The Executive Committee shall establish and set budget priorities and direct the Court Administrator to prepare the budget proposal for submission to the City–County Council.

C. Allocation of Resources. The Executive Committee shall establish guidelines for allocation of individual line items in the yearly budget approved by the City-County Council. Each judge shall be allocated an adequate amount at the beginning of the year for office expenses, including supplies, stationery, equipment, association dues, disciplinary fees and travel.

D. Claims. All claims shall be submitted to the Court Administrator for review to determine compliance with budgetary policies and guidelines approved by the Executive Committee. The Court Administrator shall then forward all approved claims consistent with the Executive Committee's policies and guidelines to the Marion County Auditor for payment. Any claim or expenditures exceeding or otherwise inconsistent with budgetary policies or guidelines must be submitted to the Executive Committee for approval prior to incurring any such expense. No judge may individually approve any claim or expenditure, which exceeds the amount allocated to each judge.

E. Transfers within Budget Character. If the Court Administrator, with the approval of the judge, or a judge, determines that a transfer is necessary within budget characters and within division, they shall have the authority to sign off on that transfer for submittal to the Marion County Auditor.

F. Transfers between Budget Characters. If the Court Administrator, with the approval of the judge, or a judge, determines that a transfer between budget characters is necessary, a written proposal with explanation shall be submitted to the Executive Committee for approval. Upon approval, determination will be made if a transfer is possible. This action requires the approval of both division heads, and action by the City-County Council. If no transfer is possible, a "Request for Fiscal Ordinance" will then be presented to the Marion County Auditor for submission to the City-County Council.

G. Additional Appropriation. If the Court Administrator, with the approval of the judge, or a judge, determines that an additional appropriation is necessary, a written proposal shall be submitted to the Executive Committee for approval. Upon approval, determination will be made if a transfer is possible. This action also requires the approval of both division heads. If no transfer is possible, a "Request for Fiscal Ordinance" will be presented to the Marion County Auditor for submission to the City-County Council.

H. Mandate. The Executive Committee shall exercise all mandates for the adequate provision of court services, personnel or other expenditures.

I. Compliance with Laws. The Executive Committee and the Court Administrator shall closely monitor all budget submissions, claims, expenditures and other financial records to assure strict compliance with all laws, rules and regulations.

Adopted as Article VIII, effective Sept. 11, 2000. Renumbered as Rule 305, and amended effective Oct. 2, 2006.

LR49–AR00 Rule 306. AMENDMENT OF ADMINISTRATIVE RULES

A. The Administrative Rules of the Marion Superior Court may be amended by a majority vote of all qualified judges.

B. Any judge who wishes to propose an amendment to the Administrative Rules shall submit the proposed amendment to the Presiding Judge.

C. After receiving a proposed amendment, the Presiding Judge shall distribute copies of the proposed amendment to all judges and schedule a meeting not less than 30 days later to discuss and vote on the amendment.

Adopted as Article IX, effective Sept. 11, 2000. Renumbered as Rule 306, and amended effective Oct. 2, 2006.

LR49–AR15 Rule 307. COURT REPORTER SERVICES

The undersigned Courts comprise all of the Courts of record of Marion County, Indiana and hereby adopt the following local rule by which Court Reporter services shall be governed.

A. Definitions. The following definitions shall apply under this local rule:

1. A *Court Reporter* is a person who is specifically designated by a Court to perform the official court reporting services for the Court including preparing a transcript of the record.

2. *Equipment* means all physical items owned by the Court or other governmental entity and used by a Court Reporter in performing court-reporting services. Equipment shall include, but not be limited to, telephones, computer hardware, software programs, disks, tapes, and any other device used for recording and storing, and transcribing electronic data.

3. *Work Space* means that portion of the Court's facilities dedicated to each Court Reporter, including but not limited to actual space in the courtroom and any designated office space.

4. *Page* means the page unit of transcript, which results when a recording is transcribed in the form required by Indiana Rule of Appellate Procedure 7.2.

5. *Recording* means the electronic, mechanical, stenographic or other recording made as required by Indiana Rule of Trial Procedure 74.

6. *Regular hours worked* means those hours which the Court is regularly scheduled to work

during any given work week. Depending on the particular Court, these hours may vary from Court to Court within the county but remain the same for each work week.

7. *Gap hours worked* means those hours worked that are in excess of the regular hours worked but are hours not in excess of forty (40) hours per work week.

8. *Overtime hours worked* means those hours worked in excess of forty (40) hours per workweek.

9. *Compensatory Time* means that time off to which an employee may be entitled by reason of the employee having worked gap hours and/or overtime hours as defined herein, and for which an employee would otherwise be entitled to receive regular pay and/or overtime pay. An employee's compensatory time off for gap hours worked shall be computed at an hour for hour basis. Compensatory time off for overtime hours worked shall be computed at a rate of one and one half compensatory time for each hour of overtime hours accrued. An employee shall receive compensatory time off for gap hours and/or overtime hours in lieu of gap and/or overtime pay.

10. *Work week* means a seven (7) consecutive day week that consistently begins and ends on the same days throughout the year; i.e. Sunday through Saturday, Wednesday through Tuesday, Friday through Thursday.

11. *Court* means the particular Court for which the Court Reporter performs services. Court may also mean the Marion Superior Court.

12. *Indigent transcript* means a transcript that is paid for from state or county funds and is for the use on behalf of a litigant who has been declared indigent by a court.

13. *Private transcript* means a transcript, including but not limited to a deposition transcript that is paid for by a private party.

14. *Expedited Transcript* means a transcript that is to be completed within seven (7) days of the request for the transcript.

15. *Daily Transcript* means a transcript that is to be completed within twenty-four (24) hours of the request for the transcript.

16. *Schedule of Transcript Supplies* means those supplies and or services necessary for the binding of the transcript and exhibit binders pursuant to Appellate Rules 28 and 29. Transcript supplies shall include, but not be limited to, CD-Rom disks, software disks, tabs and binders

17. *Minimum Transcript Fee* means the minimum fee charged for the preparation of a transcript or any portion thereof.

B. Salaries and Per Page Fees.

1. Court Reporters shall be paid an annual salary for time spent working under the control, direction and direct supervision of their supervising Judge during any regular work hours, gap hours or overtime hours. The Marion Superior Court, by and through its Executive Committee and the Supervising Judge, shall enter into a written agreement with the Court Reporter which outlines the manner in which the Court Reporter is to be compensated for gap and overtime hours; i.e. monetary compensation or compensatory time off regular work hours.

2. The maximum per page fee a Court Reporter may charge for the preparation of a county indigent transcript made at the request of the indigent shall be Three Dollars ($3.00); the Court Reporter shall submit a claim directly to the Office of the Public Defender, or the Office of Court Administration as the case may be.

3. The maximum per page fee a Court Reporter may charge for the preparation of a indigent transcript for the State Public Defender shall be Three Dollars and Fifty Cents ($3.50); the Court Reporter shall submit a claim for services directly to the Office of the State Court Administration or the Office of Court Administration as the case may be.

4. The maximum per page fee a Court Reporter may charge for preparation of a transcript for the County Prosecuting Attorney shall be Four Dollars ($4.00); the Court Reporter shall submit a claim for payment of services directly to the Office of the Prosecuting Attorney.

5. The maximum per page fee a Court Reporter may charge for the preparation of all other regular transcripts shall be Four Dollars and Fifty Cents ($4.50).

6. The maximum per page fee a Court Reporter may charge for all expedited transcripts, (those to be completed within seven days of the date of the request) shall be Five Dollars and Fifty Cents ($5.50).

7. The maximum per page fee a Court Reporter may charge for the preparation of all daily transcripts, (those to be completed within 24 hours of the request) shall be Eight Dollars ($8.00).

8. A Court Reporter may charge a minimum transcript fee of Fifty Dollars ($50.00).

9. The Court Reporter's time spent assembling the transcript and exhibit binders shall be set forth and charged at the Court Reporter's regular hourly rate based upon the court reporter's annual compensation.

10. For copies of any transcript, the charge shall be One Dollar ($1.00) per page.

11. The maximum fee a Court Reporter may charge for preparing a Compact Disc recording of a proceeding is Twenty-five Dollars ($25.00).

12. The transcript supplies used in the preparation and assembly of the transcript and exhibit

binders shall be itemized and charged in accordance with the fee schedule set out in the Schedule of Transcript Supplies and Fees on the file in the Court Administrator's office.

13. Each Court Reporter shall, on a annual basis, file a written report with the Indiana Supreme Court, Office of State Court Administration disclosing all transcript fees received by the Court Reporter for the preparation of County indigent, State indigent or private transcripts. The report shall be made on forms prescribed by the Division of State Court Administration and timely filed with that office.

C. Private Practice.

1. If a Court Reporter elects to engage in private practice through the recording of a deposition and/or preparing of a deposition transcript, and the Court Reporter desires to utilize the Court's equipment, work space and supplies, and the Court agrees to the use of the Court equipment for such purpose, the Marion Superior Court, by and through its Executive Committee and the Court Reporter's Supervising Judge, and the Court Reporter shall enter into a written agreement which must, at a minimum, designate the following:

(a) The reasonable market rate for the use of equipment, workspace and supplies.

(b) The method by which records are to be kept for the use of equipment, work space and supplies; and

(c) The method by which the Court Reporter is to reimburse the Court for the use of the equipment, workspace and supplies.

D. Miscellaneous.

1. If a recording of a Court proceeding is made and a Court Reporter was not available a the time the recording was made, and a transcript of the hearing is requested, the duly qualified Court Reporter to which the case is transferred pursuant to Local Rule shall transcribe the proceeding in accordance with these Rules and terms and conditions of the Court Reporter Agreement.

Adopted as Article X, effective May 6, 2002. Renumbered as Rule 307, and amended effective Oct. 2, 2006. Amended effective May 14, 2008.

[1]LR49–AR00 Rule 308. PURCHASES MADE WITH FEDERAL GRANT FUNDS

The Court may, from time to time, receive federal funds through grant programs or other initiatives. Pursuant to federal regulations *(including the Office of Management and Budget's Circular A–102, United States Department of Justice Common Rule 28 CFR 66.36 and any other agency common rules associated with procurement)* on sub-awards and procurement that restrict certain activities with entities that have been debarred or suspended from federal funding, the Court adopts the following rule.

A. Purchases using Federal Funds. Purchase orders through City Purchasing shall be required for all *grant funded purchases*. These purchases would include without limitation equipment and supplies.

B. Contractual Agreements. Services purchased from any entity with federal grant dollars shall require a contract executed by the Executive Committee. All such contracts shall then be forwarded to the City Purchasing Department, and purchase orders would then be issued for services to be performed under the terms of the contract.

C. Other Expenditure of Federal Funds. Any expenditure of federal funds other than salaries shall be subject to the procedures and requirements of the City Purchasing Department.

D. With the exception of federal fund expenditures provided for in this rule, other expenditures and purchasing procedures followed by the court are not subject to the procedures and requirements of the City Purchasing Department, except as otherwise required by statute.

Adopted effective Jan. 1, 2008.

LR49–AR00 Rule 309. EX PARTE COMMUNICATION IN PROBLEM SOLVING COURTS

In order to effectively monitor participant progress, a judge may initiate, permit, or consider ex parte communications when serving on therapeutic or problem-solving courts, mental health court, or drug treatment court. In this capacity, judges may assume a more interactive role with parties, treatment providers, probation officers, social workers, and others. All such communication will be promptly disclosed to all parties.

Adopted effective April 4, 2009. Amended effective March 29, 2010.

LR49–AR00 Rule 310. LATE FEES

In accordance with IC 33–37–5–22 the Marion Superior Court may impose a late payment fee of $25.00 for failing to pay costs, fines or civil penalties.

Adopted effective June 12, 2009.

LR49–AR16 Rule 311. ELECTRONIC FILING

1. General Provisions.

1–101 *Short Title.* These rules may be cited as "E-filing rules."

1–102 *Definitions.* The following terms in this Rule shall be defined as follows:

(1) "Electronic Filing Service Provider" (EFSP) means the service provided by Lexis-Nexis or a similar provider for E-filing and E-service of documents via the Internet. The service may be accessed via Internet or in person at the courthouse using a Public Access Terminal.

(2) "Public Access Terminal" means a publicly accessible computer provided for the purposes of

allowing E–filing and viewing of public court records. The public access terminal shall be located in the Marion County Clerk's office at the courthouse and made available during normal business hours.

(3) "Electronic Filing" (E–file) means the electronic transmission of documents to the Court, and from the Court, for the purposes of filing.

(4) "Electronic Service" (E-service) means the electronic transmission of documents to a party, attorney or representative under these rules. Electronic service does not include service of process or summons to gain jurisdiction over persons or property.

1–103 *Authority.* Electronic filing and electronic service pilot projects are authorized pursuant to Indiana Rules of Court Administrative Rule 16 and approved by the Division of State Court Administration. The rules in this section are adopted by the Marion Superior Court and the Marion County Circuit Court.

1–104 *Scope of Rules.*

(1) All Marion County Circuit and Superior civil courts may accept electronic filing and service of pleadings and other documents designated in this rule in mortgage foreclosure (hereinafter referred to as "MF"), civil collection(hereinafter referred to as "CC"), and individual cases that have been approved for electronic filing and service.

(2) At the request of a civil division superior court, any case that will involve multiple litigants, legally intricate issues, and an extensive number of documents may be designated a mass tort or complex litigation case by the Executive Committee of the Marion Superior Court. Cases so designated shall be subject to electronic filing and service using the county's approved Electronic Service Provider.

(3) The Marion County Circuit Court may, upon the motion of a party or its own motion, designate a case that will involve multiple litigants, legally intricate issues, and an extensive number of documents a mass tort or complex litigation case. Any case so designated shall be subject to electronic filing and service using the county's approved Electronic Service Provider.

(4) The Court and the Clerk's Office may issue, file, and serve notices, orders, and other documents electronically, subject to the provision of these rules.

(5) The filing of electronic pleadings and other documents in MF and CC cases is entirely voluntary; however, once the case is initially filed electronically, all subsequent filings in the case shall remain in electronic format until the time for appeal is exhausted.

(6) All pleadings and other documents designated in this rule shall be filed and served electronically in any individual case which has been approved for electronic filing and service.

(7) The Court shall publish and maintain a list of Courts and cases where E-filing and E-service is permitted and required.

(8) The following pleadings may be filed and served electronically:

a) New case complaint and petitions

b) Original Answers

c) Any other pleadings or document including but not limited to motions and appearance forms.

(9) Sealed documents may not be E-filed and shall be filed conventionally. No document will be maintained under seal in the absence of the authorizing statute, court rule, or court order.

(10) Parties shall E–file a document either:

(a) By registering to use the EFSP; or

(b) In person at the Marion County Clerk's office, by electronically filing through the Public Access Terminal. Parties filing in this manner shall be responsible for furnishing the document in an electronic format that will be compatible with the clerk's office-system to be uploaded in person.

(11) All filing shall comply with the requirements of Administrative Rules 9 and 16; and the Indiana Rules of Court, State and Local.

(12) Parties shall comply with the procedures and requirements of the Electronic Filing Pilot Project Plan which has been filed with State Court Administration as required by Administrative Rule 16, and which is incorporated in this rule by reference.

1–105 *Authorized Users.* For the purposes of accessing the EFSP over the Internet, the following users are authorized to register as EFSP users:

a) Licensed attorneys and their staff, including paralegals, secretaries

b) Pro hac vice attorneys

c) Judges and their staff

d) Court administrative staff, including technical support staff

e) Self-represented litigants

f) Other public users, including media representatives

1–106 *Electronic Case File.* The Clerk may maintain the original and official case file in electronic format.

2. Filing and Service Procedure.

2–101 *Registration Requirements.*

(1) Persons who are authorized users and who desire to E–file or E–serve shall register with the EFSP. Upon receipt by the EFSP of a properly executed click-through user agreement, the EFSP shall assign to the user a confidential login and password to the system. Additional author-

ized users may be added at any time. No attorney or other user shall knowingly authorize or permit his or her user name or password to be utilized by anyone.

(2) Registered users of the system shall notify the EFSP within 10–days of any change in firm name, delivery address, fax number or e-mail address.

2–102 *Time and Effect of E-Filing.* Any pleading filed electronically shall be considered as filed with the court when the transmission to the EFSP is complete. Any document E–filed by 11:59 p.m. local Indianapolis, Indiana time shall be deemed filed on that date. The EFSP is an agent of the Court for the purpose of electronic filing, receipt, service and retrieval of electronic documents. Upon completion of filing, the EFSP shall issue a confirmation receipt that includes the date and time of receipt. The confirmation receipt shall serve as proof of filing. In the event the Court rejects the submitted documents following review, the documents shall not become part of the official Court record and the filer will receive notification of the rejection. Users may be required to refile the instruments to meet necessary filing requirements. Documents may be filed through an E–filing system at any time that the Clerk's office is open to receive the filing or at such other times as may be designated by the clerk and posted publicly. Documents filed through the E–filing system are deemed filed when received by the Clerk's office, except that documents received at times that the Clerk's office is closed shall be deemed filed the next regular time when the Clerk's office is open for filing. The time stamp issued by the E–filing system shall be presumed to be the time the document is received by the Clerk.

2–103 *Format of Documents.*

(1) All electronically filed and served pleadings shall, to the extent practicable, be formatted in accordance with the applicable rules governing formatting of paper pleadings.

(2) The electronic document title of each pleading or other document shall include:

(a) Party or parties filing/serving the document,

(b) Nature of the document,

(c) Party or parties against whom relief, if any, is sought, and

(d) Nature of the relief sought (e.g., Defendant ABC Corporation's Motion for Summary Judgment)

2–104 *Payment of Filing Fees.*

(1) Registered users shall pay statutory filing fees for E–filed documents electronically to the Court through their EFSP. Filing fees are due and payable at the time of filing.

(2) An EFSP may charge registered users additional fees to deliver, access and use the service. These fees shall be payable to the EFSP at the time of filing and are in addition to statutory filing fees.

(3) An electronic E–filing system fee may be established by the City of Indianapolis and Marion County City–County Council as provided in Administrative Rule 16(D).

2–105 *Signatures.* Every pleading, document, and instrument electronically filed or served shall be deemed to have been signed by the judge, clerk, attorney or declarant and shall bear a facsimile or typographical signature of such person, along with the typed name, address, telephone number, and Bar number of a signing attorney. Typographical signatures shall be treated as personal signatures for all purposes under these rules. Documents containing signatures of third-parties (i.e., unopposed motions, affidavits, stipulations, etc.) may also be filed electronically by indicating that the original signatures are maintained by the filing party in paper-format. Unless otherwise ordered by the Court or Clerk, a printed copy of all documents filed or served electronically, including original signatures, shall be maintained by the party filing the document and shall be made available, upon reasonable notice, for inspection by other counsel, the Clerk or Court. Parties shall retain originals until two (2) years after all time periods for appeal have expired. From time to time, it may be necessary to provide the Clerk or Court with a hard copy of an electronically filed document.

2–106 *Electronic Orders.* All orders shall be filed electronically. Immediately upon the entry of an order of judgment in an action assigned to the electronic filing system, a notice of electronic filing will be transmitted to registered filing users in the case, in electronic form. Electronic transmission of the notice of electronic filing constitutes the notice required by Indiana Rule of Trial Procedure 77 (d). Any order entered electronically without the original signature of a judicial officer has the same force and effect as if the judicial officer had affixed the judicial officer's signature to a paper copy of the order and it had been entered on the docket in a conventional manner. The judicial officer may grant routine orders by way of a text entry upon the CCS. In such a case, no further document will issue and the CCS entry shall indicate that the Court will issue no further written order. The CCS order shall carry the same weight and authority as a written order signed by the judicial officer. If a party is not represented by at least one attorney who is a registered user, the Court must give notice in paper form in accordance with the Indiana Rules of Court. All orders, decrees, judgments, and proceedings of the Court filed electronically will constitute entry on the Court's docket. A hard copy version of all judgments shall be entered in the Court's Record of Judgments and Orders, pursuant to Trial Rule (D).

2-107 *Electronic Service.*

(1) Delivery of E–service documents through the EFSP to other registered users shall be considered as valid and effective service and shall have the same legal effect as an original paper document. Recipients of E–service documents shall access their documents through the EFSP.

(2) E-service shall be deemed complete when the transmission to the EFSP is completed.

(3) For the purpose of computing time to respond to documents received via E-service, any document served on a day or at a time when the Clerk's office is not open for business shall be deemed served at the time of next opening of the Clerk's office for business.

(4) Parties who register with the EFSP may consent to receive E–service documents, other than service of subpoenas or summons.

2-108 *System or User Filing Errors.* The Court shall deem the E–filing Internet site to be subject to a technical failure on a given day if the site is unable to accept filings or provide access to filed documents continuously or intermittently over the course of any period of time greater than one hour after 12:00 noon of that day. The Clerk shall document any technical failures on the site. When filing by electronic means is hindered by a technical failure, a party may file with the Clerk of Marion County in hard copy. With the exception of deadlines that by law cannot be extended, the time for filing of any paper that is delayed due to technical failure of the site shall be extended for one day for each day on which such failure occurs, unless otherwise ordered by the Court.

Adopted effective March 29, 2010. As amended effective January 1, 2013.

MARION COUNTY SMALL CLAIMS RULES

Adopted Effective March 1, 2013

Including Amendments Received Through November 1, 2013

General Comments to the Rule

The Circuit Court is charged by Ind. Code § 33–34–3–6 and 7 to "make and adopt uniform rules for conducting the business of the small claims court . . . according to a simplified procedure to enable any person either to seek or to defend against a small claim without consulting or being represented by an attorney." In discharging this responsibility, the Court has decided to enhance the normal opportunity for comment by laying these proposed rules before an Advisory Committee.[1] The Court has also attended all of the public hearings of the Supreme Court Task Force on Marion County Small Claims Court and has carefully read its Report of May 1, 2012. Finally, the Court has elicited the advice and assistance of the nine sitting Small Claims Court judges.

At the end of the text of each proposed rule, the reader will find citations to any relevant Task Force finding or recommendation, as well as to relevant passages of a February 2012 report on "Landlord–Tenant Court Proceedings in Indiana" co-authored by Professor Florence Wagman Roisman of the Robert H. McKinney School of Law and Brienne Delaney, a 2012 graduate of the law school. Occasionally, the citations are supplemented by brief comments.

It should be noted that these Rules necessarily have a limited function. Most importantly, these Rules may not conflict with the Indiana Small Claims Rules. These rules may supplement, but not supplant the State rules.

Adopted Oct. 15, 2012, effective March 1, 2013.

100. GENERAL PROVISIONS

LR49–SC01 Rule 101. Purpose, Scope and Authority

A. The purpose of these rules is to promote uniformity and fairness of practice and procedure among the township divisions of the Marion County Small Claims Court.

B. These rules are intended to supplement the Indiana Rules for Small Claims. In the event of a conflict between these rules and the Indiana Rules, the latter shall govern.

C. These rules shall apply to all divisions of the Marion County Small Claims Court and to all Judges serving in that Court, regardless of their formal designation as part-time or full-time.

D. The Circuit Court is authorized to promulgate these rules by Ind. Code §§ 33–34–3–6—7.

Adopted Oct. 15, 2012, effective March 1, 2013.

LR49–SC01 Rule 102. Citation

These rules may be cited as LR49–SC ___.

Adopted Oct. 15, 2012, effective March 1, 2013.

LR49–SC00 Rule 103. Definitions

Court. "Court" shall mean all of the Marion County Small Claims Courts, unless the context indicates otherwise.

Court website. "Court['s] website" shall mean a website that contains Court information including a calendar and forms, with its URL location to be determined by March 01, 2013.

Judge. "Judge" means the sitting Judge or Judge *pro tempore* of a division of the Marion County Small Claims Court, unless the context indicates otherwise.

SCR. "SCR" shall mean Small Claims Rule of the State of Indiana.

Session. "Session" shall mean periods during which the Judge is scheduled to take the bench to transact the business of the court, in the morning between 9:00 A.M. and 12:00 P.M. and afternoon between 1:30 P.M. and 4:30 P.M.

Adopted Oct. 15, 2012, effective March 1, 2013.

LR49–SC00 Rule 104. Court Hours

The Court shall be open to accept pleadings and conduct any other business during "regular office hours" of 8:30 a.m. to 4:30 p.m. Monday through Friday of each week, except for holidays as recognized by the Circuit Court. For the convenience of the public, the Court may also arrange for sessions outside regular office hours.

Adopted Oct. 15, 2012, effective March 1, 2013.

LR49–SC00 Rule 105. Court Sessions

The Judge shall schedule as many sessions as necessary to transact the business of the Court in a reasonably prompt manner in compliance with these Rules. The Court shall post the Court calendar both in the Court and on the Court website.

Adopted Oct. 15, 2012, effective March 1, 2013.

200. COMMENCEMENT OF CASE

LR49–SC02 Rule 201. Forms

A. For the purpose of this section, a "form" shall mean any standardized pleading or order or document approved for use in the Small Claims Courts by the Circuit Court.

B. For the purpose of this section, a "required form" is a form which must be used by litigants and the Court.

C. For the purpose of this section, a "suggested form" is a form which will be deemed acceptable by the Court but need not be used by litigants and the Court.

D. Before a form is deemed required, it must be presented to the various Small Claims Courts and the State Court Administration for comment. When a proposed required form is for the use of litigants, the Circuit Court shall also solicit comment from bar associations and organizations described in LR49–SC00–202(B) before adopting the same.

E. The Court shall maintain a supply of preprinted required forms. Required forms shall be posted on the Court website and the Indiana Judiciary website. The Court may charge a fee, not to exceed the cost to the Court, for providing a form subject to a waiver of such costs pursuant to LR49–SC00–202.

F. The Court may, in its discretion, maintain a supply of suggested forms. Suggested forms shall be available at each Court in a binder for inspection and copying. Suggested forms shall be posted on the Court website and the Indiana Judiciary website.

G. The Clerk shall assist unrepresented litigants in completing a form, but shall not provide advice as to the use or effect of the form.

Comment: The intent of LR49–SC02–201(G) is to encourage the provision of clerical assistance to unrepresented litigants in completing Court forms. It is not intended to encourage the provision of advice that could be considered the unauthorized practice of law. For instance, it is permissible to indicate that a form is asking for the facts of the case. It would not be permissible to suggest what facts should be included on the form or how those facts should be presented.

Citation(s):

REPORT ON THE MARION COUNTY SMALL CLAIMS COURT, FINDINGS OF FACT C(34), p. 11; D(51)–(52), p. 13.

REPORT ON THE MARION COUNTY SMALL CLAIMS COURT, PART C COMPLEMENTARY REFORM 3(a), p. 28; 4, p. 29.

REPORT #1 ON LANDLORD-TENANT COURT PROCEEDINGS IN INDIANA III(B), p. 17.

Adopted Oct. 15, 2012, effective March 1, 2013.

LR49–SC00 Rule 202.   Waiver of Filing Fees and Costs

A. Upon filing a Waiver of Filing Fee and Costs form and a showing of the present inability to pay the filing fee and costs, the Court may waive the filing fee and costs in full or in part.

B. The Court may presume that an applicant is unable to pay the filing fee and costs if the applicant is represented by an attorney of an organization that uses generally accepted standards of poverty to determine eligibility for its services. Persons whose filing fees and costs have been waived are not required to pay Required Form fees as indicated in LR49–SC02–201(E).

> *Comment: For example, Indiana Legal Services uses objective financial criteria typically requiring eligible clients to have income at or below one hundred and twenty-five percent (125%) of the U.S. Census Poverty Guidelines.*

Citation(s):

Ind. Code § 33–37–3–2

REPORT ON THE MARION COUNTY SMALL CLAIMS COURT, FINDINGS OF FACT D(45), p. 12.

Adopted Oct. 15, 2012, effective March 1, 2013.

LR49–SC03 Rule 203.   Timeliness of Service

Service shall be effected no fewer than twenty (20) days before the initial hearing, except when possession of real estate is sought. When possession of real estate is sought, service shall be effected no fewer than ten (10) days before the initial hearing, except in those instances consistent with Ind. Code § 32–30–3–4 and § 32–31–6–7.

> *Comment: In emergency situations, the Court may reduce the Timeliness of Service requirement to a period of time less than ten (10) days. Consistent with Ind. Code § 32–31–6–7, failure to pay rent is not considered an emergency situation.*

Citation(s):

REPORT ON THE MARION COUNTY SMALL CLAIMS COURT, FINDINGS OF FACT G, p. 15–16.

REPORT ON THE MARION COUNTY SMALL CLAIMS COURT, PART C COMPLEMENTARY REFORM 1(b), p. 27.

Adopted Oct. 15, 2012, effective March 1, 2013.

LR49–SC03 Rule 204.   Explanation of Service Options

At the time of filing a claim, the Clerk shall explain to unrepresented litigants their options for serving the Notice of Claim and Summons. Should the litigant fail to designate a preference, service shall be by certified mail.

Citation(s):

REPORT ON THE MARION COUNTY SMALL CLAIMS COURT, FINDINGS OF FACT G, p. 15–16.

REPORT ON THE MARION COUNTY SMALL CLAIMS COURT, PART C COMPLEMENTARY REFORM 1(b), p. 27.

INDIANA SMALL CLAIMS RULE 3(C).

Adopted Oct. 15, 2012, effective March 1, 2013.

300. MOTIONS

LR49–SC09 Rule 301.   Continuances

A. Absent a Motion for Continuance, parties shall be ready for a trial on the merits at the initial hearing. Motions for Continuance of the initial hearing shall be granted liberally, except for hearings for possession of real estate. Motions for Continuance of the initial hearing joined by all parties shall be automatically granted. Motions for Continuance of hearings set after the initial hearing shall be granted only for good cause shown.

B. If the parties at the initial hearing declare that they desire to proceed to trial, the Court shall try the case during that session, provided that the Court may continue the case due to congestion on the Court docket. The Court shall reserve a reasonable portion of the Court's docket for contested matters on any day during which it holds initial hearings.

C. If a case is continued, the Court shall determine from the litigants the time needed for trial and the Court shall endeavor to schedule contested matters and keep its docket in such a manner as to avoid unnecessary delay and inconvenience to the parties.

Citation(s):

REPORT ON THE MARION COUNTY SMALL CLAIMS COURT, PART C COMPLEMENTARY REFORM 2(c), p. 27.

Adopted Oct. 15, 2012, effective March 1, 2013.

LR49–SC12 Rule 302.   Change of Venue From the Court

In addition to a Motion to Correct Venue, as provided at SCR 12 either party may move for a change of venue from the Court, except in cases in which there is a claim between a landlord and tenant. The Court shall grant Motions for Change of Venue upon a showing of good cause. Motions for Change of Venue and Motions to Correct Venue shall be filed within ten (10) days of the service of the Notice of Claim or objections to venue will be deemed waived.

Comment: More than one Court may be considered proper venue. As a result, it may be appropriate to allow for a Motion for Change of Venue even though the Court granting the motion is considered a proper venue for the matter.

Citation(s):

REPORT ON THE MARION COUNTY SMALL CLAIMS COURT, FINDINGS OF FACT E, p. 13—14.

Adopted Oct. 15, 2012, effective March 1, 2013.

LR49–TP38 Rule 303.   Jury Demand

A demand for trial by jury must be filed with the Court no fewer than ten (10) days after the first setting of the initial hearing.

Comment: This Rule implements Ind. T. R. 38(B) which governs the timeliness of a Jury Demand. A jury must be demanded no later than ten (10) days after the deadline for filing a responsive pleading or in most cases about thirty (30) days after service. When as in Small Claims cases, no responsive pleading is required, the deadline for demanding a jury is "within ten (10) days after the time such pleading otherwise would have been required."

The right to a jury trial in most civil cases is a right protected by both the Indiana and U.S. Constitutions. Pro se litigants in small claims cases may first become aware of this important right by receiving a pamphlet or talking with court staff at the initial hearing. Imposing a deadline of ten (10) days after service, as is required by Ind. Code § 33–29–2–7 for small claims courts which are a division of a Superior Court, would result in some defendants inadvertently losing this right before their initial hearing. This Court believes that LR49–TP38–303 is more consistent with Ind. T. R. 38(B) and the constitutional status of the right to a trial by jury.

Adopted Oct. 15, 2012, effective March 1, 2013.

400.   HEARING PROCEDURES

LR49–SC11 Rule 401.   Non–Delegable Duties

The Judge shall review all tendered Judgments and Orders, but may delegate to Court staff related clerical functions not requiring the exercise of judicial discretion. In no event may any official duty of the Court be delegated to persons not sitting as *pro tempore* Judges or not employed as staff.

Comment: Court staff may only use a stamp bearing the Judge's signature when specifically directed to do so by the Judge. Standing policies regarding the use of such a stamp by Court staff other than the Judge are not permitted except regarding the use of the stamp for copies of Orders which bear the Judge's original signature.

Citation(s):

REPORT ON THE MARION COUNTY SMALL CLAIMS COURT, FINDINGS OF FACT C(32)—(33), p. 11; C(35), p. 11.

REPORT ON THE MARION COUNTY SMALL CLAIMS COURT, PART C COMPLEMENTARY REFORM 2(c)–(d), p. 27–28.

REPORT #1 ON LANDLORD-TENANT COURT PROCEEDINGS IN INDIANA I(A), p. 6.

INDIANA SMALL CLAIMS RULE 11(A).

Reynolds v. Capps, 968 N.E.2d 789 (Ind. Ct. App. 2012).

Adopted Oct. 15, 2012, effective March 1, 2013.

LR49–SC00 Rule 402.   Notice of Litigant's Rights

At the beginning of each session, the Court shall notify litigants of their rights as described in the Notice of Claim including but not limited to the following:

A. Litigants are encouraged to settle their disputes;

B. Litigants are also free to refuse to speak or provide information to the opposing party or its attorney;

C. At the initial hearing, the Court will consider Motions to Continue the trial;

D. When the session resumes, a litigant may speak with the Judge in open Court;

E. If no Motions to Continue the trial are made, the case will be tried during the session, unless the Court's docket is congested, in which case the matter will be continued to a later date.

The above information will be included in a video provided by the Circuit Court which may be used instead of an oral notification. The video shall be subtitled in Spanish.

Citation(s):

REPORT ON THE MARION COUNTY SMALL CLAIMS COURT, FINDINGS OF FACT C(34), p.11; C(40), p. 12; C(43), p. 12; D(44), p. 12; D(49), p. 13; D(53), p. 13.

REPORT ON THE MARION COUNTY SMALL CLAIMS COURT, PART C COMPLEMENTARY REFORM 2(b), p. 27; 3(a), p. 28.

REPORT #1 ON LANDLORD-TENANT COURT PROCEEDINGS IN INDIANA III(B), p. 17; III(C), p. 18.

Adopted Oct. 15, 2012, effective March 1, 2013.

LR49–SC00 Rule 403.   Access to Court Files

Court files shall be under the control of the Court at all times. To facilitate trial preparation and/or negotiations, the Court may allow a party or its counsel to review or possess on the Court premises one or more files for a short period of time before and after the session and during the session. The opposing party shall have reasonable access to the file when in the possession of the other party.

Citation(s):

REPORT ON THE MARION COUNTY SMALL CLAIMS COURT, FINDINGS OF FACT C(29)—(30), p. 10—11.

REPORT ON THE MARION COUNTY SMALL CLAIMS COURT, PART C COMPLEMENTARY REFORM 2(f), p. 28.

Adopted Oct. 15, 2012, effective March 1, 2013.

LR49–SC11 Rule 404. Agreed Judgments and Post–Judgment Payment Plans

Agreed Judgments and payment plans shall be reviewed for approval by the Court. In determining whether to approve the proposed judgment or payment plan, the Court shall consider in addition to the requirements of SCR 11 whether the judgment requires payment from income or assets which would be exempt from execution and if so whether the Defendant was informed of such exemption rights before signing the agreement. A debtor's signature on a Court-prescribed Notice of Exemption Rights Form shall give rise to a rebuttable presumption that the debtor was informed of his/her exemption rights. The absence of the same shall give rise to a rebuttable presumption the debtor was not informed of his/her exemption rights.

> *Comment: This provision is consistent with Branham v. Varble, which indicates that it is appropriate for Judges in small claims proceedings to advise pro se litigants of their exemption rights, at least as it pertains to the general wage and SSI exemptions. Branham v. Varble, 952 N.E.2d 744, 748 (Ind. 2011).*

Citation(s):

REPORT ON THE MARION COUNTY SMALL CLAIMS COURT, FINDINGS OF FACT C(35)—(36), p. 11; E(61), p. 14.

REPORT ON THE MARION COUNTY SMALL CLAIMS COURT, PART C COMPLEMENTARY REFORM 2(c), p. 27; 2(e), p. 28.

REPORT #1 ON LANDLORD-TENANT COURT PROCEEDINGS IN INDIANA I(A), p. 6.
Adopted Oct. 15, 2012, effective March 1, 2013.

LR49–SC00 Rule 405. Notice of Appeal Rights

At the time that the Court announces its decision in a contested matter, the Court shall advise the losing party of his/her right to appeal. In the event that the Court enters judgment outside the presence of the parties, said advice shall be included in the Entry served on the parties.
Adopted Oct. 15, 2012, effective March 1, 2013.

LR49–SC00 Rule 406. Bifurcation of Proceedings

When a claim for possession of real or personal property is joined with a claim for damages, the Court may bifurcate the proceedings. The initial hearing may be restricted to the issue of whether the Plaintiff is entitled to possession, provided that the Defendant may introduce evidence in the form of testimony, affidavits or certified records or other reliable evidence constituting a defense under Indiana statutes or common law. All remaining issues, including damages, may be tried at a subsequent hearing.

> *Comment: The intent of this section is to give effect to Ind. Code § 32–30–3–5 as to the form of permissible evidence. See Morton v. Ivacic, 898 N.E.2d 1196, 1199 (Ind. 2008). It is also intended to recognize defenses in addition to a denial that the rent was not paid. See Theis v. Heuer, 264 Ind. 1, 280 N.E.2d 300 (Ind. 1972); Barnes v. Mac Brown & Co., Inc., 264 Ind. 227, 342 N.E.2d 619 (Ind. 1976). Such defenses include, but are not limited to, constructive eviction, violations of warranties of habitability, and the Protecting Tenants at Foreclosure Act of 2009, 12 U.S.C. § 5220.*

Citation(s):

REPORT #1 ON LANDLORD-TENANT COURT PROCEEDINGS IN INDIANA II(B)(1), p. 12—13.

Protecting Tenants at Foreclosure Act of 2009, 12 U.S.C. § 5220
Adopted Oct. 15, 2012, effective March 1, 2013.

500. DEFAULT JUDGMENTS

LR49–SC03 Rule 501. Required Findings for Default Judgment

Before entering a default judgment, the Court shall make the following specific findings:

A. The Court has jurisdiction over the Defendant(s) and that the requirements of SCR 3(D) have been met.

B. The Plaintiff has complied with Ind. Trial Rule 9.2.

C. The Defendant(s) is not a member(s) of the United States Armed Forces in accordance with the Servicemembers Civil Relief Act.

Citation(s):

REPORT ON THE MARION COUNTY SMALL CLAIMS COURT, PART C COMPLEMENTARY REFORM 1(b), p. 27.

REPORT ON THE MARION COUNTY SMALL CLAIMS COURT, FINDINGS OF FACT G, p. 15—16.

Servicemembers Civil Relief Act, 50 U.S.C. §§ 501 *et seq.*
Adopted Oct. 15, 2012, effective March 1, 2013.

LR49–SC10 Rule 502. Attorney's Fees

No judgment shall include attorney's fees unless such fees are authorized by law or by contract between the parties. The party seeking attorney's fees shall support its request with evidence which may be in the form of an affidavit setting forth the legal authority for the awarding of attorney's fees, the number of hours reasonably spent on the case and the hourly rate of those persons providing legal services.

Adopted Oct. 15, 2012, effective March 1, 2013.

LR49–SC10 Rule 503.   Recoverable Damages

A judgment may not exceed the relief specifically requested in the Notice of Claim, except that a Notice of Claim generally seeking unpaid rents for real estate shall be deemed to include a request for rents accruing after filing through the date of judgment. Furthermore, a landlord may seek damages to the extent that notice of such damages has been given to the tenant in compliance with Ind. Code § 32–31–3–1 *et seq.* no fewer than five (5) days before the hearing. The Court may allow an amendment of the Notice of Claim and/or a continuance to file the same at any time before the damages hearing, if it finds that the Defendant(s) have or will receive reasonable notice of said amendment before the damages hearing.

> *Comment*: The problem addressed in this rule is that of a Defendant not being made aware of the full extent of the landlord's alleged damages. A catch phrase of "all other available relief" or "compensation for any waste committed on the premises" is insufficient to alert an unrepresented Defendant

in a small claims setting. By incorporating the requirements of the Indiana Security Deposit Act, specific and timely notice of the landlord's claims will be assured.

Citation(s):

REPORT ON THE MARION COUNTY SMALL CLAIMS COURT, FINDINGS OF FACT D(48), p. 12.

REPORT ON THE MARION COUNTY SMALL CLAIMS COURT, PART C COMPLEMENTARY REFORM 2(h), p. 28.

Adopted Oct. 15, 2012, effective March 1, 2013.

LR49–SC00 Rule 504.   Dismissal of Plaintiff's Claim

Upon the failure of a Plaintiff to appear at the initial hearing or at a trial on the merits, the cause may be dismissed without prejudice, provided that the dismissal may be with prejudice if the same cause of action was previously dismissed for failure to prosecute or was voluntarily dismissed by the Plaintiff. Further, default judgment may be entered in favor of Defendant on any counterclaim.

Adopted Oct. 15, 2012, effective March 1, 2013.

600.   POST JUDGMENT PROCEEDINGS

LR49–SC00 Rule 601.   Court's Jurisdiction Pending Docketing in a New Court

Nothing in these rules shall be construed as divesting the Court of jurisdiction to hear matters arising between the date of filing of a Motion for Change of Venue or a Jury Demand or a Notice of Appeal and the date the case is docketed in the receiving Small Claims or Superior or Circuit Court.

Adopted Oct. 15, 2012, effective March 1, 2013.

LR49–SC00 Rule 602.   Proceedings Supplemental

A.   General Procedure. Proceedings supplemental to execution shall be governed by Ind. T. R. 69(E) and applicable statutes, and subject to the approval of the Court.

B.   Thirty–Day Rule. A Motion for Proceedings Supplemental shall not be set until thirty (30) calendar days after the date of judgment, except by order of the Court for good cause shown.

C.   Hearings. A Proceedings Supplemental shall be dismissed if the Court finds that the judgment creditor has had a reasonable opportunity to discover and/or execute on non-exempt assets or income. Except when the dismissal is due to the failure of the judgment debtor to appear at a Proceeding Supplemental hearing after due notice, subsequent Motions for Proceedings Supplemental shall only be granted upon a showing of a material change in the judgment debtor's financial circumstances or that a sufficient period of time has lapsed to justify a subsequent proceeding.

> *Comment: This provision is consistent with Carter v. Grace Whitney Properties, which holds that future proceedings supplemental "must be supported by a showing [by the creditor] that new facts justifying a new order or examination have come to its knowledge." Carter v. Grace Whitney Properties, 939 N.E.2d 630, 637 (Ind. App. 2010); See also, Button v. James, 909 N.E.2d 1007, 1009 (Ind. App. 2009); Kirk v. Monroe County Tire, 585 N.E.2d 1366, 1369 (Ind. Ct. App. 1992).*

Citation(s):

REPORT ON THE MARION COUNTY SMALL CLAIMS COURT, FINDINGS OF FACT C(35)—(36), p. 11; E(61), p. 14.

REPORT ON THE MARION COUNTY SMALL CLAIMS COURT, PART C COMPLEMENTARY REFORM 2(c), p. 27; 2(e), p. 28.

REPORT #1 ON LANDLORD-TENANT COURT PROCEEDINGS IN INDIANA I(A), p. 6.

Adopted Oct. 15, 2012, effective March 1, 2013.

LR49–SC11 Rule 603.   Garnishment of Wages

The Court may set the amount of a wage garnishment at less than the maximum imposed by Ind. Code § 24–4.5–5–105, if it determines that Defendant will be deprived of income necessary for Defendant's support and/or the support of those legally dependent on the Defendant. The Defendant bears the burden of proving the above financial circumstances.

> *Comment: This provision is consistent with SCR 11(C), which authorizes the Court to specify the method of payment when ordering a judgment.*

Citation(s):

Ind. Code § 24–4.5–5–105.

Adopted Oct. 15, 2012, effective March 1, 2013.

700. MISCELLANEOUS

LR49–SC00 Rule 701. Staff Identification

Court staff and the Constable and his/her deputies are to display identification by name and title at all times as prescribed by the Judge. When conducting Court business by phone, staff shall also identify themselves.

Citation(s):

REPORT ON THE MARION COUNTY SMALL CLAIMS COURT, FINDINGS OF FACT C(31), p. 11.

REPORT ON THE MARION COUNTY SMALL CLAIMS COURT, PART C COMPLEMENTARY REFORM 2(a), p. 27.

Adopted Oct. 15, 2012, effective March 1, 2013.

LR49–SC00 Rule 702. Court Facilities

Court facilities shall be available on an equal basis to all persons having business with the Court, provided that the Court may reserve facilities for the purpose of conducting settlement conferences during Court sessions and for a reasonable period of time before and after each session. The Courtroom may be used for conferences, if other areas on the premises are unavailable or insufficient. If it is necessary to use the Courtroom, oral and/or written notice shall be given that the use of the Courtroom is not an endorsement or approval of the positions of any party and that the Court will independently review any agreement reached by the parties.

Citation(s):

REPORT ON THE MARION COUNTY SMALL CLAIMS COURT, FINDINGS OF FACT C(30), p. 11.

Adopted Oct. 15, 2012, effective March 1, 2013.

LR49–SC00 Rule 703. Wedding Fees

A. The Judge may charge a reasonable fee for weddings. The fee for weddings performed on the Court premises or during the "regular office hours" of the Court shall be $80.

B. The fee shall be deposited in the Township General Fund when the Judge performs a wedding:

1. on Court premises; or

2. during "regular office hours" of the Court for a full-time Judge, pursuant to Rule LR49–SC00–104; or

3. during a scheduled session for a part-time Judge, pursuant to Rule LR49–SC00–103 and 105.

C. The Judge shall keep a record of each wedding performed and shall report annually to the Township

LR49–SC00 Rule 604. Appeals

The provisions of LR49–TR79.1–228(C) of the Marion County Civil Rules shall govern all appeals from a Small Claims Court.

Adopted Oct. 15, 2012, effective March 1, 2013.

Advisory Board the number of weddings performed on Court premises, during the "regular office hours" of the Court, or during a scheduled session.

Citation(s):

REPORT ON THE MARION COUNTY SMALL CLAIMS COURT, FINDINGS OF FACT F(64)—(65), p. 15.

REPORT ON THE MARION COUNTY SMALL CLAIMS COURT, PART C COMPLEMENTARY REFORM 9, p. 30.

Comment: Officiating at weddings is a minor activity in all of the Small Claims Courts, except in Center Township. Wedding fees have been a substantial source of personal income for Center Township judges since the inception of the Small Claims system more than forty (40) years ago. Moreover, Justices of the Peace performed weddings for a fee for many years before they were replaced by the current system. Changing views on the propriety of public officials accepting fees as compensation and increases in the revenue derived from wedding fees require a reevaluation of this practice. For these reasons, the Rule follows the Task Force recommendation and requires that wedding fees for weddings performed in the Court or on Court time be deposited in the Township General Fund.

Adopted Oct. 15, 2012, effective March 1, 2013.

LR49–SC00 Rule 704. Law Practice of Judges

A Judge shall not practice law before another Small Claims Court Judge.

Citation(s):

REPORT ON THE MARION COUNTY SMALL CLAIMS COURT, FINDINGS OF FACT F(68)—(70), p. 15.

REPORT ON THE MARION COUNTY SMALL CLAIMS COURT, PART C COMPLEMENTARY REFORM 8, p. 30.

Adopted Oct. 15, 2012, effective March 1, 2013.

LR49–SC00 Rule 705. Compliance with the Americans With Disabilities Act ("ADA")

The Court shall arrange for an evaluation of the compliance of Court facilities with the ADA. By April 1, 2013, the Court shall provide to the Township Advisory Board a copy of the evaluation and request the Board to correct violation(s).

Citation(s):

REPORT #1 ON LANDLORD-TENANT COURT PROCEEDINGS IN INDIANA I(C), p. 6—7.

Title VII Civil Rights Act of 1964, 42 U.S.C. §§ 2000 *et seq.*

Adopted Oct. 15, 2012, effective March 1, 2013.

LR49–SC00 Rule 706. Availability of Rules and Other Legal Reference Material

A. Sufficient copies of these Rules, the Indiana Small Claims Rules, the Small Claims Litigant's Manual and the brochure entitled Rights and Responsibilities shall be available at the Court. The above materials shall be in English and Spanish. The Court may supplement the above materials as it sees fit.

B. The Circuit Court shall be responsible for making the above materials available to locations other than the Small Claims Court. These locations include, but are not limited to, the Court's website and Indianapolis Marion County Public Library branches.

Citation(s):

REPORT ON THE MARION COUNTY SMALL CLAIMS COURT, PART C COMPLEMENTARY REFORM 3(d), p. 28.

REPORT #1 ON LANDLORD-TENANT COURT PROCEEDINGS IN INDIANA I(D), p. 8—7.

REPORT #1 ON LANDLORD-TENANT COURT PROCEEDINGS IN INDIANA III(A), p. 16.

Adopted Oct. 15, 2012, effective March 1, 2013.

LR49–SC00 Rule 707. Availability of Interpreter Services

Upon a showing that a party has limited English proficiency to understand and/or effectively participate in the proceedings, the Court shall provide a certified interpreter at no cost to the party. The Court shall provide an American Sign Language interpreter at no cost to parties with hearing disabilities.

Citation(s):

REPORT ON THE MARION COUNTY SMALL CLAIMS COURT, FINDINGS OF FACT D(46)—(48), p. 12.

REPORT ON THE MARION COUNTY SMALL CLAIMS COURT, PART C COMPLEMENTARY REFORM 3(d), p. 28.

REPORT #1 ON LANDLORD-TENANT COURT PROCEEDINGS IN INDIANA I(D), p. 8—7.

Adopted Oct. 15, 2012, effective March 1, 2013.

MONROE CIRCUIT COURT RULES OF ADMINISTRATION

Adopted Effective January 1, 1991

Including Amendments Received Through November 1, 2013

Research Notes

These rules may be searched electronically on Westlaw *in the* IN-RULES *database; updates to these rules may be found on* Westlaw *in* IN-RULESUPDATES. *For search tips and a summary of database content, consult the Westlaw Scope Screens for each database.*

LR53–AR00 Rule 0100. EXECUTIVE ORGANIZATION

A. Board of Judges. The nine (9) judges of the Monroe Circuit Court shall constitute the Board of Judges.

B. Presiding Judge and Vice Presiding Judge of Board of Judges: The Board of Judges at the November meeting shall select from amongst them a Presiding Judge whose two-year term shall begin January 1st and a Vice Presiding Judge who shall serve a two year term beginning January 1st. Regardless of these provisions for terms of office, the Presiding Judge and the Vice Presiding Judge shall serve at the pleasure of the majority of the Board of Judges. The Presiding Judge shall:

1. Provide general administrative direction and supervision of the operation of the court consistent with the policies, priorities and goals of the Court;

2. Preside over the Board of Judges meetings and direct the preparation of the agenda and minutes of the meetings;

3. Provide liaison between the Court, government, and civic agencies;

4. Submit a proposed annual budget for the court system to the Board of Judges for approval;

5. Insure efficient operation of the court system and compliance with local rules;

6. Allocate courtrooms and ancillary space for efficient administration of court business;

7. Prepare proposed local rules to expedite and facilitate the court business;

8. Review annually the bail schedule, caseload allocation plan, juror policies and other issues bearing on the operation of the court system and present any proposed changes to the Board of Judges;

9. Recommend appointments as specified in IC 33–4–10–5(1) and by local ordinance for approval by the Board of Judges;

10. Develop and implement an orientation program for new judges and magistrates;

11. Establish and maintain a plan for continuity of operations.

12. Perform other duties as directed by the Board of Judges, or as set out in these Rules.

C. Vice Presiding Judge: When the Presiding Judge is unavailable the Vice Presiding Judge, if available, will serve as the acting Presiding Judge. If Vice Presiding Judge is unavailable, the Presiding Judge shall designate one of the other judges as acting Presiding Judge;

D. Executive Management Team: The Executive Management Team shall consist of the Presiding Judge, the Vice Presiding Judge, Director of Court Services, Chief Probation Officer, Youth Services Bureau Executive Director and designees of the Presiding Judge. The Executive Management Team directed by the Presiding Judge shall be responsible for implementing the policies, priorities and goals of the Board of Judges. Members of the Board of Judges shall be advised of the time and place of meetings and may attend.

Proposed programs, projects, and services utilizing system resources shall be presented to the Executive Management Team and be consistent with the established priorities and goals of the Board of Judges.

Adopted effective Jan. 1, 1991. Amended effective Oct. 4, 2000; renumbered as Rule 0100, and amended effective Feb. 7, 2007. Amended effective Jan. 1, 2008; Jan. 1, 2012.

LR53–AR00 Rule 0101. PROCEDURE FOR LOCAL RULES

A. The Presiding Judge shall submit proposed rules to the Monroe County Bar for consideration and recommendation.

B. After adoption by the Board of Judges the rules shall be published and distributed to:

1. The Board of Judges of the Monroe Circuit Court;

2. The Clerk of the Supreme Court and the Court of Appeals of Indiana;

3. The Indiana State Court Administrator;

4. The Clerk of the Monroe Circuit Court;

5. Members of the Monroe County Bar Association.

Adopted effective Jan. 1, 1991. Amended effective Oct. 4, 2000; renumbered as Rule 0101, and amended effective Feb. 7, 2007. Amended effective May 27, 2009.

LR53–AR00 Rule 0102. EXPENDITURES

The Presiding Judge may approve capital expenditures up to $1,500 without further consideration by the Board of Judges.

Adopted effective Jan. 1, 1991. Amended effective Oct. 4, 2000; renumbered as Rule 0102, and amended effective Feb. 7, 2007; Jan. 1, 2012.

LR53–AR00 Rule 0103. MEETINGS

A. Monthly Meeting. The Board of Judges shall meet at least monthly to make policy decisions, provide education reports, and review operations of the court system. The Director of Court Services, the Chief Probation Officer, and the Youth Services Bureau Executive Director shall be required to attend these meetings and participate in discussions.

B. February Meeting. In February the Board of Judges, the Director of Court Services, the Chief Probation Officer, and the Youth Services Bureau Executive Director shall attend an extended meeting to discuss:

1. Budget requests for the next annual budget;

2. Allocation of caseload;

3. An assessment of the Monroe Circuit Court prepared by the Presiding Judge, identifying the issues and opportunities which the Court will confront during the year and proposing priorities and goals for the year.

C. September Meeting. In September the Board of Judges and the Director of Court Services, the Chief Probation Officer, and the Youth Services Bureau Executive Director shall attend an extended meeting to discuss:

1. The Annual Report;

2. Performance of the Office of Court Services, the Probation Department, the Youth Services Bureau and Division updates including Specialty Courts;

3. *Decisions:* Decisions on all court system issues and these rules but for the selection of the Presiding Judge and Vice Presiding Judge shall be

made by a vote of the majority of the Board of Judges then in attendance.

Adopted effective Jan. 1, 1991. Amended effective Oct. 4, 2000; renumbered as Rule 0103, and amended effective Feb. 7, 2007; Jan. 1, 2012.

LR53–AR00 Rule 0104. ATTENDANCE AT MEETINGS

The Presiding Judge shall be responsible for attending meetings of the Monroe County Council and the Monroe County Commissioners.

Adopted effective Jan. 1, 1991. Amended effective Oct. 4, 2000; renumbered as Rule 0104, and amended effective Feb. 7, 2007. Amended effective May 27, 2009.

LR53–AR00 Rule 0105. BOARD OF JUDGES MEETING PROCEDURES

A. The Board of Judges will follow the Robert's Rules of Order during their meetings.

B. Issues will be tabled after first discussion and voted upon at the next meeting. This procedure may be suspended by a vote of the Board.

C. The Presiding Judge and the Court Administrator will determine agenda items. Any member of the Board of Judges can place an item on the agenda. The agenda should be distributed to the members no later than two days prior to the meeting.

D. Any policies established by external committees of which Judges are members and which may affect or concern court procedures, should be reported to the Board of Judges.

E. The minutes will reflect an ongoing list of unresolved issues or a method to track projects/issues.

F. Meetings will be held on the first and third Wednesday of each month and at such other times as the Board may agree.

G. There will be at least 2 in-service meetings per year.

Adopted effective Jan. 1, 1991. Amended effective Oct. 4, 2000; renumbered as Rule 0105, and amended effective Feb. 7, 2007. Amended effective Jan. 1, 2008; Jan. 1, 2012.

LR53–AR00 Rule 0106. EMERGENCY CLOSING

A. The Presiding Judge, after consultation with the Board of Judges, if practical may determine that the Courts are closed due to a temporary emergency (i.e. snow, breakdown in facility utilities, etc.) Any judge, notwithstanding that authority, may require his or her court reporters to work.

B. The County Commissioners have the authority to close the Justice Building.

Adopted effective Jan. 1, 1991. Amended effective Oct. 4, 2000; renumbered as Rule 0106, and amended effective Feb. 7, 2007. Amended effective May 27, 2009; May 31, 2011.

LR53–AR00 Rule 0107. CRIMINAL DUTY JUDGE RESPONSIBILITIES

A. The Criminal Duty Judge shall review affidavits for probable cause submitted by the duty prosecutor each Saturday evening and submit an order no later than 10:30 PM, by electronic or written means, to the Monroe County Correctional Center, and others on an approved distribution list, finding probable cause and setting bail for those "affected persons" arrested from Thursday night at midnight until Saturday at 2:00PM, and the arrest was made without a warrant. A signed written order shall be issued on Monday morning for each determination. The schedule is adjusted on holiday weekends so that no person is held longer than twenty-four hours without a finding of probable cause.

B. The Criminal Duty Judge shall be responsible for initial hearings, probable cause determinations, restraining orders, and other judicial issues requiring immediate action.

C. The Criminal Duty Judge shall request incarcerated felony defendants to appear in court within 24 hours of their arrest, excluding weekends, to inform them of the reason for their hold. Each day the Office of Court Services staff will review the arrest list and inform the Criminal Duty Judge of these defendants.

Adopted effective Jan. 1, 1991. Amended effective Oct. 4, 2000; renumbered as Rule 0107, and amended effective Feb. 7, 2007. Amended effective May 27, 2009; Jan. 1, 2012.

LR53–AR00 Rule 0108. CASELOAD ALLOCATION

A. Procedure. The Board of Judges shall:

1. Review and comply with current caseload allocation orders of the Indiana Supreme Court.

2. Review and assess literature from the Indiana State Bar Association, the American Bar Association, and the National Center for State Courts.

3. Review and consider suggestions made by the Monroe County Bar, the Prosecuting Attorney, and the Public Defender.

4. Review and analyze the statistics on current workload and caseflow within the Monroe Circuit Court.

5. Analyze whether the current allocation is providing quality public service. There shall be a presumption in favor of the current allocation in order to preserve public confidence in the system, promote stability for the employees of the court system, and avoid inefficient use of personnel, time, and resources to effectuate change. Caseload allocation shall be determined by judicial seniority.

B. Implementation. The Clerk of Monroe County shall maintain a random filing system, by computer or otherwise, implementing the caseload allocation approved by the Board of Judges. If the caseload allocation is changed by order of the Board of Judges, the Presiding Judge shall forward the amended allocation to the Clerk of the Supreme Court and Court of Appeals, the State Court Administrator, the Clerk of the Monroe Circuit Court, and the President of the Monroe County Bar Association. The current allocation is as follows:

1. *Case Assignment.* The Clerk shall assign cases as from time to time directed by the Board of Judges.

a. The Clerk shall randomly assign all murder, A, B, C, D felony and misdemeanor cases to Divisions II, III, V, and IX.

b. Domestic relations cases shall be assigned randomly to Division I, IV, VI and VIII, unless consolidated with an active protection order case as provided in section c.

c. Protective order cases shall be randomly assigned to Division I, IV, VI, and VIII. If however; the parties of the protection order have an active or closed domestic relations (DR) case or an active child in need of services (CHINS) case, the protection order will be assigned to the Division with the DR or CHINS case. Domestic relations cases shall be assigned to the Division with an active protection order case involving the same parties

d. The Clerk shall randomly assign Civil cases to Division I and to Division VI.

e. Juvenile delinquencies, juvenile status, juvenile miscellaneous resulting from delinquent acts, juvenile paternity, adoptions, mental health and guardianship cases shall be assigned to Division VII.

f. Juvenile CHINS, juvenile miscellaneous filed by the Office of Family and Children, and juvenile terminations shall be assigned to Division VII.

g. Estate cases shall be assigned to Division I

h. Small claims cases shall be randomly assigned 50% to Division IV and 50% to Division VIII.

i. Infraction cases shall be randomly assigned to Divisions II, III, V, and IX.

j. Reciprocal support cases shall be assigned to Divisions I, IV, VI, and VIII.

k. A redocketed case bearing a 1992 or earlier cause number shall be assigned to the court of original jurisdiction if that division in the reallocation of cases is assigned that case type, otherwise it will be randomly assigned to a division with that jurisdiction.

l. A redocketed case bearing a 1993 or later cause number shall be assigned to the court of original jurisdiction if that division in the reallocation of cases is assigned that case type, otherwise it will be randomly assigned to a division with that jurisdiction.

m. The Clerk shall use the related case function in the Odyssey Case Management System in protection order (PO) and juvenile paternity (JP) cases involving the same parties to facilitate coordination, consistency, and efficiency within judicial orders.

n. The Clerk shall use the related case function in the Odyssey Case Management System if an active CHINS case pending in Division VII involves the same parties to a new or pending domestic relations, support, or custody case.

2. *Case Refiled.* If a case is dismissed without prejudice on a plaintiff's motion and the same case is subsequently refiled by a plaintiff, the refiled case shall be assigned to the same Division of the Monroe Circuit Court in which the dismissed case was originally filed providing that division is overseeing that case type. If that division is no longer hearing that case type, then the Clerk will randomly assign that case to a division with jurisdiction. "Same case" shall mean substantially the same cause of action, arising out of the same transaction or occurrence, and between substantially the same parties. If such a refiled case is not initially refiled in the same division of the Monroe Circuit Court, then upon motion of any party or Court, it shall be transferred to the Division of the Monroe Circuit Court in which is was originally filed.

3. *Case Recusal.* The Court Reporter shall notify the Clerk of the cases in which judges recuse themselves. When a judge disqualifies and recuses in a case pursuant to Trial Rule 79 (C), the clerk shall randomly reassign the case to another Division currently receiving new filings of that case type pursuant to Caseload Allocation Rule LR 53–AR00108. Credit will be provided to the new division assigned.

C. Case Consolidation.

1. *Civil Cases.* Civil cases filed against different defendants that arise out of the same occurrence, or multiple cases filed against the same defendant may be consolidated and assigned to the division with the oldest case number.

2. *Criminal Cases.* All criminal cases against a defendant shall be consolidated in the Division with the oldest pending case number. A new case shall be filed in that Division, or transferred to that Division. Pending cases include defendants on Probation and in the Pre–Trial Diversion Program.

D. Case Transfer.

1. Nothing in this Rule shall preclude the transfer of case from one Division of the Circuit Court to another Division to promote efficiency and provide for timely resolution of cases. Upon transfer, credit will be given to the new Division assigned by the Odyssey Case Management System.

Adopted effective Jan. 1, 1991. Amended effective Oct. 4, 2000. Renumbered as Rule 0108, and amended effective Feb. 7, 2007. Amended effective Jan. 1, 2009; Jan. 1, 2010; Jan. 1, 2012.

LR53–AR00 Rule 0109. SPECIAL JUDGES IN CIVIL CASES PURSUANT TO TRIAL RULE 79(H)

When it is necessary to appoint a special judge pursuant to Trial Rule 79 (H), it shall be done in accordance with District 20 Rule on appointment of special judge in civil cases at DR20–TR79–000.DR 20–TR79–000 APPOINTMENT OF SPECIAL JUDGE IN CIVIL CASES

A. Eligibility for Special Judge Service:

1. *Agreement to Serve.* Pursuant to Trial Rule 79(H), the full-time Judicial Officers of Administrative District 20 shall be deemed in agreement to serve as a Special Judge only for those case type(s) which compose that Judicial Officer's typical caseload, as determined by the Local County Caseload Allocation Plan.

2. *Prior Service Excluded.* The appointment as Special Judge shall apply unless the appointed Judicial Officer has previously served as Judge or Special Judge in the case, is disqualified by interest or relationship, or is excused from service as a Special Judge by the Indiana Supreme Court.

B. Appointment of a Special Judge: In the event of the need for the regular, sitting Judicial Officer to recuse herself/himself from a normally assigned case, or should the appointment of a Special Judge through agreement by the Parties fail, the Special Judge appointment shall be made by the Administrative District 20 Facilitator:

1. *Priority Given to Local County Appointments.* Special Judge appointments shall be made within the Local County, on a rotating basis so long as a Judicial Officer within the County who has jurisdiction for the type of case remains eligible for Special Judge service. Following the appointment of the Special Judge, the Special Judge may request that the case be transferred to the court of the Special Judge.

2. *District (Outside County) Appointments.* In the event that no Local Judicial Officer is available, the case will be forwarded to the District 20 Facilitator who will appoint a Special Judge on a rotating basis, from the available Judicial Officers within the Administrative District who have jurisdiction for the type of case.

C. Acceptance of Appointment:

1. *Acceptance Mandatory.* Pursuant to Trial Rule 79(H), a person appointed to serve as Special Judge under these rules must accept jurisdiction in the case, unless the appointed Special Judge is disqualified pursuant to the Code of Judicial Conduct, ineligible for service under these rules, or excused from service by the Indiana Supreme Court.

2. *Documentation.* An oath or additional evidence of acceptance of jurisdiction is not required.

D. Supreme Court Certification. In the event that no Judicial Officer in the Administrative District is eligible to serve as a Special Judge, or the regular, sitting Judicial Officer in the court in which the case is pending sets out particular circumstances why appointment under these rules should not be made, then the regular, sitting Judicial Officer shall certify the same to the Indiana Supreme Court for appointment of a Special Judge.

E. Discontinuation of Special Judge Service. The provisions of T.R. 79(I) apply if a Special Judge ceases to serve following assumption of jurisdiction.

F. Method of Assignment and Related Records. The District Facilitator has maintained a method for rotation for appointments and maintained records related thereto which will be continued. Any amendments to the method will be made by votes cast by the Judicial Officers of Administrative District 20.

Adopted effective Jan. 1, 1991. Amended effective Oct. 4, 2000. Renumbered as Rule 0109, and amended effective Feb. 7, 2007. Amended effective Jan. 1, 2008; Jan. 1, 2012; Aug. 15, 2013.

LR53–AR00 Rule 0110. REQUIRED COMPLETION OF THE FAMILY LAW INFORMATION SHEET AND GUARDIANSHIP CHILD AND INCAPACITATED ADULT INFORMATION SHEET

Pursuant to Trial Rule 3.1 (A) (7), all parties are required to fully complete the Family Law Information Form and the Guardianship Child and Incapacitated Adult Information Sheet.

Adopted effective Jan. 1, 1991. Amended effective Oct. 4, 2000; renumbered as Rule 0110, and amended effective Feb. 7, 2007; Jan. 1, 2012.

LR53–AR00 Rule 0111. ALLOCATION OF SMALL CLAIMS/EVICTIONS/ORDINANCE VIOLATIONS/PROCEEDINGS SUPPLEMENTAL/INFRACTIONS

Updated 01/01/08

A. Small Claims: Small Claims are filed randomly between two of the court divisions. A maximum of 150 new Small Claims will be filed during a week. The Clerk will set hearings on the claims by filling the time slots as they appear on a calendar at the rate 25 cases per hour. These hearings are set on the first available date within 30–45 days of the filing date. The Clerk will enter the case electronically and issue the service before sending the file to the Court.

B. Bulk Filings: Bulk filings are limited to 25 a day and 50 a week.

C. Evictions: Eviction cases are randomly assigned by the Clerk to Division IV and Division VIII. The Clerk will enter the case data in JTS, issue a cause number and receipt for the plaintiff, mark the file as an eviction, tag the file with a marker requesting the Court to "Please set for hearing and return to Clerk." The Court sets the time within 15 to 45 days from the filing date. The case file is returned to the Clerk who issues service and completes the data entry in JTS.

D. Ordinance Violation: Ordinance Violation filings are limited to 25 a day and 50 a week. The City attorney will set their own hearing date and times in accordance with the Court docket.

E. Proceedings Supplemental: Proceedings Supplemental are filed at the maximum rate of 75 cases per week. The Clerk will set all proceedings supplemental complying with the 21 to 45 day service requirements. The Clerk will execute the order to appear, input data into JTS, issue the service and send the file to the Court. Ordinance Violation Proceedings Supplementals are processed like small claims proceedings supplemental.

F. Infractions: Traffic tickets are filed in the Clerks Office by law enforcement. Traffic violations are assigned randomly to Division II, III, V, and IX. The Prosecutor and Clerk hold initial hearings each Thursday at 1:00 p.m. in the Clerk's office.

G. At initial hearing, defendants either pay the citation, enroll in the Infraction Diversion Program, or are assigned a bench trial date. Jury trials are assigned to the Division of the initial case filing.

Adopted effective Jan. 1, 1991. Amended effective Oct. 4, 2000; renumbered as Rule 0111, and amended effective Feb. 7, 2007. Amended effective Jan. 1, 2008; Jan. 1, 2012.

LR53–AR79 Rule 0112. SPECIAL JUDGES IN CRIMINAL CASES

When it is necessary to appoint a special judge pursuant to Criminal Rule 13, it shall be done in accordance with District 20 Rule on appointment of special judge in criminal cases at **DR20–CR13–000.**

DR 20–CR13–000 APPOINTMENT OF SPECIAL JUDGE IN CRIMINAL CASES

Each county within the Administrative District shall amend its local rules, pursuant to Criminal Rule 2.2 and 13, to allow for appointment of Special Judges utilizing the following elements.

A. Eligibility for Special Judge Service.

1. *Available to Serve.* Pursuant to Criminal Rule 13(C), the Judicial Officers of Administrative District 20 shall be deemed in agreement to serve as a Special Judge only for those case type(s) which compose that judicial officer's typical caseload, as determined by the local Caseload Allocation Plan.

2. *Prior Service Excluded.* The appointment of Special Judge shall apply unless the appointed Judicial Officer has previously served as Judge or Special Judge in the case, is disqualified by interest or relationship, or is excused from service as a Special Judge by the Indiana Supreme Court.

B. Appointment within the Administrative District. In order to improve the coordination within the Administrative District, and pursuant to Criminal

Rule 13(C), appointments of a Special Judge in criminal cases shall be made among the Judicial Officers of the Administrative District.

C. Appointment of a Special Judge. In the event of the need for the regular, sitting Judicial Officer to recuse herself/himself from a normally assigned case, Special Judge appointment shall be made by the Administrative District 20 Facilitator.

1. *Priority Given to Local County Appointments.* Pursuant to Criminal Rule 2.2, appointments of a Special Judge shall be made in the same manner as set forth within the Local Rules of the Local County, so long as a Judicial Officer with criminal jurisdiction remains available within the Local County for appointment. Following the appointment of the Special Judge, the Special Judge may request that the case be forwarded to the court of the Special Judge.

2. *District (Outside County) Appointments.* In the event that no Local Judicial Officer is available, a Special Judge shall be appointed, on a rotating basis, from the available Judicial Officers within the Administrative District.

D. Acceptance of Appointment.

1. *Acceptance Mandatory.* Pursuant to Criminal Rule 13(C), a person appointed to serve as Special Judge under these rules must accept jurisdiction in the case, unless the appointed Special Judge is disqualified pursuant to the Code of Judicial Conduct, ineligible for service under these rules, or excused from service by the Indiana Supreme Court.

2. *Documentation.* An oath or additional evidence of acceptance of jurisdiction is not required.

E. Supreme Court Certification. In the event that no Judicial Officer in the Administrative District is eligible to serve as a Special Judge, or the regular, sitting Judicial Officer in the court in which the case is pending sets out particular circumstances why appointment under these rules should not be made, then the regular, sitting Judicial Officer shall certify the same to the Indiana Supreme Court for appointment of a Special Judge.

F. Discontinuation of Special Judge Service. The provisions of C.R. 13(F) if a Special Judge ceases to serve following assumption of jurisdiction.

G. Method for Assignment and Related Records. The District Facilitator has maintained a method for rotation for appointments and maintained records related thereto which will be continued. Any amendments to the method will be made by votes cast by the Judicial Officers of Administrative District 20.

Adopted effective Jan. 1, 1991. Amended effective Oct. 4, 2000. Renumbered as Rule 0112, and amended effective Feb. 7, 2007. Amended effective Aug. 15, 2013.

LR53–AR01   Rule   0113.   MONROE   CIRCUIT COURT PLAN FOR ALLOCATION OF JUDICIAL RESOURCES

A. Cases shall be assigned in accordance with LR53–AR01–108, Caseload Allocation, and related procedures of the Monroe Circuit Court.

B.   The Presiding Judge shall:

1. Review and evaluate the caseload allocation data as reported by the Division of State Court Administration.

2. Submit the initial evaluation and report with necessary recommendations to the Board of Judges for review and analysis in accordance with the Monroe Circuit Court local rules.

C.   The Board of Judges shall:

1. Review and analyze the report and other available data as enumerated in LR53–AR01–108, Caseload Allocation and implement any necessary actions to ensure the random and equal caseload allocation as established in the Monroe Circuit Court rules and procedures.

Adopted effective Jan. 1, 1991. Amended effective Oct. 4, 2000; renumbered as Rule 0113, and amended effective Feb. 7, 2007; amended effective Jan. 19, 2010; Jan. 1, 2012.

LR53–AR00 Rule 0114.   FISCAL MANAGEMENT

A.   Board of Judges.

1. *Budgets.* The Board of Judges shall direct the preparation of a unified budget for all divisions of the Court, the Probation Department, and the Office of Court Services to be funded from the county general fund upon approval of the County Council. The Board of Judges shall further direct the preparation of additional budgets for programs funded by user fee income and grants, including all Youth Services Bureau budgets, for approval by the County Council.

2. *Annual Procedure.* Each year the Board of Judges shall establish a schedule for budget preparation, review, and submission with the goal of providing for the effective functioning of the court as follows:

a. Each judge, the Chief Probation Officer, and the Director of Court Services shall submit written budget requests to the Financial Coordinator in the Office of Court Services. These requests shall be specific and well-justified in light of the past year's expenditures and the future needs of the offices.

b. The Board of Judges shall meet to review the budget requests and may request further discussion from the chief Probation Officer, the Director of Court Services, or any other employee.

c. The Board of Judges shall establish budget priorities and guidelines for allocation of individual line items in the budget and shall direct the

Director of Court Services to prepare budget proposals for submission to the County Council.

B.   Office of Court Services/Probation/Youth Services Bureau.

1. *Budgets.* The Director of Court Services, the Chief Probation Officer, and the Youth Services Bureau Executive Director shall prepare budget proposals established by the Board of Judges for submission to the County Council for approval.

2. *Claims.* All claims shall be submitted to the Financial Coordinators after review by the Director of Court Services, the Chief Probation Officer, and the Youth Services Bureau Executive Director for compliance with the budgetary polices [1] and guidelines of the Board of Judges. The Financial Coordinators shall forward all payroll claims and all purchase, travel, and training claims consistent with the Board's policies and guidelines as authorized by the Director of Court Services, the Chief Probation Officer, and the Youth Services Bureau Executive Director to the Auditor's Office for payment. The Director of Court Services, the Chief Probation Officer, and the Youth Services Bureau Executive Director must submit any claim exceeding budgetary guidelines or otherwise inconsistent with the Board's policies to the Board for approval.

3. *Transfers within Budget Categories.* The Director of Court Services, the Chief Probation Officer, and the Youth Services Bureau Executive Director with the assistance of the Financial Coordinators may determine that a transfer is necessary within budget categories.

4. *Transfers between Budget Categories.* The Presiding Judge should approve transfers between budget categories as necessary. A written proposal shall be submitted to the to the County Council for approval.

5. *Additional Appropriations.* If the Director of Court Services, the Chief Probation Officer, or the Youth Services Bureau Executive Director with the assistance of the Financial Coordinators determines that an additional appropriation is necessary, a written proposal shall be submitted to the Presiding Judge prior to submission to the County Council.

6. *Mandate.* No individual judge shall exercise mandates for the adequate provision of court services, personnel, or other expenditures.

7. *Compliance With Laws.* The Presiding Judge, the Director of Court Services, the Chief Probation Officer, the Youth Services Bureau Executive Director and the Financial Coordinators shall closely monitor all budget submissions, claims, expenditures, and other financial records to assure

strict compliance with all laws, rules, and regulations.

Adopted effective Jan. 1, 1991. Amended effective Oct. 4, 2000; renumbered as Rule 0114, and amended effective Feb. 7, 2007; Jan. 1, 2012.

1 So in original.

LR53–AR00 Rule 0115. BOARD OF JUDGES CHECKING ACCOUNT

The Board of Judges will maintain a checking account administered by the Director of Court Services to be used for flowers, contributions, or cards on behalf of the Board of Judges as follows:

A. For court system staff, flowers or a contribution will be sent upon the death of a spouse, child, or parent.

B. For members of the Monroe County Bar Association, flowers or a contribution will be sent upon the death of a spouse or child, and a sympathy card will be sent upon the death of parents.

Adopted effective Jan. 1, 1991. Amended effective Oct. 4, 2000; renumbered as Rule 0115, and amended effective Feb. 7, 2007. Amended effective May 27, 2009.

LR53–AR00 Rule 0116. PERSONNEL

A. General Organization. The Monroe Circuit Court employs personnel as follows:

1. *Court Division:*
    Commissioner
    Official Court Reporters
    Associate Court Reporters
    Law Clerks
2. *Probation Department:*
    Chief Probation Officer
    Deputy Chief Probation Officers
    Probation Supervisor
    Probation Officers
    Program Staff
    Field Officers
    Clerical Staff
3. *Office of Court Services:*
    Director of Court Services
    Deputy Court Administrator
    Case Management Coordinator
    Financial Coordinator
    Public Service Coordinator
    Family Court Coordinator
    Shared Court Reporters
    Bailiffs
4. *Youth Services Bureau:*
    Executive Director
    Assistant Director
    Shelter Care Coordinator
    Residential Coordinators
    Residential Specialists
    Health and Wellness Specialists
    Clinical Coordinator Youth

Support Specialist Project Safe
Place Coordinator Clinicians
Financial Manager
Secretary/Receptionist

B. Court Divisions. The Monroe Circuit Court shall have 9 court divisions. The judge of each court division shall have the sole authority to employ an Official Court Reporter, two Associate Court Reporters, and a Law Clerk, to serve at the pleasure of the judge. The Official Court Reporter of a division shall supervise the Associate Court Reporters and Law Clerks if so directed by the division's presiding judge.

C. Probation Department. The Board of Judges shall have the sole authority to employ Probation Department personnel and to terminate their employment. All employees of the Probation Department serve at the pleasure of the Board of Judges. The Board of Judges shall advertise the position of Chief Probation Officer and interview and screen applicants for that position. The Chief Probation Officer shall advertise any other available probation position and interview and screen applicants as directed by the Board of Judges. The Board of Judges has authorized the Chief Probation Officer to make final hiring decisions regarding Probation Department positions. As directed by the Board of Judges, the Chief Probation Officer shall supervise employees of the Probation Department and may delegate certain supervisory responsibilities to the staff and other employees.

D. Office of Court Services. The Board of Judges shall have the sole authority to employ personnel for the Office of Court Services and to terminate their employment. All employees of the Office of Court Services serve at the pleasure of the Board of Judges. The Director of Court Services shall advertise an available position and interview and screen applicants as directed by the Board of Judges. The Board of Judges has authorized the Director of Court Services to make final hiring decisions regarding Office of Court Services positions. Employees of the Office of Court Services shall be supervised by the Director of Court Services.

E. Youth Services Bureau Executive Director. The Board of Judges shall have the sole authority to employ personnel for the Youth Services Bureau and to terminate their employment. All employees of the Youth Services Bureau serve at the pleasure of the Board of Judges. The Youth Services Bureau Executive Director shall advertise an available position and interview and screen applicants as directed by the Board of Judges. Employees of the Youth Shelter Bureau shall be supervised by the Youth Shelter Bureau Executive Director.

Adopted effective Jan. 1, 1991. Amended effective Oct. 4, 2000; renumbered as Rule 0116, and amended effective Feb. 7, 2007. Amended effective May 27, 2009; Jan. 1, 2012.

LR53–AR00 Rule 0117. STAFF INTRODUCTIONS

The Director of Court Services, the Chief Probation Officer, and the Youth Services Bureau Executive Director shall introduce new staff to the Board of Judges and submit copies of their resumes to the Board upon request.

Adopted effective Jan. 1, 1991. Amended effective Oct. 4, 2000; renumbered as Rule 0117, and amended effective Feb. 7, 2007. Amended effective Oct. 26, 2010.

LR53–AR00 Rule 0118. EVALUATIONS

A. Staff of the Probation Department is evaluated on an annual basis. The evaluation includes a job performance development plan for each employee.

B. New probation department employees are on a probationary status for 6 months and are evaluated monthly. At the end of the probationary period, a formal job performance appraisal is conducted to determine employment, training needs, or other concerns.

C. The staff of the Office of Court Services will be evaluated in the spring of each year by the Director of Court Services.

D. The Director of Court Services, the Chief Probation Officer, and the Youth Services Bureau Executive Director will be evaluated annually by the Board of Judges.

Adopted effective Jan. 1, 1991. Amended effective Oct. 4, 2000; renumbered as Rule 0118, and amended effective Feb. 7, 2007. Amended effective May 27, 2009; Jan. 1, 2012.

LR53–AR00 Rule 0119. AUDIT OF PROBATION ACCOUNTS

An internal audit will be completed whenever a collections clerk terminates employment.

Adopted effective Jan. 1, 1991. Amended effective Oct. 4, 2000; renumbered as Rule 0119, and amended effective Feb. 7, 2007.

LR53–AR00 Rule 0120. STAFF HIRING

A. The Board of Judges has authorized the Chief Probation Officer to make final hiring decisions regarding Probation Department positions.

B. The Board of Judges has authorized the Director of Court Services to make final hiring decisions regarding Office of Court Services positions.

C. After the Director of Court Services, the Chief Probation Officer, and the Youth Services Bureau Executive Director interview applicants and choose the final candidate for a position, they shall notify the Board of Judges in writing or by electronic mail of applicant's hiring, including a copy of the applicant's resume upon request.

Adopted effective Jan. 1, 1991. Amended effective Oct. 4, 2000; renumbered as Rule 0120, and amended effective Feb. 7, 2007. Amended effective May 27, 2009; Jan. 1, 2012.

LR53–AR00 Rule 0121. PERSONNEL RECORDS

A. The Director of Court Services shall maintain a personnel file on each court staff member and judges which would include, but not be limited, to hire date, pay rate, and emergency information.

B. The Judges, Director of Court Services, Chief Probation Officer, and the Youth Services Bureau Executive Director shall maintain personnel records.

Adopted effective Jan. 1, 1991. Amended effective Oct. 4, 2000; renumbered as Rule 0121, and amended effective Feb. 7, 2007. Amended effective May 27, 2009; Jan. 1, 2012.

LR53–AR00 Rule 0122. PROBATIONARY STATUS

New employees shall be on probationary status for a minimum of 3 months and a maximum of 6 months, the specific duration of which is at the discretion of the department head. The period may be extended at the discretion of the department head. An employee is not eligible for vacation while on probationary status.

Adopted effective Jan. 1, 1991. Amended effective Oct. 4, 2000; renumbered as Rule 0122, and amended effective Feb. 7, 2007.

LR53–AR00 Rule 0123. LONGEVITY FORMULA FOR COURT STAFF

The effective date for longevity is the date an individual began full-time employment with the County. People cannot go back and claim days that would be affected by interrupted service. All records must be verified by the Auditor's Office. Longevity pay is based on the following schedule of complete and uninterrupted years of service:

YEARS	AMOUNT
>1	$ 0
1	200
2	400
5	600
10	800
15	1,200
20	1,400
25	1,700
30	2,000

Adopted effective Jan. 1, 1991. Amended effective Oct. 4, 2000; renumbered as Rule 0123, and amended effective Feb. 7, 2007. Amended effective May 27, 2009.

LR53–AR00 Rule 0124. AFTER HOURS SIGN–IN

All employees entering the Justice Building after work hours shall personally sign themselves in.

Adopted effective Jan. 1, 1991. Amended effective Oct. 4, 2000; renumbered as Rule 0124, and amended effective Feb. 7, 2007.

LR53–AR00 Rule 0125. LAW CLERKS

Each judge is allocated an average of 40 hours of Law Clerk work per pay period.

Adopted effective Jan. 1, 1991. Amended effective Oct. 4, 2000; renumbered as Rule 0125, and amended effective Feb. 7, 2007. Amended effective May 27, 2009.

LR53–AR00 Rule 0126. TRAVEL POLICY

The Director of Court Services, the Chief Probation Officer, and the Youth Services Bureau Executive Director may approve training requests not exceeding $500/person/training. Any request above $500 must be approved by the Presiding Judge.

Adopted effective Jan. 1, 1991. Amended effective Oct. 4, 2000; renumbered as Rule 0126, and amended effective Feb. 7, 2007.

LR53–AR00 Rule 0127. ADMINISTRATIVE PROCEDURES

Updated 10/26/10

A. Executive Management Team. The Director of Court Services, the Chief Probation Officer, the Youth Services Executive Director and the Presiding Judge, shall constitute a management team for administrative issues. The team shall coordinate personnel policy and fiscal issues, identify issues or procedures that may impact outside specific divisions, maintain consistency on administrative issues among the divisions, and addresses other issues and projects consistent with the policies, priorities and goals of the Board of Judges.

B. Purpose. The Executive Management Team shall advise the Board of Judges on administrative procedures and policy matters. The Executive Management Team is responsible for full communication between the Board of Judges and the employees of the Monroe Circuit Court on issues affecting the court system.

Adopted effective Jan. 1, 1991. Amended effective Oct. 4, 2000; renumbered as Rule 0127, and amended effective Feb. 7, 2007; Jan. 1, 2012.

LR53–AR00 Rule 0128. CLERK FILES—ACCESS

Members of the public and attorneys shall not be permitted to remove court files from the Clerk's Office.

Adopted effective Jan. 1, 1991. Amended effective Oct. 4, 2000; renumbered as Rule 0128, and amended effective Feb. 7, 2007.

LR53–AR00 Rule 0129. COPYING OF COURT TAPES

A. Audio copies of court proceedings will be provided to attorneys only. However, any person may listen to a tape or CD by scheduling a time with the Office of Court Services.

B. Copies for attorneys of taped court proceedings will be provided by the Office of Court Services. The court reporter from the originating court will index and deliver the tapes to the Office of Court Services. The Office of Court Services staff will duplicate the tapes for the requesting attorney. The requesting attorney must provide blank tapes (brand new, high quality). Requests from attorneys of court proceedings on disc will be provided by the court reporter.

The requesting attorney must provide blank CD's. The service is provided at no cost.

C. Attorneys shall not transfer possession of a tape or CD or make another coy of the tape or CD for another person except as necessary for transcription. This rule does not prohibit an attorney from playing a tape or CD for a client.

Adopted effective Jan. 1, 1991. Amended effective Oct. 4, 2000; renumbered as Rule 0129, and amended effective Feb. 7, 2007. Amended effective May 27, 2009; May 31, 2011.

LR53–AR00 Rule 0130. EQUIPMENT USE

A. Use of county equipment for non-court related business in which actual expense is incurred by the County is prohibited unless the staff member has prior written judicial approval <u>and</u> any actual expense incurred by the County is reimbursed to the County.

B. With the exception of vehicles, laptop computers, and transcribers, County equipment may not be taken home.

Adopted effective Jan. 1, 1991. Amended effective Oct. 4, 2000; renumbered as Rule 0130, and amended effective Feb. 7, 2007. Amended effective May 27, 2009.

LR53–AR00 Rule 0131. COURT RECORDS

Original court records shall not be removed from the Justice Building, except by written permission of the judge.

Adopted effective Jan. 1, 1991. Amended effective Oct. 4, 2000; renumbered as Rule 0131, and amended effective Feb. 7, 2007.

LR53–AR15 Rule 0132. TRANSCRIPTS

Updated 1–1–10

A. Definitions. The following definitions shall apply under this local rule:

1. A Court Reporter is a person who is specifically designated by a court to perform the official court reporting services for the court including preparing a transcript of the record in a given case before the court.

2. Equipment means all physical items owned by the court or other governmental entity used by a court reporter in performing court reporting services. Equipment shall include, but not be limited to, telephones, computer hardware, software programs, disks, tapes and any other device used for recording, storing, and transcribing electronic data.

3. Work space means that portion of the court's facilities dedicated to each court reporter, including but not limited to, actual space in the courtroom and any designated office space.

4. Page means the page unit of transcript which results when a recording is transcribed in the form required by Indiana Rule of Appellate Procedure 7.2.

5. Recording means the electronic, mechanical, stenographic, or other recording made as required by Indiana Rule of Trial Procedure 74.

6. Regular hours worked means those hours which a division of the court is regularly scheduled to work during any given work week. Depending on the schedule of the court and its flex schedule for court reporters, these hours may vary from division to division of the court, within the county but remain the same for each work week.

7. Gap hours worked means those hours worked that are in excess of the regular hours worked but hours not in excess of 40 hours per work week.

8. Overtime hours means those hours worked in excess of 40 hours per work week.

9. Work week means a 7 consecutive day week defined by the County's payroll schedule which consistently begins and ends on the same day throughout the year; i.e. Sunday through Saturday, Wednesday through Tuesday, or Friday through Thursday.

10. Court means the Monroe Circuit Court and Division means the particular division of the Court for which the court reporter performs services. Court may also mean all of the divisions of the Monroe Circuit Court.

11. County indigent transcript means a transcript that is paid for from county funds and is for the use on behalf of a litigant who has been declared indigent by a court.

12. State indigent transcript means a transcript that is paid for from state funds and is for the use on behalf of a litigant who is declared indigent by a court.

13. Private transcript means a transcript, including but not limited to, a deposition transcript that is paid for by a private party. A transcript required within 14 days of the request is a category 1 expedited private transcript. A transcript required within 30 days of the request is a category 2 expedited private transcript. A transcript required within 45 days of the request is a category 3 expedited private transcript.

14. Volume applies to Appellate Court bound transcripts. Each volume is to be limited to 250 pages. The table of contents is to be a separate volume and the exhibits are to be included in a separate bound volume (or volumes if more than 250 pages).

A. Section Two. Salaries and Per Page Fees.

1. Court Reporters shall be paid an annual salary for time spent working under the control, direction and direct supervision of their supervising Judge during any regular work hours, gap hours or overtime hours. The Monroe Circuit Court shall enter into a written agreement with the court reporters which outlines the manner in which the court reporter is to be compensated for gap and overtime hours; i.e. monetary compensation or compensatory time off regular work hours.

2. The maximum per page fee a court reporter may charge for the preparation of a routine county indigent transcript shall be $3.00. The court reporter shall submit a claim directly to the county for the preparation of any county indigent transcripts. The court reporter shall not charge a fee for copies of an indigent transcript when the preparation of same has already been paid by the county. The court reporter shall not charge for copies of a prepared indigent transcript requested by a Court appointed entity (i.e. CASA, GAL) when the preparation of same has already been paid by the county.

3. The maximum per page fee a court reporter may charge for the preparation of a non-appellate state indigent transcript shall be $3.00.

4. The maximum per page fee a court reporter may charge for the preparation of a non-appellate private transcript shall be $4.00. The per page fee a court reporter may charge for a copy of a prepared transcript shall be $2.00. The maximum per page fee a court reporter may charge for the preparation of a category 1 expedited private transcript shall be $7.50. The maximum per page fee a court reporter may charge for the preparation of a category 2 expedited private transcript shall be $6.50. The maximum per page fee a court reporter may charge for the preparation of a category 3 expedited private transcript shall be $5.50. Category 1, category 2 and category 3 expedited private transcripts are defined in Section 1, definition #13.

5. Each court reporter shall report, at least on an annual basis, all transcript fees received for the preparation of county indigent, state indigent, or private transcripts to the Indiana Supreme Court Division of State Court Administration. The reporting shall be made on forms prescribed by the Division of the State Court Administration.

B. Section Three. Private Practice.

1. If a court reporter elects to engage in private practice by recording a deposition and/or preparing a deposition transcript, outside of and in addition to his or her official duties for the court, and the court reporter desires to utilize the court's equipment, work space and supplies, and the court agrees to the use of the court equipment for such purpose, the court and the court reporter shall enter into a written agreement which must, at a minimum, designate the following:

a. The reasonable market rate for the use of equipment, work space and supplies;

b. The method by which records are to be kept for the use of equipment, work space and supplies; and

c. The method by which the court reporter is to reimburse the court for the use of the equipment, work space and supplies.

2. If a court reporter elects to engage in private practice though the recording of a deposition and/or preparing of a deposition transcript, all such private practice work shall be conducted outside of regular working hours.

C. Section Four. Appellate Court Transcripts.

1. The maximum per page a court reporter may charge for the preparation of an appellate indigent transcript is $3.50.

2. The maximum per page fee a court reporter may charge for the preparation of an appellate private transcript shall be $4.50.

3. A minimum fee of $35.00 per transcript may be charged for small transcripts but not in addition to the per page fee.

4. The Index and Table of Contents shall be charged at the same per page rate as the body of the transcript.

5. Labor charge may be assessed at the same rate as the Official Court Reporter's hourly salary for time spent binding the transcript and exhibits.

6. In addition, a reasonable market rate for office supplies may be charged for private appellate transcripts as designated in the Schedule of Supplies.

Adopted effective Jan. 1, 1991. Amended effective Oct. 4, 2000; renumbered as Rule 0132, and amended effective Feb. 7, 2007. Amended effective May 27, 2009; amended Aug. 20, 2010, effective Jan. 1, 2011; Jan. 1, 2012.

LR53–AR00 Rule 0133. DISCLOSURE OF PENDING CASE INFORMATION

The staff of the Probation Department shall not disclose any information regarding a pending case to the media. The media shall have access to information through court personnel in compliance with both the Indiana Rules of Court: Administrative Rule #9–Confidentiality of Court Records and the Code of Judicial Conduct, CANON 3, B. #10.

Adopted effective Jan. 1, 1991. Amended effective Oct. 4, 2000; renumbered as Rule 0133, and amended effective Feb. 7, 2007.

LR53–AR00 Rule 0134. OFFICE OF COURT SERVICES

A. **Establishment and Purpose.** The Board of Judges has established an Office of Court Services to coordinate jury management, automation, statistics, system analysis, court security, fiscal management, caseflow management, and public service for the Monroe Circuit Court.

B. **Director of Court Services.** As directed by the Board of Judges, the Director of Court Services shall implement, supervise and evaluate the administrative functions and court staff; prepare and monitor the court's budgets; coordinate training for court personnel; assist in the hiring and discharge of personnel; research, develop and implement efficient programs and procedures; attend and coordinate Board of Judges meetings; and perform other duties as required.

C. **Other Personnel.** The Board of Judges, through the Director of Court Services, shall hire administrative, clerical staff, and bailiffs as needed to provide services to the Court.

D. **Financial Planning and Budget Management.** The Office of Court Services shall be responsible for the preparation, monitoring, and analysis of all budgets of the Monroe Circuit Court. All required fiscal reports are prepared for review by the Board of Judges. This office serves as primary liaison with the Auditor's Office, and prepares and submits payroll, claims, and employee information as required. This office orders supplies and equipment and oversees maintenance and service of equipment.

E. **Jury Management.** The Office of Court Services is responsible for the summoning, impaneling, orientation, and payment of jurors needed for the Court.

F. **Statistical Analysis.** The Office of Court Services is responsible for compiling, analyzing, and reporting statistical case data in the divisions of the Court.

G. **Court Security.** The Office of Court Services provides security for the judges, court staff, attorneys, and the public in the courtrooms and court offices.

H. **Caseflow Management.** The Office of Court Services is responsible for assessing caseflow in the divisions of the Court and recommending improvements to the Board of Judges.

I. **Court Support Programs.** The Office of Court Services coordinates and provides statistical information on court support programs, coordinates referrals and communications to the Mental Health Center, and insures compliance with the American with Disabilities Act.

J. **Public Service.** The Office of Court Services provides public service to the citizens of Monroe County by providing case information, public use of courtrooms, and educational tours.

Adopted effective Jan. 1, 1991. Amended effective Oct. 4, 2000; renumbered as Rule 0134, and amended effective Feb. 7, 2007; Jan. 1, 2012.

LR53–AR00 Rule 0135. ACCESS TO SECURE HALLWAY

Access to the Secure Hallway will be provided by the Office of Court Services. Staff will allow entry to the following individuals:

A. Court Staff.

B. Members of the Bar and Bench.

C. The public with prior permission of a judge's staff.

Adopted effective Jan. 1, 1991. Amended effective Oct. 4, 2000; renumbered as Rule 0135, and amended effective Feb. 7, 2007.

LR53–AR00 Rule 0136. COPY OF DOCUMENT CHARGES

The cost for copies of court documents to the public is set by statute and payable in the Clerk's Office.

Adopted effective Jan. 1, 1991. Amended effective Oct. 4, 2000; renumbered as Rule 0136, and amended effective Feb. 7, 2007. Amended effective May 27, 2009.

LR53–AR00 Rule 0137. NON–JUDICIAL COURTROOM USE

The use of courtrooms for rehearsals by attorneys during working hours may be coordinated through the Office of Court Services.

Adopted effective Jan. 1, 1991. Amended effective Oct. 4, 2000; renumbered as Rule 0137, and amended effective Feb. 7, 2007.

LR53–AR00 Rule 0138. LAW LIBRARY

The Law Library may be used by the judges, court staff, Bar members, and when space is available, the general public.

Adopted effective Jan. 1, 1991. Amended effective Oct. 4, 2000; renumbered as Rule 0138, and amended effective Feb. 7, 2007.

LR53–AR00 Rule 0139. POSTING OF NON–COURT RELATED ANNOUNCEMENTS

Public announcements may not be posted on walls and windows. They may be placed in attorney mailboxes.

Adopted effective Jan. 1, 1991. Amended effective Oct. 4, 2000; renumbered as Rule 0139, and amended effective Feb. 7, 2007.

LR53–AR00 Rule 0140. BAILIFF DUTIES

A. The bailiffs shall deliver transport orders and commitment orders to the booking division of the Jail, and warrants and writs to the records division of the Sheriff's Office.

B. All bailiffs shall carry a radio for emergency situations.

C. The bailiffs shall unlock and check the courtrooms that will be in use at the time indicated on the court calendar. At the completion of courtroom proceedings, the bailiffs should lock the courtrooms. If a bailiff is not present, the court reporter should lock the courtroom.

Adopted effective Jan. 1, 1991. Amended effective Oct. 4, 2000; renumbered as Rule 0140, and amended effective Feb. 7, 2007. Amended effective May 27, 2009.

LR53–AR00 Rule 0141. QUARTERLY STATISTICS

The office of Court Services staff is responsible for preparing and reporting required case statistics to the State Court Administrator's office quarterly.

Adopted effective Jan. 1, 1991. Amended effective Oct. 4, 2000; renumbered as Rule 0141, and amended effective Feb. 7, 2007.

LR53–AR00 Rule 0142. PROBATION DEPARTMENT

Updated 08/01/09

A. **Establishment and Purpose.** As required by Indiana law, the Board of Judges has established a Probation Department to serve all divisions of the Monroe Circuit Court. The Probation Department shall comply with all laws of the State of Indiana and all standards put forth by the Judicial Conference of Indiana. The Probation Department staff conducts interviews and investigations, prepares pre-sentence and juvenile reports, and oversees probationers and juveniles for compliance with court orders. These activities are conducted with the goals of rehabilitating offenders and protecting society. Further, the Probation Department develops and maintains community-based alternative correction programs.

B. **Chief Probation Officer.** As directed by the Board of Judges, the Chief Probation Officer shall oversee the efficient operation of the department; assist in the hiring and discharge of personnel; ensure the proper evaluation and training of department employees; compile statistics and create required reports; monitor budget expenditures and outline budget requests; maintain written policies and procedures for the department; and perform other duties as required.

C. **Probation Department Management Team.** The Chief Probation Officer, Assistant Chief Probation Officers, and the Division Supervisors shall constitute the Probation Department Management Team. This team shall meet frequently to oversee operation of the Department and to formulate proposed changes to department policy and operation. Each Division Supervisor shall meet regularly with division staff and shall communicate staff concerns to the Probation Management Team.

D. **Procedures.** The Probation Department shall maintain a written policy, procedure, and training manual which sets forth the manner of operation of the Department and the duties of each officer or staff member.

E. Caseload Allocation. The Chief Probation Officer, with the assistance of the Probation Department Management Team, shall maintain a written caseload allocation policy for probation officers. This policy shall reflect a plan for equitable distribution of cases to officers based on workload, staff expertise, and training.

F. Statistics and Reports. The Probation Department shall maintain all statistical reports and records required by law and necessary for compliance with grant or program authorities. A written report summarizing the activity and operation of the Probation Department shall be delivered to the Board of Judges by March 31st of each year.

G. Fees and Costs. Court-ordered supervision fees shall be collected by designated staff pursuant to an established system of financial records management. This system, subject to a State Board of Accounts audit, shall delineate special funds accounts, maintenance of daily collections and ledgers, and proper deposit and disbursement of funds. An internal audit will be conducted any time the collection clerk or staff responsible for the collection of fees terminates employment.

Adopted effective Jan. 1, 1991. Amended effective Oct. 4, 2000; renumbered as Rule 0142, and amended effective Feb. 7, 2007. Amended effective May 27, 2009; Jan. 1, 2012.

LR53–AR00 Rule 0143. COMMUNITY ALTERNATIVE SUPERVISION PROGRAM (CASP) VIOLATIONS

A. The CASP case manager (probation officer) will file a Notice of Noncompliance/Petition to Revoke Suspended Sentence for technical and/or new offense violation(s) that occur while participating on CASP and are specific to that program. The officer will provide probable cause information for the issuance of a warrant to the Sentencing Court, Duty Court, or Duty Judge if requested after hours. The CASP officer will continue to supervise the offender until the offender's CASP obligations are terminated or completed.

B. A probable cause hearing and a request for warrant should be pursued on PTRs that allege serious or multiple home detention or CASP violations.

Adopted effective Jan. 1, 1991. Amended effective Oct. 4, 2000; renumbered as Rule 0143, and amended effective Feb. 7, 2007. Amended effective May 27, 2009; Jan. 1, 2010.

LR53–AR00 Rule 0144. ADMINISTRATIVE PROBATION MODIFICATION MEETINGS

A. The Board of Judges has authorized the Probation Department to conduct Administrative Probation Modification (APM) meetings to address minor technical violations of probation. During the APM meeting, a Probation Supervisor and the supervising Probation Officer are authorized to resolve minor technical violations of probation via agreement with the probationer. Upon agreement with probationer, during this APM

meeting, a Probation Supervisor may impose minor consequences for said technical violations as follows: up to 50 hours of Community Service (Public Restitution or Road Crew) may be added to the probation conditions; the supervised term of probation may be extended up to the date of discharge from probation; the probationer may be required to submit to a mental health or substance abuse evaluation and participate in treatment as directed; the probationer may be required to participate in the Day Reporting Program up to 60 days and pay all corresponding fees upon agreement, and without the filing of a Petition to Modify or Notice of Noncompliance. Written judicial approval and an order are necessary only when conditions of probation have been modified. If a specific condition is not modified, a Judge's signature is not required.

B. Probationers do not have a right to an attorney for an Administrative Probation Modification meeting and may refuse to participate.

Adopted effective Jan. 1, 1991. Amended effective Oct. 4, 2000; renumbered as Rule 0144, and amended effective Feb. 7, 2007. Amended effective May 27, 2009.

LR53–AR00 Rule 0145. RECOMMENDATION TO THE COURT FOR DISMISSAL

Probation Officers can file "Recommendation to the Court for Dismissal" but may not file motions.

Adopted effective Jan. 1, 1991. Amended effective Oct. 4, 2000; renumbered as Rule 0145, and amended effective Feb. 7, 2007.

LR53–AR00 Rule 0146. PETITION TO REVOKE

A. Probation Officers may file a PTR when the preponderance of evidence shows a new offense has been committed even if charges are not filed.

B. Petitions to Revoke may be filed if violators fail to complete Public Restitution by deadline.

Adopted effective Jan. 1, 1991. Amended effective Oct. 4, 2000; renumbered as Rule 0146, and amended effective Feb. 7, 2007. Amended effective May 27, 2009.

LR53–AR00 Rule 0147. COMMUNITY CORRECTIONS PROGRAM POLICY

The Monroe County Community Corrections Program will not compete with not-for-profit organizations for remuneration which could be fund-raising events for those agencies.

Adopted effective Jan. 1, 1991. Amended effective Oct. 4, 2000; renumbered as Rule 0147, and amended effective Feb. 7, 2007.

LR53–AR00 Rule 0148. ROAD CREW AND PUBLIC RESTITUTION AGENCY APPROVAL

A. Any governmental or not-for-profit agency wishing to receive Road Crew services and/or Public Restitution workers from the Monroe Circuit Court Probation Department shall make application for "Approved Provider" status through the Community Corrections Director. The agency shall complete the "Monroe County Community Corrections Agency Agreement for Community Service Workers" form and submit this form to the Community Corrections Director. The agency shall also provide any additional information requested by the Community Corrections Director.

B. Upon receipt of this completed form, the Community Corrections Director will present this application for "Approved Agency" status to the Chief Probation Officer.

C. The Chief Probation Officer, or designee, will inform the applicant agency of the decision regarding approval status.

Adopted effective Jan. 1, 1991. Amended effective Oct. 4, 2000; renumbered as Rule 0148, and amended effective Feb. 7, 2007. Amended effective May 27, 2009. Amended effective Jan. 19, 2010.

LR53–AR00 Rule 0149. PROBATION FEES

Updated 01/01/10

A. The Board of Judges shall set/approve a schedule of fees for the Probation Department. This fee schedule will be updated annually or as needed.

B. The Probation Department Fee Schedule will be recorded on an Order, to be filed with the Clerk in the General Order Book under "Establishing Fees For The Monroe County Probation Department."

Adopted effective Jan. 1, 1991. Amended effective Oct. 4, 2000; renumbered as Rule 0149, and amended effective Feb. 7, 2007. Amended effective May 27, 2009; Jan. 1, 2012.

LR53–AR00 Rule 0150. UNSUPERVISED PROBATION

Updated 01/01/10

A. If a person is placed on unsupervised probation, no responsibility of supervision will be placed on the Probation Department. The sentencing court shall execute an Order of Unsupervised Probation. If a person is placed on unsupervised probation, the court reporter shall forward a copy of the Chronological Case Summary (CCS) entry and Order of Unsupervised Probation to the Probation Department. The name of the probationer will be placed in the case management database by the Probation Department, but no further contact or supervision of the "probationer" will be required. The Probation Department will advise the sentencing court if the unsupervised "probationer" has been arrested on another charge.

B. Persons placed on unsupervised probation with no term of supervised probation shall be assessed an administrative fee and an initial Probation user fee as set by the current Probation Department Fee Schedule. Persons placed on any term of supervised probation with an allowance for unsupervised probation

shall be responsible for all fees imposed including monthly fees during any unsupervised period.

Adopted effective Jan. 1, 1991. Amended effective Oct. 4, 2000; renumbered as Rule 0150, and amended effective Feb. 7, 2007. Amended effective May 27, 2009; Jan. 1, 2012.

LR53–AR00 Rule 0151. WORK RELEASE PROGRAM

Updated 01/01/10

A. The local Work Release Program which operated out of the Monroe County Jail officially terminated on April 3, 2009.

B. Defendants to be considered for placement in a work release facility (local or out–of–county) must be referred to the Community Corrections Program for program eligibility determination.

C. Defendants must meet eligibility for the local Community Alternative Supervision Program (CASP) before being considered for work release placement (local or out–of–county), including the requirement that delinquent local Community Corrections fees must be paid in full.

D. Offenders must have an actual 30 days to serve to qualify for the Work Release Program but exceptional cases will receive consideration.

Adopted effective Jan. 1, 1991. Amended effective Oct. 4, 2000; renumbered as Rule 0151, and amended effective Feb. 7, 2007. Amended effective May 27, 2009; Jan. 1, 2010.

LR53–AR00 Rule 0152. ALCOHOL EDUCATION SCHOOL ATTENDANCE

All persons charged with an alcohol related offense may be required to attend alcohol education classes or to complete substance abuse treatment. Persons referred to Alcohol Education School (AES) by the Pretrial Diversion Program (PDP) who fail to attend AES should be reported by the Probation Department to PDP and at that time have their case re-instated as determined by the Monroe County Prosecutor.

Adopted effective Jan. 1, 1991. Amended effective Oct. 4, 2000; renumbered as Rule 0152, and amended effective Feb. 7, 2007. Amended effective May 27, 2009.

LR53–AR00 Rule 0153. COURT ALCOHOL AND DRUG PROGRAM USER FEES

A. The Criminal Division of the Monroe Circuit Court has set the following schedule of fees pursuant to the authority granted by IC 12–23–14.

B. Court Alcohol and Drug Program Schedule of Fees:

1. Assessment, Referral, and Monitoring: $300 for misdemeanor conviction; $400 for felony conviction.

2. Assessment, Referral, and Monitoring for other jurisdictions: $300 for misdemeanor conviction; $300 for felony conviction.

3. Transfer out fee: $100.

4. Alcohol Education School fee: $75.

5. Prime for Life Course: $12 Hour—$170.00, 16 Hour—$220.00.

C. All Court Alcohol and Drug Program Fees are payable to Clerk of the Court.

Adopted effective May 27, 2009.

LR53–AR00 Rule 0154. DRUG TREATMENT COURT USER FEES

A. The Criminal Division of the Monroe Circuit Court has set the following schedule of fees pursuant to the authority granted by IC 33–23–16–23 and in accordance with the rules adopted by the Indiana Judicial Conference on June 16, 2011 effective July 1, 2011;

B. Drug Treatment Court Administration Fee: Not more than $100.00 per admission

C. Drug Treatment Court User Fee: Fifty dollars ($50) or less will be collected monthly beginning with the second month of participation and continuing for each month thereafter for the duration of participation in the problem-solving court.

D. Drug Treatment Court User Fees are payable to Clerk of the Court.

Adopted effective May 27, 2009. Amended effective Jan. 1, 2012.

LR53–AR00 Rule 0155. YOUTH SERVICES BUREAU

A. Establishment. The Monroe County Youth Services Bureau was established in compliance with IC 31–31–8.

B. Transfer of Authority. The Monroe County Board of Commissioners transferred its authority regarding the Youth Services Bureau to the Monroe County Board of Judges effective July 5, 2010. Monroe County Code 420–1.

C. Youth Services Bureau Executive Director. The Executive Director for the Youth Services Bureau is responsible for implementing the policy directions and goals of the Youth Services Bureau, including securing and administering department funds, supervising development and operations of programs and services, and supervising personnel.

D. Citizen Advisory Board. A Citizen Advisory Board representing the needs of children and youth will meet with the Judge of the Monroe Circuit Court and/or the Youth Services Bureau Executive Director on a regular basis in accordance with IC 31–31–8–6. This Board shall be advisory in nature and have no legal authority or responsibility for the operation of the Bureau.

Adopted effective Jan. 1, 2010. Amended effective Jan. 1, 2012.

MONROE CIRCUIT COURT LOCAL TRIAL RULES OF PRACTICE AND PROCEDURE

Adopted Effective January 1, 1991

Including Amendments Received Through November 1, 2013

Research Notes

These rules may be searched electronically on Westlaw *in the* IN-RULES *database; updates to these rules may be found on* Westlaw *in* IN-RULESUPDATES. *For search tips and a summary of database content, consult the Westlaw Scope Screens for each database.*

LR53–TR00 Rule 0200. SCOPE OF LOCAL RULES OF TRIAL PROCEDURE

These rules shall apply in all cases in the Monroe Circuit Court. If there is a conflict between a Local Rules of Trial Procedure and another, more specific Monroe County Local Rule, that more specific rule shall control.

Adopted effective Jan. 1, 1991. Amended effective Oct. 4, 2000; renumbered as Rule 0200, and amended effective Feb. 7, 2007; Jan. 1, 2012.

LR53–TR00 Rule 0201. SERVICE TO ATTORNEY'S JUSTICE BUILDING MAILBOX

An attorney who has a mailbox in the Justice Building Court Services office consents to service of pleadings to that mailbox. Such service shall be deemed equivalent to service by United States mail.

Adopted as Rule 1, effective Jan. 1, 1991. Amended effective Oct. 4, 2000; renumbered as Rule 0201, and amended effective Feb. 7, 2007; Jan. 1, 2012.

LR53–TR00 Rule 0202. SERVICE OF EMERGENCY MOTIONS

A motion seeking judicial action in three days or less shall be served on opposing parties by FAX, email, or personal service. The attorney or party filing of such a motion shall also inform the other parties of the filing by telephone at the time the motion is delivered to the court.

Adopted as Rule 2, effective Jan. 1, 1991. Amended effective Oct. 4, 2000; renumbered as Rule 0202, and amended effective Feb. 7, 2007; Jan. 1, 2012.

LR53–TR05 Rule 0203. PREPARATION OF PLEADINGS AND ORDERS

A. Proposed Orders. A party or attorney filing a motion shall, at the time of filing, provide the court with an original proposed order and sufficient copies for each party, and an extra copy for the court. Proposed orders shall include a full distribution list of attorneys or parties to whom the order should be sent.

B. Filing by Electronic Facsimile Transmission. Pleadings not exceeding ten (10) pages in length, may be filed by facsimile (FAX) as provided in Administrative Rule 12. Facsimile filing does not require follow up filing of duplicate original documents.

Adopted as Rule 3, effective Jan. 1, 1991. Amended effective Oct. 4, 2000; renumbered as Rule 0203, and amended effective Feb. 7, 2007; Jan. 1, 2012.

LR53–TR00 Rule 0204. MOTIONS

A. Enlargement of Time to Answer. An initial written motion for enlargement of time to file an answer or other responsive pleadings shall be automatically allowed for an additional 30 days from the original due date without order of the court. Said motion shall state the original date when the response was due and the date to which that time is enlarged. For this rule to be applicable, the motion must be filed on or before the original due date.

B. Accompanying Legal Memorandum. A separate legal memorandum shall be filed with any motion to dismiss a TR 12(b)(6) motion for judgment on the pleadings, a motion for more definite statement, or a motion to strike. A party opposing such a motion shall file a response memorandum within 20 days of the filing of the motion or the motion shall be subject to summary ruling without further notice and without a hearing.

Adopted as Rule 4, effective Jan. 1, 1991. Amended effective Oct. 4, 2000; renumbered as Rule 0204, and amended effective Feb. 7, 2007. Amended effective Jan. 19, 2010; Jan. 1, 2012.

LR53–TR00 Rule 0205.   INTERROGATORIES

A.   Number of Interrogatories. The number of interrogatories which may be served pursuant to Rule 33 shall be limited so as to require the answering party to make no more than 50 answers. Waiver of this limitation by order of the court will be granted in cases in which such limitation would work a manifest injustice or would be impractical because of the complexity of the issues of the case.

B.   Form of Answers or Objections. Answers or objections to interrogatories shall set forth in full the interrogatory being answered or objected to immediately preceding the answer or objection.

Adopted as Rule 5, effective Jan. 1, 1991. Amended effective Oct. 4, 2000; renumbered as Rule 0205, and amended effective Feb. 7, 2007. Amended effective Jan. 19, 2010; Jan. 1, 2012.

LR53–TR00 Rule 0206.   DEPOSITIONS

A.   This rule shall not apply in criminal or juvenile delinquency cases.

B.   Video Recordings of Depositions. A transcript of a video recording of deposition testimony shall be tendered to the court when the deposition is offered into evidence.

C.   Depositions of Experts. Depositions of experts shall be admissible at trial regardless of the availability of the witness or other limitations in Trial Rule 32(A), unless objection to the admissibility is made in writing 5 days prior to the taking of said deposition or within 10 days subsequent to notice of the deposition, whichever deadline occurs first. A copy of the notice shall be tendered to the reporter at the time of taking the deposition for inclusion with the deposition. In the absence of such written objection, the deposition of an expert may be admitted by stipulation.

D.   Copy of Deposition. Any party or counsel to an action may obtain a photocopy of a deposition on file with the Clerk of the Court upon tender of a receipt showing payment to the deposing party of 50% of the cost of said deposition. In addition, the requesting party of counsel shall tender to the Clerk the present statutory rate per page for the copying service.

Adopted as Rule 6, effective Jan. 1, 1991. Amended effective Oct. 4, 2000; renumbered as Rule 0206, and amended effective Feb. 7, 2007; Jan. 1, 2012.

LR53–TR53 Rule 0207.   CONTINUANCES

A.   Information in Motion. A motion to continue a hearing or trial shall contain the following:

1.   The date and time of the hearing or trial for which a continuance is sought;

2.   The reason for the continuance;

3.   A motion for continuance shall not contain any other requests;

4.   A good-faith estimate of the time needed for such hearing or trial when rescheduled;

5.   The date and time opposing counsel/party was notified that the party would seek a continuance;

6.   Whether opposing counsel /party agrees with or objects to the continuance; and

7.   Contact information, including at least one telephone number, for any unrepresented opposing party, or an explanation of why that information is not available on diligent inquiry.

B.   Continuances Sought for Conflicts:

1.   *Scheduling Conflicts.* A motion for continuance based on a conflict with a previously scheduled vacation shall state the date the vacation was set. A motion for continuance based upon a scheduling conflict with a another case shall specify the other case name and number, the date on which the conflicting hearing or trial date was set by the other court, and the type of hearing or trial. Any such motion for continuance shall be filed within 7 days of the scheduling conflict becoming apparent.

C.   Objections:

1.   If there is an objection to a continuance, the objecting party may ask the court to set a telephone conference to consider the objection.

Adopted as Rule 7, effective Jan. 1, 1991. Amended effective Oct. 4, 2000; renumbered as Rule 0207, and amended effective Feb. 7, 2007; Jan. 1, 2012.

LR53–TR00 Rule 0208.   [Deleted eff. Jan. 1, 2012.]

MONROE CIRCUIT COURT RULES OF CRIMINAL PROCEDURE

Adopted Effective January 1, 1991

Including Amendments Received Through November 1, 2013

Research Notes

These rules may be searched on Westlaw *in the* IN-RULES *database; updates to these rules may be found on* Westlaw *in IN-RULESUPDATES. For search tips and a summary of database content, consult the* Westlaw *Scope Screens for each database.*

LR53–CR00 Rule 0300. STATEMENT OF PRINCIPLES

The Criminal Rules of the Monroe Circuit Court are intended:

A. To promote a fair and expeditious determination of the charges, whether by plea or trial;

B. To provide the defendant with sufficient information to make an informed plea;

C. To permit thorough preparation for trial and minimize surprise at trial;

D. To avoid unnecessary and repetitious trials by identifying any latent procedural or constitutional issues and affording remedies therefore prior to trial;

E. To reduce interruptions and complications of trials by identifying collateral issues and determining them prior to trial; and

F. To effect economies of time, money, and judicial and professional talents by minimizing paperwork, repetitious asserts of issues, and the number of separate hearings.

Adopted as Rule CR-1, effective Jan. 1, 1991. Amended effective Oct. 4, 2000; renumbered as Rule 0300, and amended effective Feb. 7, 2007; Jan. 1, 2012.

LR53–CR00 Rule 0301. DISCLOSURE BY THE PROSECUTING ATTORNEY

A. Scope. The prosecuting attorney shall, except as otherwise provided by these rules, disclose and provide to the defendant the following information:

1. The names, addresses, and telephone numbers of all persons who may be called as witnesses in the case, together with copies of their written or recorded statements and any record of their prior criminal convictions;

2. Copies of any written or recorded statements and a written summary of any oral statements, related to the case, made by the defendant or made by a co-defendant;

3. A copy of the grand jury minutes containing testimony of any person from whom testimony was taken in the case;

4. Copies of any reports or statements of expert or skilled witnesses related to the case, including results of physical or mental examinations, scientific tests, experiments, or comparisons;

5. The terms of any agreements made with co-defendants or other witnesses to secure their testimony, including any written documentation thereof;

6. Identification of any books, papers, documents, photographs, or other tangible objects which may be offered as evidence in the case or which were obtained from or belong to the defendant;

7. Copies of affidavits for search warrants, search warrants, and returns made on search warrants;

8. Whether any relevant grand jury testimony has not been transcribed;

9. Whether any existing material or information subject to these rules is not then available to the prosecuting attorney for disclosure to the defendant;

10. Whether any material or information related to the case has been provided by an informant;

11. If there has been any electronic surveillance or wiretapping of the defendant's premises or conversations to which the defendant was a party; and

12. If requested by the defendant, any relationship of specified persons to the prosecuting attorney.

B. Exculpatory or Mitigating Information. The prosecuting attorney shall disclose to the defendant any material or information known to the prosecuting attorney which would tend to negate the guilt of the defendant as to the offense charged or which would tend to mitigate any sentence imposed in the event of a conviction.

C. Examination of Evidence. The prosecuting attorney's duties to disclose information and evidence under this rule include material and information in the possession and control of the prosecuting attorney's staff and employees, of any other persons who have participated in the investigation and evaluation of the case, of any other persons who regularly report to the prosecuting attorney, and of any other persons who have reported to the prosecuting attorney with reference to the charge filed.

Adopted as Rule CR-2, effective Jan. 1, 1991. Amended effective Oct. 4, 2000; renumbered as Rule 0301, and amended effective Feb. 7, 2007. Amended effective May 27, 2009; Jan. 1, 2012.

LR53–CR00 Rule 0302. DISCLOSURE BY THE DEFENDANT

A. Scope. The defendant shall, subject to constitutional limitations and except as otherwise provided by these rules, disclose to the prosecuting attorney:

1. The names, addresses and telephone numbers of all persons who may be called as witnesses in the case, together with copies of their written or recorded statements;

2. Copies of any reports or statements of expert or skilled witnesses related to the case, including results of physical or mental examinations, scientific tests, experiments, or comparisons, intended to be offered as evidence in the case;

3. Identification of any books, papers, documents, photographs, or other tangible objects which may be offered as evidence in the case; and

4. Identification of any affirmative defenses upon which the defendant intends to rely in the case.

B. Examination of Evidence. The defendant shall permit inspection, copying, photographing, and testing of all evidence disclosed under these rules at reasonable times and places and under reasonable terms and conditions to insure against loss of, damage to, or alteration of the character or integrity of the evidence.

C. Additional Disclosure upon Order of Court. The Court may, subject to constitutional limitations, require a defendant or a suspect in an investigation:

1. To appear in a line-up;

2. To speak, and to speak specific words, within the hearing of witnesses to an alleged offense;

3. To pose for photographs not involving the reenactment of alleged events;

4. To provide handwriting specimens;

5. To be fingerprinted;

6. To don specified articles of clothing;

7. To submit to reasonable physical or medical inspections;

8. To submit to the taking of specimens of material from under fingernails and toenails; and

9. To submit to the taking of sample of blood, hair, and other bodily substances and materials.

D. Reasonable Cause and Notice. A suspect not charged with an offense shall be required to appear pursuant to Section (C) only after a determination by the Court that there is reasonable cause to require the person to appear for the specified purpose. A defendant or suspect ordered to appear for a purpose specified in Section (C) shall be given reasonable advance written notice specifying the purpose of the appearance, the place at which the person must appear, and the date, time, and length of time required for the appearance. Such notice shall be provided to the person and the person's attorney, if any, and the attorney shall have the right to the present.

Adopted as Rule CR-3, effective Jan. 1, 1991. Amended effective Oct. 4, 2000; renumbered as Rule 0302, and amended effective Feb. 7, 2007; Jan. 1, 2012.

LR53–CR00 Rule 0303. GENERAL RULES PERTAINING TO DISCOVERY

A. Requirement of Court Order. No written motion to, or order of, the Court shall be required to obtain discovery pursuant to these rules, except:

1. For additional discovery or disclosure not specifically required by these rules;

2. For an extension of time within which to comply with these rules, specifying the reasons for the extension;

3. For a protective order; or

4. To complete compliance with these rules.

B. Time of Disclosure. The prosecuting attorney shall provide full discovery to the defendant:

1. Within 21 days after the initial hearing in a felony case, or

2. Within 15 days:

   a. After an attorney's appearance for the defendant; or

   b. After a pro se defendant's request in a misdemeanor case.

The defendant shall provide full discovery to prosecuting attorney:

1. Within 21 days after disclosure by the prosecuting attorney in a felony case; and

2. Within 15 days after disclosure by the prosecuting attorney in a misdemeanor case.

C. Continuing Duty. The duty of disclosure pursuant to these rules continues until dismissal, acquittal, or conviction and a party shall disclose all information and material subject to these rules or other order of the Court promptly after discovery thereof, notwithstanding any prior compliance with these rules.

D. Manner of Disclosure. All disclosures required by these rules shall be made in writing or, if first discovered during hearing or trial, on the record in open court.

E. Work Product. Neither party shall be required to disclose work product.

F. Excision. Tangible items which are in part subject to these rules and in part beyond the scope of these rules shall be excised and produced to the extent required by these rules, with notice to the other party that portions thereof have been excised.

G. Protective Orders. Disclosure required by these rules may be denied or subjected to reasonable limitations if the Court, after motion by either party determines that any benefit of the disclosure is outweighed by a substantial risk to any person of physical harm, non-physical injury or damage, undue embarrassment, or other compelling factor.

H. In Camera Examination. Any tangible item or information which becomes the subject of a motion for protective order may be examined, inspected, or otherwise evaluated, by the Court in camera. Upon order of the Court granting such relief, a summary of the protected information, shall be sealed and preserved in the record of the case.

I. Impeding Investigation Prohibited. Neither party shall, directly or indirectly, advise any person to refuse to discuss the case with the other party, advise any person to refuse to disclose any relevant information or material to the other party, or otherwise impede the other party's investigation of the case, except as may be authorized by constitutional provision, the statues of this State, or common law privilege.

J. Sanctions. Upon failure or refusal of either party to comply with these rules or other discovery orders of the Court, the Court may impose sanctions.

Adopted as Rule CR-4, effective Jan. 1, 1991. Amended effective Oct. 4, 2000; renumbered as Rule 0303, and amended effective Feb. 7, 2007. Amended effective May 27, 2009; Jan. 1, 2012.

LR53–CR16 Rule 0304. PRETRIAL CONFERENCES

A. Number; Orders and Reports. One or more pretrial conferences may be required at the discretion of the Court. All attorneys of record are required to appear at and participate in all required pretrial conferences. The Court shall make or require an appropriate order or report after a required pretrial conference.

B. Presence of Defendant. The defendant may be required, by order of the Court, to attend pretrial conferences.

C. Scope. All pretrial conferences shall address with specificity:

1. The names of all persons, including addresses and telephone numbers upon request of the opposing party, intended to be called to testify at pretrial hearings or at trial;

2. The identification of all tangible items intended to be offered as exhibits at pretrial hearings or at trial;

3. All stipulations of testimony and fact concerning matters not in material dispute which may aid in expediting pretrial hearings or the trial;

4. The identification of all motions to dismiss, motions to suppress evidence, questions of law, and procedural issues which can and should be resolved prior to trial to expedite the trial of the case;

5. The anticipated necessity of further discovery by either party and the reasonable length of time required to complete it; and

6. The tender of any proposed plea and/or sentencing agreement by the prosecuting attorney and the response of the defendant thereto.

D. Waiver of Issues. All motions to dismiss, motions to suppress evidence, question of law, and procedural issues known to the parties on the basis of the information then available and not specifically identified for pretrial resolution in the pretrial order are waived.

Adopted as Rule CR-5, effective Jan. 1, 1991. Amended effective Oct. 4, 2000; renumbered as Rule 0304, and amended effective Feb. 7, 2007.

LR53–CR00 Rule 0305. TRIAL SCHEDULE

Except as may be required for compliance with Criminal Rule 4 of the Indiana Rules of Criminal Procedure or other just cause determined by the Court, cases will be scheduled and called for trial according to the earliest date of filing. However, all cases scheduled for trial remain on the trial docket, unless continued on order of the Court.

Adopted as Rule CR-6, effective Jan. 1, 1991. Amended effective Oct. 4, 2000; renumbered as Rule 0305, and amended effective Feb. 7, 2007.

LR53–CR53 Rule 0306. CONTINUANCES

A. Requirement of Motions. All motions for continuance shall be requested, and will be granted by the Court only for good cause.

B. Conflicting Settings. All motions for continuance based on conflicting case settings shall be filed within 14 days after notice of the conflict and shall specify:

1. The court in which the conflicting case is pending;

2. The name and cause number of the case;

3. The nature of the conflicting hearing or trial; and

4. The date upon which the other court scheduled the conflicting setting.

C. Further Discovery. Continuances for the purpose of conducting further discovery may be granted for good cause shown. However, no continuances for the purpose of discovery filed more than 6 months after the initial hearing will be granted by the Court, absent demonstration by the moving party that need for the additional discovery could not have been anticipated, or that the discovery could not have been completed by the exercise of due diligence.

D. Unavailability of Witnesses. Any motion for continuance based on the unavailability of a witness shall be filed at least 7 days before the scheduled trial date. Any such motion filed more than 6 months after the initial hearing, or any such motion to which an objection is filed, must comply with IC 35–36–7–1 or IC 35–36–7–2.

Adopted as Rule CR-7, effective Jan. 1, 1991. Amended effective Oct. 4, 2000; renumbered as Rule 0306, and amended effective Feb. 7, 2007; Jan. 1, 2012.

LR53–CR00 Rule 0307. APPEARANCE OF DEFENSE COUNSEL

A. Written Appearance. An attorney must file a written appearance for the defendant at the earliest possible time after being retained by the defendant or appointed by the Court to represent the defendant.

B. Withdrawal of Appearance. An attorney's appearance on behalf of a defendant may be vacated or withdrawn only after a hearing in the presence of the defendant. The defendant's presence will not be required upon the attorney's demonstration at the hearing of the inability to locate the defendant.

C. Waiver of Hearing. The hearing required in Section (B) is waived if another attorney has entered a written appearance on behalf of the defendant.

D. Withdrawal Based on Nonpayment of Fees. An attorney's motion to vacate or withdraw his appearance on behalf of a defendant based solely upon the defendant's failure to pay the attorney's fee, will not be granted:

1. If filed more than 6 months after the initial hearing; or

2. If filed more than 30 days before a trial date scheduled within the first 6 months after the initial hearing.

E. Duration of Appearance. An attorney's appearance on behalf of a defendant is deemed to be vacated or withdrawn after the time permitted to file a Notice of Appeal for the purposes of appealing a disposition on the merits has elapsed and an appeal has not been initiated. If an appeal is initiated, the attorney remains of record for the defendant until the appeal is concluded or the appearance is otherwise vacated pursuant to this rule.

Adopted as Rule CR-8, effective Jan. 1, 1991. Amended effective Oct. 4, 2000; renumbered as Rule 0307, and amended effective Feb. 7, 2007; Jan. 1, 2012.

LR53–CR00 Rule 0308. PRE–SENTENCE INVESTIGATIONS

Court Reporters are to return Pre–Sentence Investigations to the Probation Department at the conclusion of the case.

Adopted effective Jan. 1, 1991. Amended effective Oct. 4, 2000; renumbered as Rule 0308, and amended effective Feb. 7, 2007.

LR53–CR00 Rule 0309. BONDS

All bonds shall be delivered by the Monroe County Sheriff's Office to the Clerk for posting. The Clerk shall deliver the bonds to the appropriate court division prior to the time of Initial Hearing.

Adopted effective Jan. 1, 1991. Amended effective Oct. 4, 2000; renumbered as Rule 0309, and amended effective Feb. 7, 2007.

LR53–CR00 Rule 0310. BAIL BOND SCHEDULE

IN THE CIRCUIT COURT
FOR THE COUNTY OF MONROE AND STATE OF INDIANA

ORDER ESTABLISHING BAIL SCHEDULE

Pursuant to the provisions of IC 35–33–8–4, the Circuit Court of Monroe County, Indiana, enters the following order establishing the amount of bail for those persons charged with the commission of criminal offenses by information; arrest on probable cause, or indictment.

IT IS THEREFORE ORDERED, ADJUDGED, AND DECREED by the Court that effective immediately and until further order of the Court, bail shall be as follows for all individuals charged with the commission of criminal offenses in the Monroe Circuit Court:

SECTION 1. FELONIES

A. For a person charged with murder or attempted murder, a person who is a sexually violent predator under IC 35–38–1–7.5, and who is arrested or charged with the commission of an offense that would classify the person as a sex or violent offender as defined by IC 11–8–8–5, or for a person charged with Child Molesting or Child Solicitation, no bail shall be set except by a judge at a preliminary hearing;

B. For a person charged with being a habitual offender; bail shall be $50,000 surety and $500 cash, or a habitual substance offender; bail shall be $25,000 surety and $500 cash;

C. For any Class A felony offense, bail shall be $50,000 surety and $500 cash;

D. For any Class B felony offense, bail shall be $20,000 surety and $500 cash;

E. For any Class C felony offense, bail shall be $5,000 surety and $500 cash;

F. For any Class D felony offense, bail shall be $2,000 surety and $500 cash.

SECTION II. MISDEMEANORS

A. Any person arrested for a misdemeanor offense other than battery, domestic battery, invasion of privacy, resisting law enforcement, possession of a handgun without a license, operating a vehicle while intoxicated operating with either a .08 or .15 ACE or dealing marijuana or hashish, shall be released from jail to appear in court on that person's own recognizance, subject to the following conditions:

1. At the time such a person is released on recognizance, the person shall be required to furnish a present residential and mailing address, telephone number, social security number, and employer's name and address. The identifying data of any full-time or part-time student at Indiana University—Bloomington shall include a student's permanent address and telephone number as well as the student's local address and telephone number.

2. If the person arrested is under 21 years of age, the information shall also include parents' names, addresses, and telephone numbers.

3. If the person agrees to provide the data required in Section II, A (1), but is unable to provide a social security number, driver's license, photo identification card, or employer information, the person may be released to the custody of a resident of Monroe County over 18 years of age who can provide such data on themselves.

4. Upon refusal to provide the information required under this Section, the person shall be held until brought before a judge.

B. A person shall not be released on recognizance if the person:

1. Has any conviction with the last 5 years;

2. Has failed to appear in any court within the last 5 years;

3. Has pending criminal charges; or

4. Is on probation or parole at the time of arrest.

C. If the provisions of this Section do not authorize the release of the person on recognizance, bail shall be as follows:

1. For any Class A misdemeanor, bail shall be $1,000 surety and $500 cash;

2. For any Class B misdemeanor, bail shall be $500 surety and $500 cash;

3. For any Class C misdemeanor, bail shall be $500 surety and $500 cash.

SECTION III. MISCELLANEOUS PROVISIONS

A. Promise to Appear.

1. Any person, whether released on recognizance or bail for a misdemeanor or felony offense, shall be required to execute a written Promise to Appear in the appropriate court at the designated date and time. The Promise to Appear form shall be immediately forwarded to the appropriate court by the Sheriff.

B. Intoxication. No person shall be released by the Sheriff of Monroe County, regardless of the provisions of this Order, unless such person clearly manifests a state of sobriety at the time the provisions of this Order would otherwise permit release.

1. The Sheriff shall hold in custody any person who is under the influence of alcohol or controlled substances until such time it is determined, at the Sheriff's discretion, that the individual may be safely released without danger to self or others.

2. When information is available concerning the blood-alcohol content of an intoxicated person due to the administration of blood tests, breath tests, or other chemical tests, no intoxicated person shall be released by the Sheriff except as provided by IC 35–33–1–6.

3. When no information is available concerning the blood-alcohol content of a person charged with operating while intoxicated, such person shall not be released for a period of 24 hours, unless ordered by a judge.

4. When no information is available concerning the blood-alcohol content of a person charged with public intoxication, such person shall not be released for a period of 4 hours, unless ordered by a judge.

C. Battery. A person arrested on a charge involving battery or domestic battery, shall not be released until 24 hours have elapsed, unless ordered by a judge. The person may then post bail:

1. Pursuant to other sections of this Bail Order; and

2. If the person agrees in writing to initiate no contact with the victim.

Upon refusal to sign a No Contact Agreement, the person shall be held without bail until brought before a judge.

D. Extradition. Any person extradited to Monroe County shall be held without bail until brought before a judge.

E. Overweight Trucking Violations. The bail schedule as set out in this Order shall not apply to trucking violations. Bail for such offenses shall be determined pursuant to the provisions of IC 9–20–18–1, et seq.

F. Combination of Charges. If a person is charged with the commission of more than one offense arising out of a single incident, whether the offenses are felonies or misdemeanors, bail shall be in one amount for all charges, and shall be in the amount established for the most serious offense charged.

G.   Double Bond.   The specified surety bond for felonies or misdemeanors shall be doubled in the event the person has a pending case, has been convicted of a felony within the last 5 years, or is a habitual substance offender.

H.   Cash Bond.   After normal business hours the Sheriff shall accept a bond made in cash or by certified check and shall issue a receipt.   A cash bond must be posted in the name of the Defendant.   Thereafter, as soon as is practicable, the Sheriff shall deposit the cash or certified check with the Monroe County Clerk.

I.   10% Cash Deposit or Full Cash Bond.   The Clerk or Sheriff may not accept 10% cash deposit or full cash bond in lieu of the bond otherwise required herein except upon express written order of a judge. In the event a 10% cash bond is approved by a Court, the Clerk may retain as a service fee 10% of the amount deposited when the bond is released at the conclusion of the case.

J.   Probation/Parole Hold.   A person charged with the commission of a crime while on probation or parole shall be held without bail until brought before a judge.

K.   Release of Bond.   No cash bond may be released by the Monroe County Clerk except upon written order of a judge after judgment has been entered and any fines, fees, and costs imposed by the Court have been paid and satisfied.

L.   Amount of Bail on Warrant.   If bail is set at a probable cause hearing, the amount of bail set by the judge shall be endorsed upon the arrest warrant and shall supersede conflicting provisions of this order.

Adopted effective Jan. 1, 1991.   Amended effective Oct. 4, 2000; renumbered as Rule 0310, and amended effective Feb. 7, 2007.   Amended effective May 27, 2009; Jan. 1, 2012.

LR53–CR00 Rule 0311.   PUBLIC DEFENDER APPOINTMENT

Public Defender appointments continue for 30 days beyond conviction in criminal cases or disposition in Juvenile Delinquency cases.

Adopted effective Jan. 1, 1991.   Amended effective Oct. 4, 2000; renumbered as Rule 0311, and amended effective Feb. 7, 2007.   Amended effective May 27, 2009.

LR5S–CR00 Rule 0312.   TRANSPORTING PRISONERS FOR MENTAL HEALTH EVALUATIONS[1]

A.   The Monroe County Sheriff will provide transportation of prisoners to the Bloomington Hospital or Centerstone, or other agency determined as appropriate for competency or sanity evaluations.

B.   Emergency evaluations and dispositional reports may be conducted in jail.

Adopted effective Jan. 1, 1991.   Amended effective Oct. 4, 2000; renumbered as Rule 0312, and amended effective Feb. 7, 2007; Jan. 1, 2012.

[1] So in original.

LR53–CR00 Rule 0313.   LATE PAYMENT FEE

The Court may impose a late payment fee of $25 pursuant to IC 33–37–5–22.

Adopted effective Jan. 1, 1991.   Amended effective Oct. 4, 2000; renumbered as Rule 0313, and amended effective Feb. 7, 2007; Jan. 1, 2012.

LR53–CR00 Rule 0314.   MENTAL HEALTH EVALUATIONS

The Office of Court Services staff will coordinate referrals and communications with the Bloomington Hospital, Centerstone or other agency directed by the Court.

Adopted effective Jan. 1, 1991.   Amended effective Oct. 4, 2000; renumbered as Rule 0314, and amended effective Feb. 7, 2007; Jan. 1, 2012.

MONROE COUNTY FAMILY LAW RULES

Adopted Effective January 1, 1991

Including Amendments Received Through November 1, 2013

Research Notes

These rules may be searched electronically on Westlaw *in the* IN-RULES *database; updates to these rules may be found on Westlaw in* IN-RULESUPDATES. *For search tips and a summary of database content, consult the Westlaw Scope Screens for each database.*

LR53–FL00 Rule 0400. FAMILY LAW RULES SCOPE AND TITLE

A. Scope. These Rules shall apply in the Monroe Circuit Court in all domestic relations, paternity, and child support cases in the Monroe Circuit Court unless otherwise ordered by a judge presiding in a specific case. These Rules are in addition to, and are not intended to replace, the Local Rules of Practice and Procedure for the Monroe Circuit Court. In the event of a conflict in a family law matter, these Rules shall apply. These Family Law Rules shall be effective on January 1, 2012.

B. Title. These Rules shall be known as the "Monroe County Family Law Rules" and shall be referred to as LR53–FL00–04**.

C. Duties of Pro se Parties and Attorneys.

1. The Monroe Circuit Court expects and requires good faith cooperation and communication between parties. This is especially important in cases involving minor children.

2. Parents shall make every reasonable effort, through discussion and communication, to reach agreements that serve the best interests of children before seeking court intervention.

3. Attorneys shall help their clients reach just agreements, and shall use all available means of communication to fairly resolve disputes and misunderstandings between the parties.

4. Whenever possible opposing attorneys in a family law case should communicate with each other to resolve pending matters and avoid unnecessary court action.

5. Attorneys shall at all times observe the obligation of a lawyer to maintain a professional, courteous and civil attitude toward all persons involved in the legal system.

6. This rule is not intended to impede the obligation of an attorney to act as an advocate, or to affect a lawyer's duty to act promptly and diligently in the representation of a family law client.

Adopted as Rule 1, effective Jan. 1, 1991. Amended effective Oct. 4, 2000; amended June 2, 2003, effective July 1, 2003; renumbered as Rule 0400, and amended effective Feb. 7, 2007. Amended effective May 27, 2009; Jan. 1, 2012.

LR53–FL00 Rule 0401. UNREPRESENTED (PRO SE) PARTIES

A. The same court rules of evidence and procedure apply to parties who are represented by lawyers and parties without lawyers (pro se). The court is required to hold all parties to the same standards.

B. Unrepresented parties are required to file appropriate pleadings to initiate court action. The court will accept form pleadings approved by the Indiana Supreme Court. (www.in.gov/judiciary/selfservice/forms/) The court has the discretion to reject incomplete pleadings and other form pleadings that do not satisfy Indiana law. Unrepresented pro se parties may access the Monroe County Government web site and click on the "Justice" tab for additional resources and information. http://www.co.monroe.in.us/tsd/

C. Any document filed with the court shall at a minimum, contain a "certificate of service" that states that the document was provided to the other party; the address of both parties; and the date of delivery.

Adopted effective Jan. 1, 2012.

LR53–FL00 Rule 0402. ALTERNATIVE DISPUTE RESOLUTION

A. Mediation is a preferred way to resolve family law issues. Parties shall attend mediation before any of the following contested court hearings, unless excused by the court:

1. final hearings;

2. post-decree hearings about child custody or parenting time.

C.[1] Parties may either select a mediator by agreement or ask the court to appoint a panel of mediators.

D. Parties of limited means may request the service of the Family Court Mediation Program. Nominal charges for this program are assessed on a sliding fee scale, based upon income.

E. This rule does not require mediation of contempt motions that allege the failure to pay child support or interference with court ordered parenting time.

C. [1] A party may request to be excused from mediation in cases involving domestic violence, or for other good reason.

Adopted effective Jan. 1, 2012. Amended effective Aug. 15, 2013.

[1] So in original.

LR53–FL00 Rule 0403. CONFERENCES

A conference with the court may be set at any stage of the litigation. The court will not take testimony or admit exhibits at conferences. Conferences are not recorded. Parties may request that conferences be conducted telephonically. If the parties are not represented by counsel (pro se), the conference may be used to assess and clarify the issues, advise the parties of required documentation (i.e. child support worksheets, financial declaration, etc), to refer the case to mediation, and/or to assign a hearing date. If the parties are represented by counsel, the conference may also address case management deadlines, witness and exhibit lists, and other matters. Clients are not required to attend conferences with counsel unless the court directs otherwise.

A. Expedited Conferences. The court may set a conference at any time to address a motion to continue or other motion that requires a prompt response. An expedited conference may be set to schedule a requested emergency hearing.

B. Attorney Conferences. The court may order attorneys to conduct an attorney conference at any time to address specific issues, or in preparation for a hearing. Counsel shall file an attorney conference report following the conference to report stipulations, agreements, or other action taken.

Adopted effective Jan. 1, 2012.

LR53–FL00 Rule 0404. PRELIMINARY HEARINGS

At or after the filing of a Petition for Dissolution of Marriage, a party may request a hearing on temporary maintenance, child support, child custody, possession of marital property, or counseling. The motion shall follow the requirements of the statute (IC 31–15–4) and be accompanied by an affidavit setting forth the factual basis for the relief requested. Each party shall file a completed Financial Declaration no later than the time of the hearing (Appendix E)

Adopted effective Jan. 1, 2012.

LR53–FL00 Rule 0405. ADMINISTRATIVE PROCEDURES

A. Information Sheet: Every party initiating a family law case shall complete a Family Law Information Sheet on green paper and file it with the initial pleadings. Each time a party initiates a modification, that party shall complete a new party Information Sheet on green paper and file it with the modification pleadings. The information provided shall include notice of any other pending legal proceeding involving child abuse and neglect, paternity, a protective order, and criminal charges. It shall include the name and location of the court in which the case is pending, the case number, the names of the parties involved, and a brief summary of the nature of the legal proceeding.

B. Request for Hearing: Every request for a hearing shall include a brief statement of the issues to be decided at the hearing; whether or not an emergency exists that requires immediate court action; and an estimate of the time the court should allow for the hearing.

C. Summary Presentation: By agreement of the parties, all issues and evidence relevant to a domestic relations case may be presented in summary fashion by counsel.

D. Summons Form: In all new cases relevant to family law matters, the petitioner shall use the Summons Forms set forth in Appendix A or B.

Adopted as Rule 2, effective Jan. 1, 1991. Amended effective Oct. 4, 2000; amended June 2, 2003, effective July 1, 2003; renumbered as Rule 0401, and amended effective Feb. 7, 2007. Amended effective May 27, 2009; Jan. 1, 2012.

LR53–FL00 Rule 0406. CONTINUANCES

A. Information in Motion. A motion to continue a hearing or trial shall contain the following:

1. The date and time of the hearing or trial for which a continuance is sought;

2. The reason for the continuance;

3. A good-faith estimate of the time needed for such hearing or trial when rescheduled;

4. The date and time opposing counsel/party was notified that the party would be seeking a continuance;

5. Whether opposing counsel /party agrees with or objects to the continuance; and

6. Contact information, including at least one telephone number, for any unrepresented opposing party, or an explanation of why that information is not available on diligent inquiry.

B. Continuances Sought for Conflicts:

1. *Scheduling Conflicts.* A motion for continuance based upon a scheduling conflict with a previously scheduled vacation shall state the date the vacation was set. A motion for continuance based upon a scheduling conflict with a another case shall specify the other case name and number, the date on which the conflicting hearing or trial date was set by the other court, and the type of hearing or trial. Any such motion for continuance shall be filed within 7 days of the scheduling conflict becoming apparent.

C. Objections:

2. If there is an objection to a continuance, the objecting party may ask the court to set a telephone conference to consider the objection.

Adopted as Rule 3, effective Jan. 1, 1991. Amended effective Oct. 4, 2000; amended June 2, 2003, effective July 1, 2003; renumbered as Rule 0402, and amended effective Feb. 7, 2007. Amended effective May 27, 2009; Jan. 1, 2012.

LR53–FL00 Rule 0407. SUBMISSION OF AGREEMENTS

A. Written Agreements and Orders Required. No agreed matter shall be submitted unless accompanied with a signed agreement and a proposed order or decree.

B. Copies. When submitting an Agreement or proposed order, the parties shall submit two (2) copies for the court and a copy for each party.

Adopted as Rule 4, effective Jan. 1, 1991. Amended effective Oct. 4, 2000; amended June 2, 2003, effective July 1, 2003; renumbered as Rule 0403, and amended effective Feb. 7, 2007. Amended effective May 27, 2009; Jan. 1, 2012.

LR53–FL00 Rule 0408. CHILD SUPPORT

A. Worksheet Required. In all proceedings involving child support, each party shall file one or more completed Indiana Child Support Obligation Worksheet, Health Insurance Worksheet (not required if parties agree that one parent will carry insurance), and Post Secondary Worksheet (if applicable) with every agreed order, and at every hearing or trial. Worksheet and child support guideline information is available at: www.in.gov/judiciary/rules/child_support.

B. Deviations from Child Support Guidelines. If an agreed amount of child support deviates from the Guidelines, the agreement shall set out the reasons for the deviation.

C. Income Withholding Order Required. In all proceedings involving child support, the Income Withholding Order required by IC 31–16–15–0.5 shall be submitted to the court with any agreement or proposed order. A sample Income Withholding Order is attached as Appendix F

D. Child Support Arrearage Calculation Form. In all proceedings involving a child support arrearage, including contempt hearings, the party alleging the child support arrearage shall file a completed Child support Arrearage Calculation Form with the court at the hearing. The form is located at Appendix D to these Rules.

Adopted as Rule 5, effective Jan. 1, 1991. Amended effective Oct. 4, 2000; amended June 2, 2003, effective July 1, 2003; renumbered as Rule 0404, and amended effective Feb. 7, 2007. Amended effective May 27, 2009; Jan. 1, 2012.

LR53–FL00 Rule 0409. CHILDREN IN FAMILY LAW CASES

A. Cope: (http://www.vnsi.org/chil.asp) The best interest of children of divorcing parents and parents involved in paternity proceedings will be served by requiring parental participation in an education workshop entitled "Children Cope with Divorce". Participation will:

• Improve post-separation parenting; and

• Encourage agreements between the parties concerning their child(ren).

These same interests will be served by requiring attendance at the workshop by some parents involved in post-dissolution proceedings.

Both parents in domestic relations and juvenile paternity cases involving children under the age 18 years shall attend the parenting education workshop. The workshop must be completed prior to final hearing. Parents in cases seeking modification of custody and visitation orders may be ordered to attend the parenting education workshop. Each parent is responsible for the fee ($50.00/person), though an allowance for indigent fee waiver may be available. The Petitioner shall register for the workshop within 30 days of filing the petition. A copy of the Standing Order that requires attendance shall be served on the Respondent with petition. The Respondent shall register for the workshop within 30 days after receiving the Standing Order. Said registration can be completed on line at: (http://www.vnsi.org/chil.asp or made through:

CHILDREN COPE WITH DIVORCE

Call Tuesday through Friday   Send completed registration cards to:

9:00 am to 6:00 pm

(877) 840–2673 or (317)722–8201   Children Cope With Divorce, Registrar

Ask for Children Cope With Divorce   4701 N. Keystone Avenue

Seminar Registration   Indianapolis, IN 46205

B. If the court finds that it would be in the best interests of a child in a family law case, the court may order the parents or other involved parties to participate in Up to Parents or Proud to Parent, or other resource not listed below as follows:

1. *Marital Dissolution and Separation Cases:* Parties so ordered shall complete the website work on www.UpToParents.org within 30 days of being so ordered. Parties shall file a copy of the "conclusion page" (which appears as the final page of the website work) to the court as documentation

2. *Paternity Cases:* Parties so ordered shall complete the website work at www.ProudToParent. org within thirty (30) days of being so ordered. Parents shall file a copy of "The Conclusion Page" (which appears as the final page of the website work) to the court as documentation.

C. Resources in Cases Involving Risk to Child Safety. If the parties allege that current custody or parenting time orders present a risk to the safety of the child, the parties may request appointment of a guardian ad litem or custody evaluator. The request shall contain the availability, name, address, and phone number of the recommended professional and the cost of services, and how the costs will be divided between the parities. With reduced income parties the parties may request a Civil Investigation to be conducted by a probation officer.

Adopted as Rule 6, effective Jan. 1, 1991. Amended effective Oct. 4, 2000; amended June 2, 2003, effective July 1, 2003; renumbered as Rule 0405, and amended effective Feb. 7, 2007. Amended effective May 27, 2009; Jan. 1, 2012.

LR53–FL00 Rule 0410. FINANCIAL DECLARATION FORM

A. Required Exchange of Financial Declaration Form: In a dissolution of marriage or legal separation case, either party may request the exchange of the Financial Declaration Forms attached at Appendix E by filing a written notice with the court. Each party, except the State of Indiana when it is a party for child support purposes, shall provide to each other party a completed Financial Declaration Form and supporting documents within forty-five (45) days after service of the written notice. No court order for such exchange shall be required. The court may also order this exchange without a request from a party. If the court does order the exchange of Financial Declaration Forms, the court shall specify the deadline for the exchange.

B. Required Filing with Court: Each party, except the State of Indiana when it is a party for child support purposes, shall file with the court a completed Financial Declaration Form and supporting documents at or before the time of any contested preliminary or final hearing in a dissolution of marriage or legal separation case

C. Admissibility. Unless a party makes a specific objection to the admission of the other party's completed Financial Declaration Form, the Form shall be admitted into evidence. Any objection shall be made only to that part of the other party's completed Financial Declaration Form that is deemed objectionable and not to the entire completed Form. A party does not waive the right to challenge the accuracy of the other party's completed Form by failing to object to the admissibility of the completed Form.

D. Supporting Documents. For the purpose of providing a full and complete verification of assets, liabilities and values, at the time of the initial exchange, each party shall attach to the Form the supporting information that is reasonably available. This shall include recent bills, wage and tax records, credit card statements, and blank pension and year-end mortgage statements. "Reasonably available" means material which may be obtained by letter accompanied with an authorization, but does not mean material that must be subpoenaed, or is in the possession of the other party. Appraisals of real estate and pensions, or of personal property such as jewelry, antiques or special collections (i.e. stamps, coins, or guns), are not required. However, once an appraisal is obtained, it must be exchanged

E. Financial Declaration—Mandatory Discovery. Once requested by notice to the court by either party, or by an order of the court, the exchange of forms constitutes mandatory discovery; thus, Indiana Trial Rule 37 sanctions apply. Additionally, pursuant to Indiana Trial Rule 26(E) (2) and (3), the form must be supplemented if additional material becomes available.

F. Confidentiality of Financial Declaration. Financial Declaration Forms may be withdrawn by the parties at the conclusion of the case with the agreement of all parties and the approval of the judge presiding in the case. Financial Declaration forms and any supporting documents shall be maintained as confidential documents pursuant to Administrative Rule 9 (G), and shall be submitted on light green paper.

Adopted as Rule 7, effective Jan. 1, 1991. Amended effective Oct. 4, 2000; amended June 2, 2003, effective July 1, 2003; renumbered as Rule 0406, and amended effective Feb. 7, 2007. Amended effective May 27, 2009; Jan. 1, 2012.

LR53–FL00 Rule 0411. TEMPORARY RESTRAINING ORDERS

Temporary restraining orders will be issued only in strict compliance with Trial Rule 65 (B).

Adopted as Rule 9, effective Jan. 1, 1991. Amended effective Oct. 4, 2000; amended June 2, 2003, effective July 1, 2003; renumbered as Rule 0408, and amended effective Feb. 7, 2007. Amended effective May 27, 2009; Jan. 1, 2012.

LR53–FL00 Rule 0412. CONTEMPT ACTIONS

All petitions for contempt shall state the date of each order and the specific provisions thereof that are violated. The petition for contempt must be verified, state whether incarceration is a requested remedy and must be in compliance with IC 34–47–3–5.

Adopted as Rule 10, effective Jan. 1, 1991. Amended effective Oct. 4, 2000; amended June 2, 2003, effective July 1, 2003; renumbered as Rule 0409, and amended effective Feb. 7, 2007; Jan. 1, 2012.

LR53–FL00 Rule 0413. ATTORNEY FEES

Attorney fees may be awarded based on evidence presented by way of Affidavit (or oral testimony if the Court shall allow) at the final or other hearing.

Adopted as Rule 11, effective Jan. 1, 1991. Amended effective Oct. 4, 2000; amended June 2, 2003, effective July 1, 2003; renumbered as Rule 0410, and amended effective Feb. 7, 2007. Amended effective May 27, 2009; Jan. 1, 2012.

LR53–FL00 Rule 0414. ORDER FOR LAW ENFORCEMENT ASSISTANCE

An order directing the Bloomington Police Department, Monroe County Sheriff's Office, or other appropriate law enforcement agency, to accompany a party to his or her residence to obtain possession of property should read substantially as follows:

The _____ (name of agency) is hereby ordered to assist _____ (name) in taking possession of his/her personal property specified above at _____ (address) as soon as possible.

Adopted as Rule 12, effective Jan. 1, 1991. Amended effective Oct. 4, 2000; amended June 2, 2003, effective July 1, 2003; renumbered as Rule 0411, and amended effective Feb. 7, 2007; Jan. 1, 2012.

LR53–FL00 Rule 0415. WITHDRAWL OF COUNSEL

Upon conclusion of a matter, the appearance of an attorney may be withdrawn by motion of that attorney. Such Motion to Withdraw must comport with TR 3.1(E). There is no automatic withdrawal of representation in Family Law matters.

Adopted as Rule 15, effective Jan. 1, 1991. Amended effective Oct. 4, 2000; amended June 2, 2003, effective July 1, 2003; renumbered as Rule 0414, and amended effective Feb. 7, 2007. Amended effective May 27, 2009; Jan. 1, 2012.

LR53–FL00 Rule 0416. COLLABORATIVE LAW

If the parties are both represented by attorneys trained in Collaborative Law, and have signed retainer agreements with those attorneys to participate in a Collaborative Law family law matter, they may file a Joint Petition for Dissolution, and may file a stipulation asking among other things that the case not be set for conference or hearing. If either party violates the agreement to proceed in the Collaborative Law process, the court may allow withdrawal of representation of both attorneys if so requested.

Adopted effective Jan. 1, 2012.

APPENDICES

APPENDIX A. SUMMONS DISSOLUTION OF MARRIAGE OR LEGAL SEPARATION

STATE OF INDIANA

MONROE CIRCUIT COURT
301 North College Avenue, PO Box 547
Bloomington, Indiana 47402
(812) 349–2601

IN RE THE MARRIAGE OF   CASE NO. 53C0 _____ DR _____

_____,
Petitioner

and

_____,
Respondent

SUMMONS
Dissolution of Marriage or Legal Separation

To: _____
_____
_____

The Petitioner has filed an action to dissolve your marriage or for legal separation. The issues raised in this action are stated in the petition which is attached to this summons. The petition also states the relief sought by the Petitioner.

You may file a counter petition if you wish to raise any issues not raised in the petition.

You will be notified by first-class mail of the date and time of the final hearing and any preliminary hearing(s). If you do not file any response, or appear in court at the scheduled hearings, the issues raised in the petition will be heard and decided by the court in your absence without any further notice to you. You must inform the court in writing if your mailing address on this Summons is not correct, or if you change your mailing address before a final order is entered in this case.

A final hearing may not be conducted earlier than 60 days after the filing of the petition.

_____   _____
Date   Clerk, Monroe Circuit Court

A copy of the above summons and a copy of the complaint attached thereto were received by me this ___ day of
_____, 2 ___.

_____
Signature of Respondent

PRAECIPE: I designate the following mode of service to be used by the clerk:

___ By Certified or Registered Mail with return receipt to above address.

___ By Sheriff delivering a copy of summons and complaint personally to Respondent or by leaving a copy of the summons and complaint at his/her dwelling house or usual place of abode.

___ By Personal Service delivering a copy of summons and complaint personally to Respondent.

___ By Serving an Agent as provided by rule, statute, or valid agreement.

Signed: _____   Attorney/Petitioner
Printed: _____   Attorney# _____

Address: _____

_____

Telephone: _____

RETURN OF SUMMONS

This Summons came to hand on the _____ day of _____, 2 _____ and I served the same on the _____ day of _____, 2 _____.

1. By delivering a copy of summons and complaint personally to _____ on this _____ day of _____, 2 _____.

2. By leaving a copy of summons and complaint personally with _____ on this _____ day of _____, 2 _____.

3. By mailing by first-class a copy of summons and complaint on this _____ day of _____, 2 _____ to _____ respondent's last known address.

4. Respondent cannot be found in my bailiwick and summons was not served.

And I now return this writ this _____ day of _____, 2 _____.

_____ Sheriff

_____ Deputy

Adopted effective Jan. 1, 1991. Amended effective Oct. 4, 2000; amended June 2, 2003, effective July 1, 2003; amended effective Feb. 7, 2007; Jan. 1, 2012.

APPENDIX B. SUMMONS PATERNITY ACTION

STATE OF INDIANA
MONROE CIRCUIT COURT
301 North College Avenue, PO Box 547
Bloomington, Indiana 47402
(812) 349–2601

IN THE MATTER OF   CASE NO. 53C0 _____ JP _____
THE PATERNITY OF:

_____,

_____,

Petitioner

SUMMONS
Paternity Action

To: _____

_____

_____

The Petitioner has filed a petition to establish paternity. The issues raised in this action for paternity are stated in the petition which is attached to this summons. The petition also states the relief sought by the Petitioner.

You may file a counter petition if you wish to raise any issues not raised in the petition.

You will be notified by first-class mail of the date and time of any hearings. If you do not appear in court at the scheduled hearings, the issues raised in the petition will be heard and decided by the court in your absence without any further notice to you. You must inform the court in writing if your mailing address on this Summons is not correct, or if you change your mailing address before a final order is entered in this case.

_____   _____

Date   Clerk, Monroe Circuit Court

A copy of the above summons and a copy of the complaint attached thereto were received by me this ___ day of _____, 2 ___.

_____

                Signature of Respondent

PRAECIPE: I designate the following mode of service to be used by the clerk:

___ By Certified or Registered Mail with return receipt to above address.

___ By Sheriff delivering a copy of summons and complaint personally to Respondent or by leaving a copy of the summons and complaint at his/her dwelling house or usual place of abode.

___ By Personal Service delivering a copy of summons and complaint personally to Respondent.

___ By Serving an Agent as provided by rule, statute, or valid agreement.

                Signed: _____   Attorney/Petitioner
                Printed: _____   Attorney# _____
                Address: _____
                              _____
                Telephone:

RETURN OF SUMMONS

    This Summons came to hand on the ____ day of _____, 2 ____ and I served the same on the ____ day of _____, 2 ____.

    1.   By delivering a copy of summons and complaint personally to _____ on this ____ day of _____, 2 ____.

    2.   By leaving a copy of summons and complaint personally with _____ on this ____ day of _____, 2 ____.

    3.   By mailing by first-class a copy of summons and complaint on this ____ day of _____, 2 ____ to _____ respondent's last known address.

    4.   Respondent cannot be found in my bailiwick and summons was not served.

And I now return this writ this ____ day of _____, 2 ____.

                       _____   Sheriff

                       _____   Deputy

Adopted effective Jan. 1, 1991. Amended effective Oct. 4, 2000; amended June 2, 2003, effective July 1, 2003; amended effective Feb. 7, 2007; Jan. 1, 2012.

APPENDIX C. ACKNOWLEDGMENT OF RECEIPT OF INDIANA PARENTING TIME GUIDELINES

Suggested acknowledgment for use under LR53–FL00–0410

[Caption]

ACKNOWLEGMENT[1] OF RECEIPT OF
INDIANA PARENTING TIME GUIDELINES

    The Petitioner and the Respondent acknowledge that they have received a copy of the Indiana Parenting Time Guidelines consisting of 28 typewritten pages as adopted by the Indiana Supreme Court on December 22, 2000 with an effective date of March 31, 2001.

    Acknowledged this ___ day of _____, 2 ___.

_____	_____
Petitioner	Respondent
_____	_____
Attorney for Petitioner	Attorney for Respondent

ACKNOWLEDGMENT OF USE

The parties further acknowledge that they have made reference to these Parenting Time Guidelines in the entry submitted in this cause and that these Guidelines will be used by the parties for the purpose of parenting time and in the resolution of any disputes on parenting time issues until further order of the Court.

Acknowledged this ___ day of _____, 2 ___.

_____	_____
Petitioner	Respondent
_____	_____
Attorney for Petitioner	Attorney for Respondent

Adopted effective Jan. 1, 1991. Amended effective Oct. 4, 2000; amended June 2, 2003, effective July 1, 2003; amended effective Feb. 7, 2007; Jan. 1, 2012.

APPENDIX D.   CHILD SUPPORT ARREARAGE CALCULATION

STATE OF INDIANA   )   IN THE MONROE CIRCUIT COURT
)SS:
COUNTY OF MONROE   )   CAUSE NO. 53C0 _____

IN RE THE MARRIAGE/PATERNITY
SUPPORT OF

_____

and

_____

CHILD SUPPORT ARREARAGE CALCULATION

Weekly child support amount   _____

Date of child support order   _____

Prior findings of arrearage and date of finding   _____

Support owed [number of weeks X weekly amount]   _____

LESS

Support paid through the Clerk's Office   _____

Support paid directly   _____

TOTAL ARREARAGE   _____

DATE   _____

I affirm under the penalties for perjury that the foregoing information is true and accurate to the best of my knowledge and belief.

_____	_____
Date	Signature

Adopted effective Jan. 1, 1991. Amended effective Oct. 4, 2000; amended June 2, 2003, effective July 1, 2003; amended effective Feb. 7, 2007; Jan. 1, 2012.

APPENDIX E. FINANCIAL DECLARATION FORM

MONROE CIRCUIT COURT FAMILY LAW RULES
FINANCIAL DECLARATION FORM

ALL PARTIES, INCLUDING PARTIES NOT REPRESENTED BY COUNSEL, ARE REQUIRED TO COMPLY WITH THE FAMILY LAW RULES AND TO COMPLETE AND EXCHANGE THIS FORM.

THIS DECLARATION IS MANDATORY DISCOVERY AND MUST BE COMPLETED AND PROVIDED TO THE OTHER PARTY WITHIN THE TIME PRESCRIBED BY MONROE COUNTY FAMILY LAW RULE LR53–FL00–0410.

FAILURE BY A PARTY TO COMPLETE, EXCHANGE, AND FILE THIS FORM AS REQUIRED MAY RESULT IN THE IMPOSITION OF COSTS, ATTORNEY FEES, AND OTHER SANCTIONS DETERMINED BY THE COURT.

A "LIVE" VERSION OF THE FINANCIAL DECLARATION FORM IS AVAILABLE AT: www.co.monroe. in.us Choose the Justice tab, Circuit Court, and on the left, select "Local Rules."

Adopted effective Jan. 1, 1991. Amended effective Oct. 4, 2000; amended June 2, 2003, effective July 1, 2003; amended effective Feb. 7, 2007; Jan. 1, 2012.

APPENDIX F. INCOME WITHHOLDING FOR SUPPORT

INCOME WITHHOLDING FOR SUPPORT
○ ORIGINAL INCOME WITHHOLDING ORDER/NOTICE FOR
   SUPPORT (IWO)
○ AMENDED IWO
○ ONE–TIME ORDER/NOTICE FOR LUMP SUM PAYMENT
○ TERMINATION of IWO   Date: _____

_____

   ○ Child Support Enforcement (CSE) Agency ○ Court ○ Attorney ○ Private Individual/ Entity (Check One)

NOTE: This IWO must be regular on its face. Under certain circumstances you must reject this IWO and return it to the sender (see IWO instructions http://www. acf.hhs.gov/programs/cse/newhire/ employer/publication/publication.htm#forms).   If you receive this document from someone other than a State or Tribal CSE agency or a Court, a copy of the underlying order must be attached.

State/Tribe/Territory	Remittance Identifier (include w/ payment)
City/County/Dist./Tribe	Order Identifier
Private Individual/Entity	CSE Agency Case Identifier

_____

	RE:
Employer/Income Withholder's Name	Employee/Obligor's Name (Last, First, Middle)
Employer/Income Withholder's Address	Employee/Obligor's Social Security Number
	Custodial Party/Obligee's Name (Last, First, Middle)

Employer/Income Withholder's FEIN ____

Child(ren)'s Name(s) (Last, First, Middle)	Child(ren)'s Birth Date(s)

ORDER INFORMATION: This document is based on the support or withholding order from (State/Tribe). You are required by law to deduct these amounts from the employee/obligor's income until further notice.

$ _____ Per _____ current child support

$ _____ Per _____ past-due child support—**Arrears greater than 12 weeks?** ○ Yes ○ No

$ _____ Per _____ current cash medical support

$ _____ Per _____ past-due cash medical support

$ _____ Per _____ current spousal support

$ _____ Per _____ past-due spousal support

$ _____ Per _____ other (must specify) _____

for a **Total Amount to Withhold** of $ _____ per _____.

AMOUNTS TO WITHHOLD: You do not have to vary your pay cycle to be in compliance with the Order Information. If your pay cycle does not match the ordered payment cycle, withhold one of the following amounts:

$ _____ per weekly pay period

$ _____ per semimonthly pay period (twice a month)

$ _____ per biweekly pay period (every two weeks)

$ _____ per monthly pay period

$ _____ **Lump Sum Payment:** Do not stop any existing IWO unless you receive a termination order.

REMITTANCE INFORMATION: If the employee/obligor's principal place of employment is (State/Tribe), you must begin withholding no later than the first pay period that occurs __ days after the date of _____. Send payment within __ working days of the pay date. If you cannot withhold the full amount of support for any or all orders for this employee/obligor, withhold up to __ % of disposable income for all orders. If the employee/obligor's principal place of employment is not _____ (State/Tribe), obtain withholding limitations, time requirements, and any allowable employer fees at http://www.acf.hhs.gov/ programs/cse/ newhire/employer/contacts/contact for the employee/obligor's principal place of employment. For electronic payment requirements and centralized payment collection and disbursement facility information (State Disbursement Unit [SDU]), see http://www.acf.hhs.gov/programs/ cse/ newhire/employer/contacts/contact

Include the **Remittance Identifier with the payment** and if necessary this FIPS code:

_____.

Remit payment to _____ (SDU/Tribal Order Payee) at _____ (SDU/Tribal Payee Address)

○ **Return to Sender [Completed by Employer/Income Withholder].** Payment must be directed to an SDU in accordance with 42 USC § 666(b)(5) and (b)(6) or Tribal Payee (see Payments to SDU below). If payment is not directed to an SDU/Tribal Payee or this IWO is not regular on its face, you must check this box and return the IWO to the sender.

Signature of Judge/Issuing Official (if required by State or Tribal law): _____

Print Name of Judge/Issuing Official: _____

Title of Judge/Issuing Official: _____

Date of Signature: _____

If the employee/obligor works in a State or for a Tribe that is different from the State or Tribe that issued this order, a copy of this IWO must be provided to the employee/obligor. ○ If checked, the employer/income withholder must provide a copy of this form to the employee/obligor.

ADDITIONAL INFORMATION FOR EMPLOYERS/INCOME WITHHOLDERS

State-specific contact and withholding information can be found on the Federal Employer Services website located at: http:// www.acf.hhs.gov/programs/cse/newhire/employer/ contacts/contact_map.htm

Priority: Withholding for support has priority over any other legal process under State law against the same income (USC 42 § 666(b)(7)). If a Federal tax levy is in effect, please notify the sender.

Combining Payments: When remitting payments to an SDU or Tribal CSE agency, you may combine withheld amounts from more than one employee/obligor's income in a single payment. You must, however, separately identify each employee/obligor's portion of the payment.

Payments To SDU: You must send child support payments payable by income withholding to the appropriate SDU or to a Tribal CSE agency. If this IWO instructs you to send a payment to an entity other than an SDU (e.g. , payable to the custodial party, court, or attorney), you must check the box above and return this notice to the sender. Exception: If this IWO was sent by a Court, Attorney, or Private Individual/Entity and the initial order was entered before January 1, 1994 or the order was issued by a Tribal CSE agency, you must follow the "Remit payment to" instructions on this form.

Reporting the Pay Date: You must report the pay date when sending the payment. The pay date is the date on which the amount was withheld from the employee/obligor's wages. You must comply with the law of the State (or Tribal law if applicable) of the employee/obligor's principal place of employment regarding time periods within which you must implement the withholding and forward the support payments.

Multiple IWOs: If there is more than one IWO against this employee/obligor and you are unable to fully honor all IWOs due to Federal, State, or Tribal withholding limits, you must honor all IWOs to the greatest extent possible, giving priority to current support before payment of any past-due support. Follow the State or Tribal law/procedure of the employee/obligor's principal place of employment to determine the appropriate allocation method.

Lump Sum Payments: You may be required to notify a State or Tribal CSE agency of upcoming lump sum payments to this employee/obligor such as bonuses, commissions, or severance pay. Contact the sender to determine if you are required to report and/or withhold lump sum payments.

Liability: If you have any doubts about the validity of this IWO, contact the sender. If you fail to withhold income from the employee/obligor's income as the IWO directs, you are liable for both the accumulated amount you should have withheld and any penalties set by State or Tribal law/procedure.

_____
_____
_____

Anti-discrimination: You are subject to a fine determined under State or Tribal law for discharging an employee/obligor from employment, refusing to employ, or taking disciplinary action against an employee/obligor because of this IWO.

_____
_____

Withholding Limits: You may not withhold more than the lesser of: 1) the amounts allowed by the Federal Consumer Credit Protection Act (CCPA) (15 U.S.C. 1673(b)); or 2) the amounts allowed by the State or Tribe of the employee/obligor's principal place of employment (see REMITTANCE INFORMATION). Disposable income is the net income left after making mandatory deductions such as: State, Federal, local taxes; Social Security taxes; statutory pension contributions; and

Medicare taxes. The Federal limit is 50% of the disposable income if the obligor is supporting another family and 60% of the disposable income if the obligor is not supporting another family. However, those limits increase 5%—to 55% and 65%—if the arrears are greater than 12 weeks. If permitted by the State or Tribe, you may deduct a fee for administrative costs. The combined support amount and fee may not exceed the limit indicated in this section.

For Tribal orders, you may not withhold more than the amounts allowed under the law of the issuing Tribe. For Tribal employers/income withholders who receive a State IWO, you may not withhold more than the lesser of the limit set by the law of the jurisdiction in which the employer/income withholder is located or the maximum amount permitted under section 303(d) of the CCPA (15 U.S.C. 1673 (b)).

Depending upon applicable State or Tribal law, you may need to also consider the amounts paid for health care premiums in determining disposable income and applying appropriate withholding limits.

Arrears greater than 12 weeks? If the Order Information does not indicate that the arrears are greater than 12 weeks, then the Employer should calculate the CCPA limit using the lower percentage.

Additional Information: _____
_____
_____

NOTIFICATION OF EMPLOYMENT TERMINATION OR INCOME STATUS: If this employee/obligor never worked for you or you are no longer withholding income for this employee/obligor, an employer must promptly notify the CSE agency and/or the sender by returning this form to the address listed in the Contact Information below:
○ This person has never worked for this employer nor received periodic income.
○ This person no longer works for this employer nor receives periodic income.
Please provide the following information for the employee/obligor:
Termination date: _____ Last known phone number: _____

Last known address: _____

Final payment date to SDU/ Tribal Payee: _____ Final payment amount: _____

New employer's name: _____

New employer's address: _____

_____

CONTACT INFORMATION:
To Employer/Income Withholder: If you have any questions, contact _____ (Issuer name) by phone at ___, by fax at ___, by email or website at: _____. Send termination/income status notice and other correspondence to: _____ (Issuer address).
To Employee/Obligor: If the employee/obligor has questions, contact _____ (Issuer name) by phone at _____, by fax at _____, by email or website at _____. Monroe Circuit Jury Management Rules 59

Adopted effective Jan. 1, 2012.

MONROE CIRCUIT COURT JURY MANAGEMENT RULES

Adopted Effective January 1, 1991

Including Amendments Received Through November 1, 2013

Research Notes

These rules may be searched electronically on Westlaw in the IN-RULES database; updates to these rules may be found on Westlaw in IN-RULESUPDATES. For search tips and a summary of database content, consult the Westlaw Scope Screens for each database.

Rule
LR53–JR00 Rule 0500.   Jury Management

LR53–JR00 Rule 0500.   JURY MANAGEMENT

A.   The Judge or Court Reporter in each division will inform the Jury Coordinator of the status of scheduled jury trials.

B.   The Jury Coordinator will use the jury message line on a daily basis to indicate to jurors the status of trials.   Jurors are instructed to call the jury message line after 7 pm during their scheduled weeks of service.

C.   If a jury is canceled after work hours (including a weekend or holiday), the Judge or Court Reporter will call the Office of Court Services staff at home in order to change the jury message line.

D.   Meals for jurors will be provided on the last day of trial immediately prior to or during deliberations.

E.   Miscellaneous civil files will be opened for individuals who fail to comply with jury service.

F.   The Office of Court Services staff will provide the Judge with the names and addresses of those individuals who fail to comply.   A 15 minute rule to show cause hearing will be set.   The Office of Court Services staff will prepare the rule to show cause order and file it in the Clerk's Office with a judge's cause number which will be recorded in the Miscellaneous Civil Book.   The caseload will not be affected.

Adopted effective Jan. 1, 1991.   Amended effective Oct. 4, 2000; renumbered as Rule 0500, and amended effective Feb. 7, 2007.   Amended effective May 27, 2009.

MONROE CIRCUIT COURT FAMILY COURT RULES

Adopted Effective January 1, 1991

Including Amendments Received Through November 1, 2013

Research Notes

These rules may be searched electronically on Westlaw in the IN-RULES database; updates to these rules may be found on Westlaw in IN-RULESUPDATES. For search tips and a summary of database content, consult the Westlaw Scope Screens for each database.

LR53–FC00 Rule 0600. DEFINITIONS

A. Family Court. "Family Court" is the court, or courts, before which cases involving a family or household are linked together for purposes of case coordination. The individual cases maintain their separate integrity and separate docket number, but may be given a common family court designation. The individual cases may all be transferred to one judge, or may remain in the separate courts in which they were originally filed.

B. Family Court Proceeding. A "Family Court Proceeding" is comprised of the individual cases of the family or household which have been assigned to Family Court.

Adopted as Definitions, effective Jan. 1, 1991. Amended effective Oct. 4, 2000; Dec. 14, 2005; renumbered as Rule 0600, and amended effective Feb. 7, 2007; Jan. 1, 2012.

LR53–FC00 Rule 0601. EXERCISE OF JURISDICTION

The Family Court may exercise jurisdiction over any case involving the family at the same time it exercises jurisdiction over a juvenile case (Child in Need of Services, Delinquency, Status, and Paternity) involving the family.

Adopted as Rule 1, effective Jan. 1, 1991. Amended effective Oct. 4, 2000; Dec. 14, 2005; renumbered as Rule 0601, and amended effective Feb. 7, 2007.

LR53–FC00 Rule 0603. DESIGNATION OF FAMILY COURT CASE AND CHANGE OF JUDGE

A. Once notice is sent to the parties that a case has been selected for Family Court, no motion for change of venue from the judge may be granted except to the extent permitted by Indiana Trial Rule 76.

B. Within 10 days after notice is sent that a case has been selected for Family Court, a party may object for cause to the Family Court designation.

C. A motion for change of venue from the judge in any matters arising in the Family Court proceeding or any future cases joined in the Family Court proceeding after the initial selection of cases, shall be granted only for cause.

D. If a special judge is appointed, all current and future cases in the Family Court proceeding may be assigned to the special judge.

Adopted as Rule 3, effective Jan. 1, 1991. Amended effective Oct. 4, 2000; Dec. 14, 2005; renumbered as Rule 0603, and amended effective Feb. 7, 2007. Amended effective Jan. 19, 2010.

LR53–FC00 Rule 0604. JUDICIAL NOTICE AND ACCESS TO RECORDS

A. Notice of Case Assignment. Within a reasonable time after a case is assigned to Family Court, the court shall provide to all parties in the Family Court proceeding a list of all cases that have been assigned to that Family Court proceeding.

B. Judicial Notice. Any court having jurisdiction over a case assigned to Family Court may take judicial notice of any relevant orders or Chronological Case Summary (CCS) entry issued by any Indiana Circuit, Superior, County, or Probate Court.

1. If a court takes judicial notice of:

a. A court order, the court shall provide a copy of that court order; or

b. A CCS or CCS entry(s), the court shall provide a copy of the entire CCS.

2. The court shall provide copies of the order or CCS to the parties to the case at or before the time judicial notice is taken.

C. Access to Records. Parties to a Family Court proceeding shall have access to all cases within the Family Court proceeding, with the exception of confidential cases or records to which they are not a party. Parties may seek access to the confidential cases or records in another case within the Family Court proceeding in which they are not a party, by written petition based on relevancy and need. Confidential records shall retain their confidential status and the Family Court shall direct that confidential records not be included in the public record of the proceedings.

Adopted as Rule 4, effective Jan. 1, 1991. Amended effective Oct. 4, 2000; Dec. 14, 2005; renumbered as Rule 0604, and amended effective Feb. 7, 2007. Amended effective Jan. 19, 2010; Jan. 1, 2012.

MONROE CIRCUIT COURT SMALL CLAIMS RULES AND PROCEDURES

Adopted Effective January 1, 1991

Including Amendments Received Through November 1, 2013

Research Notes

These rules may be searched electronically on Westlaw in the IN-RULES database; updates to these rules may be found on Westlaw in IN-RULESUPDATES. For search tips and a summary of database content, consult the Westlaw Scope Screens for each database.

LR53–SC00 Rule 0700. SCOPE

A. Scope. These rules shall govern the procedure and practice of the Small Claims Division, Monroe Circuit Court.

B. Citation. These rules may be cited as LR53–SC00–07 **–

Adopted as Rule SC-1, effective Jan. 1, 1991. Amended effective Oct. 4, 2000; renumbered as Rule 0700, and amended effective Feb. 7, 2007; Jan. 1, 2012.

LR53–SC00 Rule 0701. COMMUNICATIONS WITH THE COURT

A. Written Communications. Any matter communicated to the court, outside of the courtroom, must be in writing and signed by the communicating party.

B. Case Identification and Duty to Serve. The communication shall contain the cause number of the case. The person filing the communication shall certify in writing that he or she has sent a copy of the communication to all parties.

Adopted as Rule SC-2, effective Jan. 1, 1991. Amended effective Oct. 4, 2000; renumbered as Rule 0701, and amended effective Feb. 7, 2007.

LR53–SC00 Rule 0702. SCHEDULING

A. Initial Hearing. Upon the filing of a complaint, an initial hearing shall be scheduled by the Clerk of the court. Parties are not expected to be fully prepared for trial at the initial hearing, but must be prepared to present a prima facie case through direct testimony or affidavit in the event an opposing party fails to appear, in accordance with Indiana Small Claims Rule 10(b). The failure to appear at an initial hearing shall result in a judgment being entered upon the presentation of a prima facie case by the claimant present. If the plaintiff fails to appear at the time and place specified for the trial, or for any continuance thereof, the court may dismiss the action without prejudice.

B. Contested Hearing. If both parties appear at the initial hearing, the judge shall encourage the parties to resolve their dispute. If the parties are unable to achieve a resolution, they shall inform the judge of the need to schedule a trial and indicate the amount of time needed to present their respective cases.

C. Waiver of Initial Hearing. If the parties know prior to the initial hearing that the matter will be contested, a motion may be filed to vacate the initial hearing and schedule a contested hearing. The motion shall estimate the time needed to present the petitioner's case-in-chief and the time needed to present the case in opposition if that can be reasonably ascertained.

Adopted as Rule SC-3, effective Jan. 1, 1991. Amended effective Oct. 4, 2000; renumbered as Rule 0702, and amended effective Feb. 7, 2007; Jan. 1, 2012.

LR53–SC00 Rule 0703. CONTINUANCES

A. Written Motion Required. Continuances may be granted only upon good cause shown in a written motion signed by the moving party. A copy of motion must be mailed or delivered to the opposing party by the party requesting the continuance.

B. Advance Notice. A continuance will not be granted within 72 hours of the trial unless the opposing party agrees to the continuance or the judge determines a continuance is necessary

Adopted as Rule SC-4, effective Jan. 1, 1991. Amended effective Oct. 4, 2000; renumbered as Rule 0703, and amended effective Feb. 7, 2007; Jan. 1, 2012.

LR53–SC00 Rule 0704. DISCOVERY

A. Prior Informal Discovery Required. The parties must pursue informal discovery prior to petitioning the court for an order compelling discovery.

B. Relevant Formal Discovery. Upon a showing that informal discovery has failed and that the discovery requested is relevant and not unduly burdensome, the court may grant an order compelling discovery.

Adopted as Rule SC-5, effective Jan. 1, 1991. Amended effective Oct. 4, 2000; renumbered as Rule 0704, and amended effective Feb. 7, 2007; Jan. 1, 2012.

LR53–SC00 Rule 0705. DISMISSAL OF ACTIONS

A. Motion Required. A claim, counterclaim or cross-claim may be dismissed by filing a written pleading at any time before judgment.

B. Dismissals. If a counterclaim or cross-claim has been filed, the dismissal of the original claim will not result in the cancellation of the hearing unless the counterclaim or cross-claim has been dismissed.

Adopted as Rule SC-6, effective Jan. 1, 1991. Amended effective Oct. 4, 2000; renumbered as Rule 0705, and amended effective Feb. 7, 2007; Jan. 1, 2012.

LR53–SC00 Rule 0706. PROCEEDINGS SUPPLEMENTAL

A. Timing. A prevailing party may file a motion for proceedings supplemental after entry of the judgment in the Clerk's Record of Judgments and Orders. The judgment creditor must be present to enforce a monetary judgment.

B. Change of Circumstances. After a determination by the court that there is no income or property which may be applied to the judgment, the case will be redocketed for proceeding supplemental only if the judgment creditor can show that income or property has been discovered which may be applied to the judgment

Adopted as Rule SC-7, effective Jan. 1, 1991. Amended effective Oct. 4, 2000; renumbered as Rule 0706, and amended effective Feb. 7, 2007; Jan. 1, 2012.

LR53–SC00 Rule 0707. BANKRUPTCY STAY

Any party seeking a stay of the proceedings as a result of a bankruptcy proceeding shall petition the court, attaching to the petition a copy of the Bankruptcy Cover Petition and the Schedule of Creditors.

Adopted as Rule SC-8, effective Jan. 1, 1991. Amended effective Oct. 4, 2000; renumbered as Rule 0707, and amended effective Feb. 7, 2007.

MONROE CIRCUIT COURT PROBATE RULES

Adopted Effective January 1, 1991

Including Amendments Received Through November 1, 2013

Research Notes

These rules may be searched electronically on Westlaw in the IN-RULES database; updates to these rules may be found on Westlaw in IN-RULESUPDATES. For search tips and a summary of database content, consult the Westlaw Scope Screens for each database.

LR53–PR00 Rule 0801.   EFFECT ON OTHER LOCAL RULES

These Rules apply in estate cases in the Monroe Circuit Court. They are in addition to the Local Rules of Trial Procedure. If there is a conflict between these rules and the Local Rules of Trial Procedure, these rules shall prevail.

Adopted as Rule 1, effective Jan. 1, 1991. Amended effective Oct. 4, 2000; renumbered as Rule 0801, and amended effective Feb. 7, 2007; Jan. 1, 2012.

LR53–PR00 Rule 0802.   FILING OF PLEADINGS

A. Mail Copies. When pleadings are filed by mail or left with the court for filing by attorneys who do not have distribution boxes in the Office of Court Services, a stamped self-addressed envelope shall be included for return of the pleadings to the party or attorney.

B. Preparation of Orders. A party filing a motion or petition shall provide the court with an appropriate proposed order at the time of the filing

C. Initial Petition. The initial petition opening the estate shall be accompanied by a completed Fiduciary Information Form that contains identifying information for the proposed personal representative, or other fiduciary. The Form will be available in the Clerk's office and on the court's website. The court will maintain the Fiduciary Information Form as a confidential court record pursuant to Administrative Rule 9.

Adopted as Rule 2, effective Jan. 1, 1991. Amended effective Oct. 4, 2000; renumbered as Rule 0802, and amended effective Feb. 7, 2007; Jan. 1, 2012.

LR53–PR00 Rule 0803.   BOND

A. Corporate Surety Bond in Estates. In every estate, the fiduciary, prior to the issuance of letters, shall file a corporate surety bond in such amount as shall be set by the court, except as hereafter provided:

1. Where, under the terms of a will, the testator expresses an intention that the bond be waived, the court shall set a bond in an amount adequate to protect creditors, tax authorities, and devisees. This bond shall be a minimum of Twenty–Five Thousand Dollars ($25,000.00), unless otherwise ordered.

2. Where the fiduciary is an heir or legatee of the estate, the court may reduce the bond by the amount of the fiduciary's share of the estate.

3. Where the heirs or legatees have filed a written request that the fiduciary serve without bond, the bond may be set in an amount adequate to protect the rights of the creditors and tax authorities only.

4. In an unsupervised estate, bond may be set at the discretion of the Court, and, unless otherwise ordered, shall be in the amount of Twenty–Five Thousand Dollars ($25,000.00)

5. No bond shall be required in any supervised estate in which a corporate fiduciary, qualified by law to serve as such, is a personal representative.

6. No bond shall ordinarily be required in an estate when the surviving spouse is the personal representative and is also the only heir or legatee, and the estate is solvent.

B. Transfer in Lieu of Bond. In lieu of a bond as required by Local Probate Rule 3(A), a fiduciary may restrict transfer of all or part of the estate liquid assets by placing those assets in a federally insured financial institution with the following restriction placed on the face of the account or document: NO

PRINCIPAL OR INTEREST SHALL BE WITHDRAWN WITHOUT WRITTEN ORDER OF A JUDGE OF THE CIRCUIT COURT OF MONROE COUNTY, INDIANA.

C. Inclusion of Agency Identification. The name, address, and telephone number of the insurance agency providing the corporate surety shall be typed or printed on all corporate bonds in any estate.

Adopted as Rule 3, effective Jan. 1, 1991. Amended effective Oct. 4, 2000; Aug. 28, 2001; renumbered as Rule 0803, and amended effective Feb. 7, 2007; Jan. 1, 2012.

LR53–PR00 Rule 0804. INVENTORY AND DOCUMENTS SHOWING VALUE

A. Supervised Estates. An inventory shall be filed with the court in a supervised estate. The court will maintain the inventory as a confidential court record pursuant to Administrative Rule 9.

B. Unsupervised Estates. The court may require an inventory to be filed in unsupervised estates as a condition of continuing that status. If an inventory is filed with the court, it shall be maintained by the court as a confidential court record pursuant to Administrative Rule 9.

Adopted as Rule 4, effective Jan. 1, 1991. Amended effective Oct. 4, 2000; renumbered as Rule 0804, and amended effective Feb. 7, 2007; Jan. 1, 2012.

LR53–PR00 Rule 0805. REAL ESTATE

A. Filing of Appraisal. Any real estate appraisal filed with the court shall be maintained by the court as a confidential court record pursuant to Administrative Rule 9

B. Time of Appraisal. All appraisals shall be made within one year of the date of the filing of the petition for sale of the real estate.

C. Deeds. Deeds submitted to the court for approval in estate proceedings shall be signed by the fiduciary before a notary public prior to its submission.

D. Recording of Final Decree. Whenever a final decree reflects vesting of real estate in heirs or beneficiaries, the decree shall be recorded with the Recorder of the county where the real estate is located, and evidence of such recording shall be provided to the court with the supplemental report.

Adopted as Rule 5, effective Jan. 1, 1991. Amended effective Oct. 4, 2000; renumbered as Rule 0805, and amended effective Feb. 7, 2007; Jan. 1, 2012.

LR53–PR00 Rule 0806. SALE OF PROPERTY

A. Appraisal of Personal Property. In all supervised estates, no petition for sale of personal property shall be granted unless a written appraisal, prepared by a person competent to appraise such property and setting forth the fair market value of the property to be sold is filed with the court, either at the time of filing of the petition to sell or at the time the inventory is filed. This rule shall not apply if the property is sold at a public auction by written approval of the court. Upon request, the written appraisal shall be maintained by the court as a confidential court record pursuant to Administrative Rule 9.

B. Time of Appraisal. All appraisals shall be made within one year preceding the date of the petition to sell personal property.

C. Sale of Property at Market Value. No written appraisal shall be required for the sale of property traded in an open market when the value of that property is readily ascertainable. Such assets include, but are not limited to, stocks, bonds, mutual funds, commodities, precious metals and motor vehicles.

D. Unsupervised Administration. The court will not authorize or approve the sale of property in an unsupervised estate.

Adopted as Rule 6, effective Jan. 1, 1991. Amended effective Oct. 4, 2000; renumbered as Rule 0806, and amended effective Feb. 7, 2007; Jan. 1, 2012.

LR53–PR00 Rule 0807. CLAIMS

A. Examination of Claim Docket. Three months and fifteen days after the date of the first published notice to creditors, the fiduciary or the fiduciary's attorney, shall examine the Claim Docket and shall allow or disallow each claim filed against the estate, and file a notice with the court stating the action taken.

Adopted as Rule 7, effective Jan. 1, 1991. Amended effective Oct. 4, 2000; renumbered as Rule 0807, and amended effective Feb. 7, 2007; Jan. 1, 2012.

LR53–PR00 Rule 0808. ACCOUNTINGS

A. Intermediate Accounting. Whenever supervised estate cannot be closed within one year, an intermediate account shall be filed with the court within thirty days after the expiration of one year and each succeeding year thereafter. Such accounting shall comply with the provisions of Indiana Code Sections 29–1–16–4 and 29–1–16–6, and

1. Shall state facts showing to the court the reasons the estate cannot be closed and providing the court with an estimated date of closing;

2. Shall propose partial distribution of the estate to the extent that partial distribution can be made without prejudice to distributees, claimants, and taxing authorities.

B. Vouchers and Cancelled Checks. In all supervised estate accountings, vouchers or cancelled checks for the expenditures claimed shall be filed with the accounting. An affidavits in lieu of vouchers or cancelled checks may be accepted from the fiduciary provided the fiduciary retains the vouchers or cancelled checks on file or by a digital image, and is able to, and will

C. Expenditure Notation. In all supervised estate accountings, a notation shall be placed by each reported expenditure indicating the check number, date, payee, and reason for, or nature of the expenditure. Missing checks shall be accounted for

D. Itemized Statement of Assets. All accountings to the court shall contain an itemized statement of all assets on hand.

E. Payment of Costs and Claims. All court costs shall be paid and all claims satisfied and released before the hearing on the final account, and a Clerk's Certification (attached form at Appendix A) shall be filed with the Court before the final account will be approved.

F. Tax Closing Letters. The Federal Estate Tax Closing letter and the Indiana Inheritance Tax Closing letter showing payment of all Federal estate and Indiana inheritance tax liability in the estate shall be attached to the final report at the time of filing, unless previously filed.

Adopted as Rule 8, effective Jan. 1, 1991. Amended effective Oct. 4, 2000; renumbered as Rule 0808, and amended effective Feb. 7, 2007; Jan. 1, 2012.

LR53–PR00 Rule 0809. FEES OF ATTORNEYS AND FIDUCIARY

A. Order Approving Fees. No fees for attorneys or fiduciaries shall be paid out of any supervised estate without prior written order of the court. Appropriate proposed orders should be submitted to the court at the time a petition to approve fees is filed.

All proposed orders for approval of fees for attorneys or fiduciaries shall provide that such fees are not to be paid until the interim account or the final account has been approved by the court. Fees based on the value of the estate will not ordinarily be approved by the court.

B. Unsupervised Administration. The court will not decide, authorize or approve the payment of attorney fees or fiduciary fees in an unsupervised estate.

Adopted as Rule 9, effective Jan. 1, 1991. Amended effective Oct. 4, 2000; renumbered as Rule 0809, and amended effective Feb. 7, 2007; Jan. 1, 2012.

LR53–PR00 Rule 0810. UNSUPERVISED ADMINISTRATION

A. Statutory Requirements. A petition for administration without court supervision may be granted if the requirements of Indiana Code 29–1–7.5–2(a)(4) are met, and there is compliance of all other requirements of Indiana Code 29–1–7.5–2(a).

B. Costs and Claims Paid. All court costs shall be paid and all claims satisfied and released on or before the date of the filing of the closing affidavit, and a Clerk's certification thereof (see Appendix A) shall be filed with the court at the time such closing affidavit is filed with the court evidencing payment of court costs and all claims have been filed.

Adopted as Rule 10, effective Jan. 1, 1991. Amended effective Oct. 4, 2000; Aug. 28, 2001; renumbered as Rule 0810, and amended effective Feb. 7, 2007; Jan. 1, 2012.

APPENDICES

APPENDIX A.   CLERK'S CERTIFICATE AS TO COSTS/CLAIMS

STATE OF INDIANA   )   IN THE MONROE CIRCUIT COURT
)
COUNTY OF MONROE   )   CAUSE NO. _____

IN THE MATTER OF
THE ESTATE OF

CLERK'S CERTIFICATE AS TO COSTS/CLAIMS

___ This is to certify that all costs have been paid in this proceeding through _____

(Date)

  In addition, all claims filed in this proceeding have been satisfied and shown released. _____

          Yes/No

  If no, list the claims that remain pending: _____

_____

_____

Date: _____

                              Clerk, _____ County

Adopted effective Jan. 1, 1991. Amended effective Oct. 4, 2000; Feb. 7, 2007; effective Jan. 1, 2012.

MONROE CIRCUIT COURT
GUARDIANSHIP
RULES

Adopted Effective January 1, 2012

Including Amendments Received Through November 1, 2012

Research Notes

These rules may be searched electronically on Westlaw in the IN-RULES database; updates to these rules may be found on Westlaw in IN-RULESUPDATES. For search tips and a summary of database content, consult the Westlaw Scope Screens for each database.

Rule
LR53–GU00 Rule 0800. Guardianships
LR53–GU00 Rule 0801. Emergency Detention Procedure
Appendix
A Certification by Financial Institution
B Physician's Report

LR53–GU00 Rule 0800. GUARDIANSHIPS

A. Presence of Incapacitated Person. In all guardianship proceedings seeking to declare an adult incapacitated for any reason, the incapacitated person shall be present at the hearing or there shall be sufficient evidence presented showing that the alleged incapacitated person is unable to appear.

B. Appointment of Guardian Ad Litem or Attorney. The Court may in its discretion determine that the alleged incapacitated person should have a guardian ad litem or attorney appointed to represent his or her interests, and the hearing for appointment of a guardian for the alleged incapacitated person may be continued by the Court for that purpose.

C. Physician's Report. In all guardianship proceedings seeking to declare an adult incapacitated, a physician's report by the doctor treating the alleged incapacitated person, or such additional evidence as the Court may require, shall be presented to the Court at the time the petition is filed or on the date of the hearing. No determination will be made without a supporting medical report or testimony at hearing. (See Appendix B.)

D. Current Reports. Current reports filed by a guardian of the person shall state the present residence of the incapacitated person and a statement of the incapacitated person's current condition and general welfare. If the incapacitated person is an adult, a report of a treating physician shall be filed with the current report verifying that the incapacity of the person remains unchanged since the date the guardianship was established or the date of the last current report.

E. Biennial Reports and Bond Premium Payment. The guardian of the incapacitated person shall file current reports biennially or at such other times as ordered by the Court. If a guardian's bond is required, the guardian of the incapacitated person shall submit to the Court proof of payment of current premiums due on said bond. Failure to comply with this section may result in removal of the guardian.

F. Petition for Guardianship of a Minor. In every petition for the appointment of a guardian of the person of a minor child, the following information shall be contained in the petition:

1. The present address of the child.

2. The places where the child has resided during the past two years, and the names and present addresses of the persons with whom the child has lived during that period. If such information is not available, the petition should state the reason for such unavailability.

3. Whether, to petitioner's knowledge, any other litigation is pending in this state or in any other state concerning the custody of the child.

4. Whether, to petitioner's knowledge, any person not a party to the guardianship proceeding has physical custody of the child or claims to have custody or visitation rights with respect to the child.

G. Hearings. Hearing shall be scheduled by the Court on any petition seeking guardianship over an adult alleged to be an incapacitated person. Hearings shall be held on any petition seeking a guardianship over a child unless the guardianship is being established for school purposes only. If the guardianship is being established for school purposes only, the Court may waive the necessity of hearing.

H. Rules of the Veteran's Administration. Nothing contained in these rules shall amend or supersede the Probate Rules and Regulations promulgated by the Veteran's Administration of the United States, and every guardian appointed by the Court or the attorney for such guardian shall comply with those Rules and Regulations, if applicable

Adopted effective Jan. 1, 2012.

LR53–GU00 Rule 0801. EMERGENCY DETENTION PROCEDURE

A. In order to hospitalize a person on an emergency detention order, staff of the health care facility shall:

1. Complete the necessary commitment forms with the signatures of the petitioner and the physician.

2. During working hours call Circuit Judge, Division VII, to obtain verbal authorization. Fax a judicial endorsement form to the Judge for signature.

3. After working hours, call the duty judge to obtain verbal authorization. On the signature line of the judicial endorsement for write: per verbal order, date and time.

4. The next business day, fax a judicial endorsement form to the court reporter, Division VII, for judge's signature. The completed form shall be faxed back to the health care facility.

B. The court reporter, Division VII, shall file the original signed judicial endorsement form in the RJO and a copy of the form in the case file.

Adopted effective Jan. 1, 2012.

APPENDIX A. CERTIFICATION BY FINANCIAL INSTITUTION

TO: _____

FROM: _____
              (Guardian's Name)

RE: Guardianship of _____

In order to comply with the rule of the Monroe Circuit Probate Court, I am required to file a certification of Account Balances. Please certify the balances and names on the accounts I have listed below.

DATED: _____   _____
                                                          Guardian's Signature)

For Bank Use Only:

I certify that on the ___ day of _____, 20 ___, the last day of the period covered by this accounting, there was on deposit in this institution to the credit of the Guardian, the following balance:

Name on Account	Account Number	Balance	Date
_____	_____	_____	_____
_____	_____	_____	_____
_____	_____	_____	_____
_____	_____	_____	_____

Name and Address of Institution: _____
_____
_____

Signature of Certifying Officer: _____
                            Printed: _____
                              Title: _____
                               Date: _____

Adopted effective Jan. 1, 2012.

APPENDIX B. PHYSICIAN'S REPORT

STATE OF INDIANA   )   IN THE MONROE CIRCUIT COURT
)
COUNTY OF MONROE   )   CAUSE NO. _____

IN THE MATTER OF THE
GUARDIANSHIP OF
_____

PHYSICIAN'S REPORT

_____, a physician licensed to practice medicine in all its branches in the State of Indiana, submits the following report on _____, alleged incapacitated person, based on an examination of said person on the _____ day of _____, 20 ___.

1. Describe the nature and type of the incapacitated person's disability:

_____

_____

2. Describe the incapacitated person's mental and physical condition; and, when it is appropriate, describe educational condition, adaptive behavior and social skills:

_____

3. State whether, in your opinion, the incapacitated person is totally or only partially incapable of making personal and financial decisions; and, if the latter, the kinds of decisions which the incapacitated person can and cannot make. Include the reason or reasons for this opinion.

_____

_____

_____

4. What in your opinion is the most appropriate living arrangement for the incapacitated person; and, if applicable, describe the most appropriate treatment or rehabilitation plan. Include the reason or reasons for your opinion.

_____

_____

5. Can the incapacitated person appear in court without injury to his/her health? _____. If the answer is no, explain the medical reasons for your answer.

_____

_____

I affirm, under the penalties for perjury, that the foregoing representations are true.

Signature: _____

Printed: _____

Address: _____

City/State/Zip: _____

Telephone: _____

This report must be signed by a physician. If the description of the incapacitated person's mental, physical and education condition, adaptive behavior or social skills is based on evaluations by the professionals, all professionals preparing evaluations must sign the report. Evaluations on which the report is based must have been performed within three (3) months of the date of the filing of the petition.

Names and signatures of other persons who performed evaluations upon which this report is based:

Name: _____

Address: _____

Signature: _____

Date: _____

Name: _____

Address: _____

Signature: _____

Date: _____

Adopted effective Jan. 1, 2012.

PORTER COUNTY LOCAL SMALL CLAIMS RULES

Adopted August 4, 2006, Effective January 1, 2007

Including Amendments Received Through November 1, 2013

Research Notes

Use Westlaw *to find cases citing or applying specific rules.* Westlaw *may also be used to search for specific terms in court rules or to update court rules. See the IN-RULES and IN-RULESUPDATES Scope Screens for detailed descriptive information and search tips.*

LR64–SC00 Rule 1000. GENERAL PROCEDURE

1000.10 Conflict of Rules. All small claim proceedings in the Porter Superior Court, County Division shall be governed by the Small Claims Rules promulgated from time to time by the Indiana Supreme Court, and these published herein. In any instance where these rules conflict with the rules of the Indiana Supreme Court, the latter shall control.

1000.20 Tender of Completed Documents and Proper Costs. Parties or their attorneys are solely responsible for tender to the Court of any documents desired to be filed in complete and correct form, together with proper costs and the correct number of copies, as determined by the Clerk. Neither the Court nor the Clerk will be responsible for delays or deadlines missed due to the tender of incomplete or incorrect documents, improper costs, or insufficient number of copies.

1000.30 Appearance by Husband or Wife. Except for hearing on proceedings supplemental or by contrary order of the Court, appearances by a party's spouse shall be considered the appearance of the party upon said spouse's representation on the record that the party and the appearing spouse are currently married and cohabiting.

1000.40 Parties Current Addresses. Notices from the Court will be sent to the parties at the most recent address in the Court's possession. The parties are solely responsible to advise the Court in writing of any change of address. Failure of plaintiff to notify the Court of his/her current address may result in the dismissal of the claim.

Adopted Aug. 4, 2006, effective Jan. 1, 2007. Amended effective Jan. 1, 2012; effective Oct. 1, 2012.

LR64–SC2 Rule 1100. FORMS

1100.10 Court's Forms. The Court shall from time to time, and through consultation with the Clerk, draft forms for use of litigants, the Clerk, and the Court in small claims actions. All small claims shall be filed on forms furnished by the Clerk of the Court.

1100.20 No Other Forms. Originals or photocopies of the forms described in LR64–SC2–1100.10 shall be acceptable for filing. Any other form, photocopy or computer generated copy thereof presented to the Clerk shall be accepted for filing upon approval of the Judge to whom the case is assigned.

1100.30 Production and Form. All filings shall be placed on white, 8-1/2″ × 11× paper, with printing or writing on one side only

Adopted Aug. 4, 2006, effective Jan. 1, 2007. Amended effective Jan. 1, 2012; effective Oct. 1, 2012.

LR64–SC00 Rule 1200. HEARING CALENDARS

1200.10 General Procedure. Upon the filing of a notice of claim, the Clerk shall schedule an initial hearing for the purpose of determining whether the matter is settled, contested, uncontested or to be dismissed. If uncontested, the Court or parties shall prepare Agreed Judgment forms. If contested, the Court shall set the matter for trial or mediation. The parties need not bring their exhibits or witnesses to the initial hearing, except in eviction hearings. In order to expedite the process, any County Division Judge may direct the Clerk to inform and instruct (in writing) the litigants that the bench trial shall proceed at Initial Hearing.

1200.20 Change of Calendar. Should any party file a motion to continue the initial hearing, the Court may grant or deny the motion, or strike the initial hearing and set the matter for bench trial at a later date. The moving party must notify the other party of the continuance motion and serve notice thereon.

1200.30 Alternative Dispute Resolution in SC Cases. The Court may order Alternative Dispute Resolution (ADR) in the form of mediation at the request of either party or in the discretion of the Court.

Adopted Aug. 4, 2006, effective Jan. 1, 2007. Amended effective Jan. 1, 2012; Oct. 1, 2012; Jan. 1, 2013.

LR64–SC9 Rule 1300.   CONTINUANCES

1300.10 General Rule. With appropriate verified written motion and for good cause only, any party may file a motion to continue the initial hearing, eviction hearing, bench trial, motions hearing or proceedings supplemental to judgment, stating cause for such continuance. Continuances are highly disfavored and interfere with the general principle of quick and speedy justice in the Small Claims Rules. A continuance under this subsection may not be granted within 24 hours of the trial, unless approved by a Judge. All motions for continuance must be made in person or by the party's attorney who has filed a written appearance on behalf of said party. The party or attorney obtaining the continuance shall notify any opposing party in a timely fashion.

1300.20 No Delay Beyond Nine (9) Months. No case shall be continued for trial beyond nine (9) months from the date the action is filed. Only extreme hardship or emergency shall serve as an exception. Any continuance shall be granted only by the Court upon due showing of extreme hardship or emergency by either party. Said hardship condition shall be reported to the Court immediately upon learning of the hardship. In the event such extreme hardship or emergency is shown, the Court will grant an additional continuance for a period not longer than necessary.

1300.30 Possession of Real Estate. No continuance shall be granted to a defendant where the action involves the issue of possession of real estate, except for good cause shown and upon approval by the Court.

1300.40 Sanctions for Failure to Notify. Where notice of continuance has not been timely given, the Court may assess sanctions which may include, but are not limited to, reasonable attorney's fees, lost wages and other costs for each party and necessary witness appearances due to lack of notice. Motions for sanctions shall be heard as a part of the trial on the merits.

Adopted Aug. 4, 2006, effective Jan. 1, 2007. Amended effective Jan. 1, 2012; Oct. 1, 2012; Jan. 1, 2013.

LR64–SC10 Rule 1400.   DISMISSAL OF ACTIONS

1400.10 Dismissal by Plaintiff. Any claim may be dismissed by the plaintiff at any time before judgment has been entered unless a counterclaim has been filed by a defendant. The Court may dismiss any Notice of Claim, subject to amendment, which is so vague or ambiguous as not to state a proper cause of action.

1400.20 Dismissal by Stipulation. Any claim may be dismissed by filing a stipulation of dismissal signed by all parties to the claim.

1400.30 Conversion of Action from Small Claims to Plenary Docket. Should any party seek to have a small claims case converted to the plenary docket, the party shall first pay the difference in filing fee between small claims and the plenary docket. Should a case be filed on the plenary docket seeking less than the statutory maximum damages of small claims court, the plenary court may have the matter transferred to small claims court without reimbursement of any difference in filing fees. The Clerk shall then assign an SC designation to the caption and file. If any pending case having an SC designation is converted or transferred to the plenary docket and is given a PL, CT, or CC case designation, the Clerk shall affix the appropriate new designation to the caption and file and the case shall remain in the same court as the original SC designation. A party plaintiff may not file consecutive cases against the same defendant to bypass a plenary designation or to avoid Small Claims Rule 8 requiring an attorney appearing for a corporate party.

1400.40 Request for Jury Trial. No request for a jury trial by Plaintiff shall be granted. Upon request by Defendant, a verified statement of the factual issues to be determined must be made contemporaneously with the request for jury trial.

Adopted Aug. 4, 2006, effective Jan. 1, 2007. Amended effective Jan. 1, 2012; Oct. 1, 2012; Jan. 1, 2013.

LR64–SC10 Rule 1500.   DEFAULT

1500.10 Grace Period. The Court shall permit each party a ten (10) minute grace period to appear for any proceeding.

1500.20 Default of Defendant. Upon the failure of a defendant to appear at any hearing, or trial, judgment may be entered against said defendant on the merits.

1500.30 Default of Plaintiff. Upon the failure of a plaintiff to appear at any hearing or at a trial on the merits, the cause may be dismissed without prejudice. Further, default judgment may be entered for the defendant against the plaintiff on any timely-filed counterclaim. Upon plaintiff's failure to appear at the initial hearing or at a trial on the merits in a subsequent cause based on the same facts as the cause earlier dismissed without prejudice, the cause may be dismissed with prejudice and a default judgment may be entered for the defendant against the plaintiff on any timely-filed counterclaim.

1500.40 Notice in the Event of Inadequate Service. Where the Court has received return of service which discloses less than ten (10) days notice to any defendant of a hearing set pursuant to LR64–SC00–1200, and the defendant fails to appear for said hearing, the plaintiff shall not be entitled to entry of default. If the plaintiff wishes to proceed, the Clerk shall notify the defendant of a new calendar setting by first class mail to the address at which service was obtained. Such notice is sufficient if said notice is sent and the hearing set so as to comply with T.R. 6 and S.C. 2.

1500.50 Setting Aside Default Judgment. A default judgment may be set aside according to the procedure set forth in S.C. 10(C).

(1) *Expedited Hearing.* An expedited hearing on such a motion to set aside default judgment shall be set on the Judge's calendar.

(2) *Stay of Collection Proceedings.* In any cause in which a motion to set aside default judgment has been filed, collection proceedings as to the judgment debtor filing the motion will not be stayed unless a motion to stay such proceedings is filed and granted.

1500.60 Default on Proceedings Supplemental. The Court may permit the parties a ten (10) minute grace period to appear for any proceeding supplemental hearing. After the ten (10) minute grace period has elapsed the court may issue appropriate orders including dismissal of the hearing, or default orders against a judgment debtor.

Adopted Aug. 4, 2006, effective Jan. 1, 2007. Amended effective Jan. 1, 2012; Oct. 1, 2012; Jan. 1, 2013.

LR64–SC00 Rule 1600. ATTORNEY FEES

Evidence Required to Support Award. The amount of attorney fees awarded shall be within the sound discretion of the Court. No attorney fees shall be requested unless provided for by written agreement between the parties, applicable statute or common law. In the event attorney fees are requested pursuant to a written agreement a copy of said agreement shall be filed with the Court.

Absent the filing of an appropriate fee affidavit, attorney fees for an NSF check shall be based upon the actual amount of the check.

Adopted Aug. 4, 2006, effective Jan. 1, 2007. Amended effective Jan. 1, 2012; Oct. 1, 2012.

LR64–SC00 Rule 1700. JUDGMENTS FOR POSSESSION OF REAL ESTATE

1700.10 Bifurcated Hearing and Expedited Hearing on Possession. Hearings in actions involving the issue of possession of real estate shall be bifurcated. The possession hearing shall be set in an expedited setting as an initial hearing to determine whether a breach of any lease term has occurred. A final judgment for the possession of the real estate shall be entered at the initial hearing and a judgment for back rent and/or other damages, if any, shall be entered at a separate damages hearing. Prior to or at the damages hearing, the landlord shall have completed for tender to the Court the Landlord Computation of Damages Form (See Appendix). At the damages hearing, the parties shall be required to advise the Court of any subsequent change of address during the pendency of the action.

1700.20 Notice to Tenant. Unless the landlord shall file the pleading and bond set forth in I.C. 32–6–1.5–1, et seq., notice of the possession hearing shall be served on a tenant not less than ten (10) days prior to the possession hearing. Should a landlord request a continuance of the possession hearing, the landlord must serve new notice to the tenant of the possession hearing. A landlord may not utilize the damage hearing to seek ejectment, unless tenant is aware of the issue and possibility of ejectment and has received proper notice.

1700.30 Disposition of Tenant's Remaining Personal Property. If a tenant leaves personal property of value in or about the demised premises under circumstances which reasonably show abandonment of said personal property, the landlord shall follow the provisions of I.C. 32–31–4–3 et. seq. for removal of same.

1700.40 Landlord Computation of Damages Form. Prior to the calling of the case by the Court, the Landlord shall tender to the Tenant a copy of the Landlord Computation of Damages Form, so that the Tenant may review the form and appropriately respond to the Court's inquiry whether the Damages Hearing is contested or uncontested. Also, it is expected that the parties meet in civil and orderly fashion prior to the hearing to determine whether an agreement or stipulation can be made on any damages. The Landlord need not tender the form to a tardy or non-appearing Tenant.

Adopted Aug. 4, 2006, effective Jan. 1, 2007. Amended effective Jan. 1, 2012; Oct. 1, 2012; Jan. 1, 2013.

LR64–SC12 Rule 1800. VENUE

Local Small Claims Venue. When Porter County is the proper venue for a small claims action under S.C. 12, said action shall be filed as follows:

A. Small claims from Washington, Boone, Pleasant, Center, and Morgan Townships shall be filed in Porter Superior Court #4, sitting in Valparaiso, Indiana.

B. Small claims from Jackson, Liberty, Pine, Portage, Porter, Union and Westchester Townships shall be filed in Porter Superior Court #3, sitting in Portage, Indiana. However, Porter Superior Court #6 shall receive small claims filings if proper venue would lie in Porter Superior Court #3 and the last digit of the assigned cause number is 1,3,5,7,or 9. Where proper venue for small claims cases would lie in either Porter Superior Court #3 or Porter Superior Court #6, uncontested collection cases filed in volume by an individual plaintiff or an attorney representing several plaintiffs may be filed in a group in the court that would be next available by cause number. The Clerk shall at all times keep the next available cause number confidential.

Upon the implementation of I.C. 33–4–3–7 (effective 07/05), and in the event the filing of cases pursuant to this Rule shall result in a disparity of small claims filings reflected by the Quarterly Case Status Report (QCSR), the judges of the Superior Court County Division may jointly direct the Clerk of the Court to assign case filings in the County Division, so as to eliminate the disparity. Small Claims cases involving jurisdictional amounts between $3000 and $6000 may be transferred to a different venue within Porter County upon agreement of the courts involved.

Adopted Aug. 4, 2006, effective Jan. 1, 2007. Amended effective Jan. 1, 2012; Oct. 1, 2012.

LR64–TR69 Rule 1900. PROCEEDINGS SUPPLEMENTAL

1900.10 General Procedure. Proceedings supplemental to execution shall be governed by T.R. 69(E) and applicable statutes, and subject to the approval of the Court which entered judgment.

1900.20 Thirty Day Rule. A motion for proceedings supplemental may not be filed until thirty (30) calendar days have elapsed since the date of judgment except by order of the Court for good cause shown.

1900.30 Hearing. Unless a party specifically requests otherwise and sets the hearing accordingly, all hearing on proceedings supplemental will be set on the uncontested calendar.

1900.40 Conduct of Hearings. Unless the judgment creditor is represented by an attorney at the proceeding supplemental hearing, said hearing may be conducted by an officer of the Court. However, an officer of the Court shall advise the judgment debtor from the outset that he/she has a right to a hearing in the presence of the judge.

Adopted Aug. 4, 2006, effective Jan. 1, 2007. Amended effective Jan. 1, 2012; Oct. 1, 2012; Jan. 1, 2013.

LR64–SC00 Rule 1010. COURT ORDERS TO APPEAR (COTA)

1010.10 General Rule. A judgment creditor may request that the Court issue an order to appear (COTA) to a judgment debtor when an active proceeding supplemental is pending against the judgment debtor. The first hearing date set for a COTA shall be set within sixty (60) days of the date on which the COTA is issued.

1010.20 Failure to Appear on a COTA. Upon a judgment debtor's failure to appear on the date and time set by the COTA, the Court may order any appropriate remedy including the issuance of a contempt citation to the judgment debtor.

1010.30 Status Compliance Hearings. Unless good cause shown, a judgment creditor may not schedule a Status Hearing for Compliance and Order to Appear (COTA) within 100 days of any previous setting.

Adopted Aug. 4, 2006, effective Jan. 1, 2007. Amended effective Jan. 1, 2012; Oct. 1, 2012; Jan. 1, 2013.

LR64–SC00 Rule 1020. CONTEMPT/RULE TO SHOW CAUSE/BODY ATTACHMENT

1020.10 Contempt. Upon failure of a judgment debtor or garnishee defendant to appear as ordered for a scheduled hearing, the Court may issue a contempt citation to said person.

1020.20 Body Attachment. Body attachment shall be requested and issued only when:

(1) any party contemptuously fails to comply with a court order, or;

(2) the judgment debtor or garnishee defendant previously ordered to appear for a scheduled hearing was served with a contempt citation and failed to appear for the contempt hearing, and;

(3) the judgment creditor or attorney for judgment creditor has filed a form entitled "Affidavit in Support of Bench Warrant" which affirmatively shows the Court that notice and service has been obtained upon the judgment debtor, that the address being utilized is current and good, and that sufficient assets exist upon which a levy can be made; and

(4) counsel has filed an accounting of all payments on judgments received exclusive of payments made through the Clerk, together with a balance due on the account; and

(5) the judgment creditor or attorney has supplied the Clerk of Court with sufficient identifiers to allow the civil sheriff to proceed with body attachment.

1020.30 Procedure for Contacting Judgment Creditor When Attached Person is in Custody. Whenever a judgment defendant has been arrested on a Writ of Body Attachment, a hearing shall be conducted at the earliest convenience of the court. When creditor/plaintiff is unrepresented, the Court shall conduct hearing without notice to all parties. If creditor is represented, counsel for creditor shall be given the opportunity to appear and conduct proceedings supplemental to judgment. Should counsel waive appearance or fail to appear, the Court shall set bond, if appropriate, and issue an order for debtor to appear at future court hearings.

1020.40 Judgment Debtor in Jail. No bench warrant or body attachment shall issue for a judgment debtor already incarcerated on an unrelated matter. A Judgment Debtor shall check the Department of Correction Locator Website to determine whether the debtor is incarcerated in Indiana. If incarcerated in the Porter County Jail, the judgment creditor or attorney shall proceed to the jail to conduct proceedings supplemental to judgment.

1020.50 Setting of Cash Bond. The Court shall set an appropriate bond for the release of the judgment defendant from incarceration and upon promise to appear for future court proceedings. The Courts shall agree upon the appropriate cash bond to guarantee future appearance, which shall not be in the amount of the judgment due.

1020.60 Recall of Body Attachments. A judgment creditor or attorney must timely seek to have a bench warrant or body attachment recalled, when appropriate. Upon timely filing of a Motion to Recall Warrant or Body Attachment, the Court shall notify the Civil Bureau of the Sheriff to recall the warrant.

Adopted Aug. 4, 2006, effective Jan. 1, 2007. Amended effective Jan. 1, 2012; Oct. 1, 2012; Jan. 1, 2013.

LR64–SC00 Rule 1030. GARNISHMENT

1030.10 General Procedure. All garnishment proceedings shall be subject to the approval of the Court.

1030.20 Requirements for Garnishment Order to Issue. A garnishment order shall not issue with respect to a judgment debtor's wages or other property without:

(1) an active proceeding supplemental as to the judgment debtor;

(2) service on the garnishee-defendant of the proceeding supplemental by:

    (a) first-class mail, certified mail, or refusal thereof,

    (b) Sheriff's service, or;

    (c) private process server; and

(3) return of answered interrogatories, other verification of employment by the garnishee-defendant, or failure to answer interrogatories after notice.

1030.30 Voluntary Garnishments. In instances where a judgment debtor has entered a voluntary agreement for periodic payments to satisfy the judgment and has further consented to garnishment upon default, notwithstanding the terms of the agreement, no garnishment order shall issue unless an active proceeding supplemental is pending against the judgment debtor and the garnishee-defendant.

1030.40 Release. Upon receipt by the judgment creditor, or by the Clerk on the judgment creditor's behalf, of monies sufficient to fully satisfy the judgment, and any accrued interest and costs, the judgment creditor shall immediately obtain a Court order releasing the applicable garnishment order and shall forward a copy to the garnishee-defendant.

Adopted Aug. 4, 2006, effective Jan. 1, 2007. Amended effective Jan. 1, 2012; Oct. 1, 2012.

LR64–SC00 Rule 1040. BANKRUPTCY OF JUDGMENT DEBTOR

1040.10 Motion to Stay Proceedings Per Bankruptcy Filing. All actions, including pending collection proceedings, shall be stayed as to any judgment debtor who files with the Court in each relevant action one (1) copy of the Bankruptcy Court's notice of relief (or Bankruptcy Cover sheet showing date of filing, cause number, applicable bankruptcy chapter) or who files with the Court in each relevant action a Motion to Stay reciting the filing of bankruptcy by the judgment debtor and resultant stay of all proceedings by the Bankruptcy Court, including the cause number, date of filing, bankruptcy chapter, and attaching a copy of the applicable address matrix or schedule showing the listing of the creditor, and the name of the Bankruptcy Court. Debtor's counsel shall file a Proposed Order of Stay with the Court which shall include a provision to recall any and all outstanding bench warrants.

1040.20 Notice of Dismissal of Chapter 7 or 13 Bankruptcy. A Motion to Dissolve Bankruptcy Stay on account of dismissal of a bankruptcy must include the Order from the United States Bankruptcy Court showing dismissal.

Adopted Aug. 4, 2006, effective Jan. 1, 2007. Amended effective Jan. 1, 2012; Oct. 1, 2012; Jan. 1, 2013.

LR64–SC11 Rule 1050. RELEASE OF JUDGMENT

Upon Defendant's payment of the judgment together with interest and costs in full the plaintiff shall, upon receipt of said funds, promptly release the judgment. Should the plaintiff fail to release the judgment the Court may order the judgment released.

Adopted Aug. 4, 2006, effective Jan. 1, 2007. Amended effective Jan. 1, 2012; Oct. 1, 2012.

APPENDIX 1. COMPUTATION OF DAMAGES/UNPAID RENT BY LANDLORD
SMALL CLAIMS RULES APPENDIX 1

STATE OF INDIANA	)	IN THE PORTER SUPERIOR COURT
	) SS:	
COUNTY OF PORTER	)	_____, INDIANA
	)	
_____	)	
PLAINTIFF	)	
	)	
vs.	)	CAUSE NO. 64D0 ___—_____
	)	
_____	)	
DEFENDANT	)	

COMPUTATION OF DAMAGES/UNPAID RENT BY LANDLORD

The Plaintiff(s)/Landlord, under the penalties for perjury states that the following computations represent the damages incurred as a result of a breach of the lease agreement and/or tenancy by the Defendant/Tenant:

[Ordinary wear and tear is not a compensable damage and will be subtracted by the Court in many instances. Also, labor costs for cleanup by the Landlord are normally disfavored]

I. UNPAID RENT: __ MONTHS @ $ __ PER MONTH = $ _____
   LESS SECURITY DEPOSIT (if applicable) - $ _____
   Sub–Total Due $ _____

II. DAMAGES TO PREMISES
   1. Paint, cleaning products $ _____
   2. Physical damage to walls, etc. $ _____
   3. Removal of personal property $ _____
   4. OTHER $ _____
   5. OTHER $ _____

   Total Physical Damages $ _____

GRAND TOTAL OF DAMAGES DUE $ _____

This form can be utilized when requesting a default judgment for damages, post-eviction, or as a summary exhibit at a contested trial or damages hearing. Plaintiff must return this form personally or by first class mail to the Clerk's Office on or before seven (7) calendar days before the scheduled trial. Failure to timely return this claim form to the Clerk's Office may result in the granting of a continuance to the Defendant.

PLEASE SIGN: _____

Adopted Aug. 4, 2006, effective Jan. 1, 2007. Amended effective Jan. 1, 2012; Oct. 1, 2012; Jan. 1, 2013.

PORTER COUNTY LOCAL FAMILY LAW RULES

Adopted August 4, 2006, Effective January 1, 2007

Including Amendments Received Through November 1, 2013

Research Notes

These rules may be searched electronically on Westlaw *in the* IN-RULES *database; updates to these rules may be found on Westlaw in* IN-RULESUPDATES. *For search tips and a summary of database content, consult the Westlaw Scope Screens for each database.*

LR64–TR16 Rule 2000. ALTERNATIVE DISPUTE RESOLUTION (ADR) AND CASE MANAGEMENT

2000.1 ADR. In all contested family law matters, including dissolutions, separations, custody disputes, post-decree and support proceedings, the parties may be required to comply with the requirements of ADR.

2000.2 Case Management.

(1) The Domestic Relations Case Management Order (see Appendix A) shall apply to the following contested causes of action:

(a) Petition for Dissolution of Marriage;

(b) Petition for Legal Separation.

(2) The Domestic Relations Case Management Order may, at the Court's discretion, apply to the following contested causes of action:

(a) Petition for Modification of an existing court order;

(b) Petition for Rule to Show Cause;

(c) Any other cause of action the Court deems appropriate.

Adopted Aug. 4, 2006, effective Jan. 1, 2007. Amended effective Jan. 1, 2012; Oct. 1, 2012.

LR64–TR35 Rule 2100. FINANCIAL DECLARATION FORM

2100.1 Requirement. In all family law matters, including dissolutions, separations, post-decree and support proceedings, each party shall prepare and exchange, respectively, within 45 days of the initial filing of the action or within 30 days of the filing of any post-decree matters, a Financial Declaration Form (see Appendix B and C). These time limits may be extended or shortened by court order for good cause shown. In those cases where there is service, but no appearance by counsel, it is the responsibility of the moving party to serve the completed Form on the other party and to notify that party of the duty to prepare and serve one as well.

2100.2 Exceptions. The Form need not be exchanged if:

(1) the parties agree in writing within 30 days of the initial filing to waive exchange, **and**;

(2) the parties have executed a written agreement which settles all financial issues, **or**;

(3) the proceeding is merely at a provisional or emergency relief stage, **or**;

(4) the proceeding is one in which the service is by publication and there is no response, **or**;

(5) the proceeding is post-decree and concerns issues without financial implications. Provided, however, when the proceeding is post-decree and concerns an arrearage, the alleged delinquent party shall complete the entire Form, while the support recipient need complete merely that portion thereof which requires specification of the basis of the arrearage calculation (with appropriate supporting documentation).

2100.3 Use at Trial. The Form is intended primarily as discovery although, subject to appropriate objection, it shall be admissible at the request of any party. Therefore, particularly in view of the presumptive nature of the Support Guidelines, direct examination on Form data shall address only unusual factors which require explanation, or corrections, and shall not, particularly with respect to issues of support, be routinely permitted. For evidentiary purposes, the pages of the Form shall be deemed severable.

2100.4 Supporting Documents. For the purposes of providing a full and complete verification of assets, liabilities and values, each party shall attach to the Form all information reasonably required and reasonably available. This shall include recent bills, wage and tax records, and bank, pension and year-end mortgage statements. "Reasonably available" means that material which may be obtained by letter accompanied with an authorization, but does not mean material that must be subpoenaed or is in possession of the other party. Appraisals of real estate and pensions, or of personal property such as jewelry, antiques or special collections (stamps, coins or guns, for example), are not required. However, once an appraisal is obtained, it must be exchanged. Moreover, the Court may direct that an appraisal be obtained, and may designate the appraiser.

2100.5 Privacy—Sealing of Forms. Whenever the interest of privacy so requires, the Court may, upon motion, direct the admitted Forms sealed until further order. However, such requests shall not be made as a matter of course. When ordered sealed, the court reporter shall take custody of the Forms and place them in a flat manner in an envelope of sufficient size, seal the envelope and affix a copy of the order. Forms may be withdrawn at the conclusion of the case on such terms as the Court allows.

2100.6 Final Declaration—Mandatory Discovery. The exchange of Forms constitutes mandatory discovery. Thus, Indiana Rules of Trial Procedure, Rule 37 sanctions apply. Additionally, pursuant to Trial Rule 26(E)(2) and (3), the Form shall be supplemented if additional material becomes available. Further, any additional discovery such as a motion to produce, interrogatories, or depositions of the parties shall not commence until the Forms are exchanged.

Adopted Aug. 4, 2006, effective Jan. 1, 2007. Amended effective Jan. 1, 2012; Oct. 1, 2012.

LR64–FL00 Rule 2200. CHILD SUPPORT GUIDELINES

2200.1 Worksheet Required. In all proceedings involving child support, each party shall file with any settlement, or enter into evidence during any trial, Indiana Child Support Guidelines worksheets—one or more depending on the facts. Further, the worksheet(s) shall, when reasonably possible, be delivered to the other party simultaneously with the Financial Declaration Form, but, in any event, within ten (10) days of receiving the other party's Form. The worksheet(s) shall be promptly supplemented if any changes occur prior to resolution.

2200.2 Support Settlement Agreements. If an agreement concerning support contains deviation ten percent (10%) or more from the Guidelines, the par-

ties shall present to the Court a written explanation, with supporting documents, justifying the deviation.

Adopted Aug. 4, 2006, effective Jan. 1, 2007. Amended effective Jan. 1, 2012; Oct. 1, 2012.

LR64–FL00 Rule 2300. CHILD CUSTODY

In all proceedings regarding custody of minor children which remain contested after ADR, the Court may appoint a qualified family therapist to make a recommendation as to custody, and the Court may allocate the cost thereof as it deems reasonable.

Adopted Aug. 4, 2006, effective Jan. 1, 2007. Amended effective Jan. 1, 2012; Oct. 1, 2012.

LR64–TR17 Rule 2400. GUARDIANS AD LITEM

2400.1 Definition. An individual appointed by the Court under I.C. 31–1–11.5–28(b); I.C. 31–15–6–1; I.C. 31–17–6–1 or by Order of Court.

2400.2 When appointed. Whenever the Court is required to do so by statute, and whenever the Court finds, in its discretion, that it is appropriate to appoint a guardian ad litem. The guardian ad litem then becomes a party and anything to be served on the opposing party shall also be served on the guardian ad litem.

2400.3 Duties. Guardian Ad Litem shall:

(1) Perform all duties required by law which includes to protect the best interests of the child(ren); and

(2) Submit a written report of his or her finding to the Court prior to the matter being heard by the Court. The attorneys and pro-se litigants shall receive notice of the filing of the report and may inspect same upon notice to the Court.

2400.4 How appointed.

(1) Where the parties or either of them request and/or where the Court had determined a guardian ad litem should be appointed to protect the best interest of the child, the parties shall within the time set by the Court, select a guardian ad litem.

(2) In the event the parties fail to select a guardian ad litem within the time determined by the Court, the Court shall name a three-person panel.

(3) After the Court has named the panel, the party listed on the case caption as Petitioner, shall within three (3) days, strike first. Respondent shall, within three (3) days thereafter, strike from the remaining two (2) persons. The remaining person is the court appointed guardian ad litem, subject to that person's acceptance.

(a) in the event either party should fail to strike within the time frame provided, they have waived their opportunity to strike and the other party may strike in their place.

(b) Should both parties fail to strike, then the first named person on the list is appointed guardian ad litem, subject to acceptance.

2400.5 Fees.

(1) When a guardian ad litem is selected, the Court shall order each party to pay a lump sum, in an amount not less than $350.00, into the Clerk of the Porter Superior Court to be held for payment of guardian ad litem fees. The guardian ad litem shall periodically file a fee affidavit with the Court and request that the Clerk be ordered to release sums in an appropriate amount to pay fees current to date. To insure payment to the guardian ad litem, the Court may Order additional monies to be paid into the Court as it becomes necessary. The Court may reapportion the total costs at the time of disposition.

2400.6 Term of Service.

(1) The guardian ad litem shall serve in such capacity until such time as discharged by the Court.

(2) The guardian ad litem may, at anytime, request that he or she be relieved of their duties.

(3) The parties may request that a guardian ad litem be removed and it will be within the Court's discretion whether just cause exists for such removal.

2400.7 Form of Order.

(1) Whenever a guardian ad litem is appointed, the Appointment of Guardian Ad Litem Order (See Appendix D) shall be prepared and submitted for approval of the Court.

Adopted Aug. 4, 2006, effective Jan. 1, 2007. Amended effective Jan. 1, 2012; Oct. 1, 2012.

LR64–FL00 Rule 2500. VISITATION ORDERS

2500.1 Visitation. Visitation shall be governed by the Indiana Parenting Time Guidelines.

Adopted Aug. 4, 2006, effective Jan. 1, 2007. Amended effective Jan. 1, 2012; Oct. 1, 2012.

LR64–TR52 Rule 2600. PREPARATION OF ORDERS

2600.1 Exchange. It shall be the duty of the parties' attorneys to prepare decrees and other orders as directed by the Court. The attorney so directed shall first submit them to all other attorneys of record, within fourteen (14) days, to enable them to challenge any provision thereof before submission to the Court for entry.

2600.2 Additions. If the preparing attorney believes the receiving attorney is unreasonably withholding approval as to the form of order, or if either attorney believes the other is attempting to make additions not addressed by the Court, either may submit a proposed form of order to the Court, and shall attach thereto a written explanation of the dispute. Either attorney shall have seven (7) days to respond before the Court enters any order. The Court may enter sanctions against a party who has

unreasonably withheld approval or attempted to make additions not addressed by the Court.

2600.3 Required Number of Copies. In all cases that been assigned to the Porter County Family Court, it shall be the responsibility of the parties to make sure that Family Court receives a copy of all Orders. Therefore, all orders submitted to the Court shall be accompanied by a sufficient number of copies and the same number of postage paid addressed envelopes, so that a copy may be mailed to each party or counsel of record and a copy to the Family Court. The original and one copy of all orders shall be retained by the Clerk.

Adopted Aug. 4, 2006, effective Jan. 1, 2007. Amended effective Jan. 1, 2012; Oct. 1, 2012.

LR64–TR37 Rule 2700. SANCTIONS

If a party or counsel fails to timely prepare, exchange or file a Financial Declaration Form or Child Support Worksheet(s), or fails to cooperate in providing information relevant thereto in a timely manner, either is subject to sanctions under Trial Rule 37.

Adopted Aug. 4, 2006, effective Jan. 1, 2007. Amended effective Jan. 1, 2012; Oct. 1, 2012.

LR64–FL00 Rule 2800. ATTORNEY FEE REQUESTS

2800.1 Affidavits. When attorney fees, except those sought provisionally, are requested from the opposing party, the requesting attorney shall submit an appropriate affidavit, which the Court may admit as an exhibit.

2800.2 Written Requirements. The affidavit shall indicate the:

(1) requested fee and the basis thereof;

(2) amount counsel has billed, contracted for or been promised, and;

(3) amount counsel has received from all sources.

A copy of the written fee contract, if any, shall be attached to the affidavit and be deemed as part thereof.

Opposing counsel may cross-examine the requesting attorney as to any of the submitted material.

Adopted Aug. 4, 2006, effective Jan. 1, 2007. Amended effective Jan. 1, 2012; Oct. 1, 2012.

LR64–FL00 Rule 2900. AGREED MATTERS— SUBMISSION

No agreed matter shall be submitted unless accompanied by a signed agreement, and other appropriate documents, such as a decree, a wage-withholding order, or a Qualified Domestic Relations Order. However, if the parties reach an agreement "on the courthouse steps", then the Court will accept evidence of that settlement on the record.

Adopted Aug. 4, 2006, effective Jan. 1, 2007. Amended effective Jan. 1, 2012; Oct. 1, 2012.

LR64–TR65 Rule 2910. RESTRAINING ORDERS

2910.1 Restraining Orders. Temporary Restraining Orders Without Notice will only be issued upon a showing of **strict** compliance with T.R. 65(B)(1) & (2). In Re: Anonymous, 729 N.E. 2nd 566 (Ind. 2000).

Adopted Aug. 4, 2006, effective Jan. 1, 2007. Amended effective Jan. 1, 2012; Oct. 1, 2012.

LR64–FL00 Rule 2911. CHILD COUNSELING SESSION

2911.1 General Requirements. In all proceedings involving minor children, attendance at a four (4) hour educational seminar, hereinafter referred to as *Trans*Parenting, is required of all parties in all dissolution of marriage and legal separation proceedings and shall be successfully completed within sixty (60) days of service of the original petition. Administration of the program shall be by agencies appointed by the Court using qualified counselors, trainers and educators. Participants shall pay a fee to cover the total cost of the seminar. A copy of the *Trans*Parenting certificate shall be filed with the Court prior to the final hearing or shall be attached to the final decree as an exhibit thereto. For good cause shown, the Court may waive the requirement of completion of this program in individual cases.

2911.2 Attendance. Attendance at the seminar shall be required of all parties to a case where the interests of children under the age of 18 years are involved. The Court's action on a petition shall not be delayed by a non-moving party or responding party's failure to complete or delay in completing the seminar. An equivalent counseling program may be substituted for the seminar if satisfactory written verification is provided to the Court by a third party indicating that the specific issues covered in the *Trans*Parenting program have been addressed in another forum through professional or pastoral counseling, mediation or other similar educational program.

2911.3 Fees. A fee determined annually and payable per party is required and is used to cover all costs of the program including the presenter's fees, handouts, applications and program administration. The fee may be waived if a party presents a verified affidavit of poverty and it appears upon investigation that the party is indigent.

2911.4 Application Process. Notification to the parties of their responsibility to complete the seminar or provide alternative verification shall be provided at the time of the filing of the pleadings. Applications may be obtained from the court administrator or from the Clerk of the Court. The application and fee must be returned to the agency conducting the seminar.

Adopted Aug. 4, 2006, effective Jan. 1, 2007. Amended effective Jan. 1, 2012; Oct. 1, 2012.

LR64–TR16 Rule 2912. AGREEMENT WITH COURT DATE PENDING

In all proceedings where a court date is pending and the parties reach an agreement between themselves, the parties shall notify the Court in a timely manner. Failure to do so may result in sanctions being imposed against either or both parties and/or their attorneys.

Adopted Aug. 4, 2006, effective Jan. 1, 2007. Amended effective Jan. 1, 2012; Oct. 1, 2012.

APPENDIX A.   DOMESTIC RELATIONS CASE MANAGEMENT ORDER

STATE OF INDIANA   )
PORTER SUPERIOR COURT   ) SS:
SITTING IN VALPARAISO, INDIANA)
COUNTY OF PORTER   )

CONTINUOUS TERM 200 _____

IN RE THE MARRIAGE/PATERNITY OF:)
)
           , Petitioner   )   CAUSE # _____
    v,   )
)
          , Respondent   )

DOMESTIC RELATIONS CASE MANAGEMENT ORDER

The Court, in the exercise of its discretion under Trial Rule 16 (A), now orders the parties, including pro se litigants, and their respective attorneys to comply with the following orders:

    A.   Financial Declaration Forms, complete with supporting exhibits, shall be exchanged between the parties within forty five (45) days from the date the Petition for Dissolution of Marriage or Petition for Legal Separation is filed, and within thirty (30) days from the date that a Petition for Modification or Petition for Rule to Show Cause is filed, provided said petitions address the financial obligations of the parties, i.e. child support, including but not limited to, educational expenses or the payment of marital debt.

    B.   Within forty-five (45) days from the date either party filed their petition, the parties shall be required to appear in person, if they are proceeding pro se, or by their respective attorneys, for an Initial Pre–Trial Conference.   Said conference is hereby scheduled before this court on the ___ day of ___, 200 ___, at _____ m.

Each party shall be prepared to address the following issues:

    i.   Identification of the issues pending before the court;

    ii.   Identification of issues which have been amicably resolved between the parties, together with the terms of said resolution;

    iii.   Identification of the remaining contested issues;

    iv.   Estimated time required to complete discovery relative to the contested issues;

    v.   If not addressed at the Provisional Hearing, the identification or appointment of experts who shall assist the parties or the court in the resolution of the contested issues, including the appointment of a Guardian-ad-Litem, custodial evaluator or a property evaluator;

    vi.   The possibility of settlement on all or a portion of the contested issues through mediation, settlement conference or the implementation of another Alternative Dispute Resolution method;

    vii.   The estimated time required to present the contested issues before the court, including the possibility of disposing of all or a portion of the contested issues in summary fashion;

    viii.   The parties' attendance and completion of the Trans–Parenting Class as required by Local Rule ___;

    ix.   AT THE CONCLUSION OF THE INITIAL PRE–TRIAL CONFERENCE, THE COURT SHALL SCHEDULE THE CASE FOR A FINAL PRE–TRIAL CONFERENCE.   **NO FINAL HEARINGS SHALL BE SCHEDULED UNTIL THE CONCLUSION OF THE FINAL PRE–TRIAL CONFERENCE.**

C. Within ninety (90) days from the conclusion of the Initial Pre–Trial Conference, the parties shall be required to appear in person, if they are proceeding pro se, or by their respective attorneys, for a Final Pre–Trial Conference. Said conference is hereby scheduled before this court on the ___ day of _____, 200 ___, at _____ m. Provided, however, the court shall be permitted schedule the Final Pre–Trial Conference later than ninety (90) days from the date of the Initial Pre–Trial Conference if it determines that additional time is required by the parties to complete the discovery identified at the Initial Pre–Trial Conference or if additional time is required to complete the Guardian-ad-Litem's investigation and report, the custodial evaluations, the real and personal property evaluations and/or mediation, or if the parties intend to attempt counseling and/or reconciliation.

D. That counsel, or party/parties, if pro-se, shall confer in person at a Preliminary Conference at least ten (10) days before the scheduled Final Pre–Trial Conference. The moving party shall undertake the responsibility of arranging the aforementioned conference at a time and location which is mutually agreeable between the parties. In preparation for the Final Pre–Trial Conference, the parties shall address the following issues at their Preliminary Conference:

i. The possibility of reaching an agreement regarding the contested issues;

ii. The possibility of disposing of the cause in summary fashion as to some or all of the issues;

iii. The identification and exchange of exhibits which the parties intend to introduce into evidence at the Final Hearing;

iv. The possibility of stipulating to the authenticity or admissibility of each parties' exhibits to avoid unnecessary delays at the Final Hearing;

v. The exchange of each parties' witness lists, including expert witnesses, and the nature of the testimony that each witness shall be expected to testify to at the Final Hearing;

vi. The preparation of a master list of the parties' real and personal property, which list shall be submitted by the parties to the court as a joint exhibit at the Final Pre–Trial Conference. Said exhibit shall be presented to the court in the following form and shall include all assets of the parties subject to division by the court:

EXAMPLE ASSET FORM

ASSET NUMBER	ASSET NAME	WIFE'S VALUE	HUSBAND'S VALUE	AGREED VALUE	COURT'S VALUE
1	Marital Residence 11 River Drive Valparaiso, IN Titled: Jointly	$150,000.00	$175,000.00		
2	2002 Jeep Cherokee Titled: Jointly			$ 12,500.00	
3	Joint Checking Acct. Bank One Account # 1234	$ 1,500.00	$ 2,500.00		
4	Antique Rocker	$ 500.00	$ 750.00		

vii. The preparation of a master debt list, which shall be submitted by the parties to the court as a joint exhibit at the Final Pre–Trial Conference. Said exhibit shall be presented to the court in the following form:

EXAMPLE DEBT FORM

DEBT NUMBER	ACCOUNT NAME AND NUMBER	DATE OF SEPARATION BALANCE	CURRENT BALANCE
1	SEARS MASTERCARD ACCOUNT # 1234 5678–9876 TITLED: JOINTLY	$5,250.00	$5,210.00

2   MBNA VISA
       ACCOUNT # 9876 5432–0987 $500.00 $475.00
       TITLED: HUSBAND

E. The parties shall be prepared to address the following issues at their Final Pre–Trial Conference:

vi.[1] The status of discovery;

vii. The results of mediation or settlement conference;

viii. Identification of the issues resolved by agreement, together with the terms of said agreement;

ix. Identification of the remaining contested issues;

x. The parties' final witness and exhibit lists, together with stipulations regarding the admissibility of any exhibits;

xi. A brief summary regarding the parties' contentions relative to the contested issues;

xii. The presentation of the parties' joint asset list;

xiii. The presentation of the parties' joint debt list; and

xiv. Anticipated time required to litigate the contested issues.

F. At the conclusion of the Final Pre–Trial Conference, the court shall schedule the cause of action for final hearing, and shall enter additional orders, if required, regarding Pre–Trial motions presented by the parties.

G. Pursuant to Trial Rule 16(K) and Trial Rule 41(E), failure to attend the Initial Pre–Trial Conference or the Final Pre–Trial Conference, may result in the entry of an order of dismissal or default against the party or parties who fail to appear. In addition, the court may impose sanctions against any party or attorney of record who fails to attend the preliminary conference; is unprepared to participate in either the Initial Pre–Trial Conference or Final Pre–Trial Conference, or who refuses, in bad faith, to enter into stipulations regarding the facts, the law, or the exhibits. Said sanctions may include costs associated with rescheduling any of the three conferences identified herein, and attorney fees.

No continuances of the Provisional Hearing, Initial Pre–Trial Conference, Final Pre–Trial Conference, or Final Hearing may be obtained without strict compliance with the provisions outlined in Trial Rule 53.5 and Local Rule 3500. If a continuance is requested and granted, said continuance shall be charged against the party requesting same. The existence of charged continuances, whether or not in good faith, may be considered by the court in its ruling regarding the payment of attorney fees or other costs of the action.

ALL OF WHICH IS FOUND AND RECOMMENDED THIS ___ DAY OF _____, 20 ___.

_____

MAGISTRATE, PORTER SUPERIOR COURT

ALL OF WHICH IS ORDERED, ADJUDGED AND DECREED THIS ___ DAY OF _____, 20 ___.

_____

JUDGE, PORTER SUPERIOR COURT

Adopted Aug. 4, 2007, effective Jan. 1, 2007. Amended effective Jan. 1, 2012; Oct. 1, 2012.

APPENDIX B. FINANCIAL DECLARATION FORM
STATE OF INDIANA: CIRCUIT AND SUPERIOR COURTS
OF PORTER COUNTY

IN RE: THE MARRIAGE OF: Cause No: _____

_____

_____ Petitioner

and

_____
_____ Respondent

In accordance with Local Rule 2200.1 of the Porter Superior Court and Indiana Trial Rules 26, 33, 34, 35 and 37, the undersigned, Petitioner or Respondent, hereby submits the following VERIFIED FINANCIAL DISCLOSURE STATEMENT:

FINANCIAL DECLARATION OF __

I. PRELIMINARY INFORMATION

Husband* _____   Wife* _____
Address: _____   Address: _____
_____   _____

Soc. Sec. No. _____   Soc. Sec. No. _____

Badge/Payroll No: _____   Badge/Payroll No: _____

Occupation: _____   Occupation: _____

Employer _____   Employer: _____
_____   _____
_____   _____

Birth Date: _____   Birth Date: _____

*   Itemize at bottom of page

Date of Marriage: _____
Date of Physical Separation: _____
Date of Filing: _____

Children:
Name _____ Age _____ Dob: _____ SS#: _____
Name _____ Age _____ Dob: _____ SS#: _____
Name _____ Age _____ Dob: _____ SS#: _____
Name _____ Age _____ Dob: _____ SS#: _____

II. HEALTH INSURANCE INFORMATION

Name and Address of health care insurance company: _____ .

_____

_____

Name all persons covered under Plan(s): _____

_____

Weekly cost of total health   Weekly cost of health insurance premium
   insurance premium: _____   for children only: _____
Name of the children's' health care providers: _____

_____

The names of the schools and grade level for each child are: _____

_____

List any extraordinary health care concerns of any family member:

_____

List any educational concerns of any family member: _____
_____

III. INCOME INFORMATION
A. EMPLOYMENT HISTORY

Current employer _____
Address _____
Telephone No: _____ Length of Employment _____

Job Description _____
Gross Income _____ _____ _____ _____
              Per week   bi–weekly   per month   yearly

Net Income _____ _____ _____ _____
              Per week   bi–weekly   per month   yearly

B. EMPLOYMENT HISTORY FOR LAST 5 YEARS

Employer	Dates of employment	Compensation (per wk/mo/ yr)
_____	_____	_____
_____	_____	_____
_____	_____	_____
_____	_____	_____

C. INCOME SUMMARY

1. **GROSS WEEKLY INCOME** from: Salary and wages, including commissions, bonuses, allowances and over–time $ _____

   Note: If paid monthly, determine weekly income by dividing monthly income by 4.3   _____

   Pensions & Retirement   _____

   Social Security   _____

   Disability and unemployment insurance   _____

   Public Assistance (welfare, AFDC payments, etc.)   _____

   Food stamps   _____

   Child support received for any child(ren) not born of the parties to this marriage   _____

   Dividends and Interest   _____

   Rents received   _____
   All other sources (specify)   _____

   TOTAL GROSS WEEKLY INCOME $ _____

2. **ITEMIZED WEEKLY DEDUCTIONS**
   from gross income:

State and Federal Income taxes: _____

Social Security   _____

Medical Insurance
Coverage: Health   (___)
             Dental   (___)
             Eye Care   (___)
             Psychiatric   (___)   _____

Union or other dues: _____

Retirement:
       Pension fund: Mandatory ( ) Optional ( )   _____
       Profit Sharing: Mandatory ( ) Optional ( )   _____
       401(k): Mandatory ( ) Optional ( )   _____
       SEP: Mandatory ( ) Optional ( )   _____
       ESOP: Mandatory ( ) Optional ( )   _____
       IRA: Mandatory ( ) Optional ( )   _____

Child support withheld from pay
       (not including this case)   _____

Garnishments (itemize on separate sheet)   _____

Credit Union debts   _____

Direct Withdrawals Out of Paychecks:
       Car payments   _____
       Life insurance   _____
       Disability insurance   _____
       Thrift plans   _____
       Credit union savings   _____
       Bonds   _____
       Donations   _____

       Other (specify)   _____
Other (Specify):   _____

TOTAL WEEKLY DEDUCTIONS   _____

3.   **WEEKLY DISPOSABLE INCOME**
     (A minus B: Subtract Total Weekly Deductions from Total Weekly Gross
     Income)   _____

IN ALL CASES INVOLVING CHILD SUPPORT: Prepare and attach an Indiana Child Support Guideline Worksheet (with documentation verifying your income); or, supplement with such a Worksheet within ten (10) days of the exchange of this Form.

IV.   **MONTHLY LIVING EXPENSES:**
     House
       1.   Rent(Mortgage)   _____
       2.   2nd Mortgage   _____
       3.   Line of credit   _____
       4.   Gas/Electric   _____
       5.   Telephone   _____
       6.   Water   _____
       7.   Sewer   _____
       8.   Sanitation (garbage)   _____
       9.   Cable   _____
     10.   Satellite   _____

11. Internet   _____
12. Taxes (Real Estate) (If not part of mortgage payment)   _____
13. Insurance(House) (If not part of mortgage payment)   _____
14. Lawn Care/Snow Removal   _____

Groceries
1. Food   _____
2. Toiletries   _____
3. Cleaning Products   _____
4. Paper Products   _____

Clothing
1. Clothes   _____
2. Shoes   _____
3. Uniforms   _____

Health Care
1. Health insurance not deducted from pay   _____
2. Dental insurance not deducted from pay   _____
3. Doctor Visits (non insurance covered)   _____
4. Dental Visits (non insurance covered)   _____
5. Prescription Pharmaceutical (non insurance covered)   _____
6. Over the counter medicine   _____
7. Glasses/contact lenses   _____
8. Other non-insurance covered health care*   _____

Car & Travel
1. Car Payment   _____
2. Gasoline   _____
3. Oil/Maintenance   _____
4. Insurance (Car)   _____
5. Car Wash   _____
6. Tolls   _____
7. Train/Bus   _____
8. Parking Lot Fees   _____
9. License plates   _____

Beauty Care
1. Hair Dresser/Barber   _____
2. Cosmetics   _____

School Needs
1. Lunches   _____
2. Book   _____
3. Tuition/Registration   _____
4. Uniforms   _____
5. School Supplies   _____
6. Extra curricular activities   _____

Infant Care
1. Diapers   _____
2. Baby Food   _____

Miscellaneous
1. Church Donations   _____
2. Charitable Donations   _____
3. Life Insurance   _____
4. Babysitter   _____
5. Newspapers & Magazines   _____
6. Cigarettes   _____
7. Dry Cleaning   _____

    8. Entertainment   _____
    9. Cell phone   _____
  10. Dues/subscriptions   _____
  14. Charge Cards   _____
  15. Other*   _____

Sub–Total of Expenses   _____

Average Weekly Expenses (multiply monthly expenses by 12 and divide by 52)   _____

*Itemize at bottom of page

V. PROVISIONAL ARREARAGE COMPUTATIONS.

If you allege the existence of a child support, maintenance, or other arrearage, attach all records or other exhibits regarding the payment history and compute the child support arrearages.

> You must attach a Child Support Guideline Worksheet to your Financial Declaration Form or one must be exchanged with the opposing party/counsel within 10 days of receipt of the other parties' Financial Declaration Form.

ASSETS

All property is to be listed regardless of whether it is titled in your name only or jointly or if property you own is being held for you in the name of a third party.

VI. PROPERTY

A. MARITAL RESIDENCE

Description:

_____

_____

_____

Location: _____

Date Acquired: _____

Purchase Price: _____ Down Payment: _____

Source of Down Payment:

_____

Current Indebtedness: _____

_____

Monthly Payment: _____

Current Fair Market Value: _____

B. OTHER REAL PROPERTY (Complete B, on a separate sheet of paper for each additional parcel of real estate owned, etc).

Description: _____

_____

_____

Location: _____

Date Acquired: _____

Purchase Price: _____ Down Payment: _____

Source of Down Payment:

_____

Current Indebtedness: _____

Monthly Payment: _____

Current Fair Market Value: _____

C. PERSONAL PROPERTY (motor vehicles, boats, motorcycles, furnishings, household goods, jewelry, firearms, etc. Household furnishings and household goods such as pots and pans need not be itemized.)

Description	Title	Current Value	Indebtedness	Payment	Present User
_____	_____	_____	_____	_____	_____
_____	_____	_____	_____	_____	_____
_____	_____	_____	_____	_____	_____
_____	_____	_____	_____	_____	_____
_____	_____	_____	_____	_____	_____
_____	_____	_____	_____	_____	_____
_____	_____	_____	_____	_____	_____
_____	_____	_____	_____	_____	_____
_____	_____	_____	_____	_____	_____
_____	_____	_____	_____	_____	_____
_____	_____	_____	_____	_____	_____
_____	_____	_____	_____	_____	_____

VII. BANK ACCOUNTS

Name	Type of Account (Checking, Savings, CDs, etc.)	Owner	Account No.	Balance on Date of Filing
_____	_____	_____	_____	_____
_____	_____	_____	_____	_____
_____	_____	_____	_____	_____
_____	_____	_____	_____	_____
_____	_____	_____	_____	_____

VIII NON–RETIREMENT SECURITIES (stocks, bonds, mutual funds, etc.)

Name	Type of account (Money mkt, Stocks, Bonds, Mutual Funds etc.)	Owner	Account No.	Value on date of filing
_____	_____	_____	_____	_____
_____	_____	_____	_____	_____
_____	_____	_____	_____	_____
_____	_____	_____	_____	_____

IX. LIFE INSURANCE POLICIES (whole life, variable life, annuities, term)

Company	Owner	Policy #	Beneficiary	Face Value	Loan Amount	Cash Value
_____	_____	_____	_____	_____	_____	_____
_____	_____	_____	_____	_____	_____	_____
_____	_____	_____	_____	_____	_____	_____
_____	_____	_____	_____	_____	_____	_____

X. RETIREMENT ACCOUNTS (Pension, Profit Sharing, 401(k), SEP, IRA, KEOGH, ESOP, etc).

Company Divorce	Type of Plan	Owner	Account #	Vested (Yes/No)	Value as of Date of Filing

XI. OTHER PROFESSIONAL OR BUSINESS INTERESTS

Name of Business	Type (Corp., Part., Sole Owner)	% Owned	Estimated Value

XII. MARITAL BILLS, DEBTS, AND OBLIGATIONS (list every single bill, debt and obligation regardless of whether the bill is titled in your name, your spouse's name, or jointly. Please include all mortgages, 2nd mortgages, home equity loans, charge cards, other loans, credit union loans, car payments, and unpaid medical bills, etc. Do not include monthly expenses such as utilities that are paid in full every month.)

Creditor	Description	Acct #	Monthly Payment	Balance— Date of Filing	Current Balance
Example(s):					
1st National Bank	Mortgage	87612368459	$1,530.00	$145,680.00	$145,100.00
Visa	Misc household expenses	14567865349	$300.00	$3,500.00	$3,250.00

XIII. RECAPITULATION. A summary of the marital estate is as follows:

Asset	In Name of Husband	In Name of Wife	Jointly Held	Total
Family Dwelling				
Other Real Estate				
Personal Property				
Bank Accounts				
Non–Retirement Securities				
Life Insurance Policies				
Retirement Accounts				
Other Professional/Business Interests				
Total Assets				
Liabilities				

General Creditors   _____   _____   _____   _____

Mortgage on Family Dwell-
  ing   _____   _____   _____   _____

Mortgages on other real estate   _____   _____   _____   _____

Notes to Banks and Others   _____   _____   _____   _____

Loans on Insurance Policies   _____   _____   _____   _____

Other Liabilities   _____   _____   _____   _____

    Total Liabilities   _____   _____   _____   _____

**ASSETS MINUS
LIABILITIES**   _____   _____   _____   _____

XIV. PERSONAL STATEMENT REGARDING DIVISION OF PROPERTY

Indiana law presumes that the marital property be split on a 50/50 basis. However, the Judge may order a division which may differ from an exact 50/50 division of your property. Please provide a brief statement as to your reasons, if there be any, why the Court should divide your property on anything other than a 50/50 basis.

_____

_____

_____

_____

XV. MANDATORY EXHIBITS

The following exhibits must be attached to your Financial Declaration Form:

1. The last three years of Individual State and Federal income tax returns together with all W–2 forms, 1099 forms and K–1 forms.

2. The immediate preceding six paycheck stubs showing year-to-date earnings.

3. Documents showing the amount of income received from any other source in the past three years including irregular income in an amount greater than $500 per year plus any expenses relating thereto.

4. Child support worksheet, if applicable.

5. Arrearage calculation, if applicable under V of this Financial Declaration Form.

6. With regard to all real estate listed under VI (A) and (B):

   a. The title insurance policy, if available,

   b. The deed,

   c. An amortization schedule from the lending institution, if available,

   d. Documents showing the mortgage balance as of the date of the filing of the Petition for Dissolution of Marriage,

7. As to all bank accounts identified in VII of this Financial Declaration Form:

   a. Copy of the bank statement closest to the date of the filing of the petition for Dissolution of Marriage, and

b. Copies of the bank statements for the five months immediately preceding the filing of the Petition for Dissolution of Marriage.

8. As to all Non-retirement Securities identified in VIII of this Financial Declaration Form:

a. Copy of the statement closest to the date of the filing of the petition for Dissolution of Marriage, and

b. Copies of the statements for the five months immediately preceding the filing of the Petition for Dissolution of Marriage.

9. As to all Life Insurance policies identified in IX of this Financial Declaration Form attach statements as of cash value as of the date of the filing of the Petition for Dissolution of Marriage.

10. As to all Retirement Accounts identified in X of this Financial Declaration Form attach statements showing the value of the account as of the date of the filing of the Petition for Dissolution of Marriage and for the preceding five months, if such statements are available, except for pension accounts and other defined benefit plans, in which event attach a statement from the employer describing the benefits.

11. As to all marital bills, debts and obligations identified in XII of this Financial Declaration Form, attach a statement showing the amount of each bill, debt and obligation as of the date of the filing of the divorce and for the immediately preceding five months.

XV. VERIFICATION

I declare, under the pains and penalty of perjury, that the foregoing, including statements of my income, expenses, assets and liabilities, are true and correct to the best of my knowledge and that I have made a complete and absolute disclosure of all sources of income, all assets, and all liabilities. If it is proven to the Court that I have intentionally failed to disclose all of my income, any asset, or liability, I may lose the asset and may be required to pay the liability.

Further, this Financial Declaration Form is considered as a Request for Admissions to the recipient under Trial Rule 35 and should the recipient fail to fully prepare and exchange this statement then the Court may prohibit the party who did not properly complete the Financial Declaration Form from introducing any evidence at any hearing to contradict the evidence of the other party on the issues of income, expenses, assets and liabilities.

Date: _____   _____
                                    Signature

XVI. ATTORNEY'S CERTIFICATION

I have reviewed with my client the foregoing information, including any valuations and attachments, and sign this certificate consistent with my obligation under Trial Rule 11 of the Indiana Rules of Procedure.

Date: _____   _____
                                    Attorney for the _____
                                    15 N. Washington Street
                                    Valparaiso, IN 46383
                                    219/464-3246

Adopted Aug. 4, 2007, effective Jan. 1, 2007. Amended effective Jan. 1, 2012; Oct. 1, 2012; Jan. 1, 2013.

APPENDIX C.   FINANCIAL DECLARATION FORM
STATE OF INDIANA: CIRCUIT AND SUPERIOR COURTS OF
PORTER COUNTY
(PATERNITY SHORT FORM)

IN RE: THE PATERNITY OF: CAUSE NO: _____

_____
          Petitioner

and

_____
          Respondent

In accordance with Local Rule 2200.1 of the Porter Superior Court and Indiana Trial Rules 26, 33, 34, 35 and 37, the undersigned, Petitioner or Respondent, hereby submits the following VERIFIED FINANCIAL DISCLOSURE STATEMENT:

FINANCIAL DECLARATION OF _____

I.   PRELIMINARY INFORMATION

Mother _____   Father _____
Address: _____   Address: _____
          _____   _____

Soc. Sec. No. _____   Soc. Sec. No. _____

Occupation: _____   Occupation: _____

Employer: _____   Employer: _____
          _____   _____
          _____   _____

Birth Date: _____   Birth Date: _____

Children of this action:
  Name _____ Age ____ DOB: ____ SSN: ____
  Name _____ Age ____ DOB: ____ SSN: ____
  Name _____ Age ____ DOB: ____ SSN: ____
  Name _____ Age ____ DOB: ____ SSN: ____

  For each child:

Attached copy of birth certificate: Yes   No
Attached copy of signed paternity affidavit Yes   No

  Date of filing Petition: _____
  Your other children not subject to this proceeding:

Name _____   Date of Birth _____   SSN: _____
     Lives with you: Yes No   Receives Support: Yes No   Amount of Support _____
                                Pays Support: Yes No   Amount of Support _____
Name _____   Date of Birth _____   SSN: _____
     Lives with you: Yes No   Receives Support: Yes No   Amount of Support _____
                                Pays Support: Yes No   Amount of Support _____
Name _____   Date of Birth _____   SSN: _____
     Lives with you: Yes No   Receives Support: Yes No   Amount of Support _____
                                Pays Support: Yes No   Amount of Support _____
Name _____   Date of Birth _____   SSN: _____
     Lives with you: Yes No   Receives Support: Yes No   Amount of Support _____
                                Pays Support: Yes No   Amount of Support _____

II. INCOME INFORMATION

A. EMPLOYMENT HISTORY

Current employer: _____

Address: _____

Telephone No: _____ Length of employment: _____

Job description: _____

Gross Income _____ _____ _____ _____

               Per week   Bi–weekly   Per month   Yearly

B. EMPLOYMENT HISTORY FOR LAST 5 YEARS

(Attach additional sheet if necessary)

Employer	Dates of employment	Compensation (per wk/mo/ yr)
_____	_____	_____
_____	_____	_____
_____	_____	_____
_____	_____	_____

C. INCOME SUMMARY

L.[1] GROSS WEEKLY INCOME FROM: Salary and wages, including commissions, bonuses, allowances and over-time $ _____

Note: If paid monthly, determine weekly income by dividing monthly income by 4.3   _____

Pensions & Retirement   _____

Social Security   _____

Disability and unemployment insurance   _____

Public Assistance (welfare, AFDC payments etc.)   _____

Food stamps   _____

Child support received for any child(ren) not subject to this action   _____

Dividends and Interest   _____

Rents received   _____

Income from present spouse/relationship   _____

All other sources (specify)   _____

TOTAL GROSS WEEKLY INCOME $ _____

ATTACH COPIES OF:
    Last two Federal and State Income Tax Returns
    Five of your most recent payroll stubs

[1]So in original.

III. HEALTH INSURANCE INFORMATION

Name and address of health care insurance company: _____

_____

Name all persons covered under Plan(s): _____

Weekly cost of total health insur-   Weekly cost of health insurance premium for
ance premium: _____   children only: _____

IV. MONTHLY BUDGET OF EXPENSES

		Yourself	**Children**
A.	**HOUSING**		
1.	Rent		
2.	Mortgage–principal & interest		
3.	Second Mortgage		
4.	Lot rent		
5.	Home insurance		
6.	Other (itemize) _____		
	Sub-total		
B.	**UTILITIES**		
A.	Electricity		
B.	Gas/heating Oil		
C.	Telephone		
D.	Water		
E.	Other (itemize) _____		
	Sub-total		
C.	**HOUSEHOLD MAINTENANCE**		
1.	Repairs (normal/on–going)		
2.	Cable TV		
3.	Child Support withheld from pay		
4.	Garnishments		
5.	Credit cards		
6.	Legal fines/costs		
7.	Other (itemize) _____		
	Sub–total		
D.	**OTHER EXPENSES**		
1.	Food		
2.	Clothing		
3.	Transportation		
4.	Health/medical/dental		
5.	Childcare/daycare		
6.	Personal/entertainment		
E.	**ALL OTHER EXPENSES**		

V. PROVISIONAL ARREARAGE COMPUTATIONS.

If you allege the existence of a child support, birthing expenses, past medical bills, daycare expenses, maintenance, or other arrearage, attach all records or other exhibits regarding the payment history and compute the child support arrearages.

You must attach a Child Support guideline Worksheet to your Financial Declaration From or one must be exchanged with the opposing party/counsel within 10 days of receipt of the other parties' Financial Declaration Form.

VI. VERIFICATION

I declare, under the penalties of perjury, that the foregoing, including any valuations and attachments, is true and correct and that I have made a complete and absolute disclosure of all my assets and liabilities. Furthermore, I understand that if, in the future, it is proved to this Court that I have intentionally failed to disclose any asset or liability, I may lose the asset and be required to pay the liability. Finally, I acknowledge that sanctions may be imposed against me, including reasonable attorney's fees and expenses incurred in the investigation, preparation and prosecution of any claim or action that proves my failure to disclose assets or liabilities.

Date: _____   _____

                                    PARTY'S SIGNATURE

VII. ATTORNEY CERTIFICATION

I have reviewed with my client, the foregoing information, including any valuations and attachments, and have signed this certification with my obligation under Trial Rule Eleven (11) of the Indiana Rules of Procedure.

Date: _____   _____

                                    ATTORNEY'S SIGNATURE

Adopted Aug. 4, 2007, effective Jan. 1, 2007. Amended effective Jan. 1, 2012; Oct. 1, 2012.

APPENDIX D.   APPOINTMENT OF GUARDIAN AD LITEM

STATE OF INDIANA	)	PORTER SUPERIOR COURT
	) SS:	Sitting in Valparaiso, Indiana
COUNTY OF PORTER	)	CONTINUOUS TERM 20 ___

IN RE THE MARRIAGE/PATERNITY OF:)
)
, Petitioner   )   CAUSE # _____
v   )
, Respondent   )

APPOINTMENT OF GUARDIAN AD LITEM

The Court now appoints _____ as Guardian ad Litem for the minor child(ren) of the parties, and Finds, Recommends, and Orders as follows:

1. That the GAL is appointed, pursuant to I.C. 31–15–6–1, et seq., and/or other appropriate section(s) of the Indiana Code and/or Local Rules, for the following minor children of the parties:

_____   _____
name   date of birth

_____   _____
name   date of birth

_____   _____
name   date of birth

2. That this appointment of the GAL shall become effective upon payment to the GAL of the required monetary retainer and the GAL's acceptance of the same. The issue of the retainer payment to the GAL shall be set for a review hearing within ___ days. Attorney for _____ shall coordinate such hearing date and assure that the same occurs if the GAL has not been paid in a timely manner.

Said monetary retainer shall be in the amount of $ _____. The GAL is hereby authorized to bill the parties for services rendered at the GAL's usual rate, with the understanding that said usual rate may be reduced to the county's service rate if any remainder of the GAL's bill is later submitted to Porter County for payment.

The Petitioner shall pay $ _____ toward such retainer.

The Respondent shall pay $ _____ toward such retainer.

The retainer payments shall be made within ___ days of this Order.

Further, as to future billings by the GAL, the parties will divide obligations for the same with Petitioner paying ___ % and Respondent paying ___ % of such obligations. Payment of such obligations shall be timely made. All retainer and obligations and/or payments to the GAL are subject to reallocation and/or further order of the Court.

3. That the GAL is appointed to provide the following services in this cause, with the understanding that the Court, GAL, or the parties may reasonably expand the scope of such services upon further motion, order, and/or inquiry:

{check all that apply)

___ Parenting Time/Visitation Issues

___ Child's health issues

___ Custodial Recommendation

___ Elicit child's opinion relevant to pending litigation

___ Review of home environment(s)

___ Other: _____

4. That the parties are hereby directed to provide to the GAL, within ten (10) days of the payment of the retainer, a written summary of their position on the issues pending before this court, and their requests of the GAL.

The GAL shall conduct a timely investigation of the issues the GAL deems relevant to the best interests of the child(ren).

5. That the Parties shall advise the GAL of their current residence and telephone number, as well as the residence and school (if any) of the child(ren).

6. That upon the presentation of this Order to any agency, hospital, organization, school, person, or office, including the Department of Public Welfare and mental health agencies, physicians, psychiatrists, or police departments, the aforementioned shall permit the Guardian Ad Litem to inspect and/or copy any records, reports, x-rays, photographs or other matters relevant to this case and the child that is the subject of this dissolution, custody and/or visitation proceeding. Further, the aforementioned Guardian Ad Litem may obtain any reports or examine said reports without the consent of the child(ren), his/her parents, or any other person responsible for the child's (children's) welfare;

The custodial parent(s) shall assure that the GAL is granted access to all such persons and entities and, as needed, shall sign any release necessary to facilitate the same.

7. That the Parties do hereby acknowledge that, although the GAL-child relationship is not technically an attorney-client relationship under the statute, the parties do wish to encourage the child to have open and complete discourse with the GAL. Therefore, the Guardian ad Litem assigned to this case may, at the GAL's discretion, maintain any and all information received from the child as confidential and choose not disclose same except in reports to the Court, as ordered by the Court, and/or to any party in this case;

If the GAL believes that an attorney-client relationship has been created between the child and the GAL at any time, the GAL shall promptly notify the court and the parties and set a status hearing relevant to the same;

8. That the Guardian ad Litem shall appear at all Hearings or proceedings scheduled in this case and assure proper representation for the child(ren) at said Hearings;

9. That the Guardian Ad Litem is now considered a party to this action and shall therefore be notified of any hearings, staffings, investigations, depositions, and/or other proceedings in this cause and shall be notified properly as to any action taken on behalf of the child(ren) by any party.

The scheduling of hearings requiring the GAL to be present shall be coordinated with the GAL.

Although the GAL shall be notified of all hearings, the appearance of the GAL may be waived if the issues relevant to such hearing do not reasonably involve the children.

10. That the GAL shall submit a written report to the Court no later than ten (10) days prior to any final hearing on issues, as set forth above, relevant to the children.

If such report is not submitted timely, the parties do hereby agree that there shall not be an automatic continuance of a hearing granted to either party relevant to such late report, and any party requesting such continuance shall provide notice thereof to the Court and the GAL and allow the GAL two business days to complete and submit such report. Ultimately, the Court shall have discretion to rule on the reasonableness of any continuance request.

ALL OF WHICH IS FOUND AND RECOMMENDED this ___ day of _____, 20 _____.

_____

Magistrate, Porter Superior Court

The Court having reviewed the findings and recommendations of Its Magistrate now approves and ratifies the same and adopts the same as the Order of this Court on this, the ___ day of _____, 20 ___.

SO ORDERED.

_____

Judge, Porter Superior Court

Adopted Aug. 4, 2007, effective Jan. 1, 2007. Amended effective Jan. 1, 2012; Oct. 1, 2012; Jan. 1, 2013.

APPENDIX E.   APPEARANCE FORM (CIVIL)

IN THE PORTER CIRCUIT COURT IN THE PORTER SUPERIOR COURT
APPEARANCE FORM (CIVIL)
Initiating Party

(Caption)

)
)
)   **CAUSE NUMBER:** _____

1. _____ Name of first initiating party (must include date of birth and social security number in **DR, PO, AD, GU cases)** (Supply names of additional initiating parties on continuation page.)

2. Attorney information (as applicable for service of process):

    Name: _____   Atty. Number: _____
    Address: _____   Phone: _____
    _____   Fax: _____
    _____   Computer Add: _____

    (Supply information for additional attorneys on continuation page.)

3. Case Type requested: _____
4. Will accept Fax service Yes ___ No _____
5. For all occupants of the initiating party's residence as well as any child/ren of either the petitioner or the respondent, supply the names, dates of birth and social security numbers in proceedings involving **dissolution of marriage, child custody, child support, child visitation, juvenile delinquency, CHINS, paternity, termination of parental rights, adoptions, guardianship, mental health issues, and protective orders.**

Name: _____ D.O.B. _____ SS#: _____
Name: _____ D.O.B. _____ SS#: _____
Name: _____ D.O.B. _____ SS#: _____
Name: _____ D.O.B. _____ SS#: _____
(SUPPLY ABOVE INFORMATION FOR ADDITIONAL PERSONS ON A CONTINUATION PAGE)

6. Are there now or have there been within the last twelve months pending related cases? Yes ___ No ___ If yes, list case and cause number below:

IF THE ANSWER IS YES, FILE AN <u>ADDITIONAL</u> COPY OF THE APPEARANCE FORM
(The Court has determined that the following types of matters constitute cases that are related when a named party and family or household member(s) have matters pending of the following types: **CM, or DF filings involving domestic violence or family violence related charges and/or substance abuse charges, and all cases of the following types: JM, JS, JP, JT, JD, JC, DR, GU, MH, PO and AD).**
If the caption has a name other than that of the petitioner, please describe the relationship.

Caption _____ Cause Number _____
Relationship _____

Caption _____ Cause Number _____
Relationship _____

Caption _____ Cause Number _____
Relationship _____

(Supply information for additional related cases on continuation page.)

7. Additional information required by state or local rule:
_____
_____

     Attorney at Law
     Attorney Information

PURSUANT TO TRIAL RULE 3(E), THIS APPEARANCE FORM SHALL BE UPDATED PROMPTLY SHOULD THERE BE ANY CHANGE IN OR SUPPLEMENT TO THE INFORMATION PREVIOUSLY SUPPLIED TO THE COURT

APPEARANCE FORM (CIVIL)—INTERVENING PARTY

Continuation Page

Cause Number _____

Continuation of Item 1 (Names, addresses and phone numbers of intervening parties):

Name: _____ Phone: _____
Address: _____
_____

Name: _____ Phone: _____
Address: _____
_____

Supply information for additional intervening parties.

Continuation of Item 2 (Attorney information, as applicable for service of process)

Name: _____ Atty. No: _____

Address: _____ Phone: _____

_____ Fax: _____

_____ Computer Add: _____

Authority: Pursuant to Trial Rule 3.1(C), this form shall be filed upon the first appearance in the case. In emergencies, the requested information shall be supplied when it becomes available. Parties shall advise the court of change in information previously provided to the court. This format is approved by the Division of State Court Administration. Use additional continuation pages if needed.

Adopted Aug. 4, 2007, effective Jan. 1, 2007. Amended effective Jan. 1, 2012; Oct. 1, 2012.

APPENDIX F.   APPEARANCE FORM (CIVIL)
IN THE PORTER CIRCUIT COURT IN
THE PORTER SUPERIOR COURT
APPEARANCE FORM (CIVIL)
Responding Party

(Caption)

)
)
) **CAUSE NUMBER:** _____

1. _____

   Name of first responding party (must include date of birth and social security number in **DR, PO, AD, GU cases**)

   (Supply names of additional responding parties on continuation page.)

2. Attorney information (as applicable for service of process):

   Name: _____ Atty. Number: _____

   Address: _____ Phone: _____

   _____ Fax: _____

   _____ Computer Add: _____

   (Supply information for additional attorneys on continuation page.)

3. Case Type requested: _____ 4. Will accept Fax service Yes ___ No ___

5. For all occupants of the responding party's residence as well as any child/ren of either the petitioner or the respondent, supply the names, dates of birth and social security numbers in proceedings involving **dissolution of marriage, child custody, child support, child visitation, juvenile delinquency, CHINS, paternity, termination of parental rights, adoptions, guardianship, mental health issues, and protective orders.**

   Name: _____ D.O.B. _____ SS#: _____

   Name: _____ D.O.B. _____ SS#: _____

   Name: _____ D.O.B. _____ SS#: _____

   Name: _____ D.O.B. _____ SS#: _____

   (SUPPLY ABOVE INFORMATION FOR ADDITIONAL PERSONS ON A CONTINUATION PAGE)

6. Are there now or have there been within the last twelve months pending related cases? Yes ___ No ___ If yes, list case and cause number below:

IF THE ANSWER IS YES, FILE AN <u>ADDITIONAL</u> COPY OF THE APPEARANCE FORM

(The Court has determined that the following types of matters constitute cases that are related when a named party and family or household member(s) have matters pending of the following types: **CM, or DF filings involving domestic violence or family violence related charges and/or substance abuse charges, and all cases of the following types: JM, JS, JP, JT, JD, JC, DR, GU, MH, PO and AD**).

If the caption has a name other than that of the respondent, please describe the relationship.

Caption _____ Cause Number _____
Relationship _____

Caption _____ Cause Number _____
Relationship _____

Caption _____ Cause Number _____
Relationship _____

(Supply information for additional related cases on continuation page.)

7. Additional information required by state or local rule:
_____
_____
_____

_____
Attorney at Law
Attorney Information

PURSUANT TO TRIAL RULE 3(E), THIS APPEARANCE FORM SHALL BE UPDATED PROMPTLY SHOULD THERE BE ANY CHANGE IN OR SUPPLEMENT TO THE INFORMATION PREVIOUSLY SUPPLIED TO THE COURT.
APPEARANCE FORM (CIVIL)—INTERVENING PARTY
Continuation Page

Cause Number _____
Continuation of Item 1 (Names, addresses and phone numbers of intervening parties):
Name: _____ Phone: _____
Address: _____
_____

Name: _____ Phone: _____
Address: _____
_____

Supply information for additional intervening parties.
Continuation of Item 2 (Attorney information, as applicable for service of process)
Name: _____ Atty. No: _____
Address: _____ Phone: _____
_____ Fax: _____
_____ Computer Add: _____

Authority: Pursuant to Trial Rule 3.1(C), this form shall be filed upon the first appearance in the case. In emergencies, the requested information shall be supplied when it becomes available. Parties shall advise the court of change in information previously provided to the court. This format is approved by the Division of State Court Administration. Use additional continuation pages if needed.

Adopted Aug. 4, 2007, effective Jan. 1, 2007. Amended effective Jan. 1, 2012; Oct. 1, 2012; Jan. 1, 2013; Aug. 9, 2013.

PORTER COUNTY LOCAL CIVIL RULES

Adopted August 4, 2006, Effective January 1, 2007

Including Amendments Received Through November 1, 2013

Research Notes

These rules may be searched electronically on Westlaw *in the* IN-RULES *database; updates to these rules may be found on Westlaw in* IN-RULESUPDATES. *For search tips and a summary of database content, consult the Westlaw Scope Screens for each database.*

LR64–ARO1 Rule 3000.   CASE ASSIGNMENT

3000.10 Case Type Categories PL, CT, and MF. The Clerk of the Court shall maintain an opaque container in which three black marbles, three white marbles, and three green marbles shall be placed. When a party wishes to file a new action of the case type category PL, CT, or MF, the deputy clerk receiving the filing after the costs have been paid, shall as the last function to complete the case filing, remove one marble from the opaque container without being able to see into said container. If the marble chosen is black, the case shall be filed and assigned to Superior Court #1 and shall be given a cause number beginning with 64D01. If the marble chosen is white, the case shall be filed and assigned to Superior Court #2 and shall be given a cause number beginning with 64D02. If the marble chosen is green, the case shall be filed and assigned to Circuit Court acting as Superior Court #5 and shall be given a cause number beginning with 64D05.

3000.20 The marble chosen shall be placed in an opaque container separate from the one from which it was drawn. Subsequent cases to be filed shall be assigned by the same process. Once all nine (9) marbles have been removed from the original opaque container, they shall again be placed in the original container and the same process repeated for assignment of subsequent cases.

3000.30 Case Type Category CC filings are to be assigned in increments of twenty (20) cases per Superior Division Courtroom beginning with filings for 64D01, thereafter 64D02, thereafter 64D05 and subsequently reverting to the same order.

3000.40 Case Type Categories DR, RS, ES, EU, GU, and TR. The Clerk shall maintain a second opaque container containing three marbles of one color (black) and three of a different color (white), for a total of six marbles. When a party files a new action in case type categories DR, RS, ES, EU, GU and TR in the Superior Division of the Court, the deputy clerk receiving the filing, after costs have been paid, shall as the last function to complete the case filing, remove one marble from the second opaque container without being able to see in the container. If the marble chosen is black, the case shall be assigned to Magistrate—Court I and shall be given a cause number beginning with 64D01. If the marble pulled is white, the case shall be assigned to Magistrate—Court II and shall be given a cause number beginning with 64D02. Marbles pulled for case assignment, once pulled, shall be set aside until the jar is emptied of the six marbles. The six marbles shall then be returned to the jar to start again.

3000.50 In the event the filing of cases pursuant to paragraphs 3000.10 and 3000.4 of this rule shall result in a disparity of civil filings reflected by the Quarterly Case Status Report (QCSR), the judges of the Superior Division may jointly direct the Clerk of the Court to assign case filings so as to eliminate the disparity.

3000.60 Case Type Categories MH, AD, PO, or MI. When a party wishes to file a new action of the case type categories MH, AD PO, or MI: (non-domestic relations matters), they may file it with any judge of the Court who is available. Petitions for the Issuance of a Hardship License must be filed in the Court that ordered the driver's license suspension entered if that Court is located in Porter County. A petition for relief filed pursuant to IC 35–38–9 must be filed in the Court that entered the conviction or conviction being addressed.

3000.70 Any domestic relations related matter that is required to be filed with the MI case designation is governed by Local Rule 3000.40.

3000.80 Venue Cases and Filings by Mail. For cases venued into Porter County and cases filed by mail, the Clerk shall act on behalf of the parties for purposes of case assignment procedure.

3000.90 Judicial Action before Filing. If a case being filed requires some action by a judge before filing, e.g., waiver of filing fees, the party filing the action must go to the Clerk's Office to determine case assignment before taking the case to the Judge. In such cases, no cause number will be assigned until the parties return to the Clerk after action by the Judge.

3000.100 Selection of Special Judges under Trial Rule 79(H). In case type categories CT, MH, AD, PO, MI, PL, CC, and MF, and any other civil case type designations as may hereafter be required to be reported on the Quarterly Case Status Report (QCSR), if the cause number of the case in which a special judge needs to be appointed under this section begins with 64D01, the judge of Porter Superior Court #3 shall be appointed special judge. If the cause number of the case begins with 64D02, the judge of Porter Superior Court #4 will be appointed special judge. If the cause number begins with 64D03, the judge of Porter Superior Court #1 will be appointed. If the cause number begins with 64D04, the judge of Porter Superior Court #2 will be appointed. If the cause number begins with 64D05 or 64C01, the judge of Porter Superior Court #6 will be appointed. If the cause number begins with 64D06, the judge of Porter Circuit Court, sitting as Superior Court #5 will be appointed.

3000.110 In case type categories DR, RS, ES, EU, GU and TR, and any other domestic relations or estate related civil case designations as may hereafter be required to be reported on the Quarterly Case Status Report (QCSR), if the cause number of the case in which a special judge needs to be appointed begins with 64D01, 64D03, 64D05 or 64C01, Porter County Magistrate #2 shall be appointed as special judge. If the cause number of the case begins with 64D02, 64D04 or 64D06, then Porter County Magistrate #1 shall be appointed as special judge.

Adopted Aug. 4, 2006, effective Jan. 1, 2007. Amended effective Jan. 1, 2012; Oct. 1, 2012; Aug. 9, 2013.

LR64–TR03 Rule 3100. WITHDRAWAL OF APPEARANCE

3100.10 Procedure. All withdrawals of appearances shall be in writing and by leave of Court. Permission to withdraw shall be given only after the withdrawing attorney has given the attorney's client ten (10) days written notice of the attorney's intention to withdraw and has filed a copy of such with the Court. The Court will not grant a request for withdrawal of appearance unless the same has been filed with the Court not less than 30 days prior to any scheduled hearing, except for good cause shown as determined by the Court.

(1) A withdrawal of appearance when accompanied by the appearance of other counsel shall constitute a waiver of the requirements of this Rule.

(2) All withdrawals of appearance shall comply fully with the provisions of Rules of Professional Conduct, Rule 1.16.

3100.20 Contents of Notice. The letter of withdrawal shall explain to the client that failure to secure new counsel may result in dismissal of the client's case or a default judgment may be entered against the client, whichever is appropriate, and other pertinent information such as any scheduled hearing date or trial date.

Adopted Aug. 4, 2006, effective Jan. 1, 2007. Amended effective Jan. 1, 2012; Oct. 1, 2012.

LR64–TR03 Rule 3200. PREPARATION OF FILINGS

3200.10 As used in these rules, the word "filing" shall mean and include pleadings, motions, and any other papers filed with the Court by any party to any cause. All filings shall be prepared in accordance with the provisions of the Indiana Rules of Trial Procedure. For the purpose of uniformity and convenience, the following requirements shall also be observed.

3200.20 Production and Form. Filings may be either printed or typewritten on white, 8-1/2″ × 11″ paper, with lines double spaced except for quotations, which shall be indented and single spaced and printed on one side only. Copies of filings shall likewise be printed on white paper. Legal-size paper is not permitted. Legible handwritten filings may be accepted in the discretion of the Court.

3200.30 Caption. Every filing shall contain a caption setting forth the name of the Court, the title of the action and the file or cause number. A space two inches (2″) square shall be left open for purposes of file marking each filing.

3200.40 Title. Titles on all filings shall delineate each topic included in the filing, e.g. where a filing contains an Answer, a Motion to Strike or Dismiss, and a Jury Request each shall be set forth in the title.

3200.50 Margins and Bindings. Margins shall be one inch (1″) on all four sides of the printed document. Binding or stapling shall be at the top left hand side and at no other place. Covers or backing shall not be used.

3200.60 Signature. All filings shall contain the signature of the attorney in written and typed form, the attorney's address, attorney number, telephone number, FAX number, computer address, and a designation of the party for whom the attorney appears. The following form is recommended:

_____ Jamie Doe
Indiana Attorney Number: 1234–56
Doe, Roe and Poe
Suite 1000, Blackacre Building
Valparaiso, IN 46383
Telephone #: (219) 464–1000
Fax number#: (219) 464–1001
Computer address
Attorney for Plaintiff

3200.70 Neither typewritten signatures nor facsimile signatures shall be accepted on original documents. Facsimile signatures are permitted on copies.

Adopted Aug. 4, 2006, effective Jan. 1, 2007. Amended effective Jan. 1, 2012; Oct. 1, 2012.

LR64–TR05 Rule 3300. MOTIONS

3300.10 Notice. When a motion requires notice, the serving of the copy of the motion upon the other parties in the cause shall constitute notice of filing same. If the motion requires a hearing or oral argument, the Court shall set the time and place of hearing or argument on the motion.

3300.20 Setting Motions for Hearing. Except for motions to correct error or those described in section D of this Rule, all motions shall be set for hearing at the time of their filing. It shall be the responsibility of the movant or the movant's attorney to secure the date of such hearing from the Court personnel who maintain the calendar for each of the Judges or Magistrates. It shall also be the responsibility of the movant to coordinate the hearing date with all opposing counsel.

3300.30 Motions to Correct Error. Any party may request a hearing upon a motion to correct error by filing a written request therefore by separate instrument at any time before the Court has ruled upon such motion. It shall be discretionary with the Judge before whom the cause is pending whether a hearing shall be held on such motion to correct error.

3300.40 Motions Not Likely to Require Hearing. At the time of filing, a moving party shall bring the following motions to the attention of the Judge assigned:

(1) Motion for Enlargement of Time;

(2) Motion to Reconsider;

(3) Motion for Change of Venue from County;

(4) Motion for Change of Judge;

(5) Motion to Dismiss Complaint by Plaintiff when no Answer has been filed;

(6) Motion to Dismiss Counterclaim by Defendant when no reply has been filed;

(7) Trial Rule 37 (A) Motions to Compel Responses to Interrogatories (pursuant to T.R. 33), or to Requests for Production (pursuant to T.R. 34).

3300.50 Such motions shall be summarily granted or denied ex parte unless the Judge, in the Judge's discretion, determines that a hearing should be scheduled on any such motion and schedules a hearing.

3300.60 Oral Arguments on Motions and Other Pleadings. When an oral argument is requested, the request shall be made by separate instrument and filed with the pleading to be argued. Any such oral argument requested may be heard only at the discretion of the Court, except on Motions for Summary Judgment or Motions to Dismiss pursuant to T.R. 41(E), which cannot be granted without hearing.

3300.70 Enlargement of Time. An initial written motion for enlargement of time pursuant to T.R. 6(B)(1) to respond to a claim shall be automatically allowed for an additional thirty (30) days from the original due date with a written order of the Court. Any motion filed pursuant to this Rule shall state the date when such response is due and the date to which time is enlarged. The motion must be filed on or before the original due date or this Rule is inapplicable. All subsequent motions shall be so designated and will be granted only for good cause shown.

3300.80 Briefs and Memoranda Regarding Motions. Any brief or memorandum in support of any motion shall accompany or be filed simultaneous with the motion, and a copy shall be promptly served upon the opposing party. If the opposing party desires to file a brief or memorandum, that party must do so within ten (10) days of service of the movant's brief or memorandum. If the moving party desires to file a reply brief or memorandum, that party must do so within five (5) days of service of the response, brief or memorandum.

3300.90 Motions to Strike or to Insert New Matter. Subject to T.R. 12(F) every motion to insert new matter or to strike out any part of any pleading in a cause shall be made in writing and shall set forth verbatim each set of words to be inserted or stricken. Each set of words to be inserted or stricken shall be designated in a separate specification, numbered consecutively.

3300.100 Motion to Reconsider Rulings. A motion to reconsider a ruling of the Court on any motion must be in writing and must be served personally upon the ruling Judge. A motion to reconsider must be filed within fifteen (15) days of the ruling said motion addresses.

3300.110 Motions to Compel Discovery. Upon application of any party who has served a request for discovery pursuant to T.R. 33 or T.R. 34, the Court shall, if it finds that the party to whom the interrogatories or request were directed has not responded within the time allowed, and that the moving party has complied with Trial Rule 26(F), order the nonresponding party to respond within a period of time not less than ten (10) days after entry of the Court's order. The Court may, upon written request and for good cause shown, shorten or extend such time as it deems appropriate.

3300.120 Responsibility for Notice. It shall be the responsibility of the movant to give notice to opposing parties of all hearings scheduled on motions.

3300.130 Telephone Argument. The Court, on its own motion or at a party's request, may direct argument of any motion by telephone conference. At the conclusion thereof, the Court may announce its order orally or may take the matter under advisement; but in either event, any order issued thereon shall be reduced to writing and a copy sent to the parties. The Court may further direct which party shall arrange and pay for the cost of the telephone calls.

Adopted Aug. 4, 2006, effective Jan. 1, 2007. Amended effective Jan. 1, 2012; Oct. 1, 2012.

LR64–AR00 Rule 3400. FILING PROCEDURE

3400.10 Required Number of Orders and Briefs. All orders submitted to the Court shall be accompanied by a sufficient number of copies and the same number of postage paid addressed envelopes, so that a copy may be mailed to each party or counsel of record. The original and one copy of all orders shall be retained by the Clerk.

3400.20 Flat Filing. The files of the Court shall be kept under the "flat-filing" system. All pleadings, documents and papers presented for filing to the Clerk shall be flat, unfolded, arranged in chronological order and affixed in flat file folders by standard prong fasteners.

3400.30 Court Files. No court file nor any part thereof may be removed from the custody of the Court or Clerk by any person, including any attorney, except upon authorization by a Judge of the Court and then only upon such terms and conditions as may be provided by the Judge, one unalterable and invariable condition to be the written acknowledgment of such person that they have such file in their personal possession.

3400.40 Entry Form. Every filing subsequent to the original complaint, shall be accompanied by an entry form, in duplicate, which shall contain the title and number of the case, the date, and the exact entry to appear on the Chronological Case Summary. The entry form shall be typewritten or legibly printed, and shall be signed by counsel. Hearing dates on filings requiring Court action shall be obtained from the Judge's staff. Hearing dates shall be inserted on the entry at the time of filing. All entries will be examined and approved by the Judge to whom the case is assigned, or by any other sitting Judge, if the Judge to whom the case is assigned is unavailable, prior to inclusion in the Court's entries.

3400.50 Service of Copies on Counsel and Unrepresented Parties. Every filing required to be served by T.R. 5 shall be served on all counsel of record either before it is filed or on the day it is filed with the Court. A copy of the entry form of the filing shall also be served on all counsel of record whenever the entry is the appearance of counsel or contains a setting for a Court hearing date. All proposed forms of order shall be submitted in sufficient number that distribution may be made to all parties.

3400.60 Routine Entries. Entries, either routine in nature or uncontested including, for example, those setting or continuing a hearing, shall be set out on an entry form only, which shall contain the concise substance of the entry.

3400.70 Electronic Facsimile Filing. Only parties who have agreed to accept service by electronic facsimile transmission (FAX) are permitted to file by FAX. Any filing by FAX shall not exceed ten (10) pages. FAX filings should be made to the Court in which the case is pending.

Adopted Aug. 4, 2006, effective Jan. 1, 2007. Amended effective Jan. 1, 2012; Oct. 1, 2012.

LR64–AR00 Rule 3500. CONTINUANCES AND SETTLEMENTS

3500.10 Motions for Continuance are discouraged. Neither side is entitled to an automatic continuance as a matter of right.

3500.20 Motion for Continuance. Unless made during a hearing or trial, a Motion for Continuance shall be made in writing, stating with particularity the grounds therefore and be verified, and shall state whether opposing counsel objects to the motion, and whether prior continuances have been requested by the moving party.

    (1) The Court may require any written Motion for Continuance to be signed by the party requesting the continuance in addition to the signature of the attorney so moving.

    (2) The Court may require the stipulation to continue the hearing of any pending matter to state with particularity the grounds for the continuance and be signed by all attorneys of record.

3500.30 Time for Filing. Motions or Stipulations for Continuance must be filed as soon after the cause for continuance or delay is discovered by the movant, and no later than fourteen (14) days before the date assigned for trial or hearing, unless good cause therefor is shown by affidavit to have occurred within the fourteen (14) day period.

3500.40 Court's Discretion. The Court in its discretion may grant or deny a continuance.

3500.50 Rescheduling. Unless the Court directs otherwise, all matters continued shall be rescheduled on the Court's calendar when all attorneys will be available. If all attorneys of record are not present in the Court when a matter is continued, the attorney(s) who requested such continuance shall, within ten (10) days following the granting of the continuance, reschedule the matter continued after ascertaining the availability of all attorneys of record for the rescheduled date and time.

3500.60 Costs of Delay or Continuance. Any cost or reasonable expense incurred by the Court or non-moving party as a result of the continuance or delay may be assessed against the moving party at the discretion of the Court.

3500.70 (JURY TRIALS) Costs For Late Settlement of Cause and/or Failure to Notify Court of

Settlement. Any cost or reasonable expense incurred by the Court as a result of a late settlement of the cause and/or any cost or reasonable expense incurred by the Court as a result of any failure to notify the Court of any settlement of the cause may be assessed against either party or parties or all parties, as determined by the Court in its discretion.

(1) Reasonable costs shall include, but are not limited to: costs of juror notification; and, juror per diem and mileage.

(2) All parties have the duty to notify the Court of any settlement of their cause.

(3) Late settlement of the cause means any settlement which is made within fourteen (14) calendar days of the date set for trial.

(4) Late settlement of the cause shall also mean any settlement which is made from the commencement of the trial to and including the return of a verdict by the jury.

(5) Failure to notify the Court of any settlement within five (5) calendar days of the date set for trial shall constitute failure to notify the Court of settlement.

Adopted Aug. 4, 2006, effective Jan. 1, 2007. Amended effective Jan. 1, 2012; Oct. 1, 2012.

LR64–TR35 Rule 3600. DISCOVERY

3600.10 Time Limit. Counsel are expected to begin discovery promptly. In all cases, discovery shall be completed prior to the pre-trial conference unless otherwise ordered by the Court. For good cause shown, the physical or mental examination of a party, as provided for in T.R. 35 may be ordered at any time prior to the trial.

3600.20 Extensions of Time. For good cause shown and prior to the expiration of the time within which discovery is required to be completed, time may be extended for completion of discovery. Motions and stipulations for additional time for completion of discovery must set forth reasons justifying the additional time. Stipulations extending the discovery period must be approved by the Court.

3600.30 Interrogatories.

(1) *Preparation.* Interrogatories shall be tailored specifically to each cause in which they are filed, and shall be consecutively numbered to facilitate response. All interrogatories to parties propounded pursuant to T.R. 33 shall be prepared as follows:

(a) An original and two duplicates of all interrogatories to parties shall be prepared and served on the party required to answer. Counsel for the propounder shall date and sign the interrogatories as of the date of service.

(b) After each interrogatory and every subpart requiring a separate answer, sufficient blank space shall be left by the propounder as is reasonably anticipated may be required for the responder's typewritten answer. If additional space is required for an answer, the responder shall attach supplemental pages, incorporated by reference, to comply with the spirit of T.R. 33.

(c) Additional space shall be left by the propounder at the close of the interrogatories so that a typewritten signature line and appropriate typed oath or affirmation may be inserted by the responder.

(2) *Number Limited.* Interrogatories shall be kept to a reasonable limit not to exceed a total of twenty-five (25) including subparts and shall be used solely for the purpose of discovery and shall not be used as a substitute for the taking of a deposition. For good cause shown and upon leave of Court additional interrogatories may be propounded.

(3) *Answers and Objections.* Answers or objections to interrogatories under T.R. 31 or T.R. 33 shall set forth in full the interrogatories being answered or objected to immediately preceding the answer or objections. The responding party shall type the requested answers in the space provided, as required by this Rule, shall supply the oath or affirmation, and shall serve the original and one copy upon propounding counsel.

(4) *Duplicated Forms.* No duplicated forms containing interrogatories shall be filed or served upon a party unless all interrogatories on such forms are consecutively numbered and applicable to the cause in which the same are filed and served.

(5) *Filing.* No interrogatories shall be filed with the Court except as provided in T.R. 5 E(2).

3600.40 Depositions. Depositions shall be governed by T.R. 30. Video tape or other mechanically reproduced tapes as allowed by T.R. 74, shall be admissible to the same degree as any other depositions. A transcript of the testimony elicited in the video tape shall accompany all video taped depositions filed with the Court.

Adopted Aug. 4, 2006, effective Jan. 1, 2007. Amended effective Jan. 1, 2012; Oct. 1, 2012.

LR64–AR00 Rule 3700. CASE MANAGEMENT

3700.10 Case Management Conferences. No sooner than 120 days after the filing of any complaint in a civil plenary (PL), civil tort (CT), civil collection (CC), or mortgage foreclosure (MF) case, a case management conference may be scheduled upon motion of any party or the Court. Each party shall be represented at this conference by an attorney familiar with the case, who shall be prepared to discuss and enter into stipulations concerning:

(1) the exchange of lists of witnesses known to have knowledge of the facts supporting the pleadings. The parties thereafter shall be under a con-

tinuing obligation to advise opposing parties of other witnesses as they become known;

(2) the exchange of all documents, and any other evidence reasonably available, contemplated for use in support of the pleadings;

(3) a discovery schedule;

(4) the necessity for additional conferences in complex litigation;

(5) the necessity for amendments to the pleadings and the filing or hearing of dispositive motions. Absent agreement, the Court shall schedule the filing, briefing, and hearing thereof; and

(6) settlement and the feasibility of Alternative Dispute Resolution.

3700.20 Case Management Order. At the conclusion of the case management conference, or if the Court chooses not to hold a case management conference, no sooner than 120 days after the filing of the complaint, the Court shall enter a case management order setting forth:

(1) a time limit for completion of discovery;

(2) a time limit for filing all pre-trial dispositive motions;

(3) the scheduling of a pre-trial conference;

(4) time limits for filing, and the format of proposed preliminary and final jury instructions and objections thereto;

(5) time limit(s) for filing Motions in Limine;

(6) time limit(s) for completion of Alternative Dispute Resolution (ADR) and filing of any report required by the ADR rules; and

(7) any other matters which the parties or the Court have seen fit to address.

Adopted Aug. 4, 2006, effective Jan. 1, 2007. Amended effective Jan. 1, 2012; Oct. 1, 2012.

LR64–AR00 Rule 3800. PRE–TRIAL CONFERENCES

3800.10 Mandatory Pre-trial Conferences. A pre-trial conference shall be held in every civil plenary and civil tort action, at which each party shall be represented by the attorney who will conduct the trial.

3800.20 The parties shall exchange written lists of witnesses and photocopies of exhibits, together with contentions and statements of issues of fact and law, at least thirty (30) days prior to the pre-trial conference. Counsel for the first named defendant shall prepare a pre-trial order, which shall be executed by counsel for all parties and filed not later than five (5) days prior to the pre-trial conference. The pre-trial order shall set forth in the following sequence:

(1) the jurisdiction of the Court;

(2) the pleadings raising the issues;

(3) a list of motions or other matters requiring action by the Court;

(4) a concise statement of stipulated facts, with reservations, if any;

(5) a concise statement of issues of fact which remain to be litigated;

(6) a concise statement of issues of law which remain for determination by the Court;

(7) the plaintiff's contentions;

(8) the defendant's contentions;

(9) the plaintiff's numbered list of trial exhibits;

(10) the defendant's numbered list of trial exhibits;

(11) the plaintiff's numbered list of trial witnesses, with addresses. Expert witnesses shall be so designated;

(12) the defendant's numbered list of trial witnesses, with addresses. Expert witnesses shall be so designated; and

(13) the estimated length of trial.

When, for any reason, the pre-trial order is not executed by all counsel, each shall file not later than five (5) days prior to the pre-trial conference a written statement of the reason therefore accompanied by a proposed pre-trial order.

3800.30 Pre–Trial Order. At the conclusion of the pre-trial conference, the Court shall render a pre-trial order which, when entered, shall control the course of the trial and may not be amended except by order of the Court to prevent manifest injustice.

3800.40 Memoranda of Law. Memoranda of law, addressing any unusual questions of law, shall be filed and served no later than seven (7) days prior to trial.

3800.50 Trial Setting. At the conclusion of the pre-trial conference, the cause shall be set for trial, if a trial setting has not already been made.

3800.60 Sanctions. Failure of the parties or their attorneys to be prepared for the case management conference, for the pre-trial conference, or to otherwise comply with this Rule, shall subject them to sanctions under Trial Rule 16(K).

Adopted Aug. 4, 2006, effective Jan. 1, 2007. Amended effective Jan. 1, 2012; Oct. 1, 2012.

LR64–AR00 Rule 3900. EXHIBITS

3900.10 Marking in Advance. Exhibits which are not marked at, or prior to the pre-trial conference shall be presented to the court reporter for marking prior to the beginning of the trial, where possible, or during recesses in the trial, so that the trial is not delayed for the marking of exhibits.

3900.20 Custody. After being marked for identification, models, diagrams, exhibits, and material offered or admitted into evidence in any cause pending or tried before the Court or jury shall be placed in the custody of the court reporter unless otherwise ordered by the Judge.

3900.30 Removal. After a case has been decided, unless an appeal has been taken, all models, diagrams, exhibits, or material placed in the custody of the court reporter shall be taken by the parties offering them within six (6) months after the conclusion of the case. At the time of removal, a detailed receipt shall be left with the court reporter and filed with the cause.

3900.40 Destruction of Exhibits. The court reporter shall retain the exhibits from any case for six (6) months after the conclusion of the case, including appeals. After a case is decided and no appeal taken, or after all appeals are completed, the court reporter may give notice in writing to the party introducing the exhibit giving a time within which the exhibit shall be removed from the custody of the court reporter. If the party does not recover the exhibit within the time indicated, the court reporter may dispose of same and the party shall be charged with any expenses of such disposition.

Adopted Aug. 4, 2006, effective Jan. 1, 2007. Amended effective Jan. 1, 2012; Oct. 1, 2012.

PORTER COUNTY LOCAL CRIMINAL RULES

Adopted August 4, 2006, Effective January 1, 2007

Including Amendments Received Through November 1, 2013

Research Notes

These rules may be searched electronically on Westlaw *in the* IN-RULES *database; updates to these rules may be found on Westlaw in* IN-RULESUPDATES. *For search tips and a summary of database content, consult the Westlaw Scope Screens for each database.*

LR64–CR2.2 Rule 4000. CASE ASSIGNMENT AND ALLOCATIONS

4000.10 Superior Division. The Administrator of this Court shall maintain two opaque containers. In each shall be placed four (4) black marbles, four (4) white marbles and four (4) green marbles. One container shall be designated for use in Class D felony charges to be filed in the Superior Division and the other container shall be used for all other criminal charges filed in the Superior Division. Whenever the Prosecuting Attorney of Porter County wishes to initiate a criminal action in the Superior Division of the Court, the Prosecutor shall first go to the Office of the Court Administrator for purposes of determining before which judge the case shall be filed.

The Court Administrator shall remove one (1) marble from the appropriate opaque container. If the marble chosen is black, the Prosecutor shall be directed to take the probable cause affidavit and the charging information to Porter Superior Court #1 for approval and filing. If the marble chosen is white, the Prosecutor shall be directed to Superior Court #2, and if the marble is chosen green, the Prosecutor shall be directed to Circuit Court acting as Superior Court #5. After the Prosecutor is directed to the designated court, the marble chosen shall be placed in an opaque container separate from the original container. Subsequent criminal cases shall be assigned by this same process. Once all twelve (12) marbles have been

removed from the original opaque container, they shall be replaced in the original container and the same process will be followed for assignment of subsequent cases. In addition, the Court Administrator shall remove a number of marbles of the same color which corresponds with the number of multiple defendants when the case assigned has multiple defendants.

Class D felony charges filed in the Clerk's Office shall be assigned to Superior Courts 1, 2 and 5 on a rotating basis.

Any criminal case accepted into the Porter County Adult Drug Court Program in accordance with the Drug Court's policies and procedures will be assigned to the designated Porter County Adult Drug Court for further management.

4000.20 County Division Case Assignment and Allocation. The County Division of the Court shall maintain a felony docket, a misdemeanor docket and a traffic infractions docket. Filings on the dockets shall be done in accordance with this Rule as follows:

((1) *Porter Superior Court #3*: Porter Superior Court #3 shall receive misdemeanor, felony and infraction filings from the following police departments: Indiana Department of Natural Resources; Indiana State Police Toll Road (District #11); Beverly Shores Police Department; the Department of Transportation, Northern Indiana Commuter Transit Department; Porter County Sheriff's Police; and traffic misdemeanors filed by the Porter County Sheriff. Porter Superior Court #3 shall receive filings from the first five in-custody felony case filings in each month that would have been filed in Porter Superior Court #6 pursuant to this rule.

Porter Superior Court #4: Porter Superior Court #4 shall receive filings from the following police departments: City of Valparaiso; Town of Kouts; Town of Hebron; and Valparaiso University Police Department.

Porter Superior Court #6: Porter Superior Court #6 shall receive misdemeanor, felony and infraction filings from the following police departments: Indiana State Police (District #13); Lowell Post; Portage Police Department; Chesterton Police Department; Ogden Dunes Police Department;

605

Burns Harbor Police Department; and Porter Police Department.

(2) This Rule shall also govern the filing of ordinance violation cases.

(3) The County Division of the Court will not accept the filing of Class A, B, C or D Felonies except:

(A) Class D Felony for Battery and Class D Felony for Domestic Battery and accompanying charges resulting from the same arrest where the most serious charge is a Class D felony.

(B) Class D felony cases which include a charge under Title 9. These shall be filed in the County Division.

(4) Narcotics Unit filings are treated as being filed by the Porter County Sheriff. Nothing in this section shall prevent the County Division Courts from directing filings between the Courts in order to equalize work loads of the several respective courts.

4000.30 Transfers.

(1) It shall be the policy of the Porter Superior Courts, that whenever possible consistent with good case management principles, cases involving the same defendant shall be transferred into one court for resolution of all of the pending cases.

(2) *MISDEMEANORS:* Any subsequent Misdemeanor case filed against a defendant may be transferred to the Court where the defendant's oldest existing misdemeanor case is pending. In the event the defendant has an open probation case pending in any Misdemeanor Court and is subsequently charged with a new Misdemeanor case, the new Misdemeanor case shall be transferred to the probation case, unless the new Misdemeanor case can be resolved without the resolution of the probation case. Pending as defined herein means any existing Misdemeanor case which is in pre-disposition status.

(3) *D FELONY CASES:* Any subsequent Misdemeanor or Class D Felony case may be transferred to the Court where the defendant's oldest existing Class D Felony case is pending. In the event the defendant has an open probation case pending in any court and is subsequently charged with a D Felony case, the D Felony case may be transferred to the open probation case, unless the D Felony case can be resolved without the resolution of the probation case.

(4) *MURDER, A, B, and C FELONY CASES:* Any subsequently filed Misdemeanor or D Felony case may be transferred to the court where the defendant's oldest Major Felony case is pending. However, no new Misdemeanor case involving Title 9 (traffic) may be transferred without prior agreement of both the sending and receiving court.

(5) Any Court may choose to "opt out" of transferring or receiving transferred cases by notifying the other Superior Courts of their election to not transfer or accept transferred cases.

(6) *DRUG COURT:* If accepted into the Porter County Adult Drug Court Program, qualifying criminal cases shall be transferred in accordance with the Drug Court's policies and procedures to the Superior Court designated as the Drug Court.

4000.40 Traffic Tickets.

(1) Tickets must contain specific court dates and times. Citations must contain the court date and the court times.

(2) Tickets must be turned into the Clerk's Office before the court date. Tickets turned in on the court date or thereafter will be dismissed with an Order that shows the officer has not filed the ticket with the Court on time.

4000.50 Adult Drug Court Program.

(1) Porter County Adult Drug Court Program shall be established pursuant to IC 12–23–14.5–1 to provide specialized services, including: clinical assessment, education, referral for treatment, and service coordination and case management for eligible defendants and probationers, as determined by its written policy and procedures.

(2) Those persons directed to participate in the Porter County Adult Drug Court Program shall pay the program fee, not to exceed five hundred ($500) dollars, in accordance with IC 12–23–14.5–12, as well as any additional costs associated with recommended treatment. The clerk of the court shall collect and transmit the program fee within thirty (30) days after the fees are collected, for deposit by the auditor or fiscal officer in the appropriate user fee fund established under IC 33–37–8.

(3) The day-to-day operation and management of the Porter County Adult Drug Court Program has been established in and assigned to Porter County Superior Court # 3. The Drug Court Program shall be reviewed by the Porter County Superior Court judges when necessary, and upon review and agreement by all judges, the Drug Court Program may be established in additional courts as needed.

Adopted Aug. 4, 2006, effective Jan. 1, 2007. Amended effective July 9, 2008; April 8, 2009, effective Jan. 8, 2009; April 29, 2009, effective May 1, 2009; Jan. 1, 2012; Oct. 1, 2012; Jan. 1, 2013.

LR64–CR13 Rule 4100. CHANGE OF VENUE FROM THE JUDGE, DISQUALIFICATION AND RECUSAL

4100.10 Superior Division. The Court Administrator shall maintain an opaque container in which shall be placed one black marble, one white marble and one green marble. In the event that any judge of the Superior Division of the Porter Superior Court grants a change of venue from the judge under Rule 12 of the Indiana Rules of Criminal Procedure, the Court Administrator shall select a marble from the above mentioned opaque container. The special judge shall be assigned based on the color of the marble chosen by applying LR64–CR2.2–4000.10. However, if applying LR64–CR2.2–4000.10 would result in the same judge who granted the change of venue being named as special judge, then the judge of Porter Superior Court #4 shall be named special judge in the case.

4100.20   County Division. The staff of each of the judges of the County Division of the Porter Superior Court shall maintain an opaque container in which shall be placed one blue marble, one yellow marble and one red marble. In the event that any judge of the County Division of the Porter Superior Court grants a change of venue from the judge under Rule 12 of the Indiana Rules of Criminal procedure, a staff member of that judge shall select a marble from the opaque container maintained at that Court. If the marble drawn is red, the case shall be assigned to the judge of Porter Superior Court #3 as special judge. If the marble drawn is yellow, the case shall be assigned to the judge of Porter Superior Court #4 as special judge. If the marble drawn is blue, the case shall be assigned to the judge of Porter Superior Court #6 as special judge. However, if the color of the marble drawn would result in the same judge that granted the change of venue being named as special judge, then Porter Superior Court Magistrate #2 shall be named special judge in the case.

4100.30   In the event that a special judge selected under paragraph 1 or 2 is disqualified under the Code of Judicial Conduct or excused from service by the Indiana Supreme Court, another marble shall be selected and the special judge assigned accordingly.

4100.40   For felony, misdemeanor and infraction cases filed in the County Division of the Court, if the judge to whom a case is assigned under LR64–CR2.2–4000.20 of these rules is disqualified under the Code of Judicial Conduct or recuses himself/herself for any reason, the Court, based upon caseload and geographical considerations, sets out the following reassignment schedule:

Cases from 64D03 shall be reassigned to 64D06

Cases from 64D04 shall be reassigned to 64D03

Cases from 64D06 shall be reassigned to 64D04

Adopted Aug. 4, 2006, effective Jan. 1, 2007. Amended effective Jan. 1, 2012; Oct. 1, 2012.

LR64–CR00 Rule 4200.   WITHDRAWAL OF APPEARANCE

Permission of the Court is required to withdraw the appearance of counsel for a defendant. Counsel desiring to withdraw appearance in any criminal action at any stage of the proceedings shall file a motion requesting leave to do so. Such motion shall fix a time (to be procured from the Judge's staff) when such motion shall be heard. Moving counsel shall also file with the Court satisfactory evidence of at least ten

(10) days written notice of such hearing to the attorney's client. Further, the notice to the client shall also contain notice of the next scheduled calendar setting in the cause. A withdrawal of appearance, when accompanied by the appearance of other counsel, shall constitute a waiver of this requirement.

Adopted Aug. 4, 2006, effective Jan. 1, 2007. Amended effective Jan. 1, 2012; effective Oct. 1, 2012; Jan. 1, 2013.

LR64–CR00 Rule 4300.   BOND

4300.10   Arrest Warrants. At the time a probable cause affidavit is presented to a Judge of the Court, if the Judge orders an arrest warrant issued, the Judge shall also set the amount of bond. The amount of bond for all Murder, Class A, B, C and D felonies which are presented to the Court for a finding of probable cause and issuance of an arrest warrant shall be determined on a case by case basis.

4300.20   Bond Schedule. A bond schedule applying to all Class D felonies not presented to a judge for finding of probable cause and all misdemeanors shall be adopted by the Court by general order. Said general order, when adopted or when modified shall be posted at the Porter County Jail and in each office of the Clerk of the Porter Circuit and Superior Court.

Adopted Aug. 4, 2006, effective Jan. 1, 2007. Amended effective Jan. 1, 2012; Oct. 1, 2012.

LR64–CR00 Rule 4400.   AFFIDAVIT RELATING TO PRIOR CRIMINAL RECORD

In all criminal cases submitted for disposition by plea agreement the following affidavit form shall be used and affixed to the plea agreement.

I hereby disclose the following prior criminal record including arrests:

Charge	Conviction/Sentence if any	County/ State	Year

On Probation now? ___ Yes ___ No

On Parole now? ___ Yes ___ No

OTHER PENDING CHARGES:

_____

_____

_____

Full Name _____

Birth Date _____ Social Security Number ____

I AFFIRM, UNDER PENALTIES OF PERJURY, THAT THE ABOVE DISCLOSURE IS TRUE AND COMPLETE, LISTING ALL CRIMINAL ACTIVITY WITH WHICH I HAVE BEEN CHARGED, AND LISTING ALL CHARGES NOW PENDING AGAINST ME. I UNDERSTAND THAT IN THE EVENT THIS DISCLOSURE IS INACCURATE IN ANY RESPECT, THE STATE OF INDIANA

SHALL BE PERMITTED TO REVOKE ANY
PLEA OFFER, OR WITHDRAW FROM ANY
PLEA AGREEMENT.

I UNDERSTAND THAT MY ATTORNEY IS IN
NO MANNER RESPONSIBLE FOR THE ACCU-
RACY OF THIS AFFIDAVIT.

_____   _____
Date   Defendant

*Adopted Aug. 4, 2006, effective Jan. 1, 2007. Amended
effective Jan. 1, 2012; Oct. 1, 2012.*

LR64–CR00 Rule 4500. PLEA AGREEMENT DEADLINE DATE

In all criminal prosecutions scheduled for trial by
jury the plea agreement deadline date shall be not
less than thirteen days before trial. The Court shall
not accept any plea agreements filed after this date,
except for just cause shown. Plea agreements must
be in written form and signed by the defendant and
counsel and the prosecuting attorney or his deputy.
The Court may hold the plea hearing on the plea
agreement deadline date or otherwise schedule the
hearing to another date depending upon time available. In the event the parties have no plea agreement, the Court may hold a status conference with
counsel and the defendant and prosecuting attorney
on the deadline date, in order to narrow the issues, to
discuss stipulations, and to otherwise streamline the
trial.

*Adopted Aug. 4, 2006, effective Jan. 1, 2007. Amended
effective Jan. 1, 2012; Oct. 1, 2012.*

LR64–CR00 Rule 4600. TRIAL

The Court shall control the trial calendar. The
prosecuting attorney may advise the Court of facts
relevant in determining the priority of cases on the
trial calendar. Thirty (30) days prior to trial or such
other dates as the Court may fix, the Court may order
the defendant to appear and confirm his/her plea and
desire for trial of the cause.

*Adopted Aug. 4, 2006, effective Jan. 1, 2007. Amended
effective Jan. 1, 2012; Oct. 1, 2012.*

LR64–TR07 Rule 4700. MOTIONS

4700.10 Continuance. Upon motion of any party,
the Court may grant a continuance only upon showing
of good cause and only for so long as necessary,
taking into account not only the request or consent of
the prosecution or defendant, but also the public
interest in the prompt disposition of the case. All
orders granting continuances shall indicate on which
party's motion the continuance is granted.

4700.20 Other Motions. Any application to the
Court for an order shall be made by a written motion,
unless made during the trial or the hearing, when the
Court permits it to be made orally.

(1)(1)[1] Unless otherwise provided by law or rule,
only the original copy of a motion need be filed.

The original shall state the grounds upon which the
motion is made and set forth the relief or order
sought. It may be supported by an affidavit. It
shall be accompanied by a memorandum in support
thereof.

(2) All motions shall be signed by an attorney
of record, or the defendant personally, and shall
clearly identify the attorney's printed name, their
Indiana Attorney Registration Number, and the
name, address and telephone number of the firm
with which the attorney filing same is associated.
A rubber stamp or facsimile signature on the
original shall not be acceptable.

*Adopted Aug. 4, 2006, effective Jan. 1, 2007. Amended
effective Jan. 1, 2012; Oct. 1, 2012.*

[1] So in original.

LR64–CR00 Rule 4800. WAIVERS

Whenever a defendant waives a right, the Court
shall enter of record that the defendant is present,
and after having been advised of such right, waives
the same. The Court may also require that the
waiver of a right be in writing, signed by the defendant personally and approved by the Court.

Any waiver may be set aside by the Court to
prevent any injustice.

*Adopted Aug. 4, 2006, effective Jan. 1, 2007. Amended
effective Jan. 1, 2012; Oct. 1, 2012.*

LR64–CR00 Rule 4900. FAILURE TO APPEAR

If a defendant fails to appear before the Court when
summoned or otherwise ordered by the Court to
appear, the Court may summarily issue a warrant for
the defendant's immediate arrest and appearance before the Court.

*Adopted Aug. 4, 2006, effective Jan. 1, 2007. Amended
effective Jan. 1, 2012; Oct. 1, 2012.*

LR64–TR26 Rule 4910. PRE–TRIAL DISCOV-ERY

In all criminal cases, reciprocal pre-trial discovery
shall be available to both the State and the defendant,
upon request of the opposing party, as follows:

4910.10 State. The State shall produce, upon request, the following:

(1) The names, last known addresses, dates of
birth, and social security numbers of persons whom
the State intends to call as witnesses, together with
their relevant written or recorded statements, memoranda containing substantially verbatim reports of
their oral statements and a list of memoranda reporting or summarizing their oral statements.

(2) Any written or recorded statements and the
substance of any oral statements made by the accused or by a co-defendant, and a list of witnesses
to the making and acknowledgment of such statements.

(3) A transcript of those portions of grand jury minutes containing testimony of the accused or a co-defendant, and a list of witnesses to the making and acknowledgment of such statements.

(4) Any reports or statements of experts made in connection with the particular case, including results of physical or mental examinations and of scientific tests, experiments or comparisons.

(5) Any books, papers, documents, photographs or tangible objects which the prosecuting attorney intends to use in the hearing or trial, or which were obtained from, or belong to, the accused.

(6) Any record of prior criminal convictions which may be used for impeachment of the persons whom the State intends to call as witnesses at the hearing or trial.

4910.20 Defendant. The defendant shall produce, upon request, the following:

(1) The person of the accused. Subject to Constitutional limitations the accused shall:

(a) Appear in a line-up.

(b) Speak for identification by witnesses for an offense.

(c) Be finger printed.

(d) Pose for photographs not involving re-enactment of a scene.

(e) Try on articles of clothing.

(f) Permit the taking of specimens of material from under the defendant's fingernails.

(g) Permit the taking of samples of the defendant's blood, hair or other materials of the body which involve no unreasonable intrusion.

(h) Provide a sample of the defendant's handwriting.

(1) Submit to a reasonable physical or medical inspection of the defendant's body.

(2) Whenever the personal appearance of the accused is required for the foregoing purposes reasonable notice of the time and place of such appearance shall be given by the State to the accused and the accused's counsel, who shall have a right to be present.

(3) Subject to Constitutional limitations the State shall be informed of, and permitted to inspect and copy or photograph, any report or results, or any testimony relative thereto, of physical or mental examinations or of scientific tests, experiments or comparisons, or any other reports or statements of experts which defense counsel possesses or controls, except that those portions of reports containing statements made by the defendant may be withheld if defense counsel does not intend to use any of the material contained in the report at a hearing or trial.

(4) Subject to Constitutional limitations defense counsel shall inform the State of any defenses which defense counsel intends to make at a hearing or trial and shall furnish the State with the following material and information within defense counsel's possession and control.

(a) The names, last known addresses, dates of birth and social security numbers of persons defense counsel intends to call as witnesses, together with their relevant written or recorded statements, including memoranda, reporting or summarizing their oral statements, and record of prior criminal convictions known to the defense attorney.

(b) Any papers, books, documents, photographs or tangible objects defense counsel intends to use as evidence or for impeachment at a hearing or trial.

4910.30 All Parties.

(1) If, subsequent to compliance, a party discovers additional material or information which is subject to disclosure, that party's attorney shall promptly notify the other party or the other party's counsel of the existence of such additional material, and if the additional material or information is discovered during trial, the Court shall also be notified.

(2) Any materials furnished to an attorney pursuant to this Rule shall remain in that attorney's exclusive custody and shall be used only for the purpose of conducting that attorney's side of the case, and shall be subject to such other terms and conditions as the Court may provide.

(3) Upon a showing of cause the Court may, at any time, order that specified disclosures be restricted or deferred, or make such other order as is appropriate, providing that all material and information to which a party is entitled must be disclosed in time to permit that party's counsel to make beneficial use thereof.

4910.40 Failure to Comply. If at any time during the course of the proceedings it is brought to the attention of the Court that a party has failed to comply with this Rule or an order issued pursuant thereto, the Court may order such party to permit the discovery of material and information not previously disclosed, and the Court may order a continuance, or enter such other order as it deems just under the circumstances. Willful violation by counsel of this Rule or an order issued pursuant thereto may subject counsel to appropriate sanctions.

4910.50 Discretionary Protective Order. Either side may apply for a protective order for non-disclosure of requested discovery. The Court may deny disclosure if it finds that there is a substantial risk to any person of physical harm, intimidation, bribery, economic reprisals, or unnecessary annoyance or embarrassment resulting from such disclosure which outweighs any usefulness of the disclosure to counsel.

4910.60   Matters not subject to disclosure.

(1) *Work product.* Disclosure is not required of legal research or of records, correspondence, reports or memoranda to the extent that they contain the opinions, theories, or conclusions of the State or members of its legal or investigative staffs, or of defense counsel or his/her staff.

(2) *Informants.* Disclosure of an informant's identity will not be required where there is a paramount interest in non-disclosure and a failure to disclose will not infringe upon the constitutional rights of the accused. Disclosure of the identity of witnesses to be produced at a hearing or trial will be required.

(3) Any matters protected by law.

Adopted Aug. 4, 2006, effective Jan. 1, 2007. Amended effective Jan. 1, 2012; Oct. 1, 2012.

LR64–CR00 Rule 4920. PRE–TRIAL CONFERENCE

At any time after the filing of the indictment or information, the Court upon motion of any party or upon its own motion, may order one or more conferences to consider such matters as will promote a fair and expeditious trial. In all felony cases the Court will schedule a final pre-trial conference. At the conclusion of the conference the Court may prepare and file a pre-trial conference order which documents all matters agreed upon. No admissions made by the defendant or his attorney at the conference may be used against the defendant unless the admissions are reduced to writing and signed by the defendant and his attorney.

The representative of the Prosecutor's Office having the authority to negotiate disposition of the cause and the representative of the Prosecutor's Office who will represent the State at trial of the cause shall appear at the pre-trial conference. The defense attorney and defendant shall appear for the pre-trial conference. Discovery shall be completed by the time of pre-trial. Any pre-trial motions must be submitted in writing seven (7) days prior to the pre-trial conference.

Adopted Aug. 4, 2006, effective Jan. 1, 2007. Amended effective Jan. 1, 2012; Oct. 1, 2012.

LR64–CR00 Rule 4930.   LATE PAYMENTS

(1) Any defendant found to have;

(A) committed a crime;

(B) violated a statute defining and infraction;

(C) violated an ordinance of a municipal corporation; or

(D) committed a delinquent act; and

(2) The defendant is required to pay;

(A) court costs, including fees;

(B) a fine; or

(C) a civil penalty; and

(3) The defendant is not determined by the Court imposing the court costs, fine, or civil penalty to be indigent; and

(4) The defendant fails to pay to the clerk the costs, fine, or civil penalty in full before the later of the following;

(A) The end of the business day on which the Court enters the conviction or judgment.

(B) The end of the period specified in a payment schedule set for the payment of court costs, fines, and civil penalties under rules adopted for the operation of the Court; then

The defendant shall pay an additional $25.00 fee pursuant to IC 33–37–5–22 and the Clerk of the Court shall collect the late payment fee.

Amended effective Jan. 1, 2012; Oct. 1, 2012.

PORTER COUNTY LOCAL PROBATE RULES

Adopted August 4, 2006, Effective January 1, 2007

Including Amendments Received Through November 1, 2013

Research Notes

These rules may be searched electronically on Westlaw in the IN-RULES database; updates to these rules may be found on Westlaw in IN-RULESUPDATES. For search tips and a summary of database content, consult the Westlaw Scope Screens for each database.

LR64–PR00 Rule 5000. NOTICE

5000.10 Whenever notice by publication and/or written notice by U.S. mail is required to be given, the attorney shall prepare such notice and shall ensure that such notice is properly published and/or served by certified mail, return receipt requested. The notice shall comply with all statutory requirements. It shall be the attorney's responsibility to provide proof of service prior to bringing a matter to the Court. Copies of petitions shall be sent with all notices where the hearing involved arises from the matters contained in the petition. Notice of the opening of an estate shall be sent by first class United States mail to all readily ascertainable creditors.

Adopted Aug. 4, 2006, effective Jan. 1, 2007. Amended effective Jan. 1, 2012; Oct. 1, 2012.

LR64–PR00 Rule 5100. PLEADINGS

5100.10 Filing. When pleadings are filed by mail, or left with the Court for filing, a self-addressed, stamped envelope shall be included for return of documents to the attorney. Routine pleadings, such as inventories, inheritance tax schedules, and final reports, may be filed with the Clerk for transmittal to the Court.

5100.20 Orders. All attorneys are required to prepare orders for all proceedings except when expressly directed otherwise by the Court.

5100.30 Signature and Information. Every pleading, including inventories, petitions, and accountings, filed in an estate or guardianship shall be signed and verified by the fiduciary and signed by the attorney for the fiduciary. The initial petition to open an estate or guardianship shall contain the name, address, social security number, and date of birth of the fiduciary, if a person.

Adopted Aug. 4, 2006, effective Jan. 1, 2007. Amended effective Jan. 1, 2012; Oct. 1, 2012.

LR64–PR00 Rule 5200. BOND

5200.10 Amount and Exceptions. In every estate and guardianship, the fiduciary, prior to the issuance of letters, shall file a corporate surety bond not less than the value of the personal property to be administered, plus the probable value of annual rents and profits of all property of the estate in such amount as shall be set by the Court, except as hereinafter provided:

(1) Where, under the terms of the Will, the testator expresses an intention that the bond be waived, the Court shall set a bond adequate to protect creditors and taxing authorities.

(2) Where the fiduciary is an heir or legatee of the estate, the bond may be reduced by said fiduciary's share of the estate.

(3) Where the heirs or legatees have filed a written request that the fiduciary serve without bond, the bond may be set in the amount adequate to protect the rights of the creditors and taxing authorities only.

(4) In an unsupervised estate, bond may be set at the discretion of the Court.

(5) No bond shall be required in any supervised estate or guardianship in which a corporate banking fiduciary qualified by law to serve as such is either the fiduciary or one of several co-fiduciaries.

5200.20 Restriction in Lieu of Bond. In lieu of a bond as required by Section 5200.10 of this Rule, a fiduciary may restrict transfer of all or part of the liquid assets of the estate or guardianship by placing those assets in a federally-insured financial institution with the following restriction placed on the face of the account or document: NO PRINCIPAL OR INTEREST SHALL BE WITHDRAWN WITHOUT WRITTEN ORDER OF THE CIRCUIT OR SUPERIOR COURT OF PORTER COUNTY, INDIANA. The attorney for the estate or the fiduciary shall file with the Court written acknowledgment by the federally insured financial institution of the account's restriction.

5200.30 Value. All petitions to open an estate or guardianship shall set forth the probable value of the personal property plus the estimated annual rents and profits to be derived from the property in the estate or guardianship.

5200.40 Surety. The name and address of the insurance agency providing the corporate surety bond shall be typed or printed on all corporate bonds in any estate or guardianship.

Adopted Aug. 4, 2006, effective Jan. 1, 2007. Amended effective Jan. 1, 2012; Oct. 1, 2012.

LR64–PR00 Rule 5300. INVENTORY

5300.10 No inventory shall be filed by the fiduciary in all estates and guardianships as follows: Estates (supervised and unsupervised), within sixty (60) days; Guardianships, within ninety (90) days for permanent guardians and within thirty (30) days for temporary guardians. All times relate to the date of appointment of the fiduciary. In the event a partial inventory is filed, all subsequent inventories must contain a recapitulation of prior inventories.

Adopted Aug. 4, 2006, effective Jan. 1, 2007. Amended effective Jan. 1, 2012; Oct. 1, 2012.

LR64–PR00 Rule 5400. REAL ESTATE

5400.10 Appraisals. In all supervised estates and guardianships in which real estate is to be sold, a written professional appraisal shall be filed with the Court at the time of filing the Petition for Sale unless such appraisal was filed with the Inventory. Such written appraisal shall include as a minimum the following elements:

(1) A brief description of the property interest being appraised, including the full legal description thereof.

(2) Purpose or objective of the appraisal.

(3) Date for which fair market value is determined.

(4) Data and reasoning supporting the fair market value.

(5) Fair market value determined.

(6) Statement of assumptions and special or limiting conditions.

(7) Certification of disinterest in real estate.

(8) Signature of the appraiser.

All such appraisals shall be made within one year of the date of the Petition for Sale.

5400.20 Deeds. All deeds submitted to the Court for approval in either estate or guardianship proceedings shall be signed by the fiduciary and the signature notarized prior to its submission. All such deeds shall be submitted with the Report of Sale of Real Estate or at the time of the hearing on the Final Account. Copies of such deeds shall be filed with the Court for its records.

5400.30 Recording. Whenever a final decree reflects that real estate has vested in heirs or beneficiaries, the decree shall be recorded with the recorder of the county where any such real estate is located and evidence of said recording shall be provided to the Court with the Supplemental Report.

Adopted Aug. 4, 2006, effective Jan. 1, 2007. Amended effective Jan. 1, 2012; Oct. 1, 2012.

LR64–PR00 Rule 5500. SALE OF PERSONAL PROPERTY

5500.10 Appraisals. In all supervised estates and guardianships, no Petition to Sell Personal Property shall be granted unless a written appraisal prepared by a person competent to appraise such property and setting forth the fair market value thereof, is filed with the Court at the time of the filing of the Petition to Sell, unless such appraisal was filed with the Inventory. All appraisals shall be made within one year of the date of the Petition to Sell. This rule shall not apply to personal property which is sold at public auction.

5500.20 When No Appraisal Required. No written appraisal shall be required for the sale of assets which are traded in a market and the value of which is readily ascertainable. Such assets include, but are not limited to, stocks, bonds, mutual funds, commodities, and precious metals.

Adopted Aug. 4, 2006, effective Jan. 1, 2007. Amended effective Jan. 1, 2012; Oct. 1, 2012.

LR64–PR00 Rule 5600. CLAIMS

5600.10 Five (5) months and fifteen (15) days after the date of the first published notice to creditors, the fiduciary, or the fiduciary's attorney, shall examine the Claim Docket and shall allow or disallow each claim filed against the estate.

Adopted Aug. 4, 2006, effective Jan. 1, 2007. Amended effective Jan. 1, 2012; Oct. 1, 2012.

LR64–PR00 Rule 5700. ACCOUNTINGS

5700.10 Intermediate Accounting. Whenever an estate cannot be closed within one (1) year, an intermediate accounting shall be filed with the Court within thirty (30) days after the expiration of one year and each succeeding year thereafter. Such accounting shall comply with the provisions of I.C. 29–1–16–4 and 29–1–16–6 and:

(1) Shall state facts showing why the estate cannot be closed and an estimated date of closing.

(2) Shall propose partial distribution of the estate to the extent that partial distribution can be made without prejudice to distributees and claimants.

5700.20 Form and Content. All accountings shall include the following:

(1) All guardianships accountings shall contain a certification of an officer of any financial institution in which assets are held, verifying the account balance.

(2) All Social Security or Medicare benefits received on behalf of an incapacitated person shall be included and accounted for in the guardianship accountings unless Court approval has been previously granted to allow said funds to be paid directly to a residential or health care facility.

(3) In all supervised estate and guardianship accountings, vouchers or canceled checks for the expenditures claimed shall be filed with the accounting. No affidavits in lieu of vouchers or canceled checks will be accepted from individual fiduciaries. An affidavit in lieu of vouchers or canceled checks may be accepted from a state or federally chartered financial institution who serves as a fiduciary, provided the financial institution retains the vouchers or canceled checks on file or by electronic recording device and makes same available to interested parties upon court order. The Court may require such institution to provide a certification from its Internal Audit Department verifying the accuracy of the accounting.

(4) In all supervised estate and guardianship accountings, a notation shall be placed by each expenditure indicating the reason for or nature of the expenditure.

(5) All accountings to the Court shall contain an itemized statement of the assets on hand.

(6) Receipts or canceled checks for all final distributions shall be filed either in the final report, or a supplemental report, before discharge will be granted by the Court.

(7) All accountings shall follow the prescribed statutory format. Informal, handwritten, or transactional accountings will not be accepted.

5700.30 Court Costs and Claims. All court costs shall be paid and all claims satisfied and released before the hearing on the Final Account and a Clerk's Certification thereof (see Appendix B) shall be filed with the Court before such Final Account shall be approved.

5700.40 Proof of Tax Payment. The Federal Estate Tax Closing Letter and the Indiana Inheritance Tax Closing Letter (or the counter-signed receipt) or a photocopy thereof, showing payment of all Federal Estate and/or Indiana Inheritance Tax liability in the estate, shall be attached to the Final Report at the time of filing.

Adopted Aug. 4, 2006, effective Jan. 1, 2007. Amended effective Jan. 1, 2012; Oct. 1, 2012.

LR64–PR00 Rule 5800. FEES OF ATTORNEYS AND FIDUCIARY

5800.10 Unsupervised Estates. No attorney or fiduciary fees will be determined or authorized for payment by the Court in any unsupervised administration of a decedent's estate.

5800.20 Supervised Estates and Guardianships. No fees for fiduciaries or attorneys shall be paid out of any supervised estate or guardianship without prior written order of the Court. A guardian or guardian's attorney may petition for fees at the time of filing an inventory. No further petition for fees may be filed until a biennial, annual, or final accounting has been filed.

(1) Where contracts for legal services have been entered into prior or subsequent to the opening of an estate or guardianship, the Court reserves the right to approve or disapprove the fee contracts consistent with the Court's fee guidelines.

(2) All petitions for fees for the attorney and/or fiduciary shall conform to the fee guideline set out in Appendix C and shall specifically set forth all services performed in detail as well as the amount of the fee requested and how it has been calculated.

(3) Unjustified delays in carrying out duties by the fiduciary and/or attorney will result in a reduction of fees.

Adopted Aug. 4, 2006, effective Jan. 1, 2007. Amended effective Jan. 1, 2012; Oct. 1, 2012.

LR64–PR00 Rule 5900. UNSUPERVISED ADMINISTRATION

5900.10 Consent. No petition for administration without Court supervision shall be granted unless the consent requirement of I.C. 29–1–7.5–2(a)(4) is met, along with all of the other requirements of I.C. 29–1–7.5–2(a).

5900.20 Inventory. A complete inventory of estate assets shall be filed with the Court within sixty (60) days of the appointment of the fiduciary.

5900.30 Court Costs and Claims. All Court costs shall be paid and all claims satisfied and released on or before the date of the filing of the Closing Statement and a Clerk's Certification thereof (see Appendix B) shall be filed with the Court at the time such Closing Statement is filed with the Court.

5900.40 Taxes. Every Closing Statement shall comply with Local Rule 5700.40.

Adopted Aug. 4, 2006, effective Jan. 1, 2007. Amended effective Jan. 1, 2012; Oct. 1, 2012.

LR64–PR00 Rule 5950. GUARDIANSHIPS

5950.10 Physician's Report. In all guardianship matters seeking to declare an adult incapacitated by reason of physical or mental illness, a Physician's Report (See Appendix D) by the doctor treating the alleged incapacitated person or such additional evidence as the Court shall require, shall be presented to the Court at the time the petition is filed or on the hearing date. No determination will be made without a supporting medical report or testimony.

5950.20 Guardian's Report. Current reports filed by a guardian of the person shall state the present residence and the general welfare of the incapacitated person. If the incapacitated person is an adult and the incapacity is do [1] to physical or mental illness, a Physician's Report by a treating physician shall be filed with the current report, verifying that the incapacity of the person remains unchanged since the date the guardianship was established or the date of the last current report and that the living arrangements for the incapacitated person are appropriate.

5950.30 Guardian of a Minor. In every petition for the appointment of a guardian of the person of a minor child, in addition to the information required by I.C. 29–3–5–1, the following information shall be included in the petition:

(1) The places where the child has lived within the past two years and the names and present addresses of persons with whom the child has lived during that period.

(2) Whether, to Petitioner's knowledge, any other litigation is pending concerning the custody of the child in this or any other state.

(3) Whether, to Petitioner's knowledge, any person not a party to the guardianship proceeding has physical custody of the child or claims to have custody or visitation rights with respect to the child.

Adopted Aug. 4, 2006, effective Jan. 1, 2007. Amended effective Jan. 1, 2012; Oct. 1, 2012.

1 So in original.

APPENDICES

PROBATE—APPENDIX A.   CERTIFICATION BY FINANCIAL INSTITUTION

CERTIFICATION BY FINANCIAL INSTITUTION

TO: _____

FROM: _____

(Guardian's Name)

RE: Guardianship of _____ CAUSE NO. _____

In order to comply with the rules of the Porter Superior Court, I am required to file a Certification of Account Balances. Please certify the balances and names on the accounts I have listed below.

DATED: _____   _____

(Guardian)

For Bank Use Only:

I certify that on the ___ day of _____, 20 ___, the last day of the period covered by this accounting, there was on deposit in this institution to the credit of the Guardian, the following balance:

Name on Account   Account Number Balance Date

_____   _____

_____   _____

_____   _____

Name and Address of Institution:

_____

_____

_____

Signature of Certifying Officer: _____ Date: _____

Printed: _____

Title: _____

Adopted Aug. 4, 2006, effective Jan. 1, 2007. Amended effective Jan. 1, 2012; Oct. 1, 2012.

PROBATE—APPENDIX B.   CLERK'S CERTIFICATE AS TO COSTS/CLAIMS

STATE OF INDIANA)

)

COUNTY OF PORTER)   SS:

)   CAUSE NO. _____

IN THE MATTER OF)

THE GUARDIANSHIP OF)

)

_____)

CLERK'S CERTIFICATE AS TO COSTS/CLAIMS

This is to certify that all <u>costs</u> have been paid in this proceeding through _____, 20 ___.

In addition, all <u>claims</u> filed in this proceeding have been satisfied and shown released. _____.

Yes/No

[If no, list the claims that remain pending: _____.]

_____

_____

_____.]

      Date: _____   _____

                                              Clerk of _____ County

Adopted Aug. 4, 2006, effective Jan. 1, 2007. Amended effective Jan. 1, 2012; Oct. 1, 2012.

PROBATE—APPENDIX C. MAXIMUM FEE GUIDELINES AND RULES FOR SUPERVISED ESTATES

MAXIMUM

FEE GUIDELINES AND RULES FOR SUPERVISED ESTATES

PREAMBLE

PURPOSE OF THE FEE SCHEDULE

The Probate Committee of the Indiana Judicial Conference has prepared Guidelines for Estate Fees in an effort to achieve the following objectives:

1. Establish uniformity throughout the State in determining a fair and reasonable fee for supervised estates;

2. Provide a guideline to assist the Court in determining fair and reasonable fees;

3. Furnish a guideline to attorneys so they can discuss fees that may be reasonably incurred with their clients at the onset of administration;

4. Assist the legal profession to arrive at a fair and reasonable fee for estate work.

The schedule is NOT a minimum fee schedule, but a maximum fee schedule. Every attorney and personal representative has an obligation to request a fee which is fair and reasonable for the work performed, taking into account that provisions of the Rules of Professional Conduct applicable to attorneys admitted to practice law in the State of Indiana. However, any request for fees should not exceed the guidelines set out in the schedule. In an uncomplicated estate, fees should be less than the maximum fees listed in this schedule, and fees should always bear a reasonable relationship to the services rendered.

PRINCIPLES APPLICABLE TO FEE DETERMINATIONS

Although fee guidelines have been promulgated by the Court for probate matters, it is important that your attention be directed to certain criteria as they pertain to these guideline. The existence of the guidelines does not assure that all fees allowed by the Court will adhere to them. Other factors must be considered by the attorney and his, or her, client. The same factors will also be considered by the Court in making its final determination.

The criteria to be considered including the following:

A. The time and labor required, the novelty, complexity, or difficulty of the questions involved, the skill required to perform the services properly, and shall include a determination as to how much of the attorney's time was devoted to legal matters and how much of it was devoted to ministerial functions;

B. The nature and extent of the responsibilities assumed by the attorney and the results obtained, and shall include the considerations of the identity of the personal representative and the character of the probate and non-probate transferred assets;

C. The sufficiency of assets properly available to pay for legal services, and shall consider whether the attorney's duties are expanded by the existence of non-probate assets because of their inclusion for tax purposes, both federal and state;

D. The timeliness with which the necessary services are performed consistent with statutory requirements, the Court's rules of procedure and the Rules of Professional Conduct applicable thereto.

In considering all of these factors, all attorneys are urged to discuss their fee and that of the personal representative at the time they are retained in all probate matters.

ATTORNEY FEES

I. Administration

Gross Estate services are considered to normally include: Opening of the estate, qualifying the personal representative, preparing and filing the Inventory, paying claims, collecting assets, preparing and filing non-extraordinary petitions, preparing and filing the Inheritance Tax Schedule, obtaining the Court order thereon and paying the taxes, preparing and filing the Final Report, obtaining order approving same, distributing assets, obtaining discharge of the personal representative, and preparing and serving all notices on interested parties and readily ascertainable creditors throughout the proceedings. This list shall not be considered to be exclusive.

    A. Gross Estate:

        Up to $100,000, not to exceed 6%
        Next $200,000, not to exceed 4%
        Next $700,000, not to exceed 3%
        Over $1,000,000, not to exceed 1%

    B. Miscellaneous—Extraordinary Services:

        Sale of Real Estate $500.00

    Federal Estate Tax Return:

        Basic Fee $600.00
        Assets exceeding those indicated in Inheritance
           Tax Schedule 1%

    Inheritance Tax Schedule:

    Cash, stock, bonds, other intangibles—non–probate assets 1%
    Other assets—non-probate assets 1.5%
    Petition—ex parte $175.00
    Other Than as Provided Above .... $85.00 per hour

(Attorney's expertise in probate matters will be considered by the Court in determining the applicable hourly rate.)

II. Miscellaneous

    A. Probate Will only $175.00

    B. Small Estate settlement procedure $300.00
    C. Inheritance Tax Schedule (see above)
    D. Federal Estate Tax Return (see above)

III. Wrongful Death Administration

    A. Fees not to exceed:

        Settlement prior to filing 25%

        Settlement after filing and prior to trial 33–1/3%
        Trial 40%
        Appeal, or extra work 50%

IV. General

Fees will be computed on an hourly basis only for extraordinary services or for services not specified above. Fee petitions requesting extraordinary fees must set forth services rendered with specificity. Extraordinary services, depending upon the circumstances prevailing in each individual matter, may include: sale of personal property, sale of real property, partial distribution, defending a Will, construing a Will, contesting claims, adjusting tax matters, any contested hearing, petition for instructions, heirship determination, generating additional income for the estate, federal estate tax return, etc. All fee petitions must specifically set forth the fee requested for both the personal representative and the attorney and will be set for hearing.

If all interested parties sign a waiver and consent stating that they have been advised the additional fee request exceeds the Court's guidelines and that the services as detailed are extraordinary, the Court may not require a hearing. A suggested form of acceptable waiver is attached. The Court will not determine and allow fees in an Unsupervised Administration. Fees determined on non-probate transferred assets should be charged against the transferees of these assets and not the estate.

PERSONAL REPRESENTATIVE FEES

I. Professional

Their applicable reasonable rate to be reviewed in light of all prevailing circumstances.

II. Non–Professional

An amount not in excess of one-half (1/2) of the attorney's fee.

III. Attorney

When the attorney also serves as the personal representative, an additional amount not in excess of one-third (1/3) of the attorney fee may be allowed, provided:

A. Additional services have been performed which are normally done by the personal representative; and

B. Assets of the estate warrant the allowance of additional fees.

LIMITATION ON FEES

In all instances, the combined total of the fees allowed to the personal representative and attorney for the administration of an estate shall not exceed ten percent (10%) of the decedent's gross estate.

WAIVER AND CONSENT TO ALLOWANCE OF
FEES IN EXCESS OF GUIDELINES

When an attorney reasonably believes that extraordinary circumstances exist and requests fees that exceed the Guidelines, it is suggested that all affected parties either sign a waiver and consent, or the fees be determined only after notice to the affected parties and hearing on the petition. The waiver and consent should not be merely a pro forma waiver and consent, but should be in substantially the following form:

IMPORTANT: PLEASE READ BEFORE SIGNING!
WAIVER AND CONSENT

The undersigned, an interested party in the Estate of _____, understands that:

A. The maximum fee ordinarily allowed by the Court for legal services in this estate would amount to $ ___.

B. The attorney has requested fees in the amount of $ ___, alleging that extraordinary and unusual services have been performed.

The undersigned, being fully advised, now consents to the allowance of the requested fee, waives any notice of hearing on the Petition and requests that the Court allow fees in the amount of $ ___.

Dated: _____   _____

                                                                      Devisee/Heir

Adopted Aug. 4, 2006, effective Jan. 1, 2007. Amended effective Jan. 1, 2012; Oct. 1, 2012.

PROBATE—APPENDIX D. PHYSICIAN'S REPORT

STATE OF INDIANA   )
)

COUNTY OF PORTER   ) SS:

)   CAUSE NO. ___

IN THE MATTER OF   )
THE GUARDIANSHIP OF)
)
_____)

PHYSICIAN'S REPORT

_____, a physician licensed to practice medicine in the State of Indiana, submits the following report on _____, alleged incapacitated person, based on an examination of said person on the ___ day of _____, 20 ___.

1. Describe the nature and type of the incapacitated person's disability: _____

2. Describe the incapacitated person's mental and physical condition; and, when it is appropriate, describe educational condition, adaptive behavior and social skills:

_____

3. State whether, in your opinion, the incapacitated person is totally or only partially incapable of making personal and financial decisions; and, if the latter, the kinds of decisions which the incapacitated person can and cannot make. Include the reason for this opinion. _____

4. What, in your opinion, is the most appropriate living arrangement for the incapacitated person; and, if applicable, describe the most appropriate treatment or rehabilitation plan. Include the reasons for your opinion. _____

5. Can the incapacitated person appear in court without injury to his/her health? (yes/no) If the answer is no, explain the medical reasons for your answer. _____

I affirm, under the penalties of perjury, the foregoing representations are true.

Signature: _____

Printed: _____

Street Address: _____

City/State/Zip: _____

Telephones: _____

This report must be signed by a physician. If the description of the incapacitated person's mental, physical and educational condition, adaptive behavior or social skills is based on evaluations by the professionals, all professionals preparing evaluations must sign the report. Evaluations on which the report is based must have been performed within three (3) months of the date of the filing of the petition.

Names and signatures of other persons who performed evaluations upon which this report is based:

Name: _____

Address: _____

Signature: _____

Name: _____

Address: _____

Signature: _____

Adopted Aug. 4, 2006, effective Jan. 1, 2007. Amended effective Jan. 1, 2012; Oct. 1, 2012.

PORTER COUNTY LOCAL FAMILY COURT RULES

Adopted August 4, 2006, Effective January 1, 2007

Including Amendments Received Through November 1, 2013

Research Notes

These rules can be searched electronically on Westlaw *in the* IN-RULES *database; updates to these rules may be found on Westlaw in* IN-RULESUPDATES. *For search tips and a summary of database content, consult the Westlaw Scope Screens for each database.*

LR64–FC00 Rule 6000.   CITATION

These rules shall be known as Porter County Family Court Rules and shall be cited as follows:

"PORTER COUNTY LOCAL FAMILY COURT RULE ___"(OR "LR64–FC ___—___");

Adopted Aug. 4, 2006, effective Jan. 1, 2007. Amended effective Jan. 1, 2012; Oct. 1, 2012.

LR64–FC00 Rule 6100.   OBJECTIVE

The primary objective of the Porter County Family Court is to coordinate cases among family members throughout the judicial process and to ensure the delivery of appropriate services. This allows judges to review family issues in a comprehensive manner, consolidate hearings when appropriate, issue non conflicting orders, impose sanctions to best fit family needs and instill accountability. To implement this concept, new techniques and information management systems are needed to identify family members and link their cases as they enter the judicial system. These rules are implemented only for cases assigned to Family Court.

Adopted Aug. 4, 2006, effective Jan. 1, 2007. Amended effective Jan. 1, 2012; Oct. 1, 2012.

LR64–FC00 Rule 6200.   DEFINITIONS

Family Court. "Family Court" is the court or courts before which cases involving a family or household are linked together for purposes of case coordination. The individual cases maintain their separate integrity and separate docket number, but may be given a common Family Court designation. The individual cases may all be transferred to one judge, or

may remain in the separate courts in which they were originally filed.

Family Court Proceeding. A "Family Court Proceeding" is comprised of the individual cases of the family or household which have been assigned to Family Court.

Adopted Aug. 4, 2006, effective Jan. 1, 2007. Amended effective Jan. 1, 2012; Oct. 1, 2012.

LR64–FC00 Rule 6300.   JURISDICTION AND RELATED CASES

Porter County Family Court will have jurisdiction over cases in which a family with children or household with children has involvement in multiple cases, as indicated by the Family Court matrix, of the following types: CHINS, delinquency, juvenile status offense, child support, termination of parental rights, adoption, placement of children, paternity, dissolution of marriage, mental health, domestic violence, protective order, adult criminal (intra-family) and alcohol or drug charges.

The Court has determined that the following types of matters constitute cases that are related when a named party and family or household member(s) have matters pending of the following types: CM, or DF filings involving domestic and/or family violence related charges and/or substance abuse charges, and all cases of the following types: PO, JM, JS, JP, JT, JD, JC, DR, GU, AD and MH.

The Family Court may exercise jurisdiction over any case involving the family at the same time it exercises jurisdiction over a juvenile case involving the family.

The Family Court may, in the court's discretion, set hearings on related cases to be heard concurrently, take evidence on the related cases at these hearings, and rule on the admissibility of evidence for each cause separately as needed to adequately preserve the record for appeal. This rule applies only when the cases are pending before the same judicial officer.

Adopted Aug. 4, 2006, effective Jan. 1, 2007. Amended effective Jan. 1, 2012; Oct. 1, 2012.

LR64–FC00 Rule 6400. ASSIGNMENT OF CASES, CLERKS RESPONSIBILITIES

The supervising judge of the Porter County Family Court shall approve the assignment of cases to the Family Court. The transfer and consolidation of cases assigned to Family Court are subject to the provisions of these Family Court Rules.

Upon assignment of a case to Family Court, case management procedures shall be implemented, and all parties are to be notified. The Clerk is to enter the Family Court assignment on the chronological case summary.

The Clerk of the Court shall enter the answers contained in numerical paragraphs #1, #5 and #6 of the entry of Appearance Form in the information field of the Jalen Case Management System. In Protective Order cases, the date of birth and social security number of the petitioner shall be entered as confidential information.

Notice of Case Assignment: within a reasonable time after a case is assigned to Family Court: the Court shall provide to all parties in the Family Court proceeding a list of all cases that have been assigned to that Family Court proceeding.

Adopted Aug. 4, 2006, effective Jan. 1, 2007. Amended effective Jan. 1, 2012; Oct. 1, 2012.

LR64–FC00 Rule 6500. CHANGE OF JUDGE

Change of Judge: once notice is sent to the parties that a case has been selected for Family Court, no motion for change of venue from the judge may be granted except to the extent permitted by Indiana Trial Rule 76. A motion for change of venue from the judge in any matters arising in the Family Court proceeding or any future cases joined in the Family Court proceedings after the initial selection of cases, shall be granted only for cause.

Special Judge: if a special judge is appointed, all current and future cases in the Family Court proceeding may be assigned to the special judge.

Objection to Family Court designation: within ten (10) days after notice is sent that a case has been selected for Family Court, a party may object for cause to the Family Court designation.

Adopted Aug. 4, 2006, effective Jan. 1, 2007. Amended effective Jan. 1, 2012; Oct. 1, 2012.

LR64–FC00 Rule 6600. CASE CONSOLIDATION AND TRANSFER

The supervising judge of the Porter Family Court may enter orders for the consolidation and transfer of cases assigned to Family Court when the judicial officers presiding over such cases do not object. No case shall be transferred or consolidated until the judicial officers to whom such cases have been assigned have been advised of the contemplated action. The consolidation and transfer of Family Court cases shall be accomplished by the entry of an order signed by the supervising judge.

Adopted Aug. 4, 2006, effective Jan. 1, 2007. Amended effective Jan. 1, 2012; Oct. 1, 2012.

LR64–FC00 Rule 6700. JUDICIAL NOTICE

Judicial Notice: any court having jurisdiction over a case assigned to Family Court can take judicial notice of any relevant orders or Chronological Case Summary (CCS) entry issued by any Indiana Circuit, Superior, County, or Probate Court.

Procedurally, if a court takes judicial notice of:

(1) a court order, the court shall provide a copy of that order; or

(2) a CCS or CCS entry(s), the court shall provide a copy of the entire CCS, the court shall provide copies of the order or CCS to the parties to the case at or before the time judicial notice is taken.

Adopted Aug. 4, 2006, effective Jan. 1, 2007. Amended effective Jan. 1, 2012; Oct. 1, 2012.

LR64–FC00 Rule 6800. ACCESS TO RECORDS

Access to Records: parties to a Family Court proceeding shall have access to all cases within the Family Court proceeding, with the exception of confidential cases or records to which they are not a party. Parties may seek access to confidential cases or records in another case within the Family Court proceeding in which they are not a party, by written petition based on relevancy and need. Confidential records shall retain their confidential status and the Family Court shall direct that confidential records not be included in the public record of the proceedings.

Adopted Aug. 4, 2006, effective Jan. 1, 2007. Amended effective Jan. 1, 2012; Oct. 1, 2012.

PORTER COUNTY ADMINISTRATIVE RULES

Adopted August 4, 2006, Effective January 1, 2007

Including Amendments Received Through November 1, 2013

Research Notes

These rules may be searched electronically on Westlaw in the IN-RULES database; updates to these rules may be found on Westlaw in IN-RULESUPDATES. For search tips and a summary of database content, consult the Westlaw Scope Screens for each database.

LR64–AR15 Rule 7000. COURT REPORTER SERVICES

The undersigned courts comprise all of the courts of record of Porter County, Indiana, and hereby adopt the following local rule by which court reporter services shall be governed.

7000.10 Definitions.

(1) A *Court Reporter* is a person who is specifically designated by a court to perform the official court reporting services for the court including preparing a transcript of the record.

(2) *Equipment* means all physical items owned by the court or other governmental entity and used by a court reporter in performing court reporting services. Equipment shall include, but not be limited to, telephones, computer hardware, software programs, disks, tapes, and any other device used for recording and storing, and transcribing electronic data.

(3) *Work space* means that portion of the court's facilities dedicated to each court reporter, including but not limited to actual space in the courtroom and any designated office space.

(4) *Regular Page* means the page unit of transcript which results when prepared in nonappellate fashion.

(5) *Appellate page* means the page unit of transcript which results when prepared with marginal notes, footnotes, or headers, and Table of Contents in the form required by Indiana Rules of Appellate Procedure.

(6) *Recording* means the electronic, mechanical, stenographic or other recording made as required by Indiana Rule of Trial Procedure 74.

(7) *Regular hours* worked means those hours which the court is regularly scheduled to work during any given work week. Depending on the particular court, these hours may vary from court to court within the court but remain the same for each work week.

(8) *Gap hours* worked means those hours worked that are in excess of the regular hours worked but hours not in excess of forty (40) hours per work week.

(9) *Overtime hours* worked means those hours worked in excess of forty (40) hours per work week.

(10) *Work week* means a seven (7) consecutive day week that consistently begins and ends on the same days throughout the year; i.e. Sunday through Saturday, Wednesday through Tuesday, Friday through Thursday.

(11) *Court* means the particular court for which the court reporter performs services. Court may also mean al[1] of the courts in Porter County.

(12) *County indigent transcript* means a transcript that is paid for from county funds and is for the use on behalf of a litigant who has been declared indigent by a court.

(13) *State indigent transcript* means a transcript that is paid for from state funds and is for the use on behalf of a litigant who has been declared indigent by a court.

(14) *Private transcript* means a transcript, including but not limited to a deposition transcript, that is paid for by a private party.

(15) *Expedited transcript* means any transcript requested to be delivered sooner than one week before the record is due to be filed with the Clerk of the Court of Appeals.

7000.20 Salaries and Per Page Fees.

(1) Court reporters shall be paid an annual salary for time spent working under the control, direction and direct supervision of their supervising court during any regular work hours, gap hours or overtime hours. The supervising court shall enter into written agreement with the court reporters which outlines the manner in which the court reporter is

to be compensated for gap and overtime hours; i.e. monetary compensation or compensatory time off regular work hours.

(2) The maximum per page fee a court reporter may charge for the preparation or a county indigent transcript shall be a regular page rate of $3.50 per page; $3.75 per page, appellate pay rate; and an expedited rate of $6.50 per page for expedited transcripts. The court reporter shall submit directly to the county a claim for the preparation of the county indigent transcript. In setting this rate, we take into account the use of county equipment for transcription.

(3) The maximum per page fee a court reporter may charge for the preparation of a state indigent transcript shall be a regular page rate of $4.00 per page, payable as follows: $3.50 per page directly to the court reporter and $ .50 per page paid directly to the county if county equipment is used for transcription; and $4.25 per page, appellate page rate, payable as follows: $3.75 per page payable directly to the court reporter and $ .50 per page paid directly to the county if county equipment is used for transcription; and an expedited rate of $6.50 per page for expedited transcripts, with $ .50 per page paid directly to the county if county equipment is used for transcription.

(4) The maximum per page fee a court reporter may charge for the preparation of a private transcript shall be a regular page rate of $5.00 per page, payable as follows: $4.50 per page payable directly to the court reporter and $ .50 per page paid directly to the county if county equipment is used for transcription; $5.25 per page, appellate page rate, payable as follows: $4.75 per page payable directly to the court reporter and $ .50 per page payable directly to the county if county equipment is used for transcription; and an expedited rate of $8.50 per page for expedited transcripts, with $ .50 per page paid directly to the county if county equipment is used for transcription.

(5) The maximum fee that a court reporter may charge for copies shall be $2.00 per page.

(6) The minimum fee that a court reporter may charge for transcripts is $35.00.

(7) An additional labor charge of the hourly rate based upon the court reporter's annual court compensation may be charged for the time spent binding the transcript and exhibits.

(8) Each court reporter shall report, at least on an annual basis, all transcript fees received for the preparation of either county indigent, state indigent or private transcripts to the Indiana Supreme Court Division of State Court Administration. The reporting shall be made on forms prescribed by the Division of State Court Administration.

7000.30 Private Practice.

(1) If a court reporter elects to engage in private practice through the recording of a deposition and/or preparing of a deposition transcript, and the court reporter desires to utilize the court's equipment, work space and supplies, and the court agrees to the use of the court equipment for such purpose, the court and the court reporter shall enter into a written agreement which must, at a minimum, designate the following:

(a) The reasonable market rate for the use of equipment, work space and supplies;

(b) The method by which records are to be kept for the use of equipment, work space and supplies; and

(c) The method by which the court reporter is to reimburse the court for the use of the equipment, work space and supplies.

(2) If a court reporter elects to engage in private practice through the recording of a deposition and/or preparing of a deposition transcript, all such private practice work shall be conducted outside of regular working hours.

Adopted Aug. 4, 2006, effective Jan. 1, 2007. Amended effective Jan. 1, 2012; Oct. 1, 2012.

1 So in original.

LR64–JR04 Rule 7100. PROCEDURE FOR SUMMONING JURORS

The judges of the Porter Circuit and Superior Courts adopt the two tier notice and summons procedure for summoning jurors.

Adopted Aug. 4, 2006, effective Jan. 1, 2007. Amended effective Jan. 1, 2012; Oct. 1, 2012.

LR64–AR00 Rule 7200. PORTER COUNTY ADULT DRUG COURT PROGRAM

A Porter County Adult Drug Court Program shall be established pursuant to IC 12–23–14.5–1 and in accordance with Porter County Local Rules.

Adopted and effective Feb. 7, 2007. Amended April 8, 2009, effective Jan. 8, 2009; effective Jan. 1, 2012; Oct. 1, 2012.

LR64–AR00 Rule 7300. ESTABLISHMENT OF FEE SCHEDULE FOR PORTER COUNTY ALCOHOL AND DRUG OFFENDERS SERVICE

Those persons directed to participate in the Porter County Alcohol and Drug Offenders Service (PCADOS) shall pay all applicable and necessary fees. Fees are to be determined at the time of the clinical evaluation or assessment. Fee deadlines are determined at the time of the evaluation or assessment.

Those persons directed to participate in the Porter County Alcohol and Drug Offenders Service (PCADOS) program shall pay fees in accordance with the following schedule:

LEVEL I

Basic Education Services (12 Hours) $400

LEVEL II

Advanced Education Services (20 Hours) $400

OTHER FEES

One Day Class Informational Session (8 Hours) $100

Informational Session with Assessment $200

Transfers $100

Assessment Only $100

The program fees for Porter County Alcohol and Drug Offenders Service (PCA-DOS) are payable at the Clerk's Office in the courthouse in which the sentencing Court is located. All payments must be made in cash or by money order. *(LR64–AR00–7300 effective August 30, 2009)*.

Adopted Aug. 30, 2009. Amended effective Jan. 1, 2012.

PORTER COUNTY LOCAL JUVENILE RULES

Adopted August 4, 2006, Effective January 1, 2007

Including Amendments Received Through November 1, 2013

Research Notes

These rules may be searched electronically on Westlaw in the IN-RULES database; updates to these rules may be found on Westlaw in IN-RULESUPDATES. For search tips and a summary of database content, consult the Westlaw Scope Screens for each database.

LR64–JV00 Rule 8000. CITATION

These rules shall be known as Porter County Local Juvenile Rules and shall be cited as: "PORTER COUNTY LOCAL JUVENILE RULE" (OR "LR64–JV –"); AND

Adopted Aug. 4, 2006, effective Jan. 1, 2007. Amended effective Jan. 1, 2012; Oct. 1, 2012.

LR64–JV00 Rule 8010. ASSIGNMENT OF CASES

All cases which contain a cause number of the juvenile case type shall be filed on the juvenile docket.

Adopted Aug. 4, 2006, effective Jan. 1, 2007. Amended effective Jan. 1, 2012; Oct. 1, 2012; Jan. 1, 2013.

LR64–JV00 Rule 8020. APPLICATION OF LOCAL CIVIL AND CRIMINAL RULES

The Porter County Local Civil Rules whether adopted by this Court on its own or in conjunction with the Porter Superior Court including any subsequent modifications or amendments thereto apply to all Paternity and Children in Need of Services cases, unless otherwise provided in these Porter County Local Juvenile Rules. The Porter County Local Criminal Rules whether adopted by this Court on its own or in conjunction with the Porter Superior Court including any subsequent modifications or amendments thereto apply to all Delinquency cases, unless otherwise provided in these Porter County Local Juvenile Rules. The Porter County Local Family Law Rules apply to all Juvenile cases unless there is a conflict, in which event the Porter County Local Juvenile Rules shall control.

Adopted Aug. 4, 2006, effective Jan. 1, 2007. Amended effective Jan. 1, 2012; Oct. 1, 2012; Jan. 1, 2013.

LR64–JV00 Rule 8030. REPORTS

All reports required to be filed with the Court or are filed with the Court shall be filed at least 10 days prior to the hearing and shall promptly be given to the parents, foster parents, Special Advocate, caseworker, probation officer and attorneys. If the hearing was set with less than 10 days notice then the report shall be provided to the Court and the above individuals within 4 days of the date of the hearing but no later than 2 hours prior to the hearing. Reports include DCS 310's and DCS 311's. If the child is not with parents or relatives, all reports shall state what family members have requested custody and specifically why that relative is not being considered.

Adopted effective Jan. 1, 2013.

LR64–JV00 Rule 8040. SERVICE PROVIDER REPORT

All Individuals and agencies providing service for a child or family that is the subject of a Delinquency or CHINS Petition shall provide at least monthly reports. The monthly reports shall among other things state specifically why the service should continue and whether or not there are less costly services that can be provided by the service provider or some other service provider. The monthly reports are to be provided to the Department of Child Services, Probation Department, CASA, parents, foster parents, and attorneys. The caseworker or probation officer shall keep the service providers informed of the above individuals address so that the service providers can comply with this rule.

Adopted effective Jan. 1, 2013.

LR64–JV00 Rule 8050. CASE CONFERENCE

Case Conferences are to be set at least 2 weeks in advance and cleared on the parents and the child's attorney's calendar. Notice must be given immediately to the parent, foster parents, CASA and anyone else necessary for the conference to be a success. The approved case plan must be filed with the Court.

Adopted effective Jan. 1, 2013.

LR64–JV00 Rule 8060. NOTICE OF HEARING

Proof of Notice of any hearing required to be served by the caseworker or probation worker shall be filed with the Court as soon as practicable after service has been made.

Adopted effective Jan. 1, 2013.

LR64–JV00 Rule 8070. CHILD SUPPORT WORK-SHEET

The probation officer or caseworker shall, not less than 3 days prior to an initial hearing, file a completed child support worksheet so that the Court may enter an order requiring the parents to pay for services as required by statute. The parents, under penalties for contempt, shall furnish the caseworker or officer with the necessary income information including the name and case number of any case where they are paying or receiving child support.

Adopted effective Jan. 1, 2013.

LR64–JV00 Rule 8080. SHARING OF INFORMA-TION

The Department of Child Services and the Probation Department shall freely share and exchange information, including documents, with each other concerning a child or family, upon request, regardless of the status of the case. Information deemed confidential shall be treated as such by the recipient.

Adopted effective Jan. 1, 2013.

LR64–JV00 Rule 8090. SPECIAL FINDINGS OF FACT

In all cases in which the court is required to enter special findings of fact or the parties request the Court to issue special findings of fact, counsel of record shall submit to the court in an electronic format and by hard copy filing Proposed Special Findings embracing all the facts which they allege to have been proved and relevant conclusions of law thereon. Such form of Proposed Special Findings shall be submitted to the court, pursuant to Trial Rule 52 (C), and shall be submitted within such time as the court shall direct.

Adopted effective Jan. 1, 2013.

LR64–JV00 Rule 8100. CHANGE OF VENUE FROM THE JUDGE

No change of venue from a Magistrate shall be granted. A change of venue from the Judge of the Porter Circuit Court may be sought under applicable Indiana Rules of Trial Procedure.

Adopted Aug. 4, 2006, effective Jan. 1, 2007. Amended effective Jan. 1, 2012; Oct. 1, 2012; Jan. 1, 2013.

LR64–JV00 Rule 8110. PARENTING TIME

Unless the Court enters specific orders to the contrary parenting time shall be in accordance with the Indiana Parenting Time Guidelines. For all settlement agreements in which parenting time is established, the parties shall certify in such agreement that they have received a copy of such guidelines and have read and understand the same.

Adopted effective Jan. 1, 2013.

LR64–JV00 Rule 8120. PLACEMENT ON HOUSE ARREST

Juveniles placed on House Arrest shall be subject to conditions based upon the level of House Arrest to which they are assigned.

Adopted effective Jan. 1, 2013.

LR64–JV00 Rule 8130. HOUSE ARREST LEVEL I

1. You will remain on House Arrest until you have been informed by the Juvenile Probation Department or the Court of your formal release from said conditions.

2. When at home you are to be supervised by a parent/guardian or an approved adult unless otherwise approved by the Probation Department.

3. You are to adhere to a curfew of 5:00 p.m. on weekdays and 7:00 p.m. on weekends unless otherwise approved by the Probation Department. While on House Arrest:

a. Only friends approved by your parent(s) and the Probation Department are permitted to visit you in your home and/or on your property.

b. Only one (1) approved friend is permitted to visit at any given time.

c. Visitation with said friend shall be supervised by your parent or guardian.

d. You are not allowed in anyone else's home unless accompanied by your parent and/or guardian or unless approved by your probation officer.

e. You will be allowed to participate in out of home and after school activities approved by your parent(s) and the Probation Department

4. Internet use is allowed only under your parent's direct supervision.

5. At all times your parents/guardians are to know where you are. You are not to be with any other adult without your parents and the Probation Department's permission.

6. If you are absent from school, you must report your absence to the Probation Department by 9:00 a.m. You may be required to provide a medical excuse to validate your illness.

7. At any time submit to a drug screen. Any confirmed controlled or illegal substance or substance metabolite is a violation of Court Ordered Restriction.

8. At any time allow any Juvenile Court representative or Law Enforcement Officer to enter your residence without prior notice, and to make reasonable inquiry into your activities and others in the home, and you shall at anytime submit to the reasonable search of your home, person and/or vehicle which shall relate to your compliance with these conditions of house arrest. Further, a Juvenile Court representative may visit or telephone your home or require you to attend an appointment to verify your compliance to these rules. Non–attendance will be viewed as a violation of House Arrest. You shall answer all reasonable inquires by any Juvenile Court Representatives.

9. You are not allowed to operate any motorized vehicle for the duration of House Arrest unless otherwise approved by both your parent(s) and the Probation Department.

10. **Further specific conditions:**

_____

_____

_____

Adopted effective Jan. 1, 2013.

LR64–JV00 Rule 8140. HOUSE ARREST LEVEL II

1. When at home you are to be supervised by a parent/guardian or a Court appointed adult unless otherwise approved by the Juvenile Probation Department.

2. You are not allowed to leave your property unless you are directly going to school, to work, or you are with your parents/guardians. If you are allowed to work, your hours must be approved by your Probation Officer. You must provide a written report of your work schedule each week to the Juvenile Probation Department.

3. You are not permitted to have friends in your home, on your property, or on the telephone. You are not allowed to use the Internet or a pager.

4. At ALL times your parents/guardians are to know where you are. You are not to be with any other adult without your parents' and the Probation Department's permission.

5. Obey all laws. Any tobacco products found in the possession of a child on home detention will be confiscated.

6. If you are absent from school, you must report your absence to the Juvenile Probation Department by 9:00 a.m. You may be required to provide a medical excuse to validate your illness.

7. At any time a Juvenile Court representative may visit or telephone your home or require you to attend an appointment to verify your compliance with these rules. Non-attendance will be viewed as a violation of home detention.

8. At any time submit to a drug screen. Any confirmed controlled or illegal substance or substance metabolites is a violation of home detention.

9. At any time allow any Juvenile Court representative or law enforcement officer to enter your residence without prior notice, and to make reasonable inquiry into the activities of you and others in the home. At all times you shall be subject to reasonable searches of your home, vehicle and/or person which shall relate to your compliance with these conditions of House Arrest. You shall answer all reasonable inquiries by any Juvenile Court representative.

10. You are not allowed to operate any motorized vehicle while you are on home detention without prior approval of the Court.

11. Obey all laws. Any tobacco products found in the possession of a child on home detention will be confiscated.

12. **Further specific conditions:**

_____

_____

_____

Adopted effective Jan. 1, 2013.

PORTER COUNTY LOCAL ELECTRONIC FILING RULES

(FOR JUVENILE COURT ONLY)

Adopted August 4, 2006, Effective January 1, 2007

Including Amendments Received Through November 1, 2013

Research Notes

These rules may be searched electronically on Westlaw in the IN-RULES database; updates to these rules may be found on Westlaw in IN-RULESUPDATES. For search tips and a summary of database content, consult the Westlaw Scope Screens for each database.

LR64–EF00 Rule 9000.   CITATION

These rules shall be known as Porter Electronic Filing Rules and shall be cited as:

"PORTER COUNTY LOCAL ELECTRONIC FILING RULE ___" (OR "LR64–EF ___–___");

Adopted Aug. 4, 2006, effective Jan. 1, 2007. Amended effective Jan. 1, 2012; Oct. 1, 2012.

LR64–EF00 Rule 9100.   OBJECTIVE

The primary objective of the Porter County Electronic Filing Rules is to set forth these local rules of procedure to assist the public, the bar and the court in implementing electronic filing and computer case management for Juvenile Court.

Adopted Aug. 4, 2006, effective Jan. 1, 2007. Amended effective Jan. 1, 2012; Oct. 1, 2012.

LR64–EF00 Rule 9200.   AUTHORITY

The following rules are hereby adopted and promulgated by the Porter County Juvenile Court pursuant to TR 81 of the Indiana Rules of Trial Procedure.

Adopted Aug. 4, 2006, effective Jan. 1, 2007. Amended effective Jan. 1, 2012; Oct. 1, 2012.

LR64–EF00 Rule 9300.   JURISDICTION AND RELATED CASES

These rules shall apply to all new cases filed with the court and all existing cases on file with the court. Existing cases will not be required to convert to the computer system until some activity occurs in the case. Effective January 1, 2007, all documents (other than those specifically excepted by the Court) may be filed electronically in all cases, so long as the case was initiated electronically.

Adopted Aug. 4, 2006, effective Jan. 1, 2007. Amended effective Jan. 1, 2012; Oct. 1, 2012.

LR64–EF00 Rule 9400.   ACCESS

In order to access court files electronically, a person must;

Obtain a unique password and user identification; and

Execute a user agreement with the Court.

Pay the required fee.

Adopted Aug. 4, 2006, effective Jan. 1, 2007. Amended effective Jan. 1, 2012; Oct. 1, 2012.

LR64–EF00 Rule 9500.   ELECTRONIC FILING OF PLEADINGS

New Cases

Prior to creating a new case in the court computer system ("Quest") a party must obtain a cause number from the Clerk of the Court. The cause number may be obtained upon submission of an appearance form and payment of the filing fee to the Clerk [or upon presentation to the Clerk of a court order waiving the filing fee]. Issuance of a cause number does not constitute a filing and will not toll any statute of limitations or other time limitation.

In order to create a new case in the court computer system (Quest), a person must have a password and user identification granting access to the system.

An action must be commenced in conformity with Trail Rule 3 and pursuant to Trial Rules 4 through 4.17 of the Indiana Rules of Trial Procedure.

Existing Cases

The CCS and pleadings of any existing case may be viewed on the QUEST system by use of a valid password. This does not apply to cases which are confidential by virtue of the law or court order.

To electronically file a pleading in QUEST, one must first complete an appearance form and file it with the clerk. Upon accepting the appearance form filing, the Clerk will make that case accessible for the filing of pleadings by the person who has made the appearance.

Whenever an attorney withdraws his appearance in a case, his accessibility to that case for the filing of pleadings will be removed.

Time of Filing

Documents may be filed through an E–filing system at any time that the Clerk's office is open to receive the filing or at such other times as may be designated by the Clerk and posted publicly. Documents filed through the E–filing system are deemed filed when received by the Clerk's office, except that Documents received at times that the Clerk's office is closed shall be deemed filed the next regular time when the Clerk's office is open for filing. The time stamp issued by the E–filing system shall be presumed to be the time the Document is received by the Clerk.

Notice of Filing Pleading (Manner of Service)

In addition to the usual ways of serving parties of record pursuant to TR 5, service may be made by QUEST e-mail on those parties of record or their attorneys who are current users of the QUEST system. Said notice shall indicate the name of the pleading filed, the date it was file, and any hearing date thereon, if applicable. The notified party or attorney may then access the pleading through the QUEST system. A list of current users of the QUEST system shall be maintained by the Court.

Adopted Aug. 4, 2006, effective Jan. 1, 2007. Amended effective Jan. 1, 2012; Oct. 1, 2012.

LR64–EF00 Rule 9600. PASSWORD

Access to the court case management system QUEST may occur by obtaining the password and user name through a user agreement with the QUEST Coordinator in the Porter County Juvenile Probation Office. Each person is responsible for the use of his password. No person shall knowingly utilize or cause another person to utilize the password of another without permission of the holder of the password or in violation of these rules. No attorney shall knowingly permit or cause to permit his user name and password to be utilized by anyone other than an employee of his law firm.

Adopted Aug. 4, 2006, effective Jan. 1, 2007. Amended effective Jan. 1, 2012; Oct. 1, 2012.

LR64–EF00 Rule 9700. SIGNING OF DOCU-MENTS

Documents filed through the E–filing system by use of a valid user name and password are presumed to have been signed and authorized by the User to whom that user name and password have been issued.

Adopted Aug. 4, 2006, effective Jan. 1, 2007. Amended effective Jan. 1, 2012; Oct. 1, 2012.

LR64–EF00 Rule 9800. SATISFACTION OF SIG-NATURE REQUIREMENTS

a. Where an attorney's signature is required on a pleading, the QUEST imprint of attorney's name on the pleading will satisfy said requirement.

b. Where a person's signature is required on a verified pleading or document, the QUEST imprint of the name will satisfy the requirement; however, the attorney is required to maintain an original, signed paper copy in his office.

c. A pro se litigant is required to file a signed copy with the clerk.

Adopted Aug. 4, 2006, effective Jan. 1, 2007. Amended effective Jan. 1, 2012; Oct. 1, 2012.

LR64–EF00 Rule 9900. SIGNATURE STAMPS FOR JUDICIAL OFFICERS

a. Each member of the Porter Circuit Court staff assigned to handle juvenile cases shall have their own user name and password.

b. The court staff, each using their own Quest user identification, is authorized to affix the judicial officers' electronically generated and replica signatures to all Orders approved by the appropriate judicial officer, and all CCS entries requiring a judicial officer's signature, and other documents and pleadings as directed by the judicial officer.

c. Bulk scheduling, when pre-approved by the court, can be scheduled by the agency authorized by the court to do so.

Adopted Aug. 4, 2006, effective Jan. 1, 2007. Amended effective Jan. 1, 2012; Oct. 1, 2012.

PORTER COUNTY LOCAL PROBLEM SOLVING COURT RULES

Including Amendments Posted Through November 1, 2013

Research Notes

These rules may be searched electronically on Westlaw *in the* IN-RULES *database; updates to these rules may be found on* Westlaw *in* IN-RULESUPDATES. *For search tips and a summary of database content, consult the Westlaw Scope Screens for each database.*

LR64–AR00 Rule 10000. PROBLEM SOLVING COURTS

10000.10 All Porter County "problem solving courts" shall be established pursuant to IC 33–23–16–11. A "problem solving court" is defined as it is at IC 33–23–16–8. Prior to being established as a problem solving court, a court will provide notice of intent to establish itself to the Indiana Judicial Center in accordance with IC 33–23–16–19(a). The court will submit a Petition for approval to the Indiana Judicial Center in accordance with the Rules adopted by the Board as required by 33–23–16–19(b).

10000.20   Problem Solving Court Fees

A problem solving court may require an eligible individual to pay a problem solving court administrator fee of not more than one hundred dollars ($100) per admission to a problem solving court for initial problem solving court services regardless of the length of participation in the problem solving court.

Amended effective Jan. 1, 2012; Oct. 1, 2012.

LR64–AR00 Rule 10100. ADULT DRUG COURT PROGRAM

10100.10   Establishment. The Porter County Adult Drug Court Program is established pursuant to IC 33–23–16–11(1). The objectives of the Porter County Adult Drug Court Program shall be in accordance with the definition of a "drug court" as stated at IC 33–23–16–5.

10100.20   Fees. In accordance with the Rules adopted by the Board under IC 33–23–16–23(c), those persons directed to participate in the Porter County Adult Drug Court Program shall pay a Problem–Solving Court services fee according to a schedule of fifty dollars ($50) per month for the duration of their Program participation. The Clerk of the Court shall collect and transmit the program fee within thirty (30) days after the fees are collected, for deposit by the auditor or fiscal officer in the appropriate user fee fund established under IC 33–37–8. Pursuant to 33–23–16–23(e) court services fees must be used only to fund problem solving court services.

10100.30   Assignment. The day-to-day operation and management of the Porter County Adult Drug Court Program has been established in and assigned to Porter County Superior Court # 3. The Adult Drug Court Program shall be reviewed by the Porter County Superior Court judges when necessary and upon review and agreement by all the judges, the Adult Drug Court Program may be established in additional courts as needed, subject to approval in accordance with IC 33–23–16–19.

Amended effective Jan. 1, 2012; Oct. 1, 2012.

LR64–AR00 Rule 10200. JUVENILE AND FAMILY DRUG COURT PROGRAM

10200.10   Establishment. The Porter County Juvenile and Family Drug Court Program shall be established pursuant to IC 33–23–16–11(1). The objectives of the Porter County Juvenile and Family Drug Court Program shall be in accordance with the definition of a "drug court" as stated at IC 33–23–16–5.

10200.20   Fees. In accordance with the Rules adopted by the Board under IC 33–23–16–23(c), those persons directed to participate in the Porter County Juvenile and Family Drug Court Program shall pay a Problem–Solving Court services fee according to a schedule of fifty dollars ($50) per month for the duration of their Program participation. The program fees shall be collected and transmitted within thirty (30) days after the fees are collected, for deposit by the auditor or fiscal officer in the appropriate user fee fund established under IC 33–37–8. Pursuant to 33–23–16–23(e) court services fees must be used only to fund Problem–Solving Court services.

10200.30   Assignment. The day-to-day operation and management of the Porter County Juvenile and Family Drug Court Program has been established in and assigned to Porter Circuit Court. The Juvenile and Family Drug Court Program shall be reviewed by the Porter Circuit Court judge when necessary, and upon review and agreement by all the judges with appropriate jurisdiction, the Juvenile and Family Drug Court Program may be established in additional courts as needed, subject to approval in accordance with IC 33–23–16–19.

Amended effective Jan. 1, 2012; Oct. 1, 2012.

LR64–AR00 Rule 10300. VETERANS' COURT PROGRAM

10300.10 Establishment. The Porter County Veterans' Court Program shall be established pursuant to IC 33–23–16–11(7). The objectives of the Porter County Veterans' Court Program shall be in accordance with the definition of a "veterans' court" as stated at IC 33–23–16–10.

10300.20 Fees. In accordance with the Rules adopted by the Board under IC 33–23–16–23(c), those persons directed to participate in the Porter County Veterans' Court Program shall pay a problem solving court services fee according to a schedule of fifty dollars ($50) per month for the duration of their Program participation. The Clerk of the Court shall collect and transmit the program fee within thirty (30) days after the fees are collected, for deposit by the auditor or fiscal officer in the appropriate user fee fund established under IC 33–37–8. Pursuant to 33–23–16–23(e) court services fees must be used only to fund Problem–Solving Court services.

10300.30 Assignment. The day-to-day operation and management of the Porter County Veterans' Court Program has been established in and assigned to Porter Superior Court #3. The Veterans' Court Program shall be reviewed by the Porter County Superior Court judges when necessary and upon review and agreement by all the judges, the Veterans' Court Program may be established in additional courts as needed, subject to approval in accordance with IC 33–23–16–19.

Amended effective Jan. 1, 2012; Oct. 1, 2012.

LR64–AR00 Rule 10400. REENTRY COURT PROGRAM

10300.10 [1] **Establishment.** The Porter County Re-entry Court Program shall be established pursuant to IC 33–23–16–11(5). The objectives of the Porter County Re-entry Court Program shall be in accordance with the definition of a "re-entry court" as stated at 33–23–16–9.

10300.20 [1] **Fees.** In accordance with the Rules adopted by the Board under IC 33–23–16–23(c), those persons directed to participate in the Porter County Re-entry Court Program shall pay a Problem–Solving Court services fee according to a schedule of fifty dollars ($50) per month for the duration of their Program participation. The Clerk of the Court shall collect and transmit the program fee within thirty (30) days after the fees are collected, for deposit by the auditor or fiscal officer in the appropriate user fee fund established under IC 33–37–8. Pursuant to 33–23–16–23(e) court services fees must be used only to fund Problem–Solving Court services.

10300.30 [1] **Assignment.** The day-to-day operation and management of the Porter County Re-entry Court Program has been established in and assigned to Porter Superior Court #3. The Re-entry Court Program shall be reviewed by the Porter County Superior Court judges when necessary and upon review and agreement by all the judges, the Reentry Court Program may be established in additional courts as needed, subject to approval in accordance with IC 33–23–16–19.

Amended effective Jan. 1, 2012; Oct. 1, 2012.

[1] So in original.

LOCAL GENERAL AND ADMINIS-TRATIVE RULES FOR ST. JOSEPH COUNTY

Adopted July 28, 2006, Effective January 1, 2007

Including Amendments Received Through November 1, 2013

Research Notes

Annotations to the Local General and Administrative Rules for St. Joseph County are available in West's Annotated Indiana Code, *Title 34 Appendix.*

These rules may be searched electronically on Westlaw *in the* IN-RULES *database; updates to these rules may be found on Westlaw in IN-RULESUPDATES. For search tips and a summary of database content, consult the Westlaw Scope Screens for each database.*

LR71–TR1 Rule 101. INTENT AND SCOPE OF LOCAL RULES

These local rules are adopted by the Courts of the 60th Judicial Circuit pursuant to the authority of T.R. 81, Indiana Rules of Trial Procedure, and are intended to supplement those Rules.

These local rules shall govern the practice and procedure in all cases in the following courts:

(1) St. Joseph Circuit Court (hereinafter "Circuit Court");

(2) St. Joseph Superior Court (hereinafter "Superior Court"); and

(3) St. Joseph Probate Court (hereinafter "Probate Court").

Wherever appropriate, the term "Judge" shall be construed to mean Judge, Magistrate Judge, Senior Judge or any other appropriate judicial officer of the applicable Court.

Nothing contained in these rules is intended to limit the jurisdiction and/or authority of any judge of Circuit Court, Superior Court, or Probate Court (hereinafter "Courts"); however, these rules shall control the assignment of cases within the 60th Judicial Circuit.

In an individual case, a judge of the St. Joseph Circuit, Superior or Probate courts, upon motion of any party or on the court's own motion, may suspend or modify any of these local rules should the interests of justice so require.

Adopted July 28, 2006, effective Jan. 1, 2007. Amended Aug. 2, 2007, effective Jan. 1, 2008; June 1, 2011, effective Jan. 1, 2012.

LR71–AR00 Rule 102. CONDUCT, DRESS, AND COURT HOUSE POLICIES

102.1. Professional Conduct. It is intended that the business of the Courts of the 60th Judicial Circuit will be conducted by the Judge in accordance with the Indiana Code of Judicial Conduct and that lawyers practicing in these Courts will do so in accordance with the Indiana Rules of Professional Conduct.

102.2. Behavior in the Courthouse. While in any of the courthouses within St. Joseph County, the following behavior is prohibited:

(1) Lawyers and litigants shall not lean on the bench and shall not sit or lean on counsel tables or the jury box.

(2) Lawyers, litigants, and spectators shall refrain from unnecessary conversation in the courthouse or in the courtroom that would disturb the proceedings. Any necessary conversation in the courthouse or in the courtroom shall be conducted at a sufficiently low voice level as not to interfere with the conduct of trials, hearings, or other proceedings before the court.

(3) Lawyers, litigants, or spectators shall not enter the courtroom with food or beverages. Fresh water is supplied daily and is available to lawyers and litigants at counsel tables.

(4) Lawyers, litigants, or any other person in the courtroom shall not talk to the court reporter during the hearings in which they are not participating.

(5) Lawyers, litigants, or any other person shall not chew gum or tobacco in the courthouse.

102.3. Appearance and Dress. Every person who enters a court house in St. Joseph County should be appropriately dressed. Lawyers should appear for court proceedings in professional attire; litigants, witnesses and spectators should appear in appropriate attire. Examples of clothing that is inappropriate and is prohibited from being worn during court proceedings includes, but is not limited to:

(1) Hats or caps;

(2) Outer garments such as topcoats, overcoats, jackets, or overshoes;

(3) Clothing that exposes the midriff;

(4) Shorts of any kind;

(5) Sleeveless shirts (i.e. "muscle shirts" and "tank tops");

(6) Shower shoes (i.e. rubber "flip-flops");

(7) Suggestive or otherwise inappropriate clothing (i.e. poorly fitting, slovenly, or uncleanly).

102.4. Prohibited Items. To insure compliance with state law and to promote public safety, the following rules apply to the presence or use of specific items in and around the courthouse complexes within St. Joseph County:

102.4.1. *Weapons.* No attorney, litigant, witness, or spectator may possess firearms, knives, or other deadly weapons while in or around the courthouse complexes within St. Joseph County without the prior written authorization of the Judge of the Circuit Court or Probate Court or the Chief Judge of the Superior Court. However, a law enforcement officer who is not a litigant in a pending matter and who is appearing as a witness may retain possession of their issued firearm while in the courthouse so long as he or she advises, and receives the permission of, the supervisor of the courthouse security detail upon entering the courthouse complex or has prior authorization from a Judge of one of the Courts.

102.4.2. *Cameras, Telephones, and Other Items.* Unless otherwise allowed by this Rule, and to protect the interest of privacy, safety and justice, cellular telephones, smart phones and personal digital assistants (PDA's) are not permitted in the court houses within St. Joseph County. To avoid disruption during court proceedings, the following items are prohibited in the courtrooms and the areas in or around the courtrooms during hearings or trials:

(1) Cameras, video cameras, or any devices capable of audio and/or visual recording;

(2) If allowed inside the court houses by these Rules or by order of court, a Personal Digital Assistant, electronic book, telephone, beeper, or similar electronic device capable of making an audible noise shall be disabled or switched to vibrate mode prior to entering a courtroom;

(3) Newspapers or other periodicals unrelated to the business of the Court; and

(4) Other items that may be disruptive to the court proceedings.

102.4.3. *Photographs.* The taking of photographs, sound recording (except by official court reporters in the performance of their duties), broadcasting by radio, television, telephone, or any other means, in connection with any judicial proceeding in the environs of the court houses within St. Joseph County is prohibited; provided, however, that incidental to investiture, ceremonial, training, marital, adoption or other non-judicial proceeding, a judge may permit the taking of photographs, broadcasting, televising or recording. A judge, by specific order, may allow the use of cameras or audio/visual recording equipment in his or her courtroom in an individual case so long as authorized by the Supreme Court of Indiana.

102.4.4. *Limitations on the Use of Personal Digital Assistants (PDA's) and other Electronic Devices.* To facilitate governmental efficiency and client service, the general public may bring personal digital assistants (PDA's), cellular telephones or similar electronic devices (hereinafter "electronic devices") into the portion of the St. Joseph County Courthouse complex that contains county and city governmental offices, which is located at 227 W. Jefferson Boulevard, in South Bend, Indiana. To enhance court security and the personal safety of litigants and court personnel, the general public is prohibited from bringing these electronic devices into the remainder of the St. Joseph County Courthouse complex (the portions of the Courthouse complex located at 101 South Main Street and 112 South Lafayette Street, South Bend, Indiana) as well as the Courthouse complexes located at 1000 S. Michigan Street, South Bend, Indiana, and 219 Lincoln Way West, Mishawaka, Indiana. However, attorneys, credentialed journalists, court employees, building personnel, and law enforcement officers and other government employees on official business may bring these electronic devices into Courthouse complexes. Individuals who are allowed to bring an electronic device into Courthouse complexes will insure that the device is deactivated before entering a courtroom and will not be allowed to activate the device while inside a courtroom; however, court staff, attorneys, maintenance staff and security staff may bring an activated electronic device into a courtroom to facilitate court security, safety and operations, provided that the electronic device is switched to vibrate (rather than an audible) mode prior to entering a courtroom. All persons authorized by this Rule to bring electronic devices into Courthouse complexes are strictly prohibited from using such devices for any improper or unlawful purpose, including without limitation the taking of any photographs, videos or moving pictures, recording audio or video, and texting. In the interests of privacy, safety and/or justice, a judge, a bailiff or a duly authorized court security officer may prohibit an individual who is otherwise allowed to possess an electronic device in a Courthouse complex from bringing an electronic device into any portion of a Courthouse complex; provided that if a security officer prohibits an individual from bringing an electronic device into a Courthouse complex, the security officer will prepare a written report detailing the reason(s) and/or concern(s), and shall distribute a copy to the Sheriff and to the appropriate judicial officer(s). By written authorization, a judge may permit an expert witness or other person to utilize an electronic device in a specifically designated area within a Courthouse complex. Nothing is in this rule is intended to prevent an individual from using a cellular telephone in the case of a legitimate emergency involving the personal health or safety of that individual or a third party.

102.4.5. *Enforcement.* The Sheriff of St. Joseph County (hereinafter "Sheriff"), courthouse security personnel, and the bailiffs of each of the Courts have been authorized to monitor and enforce compliance with these Rules of Conduct and Dress. Any person violating the rules regarding photography, cameras, cellular telephones, PDA's or other electronic devices shall be subject to immediate confiscation of the camera, cellular telephone, PDA or electronic device and/or a fine of up to and including $1,500.00 if a camera or device makes an audio or visual recording, or a telephone or PDA creates an audible noise, in a courtroom of a courthouse in St. Joseph County while court is in session, which penalty shall be imposed at the discretion of the judicial officer in whose courtroom the violation occurred or whose court proceeding was disrupted.

102.4.6. *Consent to Search.* All persons entering any of the courthouses within St. Joseph County are required to pass through a magnetometer/x-ray screening point and to comply with all reasonable requests of courthouse security personnel. By entering a courthouse within St. Joseph County, every person is consenting to the reasonable search of their person and effects to insure that he or she is complying with the requirements of this Rule. The Sheriff, law enforcement officers, or court security personnel may detain any person who they have reason to believe possesses any weapon or other prohibited item in violation of this Rule for a period of time sufficient to obtain name, address, date of birth, social security number, and/or to seize any weapon or other prohibited item.

Adopted July 28, 2006, effective Jan. 1, 2007. Amended Aug. 2, 2007, effective Jan. 1, 2008; June 3, 2008, effective Jan. 1, 2009; June 1, 2011, effective Jan. 1, 2012.

LR71–TR72 Rule 103.   COURT CLERK

103.1.   Clerk of the Court. The term "Clerk" means the Clerk of the Circuit Court duly elected and qualified under Article 6, Sections 2 and 4 of the Constitution of the State of Indiana. Pursuant to I.C. 33–33–2–1, the Clerk of the Circuit Court shall also serve as the *ex-officio* Clerk of the Superior and Probate Courts.

103.2.   Staffing. The Clerk shall assign sufficient staff to each court in order to effectively and efficiently manage the cases filed with and/or assigned to the respective Courts.

103.3.   Clerk's Hours of Operation. The offices of the Clerk designated to receive filings for causes pending in their respective Courts shall be open on all days that any court is in session between the hours of 8:00 a.m. and 4:30 p.m. for all purposes contemplated by these rules. Filings made by electronic filing during these regular office hours shall be considered filed on the date received; filings made after regular office hours shall be considered filed on the next business day that is not a Saturday, Sunday, or legal holiday.

Adopted July 28, 2006, effective Jan. 1, 2007. Amended August 2, 2007, effective January 1, 2008.

LR71–AR00   Rule 104.   COURT HOURS AND SCHEDULING

104.1.   Court's Hours of Operation.

104.1.1. *Judicial Days.* The Courts shall be in session Monday through Friday, legal holidays excluded, and during such other hours as each court may, from time to time, direct or otherwise post. Unless otherwise occupied by court business or the operational needs of the court, each Court will convene on each judicial day of the calendar term.

104.1.2. *Legal Holidays.* The Courts will follow the schedule for legal holidays authorized by the Board of Commissioners of St. Joseph County, subject to change due to emergencies or the operational needs of the Court.

104.1.3. *Emergency Closure.* When weather conditions or other emergencies arise, the individual court may be closed at the direction of the Judge of the Circuit Court of the Probate Court or the Chief Judge of the Superior Court. If a closing is announced, the Court and the Clerk of the Court shall make reasonable effort to notify attorneys and litigants scheduled to attend court on that date or time.

104.2.   Daily Calendar. Each regularly presiding Judge will maintain a separate calendar. The calendar of cases set for hearing on a given day will be posted in the Courthouse rotunda, on the Courtroom door, inside the Courtroom, and with the Clerk of the Court.

104.3.   Hearing on Matters Other Than Trials. Each Judge shall reserve periods of time for hearing matters other than contested trials, such as pre-trial and post-trial motions, rules to show cause, defaults, uncontested dissolutions of marriage, etc. As necessary to minimize conflicts in scheduling, the Judges shall set these schedules after consultation. Hearings shall be scheduled as follows:

104.3.1. *Scheduling Uncontested or Routine Matters.* Routine matters, procedural motions, domestic relations applications for provisional relief and contempt proceedings, uncontested petitions for dissolution of marriage, and all other matters appropriate for summary consideration and disposition will be heard on the daily calendar.

104.3.2. *Scheduling Contested or Complicated Matters.* Other matters that will require a hearing reasonably estimated to last in excess of twenty (20) minutes will be scheduled as the Court's calendar allows. Counsel or a party proceeding *pro se* should contact the chambers of the assigned judge to arrange for an appropriate hearing date and time.

104.4. Trials. Trial settings will be scheduled by the trial judge. Counsel or a party proceeding *pro se* should contact the chambers of the assigned judge to obtain a trial date, to schedule a pre-trial conference, and/or to request a copy of the trial calendar.

104.5. Prompt Appearance at Hearings and Trials. Prompt appearance at the time scheduled for all hearings and trials is enjoined upon Court, counsel, and parties. Should an occasion arise when counsel or a party proceeding *pro se* can reasonably anticipate that he or she will be tardy for a scheduled hearing, or a scheduled hearing or trial must be rescheduled due to an unanticipated emergency, counsel or the party shall notify the Court immediately.

104.6. Penalties for Failure to Comply. Unless good cause is shown, the failure of counsel or a moving party to comply with this rule or to appear for a scheduled hearing or trial may result in a default pursuant to the Trial Rules and/or may be enforced by direct contempt of court, which may result in a monetary fine or other appropriate penalty.

Adopted July 28, 2006, effective Jan. 1, 2007. Amended August 2, 2007, effective January 1, 2008.

LR71–AR00 Rule 105. COURT SESSIONS AND MANAGEMENT

105.1. Circuit Court.

105.1.1. *Court Sessions.* The calendar year term of the Circuit Court shall be divided into quarterly sessions as follows:

(1) Session I shall be conducted during the calendar months January, February, and March;

(2) Session II shall be conducted during the calendar months April, May, and June;

(3) Session III shall be conducted during the calendar months July, August, and September;

(4) Session IV shall be conducted during the calendar months October, November, and December.

105.1.2. *Grand Jury.* The Circuit Court may call a grand jury as provided by I.C. 35–34–2–2.

105.1.3. *Petit Jury.* A petit jury shall be called to serve during each of the sessions of the calendar year.

105.2. Superior Court.

105.2.1. *Division Assignments.* From time to time, the Chief Judge will publish a schedule for the calendar year of the Superior Court and its Divisions. The schedule will contain the names of the Judges who are assigned to the various divisions of the Court for each session. The schedule will be posted within the Courthouse and provided to attorneys upon request.

105.2.2. *Petit Jury.* A petit jury shall be called to serve within each Division of the Superior Court.

105.3. Probate Court.

105.3.1. *Court Sessions.* No sessions of Court shall be published; however, from time to time, the Judge will publish a schedule for the calendar year of the Probate Court and its Divisions.

105.3.2. *Petit Jury.* If needed, a petit jury shall be called to serve during each of the sessions of the calendar year. The petit jury may be called from the list maintained by the Circuit Court or Superior Court.

Adopted July 28, 2006, effective Jan. 1, 2007. Amended August 2, 2007, effective January 1, 2008.

LR71–TR40 Rule 106. CASE FLOW AND DISPOSITION

106.1. Assignment of Cases in the Circuit Court.

106.1.1. *Civil Assignment List.* The Circuit Court shall keep assignment lists for civil cases. When the issues are closed in any civil case where a trial is contemplated, that case shall be placed upon the appropriate assignment list. Cases shall be placed on the assignment lists in chronological sequence according to the date on which the issues are closed.

106.1.2. *Closing of Issues in Pending Cases.* Where a party or an attorney of a party has a good faith belief that the issues in a case have been closed by the filing of a pleading or otherwise, the party or the attorney may so inform the Court and any opposing counsel in writing and file a copy of the notice with the Clerk of the Court. Opposing counsel shall then have ten (10) days in which to file written objections to such indication that the issues are closed, unless otherwise ordered by the Court. If no such objection is filed the cause shall be placed on the appropriate assignment list.

106.2. Assignment of Cases in Superior Court. All Superior Court cases (except Small Claims and Traffic & Misdemeanor) will be assigned to a particular Judge of the Superior Court immediately upon filing. Each Judge will be responsible for the management of his or her assigned caseload, and will hear all motions, conduct pre-trial conferences, and prepare individual calendars of cases for trial.

106.2.1. *Assignment of Civil Cases in Superior Court.* All civil cases, including those transferred to the Court from other counties on change of venue, upon being filed with the Clerk, shall immediately be assigned, at random and by computer, by the Clerk to a Judge of the Court for all further action. It shall be the responsibility of the party filing the case, or the party's attorney, to ascertain the Judge to which the case has been assigned. The Chief Judge, pursuant to statute and Local Rule 109, herein, shall have the authority to transfer cases among and between the Judges or to other Judicial Officers, including Magistrate Judges, Senior Judges, Special Judges, and Temporary Judges, in order to balance the assignment of cases to the Judges of the Court and so as to comply with Indiana Supreme Court Administrative Rule 15 and Local Rule 107, that being the Local Caseload Plan for St. Joseph County.

106.2.2. *Assignment of Criminal Cases in Superior Court.* All felony criminal cases, including those transferred to this Court from other counties on change of venue, upon being filed with the clerk, shall be assigned to the Criminal Trial Division of this Court. The Chief Judge, pursuant to statute and Local Rule 109, herein, shall have the authority to transfer cases among and between the Judges or to other Judicial Officers, including Magistrate Judges, Senior Judges, and Temporary Judges in order to balance the assignment of cases to the Judges of the Court and so as to comply with Indiana Supreme Court Administrative Rule 15 and Rule LR71–AR1–107, that being the Local Caseload Plan for St. Joseph County.

106.3. All Entries by Assigned Judge. After the assignment of a case to a Judge, all entries and orders, including judgments and orders of dismissal, may be filed with the Clerk, who shall submit the same to the assigned Judge (or, if unavailable, to any sitting Judge) for approval and entry in the court records.

106.4. Listing of Assigned Cases. After the filing of the first responsive pleading, the assigned Judge will cause the case to be placed upon a list to be kept by each Judge of the Court, in which noted cases are subject to call for trial pre-trial conference. Cases may be advanced upon this list by petition to the assigned Judge for good cause shown.

Adopted July 28, 2006, effective Jan. 1, 2007. Amended August 2, 2007, effective January 1, 2008.

LR71–AR1 Rule 107. JOINT LOCAL CASELOAD ALLOCATION PLAN FOR ST. JOSEPH COUNTY

107.1. Caseload Review. Not later than October 1 of each year, a committee composed of the Judge of the Circuit Court, the Judge of the Probate Court, and the Chief Judge of the Superior Court, shall meet in person, telephonically, or by other means and shall evaluate each court's caseload data, as reported by the Division of the State Court Administration.

107.2. Special Circumstances. The committee shall consider in addition to the actual caseload data, any special circumstances relevant to evaluating the various caseloads of the various Courts and Judges in St. Joseph County. These special circumstances shall include such matters as death penalty cases, administrative and special Judge service, availability of physical resources, and any other relevant factors.

107.3. Statistical Deviation. Based upon the foregoing caseload evaluation for each Court within the County, the committee shall determine whether or not a sufficient statistical deviation occurs between the Courts which would warrant a transfer of cases within St. Joseph County from one court to another or a limitation during the following year upon what case types may be filed in certain courts or before certain Judges in order to more effectively and efficiently provide services to the citizens of St. Joseph County.

107.4. Caseload Allocation Plan and Transfer of Cases. In the event the committee determines a significant statistical deviation exists and is likely to continue to exist the following year, the committee shall unanimously adopt a written plan providing for the assignment of cases and/or for the transfer of cases from one Court to another in order to more equally distribute cases among and between the various Courts within St. Joseph County or requiring that certain types of cases only be filed in certain courts or assigned to certain Judges therein. Such transfer of cases or limitation on filing shall take into consideration the specialized jurisdictional attributes of the Probate Court and endeavor to transfer cases that fit within a receiving Judge's statutory jurisdiction. In the event that either cases transferring in or out of Probate Court are outside the normal statutory jurisdiction of the receiving Judge, the committee shall designate the receiving Judge as a special Judge of the court that retains jurisdiction over the original proceeding. The committee shall also take into consideration the impact of such transfer upon other local agencies such as the Prosecutor's Office, Public Defender's Office, Sheriff's Department, Local Law Enforcement, County Clerk's Office, Probation Departments, as well as the general citizenry and the cost of such transfers. The caseload allocation plan may be memorialized as an appendix to this rule.

107.5. Procedures Following Transfer. Once a case is assigned or transferred pursuant to the caseload allocation plan adopted by the committee into another Court, the case shall be heard and processed as all other cases originally filed within that Court.

Adopted July 28, 2006, effective Jan. 1, 2007. Amended August 2, 2007, effective January 1, 2008. Amended June 3, 2007, effective January 1, 2009.

LR71–AR00 Rule 108. ORGANIZATION OF THE CIRCUIT COURT

108.1. General Organization. The Circuit Court shall be divided into two divisions, which shall be known as the South Bend and Mishawaka Divisions.

108.2. Magistrate Judges. Magistrate judges appointed pursuant to statute or otherwise shall hold office at the pleasure of the Judge of the Circuit Court and shall perform such judicial duties as may be allowed by law, as set out in these rules, or as may be assigned by the Judge of the Circuit Court.

Adopted July 28, 2006, effective Jan. 1, 2007. Amended August 2, 2007, effective January 1, 2008.

LR71–AR00 Rule 109. ORGANIZATION OF THE SUPERIOR COURT

109.1. General Organization. The Superior Court shall be divided into five divisions, which shall be known as the Criminal Trial, Civil Trial, Small Claims, Traffic and Misdemeanor, and Mishawaka Divisions. Each of the Judges of the Superior Court is permanently assigned to the Civil or Criminal Divisions of the Court. Regardless of such assignment under these Rules, each Judge is authorized at all times to conduct hearings and trials in all matters, and to exercise the full jurisdiction of the St. Joseph Superior Court.

109.2. Criminal Trial Division. The Chief Judge shall determine the Judges assigned to the criminal division. All felony cases, as well as all traffic and misdemeanor cases in which a demand has been made for trial by jury, shall be tried in the Criminal Trial Division. The Judge assigned to the Mishawaka Division shall be responsible for the trial of all cases assigned to that Judge. The Chief Judge shall prepare an annual schedule indicating which Judge will be available in felony cases to approve requests for warrants, to fix bonds, and to conduct arraignments.

109.2.1. *Drug Treatment Court.* Within the Criminal Division there may be established a Drug Treatment Court for which one or more Judges of the court shall be responsible. Eligibility for the drug treatment court shall be determined by written criteria currently in place, or as hereafter modified. Cases may be assigned to the Drug Treatment Court only upon the consent of the Prosecuting Attorney, defendant, and the Judge assigned to the court, and upon the continuance of the case pursuant to the filing of a standard written agreement for such purposes.

109.3. Civil Trial Division. The Chief Judge shall determine the Judges assigned to the Civil Trial Division. Trials of civil cases, whether by court or by jury (except such cases as are pending in Small Claims Division), ordinarily shall be conducted in the Civil Trial Division. Petitions for temporary or regular civil commitments and for emergency detentions shall be heard in this Division. The Judge assigned to the Mishawaka Division shall be responsible for the trial of all cases assigned to that Judge.

109.4. Traffic and Misdemeanor Division. The Chief Judge shall determine the judicial officers to assign to the Traffic & Misdemeanor Division. This Division shall be responsible for the trial and disposition of traffic violations, criminal misdemeanors, infractions, and city ordinance violations. This Division is further responsible for such classes of violations as may be designated for disposition upon a plea of guilty in a violations bureau. Cases pending in the Traffic & Misdemeanor Division shall not be deemed assigned to the judge sitting therein, nor any other Judge, except upon proper motion for change of venue.

109.5. Small Claims Division. The Chief Judge shall determine the judicial officer to assign to the Small Claims Division. This division shall be responsible for the trial and disposition of all cases filed in its individual docket and falling within the jurisdiction of the division pursuant to I.C. 33–29–2–1, et seq. This division may publish its own rules of procedure. Cases pending in this division shall not be deemed assigned to the Judge sitting therein, nor to any other Judge, except upon proper motion for change of venue.

109.6. Mishawaka Division. The Chief Judge shall assign at least one Judge to this division, but may assign other judicial officers. The length of service shall be determined by the Chief Judge. The appointment shall not be considered permanent; the Chief Judge shall retain discretionary assignment authority pursuant to I.C. 33–5–40–23, as may be amended from time to time. The Mishawaka Division shall be responsible for the disposition of all cases assigned to it or that Judge. In the event that a Judge is reassigned from this division to the South Bend Division or to any other division of the court, the cases shall remain in Mishawaka and be assigned to the succeeding Judge or Magistrate Judge.

109.7. Magistrate Judges. Magistrate Judges appointed pursuant to statute or otherwise shall hold office at the pleasure of the court and shall perform such judicial duties as may be allowed by law, as set out in these rules, or as may be assigned by the Chief Judge.

109.8. Chief Judge of the Superior Court.

109.8.1. *Election of Chief Judge.* A Chief Judge, as provided for by I.C. 33–5–40–23, shall be elected for a term of two years by a majority vote of the Judges of the Court. Such elections shall be held no later than the last regularly scheduled Judges meeting in even numbered years. The term of the Chief Judge shall begin on January 1, following his or her election. A vacancy in the office of the Chief Judge shall be filled by a majority vote of the remaining Judges of the court. A Judge may resign the office of the Chief Judge without resigning from the Court and shall be eligible to vote in the election to select a successor.

109.8.2. *General Authority and Duties of Chief Judge.* The Chief Judge shall have such authority and responsibilities as conferred by statute, Supreme Court Rule, or Local Rule and shall be responsible for the efficient operation of the Court and management of its business. The Chief Judge shall have the authority to assign and reassign Judges between the divisions of the Court and to reassign cases previously assigned. The Chief Judge shall designate another Judge of the Court as acting Chief Judge during any period of the Chief Judge's unavailability or to assist the Chief Judge as may be necessary. The Chief Judge may make various assignments and appointments to boards, commissions, committees, or other such organizations as may be required or in the best interests of the Court.

109.8.3. *Specific Authority to Transfer Cases.* The Chief Judge may, in addition to the general authority otherwise granted, and in order to effectively and efficiently manage the Court, transfer cases between the Judges and magistrate judges in order to accommodate speedy trial requests in criminal cases, to handle emergency matters, to join codefendants or related cases, to transfer all cases pending against a defendant or filed by a plaintiff to a single Judge, to hear dispositive motions, to transfer cases to a Senior Judge, Magistrate Judge, Special Judge, or Temporary Judge, and to make such other transfers and assignments as may be in the best interests of the Court.

Adopted July 28, 2006, effective Jan. 1, 2007. Amended August 2, 2007, effective January 1, 2008.

LR71–AR00 Rule 110. ORGANIZATION OF THE PROBATE COURT

110.1. General Organization. The Probate Court shall be divided into two divisions, which shall be known as the Probate and Juvenile Divisions.

110.2. Magistrate Judges. Magistrate Judges appointed pursuant to statute or otherwise shall hold office at the pleasure of the Judge of the Probate Court and shall perform such judicial duties as may be allowed by law, as set out in these rules, or as may be assigned by the Judge of the Probate Court.

Adopted July 28, 2006, effective Jan. 1, 2007. Amended August 2, 2007, effective January 1, 2008.

LR71–AR15 Rule 111. Court Reporter Services

111.1. Definitions.

111.1.1. *Court Reporter.* A Court Reporter is a person who is specifically designated by a Court to perform the official court reporting services for the Court including preparing a transcript of the record.

111.1.2. *Equipment.* Equipment means all physical items owned by the Court or other governmental entity and used by a court in performing court reporter services. Equipment shall include, but not be limited to, telephones, computer hardware, software programs, disks, tapes, and any other device used for recording, storing, and transcribing electronic data.

111.1.3. *Work Space.* Work space means that portion of the Court's facilities dedicated to each court reporter, including but not limited to actual space in the courtroom and any designated office space.

111.1.4. *Page.* Page means the page unit of transcript that results when a recording is transcribed in the form required by Indiana Rule of Appellate Procedure 7.2.

111.1.5. *Recording.* Recording means the electronic, mechanical, stenographic, or other recording made as required by Indiana Rule of Trial Procedure 74.

111.1.6. *Regular Hours Worked.* Regular hours worked means those hours during which the Court is regularly scheduled to work during any given workweek. Depending on the particular Court, these hours may vary from court to court within the County but remain the same for each workweek.

111.1.7. *Gap Hours Worked.* Gap hours worked means those hours worked that are in excess of the regular hours worked but hours not in excess of forty (40) hours per workweek.

111.1.8. *Overtime Hours Worked.* Overtime hours worked means those hours worked in excess of forty (40) hours per workweek.

111.1.9. *Workweek.* Workweek means a five (5) consecutive day week that consistently begins on Monday and ends on Friday.

111.1.10. *Court.* Court means the particular court for which the court reporter performs services.

111.1.11. *County Indigent Transcript.* County indigent transcript means a transcript that is paid for from County funds and is for the use on behalf of a litigant who has been declared indigent by a Court.

111.1.12. *State Indigent Transcript.* State indigent transcript means a transcript that is paid for from state funds and is for the use on behalf of a litigant who has been declared indigent by a Court.

111.1.13. *Private Transcript.* Private transcript means a transcript, including but not limited to, a deposition transcript that is paid for by a private party.

111.2. Salaries and Per–Page Fees.

111.2.1. *Annual Salary.* A court reporter shall be paid an annual salary for time spent working under the control, direction, and direct supervision of the Court during any regular work hours, gap hours, or overtime hours.

Text of Rule 111.2.2 effective until January 1, 2013.

111.2.2. *Non–Expedited County Indigent Transcript.* The per page fee for one original and one additional copy of a non-expedited county indigent transcript preparation shall be $3.00 plus a fee of $10 per 100 pages containing marginal or header notations (e.g. $10 per 100 pages, $20 per 200 pages), which fee will be subject to review at a time that rates for federal reporters are increased. Re-orders of an existing transcript shall be one-half price (e.g. $1.50 per page, with a cost of $5 per 100 pages containing marginal or header notations).

Text of Rule 111.2.2 effective January 1, 2013.

111.2.2. *Non-expedited County Indigent Transcript.* The per page fee for one original and one additional copy of a non-expedited county indigent transcript preparation shall be $3.50 with a minimum fee of thirty-five dollars ($35.00). Re-orders of an existing transcript shall be $1.50 per page.

111.2.3. *Claim for Preparation.* The court reporter shall submit directly to the County a claim for the preparation of a county indigent transcript.

Text of Rule 111.2.4 effective until January 1, 2013.

111.2.4. *Non–Expedited State Indigent Transcript.* The maximum per page fee that a court reporter may charge for one original and one additional copy of a non-expedited state indigent transcript shall be $3.00 plus a fee of $10 per 100 pages containing marginal or header notations (e.g. $10 per 100 pages, $20 per 200 pages), which fee will be subject to review at a time that rates for federal reporters are increased. Re-orders of an existing transcript shall be one-half price (e.g. $1.50 per page, with a cost of $5 per 100 pages containing marginal or header notations).

Text of Rule 111.2.4 effective January 1, 2013.

111.2.4. *Non-expedited State Indigent Transcript.* The maximum per page fee that a court reporter may charge for one original and one additional copy of a non-expedited state indigent transcript shall be $3.50 with a minimum fee of thirty-five dollars ($35.00). Re-orders of an existing transcript shall be $1.50 per page.

Text of Rule 111.2.5 effective until January 1, 2013.

111.2.5. *Non–Expedited Private Transcript.* The maximum per page fee that a court reporter may charge for one original and one additional copy of a non-expedited private transcript shall be $3.00 plus a fee of $10 per 100 pages containing marginal

or header notations (e.g. $10 per 100 pages, $20 per 200 pages), which fee will be subject to review at a time that rates for federal reporters are increased. Re-orders of an existing transcript shall be one-half price (e.g. $1.50 per page, with a cost of $5 per 100 pages containing marginal or header notations).

Text of Rule 111.2.5 effective January 1, 2013.

111.2.5. *Non-expedited Private Transcript.* The maximum per page fee that a court reporter may charge for one original and one additional copy of a non-expedited private transcript shall be $3.50 with a minimum fee of thirty-five dollars ($35.00). Re-orders of an existing transcript shall be $1.50 per page.

Text of Rule 111.2.6 effective until January 1, 2013.

111.2.6. *Expedited Transcript.* The maximum per page fee that a court reporter may charge for an expedited transcript shall be as follows, subject to review at a time that rates for federal reporters are increased:

(1) Overnight: $6.00 per page;

(2) Within three (3) working days: $4.50 per page.

Text of Rule 111.2.6 effective January 1, 2013.

111.2.6. *Expedited Transcript.* The maximum per page fee that a court reporter may charge for an expedited transcript shall be as follows:

(1) Overnight: $6.00 per page;

(2) Within three (3) working days: $4.50 per page.

111.2.7. *Reporting of Transcript Fees.* Each court reporter shall report at least on an annual basis to the Indiana Supreme Court, Division of State Court Administration, on forms prescribed by the Division, all transcript fees (either county indigent, state indigent, or private) received by the court reporter.

111.3. Private Practice. If a court reporter elects to engage in private practice through recording of a deposition and/or preparing of a deposition transcript and desires to utilize the Court's equipment and work space, and the Court agrees to use of the Court equipment and work space for such purpose, the Court and the court reporter shall enter into a written agreement which must, at a minimum, designate the following:

(1) The court reporter shall at his or her own expense supply paper and covers for the preparation of such deposition transcript;

(2) The reasonable market rate for the use of equipment, work space, and supplies and the method by which the court reporter is to reimburse the court for the use of said equipment, work space, and supplies;

(3) That if a court reporter elects to engage in private practice through recording of a deposition and/or the preparing of a deposition transcript, that such private practice shall be conducted outside of regular working hours, unless the time is considered as compensatory time off from regular work hours;

(4) That the court reporter is to be compensated for gap and overtime hours by compensatory time off regular work hours only when the judge to whom the court reporter is assigned is not performing duties requiring the court reporter's presence;

(5) It shall be the responsibility of the court reporter to keep accurate time records of regular work hours, gap, and overtime hours to justify their compensatory hours. Hours spent in transcript preparation are not to be counted toward regular hours worked;

(6) Guilty plea and sentencing hearings shall be reported by computer-aided transcription (CAT) and preserved in accordance with the criminal rules for record retention.

Adopted July 28, 2006, effective Jan. 1, 2007. Amended Aug. 17, 2009, effective Jan. 1, 2010; Sept. 29, 2012, effective Jan. 1, 2013.

Appendix A. Caseload Allocation Plan

FOR COURTS IN ST. JOSEPH COUNTY, INDIANA

I. Organization of the Courts of St. Joseph County:

As of January 1, 2011, the Courts of St. Joseph County are organized and assigned judicial officers as follows:

(1) St. Joseph Circuit Court—one (1) judge and two (2) magistrate judges;

(2) St. Joseph Superior Court—eight (8) judges and two (2) magistrate judges; and

(3) St. Joseph Probate Court—one (1) judge and three (3) magistrate judges.

II. Designation of Judicial Officers to Hear Civil, Criminal and Juvenile Cases:

(1) Judicial Officers Designated to Hear Civil Cases: Civil Cases (other than small claims matters) shall be heard by the judge and the magistrate judges of the Circuit Court and by the judges and/or magistrate judges of the Superior Court designated by the Chief Judge of the Superior Court to hear civil cases;

(2) Judicial Officers Designated to Hear Felony Criminal Cases: Felony criminal cases shall be heard by the judges and/or magistrate judges of the Superior Court designated by the Chief Judge of the Superior Court to hear felony criminal cases;

(3) Judicial Officers Designated to Hear Small Claims Cases: Small claims matters shall by heard by the judges and/or magistrate judges of the Superior Court designated by the Chief Judge of the Superior Court to hear small claims matters;

(4) Judicial Officers Designated to Hear Traffic and Misdemeanor Cases: Unless otherwise assigned to a felony criminal court for judicial economy because a defendant has pending felony, misdemeanor and/or probation revocation matters, traffic and misdemeanor matters shall by heard by the judges and/or magistrate judges of the Superior Court designated by the Chief Judge of the Superior Court to hear traffic and misdemeanor matters.

(5) Judicial Officers Designated to Hear Paternity, Delinquency, Dependency, and Adoption Cases: Paternity, delinquency, dependency, and adoption matters shall be assigned to the Judge of the Probate Court unless the Judge assigns the matter to be heard by a magistrate judge of the Probate Court.

(6) Judicial Officers Designated to Hear Title IV–D Cases: Pursuant to LR71–FL00–430 et seq., Title IV–D Cases may be assigned to the Title IV–D Court and heard by a magistrate judge of the Probate Court designated to preside over Title IV–D hearings.

III. Protocol for Assignment of Cases Among the Courts of St. Joseph County:

(1) Civil cases (other than small claims): With the exception of cases that must be assigned statutorily to the Probate Court because of its designation as the court with exclusive jurisdiction over juvenile cases (paternity, delinquency, dependency, adoption, etc.) or to the Circuit Court (license reinstatement, name changes, etc.), civil cases (other than small claims cases) shall be assigned randomly among the judges and/or magistrate judges of the Circuit Court and the Superior Court designated to hear civil matters as follows:

A. Circuit Court shall receive a total of 42.85% (3/7ths) of all upper civil filings and Superior Court shall receive 57.15% (4/7ths) of all upper civil filings.

B. Four (4) civil judges in Superior Court shall each receive 1/4 (25%) of the 57.15% of the upper civil filings, which also means each judge shall receive 14.29% of the total civil filings.

C.   Circuit Court shall have a Mishawaka Division with one (1) Circuit Court magistrate judge presiding and a South Bend Division with the Circuit Court judge and one (1) magistrate presiding.

D.   Superior Court shall have Mishawaka Division with one (1) Superior Court judge presiding and a South Bend Division with three (3) Superior Court judges and two (2) magistrate judges presiding.

E.   Civil cases (other than small claims cases) may be files in Circuit Court and Superior Court in South Bend or Mishawaka, Indiana as follows:

(a) The City of Mishawaka, the School City of Mishawaka, or a resident of the City of Mishawaka where all defendants are residents of the City of Mishawaka shall file all of their cases with the Mishawaka Clerk's office, and those cases shall be assigned to the Mishawaka Division of Superior and Circuit Courts on an alternating basis to ensure equal distribution of those filings between the Mishawaka Divisions of those courts

(b) All attorneys and business entities with their principal places of business and all individuals with their principal residences located east of Logan Street but within St. Joseph County may either file their civil cases (other than small claims cases) at the South Bend Clerk's office and have them assigned randomly to the Mishawaka Division of the Superior and Circuit Courts or to one (1) of the three (3) judges of the civil division of the Superior Court of the judge of the Circuit Court or file their civil cases (other than small claims cases) with the Mishawaka Clerk's office and those cases shall be assigned to the Mishawaka Division of Superior and Circuit Courts on an alternating basis to ensure equal distribution of those filings between the Mishawaka Divisions of those courts.

F.   For all civil case filings with the Clerk's office in South Bend, a forty (40) case assignment rotation cycle shall be utilized with each forty (40) cases assigned as follows:

Seventeen (17) cases for Circuit Court (approximately 43%)

Twenty-three (23) for Superior Court (approximately 57%)

Circuit Court shall from time to time designate three (3) cases (17.65% of the Circuit cases) or four (4) cases (23.53% of the Circuit cases) of each of the seventeen (17) Circuit Court cases in each assignment rotation cycle to go to the Circuit Court magistrate judge sitting in Mishawaka to which direct filings will be added in order to achieve whatever total percentage of cases the Circuit Court judge wants in the Circuit Court Mishawaka Division

Superior Court shall from time to time designate three (3) cases (13.04% of the Superior cases) or four (4) cases (17.39% of the Superior cases) of each of the twenty-three (23) Superior Court cases in each assignment rotation cycle to go to Superior Court in Mishawaka to which direct filings will be added in order that Mishawaka Superior Court handles 25% of all Superior Court civil cases.

(2) Felony Criminal Cases: With the exception of criminal cases that must be assigned to the Circuit Court by L71–CR2.2–303.1 or –303.2, felony criminal cases shall be assigned randomly among the judges and/or magistrate judges of the Superior Court designated to hear criminal cases as follows:

A.   The Superior Court judge assigned to Drug Court will be assigned all D felony drug cases (given a "D01" designation) but no other D felonies.

B.   The remaining D felonies will be randomly and evenly assigned to the other three (3) Superior Court criminal judges.

C.   All other felony cases (MR, A, B and C Felonies) will be randomly and evenly assigned to the four (4) Superior Court criminal judges.

However, and notwithstanding this method of random assignment, in all felony criminal cases, except MR cases, where co-defendants are charged, cases shall be reassigned to a single judge or magistrate judge, as follows: (a) where co-defendants have been equally assigned to different judges, the judge having the lowest assigned cause number shall be assigned/reassigned all co-defendant cases; or (b) in the event that co-defendants have been unequally assigned to different judges, the judge having the greatest number of co-defendants shall be assigned/reassigned all co-defendant cases. Further, the Chief Judge of the Superior Court may reassign cases involving a defendant who has a pending case to the judge presiding over the earliest assigned cause number. The Chief Judge of the Superior Court may reassign MR cases or other felony cases where such reassignment is in the interest of judicial economy or dictated by the weighted caseload balancing requirements.

(3) Small Claims Cases: Superior Court has a Small Claims Division with two (2) locations: South Bend and Mishawaka. All small claims cases shall be filed with the Clerk's Office of the Small Claims Division in South bend and assigned to that Division at the South Bend location, except for the following:

A. All small claims cases filed by the City of Mishawaka, the School City of Mishawaka, or a resident of the City of Mishawaka where all defendants are residents of the City of Mishawaka, shall be filed with the Mishawaka Clerk's office, and assigned to the Small Claims Division of Superior Court in Mishawaka.

B. All small claims cases filed at the Mishawaka Clerk's office by attorneys and business entities with their principal places of business and individuals with their principal residences located east of Logan Street but within St. Joseph County may, at the filer's direction, be assigned to the Small Claims Division in Mishawaka or the Small Claims Division in South Bend.

C. For convenience of parties, a small claims case that must be assigned to the Small Claims Division in South Bend, may be filed in the Mishawaka Clerk's Office, but the filing party or counsel shall indicate to the Clerk on a Chronological Case Summary Entry that the matter must be docketed in the Small Claims Division in South Bend, and the Clerk shall promptly forward the pleadings to the Small Claims Division in South Bend for filing and processing.

D. The two (2) Superior Court magistrates work equally for each one of the eight (8) Superior Court judges; therefore, their handling of all small claims cases shall be assigned as follows for case allocation reporting purposes:

a. Each Superior Court judge is assigned:

1/8th of all small claims cases filed in South Bend

1/8th of all protective order cases filed in South Bend Small Claims.

Each Superior Court civil judge will add 1/8th of the South Bend small claims protective order cases to the number of protective order cases directly filed with each individual Superior Court civil judge

b. The Superior Court civil judge sitting in Mishawaka is also assigned all protective order cases directly filed in Mishawaka Small Claims and all protective order cases directly filed in Mishawaka Superior Court Civil Division, if any, in addition to 1/8th of the protective order cases filed in South Bend Small Claims Division.

(4) Traffic and Misdemeanor Cases: Superior Court has a Traffic and Misdemeanor Division located in South Bend. All traffic and misdemeanor cases shall be filed in and assigned to the Traffic and Misdemeanor Division. All misdemeanor cases in which a jury demand is granted shall be assigned to the Superior Court in Mishawaka for all further proceedings.

The two (2) Superior Court magistrates work equally for each one of the eight (8) Superior Court judges; therefore, their handling of all traffic and misdemeanor cases shall be assigned as follows for case allocation reporting purposes:

a. 1/8th of all CM, IF, and OV cases filed in South Bend Traffic and misdemeanor (less new misdemeanor cases sent to Mishawaka Traffic and Misdemeanor due to jury trial requests) will be assigned equally to each of the eight (8) Superior Court judges.

b. In addition, the Superior Court judge in Mishawaka will also be assigned, for case allocation purposes, all misdemeanor cases sent to Mishawaka Division Superior Court due to jury trial requests.

(5) Mental Health Cases: All Mental Health cases will be divided equally between four (4) Superior Court civil judges.

(6) Paternity, Delinquency, Dependency, and Adoption Cases: All paternity, delinquency, dependency, and adoption cases shall be filed in Probate Court.

IV. Exceptions to the Protocol for Assignment of Cases:

(1) Mass Filing of Collection Cases (other than small claims): Upon request and designation by the Judge of the Circuit Court and the Chief Judge of the Superior Court, a lawyer or law firm may be approved to make mass filing of collection cases (other than small claims). Unless otherwise directed by the Judge of the Circuit Court or the Chief Judge of the Superior Court based on weighted caseload balancing requirements or otherwise, cases filed by a lawyer or law firm approved for mass filing shall be assigned to the Circuit Court.

(2) Special Judge or Transfer: Nothing in these local rules shall be interpreted to prevent a party from taking a change of judge or requesting transfer of a case as otherwise authorized by statute or rule of court.

(3) Temporary or Permanent Assignment of Cases: Nothing in these local rules shall be interpreted to prevent the regularly presiding judge of a Court from assigning a case on a temporary or permanent basis to a Magistrate Judge, Special Judge, Senior Judge, Temporary Judge, Judge Pro Tem, Referee, or other duly appointed judicial officer.

(4) Caseload Balancing: Nothing in these local rules shall be interpreted to prevent the Judge of the Circuit Court, the Chief Judge of the Superior Court or the Judge of the Probate Court, either jointly or individually, from reassigning a case for the purpose of caseload balancing based on the weighted caseload criteria or other caseload balancing criteria.

(5) Emergency or Exigent Circumstances: Nothing in these local rules shall be interpreted to prevent the Judge of the Circuit Court, the Chief Judge of the Superior Court, or the Judge of the Probate Court, either jointly or individually, from assigning a case based on emergency or exigent circumstances.

V. Authority and Effective Date:

(1) This Caseload Allocation Plan is adopted pursuant to the requirements of A.R. 1 (E) and LR71–AR1–107.1

(2) The effective date of this Caseload Allocation Plan is January 1, 2011.

Adopted Aug. 27, 2008, effective Jan. 1, 2009. Amended Oct. 3, 2011, effective Jan. 1, 2011; Jan. 1, 2011; July 26, 2012, effective Jan. 1, 2013.

LOCAL CIVIL RULES FOR ST. JOSEPH COUNTY

Adopted July 28, 2006, Effective January 1, 2007

Including Amendments Received Through November 1, 2013

Research Notes

Annotations to the Local Civil Court Rules for St. Joseph County are available in West's Annotated Indiana Code, Title 34 Appendix.

These rules may be searched electronically on Westlaw in the IN-RULES database; updates to these rules may be found on Westlaw in IN-RULESUPDATES. For search tips and a summary of database content, consult the Westlaw Scope Screens for each database.

LR71–TR77 Rule 201. FILING, PLEADING, AND MOTIONS

201.1. Flat Filing. In order that the Clerk's files may be kept under the system commonly known as "flat filing," all papers presented to the Clerk for filing shall be flat and unfolded. Pleadings shall have no covers or backs and shall be fastened together at the top left-hand corner only.

201.2. Filing with the Clerk. All pleadings shall be filed with the Clerk, not directly with the Court, unless otherwise required by the Indiana Rules of Court. The entry of appearances and the filing of pleadings or other matters not requiring immediate Court action shall be filed with the Clerk and not in open Court. A Judge may permit papers to be filed in chambers, in which event he or she shall note thereon the filing date and transmit the papers to the Clerk. Unless otherwise authorized by LR 701 et seq., electronic filing of pleadings by computerized or facsimile transmission is not permitted.

201.3. Format of Pleadings. All pleadings, motions, and other papers shall be prepared in accordance with the applicable provisions of the Indiana Rules of Trial Procedure. For the purpose of uniformity and convenience, the following requirements shall also be observed:

201.3.1. *Paper.* Pleadings, motions, and other papers shall be either legibly printed or typewritten on white opaque paper of good quality at least sixteen (16) pound weight, eight and one-half inches (8 ½″) in width and eleven inches (11″) in length as required by A.R. 11. All copies shall likewise be on white paper of sufficient strength and durability to resist normal wear and tear.

201.3.2. *Style, Margins, Spacing, and Font.* Printing shall be on one side of the paper. Margins shall be at least one inch (1″). If typewritten, the lines shall be double spaced except for quotations, which shall be indented and single-spaced. Type face shall be 12 font size or larger within the body of the document and 10 font size or larger in the footnotes. The font type must be legible and script type shall not be used. Italicized type may be used for quotations, references, or case citations.

201.3.3. *Caption.* Every pleading shall contain a caption setting forth the name of the Court, the title of the action and the cause number. Where applicable, the pleading shall also contain a Quest or other CMS file number. If a special judge has been assigned to the case, the pleading should also identify the special judge.

201.3.4. *Title.* All pleadings or motions shall include a title, which shall delineate each topic included in the pleading. For example, where a pleading contains an answer, a motion to dismiss, and a jury request, each topic shall be set forth in the title.

201.3.5. *Format and Layout.* The separate Court may designate the form and/or layout for pleadings and motions to promote clarity, efficiency, and judicial economy, and to ensure compatibility and appropriate interface with the Odyssey and Quest case management systems. Pleadings not conforming to the designated form or layout may be stricken by the Court.

201.3.6. *Signature, Verification, and Other Requirements.* Parties and their counsel are enjoined to comply with the verification requirements of T.R. 11, and either the moving party or the party's attorney of record shall sign all pleadings and motions before filing with the Clerk of the Court. Every motion, petition, or other pleading filed with the Clerk shall contain the name, organization, physical address, telephone number, and facsimile number of the filing party or an attorney for that party. The Clerk shall not accept any motion, petition, notice or other pleading or a CCS entry form for filing from an unrepresented litigant unless the unrepresented litigant's current address and phone number appear on the pleading, and an opposing party may service notices and responses on an unrepresented litigant at any address he or she has provided on a pleading.

201.3.7. *Restricted Access.* Where a motion, petition, or other pleading is excluded from public access under A.R. 9(G), the parties and their counsel are enjoined to comply with the filing requirements of T.R. 5(G).

201.4. Chronological Case Summary Entry Form. Every written motion, petition, or other pleading subsequent to the original complaint presented to the Clerk for filing shall be accompanied by a Chronological Case Summary (CCS) entry form in duplicate which shall contain the title and cause number of the action, the date, and the proposed entry to appear on the docket. The CCS entry form shall identify the party making the filing, designate each pleading being filed, and shall be signed by counsel of record or the unrepresented litigant. The form shall be date stamped and presented to the Court Clerk, who shall initial the form and return the duplicate to the filing party. Hearing dates for filings requiring Court action shall be obtained from the Court Clerk and incorporated in the CCS entry at the time the motion or other pleading is filed. If no date is obtained prior to the filing, the fact of the hearing should be noted with the date and time left blank. All proposed CCS entries must be examined and approved by the Judge before becoming part of the record. The Judge may modify or amend any proposed CCS entry and will notify counsel of any substantial modification or amendment of a proposed CCS entry.

201.5. Service of Copies.

201.5.1. *Service Generally.* Every motion, petition, notice, or other pleading required to be served by T.R. 5 of the Indiana Rules of Trial Procedure, shall be served on all counsel of record or unrepresented parties either before it is filed or on the day it is filed with the Court, and the date of filing shall be indicated on the Certificate of Service. A copy of the Clerk's CCS entry form of the filing shall also be served on all counsel of record and/or each unrepresented party whenever it contains an appearance of counsel or contains a date for Court hearing of the matter.

201.5.2. *Proposed Forms of Order.* All proposed forms of order left with the Clerk when the Judge is not available shall be submitted in sufficient number so that distribution may be made to all affected parties.

201.5.3. *Distribution.* Counsel or an unrepresented party submitting a motion, petition, notice, pleading or proposed order shall indicate the method of distribution desired on the Clerk's CCS entry form. The Clerk will not return or distribute copies of motions, petitions, pleadings, notices or proposed orders, other than those originated by the Court, by mail unless the Clerk is provided with stamped, addressed envelopes. As a matter of convenience to attorneys, each court provides a mailbox for the distribution filings and orders generated by the Court, and it is the responsibility of each attorney to periodically check these mailboxes for service and distribution of court-generated filings and orders.

201.5.4. *Service by the Clerk.* Whenever the Clerk is required by rule or statute to give notice, the party or parties requesting such notice shall furnish the Clerk with sufficient copies of the notice to be given, along with stamped, addressed envelopes with the names and the addresses of the parties or their counsel to whom such notice is to be given.

201.5.5. *Service on the Court.* Service on a Judge may be made by delivering a copy to the Judge's secretary or mailing a copy to the Judge at his or her chambers. Service on a Judge may not be accomplished by facsimile transmission; however, a courtesy copy may be sent to the Judge's chambers by electronic mail or facsimile transmission contemporaneously with service by mail or otherwise.

201.6. Numbers of Copies and Orders. The Clerk shall retain the original of all filings. In cases in which a party or counsel supplies the proposed order or decree, a sufficient number shall be prepared and filed as to provide the Clerk to retain two (2) copies, which shall be filed in the flat file and the record of judgments and orders. Should the party or counsel desire additional copies, a sufficient number of copies should be filed to effectuate that purpose.

201.7. Reports. Reports of appraisers, masters, and commissioners shall be filed with the Court in triplicate. Unless otherwise authorized by the Court, a copy of the report shall be provided on either a floppy disk or an electronic mail message with a copy of the request attached in digital format.

201.8. Court Files. No Court file nor any part thereof may be removed from the custody of the Court Clerk by any person, including any attorney or Judge of this or any other Court, except upon authorization by the regularly presiding Judge to which the case is assigned and then only upon such terms and conditions as may be provided by him in the Order for authorization. One unalterable and invariable condition of this Order is the written acknowledgment of the authorized person that he has such file in his personal possession.

201.9. Motions.

201.9.1. *Scheduling Motions for Hearings.* Except for motions to correct error or not likely to require a hearing (as described below), all motions shall be scheduled for hearing at the time they are filed. It shall the responsibility of the moving party or counsel for the moving party to secure the date and time of the hearing from the Clerk or Court personnel who maintain the calendar for each Judge or Magistrate Judge. It shall also be the responsibility of the moving party or counsel for the moving party to coordinate the hearing date with all opposing counsel or unrepresented parties.

201.9.2. *Motions Not Likely to Require Hearing.* At the time of the filing, a moving party shall bring the following motions to the attention of the assigned judge:

(1) Motion for Enlargement of Time;

(2) Motion for Change of Judge;

(3) Motion for Change of Venue from the County;

(4) Motion to Dismiss Complaint by Plaintiff when no Answer has been filed;

(5) Motion to Dismiss Counterclaim by Defendant when no Reply has been filed;

(6) Motion to Compel Responses to Interrogatories or Requests for Production;

(7) Motions to Reconsider Such motions may be summarily granted or denied ex parte and without the necessity for hearing, unless the Judge, in his or her discretion, determines that a hearing should be scheduled on any such motion and schedules a hearing on the Court's own motion.

201.9.3. *Motions to Correct Error.* It is within the sound discretion of the assigned Judge whether a hearing shall be held on a motion to correct error; however, any party may request a hearing upon a motion to correct error by filing a written request by separate motion at any time before the Court has ruled upon such Motion.

201.9.4. *Oral Arguments on Motions and Other Pleadings.* Unless otherwise required by these rules or Indiana Trial Rules, it is within the sound discretion of the assigned Judge whether to allow oral argument; however, any party may file a request for oral argument by filing a written request by separate motion contemporaneously or at any time before the Court has ruled upon the motion or pleadings to be argued.

201.9.5. *Motion for Enlargement of Time.* An initial written motion for enlargement of time pursuant to Indiana Trial Rule 6(B)(1) to answer a claim shall be routinely granted for an additional thirty (30) days from the original due date or other period the assigned Judge deems reasonable by written order of the Court. Any motion for enlargement of time shall state the date when such response is due and the date to which time is requested to be enlarged. The motion must be filed on or before the original due date or this Rule shall be inapplicable. All subsequent motions for enlargement of time shall be so designated and will only be granted for good cause shown or in the interest of justice.

201.9.6. *Motions for Summary Judgment and for Dismissal.* Motions for summary judgment or motions to dismiss pursuant to Indiana Trial Rule 12 or 41 shall be scheduled for hearing, unless the Court issues a written scheduling order providing otherwise. (See Local Rule 206 for specific requirements for Pleadings and Motions under Trial Rule 12 and 56.)

Adopted July 28, 2006, effective Jan. 1, 2007. Amended Aug. 2, 2007, effective Jan. 1, 2008; June 1, 2011, effective Jan. 1, 2012.

LR71–AR8 Rule 202. UNIFORM COURT AND CASE NUMBER DESIGNATION

All filings shall conform to the requirements for uniform court and case number designation set by Admin. Rule 8. In addition, all filings shall contain the proper court and case designation as described below.

202.1. Court Designation. Pursuant to Indiana Code 33–33–71–2, St. Joseph County, Indiana, constitutes the Sixtieth (60th) Judicial Circuit. The legal names of the courts within the 60th Judicial Circuit are the St. Joseph Circuit Court, the St. Joseph Superior Court, and the St. Joseph Probate Court. All filings shall properly reflect the legal name of the applicable court. Any filing may be amended, rejected, or stricken if it does not contain the proper case name and/or the legal name of the court.

202.2. Case Designation. At the time of filing, the party initiating the case should properly designate the case type.

202.2.1. *Designation Upon Filing.* The filing party (or the attorney for the filing party) shall designate the correct case type in the cause number line of each summons and complaint before presenting a new filing to the Clerk.

202.2.2. *Proper Designations.* Case type designations must conform to the requirements of Ind. Admin. Rules 8(B)(3). Since January 1, 2003, "CP" is no longer allowed as a designator for civil plenary cases; "PL" is now the proper designation for these types of cases.

202.2.3. *Failure to Designate.* If a filing is presented without a case type designation on each summons and complaint, the entire filing may be rejected or stricken. Should a case be accepted with an incorrect designation, the court may order the matter to be redocketed with the correct case type designation and may require that the filing party pay a redocketing fee.

202.2.4. *Advice and Assistance.* The Clerk or her deputies may provide assistance to the filing party in this regard, but should not be required to make a legal judgment as to the correct case type designation. Any questions or doubts should be referred to a judge or a magistrate judge in the court receiving the filing.

Adopted July 28, 2006, effective Jan. 1, 2007. Amended August 2, 2007, effective January 1, 2008.

LR71–AR9 Rule 203. ACCESS TO COURT RECORDS

203.1. Confidential Records. The following information is excluded from public access and is confidential:

(1) Information that is excluded from public access under Federal Law;

(2) Information that is excluded from public access under Indiana statute or Court rule;

(3) Records that are sealed by Federal or state law or by court order;

(4) All personal notes and email deliberative material of judges, jurors, court staff, and judicial agencies, including without limitation the Adult Probation Department, the Juvenile Probation Department, and the Domestic Relations Counseling Bureau, whether maintained in electronic or paper format;

(5) All information recorded in a personal data assistant (PDA) or other electronic organizer or calendar system, whether maintained in electronic or paper format;

(6) Diaries, journals, or other personal notes serving as the functional equivalent of a diary or journal under Ind. Code 5–14–3–4(b)(7);

(7) Advisory or deliberative material created, collected, or exchanged by, between, or among Judges, including notes, journals, or minutes of Judge's Meetings;

(8) Information excluded from public access by a specific court order.

203.2. Access to Confidential Records. Information that is excluded from public access and is confidential may not be accessed without prior written authorization of the Judge who is assigned to a particular matter or is responsible for supervising that office or department that created, maintained, or archived the information. In some instances, access will require prior written authorization from the Judges of the Circuit Court and the Probate Court and the Chief Judge of the Superior Court; in other instances, access will require written authorization from all the Judges of the Circuit, Probate, and Superior Courts.

Adopted July 28, 2006, effective Jan. 1, 2007. Amended August 2, 2007, effective January 1, 2008.

LR71–TR3.1 Rule 204. APPEARANCE AND WITHDRAWAL OF APPEARANCE OF COUNSEL

204.1. Appearances. Counsel and unrepresented parties appearing after the filing of the original complaint shall forthwith notify all other counsel of record and unrepresented parties of such appearance and file proof of such notice. Each counsel or party shall file an appearance form (or its equivalent) that includes a mailing address and telephone number. The notice may include a post office box, but must include a physical street address to allow for proper service of process or other notification by the Court.

204.2. Withdrawal of Appearance. Unless authorized by the party in open Court or in writing or upon appearance of other counsel, an attorney will be permitted to withdraw his appearance for a party only after filing a Motion to Withdraw and setting the matter for hearing not fewer than fourteen (14) days from the date of filing. If a trial date has already been set, a motion to withdraw appearance must be filed at least thirty (30) days prior to that date unless the attorney has leave of the court to file in a shorter amount of time.

204.3. Service of Notice to Withdraw. The attorney must present to the Court adequate proof of notice to his client, as well as all other counsel and unrepresented litigants, of the intent to withdraw and of any impending pre-trial, hearing, or trial dates. The notice to his client shall be by postage prepaid, certified mail, return receipt requested and received or returned by the Postal Service undeliverable or refused addressed to the last known address of the client.

204.4. Contact Information. In cases where the withdrawal of appearance shall leave the client unrepresented, the Motion to Withdraw must contain the address and, if known, telephone number of the client where service of documents can be delivered or other notice can be provided. As required by AR 9(G), this contact information may be designated as confidential and excluded from public access.

Adopted July 28, 2006, effective Jan. 1, 2007. Amended August 2, 2007, effective January 1, 2008.

LR71–TR41(E) Rule 205.   DISMISSAL FOR LACK OF PROSECUTION

205.1. Initiated by Court. Rules to show cause why a cause should not be dismissed for lack of prosecution pursuant to T.R. 41(E) will be routinely issued and served upon affected parties and counsel by ordinary mail or by personal delivery in all cases in which no entry has been made for six months. Records of the setting of cases for trial and motions for continuance will not be considered as entries tolling the time.

205.2. Initiated by Parties. Nothing in Rule 205.1 above shall affect the right of any party to file a motion pursuant to T.R. 41. Unless otherwise directed by the regularly presiding Judge, a party filing a motion for dismissal pursuant to T.R. 41 shall request that the Court set the matter for hearing.

Adopted July 28, 2006, effective Jan. 1, 2007. Amended August 2, 2007, effective January 1, 2008.

LR71–TR12 Rule 206.   PLEADING AND MOTIONS UNDER TRIAL RULES 12 AND 56

206.1. Supporting Memorandum of Law. All pleadings and motions filed pursuant to Trial Rules 12 and 56 shall be accompanied by a separate supporting brief. An adverse party shall have thirty (30) days after service of the motion in which to serve and file an answer brief. Subject to Court approval, the moving party may file a reply brief. With regard to all other motions or matters submitted to the Court, and so long as consistent with Indiana Rules of Procedure, an adverse party wishing to respond shall do so within fifteen (15) days of service. Each motion shall be separate, while alternative motions filed together shall each be identified on the caption. Failure to file an answer brief or reply brief within the time prescribed shall be deemed a waiver of the right thereto and shall subject the motion to summary ruling.

206.2. Hearing; Hearing Date; Opposing Memorandum. Notwithstanding any other rule of court, all T.R. 12 and 56 motions shall be set for hearing by the moving party at the time of filing unless otherwise ordered by the Court. Unless other authorized by the Court, the hearing shall be scheduled for a day not fewer than fourteen (14) days after the time period allowed for filing of briefs as specified in Rule 206.1 *supra.*

206.3. Waiver of Hearing; Stipulation of the Parties. Adverse parties may stipulate that a T.R. 12 or 56 motion may be ruled upon by the Court without a hearing thereon, in which event the motion and stipulation shall be brought to the personal attention of the Judge by counsel or by a party proceeding *pro se.*

206.4. Required Notices to Parties.

206.4.1. *Notice to Parties in Mortgage Foreclosure (MF) Causes of Action.* A party filing a mortgage foreclosure (MF) cause of action shall cause to be served on the resident a copy of the Notice Concerning Mortgage Foreclosure, which is attached hereto and made a part hereof as Appendix A. Should the plaintiff fail to comply with the rule, the Court may refuse to enter default judgment, refuse to grant judgment on the pleadings or take similar action until compliance is demonstrated. Additionally, should plaintiff's failure to comply with this rule result in additional costs to the defendant, the Court may order the plaintiff to pay reasonable expenses, including attorney fees, that are related to the plaintiff's noncompliance. See also, Ind. Code 32–30–10.5 et seq.

206.4.2. *Notice to Unrepresented Parties Regarding Trial Rule 56 Motions.* Notwithstanding any other rule of court, if a party is proceeding *pro se* and an opposing party files a motion for summary judgment, counsel for the moving party must serve a notice upon the unrepresented party as set forth in Appendix B, which is attached hereto and made a party hereof.

206.5. Appearance by Counsel at Scheduled Hearings. Whenever the Court schedules a hearing on a motion pursuant to Trial Rule 12 and/or 56, counsel for all represented parties shall appear in person or by local co-counsel at such hearing.

Adopted July 28, 2006, effective Jan. 1, 2007. Amended August 2, 2007, effective January 1, 2008; amended 2008, effective Jan. 1, 2009; amended July 1, 2009, effective Jan. 1, 2010; amended July 18, 2011, effective Jan. 1, 2012.

LR71–TR55 Rule 207.   DEFAULT JUDGMENTS

207.1. Proper Service. At the time of the request for entry of a default judgment under T.R. 55, the moving party must demonstrate that service has been perfected on the party or parties against whom default is sought.

207.2. Affidavit for Judgment by Default. At the time of filing of a motion for default judgment or at the time of a hearing scheduled for entry of a default judgment, the moving party shall file an affidavit indicating that the party or parties against whom default is sought is not a member of the military service, is neither a minor nor incompetent, and is not institutionalized.

207.3. Affidavit of Attorney Fees. At the time of filing of a motion for default judgment or at the time of a hearing scheduled for entry of a default judgment, a moving party who is requesting an allowance of attorney's fees shall file an affidavit executed by the attorney requesting the fee. The affidavit shall be in a form and substance to enable the Court to determine if attorney's fees are appropriate, and if so the reasonable amount of fees. The affidavit shall set forth the authority for the Court to award attorney's fees (i.e., statute, contract, etc.) and the basis upon which the proposed fees were computed (i.e., the hourly rate, the number of hours employed or anticipated to be employed in obtaining and enforcing a judgment herein). In the absence of an affidavit or sworn testimony in lieu thereof, no attorney's fees shall be allowed.

Adopted July 28, 2006, effective Jan. 1, 2007. Amended August 2, 2007, effective January 1, 2008.

LR71–TR26 Rule 208. DISCOVERY REQUESTS

208.1. Filing with the Court. As envisioned by the Trial Rules, requests for discovery shall be served upon the parties and should not be filed with the Court unless in connection with a dispute concerning compliance with prior discovery requests. The procedure for addressing discovery disputes is outlined in Rule 208.4 below.

208.2. Format of Discovery Requests. Whenever agreed by the parties or otherwise ordered by the Court, a party shall forward simultaneously with the hard copy discovery request (interrogatories, requests for production, requests for admissions, or other requests for discovery) either a floppy disk or an electronic mail message with a copy of the request attached in digital format. Otherwise, an original and two duplicate copies shall be prepared and served on the party required to answer.

208.3. Interrogatories. All interrogatories to parties propounded pursuant to T.R. 33 shall be prepared as follows:

(1) The propounding party or the attorney of record for the propounding party shall sign and date the interrogatories as of the date of service;

(2) After each interrogatory, sufficient blank space shall be left by the propounding party as is reasonably anticipated may be required for the responder's typewritten answer. If additional space is required for an answer, the responder shall attach supplemental pages, incorporated by reference, to comply with the spirit of T.R. 33.

(3) Additional space shall be left by the propounding party at the close of the interrogatories for the signature and appropriate typed oath or affirmation to be supplied by the responder.

(4) The responding party shall type the requested answers, supply the jurat, and serve the original and one duplicate on propounding counsel.

208.4. Scheduling of Depositions. Pursuant to their obligations under the Indiana Rules of Professional Conduct and as officers of the St. Joseph Circuit, Superior or Probate courts, attorneys shall make a good faith effort to schedule depositions in a manner in which avoids scheduling conflicts. Unless agreed by counsel or otherwise authorized by the court, no deposition shall be scheduled on less than ten (10) days notice.

208.5. Discovery Disputes. To promote the orderly and expeditious handling of cases to trial readiness, counsel shall attempt in good faith to resolve all disagreements between or among themselves concerning the necessity for and scope of discovery, the necessity to seek sanctions, and/or protection against discovery under T.R. 26 through T.R. 37. After personal consultation and good faith attempts to resolve differences as to the foregoing matters, counsel for any or all parties may move to compel discovery, invoke sanctions, or seek protection against discovery as aforesaid. As a part of such motion, the party shall recite the date, time, and place of the personal consultations and the names of the participants. If counsel for any party advises the Court in writing that counsel for any other party has refused or delayed consultation hereby contemplated, the Court shall take such action as is appropriate to preclude, obviate, or avoid further delay. Where an objection is raised during the taking of a deposition which threatens to prevent the completion of the deposition and which counsel have a good faith belief is susceptible to resolution by the court without the submission of written materials, any party may recess the deposition for the purpose of submitting the objection by telephone to a judge for a ruling instanter, subject to the availability of and within the discretion of the judge. Prior to contacting a judge for such a ruling, all parties shall in good faith confer or attempt to confer in an effort to resolve the matter without court intervention and, if court action is still necessary, the parties shall inform the judge of the efforts taken to attempt to resolve the matter.

Adopted July 28, 2006, effective Jan. 1, 2007. Amended Aug. 2, 2007, effective Jan. 1, 2008; June 1, 2011, effective Jan. 1, 2012.

LR71–TR16 Rule 209. PRE–TRIAL PROCEDURES

209.1. Purpose of Pre-trial Procedure. This rule is intended to accomplish the original purpose of pretrial procedure—to simplify the issues, make cases easier, quicker, and less expensive for the Court, lawyer, and litigant and to alleviate the burden of ceremonial detain and to aid the efficient preparation of a case.

209.2. Pre-trial Conference. A pre-trial conference of Court and counsel may be scheduled by the Court on its own motion or at the request of counsel for any party in any civil case in which, in the discretion of the Court, possible problems can be identified, the course and progress of the case, the necessity, sequence, and scope of discovery should be anticipated, planned, scheduled, or estimated for the orderly and expeditious handling of it by Court and counsel. At the pre-trial conference, the Court may designate deadlines for discovery, dispositive motions, or alternative dispute resolution. The Court may also provide the parties with proposed dates for trial, additional pre-trial conferences, and/or require the filing of a pre-trial order. The Clerk shall endeavor to give at least thirty (30) days notice of the initial pre-trial conference to the parties.

209.3. Alternative Dispute Resolution. On the Court's own motion or initiative, the parties may be required to attempt alternative dispute resolution (ADR). Such ADR efforts may include, at the Court's discretion, mediation and/or settlement conferences and may require one or more sessions or sessions lasting a specific amount of time.

One or more of the parties may request that the Court order the parties engage in ADR. Such a request must be in writing and must be accompanied by a memorandum informing the Court of the nature of the case, the attorneys or unrepresented litigants involved, and a history of the settlement negotiations that have taken place to that date and that the previous settlement negotiations made in good faith have failed.

At any mediation or settlement conference, counsel for each party shall be present, in person, and each party or a designated representative having complete authority to settle the matter in question shall be present in person. Upon request and by leave of court, a party or representative of a party may be allowed to participate in said settlement conference by telephone in lieu of a personal appearance. Should any party or counsel for any party violate the requirements of this rule concerning attendance, the Court may impose sanctions.

209.3.1. *Mortgage Foreclosures on Real Estate.* Effective April 15, 2010, Plaintiffs filing new mortgage foreclosure (MF) actions in the St. Joseph Circuit Court or the St. Joseph Superior Court will be required to provide to the Clerk of the Court:

  • One (1) additional stamped, addressed envelope, with no return address information, for each individual (but not including any corporation or entity) named as a defendant,

  AND

  • A service list, including the name, address and, if available, the telephone number of each defendant.

This rule is adopted by the St. Joseph Circuit Court and the St. Joseph Superior Court pursuant to an initiative of the Indiana Supreme Court and the Indiana Housing and Community Development Authority to train and recruit volunteer lawyers to assist homeowners facing foreclosure and in furtherance of the purposes underlying Senate Enrolled Act No. 492 (2010).

All MF actions filed on or after April 15, 2010, in the St. Joseph Circuit Court or the St. Joseph Superior Court, in which a timely request for settlement conference is made pursuant to Ind. Code 32–30–10.5–10, shall be the subject of an administrative transfer to the St. Joseph Superior Court, Mishawaka Division, for purposes of the scheduling and conduct of such settlement conference.

Failure to comply with this rule will delay the processing of the case by the Clerk until compliance is achieved. Unless extended by the St. Joseph

Circuit Court and/or the St. Joseph Superior Court, this Rule expires on December 31, 2014.

209.4. Adequate Preparation for Pre-trial Conference. The purpose of the pre-trial conference being to narrow and simplify the issues for trial and to expedite the trial, counsel shall report for such conference with the Judge after full preparation including an adequate meeting of counsel as contemplated by T.R. 16(c). In all cases counsel shall be prepared to indicate to the Court whether the case may be tried to a jury of six and whether the Judge may conduct all of the voir dire examination of prospective jurors or the initial voir dire examination with supplemental inquiry by counsel.

209.5. Completion of Discovery. In cases in which a preliminary pre-trial conference has been held under Rule 12(b), discovery shall be made in accordance with the scheduling thereof then ordered. In cases in which no preliminary pre-trial conference has been held, all discovery shall be completed prior to the pre-trial conference and no discovery shall be conducted thereafter unless, upon motion or stipulation showing good cause therefore, an order is entered permitting further discovery within time to be prescribed by the Court.

209.6. Pre-trial Readiness Conference. At least ten (10) days prior to trial, the Court may set a Readiness Conference. In addition to each party proceeding *pro se* and counsel for each of the parties, the Court may order that one or more of the parties themselves attend the Readiness Conference. The purpose of the Readiness Conference is to simplify the issues anticipated at trial, and the Conference will include a determination of the parties' readiness to proceed to trial, the progress of the parties in obtaining stipulations of fact and authenticity of exhibits and, if appropriate, the willingness of the parties to waive jury trial. Where the parties have filed a written stipulation signed by all parties addressing these issues and confirming the trial date, the Court in its discretion may vacate the Readiness Conference.

209.7. Attendance by Trial Counsel Required. Unless otherwise directed by the Court, each pre-trial conference shall be attended without exception by any party proceeding *pro se* and at least one of the attorneys for each of the parties who will participate in the trial of the case and who shall be authorized to deal comprehensively with all subjects on the agenda. With prior approval of the presiding Judge, an attorney may appear telephonically. Sanctions for failure to comply with this rule shall be deemed appropriate.

209.8. Failure to Attend. Failure to attend and adequately participate in pre-trial conferences as intended by T.R. 16 may result in reassignment of the cause to the bottom of the appropriate assignment list, issuing an order pursuant to T.R. 41(E), and/or the imposition of appropriate sanctions.

209.9. Setting for Trial. Civil cases may be set for trial at the pre-trial conference or as otherwise directed by the assigned Judge.

Adopted July 28, 2006, effective Jan. 1, 2007. Amended August 2, 2007, effective January 1, 2008; July 26, 2012, effective Jan. 1, 2013.

LR71–TR39 Rule 210. SCHEDULING TRIALS

210.1. Trial Settings. All cases scheduled for trial shall be ready for trial on the date scheduled unless otherwise directed by the Court. Where multiple trials are set on one day, all trial settings shall be considered first settings and the parties shall be ready for trial on the date scheduled unless the parties have been advised of a notice of priority as described in Rule 210.2 below.

210.2. Notice of Priority. At the time of setting the case for trial, upon motion of either party and for good cause shown, the Court may order that the parties are entitled to notice of priority. Where notice of priority has been ordered for multiple trials set on the same day, the case assigned a second setting shall stand for trial if the parties are given forty-eight (48) hours prior notice and cases assigned a third subsequent setting shall stand for trial if the parties are given seven (7) days notice.

210.3. Continuances. All motions for continuances shall be in writing and shall set forth specifically the grounds asserted for such motion. Unless otherwise directed or excused by the Court, all attorneys of record and parties proceeding *pro se* shall appear before the Court on the date of the trial setting. The Court may assign a new trial setting on the date of the original trial setting, or on the date a continuance is granted, or as otherwise directed by the Court.

210.4. Imposition of Costs for Late Settlement. If a civil case is settled less than forty-eight (48) hours prior to the time it is scheduled for trial, or is settled after 10:00 a.m. on the Friday prior to a Monday trial setting (or a Tuesday setting if the intervening Monday is a legal holiday), any costs incurred by the Court as a result of the late settlement of the case shall be divided evenly among the parties and ordered to be paid by them.

Adopted July 28, 2006, effective Jan. 1, 2007. Amended August 2, 2007, effective January 1, 2008.

LR71–TR47 Rule 211. JURORS

211.1. Jury Lists. The Court will maintain lists of petit jurors who are subject to call during any session of the Court's calendar year term. Such juror lists will contain brief biographical data concerning each member of the panel. Prior to trial, the Judge will provide counsel with a list of the petit jurors called for the trial of that particular case, juror biographical data, and a juror seating chart. Juror lists and biographical information shall be confidential.

211.2. Alternate Jurors. By agreement of the parties or on order of the Court, alternative jurors may be selected and seated, selection thereof to be made after the jury itself has been selected. All jurors, both regular and alternate, shall be sworn as a panel. The parties may also agree to waive the selection of alternate jurors.

211.3. Special Venire. The Court may call a special venire as provided by statute.

211.4. Voir Dire Examination. The Court may conduct the entire voir dire examination of prospective jurors or may permit counsel to do so. The Court shall conduct such portion of the voir dire examination as the parties shall stipulate. If the Court conducts the entire examination, counsel shall be given an opportunity to suggest supplemental questions or lines of inquiry. Further voir dire examination shall be conducted pursuant to the Indiana Jury Rules.

211.5. Passing and Acceptance of Jurors. Unless otherwise approved or directed by the Court, the one pass rule shall be followed; that is, the passing of an individual juror following the voir dire examination of a panel of prospective jurors of which that juror was a member shall constitute an acceptance of that juror by the party so passing. Challenges shall be made at the bench outside the hearing of the prospective jurors and may be made by use of slips of paper of uniform size or as otherwise directed by the Court.

Adopted July 28, 2006, effective Jan. 1, 2007. Amended August 2, 2007, effective January 1, 2008.

LR71–TR51 Rule 212. TRIAL PROCEDURES

212.1. Exhibits.

212.1.1. *Marking in Advance.* All exhibits shall be marked in advance of trial or during recesses in the trial in accordance with the practice of the court reporter so that the trial is not delayed for the marking of exhibits.

212.1.2. *Custody of Court Reporter.* After being marked for identification and offered into evidence, whether or not admitted into evidence, all exhibits and proposed exhibits necessary to the record on appeal shall be placed in the custody of the Official Court Reporter who shall be responsible for their safekeeping until otherwise ordered by the Judge.

212.1.3. *Return to Parties.* Any model, diagram, exhibit, or proposed exhibit shall be returned to the party offering it upon request to the reporter after the time for appeal has elapsed or the possibility of further appeal is exhausted, unless the Court otherwise orders.

212.1.4. *Disposal.* Where no request for the return of exhibits or proposed exhibits is made within ninety (90) days of final judgment, the same may be disposed of by the reporter as the Court may direct.

212.2. Instructions Requested at Commencement of Trial. All requests for special instructions tendered in accordance with T.R. 51 shall be submitted to the Court not later than the commencement of

(c) the parties stipulate to the random selection of a special judge, or

(d) the judge before whom the case was pending has recused or disqualified,

the regularly presiding judge shall direct the Clerk to randomly select a successor special judge from a list of eligible judicial officers, which may include judges, magistrate judges or senior judges.

216.4. Acceptance; Disqualification; Ineligibility. A special judge selected pursuant to § 216.3. of this rule must accept jurisdiction unless disqualified pursuant to the Code of Judicial Conduct or excused from service by the Supreme Court of Indiana. In the event no judicial officer within Administrative District 4 is eligible to serve as special judge or the particular circumstances dictate the selection of a special judge by the Supreme Court of Indiana, a regularly presiding judge of the court in which the matter is pending shall certify the matter to the Supreme Court of Indiana for appointment of a special judge.

216.5. Discontinuation of Service as Special Judge. In the event a special judge who has assumed jurisdiction thereafter fails to act or notifies the parties that he or she no longer can serve as special judge, a regularly presiding judge of the court in which the case is pending shall assume jurisdiction; provided such judge has not previously served in the case and is otherwise eligible to serve. If the regularly presiding judge cannot assume jurisdiction under this section, selection of a successor special judge shall proceed pursuant to T.R. 79(D) and this rule.

Adopted July 28, 2006, effective Jan. 1, 2007. Amended August 2, 2007, effective January 1, 2008; Aug. 9, 2013.

LR71–TR63 Rule 217. SENIOR JUDGES, TEMPORARY JUDGES, AND JUDGES PRO TEMPORE

All routine appointments of Senior Judges, Temporary Judges, and Judges Pro Tempore shall be made by the Judge of the Circuit Court or the Probate Court, or the Chief Judge of the Superior Court.

Adopted July 28, 2006, effective Jan. 1, 2007. Amended August 2, 2007, effective January 1, 2008.

LR71–AP9 Rule 218. APPELLATE RECORDS

When an appeal is initiated by the filing of a Notice of Appeal pursuant to Appellate Rule 2, Indiana Rules of Appellate Procedure, and a transcript of all or any part of the evidence is sought for the record on appeal, the party or counsel filing the Notice shall contemporaneously personally deliver a copy of the Notice to the court reporter, shall advise the reporter of the deadline for preparation of the record, and shall arrange to pay the reporter for the preparation of the transcript.

Adopted July 28, 2006, effective Jan. 1, 2007. Amended August 2, 2007, effective January 1, 2008.

LR71–TR69 Rule 219. PROCEEDINGS SUPPLEMENTAL; OTHER COLLECTION REMEDIES

219.1. Post–Judgment Proceedings. Post-judgment proceedings shall not be instituted until ten (10) calendar days have elapsed since the entry of a final decree or judgment in the records of the Clerk of the Court. The Court may waive this requirement where it is shown that a party will be unduly harmed by its enforcement or where a rule of court or statute specifically provides otherwise.

219.2. Notification of Appearance; Local Counsel. If at the time of filing of a proceedings supplemental or any time thereafter, counsel for the moving party or a party proceeding pro se determines that he or she will not attend the hearing in person, the counsel or the moving party shall notify the Court in writing of the substitute or local counsel who will be in attendance at the hearing. Failure to comply with these notification procedures may be enforced by direct contempt of court.

219.3. Special Post–Judgment Procedures. Unless an emergency or other good cause is shown, any party filing for an extraordinary collection remedy (e.g., account freeze, employment information, or garnishment) shall have filed previously a proceedings supplemental and interrogatories responses, as appropriate.

219.4. Penalties for Failure to Comply. Unless good cause is shown, the failure of counsel or a moving party to comply with this rule or to appear for a scheduled hearing on proceedings supplemental may be enforced by contempt of court, and may result in a monetary fine or other appropriate penalty.

Adopted July 28, 2006, effective Jan. 1, 2007. Amended August 2, 2007, effective January 1, 2008.

Appendix A. NOTICE REGARDING MORTGAGE FORECLOSURE

GET HELP. GET HOPE.

FROM THE
INDIANA HOUSING & COMMUNITY DEVELOPMENT AUTHORITY
AND ITS
INDIANA FORECLOSURE PREVENTION NETWORK

Your mortgage lender has filed to foreclose on your home. According to Indiana law, you *may* be entitled to a court-ordered settlement conference. This provides an opportunity for you and your lender to negotiate a "foreclosure prevention agreement" that may allow you to keep your home.

If you want to take advantage of this right, you must notify the Court of your intention no more than 30 days after this Notice was served. You may, but are not required to, notify the Court by signing this Notice where indicated and mailing or delivering it to the appropriate Court at either 101 S. Main Street, South Bend, IN 46601 or 219 Lincolnway West, Mishawaka, IN 46544, as indicated on the Summons. You should also send a copy of the signed Notice to the lender's attorney at the address shown in the Summons.

If you choose to participate in a settlement conference, the Court will schedule it to take place at least 25 days, but no more than 60 days after the date of this Notice. You have the right to be represented by an attorney or assisted by a mortgage foreclosure counselor, either in person or by telephone, at the settlement conference.

We urge you to contact the Indiana Foreclosure Prevention Network (the "Network") to assist you in this process. The Network will help you find a foreclosure prevention counselor and/or an attorney who is knowledgeable in the foreclosure process. This is a **free and confidential** service that is provided by the State of Indiana and coordinated by the Indiana Housing and Community Development Authority. You can reach the Network by calling **1–877–GET–HOPE (1–877–438–4673)** or by visiting www.877GetHope.org.

Mortgage foreclosure is a complex process. People may approach you about "saving" your home. You should be careful about any such promises, **especially if you are asked to pay for their services**. If you believe that you have been a victim of a "foreclosure rescue scam," you should contact the Office of the Attorney General's Home Owner Protection Unit by calling 1–800–382–5516.

Date of Notice: _____

I want to participate in a foreclosure prevention settlement conference:

Sign Here: _____

Printed Name: _____

Date Signed: _____

Case No. _____ *(please insert # from Complaint)*

Developed and prescribed by IHCDA as required by P.L. 105–2009r (St. Joseph County Version, 8/1/2009)

Adopted effective Jan. 1, 2012.

Appendix B. NOTICE REGARDING SUMMARY JUDGMENT MOTION

READ THIS NOTICE AND THE ENCLOSED PAPERS—A MOTION FOR SUMMARY JUDGMENT HAS BEEN FILED AND, IF UNOPPOSED, THIS MOTION MAY RESULT IN JUDGMENT BEING ENTERED AGAINST YOU WITHOUT A HEARING OR TRIAL.

The Courts of St. Joseph County, Indiana require that this notice be sent to you about the motion for summary judgment that was filed by the opposing party. This notice does not contain legal advice, but does provide important information about your legal options. Please read it carefully.

The opposing party has filed a motion for summary judgment pursuant to Indiana Trial Rule 56(C). The motion alleges that the facts are not in dispute and the Court can rule as a matter of law. The motion asks the Court to enter judgment in favor of the opposing party without a trial.

As you are not represented by counsel, you are hereby advised of your obligation to respond to the summary judgment motion. Your previous answer, denial or even counter-claim in response to the original complaint is not sufficient to defend a motion for summary judgment. Unless you submit your own affidavits (or other documentary evidence) or a response that specifically identifies information within the existing court records that contradict the factual assertions of the evidence designated in the motion for summary judgment and supporting materials, any factual assertions in our motion and supporting documentation will be accepted by the Court as true. In essence, your failure to respond to the pending motion for summary judgment would be equivalent to failing to present any evidence in your favor at a trial.

If you wish to file a response to the motion, the Court must receive your response within thirty-three (33) days after your opponent's motion was mailed to you. Failure to meet this timeframe will result in the Court being unable to consider your response or any attachments thereto.

Either party may request a court hearing on the summary judgment motion. A written request for a hearing must be received by the Court no later than ten (10) days after the response was filed or is due. The hearing will not be a trial, and neither party will be able to present evidence at the hearing. However, either party may make legal argument and refer to the evidence designated with the summary judgment motion or with any response. If no request for a hearing is filed with the Court, the Court may decide the motion without a hearing based on the affidavits and documents filed by the parties.

Any response or request for hearing must be served (or mailed) on the attorney for the opposing party. A response (or other pleading) filed with the Court must include a statement that you have complied with this requirement. Your statement may be in the following form: "I delivered a copy of this response to (Attorney Name) by United States Mail on this ____ day of _____, 20 ___."

As with any legal matter, you may wish to consult with and/or retain an attorney to represent you in this lawsuit and to assist you in responding to our motion for summary judgment.

[If appropriate under the Federal Fair Debt Collection Act, the following identifying information should be included with the Notice:

Notice Provided by:

Attorney Name

Law Firm (if any)
Address
Telephone Number
Our Law Firm is a debt collector. This Notice is
provided as part of an attempt to collect a debt, and
any information obtained by us will be used for that
purpose. As we represent an opposing party, we
cannot provide you with legal advice.]

Adopted effective Jan. 1, 2012.

LOCAL CRIMINAL RULES FOR ST. JOSEPH COUNTY

Adopted July 28, 2006, Effective January 1, 2007

Including Amendments Received Through November 1, 2013

Research Notes

Annotations to the Local Criminal Rules for St. Joseph County are available in West's Annotated Indiana Code, *Title 34 Appendix.*

These rules may be searched electronically on Westlaw *in the* IN-RULES *database; updates to these rules may be found on* Westlaw *in* IN-RULESUPDATES. *For search tips and a summary of database content, consult the Westlaw Scope Screens for each database.*

LR71–CR00 Rule 301.   CRIMINAL CASES

301.1.   Intent of the Local Criminal Rules. Criminal cases shall be governed by this rule which is adopted to conserve the time of Court and counsel and to expedite and assure the disposition of criminal cases within the constraints imposed by C.R. 4 and is intended to provide a routine procedure for the advancement of cases from filing to disposition.

301.2.   Balancing of Interests. The legitimate interests of all civil litigants and the prompt and orderly dispatch of all civil litigation in the Circuit Court will be given preference subject only to such priority of disposition as is from time to time required for criminal cases by applicable rules of Indiana Trial Procedure, rules of the Indiana Supreme Court, and the requirements of the Constitutions of the United States and the State of Indiana to preserve to criminal case defendants all rights thereby conferred or guaranteed.

Adopted July 28, 2006, effective Jan. 1, 2007. Amended August 2, 2007, effective January 1, 2008.

LR71–CR21 Rule 302.   APPLICATION OF LOCAL RULES

The local administrative and trial rules shall apply to all criminal proceedings so far as they are not in conflict with any specific local rule adopted for the conduct of criminal proceedings, which are enumerated hereafter.

Adopted July 28, 2006, effective Jan. 1, 2007. Amended August 2, 2007, effective January 1, 2008.

LR71–CR2.2 Rule 303.   ASSIGNMENT OF CRIMINAL CASES

303.1.   Grand Jury Proceedings and Indictments.

303.1.1.   *Convening a Grand Jury.* The Circuit Court shall call and conduct all Grand Jury proceedings.

303.1.2.   *Docketing Grand Jury Proceedings.* Each newly impaneled grand jury shall be assigned a cause number on the miscellaneous criminal docket. All pre-indictment motions, orders and other filings pertaining to matters before that grand jury shall bear that particular docket number and shall be maintained by the Clerk under seal if so ordered by the Court.

303.1.3.   *Pre-indictment Challenges to Subpoenas or Proceedings.* All pre-indictment challenges to grand jury subpoenas or grand jury proceedings shall be made in writing and filed with the clerk, and shall recite all pertinent facts including the grand jury number, the date of service of the subpoena, the appearance or production date of the subpoena, and the law. Motions to quash or limit a grand jury subpoena shall be filed and served upon the Prosecuting Attorney no later than seven (7) days prior to the appearance or production date unless good cause exists for a later filing. Upon the filing of any motion to quash or limit a grand jury subpoena, the court will endeavor to rule upon the motion on or prior to the return date of the subpoena.

303.1.4.   *Persons Authorized to Appear before Grand Jury.* No person shall be present in the hall adjacent to the area or rooms utilized by a grand jury in the process of performing its function. In addition, while a grand jury is in the process of performing is function, no person shall remain in an area in which persons who are appearing before the grand jury can be monitored or observed. This rule shall not apply to grand jurors; witnesses; prosecuting attorneys, law enforcement officers, and employees; court personnel concerned with grand jury proceedings; private attorneys whose clients have been called to appear as a witness at a session of the grand jury then in progress or about to commence; and others specifically authorized to be present at the grand jury proceedings.

303.1.5. *Assignment of Grand Jury Indictments.* Except as provided in Rule 303.2 below, indictments issued by the Grand Jury shall be filed on a random basis in equal numbers between the Circuit and Superior Courts.

303.2. Felony Nonsupport and Welfare Fraud. All criminal proceedings, whether by information, indictment, or by transfer from another county, alleging violation of I.C. 35–43–5–7 (welfare fraud), I.C. 35–43–5–7. 1 (Medicaid fraud), I.C. 35–43–5–7.2 (children's health insurance fraud), or I.C. 35–46–1–5 (nonsupport of a dependant child), shall be assigned to the Circuit Court. To effectuate caseload balancing and judicial economy, other criminal proceedings may be assigned to the Circuit Court by written order signed by the Judge of the Circuit Court and the Chief Judge of Superior Court.

303.3. Other Criminal Proceedings. This Rule applies to all criminal cases filed with the Superior Court, whether initiated by information, indictment (pursuant to Local Rule 302.1), or by transfer from another county. Pursuant to Rule 2.2, Indiana Rules of Criminal Procedure, criminal felony and misdemeanor cases filed in the Superior Court will be assigned as follows:

(1) Misdemeanor cases will not be assigned to a particular Judge (except as provided in Local Rule 107, but rather shall be heard by the judicial officer then sitting in the Traffic and Misdemeanor division of the court on the date such misdemeanor is to be heard.

(2) Each of the Judges of the court shall be assigned by the Chief Judge, responsibility for the finding of probable cause in new criminal felony and misdemeanor filings.

(3) Upon the finding of probable cause on a felony charge, the prosecutor shall submit to the clerk of the court the charges and court's finding of probable cause. The clerk shall not assign a Judge or cause number to any new criminal felony filings in advance of a judicial finding of probable cause. Further, in the event that the prosecuting attorney shall elect to file a case and request that the clerk issue a summons, without first submitting the case for a finding of probable cause, or after a finding of no probable cause, the clerk shall assign the case as provided herein.

(4) The clerk shall, upon filing, whether by indictment or information, randomly assign, by computer, all criminal felony cases to the Judges of the criminal division. Should there be a Drug Treatment Court established pursuant to Local Rule 109.2 herein, all cases assigned to that Court shall be done in accordance with an assignment order entered by the Chief Judge. The Chief Judge shall thereafter have authority to transfer such felonies to other Judges of the court, so as to comply with Rule LR71–AR1–107, that being the Local Caseload Plan for St. Joseph County.

(5) Notwithstanding the subparagraph above, the Chief Judge may reassign a case to any other Judge of the court for good cause shown by any judge of the court, by agreement between judges of the court, or as may be determined to be in the best interests of the court pursuant to Rule LR71–AR00107, herein.

(6) Any dismissed felony charges shall, if re-filed, be assigned to the original Judge, notwithstanding paragraph (4) above.

(7) Upon a change of Judge under C.R. 12, the case shall be reassigned pursuant to C.R. 13. In the event that sufficient criminal division Judges are not available, Judges assigned to the civil division shall be available for assignment to the case.

Adopted July 28, 2006, effective Jan. 1, 2007. Amended Aug, 2, 2007, effective Jan. 1, 2008; June 1, 2011, effective Jan. 1, 2012; July 26, 2012, effective Jan. 1, 2013.

LR71–CR00 Rule 304. APPEARANCE AND PRESENCE OF DEFENDANTS

304.1. Personal Presence of Defendants. All defendants shall be present in Court at every stage of the proceedings conducted in open Court. All defendants shall be personally present at every stage of the proceedings including hearing on motions.

Adopted July 28, 2006, effective Jan. 1, 2007. Amended August 2, 2007, effective January 1, 2008.

LR71–CR00 Rule 305. DISCOVERY

305.1. Motions and Orders.

305.1.1. *Automatic Order to Produce.* At the initial hearing or at any time thereafter, the Court will automatically order the State to disclose and furnish all relevant items and information under this rule to the defendants within fifteen (15) days from the date of the initial hearing, subject to Constitutional limitations and protective orders. Likewise, the Court will order the defendant(s) to provide the State with discovery within thirty (30) days of the initial hearing or other date specified by the Court.

305.1.2. *Discovery Production and Certification.* At the time of production of discoverable material by either of the parties, the producing party shall in writing enumerate all material produced and shall certify to the Court in writing that it comprises all discoverable material then available and the party to whom it is supplied shall acknowledge receipt thereof in writing to be filed with the Court.

305.1.3. *Written Motion.* No written motion is required, except:

(1) To compel compliance under this Rule;

(2) For additional discovery not covered under this Rule;

(3) For a protective order; or

(4) For an extension of time.

305.2. Discovery Deadlines. All discovery shall be completed by the Omnibus date unless extended for good cause shown. However, the parties shall have a continuing obligation to disclose evidence and discovery required by these rules or by law.

305.3. Notice Required. Each side, within the time allowed for compliance with discovery under this Rule, shall provide the other with notice of its intent to introduce evidence pursuant to Indiana Rule of Evidence 404(b), 609(b), or any other Rule which requires notices as a prerequisite to the admission of evidence.

305.4. Waiver. Although each side has a right to full discovery under this Rule, each side has a corresponding duty to seek out discovery. Failure to do so may result in the waiver of this right.

305.5. State's Disclosure. The State shall disclose the following material and information within its possession or control:

(1) The names and last known addresses of persons whom the State intends to call as witnesses, with their relevant written or recorded statements;

(2) Any written, oral, or recorded statements made by the accused or by a co-defendant and a list of witnesses to the making and acknowledgment of such statements;

(3) A transcript of those portions of grand jury minutes containing testimony of persons whom the prosecuting attorney intends to call as witnesses at the hearing or trial;

(4) Any reports or statements of experts, made in connection with the particular case, including results of physical or mental examinations and of scientific tests, experiments, or comparisons;

(5) Any books, papers, documents, photographs, or tangible objects that the prosecuting attorney intends to use in the hearing or trial or which were obtained from or belong to the accused;

(6) Any record of prior criminal convictions that may be used for impeachment of the persons whom the State intends to call as witnesses at the hearing or trial;

(7) Any police reports concerning the investigation of the crime or crimes with which the defendant is charged.

The State shall also disclose to defense counsel any material or information within its possession or control that tends to negate the guilt of the accused as to the offense charged or would tend to reduce the punishment therefore. The State may perform these obligations in any manner mutually agreeable to the prosecutor and defense counsel.

305.6. Defendant's Disclosure. Defendant's counsel shall furnish the State with the following material and information within his/her possession or control:

(1) Any defense that he/she intends to make at a hearing or trial;

(2) The names and last known addresses of persons he/she intends to call as witnesses, with their relevant written or recorded statements and any record of prior criminal convictions known to him/her;

(3) Any books, papers, documents, photographs, or tangible objects he/she intends to use as evidence;

(4) Medical, scientific, or expert witness evaluations, statements, reports, or testimony that may be used at a hearing or trial.

After the formal charge has been filed, upon written motion by the State, the Court may require the accused, among other things, to:

(1) Appear in a lineup;

(2) Speak for identification by witnesses to an offense;

(3) Be fingerprinted;

(4) Pose for photographs not involving re-enactment of a scene;

(5) Try on articles of clothing;

(6) Allow the taking of specimens of material from under his/her fingernails;

(7) Allow the taking of samples of his/her blood, hair, and other materials of his/her body that involve no unreasonable intrusion;

(8) Provide a sample of his/her handwriting;

(9) Submit to a reasonable physical or medical inspection of his/her body.

Whenever the personal appearance of the accused is required for the foregoing purposes, reasonable notice of the time and place of such appearance shall be given by the State to the accused and his/her counsel, who shall have the right to be present. Provision may be made for appearances for such purposes in an order admitting the accused to bail or providing for his/her release.

305.7. Additions, Limitations, and Protective Orders.

305.7.1. *Discretionary Disclosures.* Upon a showing of materiality to the preparation of the defense, and if the request is reasonable, the court, in its discretion, may require disclosure to defense counsel of relevant material and information not covered by this Rule.

305.7.2. *Denial of Disclosure.* The court may deny disclosure authorized by this Rule if it finds that there is a substantial risk to any person of physical harm, intimidation, bribery, economic reprisals, or unnecessary annoyance or embarrassment resulting from such disclosure to counsel.

305.7.3. *Matters Not Subject to Disclosure.*

305.7.3.1. Work Product. Disclosure hereunder shall not be required of legal research of records, correspondence, reports, or memoranda to the extent that they contain the opinions, theories, or conclusions of the State or members of its legal or investigative staffs, or of defense counsel or his/her staff.

305.7.3.2. Informants. Disclosure of an informant's identity shall not be required where there is a paramount interest in non-disclosure and a failure to disclose will not infringe the Constitutional rights of the accused. Disclosure shall not be denied hereunder of the identity of witnesses to be produced at a hearing or trial.

305.7.4. *Protective Orders.* Either side may apply for a protective order for non-disclosure of requested discovery.

Adopted July 28, 2006, effective Jan. 1, 2007. Amended August 2, 2007, effective January 1, 2008.

LR71–CR00 Rule 306. DISPOSITIVE MOTIONS, MOTIONS TO SUPPRESS, OTHER MOTIONS

306.1. Motions to be in Writing. Unless a party has prior, written leave of Court, all pre-trial motions shall be filed in writing with adequate notice provided to opposing counsel and to the Court.

306.2. Hearings on Motions. The court will not ordinarily set for hearing any motion to dismiss, motion to suppress, motion in limine (where the grounds therefore are known prior to trial), or other such dispositive motion, unless the motion contains a factual explanation as to why the granting of such is appropriate and is accompanied by a sufficient memorandum of law. Such motions, filed after the omnibus date, may not be given a hearing prior to trial.

Adopted July 28, 2006, effective Jan. 1, 2007. Amended August 2, 2007, effective January 1, 2008.

LR71–CR00 Rule 307. PLEA AGREEMENT DEADLINES

307.1. Plea Agreement Date—Felony Cases. In all criminal prosecutions, the Judge may assign a date that will serve as the plea bargain deadline date. The Judge may also assign a record date, trial date, and other dates as may be appropriate. If the parties have not reached a plea agreement by the omnibus date, the court may hold a pre-trial conference as early as that day.

307.2. Plea Agreement Date—Traffic and Misdemeanor Division. The judicial officer presiding over criminal prosecutions in the Traffic & Misdemeanor Division may assign an omnibus date, record date, trial date, and other dates as may be appropriate. If the parties have no plea agreement, the court may hold a pre-trial conference on the plea agreement deadline date.

Adopted July 28, 2006, effective Jan. 1, 2007. Amended August 2, 2007, effective January 1, 2008.

LR71–CR00 Rule 308. MISCELLANEOUS CRIMINAL RULES

308.1. Determination of Probable Cause. In the even that any charging instrument, search warrant, subpoena, or other document, the issuance of which requires a finding of probable cause, or similar factual and legal finding, shall be submitted to a judge and that judge finds that no probable cause exists or that the submission is in any other way insufficient, any resubmission shall be made to the original judge, unless the original judge agrees that it may be submitted to another judge for his or her consideration.

308.2. Dismissal. Any dismissed felony shall be assigned to the original Judge if re-filed, notwithstanding any other assignment rule herein.

308.3. Bond Schedule. Each of the Courts, individually or in concert, may establish a presumptive bond schedule for criminal cases. The schedule is attached hereto as Appendix A.

308.4. Subsequent Arrest of a Person Already Released on Bail. Any person arrested for either a felony or misdemeanor, without a warrant, while already admitted to bail on a pending criminal charge, either felony or misdemeanor, shall not be eligible for pre-trial release pursuant to the presumptive bond schedule for St. Joseph County, Indiana contained in Rule LR71–CR00–308.3 (Appendix A), but shall instead remain in custody until a determination of probable cause shall be made at or before an initial hearing before a judicial officer pursuant to I.C. § 35–33–7–1 and § 35–33–7–2. If probable cause is found, bail shall be determined pursuant to I.C. § 35–33–8–1 et seq. If probable cause is not found the arrested person shall be immediately released.

Adopted July 28, 2006, effective Jan. 1, 2007. Amended August 2, 2007, effective January 1, 2008; amended July 1, 2009, effective Jan. 1, 2010.

Appendix A. PRESUMPTIVE BOND SCHEDULE

PRESUMPTIVE BOND SCHEDULE

FOR COURTS IN ST. JOSEPH COUNTY, INDIANA

Offense	Bond Amount
Murder	None
Attempted Murder	$100,000/$10,000
A felony	$50,000/$5,000
B felony— crimes of violence	$50,000/$5,000
B felony— dealing drugs (except "possession with intent")	$50,000/$5, 000
B felony	$30,000/$3,000
C felony— crimes of violence	$30,000/$3,000
C felony— dealing drugs (except "possession with intent")	$30,000/$3, 000
C felony	$10,000/$1,000
D felony— crimes of violence & stalking, intimidation, invasion of privacy, and residential entry	$10,000/$1,000
D felony— DUI & Drug Cases	$7,500/$750
D felony	$5,000/$500
A misdemeanor— DV battery, invasion of privacy, intimidation & DUI (A & C misdemeanor)	$5,000/$500
A misdemeanor	$250, cash
B misdemeanor	$150, cash
C misdemeanor	$150, cash

Adopted July 28, 2006, effective Jan. 1, 2007. Amended August 2, 2007, effective January 1, 2008; July 26, 2012, effective Jan. 1, 2013.

LOCAL RULES FOR FAMILY COURT AND ORDERS OF PROTECTION FOR ST. JOSEPH COUNTY

Adopted July 28, 2006, Effective January 1, 2007

Including Amendments Received Through November 1, 2013

Research Notes

Annotations to the Local Court Rules for Family Court and Orders of Protection for St. Joseph County are available in West's Annotated Indiana Code, *Title 34 Appendix.*

These rules may be searched electronically on Westlaw *in the IN-RULES database; updates to these rules may be found on* Westlaw *in IN-RULESUPDATES. For search tips and a summary of database content, consult the Westlaw Scope Screens for each database.*

LR71–FL00 Rule 401. DOMESTIC RELATIONS AUTHORITY

401.1. Authority. These rules are adopted pursuant to the authority of T.R. 81 of the Indiana Rules of Trial Procedure and are intended to supplement those rules. These rules shall govern the practice and procedure in all domestic relations cases in the St. Joseph Circuit, Superior, and Probate Courts and are created to foster the healthy and child-sensitive functioning of families.

401.2. Definition of Family Cases. "Family cases" means all marital dissolution, annulment, legal separation, child custody, child parenting time and visitation, child support, paternity, guardianship, and adoption cases.

401.3. Liberal Construction and Application. The St. Joseph Circuit, Superior, and Probate Courts are committed to a cooperative model for handling family cases. These rules will be liberally construed and applied to serve the ends of (a) ensuring safety, (b) reducing conflict, (c) building cooperation, and (d) protecting children and (e) promoting healthy relationships within families.

401.4. Intent and Best Practices. The judicial officers of the St. Joseph Circuit, Superior, and Probate Courts believe that conflict between parties can easily escalate and in some cases end tragically. To avoid such escalation and possible tragic results, the judicial officers of these Courts remind attorneys and parties that:

(1) Actions taken at any time in family cases, including the earliest stages, will often define much of the future of the case and the family's ability to function without the constant intervention of the Court.

(2) While courts are largely powerless to affect cases before they are filed, attorneys can set a tone of either beneficial cooperation or destructive conflict for families in those cases.

(3) Therefore, attorneys' language and conduct in family cases, including before they are filed, should be governed by a commitment to ensure safety, reduce conflict, build cooperation, protect children,

and promote the healthy family relationships that children depend on.

(4) The St. Joseph Circuit, Superior, and Probate Courts, therefore, expect and will continuously encourage attorneys to conduct themselves at all times, including before cases are filed, in ways that ensure safety, reduce conflict, build cooperation, protect children and promote healthy relationships within families.

(5) At all times, the attorney's commitment to those ends should include the following:

(a) Assessment of Case and Safety Considerations. Counsel meeting with a person involved in or contemplating a family case should promptly assess whether the case can safely be handled cooperatively and without adversarial motions or hearings. Unless safety, a history of family violence (including requests for protective orders) or other exceptional circumstances make cooperation unreasonable, counsel should handle the case in ways that avoid court and maximize the prospective parties' and other family members' development of cooperative problem-solving, childrearing, and child protection.

(b) Cooperation between Counsel before Initial Filings. Counsel representing persons anticipating a family case should make reasonable efforts to determine if the other possible parties have or may be seeking representation. Unless doing so would be dangerous or otherwise unreasonable, counsel should:

(i) consult and cooperate with each other;

(ii) attempt in good faith to find cooperative resolutions to provisional matters so that unnecessary provisional filings and hearings can be avoided and early family cooperation can be encouraged;

(iii) refer parents to resources such as co-parenting education, counseling, and mediation that can help them, their children, and the relationships within the family.

(c) Cooperation with Self-Represented Parties before Initial Filings. Unless doing so would be dangerous or otherwise unreasonable, counsel should employ these same efforts at consultation and cooperation with self-represented persons prior to the filing of any family case. When safe to do so, counsel should (i) communicate directly with such persons (including a self-represented spouse, parent, putative parent, or guardian), and (ii) take all reasonable measures to avoid provisional filings and hearings on matters that could be resolved by cooperative measures such as discussion, counseling, and mediation. Counsel should be sensitive to the special needs of victims of family violence, and nothing in these rules should be construed to require a victim of family violence to engage in pre-suit negotiations with an alleged perpetrator or to feel pressure to settle because of perceived or implied physical or mental coercion.

(d) Cooperation after Initial Filings. The principles set forth in paragraphs (b) and (c) above should be observed and implemented where appropriate in all matters arising after initial filings.

401.5. Duties of Attorneys and Parties in Family Cases involving Children.

(1) Attorneys and parties in family cases shall be responsible to act with the Courts as co-problem-solvers, not mere problem-reporters. Unless safety or a history of family violence requires otherwise, attorneys should:

(a) counsel clients, as soon as possible and as often as necessary, about the advantages and judicial expectations of safe cooperation in family cases;

(b) refer clients to all co-parenting classes, counseling, mediation, and other problem-solving processes required by the court or that appear to counsel to be promising resources for good family functioning;

(c) work with other counsel to ensure safety in families where domestic violence has been, or reasonably could be, an issue;

(d) work with all counsel to reduce conflict, build cooperation, and protect children;

(e) avoid unnecessary motions and hearings; and

(f) use the least divisive processes in pursuing safety, fairness, cooperation, and the best interests of children (where reasonably possible, for example, consulting with other counsel as early and often as necessary to find cooperative resolutions, using service by mail or acknowledgement of service instead of service of process by sheriff, encouraging restraint and safe cooperation between family members, and exhausting all viable cooperative measures before requesting relief from court).

(2) The Courts will expect all parties and attorneys to consistently pursue:

(a) personal responsibility by acting on one's own opportunities to solve problems and improve families' circumstances rather than merely reporting on the alleged fault in others;

(b) cooperation by sensibly defining and pursuing the best interests of all family members, especially children;

(c) courtesy by consistent observance of respectful language and behavior; and

(d) focused attention on children's needs, including awareness (i) that parent conflict is gravely dangerous to children and (ii) that the good future relationships between and among all parents, grandparents, and other adults in children's lives must be protected and nurtured in all family cases.

Adopted July 28, 2006, effective Jan. 1, 2007. Amended August 2, 2007, effective January 1, 2008; July 26, 2012, effective Jan. 1, 2013.

LR71–FL00 Rule 402. CASE CAPTIONING OF FAMILY CASES

402.1. Dissolution, Separation, Custody and Support Cases. Pleadings in dissolution, separation, custody, and support proceedings shall be captioned as required by statute. Parents and counsel representing parents and grandparents in family cases are encouraged to use non-adversary language in case captioning and pleadings. To facilitate respect, harmony and collegiality, parties shall be referred to using non-adversarial language whenever possible. For example, "child" "mother," "father," "putative father," "guardian," and similar non-adversarial language should be used instead of "petitioner," "respondent," "plaintiff," or "defendant," and "versus" should not be used in the captions of any family cases involving children.

All pleadings in marital dissolution and separation cases in which the parties have one or more children under the age of 22 on the date of the initial filing may be captioned, "In Re the Marriage of _____, Petitioner, Father, or Mother, and _____, Respondent, Mother, or Father."

All pleadings in marital dissolution and separation cases without children may be captioned, "In Re the Marriage of _____, Petitioner, or Husband or Wife, or Former Husband or Former Wife, and _____, Respondent, or Husband or Wife, or Former Husband or Former Wife."

402.2. Paternity and Paternity-related Cases. Pleadings in paternity proceedings will be captioned as required by statute; however, parents in paternity cases shall not be referred to as petitioner or respondent and, as appropriate, shall be referred to as Mother, Father, or Putative Father. Captions in paternity cases will be in the form of "In Re the Matter of the Paternity of _____, a Child Born Out of Wedlock," and shall also include all adult parties such as parents, alleged parents, de facto custodians, guardians, intervenors, etc. If the case is filed on an "ex rel" basis as contemplated by Trial Rule 19(A)(2) or as allowed by statute—this includes actions by the state (i.e., IV–D and DCS filings)—then the caption shall disclose that fact.

Adopted July 28, 2006, effective Jan. 1, 2007. Amended August 2, 2007, effective January 1, 2008; July 18, 2011, effective January 1, 2012; July 26, 2012, effective Jan. 1, 2013.

LR71–FL00 Rule 403. FAMILY CASES INVOLVING UNEMANCIPATED CHILDREN

403.1. Contested Matters.

403.1.1. *Referrals for Investigation and Report.* A Court may refer contested matters involving child custody and parenting to the Domestic Relations Counseling Bureau (DRCB) or another service provider for screening, investigation, and/or report. A referral may be made prior to hearing, both before and after a final decree, on motion of either party with the consent of the Court, or on the Court's own motion.

403.1.2. *Definition.* "Contested matters," for purposes of this rule, shall include issues involving child custody and parenting time, which may exist both before and after the entry of a final decree.

403.1.3. *Cooperation of Parties.* The parties to contested matters shall meet, and cooperate, with the DRCB or other service provider as required.

403.1.4. *DRCB Recommendations.* Upon referral, the DRCB may recommend either that the parties be referred for interventions (such as mediation, counseling, or case management), or that the parties proceed to an investigation and evaluation. Unless otherwise order by the Court, a DRCB investigation and evaluation of contested matters involving child custody and parenting time will not be conducted by the DRCB unless the above-mentioned interventions have failed or are found to be inadequate to protect the physical safety or emotional well-being of a minor child.

403.1.5. *DRCB Reports.* The DRCB shall report to the Court on all contested matters referred to its attention. The DRCB shall file its original report with the Court, which shall distribute copies to counsel or to a party no represented by counsel.

403.1.6. *Confidentiality of DRCB Records.* The records and reports of the DRCB contain information of a private and personal nature, and the release of that information, without court approval and supervision, could result in intentional mischief or unintentional injury to the parties, their children or relatives. As such, the records and reports of the DRCB are confidential, and that any and all access to the notes, records, or reports of the DRCB shall by allowed only by order of the Court that has jurisdiction over the relevant parties and cause of action.

403.2. Uncontested Matters. The parents of unemancipated children are encouraged to develop a parenting plan that is mutually acceptable to the parents and their children. Where practicable and appropriate for all concerned, the Court shall give due consideration to agreements between parents.

Adopted July 28, 2006, effective Jan. 1, 2007. Amended August 2, 2007, effective January 1, 2008.

LR71–FL00 Rule 404. CONDUCT OF THE PARTIES AND COUNSEL IN FAMILY CASES

404.1. Generally. Fault of one or both parties in the breakdown of a marriage is not at issue in a dissolution of marriage action under Indiana law. Likewise, fault is not typically an issue in other types of "family cases" covered by these rules. Parties and counsel are required to focus of on the relevant issues in the case and to avoid assigning fault to an opposing party or counsel in family cases.

At all times, the parties to family law cases covered by these rules and their attorneys are to conduct themselves in a manner consistent with Indiana law and rules of court. The Court will not permit unsolicited argument, name calling by anyone, needless accusations, or irrelevant or immaterial evidence to be submitted at these hearings. In its discretion, the Court may sanction violations of this rule.

404.2. Giving Rules to Clients. Attorneys appearing in family cases shall (a) furnish their family clients with a copy of these Rules at the earliest reasonable opportunity and (b) review all pertinent parts with their clients, and (c) assist clients in fully understanding and observing their provisions.

Adopted July 28, 2006, effective Jan. 1, 2007. Amended August 2, 2007, effective January 1, 2008; July 26, 2012, effective Jan. 1, 2013.

LR71–FL00 Rule 405. EXPECTATIONS OF PARENTS AND REQUIREMENTS FOR ATTORNEYS

405.1. Expectations of Parents and Attorneys.

a. Parents and attorneys in family cases will conduct themselves in concert with the courts to serve as co-problem solvers.

b. Parents and attorneys shall pursue the best interests of all family members with particular deference to the needs and welfare of the children.

c. Parents and attorneys will pursue all opportunities to resolve disputes and conflicts before relying on the Court for a determination.

d. Parents and attorneys will treat one another with courtesy and respect.

405.2. Requirements for Initial, Provisional and Other Hearings.

405.2.1. *Pre-Hearing Meeting Requirements, Exceptions.* It is required that, unless considerations of safety or other good cause make it unreasonable, before the date and time set for an initial, provisional or other hearing, attorneys and pro se parties shall meet with each other in a good-faith attempt to resolve all issues. Attorneys and pro se parties contacted for this purpose shall make themselves reasonably available for consultation.

Prior to commencement of a hearing or trial the attorneys and pro se parties shall certify to the court that they have complied with this rule. The duty of consultation shall be continuing.

405.2.2. *Resolution of Parenting Time Problems and Disputes.*

405.2.2.1. Disagreements Generally. When a disagreement occurs regarding parenting time and the requirements of the Indiana Parenting Time Guidelines, both parents shall make every effort to discuss options, including mediation, in an attempt to resolve the dispute before going to court.

405.2.2.2. Mediation. If court action is initiated, the parents shall enter into mediation pursuant to Rule 411.1 unless otherwise ordered by the court.

405.2.2.3. Child Hesitation. If a child is reluctant to participate in parenting time, each parent shall be responsible to ensure the child complies with the scheduled parenting time. In no event shall a child be allowed to make the decision on whether scheduled parenting time takes place.

405.2.2.4. Relocation. When either parent considers a change of residence, reasonable advance notice of the intent to move in accord with Indiana Code provisions shall be given to the other parent. Parents are expected to discuss necessary changes in the parenting schedule as well as the allocation of transportation costs in exercising parenting time which may result from the move.

405.2.2.5. Withholding Support or Parenting Time. Neither parenting time nor child support shall be withheld because of either parent's failure to comply with a court order. Only the court may enter sanctions for noncompliance. A child has the right both to support and parenting time, neither of which is dependent upon the other. If there is a violation of either requirement, the remedy is to apply to the court for appropriate sanctions.

405.2.2.6. Enforcement of Parenting Time.

a) Contempt Sanctions. Court orders regarding parenting time must be followed by both parents. Unjustified violations of any of the provisions contained in the order may subject the offender (noncompliant party) to contempt sanctions. These sanctions may include fine, imprisonment and/or community service.

b) Injunctive Relief. Under Indiana law, a non-custodial parent who regularly pays support and is barred from parenting time by the custodial parent may file an application for an injunction t enforce parenting time under Indiana law.

c) Criminal Penalties. Interference with custody or visitation rights may be a crime under Indiana law.

405.2.2.7. Attorney Fees. In any court action to enforce an order granting or denying parenting time, a court may award reasonable attorney fees and expenses of litigation. In awarding fees, a court may consider whether the parent seeking attorney fees substantially prevailed and whether the parent violating the order did so knowingly or intentionally. A court can also award attorney fees and expenses against a parent who pursues a frivolous or vexatious court action.

405.2.3. *Inapplicability to the Title IV–D Agency.* As the State of Indiana does not represent either of the parents in a Title IV–D child support case, this rule does not apply to petitions or rules to show cause filed by the Title IV–D agency; however, the attorney for the Title IV–D agency and the parent(s) and their counsel, if any, are encouraged to meet and discuss resolution of these matters in advance of any hearing.

405.3. Attorneys to Provide Copies of Rules to Clients. It is required that attorneys will furnish their family clients with copies of these rules and assist them in fully understanding and observing both their spirit and intent.

Adopted July 28, 2006, effective Jan. 1, 2007. Amended Aug. 2, 2007, effective Jan. 1, 2008; amended June 3, 2008, effective Jan. 1, 2009; amended July 1, 2009, effective Jan. 1, 2010; July 18, 2011, effective Jan. 1, 2012.

LR71–FL00 Rule 406. PROTECTIVE ORDERS; RESTRAINING ORDERS

No petition for a protective order or other restraining order of the Court as defined by I.C. 34–26–5 & 6 shall be accepted for filing or considered by the Court without three copies of a fully executed Notice of Filing of Protective Order on a form as prescribed by the Court. Such forms shall be given to the Clerk at the time of the filing of the request for restraining order or protective order and shall be utilized by the Clerk of the Court for insuring compliance with all relevant statutes. Counsel shall be responsible for assuring that the correct police agency receives a copy of any protective order. Counsel shall be responsible for filing any notice of termination of protective orders as required by statute.

A Petition for Protective Order filed by a party who has an open dissolution, separation, or paternity case shall be assigned to the judge handling the dissolution, separation, or paternity case. A Petition for Protective Order that is filed contemporaneously with a dissolution, separation, or paternity case shall be assigned a separate cause number but shall be assigned to the judge to whom the dissolution, separation, or paternity case is assigned.

No application for a temporary restraining order not authorized pursuant to I.C. 34–26–5 or 6 shall issue without strict compliance with the requirements of T.R. 65.

Adopted July 28, 2006, effective Jan. 1, 2007. Amended August 2, 2007, effective January 1, 2008.

LR71–FL00 Rule 407. DISCOVERY

407.1. Disclosure by the Parties. Upon the filing of a petition for dissolution of marriage or paternity action, the parties shall have a duty of reciprocal discovery and, unless otherwise ordered by the Court, shall provide the other party with copies of the following documents and things within thirty (30) days:

(1) Personal, federal and state, tax returns for three (3) years preceding the filing of the petition for dissolution of marriage with all pertinent forms W–2, 1099, K–1 and other schedules, and the most recent employment pay stub, with year-to-date gross earnings and written employment contract(s), if any;

(2) Tax returns and financial statements for five (5) years preceding the filing of the petition for dissolution of marriage for all corporations, or partnerships, or other business entities in which either marital partner has any ownership or membership interest;

(3) Statements from all banks, brokerage firms, investments firms, or mutual funds for three (3) months prior to and including the month in which the petition for dissolution of marriage is filed in which either marital partner has any interest, either alone or together with any other person, to include all checking, savings, certificate of deposit, treasury bills, stocks, bonds, or other forms of intangible assets;

(4) Copy of deed to marital residence, or any other real estate in which a marital partner has any legal or equitable interest, whether alone or with others, including but not limited to any corporate deeds;

(5) Amortization schedule or statement of balance for month in which the petition for dissolution of marriage was filed for any mortgage, land contract, or other lien on any real estate in the name of a marital partner, whether or not the marital partner has a sole or partial ownership interest;

(6) Copies of appraisals of real estate, or personal property in which a marital partner holds an interest, prepared within two (2) years from date of petition for dissolution of marriage;

(7) Statement of pension, profit sharing, individual retirement account, ESOP, or other form of tax deferred compensation plan maintained by or for a marital partner, for the month in which the petition for dissolution of marriage was filed;

(8) Declaration sheet and schedule of cash value for all insurance policies owned by or for which any marital partner is the beneficiary which have a cash surrender value;

(9) Copies of the most current statements of debt for the three (3) months preceding and including the month in which the petition was filed.

Each party shall make his or her initial disclosures based on information reasonably available to him or her and no party is excused from making disclosures because he or she has not fully completed his or her investigation of the case or because he or she challenges the sufficiency of the other party's disclosure or because the other party has not made the required disclosure.

407.2. Continuing Duty to Disclose. Duties of disclosure set forth by the Court's reciprocal discovery order shall be continuous. Supplementation shall be required not fewer than ten (10) days prior to trial showing any changes in the status of assets and debts as of the month of or one (1) month prior to trial, the most recent of which documents and things are available.

407.3. Utilization of Indiana Rules of Trial Procedure. The parties may utilize all remedies available in the Indiana Rules of Trial Procedure to enforce, modify, or extend the time within which to comply with the Court's reciprocal discovery order. The reciprocal discovery order does not preclude either party from utilizing the provisions governing requests for discovery provided for in the Indiana Rules of Trial Procedure to the full extent permitted by said rules.

Adopted July 28, 2006, effective Jan. 1, 2007. Amended August 2, 2007, effective January 1, 2008.

LR71–FL00 Rule 408.   STATUS CONFERENCES

A status conference may be requested at any time and one may be set by the Court on its own motion after the filing of the initial petition for dissolution.

The primary purpose of the status conference will be for attorneys and unrepresented parents to review with the Court the progress being made as it pertains to the resolution of outstanding issues. Attorneys and parents are expected to assist by informing the Court of all efforts being made to resolve the conflicts in order to protect and serve the immediate and long term best interests of the children.

Counsel and parents should be ready to provide to and discuss with the Court:

(1) The parents most current *Parenting Plan Worksheet (PPW)*. If the parents have not completed a joint parenting plan, each parent is expected to prepare and provide his or her own *PPW*.

(2) A list of community resources the parents could use to assist them in resolving their parenting issues.

(3) A copy of the parents' *Agreed Commitments* from their website work as provided in Rule LR71–FL00–413.

Adopted July 28, 2006, effective Jan. 1, 2007. Amended August 2, 2007, effective January 1, 2008.

LR71–FL00 Rule 409.   HEARINGS

409.1. Summary Considerations. Hearings on uncontested petitions for dissolution, applications for provisional relief, rules to show cause, petitions to modify, and other matters appropriate for summary consideration and disposition and uncontested petitions for dissolution of marriage shall be set for summary disposition on each judicial day or at other available times upon request as the calendar of the Court permits. Hearings on contested matters shall be set no earlier than ten (10) days after the filing of the report of the DRCB, as the calendar of the Court will permit. Dissolution petitions will not be considered uncontested if any issue remains unresolved between the parties.

409.2. Parenting Issues. Parents and attorneys are reminded of their obligation to avoid the use of exaggeration and unnecessarily harsh criticism in their motions and pleadings. Hearings on motions and pleadings filed with the Court in matters involving parenting time and parenting concerns may only be scheduled after first attempting to resolve the issue(s) by reaching agreements that best serve the interest of all family members with particular regard to the best interest of the children. Except in instances where it would be dangerous (i.e. past or present domestic violence; abuse or neglect of children) or otherwise unreasonable to do so, if both parents are represented by counsel, attorneys are expected to use personal or telephonic consultation to resolve any issue before seeking relief from the Court. In that consultation, it is expected that counsel will cooperate to:

(1) Attempt to resolve the matter(s) at issue;

(2) Discuss the alternative resources (including but not limited to counseling, mediation, support from the DRCB, etc.) that could be used to resolve the conflict and foster cooperation further serving the best interests of the children;

(3) Confirm that the parents have completed their mandatory website work and attended the co-parenting classes, and review with them their *Agreed Commitments* from the website discussed below in Rule LR71–FL00–413;

(4) Attempt to resolve ongoing conflict by assisting their clients in the development of, with their clients, a *Parenting Plan* (forms are available from the DRCB) to serve all family members with particular regard for the best interest of the children.

Adopted July 28, 2006, effective Jan. 1, 2007. Amended August 2, 2007, effective January 1, 2008.

LR71–FL00 Rule 410.   TRIALS AND PRE-TRIAL CONFERENCES

410.1. Trial Settings. A scheduling order, setting for trial, pre-trial conference, and discovery cut-off dates may be entered by the Court after the filing of the Petition. Each case in which a trial has been set must be ready on at least three (3) days' notice by the Court to the attorneys of record. Petitions for dissolution will be set by the Court as early as the Court's calendar permits. Contested matters that are ready for trial in less time than provided herein may be set for trial at the request of one or both of the parties as the calendar of the Court permits. Cases in which request for trial has been made must be ready on at least three (3) days' notice by the Court to the attorneys of record.

410.2. Pre-trial Conferences. On request of any party, a pre-trial conference shall be set by the Court prior to the trial date. Not fewer than five (5) days prior to the pre-trial conference, the parties shall exchange Pre-trial Statements.

410.3. Pre-trial Order and Required Pretrial Meeting. In each family law case expected to proceed to trial on any contested matter, at least twenty-one days prior to the trial date, the parties and their respective counsel (if any) shall meet in person. The purpose of this meeting shall be (a) to explore whether settlement is possible, and if so, to attempt to reach a settlement; and (b) if settlement is not possible or efforts to reach a settlement are fruitless, to prepare a joint pretrial order containing:

(1) All stipulations.

(2) Each party's contentions of facts that are in dispute and require resolution by the court.

(3) Where applicable, each party's statement of marital assets and debts, including any exhibits that will be offered in support of these figures.

(4) The identity of each witness and the factual issue(s) about which the witness is expected to testify.

(5) The expected length of trial.

(6) Whether mediation, arbitration, or another form of alternative dispute resolution may be appropriate in the opinion of either party.

The pretrial order shall also contain any information required elsewhere in these rules. The pretrial order shall be prepared as follows:

● In cases where counsel have appeared for both parties, counsel shall prepare and jointly sign the proposed pretrial order.

● In cases where counsel has appeared for only one party, he or she shall prepare the proposed pretrial order and secure the signature of the party appearing pro se.

● In cases where both parties proceed pro se, they shall jointly prepare and sign the proposed pretrial order.

● In the event one party or counsel refuses or fails to sign the proposed pretrial order, the party or counsel filing the order shall certify to the court in writing at the time of filing the order the circumstances surrounding the refusal or failure of the other party or counsel to sign the order.

The pretrial order required by this rule shall be filed with the Court no later than fourteen days before the scheduled trial date.

410.4. Pre-trial Statements. Pre-trial Statements shall be prepared by each party prior to the pre-trial conference and shall address the following:

(1) Preliminary Financial Statement, which shall include:

(a) Identification and valuation of assets;

(b) Identification and valuation of liabilities;

(2) Identification of other contested issues, including custody, parenting time, support, post-secondary educational assistance, and rehabilitative maintenance;

(3) Preliminary proposal for resolution of contested issues;

(4) The possibility of obtaining admissions of fact and of documents which will avoid unnecessary proof;

(5) The names of witnesses to be called during the trial and the general nature of their expected testimony;

(6) Such other matters as may aid in the disposition of the action.

At the conclusion of the pre-trial conference, the Court shall order the case to proceed to trial or continue the trial setting and order the parties to mediation if the Court determines mediation will assist in the resolution of contested matters.

410.5. Trial Submissions. Each party's final verified financial statement and contentions must be filed with the Court at least five (5) days before the date of trial. No case shall be considered ready for trial, or be tried, unless the report of the DRCB (where appropriate) has been filed with the Court.

Adopted July 28, 2006, effective Jan. 1, 2007. Amended August 2, 2007, effective January 1, 2008; July 18, 2011, effective January 1, 2012.

LR71–FL00 Rule 411. MEDIATION OR ALTERNATIVE DISPUTE RESOLUTION

411.1 Mandatory Mediation. In any case involving unemancipated children, prior to any contested hearing or trial, either before or after the issuance of a final decree of dissolution, on the parents shall participate in mediation pursuant to Ind. ADR Rule 2 et seq., or, in lieu of the foregoing mediation requirement, the parties may participate in another method of alternative dispute resolution (ADR) as outlined in Ind. ADR Rule 1.1. Unless excused by court order after certification by counsel or by an unrepresented party of an emergency or another reason indicating that mediation would be detrimental or counterproductive to one or more of the parents or children, parents shall mediate contested matters, both before provisional hearings involving unemancipated children and after a final decree.

411.2 Exceptions. The Court may excuse the parents from this requirement if an attorney for one of the parents or an unrepresented parent certifies in writing pursuant to Ind. TR 11 that an emergency exists or some other reason exists that justifies a conclusion that mediation would be detrimental or counterproductive to one or more of the parents or children. The certification shall include a statement of facts sufficient to enable the Court to determine whether waiver of the mediation or ADR requirements of this rule is appropriate under the circumstances. Counsel and parents are advised that the Courts do not favor requests for waiver from the requirements of this rule, and that waiver requests should be sought only in exceptional instances and not as a matter of course.

Adopted July 28, 2006, effective Jan. 1, 2007. Amended Aug. 2, 2007, effective Jan. 1, 2008; amended June 3, 2008, effective Jan. 1, 2009; amended July 1, 2009, effective Jan. 1, 2010; July 18, 2011, effective January 1, 2012.

LR71–FL00 Rule 412. CHILD SUPPORT WORKSHEET

At the time of the hearing in all matters regarding child support issues, the parties shall file:

(1) A Verified Child Support Worksheet with the Court; and

(2) Such supporting documentation as the Court may require to establish current income and income earned during the prior tax year, work-related child care expenses, if any, and the children's portion of health care expense.

A party seeking an order for child support shall cause a Notice of Hearing and Order to Disclose Information, with a Child Support Worksheet, and a copy of the Petition to be served upon the opposing party in a manner complying with the Indiana Rules of Civil Procedure. Blank copies of the worksheet may be obtained from the Clerk.

Adopted July 28, 2006, effective Jan. 1, 2007. Amended August 2, 2007, effective January 1, 2008.

LR71–FL00 Rule 413. MANDATORY WEBSITE WORK AND CO–PARENTING PROGRAMS

413.1. Co–Parenting Programs in Marital Dissolution and Separation Cases. In marital dissolution and separation cases, parents with one or more children under the age of eighteen (18) on the date of their initial petition shall attend a co-parenting program as assigned by the Domestic Relations Counseling Bureau (DRCB). Each parent shall contact the DRCB within twenty (20) days of the filing of the initial petition in their case to schedule attendance at a Co–Parenting program. Parents shall complete the program within 60 days of the initial petition, unless otherwise authorized by the Court.

413.2. Website Work in Marital Dissolution and Separation Cases. In marital dissolution and separation cases, parents with children under the age of eighteen (18) on the date of their initial petition shall complete the website work on www.UpToParents.org, or a similar website program approved by the Court, within thirty (30) days of the filing of the action. Parents should take a completed copy of their work to their co-parenting class(es). Parents shall submit a copy of "The Conclusion Page" (which appears as the final page of the website work) to the DRCB for filing with the Court to verify completion of the website work. Parents may also file a copy directly with the Clerk of the Court.

413.3. Paternity Cases. In paternity cases, parents shall attend the co-parenting class ordered by the Probate Court. Each parent shall contact the DRCB within twenty (20) days of the filing of the initial petition in their case to schedule attendance at co-parenting classes. Parents shall complete the classes within 60 days of the finding of paternity in any paternity case, unless otherwise authorized by the Court. Parents in paternity cases shall complete the website work at www.ProudToParent.org or a similar website approved by the Court and take their completed website work to their co-parenting classes.

413.4. Website Assistance. Parents may find forms (e.g. parenting plan worksheet) to develop an agreed parenting plan on the website www.UpToParents.org, www.in.gov/judiciary, or a similar website program approved by the Court. Parents open to the possibility of reconciliation may wish to substitute the website work from www.WhileWeHeal.org or a similar website program approved by the Court or recommended by the DRCB.

413.5. Website Work Brought to Hearing. Parents may be asked by the Court to produce their completed website work (Exercises and Agreed Commitments) to any hearing. If a hearing is scheduled in a dissolution, separation, or paternity case, the parents shall merge their chosen Commitments from their website work into a set of Agreed Commitments, review those Agreed Commitments before each hearing, and take copies of them to all hearings. If more than a year has passed since the parents' completion of the website work, they shall redo the work, merge their Commitments into a set of Agreed Commitments, and bring those Agreed Commitments to all hearings.

Adopted July 28, 2006, effective Jan. 1, 2007. Amended August 2, 2007, effective January 1, 2008; July 26, 2012, effective Jan. 1, 2013.

LR71–FL00 Rule 414. EXCHANGE OF INCOME INFORMATION, POST–DECREE

All decrees issued by the Court which provide for the payment of child support shall include a requirement that the parties exchange not later than April 30th of each alternating year after the year the decree is entered, income information for the previous tax years, and a copy of the most recent employment check stub showing year-to-date gross earnings, until such time as all children whose support is the subject of the decree are emancipated. The income information to be exchanged shall include personal tax returns with all pertinent forms, W–2, 1099, K–1, and other schedules and corporate, partnership, and/or sole pro-prietorship tax returns for the two (2) prior tax years.

Adopted July 28, 2006, effective Jan. 1, 2007. Amended August 2, 2007, effective January 1, 2008.

LR71–FL00 Rule 415. SANCTIONS

A party that fails to comply with these rules is subject to sanctions, upon motion of a party, pursuant to T.R. 37, Indiana Rules of Trial Procedure.

Adopted July 28, 2006, effective Jan. 1, 2007. Amended August 2, 2007, effective January 1, 2008.

LR71–FL00 Rule 416. STANDING ORDER FOR PARENTAL EDUCATION PROGRAM IN ST. JOSEPH CIRCUIT AND SUPERIOR COURTS

416.1. Findings. The Judges of the St. Joseph Superior and Circuit Courts find that it would be in the best interest of society, of children, and of the Courts to encourage cooperation and mediation between separating and divorcing parents. The Judges further find that a mandatory parental education program will:

(1) Aid the children of divorcing parents;

(2) Aid the parents in post separation parenting;

(3) Encourage agreements between litigating parents in the best interests of their children; and

(4) Conserve Court time by reducing repetitive petitions over child custody, visitation, and support.

416.2. Selection of Provider(s). The Judges of the St. Joseph Superior and Circuit Courts shall approve, annually, by order of the Court, one or more providers of a parental education program for the Courts. Approved program brochures shall be provided by the Clerk of the Court to petitioners and served with the summons upon each respondent by the Sheriff.

416.3. Attendance. In all dissolution of marriage or separation actions filed in the St. Joseph Superior and Circuit Courts, both parties shall attend a parental education program approved by the Courts if the parties have a minor child or children less than the age of eighteen (18) as of the date of filing of the action. The parties are responsible to pay the cost of attending the program. All or a portion of the attendance fee may be waived for indigence by the assigned Judge. Waiver of attendance for completion of a similar program, individual counseling, or for other good cause is available from the assigned Judge in individual cases. Each parent must attend and complete the program within sixty (60) days of the submission of his or her registration form with the DRCB. The program provider will furnish each participant and the Court with a certificate of completion of the program. A party that fails to complete the program within the required time period may be subject to a finding of contempt by the Court and appropriate sanctions.

416.4. DRCB Registration. Each parent in a dissolution or separation action involving a child or children under the age of eighteen (18) shall, within fifteen (15) days of the filing of the action, appear at the offices of the DRCB to complete a registration form. The offices of the DRCB are located on the 8th floor of the County–City Building, 227 W. Jefferson Boulevard, South Bend, Indiana 46601. Forms may be submitted between 8:30 a. m. and 4:00 p.m., Monday through Friday. Parents must provide the DRCB with the cause number of the dissolution or separation action at issue at the time they pre-register. Each parent will, at that time, be assigned to parental education class(es). The DRCB will document registration and class attendance in the Clerk's file.

Adopted July 28, 2006, effective Jan. 1, 2007. Amended August 2, 2007, effective January 1, 2008; July 26, 2012, effective Jan. 1, 2013.

LR71–FL00 Rule 417. ADDITIONAL SUPPORT FOR FAMILIES

At any time parents need assistance to reduce their conflict, foster cooperation, and more cooperatively respond to the needs of their children, they and their attorneys (if any) are expected to seek out the resources that could provide help. The DRCB is available to assist parents and attorneys in identifying alternative community resources, including but not limited to counseling and mediation resources. If attorneys and parents are not able to agree on the alternative resource(s) to use in an effort to resolve the immediate issue and conflict, the Court may select the resource(s) the parents will be ordered to use.

Adopted July 28, 2006, effective Jan. 1, 2007. Amended August 2, 2007, effective January 1, 2008.

LR71–FL00 Rule 418. ALTERNATIVE DISPUTE RESOLUTION FEE

The Clerk of the Court shall collect from every party filing a petition for legal separation, paternity, or dissolution of marriage action under I.C. 31 an alternative dispute resolution fee of twenty dollars ($20); as such amount may be modified from time to time.

Adopted July 28, 2006, effective Jan. 1, 2007. Amended August 2, 2007, effective January 1, 2008.

LR71–FL00 Rule 419. LOCAL RULES FOR FAMILY COURT PROJECT

419.1. Creation of Family Court. With the adoption of this rule, the Circuit, Probate, and Superior Courts establish a Family Court Project within St. Joseph County, Indiana.

419.2. St. Joseph Family Court. The Family Court Project within St. Joseph County shall be known as the St. Joseph Family Court.

419.3. Objective of Family Court. The primary objective of the St. Joseph Family Court is to coordinate cases among Family members throughout the judicial process. This allows judges to review issues in a comprehensive manner, consolidate hearings when appropriate, issue non-conflicting orders, impose sanctions to best fit Family needs, and encourage accountability.

419.4. Scope of Family Court Rules. These rules are implemented only for cases assigned to the St. Joseph Family Court. These rules are in addition to the local administrative, civil, and family law rules, and in the event of a conflict the specific rules of the Family Court shall control.

419.5. Definitions.

419.5.1. *Family.* For purposes of these rules, "Family" includes parents and their child or children, whether all of these individuals reside together or not, or a household comprised of adults and a child or children, whether all of the adults are related by blood or marriage to any of the child or children.

419.5.2. *Family Court.* "Family Court" is the designation given the coordinated effort to link together for purposes of case coordination all courts before which cases involving a family or household with children (hereinafter a "Family") are pending. The individual cases maintain their separate integrity and separate docket number, but may be given a common Family Court designation. Individual cases may all be transferred to one Judge, or may remain in the separate courts in which they were originally filed.

419.5.3. *Family Court Proceeding.* A "Family Court Proceeding" refers to all proceedings of each individual case pertaining to a Family that has been assigned to Family Court.

419.5.4. *Related Case.* Related cases, for purposes of the St. Joseph Family Court, include the following types of cases involving one or more members of a Family: CM, or DF filings involving domestic and/or family violence related charges and/or substance abuse charges, and all cases of the following types: PO, JM, JS, JP, JT, JD, JC, DR, GU, AD, and MH.

Adopted July 28, 2006, effective Jan. 1, 2007. Amended August 2, 2007, effective January 1, 2008.

LR71–FL00 Rule 420. JURISDICTION AND RELATED CASES

420.1. Related Cases. The following types of cases in which a Family has involvement in multiple court proceedings are within the jurisdiction of the St. Joseph Family Court: CHINS, delinquency, juvenile status offense, child support, termination of parental rights, adoption, placement of children, paternity, dissolution of marriage, legal separation, mental health, domestic violence, protective order, adult criminal (intra-family), and alcohol or drug charges.

420.2. Concurrent Jurisdiction. Concurrent Family Court jurisdiction over any Related Case may be exercised by a court exercising jurisdiction over a juvenile case involving the Family.

420.3. Concurrent Hearings. A judicial officer exercising Family Court jurisdiction over a number of cases involving a Family may, in its discretion, conduct concurrent hearings in related cases, take evidence on the related cases at these hearings, and rule on the admissibility of evidence for each case separately, as needed to adequately preserve the record for appeal.

Adopted July 28, 2006, effective Jan. 1, 2007. Amended August 2, 2007, effective January 1, 2008.

LR71–AR00 Rule 421. ASSIGNMENT OF CASES AND CLERK'S RESPONSIBILITIES

421.1. Approval of Assignment. Assignment of Family Court designation and jurisdiction to all cases involving a Family shall require the approval of the Judge of the St. Joseph Circuit Court, St. Joseph Probate Court, or St. Joseph Superior Court to which the case has been assigned. The transfer and consolidation of cases assigned to Family Court are subject to the provisions of Rule LR71–TR42–424 of these Family Court Rules.

421.2. DRCB Referral. Upon assignment of a case to Family Court, case management procedures shall be implemented, including referral to the DRCB for coordination services. The DRCB may undertake the following, as appropriate:

(1) Assess family situations and need for type of parenting intervention through screening intakes;

(2) Conduct cross-reference checks with other Court agencies for multiple-case families;

(3) Notify appropriate Courts of all legal interventions involving the family;

(4) Make referrals or recommend referrals to the Courts regarding the appropriate parental education, mediation, facilitation, high conflict co-parenting education, counseling, or evaluation service;

(5) Monitor compliance with referrals and Court orders;

(6) Coordinate other needed services for families;

(7) Provide varied levels of direct case management services for at-risk families.

Adopted July 28, 2006, effective Jan. 1, 2007. Amended August 2, 2007, effective January 1, 2008.

LR71–TR72 Rule 422. CLERK'S RESPONSIBILITIES; NOTICE

422.1. Notification of Assignment. Notification of assignment to Family Court shall be provided to all parties and counsel. The Clerk is to enter the Family Court assignment on the chronological case summary.

422.2. Service Lists. The DRCB shall confirm the entry of appearances of any counsel in any Family

Court case and shall create service lists for the judicial officer to which each case is assigned.

422.3. Notice of Related Case Assignment. The parties, within a reasonable time after a case is assigned to Family Court jurisdiction, shall provide to the DRCB a list of all Related Cases.

Adopted July 28, 2006, effective Jan. 1, 2007. Amended August 2, 2007, effective January 1, 2008.

LR71–TR76 Rule 423.   CHANGE OF JUDGE

423.1. Change of Judge. Once notice is sent to the parties that a case has been selected for Family Court, no motion for change of venue from the judge may be granted except to the extent permitted by Indiana Trial Rule 76. A motion for change of venue from the judge in any matters arising in the Family Court proceeding or any future cases joined in the Family Court proceedings after the initial selection of cases shall be granted only for cause.

423.2. Special Judge. If a special judge is appointed, all current and future cases in the Family Court proceeding may be assigned to the special judge.

423.3. Objection to Assignment to Family Court Jurisdiction. A party may object to the assignment of a case to Family Court jurisdiction. Any such objection must be filed within ten (10) days after notice is sent that a case has been assigned to Family Court and shall set forth the basis of the objection. An objection to the assignment of a case to Family Court jurisdiction may be granted for good cause shown only.

Adopted July 28, 2006, effective Jan. 1, 2007. Amended August 2, 2007, effective January 1, 2008.

LR71–TR42 Rule 424.   CASE CONSOLIDATION AND TRANSFER

The supervising judge of the St. Joseph Family Court may enter orders for the consolidation and transfer of Related Cases to Family Court jurisdiction when the judicial officers presiding over such cases do not object. No case shall be transferred or consolidated until the judicial officers to whom such cases have been assigned have been advised of the contemplated action. The consolidation and transfer of Family Court cases shall be accomplished by the entry of an order signed by the Presiding Judge of the St. Joseph Family Court.

Adopted July 28, 2006, effective Jan. 1, 2007. Amended August 2, 2007, effective January 1, 2008.

LR71–EV201 Rule 425.   JUDICIAL NOTICE AND ACCESS TO RECORDS

425.1. Judicial Notice. Any court having jurisdiction over a case assigned to Family Court jurisdiction may take judicial notice of any relevant orders or Chronological Case Summary (CCS) entries issued by any Indiana Circuit, Superior, County, or Probate Court.

425.2. Notice to Parties. If a court takes judicial notice of:

(1) A court order, the court shall provide a copy of that order; or

(2) A CCS entry(s), the court shall provide a copy of the entire CCS.

The court shall provide copies of the order or CCS to the parties to the case at or near the time judicial notice is taken.

425.3. Access to Records. Parties to a Family Court proceeding shall have access to all Related Cases, with the exception of confidential cases or records to which they are not a party. Parties may seek access to confidential cases or records in another case within the Family Court proceeding in which they are not a party, by written petition based on relevancy and need. Confidential records shall retain their confidential status and shall not be included in the public record of the proceedings. The DRCB shall be given access to all records for the purpose of maintaining their records and producing reports regarding its investigations. The records and reports of the DRCB shall be considered confidential, and all access to the records and reports of the DRCB shall be allowed only by order of the Court that has jurisdiction over the relevant parties and cause of action.

Adopted July 28, 2006, effective Jan. 1, 2007. Amended August 2, 2007, effective January 1, 2008.

LR71–AR00 Rule 426.   REQUIREMENT TO UPDATE INFORMATION

When a Family member leaves the residence of a Family member whose case has been assigned to Family Court jurisdiction, the DRCB shall be notified within three (3) business days by the party or counsel, and the new address is to be provided to the DRCB.

Adopted July 28, 2006, effective Jan. 1, 2007. Amended August 2, 2007, effective January 1, 2008.

LR71–TR3.1 Rule 427.   ENTRY OF APPEARANCE FORMS

427.1. Appearance Form. Entry of Appearance Forms as approved by the St. Joseph Circuit, Probate, and Superior Courts shall be utilized. An entry of Appearance Form that does not comply with these rules is subject to being stricken.

427.2. Appearance Form by Petitioner. The Clerk shall place the entry of Appearance Form filed by the petitioner in a Protective Order case in the confidential file.

427.3. Report. The report of a guardian ad litem or CASA shall be available to DRCB staff under the same rules of confidentiality which apply to submission of such reports to judicial officers.

Adopted July 28, 2006, effective Jan. 1, 2007. Amended August 2, 2007, effective January 1, 2008.

LR71–AR00 Rule 428. ADMINISTRATIVE MATTERS

Judicial Oversight Committee. A Judicial Oversight Committee, composed of three judges selected as follows: one of the civil judges on the St. Joseph Superior Court, the St. Joseph Circuit Court Judge, and the St. Joseph Probate Court Judge, or other judicial officer designated by each of these Courts, shall be selected by the judges of the St. Joseph Circuit, Probate, and Superior Courts. The members of the Judicial Oversight Committee shall select one of their members to serve as supervising judge of the St. Joseph Family Court. The supervising judge shall serve for a term of two years. The supervising judge can be reelected.

Supervising Judge. The supervising judge of the St. Joseph Family Court shall have the responsibility of administering Family Court, in consultation with the Judicial Oversight Committee. This shall include the employment and supervision of DRCB personnel with respect to Family Court jurisdiction only. The implementation of rules for Family Court shall be done only after consultation with and approval by a majority of St. Joseph County judicial officers, including judges and magistrate judges.

Case Management Reporting. The supervising judge of the Family Court and/or its coordinator may report and discuss case procedure with, and report case management status to, any judicial officer presiding over that case regarding the Family Court case assignment.

Adopted July 28, 2006, effective Jan. 1, 2007. Amended Aug. 2, 2007, effective Jan. 1, 2008; July 18, 2011, effective Jan. 1, 2012.

LR71–FL00 Rule 429. RESERVED

LR71–FL00 Rule 430. TITLE IV–D COURT

These local rules are adopted by the Courts of the 60th Judicial Circuit to govern the practice and procedures in the Title IV–D Court, funded by an Ordinance of the St. Joseph County Council.

430.1 Organization of Title IV–D Child Support Court. Pursuant to I.C. 31–25–4–15, the Judges of the Circuit, Superior, and Probate Courts hereby establish a Title IV–D Court to establish and enforce paternity and child support orders under federal and state law.

430.1.1 *Assignment of Magistrate Judge(s) to IV–D Court.* The Judges of the Circuit, Superior, and Probate Courts shall appoint jointly one or more magistrate judges to the IV–D Court. A magistrate judge so appointed shall be designated as a IV–D Magistrate Judge.

430.1.2 *Responsibilities of IV–D Magistrate Judges.* A IV–D magistrate judge jointly appointed by the Judges and assigned to the IV–D Court pursuant to Rule 430.1.1 has the authority to preside over, make findings of fact and recommendations for the approval of the Judges of Circuit, Superior and Probate Courts in actions arising under Title IV–D of the Social Security Act. In addition, the IV–D magistrate judge has the authority to provide such assistance as may be required in making these findings of fact and recommendations.

430.1.3 *Temporary Absence of IV–D Magistrate Judge.* During the temporary absence of the duly appointed IV–D Magistrate Judge, any magistrate judge of the St. Joseph Circuit Court, St. Joseph Superior Court, or St. Joseph Probate Court may hear and make recommendations upon assignment to the Title IV–D Court by the regularly presiding judge.

430.1.4 *Supervision of the IV–D Court.* The Title IV–D Court shall be operated under the auspices and supervision of the Judge of the St. Joseph Probate Court. The Judge of the St. Joseph Probate Court may assign such juvenile or probate magistrate judges as are necessary to handle the caseload assigned to the Title IV–D Court.

430.2 Reciprocal Support Paternity Cases.

430.2.1 *Transfer of Existing Reciprocal Cases.* All reciprocal support paternity cases previously filed in Circuit Court under UIFSA and its predecessors, regardless of the stage in the proceedings, shall be permanently transferred by written ORDER OF TRANSFER to the Probate Court and assigned to the IV–D Court. Currently, the court identifier is 71C01 and the case type is either RS or MI. The cause numbers shall remain the same upon the transfer

430.2.2 *Filing of New Reciprocal Cases.* All new reciprocal support paternity cases shall be directly filed in Probate Court and assigned to the IV–D Magistrate Judge. The court identifier for these cases will be 71J01 and the case type will be RS.

430.3 IV–D Petitions for Support in Favor of Third Party Custodian.

430.3.1 *Existing Petitions for Support for Child Born Out of Wedlock.* All IV–D Petitions for Support in favor of a third party custodian (i.e. child resides with someone other than parent) wherein the child is born out of wedlock and the action has arisen under Title IV–D previously filed in Circuit Court, shall be permanently transferred to the Probate Court by a written ORDER OF TRANSFER and assigned to the IV–D Magistrate Judge. The cause numbers shall remain the same upon the transfer of these cases, with the court identifier being 71C01 and the case type DR.

430.3.2 *New Petitions for Support for Child Born Out of Wedlock.* All new IV–D Petitions for Support in favor of a third party custodian wherein the child is born out of wedlock and the action has arisen under Title IV–D shall be directly filed in Probate Court and assigned to the IV–D Magistrate

Judge. The court identifier for these cases will be 71J01 and the case type will be DR.

430.4 IV–D Petitions for Support for Child of a Marriage.

430.4.1 *Existing Petitions for Support for Child Born of a Marriage.* All IV–D Petitions for Support wherein the support sought is for a child born of a marriage and the action has arisen under Title IV–D, may be assigned by a written ORDER OF ASSIGNMENT issued by the Judge of the Superior or Circuit Court to the IV–D Magistrate Judge upon a written finding that there is a IV–D support issue to be resolved.

430.4.2 *New Petitions for Support for Child Born of a Marriage.* New IV–D Petitions for Support for a child born of a marriage will continue to be filed in Circuit Court but the action may be assigned immediately to the IV–D Magistrate Judge by a written ORDER OF ASSIGNMENT issued by the Judge of the Circuit or Superior Court.

430.5 IV–D Child Support Issues arising out of Legal Separation Decree or Dissolution of Marriage Provisional Orders

430.5.1 *Pending Child Support Orders Arising from Legal Separation or Provisional Orders.* All IV–D child support issues arising out of a Legal Separation Decree or out of a provisional order in a Dissolution of Marriage proceeding will NOT be assigned to the IV–D Magistrate Judge.

430.5.2 *Arrearages from Child Support Orders Arising from Legal Separation or Provisional Orders.* Once a Legal Separation Decree expires by order or operation of law or once a Dissolution of Marriage Decree is granted, arrearage issues arising out of the provisional order or the Legal Separation Decree may then be assigned to the IV–D Magistrate Judge by written ORDER OF ASSIGNMENT issued by the Judge of the Circuit or Superior Court upon a written finding that there is a IV–D support issue to be resolved.

430.6 IV–D Child Support Issues arising out of Dissolution Decrees or Post–Dissolution Orders.
All IV–D child support issues arising out of a Dissolution Decree or a Post–Dissolution Order may be assigned to the IV–D Magistrate Judge by written ORDER OF ASSIGNMENT issued by the Judge of the Circuit or Superior Court upon a written finding that there is a IV–D support issue to be resolved or upon a finding that the only remaining matters involved in the case are properly within the jurisdiction of the IV–D judicial officer.

430.7 IV–D Child Support Issues arising out of Paternity Actions.
All IV–D child support issues arising out of a Paternity Action or post-paternity proceedings may be assigned to the IV–D Magistrate Judge by written ORDER OF ASSIGNMENT issued by the Judge of the Probate Court.

430.8 Procedure for Transfer of Cases to Probate Court.
Once a Judge of the Circuit or Superior Court has permanently transferred a case involving IV–D issues to the Probate Court, the Local Probate Rules and the Local Rules for Electronic Filing will control. To effectuate the transfer, the following procedure will be followed:

(7) The ORDER OF TRANSFER will be entered onto the original physical docket sheet as well as a notation that the case transferred into *QUEST*. No further entries shall be made on the original docket sheet. The flat file and original docket sheet shall be stored in the clerk's office of the court of origin.

(8) A copy of that ORDER OF TRANSFER, a copy of the docket sheet, and copies of any relevant pleadings including but not limited to the initial pleadings on any pending IV–D matters and all orders entered regarding any previous IV–D matter shall be compiled by the IV–D Clerk.

(9) Upon receipt of the ORDER OF TRANSFER being received, the IV–D Clerk shall enter the referred case into *QUEST*, and scan all orders, pleadings, and the docket sheet into *QUEST*. All court filings shall be done on *QUEST* pursuant to the Local Rules for Electronic Filings.

(10) The ORDER OF TRANSFER will be served upon all parties by the Child Support Division of the Prosecutor's Office. If a pending issue requires an immediate setting of a hearing, the Child Support Division shall also be responsible for coordinating the hearing date and time and notifying all parties.

430.9 Procedure for Assignment of IV–D Matters to IV–D Court.
Once a Judge of the Circuit, Superior or Probate Court has assigned a case involving IV–D issues to the IV–D Magistrate Judge for the resolution of IV–D issues, the following procedure will control:

(1) Cases may be considered for assignment at the oral or written request of any party or sua sponte by the assigning Judge.

(2) The Judge may issue a written ORDER OF ASSIGNMENT upon a finding that a IV–D support issue needs to be resolved or upon a finding that the only remaining matters involved in the case are properly within the jurisdiction of the IV–D Court. The ORDER OF ASSIGNMENT will be entered onto the original physical chronological case summary (CCS) or docket sheet.

(3) A copy of that ORDER OF ASSIGNMENT, a copy of the CCS, and copies of any relevant pleadings including but not limited to the initial pleadings on any pending IV–D matters and all orders entered regarding any previous IV–D matter shall be compiled by the clerk of the court of origin upon request of the Child Support Division of the Prosecutor's Office and these documents shall be forwarded to the IV–D Clerk located at the Probate Court.

(4) Upon an ORDER OF ASSIGNMENT being entered, the Child Support Division of the Prosecutor's Office shall provide an *ISETS & QUEST* Information Form to the IV–D Clerk located at the Probate Court.

(5) Upon receipt of the ORDER OF ASSIGNMENT being received, the IV–D Clerk shall enter the referred case into *QUEST*, and *ISETS* if necessary, and scan all orders, pleadings, and the docket sheet into *QUEST*. All court filings shall be done on *QUEST* pursuant to the Local Rules for Electronic Filings; however, for cases assigned by the Circuit or Superior Court, a copy of all pleadings will be maintained in the original flat file and an entry shall be made on the CCS unless otherwise ordered by the assigning court.

(6) The ORDER OF ASSIGNMENT will be served on all parties by the Child Support Division of the Prosecutor's Office. If a pending issue requires an immediate hearing, the Child Support Division shall also be responsible for coordinating the hearing date and time and notifying all parties.

(7) All non-IV–D matters that arise following an assignment to the IV–D Magistrate Judge shall be filed with the Clerk of the originating Circuit or Superior Court. Assigned IV–D issues may be recalled by the assigning judge at any time and the IV–D Magistrate Judge shall send back the assigning judge any assigned issues that require the consideration of non-IV–D matters.

(8) All findings and recommendations of the IV–D Magistrate Judge shall become orders upon approval and adoption by the originating Judge. Proposed orders shall be prepared in *QUEST* and transmitted electronically along with a proposed Chronological Case Summary to the originating Judge for possible approval and adoption. The receiving Judge shall receive the electronic proposed orders by email and shall be responsible for periodically checking email for said proposed orders. Said orders will appear on the *QUEST* Documents to approve screen of the judge who signed the assignment order so that said judge may approve or reject the order proposed by the IV–D Magistrate Judge. Upon approval of the order, the Judge shall print out the order and CCS and provide this to the assigned Clerk who will make it a part of the flat file and add the CCS entry to the docket sheet.

(9) A transfer, assignment, or recall of cases shall be done by separate order of the sending or recalling judicial officer.

(10) Procedure for Objection to Assignment: Assignment to the Title IV–D Court is within the sole discretion of the regularly presiding judge to whom the case has been venued. A change of venue from the regularly presiding judge may be made under applicable Indiana Trial Rules or statutes. An objection to assignment to the Title IV–D court shall be made to the regularly presiding judge and is within his or her discretion to grant or deny.

Adopted July 28, 2006, effective Jan. 1, 2007. Amended August 2, 2007, effective January 1, 2008.

LOCAL RULES FOR SMALL CLAIMS FOR ST. JOSEPH COUNTY

Adopted July 28, 2006, Effective January 1, 2007

Including Amendments Received Through November 1, 2013

Research Notes

Annotations to the Local Rules for Small Claims for St. Joseph County are available in West's Annotated Indiana Code, *Title 34 Appendix.*

These rules may be searched electronically on Westlaw *in the* IN-RULES *database; updates to these rules may be found on* Westlaw *in* IN-RULESUPDATES. *For search tips and a summary of database content, consult the Westlaw Scope Screens for each database.*

Rule

LR71–TR1 Rule 501.   INTENT AND SCOPE

These local rules are adopted by the Courts of the 60th Judicial Circuit to govern the practice and procedure in Small Claims proceedings.

Adopted July 28, 2006, effective Jan. 1, 2007. Amended August 2, 2007, effective January 1, 2008.

LR71–AR00 Rule 502.   APPEARANCE IN COURT

502.1.   Verification of Presence. All counsel and litigants must verify their presence for any scheduled hearing or trial by checking in with the bailiff and signing his or her name to the bailiff's daily log.

502.2.   Prompt Appearance at Hearings and Trials. Prompt appearance at the time scheduled for all hearings and trials is enjoined upon Court, counsel and parties. Should an occasion arise when counsel or a party proceeding *pro se* can reasonably anticipate that he or she will be tardy for a scheduled hearing or trial, or a scheduled hearing or trial must be rescheduled due to an unanticipated emergency, counsel or the party shall notify the Court immediately.

502.3.   Requirements for Parties and Attorneys. All parties and counsel shall pursue all reasonable opportunities to resolve disputes and conflicts before relying on the court for a determination. It is required that, except for cases involving orders of protection for a person, all parties and counsel shall meet and discuss resolution of their dispute and conflicts prior to any hearing or trial. Failure to comply with this requirement may result in possible delay or cancellation of the hearing or trial. Prior to the commencement of any hearing or trial, the parties shall certify to the Court that they have complied with this requirement.

Adopted July 28, 2006, effective Jan. 1, 2007. Amended Aug. 2, 2007, effective Jan. 1, 2008; amended July 1, 2009, effective Jan. 1, 2010.

LR71–SC15 Rule 503.   COURT REPORTING

503.1.   Recording. Proceedings in Small Claims—South Bend and in Small Claims—Mishawaka shall be recorded by the Court by means of audiotape recording only. The official court record shall remain under the control of the Official Court Reporter or the Court unless otherwise ordered by the Court or an Indiana appellate court.

Adopted July 28, 2006, effective Jan. 1, 2007. Amended August 2, 2007, effective January 1, 2008.

LR71–SC2 Rule 504.   FILING, FORMS.

504.1.   Use of Forms. Counsel and parties filing a claim or counterclaim must use the claim form provided by the Clerk or a substantially similar form, if approved by the Court. Forms for other routine matters are available from the Clerk. All motions must be accompanied by an appropriate order for the Court's consideration and use.

504.2.   Restricted Access. Where a motion, petition, or other pleading is excluded from public access under A.R. 9(G), the parties and their counsel are enjoined to comply with the filing requirements of T.R. 5(G).

504.3.   Minute Entry Codes. The Court's Minute Entry Codes shall be used by counsel and litigants for summarizing standard entries on the Chronological Case Summary (CCS).

504.4.   Court Files. No Court file nor any part thereof may be removed from the custody of the Court Clerk by any person, including any attorney or Judge of this or any other Court, except upon authorization by the regularly presiding Judge to which the case is assigned and then only upon such terms and conditions as may be provided by him in the Order for authorization. One unalterable and invariable condition of this Order is the written acknowledgment of the authorized person that he has such file in his personal possession.

Adopted July 28, 2006, effective Jan. 1, 2007. Amended August 2, 2007, effective January 1, 2008.

LR71–SC6 Rule 505. DISCOVERY

Discovery may be undertaken only upon written motion, with a copy of the proposed limited discovery sought to be attached, and approval by the Court. Requests for third party discovery in aid of collection on a judgment shall not be approved, without good cause, prior to at least one unsuccessful attempt to gain information through proceedings supplemental.

Adopted July 28, 2006, effective Jan. 1, 2007. Amended August 2, 2007, effective January 1, 2008.

LR71–SC12 Rule 506. CHANGE OF VENUE

506.1. Payment of Transfer Fee. When a change of venue from the County is granted, all accrued costs and the fee for transfer must be paid to the clerk by the moving party within ten (10) days after the transfer order is entered.

506.2. Failure to Pay Fee. In the absence of such payment, the movant will be deemed to have abandoned the motion so the Clerk will not perfect the change, the cause will be restored to the docket of this Court, and this Court shall resume general jurisdiction of the cause in accordance with T.R. 76.

Adopted July 28, 2006, effective Jan. 1, 2007. Amended August 2, 2007, effective January 1, 2008.

LR71–AR00 Rule 507. TRANSFER THE COURT'S PLENARY DIVISION

507.1. South Bend. Cases pending in Small Claims—South Bend and on which transfer to the plenary calendar of the St. Joseph Superior Court has been sought and granted shall be re-assigned by the Clerk pursuant to the Clerk's random case assignment.

507.2. Mishawaka. Cases pending in Small Claims—Mishawaka and on which transfer to the Court's plenary calendar of the St. Joseph Superior Court has been sought and granted shall be re-assigned by the Clerk to the plenary calendar of the judge of the St. Joseph Superior Court assigned to the Mishawaka Division of the St. Joseph Superior Court.

Adopted July 28, 2006, effective Jan. 1, 2007. Amended August 2, 2007, effective January 1, 2008.

LR71–AR00 Rule 508. INCORPORATION OF SMALL CLAIMS MANUAL

The July 2005 Small Claims Manual, published by the Indiana Judicial Center, is adopted and incorporated herein, as the same may be amended from time to time.

Adopted July 28, 2006, effective Jan. 1, 2007. Amended August 2, 2007, effective January 1, 2008.

LOCAL PROBATE RULES FOR ST. JOSEPH COUNTY

Adopted July 28, 2006, Effective January 1, 2007

Including Amendments Received Through November 1, 2013

Research Notes

Annotations to the Local Probate Rules for St. Joseph County are available in West's Annotated Indiana Code, *Title 34 Appendix.*

These rules may be searched electronically on Westlaw *in the IN-RULES database; updates to these rules may be found on Westlaw in IN-RULESUPDATES. For search tips and a summary of database content, consult the Westlaw Scope Screens for each database.*

LR71–PR00 Rule 601.   NOTICE

601.1.   Attorney Responsibilities. Whenever notice by publication and/or written notice by U.S. Mail is required to be given, the attorney shall prepare such notice and shall ensure that such notice is properly published and/or served by certified mail, return receipt requested. In all respects, the notice shall comply with all statutory requirements. It shall be the attorney's responsibility to ascertain and provide adequate proof thereof regarding whether notice was properly served prior to bringing a matter to the Court.

601.2.   Petitions to Accompany Notice. Copies of petitions or motions shall be sent with all notices where the hearing involved arises from the matters contained in the petition or motion.

601.3.   Service of Notice of Hearing. Whenever any estate or guardianship account (including a final account in a supervised estate) is set for hearing, copies of the account must be served with the notice of hearing.

601.4.   Notice of Opening of Estate. Notice of the opening of an estate shall be sent by First Class United States Mail to all reasonably ascertainable creditors; however, the use of "certified mail, return receipt requested," to serve such notice is recommended.

601.5.   Notice of Insolvent Estate. Notice of the hearing to be held on a Petition to determine an estate insolvent shall be served on all interested parties, including the local representative of the Inheritance Tax Division of the Indiana Department of Revenue.

601.6.   Electronic Filing. Notice requirements in the Probate Court must also comply with the Local Rules for Electronic Filing.

Adopted July 28, 2006, effective Jan. 1, 2007. Amended August 2, 2007, effective January 1, 2008.

LR71–PR00 Rule 602.   FILING OF PLEADINGS

602.1.   Compliance. All filings in the Probate Court must comply with the Local Rules for Electronic Filing.

602.2.   Routine Pleadings. Routine pleadings, such as Inventories, Inheritance Tax Schedules, and Final Reports, may be filed with the Clerk for transmittal to the Court.

602.3.   Preparation of Orders. All attorneys are required to prepare orders for all proceedings except when expressly directed otherwise by the Court.

602.4.   Guardianships. Guardianships shall be signed and verified by the fiduciary and signed by the attorney for the fiduciary.

602.5.   Attorney Information. All pleadings filed shall contain the attorney's name, address, telephone number, and registration number.

602.6.   Initial Petition. The initial petition to open an estate or guardianship shall contain the name, address, social security number, birth date, and telephone number of the personal representative or guardian, if a person.

602.7.   Affidavit of Compliance. The affidavit of compliance with the notice provisions directed to creditors in an estate proceeding shall be timely filed with the Clerk of the Court.

Adopted July 28, 2006, effective Jan. 1, 2007. Amended August 2, 2007, effective January 1, 2008.

LR71–PR00 Rule 603.   BOND

603.1.   Bond Waived by Will. Where, under the terms of the Will, the testator expresses an intention that the bond be waived, the Court shall set a bond adequate to protect creditors, tax authorities, and devises.

603.2. Heir or Legatee Fiduciary. Where the fiduciary is an heir or legatee of the estate, the bond may be reduced by said fiduciary's share of the estate, or the value of real estate, or other assets that cannot be transferred or accessed without court approval or order. The Court shall have the right to review the amount of bond if the Court should grant access to such property or asset.

603.3. Request for Service Without Bond. Where the heirs or legatees have filed a written request that the fiduciary serve without bond, the Court may set bond in an amount adequate to protect the rights of the creditors and tax authorities only.

603.4. Unsupervised Estate. In an unsupervised estate, bond may be set at the discretion of the court. In the Probate Court, bond will be required unless the personal representative is the sole beneficiary.

603.5. Corporate Banking Fiduciary. No bond shall be required in any estate or guardianship in which a corporate banking fiduciary qualified by law to serve as such is either the fiduciary or one of several co-fiduciaries.

603.6. Petition to Open Estate. All petitions to open an estate or guardianship shall set forth the probable value of the personal property.

603.7. Insurance Agency. The name and address of the insurance agency providing the corporate surety shall be typed or printed on all corporate bonds in any estate or guardianship.

Adopted July 28, 2006, effective Jan. 1, 2007. Amended August 2, 2007, effective January 1, 2008.

LR71–PR00 Rule 604.   INVENTORY

604.1. Time Period for Preparation. An inventory shall be prepared by the fiduciary in estates and guardianships as follows: Supervised estate, within sixty (60) days; guardianships, within ninety (90) days for permanent guardians and within thirty (30) days for temporary guardians. All times relate to the date of appointment of the fiduciary.

604.2. Partial Inventory. In the event a partial inventory is prepared, all subsequent inventories must contain a recapitulation of prior inventories.

604.3. Sealed Inventory. In the event that the personal representative should request that an inventory be sealed, the Court may, in its sole discretion, seal such inventory. If an inventory is sealed, it shall be maintained in the court reporter's evidence file in the Court in which such estate is filed.

Adopted July 28, 2006, effective Jan. 1, 2007. Amended August 2, 2007, effective January 1, 2008.

LR71–PR00 Rule 605.   REAL ESTATE

605.1. Deed Requirements. All deeds submitted to the Court for approval in either estate or guardian-ship proceedings shall be signed by the fiduciary and the signature notarized prior to its submission unless the court permits otherwise. All such deeds shall be submitted with the or at the time of the hearing on the Final Account unless the Court permits otherwise.

605.2. Unsupervised Estates. No Personal Representative's Deed shall be approved in unsupervised estates.

Adopted July 28, 2006, effective Jan. 1, 2007. Amended August 2, 2007, effective January 1, 2008.

LR71–PR00 Rule 606.   ACCOUNTING

606.1. Failure to Close Within One Year. Whenever an estate cannot be closed within one (1) year, the personal representative shall file a statement with the Court stating the reasons why the estate has not been closed if requested by the Court. In addition, the Court reserves the power to require the personal representative to file an intermediate accounting with the Court.

606.2. Guardianship. All guardianship accountings shall contain a certification of an officer of any financial institution in which guardianship assets are held, verifying the account balance.

606.3. Social Security/Medicare Benefits. All social security or Medicare benefits received on behalf of an incapacitated person shall be included and accounted for in the guardianship accounting unless court approval has been previously granted to allow said funds to be paid directly to a residential or health care facility, or because of the amount of such funds, the Court finds that such funds can only be used by the guardian or designated person for the benefit of use of such incapacitated person.

606.4. Statutory Format. All accounts shall follow the prescribed statutory format. Informal, handwritten, or transactional accountings will not be accepted.

606.5. Payment of Court Costs. All court costs shall be paid and all claims satisfied and released before the hearing on the Final Account, and a Clerk's Certification thereof shall be filed with the Court before such Final Account shall be approved.

606.6. Closing Letters. The Federal Estate Tax Closing letter and the Indiana Inheritance Tax Closing letter (or the countersigned receipt) or a photocopy thereof, showing payment of all Federal Estate and/or Indiana Inheritance Tax liability in the estate, executed by the Internal Revenue Service or the Indiana Department of State Revenue, shall be attached to the Final Accounting at the time of filing, unless the Court has given prior written approval to attach such letter to the Final Report, after filing but prior to the hearing on the Final Accounting.

Adopted July 28, 2006, effective Jan. 1, 2007. Amended August 2, 2007, effective January 1, 2008.

LR71–PR00 Rule 607.   UNSUPERVISED ADMIN-ISTRATION

607.1.   Payment of Court Costs. All court costs shall be paid and all claims satisfied and released on or before the date of the filing of the Closing Statement and a Clerk's Certification thereof shall be filed with the Court at the time such Closing Statement is filed with the Court.

607.2.   Closing Statement. The Court may enter an order approving the Closing Statement.

Adopted July 28, 2006, effective Jan. 1, 2007. Amended August 2, 2007, effective January 1, 2008.

LR71–PR00 Rule 608.   MISCELLANEOUS

608.1.   Inheritance Tax Schedule. If the Court determines that no Inheritance Tax Schedule is required to be filed, a copy of the Court's order shall be served on the local representative of the Inheritance Tax Division of the Indiana Department of Revenue.

608.2.   Implementation of Rules. The court may adapt procedures by standing order to effectuate implementation of these rules, and may deviate from these rules when justice requires, but only upon showing of severe prejudice or hardship.

Adopted July 28, 2006, effective Jan. 1, 2007. Amended August 2, 2007, effective January 1, 2008.

LR71–PR00 Rule 609.   GUARDIANSHIPS

609.1.   Filing of Current Reports. Current reports filed by a guardian of the person shall state the present residence of the incapacitated person and his or her general welfare. If the incapacitated person is an adult, a report of a treating physician shall be filed with the current report, verifying that the incapacity of the person remains unchanged since the date the guardianship was established or the date of the last current report and that the living arrangements for the incapacitated person are appropriate.

609.2.   Compliance with Other Rules. Nothing herein shall be deemed as amending, superseding, or altering the Probate Rules and Regulations promulgated by the Veteran's Administration of the United States of America, and every fiduciary and attorney shall comply with same, if applicable.

609.3.   Financial Matters. Other than for routine matters, the guardian shall obtain court approval prior to taking any action on any financial matter pertaining to carrying out the guardian's duties and responsibilities for the protected person.

Adopted July 28, 2006, effective Jan. 1, 2007. Amended August 2, 2007, effective January 1, 2008.

LR71–TR66 Rule 610. RECEIVERSHIP ESTATES

610.1.   Proceedings to Which This Rule is Applicable. This rule is promulgated, for the administration of estates by receivers or by other officers appointed by the court pursuant to Indiana Trial Rule 66.

610.2.   Inventory and Appraisal. Unless the Court otherwise orders, a receiver or similar officer, as soon as practicable after appointment and not later than twenty-eight (28) days after he or she has taken possession of the estate, shall file an inventory and an appraisal of all the property and assets in the receiver's possession or in the possession of others who hold possession as his or her agent, and in a separate schedule, and inventory of the property and assets of the estate not reduced to possession by the receiver but claimed and held by others.

610.3.   Periodic Reports. Within twenty-eight (28) days after the filing of inventory, and at regular intervals of three (3) months thereafter until discharged, unless the Court otherwise directs, the receiver or other similar officer shall file reports of the receipts and expenditures and of his or her acts and transactions in an official capacity.

610.4.   Compensation of Receiver, Attorneys and Other Officers. In the exercise of its discretion, the Court shall determine and fix the compensation of receivers or similar officers and their counsel and the compensation of all others who may have been appointed by the Court to aid in the administration of the estate, and such allowances or compensation shall be made only on petition therefore and on such notice, if any, to creditors, and other interested persons as the Court may direct.

Adopted June 1, 2011, effective Jan. 1, 2012.

LOCAL RULES FOR ELECTRONIC FILING FOR ST. JOSEPH COUNTY

Adopted July 28, 2006, Effective January 1, 2007

Including Amendments Received Through November 1, 2013

Research Notes

Annotations to the Local Rules for Electronic Filing for St. Joseph County are available in West's Annotated Indiana Code, *Title 34 Appendix.*

These rules may be searched electronically on Westlaw *in the* IN-RULES *database; updates to these rules may be found on Westlaw in IN-RULESUPDATES. For search tips and a summary of database content, consult the Westlaw Scope Screens for each database.*

Rule

LR71–AR16 Rule 701. ELECTRONIC FILING OF CASES IN ST. JOSEPH COUNTY

701.1. Purpose. The Courts in St. Joseph County, generally, and the St. Joseph Probate Court, specifically, intend to use current technology to improve efficiency, public access, and ease of use. With the approval of the Supreme Court of Indiana pursuant to T.R. 77, the Courts set forth these local rules of procedure to assist the public, the bar, and the courts in implementing electronic filing and computer case management for the Circuit, Superior, and Probate Courts.

701.2. Authority. The following rules are hereby adopted and promulgated pursuant to T.R. 81 of the Indiana Rules of Trial Procedure.

701.3. Control. If any local rule shall conflict with, or be inconsistent with the Indiana Rules of Trial Procedure, the latter shall control.

Adopted July 28, 2006, effective Jan. 1, 2007. Amended August 2, 2007, effective January 1, 2008.

LR71–AR16 Rule 702. FILING OF CASES IN THE ST. JOSEPH PROBATE COURT

702.1. Application. These rules apply to all new cases filed with the Probate Court and all old cases already filed with the Probate Court. Old cases will not be required to convert to the computer system until some activity occurs in the case. As of January 1, 2006, all documents (other than those specifically excepted by the Probate Court) shall be filed electronically in all cases.

702.2. Case Management System. The Probate Court is utilizing a computer case management system known as "*QUEST*". A filing in *QUEST* or a *QUEST* filing is a filing in the Probate Court's computer system.

702.3. Electronic Court Files. Probate Court files kept electronically shall be available for inspection by the public and the bar except for those files that are deemed confidential by statute or court order.

702.4. Electronic Filing of Pleadings.

702.4.1. *New Cases.* Prior to creating a new case in the *QUEST* system, a party must obtain a cause number from the Clerk of the Court. The cause number may be obtained upon submission of an appearance form and payment of the filing fee to the Clerk [or upon presentation to the Clerk of a court order waiving the filing fee]. Issuance of a cause number does not constitute a "filing" and will not toll any statute of limitations or other time limitation. In order to create a new case in the court computer system (*QUEST*), a person must have a password and user identification granting access to the system. An action must be commenced in conformity with Trial Rule 3 and pursuant to Trial Rules 4 through 4.17 of the Indiana Rules of Trial Procedure.

702.4.2. *Existing Cases.* The CCS and pleadings of any existing case may be viewed on the *QUEST* system by use of a valid password. This does not apply to cases that are confidential by virtue of the law or court order. To electronically file a pleading in *QUEST*, one must first complete an appearance form and file it with the clerk. Upon accepting the appearance form filing, the Clerk will make that case accessible for the filing of pleadings by the person who has made the appearance. Whenever an attorney withdraws his appearance in a case, his accessibility to that case for the filing of pleadings will be removed.

702.4.3. *Time of Filing.* Document may be filed through an E-filing system at any time that the Clerk's office is open to receive the filing or at such other times as may be designated by the Clerk and posted publicly. Documents filed through the E-filing system are deemed filed the next regular time when the Clerk's office is open for filing. The time stamp issued by the E-filing system shall be presumed to be the time the Document is received by the Clerk.

702.4.4. *Notice of Filing of Pleading (Manner of Service)*. In addition to the usual ways of serving parties of record pursuant to T.R. 5, service may be made by *QUEST* e-mail on those parties of record or their attorneys who are current users of the *QUEST* system. Said notice shall indicate the name of the pleading filed, the date it was filed, and any hearing date thereon, if applicable. The notified party or attorney may then access the pleading through the *QUEST* system. The Clerk of the Probate Court shall maintain a list of current users of the *QUEST* system.

702.5. System Access.

702.5.1. *Password*. In order to access Probate Court files electronically on the *QUEST* case management system, a person must obtain a unique user name and password. Prior to being assigned a user name and password, the requesting individual must execute a user agreement with the Probate Court. Upon receipt of the signed user agreement, the *QUEST* system administrator will issue a unique user identification and password.

702.5.2. *Security*. Each person is responsible for the use of his password. No person shall knowingly utilize or cause another person to utilize the password of another without permission of the holder of the password or in violation of these rules. No attorney shall knowingly permit or cause to permit his user name and password to be utilized by anyone other than an employee of his law firm.

702.5.3. *Fees and Waiver*. The user agreement requires parties to pay a nominal fee. However, access shall be free of charge for parties or litigants claiming indigence.

702.5.4. *Training and Assistance*. The Court will provide assistance and/or instruction to individuals utilizing the electronic filing system. Provisions will be made to ensure access to the system by disabled or self-represented parties or litigants.

702.6. Electronic Signature of Documents. Documents filed through the E-filing system by use of a valid user name and password are presumed to have been signed and authorized by the user to whom that user name and password have been issued. The following will meet the signature requirements:

(1) Where a person's signature is required on a verified pleading or document, the *QUEST* imprint of the name will satisfy the requirement; however, the attorney is required to maintain an original, signed paper copy in his office. Said pleading or document must be maintained for as long as required by the Administrative Rules of the Supreme Court of Indiana.

(2) A *pro se* litigant is required to file a signed paper copy with the clerk unless he is able to sign the pleading or document electronically at the clerk's office.

(3) An attorney will not be required to maintain an original, signed paper copy of a verified pleading or document if the attorney has a Court approved signature pad which enables electronic signatures to be entered on the verified pleading or document, and the pleading or document which is being filed has an electronic signature affixed to it.

702.7. Format of Pleadings. Pleadings shall conform to form or layout designed by the Court pursuant to LR71–TR77–201.3.5. The Court reserves the right to strike any pleading that does not conform to the requirements of the Quest or Odyssey case management systems or that create an undue hardship of Court staff who are assigned to prepare and/or complete entries and orders in those case management systems.

Adopted July 28, 2006, effective Jan. 1, 2007. Amended August 2, 2007, effective January 1, 2008; July 18, 2011, effective Jan. 1, 2012; July 26, 2012, effective Jan. 1, 2013.

LOCAL JURY RULES FOR ST. JOSEPH COUNTY

Adopted Effective July 28, 2006

Including Amendments Received Through November 1, 2013

Research Notes

Annotations to the Local Jury Rules for St. Joseph County are available in West's Annotated Indiana Code, Title 34 Appendix.

These rules may be searched electronically on Westlaw in the IN-RULES database; updates to these rules may be found on Westlaw in IN-RULESUPDATES. For search tips and a summary of database content, consult the Westlaw Scope Screens for each database.

LR71–AR00 Rule 801. DEFINITIONS

801.1. Court. The term "Court" or "Courts" shall mean the St. Joseph Circuit, Superior, and Probate Courts.

801.2. Judge. The term "Judge" or "Judges" shall mean the Judge of the Circuit Court, the Judge of the Probate Court, and the Chief Judge of the Superior Court.

801.3. Jury Administrator. The term "Jury Administrator" shall mean a person so appointed to administer and manage the jury process to the extent permitted by Indiana Law.

801.4. Jury Pool. The term "Jury Pool" shall mean a list of names, the number of which is to be determined annually by the Judges, drawn in accordance with this rule, from the list of names supplied by the Indiana Supreme Court, pursuant to statute and the Indiana Jury Rules.

801.5. Notice of Jury Service. The term "Notice of Jury Service" shall mean a written document which accompanies the Juror Qualification and Questionnaire Form and provides general information regarding the juror selection process of the St. Joseph County Courts.

801.6. Juror Qualification and Questionnaire Form. The term "Juror Qualification and Questionnaire Form" shall mean a written document which solicits information from prospective jurors regarding statutory qualification and exemptions.

801.7. Summons. The term "Summons" shall mean a written document which notifies a prospective juror of the dates and details of their jury service.

801.8. Bi-Monthly List. The term "Bi-monthly List" shall mean a random sub-set of the Jury Pool which shall be requested from the Clerk of Court by the Jury Administrator. Unless otherwise directed by the Judges, the bi-monthly Venire List shall be composed of one-sixth (⅙) of the Jury Pool.

Adopted effective July 28, 2006. Amended August 2, 2007, effective January 1, 2008.

LR71–AR00 Rule 802. EFFECTIVE DATE

In compliance with the Indiana Jury Rules, these rules shall become effective immediately.

Adopted effective July 28, 2006. Amended August 2, 2007, effective January 1, 2008.

LR71–AR00 Rule 803. SCOPE

The rules shall govern petit jury assembly, selection, and management in the Courts.

Adopted effective July 28, 2006. Amended August 2, 2007, effective January 1, 2008.

LR71–AR00 Rule 804. INITIAL APPOINTMENT OF JURY ADMINISTRATORS

The following are hereby appointed to act as Jury Administrators, to administer the jury assembly process:

(1) A sufficient number of Jury Commissioners as appointed by the Courts pursuant to the Indiana Code.

(2) At least one (1) Jury Clerk from the St. Joseph County clerk's office.

(3) The bailiff of each Court and judge thereof.

Adopted effective July 28, 2006. Amended August 2, 2007, effective January 1, 2008.

LR71–AR00 Rule 805. ADDITIONAL MODIFICATION OF APPOINTMENTS

Appointments made pursuant to this rule shall be updated or modified, from time to time, as deemed necessary.

Adopted effective July 28, 2006. Amended August 2, 2007, effective January 1, 2008.

LR71–AR00 Rule 806. ASSEMBLY OF THE JURY POOL

No later than November 1 of each calendar year, the Jury Pool shall be assembled for the next calendar year by randomly selecting names from the appropriate lists as may be required and supplied by the Indiana Supreme Court and/or appropriate statute.

Adopted effective July 28, 2006. Amended August 2, 2007, effective January 1, 2008.

LR71–AR00 Rule 807. SUMMONING JURORS

Jurors shall be summoned using a Two Tier Notice and Summons procedure, as follows:

(1) At least bi-monthly, the Jury Administrator shall randomly draw the bi-monthly Venire List from the Jury Pool and mail, or cause to be mailed, the Notice of Jury Service and Juror Qualification and Questionnaire Form. The bi-monthly lists may be drawn prior to each two-month jury service period or at any other time as may be appropriate.

(2) Not later than one (1) week before a jury panel for jury selection is needed, the Jury Administrator or Bailiff assigned to each court shall mail, or cause to be mailed, the Summons of Jury Service which shall specify the specific dates for which the prospective juror shall remain on call for jury service.

(3) Each Judge may implement such additional procedures as he or she may believe will best ensure compliance with the Summons for Jury Service.

Adopted effective July 28, 2006. Amended August 2, 2007, effective January 1, 2008.

LR71–AR00 Rule 808. ASSISTANCE OF THE CLERK OF COURT

At the discretion of the Court, the Jury Administrator may receive technical, administrative, or clerical assistance in summoning prospective jurors from the Office of the St. Joseph County Clerk.

Adopted effective July 28, 2006. Amended August 2, 2007, effective January 1, 2008.

LR71–AR00 Rule 809. CRITERIA FOR DISQUALIFICATION

Prospective jurors shall be found disqualified from jury service using only those criteria which is expressly provided in the Indiana Code and/or the Indiana Jury Rules.

Adopted effective July 28, 2006. Amended August 2, 2007, effective January 1, 2008.

LR71–AR00 Rule 810. CRITERIA FOR EXEMPTION

Prospective jurors shall be exempted from jury service using only those exemptions expressly provided in the Indiana Code and/or the Indiana Jury Rules.

Adopted effective July 28, 2006. Amended August 2, 2007, effective January 1, 2008.

LR71–AR00 Rule 811. DOCUMENTATION OF DISQUALIFICATION, EXEMPTION, OR DEFERRAL

Facts supporting disqualification, exemption, or deferral from jury service shall be provided to the Court, in writing, under oath or affirmation.

Adopted effective July 28, 2006. Amended August 2, 2007, effective January 1, 2008.

LR71–AR00 Rule 812. TERM OF JURY SERVICE

The term of jury service shall be that as set forth in Indiana Jury Rule 9.

Adopted effective July 28, 2006. Amended August 2, 2007, effective January 1, 2008.

LR71–AR00 Rule 813. RECORD KEEPING

813.1. Format. Records of the jury management in the Courts shall be maintained, in written format, electronic format, or both, by the Jury Administrator.

813.2. Items Included. Records shall include, but are not limited to:

(1) Annual jury pool;

(2) Periodic list;

(3) Jurors qualified;

(4) Exemptions granted;

(5) Deferrals granted;

(6) Jurors who served; and

(7) Terms of service.

813.3. Protocols. The protocols for record keeping and retention established in each Court shall comply strictly with the standards established in the Indiana Code, Indiana Jury Rules, Indiana Administrative Rules, or otherwise provided by Indiana Law.

Adopted effective July 28, 2006. Amended August 2, 2007, effective January 1, 2008.

LR71–AR00 Rule 814. JUROR PRIVACY

In addition to, and to the extent that it is not contrary to disclosure either permitted or prohibited by Indiana Supreme Court Administrative Rule 9:

(1) Personal information relating to a juror or prospective juror not disclosed in open court is

confidential, other than for the use of the parties and counsel.

(2) Upon request, copies of the Juror Qualification and Questionnaire Form may be made available to counsel on the date of trial.

(a) All copies of the Juror Qualification and Questionnaire Form so provided shall be returned to the Court at the completion of the jury selection process.

(b) No photocopies or duplicates of the Juror Qualification and Questionnaire Form shall be made without specific Court authorization.

(3) Each Court shall take steps to protect and maintain juror privacy and the confidentiality of juror information.

Adopted effective July 28, 2006. Amended August 2, 2007, effective January 1, 2008.

LR71–AR00 Rule 815.   MISCELLANEOUS

All other proceedings involving the assembly, selection, and management of petit juries in the Courts shall be conducted as required by the Indiana Jury Rules.

Adopted effective July 28, 2006. Amended August 2, 2007, effective January 1, 2008.

LOCAL RULE FOR COURT FEES
FOR ST. JOSEPH COUNTY

Adopted June 3, 2008, Effective January 1, 2009

Including Amendments Received Through November 1, 2013

Research Notes

Annotations to the Local Rules for Court Fees for St. Joseph Circuit Court are available in West's *Annotated Indiana Code, Title 34 Appendix.*

These rules may be searched electronically on Westlaw *in the* IN-RULES *database; updates to these rules may be found on Westlaw in* IN-RULESUPDATES. *For search tips and a summary of database content, consult the Westlaw Scope Screens for each database.*

Rule

LR71–AR00 Rule 901. INTENT AND SCOPE OF FEE SCHEDULE

The Courts adopt the following schedule of fees for referrals to offset the costs of court services and to reduce the burden on the county taxpayer. The Courts find that the following rules establish a reasonable schedule of user fees for the Courts of St. Joseph County.

Formerly Rule 1001. Renumbered and amended June 3, 2008, effective Jan. 1, 2009.

LR71–AR00 Rule 902. FEE SCHEDULE FOR CSAP AND DRUG COURT

The Courts adopt the following schedule of fees for referrals to the Court Substance Abuse Program (CSAP) and Drug Court.

902.1. CSAP User Fee. A party referred to CSAP shall pay a user fee of $400.00, which is payable to the Clerk of the Court. This CSAP user fee will include an assessment, participation in drug education, if recommended, case monitoring and case closure.

902.2. Drug Court User Fee. A person participating in Drug Court shall pay a problem-solving court administration fee of one hundred dollars ($100.00). In addition, each participant in Drug Court shall be assessed a services fee of fifty dollars ($50.00) per month beginning with the second month of participation and for each month thereafter for the duration of participation in the problem-solving court. Provided further, however, that the aggregate of fees paid under this section by any participant shall not exceed five hundred dollars ($500.00). [This Emergency Local Rule supersedes LR71–AR00–902.2, which was adopted originally on June 3, 2008.]

902.3. Urine Drug Screening Fees. Urine Drug Screening Fees payable to the Court Substance Abuse Program laboratory for deposit with the auditor as follows:

(a) Drug Court Urine Drug Screening Fees: $20.00 for positive drug screens, $15.00 for negative drug screens, $3.00 for no specimen fees, $2.00 for breathalyzer fee, and $45.00 for confirmation testing at an off-site laboratory.

(b) CSAP Urine Drug Screening Fees: $15.00 for drug screens, $3.00 for no specimen fees, $2.00 for breathalyzer fee, and $45.00 for confirmation testing at an off-site laboratory.

902.4. Transfer Fees. Transfer fees shall be payable to the Clerk of the Court as follows:

(a) Transfer to another jurisdiction: A transfer fee of $75.00 shall be paid to the Clerk of the Court to transfer a case to another state or in-state jurisdiction, or to transfer directly to an in-state or out-of-state treatment provider without alcohol and drug assessment.

(b) Transfer from another jurisdiction: A transfer fee of $150.00 shall be paid to the Clerk of the Court for cases transferred from another jurisdiction.

902.5. Case Monitoring Fees. A party referred for case monitoring only shall pay a fee of $75.00, which includes monitoring compliance with treatment at a court-ordered treatment provider and for monitoring of urine drug screens.

902.6. Alcohol and Drug Assessments. A party referred for an alcohol and drug assessment without other services shall pay a fee of $150.00.

Formerly Rule 1001. Renumbered and amended June 3, 2008, effective Jan. 1, 2009. Amended effective July 26, 2012, effective Jan. 1, 2013.

LR71–AR00 Rule 903. LATE PAYMENT FEE FOR COURT COSTS, FINES AND CIVIL PENALTIES

Pursuant to Indiana Code 33–37–5–22, the Courts of St. Joseph County adopt a late payment fee in the sum of twenty-five ($25.00) for defendants who have not tendered timely payment of costs, fines or civil penalties.

903.1 Definitions.

903.1.1.1 Definition of Defendant. For the purposes of this local rule, an individual who has committed a crime, violated a statute defining an infraction, violated an ordinance of a municipal corporation, or committed a delinquent act, is defined as a "defendant."

903.1.1.2 Definition of Costs. For the purposes of this local rule, costs includes court costs and fees assessed by a Court.

903.2 Assessment of Late Payment Fee.

A defendant who is required to pay court costs (including fees), a fine, or civil penalty and who has not been determined by the Court imposing the costs, fine or civil penalty to be indigent shall pay, in addition to the costs, fine or civil penalty, a late payment fee in the sum of $25.00 to the Clerk of the Court if the defendant fails to pay the costs, fine or civil penalty in full before the later of the following: (a) the end of the business day on which the Court enters the conviction or judgment; or (b) the end of the period specified in a payment schedule set for the payment of court costs, fines, and civil penalties adopted for the operation of the Courts of St. Joseph County.

903.3 Clerk to Assess and Collect Late Payment Fee.

When a defendant meets the criteria described in LR71–AR00–903.2, the Clerk shall assess and collect a late payment fee in the sum of $25.00, unless the late payment fee is suspended by Court order as provided by LR71–AR00–903.4. The Clerk may take all appropriate steps to collect late payment fees, including without limitation the retention of legal counsel to effectuate collection proceedings.

903.4 Court May Suspend Late Payment Fee.

Notwithstanding LR71–AR00–903.2, the Court that imposed the costs, fine or civil penalty may suspend the late payment fee required by this Rule if the Court finds that the Defendant has demonstrated good cause for failure to make a timely payment of the previously assessed costs, fine or civil penalty and issues an order to that effect directing the Clerk of the Court to suspend the assessment and collection of the Late Payment Fee.

Adopted June 3, 2008; effective Jan. 1, 2009.

LOCAL EMERGENCY COURT RULES FOR ST. JOSEPH COUNTY

Adopted July 28, 2006, Effective January 1, 2007

Including Amendments Received Through November 1, 2013

Research Notes

Annotations to the Local Emergency Court Rules for St. Joseph County are available in West's Annotated Indiana Code, *Title 34 Appendix.*

These rules may be searched electronically on Westlaw *in the* IN-RULES *database; updates to these rules may be found on* Westlaw *in* IN-RULESUPDATES. *For search tips and a summary of database content, consult the* Westlaw Scope Screens *for each database.*

Rule

LR71–AR00 Rule 1101. INTENT AND SCOPE OF LOCAL EMERGENCY COURT RULES

Local Emergency Court Rules are temporary in nature and shall only remain in effect until January 1 of the next odd numbered calendar year (e.g. 2009, 2011, etc.) unless converted into a permanent local rule.

Adopted as Rule 1001 July 28, 2006, effective Jan. 1, 2007. Renumbered as Rule 1101, and amended August 2, 2007, effective Jan. 1, 2008.

LR71–TR4.9 Rule 1102. TEMPORARY RULE CONCERNING MORTGAGE FORECLOSURES ON REAL ESTATE

Effective April 15, 2010, Plaintiffs filing new mortgage foreclosure (MF) actions in the St. Joseph Circuit Court or the St. Joseph Superior Court will be required to provide to the Clerk of the Court:

• One (1) additional stamped, addressed envelope, with no return address information, for each individual (but not including any corporation or entity) named as a defendant,

AND

• A service list, including the name, address and, if available, the telephone number of each defendant.

This rule is adopted by the St. Joseph Circuit Court and the St. Joseph Superior Court pursuant to an initiative of the Indiana Supreme Court and the Indiana Housing and Community Development Authority to train and recruit volunteer lawyers to assist homeowners facing foreclosure and in furtherance of the purposes underlying Senate Enrolled Act No. 492 (2010).

Failure to comply with this rule will delay the processing of the case by the Clerk until compliance is achieved.

All MF actions filed on or after April 15, 2010, in the St. Joseph Circuit Court or the St. Joseph Superior Court, in which a timely request for settlement conference is made pursuant to Ind. Code 32–30–10.5–10, shall be the subject of an administrative transfer to the St. Joseph Superior Court, Mishawaka Division, for purposes of the scheduling and conduct of such settlement conference.

Unless extended by the St. Joseph Circuit Court and/or the St. Joseph Superior Court, this Temporary Rule expires on December 31, 2012.

Adopted July 18, 2011, effective Jan. 1, 2012.

SHELBY COUNTY LOCAL ADMINISTRATIVE RULES

Amended September 30, 2005, Effective October 11, 2005

Including Amendments Received Through November 1, 2013

Research Notes

These rules may be searched electronically on Westlaw *in the* IN-RULES *database; updates to these rules may be found on Westlaw in* IN-RULESUPDATES. *For search tips and a summary of database content, consult the Westlaw Scope Screens for each database.*

LR73–AR15 Rule 1. COURT REPORTER SERVICES[1]

1.1 Definitions. The definitions contained in Administrative Rule 15(B) are adopted for use in this Rule and control any question of interpretation. For the purposes of this Rule, the Regular Hours worked by the Court Reporting Staff shall be Monday through Friday from 8:00 a.m. until 12:00 noon and from 1:00 p.m. until 4:00 p.m. or as otherwise ordered by the Court. The Work Week shall be a seven day period beginning on Sunday and ending on Saturday of each week and shall contain thirty-five (35) hours for which salaried compensation shall be paid.

1.2 Compensation. The Court Reporter shall work under the control, direction and direct supervision of the Court during all hours of employment and shall be paid an annual salary for regular hours worked during a Work Week. The salaries shall be set by the Court and approved by the County Council. Gap Hours (the 5 hours between 35 and 40 hours per week) shall be compensated in time off from work in an amount equal to the number of Gap Hours worked or by payment of regular time as directed by the court. Overtime Hours shall be compensated in an amount equal to one and one-half (1 ½) times the number of Overtime Hours worked in excess of 40 hours per week.

1.3 Duties And Responsibilities. The duties of a Court Reporter shall include Reporting the evidence presented in Court proceedings; Preservation and storage of reported testimony and any physical evidence presented in Court proceedings; Preparation of Chronological Case Summary entries at the direction of the Court and providing notice thereof as required by the Rules of Trial Procedure; Preparation of written documents to effectuate the rulings, orders and judgments of the Court or to comply with the Rules of the Indiana Supreme Court; Preparation of transcripts of evidence presented in Court proceedings requested pursuant to the Rules of Trial Procedure; and, Such other functions and responsibilities as required by law or the Court for its effective administration.

1.4 Maximum Per Page Fee.

1.4.1 A Court Reporter shall not charge more than the following per page:

1.4.1.1 $5.00 for a transcript of evidence for appealed cases. The Court Reporter shall submit a claim directly to the county for the preparation of any county indigent transcripts of evidence.

1.4.1.2 $5.00 for state/county indigent transcript of evidence for appealed cases;

1.4.1.3 $5.00 for civil transcripts of evidence for appealed cases;

1.4.1.4 $5.00 for non-appeal transcripts:

1.4.1.5 $4.00 for deposition transcripts and $1.50 for copies if Reporter elects to use Court facilities, equipment and/or supplies in the exercise of her private practice;

1.4.1.6 $7.25 for expedited transcripts

1.4.1.7 $1.75 for copies of transcripts.

2. Court Reporter shall be allowed $5.00 for each transcript disk provided.

3. Court Reporter's Certification fee for transcripts shall be $10.00.

4. Each Court Reporter shall annually report all compensation received for transcripts to the Indiana Supreme Court Division of State Court Administration.

1.5 Private Practice.

5.1 A Court Reporter may elect to engage in the private practice of recording of and preparation of deposition transcripts. Such activity, regardless of whether the deposition concerns a case pending before the Court, shall be conducted outside of regular working hours. If a Reporter, in the exercise of such private practice, utilizes, with the consent of the Court, Court facilities, equipment and/or supplies, the Reporter shall reimburse the Court for such usage pursuant to a written agreement between the Court and Reporter.

5.2. Such agreement shall establish the:

5.2.1 Reasonable market rate for the use of equipment, facilities and supplies;

5.2.2 Method by which records are kept for the use of the same; and,

5.2.3 Method by which the Reporter shall reimburse the Court for such usage.

Adopted May 28, 1998, effective June 1, 1998. Amended and renumbered as Rule 1, Sept. 30, 2005, effective Oct. 11, 2005. Amended Nov. 7, 2007, effective Dec. 17, 2007; April 12, 2011, effective Jan. 1, 2012; effective May 1, 2013.

1 See, also Rule 2

LR73–AR00 Rule 2. LOCAL CASELOAD PLANS

2.1 Caseload Allocation.

2.1.1 *Criminal Cases.* Criminal case allocation shall continue to operate as specified in LR73–AR00 Rule 3 Local Caseload Plans

2.1.2 *Civil Cases*

2.1.2.1. Juvenile Cases. All Juvenile cases (JC, JT, JD, JS, JM, and JP) shall continue to be filed in Shelby Superior Court No. 1

2.1.2.2 Remaining Civil Cases

2.1.2.2.1 All Plenary (PL) cases shall be filed 50/50 on a random basis in Shelby Circuit Court and Shelby Superior Court No. 1

2.1.2.2.2 All Domestic Relations (DR) cases shall be filed 50/50 on a random basis in Shelby Circuit Court and Shelby Superior Court No. 1

2.1.2.2.3 All Reciprocal Support (RS) cases shall be filed in Shelby Circuit Court.

2.1.2.2.4 All Protective Orders (PO) cases shall be filed in Shelby Circuit Court

2.1.2.2.5 All Small Claims (SC) shall be filed in Shelby Superior Court No. 2

2.1.2.2.6 All remaining types of civil cases (AD, AH, CT, ES, EU, GU, MH, MI and TR) shall be filed as requested by the initiating party.

2.2 Evaluation of Caseload Allocation.

A. The Allocation of Judicial Resources described herein should place the Shelby County Courts in compliance with guidelines issued by the Indiana Supreme Court's Order for Development of Local Caseload Plans. No later than March 1 of each year, the judges of the courts of record in Shelby County shall meet and evaluate the caseload data as reported to the Indiana Supreme Court Administration.

B. The caseload evaluation shall factor in the allocation of administrative duties among the judges

as well as any special circumstances such as death penalty cases.

C. Special service by Shelby County judges outside their own courts or special, senior judges or transfer judges serving in the Shelby County Courts shall also be considered. Such service shall be calculated in accordance with the weighted caseload worksheet and criteria established by the Indiana Supreme Court Division of State Court Administration.

D. Modification or changes necessary for the Shelby County Courts to remain in compliance with the Order for Development of Local Caseload Plans shall be developed and approved by a majority vote of the judges and shall become effective on April 1 of each year.

Adopted as local Rule 1991–1, September 8, 1999, effective November 1, 1999. Amended and renumbered as Rule 3, September 30, 2005, effective October 11, 2005. Amended and renumbered as LR73–AR00 Rule 2 effective Sept 1, 2011.

LR73–AR00 Rule 3. LOCAL CASELOAD PLANS

Criminal Cases

All A, B & C pool felonies and murder as defined in Local Rule 73–CR2.2–1, shall be filed in the respective courts in the following percentages:

45% in Shelby Circuit Court

45% in Shelby Superior Court No. 1

10% in Shelby Superior Court No. 2

All misdemeanor and D felonies under 9–30–5 shall be filed in Shelby Superior Court No. 2. The remaining D felonies shall be filed in the respective courts in the following percentages:

45% in Shelby Circuit Court

10% in Shelby Superior Court 1

45% in Shelby Superior Court 2

Civil Cases

Small claims and Infractions shall be filed in Shelby Superior Court No. 2.

Protective orders shall be filed in Shelby Circuit Court unless there is a related case in one of the other courts in which case the Protective Order case would be filed in the other court along with the related case.

Mortgage Foreclosure (MF), Plenary (PL), Civil Collections (CC), and Domestic Relations (DR) cases shall be filed on a 50/50 random basis between Shelby Circuit Court and Shelby Superior Court No. 1.

All other civil actions shall be filed in the court chosen by the initiating party.

Juvenile Cases

All juvenile cases shall be filed in Shelby Superior Court No. 1

The revised Caseload Allocation Plan is the current caseload plan with the only modification the assignment of pool felonies between Circuit and Superior

Court 1 courts. This modification will bring the Shelby County Courts within the forty (40%) percent variance based on the weighted caseload measures system.

Effective September 1, 2011.

LR73–AR7 Rule 4. EVIDENCE HANDLING, RETENTION AND DESTRUCTION

In all cases, the Court shall proceed pursuant to these Rules unless the Court directs a longer retention period after motion by any party or on its own motion. This section shall not apply to exhibits that are on 8.5 × 11 inch paper or that can otherwise be easily stored in a flat court file.

4.1 Civil Cases, Including Adoption, Paternity, and Juvenile Proceedings. All models, diagrams, documents, or material not on 8 ½ by 11 paper admitted in evidence or pertaining to the case placed in the custody of the court reporter as exhibits shall be taken away by the parties offering them in evidence, except as otherwise ordered by the Court, four (4) months after the case is decided unless an appeal is taken. If an appeal is taken, all such exhibits shall be retained by the court reporter for two (2) years from termination of the appeal, retrial, or subsequent appeal and termination, whichever is later. The court reporter shall retain the mechanical or electronic records or tapes, shorthand or stenographic notes as provided in Indiana Administrative Rule 7.

4.2 Retention Periods for Evidence Introduced in Criminal Misdemeanor, Class D and Class C Felonies and Attempts. Unless otherwise agreed to by the parties, and except for deoxyribonucleic acid (DNA) evidence, all models, diagrams, documents, or material not on 8 ½ by 11 paper and admitted in evidence or pertaining to the case placed in the custody of the court reporter as exhibits shall be taken away by the parties offering them in evidence except as otherwise ordered by the Court, three (3) years after the case is dismissed, the defendant is found not guilty, or the defendant is sentenced, unless an appeal is taken. If an appeal is taken, all such exhibits shall be retained by the court reporter for three (3) years from termination of the appeal, retrial, or subsequent appeal and termination, whichever is later, unless an action challenging the conviction or sentence, or post-conviction action, is pending. The court will notify the parties at their last known address when the items need to be removed. The court will destroy or otherwise dispose of items not removed by the parties within a reasonable time of the notice. The parties may substitute photographs for the actual exhibits if approved by the court. The court reporter shall retain the mechanical or electronic records or tapes, shorthand or stenographic notes as provided in Indiana Administrative Rule 7.

4.3 Retention Periods for Evidence Introduced in Criminal Class B and A Felonies. Unless otherwise agreed to by the parties, and except for deoxyribonu-

cleic acid (DNA) evidence, all models, diagrams, documents, or material not on 8 ½ by 11 paper and admitted in evidence or pertaining to the case placed in the custody of the court reporter as exhibits shall be taken away by the parties offering them in evidence, except as otherwise ordered by the Court, twenty (20) years after the case is dismissed, the defendant found not guilty, or the defendant is sentenced, unless an appeal is taken. If an appeal is taken, all such exhibits shall be retained by the court reporter for twenty (20) years from termination of the appeal, retrial, or subsequent appeal and termination, whichever is later, unless an action challenging the conviction or sentence, or post-conviction action, is pending. The court will notify the parties at their last known address when the items need to be removed. The court will destroy or otherwise dispose of items not removed by the parties within a reasonable time of the notice. The court reporter shall retain the mechanical or electronic records or tapes, shorthand or stenographic notes as provided in Indiana Administrative Rule 7. Courts should be encouraged to photograph as much evidence as possible and courts and parties reminded of the requirements of Appellate Rule 29(B).

4.4 Non-documentary and Oversized Exhibits. Non-documentary and oversized exhibits shall not be sent to the Appellate level Court, but shall remain in the custody of the trial court or Administrative Agency during the appeal. Such exhibits shall be briefly identified in the Transcript where they were admitted into evidence. Photographs of any exhibit may be included in the volume of documentary exhibits. Under no circumstances should drugs, currency, or other dangerous or valuable items be included in appellate records.

4.5 Notification and Disposition In all cases, the Court shall provide actual notice, by mail or through the Shelby County Courthouse mailbox system, to all attorneys of record and to parties if unrepresented by counsel, that the evidence will be destroyed by a date certain if not retrieved before that date. Counsel and parties have the duty to keep the Court informed of their current addresses and notice to the last current address shall be sufficient. Court reporters should maintain a log of retained evidence and scheduled disposition date and evidence should be held in a secure area. At the time of removal, the party receiving and removing the evidence shall give a detailed receipt to the court reporter, and the receipt will be made part of the court file. In all cases, the Court, or the sheriff on the Court's order, should dispose of evidence that is not retaken after notice. The sheriff should be ordered to destroy evidence if its possession is illegal or if it has negligible value. The sheriff should auction evidence of some value with proceeds going to the county general fund. These Rules and their retention periods will take precedence over inconsistent language in statutes. I.C. 35–33–5–5(c)(2).

4.6 Biologically Contaminated Evidence A party who offers biologically contaminated evidence should notify the trial court that the evidence may be biologically contaminated prior to offering the evidence at trial. A party can show contaminated evidence or pass photographs of it to jurors, but no such evidence, however contained, shall be handled or passed to jurors or sent to the Jury Room unless specifically ordered by the Court.

LR73–AR10 Rule 5. AUDIO AND/OR VIDEO RECORDINGS OF COURT PROCEEDINGS

5.1 As proscribed by Indiana Judicial Conduct rule 2.17 and because the court is further required to prohibit broadcasting or televising court proceedings, any distribution of audio and video recordings of court proceedings shall not occur without explicit leave of court and accompanying protective orders regarding such recordings. Unauthorized distribution of such recordings may be punishable as a contempt of court matter.

5.2 Except for an authorized court reporter, Audio and/or video recording of any court proceeding by any person for any reason without pre-approved leave of court is punishable by contempt of court. A person that aids, induces, or causes the unauthorized recording of court proceedings or a person that possesses or distributes an unauthorized recording of a court proceeding is also subject to contempt of court proceedings.

SHELBY COUNTY LOCAL TRIAL RULES

Amended September 30, 2005, Effective October 11, 2005

Including Amendments Received Through November 1, 2013

Research Notes

These rules may be searched electronically on Westlaw in the IN-RULES database; updates to these rules may be found on Westlaw in IN-RULESUPDATES . For search tips and a summary of database content, consult the Westlaw Scope Screens for each database.

LR73–TR45 Rule 1. POOL FELONY

1.1 All A, B, & C felonies, (hereafter "pool" felonies), shall be assigned on a random basis among the three courts by the Shelby County Clerk with Shelby Superior No. 1 receiving forty-five percent (45%), Shelby Circuit Court forty-five percent (45%) and Shelby Superior No. 2 receiving ten percent (10%) of said cases;

1.1.2 All co-defendants in "pool" felony cases shall be assigned to the same court, based upon a single random draw by the Shelby County Clerk.

1.1.3 The Shelby County Prosecutor's Office shall notify the Clerk at the time of filing if the cases involve co-defendant. Each co-defendant case will be assigned an individual cause number. For purposes of this Rule, the cases involve co–defendants: as provided by I.C. 35–34–1–9 and amendments thereto.

1.1.4 Except in felony cases involving co-defendants under 1.1.3 above, any new "pool" felony case filed against a defendant who has an open "pool" felony case already pending in any Court, shall be assigned to the Court where the current case is pending. The Shelby County Prosecutor's Office shall notify the Clerk at the time of filing if the defendant has a pending pool felony case.

1.2 All misdemeanor cases and D felonies under Indiana Code 9–30–5 shall be filed in Shelby Superior Court No. 2. The remaining D felonies (hereinafter "pool felonies" shall be filed in the respective courts in the following percentages:

45% in Shelby Circuit Court

10% in Shelby Superior Court 1

45% in Shelby Superior Court 2.

Joint Local Rule No. 1, amended effective October 1, 2001. Amended and renumbered as Rule 1, September 30, 2005, effective October 11, 2005. Amended September 1, 2011, effective Jan 1, 2012.

LR73–TR79 Rule 2. SELECTION OF SPECIAL JUDGE

2.1 Selection of a Special Judge in a Civil Case shall be conducted pursuant to Indiana Judicial Administrative District Rule DR17—TR79—00002.

2.2–Reserved.

2.3–Reserved.

2.4 Reserved.

2.5 Reserved.

Adopted as Coordinated Local Rule, 1995. Amended and renumbered as Rule 2, September 30, 2005, effective October 11, 2005. Amended effective April 8, 2009. Amended December 4, 2012; Approved May 13, 2012; Effective May 1, 2013.

LR73–TR33 Rule 3. INTERROGATORIES

3.1 Number Limited. Interrogatories shall be limited to a total of 25 including subparts and shall be used solely for the purpose of discovery and shall not be used as a substitute for the taking of a deposition. For good cause shown and upon leave of Court additional interrogatories may be propounded.

3.2 Answers and Objections. Answers or objections to interrogatories under Rule TR 31 or 33 shall set forth in full the interrogatories being answered or objected to immediately preceding the answer or objection.

3.3 Duplicated Forms. No duplicated forms containing interrogatories shall be filed or served upon a party unless all interrogatories on such forms are consecutively numbered and applicable to the cause in which the same are filed and served.

LR73–TR05 Rule 4. MAILBOX SERVICE

Pursuant to Trial Rule 5(B)(1)(d), the Circuit and Superior Courts of Shelby County hereby designate the courthouse mailboxes located in each respective court for service of pleadings upon attorneys/ law firms who have such boxes. Each law firm must notify each court if they wish to establish a mailbox in the court. Each law firm must notify the court in writing if they wish to terminate the use of the courthouse mailbox. If an attorney or law firm declines to consent to receiving service by courthouse mailbox, then they are prohibited from using courthouse mailboxes to serve other attorneys. To the extent that an Attorney or firm designates an electronic mail box for purposes of having the court send orders to such electronic mailbox, **the courts** reserve the right to send such court orders electronically. However, the court does not accept electronic filing by attorneys at this time.

SHELBY COUNTY LOCAL FAMILY LAW RULES

Amended September 30, 2005, Effective October 11, 2005

Including Amendments Received Through November 1, 2013

Research Notes

These rules may be searched electronically on Westlaw in the IN-RULES database; updates to these rules may be found on Westlaw in IN-RULESUPDATES. For search tips and a summary of database content, consult the Westlaw Scope Screens for each database.

LR73–FL00 Rule 1. DISSOLUTION EDUCATION WORKSHOP

Pursuant to I.C. 31–1–11.5–19, Shelby Circuit Court, Shelby Superior Court I and Shelby Superior Court II find that the best interests of the minor child or children of the parties shall be served by encouraging mediation and cooperation between divorcing parents prior to and after the dissolution of their marriage.

The Courts further find that the Mandatory Divorce Workshop will:

1. Aid parents in post-separation parenting;

2. Encourage agreements between parties concerning child related matters; and,

3. Aid Courts in maximizing the use of Court time.

THEREFORE, Shelby Circuit Court, Shelby Superior Court I and Shelby Superior Court II now Order both parties in any Dissolution of Marriage cause of action in which there are minor children to attend the workshop entitled "Children Cope With Divorce". Attendance shall be mandatory for all parties in any Dissolution of Marriage filed on or after April 1, 1994, if there are unemancipated children under eighteen (18) years of age.

Each party must complete the four-hour course prior to the Final Hearing. The parties shall be responsible for paying the cost of the program, currently Thirty-five Dollars ($35.00) per person; waiver of the fee for indigency may be allowed.

The parties in this cause of action are ordered to contact:

The Visiting Nurse Service

4701 N. Keystone Avenue

Indianapolis, IN 46205

(317) 722–8201

1–800–248–6540

http://www.vnsi.org/chil.asp

within fifteen (15) days of their notice of this Order to make an appointment to attend the workshop without further notice. Failure to complete the workshop may result in a party having to show cause why he/she should not be held in contempt of Court. The Sheriff of Shelby County is ordered to make due service of the Notice of Order on the Respondent when the Petition for Dissolution is served and make due return thereon.

Adopted and effective April 9, 1996. Amended and renumbered as Rule 1, September 30, 2005, effective October 11, 2005; Amended and effective Jan 1, 2012.

LR73–FL00 Rule 2. ALTERNATIVE DISPUTE RESOLUTION (ADR) IN DOMESTIC RELATIONS

2.1 Program Overview. The purpose of the ADR Plan is to provide alternative dispute resolution opportunities to litigants involved in dissolution of marriage, legal separation and paternity cases. The goal is to offer litigants the opportunity to resolve conflict amicably, arrive at acceptable resolutions, have ownership of outcomes, and provide a basis upon which to resolve later issues all with the overriding goal of furthering the best interests of children. A primary aspect of the program is to provide alternative dispute services to litigants of modest means.

The forms of alternative dispute to be used are mediation, arbitration and family counseling in high conflict cases. Mediation will be the favored process. The parties may agree to submit to non-binding arbitration. Courts may require the parties submit to non-binding arbitration.

Court may require the parties to participate in counseling in high conflict matters. If mediation or arbitration are used, the Indiana Rules for Alternative Dispute Resolution apply.

The ADR Plan is to be effective with cases filed after September 1, 2005. The Clerk of Shelby County shall commence collecting the additional $20.00 alternative dispute resolution fee, pursuant to Indiana Code 33–4–13–1, on September 1, 2005.

2.2 Eligibility Criteria. All domestic relations litigants with custody and/or visitation disputes reasonably expected to take one hour or more of court time to litigate their custody and/or visitation dispute shall be required to participate in the ADR Plan. A party currently charged with or convicted of a crime under Indiana Code 35–42—et seq. Or a substantially similar crime in another jurisdiction may not participate in the ADR Plan.

2.3 Financial Qualifications. Litigants whose income is less than 125% of the federal poverty guidelines and have less than $10,000.00 of assets will participate without cost. Litigants whose income is between 125% and 175% of the federal poverty guidelines and have less than $20,000.00 of assets will pay a co-payment of $50.00 per hour for the services of the mediator. Litigants whose income is less than 125% and have $20,000.00 or more in assets will co-pay $50.00 per hour for the services of the mediator. Litigants whose income is greater than 175% of the federal poverty guidelines or who own more than $20,000.00 in assets will pay the mediator the normal hourly rate of the mediator.

2.4 Referral and Plan Administration. The administrator of the Shelby County Public Defender Program and Pro Bono Program will be the Plan Administrator. She will be responsible for the initial intake of litigants. If a litigant is determined to qualify for no-cost or reduced rate mediation, they will be referred to a volunteer mediator through the Shelby County Pro Bono Program. If the litigant is determined not to qualify for no-cost or reduced rate mediation, the litigant may choose the alternative dispute resolution facilitator of their choice. If one party qualifies but one does not, they shall be referred to a volunteer mediator and the non-qualifying party shall pay the mediator the normal hourly charge of the mediator. Attorneys and Judges shall refer the appropriate cases to the ADR Plan. All registered domestic law mediators, including Senior Judges, are eligible to act as mediators under the plan. Funds generated by the Plan shall be managed by the Shelby County Auditor.

2.5 Plan Education. Information about the Plan, including the additional $20.00 filing fee, its implementation, purpose and goals will be presented to the Shelby County Bar Association, the Shelby County Clerk, and local mental health counselors. The general public will be advised through newspaper and radio outlets.

2.6 Plan Coordination. The ADR Plan will work closely with the Shelby County Pro Bono Program to facilitate the resolution of domestic relations cases without the necessity of extended court hearings. Participants in the Pro Bono Program in domestic relations cases will be required to participate in the ADR Plan to attempt an amicable resolution of the case. The ADR Plan will provide a funding source for resolution of high conflict disputes for litigants of modest means.

2.7 Projected Budget. The Shelby Circuit Court estimates $3,000.00 will be collected annually. These figures are based on the total number of domestic cases filed in 2004 in Shelby Circuit Court (160) and Shelby Superior Court No. 1 (158). There were approximately 5 private paternity actions filed in 2004. There were approximately 20 domestic relation cases filed in which the filing fee was waived or reduced.

2.8 Projected Annual Budget.

Income $6,200.00

Expenses 6,200.00

Compensation for intake and referral

Coordinator $13.28/hour × 5 hours/week × 52 weeks = 3,452.80

Publicity regarding program 250.00

High conflict counseling 1,497.20

Mediation* 1,000.00

$6,200.00

*Mediation costs are low because most mediators will serve on pro bono basis as part of their voluntary participation in Shelby County Pro Bono Plan.

2.9 Program Evaluation and Reporting. An annual Report containing data related to the Plan shall be submitted to the judicial Conference by December 31 of each year. It shall be the responsibility of the Judge of Shelby Superior No. 1 to prepare and submit the Annual Report. The Annual Report shall be used to evaluate the program in conjunction with ongoing discussions with the Plan Administrator and representatives from the Pro Bono Program. The Judges and representatives from the Pro Bono Program will also evaluate the Plan on an ongoing basis by reviewing exit surveys which each participant will be asked to complete.

Adopted as ADA Plan. Amended and renumbered as Rule 2, September 30, 2005, effective October 11, 2005.

LR73–FL00 Rule 3. GUARDIAN AD LITEM FEES

The Shelby County Courts, recognizing it is appropriate to require parents and custodians of children who are involved in litigation and use the services[1] of the Shelby County Guardian Ad Litem to be financially responsible for those services, hereby establishes a standard fee schedule for the services[1] of the Shelby County Guardian Ad Litem in cases other than Child in Need of Services cases.

1) For custody and/or visitation evaluations, each parent/custodian shall pay the sum of $200.00.

2) For cases in which the services of the Guardian Ad Litem is required on an ongoing basis, each parent/custodian shall pay the sum of $75. 00 per month. The Court in which the case is pending retains the discretion to deviate from the schedule in a particular case based upon the circumstances of the parties.

Adopted effective November 18, 1997. Amended and renumbered as Rule 3, September 30, 2005, effective October 11, 2005.

LR73–FL00 Rule 4. AUTOMATIC WITHDRAWAL OF APPEARANCE

In Domestic Relation (DR) cases and Paternity (JP) cases, an attorney's Appearance in the case shall automatically be deemed to be withdrawn thirty-five (35) days after the conclusion of the pending action, i.e., Final Decree, Modification, or Citation. If a new action, i.e., Modification or Citation, is filed more than thirty-five (35) days after the conclusion of a prior action, an attorney will need to re-enter his or her Appearance to represent a party in the new action.

SHELBY COUNTY LOCAL CRIMINAL RULES

Amended September 30, 2005, Effective October 11, 2005

Including Amendments Received Through November 1, 2013

Research Notes

These rules may be searched electronically on Westlaw in the IN-RULES database; updates to these rules may be found on Westlaw in IN-RULESUPDATES. For search tips and a summary of database content, consult the Westlaw Scope Screens for each database.

LR73–CR2.2 Rule 1. CRIMINAL CASELOAD ASSIGNMENT

1.1 All misdemeanors and class D Felony cases under Indiana Code 9–30–5 *et seq* shall be filed in Shelby Superior No. 2;

1.2 All A, B, & C felonies (including murder) shall be assigned on a random basis among the three courts by the Shelby County Clerk with Shelby Superior No. 1 receiving forty-five percent (45%) of said cases, Shelby Circuit receiving forty-five percent (45%) of said cases and Shelby Superior No. 2 receiving ten percent (10%) of said cases. Except for the D felony cases under Indiana Code 9–30–5 *et seq*, the remaining D felony cases shall be allocated 45% each to Superior Court 2 and Circuit Court and the remaining 10% to Shelby Superior Court I.

1.3 The most serious level of charge filed determines if the case is assigned automatically to Shelby Superior No. 2 or if the case is randomly assigned by the Shelby County Clerk;

1.4 When the State of Indiana dismisses a pool felony case and chooses to refile that case, the case shall be assigned to the court from which dismissal was taken;

1.5 All co-defendants in pool felony cases shall be assigned to the same court based upon a single random draw by the Shelby County Clerk;

1.5.1 The Shelby County Prosecutor's Office shall notify the Clerk at the time of filing if the cases involve co-defendants. Each case will be assigned an individual cause number. For purposes of this Rule, the cases involve codefendants as provided by I.C. 35–34–1–9 and amendments thereto.

1.6 Except in felony cases involving co-defendants as defined above, any new pool felony case filed against a defendant who has an open pool felony case already pending in any Court, shall be assigned to the Court where the current case is pending. The Shelby County Prosecutor's Office shall notify the Clerk at the time of filing if the defendant has a pending pool felony case.

1.7 A judge of Shelby Circuit or a Superior Court may, by appropriate order entered in the Record of Judgments and Orders, transfer and reassign to any other court of record in the county with jurisdiction to hear the charged offense(s), any pending case subject to acceptance by the receiving court, where the interests of justice or the interest of judicial economy so require.

1.8 The prosecuting attorney or the defendant may seek to transfer a case, and upon good cause shown, a case may be transferred to any of the other courts for consolidation with a companion case, or with other cases pending in that court against the defendant with the acceptance of the judge of the receiving court.

1.9 In the event a motion for change of judge is granted or it becomes necessary to reassign a felony or misdemeanor case in Shelby Circuit or Shelby Superior Courts, the Clerk shall maintain a list containing the names of the judges of the Shelby County Courts and the names of the judges of the circuit and superior courts of Hancock, Rush, Decatur, Bartholomew and Johnson Counties, who have agreed to serve. Whenever an appointment of a successor judge becomes necessary the case shall be reassigned to one of the judges on the Clerk's list on a rotation basis.

1.10 Should a judge not be available for assignment from the Clerk's list or the particular circumstances of the case require a selection of a special judge by the Indiana Supreme Court, the case shall be certified to the Indiana Supreme court pursuant to Criminal Rule 13(d).

Adopted as Joint Local Rule No. 1, effective October 11, 2001. Amended and renumbered as Rule 1, September 30, 2005, effective October 11, 2005. Amended on April 8, 2009. Amended 06–14–2011; effective September 1, 2011.

73–CB00 Rule 2.   BOND SCHEDULE

THE FOLLOWING IS THE PRESUMPTIVE BOND SCHEDULE FOR ALL SHELBY COUNTY COURTS:

2.1 Bond Schedule. Unless otherwise ordered by the Court, the following shall be the amounts set for the bail bonds:

a.	Charge		Bond Amount
	Class C Misdemeanors	$2,000	10% Cash
	Class B Misdemeanors	$3,000	10% Cash
	Class A Misdemeanors	$5,000	10% Cash
	Class D Felony	$7,500	10% Cash
	Class C, B, A Felony		NO BOND
	Murder		NO BOND

b. In the event that an arrest is made without a warrant signed by a judge endorsing a specific bond, the charts above shall establish the bond for a "preliminary charge". In the event that the individual is arrested on more than one "preliminary charge", the bond shall be set in the amount of bond for the most serious offense

2.2 In the event that the arresting officer believes that the above schedule is not appropriate for a specific arrest based upon facts known to the officer or surrounding circumstances, the officer may complete an affidavit in a form substantially conforming to the form attached hereto (Form A) and provide it to the Sheriff's Department and the Sheriff is authorized to hold such arrestee until the sooner of forty-eight (48) hours (excluding weekends and holidays) or until further order of a Judge.

2.3 No bond: this bond schedule shall not be used for nor applicable to the following cases:

2.3.1 A person arrested for a crime while on probation, parole, bond, or while released on their own recognizance. Persons on parole or probation shall have an immediate 15 day probation/parole hold placed upon them by jail staff, including but not limited to persons arrested pursuant to a warrant.

2.3.2 any person arrested on a charge of Invasion of Privacy, Domestic Battery, or Stalking.

2.4 Court Assignments.

a. All misdemeanor and/or class D felony Driving While Intoxicated arrestees will be scheduled by jail personnel·into Superior Court 2.

b. All other D, C, B, and A felonies arrestees are pool felonies and the court will be determined by a pool drawing. Such arrestees shall report to the Shelby County Clerk at the date and time designated by the jail staff when released for information regarding their assigned court, failure to do so may be punished by contempt or additional criminal charges including but not limited to escape.

2.6 Subject to paragraph 2.3, the bond stated on a warrant shall be allowed in all warrant arrests and the arrested person shall report to the appropriate court as instructed by the jail staff.

2.7 Nolle Pros–Upon notification by an authorized representative of the Shelby County Prosecutor's Office that no charges will be filed in the immediate future, the jail may release any person upon their own recognizance. If the prosecutor's office notifies the jail or the court after the arrestee has already posted bond, then such bond shall be held by the clerk until further order of the court.

FORM A

AFFIDAVIT FOR HOLD FOR PRELIMINARY CHARGE

Arrestee Name: _____

Arrestee   DOB: _____ __ _____
_____ Arrestee OLN/ID Card _____

Arrestee Home address: _____

Street: _____

Arrestee City State Zip Code _____

The undersigned law enforcement officer makes this affidavit for the purpose of requesting that the Shelby County Sheriff hold the named arrestee, and that said arrestee shall not be allowed to post bond pursuant to the schedule set by the judges of this county. In support the undersigned states the bond schedule is not appropriate for:

Name _____ (hereinafter arrestee) in that said arrestee:

____ is not a resident of this community and/or appears to have no significant ties to the community and /or appears to the undersigned to present a higher than normal risk to fail to return; or

____ has made threats of violence to this officer or to another person which if carried out would warrant a substantially higher charge and bond, and it appears likely to the undersigned that the arrestee would carry out these threats if permitted to post the standard bond; or

____ is suspected of additional or more serious charges which will require further investigation, and the bond for the offense for which the arrestee is now held is not likely to be sufficient to assure attendance at proceedings for the suspected offense; or

____ other grounds not set forth above: _____
_____
_____
_____.

I affirm under penalties for perjury that the above is true to the best of my knowledge this ___ day of _____, 20 ___ at _____ o'clock ___ m.
_____

Signature

Adopted as Joint Local Rule No. 8, effective Feb. 22, 2000. Amended and renumbered as Rule 2, Sept. 30, 2005, effective Oct. 11, 2005.

73–CR00 Rule 3. AUTOMATIC DISCOVERY IN FELONY CASES

3.1 General Provisions–Felony Cases:

3.1.1 Within thirty (30) days from the entry of an appearance by an attorney for a defendant, or from the formal filing of charges, whichever occurs later, the State shall disclose in all felony cases all relevant items and information under this rule to the defendant, subject to Constitutional limitations and such other limitation as the Court may specifically provide by separate order, and the defendant shall disclose all relevant items and information under this rule to the State within thirty (30) days after the State's disclosure. Both parties shall furnish items disclosed and required to be furnished under this Rule within a reasonable time thereafter.

3.1.2 No written motion is required, except:

3.1.2.1 To compel compliance under this rule;

3.1.2.2 For additional discovery not covered under this rule;

3.1.2.3 For a protective order seeking exemption from the provisions of this rule; or,

3.1.2.4 For an extension of time to comply with this rule.

3.1.3 Although each side has a right to full discovery under the terms of this rule, each side has a corresponding duty to seek out the discovery. Failure to do so may result in the waiver of the right to full discovery under this rule.

3.1.4 The parties may perform these disclosure obligations in any reasonable manner including by delivery in electronic format. If the discovery is in an electronic format, the party offering the discovery must make a reasonable effort to ensure the discovery is in a format that is readily accessible by the other party. Portable Document Format (PDF) and audio mp3 or .wav files are presumptively readily accessible. Alternative compliance with these rules may include a notification to the defendant or defense counsel that material and information being disclosed may be inspected, obtained, tested, copied, or photographed at a specified reasonable time and place.

3.1.5 Discovery shall not be filed with the court.

3.2 State Disclosures:

3.2.1 The State shall disclose the following materials and information within its possession or control: The names and last known addresses of persons whom the State intends to call as witnesses along with copies of their relevant written and recorded statements. However, addresses and other confidential information is subject to the disclosure limitations in Indiana Admin Rule 9 and the Indiana Access to Public Records Act Indiana Code § 5–14–3–1. In lieu of providing an address or phone number, the Prosecutor's Office may designate their office as a contact point for their listed witnesses.

3.2.2 Any written or recorded statements and the substance of any oral statements made by the accused or by a codefendant and a list of witnesses to the making and acknowledgment of such statements.

3.2.3 If applicable, the State shall disclose the existence of grand jury testimony of any person whom the prosecuting attorney may call as a witness at any trial or hearing in the case. In addition, the State shall provide a copy of those portions of any transcript of grand jury minutes, within the State's possession, which contain the testimony of such witness or witnesses. If such transcripts do not exist, the defendant may apply to the Court for an order requiring their preparation;

3.2.4 Any reports or statements of experts, made in connection with the particular case, including results of physical or mental examinations and of scientific tests, experiments or comparisons;

3.2.5 Any books, papers, documents, photographs, or tangible objects that the prosecuting attorney intends to introduce as an exhibit in the hearing or trial or which were obtained from or belong to the accused; and

3.2.6 Any record of prior criminal convictions that may be used for impeachment of the persons whom the State intends to call as witnesses at any hearing or trial.

3.2.7 The State shall disclose to the defendant(s) any material or information within its possession or control that tends to negate the guilt of the accused as to the offenses charged or would tend to reduce the punishment for such offenses.

3.3 Defendant Disclosures: Defendant's counsel (or defendant where defendant is proceeding pro se) shall furnish the State with the following material and information within his or her possession or control:

3.3.1 The names and last known addresses of persons whom the defendant intends to call as witnesses along with copies of their relevant written and recorded statements and the substance of any oral statements made by them;

3.3.2 Any books, papers, documents, photographs, or tangible objects defendant intends to use as evidence or an exhibit at any trial or hearing;

3.3.3 Any medical, scientific, or expert witness evaluations, statements, reports, or testimony which may be used at any trial or hearing;

3.3.4 Any defense, procedural or substantive, which the defendant intends to make at any hearing or trial; and

3.3.5 Any record of prior criminal convictions known to the defendant or defense counsel that may be used for impeachment of the persons whom the defense intends to call at any hearing or trial.

3.4 Defendant's Obligations Upon Request of the State. Upon request by the State, the defendant must produce the person of the accused, subject to constitutional and statutory limitations, for purposes of: appearing in a line-up; speaking for identification by witnesses to an offense; being fingerprinted; posing for photos not involving reenactment of a scene; trying on an article of clothing; permitting samples of blood, hair, or other materials of his body, which involve no unreasonable intrusion; providing a sample of the defendant's handwriting; and submitting to a reasonable physical or medical inspection of the defendant's body.

3.5 Additions, Limitation, And Protective Orders:

3.5.1 *Discretionary Disclosures*: Upon written request and a showing of materiality, the Court, in its discretion, may require additional disclosure not otherwise covered by this rule.

3.5.2 *Denial of Disclosure*: The Court may deny disclosure required by this rule upon a finding that there is substantial risk to any person of physical harm, intimidation, bribery, economic reprisals, or unnecessary annoyance or embarrassment resulting from such disclosure to defendant or counsel.

3.6 Matters Not Subject to Disclosure.

3.6.1 *Work Product*: Disclosure hereunder shall not be required of legal research or records, correspondence, reports, or memoranda to the extent that they contain the opinions, theories, or conclusions of the State or members of its legal or investigative staff, or of defense counsel or counsel's legal or investigative staff; and

3.6.2 *Informants*: Disclosure of an informant's identity shall not be required where there is a paramount interest of non-disclosure and where a failure to disclose will not infringe upon the Constitutional rights of the accused.

3.6.3 *Protective Orders*: Either the State or defense may apply for a protective order for non-disclosure of discovery required hereunder or any additional requested discovery.

3.7 Duty to Supplement Responses: The State and the defendant are under a continuing duty to supplement the discovery disclosures required hereunder as required upon the acquisition of additional information or materials otherwise required to be disclosed hereunder. Supplementation of disclosures shall be made within a reasonable time after the obligation to supplement arises.

3.8 Sanctions Upon Failure to Comply: Failure of a party to comply with either the disclosure requirements or the time limits required by this rule may result in the imposition of sanctions against the noncompliant party. These sanctions may include, but are not limited to, the exclusion of evidence at a trial or hearing, contempt of court, and/or financial sanctions.

LR73–CR02 Rule 4.   SERVICE OF SUBPOENAS IN CRIMINAL CASES

The Shelby County Sheriff's Department shall serve subpoenas without cost in criminal cases where a defendant is represented by a public defender. Personal service on a individual means physically handing the subpoena to the person named on the subpoena.

Adopted as Joint Local Rule No. 8, effective February 22, 2000.   Amended and renumbered as Rule 2, September 30, 2005, effective October 11, 2005.

LR73–CR00 Rule 5.   COMMUNITY TRANSITION VIOLATIONS

Pursuant to Indiana Code 11–10–11.5–11.5 regarding the procedure for offenders who have violated the rules of the Community Transition Program, the Judges of Shelby County authorize the detention of an offender who has violated the rules of the Shelby County Transition Program in the Shelby County Criminal Justice Center pending their return to the Department of Correction upon request of the Director of Shelby County Community Corrections or the Shelby County Prosecutor or Deputy thereof.

Adopted effective June 5, 2003.   Amended and renumbered as Rule 2, September 30, 2005, effective October 11, 2005. Amended and Renumbered as LR73–CR–00–Rule 4, March 16, 2011.

LR73–CR00 Rule 6.   PROBATION FEES

6.1 Any probationer who requests their probation be transferred to a department outside the state of Indiana shall pay a $125 fee to the Shelby County Probation Department through the Clerk of Shelby County.

6.2 Any probationer who lives in Indiana and outside Shelby County for whom a transfer of probation is sought to another probation department in Indiana by the Shelby County Probation Department or the probationer, shall pay a $25.00 fee to Shelby County Probation through the Clerk of Shelby County.

6.3 Each person who is placed on probation as a result of a felony conviction shall pay a $100.00 administrative fee. Each person who is placed on probation as a result of a misdemeanor conviction shall pay a $50.00 administrative fee. Said fees shall be paid to the Shelby County Probation Department through the Clerk of Shelby County and shall be applied first before all other fees.

6.4 The parents of each child adjudicated a delinquent and placed on probation shall be required to pay a $100.00 administrative fee to Shelby County Probation through the Clerk of Shelby County.

6.5 The above fees are in addition to the probation user fees.

Adopted effective July 30, 2003. Amended and renumbered as Rule 3, September 30, 2005, effective October 11, 2005. Renumbered as LR73–CR00 Rule 4 March 16, 2011.

LR73–CR00 Rule 7. LATE PAYMENTS–ADDITIONAL FEE

7.1 Any defendant found to have committed a crime; violated a statute defining an infraction; violated an ordinance of a municipal corporation; or committed a delinquent act; and the defendant is required to pay: court costs, including fees; a fine; or a civil penalty; and the defendant is not determined by the Court imposing the court costs, fine, or civil penalty to be indigent; and the defendant fails to pay to the clerk the costs, fine, or civil penalty in full before the later of the following:

(1) The end of the business day on which the Court enters the conviction or judgment.

(2) The end of the period specified in a payment schedule set for the payment of court costs, fines, and civil penalties under rules adopted for the operation of the Court; then the defendant shall pay an additional $25.00 late payment fee pursuant to IC 33–37–5–22 and the Clerk of the Court shall collect the late payment fee.

7.2 The late payment fees imposed under this rule are authorized for deposit in the clerk's record perpetuation fund under IC 33–37–7–2 and the clerk may use any money in the fund for the following purposes: (1) The preservation of records. (2) The improvement of record keeping systems and equipment.

LR73–CR00 Rule 8. SCHEDULE OF FEES FOR COURT ALCOHOL AND DRUG PROGRAM SERVICES

The schedule of fees set forth under Indiana Code 33–37–4–1 and Indiana Code 35–38–2–1 shall be applicable in all court alcohol and drug program services and shall not exceed $400.00.

LR73–CR00 Rule 9. AUTOMATIC WITHDRAWAL OF APPEARANCE

In all criminal cases, an attorney's Appearance in the case shall automatically be deemed to be withdrawn thirty-five (35) days after the conclusion of the pending action, i.e., not guilty verdict, sentencing. If a new action, i.e., Modification or probation violation, is filed more than thirty-five (35) days after the conclusion of a prior action, an attorney will need to re-enter his or her Appearance to represent a party in the new action.

SHELBY COUNTY LOCAL SMALL CLAIMS RULES

Amended September 30, 2005, Effective October 11, 2005

Including Amendments Received Through November 1, 2013

Research Notes

These rules may be searched electronically on Westlaw *in the* IN-RULES *database; updates to these rules may be found on Westlaw in IN-RULESUPDATES. For search tips and a summary of database content, consult the Westlaw Scope Screens for each database.*

LR73–SC8 Rule 1. POLICIES AND PROCEDURES FOR IMPLEMENTATION OF SMALL CLAIMS RULE 8

The following policies and procedures will be utilized in order to properly implement Small Claims Rule 8:

1.1 A natural person may appear pro se or by counsel.

1.2 A sole proprietor may appear by the sole owner or by counsel.

1.3 A partnership may appear by a general partner or by counsel.

1.4 A sole proprietor or partnership may appear by a full-time employee if the claim does not exceed $1,500.00 and proper filings have been made.

1.5 A corporation or limited liability corporation, (LLC), must appear by counsel if the claim exceeds $1,500.00.

1.6 A corporation or LLC may appear by a full-time employee if the claim does not exceed $1,500.00 and proper filings have been made.

1.7 The filings required for an employee to appear in a small claims proceedings are as follows:

a. A corporation or LLC must have filed a resolution designating the employee and expressing compliance with Small Claims Rule 8.

b. A sole proprietor or partnership must have filed a certificate by the owner or each of the partners designating the employee and expressing compliance with Small Claims Rule 8.

c. Each designated employee must have filed an affidavit affirming that he or she is a full-time employee and that they have not been suspended or disbarred from the practice of law in Indiana.

1.8 The filings noted above shall be filed in Shelby County Superior Court II prior to any action being undertaken by the party. If an action is already filed, it will not proceed, and may be dismissed or defaulted if proper filings are not submitted.

a. Miscellaneous entries shall be made for each filing in the Clerk's Office. Superior Court II staff shall provide minutes to the Clerk for those entries.

b. A master list of filings shall be maintained by Superior Court II and provided to the Clerk.

c. Basic forms will be available from Superior Court II and the Clerk's Office. Copies are attached as part of this rule.

1.9 Filings shall expire after five years and must be re-filed after that period.

1.10 Pursuant to rule 2(b) (4) (a) of the Indiana rules for small claims if a claim involves a written contract, which would include a written lease, it must be attached to the notice. One copy for all defendants and one copy for the court must be provided to the clerk. The clerk has been instructed not to accept filing of a small claim that does not comply with this rule.

Adopted effective October 8, 2004. Amended and renumbered as Rule 1, September 30, 2005, effective October 11, 2005. Amended Jan 1, 2012.

LR73–SC00 Rule 2. SEQUENTIAL NUMBERING OF PROCEEDINGS SUPPLEMENTAL AND GARNISHMENT PETITIONS

All Proceedings Supplemental and Garnishment pleadings shall be numbered sequentially in the title. Eg. 1st Proceeding Supplemental, 2nd Proceeding Supplemental; 1st Verified Motion to Establish Garnishment, 2nd Verified Motion to Establish Garnishment, etc.

TIPPECANOE COUNTY LOCAL RULES OF COURT

Adopted August 1, 2006, Effective January 1, 2007

Including Amendments Received Through November 1, 2013

Research Notes

These rules may be searched electronically on Westlaw *in the* IN-RULES *database; updates to these rules may be found on* Westlaw *in* IN-RULESUPDATES. *For search tips and a summary of database content, consult the Westlaw Scope Screens for each database.*

LR79–AR 1(E) Rule 1. COUNTY CASELOAD PLAN

As of the date of the Order adopting these Rules, and subject to any modifications which may subsequently be made, the Tippecanoe County Caseload Plan reads as follows:

All cases wherein the most serious charge alleged is Murder, a Class A, B, or C felony and those Class D felonies specified below shall be assigned to Tippecanoe Circuit Court, Superior Court of Tippecanoe County, and Superior Court No. 2 of Tippecanoe County, on a random basis according to the following ratio:

Court	Ratio
Tippecanoe Circuit Court	2
Superior Court of Tippecanoe County	4
Superior Court No. 2 of Tippecanoe County	4

For any defendant who has a Class A, B, or C felony case pending or who is serving a Class A, B, or C felony sentence, whether executed or suspended, any new case in which the most serious charge alleged is a Class A, B, or C felony shall be filed in the court having jurisdiction of the oldest such prior case.

Upon learning that such a case has been filed in the wrong court, the prosecutor shall within 14 days move to transfer the case to the proper court.

Class D felony cases assigned to Tippecanoe Circuit Court, Superior Court of Tippecanoe County, and Superior Court No. 2 of Tippecanoe County are as follows:

I.C. 35–42–2–1 (a) (2) (b)	Battery on a Child
I.C. 35–42–4–4 (b) (1) and (2)	Possession of Child Pornography; Child Exploitation
I.C. 35–42–4–5 (a)	Vicarious Sexual Gratification
I.C. 35–42–4–6	Child Solicitation
I.C. 35–42–4–7	Child Seduction
I.C. 35–42–4–9 (b)	Sexual Misconduct with a Minor
I.C. 35–49–3–3	Dissemination of Matter Harmful to Minors
I.C. 35–46–1–4	Neglect of a Dependent
I.C. 35–43–1–1 (d)	Arson
I.C. 35–48–4–4	Dealing in Schedule V Controlled Substance

All Class D felonies, misdemeanors, and infractions alleging a violation of Indiana Code Title 9, Traffic Code, and only those civil plenary cases with claims up to $10,000 shall be assigned to Superior Court No. 6 of Tippecanoe County.

All Class D felonies, misdemeanors, and infractions alleging a violation of Indiana Code Title 35, Article 48, Controlled Substances, and not set forth in paragraph 2 above, and only those civil cases involving small claims and landlord tenant's claims, shall be filed in Superior Court No. 4 of Tippecanoe County. Glue Sniffing, in violation of Indiana Code 35–46–6–2, and Public Intoxication cases shall be filed in Superior Court No. 4 of Tippecanoe County.

All remaining Class D felonies, misdemeanors, and infraction cases not specifically set forth above shall be filed in Superior Court No. 5 of Tippecanoe County.

Superior Court No. 3 of Tippecanoe County exercises juvenile jurisdiction and will not receive filings of felony or misdemeanor cases. A case wherein juvenile jurisdiction is waived may be assigned to a court by agreement of the parties. In the absence of such agreement, the case shall be filed in accordance with the Local Rule on Assignments of Criminal Cases.

When it is alleged that defendants jointly commit a crime or crimes and the most serious charge alleged is Murder, the cases shall be assigned together to Tippecanoe Circuit Court, Superior Court of Tippecanoe County or Superior Court No. 2 of Tippecanoe County on a random basis in the ratio of 2:4:4 set forth above.

Where it is alleged that defendants jointly commit a crime or crimes, and the most serious charge alleged is a Class A, B or C felony, their cases shall be filed together in the same court. In any such cases where one or more of the defendants has a Class A, B or C felony case pending or is serving a Class A, B, or C felony sentence, whether executed or suspended, all the cases shall be filed in the court having jurisdiction of the oldest such prior case.

Any case in which the most serious charge is a Class D felony, misdemeanor or infraction shall be filed as specified above, notwithstanding any charges against co-defendants.

A judge, by appropriate order may transfer and reassign to any other court of record in the county, any pending case, subject to acceptance by the receiving court.

A case transferred to Tippecanoe County by reason of change of venue from another county may be assigned to a court by agreement of the parties. In the absence of such an agreement, the case shall be filed in accordance with this Local Rule on Case Assignments.

When the State of Indiana dismisses a case and chooses to re-file that case, the case shall be assigned to the court from which dismissal was taken.

All petitions for civil orders of protection shall be filed initially in Superior Court No. 5 of Tippecanoe County.

The first eight (8) pro se dissolution petitions in which a fee waiver is requested each month shall be assigned to Superior Court No. 2. If more than eight such petitions are filed in a given month, the remaining petitions shall be assigned in rotation to the Circuit Court, Superior Court and Superior Court No. 2, in that order.

The Presiding Judge of the Superior Courts 4, 5, and 6 shall assign the Magistrate to serve any of the Tippecanoe Circuit or Superior Courts in a manner which provides the greater assistance to the courts with greater caseloads. Considering the 2010 caseloads, the Superior Court No. 4 will be limited to one-half day each week and the Circuit Court to two one-half days each week. The balance of the Magistrate's time will be allocated to the courts as set forth above.

In all other civil cases, parties may file in the court of their choosing.

Adopted Aug. 1, 2006, effective Jan. 1, 2007; amended Nov. 30, 2007, effective Jan. 1, 2008; amended Jan. 6, 2010, effective Jan. 1, 2010; amended Oct. 10, 2011, effective retroactive to Jan. 1, 2011; amended effective September 1, 2012.

LR79–TR 5(E) Rule 2.   FILING

A. Flat Filing. All papers presented for filing with the Clerk or Court shall be flat and unfolded.

B. Number of Copies. All Orders submitted to the Court shall be in sufficient number so that the original and one copy may be retained by the clerk and a copy mailed to each party.

C. Proposed Orders Required. The moving party, unless the Court directs otherwise, shall furnish the Court with proposed Orders in the following matters: motions for enlargement of time, for continuance, for default or default judgment, to compel discovery, for restraining order or injunction, for immediate possession of real estate or personal property, for appointment of receiver, for findings of fact and conclusions of law, for dismissal of an action, for judgment in a collection matter or mortgage or lien foreclosure, and in such other matters as the Court directs.

Adopted Aug. 1, 2006, effective Jan. 1, 2007. Amended effective Jan. 1, 2012.

LR79–TR 5(E) Rule 3.   MOTION HOUR

If the Court conducts motion hour, the same shall be for the consideration of routine matters, procedural motions, setting dates for trials, pre-trial conferences, and hearings and for other matters which can ordinarily be heard without evidence or argument. Attorneys shall notify opposing counsel in advance before approaching the Judge at motion hour for any matter requiring action to be taken by the Court.

Adopted Aug. 1, 2006, effective Jan. 1, 2007. Amended effective Jan. 1, 2012.

LR79–TR 6(B) Rule 4.   EXTENSIONS OF TIME

(1) Initial Extension. In a civil action where a party desires an initial 30—day extension of time to file a responsive pleading or to respond to a discovery request, the party shall contact opposing counsel before the due date and solicit agreement to the extension. If there is no objection or opposing counsel cannot with due diligence be reached, the party seeking the extension shall file a notice with the Court reciting the lack of objection to the extension or that opposing counsel could not with due diligence be reached. No further filings with the Court nor action by the Court shall be required for the extension. If opposing counsel objects to the request for extension, the party seeking the extension shall file a formal motion for such extension and shall recite in the motion the efforts to obtain agreement.

(2) Other Extensions. Any other request for an extension of time, unless made in open Court or at a conference, shall be made by written motion. If opposing counsel objects to the request for extension, the party seeking the extension shall recite in the motion the effort to obtain agreement; or recite that there is no objection.

(3) Due Dates. Any notice or motion filed pursuant to this rule shall state the date such response was initially due and the date on which the response will be due after the extension.

Adopted Aug. 1, 2006, effective Jan. 1, 2007. Amended effective Jan. 1, 2012.

LR79–TR73 Rule 5. TELEPHONE CONFERENCING

A. Purpose. To expedite the Court's business, the Court encourages telephone conferencing for the hearing of motions, for pre-trial and status conferences, and for other matters which may reasonably be conducted by telephone.

B. Hearing on Motions or Status Conferences. Within five (5) days after receipt of notice of hearing on a motion, any party or attorney may request that the Court conduct the hearing by telephone conference with the Court. If the Court sets the hearing for telephone conference, the party requesting the telephone conference shall arrange and place the call, unless otherwise ordered by the Court.

Adopted Aug. 1, 2006, effective Jan. 1, 2007. Amended effective Jan. 1, 2012.

LR79–TR12 Rule 6. MOTIONS

A. Applicability. This rule shall apply to motions under Trial Rule 12, contested motions to continue hearings or trials, discovery motions, and any other contested motions.

B. Briefs and Memoranda. Unless the procedure for a motion is governed otherwise by the Indiana Rules of Trial Procedure, an adverse party shall have fifteen (15) days after service of a motion in which to file a response, and the moving party shall have seven (7) days in which to file a reply. The court may in its discretion shorten or lengthen the time for a response or a reply. Failure to file a response or reply within the prescribed time shall subject such motions to summary ruling. Any party may request the court hold a hearing on a motion.

C. Notice of hearing. If the movant procures a date for hearing on a motion, the movant shall promptly give notice to all adverse parties of the date and time of such scheduled hearing.

Adopted Aug. 1, 2006, effective Jan. 1, 2007. Amended effective Jan. 1, 2012.

LR79–TR–53.5 Rule 7. CONTINUANCES

Before requesting a continuance of a matter, the moving party shall confer with the other parties to determine any objections and dates for rescheduling when all parties are available. Such objections and alternative dates shall be reported in the motion for continuance.

Adopted Aug. 1, 2006, effective Jan. 1, 2007. Amended effective Jan. 1, 2012.

LR79–TR–3.1 Rule 8. WITHDRAWAL OF APPEARANCE

Motions to withdraw an appearance shall be in writing with an attached notice to the client of intention to withdraw. The notice to the client of the intention to withdraw shall include an explanation to the client of (i) the present status of the case; (ii) the dates of scheduled hearings or other pending matters in the case; and (iii) the potential consequences to the client's case resulting from failure of the client to act promptly or to secure new counsel.

Adopted Aug. 1, 2006, effective Jan. 1, 2007. Amended effective Jan. 1, 2012.

LR79–TR79 Rule 9. WITHDRAWAL OF ORIGINAL RECORDS

Original pleadings, papers, exhibits or other official materials in the custody of the Clerk, reporter or other officer of the Court shall not be withdrawn from the officer having custody thereof except upon (i) the Order of the Judge of the Court where the record is held, and (ii) upon leaving a proper receipt with the Clerk, reporter or officer.

Adopted Aug. 1, 2006, effective Jan. 1, 2007. Amended effective Jan. 1, 2012.

LR79–CR2.2 Rule 10. CASE REASSIGNMENT AND SPECIAL JUDGES IN CRIMINAL CASES

In the event a change of judge is granted pursuant to Indiana Criminal Rule 12 or it becomes necessary to assign another judge in any felony or misdemeanor proceeding, the case shall be returned to the Clerk of court for random selection of another court from among all the courts in Tippecanoe County other than Superior Court No. 3. On selection, the case shall be reassigned by the Clerk to the selected court.

In the event no judge is available for assignment or reassignment of a felony or a misdemeanor case, such case shall be certified to the Indiana Supreme Court for the appointment of a special judge. In the event the judge presiding in a felony or misdemeanor case concludes that the unique circumstances presented in such proceeding require appointment by the Indiana Supreme Court of a special judge, the presiding judge may request the Indiana Supreme Court for such appointment.

Adopted June 23, 2010, effective June 1, 2010. Amended effective Jan. 1, 2012.

LR79–TR79 Rule 11. SPECIAL JUDGE SELECTION IN CIVIL CASES

Juvenile Cases: To ensure the effective use of all judicial resources within this Administrative District, the juvenile court shall maintain a list of eligible judges including judges (1) regularly presiding over juvenile cases within this Administrative District and (2) from contiguous counties who have agreed to serve as special judge in juvenile court and, when required pursuant to Trial Rule 79 to assign a special judge, shall assign a judge from said list on a rotating basis.

All Other Civil Cases: The six (6) judges of Tippecanoe County (not having juvenile case load) shall maintain a computer generated random selection system among said six (6) judges, and from among eligible judges pursuant to TR 79 (J), to be managed through the County Clerk's Office and the County Data Processing Department. Whenever a special judge needs to be assigned pursuant to Trial Rule 79 (H), the judge shall direct that a judge be selected by said random process first from the eligible judges in Tippecanoe County and then from the eligible judges from within the Administrative District.

If the judge selected by this Rule is disqualified or no judge is eligible to serve as special judge, the judge having jurisdiction of the cause shall notify the Indiana Supreme Court of the circumstances relevant thereto and request that a special judge be appointed by the Supreme Court.

Adopted June 23, 2010, effective June 1, 2010. Amended effective Jan. 1, 2012; April 1, 2013.

LR–79–AR00 Rule 12. TIPPECANOE COUNTY COURT SERVICES PROGRAM

Program 575		Program 576	
Whole Program/multiple charges or felony	$350	CAT Program	$400*
Whole Program—1st time	$350	Urine Drug Screen	$ 35
Classes only	$200	Community Service	$100
Evaluation only	$150	Reschedule	$ 25
Case management only	$200		
Transfer fee	$100		
Reschedule	$ 25		
2nd case number before 1st case closed	$100		

* CAT Program with new fee includes evaluation and classes. Old CAT Program was simply monitoring.

Amended effective May 1, 2012.

LR79–AR15 Rule 13. COURT REPORTER SERVICES

Section One. Definitions. The following definitions shall apply under this local rule:

(1) A Court Reporter is a person who is specifically designated by a court to perform the official court reporting services for the court including preparing a transcript of the record.

(2) Equipment means all physical items owned by the court or other governmental entity and used by a court reporter in performing court reporting services. Equipment shall include, but not limited to, telephones, computer hardware, software programs, disks, tapes, and any other device used for recording and storing, and transcribing electronic data.

(3) Work space means that portion of the court's facilities dedicated to each court reporter, including

but not limited to actual space in the courtroom and any designated office space.

(4) Page means the page unit of transcript which results when a recording is transcribed in the form required by Indiana Rule of Appellate Procedure 7.2, and includes the index and table of contents pages.

(5) Recording means the electronic, mechanical, stenographic, digital, or other recording made as required by Indiana Rule of Trial Procedure 74.

(6) Regular hours worked means those hours which the court is regularly scheduled to work during any given work week. Depending on the particular court, these hours may vary from court to court within the county but remain the same for each work week.

(7) Gap hours worked means those hours worked that are in excess of the regular hours worked but hours not in excess of forty (40) hours per work week.

(8) Overtime hours worked means those hours worked in excess of forty (40) hours per work [1]

(9) Workweek means a seven (7) consecutive day week that consistently begins and ends on the same days throughout the year; i.e. Sunday through Saturday, Wednesday through Tuesday, Friday through Thursday.

(10) Court means the particular court for which the court reporter performs services. Court may also mean all of the courts in Tippecanoe County.

(11) County indigent transcript means a transcript that is paid for from county funds and is for the use on behalf of a litigant who has been declared indigent by a court.

(12) State indigent transcript means a transcript that is paid for from state funds and is for the use on behalf of a litigant who has been declared indigent by a court.

(13) Private transcript means a transcript, including but not limited to a deposition transcript that is paid for by a private party.

Section Two. Salaries and Per Page Fees.

(1) Court Reporters shall be paid an annual salary for time spent working under the control, direction and direct supervision of their supervising court during any regular work hours, gap hours or overtime hours. The supervising court shall enter into a written agreement with the court reporters which outlines the manner in which the court reporter is to be compensated for gap and overtime hours; i.e. monetary compensation or compensatory time off regular work hours.

(2) Court reporters may contract to prepare transcripts outside the hours in which their attendance is required and outside hours they perform other work pursuant to their employment relationship.

(a) The maximum per page fee a court reporter may charge for the preparation of a county indigent transcript shall be $4.00; the court reporter shall submit a claim to the ancillary court reporter, who shall submit the claim to the county for the preparation of any county indigent transcripts. The ancillary court department shall have the responsibility of maintaining the budget for county indigent transcripts.

(3) The maximum per page fee a court reporter may charge for the preparation of a state indigent transcript shall be $4.00. The court reporter shall submit the invoice for state indigent transcripts directly to the state.

(4) The maximum per page fee a court reporter may charge for the preparation of a private transcript shall be $4.00. The court reporter shall submit the invoice for private transcripts directly to the attorney requesting the transcription. A deposit in the amount of the estimated work shall be required from the attorney making a private transcript request.

(5) The per page fee for expedited transcripts shall be $6.50 within 24 hours notice and $5.00 within three (3) days notice.

(6) An additional labor charge may be assessed in the amount of the court reporter's hourly rate based upon the court reporter's annual court compensation or $15.00 per hour, whichever is greater, for the time spent binding the transcript and the exhibit binders. An additional charge shall be assessed for the office supplies required and utilized for the binding and the electronic transmission of the transcript, pursuant to Indiana Rules of Appellate Procedure 28 and 29, pursuant to a Schedule of Transcript Supplies published annually by the Judges of the County.

(7) Each court reporter shall report, at least on an annual basis, all transcript fees received for the preparation of county indigent, state indigent or private transcripts to the Indiana Supreme Court Division of State Court Administration. The reporting shall be made on forms prescribed by the Division of State Court Administration.

Section Three.   Private Practice.

(1) If a court reporter elects to engage in private practice through the recording of a deposition and/or preparing of a deposition transcript, and the court reporter desires to utilize the court's equipment, work space and supplies, and the court agrees to the use of the court equipment for such purpose, the court and the court reporter shall enter into a written agreement which must, at a minimum, designate the following:

(a) The reasonable market rate for the use of equipment, work space and supplies;

(b) The method by which records are to be kept for the use of equipment, work space and supplies; and

(c) The method by which the court reporter is to reimburse the court for the use of the equipment, work space and supplies.

(2) If a court reporter elects to engage in private practice through the recording of a deposition and/or preparing of a deposition transcript, all such private practice work shall be conducted outside of regular working hours.

Adopted as Local Rule 2003–I. Amended and renumbered as Administrative Rule 1, Aug. 1, 2006, effective Jan. 1, 2007. Amended and renumbered as Local Rule 13 effective Jan. 1, 2012.

1 So in original. Probably should read "week".

LR79–AR15 Rule 14.   ASSIGNED COUNSEL AND GUARDIAN AD LITEM FEES

1.   Assigned Counsel Fees.

a.   Assigned counsel in pauper cases shall be paid by the court at the rate of $75.00 per hour, unless state law requires a different rate of payment.

b.   Assigned counsel shall submit verified, itemized claims using units of time no larger than one-quarter hour, detailing the work for which they seek payment.

2.   Guardian Ad Litem Fees.

a.   The order appointing a guardian ad litem shall specify the guardian's hourly fee, the amount of the retainer, and the allocation of the guardian's fee between the parties.

b.   Guardians ad litem may agree with the parties to a case upon the fee they will charge.

c.   If there is a written agreement signed by the parties, or a court order entered at the time of appointment establishing the guardian's fees, the court will approve an agreed fee no greater than $200.00 per hour.

d.   A fee established by court order entered at the time of appointment or by written agreement may be enforced by judgment and supplemental proceedings.

e.   In the absence of a written agreement or court order entered at the time of appointment, the court shall enforce payment at the assigned counsel rate established by section 1 (a) of this order.

f.   If the guardian is unable to collect his or her fee from the parties, the guardian may apply for payment to the court. The court shall then conduct a hearing to determine if the delinquent party is indigent. If the court finds that the delinquent party is indigent, the court shall order payment of the guardian's fee from the Family Relations Fund. The payment from the Family Relations Fund shall be calculated by multiplying the total hours billed by the guardian by the assigned counsel rate and subtracting the total amount previously received by the guardian.

Adopted as Local Rule 2003–2. Amended and renumbered as Administrative Rule 2, Aug. 1, 2006, effective Jan. 1, 2007. Amended and renumbered as Local Rule 14, effective Jan. 1, 2012.

LR79–JR4 Rule 15.   LOCAL RULE REGARDING JURY RULES

Pursuant to the Order of the Supreme Court of Indiana, adopted December 31, 2001, and amended July 19, 2002, amending the Indiana Jury Rules, and in the exercise of its inherent authority to supervise the administration of all courts of this state, this Local Rule is adopted and promulgated.

Jury Rule 4, Notice of Selection of Jury Pool and Summons for Jury Service, mandates that the Judges of the Courts of Record of Tippecanoe County select by Local Rule, one of the two procedures outlined therein for summoning jurors.

The Judges of the Courts of Record of Tippecanoe County, being duly advised, hereby promulgate this Local Rule adopting the two-tier notice and summons system described in Jury Rule 4. The jury qualification form and notice will be the first tier and summoning the prospective juror at least one week before service will be the second tier.

The Bailiff of each court of record, as well as the Clerk of Tippecanoe County, is hereby designated as a Jury Administrator.

Adopted Aug. 1, 2006, effective Jan. 1, 2007. Renumbered as Local Rule 15, effective Jan. 1, 2012.

LR79–CR00 Rule 16.   BAIL SCHEDULE

Unless otherwise ordered by a judicial officer, the Sheriff of Tippecanoe County is hereby ordered to follow this bail schedule for the setting of bail for all persons arrested without warrants for criminal offenses committed in Tippecanoe County:

Murder	No Bond
Attempted Murder or Class A felony committed with deadly weapon	$50,000 surety and $5,000 cash*
Class A felony	$25,000 surety and $2,500 cash*
Class B felony	$12,500 surety and $1,250 cash*
Class C felony	$5,000 surety and $500 cash*
Escape, Habitual Substance Offender, Failure to Register (D felony)	$5,000 surety only
Class D felony	$5,000 surety or cash bond of $500*
Class A misdemeanor	$2,500 surety or cash bond of $250*
Class B misdemeanor	$2,500 surety or cash bond of $250*
Class C misdemeanor	$2,500 surety or cash bond of $250*

*   The cash amount shown represents the 10% cash bond amount.

   A.   Multiple offenses. If a person is arrested for allegedly committing more than one offense, bail shall be in the amount established for the most serious offense.

   B.   Posting Bond. The total surety and total cash (100% of cash) amounts may be paid in full with cash only or surety only. Property bonds must first be approved by a Judge. When a 10% cash bond is posted with the Clerk, the arrested person and depositor must sign an Agreement on Disposition of cash bond, and the 10% cash bond must be posted in the arrested person's name only. Upon non-filing, dismissal, or acquittal, the 10% cash bond posted may be returned less publicly paid costs of representation and the administration fee. Otherwise, after the sentencing of an arrested person, the 10% cash bond will be retained by the Clerk to pay public defender fees, restitution, court costs, fines or other fees ordered by the Court.

   C.   No bond until seen by judicial officer. This bail schedule shall not be used for any person arrested for committing an offense, attempting to commit an offense, or conspiracy to commit an offense, listed below:

1. Child Molesting
2. Child Solicitation
3. Rape
4. Criminal Deviate Conduct
5. Vicarious Sexual Gratification
6. Sexual Conduct in Presence of Minor
7. Child Exploitation
8. Child Seduction
9. Sexual Battery
10. Kidnapping of Minor
11. Criminal Confinement of Minor
12. Possession of Child Pornography
13. Promoting Prostitution
14. Promoting Human Trafficking of Minor
15. Sexual Misconduct with a Minor
16. Incest

In these cases, the amount and conditions of bail will be set by a judicial officer following a bail hearing in open court not more than forty-eight (48) hours after the person has been arrested, except if the person is arrested when the courthouse is closed, then the bail hearing will be held on the next working day. The Sheriff shall notify the Magistrate's Court and the Prosecuting Attorney's Office of any persons held without bail pursuant to this provision.

C.[1] Crimes resulting in bodily injury or alleging domestic violence. If a person is arrested for a crime (other than a driving offense) that results in bodily injury to a victim or that alleges domestic violence, the person shall be detained for twelve (12) hours without the opportunity to post bond. After the expiration of twelve (12) hours, the person may be released upon the posting of bond in the amount set forth in the bond schedule above, and by signing and agreeing to follow a "10 DAY NO-CONTACT ORDER AS A CONDITION OF PRE-TRIAL RE-LEASE" as to the alleged victim(s), as set forth in Appendix A below. The person shall not be released without their signature, even if they post the monetary bond. When the person is released, the Sheriff shall provide notification to any alleged victims if so requested.

D. Exceptions to the bail schedule. All persons living outside Tippecanoe County or its adjacent counties (including Benton, Carroll, Clinton, Fountain, Montgomery, Warren and White) must post bond pursuant to the bail schedule above. However, the following exceptions apply to persons living in Tippecanoe County and its adjacent counties:

1. *Public Intoxication*: Hold 12 hours, then release on own recognizance if not impaired.

2. *Operating While Intoxicated or Operating Over Legal Limit (Misdemeanor)*: Hold for time period specified below, then release on own recognizance.

.08 - .09	3 hours
.10 - .11	4 hours
.12 - .13	5 hours
.14	6 hours
.15 - .16	7 hours
.17	8 hours
.18 - .19	9 hours
.20	10 hours
.21 - .22	11 hours
.23 or breath test refusal	12 hours
.24 - .25	13 hours
.26	14 hours
.27 - .28	15 hours
.29	16 hours
.30	17 hours
.31 or above	24 hours

3. *Minor Consuming (Class C Misdemeanor), Possession of Marijuana (Class A Misdemeanor), Possession of Paraphernalia (Class A Misdemeanor)*: If not impaired at time of arrest, book-in and immediately release on own recognizance. If impaired or actively using at the time of arrest, book-in, hold a minimum of four hours (and longer if still impaired after four hours) and then release on own recognizance.

4. *Operating While Suspended (Class A Misdemeanor) or Operating While Never Receiving a License (Class C Misdemeanor)*: Release on own recognizance.

E. Deviations from Bail Schedule.

1. *Before Initial Hearing*: A judicial officer may deviate from the Bail Schedule, or order that the arrested person be held without bail until seen by a judicial officer, upon reviewing a verified motion concerning safety or flight.

2. *At Initial Hearing*: A judicial officer may deviate from the Bail Schedule, and may order other conditions of pre-trial release, after considering evidence at the Initial Hearing.

3. *After Initial Hearing*: Once a judicial officer has set the amount of bail or other conditions of pre-trial release after the Initial Hearing, motions to modify the order shall be presented to the respective court in writing, and proper notice of the hearing shall be given to the parties and attorneys of record.

F. Waiver from Juvenile Court. When a child is waived to adult court, the initial bail amount set in the juvenile court shall remain in effect unless and until it is modified in the adult court.

G. Conditions of Pre–Trial Release. Whether released after posting bond, or released on their own recognizance, the arrested person's pre-trial release is conditioned upon maintaining good and lawful behavior, appearing in court for all court appearances, informing the respective court in writing of any change of address within 48 hours, not using or possessing illegal drugs or alcohol, and complying with all other conditions of pre-trial release set by a judicial officer. For all felony offenses, the arrested person may not leave the State of Indiana without prior approval of the court. A violation of any condition of pre-trial release may result in the court revoking the arrested person's bond and the issuing a warrant for arrest.

Adopted April 1, 2013, effective April 1, 2013.

TIPPECANOE COUNTY RULES OF FAMILY LAW

Adopted Effective January 1, 2012

Including Amendments Received Through November 1, 2013

Research Notes

These rules may be searched electronically on Westlaw *in the* IN-RULES *database; updates to these rules may be found on Westlaw in* IN-RULESUPDATES. *For search tips and a summary of database content, consult the Westlaw Scope Screens for each database.*

PREAMBLE

These local rules have been enacted to help effectuate a dignified and effective means of resolving all family law disputes, but especially those disputes involving minor children. While recognizing our adversarial system for resolving family law problems, these local rules mandate that attorneys not ignore but embrace their equally important roles as negotiators and advisors and their special responsibility for the quality of justice.

These local rules are based upon the Lake County Rules of Family Law. The Lake County Rules contain extensive commentary which is incorporated herein by reference. The Judges of Tippecanoe County are grateful to Charlie Asher for advocating the philosophy of Cooperative Divorce and developing the websites incorporated into these rules.

Adopted effective Jan. 1, 2012.

TR 79–FL00 Rule 1. SCOPE, CITATION, AND DEFINITION, COOPERATIVE APPROACH AND LIBERAL CONSTRUCTION

A. Scope. These rules shall apply to family cases in the Tippecanoe Circuit Court and all the Superior Courts, I, II, III, IV, V, and VI of Tippecanoe County.

B. Citation. These rules may be cited as the Tippecanoe County Rules of Family Law and abbreviated as F. L. R.

C. Definition. Family cases shall include all cases involving claims for or related to marital dissolution or separation, paternity, child custody, parenting time or visitation with a child, and support of a child or spouse.

Adopted effective Jan. 1, 2012.

TR 79–FL00 Rule 2. STATEMENT OF POLICY AND PURPOSE

The Circuit and Superior Courts of Tippecanoe County are committed to a cooperative model for the handling of family cases by parents, attorneys, and judges. These rules shall be liberally construed and applied to serve the healthy and child-sensitive functioning of families. In all family cases with children, the goal will be protecting the best interests of those children.

Adopted effective Jan. 1, 2012.

TR 79–FL00 Rule 3. GENERAL OBLIGATIONS OF COOPERATION OF ATTORNEYS AND PARTIES

A. Attorneys and parties in family cases are expected to act with the courts as co-problem solvers, not mere problem-reporters. Attorneys shall both inform and remind their clients about the judicial expectations of cooperation in family cases, assist their clients to understand and observe these standards, and encourage clients to participate in co-parenting classes, counseling, mediation, and other appropriate problem-solving processes.

B. To establish and maintain an atmosphere which fosters cooperative problem-solving, all parties and attorneys shall:

(1) explore resources which may reduce conflict, build cooperation, and protect children;

(2) attempt reasonable cooperative measures before resorting to the court;

(3) avoid disrespectful language and behavior; and,

(4) avoid unnecessary motions or petitions, hearing and arguments.

Adopted effective Jan. 1, 2012.

LR 79–FL00 Rule 4. INITIAL AND PROVISIONAL HEARINGS

Unless considerations of safety or other good cause make it unreasonable, before the date and time set for an initial or provisional hearing, counsel shall meet with each other (or any unrepresented party) in a good-faith attempt to resolve all matters.

Adopted effective Jan. 1, 2012.

LR 79–FL00 Rule 5. MANDATORY WEBSITE WORK FOR PARENTS

A. Dissolution of Marriage. In all dissolution cases where the parties have any children together under the age of 18, both parties shall complete the work on www.UpToParents.org within 30 days of initial filing.

B. Legal Separation. In all separation cases where the parties have any children together under the age of 18, both parties shall complete the work on www.WhileWeHeal.org within 30 days of initial filing.

C. Paternity. In all paternity cases, both parents shall complete the work on www.ProudToParent.org within 30 days of the court's finding of paternity.

D. Following completion of the website work required by this rule, the parents shall merge or exchange their chosen Commitments from their website work.

Adopted effective Jan. 1, 2012.

LR 79–FL00 Rule 6. CO–PARENTING CLASS

A. Dissolution of Marriage and Legal Separation. Mandatory Attendance. In all dissolution and separation cases where the parties have any children together under the age of 18, both parties shall complete a co-parenting class. The court may order both parties to attend additional co-parenting classes in post-decree matters.

B. Paternity. In all paternity cases the court may order the parties to attend and complete a co-parenting class.

Adopted effective Jan. 1, 2012.

LR 79–FL00 Rule 7. PROOF OF COMPLIANCE

A. Dissolution of Marriage and Legal Separation. To monitor compliance, within 60 days of the initial filing of an action for dissolution or separation, each party shall file a verified certification of their completion of the mandatory website work as required under FLR. 5, above, and of any mandatory co-parenting class as required under FLR. 6, above, a sample form of which is attached hereto as Appendix "A".

B. Paternity. To monitor compliance, within 45 days of the court's finding of paternity, each party shall file a verified certification of completion of the mandatory website work as required under FLR 5, above. A sample form is attached hereto as Appendix "B".

C. Any party failing to timely file such a certification may be subject to a hearing on such a failure.

Adopted effective Jan. 1, 2012.

LR 79–FL00 Rule 8. PARENTING PLAN PROPOSALS

A. The Indiana Parenting Time Guidelines provide useful outlines of the **minimum** time each parent should have with the children to maintain frequent, meaningful, and continuing contact with them. Any parenting time plan submitted by agreement that provides for less then the **minimum** time allowed under the Indiana Parenting Time Guidelines must contain a written explanation for deviating from those guidelines. Agreed parenting plans that exceed the **minimum** time allowed under the Guidelines will not require a written explanation.

B. Unless they have already executed an agreed parenting plan, the parties shall each prepare and exchange their written Parenting Plan Proposals utilizing the form which is attached hereto as Appendix "C". Parents, personally and with the help of counsel and all useful counseling, mediation and other problem-solving resources, shall continue to attempt to reach an agreed parenting plan. Parents shall bring their respective Parenting Plan Proposals to all hearings, mediation sessions, and settlement discussions.

Adopted effective Jan. 1, 2012.

LR 79–FL00 Rule 9. PROTOCOLS AFTER INITIAL FILING

A. Duties Regarding Consultation. Except in emergencies or when it might create a danger or substantial prejudice or is otherwise unreasonable to do so, counsel and pro se parties shall have a personal or telephonic consultation to resolve any issue before filing or seeking any other relief through the court.

Counsel and pro se parties contacted for a consultation shall make themselves reasonably available for
consultation. The duty of consultation shall be continuing.

B. Substance of Consultation. In the consultation, counsel and pro se parties shall:

(1) attempt to resolve all matters at issue;

(2) confirm the parties' compliance with FLR 5,
FLR 6, FLR 7 and FLR 8; and,

(3) discuss the resources they believe the parents
could use to resolve current and future issues and to
build cooperation.

C. Cooperation Update—Mandatory. All motions and pleadings other than the initial filings shall
include a statement confirming compliance with items
(1) through (3), above, including the date of the required personal or telephonic consultation; or, shall
recite the specific reasons for the lack of a consultation.

D. Parents shall review and bring a copy of their
website Commitments, as required by FLR 5 and the
current Parenting Plan Proposals, as required by
FLR 8, to every hearing.

Adopted effective Jan. 1, 2012.

LR 79–FL00 Rule 10. REQUIREMENTS BE-
FORE CUSTODY EVALUATIONS

All requests for custody evaluations must be (1) in
writing (2) certify that both parties and their counsel,
if any, have engaged in at least one good faith attempt
to resolve the issues through the use of a settlement
conference or mediation.

The court will not grant a request for or otherwise
order a custody evaluation except following a Status
Conference in the presence of both parties and their
attorneys, if any, during which the court has been
satisfied that:

A. both parties have completed the mandatory
website work pursuant to FLR 6, above; and,

B. both parents have completed any required
co-parenting class pursuant to FLR 7, above; and,

C. both parties have exchanged Parenting Plan
Proposals pursuant to FLR 8, above; and,

D. both parties and their attorneys, if any, have
engaged in at least one good faith attempt to resolve the issues through the use of a settlement
conference or consultation pursuant to FLR 9,
above; and,

E. the court has carefully considered and reviewed, with both parties and their attorneys, if any,
the use of other resources.

Adopted effective Jan. 1, 2012.

LR 79–FL00 Rule 11. CASE CAPTIONING

Parties in dissolution, separation, and paternity
cases shall not be captioned or designated as "petitioner", "respondent", "plaintiff", or "defendant". The
parties shall be designated as "Mother", "Father",
"Husband", or "Wife", "Former Husband", "Former
Wife", and "Putative Father". All captions shall comply with applicable statutes and case law.

Adopted effective Jan. 1, 2012.

LR 79–FL00 Rule 12. FORM OF SUMMONS

Parties in dissolution, separation, and paternity
cases shall prepare and utilize forms of summons as
set forth herein.

**A. Dissolution of Marriage and Legal Separa-
tion.** In dissolution and separation cases, the appropriate summons shall be used and shall be substantially the same as the form(s) which attached hereto as
Appendix "D" and "D–1".

B. Paternity. In paternity cases, the summons
shall be substantially the same as the form which is
attached hereto as Appendix "E".

Adopted effective Jan. 1, 2012.

LR 79–FL00 Rule 13. JUDGES' NOTICE

Whenever the initial filing is prepared by an attorney, the attorney shall also prepare and provide the
client and the Clerk with a sufficient number of copies
of the appropriate the Judges' Notice as required
herein. In cases filed by pro se parties, the Clerk
shall provide the appropriate Judges' Notice. The
Judges' Notice to Parents Going Through Divorce is
attached as Appendix "F" and Judges' Notice to Parents in Paternity Cases is attached as Appendix "G".

Adopted effective Jan. 1, 2012.

LR 79–FL00 Rule 14. FINANCIAL DECLARA-
TION FORM

A. Requirement. In all relevant cases including
dissolutions, separation, paternity, post-decree, or support proceedings and, irrespective of which court, each
party shall prepare and exchange, within 60 days of
initial filing for dissolution or separation or within 30
days of filing of any paternity or post-decree matters,
the appropriate Financial Declaration Form (see Appendix "I" and "J"). These time limits may be extended or shortened by court order for good cause
shown. In those cases where there is service, but no
appearance by counsel, it is the responsibility of the
initiating party to provide the other party with the
appropriate blank Form and to notify that party of the
duty to prepare and serve the same.

B. Exceptions. The Form need not be exchanged
if:

(1) the parties agree in writing within 60 days of
the initial filing to waive exchange;

(2) the parties have executed a written agreement which settles all financial issues;

(3) the proceeding is merely at a provisional or
emergency relief stage;

(4) the proceeding is one in which the service is by publication and there is no response; or,

(5) the proceeding is post-decree and concerns issues without financial implications.

Provided, however, when the proceeding is post-decree and concerns an arrearage, the alleged delinquent party shall complete the entire Form, while the support recipient need complete merely the portion thereof which requires specification of the basis of the arrearage calculation (with appropriate supporting documentation).

C. Use at trial. The Forms are intended primarily as mandatory discovery though, subject to appropriate objection, they shall be admissible at the request of any party. Therefore, particularly in view of the presumptive nature of the Indiana Child Support Guidelines, direct examination on form data shall address only unusual factors which require explanation or corrections and shall not, particularly with respect to issues of support, be routinely permitted. For evidentiary purposes, the pages of the Form shall be deemed severable.

D. Supporting documents. For the purposes of providing a full and complete verification of assets, liabilities, and values, each party shall attach to the form all information reasonably required and reasonably available. This shall include recent bills, wage and tax records, and bank, pension and year-end mortgage statements. "Reasonably available" means that material that may be obtained by letter accompanied with an authorization, but does not mean material that must be subpoenaed or is in the possession of the other party. Appraisals of real estate and pensions, or appraisals of personal property such as jewelry, antiques, or special collections (stamps, coins, or guns, for example) are not required. However, once an appraisal is obtained, it must be exchanged unless the appraisal was obtained in accordance with the provisions of Trial Rule 26(B) (4) (b) and is not expected to be utilized during trial. Moreover, the court may direct that an appraisal be obtained just as it may designate the appraiser.

E. Privacy—Sealing of Forms. Whenever the interest of privacy so requires, the court may, upon motion, direct the admitted Forms sealed until further order. However, such requests shall not be made as a matter of course.

When ordered sealed, the Court Reporter shall place the Forms in a flat manner in an envelope of sufficient size, seal the envelope, and affix a copy of the order. Forms may be withdrawn at the conclusion of the case on such terms as the court allows.

F. Financial Declaration Form as Mandatory Discovery. The exchange of Forms constitutes mandatory discovery. Thus, Indiana Rules of Procedure, Trial Rule 37 sanctions apply. Additionally, pursuant to Trial Rule 26(E) (2) and (3), the Form shall be supplemented if additional material becomes available.

Further, any additional discovery, such as a motion to produce, interrogatories, or depositions of the parties shall not commence until the Forms are exchanged and, once exchanged, shall not seek information already obtained.

Adopted effective Jan. 1, 2012.

LR 79–FL00 Rule 15. INDIANA CHILD SUPPORT GUIDELINES

A. Worksheet Required. In all proceedings involving child support, each party shall file with any settlement or enter into evidence during any trial Indiana Child Support Guidelines Worksheets—one or more depending upon the facts. Further, the Worksheet(s) shall, when reasonably possible, be delivered to the other parent simultaneously with the Financial Declaration Form, but, in any event, within 10 days of receiving the other parent's Form. The Worksheets shall be promptly supplemented if any changes occur prior to resolution. All Worksheets shall be signed by the party(ies) submitting the Worksheet.

B. Support Settlement Agreements. If an agreement concerning support provides any deviation from the amount calculated under the Indiana Child Support Guidelines, the parents shall present the court with a written explanation justifying the deviation.

Adopted effective Jan. 1, 2012.

LR 79–FL00 Rule 16. PREPARATION OF ORDERS

A. Exchange. It shall be the duty of the parties' attorneys to prepare decrees and other orders as directed by the court. The attorney so directed is first to submit them to all other attorneys of record or to the unrepresented party to enable them to challenge any provision thereof before submission to the court for entry.

B. Additions. If the preparing attorney believes the other attorney or the other party, if the other party is proceeding pro se, is unreasonably withholding approval as to form, or if either believes the other is attempting to make additions not addressed by the court, either may submit a proposed form to the court and shall attach thereto a written explanation of the dispute. The other party shall have 7 days to respond before the court enters any order. The court may enter sanctions against a party who has unreasonably withheld approval or attempted to make additions not addressed by the court.

C. Signatures. The signature line for counsel or pro se litigant shall indicate Approved As To Form. Such signature indicates that the order correctly reflects the court's ruling. It does not necessarily signify that the signing party or attorney agrees with the ruling.

Adopted effective Jan. 1, 2012.

LR 79–FL00 Rule 17. SANCTIONS

If a party or counsel fails to timely prepare, exchange or file a Financial Declaration Form or Child Support Worksheet or to cooperate in providing information therefore in a timely manner, either is subject to sanctions under Trial Rule 37.

Adopted effective Jan. 1, 2012.

LR 79–FL00 Rule 18. ATTORNEY FEE REQUESTS

A. Affidavits. When attorney fees (except those sought provisionally) are requested from the opposing party, the requesting attorney shall submit an appropriate affidavit, which, if the affidavit comports with these rules, the court shall admit as an exhibit.

B. Content. The affidavit shall indicate the:

(1) requested fee and the basis thereof;

(2) amounts counsel has billed, contracted for, or been promised; and,

(3) amount counsel has received from all sources.

A copy of the written fee contract, if any, shall be attached to the affidavit and deemed a part thereof. Opposing counsel may cross examine the requesting attorney as to any of the submitted material.

Adopted effective Jan. 1, 2012.

LR 79–FL00 Rule 19. AGREED MATTERS— SUBMISSION

No agreed matter shall be submitted unless accompanied with a signed agreement, and other appropriate documents, such as the decree, a wage withholding order, or a qualified domestic relations order. However, if the parties reach a settlement on the courthouse steps, then the court shall accept evidence of that settlement on the record, and enter the appropriate order upon preparation and filing by counsel within 21 days after submission, or such additional time as the court may allow.

Adopted effective Jan. 1, 2012.

LR 79–FL00 Rule 20. ORDERS EXCLUDING PARENT FROM THE RESIDENCE

In all instances where emergency or extraordinary relief is requested including, but not limited to, excluding a parent from the residence, the court shall require full compliance with the provisions of Trial Rules 65(B) and 65(E). In situations involving allegations of physical abuse, intimidation or stalking, relief may be sought by a separate filing for an Order of Protection.

Adopted effective Jan. 1, 2012.

Appendix A. CERTIFICATION OF COMPLIANCE IN DISSOLUTION CASES

CAPTION

CERTIFICATION OF COMPLIANCE IN DISSOLUTION CASES

The undersigned, as the (select: Mother or Father) in the within cause, does hereby certify that:

1. On (type date) I did complete the mandatory website work as required by FLR 5 and have attached hereto my certificate to confirm the same; and,

2. On (type date) I did complete the mandatory co-parenting class as required by FLR 6 and have attached hereto my certificate to confirm the same.

I affirm under the penalties for perjury that the foregoing representations are true.

Date: _____   _____

(Type name), (select: Mother or Father)

Adopted effective Jan. 1, 2012.

Appendix B. CERTIFICATION OF COMPLIANCE IN PATERNITY CASES

CAPTION

CERTIFICATION OF COMPLIANCE IN PATERNITY CASES

The undersigned, as the (select: Mother or Father) in the within cause, does hereby certify that:

On (type date) I did complete the mandatory website work as required by the FLR 5 and have attached hereto my certificate to confirm the same.

I affirm under the penalties for perjury that the foregoing representations are true.

Date: _____   _____

(Type name), (select: Mother or Father)

Adopted effective Jan. 1, 2012.

Appendix C. PARENTING PLAN PROPOSAL

In Re The (select: Marriage/Paternity) of:
_____

Cause No.: _____

(Select: Mother's/Father's) Parenting Plan Proposal

Parent's Affirmation

I hereby affirm, under the penalties for perjury, that **before** preparing this proposal I have:

1. carefully read the Indiana Parenting Time Guidelines, including the Preamble and General Rules and understand that they reflect the **minimum** parenting time; and,

2. completed all the work assignments for parents at (select: www.UpToParents.org/www.ProudTo Parent.org [delete paragraph # 3 in paternity cases]; and,

3. completed the co-parenting class required by the court.

Dated: _____   _____

(Select: Mother/Father)

Terms of This Proposal

The following proposal for the parenting plan for our children was prepared and is submitted in compliance with the Tippecanoe County Rules of Family Law and is part of the effort of both parents to devise a parenting plan to include the decision making and living arrangements that will serve to nurture and protect our children as the years progress. As stated in the Tippecanoe County Rules of Family Law, the following proposal was prepared and is submitted as part of the effort to compromise and settle these and other issues which now exist between the parents and, as a result, unless all of the terms of the following proposal are accepted as shown by the signature of both parents on page four (4) hereof, the following proposal and all of its terms, constitute privileged communications which are inadmissible for any purposes.

1. As the parents, important decisions in our children's lives (such as place of residence, school selection and other educational decisions, healthcare and religious upbringing) will be made as follows:

_____
_____
_____
_____
_____

2. The declared legal residence of our children for school and legal purposes will be:

_____
_____
_____
_____

3. Due to the circumstances of the lives of the members of our family, including work schedules and the like, our parenting time schedule for our children to be with each of us will vary from the **minimum** set forth in the Indiana Parenting Guidelines, as follows:

Weekdays: _____
_____
_____

Weekends: _____
_____
_____

Holidays and Special Days: _____
_____
_____

Extended Parenting Time/Summer Vacation: ____
_____
_____

4. In the event of disagreement, we will speak to one another first to try to resolve any parenting issues. If we are unable to resolve all the issues, then we will utilize the following: (Circle all that apply and add any additional ones.)

A. Redoing the (select: www.UpToParents.org/ www.ProudToParent.org) website work.

B. Additional co-parenting classes, including re-attending the basic class or attending high-conflict classes.

C. Mediation.

D. Arbitration.

E. Individual, joint, family, or child counseling.

F. Appointment of a parenting time coordinator (PTC) to work with us.

G. Appointment of a guardian ad litem (GAL) for our children.

H. Other (specify): _____
_____
_____

5. Other provisions of our parenting plan would be: _____
_____
_____
_____

Dated: _____   _____
                  (Select: Mother/Father)

                  _____
                  (attorney's name)
                  Indiana Attorney No.: _____
                  (firm name)
                  Attorney for (select: Mother/Father)
                  (address)
                  (phone number)

ACCEPTANCE

By our signatures, we, as the parents, now agree to all of the terms set forth above as our Parenting Agreement and that this document is now admissible in to evidence in court.

_____
(Select: Mother/Father) (Select: Mother/Father)

Date: _____, 20 ___. Date: _____, 20 ___.

_____
(attorney's name) (attorney's name)

Indiana Attorney No.:   Indiana Attorney No.:
_____

(firm name) (firm name)

Attorney for (select: Mother/Father) Attorney for (select: Mother/Father)

(address) (address)

(phone number) (phone number)

As dedicated parents, we will do our best to:

Remember that our children's only job is to be children, not our messengers, spies, counselors, confidants, or carriers of our hurt.

Be sure to remember that our love for our children is greater than any issue we could have with each other.

Respect each other's parenting time while also being flexible, so the children's lives can be as normal as possible.

Educate our extended families and close friends that they need to make peace as well.

Pay special attention to keep our appointments and schedules with each other and calling promptly if any problems come up.

Adopted effective Jan. 1, 2012.

Appendix D. SUMMONS AND NOTICE OF HEARING IN PROCEEDINGS FOR DISSOLUTION OF MARRIAGE

STATE OF INDIANA) IN THE (Title, Address and Phone
COUNTY OF TIPPECANOE) SS: Number of Court)

IN RE: THE MARRIAGE OF
(Name of Filing Party),
(select: Mother, Wife, Father, Husband) Cause No. _____
and
(Name of Spouse),
(select: Mother, Wife, Father, Husband)

SUMMONS AND NOTICE OF HEARING IN PROCEEDINGS FOR DISSOLUTION OF MARRIAGE

THE STATE OF INDIANA TO: (name of spouse being served)
(address)

Your spouse has filed an action for dissolution of marriage in the Court stated above. A copy of the Petition (and, in some cases, other documents) together with a separate Notice from the Court which is printed on yellow paper are attached to or otherwise served with this Summons and contain important details regarding the nature of these proceedings. Local Rules in Tippecanoe County require that both you and your spouse complete certain, specific tasks and you should immediately and carefully review those requirements.

THIS IS YOUR OFFICIAL NOTICE that a hearing on Provisional Orders has been scheduled for _____, 20 ___, at _____ M. before this Court, in (room number) which is located on the (floor), at the address listed in the upper right hand corner of this Summons. If you wish to hire an attorney to represent you in this matter, it is advisable to do so before that date. If you do not appear for that hearing, a provisional order could be entered by default which could remain in effect until this action is concluded.

THIS IS YOUR OFFICIAL NOTICE that a final hearing has been scheduled for _____, 20 ___, at _____.M. before this Court, in (room number) which is located on the (floor), at the address listed in the upper right hand corner of this Summons. If you do not file a written appearance with the Clerk and serve a copy on your spouse's attorney, you may not receive notice of any further proceedings in this action. If you do not make such an appearance, a final decree could be entered by default which grants the relief sought in your spouse's Petition after the expiration of sixty (60) days from the date of the filing of the Petition. You are not required to file any written Answer to respond to the Petition; however, certain grounds for dismissal must be asserted in a timely fashion or are waived; and, if you have a claim for relief against your spouse you may be required to assert such a claim in a written pleading which must be filed with the Clerk and served on your spouse's attorney.

The following manner of service of this SUMMONS is hereby designated:

Date:

(Name of attorney for Filing Party)

Indiana Attorney No: (insert)

(firm name)

Attorney for (select: Mother, Wife, Father, Husband)

(address)

(phone number)

CHRISTA COFFEY
CLERK, TIPPECANOE
CIRCUIT/SUPERIOR
COURTS
By: _____
Deputy Clerk

PREPARATION DATA:

All summons are to be prepared in triplicate with the original of each to be placed in the Court file with two copies available for service.

If service is by certified mail a properly addressed envelope shall be provided for the party being served. Certified mail labels and return receipts must also be furnished for each mailing and the cause number must appear on each return receipt, which shall be returnable to the Clerk at the address of the Court.

CLERK'S CERTIFICATE OF MAILING

I hereby certify that on the ___ day of _____, 20 ___, I mailed a copy of this Summons and a copy of the Petition to the party being served, by mail, requesting a return receipt, at the address furnished by the filing party.

CHRISTA COFFEY
CLERK, TIPPECANOE
CIRCUIT/SUPERIOR
COURTS

Dated: _____ BY: _____
Deputy Clerk

RETURN ON SERVICE OF SUMMONS BY MAIL

I hereby certify that the attached return receipt was received by me showing that the Summons and a copy of the Petition mailed to the party being served, _____, was accepted by the party being served on the ___ day of _____, 20 ___.

I hereby certify that the attached return receipt was received by me showing that the Summons and a copy of the Petition was returned not accepted on the ___ day of _____, 20 ___.

> CHRISTA COFFEY
> CLERK, TIPPECANOE
> CIRCUIT/SUPERIOR
> COURTS

Dated: ____, 20 ___.   BY: _____
                              Deputy Clerk

RETURN OF SERVICE OF SUMMONS BY SHERIFF

I hereby certify that I have served the within Summons:

1) By delivering on _____, 20 ___, a copy of this Summons and a copy of the Petition to each of the within named person(s).

2) By leaving on _____, 20 ___, for each of the within named person(s) a copy of the Summons and a copy of the Petition at the respective dwelling house or usual place of abode, in   , Indiana, with a person of suitable age and discretion residing within, whose usual duties or activities include prompt communication of such information to the person served, or by otherwise leaving such process thereat, and by mailing a copy of the Summons without the Petition to the said named person(s) at the address listed herein.

3) This Summons came to hand this date, _____, 20 ___. The within named _____ was not found in my bailiwick this date _____, 20 ___.

ALL DONE IN TIPPECANOE COUNTY, INDIANA.

TRACY BROWN

SHERIFF OF TIPPECANOE COUNTY, INDIANA

By: _____

SERVICE ACKNOWLEDGED

I hereby acknowledge that I received a copy of the within Summons and a copy of the Petition at in _____, Indiana, on this date, _____, 20 ___.

_____
Signature of Party Served

Adopted effective Jan. 1, 2012.

Appendix D–1. SUMMONS IN PROCEEDINGS FOR DISSOLUTION OF MARRIAGE

STATE OF INDIANA

COUNTY OF TIPPECANOE, SS:

IN THE (Title, Address and Phone Number of Court)

IN RE: THE MARRIAGE OF

(Name of Filing Party),

(select: Mother, Wife, Father, Husband)

and

(Name of Spouse),

(select: Mother, Wife, Father, Husband)

Cause No.

SUMMONS IN PROCEEDINGS FOR DISSOLUTION OF MARRIAGE

THE STATE OF INDIANA TO: (name of spouse being served)

(address)

Your spouse has filed an action for dissolution of marriage in the Court stated above. A copy of the Petition (and, in some cases, other documents) together with a separate Notice from the Court which is printed on yellow paper are attached to or otherwise served with this Summons and contain important details regarding the nature of these proceedings. Local Rules in Tippecanoe County require that both you and your spouse complete certain, specific tasks and you should immediately and carefully review those requirements.

If you do not file a written appearance with the Clerk and serve a copy on your spouse's attorney, you may not receive notice of any further proceedings in this action. If you do not make such an appearance, a final decree could be entered by default which grants the relief sought in your spouse's Petition after the expiration of sixty (60) days from the date of the filing of the Petition. You are not required to file any written Answer to respond to the Petition; however, certain grounds for dismissal must be asserted in a timely fashion or are waived; and, if you have a claim for relief against your spouse you may be required to assert such a claim in a written pleading which must be filed with the Clerk and served on your spouse's attorney.

The following manner of service of this SUMMONS is hereby designated:

(select: Registered or certified mail, return receipt # Sheriff of Tippecanoe County Private service by: Other (specify):)

Date:

(Name of attorney for Filing Party)

Indiana Attorney No: (insert)

(firm name)

Attorney for (select: Mother, Wife, Father, Husband)

(address)

(phone number)

CHRISTA COFFEY

CLERK, TIPPECANOE CIRCUIT/SUPERIOR COURTS

By:

Deputy Clerk

PREPARATION DATA:

All summons are to be prepared in triplicate with the original of each to be placed in the Court file with two copies available for service. If service is by certified mail a properly addressed envelope shall be provided for the party being served. Certified mail labels and return receipts must also be furnished for each mailing and the cause number must appear on each return receipt, which shall be returnable to the Clerk at the address of the Court.

Adopted effective Jan. 1, 2012.

Appendix E. SUMMONS AND NOTICE OF INITIAL HEARING IN A PATERNITY CASE

STATE OF INDIANA IN THE SUPERIOR COURT OF TIPPECANOE COUNTY

JUVENILE DIVISION, 301 Main Street

COUNTY OF TIPPECANOE Lafayette, Indiana 47901 (765) 423–9295

IN THE MATTER OF THE PATERNITY OF: _____

CAUSE NO. 79D03–0107–JP–0000

(Name of Child)

(Gender and Date of Birth)

(Name of Father),

Putative Father,

and

(Name of Mother).

Mother

(Name of Child) b/n/f (Name of Petitioner)

SUMMONS AND NOTICE OF INITIAL HEARING IN A PATERNITY CASE

THE STATE OF INDIANA TO: (Name of Respondent)

(Address of Respondent)

A paternity action has been filed in the Court stated above. A copy of the Petition (and, in come cases, other documents) together with a separate Notice from the Court which is printed on yellow paper are attached to or otherwise served with this Summons and contain important details regarding the nature of these proceedings. Local Rules in Tippecanoe County require that both parties to this case complete certain specific tasks. You should immediately and carefully review those requirements.

THIS IS YOUR OFFICIAL NOTICE that an Initial Hearing to Establish Paternity is scheduled for **the ___ day of _____, 20 ___, at ___ o'clock _____.m.** at the address listed in the upper right hand corner of this Summons. If you wish to hire an attorney to represent you in this matter, it is advisable to do so before that date. **If you do not appear for that hearing, a final order could be entered by default determining paternity, custody, parenting time and child support.**

If you do not file a written appearance with the Clerk and serve a copy on the attorney whose name and address is set forth at the bottom of this page, you may not receive notice of any further proceedings in this action. You are not required to file any written Answer to respond to the Petition; however, certain grounds for dismissal must be asserted in a timely fashion or are waived; and, if you have a claim for relief against the person who filed the Petition, you may be required to assert such a claim in a written pleading which must be filed with the Clerk and served upon the attorney whose name and address is set forth at the bottom of this page.

The following manner of service is designated: **Sheriff (or CMRRR, or Private Server etc.)**

Date: CHRISTA COFFEY

CLERK, SUPERIOR COURT OF TIPPECANOE COUNTY

Attorney   for   Putative   Father   By: _____

(Address of Attorney)

CLERK'S CERTIFICATE OF MAILING

I hereby certify that on the day of _____, 20 ___ , I mailed a copy of this Summons and a copy of the Petition to the party being served, by mail, requesting a return receipt, at the address furnished by the filing party.

CHRISTA COFFEY
CLERK, TIPPECANOE CIRCUIT/SUPERIOR COURTS
Dated: _____, 20 ___. BY: _____
Deputy Clerk

RETURN ON SERVICE OF SUMMONS BY MAIL

I hereby certify that the attached return receipt was received by me showing that the Summons and a copy of the Petition mailed to the party being served, was accepted by the party being served on the ___ day of _____, 20 ___.

I hereby certify that the attached return receipt was received by me showing that the Summons and a copy of the Petition was returned not accepted on the ___ day of _____, 20 ___.

CHRISTA COFFEY
CLERK, TIPPECANOE CIRCUIT/SUPERIOR COURTS
Dated: _____, 20 ___. BY: _____
Deputy Clerk

RETURN OF SERVICE OF SUMMONS BY SHERIFF

I hereby certify that I have served the within Summons:

1. By delivering on _____, 20 ___, a copy of this Summons and a copy of the Petition to each of the within named person(s).

2. By leaving on _____, 20 ___, for each of the within named person(s) a copy of the Summons and a copy of the Petition at the respective dwelling house or usual place of abode, in , Indiana, with a person of suitable age and discretion residing within, whose usual duties or activities include prompt communication of such information to the person served, or by otherwise leaving such process thereat, and by mailing a copy of the Summons without the Petition to the said named person(s) at the address listed herein.

3. This Summons came to hand this date, _____, 20 ___. The within named _____ was not found in my bailiwick this date, _____, 20 ___.

ALL DONE IN TIPPECANOE COUNTY, INDIANA.

TRACY BROWN

SHERIFF OF TIPPECANOE COUNTY, INDIANA

By: _____

SERVICE ACKNOWLEDGED

I hereby acknowledge that I received a copy of the within Summons and a copy of the Petition at in _____, Indiana, on this date, _____, 20 ___.

_____

Signature of Party Served
Adopted effective Jan. 1, 2012.

Appendix F. JUDGES' NOTICE TO PARENTS GOING THROUGH DIVORCE

JUDGES' NOTICE TO PARENTS GOING THROUGH DIVORCE

We, the Judges and Magistrates of Tippecanoe County, share the following information so that you will know of our commitment to the best interests of children. *Please read this information carefully, as we expect you and all other persons involved in your case to be partners in serving those best interests.*

1. As soon as possible, read the Tippecanoe County Rules of Family Law for important information about how divorce cases will be handled to:

ensure safety;

reduce conflict;

build cooperation; and,

protect the best interests of all family members, especially all children.

2. If you and your spouse have any children under the age of 18, you **must** do the following within 30 days:

a. Register for a co-parenting class.

b. Complete the work on www.UpToParents. org, and take your completed work to your co-parenting class, give a copy to your attorney, and bring it with you to all court appearances and other meetings.

3. If you and your spouse have any children under the age of 18, you should attempt to establish your own plan for the decision making and living arrangements that will serve to nurture and protect your children. A plan which is worked out between the parents to fit the needs of their children and family is almost always the best. You should review the Indiana Parenting Time Guidelines. The Court considers those Guidelines to be the **minimum** parenting time for each parent to have frequent, meaningful, and continuing contact with their children.

4. You and your spouse must complete and exchange Financial Declaration Forms with all required attachments.

Adopted effective Jan. 1, 2012.

Appendix G. JUDGES' NOTICE TO PARENTS IN PATERNITY CASES

JUDGES' NOTICE TO PARENTS IN PATERNITY CASES

We, the Judges and Magistrates of Tippecanoe County, share the following information so that you will know of our commitment to the best interests of children. *Please read this information carefully, as we expect you and all other persons involved in your case to be partners in serving those best interests.*

1. **If either of you question whether or not the man named as the father in this case is the father, and the man named as the father has not signed a paternity affidavit admitting paternity of the child at issue,** the Court will order genetic testing at the initial hearing to establish paternity. If the man named as father is found not to be the father by genetic testing, the case will be dismissed.

2. **If paternity is established,** whether by agreement or otherwise, or following genetic testing, the Local Rules of the Circuit and Superior Court of Tippecanoe County, Indiana, require you to do the following:

A. **Complete the work on www.ProudTo Parent.org** and furnish the Court with a certification that you have done so.

B. **Complete and exchange Financial Declaration Forms with all required attachments.**

3. **In addition, if paternity is established,** whether by agreement or otherwise, or following genetic testing, you will be expected to do the following:

A. **Devise a Parenting Plan for your children.** A Parenting Plan consists of the decision making and living and financial arrangements that will serve to nurture and protect your children as the years progress. A plan which is worked out between the parents to fit the needs of their children and family is almost always best. You should review the Indiana Parenting Time Guidelines. The Court considers those Guidelines to be the **minimum** parenting time for each parent to have frequent, meaningful, and continuing contact with their children. If you fail to devise a successful Parenting Plan for your children, this Court may require you to attend and complete, at your own expense, a co-parenting class.

B. Read the Tippecanoe County Rules of Family Law and the Indiana Parenting Time Guidelines for additional important information on the Court's expectation that everyone involved in your case will be a partner in:

    ensuring safety;

    reducing conflict;

    building cooperation; and,

    protecting the best interests of all family members, especially all children.

Adopted effective Jan. 1, 2012.

Appendix H. FINANCIAL DECLARATION FORM: DISSOLUTION OF MARRIAGE

DISSOLUTION OF MARRIAGE: FINANCIAL DECLARATION FORM STATE OF INDIANA: CIRCUIT AND SUPERIOR COURTS OF TIPPECANOE COUNTY

IN RE THE MARRIAGE OF: Cause No. _____

_____

(select: Mother, Wife, Father, Husband) and

_____

(select: Mother, Wife, Father, Husband)
FINANCIAL DECLARATION OF: _____

This declaration is considered mandatory discovery and must be exchanged between the parties within 60 days of the initial filing of the Dissolution of Marriage. Parties not represented by counsel are required to comply with these practices. Failure by either party to complete and exchange this form as required will authorize the court to impose sanctions set forth in Rule 6 of the Tippecanoe County Rules of Family Law. If appraisals or verifications are not available within 60 days the from must be exchanged within 60 days with a notation that appraisals or verifications are being obtained and then the Declaration shall be supplemented within 30 days thereafter.

Husband: _____ Wife: _____
Address: _____ Address: _____
_____ _____

Soc. Sec. No.: _____ Soc. Sec. No.: _____
Badge/Payroll No.: _____ Badge/Payroll No.: _____
Occupation: _____ Occupation: _____
Employer: _____ Employer: _____
Date started this employment: _ Date started this employment: _
Birth Date: _____ Birth Date: _____
Date of Marriage: _____
Date of Physical Separation: _____
Date of Filing: _____
List Names, dates of birth, and social security numbers of all children of this relationship, whether by birth or adoption:

_____ _____
_____ _____
_____ _____

List Names and dates of birth of any other children living at the residence of the person responding (identify if these are children of the responding party) and for each such person indicate the amount of support, if any, that is received:

_____ _____
_____ _____
_____ _____

Part I. INCOME AND EXPENSES STATEMENT

Attach COMPLETE copies of your Federal Income Tax Returns for the last three taxable years including all W2's and 1099's. Also attach proof of all wages earned in the present year up to the date of your response. If current wage statement shows year to date wages and itemized deductions this is sufficient. If current wage statement does not indicate year to date earnings and deductions attach the 8 most recent pay stubs.

Person Responding

A. Gross yearly income from Salary and Wages, including commissions, bonuses, allowances and overtime received in most recent year. _____

Average gross pay per pay period (indicate whether you are paid weekly each 2 weeks or twice per month) _____

B. Gross Monthly Income From Other Sources[1]

List and explain in detail any Rents received, Dividend income, or Pension, Retirement, Social Security, Disability and/or Unemployment Insurance benefits—or any other source including Public assistance, food stamps, and child support received for any child not born of the parties of this marriage.

_____

_____

_____

    1.   Some of these items may not apply to support or maintenance computations.

C. SELECTED LIVING EXPENSES: List names and relations of each member of the household of the Responding party whose expenses are included.

_____ _____

_____ _____

_____ _____

For each expense attach verification of payment even if it is not specifically requested on this form—please note that Indiana uses an Income Shares model for determining support and thus in most cases the expenses that a party has or does not have are not relevant in determining support under the Indiana Support Guidelines.

However if you claim your expenses justify a deviation from the support guidelines attach a detailed list of expenses together with verification of same.

Person Responding

Rent or Mortgage payments (residence) _____

Real Property Taxes (residence) if not included in mortgage payment _____

Real Property Insurance (residence) if not included in mortgage payment _____

Cost of **all** Medical Insurance—specify time period—Attach verification of payment if not on pay stub _____

Cost of **only** that medical insurance that is related to the children of this action—specify time period—attach verification from employer or insurance company _____

Child care costs—**to permit work**—specify time period (per day, week, month)—attach verification _____

Pre–School Costs (specify time period week, semester or year) _____

School Tuition—per semester (Grade or High School) _____

Book Costs—per semester (Grade or High School) _____

For Post High School Attach separate list with explanation of loans and scholarships and grants _____

Child support paid for children other than those involved in this case—attach proof of payment _____

D. IN ALL CASES INVOLVING CHILD SUPPORT: Prepare and attach any Indiana Child Support Guideline Worksheet (with documentation verifying your income); or, supplement with such a Worksheet within ten (10) days of the exchange of this Form.

Further, if there exists a parenting plan or pattern then state the number of overnights the non-custodial parent will have the child during the year.

The yearly number of overnights is _____

E. POST HIGH SCHOOL EDUCATION EXPENSE

If any of the children subject to this case are attending post high school classes, or will attend within the next six months list the following information for each such student. **Further attach to this financial affidavit any documentation you have in support of these answers.**

Name of Student _____

Name of School _____

Cost of School per year—If applicable, include room and board _____

Identify all student financial aid including grants, scholarships, and loans and for each indicate what it is and how much will be received: _____

_____

Note in those cases where it is appropriate parties may want to engage in additional discovery concerning assets that might be applied to education such as IRA's, 401 K's etc. Note further that withdrawals from IRA's for educational expenses do not suffer a 10% penalty (IRC code sec 72 (t) 2 (e).

F. Debts And Obligations: (Include credit union) attach additional sheets as needed. Indicate any special circumstances, i.e., premarital debts, debts in arrears on the date of physical separation, or date of filing and the amount or number of payments in arrears.

ATTACH A COPY OF THE MOST RECENT STATEMENT FOR EACH LISTED DEBT

Creditor's Name & Persons on

Account

Balance

Monthly Payment

PART II. NET WORTH—ATTACH ALL AVAILABLE DOCUMENTATION TO VERIFY VALUES—

List all property owned either individually or jointly. Indication who holds or how the title is held: (H) Husband, (W) Wife, or (J) Jointly or other appropriate indication. WHERE SPACE IS INSUFFICIENT FOR COMPLETE INFORMATION OR LISTING PLEASE ATTACH SEPARATE PAGE.

A. Household Furnishings: (Value of Furniture, Appliances, and Equipment, as a whole—You need not itemize—indicate whether you use replacement cost or garage sale value) _____

B. Automobiles, Boats, Snowmobiles, Motorcycles, Etc.:

Year—Make & Present Value

Titled Owner

Balance Owed

C. Cash and Deposit Accounts: (including **ALL** banks, savings and loan associations, credit unions, thrift plans, mutual funds, certificate of deposit, savings and/or checking accounts, IRA's and annuities).

This also includes listing the contents of any safety deposit boxes. Use additional page if necessary.

Name of Institution & Type of Account

Owners

Account No.

Balance

D. Securities: (Stocks, Bonds, Etc)—use additional page if necessary

Company Name

Owner

Shares

Value

E. Real Estate: (attach separate sheet with the following information for each separate piece of real estate).

Address: _____ Type of Property: _____
_____ Date of Acquisition: _____
Original Cost: _____ Present Value: _____
Basis for Valuation: _____
(Attach appraisal if obtained)
1st MORTGAGE BALANCE AS OF DATE OF ANSWER: _____
Other liens (amount and type): _____
Monthly payment on each mortgage: 1st: _____ 2nd: ____
To whom paid: _____
Taxes (if not included in Mtg. payment): _____
Insurance (if not included in Mtg. payment): _____
Special Assessments (including utility or condo assessments): _____
Identify Individual contributions to the real estate (for example, inheritance, pre-marital assets, personal loans, etc.): _____
_____
_____

F. Retirement Plans: List monthly amount you would be entitled to at earliest retirement date (indicating that date) if you stopped work today. Your response should indicate date of valuation. Further, if it is a defined interest plan list present amount in plan and date of valuation.

Also, identify whose plan it is and list both the name and the address of administrator of plan—indicate whether plan is vested—if not vested, indicate when it will vest:

_____
_____
_____

Attach documents from each plan verifying information. If not yet received, attach a copy of your written request to the plan(s).

G. Life Insurance: Give name of insured, beneficiary, company issuing, policy #, type of insurance (term, whole life, group), face value, cash value and any loans against—include plans provided by employer:

_____
_____
_____

H. Business or Professional Interests: Indicate name, share, type of business, value less indebtedness, etc.:

_____
_____
_____

I. Other Assets: (this includes coin, stamp or gun collections or other items of unusual value). Use additional pages as needed:

_____
_____
_____

PART III.   VERIFICATION

I declare, under the penalty of perjury, that the foregoing, including any valuations and attachments, is true and correct and that I have made a complete and absolute disclosure of all of my assets and liabilities. Furthermore, I understand that if, in the future, it is proven to this court that I have intentionally failed to disclosure any asset or liability, I may lose the asset and may be required to pay the liability. Finally, I acknowledge that sanctions may be imposed against me, including reasonable attorney's fees and expenses incurred in the investigation, preparation and prosecution of any claim or action that proves my failure to disclose income, assets or liabilities.

DATE: _____

PARTY'S SIGNATURE

PART IV.   ATTORNEY'S CERTIFICATION

I have reviewed with my client the foregoing information, including any valuations and attachments, and sign this certificate consistent with my obligation under Trial Rule 11 of the Indiana Rules of Procedure.

DATE: _____

_____

(attorney's name)
Indiana Attorney No.:
(firm name)
Attorney for (select: Mother/Father)
(address)
(phone number)
Adopted effective Jan. 1, 2012.

Appendix I.   PATERNITY AND POST–DECREE: FINANCIAL DECLARATION FORM

PATERNITY & POST DECREE: FINANCIAL DECLARATION FORM STATE OF INDIANA: CIRCUIT AND SUPERIOR COURTS OF TIPPECANOE COUNTY

IN RE THE MARRIAGE OF: Cause No. _____

(select: Mother, Wife, Father, Husband)
and

(select: Mother, Wife, Father, Husband)
FINANCIAL DECLARATION OF: _____

This declaration is considered mandatory discovery and must be exchanged between the parties within 30 days of the filing of any paternity case or any post decree matter. Parties not represented by counsel are required to comply with these practices. Failure by either party to complete and exchange this form as required will authorize the court to impose the sanctions set forth in Rule 6 of the Tippecanoe County Rules of Family Law, these include costs and attorney fees.

Father: _____   Mother: _____
Address: _____   Address: _____

Soc. Sec. No.: _____   Soc. Sec. No.: _____
Badge/Payroll No.: _____   Badge/Payroll No.: _____
Occupation: _____   Occupation: _____

Employer: _____   Employer: _____
Date stated[1] this employment: __   Date started this employment: __
Birth Date: _____   Birth Date: _____
List the following Dates as Applicable:
Date of Dissolution: _____   Date of most recent support or-
                                    der: _____
Date of Filing of this paternity action: _____
Date of Filing of this post decree action: _____
List Names, dates of birth, and social security numbers of all children
of this relationship, whether by birth or adoption:

_____   _____
_____   _____
_____   _____

List Names and dates of birth of any other children living at the
residence of the person responding (identify if these are children of
the responding party) and for each such person indicate the amount of
support, if any, that is received:

_____   _____
_____   _____
_____   _____

1 So in original.

Part I.   INCOME AND EXPENSES STATEMENT

Attach COMPLETE copies of your Federal Income Tax Returns for the last three taxable years including all W2's and 1099's. Also attach proof of all wages earned in the present year up to the date of your response. If current wage statement shows year to date wages and itemized deductions this is sufficient. If current wage statement does not indicate year to date earnings and deductions attach the 8 most recent pay stubs.

Person Responding

A. Gross yearly income from Salary and Wages, including commissions, bonuses, allowances and overtime received in most recent year. _____

Average gross pay per pay period (indicate whether you are paid weekly each 2 weeks or twice per month)

_____

B.   Gross Monthly Income From Other Sources[2]

2.   Some of these items may not apply to support or maintenance computations.

List and explain in detail any Rents received, Dividend income, or Pension, Retirement, Social Security, Disability and/or Unemployment Insurance benefits— or any other source including Public assistance, food stamps, and child support received for any child not born of the parties of this marriage.

_____
_____
_____

C. SELECTED LIVING EXPENSES: List names and relations of each member of the household of the Responding party whose expenses are included.

_____   _____
_____   _____
_____   _____

For each expense attach verification of payment even if it is not specifically requested on this form— please note that Indiana uses an Income Shares model

for determining support and thus in most cases the expenses that a party has or does not have are not relevant in determining support under the Indiana Support Guidelines.

However if you claim your expenses justify a deviation from the support guidelines attach a detailed list of expenses together with verification of same.

Person Responding

Rent or Mortgage payments (residence) _____

Real Property Taxes (residence) if not included in mortgage payment _____

Real Property Insurance (residence) if not included in mortgage payment _____

Cost of **all** Medical Insurance—specify time period—

Attach verification of payment if not on pay stub

_____

Cost of **only** that medical insurance that is related to the children of this action—specify time period—attach verification from employer or insurance company

_____

Child care costs—**to permit work**—specify time period (per day, week, month)—attach verification _____

Pre–School Costs (specify time period week, semester or year) _____

School Tuition—per semester (Grade or High School) _____

Book Costs—per semester (Grade or High School)

_____

For Post High School Attach separate list with explanation of loans and scholarships and grants

_____

Child support paid for children other than those involved in this case—attach proof of payment

_____

D.   IN ALL CASES INVOLVING CHILD SUPPORT: Prepare and attach any Indiana Child Support Guideline Worksheet (with documentation verifying your income); or, supplement with such a Worksheet within ten (10) days of the exchange of this Form.

Further, if there exists a parenting plan or pattern then state the number of overnights the non-custodial parent will have the child during the year.

The yearly number of overnights is _____

PART II.   ARREARAGE COMPUTATION

If case involves a claim of a support or other arrearage, attach all records or other exhibits regarding payment history and compute the arrearage as of the date of the filing of the petition or motion which raises that issue. Explain in detail how arrearage is calculated.

_____
_____

PART III. POST HIGH SCHOOL EDUCATION EXPENSE

If any of the children subject to this case are attending post high school classes, or will attend within the next six months list the following information for each such student. **Further attach to this financial affidavit any documentation you have in support of these answers.**

Name of Student _____

Name of School _____

Cost of School per year—If applicable, include room and board _____

Identify all student financial aid including grants, scholarships, and loans and for each indicate what it is and how much will be received:

_____

_____

_____

_____

Note in those cases where it is appropriate parties may want to engage in additional discovery concerning assets that might be applied to education such as IRA's, 401 K's etc. Note further that withdrawals from IRA's for educational expenses do not suffer a 10% penalty (IRC code sec 72 (t) 2 (e).

PART IV. VERIFICATION

I declare, under the penalty of perjury, that the foregoing, is true and correct and that I have made a complete and absolute disclosure of all of my income and expenses as asked. I acknowledge that sanctions may be imposed against me, including reasonable attorney's fees and expenses incurred in the investigation, preparation and prosecution of any claim or action that proves my failure to disclose income or liabilities.

DATE: _____   _____
                                                        PARTY'S SIGNATURE

PART V. ATTORNEY'S CERTIFICATION

I have reviewed with my client the foregoing information, including any valuations and attachments, and sign this certificate consistent with my obligation under Trial Rule 11 of the Indiana Rules of Procedure.

DATE: _____   _____

(attorney's name)

Indiana Attorney No.:

(firm name)

Attorney for (select: Mother/Father)

(address)

(phone number)

Adopted effective Jan. 1, 2012.

TIPPECANOE CIRCUIT COURT PROBATE RULES

Adopted August 1, 2006, Effective January 1, 2007

Including Amendments Received Through November 1, 2013

Research Notes

These rules may be searched electronically on Westlaw *in the* IN-RULES *database; updates to these rules may be found on Westlaw in* IN-RULESUPDATES. *For search tips and a summary of database content, consult the Westlaw Scope Screens for each database.*

LR79–PR Rule 1. SCOPE AND TITLE

1.1. These Rules shall apply in the Tippecanoe Circuit Court (hereafter referenced as "the Court") and shall be applicable as guidelines in all probate matters.

1.2. These Rules are intended to be interpreted consistent with State statutes and any applicable regulations and Indiana Common Law as now existing and as may hereafter develop.

1.3. These Rules shall be known as the "Tippecanoe Circuit Court Probate Rules" and are occasionally referenced herein as "these rules"

Adopted Aug. 1, 2006, effective Jan. 1, 2007. Amended effective Jan. 1, 2012.

LR79–PR Rule 2. ACCESS TO COURT AND REPRESENTATION

2.1. The Court maintains regular business hours of 8:00 a.m.—Noon and 1:00 p.m.–4:30 p.m., Monday through Friday, and is open to the public. Motion Hour is conducted each day from 8:30–9:00 a.m., unless pre-empted due to a trial. Motion Hour is the time set aside by the Court to schedule contested hearings and consider routine motions. Counsel is encouraged to contact opposing counsel to arrange a mutually agreeable date and time to meet at Motion Hour rather than ask the court to order counsel to appear. Matters relevant to these rules (such as estates, guardianships, and adoptions) are complicated proceedings normally requiring the assistance of an attorney. Therefore, these Rules are adopted in the belief that an experienced attorney will represent parties before the Court. The Court and its employ-ees can not give legal advice or refer unrepresented persons to attorneys.

2.2. All probate filings shall be typewritten or word processed and shall be consistent with these rules. Any deviation from these rules shall be brought to the Court's attention when any document is submitted. When documents are filed by mail, or left with the Court for filing, a self-addressed, stamped envelope shall be included for return of documents unless other arrangements for document return are made.

2.3. Routine pleadings such as Inventories, Inheritance Tax Schedules, and Final Reports may be filed with the Probate Commissioner for transmittal to the Court. Pro-forma hearings may also be set with the Commissioner.

Adopted Aug. 1, 2006, effective Jan. 1, 2007. Amended effective Jan. 1, 2012.

LR79–PR Rule 3. NOTICE

3.1. Whenever notice by publication or written notice by U.S. Mail is required to be given, the attorney shall prepare such notice and mailing envelopes (including postage) and shall ensure that such notice is properly published or served. In all respects, the notice shall comply with all statutory requirements. It shall be the attorney's responsibility to ascertain and provide adequate proof that notice was properly served prior to bringing a matter to Court or that notice will be properly served as part of any proceeding.

3.2. Copies of petitions shall be sent to interested parties along with all notices of hearings.

3.3. Notice of the opening of an estate shall be sent by First Class United States Mail to all reasonably ascertainable creditors; however, the use of certified mail, return receipt requested, to serve such notice is recommended.

3.4. Notice of the hearing to be held on a Petition to determine if an Estate is insolvent shall be served on all interested parties, including the local representative of the Inheritance Tax Division of the Indiana Department of Revenue.

Adopted Aug. 1, 2006, effective Jan. 1, 2007. Amended effective Jan. 1, 2012.

LR79–PR Rule 4.   BONDS

4.1. Bonds are required by statute in some circumstances. If discretionary, the Court intends to exercise that discretion for the protection of creditors, heirs, legatees or devisees, or other interested individuals or entities.

4.2. Existing law requiring bond includes circumstances where the Will requires the execution and filing of a bond or the Court finds that a bond is necessary (see I.C. 29–1–11–1).

4.3. A non-resident individual or corporate fiduciary serving jointly with a resident personal representative or a non-resident individual qualifying to serve as a personal representative or a personal representative who becomes a non-resident of Indiana (see I.C. 29–1–10–1) requires that a bond be filed.

4.4. If the filing or amount of a bond is discretionary with the Court, the Court will consider factors such as provisions of decedent's will and any consent filed by a creditor or heir, or other interested party regarding the amount or conditions of bond.

Adopted Aug. 1, 2006, effective Jan. 1, 2007. Amended effective Jan. 1, 2012.

LR79–PR Rule 5.   INVENTORY

5.1. In supervised and unsupervised estates the personal representative shall within two months after the appointment of a personal representative furnish a copy of an Inventory complying with the requirements of I.C. 29–1–7.5–3.2 or I.C. 29–1–12–1 et. seq. to interested persons who request it unless the original of the Inventory or any supplement or amendment to it is filed with the court.

Adopted Aug. 1, 2006, effective Jan. 1, 2007. Amended effective Jan. 1, 2012.

LR79–PR Rule 6.   CONFIDENTIALITY

6.1. Most probate actions are matters of public record and the files thereof are open to review by the general public, subject to excluded and confidential information such as Indiana Tax Returns and reports thereon. Unless required by law or dictated by circumstances of the case, filings with the court need not include dates of birth, social security numbers, or other information which is not necessary for probate administration.

Adopted Aug. 1, 2006, effective Jan. 1, 2007. Amended effective Jan. 1, 2012.

LR79–PR Rule 7.   TIME GUIDELINES

7.1. Orderly administration of estates requires at a minimum compliance with notice requirements, such as notice to creditors and preparing an inventory and timely preparation of an inheritance tax return to entitle the estate to a discount for payment of inheritance tax within nine months of a decedent's death. Unless there is unavoidable delay in estate administration related to sale or making distribution of assets like real estate or a unique asset owned by a decedent or tax related matters such as awaiting an inheritance tax or estate tax closing letter, most estates should be concluded within one year.

7.2.   Closing Estates:

7.21. *Unsupervised Administration*: Unless otherwise ordered by Court in a particular proceeding, closing statements complying with requirements of I.C. 29–1–7.5–4 are sufficient to result in closing an estate. Any objections thereto will be scheduled for hearing. No orders approving closing statements will routinely be provided.

7.22. *Supervised Estates*: As part of the closing process, the Court will accept Affidavits in Lieu of Vouchers.

Adopted Aug. 1, 2006, effective Jan. 1, 2007. Amended effective Jan. 1, 2012.

LR79–PR Rule 8.   GUARDIANSHIPS

8.1. In guardianship matters seeking to declare an adult incapacitated for any reason, the incapacitated person shall be present at the hearing or sufficient evidence shall be presented showing that notice of the hearing was given and that the incapacitated person is unable to appear.

8.2. In guardianship matters seeking to declare an adult incapacitated for any reason, a report or similar statement or document from the doctor treating the alleged incapacitated person, or such additional evidence as the Court shall require, shall be presented to the Court at the time the petition is filed or on the hearing date. No determination will be made without a supporting medical report or other evidence clearly demonstrating the reasons supporting the need for a guardianship.

8.3. An inventory of property within a guardian's control shall be filed within ninety (90) days after the guardian's appointment or within thirty (30) days of the appointment of a temporary guardian. A verified account of the guardian's administration shall be filed as required by statute. In addition to the information required by law, the Court requires changes in the protected person's physical or mental condition, place of residence, and the financial status of the guardianship estate to be included in any account of administration. The current report shall also contain information indicating that the living arrangements for the incapacitated person are appropriate.

8.4. In every petition for the appointment of a guardian of the person of a minor child, the following information shall be given:

8.4.1.   The child's present address.

8.4.2. The places where the child has lived within the past two years and the names and present addresses of persons with whom the child has lived during that period.

8.4.3. Whether, to Petitioner's knowledge, any other litigation is pending concerning the custody of the child in this or any other state.

8.4.4. Whether, to Petitioner's knowledge, any person not a party to the guardianship proceeding has physical custody of the child or claims to have custody or visitation rights with respect to the child.

8.5. Nothing herein shall be deemed as amending, superseding or altering the Probate Rules and Regulations promulgated by the Veteran's Administration of the United States of America, and every fiduciary and attorney shall comply with same if applicable.

8.6. Other than for routine matters, unless permitted by law, the Guardian shall obtain Court approval prior to taking any action on any financial matter pertaining to carrying out the Guardian's duties and responsibilities for the protected person.

Adopted Aug. 1, 2006, effective Jan. 1, 2007. Amended effective Jan. 1, 2012.

LR79–PR Rule 9. PRINCIPLES APPLICABLE TO FEE DETERMINATIONS

9.1. **Attorney Fees.** Although fee guidelines have been promulgated by the Court in probate matters, those guidelines do not assure that all fees allowed by the Court will adhere to them and other factors may be considered by the Court in making any final determination which may be required. The Court may consider any of the following:

9.1.1. The skill required to perform services properly in probate matters; the attorney's expertise in probate matters; the time and labor required; the novelty, complexity, or difficulty of the questions involved; and a determination as to how much of the attorney's time was devoted to legal matters and how much of it was devoted to ministerial functions.

9.1.2. The nature and extent of the responsibilities assumed by the attorney and the results obtained; the identity of the personal representative; the character of the probate and non-probate transferred assets; and whether real estate or other assets are located outside of the State of Indiana.

9.1.3. The sufficiency of assets properly available to pay for legal services, and whether the attorney's duties are expanded by the existence of non-probate assets because of their inclusion for tax purposes, either federal or state.

9.1.4. The timeliness with which the necessary services are performed consistent with statutory requirements; whether the attorney was engaged in a timely fashion or was required to perform services close to deadlines through no fault of such attorney;

the Court's rules of procedure; and the Rules of Professional Conduct applicable thereto.

In considering all of these factors, all attorneys are urged to discuss their fee and that of the personal representative at the time they are retained in all probate matters. Further, the parties are urged to enter into a written engagement agreement which documents their understandings in this regard.

9.2. **Administration.** There are two methods by which fees are typically determined. One is on an hourly basis based upon the amount of time spent by the attorney in handling the matter. The other is based upon a percentage of the size of the gross estate.

9.2.1. *Hourly Method*: The amount of an hourly fee can vary considerably. Among the factors taken into consideration in arriving at an hourly rate are the considerations listed in the paragraphs of 9.1 above. Additional considerations include the nature and length of the professional relationship between the attorney and the client as well as the experience, reputation and ability of the attorney performing the services.

9.2.2. *Percentage Method*: In this method the fees are computed based upon the size of the gross estate. The following are typically normal services: Opening of the Estate; qualifying the Personal Representative; preparing the Inventory; paying claims; collecting assets; preparing and filing the Indiana Inheritance Tax Return IH–6; obtaining a Court Order IH–9 thereon, and paying Inheritance taxes; preparing and filing the Final Report or Closing Statement; obtaining an Order approving same; distributing assets as required; obtaining discharge of the Personal Representative; and preparing and serving all notices on interested parties and readily ascertainable creditors throughout the proceedings. Fees herein shall not include services for preparation or filing of federal or state income tax returns 1040, IT–40, 1041, IT–41, federal form 709, or forms relating to employment of third persons by the decedent or estate. This list shall not be considered to be exclusive. Percentage fees shall be computed on the Gross Estate as defined for purposes of the Indiana Inheritance Tax. The maximum fee for these normal services is computed as follows:

Up to $ 100,000, not to exceed 6%
Next $ 200,000, not to exceed. 4%
Next $ 700,000, not to exceed. 3%
Excess over $ 1,000,000, not to exceed 1%

In addition to the normal services described above, many times additional services are necessary, for which an additional fee is appropriate. Such additional services and the maximum related fees may include for example the following:

A. Sale of Real Estate. Minimum fee of $500.00 except that there shall be a fee no greater than 2½% (.025) of the gross sales price of the real estate where no real estate professional receives a commission

B. Federal Estate Tax Return Form 706. Basic Fee-the greater of $3,000.00 or .15% (.0015) of the total gross estate as shown on Form 706, Part 2, Line 1, Page 1 Additional fee for non-probate assets . . . 1.5% (.015)

9.3. Miscellaneous–Fees shall be hourly for the following services: Spreading Will of Record, small estate settlement procedure, defending a will, construing a will, contesting claims, adjusting tax matters, any contested hearing, petition for instructions, heirship determination, and fees to continue a business or to generate additional income for the estate.

9.4. Wrongful Death Administration.

Fees not to exceed:
Settlement prior to filing. 25%
Settlement after filing and prior to Trial . . .33 1/3%
Trial 40%
Appeal, or extra work 50%

The above fee schedule may be increased under circumstances where the litigation is complex and the potential for recovery is difficult, provided one of the following has occurred:

A. All of the beneficiaries who will participate in the wrongful death recovery, or their legal representative(s), sign a written contingent fee contract providing for a fee greater than above.

B. The Court, having probate jurisdiction of the estate, approves a contingent fee contract providing for a fee greater than the above.

9.5. General–Except as otherwise specified above, fees in other proceedings involving guardianship and docketed trusts and related matters, will be computed on a hourly basis. Hourly fee services shall be rendered with specificity and may include: sale of personal property, sale of real property, partial distributions, contesting claims, adjusting tax matters, any contested hearing, petition for instructions, heirship determination, and fees to continue a business or to generate additional income for the trust or guardianship.

9.6. Personal Representative Fees.

9.6.1. *Professional*: Their applicable reasonable rate to be reviewed in light of all prevailing circumstances.

9.62. *Non–Professional*: An amount not in excess of one-half (1/2) of the Attorney's fee, computed via the method being employed by the attorney handling the estate. In determining the amount of the fee, consideration shall be given to the amount of work performed by the personal representative as compared to the attorney as well as the nature of the work performed by the personal representative. For example, the hourly rate to be charged for lawn care or house cleaning should be comparable to typical laborer charges as compared to the rate for negotiating a sale of property or the transfer of securities. Further, although some consideration should be given to the compensation ordinarily earned by a personal representative in their regular employment, the fact that they miss some work in order to perform their duties as personal representative does not automatically justify them to be compensated for such at their normal pay level.

Adopted Aug. 1, 2006, effective Jan. 1, 2007. Amended effective Jan. 1, 2012.

CIVIL RULES OF THE VANDERBURGH CIRCUIT AND SUPERIOR COURTS

Adopted as Superior Court Rules July 15, 2005, Effective January 1, 2006; as
Circuit Court Rules February 1, 1999; and as Circuit and Superior
Court Rules June 29, 2006, Effective January 1, 2007

Including Amendments Received Through November 1, 2013

Research Notes

Annotations to the Rules of the Vanderburgh Circuit and Superior Courts are available in West's
Annotated Indiana Code, *Title 34 Appendix.*

These rules may be searched electronically on Westlaw *in the* IN-RULES *database; updates to these rules
may be found on Westlaw in IN-RULESUPDATES. For search tips and a summary of database
content, consult the Westlaw Scope Screens for each database.*

LR82–TR81 Rule 1.01. APPLICABILITY, EFFECTIVE DATE, AND DESIGNATIONS

These rules apply to all litigants whether or not represented by counsel. These rules shall be effective beginning January 1, 2007, and supersede all rules or parts of rules previously followed by these Courts. Each rule applies to both Circuit and Superior Courts, except where one Court's designation ("C" for Circuit and "S" for Superior) appears in the last set of characters in a rule number, in which case that rule applies only to the designated Court.

Adopted as Superior Court Rule 1.01, July 15, 2005, effective Jan. 1, 2006, and as Circuit Court Rule 1, effective Feb. 1, 1999. Amended and renumbered as Circuit and Superior Court Rule 1.01, June 29, 2006, effective Jan. 1, 2007; effective Sept. 16, 2011.

LR82–AR00 Rule 1.02. CASE ALLOCATION PLAN

(A) Balance within Superior Court. The Vanderburgh Superior Court is divided into seven Divisions as follows:

1. Division I–Civil

2. Division II–Criminal

3. Division III–Civil

4. Division IV–Domestic Relations

5. Division V–Civil

6. Division VI–Criminal, Small Claims and Misdemeanor/Traffic

7. Division VII–Juvenile and Probate

Divisions I through VI are presided over by six of the Judges who rotate through these Divisions on a monthly basis.

Division VII is presided over by a single Judge. This assignment is a one year minimum assignment.

All Felony criminal cases (MR, FA, FB, FC, FD) and civil cases (PL, MF, CC, CT, MI, PO) are assigned to one of the six rotating Judges by blind lot in the order presented for filing. The County utilizes Court View 2000 software package which evenly distributes the cases among the Judges. This software also adjusts the new case assignments to account for recusals so that every attempt is made to evenly distribute the case load among the six rotating Judges.

All miscellaneous felony criminal matters (MC) are assigned to Division II. Each Judge rotates through this Division for a one month period, according to the schedule set out in the first paragraph, so that each Judge serves two non-consecutive months a year in this Division. The Judge serving in Division VI also serves as a backup for Division II.

All Domestic Relations (DR) matters are assigned to Division IV. Each Judge rotates through this Division for a one month period according to the schedule set out in the first paragraph, so that each Judge serves two non-consecutive months a year in this Division. In addition, four Magistrates rotate through this Division so that each Magistrate presides in Division IV for three non-consecutive months a year.

Cases over which Juvenile Court has concurrent original jurisdiction involving adults charged with the crime of contributing to delinquency (IC 35–46–1–8) or adults charged with violating the compulsory school attendance law (IC 20–8.1–3) shall be assigned to the Juvenile Division of the Vanderburgh Superior Court and presided over by the Judge assigned to Juvenile Court or the Magistrate assigned thereto. All remaining Misdemeanor and Traffic (CM, IF) cases shall be assigned to Division VI. These cases are presided over by four Magistrates subject to the supervision of one of the Judges. The Magistrates rotate through on a monthly basis serving three non-consecutive months a year.

All Small Claims (SC) and Ordinance Violation (OV, OE) cases are assigned to Division VI. These cases are presided over by four Magistrates subject to the supervision of one of the Judges. The Magistrates rotate through on a monthly basis serving three non-consecutive months a year. There is an assignment of one Magistrate to hear all OE cases in a court set up and named "Housing Court".

Mental Health cases are also assigned to Division VI and are heard by the presiding Judge or Magistrate presiding in Small Claims for that month.

All Probate and Juvenile matters (JS, JT, JP, JM, AD, AH, ES, EU, GU, TR, JC, JD) are assigned to Division VII. This Court is presided over by the Judge who does not participate in the rotation schedule set out in paragraph one. There is one Magistrate assigned to Juvenile Court. This Magistrate assignment is a one year minimum assignment.

The rotating schedules and the use of the Court View 2000 software creates a nearly as is possible a completely even distribution of the work load within Superior Court.

(B) Balance between Circuit and Superior Courts. The Circuit Court hears both civil and felony criminal cases. After a review of the Weighted Caseload Study for both Circuit and Superior Courts, the Judges of both Courts have unanimously agreed that no adjustment between the Courts is necessary for the following reasons:

1. The random method of assigning newly filed felony cases to Circuit or Superior Court, as adopted by both Courts, assigns four cases to Circuit Court for every three cases that are assigned to Superior Court. This results in Circuit Court being assigned more felony cases, including more serious felony cases, than Superior Court. This results in a heavier criminal jury trial schedule in Circuit Court.

2. Circuit Court assumes responsibility for and administers all Grand Juries called to hear cases in Vanderburgh County.

3. Circuit Court administers the Adult Felony Probation Department for both Courts.

4. Circuit Court administers the Alcohol Intensive Supervision Program and the Drug Intensive Supervision Program for both Courts.

5. Recognition by the Judges of both Courts that the general administration responsibilities of Superior Court are shared by seven Judges while the Circuit Court Judge assumes the total burden of these duties for Circuit Court.

The Judges of the Vanderburgh Circuit and Superior Courts unanimously believe that the current procedures comply with the Order for Development of Local Caseload Plans.

Adopted as Superior Court Rule 1.02 July 15, 2005, effective Jan. 1, 2006. Amended and renumbered as Circuit and Superior Court Rule 1.02 June 29, 2006, effective Jan. 1, 2007. Amended May 12, 2008, effective Jan. 1, 2009; effective Sept. 16, 2011.

LR82–AR00–S Rule 1.03. ASSIGNMENT OF JUDGES WITHIN SUPERIOR COURT

(A) Chief Judge and Judges of Superior Court. There shall be a Chief Judge elected on a date between January 1 and January 31 of each year by the Judges who shall begin his/her term as the Chief Judge on the following February 1st. The Chief Judge will be primarily responsible for the efficient and expeditious operation and conduct of the Court. In the absence of the Chief Judge, the Judge sitting in Division One shall act as temporary Chief Judge.

The following Courts shall have Judges elected as supervisors on a yearly basis: drug court, misdemeanor and traffic, small claims and domestic relations. Each Judge so selected shall be responsible for the efficient and expeditious operation of that Court. Each supervisor shall report periodically to the Chief Judge and all other Judges any change in the current operations of that Court. There shall be appointed each year a Supervisor of Information and Technology to oversee and assure the Court's compliance with Administrative Rule 9.

(B) Superior Court Rotation. Superior Court Judges shall rotate their sitting in the respective

Divisions of this Court consecutively in numerical order. The rotation shall commence on the first Monday of each month. Any new Judge replacement shall sit in the Division of the Judge whom he/she replaces unless otherwise agreed by majority vote of the Court as a whole. The Court, by a date not later than the first day of December or the first business day thereafter, shall publish a schedule of the sessions of this Court for the following calendar year of the Court together with the names of the Judges who will be sitting in the Divisions of this Court during each session thereof similar to Appendix B as attached hereto.

Adopted as Superior Court Rule 1.19, July 15, 2005, effective Jan. 1, 2006. Amended and renumbered as Circuit and Superior Court Rule 1.03, June 29, 2006, effective Jan. 1, 2007. Amended May 12, 2008, effective Jan. 1, 2009; effective Sept. 16, 2011.

LR82–AR00–S Rule 1.04. ASSIGNMENT AND DISPOSITION OF CIVIL CASES IN SUPERIOR COURT

All Civil cases shall, upon being filed in the office of the Clerk, be assigned in the following manner:

(A) Assignment. Each Civil Case shall be assigned to one of the six (6) rotating Judges by blind lot in the order presented for filing. The Judge assigned to each case shall have responsibility for all proceedings in that case including hearings of all motions, arguments and petitions. All emergency matters shall be heard by the assigned judge unless he/she is unable to do so, in which case he/she may refer the matter to another Judge. Where the assigned Judge is unavailable to refer the matter, such emergency matter may be heard by any other Judge.

(B) Transfer Within County. Where a case originates in the Small Claims, Juvenile or Probate Divisions and is transferred to the Civil Division, the clerk shall assign such case to a specific Judge in the same manner as in other Civil Cases.

(C) Transfer from Another County. All Civil cases transferred to this Court from another County shall be assigned by the Clerk as provided by the rules stated herein for the assignment of Civil Cases.

Adopted as Superior Court Rule 1.03, July 15, 2005, effective Jan. 1, 2006. Amended and renumbered as Circuit and Superior Court Rule 1.04, June 29, 2006, effective Jan. 1, 2007; effective Sept. 16, 2011.

LR82–SC00–S Rule 1.05. SUPERIOR COURT SMALL CLAIMS

All Small Claims matters are assigned to Division Six wherein the following Rules will apply:

(A) Service. On first appearance the Court will not allow service of process to be sent to the defendant's employer. On Proceeding Supplemental the Court will consider proper service for the purpose of obtaining an order of garnishment when service is good upon the employer, even though service may not be good upon the defendant. When the employer refuses service, it can be considered sufficient service for the purpose of an order of garnishment only. Service may be obtained by a process server if an affidavit of service is filed.

(B) Attorney Fees. Attorney's fees are awarded solely for the principal amount of the debt.

(C) Claim for Insufficient Funds. Upon filing of a claim for insufficient funds on bad checks where multiple statutory remedies are available, the claimant should elect which remedy is being requested and list the same on the statement of claim.

(D) Proceedings Supplemental—Judgment Entry. Parties must wait seven (7) days after obtaining a judgment before filing a Proceedings Supplemental, and the Judgment Entry must be filed with the Court prior to the Proceedings Supplemental being filed.

(E) Proceedings Supplemental—Hearings. Proceedings Supplemental hearings shall not be continued for progress after an order of garnishment or a personal order of garnishment has been obtained. A subsequent Motion for Proceedings Supplemental shall only be filed if the motion sets forth circumstances that have changed since the last hearing in regard to the defendant's financial status.

(F) All Cases to Have Future Date. No cases will be continued without date.

(G) Claims for Rent and Damages. All claims for rent and damages on leased property must be documented by a back rent and damages form available in the Small Claims Office, Room 223–1. This includes "judgments on proof" taken after the tenant has vacated the property, or claims for rent & damages sought on an initial appearance on a statement of claim.

(H) Non–Parties. Non-parties may be subpoenaed for initial hearings only upon leave of court.

Adopted as Superior Court Rule 1.04, July 15, 2005, effective Jan. 1, 2006. Amended and renumbered as Circuit and Superior Court Rule 1.05, June 29, 2006, effective Jan. 1, 2007; effective Sept. 16, 2011.

LR82–TR63–S Rule 1.06. SUPERIOR COURT JUDGES PRO TEMPORE

All appointments of Superior Court Judges Pro Tempore shall be made by the Chief Judge or by the Judge assigned to the Division wherein the pro tem will sit.

Adopted as Superior Court Rule 1.20, July 15, 2005, effective Jan. 1, 2006. Amended and renumbered as Circuit and Superior Court Rule 1.06, June 29, 2006, effective Jan. 1, 2007; effective Sept. 16, 2011.

LR82–TR79 Rule 1.07. SPECIAL JUDGE

In the event a Special Judge does not accept a case under Sections D, E, F, of TR 79, or a Judge of Circuit or Superior Court disqualifies or recuses under Section C of that rule, the case shall be referred to the Court Administrator of the Vanderburgh Superior Court for random reassignment to one of the non-recusing elected Judges of Vanderburgh County in both Circuit and Superior Courts.

Adopted as Superior Court Rule 1.23, July 15, 2005, effective Jan. 1, 2006, and as Circuit Court Rule 9, effective Feb. 1, 1999. Amended and renumbered as Circuit and Superior Court Rule 1.07, June 29, 2006, effective Jan. 1, 2007; effective Sept. 16, 2011.

LR82–AR11 Rule 1.08.　FORMAT OF FILINGS

Pleadings, motions and other papers shall be either legibly printed or typewritten on white opaque paper of at least sixteen (16) pound weight, eight and one-half (8 ½) inches wide and eleven (11) inches in length. All copies shall likewise be on white paper of sufficient strength and durability to resist normal wear and tear. If typewritten, the lines shall be double spaced, except for quotations, which shall be indented and single spaced. Script type shall not be used. Margins shall be at least 1 inch. Type face shall be 12 or larger in body, text, and footnotes.

Adopted as Superior Court Rule 1.05, July 15, 2005, effective Jan. 1, 2006, and as Circuit Court Rule 2, effective Feb. 1, 1999. Amended and renumbered as Circuit and Superior Court Rule 1.08, June 29, 2006, effective Jan. 1, 2007; effective Sept. 16, 2011.

LR82–TR00 Rule 1.09.　FILING OF PLEADINGS, MOTIONS AND OTHER PAPERS

All pleadings, motions and other papers shall be prepared in accordance with the provisions of the Indiana Rules of Trial Procedure. For the purpose of uniformity and convenience, the following requirements shall also be observed:

(1) All pleadings, subsequent to the original complaint, shall be filed in the office of the Judge to whom the case is assigned at any time during the office hours established by the Court. All orders submitted to the Court shall be in sufficient number and shall be accompanied by postage paid envelopes addressed to each party or counsel of record.

(2) All appearances by attorneys shall be filed in writing, together with proof of mailing or delivery thereof on counsel of record in compliance with Indiana Rules of Procedure.

(3) All filings shall be accompanied by a minute sheet which shall contain the number of the cause, the date, the suggested docket entry and a certificate of proof of service or copies. This minute sheet shall be signed by counsel or Pro Se Party, dated, stamped and filed with the Court. The Court may in its discretion, amend any such form of entry.

(4) All order book entries shall contain in their title the date for which said entry was made. A copy of all entries, which result from a hearing or trial, shall be submitted to the opposing counsel at least three (3) days before being presented to the Court.

(5) All pleadings filed and served upon opposing parties shall be clear and legible.

(6) No pleading other than a copy thereof shall be taken from the file. Any person taking any portion of the Court's files shall be deemed to be in contempt of Court. Upon request, the Clerk or Court shall (subject to Administrative Rule 9) furnish anyone with a copy of all or any part of such files upon payment of a reasonable charge therefore.

Adopted as Superior Court Rule 1.05, July 15, 2005, effective Jan. 1, 2006. Amended and renumbered as Circuit and Superior Court Rule 1.09, June 29, 2006, effective Jan. 1, 2007; effective Sept. 16, 2011.

LR82–TR10 Rule 1.10.　FORM OF PLEADING

(A) Caption. Every pleading shall contain a caption setting forth the name of the Court, the Division and Room Number, the title of the action and the file number.

(B) Titles. Titles on all pleadings shall delineate each topic included in the pleading, where a pleading contains an Answer, a Motion to Strike or Dismiss or a Jury Request each shall be set forth in the title.

Adopted as Superior Court Rule 1.05, July 15, 2005, effective Jan. 1, 2006. Amended and renumbered as Circuit and Superior Court Rule 1.10, June 29, 2006, effective Jan. 1, 2007; effective Sept. 16, 2011.

LR82–TR5 Rule 1.11.　VERIFICATION OF SERVICE ON OPPOSING PARTY

In all cases where any pleading or other document is required to be served upon an opposing party, proof of such service shall be made either by:

(1) A certificate of service signed by counsel of record or pro se party which specifies by name and address all counsel or parties upon whom the pleading or document was served, or

(2) An acknowledgment of service signed by the party served or counsel of record.

Adopted as Superior Court Rule 1.05, July 15, 2005, effective Jan. 1, 2006. Amended and renumbered as Circuit and Superior Court Rule 1.11, June 29, 2006, effective Jan. 1, 2007; effective Sept. 16, 2011.

LR82–TR5 Rule 1.12.　VERIFICATION OF TRIAL RULE 5 PLEADINGS

All Court Records (pleadings or documents) filed by any party or their attorneys shall contain a verification certifying that the court records comply with the filing requirements of Trial Rule 5 (G) applicable to information excluded from the public record under Administrative Rule 9 (G). A certification in substantially the following language shall be sufficient:

I/We hereby certify that the foregoing or attached Court Record or document complies with the requirements of Trial Rule 5(G) with regard to information excluded from the public record under Administrative Rule 9(G).

(Signed by party or counsel
of record)

Adopted as Superior Court Rule 2.26, July 15, 2005, effective Jan. 1, 2006. Amended and renumbered as Circuit and Superior Court Rule 1.12, June 29, 2006, effective Jan. 1, 2007; effective Sept. 16, 2011.

LR82–TR6 Rule 1.13.   EXTENSIONS OF TIME

(A) Standard Time Limits Apply. The time limits set out in these local rules, where allowable under the Indiana Rules of Trial Procedure, may be extended by order of the Court.

(B) Extensions. In all civil cases, each party required to respond to a complaint, counterclaim, or cross-claim, may obtain an automatic thirty (30) day extension of time to plead or otherwise respond to such claim by filing a Notice of Extension with the Court and serving a copy of the same upon all parties. Requests for additional extensions of time must be made by motion and hearing unless agreed to by the parties.

Adopted as Superior Court Rule 1.08, July 15, 2005, effective Jan. 1, 2006, and as Circuit Court Rule 3, effective Feb. 1, 1999. Amended and renumbered as Circuit and Superior Court Rule 1.13, June 29, 2006, effective Jan. 1, 2007; effective Sept. 16, 2011.

LR82–AR00 Rule 1.14.   ATTORNEY PROMPTNESS

Attorneys are expected to be prompt in their attendance at matters assigned for hearing. Failure to appear promptly or to notify the Court of an inability to attend a hearing at the time and place indicated may result in imposition of sanctions allowable and deemed appropriate by the Court.

Adopted as Superior Court Rule 1.09, July 15, 2005, effective Jan. 1, 2006. Amended and renumbered as Circuit and Superior Court Rule 1.14, June 29, 2006, effective Jan. 1, 2007; effective Sept. 16, 2011.

LR82–TR3.1 Rule 1.15.   ATTORNEY'S WITHDRAWAL

(A) Withdrawals Must Be in Writing. All withdrawals of appearance of counsel shall be in writing and by leave of Court. Leave of Court shall be granted only upon the following circumstances:

(1) The filing of an appearance by new counsel for said client; or

(2) Upon notice and hearing of the Petition for Leave to Withdraw, which said notice of hearing shall be served on the client at least 10 days prior to the hearing on the Petition for Leave to Withdraw. The Notice to the client shall include a copy of the Petition for Leave to Withdraw. Notice to the client shall also inform the client that the client can obtain new counsel or the client can represent himself/herself, if permissible, and that the client is

required to notify the Court within 30 days of the withdrawal of the client's decision. The Notice shall also include the name of the Judge assigned to the case and the address of the Court with information sufficient to advise the client that a failure to respond may result in the dismissal of the matter before the Court. Proof of service of the Notice shall be made by certified mail, return receipt, to be filed with the court on or before the date of the hearing.

(B) Withdrawal Petition Requirements. A Petition for Leave to Withdraw shall include the following:

(1) The last known address and telephone number of the client;

(2) The date the case is assigned for trial, if any;

(3) A statement of any current motions pending before the Court and

(4) A statement of the status of the case, including a verified statement that all entries have been filed.

Adopted as Superior Court Rule 1.06, July 15, 2005, effective Jan. 1, 2006, and as Circuit Court Rule 8, effective Feb. 1, 1999. Amended and renumbered as Circuit and Superior Court Rule 1.15, June 29, 2006, effective Jan. 1, 2007; effective Sept. 16, 2011.

LR82–TR12 Rule 1.16.   MOTIONS AND PETITIONS

(A) Briefs for Motions and Petitions.

(1) A Motion to Dismiss under Rule 12 of the Indiana Rules of Trial Procedure, for Summary Judgment, for judgment on a pleading, for more definite statement, or to strike, shall be accompanied by a separate Supporting Brief. The adverse party shall have thirty (30) days after service of the initial brief within which to serve and file an Answer Brief, and the moving party shall have fifteen (15) days after service of the Answer Brief within which to serve and file a Reply Brief. With respect to all other motions, the adverse party shall have fifteen (15) days after service thereof within which to serve and file a response thereto, and the moving party shall have seven (7) days after service of such response within which to serve and file a reply thereto. If multiple motions are within the same filing, said motions shall be separated by identity in the title.

(2) The provision of this rule requiring a separate Supporting Brief shall apply to every defense asserted pursuant to Rule 12 (b) of the Indiana Rules of Trial Procedure, whether asserted in the responsive pleading or by separate motion.

(3) Each party shall supply a proposed Order with the Brief or Reply.

(B) Motions for Summary Judgment.

(1) Any Motion for Summary Judgment shall be filed no later than one hundred twenty (120) days before the trial date.

(2) In addition to a separate Supporting Brief, and a proposed Summary Judgment shall be submitted with any Motion for Summary Judgment.

Adopted as Superior Court Rule 1.12, July 15, 2005, effective Jan. 1, 2006, and as Circuit Court Rule 5, effective Feb. 1, 1999. Amended and renumbered as Circuit and Superior Court Rule 1.16, June 29, 2006, effective Jan. 1, 2007. Amended June 1, 2007, effective January 1, 2008; effective Sept. 16, 2011.

LR82–TR16 Rule 1.17. SCHEDULING CONFERENCE

(A) Scheduling Conference Meeting. Upon the closing of the issues in civil cases, the Court may order or the parties may request a Scheduling Conference. At the Scheduling Conference, the Court shall establish deadlines and time limits to ensure the progress of the litigation and will enter a Scheduling Order similar to that contained in Appendix A. To the extent that the parties are in a position to discuss and/or apprise the Court of any of the situations set forth below they should do so.

(1) Whether there is a question of jurisdiction over the person or the subject matter of the action;

(2) Whether all parties, plaintiff or defendant, have been correctly designated;

(3) Whether there are any questions concerning the joinder of parties or claims;

(4) Whether a third party complaint or impleading petition is contemplated;

(5) Whether there is a question of appointment of a guardian ad litem, next friend, administrator, executor, receiver or trustee;

(6) The time reasonably required for the completion of discovery;

(7) Whether there are pending motions;

(8) Whether a trial by jury has been timely demanded;

(9) Whether separation of claims, defenses, or issues would be desirable, and if so, whether discovery should be limited to the claims, defenses, or issues first to be tried;

(10) Whether related actions are pending or contemplated in any Court;

(11) The estimated time required for trial;

(B) Items Included in Scheduling Order. The Scheduling Order will include, among other things, a date certain for a Pre-Trial Conference. The dates contained in the Court's Scheduling Order may be amended by the Court on its own motion or at the request of one or more of the parties.

Adopted as Superior Court Rule 1.10, July 15, 2005, effective Jan. 1, 2006. Amended and renumbered as Circuit and Superior Court Rule 1.17, June 29, 2006, effective Jan. 1, 2007; effective Sept. 16, 2011.

LR82–TR16 Rule 1.18. PRE–TRIAL CONFERENCE

The normal Pre-Trial requirements are set forth in Rule 16 of the Indiana Rules of Civil Procedure. The counsel who will try the lawsuit shall attend the Pre-Trial Conference in person and be prepared to discuss the following:

(1) Whether the parties are prepared to proceed to trial;

(2) Whether mediation has occurred;

(3) Whether there are pending motions;

(4) The progress of each party in obtaining stipulations of fact and authenticity of exhibits;

(5) A statement as to whether the parties are willing to waive their jury request;

(6) Whether the Court may assist in the settlement of the case;

(7) Any significant evidentiary issues;

(8) Any other matters of which the Court should be advised.

Adopted as Superior Court Rule 1.11, July 15, 2005, effective Jan. 1, 2006. Amended and renumbered as Circuit and Superior Court Rule 1.18, June 29, 2006, effective Jan. 1, 2007; effective Sept. 16, 2011.

LR82–TR33 Rule 1.19. INTERROGATORIES

A party may, without leave of Court, serve upon another party up to thirty (30) interrogatories including sub-parts.

Any party desiring to serve additional interrogatories upon another party, shall first file a written motion with the Court, identifying the proposed additional interrogatories and setting forth the reasons demonstrating good cause for their use.

Adopted as Superior Court Rule 1.22, July 15, 2005, effective Jan. 1, 2006, and as Circuit Court Rule 4, effective Feb. 1, 1999. Amended and renumbered as Circuit and Superior Court Rule 1.19, June 29, 2006, effective Jan. 1, 2007; effective Sept. 16, 2011.

LR82–TR16 Rule 1.20. TRIAL BRIEFS AND MOTIONS IN LIMINE

Unless ordered otherwise at the scheduling conference, trial briefs and motions in limine may be furnished to the Court by the parties at least two (2) weeks prior to the Pre-Trial Conference. Copies of any such trial briefs and motions in limine shall be furnished to opposing counsel and served in the same manner as other pleadings. Opposing counsel, after having been so served, shall have seven (7) days to file any response and shall serve the other party in the same manner as other pleadings.

Adopted as Superior Court Rule 1.14, July 15, 2005, effective Jan. 1, 2006, and as Circuit Court Rule 6, effective Feb. 1, 1999. Amended and renumbered as Circuit and Superior Court Rule 1.20, June 29, 2006, effective Jan. 1, 2007; effective Sept. 16, 2011.

LR82–TR51 Rule 1.21. INSTRUCTIONS

At the pre-trial conference, counsel for each party shall tender a proposed "issues" instruction (see Indiana Pattern Jury Instruction 1.03). They shall also be prepared to present and discuss any non-routine preliminary or final instructions. Other proposed preliminary or final instructions may be presented to the Court and shall be served upon opposing counsel on the first day of trial. Additional or amended final instructions may be presented upon a showing of good cause or in order to conform the instructions to the evidence at trial.

Adopted as Superior Court Rule 1.15, July 15, 2005, effective Jan. 1, 2006. Amended and renumbered as Circuit and Superior Court Rule 1.21, June 29, 2006, effective Jan. 1, 2007; effective Sept. 16, 2011.

LR82–TR55 Rule 1.22. DEFAULT JUDG- MENTS—ATTORNEYS FEES

Application for default judgment requesting an allowance of attorney's fees shall be accompanied by an affidavit executed by the attorney requesting the fee. The affidavit shall be in a form and substance to enable the Court to determine if attorney's fees are appropriate, and if so, the reasonable amount thereof. Said affidavit shall support the request by setting forth the authority for the Court to award attorney's fees (e.g. contract, statute, etc.) and the basis upon which the proposed fees are computed, such as the number of hours employed and the number of hours anticipated that will be employed pursuing satisfaction of judgment. In the absence of an affidavit there shall be no attorney's fees allowed.

Adopted as Superior Court Rule 1.21, July 15, 2005, effective Jan. 1, 2006, and as Circuit Court Rule 7, effective Feb. 1, 1999. Amended and renumbered as Circuit and Superior Court Rule 1.22, June 29, 2006, effective Jan. 1, 2007; effective Sept. 16, 2011.

LR82–TR69 Rule 1.23. POST–JUDGMENT PRO- CEEDING

(A) Entry of Final Decree Required. No post-judgment proceedings shall be instituted until there is a final decree or judgment entered of record with the Vanderburgh County Clerk's Office. The Court may waive this requirement where it is shown a party is being unduly harmed by its enforcement.

(B) Waiting Period. After Judgment is obtained and an entry is filed with the Court, parties may file Proceedings Supplemental. Parties must wait seven (7) days after obtaining a judgment before filing Proceedings Supplemental with the Court.

(C) Hearings on Proceedings Supplemental. Proceedings Supplemental hearings shall not be continued for progress after an order of garnishment or a personal order of garnishment has been obtained. A subsequent Motion for Proceedings Supplemental shall only be filed if the motion sets forth circumstances that have changed since the last hearing in regard to the defendant's financial status. No cases will be continued without date.

Adopted as Superior Court Rules 1.03 and 1.18, July 15, 2005, effective Jan. 1, 2006. Amended and renumbered as Circuit and Superior Court Rule 1.23, June 29, 2006, effective Jan. 1, 2007; effective Sept. 16, 2011.

LR82–AR7 Rule 1.24. CUSTODY, DISPOSITION AND WITHDRAWAL OF ORIGINAL REC- ORDS AND EXHIBITS

(A) Governed by Local Rules. Except as provided for in Administrative Rule 7, the custody, distribution, and withdrawal of original records and exhibits shall be governed by this rule.

(B) Court Reporter Maintains Custody. After being marked for identification, models, diagrams, exhibits and materials offered or admitted into evidence in any cause pending or tried in this Court shall be placed in the custody of the Court Reporter, unless otherwise ordered by the Court, and shall not be withdrawn until after time for an appeal has run or the case is disposed of otherwise. Should an appeal be taken, such items shall not be withdrawn until the final mandate of the reviewing Court is filed in the office of the Clerk, and until the case is disposed of as to all issues unless otherwise ordered.

(C) Retrieval. Subject to provisions of subsection A, B and D hereof, unless otherwise ordered, all models, diagrams, documents, exhibits or material placed in custody of the Court shall be retrieved by the party offering them in evidence within ninety (90) days after the case is decided. In cases in which an appeal is taken, said items shall be removed within thirty (30) days after the case is disposed of as to all issues, unless otherwise ordered. At such time of removal, a detailed receipt shall be provided by the party retrieving the evidence and filed in the cause. No motion or order is required as a prerequisite to the removal of an exhibit pursuant to this subpart.

(D) Disposal of Unretrieved Items. If the parties or their attorneys shall neglect to remove models, diagrams, exhibits or material within sixty (60) days of when the case is disposed of, the Court may direct disposition of the same.

(E) Contraband. Contraband exhibits, such as controlled substances, money and weapons shall be released to the investigative agency at the conclusion of the trial and not placed in the custody of the Court Reporter. A receipt shall be issued and a photograph substituted when such contraband exhibits are released.

(F) Withdrawal. Except as otherwise herein provided, with respect to the dispositions of models and exhibits, no person shall withdraw any original paper, pleading, record, model or exhibit from the custody of the Clerk or other office of the Court having custody thereof except by order of the appropriate Judge.

Adopted as Superior Court Rule 1.16, July 15, 2005, effective Jan. 1, 2006. Amended and renumbered as Circuit and Superior Court Rule 1.24, June 29, 2006, effective Jan. 1, 2007; effective Sept. 16, 2011.

LR82–AR9 Rule 1.25.   ACCESS TO COURT RECORDS

(A) Information Excluded from Public Access. The following information is excluded from public access and is confidential:

(1) Information that is excluded from public access pursuant to Federal Law,

(2) Information that is excluded from public access pursuant to Indiana Statute or Court Rule,

(3) All personal notes, email and deliberative material of judges, jurors and court staff, judicial agencies, and information recorded in personal data assistants (PDA's) or organizers and personal calendars,

(4) Diaries, journals or other personal notes serving as the functional equivalent of a diary or journal, pursuant to Ind. Code 5–14–3–4(b)(7),

(5) Advisory or deliberative material created, collected or exchanged by, between or among Judges, including journals or minutes of Judge's Meetings, and

(6) Information excluded from public access by specific court order.

(B) Access to Information Excluded From Public. Access to information which is excluded from public access and is confidential may not be accessed without the prior written authorization of the Judge supervising that office or department which created or archived that information. In some instances, access will require authorization from all Judges of Vanderburgh County.

Adopted as Superior Court Rule 2.25, July 15, 2005, effective Jan. 1, 2006. Amended and renumbered as Circuit and Superior Court Rule 1.25, June 29, 2006, effective Jan. 1, 2007; effective Sept. 16, 2011.

LR82–AR15 Rule 1.26.   COURT REPORTERS

(A) Definitions. The following definitions shall apply under this Local Rule:

(1) A Court Reporter is a person who is specifically designated by a court to perform the official court reporting services for the court including preparing a transcript of the record.

(2) Equipment means all physical items owned by the court or other governmental entity and used by a court reporter in performing court reporting ser-

vices. Equipment shall include, but not be limited to, telephones, computer hardware, software programs, disks, tapes and any other device used for recording, storing and transcribing electronic data.

(3) Work space means that portion of the court's facilities dedicated to each court reporter, including but not limited to actual space in the courtroom and any designated office space.

(4) Page means the page unit of transcript which results when a recording is transcribed in the form required by Indiana Rule of Appellate Procedure 7.2.

(5) Recording means the electronic, mechanical, stenographic or other recording made as required by Indiana Trial Procedure 74.

(6) Regular hours worked means those hours which the court is regularly scheduled to work during any given work week. Depending on the particular court, these hours may vary from court to court within the county but remain the same for each week.

(7) Gap hours worked means those hours worked that are in excess of the regular hours worked but not in excess of forty (40) hours per work week.

(8) Overtime hours worked means those hours worked in excess of forty (40) hours per work week.

(9) Work week means a seven (7) consecutive day week that consistently begins and ends on the same day throughout the year; i.e. Sunday through Saturday, Wednesday through Tuesday, Friday through Thursday.

(10) Court means the particular court for which the court reporter performs services. Court may also mean all of the courts in Vanderburgh County.

(11) County indigent transcript means a transcript that is paid for from county funds and is for the use on behalf of a litigant who has been declared indigent by a court.

(12) State indigent transcript means a transcript that is paid for from state funds and is for the use on behalf of litigant who has been declared indigent by a court.

(13) Private transcript means a transcript, including but not limited to a deposition transcript that is paid for by a private party.

(B) Salaries and Per Page Fees.

(1) Court reporters shall be paid an annual salary for time spent working under the control, direction and direct supervision of their supervising court during any regular work hours, gap hours, or overtime hours. The supervising court shall enter into a written agreement with the court reporters which outlines the manner in which the court reporter is to be compensated for gap and overtime hours; i.e. monetary compensation or compensatory time off regular work hours.

(2) The maximum per page fee a court reporter may charge for the preparation of a county indigent transcript shall be Four Dollars and Twenty-five Cents ($4.25) for appellate transcripts and Three Dollars and Seventy-five Cents ($3.75) for all other transcripts. The Court Reporter shall, after approval by the Court, submit a claim directly to the county for the preparation of any county indigent transcripts. All transcripts will be subject to a minimum fee of Thirty-five Dollars ($35.00).

(3) The maximum per page fee a court reporter may charge for the preparation of a state indigent transcript shall be Four Dollars and Twenty-five Cents ($4.25) for appellate transcripts and Three Dollars and Seventy-five Cents ($3.75) for all other transcripts. All transcripts will be subject to a minimum fee of Thirty-five Dollars ($35.00).

(4) The maximum per page fee a court reporter may charge for the preparation of a private transcript shall be Four Dollars and Twenty-five Cents ($4.25) for appellate transcripts and Three Dollars and Seventy-five Cents ($3.75) for all other transcripts. All transcripts will be subject to a minimum fee of Thirty-five Dollars ($35.00).

(5) The maximum per page fee a court reporter may charge for the preparation of copies of a transcript shall be One Dollar and Fifty Cents ($1.50).

(6) An additional labor charge of Twenty Dollars ($20.00) per hour may be charged for the time spent binding the transcript and exhibit binders which reflect an approximate average of the annual Court Reporters' salaries in Vanderburgh County.

(7) An additional $1.50 per page fee may be charged for the preparation of an expedited transcript (one which is to be completed within 10 calendar days).

(8) Each court reporter shall report, at least on annual basis all transcripts to the Indiana Supreme Court Division of State of Court Administration. The reporting shall be made on forms prescribed by the Division of State of Court Administration.

(C) Private Practice.

(1) If a court reporter elects to engage in private practice through the recording of a deposition and/or preparing of a deposition transcript, the court reporter desires to utilize the court's equipment, work space and supplies, and the court agrees to the use of the court equipment for such purpose, the court and the court reporter shall enter into a written agreement which must, at a minimum, designate the following:

(a) The reasonable market rate for the use of equipment, work space and supplies,

(b) The method by which records are to be kept for the use of equipment, work space and supplies, and

(c) The method by which the court reporter is to reimburse the court for the use of the equipment, work space and supplies.

(2) If a court reporter elects to engage in private practice through the recording of a deposition and/or preparing of a deposition transcript, all such private practice work shall be conducted outside of regular working hours.

Adopted as Superior Court Rule 2.24, July 15, 2005, effective Jan. 1, 2006. Amended and renumbered as Circuit and Superior Court Rule 1.26, June 29, 2006, effective Jan. 1, 2007. Amended June 1, 2007, effective January 1, 2008; effective Sept. 16, 2011.

Appendix A. SCHEDULING CONFERENCE ORDER

The parties, by their respective attorneys, reviewed the issues of the cause with the Court at a scheduling conference, and it appearing that the above litigation is at issue, the Court enters the following Order.

1. ___ shall be the date by which all parties shall have completed discovery of the issues in this cause or shall have filed their Motion to Compel Discovery.

2. ___ shall be the date when plaintiff shall have filed with the Court, and served upon opposing counsel, the specific acts of alleged negligence and/or other specific acts of breach or otherwise that the plaintiff intends to produce evidence upon at the trial.

3. ___ shall be the date by when the plaintiff shall file with the Court and serve on opposing counsel a list of plaintiff's prospective witnesses and exhibits together with an itemization of damages the plaintiff intends to produce evidence upon at the time of trial.

4. ___ shall be the date by when the defendant shall file with the Court and serve upon opposing counsel the specific acts constituting defenses alleged by the defendant that the defendant intends to produce evidence upon at the time of trial.

5. ___ shall be the date by when the defendant shall file with the Court and serve upon opposing counsel a list of defendant's prospective witnesses and exhibits together with an itemization of damages, if any, upon any Counterclaim which the defendant intends to produce evidence upon at the time of trial.

6. ___ shall be the date by when the plaintiff supplements or amends any data furnished as required above.

7. ___ shall be the date when any party may file a Motion for Summary Judgment upon pleadings and issues for trial.

8. ___ shall be the date when each party shall notify the Court that a settlement of issues is not successful and the trial date is confirmed.

9. ___ shall be the date when any party is to update their itemization of damages they intend to present evidence upon at the time of trial and for the filing of any Motions in Limine.

10. ___ shall be the date by when each party shall submit to the Courts its Proposed Preliminary, if any, and its Final Instructions for the Jury.

11. ___ shall be the date on which this cause shall be submitted to trial by jury or by Court.

12. ___ shall be the alternate date which this cause may be tried by jury.

13. ___ shall be the date on which the counsel for the parties attend a conference of attorneys as contemplated by Indiana Rules of Trial Procedure.

14. ___ shall be the date on which the Court will hold its Pre–Trial conference pursuant to Trial Rule 16 of the Indiana Rules of Trial Procedure.

15. ___ shall be the date to give Statement of Facts to Court.

Adopted as Superior Court App. A, July 15, 2005, effective Jan. 1, 2006. Amended and renumbered as Circuit and Superior Court App. A, June 29, 2006, effective Jan. 1, 2007; effective Sept. 16, 2011.

Appendix B. SCHEDULE OF ASSIGNMENT

IN THE VANDERBURGH SUPERIOR COURT

2011 TERM

The Judges of the Vanderburgh Superior Court have fixed and now publish the following schedule of assignment for the 2011 Term of the Court.

Week of		Div. I Civil	Div. II Crim.	Div. III Civil	Div. IV Dom. Rel.	Div. V Civil	Div. VI Crim.
Jan.	3	Pigman	Kiely	Trockman	Tornatta	D'Amour	Lloyd
	10	Pigman	Kiely	Trockman	Tornatta	D'Amour	Lloyd
	17	Pigman	Kiely	Trockman	Tornatta	D'Amour	Lloyd
	24	Pigman	Kiely	Trockman	Tornatta	D'Amour	Lloyd
	31	Pigman	Kiely	Trockman	Tornatta	D'Amour	Lloyd
Feb.	7	Lloyd	Pigman	Kiely	Trockman	Tornatta	D'Amour
	14	Lloyd	Pigman	Kiely	Trockman	Tornatta	D'Amour
	21	Lloyd	Pigman	Kiely	Trockman	Tornatta	D'Amour
	28	Lloyd	Pigman	Kiely	Trockman	Tornatta	D'Amour
Mar.	7	D'Amour	Lloyd	Pigman	Kiely	Trockman	Tornatta
	14	D'Amour	Lloyd	Pigman	Kiely	Trockman	Tornatta
	21	D'Amour	Lloyd	Pigman	Kiely	Trockman	Tornatta
	28	D'Amour	Lloyd	Pigman	Kiely	Trockman	Tornatta
Apr.	4	Tornatta	D'Amour	Lloyd	Pigman	Kiely	Trockman
	11	Tornatta	D'Amour	Lloyd	Pigman	Kiely	Trockman
	18	Tornatta	D'Amour	Lloyd	Pigman	Kiely	Trockman
	25	Tornatta	D'Amour	Lloyd	Pigman	Kiely	Trockman
May	2	Trockman	Tornatta	D'Amour	Lloyd	Pigman	Kiely
	9	Trockman	Tornatta	D'Amour	Lloyd	Pigman	Kiely
	16	Trockman	Tornatta	D'Amour	Lloyd	Pigman	Kiely
	23	Trockman	Tornatta	D'Amour	Lloyd	Pigman	Kiely
	30	Trockman	Tornatta	D'Amour	Lloyd	Pigman	Kiely
June	6	Kiely	Trockman	Tornatta	D'Amour	Lloyd	Pigman
	13	Kiely	Trockman	Tornatta	D'Amour	Lloyd	Pigman
	20	Kiely	Trockman	Tornatta	D'Amour	Lloyd	Pigman
	27	Kiely	Trockman	Tornatta	D'Amour	Lloyd	Pigman
July	4	Pigman	Kiely	Trockman	Tornatta	D'Amour	Lloyd
	11	Pigman	Kiely	Trockman	Tornatta	D'Amour	Lloyd
	18	Pigman	Kiely	Trockman	Tornatta	D'Amour	Lloyd
	25	Pigman	Kiely	Trockman	Tornatta	D'Amour	Lloyd
Aug.	1	Lloyd	Pigman	Kiely	Trockman	Tornatta	D'Amour
	8	Lloyd	Pigman	Kiely	Trockman	Tornatta	D'Amour
	15	Lloyd	Pigman	Kiely	Trockman	Tornatta	D'Amour
	22	Lloyd	Pigman	Kiely	Trockman	Tornatta	D'Amour
	29	Lloyd	Pigman	Kiely	Trockman	Tornatta	D'Amour
Sept.	5	D'Amour	Lloyd	Pigman	Kiely	Trockman	Tornatta
	12	D'Amour	Lloyd	Pigman	Kiely	Trockman	Tornatta
	19	D'Amour	Lloyd	Pigman	Kiely	Trockman	Tornatta
	26	D'Amour	Lloyd	Pigman	Kiely	Trockman	Tornatta
Oct.	3	Tornatta	D'Amour	Lloyd	Pigman	Kiely	Trockman
	10	Tornatta	D'Amour	Lloyd	Pigman	Kiely	Trockman
	17	Tornatta	D'Amour	Lloyd	Pigman	Kiely	Trockman
	24	Tornatta	D'Amour	Lloyd	Pigman	Kiely	Trockman
	31	Tornatta	D'Amour	Lloyd	Pigman	Kiely	Trockman
Nov.	7	Trockman	Tornatta	D'Amour	Lloyd	Pigman	Kiely
	14	Trockman	Tornatta	D'Amour	Lloyd	Pigman	Kiely
	21	Trockman	Tornatta	D'Amour	Lloyd	Pigman	Kiely
	28	Trockman	Tornatta	D'Amour	Lloyd	Pigman	Kiely
Dec.	5	Kiely	Trockman	Tornatta	D'Amour	Lloyd	Pigman
	12	Kiely	Trockman	Tornatta	D'Amour	Lloyd	Pigman
	19	Kiely	Trockman	Tornatta	D'Amour	Lloyd	Pigman
	26	Kiely	Trockman	Tornatta	D'Amour	Lloyd	Pigman

2011 MAGISTRATE SCHEDULE

MONTH	MISDEMEANOR COURT	SMALL CLAIMS	DIVISION IV	OTHER	JUVENILE COURT
JANUARY	MARCRUM	HAMILTON	MAURER	CORCORAN	FERGUSON
FEBRUARY	MAURER	MARCRUM	HAMILTON	CORCORAN	FERGUSON
MARCH	MAURER	CORCORAN	MARCRUM	HAMILTON	FERGUSON
APRIL	HAMILTON	MAURER	CORCORAN	MARCRUM	FERGUSON
MAY	MARCRUM	HAMILTON	MAURER	CORCORAN	FERGUSON
JUNE	CORCORAN	MARCRUM	HAMILTON	MAURER	FERGUSON
JULY	MAURER	CORCORAN	MARCRUM	HAMILTON	FERGUSON
AUGUST	HAMILTON	MAURER	CORCORAN	MARCRUM	FERGUSON
SEPTEMBER	MARCRUM	HAMILTON	MAURER	CORCORAN	FERGUSON
OCTOBER	HAMILTON	CORCORAN	MARCRUM	MAURER	FERGUSON
NOVEMBER	MAURER	MARCRUM	CORCORAN	HAMILTON	FERGUSON
DECEMBER	CORCORAN	MAURER	HAMILTON	MARCRUM	FERGUSON

**Housing Court is held on the 2nd Thursday of each month; the Magistrate in the Other column will switch with the presiding Housing Court Magistrate.

Adopted effective Jan. 1, 2008; amended effective Jan. 1, 2010; effective Sept. 16, 2011.

CRIMINAL RULES OF THE VANDER-BURGH SUPERIOR COURT

Adopted June 29, 2006, Effective January 1, 2007

Including Amendments Received Through November 1, 2013

Research Notes

Annotations to the Criminal Rules of the Vanderburgh Superior Court Rules are available in West's Annotated Indiana Code, *Title 34 Appendix.*

These rules may be searched electronically on Westlaw *in the* IN-RULES *database; updates to these rules may be found on* Westlaw *in* IN-RULESUPDATES. *For search tips and a summary of database content, consult the Westlaw Scope Screens for each database.*

LR82–CR2.2 Rule 2.01. ASSIGNMENT OF CRIMINAL CASES

(A) All cases in Vanderburgh County, Indiana in which the highest crime charged is a felony shall be randomly assigned (by the Clerk of Vanderburgh County) to the Circuit and Superior Courts of Vanderburgh County in the following ratio: Eight (8) cases are to be assigned to the Vanderburgh Circuit Court for each six (6) cases assigned to Vanderburgh Superior Court. Each felony cause number shall be deemed a case within the meaning of this rule, regardless of the number of counts or defendants charged in said case.

(B) All cases assigned to the Vanderburgh Circuit Court shall be tried by the Circuit Court Judge or the Magistrate of the Court as determined in the discretion of the Court.

(C) All felony cases assigned to the Vanderburgh Superior Court shall be tried in accordance with the rotation system established by the rules of that Court.

(D) All cases reassigned from the Circuit Court Judge of Vanderburgh County or the Magistrate of that Court, shall be reassigned to the Senior Judge of the Vanderburgh Circuit Court and/or any Judge of the Vanderburgh Superior Court.

(E) All cases reassigned within the Vanderburgh Superior Court shall be reassigned in accordance with the rotation system established by the rules of that Court.

(F) All criminal cases filed in the County in which the highest crime charged is a misdemeanor, shall be assigned to the Misdemeanor/Traffic Division of the Vanderburgh Superior Court.

(G) A dismissed criminal action may only be refiled in the same Court to which the case was originally assigned.

(H) The Circuit Court Judge and the Chief Judge of Superior Court may by agreement, order transfer of any felony case pending in either Court to provide consolidated legal defense for those defendants facing multiple criminal charges. Such cases shall be consolidated unless efficient case disposition may be adversely affected by transfer.

Adopted June 29, 2006, effective Jan. 1, 2007. Amended effective Sept. 16, 2011.

LR82–CR00 Rule 2.02. TRANSFER OF CASES BETWEEN VANDERBURGH CIRCUIT AND SUPERIOR COURTS

If a defendant has a pending case in the Vanderburgh Superior Court prior to the filing of a case in Circuit Court, the Circuit Court case will be transferred to Superior Court. Similarly, if a defendant has a prior pending case in Circuit Court, any newer case in Superior Court will be transferred to Circuit Court.

Adopted June 29, 2006, effective Jan. 1, 2007. Amended effective Sept. 16, 2011.

LR82–CR00 Rule 2.03.   BOND SCHEDULE

All persons charged by indictment or affidavit shall be held to bail in the amount set forth below:

(A) Felonies. No bonds shall be set in any felony matters except as determined by a Judicial Officer. The Court shall consider factors found in IC 35–33–8–4 in setting appropriate bond in all cases.

(B) Class A Misdemeanors. Unless otherwise specified, all Class A Misdemeanors shall have a bond of $100.00 for Indiana residents and $200.00 for non-residents.

Specific Exceptions for Class A Misdemeanors.

Domestic Violence Battery

> First offense: $500.00

> Second offense: $1000.00

> Third offense: $5000.00

Leaving the scene of an accident causing personal injury: $500.00.

All OMVWI bonds shall be determined by a Judicial Officer.

(C) Class B Misdemeanors. Unless otherwise specified, all Class B Misdemeanors shall have a bond of $50.00 for Indiana residents and $100.00 for non-residents.

Specific Exceptions for Class B Misdemeanors.

Invasion of Privacy involving co-habitating or formerly co-habitating adults:

> First offense: $500.00

> Second offense: $1000.00

> Third offense $5000.00

(D) Class C Misdemeanors. Unless otherwise specified, all Class C Misdemeanors shall have a bond of $50.00 for Indiana residents and 100.00 for non-residents.

Specific Exceptions for Class C Misdemeanors.

Minor possession/consumption/transport: $25.00 for Indiana resident and $50.00 for non-residents.

Adopted June 29, 2006, effective Jan. 1, 2007. Amended effective June 23, 2009; effective Sept. 16, 2011.

LR82–CR00 Rule 2.03.1.   DRUG AND ALCOHOL DEFERRAL SERVICES (DADS)—SCHEDULE OF FEES

Operating a Motor Vehicle While Intoxicated (O.M.V.W.I.) Program

$250.00—Full program fee.

$150.00—For clients referred for transfer and/or monitoring services.

$ 75.00—For clients referred from Misdemeanor Court for Possession of Marijuana u/30 grams.

Youth Alcohol Program (Y.A.P.) Violation of the Indiana State Liquor Law (V.L.L.)

$175.00—Full program fee.

$75.00—Transfer and/or monitoring services.

V.C.S.A. Program—Violation of Controlled Substance Act (V.C.S.A.)

$400.00—For clients referred for Felony offenses related to controlled substances.

The program fee for all programs covers maintenance and operating costs of the D.A.D.S. program, and is separate from the costs of referral services for education, counseling, or other treatment costs (including urine drug screens as required). The costs of referral services will be the client's responsibility.

For multiple eligible offenses, the standard fee may be levied for each additional offense.

A fee of $15.00 may be charged for each missed D.A.D.S. appointment.

Adopted effective Oct. 27, 2007. . Amended effective Sept. 16, 2011.

LR82–CR00 Rule 2.03.2. VANDERBURGH COUNTY DAY REPORTING DRUG COURT/FORENSIC DIVERSION PROGRAM

Schedule of Fees

$500—Full program fee

$100—Public Defender fee

$ 75—Evaluation fee

Drug Testing Fees

$13—urinalysis on site

$25—urinalysis by lab

$25—oral test

There is also a statutory Drug and Alcohol Interdiction Fee of $200 which is paid in the Clerk's Office.

Adopted effective Oct. 27, 2007. Amended effective Sept. 16, 2011.

LR82–CR00 Rule 2.04.   DISCOVERY

In each criminal case in the Vanderburgh Circuit and Superior Courts, the Vanderburgh County Prosecutor's Office and the law enforcement agencies which are involved in the case shall produce to the defense attorney the entire case file, including a list of all evidence held, within thirty (30) days of the defense attorney's first appearance in court. This is a continuing rule, and all additions to the case file shall be produced immediately upon their creation.

Except by order of court, a defense attorney receiving such a case file shall not reveal any victim's or witnesses' confidential identifying information, including Social Security number, driver's license number and date of birth to anyone other than an associate or employee of the attorney. In the event the defense attorney wishes to show the case file to any other person, including the defendant, the attorney shall first redact such information from the file.

Adopted June 29, 2006, effective Jan. 1, 2007. Amended June 1, 2007, effective January 1, 2008; effective Sept. 16, 2011.

LR82–CR00–S Rule 2.05. ASSIGNMENT OF CRIMINAL MATTERS

All Felony criminal matters and Misdemeanor Jury Trials are assigned to Divisions II and VI on a consolidated calendar matter, if room is taken then court sessions are held in Room 202.

Adopted as Assignment of Criminal Matters, Felony Division Rules, effective May 5, 2000. Amended and renumbered as Criminal Rule 2.05, June 29, 2006, effective Jan. 1, 2007; effective Sept. 16, 2011.

LR82–CR00–S Rule 2.06. INITIAL APPEARANCE OF THE ACCUSED

All defendants in the custody of the Sheriff at the time of the filing of a request for determination of Probable Cause or an Information or Indictment, shall appear before the Court not later than the next judicial day. All defendants arrested on warrants shall appear in open court for initial hearing not later than the next judicial day following the defendant's apprehension, or upon the date the defendant is summoned to appear, if any.

Adopted as Felony Division Rule 1, effective May 5, 2000. Amended and renumbered as Criminal Rule 2.06, June 29, 2006, effective Jan. 1, 2007; effective Sept. 16, 2011.

LR82–CR00–S Rule 2.07. CONTINUANCE OF INITIAL HEARING

The initial hearing may be continued for a period of time not to exceed twenty days to allow the defendant to obtain private counsel.

Adopted as Felony Division Rule 2, effective May 5, 2000. Amended and renumbered as Criminal Rule 2.07, June 29, 2006, effective Jan. 1, 2007; effective Sept. 16, 2011.

LR82–CR00–S Rule 2.08. TRIAL SCHEDULING

Trial shall be set not more than ten weeks form [1] the week in which Counsel first appears, or the defendant is granted leave to proceed Pro Se.

Adopted as Felony Division Rule 3, effective May 5, 2000. Amended and renumbered as Criminal Rule 2.08, June 29, 2006, effective Jan. 1, 2007; amended June 1, 2007, effective Jan. 1, 2008; effective Sept. 16, 2011.

[1] So in original. Probably should read "from".

LR82–CR00–S Rule 2.09. HOLDING DATES

The Court shall set a Holding Date at 8:30 am on the Wednesday five weeks prior to the trial. The State shall provide the Defense with a copy of the Police file and an offer of settlement (if the State intends to make such an offer on the case) not less than one week prior to the Holding Date. On the Holding Date, the Parties shall appear and report to the Court whether or not the State has provided the Police file to the Defense and whether or not the defendant has received and will accept or reject an offer by the State. If the defendant rejects the State's offer, the defense shall inform the Court and the State whether there is a counter-offer forthcoming. If the defendant fails to appear on the Holding Date without lawful justification or excuse, the Court shall modify the defendant's bond in accordance with Indiana Code 35–33–8–7 and 8, and issue a Bench Warrant for the defendant's arrest. The Judge presiding over Division II on the morning of the Holding Date or his or her designee shall take intents to plead guilty and guilty pleas, if any. That Judge shall do the sentencing on any defendant entering an intent to plead guilty or a guilty plea before him or her.

Adopted as Felony Division Rule 4, effective May 5, 2000. Amended and renumbered as Criminal Rule 2.09, June 29, 2006, effective Jan. 1, 2007; amended June 1, 2007, effective Jan. 1, 2008; effective Sept. 16, 2011.

LR82–CR00–S Rule 2.10. TRIAL DATE SELECTION

Cases in which the highest crime charged is a C felony or above shall be set on Mondays or on the first business day of the week on which the Court is open following a Monday holiday. Cases in which the highest grade of offense charged is a D felony or Misdemeanor, shall be set for trial on Thursdays. Private Counsel may not set more than two trials for the same trial date in any court.

Adopted as Felony Division Rule 5, effective May 5, 2000. Amended and renumbered as Criminal Rule 2.10, June 29, 2006, effective Jan. 1, 2007; effective Sept. 16, 2011.

LR82–CR00–S Rule 2.11. PRE–TRIAL CONFERENCE

A Pre–Trial Conference shall be set at 1:30 p.m. on the Wednesday of the week immediately after the week in which the Holding Date is set. The Judge who will preside at trial will conduct the Pre-trial conference if available; the back-up Magistrate shall attend all Pre-trial conferences. If the Judge is unavailable the back-up Magistrate shall conduct the Pre-trial. The representative or representatives of the State appearing at the Pre-trial conference on a case shall have full authority to make and accept offers and counter-offers on said case.

Adopted as Felony Division Rule 6, effective May 5, 2000. Amended and renumbered as Criminal Rule 2.11, June 29, 2006, effective Jan. 1, 2007; effective Sept. 16, 2011.

LR82–CR00–S Rule 2.12. PROGRESS DATE

The defendant shall be ordered to appear after the Pre-trial conference to indicate intent to plead guilty or to make other progress on the case.

Adopted as Felony Division Rule 7, effective May 5, 2000. Amended and renumbered as Criminal Rule 2.12, June 29, 2006, effective Jan. 1, 2007; effective Sept. 16, 2011.

LR82–CR00–S Rule 2.13. ASSIGNMENT OF TRIAL WEEKS

Unless otherwise agreed by the Division II and Division VI Judges, the Division II Judge shall be the lead trial Judge for trial weeks containing an odd numbered Monday. The Division VI Judge shall be the back-up Judge for said weeks. The Division VI Judge shall be the lead trial Judge for trial weeks containing an even numbered Monday. The Division II Judge shall be the back-up Judge for said weeks.

Adopted as Felony Division Rule 8, effective May 5, 2000. Amended and renumbered as Criminal Rule 2.13, June 29, 2006, effective Jan. 1, 2007; effective Sept. 16, 2011.

LR82–CR00–S Rule 2.14. TRIAL PRIORITIZATION

Cases in which a defendant is in custody may have priority over other cases on the docket. Otherwise, the oldest cases on the docket are to be tried first, regardless or custodial status of the accused, provided however prioritization by age may be superseded by expedited trial pursuant to Criminal Rule 4(g), or for other showing of extreme necessity. For purposes of trial priority, the age of the case will be determined from the date of filing.

Adopted as Felony Division Rule 9, effective May 5, 2000. Amended and renumbered as Criminal Rule 2.14, June 29, 2006, effective Jan. 1, 2007; effective Sept. 16, 2011.

LR82–CR00–S Rule 2.15. ADD ON MATTERS

Pre-trial appearance dates and hearings shall be scheduled not less than twenty four hours prior to said appearance or hearing, except for good cause shown.

Adopted as Felony Division Rule 10, effective May 5, 2000. Amended and renumbered as Criminal Rule 2.15, June 29, 2006, effective Jan. 1, 2007; effective Sept. 16, 2011.

LR82–CR00–S Rule 2.16. FILING PLEADINGS AND MOTIONS

All pleadings and motions in felony cases and misdemeanor cases transferred to the felony divisions of the Court other than Petitions to Revoke shall be filed in open court. For purposes of this rule a filing made at the Holding Date Conference or at the Pre-trial Conference shall be considered a filing in open court.

Adopted June 29, 2006, effective Jan. 1, 2007. Amended effective Sept. 16, 2011.

VANDERBURGH SUPERIOR COURT FAMILY LAW RULES

Adopted Effective March 6, 2000

Including Amendments Received Through November 1, 2013

Research Notes

Annotations to the Vanderburgh County Superior Court Family Law Rules are available in West's Annotated Indiana Code, Title 34 Appendix.

These rules may be searched electronically on Westlaw in the IN-RULES database; updates to these rules may be found on Westlaw in IN-RULESUPDATES. For search tips and a summary of database content, consult the Westlaw Scope Screens for each database.

DIVISION IV RULES

LR–82–FL–00 Rule 4.01. SCOPE, TITLE AND EFFECTIVE DATE

A. Scope. These rules are adopted pursuant to the authority of T.R. 81 of the Indiana Rules of Trial Procedure, and are intended to supplement those rules. These rules shall govern the practice and procedure in all domestic relations cases in the Vanderburgh Superior Courts.

B. Title. These rules will be known as the "Vanderburgh Superior Court Division IV Rules."

C. Effective Date. The effective date of these rules is January 1, 2006.

Adopted as Rule 1, effective March 6, 2000. Renumbered as Rule 4.01 and amended July 15, 2005, effective Jan. 1, 2006. Amended effective Sept. 16, 2011.

LR–82–FL–00 Rule 4.02. NOTICE

In all relevant family law matters, the moving party shall give notice of the time and place of a hearing or of a trial, by order to appear or notice of hearing, served upon the adverse party at least five (5) business days prior to the hearing or trial and file a copy of the notice with the Court on or prior to the hearing or trial.

Adopted as Rule 2, effective March 6, 2000. Renumbered as Rule 4.02 and amended July 15, 2005, effective Jan. 1, 2006. Amended effective Sept. 16, 2011.

LR–82–FL–00 Rule 4.03. PAUPER AFFIDAVITS

If a pauper affidavit is filed in lieu of Court costs, the attorney representing the party seeking pauper status shall attest on the affidavit that the attorney has made sufficient inquiry and that the attorney is of the opinion that the party requesting pauper status does qualify. In each case where a pauper affidavit has been filed and granted, the parties shall address the payment of costs in the provisional order. If one of the spouses has the means to pay Court costs, the Court may require the non-pauper party to pay costs within sixty (60) days of the filing date or prior to the final hearing, whichever occurs earlier.

Adopted as Rule 3, effective March 6, 2000. Renumbered as Rule 4.03 and amended July 15, 2005, effective Jan. 1, 2006. Amended effective Sept. 16, 2011.

LR–82–FL–00 Rule 4.04. SCHEDULING

A. Initial Meeting. All Division IV matters to be heard shall be initially set by the Clerk's Office for 8:00 A.M. Monday through Friday. All attorneys of record shall contact any other attorney of record prior to setting any matter for hearing to endeavor to set the matter on an agreeable date. If a matter is set for an initial meeting, the parties and counsel are required to attend unless excused by agreement of all counsel of record. No attorney may unilaterally excuse his/her client from the initial meeting. At that meeting, the parties and counsel shall discuss in good faith a resolution of the issues. If an agreement cannot be reached, however, a contested hearing shall be scheduled. The Court Administrator, a Magistrate or a Judge will hear uncontested matters beginning at 8:00 A.M. until 10:00 A.M.

B. Contested Hearings. Contested hearings will be scheduled beginning at 9:00 A.M. before a Judge or 10:00 A.M. before a Magistrate and may only be set on the Division IV calendar with the consent of the Court Administrator, Magistrate or Division IV Judge, and only after the matter has been set for either an uncontested setting as set forth in paragraph A above or the parties each verify that they have met and consulted in a good faith effort to reach a settlement. The parties shall verify the settlement conference, either in person on the record, or by a verified statement filed with the Court signed by the party, personally. Verification of Settlement Conference forms can be obtained from the office of any hearing officer exercising jurisdiction in Division IV. (See Appendix A) The requirement for a settlement meeting may be waived or modified for good cause shown by the judicial officer scheduled to hear the matter. Additionally, summary hearings can be scheduled for Friday mornings between 9:00 A.M. and Noon as set forth in Subpart "E" of this Rule and in Rule 4.05. No contested hearing reserving more that a half (1/2) day shall be set unless the parties either have mediated the matter or have entered into a mediation agreement that provides that the matter must be mediated at least thirty (30) days prior to any trial setting. The Court, in its discretion, may order parties to mediate their matter regardless of the time reserved for a contested hearing or trial. This mediation requirement may only be waived by a Judge or Magistrate and the waiver shall be documented in the Chronological Case Summary.

C. Reporting to Hearing. Parties and their attorneys are ordered to report to the Court no later than thirty (30) minutes prior to the time of a contested matter and shall be present at the time set for the hearing. Failure to so comply may subject any non-complying party and/or attorney to Court sanctions. Upon request of a party or *sua sponte*, a Judge may retain jurisdiction of the matter. Upon agreement of all parties, a Magistrate may retain jurisdiction of the matter.

D. Reporting of Settlements. When the parties have settled any matter which has been set for contested hearing, the parties shall immediately inform the Court that the matter has been settled so that the Court may make that time available to other parties, if possible.

E. Docket Priority. Emergency matters involving imminent threats to the health and welfare of a party, children, or the preservation of assets will be given docket priority.

1. Contested hearing times for Fridays on the Magistrate's or Judge's calendars shall be reserved for emergency matters, and provisional hearings. A Friday contested hearing will only be scheduled

with the prior consent of the Judicial Officer who shall hear the matter.

2. Emergency matters and provisional hearings may also be heard in Summary fashion before the Magistrate scheduled to hear Friday Summary Hearings. These Summary Hearings shall be set in one-half (1/2) hour increments beginning at 9:00 A.M. and ending at noon. A one-half (1/2) hour summary hearing may be scheduled by the parties in the same manner as other hearings are set. If more than one-half (1/2) hour is needed, permission must be obtained by the judicial officer scheduled to hear the matter before scheduling same.

Adopted as Rule 4, effective March 6, 2000. Renumbered as Rule 4.04 and amended July 15, 2005, effective Jan. 1, 2006. Amended effective Sept. 16, 2011.

LR–82–FL–00 Rule 4.05. SUMMARY HEARINGS

A. Purpose. By agreement of the parties all issues and evidence relevant to a domestic relations case may be presented in summary fashion. This method allows parties access to the Court relatively quickly and with less expense. While summary hearings are not appropriate for all cases, it is believed these hearings will reduce the time most cases have to wait to be heard.

B. Scheduling of Summary Hearings. Summary hearings shall be heard in increments of one-half (1/2) hour every Friday morning before a Magistrate beginning at 9:00 A.M. and ending at noon. A summary hearing may be scheduled by the parties in the same manner as other hearings are set.

C. Agreement of Parties. All parties of record must agree to set the hearing in a summary fashion and must agree to the method of conducting the same. Testimony and evidence shall be presented in a summary fashion or by such other method agreeable to the parties. At a summary hearing, each party shall be allocated equal presentation time. Time limits at summary hearings will be strictly enforced.

D. Exhibits. Any exhibits to be presented at a summary hearing shall have been exchanged prior to that hearing and stipulated to in terms of admissibility. Child support guideline worksheets shall be completed and signed by the submitting party.

E. Financial Declaration Forms. Prior to any summary hearing, each party shall complete a financial declaration form approved by the Vanderburgh Superior Court (See Appendix B). Said forms shall be exchanged at least one business day prior to the scheduled hearing. Failure to properly prepare and exchange said form shall subject the offending party to sanctions under Ind. Trial Rule 37.

F. Statement of Issues. The Court may exercise discretion at a summary hearing in approving the method of conducting the hearing and approving the means of presenting evidence and testimony. At a summary hearing, the parties will submit to the

Court, preferably in writing, or in opening statements, the issues before the Court.

Adopted as Rule 5, effective March 6, 2000. Renumbered as Rule 4.05 and amended July 15, 2005, effective Jan. 1, 2006. Amended effective Sept. 16, 2011.

LR–82–TR–65 Rule 4.06. ORDERS WITHOUT NOTICE

All requests for orders without notice must comply with Ind. Trial Rule 65 and be set with the Court in accordance with local rule 4.04(E) above.

Adopted as Rule 6, effective March 6, 2000. Renumbered as Rule 4.06 and amended July 15, 2005, effective Jan. 1, 2006. Amended effective Sept. 16, 2011.

LR–82–FL–00 Rule 4.07. AGREED MATTERS

A. Written Settlement. No agreed matter shall be submitted unless accompanied with a signed agreement stating "Agreed as to Form and Substance," and other appropriate documents, such as a decree, a Wage–Withholding Order, or a Qualified Domestic Relations Order. However, if the parties reach a settlement "on the Courthouse steps," then the parties shall recite the entire agreement for the record, and enter the appropriate order upon preparation and filing by counsel.

B. Modifying Custody. No change of custody agreement will be approved by the Court unless the party relinquishing custody either appears in open Court or fails to appear after proper notice of an uncontested Court setting.

Adopted as Rule 8, effective March 6, 2000. Renumbered as Rule 4.07 and amended July 15, 2005, effective Jan. 1, 2006. Amended effective Sept. 16, 2011.

LR–82–TR–58 Rule 4.08. PREPARATION OF ORDERS

A. Exchange. It shall be the duty of the parties' attorneys to prepare decrees and other orders as directed by the Court. The attorney so directed shall first submit them to all other attorneys of record, to enable them to challenge any provision thereof, before submission to the Court for entry.

B. Additions. If a party is withholding approval as to form or is making additions not addressed by the Court, the matter may be set for conference before the judicial officer having jurisdiction concerning the same. The party setting the conference shall provide to the Court and to the opposing party a proposed order with the notice of the scheduled conference. The Court may enter sanctions against a party who has unreasonably withheld approval or attempted to make additions not addressed by the Court.

C. Signatures. The signature line for each counsel or pro se litigant on orders arising from contested matters shall indicate "Approved As to Form Only". Such signature indicates that the order correctly reflects the Court's ruling. It does not necessarily signify that the signing party or attorney agrees with that ruling.

Adopted as Rule 9, effective March 6, 2000. Renumbered as Rule 4.08 and amended July 15, 2005, effective Jan. 1, 2006. Amended effective Sept. 16, 2011.

LR–82–FL–00 Rule 4.09. STANDING ORDER FOR PARENTAL EDUCATION WORKSHOP

The Judges of the Vanderburgh Superior Courts find that it is in the best interests of society, of children and of the Courts to encourage cooperation and mediation between separating and divorcing parents. We further find that a mandatory parental education workshop will:

Aid the children of divorcing parents;

Aid the parents in post separation parenting;

Encourage agreements between litigating parents in the best interest of their children; and

Conserve the court time by reducing repetitive petitions over child custody, parenting time and support.

Therefore the Judge orders both parties to any dissolution of marriage or separation action filed in the Vanderburgh Superior Courts to attend a parental education program if the parties have a minor child or children less than the age of 17 years, 6 months at the date of filing.

The parties are responsible for paying the cost of attending the program. All or a portion of the attendance fee may be waived upon the showing of indigence.

The Lampion Center is an approved provider of a parental education program for the Vanderburgh Superior Courts. The Lampion Center's program brochures shall be provided by the Clerk of the Court to petitioners and served with the summons upon each respondent by Sheriff (See Appendix C). Other program providers are subject to approval by the Court.

The Court may waive attendance upon a showing that a party has completed a similar program, has been in individual counseling, or for other good cause in an individual case.

The workshop provider will furnish each participant and the Court with a certificate of completion of the program.

If a party fails to complete the program within seventy (70) days of service on the respondent, the Court will take appropriate action, which action may include punishment for contempt of Court.

Adopted as Rule 10, effective March 6, 2000. Renumbered as Rule 4.09 and amended July 15, 2005, effective Jan. 1, 2006. Amended effective Sept. 16, 2011.

LR–82–FL–00 Rule 4.10. CHILD SUPPORT GUIDELINES

A. Worksheet Required. In all proceedings involving child support, each party shall file with any settlement, or submit to the Court at any hearing or trial, Indiana Child Support Guidelines worksheets— one or more depending upon the facts.

B. Support Settlement Agreements. If an agreement concerning support provides any deviation from the Guidelines, the parties shall present to the Court a written explanation.

C. Income Withholding Order Required. In all proceedings involving child support, an Income Withholding Order shall be submitted with any Settlement Agreement or Final Decree pursuant to Ind. Code § 31–16–15–1(a).

Adopted as Rule 11, effective March 6, 2000. Renumbered as Rule 4.10 and amended July 15, 2005, effective Jan. 1, 2006. Amended effective Sept. 16, 2011.

LR–82–FL–00 Rule 4.11.   HEARINGS

Hearings will be limited to the time scheduled on the calendar and it shall be the responsibility of the parties to ensure adequate time for completion of a hearing. Should the parties be unable to complete the presentation within that time, the matter will be continued and reset on the calendar in the usual manner.

Adopted as Rule 12, effective March 6, 2000. Renumbered as Rule 4.11 and amended July 15, 2005, effective Jan. 1, 2006. Amended effective Sept. 16, 2011.

LR–82–TR–53.2 Rule 4.12.   CONTINUANCES

Motions for Continuances of a final hearing, unless made during trial, shall be in writing, shall state with particularity the grounds, and shall be verified, with copies of such request served upon opposing counsel. Unless such Motion is accompanied by a stipulation signed by both counsel, the Motion must be scheduled on the calendar by the moving party for argument before a ruling is made. Interlocutory or post decree matters may be continued by the petitioning party, without argument or stipulation, only on the condition that no attorney has appeared of record for the non-moving party.

Adopted as Rule 13, effective March 6, 2000. Renumbered as Rule 4.12 and amended July 15, 2005, effective Jan. 1, 2006. Amended effective Sept. 16, 2011.

LR–82–FL–00 Rule 4.13.   FINANCIAL DECLARATION FORM

A. Requirement. In all relevant family law matters, including dissolution, separation, paternity, post-decree and support proceedings and excepting Rule 4.05(E) hearings, the parties shall simultaneously exchange a Financial Declaration Form seven (7) days prior to any contested hearing and a copy of the same with a green paper cover sheet shall be filed with the Court on the date of the hearing (See Appendix B). These time limits may be amended by Court order for good cause shown.

B. Exceptions. The Financial Declaration Form need not be exchanged if:

1. The parties agree in writing to waive exchange;

2. The parties have executed a written agreement which settles all financial issues;

3. The proceeding is one in which the service is by publication and there is no response; or

4. The proceeding is post-decree and concern issues without financial implications. Provided, however, when the proceeding is post-decree and concerns only an arrearage, the alleged delinquent party shall complete the entire Form, which the support recipient needs to complete merely that portion thereof which requires specifications of the basis of the arrearage calculation (with appropriate supporting documentation).

C. Admissibility. Subject to specific evidentiary challenges, the Financial Declaration shall be admissible into evidence upon filing. The submission of the Financial Declaration Form shall not prohibit any other relevant discovery permitted under the Indiana Trial Rules.

D. Financial Declaration—Mandatory Discovery. The exchange of Forms constitutes mandatory discovery. Thus, Ind. Trial Rule 37 sanctions apply. Additionally, pursuant to Ind. Trial Rule 26(E)(2) and (3), the Form shall be supplemented if additional material becomes available.

Adopted as Rule 14, effective March 6, 2000. Renumbered as Rule 4.13 and amended July 15, 2005, effective Jan. 1, 2006. Amended effective Sept. 16, 2011.

LR–82–FL–00 Rule 4.14.   SUPPORT ARREARAGE

In all informations for contempt based upon non-payment of support, where a party was ordered to make payments through the Clerk's Office, the party claiming an arrearage shall support the testimony on that issue by filing with the Court a current support printout from the Clerk's Office at the time of the hearing.

Adopted as Rule 15, effective March 6, 2000. Renumbered as Rule 4.14 and amended July 15, 2005, effective Jan. 1, 2006. Amended effective Sept. 16, 2011.

LR–82–FL–00 Rule 4.15.   ATTORNEY FEES

A. Preliminary Attorney Fees. Attorney fees may be awarded based on evidence presented by affidavit or oral testimony at a preliminary hearing. Affidavits shall be admissible subject to cross examination. The following factors will be considered:

1. The number and complexity of the issues. (e.g., custody dispute, complex asset valuation).

2. The nature and extent of discovery.

3. The time reasonably necessary for the preparation for or the conduct of contested *pendente lite* matters or final hearings.

4. Other matters requiring substantial expenditure of attorney's time.

5. The attorney's hourly rate.

6. The amount counsel has received from all sources.

B. Preliminary Appraisal and Accountant Fees. Appraisal or accounting fees may be awarded based on evidence presented by affidavit or oral testimony at a preliminary hearing. The following factors will be considered:

1. An itemized list of property to be appraised or valued (e.g., Defined Benefit Pension, Business Real Estate, Furnishings, Vehicles, etc.).

2. An estimate of the cost of the appraisals and the basis therefore.

3. The amount of a retainer required and the reason an expert is necessary.

C. Contempt Citation Attorney Fees. An attorney may submit an affidavit, or oral testimony, along with an itemized statement of his or her requested fee. Affidavits shall be admissible into evidence by the Court.

Adopted as Rule 16, effective March 6, 2000. Renumbered as Rule 4.15 and amended July 15, 2005, effective Jan. 1, 2006. Amended effective Sept. 16, 2011.

LR–82–FL–00 Rule 4.16. APPELLATE RECORDS

When an appeal is initiated by the filing of a Notice of Appeal pursuant to Ind. Appellate Rule 9 and a transcript of all or any part of the evidence is sought for the record on appeal, the counsel filing the Notice of Appeal shall contemporaneously and personally deliver a copy of the Notice of Appeal to the Court Reporter expected to prepare the transcript of the evidence, shall advise the Reporter of the deadline for preparation of the record, and shall arrange to pay the Reporter for the preparation of the transcript.

Adopted as Rule 17, effective March 6, 2000. Renumbered as Rule 4.16 and amended July 15, 2005, effective Jan. 1, 2006. Amended effective Sept. 16, 2011.

LR–82–FL–00 Rule 4.17. TERMINATION OF REPRESENTATION

A. Termination of Representation. Upon the entry of a final Decree of Dissolution of Marriage, Legal Separation, Paternity, or an Order of permanent modification of any custody, parenting time and/or child support Order, the representative capacity of all attorneys appearing on behalf of any party shall be deemed terminated:

1. After the filing of all entries due during the period of time the attorney provided representation; And upon:

2. An Order of withdrawal granted by the Court; or

3. The expiration of time within which an appeal of such Order may be preserved or perfected pursuant to the Indiana Rules of Trial Procedure and /or the Indiana Rules of Appellate Procedure; or

4. The conclusion of any appeal of such Order commenced pursuant to the Indiana Rules of Trial Procedure and/or the Indiana Rules of Appellate Procedure.

B. Post Dissolution Service. The service of any post dissolution pleadings upon any party not represented by counsel pursuant to paragraph A above, shall be made upon that person pursuant to the Indiana Rules of Trial Procedure.

C. Professional Courtesy. Any copy served upon original counsel will be deemed to be a matter of professional courtesy only.

Adopted as Rule 18, effective March 6, 2000. Renumbered as Rule 4.17 and amended July 15, 2005, effective Jan. 1, 2006. Amended effective Sept. 16, 2011.

APPENDICES

Appendix A.   VERIFICATION OF SETTLEMENT CONFERENCE FORM

STATE OF INDIANA	)
	) SS:
COUNTY OF VANDERBURGH	)

IN THE VANDERBURGH SUPERIOR COURT
IN RE THE MARRIAGE OF:

_____,	)
Petitioner,	)
	)
And	) CAUSE NO. 82D04–_____–DR–
	)
_____,	)
Respondent,	)

VERIFICATION OF SETTLEMENT CONFERENCE FORM

Comes now the Petitioner/Respondent, in person, and by counsel/*pro se*, and hereby verifies and states to the Court that the parties in this case have met and consulted with each other in a good faith effort to reach a settlement in this matter. Furthermore, Petitioner/Respondent verifies and states that the parties were unable to reach an agreement in this matter and requests that the Court schedule the above matter for a contested hearing on the Division IV calendar.

I hereby affirm under the penalties of perjury that the above representations are true and correct to the best of my knowledge, information and belief.

Petitioner/Respondent

Adopted July 15, 2005, effective Jan. 1, 2006. Amended effective Sept. 16, 2011.

Appendix B.   FINANCIAL DISCLOSURE FORM

This Document

Not for Public Access

Pursuant to Administrative Rule 9

Cause No.

Caption:

FINANCIAL DECLARATION FORM
STATE OF INDIANA: SUPERIOR COURT: VANDERBURGH COUNTY

_____,   CAUSE NO.: _____,
Petitioner

and   Dated: _____

_____,   VERIFIED FINANCIAL DECLARATION OF
Respondent   (HUSBAND/FATHER)   (WIFE/MOTHER)

HUSBAND/FATHER: WIFE/MOTHER:

Name: _____   Name: _____
Address: _____   Address: _____
_____   _____

Occupation: _____   Occupation: _____
Employer: _____   Employer: _____
Year of Birth: _____   Year of Birth: _____

ATTORNEYS: SPACE BELOW FOR USE OF COURT CLERK ONLY
Name, Address, Telephone Number

_____   _____
_____   _____
_____   _____
_____   _____

GROSS WEEKLY INCOME—ATTACH LAST THREE (3) PAY STUBS	AMOUNTS
1. Gross Weekly SALARY, WAGES, and COMMISSIONS	
2. Gross Weekly PENSIONS/RETIREMENT/SOC. SECURITY/UNEMPLOY-MENT/WORKMEN'S COMP.	
3. Gross Weekly CHILD SUPPORT (received from any prior marriages, not this marriage)	
4. Gross Weekly DIVIDENDS and INTEREST (Attach calculations)	
5. Gross Weekly RENTS/ROYALTIES less ordinary and necessary expenses (Attach calculations)	
6. Gross Weekly BUSINESS/SELF–EMPLOYMENT INCOME less ordinary and necessary expenses (Attach calculations)	
7. ALL OTHER SOURCES (Specify*)	
8. TOTAL GROSS WEEKLY INCOME (Total of Lines 1 through 7)	

* Includes Bonuses, Alimony and Maintenance Received from Prior Marriages; Capital Gains, Trust Income, Gifts; Prizes, In–Kind Benefits from Employment such as Company Or Free Housing, Reimbursed Meals, DO NOT Include ADC, SSI, General Assistance, Food Stamps.
Monthly Expenses and Deductions from Income
Names and relations of all members of household whose expenses are included:

9. Minus Weekly COURT–ORDERED CHILD SUPPORT for prior children—amounts actually paid	
10. Minus Weekly LEGAL DUTY CHILD SUPPORT for prior children	
11. Minus Weekly HEALTH INSURANCE PREMIUMS for Children of This Marriage Only	
12. Minus Weekly ALIMONY/SUPPORT/MAINTENANCE for Prior Spouses—amounts actually paid	
13. WEEKLY AVAILABLE INCOME [Line 8 minus Lines 9 through 12)	
14. Weekly WORK RELATED CHILD CARE COSTS for Custodial Parent to work for Children of this Marriage Only	
15. Weekly EXTRAORDINARY HEALTHCARE EXPENSES (Children of this Marriage Only—Uninsured Only)	
16. Weekly EXTRAORDINARY EDUCATION EXPENSES (Children of this Marriage Only)	

1. FEDERAL INCOME TAXES (weekly deduction times 4.3)	
2. STATE INCOME TAXES (weekly deduction times 4.3)	
3. LOCAL INCOME TAXES (weekly deduction times 4.3)	
4. SOCIAL SECURITY TAXES (weekly deduction times 4.3)	
5. RETIREMENT PENSION FUND (Mandatory) (Optional) (weekly deductions times 4.3)	
6. RENT/MORTGAGE PAYMENTS (Residence)	
7. RESIDENCE/PROPERTY TAXES/INSURANCE if not included in Mortgage Payment (Total for Year divided by 12)	
8. MAINTENANCE ON RESIDENCE	
9. FOOD/HOUSEHOLD SUPPLIES/LAUNDRY/CLEANING	
10. ELECTRICITY (Total for year divided by 12)	
11. GAS (Total for year divided by 12)	
12. WATER/SEWAGE/SOLID WASTE/TRASH COLLECTION (Trash for year divided by 12)	
13. TELEPHONE (including Long distance Charges)	
14. CLOTHING	
15. MEDICAL/DENTAL EXPENSES (Not Reimbursed by Insurance)	
16. AUTOMOBILE—LOAN PAYMENT	
17. AUTOMOBILE—GAS/OIL	
18. AUTOMOBILE—REPAIRS	
19. AUTOMOBILE—INSURANCE (Total for year divided by 12)	

20.	LIFE INSURANCE
21.	HEALTH INSURANCE (exclude payments made by children on Page 2, Line 11)
22.	DISABILITY/ACCIDENT/OTHER INSURANCE (Please specify)
23.	ENTERTAINMENT (Clubs, Social Obligations, Travel, Recreation, Cable TV)
24.	CHARITABLE/CHURCH CONTRIBUTIONS
25.	PERSONAL EXPENSES (Haircuts, cosmetics, grooming, tobacco, alcohol, etc.)
26.	BOOKS/MAGAZINES/NEWSPAPERS
27.	EDUCATION/SCHOOL EXPENSES (Self and children you have custody of)
28.	DAYCARE/WORK RELATED CHILD CARE COSTS (weekly amount times 4.3)
29.	OTHER EXPENSES (Please specify)
30.	
31.	

MONTHLY LOAN/CHARGE CARD EXPENSES FOR   BALANCE   PAYMENTS
(Do not include monthly payments shown above)

32.	
33.	
34.	
35.	
36.	
37.	
38.	
39.	Total Monthly Expenses and Deductions from Income (Total of Lines 1 thru 38)
40	Average Weekly Expenses and Deductions (Total monthly expenses—4.3)

Disclose all assets known to you, even if you do not know the value. Under ownership, H=Husband; W=Wife; J=Joint. Lien amount includes only those debts secured by an item, such as a mortgage against a house, debts shown as title to a vehicle, loans against life insurance policies or loans where an item is pledged as collateral. Value assets as of the date of petition for Dissolution of Marriage was filed. New valuation date here: _____

DESCRIPTION	GROSS VALUE	LESS: LIENS/ MORTGAGES	NET VALUE	H	W	J
A. HOUSEHOLD FURNISH-INGS, FURNITURE/APPLI-ANCES						
1. In possession of Husband						
2. In possession of Wife						
B. AUTOMOBILES, TRUCKS, RECREATIONAL VEHICLES (Include make, Model and Year)						
3.						
4.						
5.						
6.						
C. SECURITIES—STOCKS, BONDS AND STOCK OP-TIONS						
7.						
8.						
9.						
10.						
D. CASH, CHECKING, SAVINGS, DEPOSIT ACCOUNTS, CDs (Include name of Bank/ Credit Union and type of account)						
11.						
12.						
13.						
14.						

DESCRIPTION	GROSS VALUE	LESS: LIENS/ MORTGAGES	NET VALUE	H	W	J
15.						
E. REAL ESTATE (Including Land Sales Contracts)						
16. Marital Residence (show address)						
Basis of Valuation:						
Name of Lender 1st Mortgage:						
Name of Lender 2nd Mortgage:						
17. Other (show address)						
Basis of Valuation:						
Name of Lender 1st Mortgage:						
Name of Lender 2nd Mortgage:						
18. Other (show address)						
Basis of Valuation:						
Name of Lender 1st Mortgage:						
Name of Lender 2nd Mortgage:						
F. CASH RETIREMENT ACCOUNTS (IRAs, SEPS, KEOUGHS, 401K Employee savings plans, stock ownership/profit sharing, etc.)						
19.						
20.						
21.						
22.						
23.						
G. RETIREMENT BENEFITS, DEFERRED COMPENSATION PLANS AND PENSIONS (Include information available on benefits whether benefits are vested or in pay status)						
24.						
25.						
H. BUSINESS INTERESTS						
26.						
27.						
28.						

I.	LIFE INSURANCE (Show Company name and Death Benefit)			
	Term and Group			
29.	Named Beneficiary	0	0	0
30.	Named Beneficiary	0	0	0
31.	Named Beneficiary	0	0	0
	Whole Life and Others (Show cash Value under Gross value)			
32.				
	Named Beneficiary			
33.				
	Named Beneficiary			
34.				
	Named Beneficiary			
J.	OTHER ASSETS include any type of assets having value, including jewelry, personal property, assets located in safety deposit boxes, accrued bonuses, etc.			
35.				
36.				
37.				
38.				
39.				
40.				
41.				

ASSETS ACQUIRED BY YOU PRIOR TO MARRIAGE OR THROUGH INHERITANCE OR GIFT
(Whether now owned or not)

SHOW SIGNIFICANT ASSETS ONLY	GROSS VALUE	LESS: LIENS/ MORTGAGES	NET VALUE	VALUATION DATE
A. ASSETS OWNED BY YOU PRIOR TO MARRIAGE (value as of date of marriage)				
1.				
2.				
3.				
4.				
5.				
B. ASSETS ACQUIRED BY YOU DURING MARRIAGE THROUGH INHERITANCE OR GIFT (value as of date of acquisition)				
6. Acquired from whom:				
7. Acquired from whom:				
8. Acquired from whom:				

I declare under the penalties of perjury that the foregoing, including any attachments, is true and correct, that this declaration was executed on the _____ day of _____, 200 ____.

Signature: _____

Printed Name: _____

You are under a duty to supplement or amend this Financial Declaration prior to trial if you learn the information provided is incorrect or the information provided is no longer true.

CERTIFICATE OF SERVICE

I hereby certify that a true, exact, and authenticate copy of the foregoing has been served upon the following, by U.S. Mail, first class postage prepaid, this ____ day of _____, 200 ____.

_____
Attorney

Adopted July 15, 2005, effective Jan. 1, 2006. Amended effective Sept. 16, 2011.

Appendix C. LAMPION CENTER

LAMPION CENTER

Counseling for Individuals & Families

"TRANSPARENTING PROGRAM"

SEMINAR FOR DIVORCING PARENTS

Divorce is a very stressful experience for parents and children. This four (4) hour educational program focuses on ways to help your children cope with your divorce. ATTENDANCE IS REQUIRED by Order of the Courts of Vanderburgh County. The seminars are presented by qualified professionals at Lampion Center (formerly Family & Children's Service), a United Way Agency.

REGISTRATION:

Arrangements are to be made directly with Lampion Center. To register, call the agency at (812) 471–1776 and ask to register for the TransParenting program. Your cause number from the divorce papers is required upon registration. You will also be asked to provide your name, phone number, and information about any restraining orders you may have pending with your spouse/former spouse.

PAYMENT:

The cost of the seminar is (forty-five dollars) $45.00 per parent payable by cash, check, or money order to Lampion Center. Payment is requested upon arrival. This fee may only be waived by way of Pauper's Orders, Legal Aid referrals, and for persons receiving TANF. Documentation for any of these situations must be provided upon arrival.

TIME:

Morning Program: Generally scheduled the 1st Thursday of every month from 8:30 a.m. to 12:30 a.m.

Evening Program: Generally scheduled the 2nd and 3rd Tuesday of every month from 6:00 p.m. to 8:00 p.m.

(Must attend *both* evening sessions to complete)

Sign-in begins one-half (1/2) hour prior to class. **No one will be allowed in late.** For holidays and other reasons, the above schedule may vary. Please verify dates of classes upon registration.

LOCATION:

Lampion Center (formerly Family & Children's Service, Inc.)

655 S. Hebron Avenue

Evansville, IN 47714

(One block west of Green River Road on Hebron between Lincoln and Bellemeade Avenue)

QUESTIONS:

Call (812) 471–1776 and ask about the Seminar for Divorcing Parents.

PLEASE NOTE: No child care is provided. Please make other arrangements for the care of your children.

655 South Hebron Avenue Evansville, Indiana 47714
Phone 812–471–1776 Fax 812–469–2000
www.lampioncenter.com
A United Way Agency
LAMPION CENTER
655 S. Hebron Avenue
Evansville IN 47714

Lincoln Avenue

Hebron Avenue

Green River Road

**Lampion Center
655 S. Hebron**

Bellemeade Avenue

Our phone number is: 812-471-1776
The fax number is: 812-469-2000

Adopted July 15, 2005, effective Jan. 1, 2006. Amended effective Sept. 16, 2011.

CRIMINAL RULES OF THE VANDERBURGH CIRCUIT COURT

Adopted as Criminal Procedure Effective December 29, 2000; and
as Criminal Rules June 29, 2006, Effective January 1, 2007

Including Amendments Received Through November 1, 2013

Research Notes

Annotations to the Criminal Rules of the Vanderburgh Circuit Court are available in West's Annotated Indiana Code, *Title 34 Appendix.*

These rules may be searched electronically on Westlaw in the IN-RULES database; updates to these rules may be found on Westlaw in *IN-RULESUPDATES.* For search tips and a summary of database content, consult the Westlaw Scope Screens for each database.

LR82–CR2.2 Rule 2.01. ASSIGNMENT OF CRIMINAL CASES

(A) All cases in Vanderburgh County, Indiana in which the highest crime charged is a felony shall be randomly assigned (by the Clerk of Vanderburgh County) to the Circuit and Superior Courts of Vanderburgh County in the following ratio: Eight (8) cases are to be assigned to the Vanderburgh Circuit Court for each six (6) cases assigned to Vanderburgh Superior Court. Each felony cause number shall be deemed a case within the meaning of this rule, regardless of the number of counts or defendants charged in said case.

(B) All cases assigned to the Vanderburgh Circuit Court shall be tried by the Circuit Court Judge or the Magistrate of the Court as determined in the discretion of the Court.

(C) All felony cases assigned to the Vanderburgh Superior Court shall be tried in accordance with the rotation system established by the rules of that Court.

(D) All cases reassigned from the Circuit Court Judge of Vanderburgh County or the Magistrate of that Court shall be reassigned to the Senior Judge of the Vanderburgh Circuit Court and/or any Judge of the Vanderburgh Superior Court.

(E) All cases reassigned within the Vanderburgh Superior Court shall be reassigned in accordance with the rotation system established by the rules of that Court.

(F) All criminal cases filed in the County in which the highest crime charged is a misdemeanor, shall be assigned to the Misdemeanor/Traffic Division of the Vanderburgh Superior Court.

(G) A dismissed criminal action may only be refiled in the same Court to which the case was originally assigned.

(H) The Circuit Court Judge and the Chief Judge of Superior Court may by agreement, order transfer of any felony case pending in either Court to provide consolidated legal defense for those defendants facing multiple criminal charges. Such cases shall be consolidated unless efficient case disposition may be adversely affected by transfer.

Adopted June 29, 2006, effective Jan. 1, 2007. Amended effective Sept. 16, 2011.

LR82–CR00 Rule 2.02. TRANSFER OF CASES BETWEEN VANDERBURGH CIRCUIT AND SUPERIOR COURTS

If a defendant has a pending case in the Vanderburgh Superior Court prior to the filing of a case in Circuit Court, the Circuit Court case will be transferred to Superior Court. Similarly, if a defendant has a prior pending case in Circuit Court, any newer case in Superior Court will be transferred to Circuit Court.

Adopted as Criminal Procedure, effective Dec. 29, 2000. Amended effective Jan. 1, 2002; Sept. 20, 2002; amended and renumbered as Criminal Rule 2.02, June 29, 2006, effective Jan. 1, 2007; effective Sept. 16, 2011.

LR82–CR00 Rule 2.03. BOND SCHEDULE

All persons charged by indictment or affidavit shall be held to bail in the amount set forth below:

(A) Felonies. No bonds shall be set in any felony matters except as determined by a Judicial Officer. The Court shall consider factors found in IC 35–33–8–4 in setting appropriate bond in all cases.

(B) Class A Misdemeanors. Unless otherwise specified, all Class A Misdemeanors shall have a bond of $100.00 for Indiana residents and $200.00 for non-residents.

Specific Exceptions for Class A Misdemeanors.

Domestic Violence Battery

First offense: $500.00

Second offense: $1000.00

Third offense: $5000.00

Leaving the scene of an accident causing personal injury: $500.00.

All OMVWI bonds shall be determined by a Judicial Officer.

(C) Class B Misdemeanors. Unless otherwise specified, all Class B Misdemeanors shall have a bond of $50.00 for Indiana residents and $100.00 for non-residents.

Specific Exceptions for Class B Misdemeanors.

Invasion of Privacy involving co-habitating or formerly co-habitating adults:

First offense: $500.00

Second offense: $1000.00

Third offense $5000.00

(D) Class C Misdemeanors. Unless otherwise specified, all Class C Misdemeanors shall have a bond of $50.00 for Indiana residents and 100.00 for non-residents.

Specific Exceptions for Class C Misdemeanors. Minor possession / consumption / transport: $25.00 for Indiana resident and $50.00 for non-residents.

Adopted June 29, 2006, effective Jan. 1, 2007. Amended effective June 23, 2009. Amended effective Sept. 16, 2011.

LR82–CR00 Rule 2.04. DISCOVERY

In each criminal case in the Vanderburgh Circuit and Superior Courts, the Vanderburgh County Prosecutor's Office and the law enforcement agencies which are involved in the case shall produce to the defense attorney the entire case file, including a list of all

evidence held, within thirty (30) days of the defense attorney's first appearance in court. This is a continuing rule, and all additions to the case file shall be produced immediately upon their creation.

Except by order of court, a defense attorney receiving such a case file shall not reveal any victim's or witnesses' confidential identifying information, including Social Security number, driver's license number, and date of birth, to anyone other than an associate or employee of the attorney. In the event the defense attorney wishes to show the case file to any other person, including the defendant, the attorney shall first redact such information from the file.

Adopted June 29, 2006, effective Jan. 1, 2007. Amended June 1, 2007, effective January 1, 2008; effective Sept. 16, 2011.

LR82–CR00–C Rule 2.05. COURT SESSIONS

Regular court sessions are held every weekday at 9 a.m. and 1 p.m. Special court sessions for petitions to revoke, motions for modification from community corrections programs, and related matters are held on Tuesday and Thursday at 11 a.m. Court sessions are held in Room 208 on the second floor of the Courts Building. If Room 208 is being used for a trial or another matter, then court sessions are held in Room 202.

Adopted as Criminal Procedure, effective Dec. 29, 2000. Amended effective Jan. 1, 2002; Sept. 20, 2002; amended and renumbered as Criminal Rule 2.05, June 29, 2006, effective Jan. 1, 2007; effective Sept. 16, 2011.

LR82–CR00–C Rule 2.06. PROBABLE CAUSE HEARINGS

If a defendant is arrested without an arrest warrant having previously been issued, a probable cause hearing will be held. The hearing will be held at the court session immediately following the arrest and booking of the defendant in the Vanderburgh County Jail. At this hearing, the Court will review the affidavit of probable cause filed by the State to decide if there is probable cause for the offense(s) alleged by the State. If the Court finds that there is not probable cause, the defendant will be discharged. If the Court finds that there is probable cause, the Court will advise the defendant of the charges and some preliminary rights and set bond. The Court will also order the defendant to appear in three business days for an initial hearing at which time the defendant should appear with an attorney if he/she intends to hire counsel and the State should file any formal charges.

Adopted as Criminal Procedure, effective Dec. 29, 2000. Amended effective Jan. 1, 2002; Sept. 20, 2002; amended and renumbered as Criminal Rule 2.06, June 29, 2006, effective Jan. 1, 2007; effective Sept. 16, 2011.

LR82–CR00–C Rule 2.07. INITIAL HEARINGS

An initial hearing will be held on the third business day after the probable cause hearing unless the defendant was arrested as a result of an arrest warrant. If an arrest warrant was issued and then the defendant was arrested, an initial hearing will be held at the next regular court session immediately following the arrest and booking of the defendant in the Vanderburgh County Jail. At the initial hearing, the Court will advise the defendant of the charges, penalties, and constitutional rights; review bond; set an omnibus date and a holding date; and appoint counsel or set an appearance date for the defendant to appear with private counsel.

Adopted as Criminal Procedure, effective Dec. 29, 2000. Amended effective Jan. 1, 2002; Sept. 20, 2002; amended and renumbered as Criminal Rule 2.07, June 29, 2006, effective Jan. 1, 2007; effective Sept. 16, 2011.

LR82–CR00–C Rule 2.08. READINESS CONFERENCES

Readiness Conferences are an opportunity for the prosecutor, the defense attorney, and the Court to discuss the case and any plea offers. Only the attorneys need to appear for these conferences. (This is not an appearance date for the defendant). The date of the initial hearing controls when the readiness conferences are set. Readiness conferences for cases with initial hearings on the 1st through the 15th of the month will be set on the first consecutive Wednesday and Thursday of the next month. Readiness conferences for cases with initial hearings on the 16th through the 31st of the month will be set on the third consecutive Wednesday and Thursday of the next month. Readiness conferences for non-drug (excluding domestic violence) cases will be held on the first and third Wednesdays beginning at 1:30 p.m. for public defenders and 2:30 p.m. for private counsel. Readiness conferences for drug and domestic violence cases will be held on the following Thursdays beginning at 1:30 p.m. for public defenders and 2:30 p.m. for private counsel. Attorneys will be advised of the readiness conference date at the time of the initial hearing. The conferences will be held in the jury or grand jury room of Circuit Court. An attorney should contact Court staff and the Prosecutor's Office if he/she is unable to appear at his/her scheduled readiness conference.

Adopted as Criminal Procedure, effective Dec. 29, 2000. Amended effective Jan. 1, 2002; Sept. 20, 2002; amended and renumbered as Criminal Rule 2.08, June 29, 2006, effective Jan. 1, 2007. Amended June 1, 2007, effective Jan. 1, 2008; effective Sept. 16, 2011.

LR82–CR00–C Rule 2.09. HOLDING DATES

Holding dates are dates for the defendant and his/her attorney to appear so that the defendant can accept or reject any offer by the State of Indiana and/or set the matter for trial. The date of the initial hearing controls when the holding date is set. Holding dates will be set six weeks after the initial hearing on the same weekday as the initial hearing. If the scheduled holding date is a holiday, then the Court will set the holding date on the business day after the

holiday if that day is in the same week. Otherwise, the holding date will be set on the business day prior to the holiday.

Adopted as Criminal Procedure, effective Dec. 29, 2000. Amended effective Jan. 1, 2002; Sept. 20, 2002; amended and renumbered as Criminal Rule 2.09, June 29, 2006, effective Jan. 1, 2007. Amended June 1, 2007, effective Jan. 1, 2008; effective Sept. 16, 2011.

LR82–CR00–C Rule 2.10. OMNIBUS DATES

The omnibus date is not an appearance date. However, it does control several legal deadlines for pleading certain matters and filing certain documents. The omnibus date is set 75 days from the initial hearing.

Adopted as Criminal Procedure, effective Dec. 29, 2000. Amended effective Jan. 1, 2002; Sept. 20, 2002; amended and renumbered as Criminal Rule 2.10, June 29, 2006, effective Jan. 1, 2007; effective Sept. 16, 2011.

LR82–CR00–C Rule 2.11. MISCELLANEOUS HEARINGS

If an attorney needs a hearing for a miscellaneous matter, including but not limited to, hearings for motions to suppress, motions to sever or join offenses or defendants, and motions for bond reduction, the attorney should contact court staff to schedule such a hearing or put the case on the court's calendar during 9 a.m. or 1 p.m. regular matters and request a hearing date.

Adopted as Criminal Procedure, effective Dec. 29, 2000. Amended effective Jan. 1, 2002; Sept. 20, 2002; amended and renumbered as Criminal Rule 2.11, June 29, 2006, effective Jan. 1, 2007; effective Sept. 16, 2011.

LR82–CR00–C Rule 2.12. ADDING CASES TO THE COURT DOCKET

If an attorney needs to add a criminal matter to the court's calendar, the attorney should advise opposing counsel and then contact court staff. If the defendant is in custody the case must be added on at least one full day prior to the appearance date. The attorney should advise the court staff if the defendant is in custody.

Adopted as Criminal Procedure, effective Dec. 29, 2000. Amended effective Jan. 1, 2002; Sept. 20, 2002; amended and renumbered as Criminal Rule 2.12, June 29, 2006, effective Jan. 1, 2007; effective Sept. 16, 2011.

LR82–CR00–C Rule 2.13. PRE–TRIAL CONFERENCES

Pre-trial conferences will be scheduled approximately three weeks prior to trial. Court staff will contact the attorneys for each case to schedule the conference. At the pre-trial conference, the court and parties will discuss the issues in the case, motions that need to be taken up in advance, possible plea agreements and any other relevant matters. (This is not an appearance date for the defendant.)

Adopted as Criminal Procedure, effective Dec. 29, 2000. Amended effective Jan. 1, 2002; Sept. 20, 2002; amended and renumbered as Criminal Rule 2.13, June 29, 2006, effective Jan. 1, 2007; effective Sept. 16, 2011.

LR82–CR00–C Rule 2.14.   TRIAL DATES

When a party requests a trial date, the Court will attempt to set the date within approximately 30 days if the defendant is in custody and 60 days if the defendant is not in custody. All trials, including court and jury trials, start at 8 a.m. unless the Court advises otherwise. Questionnaires for prospective jurors will be available approximately two days prior to the trial. If additional time is needed to review the questionnaires, the bailiff can be contacted at 812–435–5196. Preliminary instructions will be provided on the first day of trial and final instructions will be provided during the trial. If additional time is needed to review the instructions, the staff attorney can be contacted at 812–435–5312. Peremptory challenges and challenges for cause are to be in writing on a form provided by court staff on the day of trial.

Adopted as Criminal Procedure, effective Dec. 29, 2000. Amended effective Jan. 1, 2002; Sept. 20, 2002; amended and renumbered as Criminal Rule 2.14, June 29, 2006, effective Jan. 1, 2007; effective Sept. 16, 2011.

LR82–CR10–C Rule 2.15.   PLEA AND SENTENCING HEARINGS

If a defendant and the State have entered into a plea agreement, the Court will not take a guilty plea and order a pre-sentence investigation until the agreement has been reduced to writing and executed by the parties. When a defendant pleads guilty with or without a plea agreement with the State, the Court will establish a factual basis for each offense and advise the defendant of the penalties and constitutional rights. For these cases and for cases in which the defendant has been found guilty after a jury or court trial, a judgment and sentencing date will be set. The judgment and sentencing date will usually be scheduled approximately 20 days later if the defendant is in custody and approximately 40 days later if the defendant is not in custody. After a judgment and sentencing date has been set, the defendant should immediately report to the Probation Department in Room 127 of the Administration Building so that an interview can be scheduled for the defendant's pre-sentence report. If the defendant is in custody, a member of the probation staff will interview the defendant in the jail. Subject to the Court's approval, and if both parties agree, pre-sentence investigation reports may be waived in certain Class D felonies.

Adopted as Criminal Procedure, effective Dec. 29, 2000. Amended effective Jan. 1, 2002; Sept. 20, 2002; amended and renumbered as Criminal Rule 2.15, June 29, 2006, effective Jan. 1, 2007; effective Sept. 16, 2011.

LR82–CR00–C Rule 2.16.   MODIFICATION REQUESTS—COMMUNITY CORRECTIONS OR PROBATIONARY SENTENCES

Any request for modification of a community corrections or probationary sentence should be in writing and sent to the court. Hearings on such requests are set on Tuesdays and Thursdays at 11 a.m. This shall include requests for modification of driver's license suspensions.

Adopted as Criminal Procedure, effective Dec. 29, 2000. Amended effective Jan. 1, 2002; Sept. 20, 2002; amended and renumbered as Criminal Rule 2.16, June 29, 2006, effective Jan. 1, 2007; effective Sept. 16, 2011.

LR82–CR00–C Rule 2.17.   PETITIONS TO REVOKE—COMMUNITY CORRECTIONS OR PROBATIONARY SENTENCES

If a petition to revoke the sentence of a person on a community corrections program or on probation is filed, either a bench warrant will be issued or the defendant will be advised of an appearance date by summons. These hearings are set on Tuesdays and Thursdays at 11 a.m.

Adopted as Criminal Procedure, effective Dec. 29, 2000. Amended effective Jan. 1, 2002; Sept. 20, 2002; amended and renumbered as Criminal Rule 2.17, June 29, 2006, effective Jan. 1, 2007; effective Sept. 16, 2011.

LR82–CR00–C Rule 2.18.   SHOCK PROBATION HEARINGS—DEPARTMENT OF CORRECTIONS SENTENCES

Any request for modification of a sentence being served at the Indiana Department of Corrections should be in writing and sent to the court. Once a modification request is received, court staff will request a progress report from the facility where the defendant is an inmate. Once the progress report has been received by the court, a shock probation hearing will be scheduled. (If the sentence involved a plea agreement with the State, the State must agree to have a shock probation hearing before a hearing is set.) These hearings are usually held on the last Thursday of each month. If the Court is unavailable on such date, a different date will be selected. If a defendant is represented by an attorney, the attorney will be sent a notice of the hearing date. (Defendants are not transported back to Vanderburgh County for these hearings.)

Adopted as Criminal Procedure, effective Dec. 29, 2000. Amended effective Jan. 1, 2002; Sept. 20, 2002; amended and renumbered as Criminal Rule 2.18, June 29, 2006, effective Jan. 1, 2007; effective Sept. 16, 2011.

VANDERBURGH COUNTY LOCAL PROBATE RULES

Adopted Effective February 5, 2003

Including Amendments Received Through November 1, 2013

Research Notes

Annotations to the Vanderburgh County Local Probate Rules are available in West's Annotated Indiana Code, *Title 34 Appendix.*

These rules may be searched electronically on Westlaw *in the* IN-RULES *database; updates to these rules may be found on* Westlaw *in* IN-RULESUPDATES. *For search tips and a summary of database content, consult the Westlaw Scope Screens for each database.*

LR82–PR Rule 1.   NOTICE

1.1   Whenever notice is required to be given to interested persons pursuant to I.C. 29–1–1–11 through I. C. 29–1–1–18, it shall be the duty of the attorney for the person invoking the jurisdiction of the Court to prepare and give the required notice, and to provide the Court with proof thereof.

1.2   Copies of pleadings shall be served with the notice of hearing thereon.

1.3   Notice of hearing to be held on Petition to Determine an Estate Insolvent shall be served on all interested parties, including the Vanderburgh County Assessor, all claimants, and all reasonably ascertainable creditors.

Adopted effective February 5, 2003. Amended effective March 12, 2007; effective Sept. 16, 2011.

LR82–PR Rule 2.   FILING OF PLEADINGS

2.1   When pleadings are filed by mail or left with the Court for filing, a self-addressed, stamped envelope shall be included for return of documents to the attorney.

2.2   All pleadings invoking the jurisdiction of the Court in probate matters and all proceedings thereafter shall be filed in the offices of the Probate Division of the Vanderburgh Superior Court.

2.3   Until approved by the Vanderburgh Superior court pursuant to Indiana Trial Rule 5(E) (2) and Administrative Rule 12, no pleadings will be accepted as filed by electronic facsimile.

2.4   All attorneys are required to prepare orders for al[1] proceedings except when expressly directed otherwise by the Court.

2.5   Every pleading filed by or on behalf of a fiduciary in an Estate or Guardianship proceeding, including but not limited to Inventories, Petitions, and Accountings, shall be signed and verified by the fiduciary.

2.6   All pleadings filed shall contain the attorney's name, address, telephone number and registration number.

2.7   The initial Petition to open an Estate or Guardianship shall contain the name, address, social security number or date of birth and telephone number of the Personal Representative or Guardian. In the event of a change in address, the individual Personal Representative or Guardian shall immediately advise the court of the new address.

2.8   The Instructions to the Personal Representative or Guardian, executed by the fiduciary, must be filed with the court at the time letters are ordered issued in the proceeding. (See attached Instruction forms.)

Adopted effective February 5, 2003. Amended effective March 12, 2007; effective Sept. 16, 2011.

---

[1] So in original. Probably should read "all".

LR82–PR Rule 3. ATTENDANCE OF PROPOSED FIDUCIARIES

3.1 Unless waived by the court, all proposed personal representatives and guardians who are residents of Indiana shall appear before the Vanderburgh County Clerk to qualify.

3.2 Unless waived by the court, non-resident personal representatives and guardians shall appear in person before the Vanderburgh County Clerk to take their oath and submit an affidavit describing their education, employment and lack of felony convictions.

3.3 Such personal representative or guardian is under a continuing order of the Court to personally advise the Court and the attorney of record in writing as to any change of required information.

Adopted effective February 5, 2003. Amended effective March 12, 2007; effective Sept. 16, 2011.

LR82–PR Rule 4. REPRESENTATION OF FIDUCIARIES BY COUNSEL

4.1 No personal representative or guardian of an estate may proceed without counsel without Court approval.

Adopted effective February 5, 2003. Amended effective March 12, 2007; effective Sept. 16, 2011.

LR82–PR Rule 5. BOND

5.1 In every estate, the Court shall apply the provisions of I.C. 29–1–11 for fixing or waiving bond of the Indiana resident individual to serve as a personal representative, and shall apply the provisions of I.C. 29–1–10–1(d) to qualification of a non-resident individual to serve as a personal representative.

5.2 In every guardianship, the Court shall apply the provisions of I.C. 29–3–7–1 and 2 for establishing bond.

5.3 In the event the Court imposes restrictions upon access to property without a court order in a guardianship pursuant to I.C. 29–3–7–1 (c) (2), or access to property in an estate without a court order pursuant to I.C. 29–1–11–2, the fiduciary shall thereafter file with the Court within ten (10) days of the Order authorizing the creation of the restricted account or investment, evidence satisfactory to the court that the account or investment has been created, and that the account or investment is restricted as required by the Court's order.

Adopted effective February 5, 2003. Amended effective March 12, 2007; effective Sept. 16, 2011.

LR82–PR Rule 6. INVENTORY

6.1 An inventory shall be prepared by the fiduciary in all estates and guardianships. Such inventory shall be filed in supervised estates and guardianships as follows: Supervised estates, within sixty (60) days; Guardianships, within ninety (90) days for permanent guardian and within thirty (30) days for temporary guardian. The attorney for the fiduciary shall retain in his or her file the original of the inventory, or any supplement or amendment to it. In lieu of an inventory being filed in Unsupervised Estates, a personal representative may certify to the Court that an Inventory has been prepared, under the provisions of I.C. 29–1–7.5–3. 2(a) and that the same, and any supplement or amendment thereto, is available. The attorney for the personal representative shall retain in his or her file the original of the inventory, or any supplement or amendment to it. All times relate to the date of appointment of the fiduciary. (Form: Certification of Inventory Preparation is attached). Upon application by the personal representative, the Court may, in its sole discretion, order an inventory, or any supplement or amendment to it, to be sealed. If so ordered, it may not be opened without an order of the Court, after notice to the personal representative and an opportunity for hearing.

6.2 In the event a supplement or an amendment to an inventory is filed, all such subsequent inventories must contain a recapitulation of prior inventories.

Adopted effective February 5, 2003. Amended effective March 12, 2007; effective Sept. 16, 2011.

LR82–PR Rule 7. REAL ESTATE

7.1 In all supervised estates and guardianships in which real estate is to be sold a written professional appraisal prepared by a licensed real estate appraiser shall be filed with the Court at the time of filing the Petition for Sale, unless such appraisal was filed with the inventory.

7.2 All appraisals required by Rule 7.1 shall be made within one (1) year of the date of the Petition for Sale.

7.3 A copy of the deed shall be submitted with the Report of Sale of Real Estate or at the time of the hearing on the Final Account. Copies of such deeds shall be filed with the Court for its records.

7.4 Whenever a Final Decree reflects that real estate has vested in heirs or beneficiaries, evidence of recording, at the expense of the estate, a certified copy of the Final Decree in every county of this state in which any real property distributed by the decree is situated (except Vanderburgh County) shall be provided to the court with the Supplemental Report.

Adopted effective February 5, 2003. Amended effective March 12, 2007; effective Sept. 16, 2011.

LR82–PR Rule 8. SALE OF ASSETS

8.1 In all supervised estates and guardianships, no Petition to Sell Personal Property shall be granted unless a written appraisal prepared by a person competent to appraise such property and setting forth the Fair Market Value thereof, is filed with the Court at the time of the filing of the Petition to Sell, unless such appraisal was filed with the Inventory. This rule shall not apply to personal property that is sold at public auction.

8.2 All appraisals required by Rule 8.1 shall be made within one year of the date of the Petition to Sell.

8.3 No written appraisal shall be required for the sale of assets which are traded in a market and the value of which is readily ascertainable. Such assets include, but are not limited to, stocks, bonds, mutual funds, commodities, and precious metals.

Adopted effective February 5, 2003. Amended effective March 12, 2007; effective Sept. 16, 2011.

LR82–PR Rule 9. ACCOUNTING

9.1 Whenever an estate is not closed within one (1) year, the Personal Representative shall:

A. In a supervised estate, file an intermediate account with the Court within thirty days (30) after the expiration of one (1) year and each succeeding six (6) months thereafter. The accounting shall comply with the provisions of I.C. 29–1–16–4 and 29–1–16–6 and,

B. Shall state the facts showing why the estate cannot be closed and an estimated date of closing;

C. Shall purpose partial distribution of the estate to the extent that partial distribution can be made without prejudice to distributees and claimants; or,

D. In an unsupervised estate, file a statement with the Court stating the reasons why the estate has not been closed.

9.2 All accountings concerning restricted guardianship bank accounts shall contain a verification of those account balances by an officer of the financial institution in which such guardianship bank accounts are held.

9.3 All Social Security, Veterans, Retirement, or Medicare benefits received on behalf of an incapacitated person or minor shall be included and accounted for in the guardianship accountings unless Court approval has been previously granted to allow said funds to be paid directly to a residential or health care facility.

9.4 In all supervised estate and guardianship accountings, a notation shall be placed by each expenditure indicating the reason for or nature of the expenditure unless the payee name indicates the name of the expenditure.

EXAMPLE:##CVS Drug Store—Prescription Drugs for Incapacitated Person

Dr. Edward Mohlenkamp—Doctor's Appointment

Hoffman Plumbing—Plumbing repairs to ward's home

Good Samaritan Nursing Home—January Nursing Home Care

Weinbach's—Clothing for ward

9.5 All accountings shall follow the prescribed statutory format. Informal, handwritten, or transactional accountings will not be accepted.

9.6 In a supervised estate, all Court Costs shall be paid and all claims satisfied and released and proof presented to the Court before the hearing on the Final Account.

9.7 The Federal Estate Tax Closing Letter and the Indiana Inheritance Closing Letter (countersigned tax receipt), or a photocopy thereof, showing payment of all Federal Estate and/or Indiana Inheritance Tax liability shall be filed prior to entry of an order on the Final Accounting.

Adopted effective February 5, 2003. Amended effective March 12, 2007; effective Sept. 16, 2011.

LR82–PR Rule 10. FEES OF ATTORNEYS AND FIDUCIARY

10.1 No fees for personal representative, guardians or attorneys shall be paid from any guardianship or supervised estate without prior written order of the Court.

10.2 A petition for fees must be signed or approved in writing by the personal representative or guardian.

10.3 Unless otherwise ordered by the court, payment of fees in a supervised estates shall be authorized as follows:

A. One-half upon the filing of an inheritance tax return or upon a Court determination of no tax due; and

B. The remaining one-half upon approval of the final accounting.

10.4 In a guardianship an initial petition for fees may be filed upon filing the inventory.

Except as provided in paragraph 10.5, no further petition for fees will be approved until an annual, biennial or final account is approved.

10.5 When unusual circumstances require substantial work in a guardianship, the Court may award fees prior to the approval of an account.

10.6 Attorney fees for representing a minor in settlement of a claim for personal injuries are subject to Court approval. If the entire attorney fee is to be paid at the time a structured settlement is approved, the amount of the fee must be based on the present value of the settlement.

10.7 Unjustified delays in carrying out duties by the fiduciary and/or attorney may result in a reduction of fees.

Adopted effective February 5, 2003. Amended effective March 12, 2007; effective Sept. 16, 2011.

LR82–PR Rule 11. GUARDIANSHIP

11.1 A Guardian Ad Litem appointed pursuant to I.C.29–3–2–3 will be paid reasonable compensation, considering the needs of the alleged incompetent respondent, the nature and relative difficulty of the services provided, local custom, the availability or limitations of resources of the Ward's Estate, and, in the discretion of the Court, any other considerations deemed relevant under the circumstances of the case.

11.2   In all guardianship matters seeking to declare an adult incapacitated for any reason, a Physician's Report by the doctor treating the alleged incapacitated person or such additional evidence as the court shall require, shall be presented to the Court at the time the petition is filed or on the hearing date to support the findings required by I.C. 29–3–4–1(d). The Physician's Report shall be in a form substantially similar to the form provided by these Rules.

11.3   In every petition for the appointment of a guardian of the person of a minor child, in addition to the statements required by I.C. 29–3–5–1(a), the following information shall also be given.

A.   The places where the child has lived within the past two years and the names and present addresses of persons with whom the child has lived during that period.

B.   Information relevant to the child's health, education and welfare.

C.   Whether, to Petitioner's knowledge, any other litigation public or private is pending or threatened concerning the custody of the child in this or any other state.

D.   Any other matters relevant to the determination of the best interests of the person or property of the incapacitated person or minor.

E.   The Court may in its discretion initiate such further investigation, and obtain a report by the division of family and children or county office of family and children as the Court deems appropriate, pursuant to I. C. 29–3–9–11.

11.4   Current reports filed by a guardian of the person pursuant to I.C. 29–3–9–6(c) shall include the present residence of the incapacitated person and his or her general welfare; if the incapacitated person is an adult, a report of a treating physician concerning in then-current health of the adult; a statement of any changes affecting the findings of the court establishing the guardianship (including but not limited to economic changes); and the then-current living arrangements for the incapacitated person.

Adopted effective February 5, 2003. Amended effective March 12, 2007; effective Sept. 16, 2011.

LR82–PR Rule 12.   MISCELLANEOUS

12.1   Scheduled court hearings shall be taken at the time scheduled, if all parties are present and ready for hearing. Parties are to notify the bailiff of their readiness status. Those matters not ready on time shall be subject to stand-by availability after the conclusion of all hearings at which parties were ready at the scheduled time.

12.2   When opening a new cause of action in the Probate Division an attorney must file the initial pleadings.

12.3   The Court may cause a pleading to be scheduled to come before the court at a time when a contested evidentiary hearing is not possible. If so, the attorney or party filing the pleading shall serve Notice That Pleading Is Not Scheduled for Full Evidentiary Hearing (Form: Notice that Pleading is not Scheduled for Full Evidentiary Hearing is attached.) to the person or persons required by Indiana Statute or these Rules to receive notice of hearing on the pleading. The Notice That Pleading Is Not Scheduled For Full Evidentiary Hearing shall be served in addition to and in the same manner as any other notice of hearing required by Indiana statute or these Rules. However, the Notice That Pleading Is Not Scheduled For Full Evidentiary Hearing may be a separate document or may be incorporated into, and conspicuously stated as part of, any other notice required by Indiana statute or these Rules. The Court, upon application of a party and good cause shown, may grant an exception to the requirements of this Rule for a particular hearing.

12.4   The Court may adapt proceedings by standing order to effectuate the implementation of these rules, and may deviate from these rules when justice requires, but only upon showing of severe prejudice or hardship.

Adopted effective February 5, 2003. Amended effective March 12, 2007; effective Sept. 16, 2011.

LR82–PR Rule 13.   PRIVATE ADOPTIONS

13.1   Prior to filing the Petition for Adoption, if the Petitioner want temporary custody of the child, they must complete a pre-placement adoption investigation with a licensed agency. The Adoption Investigation must include the following:

A.   Home—physical description or neighborhood, house, housekeeping standards, etc.

B.   Motivation and Understanding of Adoption—reasons to adopt, understanding of adoption and responsibilities to child. How Petitioner became aware of the child.

C.   History of adoptive family members.

D.   Police record checks of household members.

E.   Information regarding marriage of adoptive parents.

F.   Child rearing attitudes.

G.   Employment and finances for household

H.   Health and medical information for household members.

I.   Information on adoptive child.

J.   Information on birth parents (non-identifying).

K.   Psychological evaluation—attach report.

L. Minimum of three references.

M. Recommendation.

N. Attorney will need to request a putative father search.

13.2 The following documents must be filed along with the Petition for Adoption:

A. A statement under oath of how and when the arrangements were made for the Adoption.

B. Consent of birth mother and father. If consent is unobtainable then notice must be given. All Consents must be dated, notarized or duly verified.

C. Written acknowledgment by birth mother of availability of up to 3 hours of counseling at adoptive parents' expense within six months following the birth of the child.

D. Financial disclosure of incurred expenses and expected expenses.

13.3 A consent hearing will be set within thirty (30) days of the filing of the Petition for Adoption, at which time the birth mother should be represented by counsel to advise her as to her rights in consenting to the adoption and executing a voluntary waiver of parental rights. This attorney would be responsible for obtaining consents of the birth mother and birth father. The payment of attorney fees is the responsibility of the adoptive parents, regardless of whether the adoption is approved. If the birth mother is represented by independent counsel as recommended, and her Consent is obtained, then the birth mother need not attend the consent hearing, so long as the court finds that the Consent is in the proper form. If she is not represented by counsel, then she must attend the Consent hearing. If she is under the age of eighteen (18) then she must attend the consent hearing and be represented by counsel. Such hearing will not be attended by the Petitioners.

The birth father will also need to attend the Consent hearing if he does not execute a written Consent and Waiver of Notice to the hearing. If he is under eighteen (18) years of age, he must be represented by counsel and must attend the Consent hearing.

13.4 If the Petitioners have met the requirements of the Court on filing the necessary documentation for a Private Adoption the court may issue an order authorizing the Petitioners to have temporary custody of the child. If the Petitioners have not met the requirements of the Court, then they may not take physical custody of the child prior to an Order of this Court authorizing such placement. Such unauthorized custody may be grounds for (i) removal of the child from the Petitioners' custody and (ii) denial of the Petition for Adoption.

13.5 There is a Court-imposed mandatory one (1) year supervision of the placement by the licensed agency. A follow-up report or reports will be filed by the licensed agency during the year of which placement is being supervised confirming that there have been no substantial changes in the Pre–Adoption or Adoption Investigation Report filed contemporaneously with the filing of the Petition for Adoption.

Adopted effective February 5, 2003. Amended effective March 12, 2007; effective Sept. 16, 2011.

LR82–PR Rule 14.   PROBATE CLERKS

The Vanderburgh County Clerk authorizes the deputizing of three (3) employees of the Vanderburgh Superior Court, Probate Division, to perform the duties in accordance with the Constitution of the United States of America and the Constitution of the State of Indiana with regard to any and all documents requiring the signature of a deputy clerk filed on behalf of Estates, Will Contests, Guardianships, Trusts, Adoptions, and any other documents in which the presiding Judge of the Vanderburgh Superior Court, Probate Division, authorizes said deputies to sign. The Vanderburgh County Clerk further authorizes said deputies to administer oaths, and two of the deputies are authorized to issue receipts for court costs and miscellaneous copies for all estates, trusts, guardianships, and adoptions filed in the Vanderburgh Superior Court, Probate Division.

Adopted effective February 5, 2003. Amended effective March 12, 2007; effective Sept. 16, 2011.

Appendix A.   INSTRUCTIONS TO PERSONAL REPRESENTATIVE OF SUPERVISED ESTATE

Read the following carefully; then, date and sign one copy and return it to the Court.   Keep a copy for your reference.

You have been appointed PERSONAL REPRESENTATIVE of the Estate of a deceased person.   It is important that you understand the significance of the appointment and your responsibilities.   This makes you what is known in law as a "fiduciary" charged with the duty to act responsibly in the best interests of the estate and impartially for the benefit and protection of creditors and beneficiaries. You may be held personally liable if you breach this trust.

This is a SUPERVISED ADMINISTRATION.   This means that your actions are supervised almost entirely by the Court; therefore, before you take any action of importance to the Estate, such as the transfer or sale of assets, you must first seek the permission of the Court.   If you have any questions as to whether to seek court permission, you should discuss this with your attorney before taking any action.

Listed below are some of your duties but not necessarily all of them.   Ask the attorney for the Estate to fully explain to you each of the items below and to tell you about any other duties you have in your particular circumstances.   Although the attorney will assist you, the ultimate responsibility to see that the estate is properly handled rests with you.

INVESTIGATE, COLLECT AND PROTECT THE PROPERTY OF THE DECEDENT

1.2   Inspect all document and personal papers of the decedent and retain anything pertinent to tax reporting, location and value of assets, debts or obligations of or to the decedent or any other items of significance to the administration of the estate of the decedent.

1.3   Complete change of address form at Post Office to have mail forwarded to you.

1.4   Keep a separate checking account or other type of transaction account for the Estate and keep a record of all receipts and disbursements.   Never commingle Estate funds with any other funds or use them for other than Estate purposes. Accounts and securities which are registered to the Estate should be in your name "as Personal Representative for the Estate of (name of Decedent)."   Retain all paid bills and canceled checks or other evidence of disbursement or distribution of any funds or assets of the Estate for the Final Report of the Court.

1.5   Locate and secure all property in which the decedent had any interest, separately or jointly.   Maintain adequate insurance coverage.

1.6   Determine the values of all assets on the date of death, obtaining appraisals if needed.

1.7   Collect any proceeds of life insurance on the life of the decedent which is payable to the Estate.   Obtain Form 712 from the insurance company, if needed for taxes.

1.8   Sign your name as "Personal Representative for the Estate of (name of decedent)" on accounts and securities which are registered to the estate.   Consent to Transfer forms are available from the County Assessor.

1.9   Within two (2) months after you qualify and receive Letters of Personal Representative, you must file with the Court an inventory of all property found belonging to the decedent on the date of death and giving values as of the date of death.

PAY VALID CLAIMS AND KEEP RECORDS OF ALL DISBURSEMENTS

1.10   Personally notify decedent's creditors whom you can reasonable ascertain. Others are notified by publication in the newspaper.   Generally, creditors have three (3) months after the date of first publication to submit their claims.

1.11 Pay legal debts and funeral bills and keep notations indicating the reason for each payment.

    A. Pay only priority claims timely filed if there is a question of solvency of the estate.

    B. Do not pay bills which are doubtful but refer them for Court determination.

1.12 Prepare and file the appropriate state and federal income, estate and inheritance tax forms in a timely manner. Pay taxes due or claim applicable refunds.

1.13 Pay court costs when due; however, attorney fee's and fiduciary fees are only paid after written Court order.

1.14 Keep records of all receipts and all paid bills and canceled checks or other evidence of distribution of any funds or assets of the estate for the Final Report to the Court.

DISTRIBUTE THE ASSETS OF THE ESTATE AND CLOSE THE ESTATE

1.15 File a Final Account with this court (with "vouchers" or canceled checks) within one year from the date you received your Letters from this Court. If you cannot meet this deadline, you must show good cause for an extension.

1.16 After Court authorization, make distributions to the proper heirs of beneficiaries and obtain receipts for these.

1.17 File a supplemental report to the Court (with "vouchers" or canceled checks) and obtain an order for closure of the estate.

      BRETT J. NIEMEIER, JUDGE
      VANDERBURGH SUPERIOR COURT
      PROBATE DIVISION

I acknowledge receipt of a copy of the above instructions and have read said instructions carefully.

Dated:

Cause Number 82D07——___—ES–

ESTATE OF:

BY:

PERSONAL REPRESENTATIVE

I hereby certify that the foregoing Court Record or document complies with the requirements of Trial Rule 5(G) with regard to information excluded from the public record under Administrative 9(G).

Counsel of Record

Adopted effective February 5, 2003. Amended effective March 12, 2007; effective Sept. 16, 2011.

Appendix B. INSTRUCTIONS TO PERSONAL REPRESENTATIVE OF UNSUPERVISED ESTATE

Read the following carefully; then, date and sign one copy and return it to the Court. Keep a copy for your reference.

You have been appointed PERSONAL REPRESENTATIVE of the Estate of a deceased person. It is important that you understand the significance of the appointment and your responsibilities.

Listed below are some of your duties but not necessarily all of them. These duties are not listed in any order of priority. Ask the attorney for the Estate to fully explain to you each of the items below and to tell you about any other duties you have in your particular circumstances. Although the attorney will probably file all papers with the Court, the ultimate responsibility to see that reports and returns are accurately prepared and filed rests with you. As PERSONAL REPRESENTATIVE, you are required to:

1.18   Locate all property owned individually or otherwise by the decedent at the date of death; and ascertain the value of such assets as of date of death.   Secure all property in safekeeping and maintain adequate insurance coverage; keep records of the assets.   If applicable, obtain an appraisal of the property.

1.19   Keep a separate checking account or other type of transaction account for the Estate and keep a record of all receipts and disbursements.   Never co-mingle Estate funds with any other funds or use them for other than Estate purposes. Accounts and securities which are registered to the Estate should be in your name "as Personal Representative for the Estate of (name of Decedent)."   Retain all paid bills and canceled checks or other evidence of disbursement or distribution of any funds or assets of the Estate for the Closing Statement to be filed with the Court.

1.20   Within two (2) months after you qualify and receive Letters of Personal Representative, you must file with the Court an inventory of all property found belonging to the decedent on the date of death and giving values as of the date of death.   In lieu of an inventory being filed a personal representative may certify to the Court that an Inventory has been prepared and the same distributed to each distributee.   (Form available in the Probate Division)

1.21   You may need to obtain Consent to Transfer forms from the county Assessor for accounts and securities in order to transfer such assets.

1.22   Collect any proceeds of life insurance on the life of the decedent which is payable to the Estate.   Obtain Form 712 from the insurance company, if needed for taxes.

1.23   Have mail forwarded; complete change of address forms at the Post Office.

1.24   Inspect all documents and personal papers of the decedent and retain anything pertinent to tax reporting, location and value of assets, debts or obligations of or to the decedent, or any other items of significance to administering the final affairs of decedent.

1.25   Pay all legal debts and funeral bills; however, pay only priority claims timely filed if there is any question of solvency of the Estate.   Do not pay bills which are doubtful but refer them for Court determination.   Do not make any distribution to any heir or beneficiary until at least five (5) months after the date of first publication by notice.

1.26   Prepare and file returns and pay taxes due (or claim any refund) for both State and Federal income taxes for the tax year in which the decedent died and any prior years, if applicable.

1.27   Prepare and file the prescribed Schedule and pay any tax due for the Indiana Inheritance Tax within nine (9) months after date of death.

1.28   Unless subject to an exception, obtain a federal tax identification number for the Estate.   Choose a tax year for the Estate; file Estate income tax returns and pay any tax due for both State and Federal income tax.

1.29   Make distribution and obtain receipts for distributions.

1.30   File a Closing Statement, with receipts for distribution if already made; send a copy thereof to all distributees of the estate and to all creditors or other claimants whose claims are neither paid nor barred; furnish a full account in writing of the administration to the distributees.   File original vouchers with the court.

1.31   Pay Court costs and expenses of administration when due.

1.32   Make payments and distributions to the right persons.   You are responsible for incorrect payments or distribution.

BRETT J. NIEMEIER, JUDGE

VANDERBURGH SUPERIOR COURT

PROBATE DIVISION

I acknowledge receipt of a copy of the above instructions and have read and will follow said instructions carefully.

Dated:

Cause Number 82D07—___—EU–

ESTATE OF:

BY:

PERSONAL REPRESENTATIVE

I hereby certify that the foregoing Court Record or document complies with the requirements of Trial Rule 5(G) with regard to information excluded from the public record under Administrative 9(G).

Counsel of Record

Adopted effective February 5, 2003. Amended effective March 12, 2007; effective Sept. 16, 2011.

Appendix C. INSTRUCTIONS TO GUARDIAN

Read carefully; date and sign one copy and return it to this Court within ten days. Keep a copy for your reference.

You have been appointed the Guardian of an individual, "Protected Person" who, because of some incapacity, is unable to care for his/her own financial and/or personal affairs. It is important that you understand the significance of this appointment and your responsibility as Guardian.

In order to qualify and have your Letters issued to you, you may be required to post a bond in the amount set by the Court and to take an oath to faithfully discharge your duties as Guardian. The Bond assures the Court that you will properly protect the assets of the Protected Person.

Listed below are some of your duties, but not necessarily all of them. You are directed to ask the Attorney for the Guardianship to fully explain to you each of the items below and to tell you about the other duties you have in your particular circumstances. Though the Attorney will file all papers with the court, the ultimate responsibility to see that all reports, etc., are accurately and timely prepared and filed, rests with you.

As GUARDIAN of the financial affairs of the Protected Person, you are required to:

1. File with the court, within ninety (90) days after your appointment, a verified Inventory and appraisement of all the property belonging to the Protected Person;

2. File with the court a verified account of all the income and expenditures of the Guardianship every two (2) years after your appointment;

3. If assets were placed in a restricted account you are to file an accounting every two (2) years, together with a statement from the financial institution showing the current balance of the funds and that the same remain in an account that is restricted;

4. Pay bond premiums as they become due;

5. File Federal and State Tax Returns for Ward and pay taxes;

6. File a final accounting, detailing all property and income received and all expenses paid with receipts to verify each expenditure with the Court upon the termination of the guardianship or upon the death of the ward;

7. Keep all of the assets of the Protect Person separate from your own;

8. Open an account where the canceled checks are returned to you, in your name as Guardian, in which all of the cash assets of the Protected Person are deposited. This account must be used for all payments or disbursements on behalf of the Guardianship and the Protected Person;

9. Obtain approval from the Court to use Guardianship assets.

It is your duty to protect and preserve the Protected Person's property, to the account for the use of the property faithfully and to perform all the duties required by law of a Guardian.

You may NOT make expenditures or investments from the Guardianship funds without court authorization.

Guardianship funds must never be co-mingled with personal funds. A separate account for all Guardianship assets must be kept in your name as Guardian. Accurate accounts must be kept and accurate reports made. Unauthorized use of Guardianship funds can result in your being personally liable for the misuse of those sums.

As GUARDIAN of the personal affairs of the Protected Person, you are required to:

    A. Make certain that the physical and mental needs of the Protected Person (food, clothing, shelter, medical attention, education, etc.) are properly and adequately provided for;

    B. File with the Court a status report as to the physical condition and general welfare of the Protected Person every two (2) years after your appointment if said Protected Person is over the age of eighteen (18).

    C. File with the Court a status report as to the physical condition and general welfare of the Protected Person yearly after your appointment of said Protected Person is a minor.

It is important to understand that you have the same duties and responsibilities concerning the Protected Person whether or not the Protected Person is your relative.

If at anytime you have a change of address, please notify the Court immediately so that we may make that change to our Court file.

If any questions arise during the Guardianship, you should consult with your Attorney immediately.

I acknowledge I have read and understand the above instructions and agree to follow them carefully, and further that I have kept a copy for my continued use and review.

    Dated:

    Cause Number:

    The Guardianship of:

    By: _____, Guardian

I hereby certify that the foregoing Court Record or document complies with the requirements of Trial Rule 5(G) with regard to information excluded from the public record under Administrative 9(G).

    Counsel of Record

Adopted effective February 5, 2003. Amended effective March 12, 2007; effective Sept. 16, 2011.

Appendix D. CERTIFICATION OF INVENTORY PREPARATION

STATE OF INDIANA   )
) SS:
COUNTY OF VANDERBURGH   )

IN THE VANDERBURGH SUPERIOR COURT
PROBATE DIVISION

82D07—_____—EU–
IN THE MATTER OF THE UNSUPERVISED   )
ESTATE OF _____,   )
DECEASED   )
_____,   )

CERTIFICATION OF INVENTORY PREPARATION

Comes now the Personal Representative of the Estate of _____, pursuant to the provisions of I.C. 29–1–7.5–3.2 (e) and certifies to the Court that (1) the

Inventory of the estate's assets, and supplement or amendment to it that is required to be prepared pursuant to the provisions of I.C.29–1–7.5–3. 2 (a) has been prepared and is available to distributees upon request made to the Personal Representative, and (2) copies of this Certification have been distributed to each of the distributees.

Dated this ___ day of _____, 20 ___.

Personal Representative

I, _____, swear and affirm under the penalties of perjury that the above and foregoing representations are true and correct to the best of my knowledge and belief.

Personal Representative

I hereby certify that the foregoing Court Record or document complies with the requirements of Trial Rule 5(G) with regard to information excluded from the public record under Administrative 9(G).

Counsel of Record

Adopted effective February 5, 2003. Amended effective March 12, 2007; effective Sept. 16, 2011.

Appendix E. NOTICE THAT PLEADING IS NOT SCHEDULED FOR FULL EVIDENTIARY HEARING

(Case Caption)

SET FOR HEARING: Date:
                                          Time:
                                          Administration Building
                                          Room 129, Probate Division
                                          Evansville IN 47708

NOTICE THAT PLEADING IS NOT SCHEDULED FOR FULL EVIDENTIARY HEARING

The pleading attached to this Notice is scheduled to come before the court on a day and time when it will not be possible to conduct a full evidentiary hearing; only a brief hearing is scheduled. A full evidentiary hearing involves questioning and cross-examination of opposing witnesses, presentation of exhibits supporting positions of two (2) or more opposing parties, and more than brief legal arguments to the Court. Therefore, you should not expect the Court to conduct a full evidentiary hearing on the date of which you are being notified.

If you oppose the action requested in the attached pleading and want the Court to conduct a full evidentiary hearing on whether the pleading should be granted, you must respond to the pleading and request a full evidentiary hearing in one (1) of the following ways. First, you may appear in person or by your attorney at the date and time of which you are now being notified and object to the pleading and request a full evidentiary hearing. Or you may state your opposition and request for a full evidentiary hearing in writing by serving it **BEFORE** the date of which you are now being notified on the Court and the party which filed the attached pleading; the writing must be signed by you or your attorney and must contain the address which you stipulate as adequate for further notice to you. In addition, statutes or court rules of Indiana or these Rules require a specific responsive pleading or specific contents in a response to the pleading attached, and the responding party shall comply therewith.

The court has the authority to order a pre-hearing conference, additional pleadings or responses, legal briefs, or alternate dispute resolution prior to scheduling a full evidentiary hearing.

Vanderburgh Superior Court
Probate Division

County Courts Building
825 Sycamore Street, Room 127
Evansville IN 47708

I hereby certify that the foregoing Court Record or document complies with the requirements of Trial Rule 5(G) with regard to information excluded from the public record under Administrative 9(G).

Counsel of Record

Adopted effective February 5, 2003. Amended effective March 12, 2007; effective Sept. 16, 2011.

VIGO COUNTY CIVIL RULES OF PROCEDURE

Adopted October 1, 2006, Effective January 1, 2007

Including Amendments Received Through November 1, 2013

Research Notes

These rules may be searched electronically on Westlaw in theIN-RULES database; updates to these rules may be found on Westlaw in IN-RULESUPDATES. For search tips and a summary of database content, consult the Westlaw Scope Screens for each database.

LR84–TR3.1 Rule 1. APPEARANCE AND WITHDRAWAL OF APPEARANCE

(A) All pleadings shall show the name and address, telephone number, fax number and attorney number of the individual attorney or attorneys filing the pleading. All attorneys for a defendant or a third party shall file a written appearance for such defendant or third party. Any pleading not signed by at least one (1) attorney appearing of record as required by T. R. 11 shall not be accepted for filing by the Clerk of the Court or, if inadvertently accepted for filing, shall, upon discovery of such omission, be stricken from the record. All appearance forms must be substantially in compliance with the requirements for appearance forms as set out by the Indiana Supreme Court.

(B) Counsel desiring to withdraw their appearance in any action shall file a written petition requesting leave of Court to do so. Permission to withdraw shall be given only after the withdrawing attorney has given his or her client ten (10) days written notice of the attorney's intention to withdraw and has filed a copy of such notice with the Court. The notice of withdrawal shall explain to the client that failure to secure new counsel may result in dismissal of the client's case or a default judgment may be entered against the client, whichever is appropriate, and other pertinent information such as trial setting date or any other hearing date. The Court will not grant a request for withdrawal of appearance unless the request has been filed with the Court at least thirty (30) days prior to any scheduled hearing or trial date, except for good cause shown as determined by the Court. All withdrawals of appearance shall comply fully with the provisions of Rules of Professional Conduct, Rule 1.16.

(C) A withdrawal of appearance when accompanied by the simultaneous entry of appearance by substitute counsel shall constitute a waiver of the requirements of Paragraph (B) of this rule.

(D) This rule shall apply to all probate pleadings.

Adopted as Circuit and Superior Court Rule 3. Amended and renumbered as Civil Rule 1, October 1, 2006, effective Jan. 1, 2007; effective Jan. 1, 2012.

LR84–TR5 Rule 2. BANKRUPTCY NOTICE OF STAY

Whenever any party receives an order from a Bankruptcy Court staying proceedings, it shall be sufficient for such party to file a notice of such order with the Court. Such notice shall contain the name of the party, the cause number in bankruptcy and the date of the issuance of the stay.

Adopted as Circuit and Superior Court Rule 16. Amended and renumbered as Civil Rule 2, October 1, 2006, effective Jan. 1, 2007; effective Jan. 1, 2012.

LR84–TR6 Rule 3. INITIAL ENLARGEMENTS OF TIME

In every civil action pending in this Court in which a party wishes to obtain an initial enlargement of time not exceeding thirty (30) days within which to file a responsive pleading or a response to a written request for discovery, the party shall contact counsel for the opposing party and solicit opposing counsel's agreement to the extension. In the event opposing counsel does not object to the extension or cannot with due diligence be reached, the party requesting the extension shall document the lack of objection by notice to opposing counsel and send a copy of the notice to the Clerk of the Court, which notice shall be filed of record in the case. No further filings with the Court nor action by the Court shall be required for the extension.

Adopted as Circuit and Superior Court Rule 5. Amended and renumbered as Civil Rule 3, October 1, 2006, effective Jan. 1, 2007; effective Jan. 1, 2012.

LR84–TR7 Rule 4. MOTION PRACTICE

(A) Form and Notice. Each motion shall be separate; alternative motions filed together shall each be named in the caption on the face. When a motion requires notice, the serving of the copy of the motion upon the other parties in the cause shall constitute notice of filing same. A movant shall file an original form of proposed order along with sufficient copies to serve all parties of record.

(B) Oral Arguments on Motions and Other Pleadings. A request for oral argument on a motion shall be by separate instrument and timely served and filed with the brief, answer brief, or reply brief, except as otherwise provided. Failure to file a timely request for oral argument will constitute a waiver of oral argument. The granting of a motion for oral argument, except as mandated by the Trial Rules Motions (e.g. summary judgment and 41(E) motions) shall be wholly discretionary with the Court. The Court, upon its own initiative, may also direct that oral argument be had. The request for oral argument shall set forth specifically the purpose of the request and an estimate of the time reasonably required for the Court to devote to the argument. An oral argument shall not include the presentation of evidence.

(C) Enlargement of Time. An initial written motion for enlargement of time pursuant to T.R.6(B)(1) to respond to a claim shall be automatically allowed for an additional thirty (30) days from the original due date without a written order of the Court. Any motion filed pursuant to this Rule shall state the date when such response is due and the date to which time is enlarged. The motion must be filed on or before the original due date or this Rule shall be inapplicable. All subsequent motions shall be so designated and will be granted only for good cause shown.

(D) Briefs and Memoranda Regarding Motions.

(1) A Motion to Dismiss under Rule 12 of the Indiana Rules of Trial Procedure, for judgment on the pleadings, for more definite statement, to strike, or motions made pursuant to Rule 37 of the trial rules shall be accompanied by a separate supporting brief. Any brief or memorandum in support of any motion shall accompany or be filed simultaneous with the motion, and a copy shall be promptly served upon the opposing party. If the opposing party desires to file a brief or memorandum, that party must do so within thirty (30) days of service of the movant's brief or memorandum. If the mov-

ing party desires to file a reply brief or memorandum, that party must do so within seven (7) days of service of the response, brief or memorandum. Time shall be computed as provided in Rule 6, Indiana Rules of Trial Procedure. Extensions of time shall be granted only by order of the assigned or presiding Judge for good cause shown. Failure to file an answer brief in opposition to a motion within the time prescribed shall subject the motion to summary ruling.

(2) Except by permission of the Court, no brief shall exceed twenty (20) pages in length (exclusive of any pages containing a table of contents, table of authorities, and appendices), and no reply brief shall exceed ten (10) pages. Permission to file briefs in excess of these page limitations will be granted only upon motion supported by extraordinary and compelling reasons. Briefs exceeding twenty (20) pages in length (exclusive of any pages containing the table of contents, table of authorities, and appendices) shall contain:

(i) a table of contents with page reference;

(ii) a statement of issues; and

(iii) a table of cases (alphabetically arranged), statutes and other authorities cited, with reference to the pages of the brief where they are cited. If a party relies upon a legal decision not published in North Eastern Reporter 2d, or on a statute or regulation not found in the current publication of the United States Code, the Indiana Code, or the Indiana Administrative Code, then the party shall furnish the Court and all counsel of record with a copy of the relied-upon decision, statute, or regulation.

(E) Motions to Strike or to Insert New Matter. Subject to T.R. 12(F) every motion to insert new matter or to strike out any part of any pleading in a cause shall be made in writing and shall set forth verbatim each set of words to be inserted or stricken. Each set of words to be inserted or stricken shall be designated in a separate specification, numbered consecutively.

Adopted October 1, 2006, effective Jan. 1, 2007. Amended effective Jan. 1, 2012.

LR84–TR16 Rule 5. PRE–TRIAL PROCEDURE

In all civil tort cases on the plenary docket, after the issues have been closed on the merits and the Court has determined jurisdiction is proper, the Court shall enter an initial pre-trial order substantially as follows:

COURT'S INITIAL PRE–TRIAL ORDER

Pursuant to Trial Rule 16 of the Indiana Rules of Trial Procedure, and LR84–TR16–5, the Court enters the following initial pre-trial order:

(A) The Court finds that the issues have been closed and makes a preliminary determination that jurisdiction is proper.

(B) The Court ORDERS the parties immediately to commence such discovery as may be needed for the parties to mediate this matter.

(C) The Court ORDERS each party to file and serve on all other parties a preliminary witness and exhibit list no later than thirty (30) days after entry of this Order. Parties not complying with this Order shall be subject to sanctions.

(D) The Court ORDERS the parties to file, either jointly or separately, a pre-trial report no later than one hundred twenty (120) days after entry of this Order. The pre-trial report shall contain the following information:

(1) A brief summary of the nature of the case (including any non-binding observations about whether liability is contested);

(2) An estimate of days required for trial;

(3) An agreement, if any exists, as to the parties' selection as mediator;

(4) An estimate as to additional time needed to complete discovery necessary for trial;

(5) An amended list of witnesses and exhibits necessary for trial;

(6) Any anticipated pre-trial motions, including dispositive motions (such as motions to dismiss or for summary judgment) and anticipated trial motions such as motions in limine);

(7) A summary of any stipulations proposed (or with respect to which the parties have agreed).

(E) The pre-trial report ordered under paragraph (D) is a prerequisite to a scheduling conference at which a trial date is assigned.

(F) Upon filing the mandatory pre-trial report, either party may request the court to schedule a telephone conference for determination of a trial date. The Court will then enter a formal pre-trial order setting forth final deadlines for discovery, disclosure of contentions, witnesses, and exhibits, pre-trial motions, and such other matters as the Court deems necessary in management of the case.

(H)[1] Nothing in this Order shall preclude the parties from accelerating discovery as appropriate or convening mediation prior to filing a pre-trial report. A party shall not, however, request a pre-trial conference or scheduling conference without complying with this Order.

(K)[1] Upon a showing to the Court that any party failed to exercise good faith within the parameters of this Order, the Court shall have the authority to enforce sanctions.

Adopted October 1, 2006, effective Jan. 1, 2007. Amended effective Jan. 1, 2012.

[1] So in original.

LR84–TR16 Rule 6.   MEDIATION

(A) In all civil tort cases on the plenary docket where a timely demand for jury trial is made, parties are required to complete mediation of the case no later than sixty (60) days before the case goes to trial.

(B) Mediator selection shall be governed by A.D.R. Rule 2.4. The Court shall maintain a roster of Mediators approved by the Indiana Supreme Court Commission for Continuing Legal Education. If the parties are unable to agree upon a mediator pursuant to A.D.R. Rule 2.4, the parties shall submit said fact to the Court and the Court shall name a panel of three (3) from which the parties shall strike. The party that initiated the action shall strike first. The parties shall have ten (10) days to strike from the panel of mediators named by the Court. In the event the parties fail to select a mediator hereunder, the Court shall name the mediator.

(C) Parties are required to have present or immediately available by telephone at the mediation all persons who have the authority to resolve the case. When a party has insurance coverage that is subject to payment of any settlement or judgment that might be had in said case, then the insurance company shall have someone present or immediately available by telephone who has the authority to settle the case.

(D) Upon a showing to the Court that any party failed to exercise good faith within the parameters of this Rule, the Court shall have the authority to enforce sanctions.

(E) Notwithstanding the foregoing, a party may file a motion reciting that mediation would be futile or non-productive, citing the reasons therefore, and requesting relief from the requirements of this rule.

Adopted October 1, 2006, effective Jan. 1, 2007. Amended effective Jan. 1, 2012.

LR84–TR26 Rule 7.   DISCOVERY IN GENERAL

(A) Time Limit. Counsel are expected to begin discovery promptly. In all cases, discovery shall be completed prior to the pre-trial conference unless otherwise ordered by the Court. Any physical or mental examination of a party pursuant to T.R. 35 must be completed no later than sixty (60) days prior to the discovery cut-off set by the Court.

(B) Extensions of Time. For good cause shown and prior to the expiration of the time within which discovery is required to be completed, time may be extended for completion of discovery. Motions and stipulations for additional time for completion of discovery must set forth reasons justifying the additional time. Stipulations extending the discovery period must be approved by the Court.

(C) Filing. All discovery requests, including third party Requests for Production under T.R. 34(C), to be served upon another party shall not be filed with the Court. The person serving such discovery requests shall notify the Court in writing of the service of such discovery requests and the date upon which answers are to be made. Answered interrogatories and any objections thereto shall be filed with the Court by the person having the burden of answering or objecting, within the time provided by Indiana Trial Rules of Procedure or within such other time as the Court may allow.

Adopted October 1, 2006, effective Jan. 1, 2007. Amended effective Jan. 1, 2012.

LR84–TR30 Rule 8. DEPOSITIONS

Depositions shall be governed by T.R. 30. Video tape or other mechanically reproduced tapes, as allowed by T.R. 74, shall be admissible to the same degree as any other depositions. A transcript of the testimony elicited in the video tape shall accompany all videotaped depositions filed with the Court. A party may take the deposition of an expert or treating physician, timely listed on a party's witness list, after the cut off of discovery if the purpose of the same is for the presentation of the deposition at trial.

Adopted October 1, 2006, effective Jan. 1, 2007. Amended effective Jan. 1, 2012.

LR84–TR32 Rule 9. DEPOSITION OF EXPERT

The deposition of an expert or treating physician taken for the purpose of presentation of the deposition at trial shall be admissible, if otherwise ruled to be admissible by the Court, without the necessity of a party showing the unavailability of the expert to personally appear at trial.

Adopted October 1, 2006, effective Jan. 1, 2007. Amended effective Jan. 1, 2012.

LR84–TR33 Rule 10. INTERROGATORIES

(A) Form. Interrogatories shall be tailored specifically to each cause in which they are filed. No fill-in the blank or photocopied forms containing interrogatories shall be filed or served upon a party unless all interrogatories on such forms are consecutively numbered and applicable to the case in which the same are filed and served. The intent and purpose of this rule is to prohibit the filing of fill-in the blank or photocopied forms of interrogatories except where the nature of the case or the number of the parties makes the use of such forms necessary and feasible.

(B) Answers and Objections. Answers or objections to Interrogatories under Trial Rule 33 shall set forth in full the interrogatory being answered or objected to immediately preceding the answer or objection. Any objection to an interrogatory must clearly state in detail the legal basis upon which it is made, or the objection will be waived.

(C) Number Limited. The number of interrogatories shall be kept to a reasonable limit and shall not require the answering party to make more than one hundred twenty-five (125) responses. For good cause shown and upon leave of Court, additional interrogatories may be propounded if the Court finds this limita-

tion would work a manifest injustice or would be impractical because of the complexity of the issues of the case. Interrogatories shall be used solely for the purpose of discovery and shall not be used as a substitute for the taking of a deposition.

Adopted October 1, 2006, effective Jan. 1, 2007. Amended effective Jan. 1, 2012.

LR84–TR37 Rule 11. MOTIONS TO COMPEL DISCOVERY

To curtail undue delay in the administration of justice, this Court shall refuse to rule on any and all motions for discovery and production of documents under T.R. 26 through T.R. 37, unless moving counsel shall first advise the Court in writing that after personal consultation and sincere attempts to resolve differences, they are unable to reach an accord. This statement shall recite, in addition, the date, time and place of such conference, and the names of all parties participating therein. If counsel for any party advises the Court in writing that opposing counsel has refused or delayed meeting and discussion of the problems covered in this subsection, the Court may take such actions as are appropriate to avoid delay.

The Court shall, if it finds that the party to whom the interrogatories or request were directed has not responded within the time allowed, and that the moving party has complied with Trial Rule 26(F) and this section, order the non-responding party to respond within a period of time not less than ten (10) days after entry of the Court's order. The Court may, upon written request and for good cause shown, shorten or extend such time as it deems appropriate.

Adopted October 1, 2006, effective Jan. 1, 2007. Amended effective Jan. 1, 2012.

LR84–TR40 Rule 12. TRIALS

(A) Setting Cases for Trial. No trial date will be set unless a pretrial report pursuant to LR84–TR16–5 has been filed.

(B) All counsel of record shall be advised promptly by the Court or Clerk of the Court as to the date and time of trial settings, either by individual notice or by providing copies of trial calendars, as the Court may direct.

(C) When more than one (1) case is set for trial on a given trial date, the case set for second or third shall be required to stand for trial if counsel are given fourteen (14) calendar days notice that the case first set has been settled.

(D) The parties shall immediately notify the Court of any reasonably anticipated settlement of a case.

Adopted October 1, 2006, effective Jan. 1, 2007. Amended effective Jan. 1, 2012.

LR84–TR51 Rule 13. JURY INSTRUCTIONS

(A) All requests for instructions submitted in accordance with Trial Rule 51 shall be submitted to the

Court and exchanged with opposing counsel not later than the beginning of trial. Any proposed instruction which is not an Indiana Pattern Jury Instruction and all 1.03 Issue instructions shall be submitted to the Court and exchanged with opposing counsel not later than five (5) days prior to trial. Counsel shall have the right to submit additional instructions during trial on matters which could not reasonably have been anticipated in advance of trial. Such requests for special instructions shall contain citations to supporting authorities. All instructions submitted to the Court shall also either be submitted on an electronic disk compatible with the Court's computer in order that the Court's staff may duplicate the instructions or with an additional set of instructions designated as Court's Instructions without showing authority for the instruction or the party submitting the instruction.

(B) Indiana Pattern Jury Instructions shall be used where applicable.

Adopted October 1, 2006, effective Jan. 1, 2007. Amended effective Jan. 1, 2012.

LR84–TR53.4 Rule 14. MOTION TO RECONSIDER RULINGS

A motion to reconsider a ruling of the Court on any motion must be in writing and must be served personally upon the ruling Judge. A motion to reconsider must be filed within fifteen (15) days of the ruling.

Adopted October 1, 2006, effective Jan. 1, 2007. Amended effective Jan. 1, 2012.

LR84–TR53.5 Rule 15. MOTIONS FOR CONTINUANCE

Motions for Continuance are discouraged. Neither side is entitled to an automatic continuance as a matter of right.

(A) Upon verified motion, civil actions may be postponed or continued in the discretion of the Court. The Court may award such costs as will reimburse the other parties for their actual expenses incurred from the delay. A motion for continuance shall state whether opposing counsel objects to the motion and whether prior continuances have been requested by the moving party. The Court may require any written Motion for Continuance to be signed by the party requesting the continuance.

A motion to postpone a civil trial based on the absence of evidence can be made only upon affidavit showing: the materiality of the evidence expected to be obtained; that due diligence has been used to obtain it; where the evidence may be; and, if it is for an absent witness, the affidavit must show the name and residence of the witness, if known, and the probability of procuring the testimony within a reasonable time, and that his/her absence has not been procured by the act or connivance of the party, nor by others at the party's request, nor with his/her knowledge or consent; and what facts the party believes to be true, and that he/she is unable to prove such facts by any

other witness whose testimony can be as readily procured.

If the adverse party will stipulate to the content of the evidence that would have been elicited at trial from the absent document or witness, the trial shall not be postponed. In the event of a stipulation, the parties shall have the right to contest the stipulated evidence to the same extent as if the absent document or witness were available at trial.

(B) Time for Filing. Motions for Continuance must be filed as soon after the cause for continuance or delay is discovered by the party seeking the continuance, and no later than fourteen (14) days before the date assigned for trial, unless the reason therefore is shown by affidavit to have occurred within the fourteen (14) day period.

(C) Title of Motion. A Motion for Continuance, whether it is plaintiff's or defendant's motion, shall denominate whether it is the First (1st), Second (2nd), Third (3rd), etc. Motion for Continuance filed by plaintiff or defendant.

(D) Dispositive Motions. The filing of a dispositive motion shall not constitute good cause for a Motion for Continuance of a trial if the time requirements governing such motion will not allow for the resolution of the motion prior to the date of trial.

Adopted as Circuit and Superior Court Rule 6. Renumbered as Civil Rule 15, and amended June 1, 2006, effective Jan. 1, 2008. Amended effective Jan. 1, 2012.

LR84–TR55 Rule 16. AFFIDAVIT OF DEBT AND ATTORNEY FEES IN DEFAULT JUDGMENTS

(A) On all default judgments relating to commercial cases (except small claims) plaintiff or his counsel must submit an affidavit of debt and an affidavit in support of attorney fees requested by counsel. The affidavit for attorney's fees shall set forth the number of hours spent on the case and the hourly charge.

(B) In small claims cases, a request for attorney fees up to $300.00 will be considered reasonable. Any request for attorney fees over that amount must be supported by an affidavit setting forth the number of hours spent on the case and the hourly charge.

Adopted October 1, 2006, effective Jan. 1, 2007. Amended effective Jan. 1, 2012.

LR84–TR73 Rule 17. TELEPHONIC CONFERENCE

Although not favored, the Court, on its own motion or at a party's request, may direct argument of any motion be by telephone conference. At the conclusion thereof, the Court may announce its order orally or may take the matter under advisement; but in either event, any order issued thereon shall be reduced to writing and a copy sent to the parties. The Court may further direct which party shall arrange and pay for the cost of the telephone calls.

Adopted October 1, 2006, effective Jan. 1, 2007. Amended effective Jan. 1, 2012.

LR84–TR79 Rule 18. LOCAL REASSIGNMENT RULES

(A) The Presiding Judge in Administrative District 19 shall administer reassignment of cases pursuant to T.R. 79(H). The Presiding Judge shall be selected from the sitting Judges and Magistrates in District 19. The initial Presiding Judge's term shall commence April 1, 2013, and terminate December 31, 2013. All subsequent terms shall be for a calendar year. Should the Presiding Judge leave the bench during the term, a successor Judge shall be selected to fulfill the balance of that term as well as the entirety of the next term. A Judge may not refuse to serve as Presiding Judge.

(B) During his or her term of service, the Presiding Judge shall maintain a record of the cause number of each case certified for reassignment and appointment of a special judge, the Judge who certified the case, and the Judge to whom the case was reassigned. The Presiding Judge shall submit a written semi-annual report to all District 19 Judges and Magistrates no more than ten (10) days following the end of the first and third quarters of each calendar year. The Presiding Judge may assign administrative duties to local court support staff to assist in fulfilling these responsibilities. The Presiding Judge shall transfer the records maintained during his or her term of service to the succeeding Presiding Judge.

(C) Pursuant to Trial Rule 79 (H), the District Judges and Magistrates shall certify to the Presiding Judge cases for reassignment and special judge appointment. The certification shall include a prepared order of appointment, as exhibited in Appendix A. When the Presiding Judge receives a certification requiring reassignment, the Presiding Judge shall appoint a Judge or Magistrate in the following manner:

(1) At the beginning of each calendar year, the Presiding Judge shall create a list of all judicial officers in District 19. The District will follow the principle that each Judge or Magistrate will receive a new case for each case from which he or she has been removed—a one-off, one-on formula. Upon receiving a certification, the Presiding Judge shall assign the case to the first eligible Judge or Magistrate on the list.

(2) Sullivan County Judges shall not be eligible for assignment to cases from Putnam County. Putnam County Judges shall not be eligible for assignment to cases from Sullivan County.

The order of appointment shall be filed in the court where the case originated. The order of appointment shall constitute acceptance, and neither oath nor additional evidence of acceptance is required.

(D) A Senior Judge may elect to participate in District 19 special judge selection by submitting a written petition to the Presiding Judge no later than January 15 of any calendar year indicating that the Senior Judge wishes to participate during the year.

(E) When a Judge or Magistrate vacates the bench and is certified as a Senior Judge, that Judge shall retain jurisdiction of all previously existing Special Judge cases as provided by Administrative Rule 5. In the event the Judge or Magistrate vacates the bench and is not certified as a Senior Judge or is unavailable as indicated under Trial Rule 79 (L), then the successor Judge shall assume jurisdiction over all previous Special Judge cases of the vacating Judge or Magistrate. The county's judicial personnel shall first attempt to absorb conflicts of interest of the Successor Judge within the county without undue hardship.

(F) If no Judge or Magistrate is eligible to serve as a Special Judge, or if the Presiding Judge determines the selection of a Special Judge by the Indiana Supreme Court is warranted under the particular circumstances of a case, the Presiding Judge shall certify the case to the Indiana Supreme Court for appointment of a Special Judge.

Adopted October 1, 2006, effective Jan. 1, 2007. Amended effective Jan. 1, 2012; May 1, 2013.

LR84–TR00 Rule 19. CUSTODY AND DISPOSITION OF MODELS AND EXHIBITS

(A) Custody. After being marked for identification, models, diagrams, exhibits and material offered or admitted in evidence shall be placed in the custody of the court reporter unless otherwise directed by the Court.

(B) Removal. All models, diagrams, exhibits or material placed in the custody of the court reporter shall be taken away by the parties offering them in evidence except as otherwise ordered by the Court within sixty (60) days after the case is decided, unless an appeal is taken. In all cases in which an appeal is taken, they shall be taken away within sixty (60) days after the appeal is concluded. At the time of removal, a detailed receipt shall be given to the court reporter and filed in the cause.

(C) Neglect to Remove. If the parties or their attorneys shall neglect to remove models, diagrams, exhibits, or material within thirty (30) days after notice from the court reporter, the items shall be sold by the Sheriff at public or private sale or otherwise disposed of as the Court may direct. If sold, the proceeds, less the expense of the sale, shall be paid into the general fund of the county.

Adopted as Circuit and Superior Court Rule 12. Amended and renumbered as Civil Rule 19, October 1, 2006, effective Jan. 1, 2007; effective Jan. 1, 2012.

LR84–TR00 Rule 20. WITHDRAWAL OF ORIGINAL RECORDS AND PAPERS

(A) No person shall withdraw any original pleading, paper, record, model or exhibit from the custody of the clerk or other officer of the Court having custody thereof except: (1) upon order of a judge of this Court, and (2) upon leaving a proper receipt with the clerk or officer.

(B) No person shall remove any books from the Court or Judge's chamber except upon leaving a proper receipt with a member of the Judge's staff.

Adopted as Circuit and Superior Court Rule 13. Amended and renumbered as Civil Rule 21, October 1, 2006, effective Jan. 1, 2007; effective Jan. 1, 2012.

VIGO COUNTY FAMILY LAW RULES

Adopted October 1, 2006, Effective January 1, 2007

Including Amendments Received Through November 1, 2013

Research Notes

These rules may be searched electronically on Westlaw *in the* IN-RULES *database; updates to these rules may be found on* Westlaw *in* IN-RULESUPDATES. *For search tips and a summary of database content, consult the Westlaw Scope Screens for each database.*

LR84–FL00 Rule 1. DISSOLUTION OF MARRIAGE WITH MINOR CHILDREN

(A) Both parties in any cause of action for Dissolution of Marriage in which there are minor children shall attend a workshop entitled "Children Cope with Divorce". Attendance is mandatory for both parties if there are unemancipated children under eighteen (18) years of age. The four-hour course must be completed prior to the final hearing. The parties are responsible for paying the costs of this program which is forty-five dollars ($45.00) per person, with an allowance for waiver of the fee for indigence.

(B) The parties are to contact the Family Service Association, 619 Cherry Street, Terre Haute, Indiana 47807, telephone (812) 232–4349, to make an appointment to attend the workshop. The petitioner shall contact the Family Service Association within fifteen (15) days of filing the Petition for Dissolution of Marriage, and the respondent shall contact the Family Service Association within fifteen (15) days of receiving notice of this rule.

(C) The Clerk shall provide a copy of this rule to petitioner at the time of filing of a petition for dissolution of marriage.

(D) Failure to complete the workshop may result in a party having to show cause why he or she should not be held in contempt of Court.

(E) The Sheriff of Vigo County shall serve a copy of this rule on the respondent when the petition is served and shall make due return thereon.

Adopted October 1, 2006, effective Jan. 1, 2007. Amended effective Jan. 1, 2012.

84LR–FL00 Rule 2. DISSOLUTION OF MARRIAGE MEDIATION WORKSHOP

(A) If the petitioner and respondent, at the time of the filing of a Dissolution of Marriage action, are proceeding without an attorney to represent them, and they have a child or children as a result of the marriage or their relationship, they shall contact the Dispute Resolution Center for the Wabash Valley, telephone (812) 235–7409, to make an appointment to attend a Mediation Consultation Workshop. The petitioner shall contact the Dispute Resolution Center within seven (7) days of filing the Petition for Dissolution of Marriage, and the respondent shall contact the Dispute Resolution Center within seven (7) days of receiving notice of this rule.

(B) There shall be no charge to the parties for participation in this workshop, the purpose of which is to acquaint the parties with the process of mediation, and to assist them in determining whether mediation could be helpful to them in identifying, addressing and resolving issues in their dissolution of marriage action.

(C) The Clerk shall provide a copy of this rule to petitioner at the time of filing of a petition for dissolution of marriage.

(D) The Sheriff of Vigo County shall serve a copy of this rule on the respondent when the petition is served and shall make due return thereon.

(E) The Dispute Resolution Center shall make due report to the Court in which the Dissolution of Marriage action is pending regarding the parties' attendance and the results of the workshop program.

Adopted October 1, 2006, effective Jan. 1, 2007. Amended effective Jan. 1, 2012.

VIGO COUNTY CRIMINAL RULES

Adopted October 1, 2006, Effective January 1, 2007

Including Amendments Received Through November 1, 2013

Research Notes

These rules may be searched electronically on Westlaw in the IN-RULES database; updates to these rules may be found on Westlaw in IN-RULESUPDATES. For search tips and a summary of database content, consult the Westlaw Scope Screens for each database.

LR84–CR2.1 Rule 1. WITHDRAWAL OF APPEARANCE

(A) Except as otherwise provided in this rule, withdrawal of representation of a defendant in criminal cases may not be granted except upon hearing conducted in open court on record in the presence of the defendant. Withdrawal of appearance will be allowed without compliance with the requirements of this rule if the reason for withdrawal is the inability to locate and communicate with the defendant; in such event, a warrant shall forthwith be issued for the arrest of the defendant.

(B) A hearing in open court will not be required where other counsel has entered an appearance, the substitution of counsel will not cause a delay in the proceedings and the defendant has either consented to or requested the substitution of counsel in writing.

Adopted as Circuit and Superior Court Rule 3. Amended and renumbered as Criminal Rule 1, October 1, 2006, effective Jan. 1, 2007; effective Jan. 1, 2012.

CR2.2 Rule 2. CRIMINAL CASE ASSIGNMENTS

(A) Except as provided in paragraph (F) and (G) below, the following rotation for felony cases, excluding Class D Felonies, is adopted for Superior Court Division 1, Circuit/Superior Court Division 3, Superior Court Division 5, and Superior Court Division 6. All felony cases, excluding Class D Felonies, will be assigned on a rotating basis beginning with Division 1, then 3, then 5, and then 6, and is based upon the time of the occurrence of the offense.

(1) Offenses occurring between 12:01 A.M. of the first day of each month through midnight on the 9th day of each month will be assigned to Superior Court Division 1.

(2) Offenses occurring between 12:01 A.M. of the 10th day of each month through midnight of the 18th day of that month will be assigned to Circuit/Superior Court Division 3.

(3) Offenses occurring between 12:01 A.M. on the 19th day of each month through midnight of the 27th day of that month will be assigned to Superior Court Division 6.

(4) Offenses occurring between 12:01 A.M. of the 28th day of each month through midnight of the last day of that month will be assigned to Superior Court Division 5.

(5) Notwithstanding the above rule, no Superior Court judge shall have more than one capital murder case pending at any one time except where multiple defendants are charged with capital murder arising out of a single episode.

(B) Assignment of Class D Felonies.

(1) Class D Felonies arising out of domestic relations shall be assigned to Superior Court Division 4.

(2) Class D Felonies relating to Operating a Motor Vehicle While Intoxicated shall be assigned to Vigo Superior Court Division 5.

(3) All other Class D Felonies shall be assigned to Vigo Superior Court Division 1, 3 and 6 on a rotating basis, beginning with Division 1, then 3, then 6, and is based upon the time of the occurrence of the offense.

  (a) Offenses occurring from the first day of the month through midnight of the 10th day of the month will be assigned to Superior Court Division 1.

  (b) Offenses occurring from 12:01 A.M. on the 11th day of each month through midnight of the 20th day of each month will be assigned to Superior Court Division 3.

  (c) Offenses occurring from 12:01 A.M. on the 21st day of each month through the end of the month will be assigned to Superior Court Division 6.

(C) All criminal misdemeanor cases shall be assigned as follows:

(1) Offenses for Operating a Vehicle While Intoxicated shall be assigned to Division 5.

(2) All criminal misdemeanors arising out of domestic violence shall be assigned to Division 4.

(3) All other misdemeanor offenses shall be assigned to Division 1, and 6 on a rotating basis.

Offenses occurring between 12:01 A.M. of the first day of each month through midnight of the 15th day of that month will be assigned to Superior Court Division 1. Offenses occurring between 12:01 on the 16th day of each month through the end of the month will be assigned to Superior Court Division 6

(D) In the case of multiple offenses, the date of the earliest offense alleged in the charging document shall assign the rotation date and assignment of the court. If a case involves both felony and misdemeanor charges, the case shall be considered a felony for application of this rule.

(E) A judge of the Circuit or Superior Courts, by appropriate order entered in the record of judgments and orders, may transfer and reassign a case to any other court of record in the county with jurisdiction to hear the charged offense subject to acceptance by the receiving court.

(F) When the State of Indiana dismisses a case and chooses to re-file that case, the case shall be assigned to the court from which the dismissal was taken, except for cases dismissed and transferred to Drug Court.

(G) With the exception of new causes of action covered under (B)(1), (B)(2), and (C) above, when a new cause of action is filed against a Defendant with an existing felony proceeding originally filed under subsection (A) or (B)(3) the new cause of action shall be assigned to the Court where the existing cause of action is pending.

(H) When a new cause of action is filed against a Defendant who is on probation or serving a direct commitment in a Community Corrections program as a result of a case originally filed under (A) or (B)(3) the new cause of action shall be filed in the Court in which the probation or Commitment is being supervised.

(I) Change of Judge.

(1) In the event a change of judge is granted or it becomes necessary to assign another judge in any criminal proceeding in Superior Court Division 1, the case shall be reassigned first to Superior Court Division 3, then to Superior Court Division 5, then to Superior Court Division 6; if the receiving judge cannot accept jurisdiction the case shall be reassigned to the alternative court in the order indicated. If the judges of Superior Court Division 3, Superior Court Division 5, or Superior Court Division 6 cannot accept jurisdiction, the case will be reassigned to Superior Court Division 4.

(2) In the event a change of judge is granted or it becomes necessary to assign another judge in any criminal proceeding in Superior Court Division 3, the case shall be reassigned first to Superior Court Division 5, then to Superior Court Division 6 then to Superior Court Division 1; if the receiving judge cannot accept jurisdiction the case shall be reassigned to the alternative court in the order indicated. If the judges of Superior Court Division 1, Superior Court Division 5, or Superior Court Divi-

sion 6 cannot accept jurisdiction, the case will be reassigned to Superior Court Division 4.

(3) In the event a change of judge is granted or it becomes necessary to assign another judge in any criminal proceeding in Superior Court Division 4, the case shall be reassigned first to the judge of Superior Court Division 5. If the judge of Superior Court Division 5 cannot accept jurisdiction, the case will be reassigned first to Superior Court Division 6, then to Superior Court Division 1, then to Superior Court Division 3; if the receiving judge cannot accept jurisdiction the case shall be reassigned to the alternative court in the order indicated.

(4) In the event a change of judge is granted or it becomes necessary to assign another judge in any misdemeanor criminal proceeding in Superior Court Division 5, the case shall be reassigned first to the judge in Superior Court Division 4. In the event a change of judge is granted or it becomes necessary to assign another judge in any felony criminal proceeding in Superior Court Division 5, the case shall be reassigned first to Superior Court Division 6, then to Superior Court Division 1, then to Superior Court Division 3; if the receiving judge cannot accept jurisdiction the case shall be reassigned to the alternative court in the order indicated. If the judges of Superior Court Division 1, Superior Court Division 3, or Superior Court Division 6 cannot accept jurisdiction, the case will be reassigned to Superior Court Division 4.

(5) In the event a change of judge is granted or it becomes necessary to assign another judge in any criminal proceeding in Superior Court Division 6, the case shall be reassigned to Superior Court Division 1, then to Superior Court Division 3, then to Superior Court Division 5; if the receiving judge cannot accept jurisdiction the case shall be reassigned to the alternative court in the order indicated. If the judges of Superior Court Division 1, Superior Court Division 3, or Superior Court Division 5 cannot accept jurisdiction, the case will be reassigned to Superior Court Division 4.

(J) In the event no judge is available for assignment or reassignment of a felony or misdemeanor case, such case shall be certified to the Indiana Supreme Court for appointment of a Special Judge. In the event the judge presiding in a felony or misdemeanor case concludes that special circumstances presented in such proceeding require appointment by the Indiana Supreme Court of a Special Judge, the presiding judge may request the Indiana Supreme Court make such appointment.

(K) This rule does not prohibit the filing of appropriate criminal offenses in the Terre Haute City Court to the extent of its jurisdiction.

Adopted as Circuit and Superior Court Rule 17. Amended Feb. 6, 2006, effective April 23, 2006; amended and renumbered as Criminal Rule 2, Oct. 1, 2006, effective Jan. 1, 2007; amended Aug. 1, 2009, effective Jan. 1, 2010; Sept. 8, 2010, effective Jan. 1, 2011; Aug. 17, 2011, effective Jan. 1, 2012; Sept. 9, 2012, effective Sept. 1, 2012; June 12, 2013, effective May 1, 2013.

LR84–CR00 Rule 3.   BAIL

(A) Persons arrested for a non-violent misdemeanor shall be released on their own recognizance unless they do not reside in the State of Indiana. Except in the case of judicial order otherwise, the Sheriff shall have the authority and discretion to detain a person under the influence of intoxicating beverages or drugs until such time as that person may be safely released.

(B) At the time each person is released on his own recognizance, he will be required to furnish data concerning his address, phone number, social security number, driver's license, employer's name and address, and, if under twenty-one (21) years of age, his parents: name, address and phone number.

(C) A person charged with a criminal offense (felony or misdemeanor) may post bond in the amount shown in the bail bond schedule, which schedule shall be posted in the jail and in the clerk's office, in one (1) of four (4) ways:

(1) Surety bond

(2) Real property bond

(3) Full cash bond, or

(4) By depositing with the Clerk of the Court, cash in the amount of ten percent (10%) of the bond set by the Court (unless the Court, in its discretion, prohibits such procedures).

(D) Except as provided in Paragraph (A), no bond may be posted without approval of a Judge of the Superior Court. If the defendant posts bail by depositing the full cash amount, the defendant and each person who makes the deposit on behalf of the defendant shall execute an agreement that allows the Court to retain all or a part of the cash to pay publicly paid costs of representation and fines, costs, fees, and restitution that the Court may order the defendant to pay if convicted.

(E) When the conditions of the bond, as provided in Paragraph (C), have been performed and an order is entered discharging the bond, if the bond has been posted under (C)(4), the Clerk shall retain ten percent (10%) of the amount deposited or fifty dollars ($50), whichever is the lesser amount, as an administrative fee, which money shall be paid into the General Fund of the County. The amount retained by the Clerk as bond costs shall be not less than Ten Dollars ($10.00). The Clerk shall also retain from the deposit such fines, costs, fees, and restitution as ordered by the court, publicly paid costs of representation as ordered by the court, and the five dollar ($5) fee required by IC.35–33–8–3.2(d). The balance of the amount of the deposit shall be remitted to the person making the deposit.

Adopted as Circuit and Superior Court Rule 8. Amended and renumbered as Criminal Rule 3, October 1, 2006, effective Jan. 1, 2007; effective Jan. 1, 2012.

LR84–CR00 Rule 4.   PUBLIC DEFENDER FEE

(A) If the Court finds that the public defender client is able to pay part of the cost of representation by the assigned counsel, the court shall order the person to pay the following:

(1) For a felony action, a fee of one hundred dollars ($100.00).

(2) For a misdemeanor action, a fee of fifty dollars ($50.00).

(B) If at any stage of prosecution for a felony or misdemeanor the court makes a finding of ability to pay the costs of reasonable representation the court shall require payment by the person or person's parent if delinquent, of the following attorney fees in addition to other costs assessed against the person:

(1) For an A felony action, a fee not to exceed one thousand dollars ($1,000.00).

(2) For a B felony action, a fee not to exceed eight hundred dollars ($800.00).

(3) For a C felony action, a fee not to exceed six hundred dollars ($600.00).

(4) For a D felony action, a fee not to exceed four hundred dollars ($400.00).

(5) For all misdemeanor actions, a fee not to exceed two hundred dollars ($200.00).

The Court will order the clerk's office to withhold the reasonable attorney fee assessed by the court from the public defender client's remaining bond deposit.

Adopted October 1, 2006, effective Jan. 1, 2007. Amended effective Jan. 1, 2012.

LR84–CR00 Rule 5.   DISCOVERY—CRIMINAL CASES

In all criminal cases, discovery shall be governed by this rule. The Court will not rule on any motion for discovery if the subject matter of the motion is covered by this rule; the Court will, however, rule on motions for discovery of specific items of evidence that are not addressed by this rule.

(A) The State shall disclose to the Defendant the following material information within its possession or control on or before thirty (30) days following the Initial Hearing:

(1) The names, last known addresses and telephone numbers of persons whom the State may call as witnesses together with

(a) their relevant written or recorded statements.

(b) memoranda containing substantially verbatim reports of their oral statements (if any memoranda exists)

(c) memoranda reporting or summarizing oral statements (if such memoranda exists),

(d) a brief statement, normally not to exceed ten words, indicating the nature of each witness' involvement in the case; such statements may be no more than a reference to statements described in paragraphs (A) (1), (a), (b), or (c) above.

(2) Any written or recorded statements and the substance of any oral statements made by the accused or by a co-defendant, and a list of witnesses to the making and acknowledgment of such statements.

(3) A transcript of the recorded grand jury testimony of persons whom the prosecuting attorney may call as witnesses at a hearing or trial. A typed transcript of said testimony shall be provided if it is available.

(4) Any reports or statements of experts, made in connection with the particular case, including results of physical or mental examinations and of scientific tests, experiments or comparisons.

(5) Any books, papers, documents, photographs, or tangible objects which the prosecuting attorney intends to use in the hearing or trial or which were obtained from or belong to the accused, together with the location of such items and an indication of appropriate means for defense counsel's examination of same. Under circumstances where chain of custody issues are readily apparent, such as drug cases, such chain shall be provided to the extent available on the disclosure date provided above and shall be supplemented:

(a) upon Defendant's written request,

(b) by pre-trial conference, and

(c) thereafter as ordered to complete such chain.

(6) Any arrest record or prior criminal convictions which may be used for impeachment of the persons whom the State intends to call as witnesses at the hearing or trial.

(7) A copy of any written agreement and the complete substance of any oral agreement made by the State with (a) any witnesses to secure their testimony or (b) any co-defendant or other person charged arising out of same incident.

(8) Any evidence which tends to negate the guilt of the accused as to the crime charged or tends to reduce the class of the act alleged or which would tend to mitigate his punishment.

(9) Evidence of other crimes which the State intends to use at trial, pursuant to Rule 404, Indiana Rules of Evidence.

(B)(1) The State shall perform these obligations in any manner mutually agreeable to the Prosecutor's Office and to defense counsel. The State shall provide legible copies of existing written statements described in paragraphs (A)(1), (2), (3), and (7). Other items shall be provided for examination, testing, copying, photographing, or other proper use either by agreement or at specified reasonable times and places. Defense counsel shall provide reasonable notice of

such examination and shall schedule these examinations in cooperation with the State. An application to the Court shall be made to obtain copies of audio or video tape. Said application shall state in specific terms the necessity for such copies.

(2) The State shall make a record of compliance with this order not more than five (5) days after the date set out in paragraph (A) above.

(C) Subject to Constitutional limitations, the defense shall disclose to the State the following material and information within its possession or control on or before thirty (30) days following the date that the State has provided to the defense the information required under this rule:

(1) The names, addresses and telephone numbers of persons whom the defendant may call as witnesses along with (a) a summary of their testimony similar to that described in (A)(1)(d), (b) record of prior criminal convictions, and (c) the relationship, if any, of the witness to the defendant or any co-defendant.

(2) Any books, papers, documents, photographs, or tangible objects which are intended to be used at a hearing or trial.

(3) Any reports or statements of experts, made in connection with the particular case, including results of physical or mental examinations and of scientific tests, experiments or comparisons insofar as permitted by law.

(4) A statement of defenses, procedural or substantive, the defendant intends to make at a hearing or trial. Such a statement shall not limit defendant's right to file any defense defined by statute, such as alibi, insanity, etc., where a specific timetable for notice to the State is statutorily described.

(D)(1) The defense shall perform these obligations in any manner mutually agreeable to the Prosecutor's Office and to defense counsel. Defense shall provide the same documents in a fashion similar to the State's obligations described in (B)(1).

(2) The defense shall make a record of compliance with this order not more than five (5) days after the date set out in paragraph (C) above.

(E) The Court anticipates that compliance will be deemed satisfactory unless failure to comply is brought to the Court's attention by Motion to Compel. Sanctions for failure of compliance or violations of orders on Motion to Compel shall be pursuant to Trial Rule 37.

(F) Nothing herein shall limit any party's right to seek protective orders to avoid destruction or other loss of evidence, or to seek deposition at such times as they may desire.

(G)(1) The Court may deny disclosure upon showing that:

(a) A substantial risk to any person of physical harm, intimidation, bribery, economic reprisals, or unnecessary annoyance or embarrassment resulting from such disclosure which outweighs any usefulness of the disclosure to counsel.

(b) There is a paramount interest in non-disclosure of an informant's identity and a failure to disclose will not infringe the Constitutional rights of the accused. Disclosure of the identity of witnesses to be produced at a hearing or trial will be required.

(2) Such determination of non-disclosure shall be by the Court and shall not be within the discretion of the State or defense. Such non-disclosure shall be sought by motion for protective order.

(H) Disclosure shall not be required of:

(1) Any matter otherwise protected by law (however disclosing the identity of juvenile co-defendants or witnesses shall not be barred because of delinquency non-disclosure statutes).

(2) Work product of counsel including memoranda of opinions, theories, or research for themselves or from their legal or in-house investigative staff.

(I) This discovery order is a continuing order through the trial of this cause and no written motion shall normally be required except to compel discovery for a protective order, or an extension of time.

(J) Failure of either party to engage in and comply with discovery shall not be excused by the parties unsuccessful or incomplete efforts to enter into a plea agreement or other resolution of the case unless both parties waive in writing (1) compliance with this order for a specified period of time and (2) any speedy trial requirements.

(K) Any cost for reproduction or transcripts under this order shall be borne by the party to whom the information is provided except that as to pauper counsel defendants the costs shall be borne by the State or County.

(L) Depositions:

(1) Unless good cause is shown, depositions of lay witnesses shall be completed not later than two (2) weeks prior to the trial date.

(2) Depositions of expert witnesses may be taken at any time.

Adopted as Circuit and Superior Court Rule 15. Amended and renumbered as Criminal Rule 5, October 1, 2006, effective Jan. 1, 2007; effective Jan. 1, 2012.

VIGO COUNTY PROBATE RULES

Adopted October 1, 2006, Effective January 1, 2007

Including Amendments Received Through November 1, 2013

Research Notes

These rules may be searched electronically on Westlaw *in the* IN-RULES *database; updates to these rules may be found on Westlaw in IN-RULESUPDATES. For search tips and a summary of database content, consult the Westlaw Scope Screens for each database.*

LR84–PR00 Rule 1. PLEADINGS AND PREPARED ORDERS

(A) Unless directed otherwise by the Court, counsel shall prepare all proposed Orders and provide sufficient copies to the Clerk.

(B) All pleadings shall be signed by the fiduciary and counsel.

Adopted October 1, 2006, effective Jan. 1, 2007. Amended effective Jan. 1, 2012.

LR84–PR00 Rule 2. CONVERSION OF UNSUPERVISED ESTATES TO SUPERVISED ESTATES

The Court shall have no involvement, other than for opening, closing, determining Indiana Inheritance Tax due and hearing Petitions regarding fees (if sought) in an Unsupervised Administration of a Decedent's Estate. If the jurisdiction of the Court is invoked for any other matter, the Administration may become a Supervised Administration from there on for all remaining matters.

Adopted October 1, 2006, effective Jan. 1, 2007. Amended effective Jan. 1, 2012.

LR84–PR00 Rule 3. INVENTORY IN ESTATES

(A) In all supervised estates, the personal representative shall file an inventory conforming with the requirements of I.C. 29–1–12–1 within two (2) months of appointment.

(B) In all unsupervised estates, the Personal Representative shall, within two (2) months of appointment, either: (1) file an inventory conforming with the requirements of I.C. 29–1–7.5–3.2(b), or (2) file a verified certification that an inventory conforming with the requirements of I.C. 29–1–7.5–3.2 has been prepared and is available to be furnished to distributees on request.

Adopted October 1, 2006, effective Jan. 1, 2007. Amended effective Jan. 1, 2012.

LR84–PR00 Rule 4. MAXIMUM FEE GUIDELINES FOR ATTORNEY AND PERSONAL REPRESENTATIVE

Attorney and personal representative fees in supervised estates shall not exceed the amounts calculated pursuant to Sections I through IV of this rule.

I. Attorney Fees for Supervised Estate Administration:

Gross estate services are considered to normally include: probating the Will, opening the estate, qualifying the personal representative, preparing and filing the Inventory, paying claims, collecting assets, preparing and filing petitions, obtaining Court Orders thereon, sale of personal property, sale of real property, partial distribution, heirship determination, preparing and filing of Fiduciary Income Tax Return, preparing and filing all tax returns and schedules including those for Indiana Inheritance Tax and Federal Estate Tax and paying the taxes, preparing and filing the Final Report, obtaining Order approving same, distributing assets, obtaining discharge of the personal representative, and preparing and serving all notices on interested parties throughout the proceedings. The list shall not be considered to be exclusive.

A. *Gross Probate Estate*—Minimum Fee of $2,000.00

First $100,000.00, not to exceed 6%

Next $100,000.00, not to exceed 5%

Next $100,000.00, not to exceed 4%

Next $700,000.00, not to exceed 3%

Excess of $1,000,000.00, not to exceed...1%

B. *Non–Probate Assets*—For handling matters concerning non-probate assets during the administration, the attorney representing the supervised estate may charge an additional fee as follows:

First $100,000.00 of such assets, not to exceed...3%

Next $100,000.00, not to exceed 2%

Excess of $200,000.00 not to exceed......1%

C. *Extraordinary Fee Requests*—Extraordinary services may include Will contest actions, contesting claims, other contested hearings, involved heirship determinations, and dealing with unusual and complex matters. The attorney must petition the Court for allowance of fees for such extraordinary services. All such petitions will be set for hearing, with notice to all interested parties. If all interested parties sign a waiver and consent stating they have been advised the additional fee request exceeds the Court's guidelines and that the services as detailed are extraordinary, the Court may, in its discretion, determine if a hearing is required.

Extraordinary fees shall be considered based on an hourly rate taking into consideration the complexity of the matter and the attorney's probate expertise.

II. Petition or Request for Attorney Fees Required in Supervised Estates.

A. No fees may be paid without first submitting a Petition or Request for fees which shall include therein a work sheet or other calculation supporting the fees requested as being in accordance with this guideline

B. No attorney fees shall be approved until and unless an Indiana Inheritance Tax Return has been filed, if such is required by law, and then no more than fifty percent (50%) of the total anticipated fee can be requested.

III. Attorney Fees in Miscellaneous Matters:

A. *Death Tax Matters Only*—When no estate administration is required, the preparation and filing of the Indiana Inheritance Tax Return and Federal Estate Tax Return, if applicable, and securing the respective clearances thereon shall entitle the attorney to a minimum fee of $500.00 and a maximum fee as follows:

First $500,000.00 of includable assets, not to exceed 2%
Excess of $500,000.00 of includable assets, not to exceed 1%
B. Other Miscellaneous matters such as spreading a will of record, petitioning for lock box opening to conduct a will search, etc. .... Hourly rate
   (Attorney's expertise and the complexity of the matter should be considered in determining the applicable hourly rate.)

IV. Personal Representative Fees.

A. *Professional*—Their applicable reasonable rate shall be reviewed in light of all prevailing circumstances.

B. *Non–Professional*—An amount not in excess of one-half (1/2) of the attorney's fees.

C. *Attorney as Personal Representative*—When the attorney also serves as the personal representative, an additional amount not in excess of one-half of the attorney fee may be allowed.

Adopted October 1, 2006, effective Jan. 1, 2007. Amended effective Jan. 1, 2012.

LR84–PR00 Rule 5. FEES IN UNSUPERVISED ESTATES

No Attorney or Personal Representative fees will be determined and authorized for payment by the Court in any Unsupervised Administration of a Decedent's Estate, unless a Petition for Fees or objection to fees is filed with the Court. If such Petition or objection is not filed, the Court will not become involved in the determination of fees in an Unsupervised Administration of a Decedent's Estate. However, the Court expects compliance with these guidelines in general.

Adopted October 1, 2006, effective Jan. 1, 2007. Amended effective Jan. 1, 2012.

LR84–PR00 Rule 6. WRONGFUL DEATH ADMINISTRATION

The Court recognizes that in most instances a retainer or contingent fee agreement is an appropriate method by which legal services can be provided in wrongful death claims. Accordingly, fees shall be allowed under such agreements if, at the time of settlement of the claim, it is shown to the Court's satisfaction:

A. That the Personal Representative was, prior to entering into such agreement, fully informed as to all aspects of the arrangement.

B. That the agreement is fair and reasonable.

C. That the fee sought is fair and reasonable.

Adopted October 1, 2006, effective Jan. 1, 2007. Amended effective Jan. 1, 2012.

LR84–PR00 Rule 7. GUARDIANSHIP ADMINISTRATION

Fees for the administration of guardianships shall be based on an hourly rate to be approved by the Court for both the attorney and the guardian. The Court will consider the attorney's and guardian's expertise in approving the hourly rate.

Adopted October 1, 2006, effective Jan. 1, 2007. Amended effective Jan. 1, 2012.

VIGO COUNTY SMALL CLAIMS RULES

Adopted June 2, 2008, Effective January 1, 2009

Including Amendments Received Through November 1, 2013

Research Notes

These rules may be searched electronically on Westlaw *in the* IN-RULES *database; updates to these rules may be found on Westlaw in IN-RULESUPDATES. For search tips and a summary of database content, consult the Westlaw Scope Screens for each database.*

LR84–SC00 Rule 1. SCOPE

A. Scope. Theses[1] rule shall govern the procedure and practice of the Small Claims Divisions of the Vigo Superior Courts.

B. Citation. These rules may be cited as L.R.S.C. ___. The small claims rules promulgated by the Indiana Supreme Court are hereinafter referred to as S.C. ___; and the Indiana Rules of Trial Procedure are hereinafter referred to as T.R. ___.

Adopted June 2, 2008, effective Jan. 1, 2009. Amended effective Jan. 1, 2012.

[1] So in original.

LR84–SC00 Rule 2. GENERAL PROCEDURES

A. Conflict of Rules. All proceedings in the Vigo Superior Courts, Small Claims Divisions, shall be governed by the Small Claims Rules promulgated by the Indiana Supreme Court and the local rules set forth herein. In instances where these local rules conflict with the rules promulgated by the Indiana Supreme Court, the latter shall control.

B. Tender of Completed Documentation and Proper Costs. Parties or their attorneys are solely responsible to tender to the Court in complete and correct form any documents desired to be filed, together with proper costs, as determined by the Clerk. Neither the Court nor the Clerk will be responsible for delays or deadlines missed due to the tender of incomplete or incorrect documents or improper costs.

C. Copies of Motions and Orders. The original and one copy of any motion and the original and three copies of the order (or sufficient copies to serve all parties) shall be filed. Excess copies of motions will not be returned to the filing party. See Rule 12–F for proceeding supplemental filing requirements.

D. Judgment Orders. All judgment orders shall include an itemization of the amounts claimed (e.g., principal, interest, attorney fees, collection agency fees) as well as the total judgment not including court costs. Court costs shall be listed separately.

E. Multiple Claims With Same Defendant. A Plaintiff shall not be allowed to file multiple cases naming the same defendant based on the same or similar transactions in order to circumvent the monetary jurisdictional limits of small claims court.

F. Appearance by Husband or Wife. In cases where husband and wife are parties, except for hearings on proceeding supplemental involving garnishment or by contrary order of the Court, appearance by a party's spouse shall be considered the appearance of the party upon the spouse's representation on the record that the party and the appearing spouse are currently married and living together.

G. Parties' Current Address. Notice from the Court will be sent to the parties at the most recent address contained in the Court's file. The parties are solely responsible to maintain their current address in all files concerning them.

Adopted June 2, 2008, effective Jan. 1, 2009. Amended effective Jan. 1, 2012.

LR84–SC00 Rule 3. FORMS

A. Court Forms. The court shall from time to time draft forms for use of the parties in small claims actions.

B. No Other Forms. Originals or photocopies of the forms described in S.C.L.R. 3A shall be acceptable for filing. Any other form or photocopy thereof presented to the Clerk shall be accepted for filing only if such form receives prior approval from the judge. In such instance, blank forms identical to that submitted and approved shall be immediately provided to the Clerk for future reference and comparison.

Adopted June 2, 2008, effective Jan. 1, 2009. Amended effective Jan. 1, 2012.

LR84–SC00 Rule 4. CHANGE OF JUDGE

A change of judge shall be granted as provided by statute and by T.R. 76 and 78.

Adopted June 2, 2008, effective Jan. 1, 2009. Amended effective Jan. 1, 2012.

LR84–SC00 Rule 5. COUNTERCLAIMS OUTSIDE SMALL CLAIMS JURISDICTION

A. Monetary Limit. A defendant who has a counterclaim in excess of the monetary jurisdiction of the Small Claims Division who does not wish to waive the excess of the claim must file a motion to move the case to the plenary docket and pay the required fee.

B. Subject Matter Jurisdiction. A defendant who has a counterclaim outside the subject matter jurisdiction of the Small Claims Division must file a motion to move the case to the plenary docket and pay the required fee.

Adopted June 2, 2008, effective Jan. 1, 2009. Amended effective Jan. 1, 2012.

LR84–SC00 Rule 6. CONTINUANCES

A. General Rule. Either party may be granted a continuance for good cause shown. Except in unusual circumstances no party shall be allowed more than (1) continuance in any case, and all continuances must have the specific approval of the court. Continuances shall be for as short period as possible, and where feasible the party not requesting the continuance shall be considered in scheduling a new hearing date. The court shall give notice of the continuance and the new date and time of trial to all parties.

B. Possession of Real Estate or Personal Property. No continuances will be granted to a defendant where the action involves the issue of possession of real estate or personal property, except for good cause approved by a judge.

C. Proceedings Supplemental. No motion for continuance of a proceedings supplemental hearing will be granted, except by agreement of the parties, or for good cause approved by the judge.

Adopted June 2, 2008, effective Jan. 1, 2009. Amended effective Jan. 1, 2012.

LR84–SC00 Rule 7. DISMISSAL OF ACTIONS

A. Dismissal by Plaintiff. Any claim may be dismissed by the plaintiff at any time before judgment has been entered unless a counterclaim has been filed by a defendant.

B. Dismissal by Stipulation. Any claim may be dismissed by filing a stipulation of dismissal signed by all parties to the claim.

C. Dismissal by the Court. The cause or any pending pleading in the cause may be dismissed with or without prejudice upon order of the Court, including by way of illustration and not limitation, as follows:

(1) the cause had not been reduced to judgment and there has been no action on the case for a period of sixty (60) days; provided however, that no such cause shall be dismissed without notice and hearing; or

(2) a proceedings supplemental pleading had been filed and there is no action on the day on which the proceedings supplemental is set for hearing, or for sixty (60) days thereafter. (Note: no 41E hearing required)

Motions to reinstate a case dismissed pursuant to this section shall be granted if filed within six months of the dismissal. Motions filed after six months shall be denied, and a new case may be filed.

Adopted June 2, 2008, effective Jan. 1, 2009. Amended effective Jan. 1, 2012.

LR84–SC00 Rule 8. DEFAULT

A. Default of Defendant and Default Affidavit. Upon the failure of a defendant to appear at the initial court trial setting or at a trial on the merits, the plaintiff shall be entitled to judgment on the merits against the defendant.

B. Default of Plaintiff. Upon the failure of a plaintiff to appear at the initial court trial setting or at a trial on the merits, the cause shall be dismissed without prejudice, and default judgment shall be entered for the defendant against the plaintiff on any timely-filed counterclaim. Upon plaintiff's failure to appear at the initial court trial setting or at a trial on the merits in the subsequence[1] cause based on the same facts as the cause earlier dismissed without prejudice, the subsequent cause shall be dismissed with prejudice and default judgment shall be entered for the defendant against the plaintiff on any timely-filed counterclaim.

C. Setting Aside Default Judgment. A default judgment may be set aside according to the procedures set for in S.C. 10(c).

Adopted June 2, 2008, effective Jan. 1, 2009. Amended effective Jan. 1, 2012.

[1] So in original.

LR84–SC00 Rule 9. ATTORNEY FEES

A request for attorney fees up to $300.00 will be deemed reasonable regardless of the amount of the judgment. Any request for attorney fees over that amount must be supported by an affidavit setting forth the number of hours spent on the case and the hourly charge. The amount of attorney fees awarded shall be within the sound discretion of the Court.

No attorney fees shall be awarded unless provided for by written agreement between the parties or according to applicable statute(s).

The Court retains the discretion to adjust attorney fees even when the defendant signs an agreed judgment.

Adopted June 2, 2008, effective Jan. 1, 2009. Amended effective Jan. 1, 2012.

LR84–SC00 Rule 10. JUDGMENT FOR POSSESSION OF REAL ESTATE OR PERSONAL PROPERTY

A. Bifurcated Judgment and Expedited Hearing on Possession. Judgment in actions involving the issue of possession of real estate or personal property shall be bifurcated. The initial hearing shall be on the possession issue. A final judgment for possession of the real estate or personal property shall be entered at the initial hearing and a judgment for back rent and/or other damages, if any, shall be entered at a subsequent hearing.

B. Disposition of Tenant's Remaining Personal Property. If a tenant leaves personal property of value in or about the premises under circumstances, which reasonably show abandonment of the personal property, the landlord may:

(1) remove the property from the premises using reasonable care and storing it in a location reasonably secure from damage of any kind; and

(2) immediately notify the tenant by first class mail to tenant's last known address, with a copy retained by the landlord, that the property is stored, that the storage charges (if any, but not to exceed $3.00 per day) are accruing, and that the property is available to tenant upon reasonable notice to landlord at a reasonable time until the date of the hearing on damages. The notice shall also contain landlord's telephone number, and an address at which and reasonable time during which the landlord can be contacted.

(3) If the tenant has not contacted landlord to arrange an imminent and mutually convenient date and time for retrieval of tenant's personal property by the date of the damage hearing, a landlord may dispose of the property in a reasonable manner, including the destruction of apparently valueless property and the private sale or donation of property of value. Proceeds from any sale and credit for any donation shall first be applied to reduce any accrued storage charges and then to reduce any alleged back rent or damages beyond normal wear and tear established by the Court.

Adopted June 2, 2008, effective Jan. 1, 2009. Amended effective Jan. 1, 2012.

LR84–SC00 Rule 11. RELEASE OF JUDGMENT

(A) Release of Judgment. Upon payment in full, including accrued interest, the clerk shall notify the judgment creditor and shall require him or her to file a release of judgment. If the judgment creditor fails to file a release within thirty (30) days of the issuance of the notice, the clerk shall enter on the Chronological Case Summary that the judgment has been satisfied, the plaintiff has failed to release judgment pursuant to court directive, and the clerk shall enter a release of judgment in the judgment docket.

(B) Failure to Release Judgment. Upon a judgment creditor's failure to release a judgment allegedly fully paid and satisfied, the affected debtor may file a motion with the Court to have the judgment deemed satisfied pursuant to T.R. 13(M).

Adopted June 2, 2008, effective Jan. 1, 2009. Amended effective Jan. 1, 2012.

LR84–SC00 Rule 12. PROCEEDING SUPPLEMENTAL

A. General Procedure. Proceedings supplemental to execution shall be governed by T.R. 69(E) of the Indiana Rules of Trial Procedure and applicable statute.

B. Thirty Day Rule. A motion for proceedings supplemental may not be filed until thirty (30) calendar days have elapsed since the date of judgment except by order of the Court for good cause shown.

C. One Year Rule. Except by order of the Court for good cause shown, no proceedings supplemental may pend for more than six (6) months from the date of its filing and no judgment creditor may file more than four (4) proceedings supplemental per year against any individual judgment debtor in a given cause. At the end of the six (6) month period, any pending proceedings supplemental shall be dismissed without prejudice.

D. Bank Interrogatories. Except by order of the Court for good cause shown, judgment creditors may not submit garnishment interrogatories to more than two (2) banking institution for each hearing on proceeding supplemental.

E. Proceedings Supplemental During Pendency of Garnishment Order. If a garnishment order has been issued, additional proceedings supplemental directed to the judgment debtor may be filed only by order of the Court for good cause shown.

F. Copies of Motion and Order. Three copies of motions for proceeding supplemental, orders and subpoenas shall be filed. If a garnishee defendant is named, then four copies of each document shall be filed. Please call the civil court reporter for the hearing date prior to filing.

Adopted June 2, 2008, effective Jan. 1, 2009. Amended effective Jan. 1, 2012.

LR84–SC00 Rule 13. BENCH WARRANTS

A. Motion for Bench Warrant. A Plaintiff may request a bench warrant if:

(1) the judgment debtor or garnishee defendant previously ordered to appear for a scheduled hearing was served with an order to appear and failed to appear for the hearing.

(2) The party requesting the warrant can provide the judgment debtor's Social Security number and/or date of birth.

B. Procedure. The Court will send a notice to the defendant that the defendant must contact the court within ten days or the warrant will be issued.

No ten-day notice will be issued if the defendant fails to appear for the rescheduled hearing.

Adopted June 2, 2008, effective Jan. 1, 2009. Amended effective Jan. 1, 2012.

LR84–SC00 Rule 14. GARNISHMENT

A. General Procedure. All garnishment proceedings shall comply with T.R. 69(e) and applicable statutes.

B. Requirements of Garnishment Order to Issue. A garnishment order shall not issue with respect to a judgment debtor's wage or other property without:

(1) an active proceedings supplemental as to the judgment debtor or waiver of notice by the judgment debtor and

(2) service on the garnishee-defendant by:

    a. certified mail, or refusal thereof, or

    b. Sheriff's service, or

    c. private process service; and

    d. return of answered interrogatories, other verification of employment by garnishee-defendant, or failure to answer interrogatories after notice.

C. Stay of Garnishment. In instances where a judgment debtor has entered a voluntary agreement for periodic payment to satisfy the judgment and has further consented to garnishment upon default of the terms of the agreement, a garnishment order will be entered but stayed pending compliance with the payment agreement. Upon notice by the judgment creditor that the judgment debtor is not in compliance, the order of garnishment will be issued.

D. Release. Upon receipt by the judgment creditor or by the Clerk on the judgment creditor's behalf of monies sufficient to fully satisfy the judgment, any accrued interest and costs, the judgment creditor shall immediately obtain a court order releasing the applicable garnishment order and shall forward a copy to garnishee-defendant(s).

Adopted June 2, 2008, effective Jan. 1, 2009. Amended effective Jan. 1, 2012.

LR84–SC00 Rule 15. BANKRUPTCY

Whenever any party receives an order from a Bankruptcy Court staying proceedings, that party shall file a notice of such order with the Court. Such notice shall contain the name of the party, the cause number in bankruptcy and the date of the issuance of the stay.

Adopted June 2, 2008, effective Jan. 1, 2009. Amended effective Jan. 1, 2012.

LR84–SC8 Rule 16. REPRESENTATION AT TRIAL–ATTORNEYS

A. Small Claims Rule 8(C) allows a person to appear at trial and, if he or she chooses, represent himself or herself and avoid the cost of hiring an attorney. However, a person is allowed to hire an attorney and have the attorney appear with him or her at trial. A person who holds a power of attorney for another person may not represent that person in court.

B. Corporations–Representation in Small Claims Court. As a general rule, a corporation must appear by counsel. S.C. Rule 8(C) provides a limited exception for certain claims. A corporation, whether as a Plaintiff of [1] a Defendant, may be represented by an employee who is not an attorney if the following conditions exist:

1. The claim (for or against the corporation) is not more than the prescribed limit set by S.C. Rule 8(C) (currently $1,500.00); and

2. The claim is not an assignment (such as a claim that has been assigned to a collection agency); and

3. There is a corporate resolution and employee affidavit on file with the clerk authorizing a full-time employee to represent the corporation. The clerk will provide the affidavit form.

C. Sole Proprietors and Partnerships (Unincorporated Businesses). As a general rule, an unincorporated business must be represented by the owner of the business or an attorney. S.C. Rule 8(C) provides a limited exception for certain claims. A business, operated as a sole proprietor or partnership, may (whether as a Plaintiff or Defendant) be represented by an employee who is not an attorney if the following conditions exist:

1. The claim (for or against the business) is not more than the prescribed limit set by S.C. Rule 8(C) (currently $1,500.00); and

2. The claim is not an assignment (such as a claim that has been assigned to a collection agency); and

3. The business has on file with the clerk an employee affidavit and certificate of compliance designating a full-time employee to represent the business. The clerk will provide the affidavit form.

The person who is named in an affidavit and files the claim must be the individual who appears in court. If circumstances dictate that another em-

ployee must make the court appearance, a resolution and .affidavit must be filed with the Clerk
before the court date and a copy made available to
the Court.

*Adopted June 2, 2008, effective Jan. 1, 2009. Amended
effective Jan. 1, 2012.*

1 So in original.

LR84–SC00 Rule 17.   PRIVATE PROCESS SERV-
ING FEES

Costs for private process servers that may be assessed against a judgment debtor are limited to the
fee approved for service by sheriff.

*Adopted June 2, 2008, effective Jan. 1, 2009. Amended
effective Jan. 1, 2012.*

VIGO COUNTY ADMINISTRATIVE RULES

Adopted October 1, 2006, Effective January 1, 2007

Including Amendments Received Through November 1, 2013

Research Notes

These rules may be searched electronically on Westlaw *in the* IN-RULES *database; updates to these rules may be found on* Westlaw *in* IN-RULESUPDATES. *For search tips and a summary of database content, consult the Westlaw Scope Screens for each database.*

LR84–AR00 Rule 1.   COURT HOURS

Each Court shall be open to the public daily during regular business days, Monday through Friday. The Presiding Judge of each respective Division shall designate a schedule of business hours for said respective Divisions as the respective Court's Docket allows and is in the best interests of the public and Court. Except when otherwise designated, the Courts shall be open until 4:00 p.m. on each business day. If any Division of the Court finds it necessary to remain in session until after 4:00 p.m., no member of the staff of that Division shall leave for the day except upon permission of the presiding Judge.

Adopted as Circuit and Superior Court Rule 2. Amended and renumbered as Administrative Rule 1, October 1, 2006, effective Jan. 1, 2007. Amended effective Jan. 1, 2009; effective Jan. 1, 2012.

LR84–AR01 Rule 2.   CASE ASSIGNMENTS

(A) Criminal Cases shall be filed pursuant to LR84–CR2.2–2.

(B) Civil Cases.

(1) *Dissolution Actions (DR).* The filing of dissolution actions shall be filed in the following proportionate rotation:

Vigo Superior Court Division Two	60%
Vigo Superior Court Division One	13.33%
Vigo Superior Court Division Three	13.33%
Vigo Superior Court Division Six	13.33%

(2) *Probate.* The filing of probate matters shall be filed in the following proportionate rotation:

Vigo Superior Court Division One	33.33%
Vigo Superior Court Division Two	33.33%
Vigo Superior Court Division Three	33.33%

(3) *Civil Tort (CT).* The filing of civil tort actions shall be filed in the following proportionate rotation:

Vigo Superior Court Division Six	20%
Vigo Superior Court Division One	20%
Vigo Superior Court Division Two	40%
Vigo Superior Court Division Three	20%

(4) *Civil Plenary (PL).* The filing of civil plenary actions shall be filed in the following proportionate rotation:

Vigo Superior Court Division One	25%
Vigo Superior Court Division Two	25%
Vigo Superior Court Division Three	25%
Vigo Superior Court Division Six	25%

(5) *Civil Collections (CC).* The filing of civil collection actions shall be filed in the following proportionate rotation:

Vigo Superior Court Division One	20%
Vigo Superior Court Division Two	20%
Vigo Superior Court Division Three	20%
Vigo Superior Court Division Four	20%
Vigo Superior Court Division Six	20%

(6) *Mortgage Foreclosures (MF).* The filing of mortgage foreclosures shall be filed in the following proportionate rotation:

Vigo Superior Court Division Three	40%
Vigo Superior Court Division One	15%
Vigo Superior Court Division Two	15%
Vigo Superior Court Division Four	15%
Vigo Superior Court Division Six	15%

(7) *Small Claims (SC).* The filing of small claims actions shall be in the following proportionate rotation:

Vigo Superior Court Division 4	66%
Vigo Superior Court Division 5	34%

(8) *Protective Orders (PO).* Petitions for protection orders and workplace restraining orders shall be filed in Vigo Superior Court Division 4 except for protection order petitions filed by a party:

1. To a pending marriage dissolution case or to a marriage dissolution case in which a decree has been entered and there are minor children to the parties. These petitions shall be filed in the Court presiding over the dissolution action.

2. To a pending paternity case or who is a juvenile or naming a juvenile as respondent. These cases shall be filed in Juvenile Court.

(9) *Mental Health Cases (MH)*. All mental health cases filed shall be in Vigo Superior Court Division 2.

(10) *Juvenile Court (JP)*. To the extent of its jurisdiction, all juvenile matters shall be filed in the Juvenile Division of the Vigo Circuit Court.

(11) *Miscellaneous (MI)*. All miscellaneous civil filings shall be filed in the following rotation:

All miscellaneous civil filings will be divided equally between Division 1, Division 2, Division 3, Division 4, Division 5, and Division 6 on a rotating basis.

As in the past, Vigo County Judges shall continue to cooperate with one another to insure the effective and efficient administration of justice by assisting one another with hearings, should they be available to do so.

Adopted as Local Rule 17, effective April 1, 2005. Amended Dec. 8, 2005, effective Jan. 1, 2006; amended and renumbered as Administrative Rule 2, Oct. 1, 2006, effective Jan. 1, 2007; amended Aug. 1, 2009, effective Jan. 1, 2010; Sept. 8, 2010, effective Jan. 1, 2011; Aug. 17, 2011, effective Jan. 1, 2012.

LR84–AR9 Rule 3. CONFIDENTIALITY OF COURT RECORDS

(A) Search Warrants. All search warrants shall be confidential prior to return of duly executed service.

(B) Arrest Warrants. All arrest warrants for criminal offenses shall be confidential prior to return of duly executed service, unless in a particular case, the State applies for an Order lifting confidentiality in order to facilitate the peaceful surrender of the person for whom the arrest warrant was issued.

(C) Indictments and Informations. Only those informations filed after, or contemporaneously with, the issuance of an arrest warrant after a finding of probable cause shall be confidential prior to duly executed service. All indictments shall be confidential prior to the return of duly executed service.

Adopted October 1, 2006, effective Jan. 1, 2007. Amended effective Jan. 1, 2012.

LR84–AR11 Rule 4. FORM AND STYLE OF PAPERS, NUMBER OF COPIES, FILING AND SERVICES

(A) In order that the files of the Clerk's office may be kept under the system commonly known as "flat filing", all papers presented to the Clerk of the Judge for filing shall be 8 ½ × 11″, flat and unfolded. (Original oversized documents may be filed as part of a pleading; however, all copies shall be reduced to 8 ½ × 11″ where possible). Typewritten pages shall have neither covers nor backs and shall be fastened together at the top and at no other place. All pleadings shall be typewritten on unlined, opaque paper, single spaced with double spacing between paragraphs. Briefs and instructions shall be double spaced.

(B) All orders submitted to the Court shall be in sufficient number that the original may be retained by the Clerk and a copy mailed to each affected party

(C) The use of fill-in the blank or photocopied forms is not encouraged and such will be accepted for filing only if legible, clearly understandable and not altered by striking over and/or erasing.

Adopted as Circuit and Superior Court Rule 4. Amended and renumbered as Administrative Rule 4, October 1, 2006, effective Jan. 1, 2007; effective Jan. 1, 2012.

LR84–AR12 Rule 5. FILING BY FACSIMILE TRANSMISSION

Pleadings, motions and other papers may be filed by Facsimile Transmission as provided by Indiana Administrative Rule 12; the Court, by Facsimile Transmission, may issue orders or other responses thereto. All Facsimile Transmissions, by a party or the Court, shall be considered as being mailed for purposes of computing time under T.R. 6(E).

Adopted as Circuit and Superior Court Rule 4(D). Amended and renumbered as Administrative Rule 5, October 1, 2006, effective Jan. 1, 2007; effective Jan. 1, 2012.

LR84–AR15 Rule 6. COURT REPORTER SERVICES

(A) Definitions. The following definitions shall apply under the local rule.

(1) A Court Reporter is a person who is specifically designated by a court to perform the official court reporting services for the court including preparing a transcript of the record.

(2) Equipment means all physical items owned by the court or other government entity and used by a court reporter in performing court reporting services. Equipment shall include, but not limited to, telephones, computer hardware, software programs, disks, tapes, and any other device used for recording and storing and transcribing electronic data.

(3) Work space means that portion of the court's facilities dedicated to each court reporter, including but not limited to actual space in the courtroom and any designated office space.

(4) Page means the page unit of transcript which results when a recording is transcribed in the form required by Indiana rule of Appellate Procedure 7.2.

(5) Recording means the electronic, mechanical, stenographic or other recording made as required by Indiana rule of Appellate Procedure 74.

(6) Regular hours worked means those hours which the court is regularly scheduled to work during any given week. Depending on the particular court, these hours may vary from court to court within the county but remain the same for each work week.

(7) Gap hours worked means those hours worked that are in excess of the regular hours worked but hours not in excess of forty (40) hours per work week.

(8) Overtime hours worked means those hours worked that are in excess of forty (40) hours per work week.

(9) Work week means a seven (7) consecutive day week that consistently begins and ends on the same days throughout the year; i.e. Sunday through Saturday, Wednesday through Thursday, Friday through Thursday.

(10) Court means the particular court for which the court reporter performs services. Court may also mean all of the courts in Vigo County.

(11) County indigent transcript means a transcript that is paid for from county funds and is on behalf of a litigant who has been declared indigent by a court.

(12) State indigent transcript means a transcript that is paid for from state funds and is for the use on behalf of a litigant who has been declared indigent by a court.

(13) Private transcript means a transcript, including but not limited to a deposition transcript that is paid for by a private party.

(14) Expedited transcript means a transcript which is requested to be prepared within three (3) working days or less.

(B) Salaries and Per Page Fees.

(1) Court Reporters shall be paid an annual salary for time spent working under the control, direction, and direct supervision of their supervising court during any regular working hours, gap hours, or overtime hours. The supervising court shall compensate court reporters for gap and overtime hours by allowing compensatory time off regular work hours.

(2) The maximum per page fee a court reporter may charge for the preparation of a county or state indigent transcript shall be $4.00 per page; the court reporter shall submit a claim directly to the county for the preparation of any county indigent transcripts.

(3) The maximum per page a court reporter may charge for the preparation of a private transcript shall be $4.00 per page for a private regular transcript. If a court reporter is requested to prepare an expedited transcript, the maximum page fee shall be $6.50 when the transcript must be prepared

within twenty-four (24) hours or less; $5.00 when the transcript must be prepared within three (3) working days. That a minimum transcript fee shall be $35.00. That said transcript fee shall be retroactive to the 25th day of July, 2001.

(4) In light of the various additional requirements under the new appeal process, the court shall provide binders for said transcripts so prepared.

(5) In the event a court reporter prepares a transcript using county owned equipment, the court reporter shall provide the paper at the court reporter's own expense and provide copies of the transcript using an outside copying service at the court reporter's own expense.

(6) Each court reporter shall report, at least on an annual basis, all transcript fees received for the preparation of either county indigent, state indigent, or private transcripts to the Indiana Supreme Court Division of State Court Administration. The reporting shall be made on forms prescribed by the Division of State Court Administration.

(C) Private Practice.

(1) If a court reporter elects to engage in private practice through the recording of a deposition and/or preparing of a deposition transcript, and the court reporter desires to utilize the court's equipment, work space, and supplies, and the court agrees to the use of the court's equipment for such purpose, the court and the court reporter shall enter into a written agreement which must, at a minimum, designate the following:

(a) The reasonable market rate for the use of equipment, work space, and supplies.

(b) The method by which records are to kept for the use of equipment, work space, and supplies.

(c) The method by which the court reporter is to reimburse the court for the use of the equipment, work space, and supplies.

(2) If a court reporter elects to engage in private practice through the recording of a deposition and/or preparing of a deposition transcript, all such private practice work shall be conducted outside of regular working hours.

Adopted as Circuit and Superior Court Rule 4. Amended and renumbered as Administrative Rule 6, October 1, 2006, effective Jan. 1, 2007; effective Jan. 1, 2012.

LR84–AR 15 Rule 7. COURT ALCOHOL AND DRUG PROGRAM FEES

All individuals ordered to enroll in the Vigo County Court Alcohol and Drug Program may be charged up to a maximum of $400.00 for program services, pursuant to Indiana Code 12–23–14–16.

Adopted June 2, 2008, effective Jan. 1, 2009. Amended effective Jan. 1, 2012.

Appendix A.   APPOINTMENT OF SPECIAL JUDGE

STATE OF INDIANA)
) SS:
COUNTY OF   )   IN THE _____ COURT
                            200 __ TERM

_____
   Plaintiff
   –VS–
_____   CAUSE NO. _____
   Defendant

APPOINTMENT OF SPECIAL JUDGE

_____, Presiding Judge for the Administrative District 7, having received certification requiring reassignment of a special judge, now appoints The Honorable _____, as Special Judge in this Cause.

SO ORDERED this __ day of _____, 20 __.

_____, Presiding Judge
Administrative District 7

Distribution:
_____, Special Judge
_____, Atty
_____, Atty

Adopted Oct. 31, 2006, effective Jan. 1, 2007. Amended effective Jan. 1, 2012.

WAYNE COUNTY ADMINISTRATIVE RULES

Passed by the Wayne County Bar Association Effective January 1, 2011

Including Amendments Received Through November 1, 2013

Rule
LR89–AR15 Rule 001.   Court Reporter Services

LR89–AR15 Rule 001.   COURT REPORTER SERVICES

The undersigned Courts comprise all of the Courts of record of Wayne County, Indiana and hereby adopt the following local rule by which Court Reporter services shall be governed.

Section One.   Definitions.   The following definitions shall apply under this local rule:

(1) *A Court Reporter* is a person who is specifically designated by a Court to perform the official court reporting services for the Court including preparing a transcript of the record.

(2) *Equipment* means all physical items owned by the Court or other governmental entity and used by a Court Reporter in performing court reporting services.   Equipment shall include, but not be limited to, telephones, computer hardware, software programs, disks, tapes, and any other devices used for recording and storing, and transcribing electronic data.

(3) *Work space* means that portion of the Court's facilities dedicated to each Court Reporter, including but not limited to actual space in the courtroom and/or any designated office space.

(4) *Page* means the page unit of transcript which results when a recording is transcribed in the form required by Indiana Rule of Appellate Procedure 7.2.

(5) *Recording* means the electronic, mechanical, stenographic or other recording made as required by Indiana Rule of Trial Procedure 74.

(6) *Regular hours worked* means those hours which the Court is regularly scheduled to work during any given work week.   Depending on the particular Court, these hours may vary from Court to Court within the County but remain the same for each work week.

(7) *Gap hours worked* means those hours worked that are in excess of the regular hours worked, but hours not in excess of forty (40) hours per work week.

(8) *Overtime hours worked* means those hours worked in excess of forty (40) hours per work week.

(9) *Work week* means a seven (7) consecutive day week that consistently begins and ends on the same days throughout the year; i.e. Sunday through Saturday, Wednesday through Tuesday, Friday through Thursday.

(10) *Court* means the particular Court for which the Court Reporter performs services.   Court may also mean all of the Courts in Wayne County.

(11) *County indigent transcript* means a transcript that is paid for from county funds and is for the use on behalf of a litigant who has been declared indigent by a Court.

(12) *State indigent transcript* means a transcript that is paid for from state funds and is for the use on behalf of a litigant who has been declared indigent by a Court.

(13) *Private transcript* means a transcript, including but not limited to a deposition transcript that is paid for by a private party.

Section Two.   Salaries and Per Page Fees.

(1) Court Reporters shall be paid an annual salary for time spent working under the control, direction, and direct supervision of their supervising Court.

(2) The fee a Court Reporter shall charge for the preparation of a **county indigent transcript** shall be as follows:

(a) A minimum fee of $44.00 for any transcript eleven pages or less;

(b) $4.00 per page, including the Index and Table of Contents;

(c) An additional labor charge approximating the hourly rate based upon the Court Reporter's annual Court compensation for the time spent proof reading, binding the transcript and preparing the exhibit binders.

(3) The fee a Court Reporter shall charge for the preparation of a **State indigent transcript** shall be as follows:

(a) A minimum fee of $44.00 for any transcript eleven (11) pages or less;

(b) $4.00 per page, including the Index and Table of Contents;

(c) An additional labor charge approximating the hourly rate based upon the Court Reporter's annual Court compensation for the time spent proof reading, binding the transcript and preparing the exhibit binders.

(4) The fee a Court Reporter shall charge for the preparation of a *private transcript* shall be as follows:

(a) A minimum fee of $44.00 for any transcript eleven (11) pages or less;

(b) $4.00 per page, including the Index and Table of Contents;

(c) An additional labor charge approximating the hourly rate based upon the Court Reporter's annual Court compensation for the time spent proof reading, binding the transcript and preparing the exhibit binders.

(5) The per page fee a Court Reporter shall charge for a COPY of any transcript shall be $1.00.

(6) Each Court Reporter shall report, at least on an annual basis, all transcript fees received for the preparation of either county indigent, state indigent, or private transcripts to the Indiana Supreme Court, Division of State Court Administration. The reporting shall be made on forms prescribed by the Division of State Court Administration.

Section Three. Private Practice—Depositions.

(1) With permission of the supervising Court, if a Court Reporter elects to engage in private practice through the recording of a deposition and/or preparing of a deposition transcript, and the Court Reporter desires to utilize the Court's equipment, work space, and supplies, and the Court agrees to the use of the Court equipment for such purpose, the Court and the Court Reporter shall enter into a written agreement which must, at a minimum designate the following:

(a) The reasonable market rate for the use of the equipment, work space, and supplies;

(b) The method by which records are to be kept for the use of equipment, work space, and supplies; and,

(c) The method by which the Court Reporter is to reimburse the Court for the use of the equipment, work space, and supplies.

(2) If a Court Reporter elects to engage in private practice through the recording of a deposition and/or preparing of a deposition transcript, all such private practice work shall be conducted outside of regular working hours.

Adopted effective Jan. 1, 2012. Amended effective Jan. 1, 2013.

WAYNE COUNTY RULES OF CIVIL PROCEDURE

Adopted Effective October 30, 1997

Including Amendments Received Through November 1, 2013

Research Notes

Annotations to the Wayne County Rules of Civil Procedure are available in West's Annotated Indiana Code, *Title 34 Appendix.*

These rules may be searched electronically on Westlaw *in the* IN-RULES *database; updates to these rules may be found on* Westlaw *in* IN-RULESUPDATES. *For search tips and a summary of database content, consult the Westlaw Scope Screens for each database.*

LR89–TR3.1 Rule 001. WITHDRAWAL OF APPEARANCE

All withdrawals of Appearance shall be in writing and by leave of court. Permission to withdraw shall be given only after the withdrawing attorney has given his or her client ten (10) days written notice of his or her intention to withdraw and has filed a copy of such with the court or upon a simultaneous entering of Appearance by new counsel for said client. The letter of withdrawal shall explain to the client that failure to secure new counsel may result in dismissal of the client's case or a default judgment may be entered against him, whichever is appropriate, and other pertinent information such as a pending trial setting date or any other hearing date. Such letter of withdrawal shall be sent to the client via both certified mail-return receipt requested and first class mail, postage pre-paid. The certificate of service attached to the required motion for leave to withdraw must indicate compliance with both forms of mail to the client and to all counsel of record or the request shall be denied. The court will not grant a request for withdrawal of appearance unless the same has been filed with the court at least ten (10) days prior to the trial date, except for good cause shown.

Adopted as Rule 3, effective Oct. 30, 1997. Renumbered as Rule 001, and amended March 29, 2007; effective Jan. 1, 2008.

LR89–TR5 Rule 002. FILING

A. Filing and Submission Only to the Clerk. All papers presented for filing shall be submitted to the Clerk and not to the court.

B. Separate Motions and Order; Order by Chronological Case Summary Entry Form; Service. Proposed orders shall be prepared and filed separately from the pleadings, petitions, motion or other papers to which they have reference.

Orders, either routine in nature or uncontested including, for example, those setting or continuing a hearing, shall be affected by the chronological case summary entry only, which shall contain the concise substance of the order.

All orders shall be accompanied with sufficient copies so that copies may be mailed to all parties.

C. Counsel to Furnish Pleadings to Special Judge. When a Special Judge who is not a Wayne County Judge is selected and qualifies in a case, copies of all filings subsequent to the qualification of such Special Judge shall be delivered in person, by mail, or by facsimile to the office of the Special Judge with certificate of forwarding same made a part of the filing.

Adopted as Rule 4, effective Oct. 30, 1997. Amended effective March 29, 2007; amended Sept. 7, 2007, effective Jan. 1, 2008.

LR89–AR12 Rule 003. FACSIMILE FILING

Facsimile filing is permitting in the Wayne Circuit and Wayne Superior Courts. If the filing requires immediate attention of the Judge, it shall be so indicated in bold letters in an accompanying transmittal memorandum. Facsimile filing must be through the Clerk's central reception number (765–973–9250). Legibility of documents and timeliness of filing is the responsibility of the sender.

Any documents filed by facsimile which seek an Order of Court must be accompanied by a copy of a proposed order. Such proposed order must contain the requesting party or attorney's facsimile number in the distribution list. If the Court adopts the proposed order and certifies that an emergency exists, the Clerk shall return such Order to sender by facsimile. Upon receipt of the Court's Order, sender shall serve it upon all parties or counsel of record by facsimile or First Class U.S. Mail and file an acknowledgment of receipt and Certificate of Service via facsimile to the Clerk's central reception number on the form below:

Cause No.

Acknowledgment and Certificate of Service:

I acknowledge receipt of the following order or request from the Court:
_____ and certify that I have served
a copy of the
Court's Order or request upon the following parties or
counsel of record:
_____ via: facsimile transmission;
First Class, U.S. Mail

Firm Name
Attorney's Name, Address &
Telephone
Attorney's Number

Adopted as Rule 4, effective Oct. 30, 1997. Renumbered as Rule 003, and amended March 29, 2007, effective Jan. 1, 2008.

LR89–TR06 Rule 004. MOTIONS

A. Preparation. All pleadings, motions, briefs, and other papers shall be prepared in accordance with the provisions of the Indiana Rules of Procedure.

B. Continuances and Enlargements of Time. All motions for continuance or enlargement of time (whether 1st, 2nd, 3rd, etc.) shall be made in writing, shall state whether or not opposing counsel objects to the motion, and shall state whether prior continuances or enlargements have been requested by either party and whether such prior request was granted. The Court may require any written motion for continuance or enlargement of time to be signed by the party requesting the continuance.

C. First Enlargement of Time. The first motion for enlargement of time to file a responsive pleading to a Complaint shall be granted summarily for up to forty-five (45) days. Any request for additional time beyond forty-five (45) days or a subsequent request for enlargement of time shall be at the discretion of the Court.

D. Title of Motion. All motions for continuance or enlargement of time shall denominate in the title of such motion whether it is the first, second, third, etc.

motion for continuance or enlargement of time; e.g. Defendant's Second Motion For Enlargement Of Time To File Answer.

E. Proposed Orders to Accompany All Motions. All motions seeking an Order of the Court shall be accompanied by a sufficient number of proposed Orders to be executed by the Court in granting the motion. Proposed Orders continuing a matter or granting an enlargement of time shall not set forth the new date but shall leave the date blank for the Court to complete.

Adopted as Rule 5, effective Oct. 30, 1997. Renumbered as Rule 004, and amended March 29, 2007, effective Jan. 1, 2008.

LR89–TR55 Rule 005. DEFAULT JUDGMENT

Upon the proper filing of a motion for default judgment pursuant to Trial Rule 55, the Court may enter default and may either: 1) enter default judgment in the amount requested if supported by proper accompanying pleadings (Affidavit of Indebtedness, etc.); or 2) set the matter for damages hearing. In the event the Court sets the matter for damages hearing, the moving party may file any Affidavit (of indebtedness or otherwise) in support of its claim for damages or judgment if said party has not already done so. In the event the Court sets the matter for damages hearing, it is not necessary that the moving party or such party's counsel attend the damages hearing. If the nonmoving party does not appear or appears and does not contest the damage or judgment amount requested, and the amount requested is supported by proper accompanying pleadings filed by the moving party, the Court may enter judgment in the amount requested. If the amount of damages or judgment is contested at the damages hearing the Court will then set the matter for further hearing at a later date and further evidence may be presented.

Adopted effective Jan. 1, 2008. Amended effective Jan. 1, 2012.

LR 89–TR56 Rule 006. MOTIONS FOR SUMMARY JUDGMENT

All Trial Rule 56 Motions for Summary Judgment shall be filed at least one hundred fifty (150) days prior to trial.

Adopted effective Jan. 1, 2012.

LR89–TR37 Rule 007. SANCTIONS

If a party who has been properly served fails to appear at a contempt hearing, the Court shall not proceed but shall upon request by the moving party cause to issue a Rule To Show Cause Order ordering the non-moving party into court to answer as to why he/she failed to appear and why he/she should not be held in contempt of court. If the non-moving party again fails to appear in court as ordered after being properly served with the Rule To Show Cause Order, a Writ Of Body Attachment shall be issued for the non-moving party.

Adopted effective Jan. 1, 2008. Amended effective Jan. 1, 2012.

LR89–TR73 Rule 008. ORAL ARGUMENT

The granting of a motion for oral argument, unless required by the Indiana Rules Of Procedure, shall be discretionary with the Court.

Adopted as Rule 5, effective Oct. 30, 1997. Amended effective March 29, 2007. Renumbered and amended as Rule 007 effective Jan. 1, 2008. Amended effective Jan. 1, 2012.

LR89–TR40 Rule 009. TRIAL READINESS CERTIFICATE (TRC)

A. TRC. Any party may request the scheduling of a bench trial by filing a Trial Readiness Certificate (TRC) that certifies that the cause is ready to be scheduled for trial, that discovery has been finalized or will be finalized by the court ordered discovery cut off date heretofore set, and that no continuance of any trial date so scheduled will be requested for the purpose of filing any pleading or motion now reasonably contemplated, pursuing further discovery proceedings, securing attendance of any witness or party, or for any reason now reasonably foreseeable.

B. Request of Response. A party filing a TRC may request that the other party file a TRC within thirty (30) days. Such request shall be made on the TRC. The party requested to file a TRC within thirty (30) days shall file a TRC within such time unless within such thirty (30) day period an application for enlargement of time showing good cause is filed.

C. Failure to Timely Respond. In the event a party requested to file a TRC within thirty (30) days fails to timely file a TRC or a motion for enlargement of time within which to file a TRC, the court may summarily proceed to schedule a pre-trial and trial date with or without a praecipe being filed by the requesting party.

D. Form. Trial Readiness Certificates (TRC's) shall be in the form set forth in Appendix "A". TRC's not in such form may be summarily denied.

Adopted effective Jan. 1, 2008. Amended effective Jan. 1, 2012.

LR89–TR16 Rule 010. PRE–TRIAL PROCEDURE

A. Setting of Pre–Trial Conference.

1. *Jury Trials.* In those cases where a jury has been requested, a preliminary pre-trial conference shall be set approximately six (6) months prior to the trial date. A preliminary pre-trial conference will be set upon the filing and approval by the court of an Agreed Case Management Order pursuant to Rule 11. A final pre-trial conference shall be set approximately thirty (30) to forty-five (45) days prior to the trial date.

2. *Bench Trials.* In those cases to be tried to the court, a preliminary pre-trial conference will not be set unless requested by a party or otherwise ordered by the court. Final pre-trial conference shall be set approximately thirty (30) to forty-five (45) days prior to the trial date as arranged by the Court.

B. Filing of Pre–Trial Statements. At least forty-eight (48) hours prior to both the preliminary and the final pre-trial conferences, counsel for each party shall file Pre–Trial Statements which shall include all matters deemed important to the trial of the cause, but must include all information set forth in Paragraph "C" below.

C. Form of Pre–Trial Statement. The pre-trial statement shall contain the following statements in separate numbered Paragraphs as follows:

1. *Jurisdiction.* Setting forth the basis of jurisdiction.

2. *Status of Record.* Setting forth the pleadings raising the issues.

3. *Pending Motions and Outstanding Discovery.* Setting forth the motions or other matters requiring action by the Court and a concise statement as to the status of discovery.

4. *Statement of Position.* Setting forth a concise statement as to each party's position.

5. *Stipulations.* Setting forth a concise statement of stipulated facts.

6. *Issues of Fact.* Setting forth a statement of the issues of fact which remain to be litigated at trial.

7. *Issues of Law.* Setting forth a concise statement of the issues of law on which there is agreement and which remain to be litigated at trial.

8. *Exhibits.* Setting forth each exhibit which shall be presented at trial.

9. *Amendments to Pleadings.* Setting forth a concise statement as to whether or not there are any amendments to the pleadings.

10. *Probable Settlement.* Setting forth a concise statement as to settlement negotiations and the likelihood of settlement.

11. *Probable Trial Time.* Setting forth a concise statement as to the anticipated length of trial.

12. *List of Witnesses.* Setting forth a numbered list of trial witnesses which shall include each witness's address. Expert witnesses shall be so designated.

D. Failure to File Pre–Trial Statement. In the event either party should fail to timely file a Pre–Trial Statement as required by this Rule, the Court shall have the right to cancel the pre-trial conference and/or the trial or to enter appropriate sanctions against the party failing to file such Pre–Trial Statement.

E. Preliminary Pre–Trial Conference. The primary purposes of the preliminary pre-trial conference are to determine whether or not the case is ready to proceed to trial by jury as scheduled and to determine the procedure to prepare the case for trial. Once a case is determined at the preliminary pre-trial conference to be ready to proceed to jury trial as scheduled, a continuance of such date will not be granted except for extraordinary circumstances which were not reasonably foreseeable at the preliminary pre-trial conference. Such reasons shall not include the need to file further pleadings or motions, pursuing or completing further discovery, securing attendance of any witness or party, or any other reasonably foreseeable reason.

F. Final Pre–Trial Conference. The primary purpose of the final pre-trial conference are to determine the procedure to prepare the case for trial and to discuss these matters set out in Rule 16 of the Indiana Rules of Trial Procedure.

G. Attendance By Trial Counsel Required. The primary purpose of the final pre-trial conference are to determine the procedure to prepare the case for trial and to discuss these matters set out in Rule 16 of the Indiana Rules of Trial Procedure.

H. Pre–Trial Order. Following the pre-trial conference, a pre-trial order shall be entered in compliance with Rule 16(J) of the Indiana Rules of Trial Procedure.

I. More Than One Pre–Trial Conference. If necessary or advisable, the Court may adjourn the pretrial conference from time to time or may order additional Pre–Trial Conferences as it deems appropriate.

Adopted as Rule 10, effective Oct. 30, 1997. Amended effective March 29, 2007. Renumbered and amended as Rule 009 effective Jan. 1, 2008. Amended effective Jan. 1, 2012.

LR89–TR40 Rule 011. CASE MANAGEMENT CONFERENCE & ORDER AND SETTING OF PRE–TRIAL AND TRIAL DATES

A. Mandatory Case Management Conference. A case management conference shall be required in all cases where a jury trial is requested.

B. Discretionary Case Management Conference. A case management conference may be ordered in any other case upon the filing of a motion by any party or on the court's own motion.

C. Conference Procedure. Within one hundred twenty (120) days of the filing of a Complaint in those cases where a case management conference is mandatory, or within thirty (30) days after otherwise being ordered to participate in a case management conference, the Plaintiff shall arrange a meeting of all parties for the following purposes:

1. *List of Witnesses.* Exchange preliminary lists of witnesses known to have knowledge of the facts supporting the pleadings. The parties shall thereafter be under a continuing obligation to advise opposing parties of other witnesses as they become known. The parties shall establish a date by which any testifying expert witness must be disclosed.

2. *Documents.* Exchange all documents which are contemplated to be used in support of the pleadings. Documents later shown to have been reasonably available to a party and not exchanged may be subject to exclusion at the time of trial.

3. *Other Evidence.* Exchange any other evidence reasonably available to obviate the filing of unnecessary discovery motions.

4. *Mediation and Settlement.* Discuss the likelihood of settlement of the action and the date, if any, by which mediation shall occur.

5. *Discovery Schedule.* Agree upon a schedule for all discovery including a date by which discovery shall be finalized and completed.

6. *Complicated Case.* Discuss whether the action is sufficiently complicated so that additional conferences may be required.

7. *Additional Parties.* Discuss the date by which any motion to join additional parties must be filed.

8. *Pre–Trial Motions.* Discuss and agree upon the dates by which any motions to dismiss, motions for summary judgment, and other motions shall be filed. It shall not be necessary to include the date for filing motions in limine as motions in limine are to be filed at least fifteen (15) days prior to trial pursuant to LR89–TR–006.

9. *Anticipated Trial Readiness Date.* Discuss the date by which the parties reasonably anticipate the case will be ready for trial.

10. *Estimated Length of Trial.* Discuss the length of time the parties reasonably anticipate the trial will take to complete.

D. Case Management Order. Within ten (10) days after meeting, but within one hundred eighty (180) days of filing the Complaint, those attending are to file an Agreed Case Management Order setting forth:

1. The likelihood of mediation and settlement;

2. A detailed schedule of discovery for each party, including an agreed upon date by which discovery shall be completed and finalized;

3. A limitation on the time to join additional parties and to amend the pleadings;

4. A limitation on the time to file all pre-trial motions, excluding motions in limine;

5. A preliminary estimate of the time required for trial;

6. The date by which the parties reasonably anticipate the case will be ready for trial; and

7. Any other matters which the parties believe may be helpful to the Court.

E. Setting of Pre–Trial and Trial Dates In Cases Where Jury Requested. Upon the filing of an Agreed Case Management Order pursuant to this Rule, which is thereafter approved by the court, preliminary pre-trial, pre-trial, and trial dates shall be set by the Wayne County Court Scheduling Office. The preliminary pre-trial conference shall be set approximately six (6) months prior to the scheduled trial date with the final pre-trial conference scheduled approximately thirty (30) to forty-five (45) days prior to the scheduled trial date. At the preliminary pre-trial conference, all counsel shall be prepared to discuss whether the case remains ready to proceed to trial.

Adopted as Rule 11, effective Oct. 30, 1997. Amended effective March 29, 2007. Renumbered and amended as Rule 010 effective Jan. 1, 2008. Amended effective Jan. 1, 2012.

LR89–TR16 Rule 012. MOTIONS IN LIMINE, JURY INSTRUCTIONS, AND JUROR QUESTIONNAIRE

A. Motions in Limine. Any Motion in Limine shall be filed so that it is actually received by the Court at least fifteen (15) days prior to trial, or longer as the Court may order.

B. Objections to Motions in Limine. Objections to any Motions In Limine shall be submitted to the Court in writing and shall be submitted at least seven (7) days prior to trial. Written objections shall be numbered and shall specify distinctly and with clarity the objectionable matter to the Motion in Limine. Each objection shall be accompanied by citations of authority.

C. Agreed Upon Fact Instruction. Counsel shall submit to the Court an agreed upon fact Instruction so that it is actually received by the Court at least fifteen (15) days prior to trial, or longer as the Court may order.

D. Proposed Jury Instructions. Counsel may submit proposed jury instructions to the Court, provided that such instructions are actually received by the Court at least fifteen (15) days prior to trial, or longer as the Court may order. Instructions covering matters occurring at the trial which could not reasonable be anticipated may be tendered and/or substituted at the conclusion of the trial. Each proposed instruction shall be accompanied by citations of authority.

E. Objections to Proposed Jury Instructions. Objections to proposed jury instructions may be submitted to the Court in writing and shall be submitted at least seven (7) days prior to trial. Written objections shall be numbered and shall specify distinctly and with clarity the objectionable matter in the proposed instruction. Each objection shall be accompanied by citations of authority.

F. Juror Questionnaires. In all cases, the Juror Questionnaire Form in Appendix B shall be used unless all parties consent to a proposed juror questionnaire which shall be tendered jointly and shall actually be received by the Court at least fifteen (15) days prior to trial, or longer as the Court may order. In no cases shall a proposed juror questionnaire be in excess of a single one-sided typed $8\frac{1}{2} \times 11$ page without leave of the Court.

Adopted as Rule 12, effective Oct. 30, 1997. Amended effective March 29, 2007. Renumbered and amended as Rule 011 effective Jan. 1, 2008. Amended effective Jan. 1, 2012.

LR89–AR1 Rule 013. RANDOM FILING OF CIVIL CASES

A. Random Filing. Civil filings in Wayne Circuit, Wayne Superior Court No. 1 and Wayne Superior Court No. 2 shall be assigned to said courts by way of random selection process but in such a way that each court receives roughly the same number of filings of each type of category (i.e., adoptions, civil miscellaneous, civil plenary, civil torts, domestic relations, estates, guardianships, mental health, protective orders, etc.)

B. Exempt Filings. Paternity filings shall be exempt from the random selection process.

C. Captions to Contain Blanks. Captions of all proposed initial pleadings shall contain blank spaces where appropriate to enable the Clerk to enter the identity of the receiving court and its cause number.

D. Transfer of Cases to Balance Case Load. The judges of the Wayne Circuit Court, Wayne Superior Court No. 1, and Wayne Superior Court No. 2 shall periodically review the filing patterns and reserve the right to transfer cases in the event of a disproportionate distribution of cases in order to balance the caseload and expedite dispositions of all pending cases.

Adopted as Rule 15, effective Oct. 30, 1997. Amended effective March 29, 2007. Renumbered and amended as Rule 012 effective Jan. 1, 2008. Amended effective Jan. 1, 2012.

LR89–TR79 Rule 014. SPECIAL JUDGE SELECTION IN CIVIL CASES

In the event a special judge is required to be selected pursuant to Rule 79(D), (E), or (F) or requiring selection pursuant to Local Rule, this Rule shall control. A special judge shall be designated by the Clerk of the Wayne Circuit and Superior Courts in sequence from the following courts, to-wit:

1. The presiding Judge of the Wayne Circuit Court;

2. The presiding Judge of the Wayne Superior Court No. 1;

3. The presiding Judge of the Wayne Superior Court No. 2;

4. The presiding Judge of the Fayette Circuit Court;

5. The presiding Judge of the Fayette Superior Court;

6. The presiding Judge of the Franklin Circuit Court No. 1;

7. The presiding Judge of the Franklin Circuit Court No. 2;

8. The presiding Judge of the Randolph Circuit Court;

9. The presiding Judge of the Randolph Superior Court;

10. The presiding Judge of the Rush Circuit Court; and

11. The presiding Judge of the Union Circuit Court.

The Clerk shall maintain such records as necessary to assure that selections are rotated in the above sequence.

Adopted as Rule 16, effective Oct. 30, 1997. Amended effective March 29, 2007. Renumbered and amended as Rule 013 effective Jan. 1, 2008. Amended effective Jan. 1, 2012.

LR89–TR00 Rule 015. ATTORNEYS FEES IN CIVIL CASES

A. General Provisions. RULE 1.5 of the Rules of Professional Conduct adopted by the Supreme Court of Indiana shall govern the awarding of attorneys fees in civil actions. All fees charged by attorneys must be reasonable. Factors which the Wayne Circuit and Superior Courts will consider in determining attorney fee awards in civil cases include:

1. The time and labor required, the novelty and difficulty of questions involved, and the skill requisite to perform the legal service properly;

2. The likelihood, if apparent to the client, that the acceptance of the particular employment will preclude other employment by the lawyer;

3. The fee customarily charged in the locality for similar legal service;

4. The amount involved and the results obtained;

5. The time limitations imposed by the client or by the circumstances;

6. The nature and length of the professional relationship with the client;

7. The experience, reputation and ability of the lawyer or lawyers performing the services.

Attorneys' fees are to be based upon those factors as set forth above and other relevant factors. At the appropriate time in the proceeding, attorneys shall submit a Verified Affidavit in support of the request for attorneys fees setting forth: facts in support of

such request; a detailed list of the services and time expended on the matter to date; the amount of time expected to be expended in the future through to completion, including collection; the attorney's customary and usual hourly fee; and all other relevant facts in support of the request. All fees, if any, shall be awarded at the time of Judgment and not at a future date unless authorized specifically by statute.

B. Mechanics Liens. In cases involving mechanics liens, the Court will find as reasonable attorney fees, unless there is evidence to the contrary, the following:

• to $1,500.00 for the first $10,000.00 of judgment (or any portion thereon);

• to 5% of the next $15,000.00;

• to 3% of the next $25,000.00;

• to 1–1/2% of the next $50,000.00;

• to 1% of the next $150,000.00;

• to 1/2% of everything over $250,000.00.

The above fees shall include conferences with client, preparation of notices, complaint and summons, obtaining judgment, and reasonable collection efforts. In instances where additional fees are requested, the attorney shall file a Verified Petition/Affidavit which details the services and times expended thereon and includes those matters referred to in Rule 1.5 of the Rules of Professional Conduct.

C. Other Written Instruments Including Leases, Notes, and Contracts. In all cases where instruments provide for attorney fees, or such fees are provided for by statute, except real estate mortgage foreclosure and mechanics liens, the Court will find as reasonable attorneys fees, unless there is evidence to the contrary, the following:

Amount of Debt	% fee to be awarded
The first $3,000.00	33–1/3%
The next $10,000.00	17%
The next $12,000.00	8%
Excess of $25,000.00	3%

The above fees shall include conferences with client, preparation of notices, complaint and summons, obtaining judgment, and reasonable collection efforts. In instances where additional fees are requested the attorney shall file a Verified Petition/Affidavit which details the services and times expended thereon and includes those matters referred to in Rule 1.5 of the Rules of Professional Conduct.

Adopted as Rule 17, effective Oct. 30, 1997. Amended effective March 29, 2007. Renumbered and amended as Rule 014 effective Jan. 1, 2008. Amended effective Jan. 1, 2012.

Appendix A. TRIAL READINESS CERTIFICATE

STATE OF INDIANA   )   IN THE WAYNE _____ COURT
)SS:

COUNTY OF WAYNE   )   20 ____ TERM

                                      CAUSE NO. 89 ___–___–___–___

_____   )
_____   )
        Plaintiff(s),   )
)
     v.   )
)
_____   )
_____   )
       Defendant(s).   )

TRIAL READINESS CERTIFICATE

As attorney for _____, I certify that this cause is ready to be scheduled for trial, and that no continuance from any trial date so scheduled will be requested by me or on behalf of _____ to file any pleading or motion, pursue further discovery proceedings, secure attendance of any witness or party, or for any reason now reasonably foreseeable.

TIME REQUIRED TO COMPLETE TRIAL: _____

Request _____ counsel to respond within thirty (30) days.

_____

Attorney for _____

CERTIFICATE OF SERVICE

I hereby certify that I have served a copy of this document, by placing the same in the United States Mail, postage prepaid, on _____, this ___ day of _____, 20 ___.

_____

Amended effective Jan. 1, 2012.

Appendix B. JUROR QUESTIONNAIRE

WAYNE COUNTY, IN   JUROR QUESTIONNAIRE

Dear Prospective Juror: Your name has been drawn by random selection for jury service from state and local government records. The full cooperation of every Citizen is necessary if our system of justice is to function fairly and efficiently. You are required to answer and return this Questionnaire within 10 days after receiving it. Refusing to answer or making untruthful answers could result in fine, imprisonment, or both for contempt of court.
PLEASE PRINT CAREFULLY

NAME: _____ DATE OF BIRTH: _____
ADDRESS: _____
HOME PHONE: _____ WORK PHONE: _____
EDUCATION: Highest grade completed/degree received _____ MIL. TO COURTHOUSE (round trip): _____

EMPLOYMENT AND/OR SCHOOL
(please check all that apply)   Current Employer (or last employer if not currently employed)

___ Employed   ___ Unemployed
___ Self–Employed   ___ Part–Time   Address
___ At Home   ___ Retired
___ Student   ___ Other

                            Your job or occupation

MARITAL STATUS: ___ Single ___ Married ___ Widowed ___ Divorced ___ Separated

Name of Spouse _____ Spouse's Occupation _____

Number of Children Living at Home _____

YOUR EXPERIENCE WITH THE LAW

Have you ever been a victim, witness, plaintiff, or defendant in a criminal or civil suit? __ Yes __ No

   If yes. explain: _____

Have you, a family member, or a close friend ever been in a serious traffic accident? __ Yes __ No

   Was alcohol involved? ___ Yes ___ No

   Who was injured? ___ Yourself ___ Family Member(s) ___ Other(s) ___ No one

Have you ever been convicted of a misdemeanor other than traffic violations? __ Yes __ No

   If yes, please state, what crime and location of conviction _____

_____

Have you ever been seated on a jury? __ Yes __ No If yes, date when last served _____

Have you or a family member ever worked for any of the following (Please check all that apply)

__ Law Enforcement Agency __ Court System __ Corrections/Detention System __ Other (law enforcement)

If so, please describe _____

BACKGROUND

Are you a United States Citizen?   YES __   NO __

Do you read, speak and understand English? _____

Are you physically or mentally able to carry out the functions of a juror? __ Yes __ No

   If no, explain: _____

Do you live in Wayne County? _____ If so, for how long? _____

If you do not live in Wayne County, do you authorize the cancellation of your voter's registration? _____

- If serving as a juror would create an extreme inconvenience or hardship, you can address that issue to the judge during the jury selection process.
- If you believe that you would be unable to be a juror for medical reasons, please send your doctor's certificate explaining why with this form.
- If you are summoned for jury service, you must appear. Failure to comply with the summons is punishable through a contempt of court action.

I affirm, under the penalties for perjury, that the foregoing representations are true.

   Date _____ Signature _____

Amended effective Jan. 1, 2012.

WAYNE COUNTY RULES OF CRIMINAL PROCEDURE

Adopted effective January 1, 2008

Including Amendments Received Through November 1, 2013

Research Notes

Annotations to the Wayne County Rules of Criminal Procedure are available in West's Annotated Indiana Code, *Title 34 Appendix.*

These rules may be searched electronically on Westlaw in the IN-RULES database; updates to these rules may be found on Westlaw in IN-RULESUPDATES. For search tips and a summary of database content, consult the Westlaw Scope Screens for each database.

LR89–CR00 Rule 001. SCOPE

These rules govern the procedure and practice of criminal cases in Wayne Circuit and Superior Courts unless otherwise provided by law or rules of the Supreme Court of Indiana or by other local rules, and are effective as of January 1, 2008.

Adopted effective Jan. 1, 2008.

LR89–CR00 Rule 002. RELEASE FROM CUSTODY—PROMISE TO APPEAR

A. A person arrested and incarcerated without a warrant shall be released from custody within forty-eight (48) hours of arrest unless a judicial determination of probable cause for arrest has been obtained.

B. A person arrested and incarcerated shall be permitted to post bail consistent with the Court's bail schedule unless otherwise ordered or communicated to the Sheriff by a judge.

C. Prior to release of a person pursuant to the 48 hour rule or upon posting bail, the person must complete a verified promise to appear, on a form approved by the courts, indicating his or her full name, date of birth, address, place of employment, home and work telephone numbers, social security number and promise to appear in the Court and at the time designated by the Sheriff. A copy of the Promise to Appear shall be provided to the arrested person and to the Court upon designation. The Promise To Appear is Form 1 in the Appendix.

D. Failure to appear as promised upon release from custody is cause for issuance of an arrest warrant.

E. All persons arrested and incarcerated shall be brought before the Court in which charges are filed within a reasonable period of time.

Adopted effective Jan. 1, 2008.

LR89–CR00 Rule 003. APPOINTED COUNSEL

A. A defendant who is financially unable to obtain counsel is entitled to appointed counsel in accordance with this rule, except in misdemeanor cases where the prosecution is not seeking a sentence of incarceration. If the court appoints counsel, the defendant will be notified of the name, address and telephone number of appointed counsel.

B. If a defendant states that he or she is financially unable to obtain counsel, the Court will examine the defendant as to financial circumstances and may require financial statements and/or investigation of the defendant's financial circumstances. If the investigation reveals that the defendant is financially unable to obtain counsel, the Court will appoint counsel.

C. At the time of the initial hearing, a defendant, for whom counsel is not appointed or for whom counsel has not entered an appearance, will be scheduled for a hearing regarding counsel and will be ordered to appear for said hearing. The defendant shall be instructed to contact attorney(s) in order to determine the costs of privately retained counsel and to report back to the Court at the time of the hearing regarding his or her efforts and progress in retaining private counsel. A list of attorneys who have notified the Courts that they may consider representing criminal defendants and receive payment in installments shall be provided to a defendant upon request. Attorneys willing to consider providing representation under such an arrangement shall advise the Court Administrator in writing so as to be included on the list.

D. If the Court finds that the defendant is able to pay part of the cost of representation by appointed counsel, the Court may order the defendant to pay an appropriate sum to the Clerk of the courts to be deposited into the county's supplemental public defender services fund.

E. The Court may order a person for whom a public defender has been appointed to perform community service during pre-trial release to compensate the county for the value of Public Defender services.

F. Notwithstanding the provisions of this rule, the Court may appoint counsel for any person at any stage of the proceedings to prevent a failure of justice.

Adopted effective Jan. 1, 2008.

LR89–CR00 Rule 004. APPEARANCE OF COUNSEL

A. Any attorney representing a defendant shall appear for such defendant immediately upon being retained or appointed by signing and filing an appearance in writing containing counsel's name, attorney number, address, telephone number, and a statement indicating whether counsel will accept service by fax. A copy of this appearance shall be served on the prosecution.

B. The Prosecuting Attorney of Wayne County may have a standing appearance form filed with the Clerk of the Wayne Circuit, Superior 1, Superior 2, and Superior 3 Courts which shall be deemed of record and applicable in all pending criminal cases, save and except when an individual appearance form is filed by the State of Indiana in a given case.

Adopted effective Jan. 1, 2008.

LR89–CR00 Rule 005. WITHDRAWAL OF COUNSEL

A. All withdrawals of Appearance by privately retained counsel shall be in writing and by leave of court. Permission to withdraw shall be given only after the withdrawing attorney has given his or her client ten (10) days written notice of his or her intention to withdraw and has filed a copy of such with the court or upon a simultaneous entering of Appearance by new counsel for said client. The letter of withdrawal shall explain to the client that failure to secure new counsel may result in dismissal of the client's case or default judgment may be entered against him, whichever is appropriate, and other pertinent information such as a pending trial setting date or any other hearing date. Such letter of withdrawal shall be sent to the client via both certified mail-return receipt requested and first class mail, postage pre-paid. The certificate of service attached to the required motion

for leave to withdraw must indicate compliance with both forms of mail to the client and to all counsel of record or the request shall be denied. The court will not grant a request for withdrawal of appearance unless the same has been filed with the court at least ten (10) days prior to the trial date, except for good cause shown. The Court shall have discretion to grant a Motion To Withdraw if the Court finds that the Defendant is properly notified although by means that are not in strict compliance with this rule.

B. If the motion to withdraw is granted, the Court will determine whether the then existing financial circumstances of the defendant necessitate the appointment of counsel. If so, counsel shall be appointed forthwith so as to obviate delay in the proceedings. If the defendant is not qualified for appointed counsel, the defendant shall be ordered to pursue the retention of alternate counsel and to report back to the Court within not less than fourteen days the results of all efforts made to retain another attorney.

Adopted effective Jan. 1, 2008.

LR89–CR00 Rule 006. INITIAL HEARING/PRE-TRIAL CONFERENCE

A.[1] Initial hearing shall be conducted in accordance with Indiana Statutes and Criminal Rules.

Adopted effective Jan. 1, 2008.

1 No "B." in original.

LR89–CR00 Rule 007. PRE-TRIAL CONFERENCE

A pre-trial conference will be scheduled at the initial hearing which shall require personal attendance by the Prosecutor's Office, defense counsel and the defendant. Failure of the defendant to appear may result in revocation of a bond, an increase in bail, and/or the issuance of a warrant.

Adopted effective Jan. 1, 2008.

LR89–CR00 Rule 008. WAIVER OF JURY TRIAL

Jury trials shall only be waived by the defendant in open Court and/or by written Waiver signed by Defendant and by defense counsel.

Adopted effective Jan. 1, 2008.

LR89–CR00 Rule 009. CRIMINAL DISCOVERY

The Wayne County Courts shall have Discovery consistent with applicable law. Neither the State nor the defense shall be required to file any Discovery documents or pleadings with the Court, but the parties are permitted to do so.

Neither the counsel for the parties nor other prosecution or defense personnel shall advise persons having properly discoverable information (except the accused) to refrain from discussing the case with opposing counsel, nor shall they otherwise impede opposing counsel's investigation of the case.

Adopted effective Jan. 1, 2008.

LR89–CR00 Rule 010.   STIPULATIONS

All stipulations shall be reduced to writing, signed by counsel and by the defendant personally, unless made during the course of a hearing or trial in open Court.

Adopted effective Jan. 1, 2008.

LR89–CR00 Rule 011. SELECTION OF JURY PANEL

A list of the petit jurors called for the trial of a particular case shall be available not less than four business days prior to the trial date.

When jury panels have been drawn, the bailiff shall cause the Court's questionnaire to be sent to each member of such panels to be answered and returned by such persons at least one business day prior to the commencement of jury selection. Such completed jury questionnaires are confidential and may only be obtained or examined by attorneys of record. Requests to supplement the Court's jury questionnaire shall be made in writing, prior to the final pretrial conference and shall include a verbatim proposed questionnaire.

Adopted effective Jan. 1, 2008.

LR89–CR00 Rule 012.   VOIR DIRE

The prosecutor and defense shall have an opportunity to question each prospective juror and observe questioning of the prospective juror by opposing counsel prior to passing or striking a prospective juror. Peremptory challenges shall be made in writing at the bench. If a prospective juror is stricken by both sides, each side is chargeable for the strike. A juror not stricken may become a member of the trial jury. A challenge for cause can be raised at any time. The Court may put time limitations on jury questioning.

Adopted effective Jan. 1, 2008.

LR89–CR00 Rule 013. FILING PROCEDURE FOR CRIMINAL CASES

A. Misdemeanors are filed in Wayne Superior Court III unless the misdemeanor accompanies a felony charge filed in Wayne Circuit Court, Wayne Superior Court I, or Wayne Superior Court II.

B. The following felonies shall be filed in Wayne Superior Court III, unless at least one Class C, B or A felony (other than those filed under I.C. 9–30–5 or 9–30–6) or Murder, is also filed against the same defendant in the same Information or Indictment:

1. Battery, a class D felony, filed under I.C. 35–42–2–1.

2. Domestic Battery, a Class D Felony, filed under I.C. 35–42–2–1.3.

3. Possession of Marijuana, Hash Oil or Hashish, a Class D Felony.

4. All offenses filed under I.C. 9–30–5.

5. All offenses involving the operation of a motor vehicle while driving privileges are suspended, restricted, or forfeited.

C. If the defendant:

1. has at least one pending criminal case, or

2. is on probation

in Circuit Court, Superior Court I or Superior Court II, then any felony charges brought against the same defendant, other than those felony charges listed at (B)(1–5), are to be filed in the court having jurisdiction over the matter referred to at (C)(1) OR (C)(2).

D. If the defendant:

1. has at least one pending felony case, and/or

2. is on formal felony probation

in Superior Court III, then any Class D Felony charges brought against the same defendant shall be filed in Wayne Superior Court III.

E. Except as otherwise dictated by paragraph (A), (B), (C) or (D), criminal cases shall be filed in a random and equal manner in Circuit Court, Superior Court I and Superior Court II.

F. If the Judge or personnel of a Court are required as witnesses in any case, the case shall not be filed in that Court, and the Clerk shall cause that case to be randomly filed in a different Court, unless otherwise excepted by this rule.

G. When the State of Indiana chooses to re-file a dismissed case, the case shall be assigned to the Court from which the dismissal was taken. This rule applies to all charges arising out of the same offense report, arrest report, or set of operative facts.

H. Upon the granting of a change of judge or the disqualification or recusal of a judge, a successor or special judge shall be assigned as follows:

Initial Judge	Successor/Special Judge
Circuit Court	Superior Court 1
Superior Court 1	Superior Court 2
Superior Court 2	Circuit Court
Superior Court 3	On an equal and rotating basis from among the Judges of Circuit Court, Superior Court 1 and Superior Court 2

I. In order to provide for an appropriately balanced case load and appropriate use of court resources, the Judges of the Wayne County Courts may, from time to time, transfer cases to other courts within Wayne County. Transfer of cases shall be by written order of the forwarding court, and shall be subject to written consent by the Judge of the receiving Court.

J. If unusual and unforeseen circumstances occur, deviation from the provisions of this rule may be obtained for a particular case with the approval of the Courts.

Adopted effective Jan. 1, 2008.

LR89–CR00 Rule 014.   BAIL

A.   Setting Bail.   The Court will set the amount of bail that the accused shall be required to post.   Warrant arrests may include the amount of the bail on the face of the warrant or on the order directing the Clerk to issue the Warrant.   Prosecution requests for arrest warrants shall include any prosecution's recommendation regarding bail amount and the reasons therefor.   Where charges are filed subsequent to arrest, the probable cause affidavit or oral probable cause submission shall include any prosecution's recommendation as to the appropriate bail.

B.   Filed motions for re-determination of bail will be given scheduling priority by the Courts.

C.   Automatic 10% Cash Bonds: A 10% cash bond is authorized by the Court for individuals charged with Class D and/or C Felonies.

A defendant charged with a misdemeanor or a Class D and/or C Felony for whom bail has been set, may satisfy the requirement of bail by depositing ten percent (10%) of the amount of the bail in cash with the clerk of the Court or the Sheriff of Wayne County as security for the full amount of the bail.

A defendant applying for 10% cash bail must make, under affirmation, an application on a form approved by the Court.   Such form is listed as Form 2 in the Appendix.

D.   CRIMINAL BAIL SCHEDULE (if bail is not otherwise set by Court):

The Bail schedule listed below is a presumptive Bail Schedule range that the Wayne Circuit, Wayne Superior Count 1 and Wayne Superior Court 2 shall use:

Offenses Against Persons: I.C. 35–42 *et seq.*

Murder		**No bail authorized**	
Class A Felony	$25,000.00	to	$75,000.00
Class B Felony	$15,000.00	to	$50,000.00
Class C Felony	$ 7,500.00	to	$25,000.00
Class D Felony	$ 5,000.00	to	$15,000.00

Offenses Against Property: I.C. 35–43 *et seq.*

Class A Felony	$15,000.00	to	$50,000.00
Class B Felony	$10,000.00	to	$35,000.00
Class C Felony	$ 5,000.00	to	$20,000.00
Class D Felony	$ 2,500.00	to	$10,000.00

Offenses Relating to Controlled Substances: I.C. 35–48–4 *et seq.*

Class A Felony	$15,000.00	to	$40,000.00
Class B Felony	$15,000.00	to	$30,000.00
Class C Felony	$ 7,500.00	to	$15,000.00
Class D Felony	$ 5,000.00	to	$ 7,500.00

Other Offenses Not Categorized Above

Class A Felony	$ 6,000.00	to	$60,000.00
Class B Felony	$ 4,500.00	to	$45,000.00
Class C Felony	$ 3,000.00	to	$30,000.00
Class D Felony	$ 1,500.00	to	$25,000.00

The scheduled above is established as a general guide for the Wayne County Courts (except Wayne Superior III) in setting bail for persons charged with bailable offenses.

The Sheriff of Wayne County shall use maximum amount for non-warrant arrests until the initial hearing, whereupon the Court has discretion to revise the amount of the bail.

Nothing in this schedule shall prevent the Court from setting above or below the range provided in this schedule or from admitting an individual defendant to release upon recognizance.

The Bail Schedule in this paragraph shall apply to all cases filed in Wayne County courts other than Wayne Superior Court 3.

Bonds shall be increased 50% for persons admitted to bail on a separate Felony case or who is charged as a Habitual Offender or a Habitual Substance Offender. The Prosecution shall include such fact in its Affidavit of Probable Cause or Charging Information.

E. The Wayne County Superior Court 3 shall post its current bond schedule in the courtroom of Wayne Superior Court 3, shall provide a copy of its current bond schedule to the Wayne County Sheriff, and such bond schedule shall be available for review in the Wayne Superior Court 3 offices.

The $5.00 bonding fee (death benefit fee) is to be added to surety and cash bonds on all misdemeanor and truck violations. The fee is not to be added to felony charges.

The Clerk shall retain from the cash bond such administrative fees as are authorized by law.

Adopted effective Jan. 1, 2008.

LR89–CR2.2 Rule 015.   SEARCH WARRANTS

Criminal cases opened for the purpose of obtaining a Search Warrant shall be assigned a new Miscellaneous Criminal case number. Cases for Search Warrants shall be assigned randomly among the Wayne Circuit, Superior No. 1, Superior No. 2, and Superior No. 3 courts in the same manner as set forth in LR 89–CR00 Rule 013. In the event there is a pending action involving the same criminal defendant for whom, or against whom, a Search Warrant is now requested that is related to such pending proceeding, a Notice Of Filing Of Request For Search Warrant shall be filed in the underlying pending action within twenty-four (24) hours after execution of the Search Warrant. Such Notice shall advise the court, counsel, and defendant that a request for a Search Warrant has been filed in a miscellaneous criminal case setting forth the caption of the case and the case number. Failure to file such a Notice is grounds for appropriate sanctions. Requests for Search Warrants are *ex parte* proceedings.

Adopted effective Jan. 1, 2013.

Appendix A. PROMISE TO APPEAR
Form 1

Date & Time Booked In ____

Date & Time Released _____

WAYNE CIRCUIT AND SUPERIOR COURTS
APPEARANCE FORM

Full Name: _____

Present Address: _____

           (Street)   (Apartment No.)

_____

      (City)   (State)   (Zip)

Phone No.: _____   Social Security No.: _____

DOB: _____   Driver's License No.: _____

Employer's Name and Address: _____

Current Charge: _____

I (am) (am not) presently on bond on another charge (of _____

_____pending in _____).

PROMISE TO APPEAR

The undersigned hereby certifies that the above information is true.

I promise to appear in the Wayne _____ Court (No. _____) on the _____ (A.M.)(P.M.). I understand that a bench warrant for my arrest will be issued if I fail to appear at said time and place.

   I affirm under the pains and penalty for perjury that the foregoing information is true.

Dated: _____   _____

                                             Signature

WITNESSES:

_____

_____

Appendix B. PERSONAL APPEARANCE BOND WITH PERCENTAGE CASH DEPOSIT
FORM 2

STATE OF INDIANA   **IN THE WAYNE _____ COURT**

VS.

_____   **CAUSE NO.**

PERSONAL APPEARANCE BOND
WITH PERCENTAGE CASH DEPOSIT

   I, the undersigned Defendant, understand that the bail has been set to assure my appearance in the above Court when ordered; I accept the option to deposit ten per cent (10%) of the amount of bail in cash with the Clerk.

   I understand that I am bound to the State of Indiana in the full amount of the bail set in the sum of _____ dollars; ($ ___). If I appear in Court as directed and comply with all conditions as ordered by the court until this case is finished, then this bond shall be released; if otherwise, the bond shall remain in full force.

   If I do not appear at any time fixed by the Court, the Court may declare this bond forfeited, and notice shall be mailed to me and _____ at the addresses given below. Unless the Court finds there was justification for my failure to appear, the Court may immediately enter judgment against me for the full amount of the bail. The cash deposit, less an administrative fee, shall be applied to the judgment, and the balance of the judgment may be enforced and collected in the same manner as a civil judgment.

If I fail to appear as required, or violate any condition of my release from custody, the release may be revoked and a warrant for my arrest may be issued immediately. I agree that, as conditions for my release from custody, I will:

(a) inform my attorney and the court of any change in address or employment within 72 hours of such change;

(b) personally appear in this cause in any Court in Wayne County at which my appearance is required by the Court. Notice by the court to my attorney of record shall constitute notice to me;

(c) comply with all other conditions of release as ordered by the Court.

When the conditions of the bond have been performed, unless the Court orders otherwise, the Clerk shall retain those fees required by the Court and return the balance of the cash deposit to the undersigned defendant. However, if judgment for fees, fines, costs, restitution or any other obligations is ordered by the court, the remaining cash bond shall be first applied by the Clerk to the payment of the above judgment, upon court order.

I affirm under the pains and penalties that the foregoing information is true and correct.

_____

Defendant's Signature

_____

Printed Name of Defendant

_____

Defendant's Address

Dated: _____

I have read and understand this agreement. I acknowledge that any monies provided by me to the defendant belong to the defendant and shall be applied as set forth above.

_____

Signature of Person Providing Cash Funds to Defendant

_____

Printed Name of Person Providing Cash Funds to Defendant

_____

Address Person Providing Cash Funds to Defendant

Dated: _____

WAYNE COUNTY RULES OF FAMILY LAW

Adopted Effective October 30, 1997

Amended effective January 1, 2008

Including Amendments Received Through November 1, 2013

Research Notes

Annotations to the Wayne County Rules of Family Law are available in West's Annotated Indiana Code, *Title 34 Appendix.*

These rules may be searched electronically on Westlaw *in the* IN-RULES *database; updates to these rules may be found on Westlaw in* IN-RULESUPDATES. *For search tips and a summary of database content, consult the Westlaw Scope Screens for each database.*

LR89–FL00 Rule 001. SCOPE AND TITLE

A. Scope. These Rules shall govern the procedure and practice of all family law and domestic relations matters in the Wayne Circuit and Superior courts unless otherwise provided by law or rules of the Supreme Court of Indiana. These Rules are in addition to and are not intended to replace the Wayne County Local Civil Rules of Court. In the event of a conflict in a family law or domestic relations matter, the Wayne County Family Law Rules shall apply.

B. Title. These Rules shall be known as the Wayne County Rules of Family Law and shall be cited as LR89–FL00–1, et. seq.

Adopted effective Oct. 30, 1997; amended effective Jan. 1, 2008.

LR89–FL00 Rule 002. ADMINISTRATIVE PROCEDURES

A. Advice of Time Required. Parties shall advise the Court in the text of any preliminary or contempt petition if the matter cannot be heard on the regularly scheduled docket and shall provide an estimate of the time required in the event that more than fifteen minutes is necessary.

B. Summary Hearing. All issues and evidence relevant to a preliminary hearing may be presented in summary fashion by each party, or by counsel, if represented. Summary provisional hearings are set in fifteen minute intervals.

C. Copies of Decree Required. When submitting a Final Decree and Property Settlement, the parties shall submit sufficient copies of each for the Court to retain an original and copy of each and provide copies to all counsel of record.

D. Bench Warrant. In order to obtain a bench warrant from the Court, a party must have personal service on the adverse party and complete a bench warrant on copy service with sworn testimony confirming actual notice to the adverse party.

E. Summons and Notice. In all relevant family law matters, the petitioner shall use the form of Summons and Notice set forth in Appendix A.

F. Notifications. In all relevant family law matters, an instruction sheet on *Parenting Together to Keep Kids First* and a cooperation notice sheet regarding cooperation in family law cases are included with the Summons and Notice set forth in Appendix A and provided to *pro se* filers. The green notice sheet is set forth in Appendix D.

Adopted effective Oct. 30, 1997. Amended effective Jan. 1, 2008; Jan. 1, 2011; Jan. 1, 2013.

LR89–FL00 Rule 003. SPECIFIC DISCLOSURE REQUIREMENTS

Prior to any preliminary hearing or within thirty days after service of any petition seeking relief in any family law matter, whichever shall first occur, each party shall provide the Court and the opposing party with written notice of any other pending legal proceeding in which such person is a party wherein the other pending legal proceeding involves an issue or allegation of domestic violence, spousal abuse, child abuse, protective order, restraining order, Child(ren) in Need of Services, Termination of Parent–Child Relationship, Juvenile Delinquency, or any criminal charges. The written notice should include the cause number of the legal proceeding, identification and location of the Court, names of the parties involved, and a brief summary of the nature of the legal proceeding.

Adopted effective Oct. 30, 1997; amended effective Jan. 1, 2008.

LR89–FL00 Rule 004. COOPERATION IN FAMILY CASES

A. Liberal Construction and Application.

1. The Courts of Wayne County are committed to a cooperative model for the handling of family cases by parents, attorneys, and judges. This Rule will be liberally construed and applied to serve the healthy and child-sensitive functioning of families.

2. "Family cases" are defined as all marital dissolution or separation, paternity, and guardianship.

3. The adoption of this Rule is not intended to affect lawyers' duty to act with reasonable diligence and promptness in representing a client. See Indiana Rule of Professional Conduct 1.3 and its commentary.

B. Case Captioning.

1. Parties in marital dissolution and separation and paternity cases shall not be captioned or designated as "petitioner," "respondent," "plaintiff," or "defendant."

2. In marital dissolution and separation cases where the parties have one or more children under the age of nineteen on the date of the initial filing, all pleadings shall be captioned, "In Re The Marriage of _____, Father [or Mother], and _____, Mother [or Father]." The party filing the initial petition shall be named first.

3. In marital dissolution and separation cases without children under the age of nineteen of the initial filing, all pleadings shall be captioned, "In Re The Marriage of _____, Wife [or Husband], and _____, Husband [or Wife]." The party

filing the initial petition shall be named first. Following dissolution, parties without children shall be captioned and designated "former husband" and "former wife."

4. Parties in paternity cases shall be captioned and designated as "mother," "putative father," and "father."

C. Duties of Attorneys and Parties in Family Cases.

1. Attorneys and parties in family cases shall be responsible to act with the Courts as co-problem solvers, not mere problem reporters.

2. The Courts expect all parties and attorneys to consistently observe:

    a. personal responsibility by acting on one's own opportunities to solve problems and improve circumstances rather than merely reporting on the alleged fault in others,

    b. cooperation by sensibly defining and pursuing the best interests of all family members,

    c. courtesy by constant observance of respectful language and behavior, and

    d. focused attention on children's needs including an awareness that parent conflict is gravely dangerous to children.

3. Attorneys appearing in family cases shall (a) furnish their family clients with a copy of this Rule and (b) assist them in fully understanding and observing its provisions.

D. Website Work.

1. In marital dissolution and separation cases, parents with one or more children under the age of twenty-one on the date of their initial petition shall be ordered to complete the work on www.UpToParents.org and take their completed work to any case-related appointment, whether it be a parenting class, attorney conference, court, mediation, etc. Parents open to the possibility of reconciliation may substitute the work from www.WhileWeHeal.org.

2. In paternity cases, parents shall be ordered to complete the work on www.ProudToParent.org and take their completed work to any case-related appointment, whether it be a parenting class, attorney conference, court, mediation, etc.

3. Parents shall merge their chosen Commitments from their website work into a set of Agreed Commitments, review those Agreed Commitments, and take copies of them to any hearing or other case-related appointment.

4. The website work and class shall be completed promptly but within forty-five days of the filing of the Petition, unless leave of court is granted.

5. The Agreed Commitments and other result generated as a result of the website work shall be inadmissible and unenforceable in the event litigation is required. The purpose of the website work

is to generate a culture of co-parenting for the long-term benefit of families.

6. The Court for good cause shown may order a waiver of completion of the website work and class.

E. Protocols for Motions and Hearings Involving Minor Children and Cooperation Update.

1. In matters involving minor children, parties and counsel shall make every reasonable effort to resolve problems by reaching agreements that serve the best interests of all family members and should appear in court on contested matters only in rare circumstances after every reasonable effort to resolve problems has been made.

2. In matters already pending before the Court, except in instances where it would be dangerous or otherwise unreasonable to do so, counsel and parties without counsel shall use good-faith personal or telephonic consultation to resolve any issue before seeking relief from a court. In that mandatory consultation, counsel shall:

a. attempt to resolve the matter at issue;

b. discuss, and make a list of, the resources they believe the parents could use to resolve current and future issues and to build cooperation (separate lists shall be made if a joint list is not agreed on);

c. if previously ordered by the Court, confirm that the parents (i) have completed the website work referred to in paragraph D, (ii) have merged their chosen Commitments into a set of Agreed Commitments, and (iii) will review and bring their Agreed Commitments and any other website work to any upcoming case-related appointment;

d. confirm the date each parent completed the assigned parenting class; and

e. discuss what the Court can do to assit[1] the parents in reaching further agreements.

3. All motions filed by counsel and parties without counsel shall include a Cooperation Update separate and apart from the underlying motion and in the form as prescribed by Appendix C of these Rules, confirming compliance with each of the requirements in paragraph E(2), including the date of each parent's attendance at the required parenting class.

4. To the extent that the filing date of a particular motion triggers certain rights and obligations, strict compliance with subsection E(2) may be excepted so long as the moving party indicates that a Cooperation Update is not included in said motion due to the importance of the filing date. In such cases, the moving party shall be required to comply with subsection E(2) and file a Cooperation Update within seven days of the date of filing.

5. Failure to comply with this section may result in the denial of relief or hearing until compliance is ensured.

6. Parents shall review and bring to every hearing a copy of their Agreed Commitments and current Parenting Planning Worksheet.

F. Status Conferences.

1. A status conference may be requested at any time, and one will ordinarily be scheduled by the Court for approximately sixty days after the filing of the initial petition for dissolution, for separation, for the establishment of paternity, and for modification, approximately sixty days after the finding of paternity. The moving party shall provide with his/her initial pleading a proposed Notice of Status Conference, leaving the date and time blank.

2. Any request for a status conference which is not the automatic sixty-day conference shall comply with subsection E(2) and contain a Cooperation Update. Said request shall further indicate the moving party's proposed agenda for such status conference.

3. The chief purposes of status conferences will be (a) for attorneys (and parties without attorneys) to report on progress in reducing conflict, building cooperation, preserving family relationships, and responding to the needs of the children, (b) for families, where required, to be referred for any necessary help, and (c) for attorneys (and parties without attorneys) to report on discovery issues.

4. Parties or their attorneys shall consult in advance of the status conference and present suggestions for the future course of the case that would serve the best interests of all family members.

5. Additional status conferences should be requested whenever parties or counsel believe they would be helpful in reducing conflict, building cooperation, preserving relationships, or protecting children.

G. Additional Assistance to Families.

1. At any time parties need resources to reduce conflict, build cooperation, preserve family relationships, or respond to the needs of their children, they and their attorneys, if any, should make arrangements to find the resources that could help them.

2. If parents nevertheless continue to have conflict and appear in court without an agreement about the resources they will use, the Court may select the resources the parents will be ordered to use.

H. Requests for Trial Settings.

1. Trial settings must be requested in writing in compliance with Wayne County Rule of Civil Procedure LR89–TR00–009. In addition to complying with the requirements of Wayne County Rule of Civil Procedure LR89–TR00–009, the trial setting request must give a detailed account of (i) all unresolved issues and (ii) what problem-solving resources (including counseling and mediation) the parties have used to reach cooperative agreements.

Failure to comply with this section may result in the denial of a trial setting.

I. Enforcement.

1. This Rule and the enforcement thereof appear contradictory. However, the benefits of the overall concepts contained in this Rule, as well as the recognized and hoped long-term advantages of implementing such a process, render its enforcement of vital importance, as families in conflict do not always fit well into the mold of the traditional adversary system. Nevertheless, it must be recognized that an attempt to reshape the model within which family law cases have traditionally occurred will require, on occasion, the use of those enforcement mechanisms which do not fall within a model of cooperation.

2. Courts may use, at their discretion, the variety of enforcement mechanisms available, including but not limited to the award of attorney's fees and sanctions, available to them in the traditional system.

J. Effective Date.

1. This Rule shall apply to all filings, in both new and pending cases, as of the effective date of the entirety of these Rules.

Amended effective Jan. 1, 2008; July 31, 2009, effective Jan. 1, 2010; Jan. 1, 2011; Jan. 1, 2013.

Commentary

Family cases of all sorts (see paragraph (A)(2)) must be handled in ways that reduce conflict, build cooperation between parents, and protect children. The Courts of Wayne County will expect parties and attorneys to give consistent attention to those ends and will liberally construe and apply this Rule to serve those ends.

This Rule provides nine measures to promote the cooperation necessary to serve the best interests of all family members involved in family cases.

Cases will be captioned and parties will be designated in ways that better convey everyone's duty of cooperation. Parents will be designated as "mother" and "father" (or in some paternity cases as "putative father"), never as "petitioner" or "respondent." See paragraph B.

Attorneys and parties will be expected to consistently observe personal responsibility, cooperation, courtesy, and focused attention on children's needs. See paragraph C.

Parties shall be referred for website work. See paragraph D.

In matters involving minor children, before filing motions or pleadings, attorneys are required to have a personal consultation on five matters: (a) an attempt to resolve by agreement the matter at issue; (b) a discussion of the resources parents could use to resolve current and future issues; (c) if ordered, confirmation that the parents have completed, and will bring to upcoming case-related appointments, their Agreed Commitments from their website work; and (d) confirmation of the

parents' attendance at the parenting class. See paragraph E.

Counsel shall including a Cooperation Update on those five matters in their pleadings. See paragraph E.

Parties must bring their Agreed Commitments and Parenting Plan Worksheet to all case-related appointments. See paragraph E.

The Courts will hold status conferences to hear counsel's suggestions for helping families cooperate and function better. Parties without attorneys will also participate in status conferences. See paragraph F.

Requests for trial settings must be in writing and substantially comply with Wayne County Local Rule of Civil Procedure LR89–TR00–009. In addition to the requirements of said rule, the request must account for past and future problem-solving alternatives to trial.

LR89–FL00 Rule 005. PROVISIONAL HEARINGS

A. In Non–Dissolution of Marriage Cases. The Court shall have the discretion to hold provisional hearings in non-dissolution of marriage cases and may grant relief where appropriate.

B. Child Support Worksheet. All Motions for Provisional Order seeking child support or a modification thereof shall be accompanied by a proposed Child Support Obligation Worksheet.

C. Cooperation. In provisional motions which involve minor children accompanying an initiating pleading, strict compliance with LR89–FL00–4 is not required; however, the moving party shall make reasonable efforts at resolving all provisional issues with the non-moving party, whether or not represented by Counsel, after service of said initiating pleading and prior to the scheduled hearing.

D. Time Allotted and Nature of Proceedings. Provisional hearings shall be held in summary fashion and shall be scheduled in fifteen-minute increments, unless either party has indicated in his/her Motion for Provisional Hearing or Response thereto that additional time is required. Such indication that additional time is required further constitutes a waiver of the three-week scheduling requirement. Said proceedings shall be held in court chambers off the record. Either party may request in his/her Motion for Provisional Order that the proceedings be held on the record, which further constitutes a waiver of the three-week scheduling requirement. The Court shall have the discretion to grant or deny in whole or in part a request for an on-the-record evidentiary hearing exceeding fifteen minutes in length.

E. Attorney's Fees. Provisional attorney fees may be awarded based on the following factors:

1. The number and the complexity of the issues (e.g. custody dispute, complex asset valuation).

2. The nature and extent of discovery.

3. The time reasonably necessary for the preparation for or the conduct of contested preliminary matters or final hearings.

4. Other matters requiring substantial expenditure of attorneys' time.

5. The attorney's hourly rate.

6. The amount counsel has received from all sources.

7. The ability of the opposing party to pay the requested fees and the disparity of income between the parties.

F. Preliminary Appraisal, Evaluator, and Accountant Fees. Appraisal, evaluator, or accounting fees may be allocated based on the following factors:

1. Itemized list of property to be appraised or valued (e.g., Defined benefit pension, business interests, business real estate, furnishings, vehicles, etc.).

2. An estimate of the cost of the appraisals and the basis therefore.

3. The amount of a retainer required and the reason an expert is necessary.

4. Whether the parties agree to a specific appraiser, evaluator, or accountant.

G. Provisional Child Support Orders. There is hereby created a rebuttable presumption that provisional child support orders shall be made retroactive to the first Friday following the date of filing of a written request for a provisional child support order. Such presumption may be rebutted upon a showing that such retroactivity is inappropriate under the facts of a particular case.

H. Exchange of Necessary Documentation. At least seven days before the scheduled provisional hearing, the parties shall exchange documentation of all year-to-date income (usually satisfied by the party's three most recent paystubs), whether there are subsequently born children, documentation of an order or duty of support for prior born children, documentation of maintenance paid, documentation of work-related child care expenses, documentation of the weekly cost of health insurance for the minor children, and a proposed child support obligation worksheet.

Amended effective Jan. 1, 2008; amended July 31, 2009, effective Jan. 1, 2010; Jan. 1, 2011.

LR89–FL00 Rule 006. ORDERS EXCLUDING A SPOUSE FROM THE RESIDENCE

A. Eviction Without Notice. A Restraining Order without notice pursuant to Ind. Trial Rule 65 which would evict a spouse from the marital residence may be issued only upon the following bases:

1. Strict compliance with Ind. Trial Rule 65; and

2. There are alleged specific facts indicating more than a generalized fear of an adverse action; and

3. There is independent, corroborated evidence of actual or threatened physical abuse sufficient to find a risk of imminent danger; and

4. The moving party is physically available to testify unless there is a showing of exceptional circumstances precluding his or her availability; and

5. The moving party certifies to the Court the reasons supporting the claim why notice cannot be given.

In addition to the foregoing criteria, the Court may consider any other relevant social or economic factors including whether either party has a reasonable alternative residence pending hearing on the provisional motion(s). In those circumstances where the Court allows a party to be heard ex parte on the record and finds an emergency exists justifying issuance of an eviction order, the cause shall heard within ten days with notice to all parties. Such an order shall, by its own terms, terminate effective the date and time of the hearing, unless extended by the Court after hearing evidence thereon. Furthermore, such an order shall terminate at the expiration of ten days from the date of said order if no hearing is held prior thereto.

B. Order. If an Order granting exclusive possession of the marital residence to one spouse is entered by the Court without hearing under this Rule, such Order shall contain the following language: "The _____ is hereby restrained from entering marital residence located at _____ and the Wayne County Sheriff's Department, Richmond Police Department, or other appropriate law enforcement agency shall use all reasonable force, including arrest, to remove a party from the premises upon presentation of such an Order."

C. Extraordinary Remedy. Any orders issued ex parte hereunder shall be considered an extraordinary remedy and should be considered only in emergency circumstances.

Adopted effective Oct. 30, 1997; amended effective Jan. 1, 2008.

LR89–FL00 Rule 007. FINANCIAL DECLARATION FORM

A. Requirement. In all relevant family law matters, including dissolution of marriage, separations, paternity, post-decree and support proceedings, each party shall prepare and exchange, respectively, within forty-five days of the initial filing of the action or within thirty days of the filing of any post-decree matters, a Financial Declaration Form (see Appendix B). These time limits may be extended or shortened by court order for good cause shown. With respect to post-decree modification actions, only Page 1 need be completed.

B. Exceptions. The Financial Declaration Form need not be exchanged if:

1. the parties agree in writing to waive exchange;

2. the parties have executed a written agreement which settles all financial issues;

3. the proceeding is one in which the service is by publication and there is no response;

4. the proceeding is post-decree and concerns issues without financial implications; provided, however, when the proceeding is a post-decree modification which necessarily implicates child support, this Rule shall still apply; or

5. the Court otherwise waives such requirement.

C. Admissibility. Subject to specific evidentiary challenges, the Financial Declaration Form shall be admissible into evidence.

D. Supporting Documents. For the purpose of providing a full and complete verification of assets, liabilities and values, each party shall attach to the Financial Declaration Form all information reasonably required and reasonably available. This shall include recent bills, wage and tax records, bank records, pension and retirement account information, and mortgage account records. The term "reasonably available" means that material which may be obtained by letter accompanied with an authorization, but such term does not mean material that must be subpoenaed or is in the possession of the other party. Appraisals of real estate or personal property, or pension valuations are not required. However, once an appraisal or valuation is obtained it must be exchanged. Further, the Court may direct than an appraisal or valuation be obtained, just as it may designate the appraiser or valuator. The Court may require either party to supplement the Financial Declaration Form with appraisals, bank records, and other evidence to support the values set forth in the Form.

E. Financial Declaration—Mandatory Discovery. The exchange of Financial Declaration Forms constitutes mandatory discovery. However, Indiana Trial Rule 37 sanctions do not automatically apply. In the event that a party does not timely submit his or her fully completed Financial Declaration Form and reasonable efforts have been made to informally resolve any such dispute, the party seeking compliance may file a Motion to Compel and [if desired] for Sanctions. If such Motion is granted, the Order shall set a deadline for compliance and schedule a hearing on potential sanctions. At said hearing, the Court may take into consideration the noncompliant party's compliance with the Order to Compel in determining whether to award sanctions to the moving party. Additionally, pursuant to Indiana Trial Rule 26(E)(2) and (3), the Financial Declaration Form shall be supplemented if information changes or is added or if additional material becomes available. Any additional discovery such as Requests For Production, Interrog-

atories, or Depositions of the parties to the action shall not commence until the Financial Declaration Forms has been exchanged; provided, however, that if a party's noncompliance has resulted in the filing of a Motion to Compel, the moving party may move forward with additional discovery reasonably necessary to obtain the information sought. Any further discovery shall not seek to obtain information already obtained by the Financial Declaration Form.

F. Privacy—Sealing Of Financial Declaration Form. Whenever the interest of privacy so requires, the Court may, upon proper Motion, direct that the Financial Declaration Form(s) be sealed until further order of the court. However, such request(s) shall not be made as a matter of course. When ordered sealed, the Court Reporter shall place the Financial Declaration Form(s) in a flat manner in an envelope of sufficient size, seal the envelope, and affix a copy of the Order directing that the Financial Declaration Form(s) be placed under seal. Financial Declaration Form(s) may be withdrawn at the conclusion of the case on such terms as the Court may allow.

G. Clerk To Provide Notice Upon Filing. Upon the pro se filing of any family law matter referred to in LR89–FL00–7(A), the Clerk shall provide to the moving party upon filing a Notice of the requirement of this Rule. Such Notice shall be in a form substantially as follows: "You are advised that each party is required to provide to the other party or his or her legal counsel, if applicable, a fully completed Financial Declaration Form with all required attachments within forty-five days of the filing of such petition/motion or, in the case of a post-decree petition/motion, within thirty days. You are further advised that copies of the Financial Declaration form may be obtained at the Clerk's Office, located on the Second Floor of the Wayne County Courthouse, 301 East Main Street, Richmond, Indiana. They may also be found online at http://www.in.gov/judiciary/localrul es/current/wayne-circuit-superior-(family)–032305.pdf. Failure to timely provide a fully completed Financial Declaration Form with all required attachments may be result in sanctions being entered against the party failing to comply with this Rule."

Adopted effective Oct. 30, 1997; amended effective Jan. 1, 2008.

LR89–FL00 Rule 008.   PARENTING CLASS

A. Attendance at Class. Before final hearing is scheduled on a petition for Dissolution of Marriage, Petition for Legal Separation, or Petition to Establish Paternity in which the parties have minor children, each party must attend not less than one parenting class session as designated by the Wayne County Circuit and Superior Courts. The Wayne County Clerk of Courts shall distribute an informational flyer, provided to it by the judges, which discloses the name and location of the class, as well as the telephone number to call to schedule the class. Said flyer shall also provide for the cost and any prerequisite rules made by the moderator of such class.

B. Certificate. The moderator of each session will provide each attendee with a certificate of attendance, unless waived, which must be filed with the Court's Clerk prior to the Court's granting the Petition for Dissolution of Marriage or Petition for Legal Separation.

C. Payment. Each party is responsible for payment of the cost of that party's participation.

D. Waiver. In those limited circumstances where it is apparent that a party's compliance with this rule cannot be compelled or is otherwise unnecessary, upon written motion, the Court may grant a waiver of its application.

E. Motion to Compel Attendance. If one party has failed to attend the class as required, the complying party may file a Motion to Compel Attendance with the Court requesting that the Court enter an Order requiring the opposing party to attend the class by a date certain or be subject to contempt of Court. Appropriate sanctions may include, but shall not be limited to, attorney's fees, incarceration, or a finding that parenting time by said party might endanger the child(ren)'s physical health or significantly impair the child(ren)'s emotional development justifying a restriction on parenting time in accordance with Ind. Code 31–17–4–1 or Ind. Code 31–14–14–1.

Adopted effective Oct. 30, 1997. Amended effective Jan. 1, 2008; amended July 31, 2009, effective Jan. 1, 2010; Jan. 1, 2011.

LR89–FL00 Rule 009. MEDIATION

No final hearing regarding dissolution of marriage, modification, custody, child support, or parenting time which is anticipated to take more than thirty minutes of court time shall be set without the parties having first submitted a Notice to the Court (which may be incorporated in the Trial Readiness Certificate required under LR89–TR00–009) that they have engaged in mediation, either formal or informal, within the last six months regarding the matters to be set for hearing. "Formal mediation" is such mediation as contemplated by the Rules of Alternative Dispute Resolution. "Informal mediation" is intended to include any face-to-face meeting between the parties, whether such meeting includes attorneys only or the involvement of the parties who may or may not be separated, depending on the circumstances. In the event the parties cannot agree as to a location for informal mediation, such informal mediation shall be conducted in Wayne County, Indiana. The Court shall have the discretion to order parties to formal mediation even if they have certified to the Court that informal mediation was unsuccessful.

Amended effective Jan. 1, 2008; Jan. 1, 2013.

LR89–FL00 Rule 010. PARENTING TIME ORDERS

The phrase "reasonable parenting time," if not specifically defined in the Court's order, is defined as the parenting time schedule outlined in the Indiana Parenting Time Guidelines. Parenting time orders may be informally adjusted by agreement of the parties without Court order to accommodate the needs of the family; however, intended long-term formal modifications should, to protect all parties, be reduced to writing and submitted to the Court by Petition or Stipulation and approved by the Court to become binding.

Amended effective Jan. 1, 2008.

LR89–FL00 Rule 011. CHILD CUSTODY AND PARENTING TIME: REFERRALS FOR INVESTIGATION AND REPORT

A. Motion. On motion of either party with the approval of the Court, or on the Court's own motion, contested matters involving child custody and parenting time may be referred to appropriate sources for investigation and report to the Court.

B. Admissibility. Subject to the provisions of Ind. Code § 31–17–2–12, all custodial evaluator reports or guardian ad litem reports which are court-ordered regarding custody and/or parenting time shall be admissible into evidence on the motion of either party without the evaluator needing to be present at the hearing. No part of this Rule is intended to supplant the right of either party to compel the attendance of the evaluator or other witnesses as set out in Ind. Trial Rule 45.

C. Physical and Mental Examination. In all contested family law matters involving child custody or visitation, the provision of Ind. Trial Rule 35 providing for the physical or mental examinations by a physician shall be extended to include examination and evaluations by a psychologist, therapist or other qualified evaluator upon order of the Court.

D. Parenting Coordinators. At the discretion of the Court and subject to availability, the Court may appoint parenting coordinators when appropriate.

E. Fees. There shall be a rebuttable presumption that the parties shall equally share the cost of any such referral ordered herein. Factors the Court may consider to deviate from an equal split of said fees include but are not limited to income disparity greater than 65%–35%, whether the referral provided the Court with information beneficial to the family as a whole, and whether the referral provided information confirming the moving party's position.

F. Termination of Guardian Ad Litem Appointment. Upon the entry of final Decree of Dissolution of Marriage, Legal Separation, Paternity, or Order of permanent modification of any custody, parenting time, and/or child support Order, the appointment of the Guardian Ad Litem shall be deemed terminated unless otherwise ordered by the Court.

Adopted effective Oct. 30, 1997; amended effective Jan. 1, 2008.

LR89–FL00 Rule 012. REQUIREMENTS BEFORE CUSTODIAL EVALUATION (NOT APPLICABLE FOR APPOINTMENT OF GUARDIAN AD LITEM)

All requests for custody evaluations must be (1) in writing, (2) certify that both parties and their counsel, if any, have engaged in at least one good faith attempt to resolve the issues through the use of a settlement conference or mediation.

The court will not grant a request for or otherwise order a custody evaluation except following a Status Conference in the presence of both parties and their attorneys, if any, during which the court has been satisfied that:

A. both parties have completed the mandatory website work;

B. both parents have completed any required co-parenting class;

C. both parties have exchanged Parenting Plan Proposals;

D. both parties and their attorneys, if any, have engaged in at least one good faith attempt to resolve the issues through the use of a settlement conference or consultation; and

E. the court has considered and reviewed with both parties and their attorneys, if any, the use of other resources.

> *Commentary: Custody evaluations are sometimes divisive and produce less, rather than more, cooperation between parents. As a result, custody evaluations will be reserved for cases where one or both parents lack the capacity to safely resolve the issues they face. No custody evaluation will be ordered or conducted unless reasonable cooperative measures have been attempted, such as co-parenting education, counseling, and mediation.*

Adopted effective Oct. 30, 1997; amended effective Jan. 1, 2008; Jan. 1, 2011.

LR89–FL00 Rule 013. CONTACT WITH CUSTODIAL EVALUATORS AND GUARDIANS AD LITEM/COURT APPOINTED SPECIAL ADVOCATES

A. **Contact with Custodial Evaluators.** In the event a custodial evaluation is ordered by the Court, the Court shall direct the parties to contact the custodial evaluator to arrange for an appointment with the custodial evaluator. Other than making contact with the office of the custodial evaluator to arrange for the client's appointment with the custodial evaluator, counsel shall not initiate contact or otherwise communicate with the custodial evaluator until the custodial evaluator's report has been issued. Prohibited contact or communication shall include the sending of

school records, medical records, affidavits, reports, or any other type of written record by the attorney to the custodial evaluator. Information which may be requested by the custodial evaluator shall be delivered or otherwise presented to the evaluator by the party and not counsel. In the event the custodial evaluator should contact counsel before the evaluator's report has been issued, such fact should be promptly conveyed to opposing counsel indicating the specific dialogue between counsel and the custodial evaluator. Following the issuance of the evaluator's report, the evaluator shall be deemed a witness and counsel shall be permitted ex parte communication with the evaluator at counsel's/client's expense.

Whenever a Court orders a custodial evaluation the Court shall attach a copy of this Rule to its order and shall have the Clerk distribute such order and attached Rule to the designated custodial evaluator.

B. **Contact with Guardians Ad Litem/Court Appointed Special Advocates.** In the event a Guardian Ad Litem/Court Appointed Special Advocate is appointed by the Court, the parties' attorneys shall not communicate with said Guardian Ad Litem/Court Appointed Special Advocate unless said communication includes all other parties to the cause of action. In the event such inclusion is not feasible, the fact that there was communication and the nature thereof shall be disclosed to all other parties within seven days of such communication.

Amended effective Jan. 1, 2008; Jan. 1, 2011.

LR89–FL00 Rule 014. CHILD SUPPORT GUIDELINES

A. **Worksheet Required.** In all proceedings involving child support, each party shall file with any settlement, or submit to the Court at any hearing or trial, an Indiana Child Support Obligation Worksheet(s)—one or more depending upon the facts. In any request for provisional order that contemplates any order for child support, a Child Support Obligation Worksheet—with supporting documentation such as a recent pay stub and/or an explanation in the body of the Motion as to how the figures were computed—shall be attached to either the Motion for Provisional Order or Affidavit in Support. A response Child Support Obligation Worksheet—with supporting documentation such as a recent pay stub and/or an explanation in the body of the Motion as to how the figures were computed—shall be provided to the other party or to opposing counsel, as the case may be, at least forty-eight hours prior to the provisional hearing, unless reasonable circumstances prevent doing so, and then such Child Support Obligation Worksheet shall be provided to the other party or to opposing counsel at the earliest opportunity. Child Support Obligation Worksheets shall be promptly supplemented if changes occur prior to trial. Child Support Obligation Worksheets intended to be introduced at trial or final hearing shall be exchanged by the parties or counsel, along with supporting documentation, at least seven days prior to trial.

B. Support Settlement Agreements. If an agreement concerning support provides any deviation from the Guidelines, the parties shall present to the Court a written explanation, with supporting documentation, justifying the deviation. The proposed Order shall specifically state that the Court is deviating from the Child Support Guidelines and set forth the reasons for such deviation.

C. Required Language. All Orders requiring the payment of child support shall include the following language:

"In the event that an Income Withholding Order is in place and has been activated, child support shall be paid to the State Central Unit and sent to: State Central Collection Unit, Post Office Box 6219, Indianapolis, Indiana 46206–6219. Payment shall include the Cause Number of this case which is _____, the ISETS number which is _____, and the last four digits of the Payor's social security number. In the event that an Income Withholding Order is not in place or has not been activated and you are paying child support directly, your child support payment shall be paid in cash or by way of a Money Order or Certified Check to the Clerk of the Court. Please note on your Money Order or Certified Check the Cause Number of this case which is _____, the ISETS number which is _____, and the last four digits of the Payor's social security number. You should retain a copy of the Money Order or Certified Check for your records as proof of payment. Any payments for support and/or arrears made in a manner which does not conform to this paragraph shall be deemed gifts and shall not be credited toward the satisfaction of any obligation for current support and/or arrears."

D. Income Withholding Order Required. In all proceedings involving child support, an Income Withholding Order shall be submitted with any Settlement Agreement or Final Decree as may be required by statute or the parties shall:

1. Submit a written agreement providing for an alternative child support arrangement; or,

2. Provide within the proposed Decree that "the Court determines that good cause exists not to require immediate income withholding" and stating the specific reasons therefore.

Amended effective Jan. 1, 2008; Jan. 1, 2011.

LR89–FL00 Rule 015. MODIFICATION OF POST–DECREE CHILD SUPPORT ORDERS

There is hereby created a rebuttable presumption that modification of post-decree child support orders shall be made retroactive to sixty days following the filing of the petition for modification.

In cases where a change of child custody is involved, there shall be a rebuttable presumption that modification of post-decree child support orders shall be made retroactive to the date of filing of the petition for modification or the date of the de facto change in custody, whichever is later.

Amended effective Jan. 1, 2008; Jan. 1, 2011.

LR89–FL00 Rule 016. AGREED ENTRIES

An agreed entry shall not be approved by the Court without a Petition or Stipulation having first been filed. A Petition or Stipulation for Agreed Entry shall specifically set forth the basis and reasons for such Petition or Stipulation which meets the statutory requirements for the same.

Amended effective Jan. 1, 2011.

LR89–FL00 Rule 017. EXHIBITS

In all family law cases, trial exhibits for the originally initiating party shall be marked as numbers and trial exhibits for the originally responding party shall be marked as letters.

Amended effective Jan. 1, 2011.

LR89–FL00 Rule 018. FEES

A. Attorney Fees. Attorney fees may be awarded based on evidence presented by way of Affidavit (or oral testimony if the Court shall allow) at the final or other hearing. The Affidavit shall include an itemized statement of the requested fee. Affidavits shall be admissible into evidence by the Court. The following factors may be considered and should be included in any Affidavit submitted to the Court:

1. The number and the complexity of the issues (e.g. custody dispute, complex asset valuation.

2. The nature and extent of discovery and the parties' cooperation therewith (or lack thereof).

3. The time reasonably necessary for the preparation for or the conduct of contested preliminary matters or final hearings.

4. The extent to which either party encouraged or discouraged settlement without protracted litigation.

5. Other matters requiring substantial expenditure of attorney's time.

6. The attorney's hourly rate.

7. The amount counsel has received from all sources.

8. The ability of the opposing party to pay the requested fees and the disparity of income between the parties.

The Court shall have the discretion to award no, partial, or full attorney's fees.

B. Contempt Citation Attorney Fees. There shall be a rebuttable presumption that attorney fees will be awarded to the prevailing party in all matters involving a contempt citation.

Amended effective Jan. 1, 2011.

LR89–FL00 Rule 019. TERMINATION OF REPRESENTATIVE CAPACITY

A. Representative Capacity Terminated. Upon the entry of final Decree of Dissolution of Marriage, Legal Separation, Paternity, or Order of permanent modification of any custody, parenting time and/or child support Order, the representative capacity of all attorneys appearing on behalf of any party shall be deemed terminated upon:

1. An order of withdrawal granted pursuant to local rule;

2. The expiration of time within which an appeal of such Order may be preserved or perfected pursuant to the Indiana Rules of Trial Procedure and/or the Indiana Rules of Appellate Procedure; or

3. The conclusion of any appeal of such Order commenced pursuant to Indiana Rules of Trial Procedure and/or the Indiana Rules of Appellate Procedure.

The failure of the Clerk of Wayne County to remove the appearance of such attorney from the Chronological Case Summary upon the occurrence of one of the above shall not affect the application of this Rule.

B. Post–Decree Service. The service of any post-decree pleadings upon any party not represented by counsel pursuant to paragraph A above, despite the possible mistaken continued appearance of said attorney on the Chronological Case Summary, shall be made upon that person pursuant to Indiana Rules of Trial Procedure.

C. Courtesy Copy. Any copy served upon original counsel will be deemed to be a matter of professional courtesy only; however, such professional courtesy is encouraged, and if a courtesy copy of such petition is sent to a representative, whether terminated or not, such shall be shown on a certificate of service.

D. Termination of Appointment of Guardian Ad Litem. Upon the entry of final Decree of Dissolution of Marriage, Legal Separation, Paternity, or Order of permanent modification of any custody, parenting time and/or child support Order, the appointment of the Guardian Ad Litem shall be deemed terminated. The Guardian Ad Litem shall be under no continuing obligation to continue work on the matter unless otherwise ordered by the Court or reappointed in later proceedings.

Adopted effective Jan. 1, 2011.

Appendix A. SUMMONS AND NOTICE

SUMMONS

IN THE WAYNE COUNTY CIRCUIT AND SUPERIOR COURTS

_____

Husband/Father

and   Cause No. _____

_____

Wife/Mother

        TO: _____

        Address: _____

        _____

    You are hereby notified that a proceeding for (Dissolution of Marriage) (Legal Separation) (Paternity) (Modification) has been initiated by (Husband/Father) (Wife/Mother) in the Court indicated above.

    You must complete the attached Financial Declaration Form and submit it to the other party within thirty days after receipt of this Summons.

    In any proceeding for Dissolution of Marriage with minor children, Legal Separation with minor children, or Paternity, you must register for one session of Helping Children Cope with Divorce within twenty days after receipt of this Summons. Failure to schedule and attend may result in sanctions. Information regarding said class is attached to this Summons.

    If this Summons is accompanied by an Order to Appear or Notice of Hearing, you must appear in Court on the date and time stated in the Order to Appear or Notice of Hearing. If you do not appear, evidence may be heard in your absence and a determination made by the Court. If a Temporary Restraining Order is attached, it is effective immediately upon your receipt or knowledge of the Order.

    If you wish to retain an attorney to represent you in this matter, it is advisable to do so before the date stated in the Order to Appear or Notice of Hearing. If you take no action in this case after receipt of this Summons, the Court can grant a (Dissolution of Marriage) (Legal Separation) (Decree of Paternity) or make a determination regarding any of the following: paternity, child custody, child support, maintenance, parenting time, real and/or personal property division, and any other distribution of assets and allocation of debts.

Dated: _____   _____

                                            Clerk, Wayne County

The following manner of service of summons is designated:

☐ Registered or Certified Mail
☐ Service on Individual
☐ Service at place of employment, to-wit: _____
☐ Private Service

_____   Address: _____

Party/Party's Attorney

                                          _____

                                          Telephone No. _____

Wayne County Circuit and Superior Courts
Wayne County Courthouse
301 East Main Street
Richmond, Indiana 47374
765.973.9220

SHERIFF'S RETURN OF SERVICE OF SUMMONS

I hereby certify that I have served this summons on the ___ day of _____, ___:

(1) By delivering a copy of the Summons and a copy of the Petition.

(2) By leaving a copy of the Summons and a copy of the Petition at the following address:

_____

which is the dwelling place or usual place of abode and by mailing a copy of said Summons to the above address.

(3) Other service or remarks: _____

_____

Sheriff

By: _____

Deputy

CLERK'S CERTIFICATE OF MAILING

I hereby certify that on the ___ day of _____, ___, I mailed a copy of this Summons and a copy of the Petition by _____ mail, requesting a return receipt, at the address furnished by the initiating party.

_____

Clerk, Wayne County

By: _____

Deputy

RETURN OF SERVICE OF SUMMONS BY MAIL

I hereby certify that the attached receipt was received by me showing that the Summons and a copy of the Petition was accepted by the party being served on the ___ day of _____, ___.

I hereby certify that the attached return receipt was received by me showing that the Summons and a copy of the Petition was returned not accepted on the ___ day of _____, ___.

I hereby certify that the attached return receipt was received by me showing that the Summons and a copy of the Petition was accepted by _____ on behalf of the party being served on the ___ day of _____, ___.

_____

Clerk, Wayne County

By: _____

Deputy

ACKNOWLEDGMENT

I hereby acknowledge that I have received this Summons and a copy of the Petition on the ___ day of _____, ___.

_____

Printed:

Appendix B. FINANCIAL DECLARATION FORM

STATE OF INDIANA—COUNTY OF WAYNE

_____	Cause No. _____
Father/Husband	Dated: _____
_____	FINANCIAL DECLARATION OF:
Mother/Wire	_____

HUSBAND/FATHER:	MOTHER/WIFE:
Name:	Name:
Address:	Address:
SSN:	SSN:
Occupation:	Occupation:
Employer:	Employer:
Date of Birth:	Date of Birth:
ATTORNEY FOR HUSBAND/FATHER:	ATTORNEY FOR WIFE/MOTHER:
Name/Atty ID:	Name/Atty ID:
Address:	Address:
Phone/Fax:	Phone/Fax:
E-mail:	E-mail:

Date of Marriage:
Date of Filing:
Children of this relationship:

Name	Date of Birth	SSN	Lives With

GROSS WEEKLY INCOME—ATTACH LAST THREE PAYROLL STUBS AND LAST THREE YEARS' TAX RETURNS	AMOUNTS
1. Gross Weekly SALARY, WAGES, and COMMISSIONS	
2. Gross Weekly—PENSION, RETIREMENT, SOCIAL SECURITY PAYMENTS	
3. Gross Weekly CHILD SUPPORT received from any prior marriage (not this marriage)	
4. Gross Weekly DIVIDENDS and INTEREST	
5. Gross Weekly RENTS/ROYALTIES less ordinary and necessary expenses (attach calculation)	
6. Gross Weekly BUSINESS/SELF–EMPLOYMENT INCOME less ordinary and necessary expenses (attach calculation)	
7. ALL OTHER SOURCES (Specify) *Includes: bonuses; alimony/maintenance received from prior marriages; capital gains; trust income; gifts; prizes; in-kind benefits from employment such as company car, free housing, reimbursed meals. DOES NOT INCLUDE government benefits.	
8. **TOTAL GROSS WEEKLY INCOME (Total of Lines 1 through 7)**	
9. Minus Weekly COURT ORDERED CHILD SUPPORT for prior children—amounts actually paid	
10. Minus Weekly LEGAL DUTY CHILD SUPPORT for prior children	
11. Minus Weekly HEALTH INSURANCE PREMIUMS for children of this marriage only	
12. Minus Weekly ALIMONY/SUPPORT/MAINTENANCE paid to prior spouses— amounts actually paid	
13. **WEEKLY AVAILABLE INCOME (Line 8 less Lines 9 through 12)**	
14. Weekly WORK RELATED CHILD CARE COSTS for custodial parent to work for children of this marriage only	
15. Weekly EXTRAORDINARY HEALTH CARE EXPENSES (children of this marriage only—uninsured only)	
16. Weekly EXTRAORDINARY EDUCATIONAL EXPENSES (children of this marriage only)	

Names and relationship of all members of household whose expenses are included:
STOP if this is a post-decree modification or paternity action.

MONTHLY EXPENSES AND DEDUCTIONS FROM INCOME

1. FEDERAL INCOME TAXES	
2. STATE INCOME TAXES	

3. LOCAL INCOME TAXES

4. SOCIAL SECURITY TAXES

5. MEDICARE TAXES

6. RETIREMENT/PENSION FUND (designate Mandatory/Optional)

7. RENT/MORTGAGE PAYMENTS (Residence)

8. RESIDENCE/PROPERTY TAXES/INSURANCE—If not included in mortgage
payment

9. MAINTENANCE ON RESIDENCE

10. FOOD/HOUSEHOLD SUPPLIES/LAUNDRY/CLEANING

11. ELECTRICITY

12. GAS

13. WATER/SEWER/SOLID WASTE/TRASH COLLECTION

14. TELEPHONE (including long distance charges)

15. CLOTHING

16. MEDICAL/DENTAL EXPENSES (not reimbursed by insurance)

17. AUTOMOBILE—LOAN PAYMENT

18. AUTOMOBILE—GAS/OIL

19. AUTOMOBILE—REPAIRS

20. AUTOMOBILE—INSURANCE

21. LIFE INSURANCE

22. HEALTH INSURANCE (designate who is covered and exclude amount for children
shown on page 1, line 11)

23. DISABILITY/ACCIDENT/OTHER INSURANCE (specify)

24. ENTERTAINMENT (clubs, social obligations, travel, recreation, cable television)

25. CHARITABLE/CHURCH CONTRIBUTIONS

26. PERSONAL EXPENSES (haircuts, cosmetics, grooming, tobacco, alcohol, etc.)

27. BOOKS/MAGAZINES/NEWSPAPERS

28. EDUCATION/SCHOOL EXPENSES (self and children of whom you have custody)

29. DAY CARE/WORK RELATED CHILD CARE COSTS

30. OTHER EXPENSES (specify)

UNSECURED MONTHLY LOAN/CHARGE CARD EXPENSES (Do not include monthly payments shown above)	FOR	BALANCE	PAYMENT
31			
32			
33			
34			
35			
36			
37			
38			
39			

**40. Total Monthly Expenses and Deductions from Income (Total of Lines 1 through
39)**

**41. Average Weekly Expenses and Deductions (Total monthly expenses divided by
4.3)**

ASSETS

Disclose all assets know to you, even if you do not know the value. Under ownership, H—Husband; W—Wife; J—Joint. Lien amount includes only those debts secured by an item, such as a mortgage against a house, debts shown on title to vehicle, loans against life insurance policies or loans where an item is pledged as collateral. Value assets as of the date the Petition for Dissolution of Marriage was filed.

DESCRIPTION	GROSS VALUE	LESS: LIENS/MORTGAGES	NET VALUE	TITLE H W J
A. HOUSEHOLD FUR-NISHINGS/FURNI-TURE/APPLIANCES				

850

DESCRIPTION	GROSS VALUE	LESS: LIENS/MORTGAGES	NET VALUE	TITLE H W J
In possession of Husband				
In possession of Wife				
B. AUTOMOBILES, TRUCKS, RECREATIONAL VEHICLES Include Make, Model, and Year				
C. SECURITIES— STOCKS, BONDS, AND STOCK OPTIONS				
D. CASH, CHECKING, SAVINGS, DEPOSIT ACCTS, CDS (Include name of bank/credit union and type of account)				
E. REAL ESTATE (including sales contracts)				
Marital residence (show address)				
Basis of Valuation: Name of lender first mortgage: Name of lender second mortgage:				
Other (show address)				
Basis of Valuation: Name of lender first mortgage: Name of lender second mortgage:				
Other (show address)				
Basis of Valuation: Name of lender first mortgage: Name of lender second mortgage:				
F. CASH RETIREMENT ACCOUNTS (IRAs, SEPs, KEOUGHS, 401(k), employee savings plans, stock owner-				

ship/profit sharing plans, etc.)

_____
_____
_____
_____
_____
_____

G. RETIREMENT BENEFITS, DE- FERRED COMPENSA- TION PLANS AND PENSIONS (include information available on benefits, whether benefits are vested or in pay status)

_____
_____
_____
_____
_____
_____

H. BUSINESS INTER- ESTS

_____
_____
_____
_____
_____

I. LIFE INSURANCE (show company name and death benefit)

Term and Group _____
Named beneficiary: _____
Named beneficiary: _____
Named beneficiary: _____
Named beneficiary: _____
Whole Life and Others (show cash value under gross value) _____
Named beneficiary: _____
Named beneficiary: _____
Named beneficiary: _____
Named beneficiary: _____

J. OTHER ASSETS Include any type of assets having value, including jewelry, personal property, assets located in safety deposit boxes, accrued bonuses, etc.

_____
_____
_____
_____
_____
_____
_____
_____
_____

ASSETS ACQUIRED BY YOU PRIOR TO THE MARRIAGE OR THROUGH INHERITANCE OR GIFT
(Whether now owned or not)

DESCRIPTION	GROSS VALUE	LESS: LIENS/MORTGAGES	NET VALUE	VALUATION DATE
ASSETS OWNED BY YOU PRIOR TO MAR- RIAGE (value as of date of marriage)				
THROUGH INHERI- TANCE OR GIFTS (val- ue as of date of acquisi- tion)				
Description: Acquired from whom:				
Description: Acquired from whom:				
Description: Acquired from whom:				

I DECLARE UNDER PENALTY OF PERJURY THAT THE FOREGOING, INCLUDING ANY ATTACHMENTS, IS TRUE AND CORRECT, THAT THIS DECLARATION WAS EXECUTED ON
_____

_____
Party

YOU MUST ATTACH DOCUMENTATION VERIFYING ALL DATA. YOU ARE UNDER A DUTY TO SUPPLEMENT OR AMEND THIS FINANCIAL DECLARATION FORM PRIOR TO TRIAL IF YOU LEARN THE INFORMATION PROVIDED IS INCORRECT OR NO LONGER TRUE.
CERTIFICATE OF SERVICE
I hereby certify that a copy of the foregoing was provided to the following by U.S. mail, postage prepaid, on _____:

_____
_____
_____
_____
_____

_____
Attorney/Pro Se Party

Appendix C. COOPERATION UPDATE FORM

COMES NOW Mother/Father, pro se/by Counsel, and respectfully submits his/her Cooperation Update Sheet and advises the Court as follows:

1. The parties attempted to resolve the matters at issue and met in person in an attempt to resolve the matters as issue on the following dates: _____.

2. The parties attempted to resolve the matters at issue and had telephone contact in an attempt to resolve the matters at issue on the following dates: .

3. The Mother/Father completed the appropriate website work required under Wayne County Local Rules on: .

4. The Mother/Father exchanged the appropriate website work required under Wayne County Local Rules on: .

5. The Mother/Father merged the appropriate website work required under Wayne County Local Rules and completed an Agreed Commitment Form on: .

6. The Mother/Father completed attendance of the co-parenting class required under the Wayne County Local Rules on: .

7. It is believed that these parents could use the following resources to assist them in resolving current and future issues and to build cooperation: .

8. It is believed that it would assist these parents if the Court would do the following: .

Respectfully submitted,

_____

Attorney for Mother/Father

_____

Mother/Father

_____

Date This Sheet Prepared

Appendix D. NOTICE

Wayne County has launched a new initiative for families that find themselves with cases in our courts. As judges responsible for these cases, we are committed to making them about ensuring safety, reducing conflict, building cooperation, and protecting children. These cases call for problem-solving in families, not more conflict. **Parents win together** or lose together. If the parents build safety and cooperation and, together, give their children a good place to live, then everyone wins. If the parents make a childhood a painful or dangerous place by remaining in conflict, then everyone loses.

If you have minor children, you are required to attend the class Parenting Together To Keep Kids First. Please refer to the yellow sheet for Instructions on completing the required web-site work and how to sign up for the class.

The Wayne County Local Rules require cooperation in family law cases. Except where it would be dangerous to do so, before **any** hearing, whether you have children or not, both parties are required to meet to discuss the matter and to try to reach an agreement. The Court will **not** hear the matter and your hearing will be cancelled unless there has been a prior, good-faith meeting to try to reach an agreement. The Wayne County Local Rules can be found at http://www.in.gov/judiciary/2882.htm.

If your case involves children and there is a request for child support, both parents are **required** to prepare an Indiana Child Support Obligation Worksheet (CSOW). In order to prepare the CSOW, please go to the child support calculator found at https://mycourts.in.gov/csc/parents/. Both parents shall bring the completed CSOW to any hearings. Failure to prepare the CSOW and to bring it with you to a child support hearing may result in the hearing being cancelled or other sanctions being entered.

With regard to parenting time, except in extraordinary circumstances, the Indiana Parenting Time Guidelines are considered the **minimum** a noncustodial parent should be awarded. You can find the Guidelines at http://www.in.gov/judiciary/rules/parenting/.

We trust that you will join us in making Wayne County a leader in protecting children and helping them to become well-adjusted, productive adults.

David A. Kolger, Judge Wayne County Circuit Court

Charles K. Todd, Jr., Judge Wayne County Superior Court I

Gregory A Horn, Judge Wayne County Superior Court II

Adopted effective Jan. 1, 2013.

WAYNE COUNTY RULES OF PROBATE

Adopted October 30, 1997, Effective November 1, 1997

Amended effective January 1, 2008

Including Amendments Received Through November 1, 2013

Research Notes

Annotations to the Wayne County Rules of Probate are available in West's Annotated Indiana Code, *Title 34 Appendix.*

These rules may be searched electronically on Westlaw *in the IN-RULES database; updates to these rules may be found on Westlaw in IN-RULESUPDATES. For search tips and a summary of database content, consult the Westlaw Scope Screens for each database.*

LR89–PR00 Rule 001. NOTICE

1.1 Whenever notice by publication and/or written notice by U.S. Mail is required to be given the attorney shall prepare such notice and shall give sufficient numbers of the same to the Clerk who shall ensure that such notice is issued as required by the Statute. It shall also be the attorney's responsibility to provide the Clerk with addressed and stamped envelopes when notice is to be made by First Class Mail.

1.2 Copies of petitions shall be sent with all notices where the hearing involved arises from the matters contained in the petition.

1.3 On the filing with the Clerk by the personal representative or guardian of any petition, application, complaint, partial report, final report, or any report that requires fixing of date and place of hearing of same by the Court and giving notice thereof to any or all interested persons as required by law or order of the Court, the Clerk shall forthwith fix the date and place of hearing, by endorsement on the same, and shall give, for such personal representative or guardian, the required notice. The Clerk shall then also make and record on the proper order book on the date of the filing of such petition or report, an order by the court fixing the date and place of hearing of such petition or report, the same as fixed thereon by the Clerk, and directing the Clerk to give for the personal representative or guardian the required notice.

1.4 The Wayne County Scheduling Clerk will accept calendaring responsibilities concerning notification to all personal representatives and guardians of the due date of any statutorily required inventory or accounting. A copy of such notice of due date will be mailed to the attorney of record for the personal representative or guardian.

Adopted Oct. 30, 1997, effective Nov. 1, 1997; amended effective Jan. 1, 2008; Jan. 1, 2013.

LR89–PR00 Rule 002. FILING OF PLEADINGS

2.1 Routine pleadings, such as Inventories, Inheritance Tax Schedules, and Final Reports, may be filed with the Clerk for transmittal to the Court.

2.2 All attorneys are required to prepare orders for all proceedings except when expressly directed otherwise by the Court.

2.3 Every pleading, including Inventories, Petitions, and Accountings, filed in an Estate or Guardianship, shall be signed and verified by the fiduciary and signed by the attorney for the fiduciary. Pleadings of a procedural nature only may be signed by only the attorney.

2.4 All pleadings filed shall contain the attorney's name, address, telephone number, and attorney's Registration Number.

2.5 The initial petition to open an Estate or Guardianship shall contain the name and address of the fiduciary.

Adopted Oct. 30, 1997, effective Nov. 1, 1997; amended effective Jan. 1, 2008.

LR89–PR00 Rule 003. BOND

3.1 The filing of any bond for a Personal Representative shall be governed by Indiana Code 29–1–11–1 (or any subsequent recodification thereof).

3.2 The filing of any bond for a guardian shall be governed by Indiana Code 29–1–7–1 and 29–1–7–2 (or any subsequent recodification thereof).

3.3 In the event that a bond is requested or anticipated, the petition to open an estate or guardianship shall set forth the probable value of the personal property plus the estimated annual rents and profits to be derived from the property in the estate or guardianship.

Adopted Oct. 30, 1997, effective Nov. 1, 1997; amended effective Jan. 1, 2008.

LR89–PR00 Rule 004.   INVENTORY

4.1   An inventory shall be filed in duplicate by the fiduciary in all estates and guardianships, except unsupervised estates, within sixty (60) days; Guardianships within ninety (90) days for permanent guardians; and, within thirty (30) days for temporary guardians. All times relate to the appointment of the fiduciary.

4.2   In the event a partial inventory is filed, all subsequent inventories must contain a recapitulation of prior inventories.

Adopted Oct. 30, 1997, effective Nov. 1, 1997; amended effective Jan. 1, 2008.

LR89–PR00 Rule 005.   SALE OF REAL ESTATE

5.1   When a Petition to Sell Real Estate is filed in a supervised estate or guardianship, it shall be accompanied by a written appraisal prepared by a person qualified to appraise such property, setting forth the fair market value of said real estate, unless such an appraisal was previously filed with the Inventory.

5.2   All appraisals required by Rule 5.1 shall be made within one (1) year of the date of a Petition to Sell Real Estate.

5.3   In a supervised estate, whenever a Final Decree contains real estate located in any county other than Wayne County, the Decree or a Personal Representative's Deed shall be recorded with the Recorder of the County in which any such real estate is located.

Adopted Oct. 30, 1997, effective Nov. 1, 1997; amended effective Jan. 1, 2008.

LR89–PR00 Rule 006. SALE OF PERSONAL PROPERTY

6.1   In all supervised estates and guardianships, no Petition to Sell Personal Property at private sale shall be granted unless a written appraisal prepared by a person competent to appraise such property and setting forth the Fair Market Value thereof, is filed with the Court at the time of the filing of the Petition to Sell, unless such appraisal was filed with the Inventory.   In the case of a motor vehicle, a valuation obtained from a nationally recognized vehicle valuation service, such as NADA or Kelly Blue Book, may, in the discretion of the court, be substituted for a written appraisal.

6.2   All appraisals required by Rule 6.1 shall be made within one (1) year of the date of the Petition to Sell.

6.3   No written appraisal shall be required for the sale of assets which are traded in a market and the value of which is readily ascertainable.   Such assets

include, but are not limited to, stocks, bonds, mutual funds, commodities, and precious metals.

Adopted Oct. 30, 1997, effective Nov. 1, 1997; amended effective Jan. 1, 2008; Jan. 1, 2013.

LR89–PR00 Rule 007.   CLAIMS

7.1   On or before three (3) months and fifteen (15) days after the date of the first published notice to creditors, the personal representative or the personal representative's attorney shall file a pleading with the court showing the personal representative's determination of either allowing a claim, or disallowing a claim, in whole or in part, as to those claims filed within three (3) months after the date of the first published notice to creditors.   A copy of this pleading shall be served upon each creditor whose claim has been disallowed in full or in part.   The Clerk shall give immediate written notice to a creditor if its claim has been disallowed in full or in part.   Such pleading shall also be filed within thirty (30) days after the filing of any subsequent claim made by other creditors beyond the initial time period of three (3) months following the first published notice of creditors, with the same service of copy and notice.   In the absence of a pleading from the personal representative during these time periods, the claim shall be deemed disallowed.   Compliance with this rule shall be deemed compliance with I.C. 29–1–14–10.

Adopted Oct. 30, 1997, effective Nov. 1, 1997; amended effective Jan. 1, 2008; Jan. 1, 2013.

LR89–PR00 Rule 008.   ACCOUNTINGS

8.1   Accountings for estates must comply with Indiana Code 29–1–16.

8.2   All guardianship accounts shall contain a certification of an officer of any financial institution in which guardianship assets are held, verifying the account balance.

8.3   All Social Security or Medicare benefits received on behalf of an incapacitated person shall be included and accounted for in the guardianship accountings unless Court approval has been previously granted to allow said funds to be paid directly to a residential or health care facility.

8.4   In all supervised estate and guardianship accountings, vouchers canceled checks, bank statements, check images provided by the financial institution, or other evidence of expenditures acceptable to the Court for the expenditures claimed shall be filed with the accounting.

8.5   In all supervised estate and guardianship accountings, a notation shall be placed by each expenditure indicating the reason for or nature of the expenditure.

EXAMPLE:

Bogata Drugs—Prescription drugs

Dr. John Jones—Medical services

Sam Smith—repair roof of home at 162 Maple

Street, Anytown, Indiana
Tendercare Nursing Home—Nursing home care

8.6   All accountings to the Court shall contain an itemized statement of the assets on hand.

8.7   Receipts canceled checks, bank statements, check images provided by the financial institution, or other evidence acceptable to the Court for all final distributions shall be filed either in the final report, or a supplemental report, before discharge will be granted by the Court.

8.8   All accountings shall follow the prescribed statutory format. Informal, handwritten, or transactional accountings will not be accepted.

8.9   All Court costs shall be paid and all claims satisfied and released before the hearing on the Final Account and a Clerk's Certification thereof shall be filed with the Court before such Final Account shall be approved.

8.10   In those estates where no Indiana inheritance tax is due, the Affidavit required to be filed with the local Assessor's Office shall also be filed under the estate's caption and cause number with the Clerk of the Court.

Adopted Oct. 30, 1997, effective Nov. 1, 1997; amended effective Jan. 1, 2008.

LR89–PR00 Rule 009.   FEES OF ATTORNEY AND FIDUCIARY

9.1   No fees for fiduciaries or attorneys shall be approved in any supervised estate or guardianship until the Court has approved a fee petition filed by the attorney for the estate.

9.2   No attorney or fiduciary fees will be determined and authorized for payment by the Court in any Unsupervised Administration of a decedent's estate.

9.3   Where contracts for legal services have been entered into prior or subsequent to the opening of an estate or guardianship, the Court reserves the right to approve or disapprove the fee contracts consistent with this Court's fee guidelines.

9.4   Rule 1.5 of the Rule of Professional Conduct has been adopted by the Supreme Court of Indiana to govern attorney fees. All fees charged by attorneys shall be reasonable. The rule further enumerates the factors to be considered, which are as follows:

   (1) the time and labor required, the novelty and difficulty of questions involved, and the skills requisite to perform the legal service properly;

   (2) the likelihood, if apparent to the client, that the acceptance of the particular employment will preclude other employment by the lawyer;

   (3) the fee customarily charged in the locality for similar legal services;

   (4) the amount involved and the results obtained;

   (5) the time limitations imposed by the client or by the circumstances;

   (6) the nature and length of the professional relationship with the client;

   (7) the experience, reputation and ability of the lawyer or lawyers performing the services.

The guidelines set forth in Appendix A to these rules are not to be used as a substitution for the attorney's determination of what a reasonable fee would be in a given situation. Rather, the guidelines are established to assist attorneys and fiduciaries by outlining what the Court will deem to be reasonable based upon the factors contained in Rule of Professional Conduct 1.5.

The basic guideline amounts are based upon usual and ordinary services. The guidelines also will assist in calculations of fees generated by the provisions of extraordinary services.

9.5   Unjustified delays in carrying out duties by the fiduciary and/or attorney may result in a reduction of fees.

Adopted Oct. 30, 1997, effective Nov. 1, 1997; amended effective Jan. 1, 2008.

LR89–PR00 Rule 010.   UNSUPERVISED ADMINISTRATION

10.1   Any petition for unsupervised administration of an estate must comply with Indiana Code 29–1–7.5.

10.2   A verified Closing Statement filed in unsupervised administrations must comply with Indiana Code § 29–1–7.5–4, and must contain statements that the Personal Representative has completed the items set forth therein.

10.3   No Orders as to attorneys fees, compliance regarding notice of administration to decedent's creditor's, or other orders shall be entered by the Court in unsupervised estates except that the Court shall enter an Order approving the verified closing statement as required by Indiana Code § 29–1–7.5–4.

Adopted Oct. 30, 1997, effective Nov. 1, 1997; amended effective Jan. 1, 2008.

LR89–PR00 Rule 011.   GUARDIANSHIPS

11.1   In all guardianship matters seeking to declare an adult incapacitated for any reason, the incapacitated person shall be present at the hearing or sufficient evidence is presented to excuse the absence of the incapacitated person pursuant to Indiana Code 29–3–5–1.

11.2   In all guardianship matters seeking to declare an adult incapacitated for any reason, a Physician's Report by the doctor treating the alleged incapacitated person, or such evidence as the Court shall require, shall be presented to the Court at the time the petition is filed or on the hearing date.

11.3   In every petition for the appointment of a guardian of the person of a minor child or an incapacitated adult, the petition shall contain the information required by Indiana Code 29–3–5.

11.4 Nothing herein shall be deemed as amending, superseding or altering the Probate Rules and Regulations promulgated by the Veteran's Administration of the United States of America, and every fiduciary and attorney shall comply with same, if applicable.

11.5 In all estate and guardianship matters involving either a claim for wrongful death or personal injury, the civil case and the corresponding guardianship or probate proceedings will be filed in the same Court without regard to the usual computer filing system which governs the filing of all other actions.

Adopted Oct. 30, 1997, effective Nov. 1, 1997; amended effective Jan. 1, 2008.

LR89–PR00 Rule 012. MISCELLANEOUS

12.1 (a) In those matters for which the Court has authority to grant an extension of time, the Court shall automatically grant one forty-five (45) day extension upon the filing of a written petition on or before the otherwise applicable deadline.

(b) Any additional extension of time may be granted only upon the filing of an additional petition setting forth such good cause.

12.2 Procedure for past-due filings and reports:

(A) *First Notice*: A notice will be mailed to the attorney when the matter becomes past due.

(B) *Second Notice*: If there is no response within thirty (30) days of the mailing of the First Notice, a letter notice from the Court will be mailed requesting compliance within fifteen (15) days.

(C) *Court Order*: If there is no response within fifteen (15) days of the mailing of the Second Notice, a Court order to show cause will be issued. Both the attorney and fiduciary must appear at the date and time specified in the Court Order.

(Note: Rule 9.5 may be invoked in any of the above circumstances.)

12.3 In all probate matters, two (2) original orders shall be presented to the Clerk at the time of filing.

Adopted Oct. 30, 1997, effective Nov. 1, 1997; amended effective Jan. 1, 2008; Jan. 1, 2013.

Appendix A. COMPUTATION OF FEES

PROBATE EXHIBIT A

COMPUTATION OF FEES

ESTATE OF _____
PROBATE NO. _____
1. Inventories Value of Estate $ _____

2. Income During Administration $ _____

3. Assets Omitted from Inventory $ _____

TOTAL $ _____
4. Total Gross Estate—Federal Estate Tax $ _____

PERSONAL REPRESENTATIVE   ATTORNEY

First $100,000—5% $ _____   6% $ _____

Next $200,000—4% $ _____   5% $ _____

Next $700,000—2% $ _____   3% $ _____

Excess of $1,000,000—1% $ _____   2% $ _____

Total $ _____ $ _____

ADDITIONAL FEES CLAIMED
Personal Representative $ _____   Attorney $ _____

EXPLANATION OF ADDITIONAL FEES CLAIMED:

If additional fees are claimed, attach a detailed statement showing the nature of the services rendered, the time involved and the reasons why the same should generate additional fees. Please provide such additional information and supportive evidence as you think will enable the Court to weigh the claim for fees.

ATTORNEY & PERSONAL REPRESENTATIVE FEE GUIDELINES

I. Estate Administration:

Gross estate services are considered to normally include: probating the Will, opening the estate, qualifying the personal representative, preparing and filing the Inventory, paying claims, collecting assets, preparing and filing non-extraordinary petitions, assisting with and/or preparing and filing of Fiduciary Income Tax Return, assisting with and/or preparing and filing all tax returns and schedules, obtaining Court Orders thereon, and paying the taxes, preparing and filing the Final Report, obtaining Order approving same, distributing assets, obtaining discharge of the personal representative, and preparing and serving all notices on interested parties throughout the proceedings. The list shall not be considered to be exclusive.

A. Gross Estate—Minimum Fee of $1,500.00

Attorney:
First $100.000.00, not to exceed 6%
Next $200.000.00, not to exceed 5%
Next $700,000,00, not to exceed 3%
Excess of $1,000,000.00, not to exceed 2%
Fiduciary:
First $100,000.00, not to exceed 5%

Next $200,000.00, not to exceed 4%
Next $700,000.00, not to exceed 2%
Excess of $1,000,000.00, not to exceed 1%

B.   Miscellaneous—Extraordinary Services:

1.   Indiana Inheritance Tax Scheduled—(preparation and filing only) (To be applied only to non-administered property):

Attorney fees shall be three percent (3%) of the first $100,000.00 of the non-administered assets of gross estate as determined for Indiana Inheritance Tax purposes plus two percent (2%) of the next $100,000.00 of the non-administered assets of the gross estate, plus one and one-half percent (1 ½%) of the next $200,000.00 of the non-administered assets of the gross estate, plus one percent (1%) of all non-administered assets of the gross estate in excess of $400,000.00. Personal Representative's fees for non-administered assets of the gross estate as determined for Indiana Inheritance Tax purposes shall be one-third (1/3) of the attorney fees for such nonadministered assets.

2.   Federal Estate Tax Returns—(To be applied only to non-administered property, to be based only on assets not listed on Indiana Inheritance Tax Schedule).

A base attorney fee of .... $750.00 or

One percent (1%) of the first $100,000.00 of the non-administered assets of the said gross estate as determined for Federal Estate Tax purposes,

PLUS, 3/4 of one percent (1%) of the next $150,000.00 of non-administered assets of said gross estate,

PLUS, 1/2 of one percent (1%) on all non-administered assets of said gross estate in excess of $250,000.00.

Personal Representative's fees shall be one-third (1/3) of attorney fees.

3.   Other than as provided above .... Hourly Rate

(Attorney's expertise in probate matters will be considered by the Court in determining the applicable hourly rate)

II.   Wrongful Death Administration:

The Court recognizes that in most instances a retainer or contingent fee agreement is an appropriate method by which legal services can be provided in wrongful death claims. Accordingly, fees shall be allowed under such agreements if, at the time of settlement of the claim, it is shown to the Court's satisfaction:

1.   That the Personal Representative was, prior to entering into such agreement, fully informed as to all aspects of the arrangement.

2.   That the agreement is fair and reasonable.

3.   That the fee sought is fair and reasonable.

III.   In General:

A.   Extraordinary Fee Requests

Fee petitions requesting extraordinary fees must set forth services rendered with specificity. Extraordinary services may include: sale of personal property, sale of real property, partial distribution, will contest actions, contesting claims, adjusting tax matters, contested hearings, petition for instructions, heirship determinations, generating additional income for the estate, etc. All such petitions will be set for hearing, with notice to all interested parties. If all interested parties sign a waiver and consent stating they have been advised the additional fee request exceeds the Court's guidelines and that the services as detailed are extraordinary, the Court may, in its discretion, determine if a hearing is required. An acceptable form of waiver is attached.

B. Unsupervised Estates

The Court will not determine fees in an unsupervised administration.

IV. Guardianship Administration:

Fees for the administration of guardianships shall be based on an hourly rate to be approved by the Court for both the attorney and the guardian. The Court will consider the attorney's and guardian's expertise in approving the hourly rate.